D0721725

RAND

# Microeconomic Theory

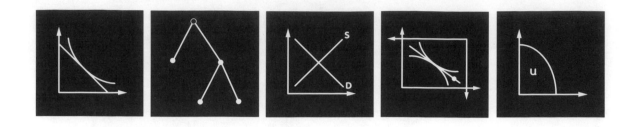

# Microeconomic Theory

Andreu Mas-Colell    Michael D. Whinston

and

Jerry R. Green

New York  Oxford  OXFORD UNIVERSITY PRESS  1995

OXFORD UNIVERSITY PRESS

Oxford   New York
Athens   Auckland   Bangkok   Bombay
Calcutta   Cape Town   Dar es Salaam   Deli
Florence   Hong Kong   Istanbul   Karachi
Kuala Lumpur   Madras   Madrid   Melbourne
Mexico City   Nairobi   Paris   Singapore
Taipei   Tokyo   Toronto

and associated companies in
Berlin   Ibadan

Copyright © 1995 by Oxford University Press, Inc.

Published by Oxford University Press, Inc.,
198 Madison Avenue, New York, New York 10016

Oxford is a registered trademark of Oxford University Press

All rights reserved. No part of this publication may be reproduced,
stored in a retrieval system, or transmitted, by any form or by any means,
electronic, mechanical, photocopying, recording, or otherwise,
without the prior permission of Oxford University Press.

Library of Congress Cataloging-in-Publication Data
Mas-Colell, Andreu.
Microeconomic theory / Andreu Mas-Colell, Michael D. Whinston, and Jerry R. Green.
p.   cm.
Includes bibliographical references and index.
ISBN 0–19–507340–1 (cloth)
ISBN 0–19–510268–1 (paper)
1. Microeconomics.   I. Whinston, Michael Dennis.   II. Green, Jerry R.   III. Title.
HB172.M6247   1995
338.5—dc20   95–18128

19   18   17   16   15   14   13   12   11

Printed in the United States of America
on acid-free paper

A Esther, por todo   A. M.-C.


To Bonnie, for keeping me smiling throughout;
to Noah, for his sweetness and joy at the book's completion;
and to Nan, for helping me get started   M. D. W.


To Pamela, for her kindness, character, strength, and spirit   J. R. G.

# Contents

# Preface

*Microeconomic Theory* is intended to serve as the text for a first-year graduate course in microeconomic theory. The original sources for much of the book's material are the lecture notes that we have provided over the years to students in the first-year microeconomic theory course at Harvard. Starting from these notes, we have tried to produce a text that covers in an accessible yet rigorous way the full range of topics taught in a typical first-year course.

The nonlexicographic ordering of our names deserves some explanation. The project was first planned and begun by the three of us in the spring of 1990. However, in February 1992, after early versions of most of the book's chapters had been drafted, Jerry Green was selected to serve as Provost of Harvard University, a position that forced him to suspend his involvement in the project. From this point in time until the manuscript's completion in June 1994, Andreu Mas-Colell and Michael Whinston assumed full responsibility for the project. With the conclusion of Jerry Green's service as Provost, the original three-person team was reunited for the review of galley and page proofs during the winter of 1994/1995.

## The Organization of the Book

Microeconomic theory as a discipline begins by considering the behavior of individual agents and builds from this foundation to a theory of aggregate economic outcomes. *Microeconomic Theory* (the book) follows exactly this outline. It is divided into five parts. Part I covers individual decision making. It opens with a general treatment of individual choice and proceeds to develop the classical theories of consumer and producer behavior. It also provides an introduction to the theory of individual choice under uncertainty. Part II covers game theory, the extension of the theory of individual decision making to situations in which several decision makers interact. Part III initiates the investigation of market equilibria. It begins with an introduction to competitive equilibrium and the fundamental theorems of welfare economics in the context of the Marshallian partial equilibrium model. It then explores the possibilities for market failures in the presence of externalities, market power, and asymmetric information. Part IV substantially extends our previous study of competitive markets to the general equilibrium context. The positive and normative aspects of the theory are examined in detail, as are extensions of the theory to equilibrium under uncertainty and over time. Part V studies welfare economics. It discusses the possibilities for aggregation of individual preferences into social preferences both with and without interpersonal utility comparisons, as well as the implementation of social choices in the presence of incomplete information about agents' preferences. A Mathematical Appendix provides an introduction to most of the more advanced mathematics used in the book (e.g., concave/convex functions, constrained optimization techniques, fixed point theorems, etc.) as well as references for further reading.

### The Style of the Book

In choosing the content of *Microeconomic Theory* we have tried to err on the side of inclusion. Our aim has been to assure coverage of most topics that instructors in a first-year graduate microeconomic theory course might want to teach. An inevitable consequence of this choice is that the book covers more topics than any single first-year course can discuss adequately. (We certainly have never taught all of it in any one year.) Our hope is that the range of topics presented will allow instructors the freedom to emphasize those they find most important.

We have sought a style of presentation that is accessible, yet also rigorous. Wherever possible we give precise definitions and formal proofs of propositions. At the same time, we accompany this analysis with extensive verbal discussion as well as with numerous examples to illustrate key concepts. Where we have considered a proof or topic either too difficult or too peripheral we have put it into smaller type to allow students to skip over it easily in a first reading.

Each chapter offers many exercises, ranging from easy to hard [graded from A (easiest) to C (hardest)] to help students master the material. Some of these exercises also appear within the text of the chapters so that students can check their understanding along the way (almost all of these are level A exercises).

The mathematical prerequisites for use of the book are a basic knowledge of calculus, some familiarity with linear algebra (although the use of vectors and matrices is introduced gradually in Part I), and a grasp of the elementary aspects of probability. Students also will find helpful some familiarity with microeconomics at the level of an intermediate undergraduate course.

### Teaching the Book

The material in this book may be taught in many different sequences. Typically we have taught Parts I–III in the Fall semester and Parts IV and V in the Spring (omitting some topics in each case). A very natural alternative to this sequence (one used in a number of departments that we know of) might instead teach Parts I and IV in the Fall, and Parts II, III, and V in the Spring.[1] The advantage of this alternative sequence is that the study of general equilibrium analysis more closely follows the study of individual behavior in competitive markets that is developed in Part I. The disadvantage, and the reason we have not used this sequence in our own course, is that this makes for a more abstract first semester; our students have seemed happy to have the change of pace offered by game theory, oligopoly, and asymmetric information after studying Part I.

The chapters have been written to be relatively self-contained. As a result, they can be shifted easily among the parts to accommodate many other course sequences. For example, we have often opted to teach game theory on an "as needed" basis,

---

1. Obviously, some adjustment needs to be made by programs that operate on a quarter system.

breaking it up into segments that are discussed right before they are used (e.g., Chapter 7, Chapter 8, and Sections 9.A–B before studying oligopoly, Sections 9.C–D before covering signaling). Some other possibilities include teaching the aggregation of preferences (Chapter 21) immediately after individual decision making and covering the principal-agent problem (Chapter 14), adverse selection, signaling, and screening (Chapter 13), and mechanism design (Chapter 23) together in a section of the course focusing on information economics.

In addition, even within each part, the sequence of topics can often be altered easily. For example, it has been common in many programs to teach the preference-based theory of consumer demand before teaching the revealed preference, or "choice-based," theory. Although we think there are good reasons to reverse this sequence as we have done in Part I,[2] we have made sure that the material on demand can be covered in this more traditional way as well.[3]

### On Mathematical Notation

For the most part, our use of mathematical notation is standard. Perhaps the most important mathematical rule to keep straight regards matrix notation. Put simply, vectors are always treated mathematically as *column vectors*, even though they are often displayed within the written text as rows to conserve space. The transpose of the (column) vector $x$ is denoted by $x^T$. When taking the inner product of two (column) vectors $x$ and $y$, we write $x \cdot y$; it has the same meaning as $x^T y$. This and other aspects of matrix notation are reviewed in greater detail in Section M.A of the Mathematical Appendix.

To help highlight definitions and propositions we have chosen to display them in a different typeface than is used elsewhere in the text. One perhaps unfortunate consequence of this choice is that mathematical symbols sometimes appear slightly differently there than in the rest of the text. With this warning, we hope that no confusion will result.

Summation symbols ($\sum$) are displayed in various ways throughout the text. Sometimes they are written as

$$\sum_{n=1}^{N}$$

(usually only in displayed equations), but often to conserve space they appear as $\sum_{n=1}^{N}$, and in the many cases in which no confusion exists about the upper and lower limit of the index in the summation, we typically write just $\sum_n$. A similar point applies to the product symbol $\prod$.

---

2. In particular, it is *much* easier to introduce and derive many properties of demand in the choice-based theory than it is using the preference-based approach; and the choice-based theory gives you *almost* all the properties of demand that follow from assuming the existence of rational preferences.

3. To do this, one introduces the basics of the consumer's problem using Sections 2.A–D and 3.A–D, discusses the properties of uncompensated and compensated demand functions, the indirect utility function, and the expenditure function using Sections 3.D–I and 2.E, and then studies revealed preference theory using Sections 2.F and 3.J (and Chapter 1 for a more general overview of the two approaches).

Also described below are the meanings we attach to a few mathematical symbols whose use is somewhat less uniform in the literature [in this list, $x = (x_1, \ldots, x_N)$ and $y = (y_1, \ldots, y_N)$ are (column) vectors, while $X$ and $Y$ are sets]:

| Symbol | Meaning |
|---|---|
| $x \geq y$ | $x_n \geq y_n$ for all $n = 1, \ldots, N$. |
| $x \gg y$ | $x_n > y_n$ for all $n = 1, \ldots, N$. |
| $X \subset Y$ | *weak* set inclusion ($x \in X$ implies $x \in Y$). |
| $X \setminus Y$ | The set $\{x : x \in X \text{ but } x \notin Y\}$. |
| $E_x[f(x, y)]$ | The expected value of the function $f(\cdot)$ over realizations of the random variable $x$. (When the expectation is over all of the arguments of the function we simply write $E[f(x, y)]$.) |

### Acknowledgments

Many people have contributed to the development of this book. Dilip Abreu, Doug Bernheim, David Card, Prajit Dutta, Steve Goldman, John Panzar, and David Pearce all (bravely) test-taught a very early version of the manuscript during the 1991–92 academic year. Their comments at that early stage were instrumental in the refinement of the book into its current style, and led to many other substantive improvements in the text. Our colleagues (and in some cases former students) Luis Corchón, Simon Grant, Drew Fudenberg, Chiaki Hara, Sergiu Hart, Bengt Holmstrom, Eric Maskin, John Nachbar, Martin Osborne, Ben Polak, Ariel Rubinstein, and Martin Weitzman offered numerous helpful suggestions. The book would undoubtedly have been better still had we managed to incorporate all of their ideas.

Many generations of first-year Harvard graduate students have helped us with their questions, comments, and corrections. In addition, a number of current and former students have played a more formal role in the book's development, serving as research assistants in various capacities. Shira Lewin read the entire manuscript, finding errors in our proofs, suggesting improvements in exposition, and even (indeed, often) correcting our grammar. Chiaki Hara, Ilya Segal, and Steve Tadelis, with the assistance of Marc Nachman, have checked that the book's many exercises could be solved, and have suggested how they might be formulated properly when our first attempt to do so failed. Chiaki Hara and Steve Tadelis have also given us extensive comments and corrections on the text itself. Emily Mechner, Nick Palmer, Phil Panet, and Billy Pizer were members of a team of first-year students that read our early drafts in the summer of 1992 and offered very helpful suggestions on how we could convey the material better.

Betsy Carpenter and Claudia Napolilli provided expert secretarial support throughout the project, helping to type some chapter drafts, copying material on very tight deadlines, and providing their support in hundreds of other ways. Gloria Gerrig kept careful track of our ever-increasing expenditures.

Our editor at Oxford, Herb Addison, was instrumental in developing the test teaching program that so helped us in the book's early stages, and offered his support throughout the book's development. Leslie Phillips of Oxford took our expression of appreciation for the look of the Feynman Lectures, and turned it into a book design that exceeded our highest expectations. Alan Chesterton and the rest of the staff at Keyword Publishing Services did an absolutely superb job editing and producing the book on a very tight schedule. Their complete professionalism has been deeply appreciated.

The influence of many other individuals on the book, although more indirect, has been no less important. Many of the exercises that appear in the book have been conceived over the years by others, both at Harvard and elsewhere. We have indicated our source for an exercise whenever we were aware of it. Good exercises are an enormously valuable resource. We thank the anonymous authors of many of the exercises that appear here.

The work of numerous scholars has contributed to our knowledge of the topics discussed in this book. Of necessity we have been able to provide references in each chapter to only a limited number of sources. Many interesting and important contributions have not been included. These usually can be found in the references of the works we do list; indeed, most chapters include at least one reference to a general survey of their topic.

We have also had the good fortune to teach the first-year graduate microeconomic theory course at Harvard in the years prior to writing this book with Ken Arrow, Dale Jorgenson, Steve Marglin, Eric Maskin, and Mike Spence, from whom we learned a great deal about microeconomics and its teaching.

We also thank the NSF and Sloan Foundation for their support of our research over the years. In addition, the Center for Advanced Study in the Behavioral Sciences provided an ideal environment to Michael Whinston for completing the manuscript during the 1993/1994 academic year. The Universitat Pompeu Fabra also offered its hospitality to Andreu Mas-Colell at numerous points during the book's development.

Finally, we want to offer a special thanks to those who first excited us about the subject matter that appears here: Gerard Debreu, Leo Hurwicz, Roy Radner, Marcel Richter, and Hugo Sonnenschein (A.M.–C.); David Cass, Peter Diamond, Franklin Fisher, Sanford Grossman, and Eric Maskin (M.D.W.); Emmanuel Drandakis, Ron Jones, Lionel McKenzie, and Edward Zabel (J.R.G.).

A.M.-C., M.D.W., J.R.G.

Cambridge, MA
*March 1995*

# Microeconomic Theory

# PART ONE

# Individual Decision Making

A distinctive feature of microeconomic theory is that it aims to model economic activity as an interaction of individual economic agents pursuing their private interests. It is therefore appropriate that we begin our study of microeconomic theory with an analysis of individual decision making.

Chapter 1 is short and preliminary. It consists of an introduction to the theory of individual decision making considered in an abstract setting. It introduces the decision maker and her choice problem, and it describes two related approaches to modeling her decisions. One, the *preference-based approach*, assumes that the decision maker has a preference relation over her set of possible choices that satisfies certain rationality axioms. The other, the *choice-based approach*, focuses directly on the decision maker's choice behavior, imposing consistency restrictions that parallel the rationality axioms of the preference-based approach.

The remaining chapters in Part One study individual decision making in explicitly economic contexts. It is common in microeconomics texts—and this text is no exception—to distinguish between two sets of agents in the economy: *individual consumers* and *firms*. Because individual consumers own and run firms and therefore ultimately determine a firm's actions, they are in a sense the more fundamental element of an economic model. Hence, we begin our review of the theory of economic decision making with an examination of the consumption side of the economy.

Chapters 2 and 3 study the behavior of consumers in a market economy. Chapter 2 begins by describing the consumer's decision problem and then introduces the concept of the consumer's *demand function*. We then proceed to investigate the implications for the demand function of several natural properties of consumer demand. This investigation constitutes an analysis of consumer behavior in the spirit of the choice-based approach introduced in Chapter 1.

In Chapter 3, we develop the classical preference-based approach to consumer demand. Topics such as utility maximization, expenditure minimization, duality, integrability, and the measurement of welfare changes are studied there. We also discuss the relation between this theory and the choice-based approach studied in Chapter 2.

In economic analysis, the aggregate behavior of consumers is often more important than the behavior of any single consumer. In Chapter 4, we analyze the extent to which the properties of individual demand discussed in Chapters 2 and 3 also hold for aggregate consumer demand.

In Chapter 5, we study the behavior of the firm. We begin by posing the firm's decision problem, introducing its technological constraints and the assumption of profit maximization. A rich theory, paralleling that for consumer demand, emerges. In an important sense, however, this analysis constitutes a first step because it takes the objective of profit maximization as a maintained hypothesis. In the last section of the chapter, we comment on the circumstances under which profit maximization can be derived as the desired objective of the firm's owners.

Chapter 6 introduces risk and uncertainty into the theory of individual decision making. In most economic decision problems, an individual's or firm's choices do not result in perfectly certain outcomes. The theory of decision making under uncertainty developed in this chapter therefore has wide-ranging applications to economic problems, many of which we discuss later in the book.

# Preference and Choice

## 1.A Introduction

In this chapter, we begin our study of the theory of individual decision making by considering it in a completely abstract setting. The remaining chapters in Part I develop the analysis in the context of explicitly economic decisions.

The starting point for any individual decision problem is a *set of possible (mutually exclusive) alternatives* from which the individual must choose. In the discussion that follows, we denote this set of alternatives abstractly by $X$. For the moment, this set can be anything. For example, when an individual confronts a decision of what career path to follow, the alternatives in $X$ might be: {go to law school, go to graduate school and study economics, go to business school, ... , become a rock star}. In Chapters 2 and 3, when we consider the consumer's decision problem, the elements of the set $X$ are the possible consumption choices.

There are two distinct approaches to modeling individual choice behavior. The first, which we introduce in Section 1.B, treats the decision maker's tastes, as summarized in her *preference relation*, as the primitive characteristic of the individual. The theory is developed by first imposing rationality axioms on the decision maker's preferences and then analyzing the consequences of these preferences for her choice behavior (i.e., on decisions made). This preference-based approach is the more traditional of the two, and it is the one that we emphasize throughout the book.

The second approach, which we develop in Section 1.C, treats the individual's choice behavior as the primitive feature and proceeds by making assumptions directly concerning this behavior. A central assumption in this approach, the *weak axiom of revealed preference*, imposes an element of consistency on choice behavior, in a sense paralleling the rationality assumptions of the preference-based approach. This choice-based approach has several attractive features. It leaves room, in principle, for more general forms of individual behavior than is possible with the preference-based approach. It also makes assumptions about objects that are directly observable (choice behavior), rather than about things that are not (preferences). Perhaps most importantly, it makes clear that the theory of individual decision making need not be based on a process of introspection but can be given an entirely behavioral foundation.

Understanding the relationship between these two different approaches to modeling individual behavior is of considerable interest. Section 1.D investigates this question, examining first the implications of the preference-based approach for choice behavior and then the conditions under which choice behavior is compatible with the existence of underlying preferences. (This is an issue that also comes up in Chapters 2 and 3 for the more restricted setting of consumer demand.)

For an in-depth, advanced treatment of the material of this chapter, see Richter (1971).

# 1.B  Preference Relations

In the preference-based approach, the objectives of the decision maker are summarized in a *preference relation*, which we denote by $\succsim$. Technically, $\succsim$ is a binary relation on the set of alternatives $X$, allowing the comparison of pairs of alternatives $x, y \in X$. We read $x \succsim y$ as "x is at least as good as y." From $\succsim$, we can derive two other important relations on $X$:

(i) The *strict preference* relation, $\succ$, defined by

$$x \succ y \iff x \succsim y \text{ but not } y \succsim x$$

and read "x is preferred to y."[1]

(ii) The *indifference* relation, $\sim$, defined by

$$x \sim y \iff x \succsim y \text{ and } y \succsim x$$

and read "x is indifferent to y."

In much of microeconomic theory, individual preferences are assumed to be *rational*. The hypothesis of rationality is embodied in two basic assumptions about the preference relation $\succsim$: *completeness* and *transitivity*.[2]

**Definition 1.B.1:** The preference relation $\succsim$ is *rational* if it possesses the following two properties:

(i) *Completeness:* for all $x, y \in X$, we have that $x \succsim y$ or $y \succsim x$ (or both).
(ii) *Transitivity:* For all $x, y, z \in X$, if $x \succsim y$ and $y \succsim z$, then $x \succsim z$.

The assumption that $\succsim$ is complete says that the individual has a well-defined preference between any two possible alternatives. The strength of the completeness assumption should not be underestimated. Introspection quickly reveals how hard it is to evaluate alternatives that are far from the realm of common experience. It takes work and serious reflection to find out one's own preferences. The completeness axiom says that this task has taken place: our decision makers make only meditated choices.

Transitivity is also a strong assumption, and it goes to the heart of the concept of

---

1. The symbol $\iff$ is read as "if and only if." The literature sometimes speaks of $x \succsim y$ as "x is weakly preferred to y" and $x \succ y$ as "x is strictly preferred to y." We shall adhere to the terminology introduced above.

2. Note that there is no unified terminology in the literature; *weak order* and *complete preorder* are common alternatives to the term *rational preference relation*. Also, in some presentations, the assumption that $\succsim$ is *reflexive* (defined as $x \succsim x$ for all $x \in X$) is added to the completeness and transitivity assumptions. This property is, in fact, implied by completeness and so is redundant.

rationality. Transitivity implies that it is impossible to face the decision maker with a sequence of pairwise choices in which her preferences appear to cycle: for example, feeling that an apple is at least as good as a banana and that a banana is at least as good as an orange but then also preferring an orange over an apple. Like the completeness property, the transitivity assumption can be hard to satisfy when evaluating alternatives far from common experience. As compared to the completeness property, however, it is also more fundamental in the sense that substantial portions of economic theory would not survive if economic agents could not be assumed to have transitive preferences.

The assumption that the preference relation $\succsim$ is complete and transitive has implications for the strict preference and indifference relations $\succ$ and $\sim$. These are summarized in Proposition 1.B.1, whose proof we forgo. (After completing this section, try to establish these properties yourself in Exercises 1.B.1 and 1.B.2.)

**Proposition 1.B.1:** If $\succsim$ is rational then:

    (i) $\succ$ is both *irreflexive* ($x \succ x$ never holds) and *transitive* (if $x \succ y$ and $y \succ z$, then $x \succ z$).

    (ii) $\sim$ is *reflexive* ($x \sim x$ for all $x$), *transitive* (if $x \sim y$ and $y \sim z$, then $x \sim z$), and *symmetric* (if $x \sim y$, then $y \sim x$).

    (iii) if $x \succ y \succsim z$, then $x \succ z$.

The irreflexivity of $\succ$ and the reflexivity and symmetry of $\sim$ are sensible properties for strict preference and indifference relations. A more important point in Proposition 1.B.1 is that rationality of $\succsim$ implies that both $\succ$ and $\sim$ are transitive. In addition, a transitive-like property also holds for $\succ$ when it is combined with an at-least-as-good-as relation, $\succsim$.

An individual's preferences may fail to satisfy the transitivity property for a number of reasons. One difficulty arises because of the problem of *just perceptible differences*. For example, if we ask an individual to choose between two very similar shades of gray for painting her room, she may be unable to tell the difference between the colors and will therefore be indifferent. Suppose now that we offer her a choice between the lighter of the two gray paints and a slightly lighter shade. She may again be unable to tell the difference. If we continue in this fashion, letting the paint colors get progressively lighter with each successive choice experiment, she may express indifference at each step. Yet, if we offer her a choice between the original (darkest) shade of gray and the final (almost white) color, she would be able to distinguish between the colors and is likely to prefer one of them. This, however, violates transitivity.

Another potential problem arises when the manner in which alternatives are presented matters for choice. This is known as the *framing* problem. Consider the following example, paraphrased from Kahneman and Tversky (1984):

> Imagine that you are about to purchase a stereo for 125 dollars and a calculator for 15 dollars. The salesman tells you that the calculator is on sale for 5 dollars less at the other branch of the store, located 20 minutes away. The stereo is the same price there. Would you make the trip to the other store?

It turns out that the fraction of respondents saying that they would travel to the other store for the 5 dollar discount is much higher than the fraction who say they would travel when the question is changed so that the 5 dollar saving is on the stereo. This is so even though the ultimate saving obtained by incurring the inconvenience of travel is the same in both cases.[3] Indeed, we would expect indifference to be the response to the following question:

> Because of a stockout you must travel to the other store to get the two items, but you will receive 5 dollars off on either item as compensation. Do you care on which item this 5 dollar rebate is given?

If so, however, the individual violates transitivity. To see this, denote

$x$ = Travel to the other store and get a 5 dollar discount on the calculator.

$y$ = Travel to the other store and get a 5 dollar discount on the stereo.

$z$ = Buy both items at the first store.

The first two choices say that $x \succ z$ and $z \succ y$, but the last choice reveals $x \sim y$. Many problems of framing arise when individuals are faced with choices between alternatives that have uncertain outcomes (the subject of Chapter 6). Kahneman and Tversky (1984) provide a number of other interesting examples.

At the same time, it is often the case that apparently intransitive behavior can be explained fruitfully as the result of the interaction of several more primitive rational (and thus transitive) preferences. Consider the following two examples

(i) A household formed by Mom ($M$), Dad ($D$), and Child ($C$) makes decisions by majority voting. The alternatives for Friday evening entertainment are attending an opera ($O$), a rock concert ($R$), or an ice-skating show ($I$). The three members of the household have the rational individual preferences: $O \succ_M R \succ_M I$, $I \succ_D O \succ_D R$, $R \succ_C I \succ_C O$, where $\succ_M$, $\succ_D$, $\succ_C$ are the transitive individual strict preference relations. Now imagine three majority-rule votes: $O$ versus $R$, $R$ versus $I$, and $I$ versus $O$. The result of these votes ($O$ will win the first, $R$ the second, and $I$ the third) will make the household's preferences $\succsim$ have the intransitive form: $O \succ R \succ I \succ O$. (The intransitivity illustrated in this example is known as the *Condorcet paradox*, and it is a central difficulty for the theory of group decision making. For further discussion, see Chapter 21.)

(ii) Intransitive decisions may also sometimes be viewed as a manifestation of a change of tastes. For example, a potential cigarette smoker may prefer smoking one cigarette a day to not smoking and may prefer not smoking to smoking heavily. But once she is smoking one cigarette a day, her tastes may change, and she may wish to increase the amount that she smokes. Formally, letting $y$ be abstinence, $x$ be smoking one cigarette a day, and $z$ be heavy smoking, her initial situation is $y$, and her preferences in that initial situation are $x \succ y \succ z$. But once $x$ is chosen over $y$ and $z$, and there is a change of the individual's current situation from $y$ to $x$, her tastes change to $z \succ x \succ y$. Thus, we apparently have an intransitivity: $z \succ x \succ z$. This *change-of-tastes* model has an important theoretical bearing on the analysis of addictive behavior. It also raises interesting issues related to commitment in decision making [see Schelling (1979)]. A rational decision maker will anticipate the induced change of tastes and will therefore attempt to tie her hand to her initial decision (Ulysses had himself tied to the mast when approaching the island of the Sirens).

It often happens that this change-of-tastes point of view gives us a well-structured way to think about *nonrational* decisions. See Elster (1979) for philosophical discussions of this and similar points.

---

## Utility Functions

In economics, we often describe preference relations by means of a *utility function*. A utility function $u(x)$ assigns a numerical value to each element in $X$, ranking the

---

3. Kahneman and Tversky attribute this finding to individuals keeping "mental accounts" in which the savings are compared to the price of the item on which they are received.

elements of $X$ in accordance with the individual's preferences. This is stated more precisely in Definition 1.B.2.

**Definition 1.B.2:** A function $u: X \to \mathbb{R}$ is a *utility function representing preference relation* $\succsim$ if, for all $x, y \in X$,

$$x \succsim y \Leftrightarrow u(x) \geq u(y).$$

Note that a utility function that represents a preference relation $\succsim$ is not unique. For any strictly increasing function $f: \mathbb{R} \to \mathbb{R}$, $v(x) = f(u(x))$ is a new utility function representing the same preferences as $u(\cdot)$; see Exercise 1.B.3. It is only the ranking of alternatives that matters. Properties of utility functions that are invariant for any strictly increasing transformation are called *ordinal*. *Cardinal* properties are those not preserved under all such transformations. Thus, the preference relation associated with a utility function is an ordinal property. On the other hand, the numerical values associated with the alternatives in $X$, and hence the magnitude of any differences in the utility measure between alternatives, are cardinal properties.

The ability to represent preferences by a utility function is closely linked to the assumption of rationality. In particular, we have the result shown in Proposition 1.B.2.

**Proposition 1.B.2:** A preference relation $\succsim$ can be represented by a utility function only if it is rational.

**Proof:** To prove this proposition, we show that if there is a utility function that represents preferences $\succsim$, then $\succsim$ must be complete and transitive.

*Completeness.* Because $u(\cdot)$ is a real-valued function defined on $X$, it must be that for any $x, y \in X$, either $u(x) \geq u(y)$ or $u(y) \geq u(x)$. But because $u(\cdot)$ is a utility function representing $\succsim$, this implies either that $x \succsim y$ or that $y \succsim x$ (recall Definition 1.B.2). Hence, $\succsim$ must be complete.

*Transitivity.* Suppose that $x \succsim y$ and $y \succsim z$. Because $u(\cdot)$ represents $\succsim$, we must have $u(x) \geq u(y)$ and $u(y) \geq u(z)$. Therefore, $u(x) \geq u(z)$. Because $u(\cdot)$ represents $\succsim$, this implies $x \succsim z$. Thus, we have shown that $x \succsim y$ and $y \succsim z$ imply $x \succsim z$, and so transitivity is established. ∎

At the same time, one might wonder, can *any* rational preference relation $\succsim$ be described by some utility function? It turns out that, in general, the answer is no. An example where it is not possible to do so will be discussed in Section 3.G. One case in which we can always represent a rational preference relation with a utility function arises when $X$ is finite (see Exercise 1.B.5). More interesting utility representation results (e.g., for sets of alternatives that are not finite) will be presented in later chapters.

# 1.C Choice Rules

In the second approach to the theory of decision making, choice behavior itself is taken to be the primitive object of the theory. Formally, choice behavior is represented by means of a *choice structure*. A choice structure $(\mathcal{B}, C(\cdot))$ consists of two ingredients:

(i) $\mathscr{B}$ is a family (a set) of nonempty subsets of $X$; that is, every element of $\mathscr{B}$ is a set $B \subset X$. By analogy with the consumer theory to be developed in Chapters 2 and 3, we call the elements $B \in \mathscr{B}$ *budget sets*. The budget sets in $\mathscr{B}$ should be thought of as an exhaustive listing of all the choice experiments that the institutionally, physically, or otherwise restricted social situation can conceivably pose to the decision maker. It need not, however, include all possible subsets of $X$. Indeed, in the case of consumer demand studied in later chapters, it will not.

(ii) $C(\cdot)$ is a *choice rule* (technically, it is a correspondence) that assigns a nonempty set of chosen elements $C(B) \subset B$ for every budget set $B \in \mathscr{B}$. When $C(B)$ contains a single element, that element is the individual's choice from among the alternatives in $B$. The set $C(B)$ may, however, contain more than one element. When it does, the elements of $C(B)$ are the alternatives in $B$ that the decision maker *might* choose; that is, they are her *acceptable alternatives* in $B$. In this case, the set $C(B)$ can be thought of as containing those alternatives that we would actually see chosen if the decision maker were repeatedly to face the problem of choosing an alternative from set $B$.

**Example 1.C.1:** Suppose that $X = \{x, y, z\}$ and $\mathscr{B} = \{\{x, y\}, \{x, y, z\}\}$. One possible choice structure is $(\mathscr{B}, C_1(\cdot))$, where the choice rule $C_1(\cdot)$ is: $C_1(\{x, y\}) = \{x\}$ and $C_1(\{x, y, z\}) = \{x\}$. In this case, we see $x$ chosen no matter what budget the decision maker faces.

Another possible choice structure is $(\mathscr{B}, C_2(\cdot))$, where the choice rule $C_2(\cdot)$ is: $C_2(\{x, y\}) = \{x\}$ and $C_2(\{x, y, z\}) = \{x, y\}$. In this case, we see $x$ chosen whenever the decision maker faces budget $\{x, y\}$, but we may see either $x$ or $y$ chosen when she faces budget $\{x, y, z\}$. ∎

When using choice structures to model individual behavior, we may want to impose some "reasonable" restrictions regarding an individual's choice behavior. An important assumption, the weak axiom of revealed preference [first suggested by Samuelson; see Chapter 5 in Samuelson (1947)], reflects the expectation that an individual's observed choices will display a certain amount of consistency. For example, if an individual chooses alternative $x$ (and only that) when faced with a choice between $x$ and $y$, we would be surprised to see her choose $y$ when faced with a decision among $x$, $y$, and a third alterative $z$. The idea is that the choice of $x$ when facing the alternatives $\{x, y\}$ reveals a proclivity for choosing $x$ over $y$ that we should expect to see reflected in the individual's behavior when faced with the alternatives $\{x, y, z\}$.[4]

The weak axiom is stated formally in Definition 1.C.1.

**Definition 1.C.1:** The choice structure $(\mathscr{B}, C(\cdot))$ satisfies the *weak axiom of revealed preference* if the following property holds:

If for some $B \in \mathscr{B}$ with $x, y \in B$ we have $x \in C(B)$, then for any $B' \in \mathscr{B}$ with $x, y \in B'$ and $y \in C(B')$, we must also have $x \in C(B')$.

In words, the weak axiom says that if $x$ is ever chosen when $y$ is available, then there can be no budget set containing both alternatives for which $y$ is chosen and $x$ is not.

---

4. This proclivity might reflect some underlying "preference" for $x$ over $y$ but might also arise in other ways. It could, for example, be the result of some evolutionary process.

Note how the assumption that choice behavior satisfies the weak axiom captures the consistency idea: If $C(\{x, y\}) = \{x\}$, then the weak axiom says that we cannot have $C(\{x, y, z\}) = \{y\}$.[5]

A somewhat simpler statement of the weak axiom can be obtained by defining a *revealed preference relation* $\succsim^*$ from the observed choice behavior in $C(\cdot)$.

**Definition 1.C.2:** Given a choice structure $(\mathscr{B}, C(\cdot))$ the *revealed preference relation* $\succsim^*$ is defined by

$$x \succsim^* y \Leftrightarrow \text{there is some } B \in \mathscr{B} \text{ such that } x, y \in B \text{ and } x \in C(B).$$

We read $x \succsim^* y$ as "$x$ is revealed at least as good as $y$." Note that the revealed preference relation $\succsim^*$ need not be either complete or transitive. In particular, for any pair of alternatives $x$ and $y$ to be comparable, it is necessary that, for some $B \in \mathscr{B}$, we have $x, y \in B$ and either $x \in C(B)$ or $y \in C(B)$, or both.

We might also informally say that "$x$ is revealed preferred to $y$" if there is some $B \in \mathscr{B}$ such that $x, y \in B$, $x \in C(B)$, and $y \notin C(B)$, that is, if $x$ is ever chosen over $y$ when both are feasible.

With this terminology, we can restate the weak axiom as follows: "*If $x$ is revealed at least as good as $y$, then $y$ cannot be revealed preferred to $x$.*"

**Example 1.C.2:** Do the two choice structures considered in Example 1.C.1 satisfy the weak axiom? Consider choice structure $(\mathscr{B}, C_1(\cdot))$. With this choice structure, we have $x \succsim^* y$ and $x \succsim^* z$, but there is no revealed preference relationship that can be inferred between $y$ and $z$. This choice structure satisfies the weak axiom because $y$ and $z$ are never chosen.

Now consider choice structure $(\mathscr{B}, C_2(\cdot))$. Because $C_2(\{x, y, z\}) = \{x, y\}$, we have $y \succsim^* x$ (as well as $x \succsim^* y$, $x \succsim^* z$, and $y \succsim^* z$). But because $C_2(\{x, y\}) = \{x\}$, $x$ is revealed preferred to $y$. Therefore, the choice structure $(\mathscr{B}, C_2)$ violates the weak axiom. ∎

We should note that the weak axiom is not the only assumption concerning choice behavior that we may want to impose in any particular setting. For example, in the consumer demand setting discussed in Chapter 2, we impose further conditions that arise naturally in that context.

The weak axiom restricts choice behavior in a manner that parallels the use of the rationality assumption for preference relations. This raises a question: What is the precise relationship between the two approaches? In Section 1.D, we explore this matter.

# 1.D The Relationship between Preference Relations and Choice Rules

We now address two fundamental questions regarding the relationship between the two approaches discussed so far:

---

5. In fact, it says more: We must have $C(\{x, y, z\}) = \{x\}$, $= \{z\}$, or $= \{x, z\}$. You are asked to show this in Exercise 1.C.1. See also Exercise 1.C.2.

(i) If a decision maker has a rational preference ordering $\succsim$, do her decisions when facing choices from budget sets in $\mathscr{B}$ necessarily generate a choice structure that satisfies the weak axiom?

(ii) If an individual's choice behavior for a family of budget sets $\mathscr{B}$ is captured by a choice structure $(\mathscr{B}, C(\cdot))$ satisfying the weak axiom, is there necessarily a rational preference relation that is consistent with these choices?

As we shall see, the answers to these two questions are, respectively, "yes" and "maybe".

To answer the first question, suppose that an individual has a rational preference relation $\succsim$ on $X$. If this individual faces a nonempty subset of alternatives $B \subset X$, her preference-maximizing behavior is to choose any one of the elements in the set:

$$C^*(B, \succsim) = \{x \in B : x \succsim y \text{ for every } y \in B\}$$

The elements of set $C^*(B, \succsim)$ are the decision maker's most preferred alternatives in $B$. In principle, we could have $C^*(B, \succsim) = \varnothing$ for some $B$; but if $X$ is finite, or if suitable (continuity) conditions hold, then $C^*(B, \succsim)$ will be nonempty.[6] From now on, we will consider only preferences $\succsim$ and families of budget sets $\mathscr{B}$ such that $C^*(B, \succsim)$ is nonempty for all $B \in \mathscr{B}$. We say that the rational preference relation $\succsim$ *generates* the choice structure $(\mathscr{B}, C^*(\cdot, \succsim))$.

The result in Proposition 1.D.1 tells us that any choice structure generated by rational preferences necessarily satisfies the weak axiom.

**Proposition 1.D.1:** Suppose that $\succsim$ is a rational preference relation. Then the choice structure generated by $\succsim$, $(\mathscr{B}, C^*(\cdot, \succsim))$, satisfies the weak axiom.

**Proof:** Suppose that for some $B \in \mathscr{B}$, we have $x, y \in B$ and $x \in C^*(B, \succsim)$. By the definition of $C^*(B, \succsim)$, this implies $x \succsim y$. To check whether the weak axiom holds, suppose that for some $B' \in \mathscr{B}$ with $x, y \in B'$, we have $y \in C^*(B', \succsim)$. This implies that $y \succsim z$ for all $z \in B'$. But we already know that $x \succsim y$. Hence, by transitivity, $x \succsim z$ for all $z \in B'$, and so $x \in C^*(B', \succsim)$. This is precisely the conclusion that the weak axiom demands.  ∎

Proposition 1.D.1 constitutes the "yes" answer to our first question. That is, if behavior is generated by rational preferences then it satisfies the consistency requirements embodied in the weak axiom.

In the other direction (from choice to preferences), the relationship is more subtle. To answer this second question, it is useful to begin with a definition.

**Definition 1.D.1:** Given a choice structure $(\mathscr{B}, C(\cdot))$, we say that the rational preference relation $\succsim$ *rationalizes* $C(\cdot)$ relative to $\mathscr{B}$ if

$$C(B) = C^*(B, \succsim)$$

for all $B \in \mathscr{B}$, that is, if $\succsim$ generates the choice structure $(\mathscr{B}, C(\cdot))$.

In words, the rational preference relation $\succsim$ rationalizes choice rule $C(\cdot)$ on $\mathscr{B}$ if the optimal choices generated by $\succsim$ (captured by $C^*(\cdot, \succsim)$) coincide with $C(\cdot)$ for

---

6. Exercise 1.D.2 asks you to establish the nonemptiness of $C^*(B, \succsim)$ for the case where $X$ is finite. For general results, See Section M.F of the Mathematical Appendix and Section 3.C for a specific application.

all budget sets in $\mathscr{B}$. In a sense, preferences explain behavior; we can interpret the decision maker's choices as if she were a preference maximizer. Note that in general, there may be more than one rationalizing preference relation $\succsim$ for a given choice structure $(\mathscr{B}, C(\cdot))$ (see Exercise 1.D.1).

Proposition 1.D.1 implies that the weak axiom must be satisfied if there is to be a rationalizing preference relation. In particular, since $C^*(\cdot, \succsim)$ satisfies the weak axiom for any $\succsim$, only a choice rule that satisfies the weak axiom can be rationalized. It turns out, however, that the weak axiom is not sufficient to ensure the existence of a rationalizing preference relation.

**Example 1.D.1:** Suppose that $X = \{x, y, z\}$, $\mathscr{B} = \{\{x, y\}, \{y, z\}, \{x, z\}\}$, $C(\{x, y\}) = \{x\}$, $C(\{y, z\}) = \{y\}$, and $C(\{x, z\}) = \{z\}$. This choice structure satisfies the weak axiom (you should verify this). Nevertheless, we cannot have rationalizing preferences. To see this, note that to rationalize the choices under $\{x, y\}$ and $\{y, z\}$ it would be necessary for us to have $x \succ y$ and $y \succ z$. But, by transitivity, we would then have $x \succ z$, which contradicts the choice behavior under $\{x, z\}$. Therefore, there can be no rationalizing preference relation. ∎

To understand Example 1.D.1, note that the more budget sets there are in $\mathscr{B}$, the more the weak axiom restricts choice behavior; there are simply more opportunities for the decision maker's choices to contradict one another. In Example 1.D.1, the set $\{x, y, z\}$ is not an element of $\mathscr{B}$. As it happens, this is crucial (see Exercises 1.D.3). As we now show in Proposition 1.D.2, if the family of budget sets $\mathscr{B}$ includes enough subsets of $X$, and if $(\mathscr{B}, C(\cdot))$ satisfies the weak axiom, then there exists a rational preference relation that rationalizes $C(\cdot)$ relative to $\mathscr{B}$ [this was first shown by Arrow (1959)].

**Proposition 1.D.2:** If $(\mathscr{B}, C(\cdot))$ is a choice structure such that

    (i) the weak axiom is satisfied,

    (ii) $\mathscr{B}$ includes all subsets of $X$ of up to three elements,

then there is a rational preference relation $\succsim$ that rationalizes $C(\cdot)$ relative to $\mathscr{B}$; that is, $C(B) = C^*(B, \succsim)$ for all $B \in \mathscr{B}$. Furthermore, this rational preference relation is the *only* preference relation that does so.

---

**Proof:** The natural candidate for a rationalizing preference relation is the revealed preference relation $\succsim^*$. To prove the result, we must first show two things: (i) that $\succsim^*$ is a rational preference relation, and (ii) that $\succsim^*$ rationalizes $C(\cdot)$ on $\mathscr{B}$. We then argue, as point (iii), that $\succsim^*$ is the unique preference relation that does so.

**(i)** We first check that $\succsim^*$ is rational (i.e., that it satisfies completeness and transitivity).

*Completeness* By assumption (ii), $\{x, y\} \in \mathscr{B}$. Since either $x$ or $y$ must be an element of $C(\{x, y\})$, we must have $x \succsim^* y$, or $y \succsim^* x$, or both. Hence $\succsim^*$ is complete.

*Transitivity* Let $x \succsim^* y$ and $y \succsim^* z$. Consider the budget set $\{x, y, z\} \in \mathscr{B}$. It suffices to prove that $x \in C(\{x, y, z\})$, since this implies by the definition of $\succsim^*$ that $x \succsim^* z$. Because $C(\{x, y, z\}) \neq \varnothing$, at least one of the alternatives $x$, $y$, or $z$ must be an element of $C(\{x, y, z\})$. Suppose that $y \in C(\{x, y, z\})$. Since $x \succsim^* y$, the weak axiom then yields $x \in C(\{x, y, z\})$, as we want. Suppose instead that $z \in C(\{x, y, z\})$; since $y \succsim^* z$, the weak axiom yields $y \in C(\{x, y, z\})$, and we are in the previous case.

**(ii)** We now show that $C(B) = C^*(B, \succsim^*)$ for all $B \in \mathscr{B}$; that is, the revealed preference relation $\succsim^*$ inferred from $C(\cdot)$ actually generates $C(\cdot)$. Intuitively, this seems sensible. Formally, we show this in two steps. First, suppose that $x \in C(B)$. Then $x \succsim^* y$ for all $y \in B$; so we have $x \in C^*(B, \succsim^*)$. This means that $C(B) \subset C^*(B, \succsim^*)$. Next, suppose that $x \in C^*(B, \succsim^*)$. This implies that $x \succsim^* y$ for *all* $y \in B$; and so for each $y \in B$, there must exist some set $B_y \in \mathscr{B}$ such that $x, y \in B_y$ and $x \in C(B_y)$. Because $C(B) \neq \varnothing$, the weak axiom then implies that $x \in C(B)$. Hence, $C^*(B, \succsim^*) \subset C(B)$. Together, these inclusion relations imply that $C(B) = C^*(B, \succsim^*)$.

**(iii)** To establish uniqueness, simply note that because $\mathscr{B}$ includes all two-element subsets of $X$, the choice behavior in $C(\cdot)$ completely determines the pairwise preference relations over $X$ of any rationalizing preference.

This completes the proof. ∎

We can therefore conclude from Proposition 1.D.2 that for the special case in which choice is defined for all subsets of $X$, a theory based on choice satisfying the weak axiom is completely equivalent to a theory of decision making based on rational preferences. Unfortunately, this special case is too special for economics. For many situations of economic interest, such as the theory of consumer demand, choice is defined only for special kinds of budget sets. In these settings, the weak axiom does not exhaust the choice implications of rational preferences. We shall see in Section 3.J, however, that a strengthening of the weak axiom (which imposes more restrictions on choice behavior) provides a necessary and sufficient condition for behavior to be capable of being rationalized by preferences.

Definition 1.D.1 defines a rationalizing preference as one for which $C(B) = C^*(B, \succsim)$. An alternative notion of a rationalizing preference that appears in the literature requires only that $C(B) \subset C^*(B, \succsim)$; that is, $\succsim$ is said to rationalize $C(\cdot)$ on $\mathscr{B}$ if $C(B)$ is a subset of the most preferred choices generated by $\succsim$, $C^*(B, \succsim)$, for every budget $B \in \mathscr{B}$.

There are two reasons for the possible use of this alternative notion. The first is, in a sense, philosophical. We might want to allow the decision maker to resolve her indifference in some specific manner, rather than insisting that indifference means that anything might be picked. The view embodied in Definition 1.D.1 (and implicitly in the weak axiom as well) is that if she chooses in a specific manner then she is, de facto, not indifferent.

The second reason is empirical. If we are trying to determine from data whether an individual's choice is compatible with rational preference maximization, we will in practice have only a finite number of observations on the choices made from any given budget set $B$. If $C(B)$ represents the set of choices made with this limited set of observations, then because these limited observations might not reveal all the decision maker's preference maximizing choices, $C(B) \subset C^*(B, \succsim)$ is the natural requirement to impose for a preference relationship to rationalize observed choice data.

Two points are worth noting about the effects of using this alternative notion. First, it is a weaker requirement. Whenever we can find a preference relation that rationalizes choice in the sense of Definition 1.D.1, we have found one that does so in this other sense, too. Second, in the abstract setting studied here, to find a rationalizing preference relation in this latter sense is actually trivial: Preferences that have the individual indifferent among all elements of $X$ will rationalize *any* choice behavior in this sense. When this alternative notion is used in the economics literature, there is always an insistence that the rationalizing preference relation should satisfy some additional properties that are natural restrictions for the specific economic context being studied.

## REFERENCES

Arrow, K. (1959). Rational choice functions and orderings. *Econometrica* **26**: 121–27.

Elster, J. (1979). *Ulysses and the Sirens.* Cambridge, U.K.: Cambridge University Press.

Kahneman, D., and A. Tversky. (1984). Choices, values, and frames. *American Psychologist* **39**: 341–50.

Plott, C. R. (1973). Path independence, rationality and social choice. *Econometrica* **41**: 1075–91.

Richter, M. (1971). Rational choice. Chap. 2 in *Preferences, Utility and Demand*, edited by J. Chipman, L. Hurwicz, and H. Sonnenschein. New York: Harcourt Brace Jovanovich.

Samuelson, P. (1947). *Foundations of Economic Analysis.* Cambridge, Mass.: Harvard University Press.

Schelling, T. (1979). *Micromotives and Macrobehavior.* New York: Norton.

Thurstone, L. L. (1927). A law of comparative judgement. *Psychological Review* **34**: 275–86.

## EXERCISES

**1.B.1$^B$** Prove property (iii) of Proposition 1.B.1.

**1.B.2$^A$** Prove properties (i) and (ii) of Proposition 1.B.1.

**1.B.3$^B$** Show that if $f: \mathbb{R} \to \mathbb{R}$ is a strictly increasing function and $u: X \to \mathbb{R}$ is a utility function representing preference relation $\succsim$, then the function $v: X \to \mathbb{R}$ defined by $v(x) = f(u(x))$ is also a utility function representing preference relation $\succsim$.

**1.B.4$^A$** Consider a rational preference relation $\succsim$. Show that if $u(x) = u(y)$ implies $x \sim y$ and if $u(x) > u(y)$ implies $x \succ y$, then $u(\cdot)$ is a utility function representing $\succsim$.

**1.B.5$^B$** Show that if $X$ is finite and $\succsim$ is a rational preference relation on $X$, then there is a utility function $u: X \to \mathbb{R}$ that represents $\succsim$. [*Hint*: Consider first the case in which the individual's ranking between any two elements of $X$ is strict (i.e., there is never any indifference), and construct a utility function representing these preferences; then extend your argument to the general case.]

**1.C.1$^B$** Consider the choice structure $(\mathscr{B}, C(\cdot))$ with $\mathscr{B} = (\{x, y\}, \{x, y, z\})$ and $C(\{x, y\}) = \{x\}$. Show that if $(\mathscr{B}, C(\cdot))$ satisfies the weak axiom, then we must have $C(\{x, y, z\}) = \{x\}, = \{z\}$, or $= \{x, z\}$.

**1.C.2$^B$** Show that the weak axiom (Definition 1.C.1) is equivalent to the following property holding:

> Suppose that $B, B' \in \mathscr{B}$, that $x, y \in B$, and that $x, y \in B'$. Then if $x \in C(B)$ and $y \in C(B')$, we must have $\{x, y\} \subset C(B)$ and $\{x, y\} \subset C(B')$.

**1.C.3$^C$** Suppose that choice structure $(\mathscr{B}, C(\cdot))$ satisfies the weak axiom. Consider the following two possible revealed preferred relations, $\succ^*$ and $\succ^{**}$:

$x \succ^* y \Leftrightarrow$ there is some $B \in \mathscr{B}$ such that $x, y \in B$, $x \in C(B)$, and $y \notin C(B)$

$x \succ^{**} y \Leftrightarrow x \succsim^* y$ but not $y \succsim^* x$

where $\succsim^*$ is the revealed at-least-as-good-as relation defined in Definition 1.C.2.

(a) Show that $\succ^*$ and $\succ^{**}$ give the same relation over $X$; that is, for any $x, y \in X$, $x \succ^* y \Leftrightarrow x \succ^{**} y$. Is this still true if $(\mathscr{B}, C(\cdot))$ does not satisfy the weak axiom?

(b) Must $\succ^*$ be transitive?

(c) Show that if $\mathscr{B}$ includes all three-element subsets of $X$, then $\succ^*$ is transitive.

**1.D.1$^B$** Give an example of a choice structure that can be rationalized by several preference relations. Note that if the family of budgets $\mathscr{B}$ includes all the two-element subsets of $X$, then there can be at most one rationalizing preference relation.

**1.D.2**[A] Show that if $X$ is finite, then any rational preference relation generates a nonempty choice rule; that is, $C(B) \neq \emptyset$ for any $B \subset X$ with $B \neq \emptyset$.

**1.D.3**[B] Let $X = \{x, y, z\}$, and consider the choice structure $(\mathscr{B}, C(\cdot))$ with

$$\mathscr{B} = \{\{x, y\}, \{y, z\}, \{x, z\}, \{x, y, z\}\}$$

and $C(\{x, y\}) = \{x\}$, $C(\{y, z\}) = \{y\}$, and $C(\{x, z\}) = \{z\}$, as in Example 1.D.1. Show that $(\mathscr{B}, C(\cdot))$ must violate the weak axiom.

**1.D.4**[B] Show that a choice structure $(\mathscr{B}, C(\cdot))$ for which a rationalizing preference relation $\succsim$ exists satisfies the *path-invariance* property: For every pair $B_1, B_2 \in \mathscr{B}$ such that $B_1 \cup B_2 \in \mathscr{B}$ and $C(B_1) \cup C(B_2) \in \mathscr{B}$, we have $C(B_1 \cup B_2) = C(C(B_1) \cup C(B_2))$, that is, the decision problem can safely be subdivided. See Plott (1973) for further discussion.

**1.D.5**[C] Let $X = \{x, y, z\}$ and $\mathscr{B} = \{\{x, y\}, \{y, z\}, \{z, x\}\}$. Suppose that choice is now stochastic in the sense that, for every $B \in \mathscr{B}$, $C(B)$ is a frequency distribution over alternatives in $B$. For example, if $B = \{x, y\}$, we write $C(B) = (C_x(B), C_y(B))$, where $C_x(B)$ and $C_y(B)$ are nonnegative numbers with $C_x(B) + C_y(B) = 1$. We say that the stochastic choice function $C(\cdot)$ can be *rationalized by preferences* if we can find a probability distribution $Pr$ over the six possible (strict) preference relations on $X$ such that for every $B \in \mathscr{B}$, $C(B)$ is precisely the frequency of choices induced by $Pr$. For example, if $B = \{x, y\}$, then $C_x(B) = Pr(\{\succ : x \succ y\})$. This concept originates in Thurstone (1927), and it is of considerable econometric interest (indeed, it provides a theory for the error term in observable choice).

(a) Show that the stochastic choice function $C(\{x, y\}) = C(\{y, z\}) = C(\{z, x\}) = (\frac{1}{2}, \frac{1}{2})$ can be rationalized by preferences.

(b) Show that the stochastic choice function $C(\{x, y\}) = C(\{y, z\}) = C(\{z, x\}) = (\frac{1}{4}, \frac{3}{4})$ is not rationalizable by preferences.

(c) Determine the $0 < \alpha < 1$ at which $C(\{x, y\}) = C(\{y, z\}) = C(\{z, x\}) = (\alpha, 1 - \alpha)$ switches from rationalizable to nonrationalizable.

# Consumer Choice

## 2.A Introduction

The most fundamental decision unit of microeconomic theory is the *consumer*. In this chapter, we begin our study of consumer demand in the context of a market economy. By a *market economy*, we mean a setting in which the goods and services that the consumer may acquire are available for purchase at known prices (or, equivalently, are available for trade for other goods at known rates of exchange).

We begin, in Sections 2.B to 2.D, by describing the basic elements of the consumer's decision problem. In Section 2.B, we introduce the concept of *commodities*, the objects of choice for the consumer. Then, in Sections 2.C and 2.D, we consider the physical and economic constraints that limit the consumer's choices. The former are captured in the *consumption set*, which we discuss in Section 2.C; the latter are incorporated in Section 2.D into the consumer's *Walrasian budget set*.

The consumer's decision subject to these constraints is captured in the consumer's *Walrasian demand function*. In terms of the choice-based approach to individual decision making introduced in Section 1.C, the Walrasian demand function is the consumer's choice rule. We study this function and some of its basic properties in Section 2.E. Among them are what we call *comparative statics* properties: the ways in which consumer demand changes when economic constraints vary.

Finally, in Section 2.F, we consider the implications for the consumer's demand function of the *weak axiom of revealed preference*. The central conclusion we reach is that in the consumer demand setting, the weak axiom is essentially equivalent to the *compensated law of demand*, the postulate that prices and demanded quantities move in opposite directions for price changes that leave real wealth unchanged.

## 2.B Commodities

The decision problem faced by the consumer in a market economy is to choose consumption levels of the various goods and services that are available for purchase in the market. We call these goods and services *commodities*. For simplicity, we assume that the number of commodities is finite and equal to $L$ (indexed by $\ell = 1, \ldots, L$).

As a general matter, a *commodity vector* (or commodity *bundle*) is a list of amounts of the different commodities,

$$x = \begin{bmatrix} x_1 \\ \vdots \\ x_L \end{bmatrix},$$

and can be viewed as a point in $\mathbb{R}^L$, the commodity *space*.[1]

We can use commodity vectors to represent an individual's consumption levels. The $\ell$th entry of the commodity vector stands for the amount of commodity $\ell$ consumed. We then refer to the vector as a *consumption vector* or *consumption bundle*.

Note that time (or, for that matter, location) can be built into the definition of a commodity. Rigorously, bread today and tomorrow should be viewed as distinct commodities. In a similar vein, when we deal with decisions under uncertainty in Chapter 6, viewing bread in different "states of nature" as different commodities can be most helpful.

---

Although commodities consumed at different times should be viewed rigorously as distinct commodities, in practice, economic models often involve some "time aggregation." Thus, one commodity might be "bread consumed in the month of February," even though, in principle, bread consumed at each instant in February should be distinguished. A primary reason for such time aggregation is that the economic data to which the model is being applied are aggregated in this way. The hope of the modeler is that the commodities being aggregated are sufficiently similar that little of economic interest is being lost.

We should also note that in some contexts it becomes convenient, and even necessary, to expand the set of commodities to include goods and services that may potentially be available for purchase but are not actually so and even some that may be available by means other than market exchange (say, the experience of "family togetherness"). For nearly all of what follows here, however, the narrow construction introduced in this section suffices.

---

# 2.C The Consumption Set

Consumption choices are typically limited by a number of physical constraints. The simplest example is when it may be impossible for the individual to consume a negative amount of a commodity such as bread or water.

Formally, the *consumption set* is a subset of the commodity space $\mathbb{R}^L$, denoted by $X \subset \mathbb{R}^L$, whose elements are the consumption bundles that the individual can conceivably consume given the physical constraints imposed by his environment.

Consider the following four examples for the case in which $L = 2$:

(i) Figure 2.C.1 represents possible consumption levels of bread and leisure in a day. Both levels must be nonnegative and, in addition, the consumption of more than 24 hours of leisure in a day is impossible.

(ii) Figure 2.C.2 represents a situation in which the first good is perfectly divisible but the second is available only in nonnegative integer amounts.

(iii) Figure 2.C.3 captures the fact that it is impossible to eat bread at the same

---

1. Negative entries in commodity vectors will often represent debits or net outflows of goods. For example, in Chapter 5, the inputs of a firm are measured as negative numbers.

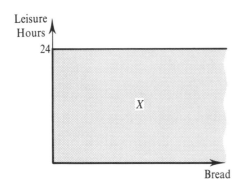

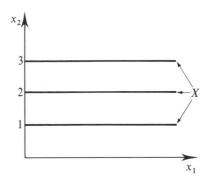

**Figure 2.C.1 (left)**

A consumption set.

**Figure 2.C.2 (right)**

A consumption set where good 2 must be consumed in integer amounts.

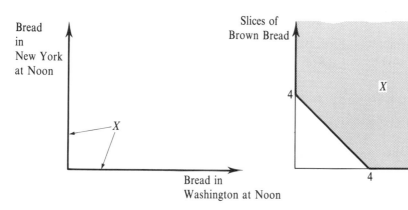

**Figure 2.C.3 (left)**

A consumption set where only one good can be consumed.

**Figure 2.C.4 (right)**

A consumption set reflecting survival needs.

instant in Washington and in New York. [This example is borrowed from Malinvaud (1978).]

(iv) Figure 2.C.4 represents a situation where the consumer requires a minimum of four slices of bread a day to survive and there are two types of bread, brown and white.

In the four examples, the constraints are physical in a very literal sense. But the constraints that we incorporate into the consumption set can also be institutional in nature. For example, a law requiring that no one work more than 16 hours a day would change the consumption set in Figure 2.C.1 to that in Figure 2.C.5.

To keep things as straightforward as possible, we pursue our discussion adopting the simplest sort of consumption set:

$$X = \mathbb{R}_+^L = \{x \in \mathbb{R}^L : x_\ell \geq 0 \text{ for } \ell = 1, \ldots, L\},$$

the set of all nonnegative bundles of commodities. It is represented in Figure 2.C.6. Whenever we consider any consumption set $X$ other than $\mathbb{R}_+^L$, we shall be explicit about it.

One special feature of the set $\mathbb{R}_+^L$ is that it is *convex*. That is, if two consumption bundles $x$ and $x'$ are both elements of $\mathbb{R}_+^L$, then the bundle $x'' = \alpha x + (1 - \alpha)x'$ is also an element of $\mathbb{R}_+^L$ for any $\alpha \in [0, 1]$ (see Section M.G. of the Mathematical Appendix for the definition and properties of convex sets).[2] The consumption sets

---

2. Recall that $x'' = \alpha x + (1 - \alpha)x'$ is a vector whose $\ell$th entry is $x''_\ell = \alpha x_\ell + (1 - \alpha)x'_\ell$.

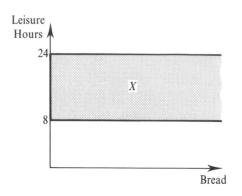

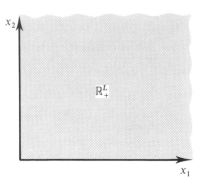

**Figure 2.C.5 (left)**

A consumption set reflecting a legal limit on the number of hours worked.

**Figure 2.C.6 (right)**

The consumption set $\mathbb{R}^L_+$.

in Figures 2.C.1, 2.C.4, 2.C.5, and 2.C.6 are convex sets; those in Figures 2.C.2 and 2.C.3 are not.

Much of the theory to be developed applies for general convex consumption sets as well as for $\mathbb{R}^L_+$. Some of the results, but not all, survive without the assumption of convexity.[3]

## 2.D   Competitive Budgets

In addition to the physical constraints embodied in the consumption set, the consumer faces an important economic constraint: his consumption choice is limited to those commodity bundles that he can afford.

To formalize this constraint, we introduce two assumptions. First, we suppose that the $L$ commodities are all traded in the market at dollar prices that are publicly quoted (this is the *principle of completeness*, or *universality, of markets*). Formally, these prices are represented by the *price vector*

$$p = \begin{bmatrix} p_1 \\ \vdots \\ p_L \end{bmatrix} \in \mathbb{R}^L,$$

which gives the dollar cost for a unit of each of the $L$ commodities. Observe that there is nothing that logically requires prices to be positive. A negative price simply means that a "buyer" is actually paid to consume the commodity (which is not illogical for commodities that are "bads," such as pollution). Nevertheless, for simplicity, here we always assume $p \gg 0$; that is, $p_\ell > 0$ for every $\ell$.

Second, we assume that these prices are beyond the influence of the consumer. This is the so-called *price-taking assumption*. Loosely speaking, this assumption is likely to be valid when the consumer's demand for any commodity represents only a small fraction of the total demand for that good.

The affordability of a consumption bundle depends on two things: the market prices $p = (p_1, \ldots, p_L)$ and the consumer's wealth level (in dollars) $w$. The consumption

---

3. Note that commodity aggregation can help convexify the consumption set. In the example leading to Figure 2.C.3, the consumption set could reasonably be taken to be convex if the axes were instead measuring bread consumption over a period of a month.

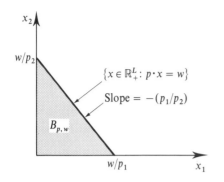

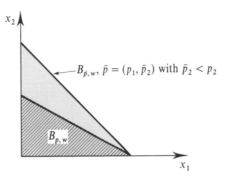

**Figure 2.D.1 (left)**

A Walrasian budget set.

**Figure 2.D.2 (right)**

The effect of a price change on the Walrasian budget set.

bundle $x \in \mathbb{R}_+^L$ is affordable if its total cost does not exceed the consumer's wealth level $w$, that is, if[4]

$$p \cdot x = p_1 x_1 + \cdots + p_L x_L \leq w.$$

This economic-affordability constraint, when combined with the requirement that $x$ lie in the consumption set $\mathbb{R}_+^L$, implies that the set of feasible consumption bundles consists of the elements of the set $\{x \in \mathbb{R}_+^L : p \cdot x \leq w\}$. This set is known as the *Walrasian*, or *competitive budget set* (after Léon Walras).

**Definition 2.D.1:** The *Walrasian, or competitive budget set* $B_{p,w} = \{x \in \mathbb{R}_+^L : p \cdot x \leq w\}$ is the set of all feasible consumption bundles for the consumer who faces market prices $p$ and has wealth $w$.

The *consumer's problem*, given prices $p$ and wealth $w$, can thus be stated as follows: *Choose a consumption bundle $x$ from $B_{p,w}$.*

A Walrasian budget set $B_{p,w}$ is depicted in Figure 2.D.1 for the case of $L = 2$. To focus on the case in which the consumer has a nondegenerate choice problem, we always assume $w > 0$ (otherwise the consumer can afford only $x = 0$).

The set $\{x \in \mathbb{R}^L : p \cdot x = w\}$ is called the *budget hyperplane* (for the case $L = 2$, we call it the *budget line*). It determines the upper boundary of the budget set. As Figure 2.D.1 indicates, the slope of the budget line when $L = 2$, $-(p_1/p_2)$, captures the rate of exchange between the two commodities. If the price of commodity 2 decreases (with $p_1$ and $w$ held fixed), say to $\bar{p}_2 < p_2$, the budget set grows larger because more consumption bundles are affordable, and the budget line becomes steeper. This change is shown in Figure 2.D.2.

Another way to see how the budget hyperplane reflects the relative terms of exchange between commodities comes from examining its geometric relation to the price vector $p$. The price vector $p$, drawn starting from any point $\bar{x}$ on the budget hyperplane, must be orthogonal (perpendicular) to any vector starting at $\bar{x}$ and lying

---

4. Often, this constraint is described in the literature as requiring that the cost of planned purchases not exceed the consumer's *income*. In either case, the idea is that the cost of purchases not exceed the consumer's available resources. We use the wealth terminology to emphasize that the consumer's actual problem may be intertemporal, with the commodities involving purchases over time, and the resource constraint being one of lifetime income (i.e., wealth) (see Exercise 2.D.1).

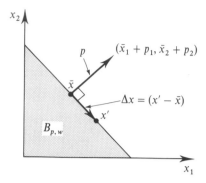

**Figure 2.D.3**

The geometric relationship between $p$ and the budget hyperplane.

on the budget hyperplane, This is so because for any $x'$ that itself lies on the budget hyperplane, we have $p \cdot x' = p \cdot \bar{x} = w$. Hence, $p \cdot \Delta x = 0$ for $\Delta x = (x' - \bar{x})$. Figure 2.D.3 depicts this geometric relationship for the case $L = 2$.[5]

The Walrasian budget set $B_{p,w}$ is a *convex* set: That is, if bundles $x$ and $x'$ are both elements of $B_{p,w}$, then the bundle $x'' = \alpha x + (1 - \alpha)x'$ is also. To see this, note first that because both $x$ and $x'$ are nonnegative, $x'' \in \mathbb{R}^L_+$. Second, since $p \cdot x \leq w$ and $p \cdot x' \leq w$, we have $p \cdot x'' = \alpha(p \cdot x) + (1 - \alpha)(p \cdot x') \leq w$. Thus, $x'' \in B_{p,w} = \{x \in \mathbb{R}^L_+ : p \cdot x \leq w\}$.

The convexity of $B_{p,w}$ plays a significant role in the development that follows. Note that the convexity of $B_{p,w}$ depends on the convexity of the consumption set $\mathbb{R}^L_+$. With a more general consumption set $X$, $B_{p,w}$ will be convex as long as $X$ is. (See Exercise 2.D.3.)

---

Although Walrasian budget sets are of central theoretical interest, they are by no means the only type of budget set that a consumer might face in any actual situation. For example, a more realistic description of the market trade-off between a consumption good and leisure, involving taxes, subsidies, and several wage rates, is illustrated in Figure 2.D.4. In the figure, the price of the consumption good is 1, and the consumer earns wage rate $s$ per hour for the first 8 hours of work and $s' > s$ for additional ("overtime") hours. He also faces a tax rate $t$

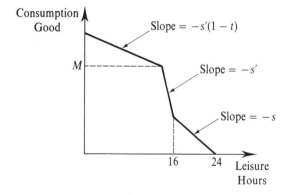

**Figure 2.D.4**

A more realistic description of the consumer's budget set.

5. To draw the vector $p$ starting from $\bar{x}$, we draw a vector from point $(\bar{x}_1, \bar{x}_2)$ to point $(\bar{x}_1 + p_1, \bar{x}_2 + p_2)$. Thus, when we draw the price vector in this diagram, we use the "units" on the axes to represent units of prices rather than goods.

per dollar on labor income earned above amount $M$. Note that the budget set in Figure 2.D.4 is not convex (you are asked to show this in Exercise 2.D.4). More complicated examples can readily be constructed and arise commonly in applied work. See Deaton and Muellbauer (1980) and Burtless and Hausmann (1975) for more illustrations of this sort.

# 2.E Demand Functions and Comparative Statics

The consumer's *Walrasian* (or *market*, or *ordinary*) *demand correspondence* $x(p, w)$ assigns a set of chosen consumption bundles for each price–wealth pair $(p, w)$. In principle, this correspondence can be multivalued; that is, there may be more than one possible consumption vector assigned for a given price–wealth pair $(p, w)$. When this is so, any $x \in x(p, w)$ might be chosen by the consumer when he faces price–wealth pair $(p, w)$. When $x(p, w)$ is single-valued, we refer to it as a *demand function*.

Throughout this chapter, we maintain two assumptions regarding the Walrasian demand correspondence $x(p, w)$: That it is *homogeneous of degree zero* and that it satisfies *Walras' law*.

**Definition 2.E.1:** The Walrasian demand correspondence $x(p, w)$ is *homogeneous of degree zero* if $x(\alpha p, \alpha w) = x(p, w)$ for any $p$, $w$ and $\alpha > 0$.

Homogeneity of degree zero says that if both prices and wealth change in the same proportion, then the individual's consumption choice does not change. To understand this property, note that a change in prices and wealth from $(p, w)$ to $(\alpha p, \alpha w)$ leads to no change in the consumer's set of feasible consumption bundles; that is, $B_{p,w} = B_{\alpha p, \alpha w}$. Homogeneity of degree zero says that the individual's choice depends only on the set of feasible points.

**Definition 2.E.2:** The Walrasian demand correspondence $x(p, w)$ satisfies Walras' law if for every $p \gg 0$ and $w > 0$, we have $p \cdot x = w$ for all $x \in x(p, w)$.

Walras' law says that the consumer fully expends his wealth. Intuitively, this is a reasonable assumption to make as long as there is some good that is clearly desirable. Walras' law should be understood broadly: the consumer's budget may be an intertemporal one allowing for savings today to be used for purchases tomorrow. What Walras' law says is that the consumer fully expends his resources *over his lifetime*.

**Exercise 2.E.1:** Suppose $L = 3$, and consider the demand function $x(p, w)$ defined by

$$x_1(p, w) = \frac{p_2}{p_1 + p_2 + p_3} \frac{w}{p_1},$$

$$x_2(p, w) = \frac{p_3}{p_1 + p_2 + p_3} \frac{w}{p_2},$$

$$x_3(p, w) = \frac{\beta p_1}{p_1 + p_2 + p_3} \frac{w}{p_3}.$$

Does this demand function satisfy homogeneity of degree zero and Walras' law when $\beta = 1$? What about when $\beta \in (0,1)$?

In Chapter 3, where the consumer's demand $x(p, w)$ is derived from the maximization of preferences, these two properties (homogeneity of degree zero and satisfaction of Walras' law) hold under very general circumstances. In the rest of this chapter, however, we shall simply take them as assumptions about $x(p, w)$ and explore their consequences.

One convenient implication of $x(p, w)$ being homogeneous of degree zero can be noted immediately: Although $x(p, w)$ formally has $L + 1$ arguments, we can, with no loss of generality, fix (*normalize*) the level of one of the $L + 1$ independent variables at an arbitrary level. One common normalization is $p_\ell = 1$ for some $\ell$. Another is $w = 1$.[6] Hence, the effective number of arguments in $x(p, w)$ is $L$.

For the remainder of this section, we assume that $x(p, w)$ is always single-valued. In this case, we can write the function $x(p, w)$ in terms of commodity-specific demand functions:

$$x(p, w) = \begin{bmatrix} x_1(p, w) \\ x_2(p, w) \\ \vdots \\ x_L(p, w) \end{bmatrix}.$$

When convenient, we also assume $x(p, w)$ to be continuous and differentiable.

---

The approach we take here and in Section 2.F can be viewed as an application of the choice-based framework developed in Chapter 1. The family of Walrasian budget sets is $\mathscr{B}^W = \{B_{p,w} : p \gg 0, w > 0\}$. Moreover, by homogeneity of degree zero, $x(p, w)$ depends only on the budget set the consumer faces. Hence $(\mathscr{B}^W, x(\cdot))$ is a choice structure, as defined in Section 1.C. Note that the choice structure $(\mathscr{B}^W, x(\cdot))$ does not include all possible subsets of $X$ (e.g., it does not include all two- and three-element subsets of $X$). This fact will be significant for the relationship between the choice-based and preference-based approaches to consumer demand.

---

*Comparative Statics*

We are often interested in analyzing how the consumer's choice varies with changes in his wealth and in prices. The examination of a change in outcome in response to a change in underlying economic parameters is known as *comparative statics* analysis.

*Wealth effects*

For fixed prices $\bar{p}$, the function of wealth $x(\bar{p}, w)$ is called the consumer's *Engel function*. Its image in $\mathbb{R}^L_+$, $E_{\bar{p}} = \{x(\bar{p}, w) : w > 0\}$, is known as the *wealth expansion path*. Figure 2.E.1 depicts such an expansion path.

At any $(p, w)$, the derivative $\partial x_\ell(p, w)/\partial w$ is known as the *wealth effect* for the $\ell$th good.[7]

---

6. We use normalizations extensively in Part IV.

7. It is also known as the *income effect* in the literature. Similarly, the wealth expansion path is sometimes referred to as an *income expansion path*.

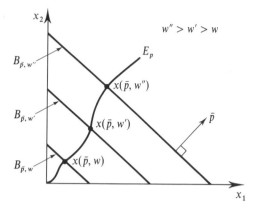

**Figure 2.E.1**

The wealth expansion path at prices $\bar{p}$.

A commodity $\ell$ is *normal* at $(p, w)$ if $\partial x_\ell(p, w)/\partial w \geq 0$; that is, demand is nondecreasing in wealth. If commodity $\ell$'s wealth effect is instead negative, then it is called *inferior* at $(p, w)$. If every commodity is normal at all $(p, w)$, then we say that *demand is normal*.

The assumption of normal demand makes sense if commodities are large aggregates (e.g., food, shelter). But if they are very disaggregated (e.g., particular kinds of shoes), then because of substitution to higher-quality goods as wealth increases, goods that become inferior at some level of wealth may be the rule rather than the exception.

In matrix notation, the wealth effects are represented as follows:

$$D_w x(p, w) = \begin{bmatrix} \dfrac{\partial x_1(p, w)}{\partial w} \\[1.5em] \dfrac{\partial x_2(p, w)}{\partial w} \\[1.5em] \vdots \\[1.5em] \dfrac{\partial x_L(p, w)}{\partial w} \end{bmatrix} \in \mathbb{R}^L.$$

*Price effects*

We can also ask how consumption levels of the various commodities change as prices vary.

Consider first the case where $L = 2$, and suppose we keep wealth and price $p_1$ fixed. Figure 2.E.2 represents the demand function for good 2 as a function of its own price $p_2$ for various levels of the price of good 1, with wealth held constant at amount $w$. Note that, as is customary in economics, the price variable, which here is the independent variable, is measured on the vertical axis, and the quantity demanded, the dependent variable, is measured on the horizontal axis. Another useful representation of the consumers' demand at different prices is the locus of points demanded in $\mathbb{R}^2_+$ as we range over all possible values of $p_2$. This is known as an *offer curve*. An example is presented in Figure 2.E.3.

More generally, the derivative $\partial x_\ell(p, w)/\partial p_k$ is known as the *price effect of $p_k$, the price of good $k$, on the demand for good $\ell$*. Although it may be natural to think that a fall in a good's price will lead the consumer to purchase more of it (as in

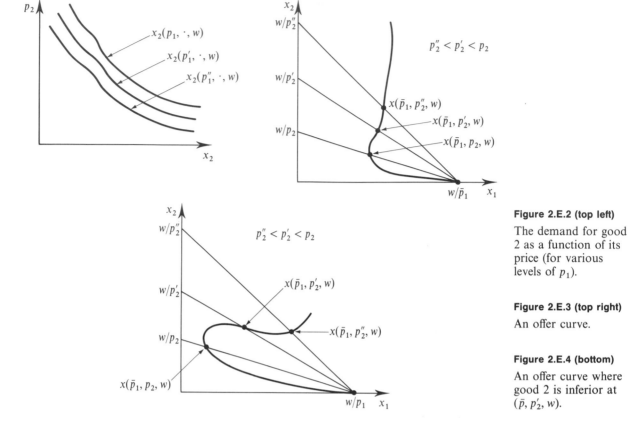

**Figure 2.E.2 (top left)**

The demand for good 2 as a function of its price (for various levels of $p_1$).

**Figure 2.E.3 (top right)**

An offer curve.

**Figure 2.E.4 (bottom)**

An offer curve where good 2 is inferior at $(\bar{p}, p_2', w)$.

Figure 2.E.3), the reverse situation is not an economic impossibility. Good $\ell$ is said to be a *Giffen good* at $(p, w)$ if $\partial x_\ell(p, w)/\partial p_\ell > 0$. For the offer curve depicted in Figure 2.E.4, good 2 is a Giffen good at $(\bar{p}_1, p_2', w)$.

Low-quality goods may well be Giffen goods for consumers with low wealth levels. For example, imagine that a poor consumer initially is fulfilling much of his dietary requirements with potatoes because they are a low-cost way to avoid hunger. If the price of potatoes falls, he can then afford to buy other, more desirable foods that also keep him from being hungry. His consumption of potatoes may well fall as a result. Note that the mechanism that leads to potatoes being a Giffen good in this story involves a wealth consideration: When the price of potatoes falls, the consumer is effectively wealthier (he can afford to purchase more generally), and so he buys fewer potatoes. We will be investigating this interplay between price and wealth effects more extensively in the rest of this chapter and in Chapter 3.

The price effects are conveniently represented in matrix form as follows:

$$D_p x(p, w) = \begin{bmatrix} \dfrac{\partial x_1(p, w)}{\partial p_1} & \cdots & \dfrac{\partial x_1(p, w)}{\partial p_L} \\ & \ddots & \\ \dfrac{\partial x_L(p, w)}{\partial p_1} & \cdots & \dfrac{\partial x_L(p, w)}{\partial p_L} \end{bmatrix}.$$

*Implications of homogeneity and Walras' law for price and wealth effects*

Homogeneity and Walras' law imply certain restrictions on the comparative statics effects of consumer demand with respect to prices and wealth.

Consider, first, the implications of homogeneity of degree zero. We know that $x(\alpha p, \alpha w) - x(p, w) = 0$ for all $\alpha > 0$. Differentiating this expression with respect to $\alpha$, and evaluating the derivative at $\alpha = 1$, we get the results shown in Proposition 2.E.1 (the result is also a special case of Euler's formula; see Section M.B of the Mathematical Appendix for details).

**Proposition 2.E.1:** If the Walrasian demand function $x(p, w)$ is homogeneous of degree zero, then for all $p$ and $w$:

$$\sum_{k=1}^{L} \frac{\partial x_{\ell}(p, w)}{\partial p_k} p_k + \frac{\partial x_{\ell}(p, w)}{\partial w} w = 0 \text{ for } \ell = 1, \ldots, L. \tag{2.E.1}$$

In matrix notation, this is expressed as

$$D_p x(p, w)p + D_w x(p, w)w = 0. \tag{2.E.2}$$

Thus, homogeneity of degree zero implies that the price and wealth derivatives of demand for any good $\ell$, when weighted by these prices and wealth, sum to zero. Intuitively, this weighting arises because when we increase all prices and wealth proportionately, each of these variables changes in proportion to its initial level.

We can also restate equation (2.E.1) in terms of the *elasticities* of demand with respect to prices and wealth. These are defined, respectively, by

$$\varepsilon_{\ell k}(p, w) = \frac{\partial x_{\ell}(p, w)}{\partial p_k} \frac{p_k}{x_{\ell}(p, w)}$$

and

$$\varepsilon_{\ell w}(p, w) = \frac{\partial x_{\ell}(p, w)}{\partial w} \frac{w}{x_{\ell}(p, w)}.$$

These elasticities give the *percentage* change in demand for good $\ell$ per (marginal) percentage change in the price of good $k$ or wealth; note that the expression for $\varepsilon_{\ell w}(\cdot, \cdot)$ can be read as $(\Delta x / x)/(\Delta w / w)$. Elasticities arise very frequently in applied work. Unlike the derivatives of demand, elasticities are independent of the units chosen for measuring commodities and therefore provide a unit-free way of capturing demand responsiveness.

Using elasticities, condition (2.E.1) takes the following form:

$$\sum_{k=1}^{L} \varepsilon_{\ell k}(p, w) + \varepsilon_{\ell w}(p, w) = 0 \quad \text{for } \ell = 1, \ldots, L. \tag{2.E.3}$$

This formulation very directly expresses the comparative statics implication of homogeneity of degree zero: An equal percentage change in all prices and wealth leads to no change in demand.

Walras' law, on the other hand, has two implications for the price and wealth effects of demand. By Walras' law, we know that $p \cdot x(p, w) = w$ for all $p$ and $w$. Differentiating this expression with respect to prices yields the first result, presented in Proposition 2.E.2.

**Proposition 2.E.2:** If the Walrasian demand function $x(p, w)$ satisfies Walras' law, then for all $p$ and $w$:

$$\sum_{\ell=1}^{L} p_\ell \frac{\partial x_\ell(p, w)}{\partial p_k} + x_k(p, w) = 0 \quad \text{for } k = 1, \ldots, L, \tag{2.E.4}$$

or, written in matrix notion,[8]

$$p \cdot D_p x(p, w) + x(p, w)^{\mathsf{T}} = 0^{\mathsf{T}}. \tag{2.E.5}$$

Similarly, differentiating $p \cdot x(p, w) = w$ with respect to $w$, we get the second result, shown in Proposition 2.E.3.

**Proposition 2.E.3:** If the Walrasian demand function $x(p, w)$ satisfies Walras' law, then for all $p$ and $w$:

$$\sum_{\ell=1}^{L} p_\ell \frac{\partial x_\ell(p, w)}{\partial w} = 1, \tag{2.E.6}$$

or, written in matrix notation,

$$p \cdot D_w x(p, w) = 1. \tag{2.E.7}$$

The conditions derived in Propositions 2.E.2 and 2.E.3 are sometimes called the properties of *Cournot* and *Engel aggregation*, respectively. They are simply the differential versions of two facts: That total expenditure cannot change in response to a change in prices and that total expenditure must change by an amount equal to any wealth change.

**Exercise 2.E.2:** Show that equations (2.E.4) and (2.E.6) lead to the following two elasticity formulas:

$$\sum_{\ell=1}^{L} b_\ell(p, w)\varepsilon_{\ell k}(p, w) + b_k(p, w) = 0,$$

and

$$\sum_{\ell=1}^{L} b_\ell(p, w)\varepsilon_{\ell w}(p, w) = 1,$$

where $b_\ell(p, w) = p_\ell x_\ell(p, w)/w$ is the budget share of the consumer's expenditure on good $\ell$ given prices $p$ and wealth $w$.

# 2.F The Weak Axiom of Revealed Preference and the Law of Demand

In this section, we study the implications of the weak axiom of revealed preference for consumer demand. Throughout the analysis, we continue to assume that $x(p, w)$ is single-valued, homogeneous of degree zero, and satisfies Walras' law.[9]

The weak axiom was already introduced in Section 1.C as a consistency axiom for the choice-based approach to decision theory. In this section, we explore its implications for the demand behavior of a consumer. In the preference-based approach to consumer behavior to be studied in Chapter 3, demand necessarily

---

8. Recall that $0^{\mathsf{T}}$ means a row vector of zeros.

9. For generalizations to the case of multivalued choice, see Exercise 2.F.13.

satisfies the weak axiom. Thus, the results presented in Chapter 3, when compared with those in this section, will tell us how much more structure is imposed on consumer demand by the preference-based approach beyond what is implied by the weak axiom alone.[10]

In the context of Walrasian demand functions, the weak axiom takes the form stated in the Definition 2.F.1.

**Definition 2.F.1:** The Walrasian demand function $x(p, w)$ satisfies the *weak axiom of revealed preference* (the WA) if the following property holds for any two price–wealth situations $(p, w)$ and $(p', w')$:

If $p \cdot x(p', w') \leq w$   and   $x(p', w') \neq x(p, w)$,   then   $p' \cdot x(p, w) > w'$.

If you have already studied Chapter 1, you will recognize that this definition is precisely the specialization of the general statement of the weak axiom presented in Section 1.C to the context in which budget sets are Walrasian and $x(p, w)$ specifies a unique choice (see Exercise 2.F.1).

In the consumer demand setting, the idea behind the weak axiom can be put as follows: If $p \cdot x(p', w') \leq w$ and $x(p', w') \neq x(p, w)$, then we know that when facing prices $p$ and wealth $w$, the consumer chose consumption bundle $x(p, w)$ even though bundle $x(p', w')$ was also affordable. We can interpret this choice as "revealing" a preference for $x(p, w)$ over $x(p', w')$. Now, we might reasonably expect the consumer to display some consistency in his demand behavior. In particular, given his revealed preference, we expect that he would choose $x(p, w)$ over $x(p', w')$ whenever they are both affordable. If so, bundle $x(p, w)$ must not be affordable at the price–wealth combination $(p', w')$ at which the consumer chooses bundle $x(p', w')$. That is, as required by the weak axiom, we must have $p' \cdot x(p, w) > w'$.

The restriction on demand behavior imposed by the weak axiom when $L = 2$ is illustrated in Figure 2.F.1. Each diagram shows two budget sets $B_{p', w'}$ and $B_{p'', w''}$ and their corresponding choice $x(p', w')$ and $x(p'', w'')$. The weak axiom tells us that we cannot have both $p' \cdot x(p'', w'') \leq w'$ and $p'' \cdot x(p', w') \leq w''$. Panels (a) to (c) depict permissible situations, whereas demand in panels (d) and (e) violates the weak axiom.

### Implications of the Weak Axiom

The weak axiom has significant implications for the effects of price changes on demand. We need to concentrate, however, on a special kind of price change.

As the discussion of Giffen goods in Section 2.E suggested, price changes affect the consumer in two ways. First, they alter the relative cost of different commodities. But, second, they also change the consumer's real wealth: An increase in the price of a commodity impoverishes the consumers of that commodity. To study the implications of the weak axiom, we need to isolate the first effect.

One way to accomplish this is to imagine a situation in which a change in prices is accompanied by a change in the consumer's wealth that makes his initial consumption bundle just affordable at the new prices. That is, if the consumer is originally facing prices $p$ and wealth $w$ and chooses consumption bundle $x(p, w)$, then

---

10. Or, stated more properly, beyond what is implied by the weak axiom in conjunction with homogeneity of degree zero and Walras' law.

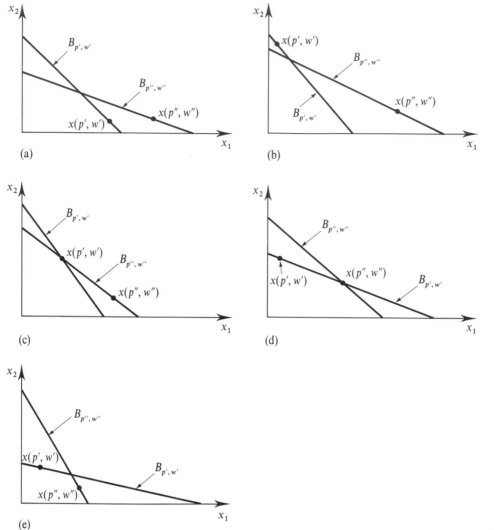

**Figure 2.F.1**

Demand in panels (a) to (c) satisfies the weak axiom; demand in panels (d) and (e) does not.

when prices change to $p'$, we imagine that the consumer's wealth is adjusted to $w' = p' \cdot x(p, w)$. Thus, the wealth adjustment is $\Delta w = \Delta p \cdot x(p, w)$, where $\Delta p = (p' - p)$. This kind of wealth adjustment is known as *Slutsky wealth compensation*. Figure 2.F.2 shows the change in the budget set when a reduction in the price of good 1 from $p_1$ to $p_1'$ is accompanied by Slutsky wealth compensation. Geometrically, the restriction is that the budget hyperplane corresponding to $(p', w')$ goes through the vector $x(p, w)$.

We refer to price changes that are accompanied by such compensating wealth changes as *(Slutsky) compensated price changes*.

In Proposition 2.F.1, we show that the weak axiom can be equivalently stated in terms of the demand response to compensated price changes.

**Proposition 2.F.1:** Suppose that the Walrasian demand function $x(p, w)$ is homogeneous of degree zero and satisfies Walras' law. Then $x(p, w)$ satisfies the weak axiom if and only if the following property holds:

For any compensated price change from an initial situation $(p, w)$ to a new price–wealth pair $(p', w') = (p', p' \cdot x(p, w))$, we have

$$(p' - p) \cdot [x(p', w') - x(p, w)] \leq 0, \qquad (2.F.1)$$

with strict inequality whenever $x(p, w) \neq x(p', w')$.

**Proof:** (i) *The weak axiom implies inequality (2.F.1), with strict inequality if $x(p, w) \neq x(p', w')$.* The result is immediate if $x(p', w') = x(p, w)$, since then $(p' - p) \cdot [x(p', w') - x(p, w)] = 0$. So suppose that $x(p', w') \neq x(p, w)$. The left-hand side of inequality (2.F.1) can be written as

$$(p' - p) \cdot [x(p', w') - x(p, w)] = p' \cdot [x(p', w') - x(p, w)] - p \cdot [x(p', w') - x(p, w)].$$

$$(2.F.2)$$

Consider the first term of (2.F.2). Because the change from $p$ to $p'$ is a compensated price change, we know that $p' \cdot x(p, w) = w'$. In addition, Walras' law tells us that $w' = p' \cdot x(p', w')$. Hence

$$p' \cdot [x(p', w') - x(p, w)] = 0. \qquad (2.F.3)$$

Now consider the second term of (2.F.2). Because $p' \cdot x(p, w) = w'$, $x(p, w)$ is affordable under price–wealth situation $(p', w')$. The weak axiom therefore implies that $x(p', w')$ must *not* be affordable under price–wealth situation $(p, w)$. Thus, we must have $p \cdot x(p', w') > w$. Since $p \cdot x(p, w) = w$ by Walras' law, this implies that

$$p \cdot [x(p', w') - x(p, w)] > 0 \qquad (2.F.4)$$

Together, (2.F.2), (2.F.3) and (2.F.4) yield the result.

(ii) *The weak axiom is implied by (2.F.1) holding for all compensated price changes, with strict inequality if $x(p, w) \neq x(p', w')$.* The argument for this direction of the proof uses the following fact: The weak axiom holds if and only if it holds for all *compensated* price changes. That is, the weak axiom holds if, for any two price–wealth pairs $(p, w)$ and $(p', w')$, we have $p' \cdot x(p, w) > w'$ whenever $p \cdot x(p', w') = w$ and $x(p', w') \neq x(p, w)$.

To prove the fact stated in the preceding paragraph, we argue that if the weak axiom is violated, then there must be a compensated price change for which it is violated. To see this, suppose that we have a violation of the weak axiom, that is, two price–wealth pairs $(p', w')$ and $(p'', w'')$ such that $x(p', w') \neq x(p'', w'')$, $p' \cdot x(p'', w'') \leq w'$, and $p'' \cdot x(p', w') \leq w''$. If one of these two weak inequalities holds with equality, then this is actually a compensated price change and we are done. So assume that, as shown in Figure 2.F.3, we have $p' \cdot x(p'', w'') < w'$ and $p'' \cdot x(p', w') < w''$.

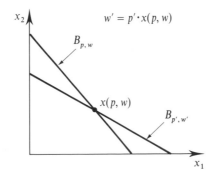

$$w' = p' \cdot x(p, w)$$

$B_{p, w}$

$x(p, w)$

$B_{p', w'}$

$x_2$

$x_1$

**Figure 2.F.2**

A compensated price change from $(p, w)$ to $(p', w')$.

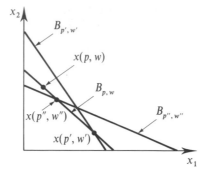

**Figure 2.F.3**

The weak axiom holds
if and only if it holds
for all compensated
price changes.

Now choose the value of $\alpha \in (0,1)$ for which

$$(\alpha p' + (1-\alpha)p'')\cdot x(p', w') = (\alpha p' + (1-\alpha)p'')\cdot x(p'', w''),$$

and denote $p = \alpha p' + (1-\alpha)p''$ and $w = (\alpha p' + (1-\alpha)p'')\cdot x(p', w')$. This construction is illustrated in Figure 2.F.3. We then have

$$\alpha w' + (1-\alpha)w'' > \alpha p'\cdot x(p', w') + (1-\alpha)p''\cdot x(p', w')$$
$$= w$$
$$= p\cdot x(p, w)$$
$$= \alpha p'\cdot x(p, w) + (1-\alpha)p''\cdot x(p, w).$$

Therefore, either $p'\cdot x(p, w) < w'$ or $p''\cdot x(p, w) < w''$. Suppose that the first possibility holds (the argument is identical if it is the second that holds). Then we have $x(p, w) \neq x(p', w')$, $p\cdot x(p', w') = w$, and $p'\cdot x(p, w) < w'$, which constitutes a violation of the weak axiom for the compensated price change from $(p', w')$ to $(p, w)$.

---

Once we know that in order to test for the weak axiom it suffices to consider only compensated price changes, the remaining reasoning is straightforward. If the weak axiom does not hold, there exists a compensated price change from some $(p', w')$ to some $(p, w)$ such that $x(p, w) \neq x(p', w')$, $p\cdot x(p', w') = w$, and $p'\cdot x(p, w) \leq w'$. But since $x(\cdot, \cdot)$ satisfies Walras' law, these two inequalities imply

$$p\cdot[x(p', w') - x(p, w)] = 0 \qquad \text{and} \qquad p'\cdot[x(p', w') - x(p, w)] \geq 0.$$

Hence, we would have

$$(p' - p)\cdot[x(p', w') - x(p, w)] \geq 0 \qquad \text{and} \qquad x(p, w) \neq x(p', w'),$$

which is a contradiction to (2.F.1) holding for all compensated price changes [and with strict inequality when $x(p, w) \neq x(p', w')$]. ∎

The inequality (2.F.1) can be written in shorthand as $\Delta p \cdot \Delta x \leq 0$, where $\Delta p = (p' - p)$ and $\Delta x = [x(p', w') - x(p, w)]$. It can be interpreted as a form of the *law of demand*: *Demand and price move in opposite directions.* Proposition 2.F.1 tells us that the law of demand holds for *compensated* price changes. We therefore call it the *compensated law of demand*.

The simplest case involves the effect on demand for some good $\ell$ of a compensated change in its own price $p_\ell$. When only this price changes, we have $\Delta p = (0, \ldots, 0, \Delta p_\ell, 0, \ldots, 0)$. Since $\Delta p \cdot \Delta x = \Delta p_\ell \Delta x_\ell$, Proposition 2.F.1 tells us that if $\Delta p_\ell > 0$, then we must have $\Delta x_\ell < 0$. The basic argument is illustrated in Figure 2.F.4. Starting at

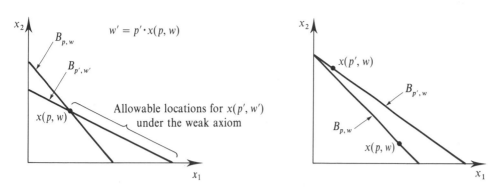

**Figure 2.F.4 (left)**

Demand must be nonincreasing in own price for a compensated price change.

**Figure 2.F.5 (right)**

Demand for good 1 can fall when its price decreases for an uncompensated price change.

$(p, w)$, a compensated decrease in the price of good 1 rotates the budget line through $x(p, w)$. The WA allows moves of demand only in the direction that increases the demand of good 1.

Figure 2.F.5 should persuade you that the WA (or, for that matter, the preference maximization assumption discussed in Chapter 3) is not sufficient to yield the law of demand for price changes that are *not* compensated. In the figure, the price change from $p$ to $p'$ is obtained by a decrease in the price of good 1, but the weak axiom imposes no restriction on where we place the new consumption bundle; as drawn, the demand for good 1 falls.

When consumer demand $x(p, w)$ is a differentiable function of prices and wealth, Proposition 2.F.1 has a differential implication that is of great importance. Consider, starting at a given price–wealth pair $(p, w)$, a differential change in prices $dp$. Imagine that we make this a compensated price change by giving the consumer compensation of $dw = x(p, w) \cdot dp$ [this is just the differential analog of $\Delta w = x(p, w) \cdot \Delta p$]. Proposition 2.F.1 tells us that

$$dp \cdot dx \le 0. \tag{2.F.5}$$

Now, using the chain rule, the differential change in demand induced by this compensated price change can be written as

$$dx = D_p x(p, w)\, dp + D_w x(p, w)\, dw. \tag{2.F.6}$$

Hence

$$dx = D_p x(p, w)\, dp + D_w x(p, w)\, [x(p, w) \cdot dp] \tag{2.F.7}$$

or equivalently

$$dx = [D_p x(p, w) + D_w x(p, w) x(p, w)^{\mathrm{T}}]\, dp. \tag{2.F.8}$$

Finally, substituting (2.F.8) into (2.F.5) we conclude that for any possible differential price change $dp$, we have

$$dp \cdot [D_p x(p, w) + D_w x(p, w) x(p, w)^{\mathrm{T}}]\, dp \le 0. \tag{2.F.9}$$

The expression in square brackets in condition (2.F.9) is an $L \times L$ matrix, which we denote by $S(p, w)$. Formally

$$S(p, w) = \begin{bmatrix} s_{11}(p, w) & \cdots & s_{1L}(p, w) \\ \vdots & \ddots & \vdots \\ s_{L1}(p, w) & \cdots & s_{LL}(p, w) \end{bmatrix},$$

where the $(\ell, k)$th entry is

$$s_{\ell k}(p, w) = \frac{\partial x_\ell(p, w)}{\partial p_k} + \frac{\partial x_\ell(p, w)}{\partial w} x_k(p, w). \qquad (2.F.10)$$

The matrix $S(p, w)$ is known as the *substitution*, or *Slutsky*, matrix, and its elements are known as *substitution effects*.

The "substitution" terminology is apt because the term $s_{\ell k}(p, w)$ measures the differential change in the consumption of commodity $\ell$ (i.e., the substitution to or from other commodities) due to a differential change in the price of commodity $k$ when wealth is adjusted so that the consumer can still just afford his original consumption bundle (i.e., due solely to a change in relative prices). To see this, note that the change in demand for good $\ell$ if wealth is left unchanged is $(\partial x_l(p, w)/\partial p_k) \, dp_k$. For the consumer to be able to "just afford" his original consumption bundle, his wealth must vary by the amount $x_k(p, w) \, dp_k$. The effect of this wealth change on the demand for good $\ell$ is then $(\partial x_\ell(p, w)/\partial w) \, [x_k(p, w) \, dp_k]$. The sum of these two effects is therefore exactly $s_{\ell k}(p, w) \, dp_k$.

We summarize the derivation in equations (2.F.5) to (2.F.10) in Proposition 2.F.2.

**Proposition 2.F.2:** If a differentiable Walrasian demand function $x(p, w)$ satisfies Walras' law, homogeneity of degree zero, and the weak axiom, then at any $(p, w)$, the Slutsky matrix $S(p, w)$ satisfies $v \cdot S(p, w)v \leq 0$ for any $v \in \mathbb{R}^L$.

A matrix satisfying the property in Proposition 2.F.2 is called *negative semidefinite* (it is negative *definite* if the inequality is strict for all $v \neq 0$). See Section M.D of the Mathematical Appendix for more on these matrices.

Note that $S(p, w)$ being negative semidefinite implies that $s_{\ell\ell}(p, w) \leq 0$: That is, *the substitution effect of good $\ell$ with respect to its own price is always nonpositive*.

An interesting implication of $s_{\ell\ell}(p, w) \leq 0$ is that a good can be a Giffen good at $(p, w)$ only if it is inferior. In particular, since

$$s_{\ell\ell}(p, w) = \partial x_\ell(p, w)/\partial p_\ell + [\partial x_\ell(p, w)/\partial w] \, x_\ell(p, w) \leq 0,$$

if $\partial x_\ell(p, w)/\partial p_\ell > 0$, we must have $\partial x_\ell(p, w)/\partial w < 0$.

For later reference, we note that Proposition 2.F.2 does *not* imply, in general, that the matrix $S(p, w)$ is symmetric.[11] For $L = 2$, $S(p, w)$ is necessarily symmetric (you are asked to show this in Exercise 2.F.11). When $L > 2$, however, $S(p, w)$ need not be symmetric under the assumptions made so far (homogeneity of degree zero, Walras' law, and the weak axiom). See Exercises 2.F.10 and 2.F.15 for examples. In Chapter 3 (Section 3.H), we shall see that the symmetry of $S(p, w)$ is intimately connected with the possibility of generating demand from the maximization of rational preferences.

Exploiting further the properties of homogeneity of degree zero and Walras' law, we can say a bit more about the substitution matrix $S(p, w)$.

---

11. A matter of terminology: It is common in the mathematical literature that "definite" matrices are assumed to be symmetric. Rigorously speaking, if no symmetry is implied, the matrix would be called "quasidefinite." To simplify terminology, we use "definite" without any supposition about symmetry; if a matrix is symmetric, we say so explicitly. (See Exercise 2.F.9.)

**Proposition 2.F.3:** Suppose that the Walrasian demand function $x(p, w)$ is differentiable, homogeneous of degree zero, and satisfies Walras' law. Then $p \cdot S(p, w) = 0$ and $S(p, w)p = 0$ for any $(p, w)$.

**Exercise 2.F.7:** Prove Proposition 2.F.3. [*Hint:* Use Propositions 2.E.1 to 2.E.3.]

It follows from Proposition 2.F.3 that the matrix $S(p, w)$ is always singular (i.e., it has rank less than $L$), and so the negative semidefiniteness of $S(p, w)$ established in Proposition 2.F.2 cannot be extended to negative definiteness (e.g., see Exercise 2.F.17).

---

Proposition 2.F.2 establishes negative semidefiniteness of $S(p, w)$ as a necessary implication of the weak axiom. One might wonder: Is this property sufficient to imply the WA [so that negative semidefiniteness of $S(p, w)$ is actually equivalent to the WA]? That is, if we have a demand function $x(p, w)$ that satisfies Walras' law, homogeneity of degree zero and has a negative semidefinite substitution matrix, must it satisfy the weak axiom? The answer is *almost, but not quite.* Exercise 2.F.16 provides an example of a demand function with a negative semidefinite substitution matrix that violates the WA. The sufficient condition is that $v \cdot S(p, w)v < 0$ whenever $v \neq \alpha p$ for any scalar $\alpha$; that is, $S(p, w)$ must be negative definite for all vectors other than those that are proportional to $p$. This result is due to Samuelson [see Samuelson (1947) or Kihlstrom, Mas-Colell, and Sonnenschein (1976) for an advanced treatment]. The gap between the necessary and sufficient conditions is of the same nature as the gap between the necessary and the sufficient second-order conditions for the minimization of a function.

---

Finally, how would a theory of consumer demand that is based solely on the assumptions of homogeneity of degree zero, Walras' law, and the consistency requirement embodied in the weak action compare with one based on rational preference maximization?

Based on Chapter 1, you might hope that Proposition 1.D.2 implies that the two are equivalent. But we cannot appeal to that proposition here because the family of Walrasian budgets does not include every possible budget; in particular, it does not include all the budgets formed by only two- or three-commodity bundles.

In fact, the two theories are not equivalent. For Walrasian demand functions, the theory derived from the weak axiom is weaker than the theory derived from rational preferences, in the sense of implying fewer restrictions. This is shown formally in Chapter 3, where we demonstrate that if demand is generated from preferences, or is capable of being so generated, then it must have a symmetric Slutsky matrix at all $(p, w)$. But for the moment, Example 2.F.1, due originally to Hicks (1956), may be persuasive enough.

**Example 2.F.1:** In a three-commodity world, consider the three budget sets determined by the price vectors $p^1 = (2, 1, 2)$, $p^2 = (2, 2, 1)$, $p^3 = (1, 2, 2)$ and wealth $= 8$ (the same for the three budgets). Suppose that the respective (unique) choices are $x^1 = (1, 2, 2)$, $x^2 = (2, 1, 2)$, $x^3 = (2, 2, 1)$. In Exercise 2.F.2, you are asked to verify that any two pairs of choices satisfy the WA but that $x^3$ is revealed preferred to $x^2$, $x^2$ is revealed preferred to $x^1$, and $x^1$ is revealed preferred to $x^3$. This situation is incompatible with the existence of underlying rational preferences (transitivity would be violated).

The reason this example is only *persuasive* and does not quite settle the question is that demand has been defined only for the three given budgets, therefore, we cannot be sure that it satisfies the requirements of the WA for all possible competitive budgets. To clinch the matter we refer to Chapter 3. ∎

In summary, there are three primary conclusions to be drawn from Section 2.F:

(i) The consistency requirement embodied in the weak axiom (combined with the homogeneity of degree zero and Walras' law) is equivalent to the compensated law of demand.

(ii) The compensated law of demand, in turn, implies negative semidefiniteness of the substitution matrix $S(p, w)$.

(iii) These assumptions do *not* imply symmetry of $S(p, w)$, except in the case where $L = 2$.

## REFERENCES

Burtless, G., and J. A. Hausman (1978). The effects of taxation on labor supply: Evaluating the Gary negative income tax experiment. *Journal of Political Economy* **86**: 1103–30.

Deaton, A., and J. Muellbauer (1980). *Economics and Consumer Behavior*. Cambridge, U.K.: Cambridge University Press.

Hicks, J. (1956). *A Revision of Demand Theory*. Oxford: Oxford University Press.

Kihlstrom, R., A. Mas-Colell, and H. Sonnenschein (1976). The demand theory of the weak axiom of revealed preference. *Econometrica* **44**: 971–78.

Malinvaud, E. (1978). *Lectures on Microeconomic Theory*. New York: Elsevier.

Samuelson, P. (1947). *Foundations of Economic Analysis*. Cambridge, Mass.: Harvard University Press.

## EXERCISES

**2.D.1**[A] A consumer lives for two periods, denoted 1 and 2, and consumes a single consumption good in each period. His wealth when born is $w > 0$. What is his (lifetime) Walrasian budget set?

**2.D.2**[A] A consumer consumes one consumption good $x$ and hours of leisure $h$. The price of the consumption good is $p$, and the consumer can work at a wage rate of $s = 1$. What is the consumer's Walrasian budget set?

**2.D.3**[B] Consider an extension of the Walrasian budget set to an arbitrary consumption set $X$: $B_{p,w} = \{x \in X: p \cdot x \le w\}$. Assume $(p, w) \gg 0$.

(a) If $X$ is the set depicted in Figure 2.C.3, would $B_{p,w}$ be convex?

(b) Show that if $X$ is a convex set, then $B_{p,w}$ is as well.

**2.D.4**[A] Show that the budget set in Figure 2.D.4 is not convex.

**2.E.1**[A] In text.

**2.E.2**[B] In text.

**2.E.3**[B] Use Propositions 2.E.1 to 2.E.3 to show that $p \cdot D_p x(p, w) p = -w$. Interpret.

**2.E.4**[B] Show that if $x(p, w)$ is homogeneous of degree one with respect to $w$ [i.e., $x(p, \alpha w) = \alpha x(p, w)$

for all $\alpha > 0$] and satisfies Walras' law, then $\varepsilon_{\ell w}(p, w) = 1$ for every $\ell$. Interpret. Can you say something about $D_w x(p, w)$ and the form of the Engel functions and curves in this case?

**2.E.5$^B$** Suppose that $x(p, w)$ is a demand function which is homogeneous of degree one with respect to $w$ and satisfies Walras' law and homogeneity of degree zero. Suppose also that all the cross-price effects are zero, that is $\partial x_\ell(p, w)/\partial p_k = 0$ whenever $k \neq \ell$. Show that this implies that for every $\ell$, $x_\ell(p, w) = \alpha_\ell w/p_\ell$, where $\alpha_\ell > 0$ is a constant independent of $(p, w)$.

**2.E.6$^A$** Verify that the conclusions of Propositions 2.E.1 to 2.E.3 hold for the demand function given in Exercise 2.E.1 when $\beta = 1$.

**2.E.7$^A$** A consumer in a two-good economy has a demand function $x(p, w)$ that satisfies Walras' law. His demand function for the first good is $x_1(p, w) = \alpha w/p_1$. Derive his demand function for the second good. Is his demand function homogeneous of degree zero?

**2.E.8$^B$** Show that the elasticity of demand for good $\ell$ with respect to price $p_k$, $\varepsilon_{\ell k}(p, w)$, can be written as $\varepsilon_{\ell k}(p, w) = d \ln (x_\ell(p, w))/d \ln (p_k)$, where $\ln(\cdot)$ is the natural logarithm function. Derive a similar expression for $\varepsilon_{\ell w}(p, w)$. Conclude that if we estimate the parameters $(\alpha_0, \alpha_1, \alpha_2, \gamma)$ of the equation $\ln (x_\ell(p, w)) = \alpha_0 + \alpha_1 \ln p_1 + \alpha_2 \ln p_2 + \gamma \ln w$, these parameter estimates provide us with estimates of the elasticities $\varepsilon_{\ell 1}(p, w)$, $\varepsilon_{\ell 2}(p, w)$, and $\varepsilon_{\ell w}(p, w)$.

**2.F.1$^B$** Show that for Walrasian demand functions, the definition of the weak axiom given in Definition 2.F.1 coincides with that in Definition 1.C.1.

**2.F.2$^B$** Verify the claim of Example 2.F.1.

**2.F.3$^B$** You are given the following partial information about a consumer's purchases. He consumes only two goods.

|        | Year 1 | | Year 2 | |
|--------|----------|-------|----------|-------|
|        | Quantity | Price | Quantity | Price |
| Good 1 | 100      | 100   | 120      | 100   |
| Good 2 | 100      | 100   | ?        | 80    |

Over what range of quantities of good 2 consumed in year 2 would you conclude:

**(a)** That his behaviour is inconsistent (i.e., in contradiction with the weak axiom)?

**(b)** That the consumer's consumption bundle in year 1 is revealed preferred to that in year 2?

**(c)** That the consumer's consumption bundle in year 2 is revealed preferred to that in year 1?

**(d)** That there is insufficient information to justify (a), (b), and/or (c)?

**(e)** That good 1 is an inferior good (at some price) for this consumer? Assume that the weak axiom is satisfied.

**(f)** That good 2 is an inferior good (at some price) for this consumer? Assume that the weak axiom is satisfied.

**2.F.4$^A$** Consider the consumption of a consumer in two different periods, period 0 and period 1. Period $t$ prices, wealth, and consumption are $p^t$, $w_t$, and $x^t = x(p^t, w_t)$, respectively. It is often of applied interest to form an index measure of the quantity consumed by a consumer. The *Laspeyres* quantity index computes the change in quantity using period 0 prices as weights: $L_Q = (p^0 \cdot x^1)/(p^0 \cdot x^0)$. The *Paasche* quantity index instead uses period 1 prices as weights: $P_Q = (p^1 \cdot x^1)/(p^1 \cdot x^0)$. Finally, we could use the consumer's expenditure change: $E_Q = (p^1 \cdot x^1)/(p^0 \cdot x^0)$. Show the following:

**(a)** If $L_Q < 1$, then the consumer has a revealed preference for $x^0$ over $x^1$.

**(b)** If $P_Q > 1$, then the consumer has a revealed preference for $x^1$ over $x^0$.

**(c)** No revealed preference relationship is implied by either $E_Q > 1$ or $E_Q < 1$. Note that at the aggregate level, $E_Q$ corresponds to the percentage change in gross national product.

**2.F.5$^C$** Suppose that $x(p, w)$ is a differentiable demand function that satisfies the weak axiom, Walras' law, and homogeneity of degree zero. Show that if $x(\cdot, \cdot)$ is homogeneous of degree one with respect to $w$ [i.e., $x(p, \alpha w) = \alpha x(p, w)$ for all $(p, w)$ and $\alpha > 0$], then the law of demand holds even for *uncompensated* price changes. If this is easier, establish only the infinitesimal version of this conclusion; that is, $dp \cdot D_p x(p, w)\, dp \leq 0$ for any $dp$.

**2.F.6$^A$** Suppose that $x(p, w)$ is homogeneous of degree zero. Show that the weak axiom holds if and only if for some $w > 0$ and all $p, p'$ we have $p' \cdot x(p, w) > w$ whenever $p \cdot x(p', w) \leq w$ and $x(p', w) \neq x(p, w)$.

**2.F.7$^B$** In text.

**2.F.8$^A$** Let $\hat{s}_{\ell k}(p, w) = [p_k / x_\ell(p, w)] s_{\ell k}(p, w)$ be the substitution terms in elasticity form. Express $\hat{s}_{\ell k}(p, w)$ in terms of $\varepsilon_{\ell k}(p, w)$, $\varepsilon_{\ell w}(p, w)$, and $b_k(p, w)$.

**2.F.9$^B$** A symmetric $n \times n$ matrix $A$ is negative definite if and only if $(-1)^k |A_{kk}| > 0$ for all $k \leq n$, where $A_{kk}$ is the submatrix of $A$ obtained by deleting the last $n - k$ rows and columns. For semidefiniteness of the symmetric matrix $A$, we replace the strict inequalities by weak inequalities and require that the weak inequalities hold for all matrices formed by permuting the rows and columns of $A$ (see Section M.D of the Mathematical Appendix for details).

**(a)** Show that an arbitrary (possibly nonsymmetric) matrix $A$ is negative definite (or semidefinite) if and only if $A + A^T$ is negative definite (or semidefinite). Show also that the above determinant condition (which can be shown to be necessary) is no longer sufficient in the nonsymmetric case.

**(b)** Show that for $L = 2$, the necessary and sufficient condition for the substitution matrix $S(p, w)$ of rank 1 to be negative semidefinite is that any diagonal entry (i.e., any own-price substitution effect) be negative.

**2.F.10$^B$** Consider the demand function in Exercise 2.E.1 with $\beta = 1$. Assume that $w = 1$.

**(a)** Compute the substitution matrix. Show that at $p = (1, 1, 1)$, it is negative semidefinite but not symmetric.

**(b)** Show that this demand function does not satisfy the weak axiom. [*Hint*: Consider the price vector $p = (1, 1, \varepsilon)$ and show that the substitution matrix is not negative semidefinite (for $\varepsilon > 0$ small).]

**2.F.11$^A$** Show that for $L = 2$, $S(p, w)$ is always symmetric. [*Hint*: Use Proposition 2.F.3.]

**2.F.12$^A$** Show that if the Walrasian demand function $x(p, w)$ is generated by a rational preference relation, than it must satisfy the weak axiom.

**2.F.13$^C$** Suppose that $x(p, w)$ may be multivalued.

**(a)** From the definition of the weak axiom given in Section 1.C, develop the generalization of Definition 2.F.1 for Walrasian demand correspondences.

**(b)** Show that if $x(p, w)$ satisfies this generalization of the weak axiom and Walras' law, then $x(\cdot)$ satisfies the following property:

(∗)    For any $x \in x(p, w)$ and $x' \in x(p', w')$, if $p \cdot x' < w$, then $p \cdot x > w$.

(c) Show that the generalized weak axiom and Walras' law implies the following generalized version of the compensated law of demand: Starting from any initial position $(p, w)$ with demand $x \in x(p, w)$, for any compensated price change to new prices $p'$ and wealth level $w' = p' \cdot x$, we have

$$(p' - p) \cdot (x' - x) \leq 0$$

for all $x' \in x(p', w')$, with strict inequality if $x' \in x(p, w)$.

(d) Show that if $x(p, w)$ satisfies Walras' law and the generalized compensated law of demand defined in (c), then $x(p, w)$ satisfies the generalized weak axiom.

**2.F.14$^A$** Show that if $x(p, w)$ is a Walrasian demand function that satisfies the weak axiom, then $x(p, w)$ must be homogeneous of degree zero.

**2.F.15$^B$** Consider a setting with $L = 3$ and a consumer whose consumption set is $\mathbb{R}^3$. The consumer's demand function $x(p, w)$ satisfies homogeneity of degree zero, Walras' law and (fixing $p_3 = 1$) has

$$x_1(p, w) = -p_1 + p_2$$

and

$$x_2(p, w) = -p_2.$$

Show that this demand function satisfies the weak axiom by demonstrating that its substitution matrix satisfies $v \cdot S(p, w) \, v < 0$ for all $v \neq \alpha p$. [*Hint:* Use the matrix results recorded in Section M.D of the Mathematical Appendix.] Observe then that the substitution matrix is not symmetric. (*Note:* The fact that we allow for negative consumption levels here is not essential for finding a demand function that satisfies the weak axiom but whose substitution matrix is not symmetric; with a consumption set allowing only for nonnegative consumption levels, however, we would need to specify a more complicated demand function.)

**2.F.16$^B$** Consider a setting where $L = 3$ and a consumer whose consumption set is $\mathbb{R}^3$. Suppose that his demand function $x(p, w)$ is

$$x_1(p, w) = \frac{p_2}{p_3},$$

$$x_2(p, w) = -\frac{p_1}{p_3},$$

$$x_3(p, w) = \frac{w}{p_3}.$$

(a) Show that $x(p, w)$ is homogeneous of degree zero in $(p, w)$ and satisfies Walras' law.

(b) Show that $x(p, w)$ violates the weak axiom.

(c) Show that $v \cdot S(p, w) \, v = 0$ for all $v \in \mathbb{R}^3$.

**2.F.17$^B$** In an $L$-commodity world, a consumer's Walrasian demand function is

$$x_k(p, w) = \frac{w}{\left( \sum_{\ell=1}^{L} p_\ell \right)} \quad \text{for } k = 1, \ldots, L.$$

(a) Is this demand function homogeneous of degree zero in $(p, w)$?

(b) Does it satisfy Walras' law?

(c) Does it satisfy the weak axiom?

(d) Compute the Slutsky substitution matrix for this demand function. Is it negative semidefinite? Negative definite? Symmetric?

# Classical Demand Theory

## 3.A Introduction

In this chapter, we study the classical, preference-based approach to consumer demand.

We begin in Section 3.B by introducing the consumer's preference relation and some of its basic properties. We assume throughout that this preference relation is *rational*, offering a complete and transitive ranking of the consumer's possible consumption choices. We also discuss two properties, *monotonicity* (or its weaker version, *local nonsatiation*) and *convexity*, that are used extensively in the analysis that follows.

Section 3.C considers a technical issue: the existence and continuity properties of utility functions that represent the consumer's preferences. We show that not all preference relations are representable by a utility function, and we then formulate an assumption on preferences, known as *continuity*, that is sufficient to guarantee the existence of a (continuous) utility function.

In Section 3.D, we begin our study of the consumer's decision problem by assuming that there are $L$ commodities whose prices she takes as fixed and independent of her actions (the *price-taking assumption*). The consumer's problem is framed as one of *utility maximization* subject to the constraints embodied in the Walrasian budget set. We focus our study on two objects of central interest: the consumer's optimal choice, embodied in the *Walrasian* (or *market* or *ordinary*) *demand correspondence*, and the consumer's optimal utility value, captured by the *indirect utility function*.

Section 3.E introduces the consumer's *expenditure minimization problem*, which bears a close relation to the consumer's goal of utility maximization. In parallel to our study of the demand correspondence and value function of the utility maximization problem, we study the equivalent objects for expenditure minimization. They are known, respectively, as the *Hicksian* (or *compensated*) *demand correspondence* and the *expenditure function*. We also provide an initial formal examination of the relationship between the expenditure minimization and utility maximization problems.

In Section 3.F, we pause for an introduction to the mathematical underpinnings of duality theory. This material offers important insights into the structure of preference-based demand theory. Section 3.F may be skipped without loss of continuity in a first reading of the chapter. Nevertheless, we recommend the study of its material.

Section 3.G continues our analysis of the utility maximization and expenditure minimization problems by establishing some of the most important results of demand theory. These results develop the fundamental connections between the demand and value functions of the two problems.

In Section 3.H, we complete the study of the implications of the preference-based theory of consumer demand by asking how and when we can recover the consumer's underlying preferences from her demand behavior, an issue traditionally known as the *integrability problem*. In addition to their other uses, the results presented in this section tell us that the properties of consumer demand identified in Sections 3.D to 3.G as *necessary* implications of preference-maximizing behavior are also *sufficient* in the sense that any demand behavior satisfying these properties can be rationalized as preference-maximizing behavior.

The results in Sections 3.D to 3.H also allow us to compare the implications of the preference-based approach to consumer demand with the choice-based theory studied in Section 2.F. Although the differences turn out to be slight, the two approaches are not equivalent; the choice-based demand theory founded on the weak axiom of revealed preference imposes fewer restrictions on demand than does the preference-based theory studied in this chapter. The extra condition added by the assumption of rational preferences turns out to be the *symmetry* of the Slutsky matrix. As a result, we conclude that satisfaction of the weak axiom does not ensure the existence of a rationalizing preference relation for consumer demand.

Although our analysis in Sections 3.B to 3.H focuses entirely on the positive (i.e., descriptive) implications of the preference-based approach, one of the most important benefits of the latter is that it provides a framework for normative, or *welfare*, analysis. In Section 3.I, we take a first look at this subject by studying the effects of a price change on the consumer's welfare. In this connection, we discuss the use of the traditional concept of Marshallian surplus as a measure of consumer welfare.

We conclude in Section 3.J by returning to the choice-based approach to consumer demand. We ask whether there is some strengthening of the weak axiom that leads to a choice-based theory of consumer demand equivalent to the preference-based approach. As an answer, we introduce the *strong axiom of revealed preference* and show that it leads to demand behavior that is consistent with the existence of underlying preferences.

Appendix A discusses some technical issues related to the continuity and differentiability of Walrasian demand.

For further reading, see the thorough treatment of classical demand theory offered by Deaton and Muellbauer (1980).

# 3.B Preference Relations: Basic Properties

In the classical approach to consumer demand, the analysis of consumer behavior begins by specifying the consumer's preferences over the commodity bundles in the consumption set $X \subset \mathbb{R}_+^L$.

The consumer's preferences are captured by a preference relation $\succsim$ (an "at-least-as-good-as" relation) defined on $X$ that we take to be *rational* in the sense introduced in Section 1.B; that is, $\succsim$ is *complete* and *transitive*. For convenience, we repeat the formal statement of this assumption from Definition 1.B.1.[1]

**Definition 3.B.1:** The preference relation $\succsim$ on $X$ is *rational* if it possesses the following two properties:

(i) *Completeness*. For all $x, y \in X$, we have $x \succsim y$ or $y \succsim x$ (or both).

(ii) *Transitivity*. For all $x, y, z \in X$, if $x \succsim y$ and $y \succsim z$, then $x \succsim z$.

In the discussion that follows, we also use two other types of assumptions about preferences: *desirability* assumptions and *convexity* assumptions.

(i) *Desirability assumptions.* It is often reasonable to assume that larger amounts of commodities are preferred to smaller ones. This feature of preferences is captured in the assumption of monotonicity. For Definition 3.B.2, we assume that the consumption of larger amounts of goods is always feasible in principle; that is, if $x \in X$ and $y \geq x$, then $y \in X$.

**Definition 3.B.2:** The preference relation $\succsim$ on $X$ is *monotone* if $x \in X$ and $y \gg x$ implies $y \succ x$. It is *strongly monotone* if $y \geq x$ and $y \neq x$ imply that $y \succ x$.

The assumption that preferences are monotone is satisfied as long as commodities are "goods" rather than "bads". Even if some commodity is a bad, however, we may still be able to view preferences as monotone because it is often possible to redefine a consumption activity in a way that satisfies the assumption. For example, if one commodity is garbage, we can instead define the individual's consumption over the "absence of garbage".[2]

Note that if $\succsim$ is monotone, we may have indifference with respect to an increase in the amount of some but not all commodities. In contrast, strong montonicity says that if $y$ is larger than $x$ for *some* commodity and is no less for any other, then $y$ is strictly preferred to $x$.

For much of the theory, however, a weaker desirability assumption than monotonicity, known as *local nonsatiation*, actually suffices.

**Definition 3.B.3:** The preference relation $\succsim$ on $X$ is *locally nonsatiated* if for every $x \in X$ and every $\varepsilon > 0$, there is $y \in X$ such that $\|y - x\| \leq \varepsilon$ and $y \succ x$.[3]

The test for locally nonsatiated preferences is depicted in Figure 3.B.1 for the case in which $X = \mathbb{R}^L_+$. It says that for any consumption bundle $x \in \mathbb{R}^L_+$ and any arbitrarily

---

1. See Section 1.B for a thorough discussion of these properties.

2. It is also sometimes convenient to view preferences as defined over the level of goods available for consumption (the stocks of goods on hand), rather than over the consumption levels themselves. In this case, if the consumer can freely dispose of any unwanted commodities, her preferences over the level of commodities on hand are monotone as long as some good is always desirable.

3. $\|x - y\|$ is the Euclidean distance between points $x$ and $y$; that is, $\|x - y\| = [\sum_{\ell=1}^{L} (x_\ell - y_\ell)^2]^{1/2}$.

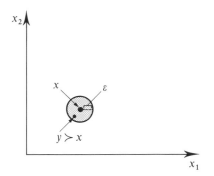

**Figure 3.B.1**
The test for local
nonsatiation.

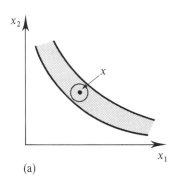

(a)

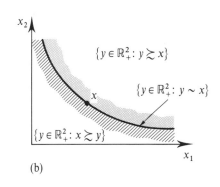

(b)

**Figure 3.B.2**
(a) A thick indifference
set violates local
nonsatiation.
(b) Preferences
compatible with local
nonsatiation.

small distance away from $x$, denoted by $\varepsilon > 0$, there is another bundle $y \in \mathbb{R}_+^L$ within this distance from $x$ that is preferred to $x$. Note that the bundle $y$ may even have less of every commodity than $x$, as shown in the figure. Nonetheless, when $X = \mathbb{R}_+^L$ local nonsatiation rules out the extreme situation in which all commodities are bads, since in that case no consumption at all (the point $x = 0$) would be a satiation point.

**Exercise 3.B.1:** Show the following:

    **(a)** If $\succsim$ is strongly monotone, then it is monotone.

    **(b)** If $\succsim$ is monotone, then it is locally nonsatiated.

Given the preference relation $\succsim$ and a consumption bundle $x$, we can define three related sets of consumption bundles. The *indifference set* containing point $x$ is the set of all bundles that are indifferent to $x$; formally, it is $\{y \in X : y \sim x\}$. The *upper contour set* of bundle $x$ is the set of all bundles that are at least as good as $x$: $\{y \in X : y \succsim x\}$. The *lower contour set* of $x$ is the set of all bundles that $x$ is at least as good as: $\{y \in X : x \succsim y\}$.

One implication of local nonsatiation (and, hence, of monotonicity) is that it rules out "thick" indifference sets. The indifference set in Figure 3.B.2(a) cannot satisfy local nonsatiation because, if it did, there would be a better point than $x$ within the circle drawn. In contrast, the indifference set in Figure 3.B.2(b) is compatible with local nonsatiation. Figure 3.B.2(b) also depicts the upper and lower contour sets of $x$.

(ii) *Convexity assumptions.* A second significant assumption, that of convexity of $\succsim$, concerns the trade-offs that the consumer is willing to make among different goods.

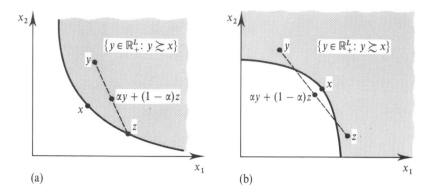

(a)                    (b)

**Figure 3.B.3**

(a) Convex preferences.
(b) Nonconvex preferences.

**Definition 3.B.4:** The preference relation $\succsim$ on $X$ is *convex* if for every $x \in X$, the upper contour set $\{y \in X : y \succsim x\}$ is convex; that is, if $y \succsim x$ and $z \succsim x$, then $\alpha y + (1 - \alpha)z \succsim x$ for any $\alpha \in [0, 1]$.

Figure 3.B.3(a) depicts a convex upper contour set; Figure 3.B.3(b) shows an upper contour set that is not convex.

Convexity is a strong but central hypothesis in economics. It can be interpreted in terms of *diminishing marginal rates of substitution*: That is, with convex preferences, from any initial consumption situation $x$, and for any two commodities, it takes increasingly larger amounts of one commodity to compensate for successive unit losses of the other.[4]

Convexity can also be viewed as the formal expression of a basic inclination of economic agents for diversification. Indeed, under convexity, if $x$ is indifferent to $y$, then $\frac{1}{2}x + \frac{1}{2}y$, the half–half mixture of $x$ and $y$, cannot be worse than either $x$ or $y$. In Chapter 6, we shall give a diversification interpretation in terms of behavior under uncertainty. A taste for diversification is a realistic trait of economic life. Economic theory would be in serious difficulty if this postulated propensity for diversification did not have significant descriptive content. But there is no doubt that one can easily think of choice situations where it is violated. For example, you may like both milk and orange juice but get less pleasure from a mixture of the two.

---

Definition 3.B.4 has been stated for a general consumption set $X$. But de facto, the convexity assumption can hold only if $X$ is convex. Thus, the hypothesis rules out commodities being consumable only in integer amounts or situations such as that presented in Figure 2.C.3.

Although the convexity assumption on preferences may seem strong, this appearance should be qualified in two respects: First, a good number (although not all) of the results of this chapter extend without modification to the nonconvex case. Second, as we show in Appendix A of Chapter 4 and in Section 17.I, nonconvexities can often be incorporated into the theory by exploiting regularizing aggregation effects across consumers.

---

We also make use at times of a strengthening of the convexity assumption.

**Definition 3.B.5:** The preference relation $\succsim$ on $X$ is *strictly convex* if for every $x$, we have that $y \succsim x$, $z \succsim x$, and $y \neq z$ implies $\alpha y + (1 - \alpha)z \succ x$ for all $\alpha \in (0, 1)$.

---

4. More generally, convexity is equivalent to a diminishing marginal rate of substitution between any two goods, provided that we allow for "composite commodities" formed from linear combinations of the $L$ basic commodities.

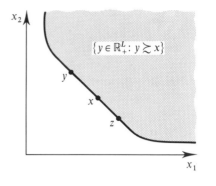

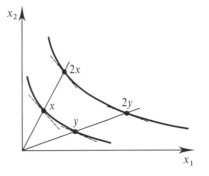

**Figure 3.B.4 (left)**

A convex, but not strictly convex, preference relation.

**Figure 3.B.5 (right)**

Homothetic preferences.

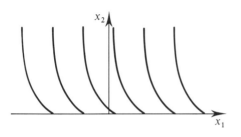

**Figure 3.B.6**

Quasilinear preferences.

Figure 3.B.3(a) showed strictly convex preferences. In Figure 3.B.4, on the other hand, the preferences, although convex, are not strictly convex.

In applications (particularly those of an econometric nature), it is common to focus on preferences for which it is possible to deduce the consumer's entire preference relation from a single indifference set. Two examples are the classes of *homothetic* and *quasilinear* preferences.

**Definition 3.B.6:** A monotone preference relation $\succsim$ on $X = \mathbb{R}_+^L$ is *homothetic* if all indifference sets are related by proportional expansion along rays; that is, if $x \sim y$, then $\alpha x \sim \alpha y$ for any $\alpha \geq 0$.

Figure 3.B.5 depicts a homothetic preference relation.

**Definition 3.B.7:** The preference relation $\succsim$ on $X = (-\infty, \infty) \times \mathbb{R}_+^{L-1}$ is *quasilinear* with respect to commodity 1 (called, in this case, the *numeraire* commodity) if[5]

    (i) All the indifference sets are parallel displacements of each other along the axis of commodity 1. That is, if $x \sim y$, then $(x + \alpha e_1) \sim (y + \alpha e_1)$ for $e_1 = (1, 0, \ldots, 0)$ and any $\alpha \in \mathbb{R}$.

    (ii) Good 1 is desirable; that is, $x + \alpha e_1 \succ x$ for all $x$ and $\alpha > 0$.

Note that, in Definition 3.B.7, we assume that there is no lower bound on the possible consumption of the first commodity [the consumption set is $(-\infty, \infty) \times \mathbb{R}_+^{L-1}$]. This assumption is convenient in the case of quasilinear preferences (Exercise 3.D.4 will illustate why). Figure 3.B.6 shows a quasilinear preference relation.

---

5. More generally, preferences can be quasilinear with respect to any commodity $\ell$.

## 3.C  Preference and Utility

For analytical purposes, it is very helpful if we can summarize the consumer's preferences by means of a utility function because mathematical programming techniques can then be used to solve the consumer's problem. In this section, we study when this can be done. Unfortunately, with the assumptions made so far, a rational preference relation need not be representable by a utility function. We begin with an example illustrating this fact and then introduce a weak, economically natural assumption (called *continuity*) that guarantees the existence of a utility representation.

**Example 3.C.1:** *The Lexicographic Preference Relation.* For simplicity, assume that $X = \mathbb{R}_+^2$. Define $x \succsim y$ if either "$x_1 > y_1$" or "$x_1 = y_1$ and $x_2 \geq y_2$." This is known as the *lexicographic preference relation*. The name derives from the way a dictionary is organized; that is, commodity 1 has the highest priority in determining the preference ordering, just as the first letter of a word does in the ordering of a dictionary. When the level of the first commodity in two commodity bundles is the same, the amount of the second commodity in the two bundles determines the consumer's preferences. In Exercise 3.C.1, you are asked to verify that the lexicographic ordering is complete, transitive, strongly monotone, and strictly convex. Nevertheless, it can be shown that no utility function exists that represents this preference ordering. This is intuitive. With this preference ordering, no two distinct bundles are indifferent; indifference sets are singletons. Therefore, we have two dimensions of distinct indifference sets. Yet, each of these indifference sets must be assigned, in an order-preserving way, a different utility number from the one-dimensional real line. In fact, a somewhat subtle argument is actually required to establish this claim rigorously. It is given, for the more advanced reader, in the following paragraph.

---

Suppose there is a utility function $u(\cdot)$. For every $x_1$, we can pick a rational number $r(x_1)$ such that $u(x_1, 2) > r(x_1) > u(x_1, 1)$. Note that because of the lexicographic character of preferences, $x_1 > x_1'$ implies $r(x_1) > r(x_1')$ [since $r(x_1) > u(x_1, 1) > u(x_1', 2) > r(x_1')$]. Therefore, $r(\cdot)$ provides a one-to-one function from the set of real numbers (which is uncountable) to the set of rational numbers (which is countable). This is a mathematical impossibility. Therefore, we conclude that there can be no utility function representing these preferences.

---

∎

The assumption that is needed to ensure the existence of a utility function is that the preference relation be continuous.

**Definition 3.C.1:** The preference relation $\succsim$ on $X$ is *continuous* if it is preserved under limits. That is, for any sequence of pairs $\{(x^n, y^n)\}_{n=1}^{\infty}$ with $x^n \succsim y^n$ for all $n$, $x = \lim_{n \to \infty} x^n$, and $y = \lim_{n \to \infty} y^n$, we have $x \succsim y$.

Continuity says that the consumer's preferences cannot exhibit "jumps," with, for example, the consumer preferring each element in sequence $\{x^n\}$ to the corresponding element in sequence $\{y^n\}$ but suddenly reversing her preference at the limiting points of these sequences $x$ and $y$.

An equivalent way to state this notion of continuity is to say that for all $x$, the upper contour set $\{y \in X : y \succsim x\}$ and the lower contour set $\{y \in X : x \succsim y\}$ are both *closed*; that is, they include their boundaries. Definition 3.C.1 implies that for any sequence of points $\{y^n\}_{n=1}^{\infty}$ with $x \succsim y^n$ for all $n$ and $y = \lim_{n \to \infty} y^n$, we have $x \succsim y$ (just let $x^n = x$ for all $n$). Hence, continuity as defined in Definition 3.C.1 implies that the lower contour set is closed; the same is implied for the upper contour set. The reverse argument, that closedness of the lower and upper contour sets implies that Definition 3.C.1 holds, is more advanced and is left as an exercise (Exercise 3.C.3).

**Example 3.C.1 continued:** Lexicographic preferences are not continuous. To see this, consider the sequence of bundles $x^n = (1/n, 0)$ and $y^n = (0, 1)$. For every $n$, we have $x^n \succ y^n$. But $\lim_{n \to \infty} y^n = (0, 1) \succ (0, 0) = \lim_{n \to \infty} x^n$. In words, as long as the first component of $x$ is larger than that of $y$, $x$ is preferred to $y$ even if $y_2$ is much larger than $x_2$. But as soon as the first components become equal, only the second components are relevant, and so the preference ranking is reversed at the limit points of the sequence. ∎

It turns out that the continuity of $\succsim$ is sufficient for the existence of a utility function representation. In fact, it guarantees the existence of a *continuous* utility function.

**Proposition 3.C.1:** Suppose that the rational preference relation $\succsim$ on $X$ is continuous. Then there is a continuous utility function $u(x)$ that represents $\succsim$.

**Proof:** For the case of $X = \mathbb{R}_+^L$ and a monotone preference relation, there is a relatively simple and intuitive proof that we present here with the help of Figure 3.C.1.

Denote the diagonal ray in $\mathbb{R}_+^L$ (the locus of vectors with all $L$ components equal) by $Z$. It will be convenient to let $e$ designate the $L$-vector whose elements are all equal to 1. Then $\alpha e \in Z$ for all nonnegative scalars $\alpha \geq 0$.

Note that for every $x \in \mathbb{R}_+^L$, monotonicity implies that $x \succsim 0$. Also note that for any $\bar{\alpha}$ such that $\bar{\alpha} e \gg x$ (as drawn in the figure), we have $\bar{\alpha} e \succsim x$. Monotonicity and continuity can then be shown to imply that there is a unique value $\alpha(x) \in [0, \bar{\alpha}]$ such that $\alpha(x)e \sim x$.

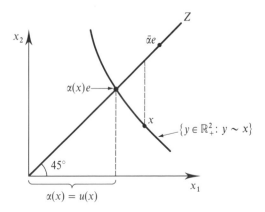

**Figure 3.C.1**

Construction of a utility function.

Formally, this can be shown as follows: By continuity, the upper and lower contour sets of $x$ are closed. Hence, the sets $A^+ = \{\alpha \in \mathbb{R}_+ : \alpha e \succsim x\}$ and $A^- = \{\alpha \in \mathbb{R}_+ : x \succsim \alpha e\}$ are nonempty and closed. Note that by completeness of $\succsim$, $\mathbb{R}_+ \subset (A^+ \cup A^-)$. The nonemptiness and closedness of $A^+$ and $A^-$, along with the fact that $\mathbb{R}_+$ is connected, imply that $A^+ \cap A^- \neq \varnothing$. Thus, there exists a scalar $\alpha$ such that $\alpha e \sim x$. Furthermore, by monotonicity, $\alpha_1 e \succ \alpha_2 e$ whenever $\alpha_1 > \alpha_2$. Hence, there can be at most one scalar satisfying $\alpha e \sim x$. This scalar is $\alpha(x)$.

We now take $\alpha(x)$ as our utility function; that is, we assign a utility value $u(x) = \alpha(x)$ to every $x$. This utility level is also depicted in Figure 3.C.1. We need to check two properties of this function: that it represents the preference $\succsim$ [i.e., that $\alpha(x) \geq \alpha(y) \Leftrightarrow x \succsim y$] and that it is a continuous function. The latter argument is more advanced, and therefore we present it in small type.

That $\alpha(x)$ represents preferences follows from its construction. Formally, suppose first that $\alpha(x) \geq \alpha(y)$. By monotonicity, this implies that $\alpha(x)e \succsim \alpha(y)e$. Since $x \sim \alpha(x)e$ and $y \sim \alpha(y)e$, we have $x \succsim y$. Suppose, on the other hand, that $x \succsim y$. Then $\alpha(x)e \sim x \succsim y \sim \alpha(y)e$; and so by monotonicity, we must have $\alpha(x) \geq \alpha(y)$. Hence, $\alpha(x) \geq \alpha(y) \Leftrightarrow x \succsim y$.

We now argue that $\alpha(x)$ is a continuous function at all $x$; that is, for any sequence $\{x^n\}_{n=1}^\infty$ with $x = \lim_{n \to \infty} x^n$, we have $\lim_{n \to \infty} \alpha(x^n) = \alpha(x)$. Hence, consider a sequence $\{x^n\}_{n=1}^\infty$ such that $x = \lim_{n \to \infty} x^n$.

We note first that the sequence $\{\alpha(x^n)\}_{n=1}^\infty$ must have a convergent subsequence. By monotonicity, for any $\varepsilon > 0$, $\alpha(x')$ lies in a compact subset of $\mathbb{R}_+$, $[\alpha_0, \alpha_1]$, for all $x'$ such that $\|x' - x\| \leq \varepsilon$ (see Figure 3.C.2). Since $\{x^n\}_{n=1}^\infty$ converges to $x$, there exists an $N$ such that $\alpha(x^n)$

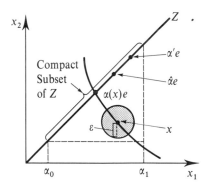

$x_2$

Compact Subset of $Z$

$\alpha'e$

$\hat{\alpha}e$

$\alpha(x)e$

$\varepsilon$

$x$

$Z$

$\alpha_0$            $\alpha_1$      $x_1$

**Figure 3.C.2**

Proof that the constructed utility function is continuous.

lies in this compact set for all $n > N$. But any infinite sequence that lies in a compact set must have a convergent subsequence (see Section M.F of the Mathematical Appendix).

What remains is to establish that all convergent subsequences of $\{\alpha(x^n)\}_{n=1}^\infty$ converge to $\alpha(x)$. To see this, suppose otherwise: that there is some strictly increasing function $m(\cdot)$ that assigns to each positive integer $n$ a positive integer $m(n)$ and for which the subsequence $\{\alpha(x^{m(n)})\}_{n=1}^\infty$ converges to $\alpha' \neq \alpha(x)$. We first show that $\alpha' > \alpha(x)$ leads to a contradiction. To begin, note that monotonicity would then imply that $\alpha'e \succ \alpha(x)e$. Now, let $\hat{\alpha} = \frac{1}{2}[\alpha' + \alpha(x)]$. The point $\hat{\alpha}e$ is the midpoint on $Z$ between $\alpha'e$ and $\alpha(x)e$ (see Figure 3.C.2). By monotonicity, $\hat{\alpha}e \succ \alpha(x)e$. Now, since $\alpha(x^{m(n)}) \to \alpha' > \hat{\alpha}$, there exists an $\bar{N}$ such that for all $n > \bar{N}$, $\alpha(x^{m(n)}) > \hat{\alpha}$.

Hence, for all such $n$, $x^{m(n)} \sim \alpha(x^{m(n)})e \succ \hat{\alpha}e$ (where the latter relation follows from monotonicity). Because preferences are continuous, this would imply that $x \succsim \hat{\alpha}e$. But since $x \sim \alpha(x)e$, we get $\alpha(x)e \succsim \hat{\alpha}e$, which is a contradiction. The argument ruling out $\alpha' < \alpha(x)$ is similar. Thus, since all convergent subsequences of $\{\alpha(x^n)\}_{n=1}^{\infty}$ must converge to $\alpha(x)$, we have $\lim_{n \to \infty} \alpha(x^n) = \alpha(x)$, and we are done.

∎

From now on, we assume that the consumer's preference relation is continuous and hence representable by a continuous utility function. As we noted in Section 1.B, the utility function $u(\cdot)$ that represents a preference relation $\succsim$ is not unique; any strictly increasing transformation of $u(\cdot)$, say $v(x) = f(u(x))$, where $f(\cdot)$ is a strictly increasing function, also represents $\succsim$. Proposition 3.C.1 tells us that if $\succsim$ is continuous, there exists *some* continuous utility function representing $\succsim$. But not all utility functions representing $\succsim$ are continuous; any strictly increasing but discontinuous transformation of a continuous utility function also represents $\succsim$.

For analytical purposes, it is also convenient if $u(\cdot)$ can be assumed to be differentiable. It is possible, however, for continuous preferences *not* to be representable by a differentiable utility function. The simplest example, shown in Figure 3.C.3, is the case of *Leontief* preferences, where $x'' \succsim x'$ if and only if Min $\{x_1'', x_2''\} \geq$ Min $\{x_1', x_2'\}$. The nondifferentiability arises because of the kink in indifference curves when $x_1 = x_2$.

Whenever convenient in the discussion that follows, we nevertheless assume utility functions to be twice continuously differentiable. It is possible to give a condition purely in terms of preferences that implies this property, but we shall not do so here. Intuitively, what is required is that indifference sets be smooth surfaces that fit together nicely so that the rates at which commodities substitute for each other depend differentiably on the consumption levels.

Restrictions on preferences translate into restrictions on the form of utility functions. The property of monotonicity, for example, implies that the utility function is increasing: $u(x) > u(y)$ if $x \gg y$.

The property of convexity of preferences, on the other hand, implies that $u(\cdot)$ is *quasiconcave* [and, similarly, strict convexity of preferences implies strict quasiconcavity of $u(\cdot)$]. The utility function $u(\cdot)$ is quasiconcave if the set $\{y \in \mathbb{R}_+^L : u(y) \geq u(x)\}$ is convex for all $x$ or, equivalently, if $u(\alpha x + (1 - \alpha)y) \geq$ Min $\{u(x), u(y)\}$ for

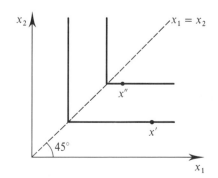

**Figure 3.C.3**

Leontief preferences cannot be represented by a differentiable utility function.

any $x$, $y$ and all $\alpha \in [0, 1]$. [If the inequality is strict for all $x \neq y$ and $\alpha \in (0, 1)$ then $u(\cdot)$ is strictly quasiconcave; for more on quasiconcavity and strict quasiconcavity see Section M.C of the Mathematical Appendix.] Note, however, that convexity of $\succsim$ does *not* imply the stronger property that $u(\cdot)$ is concave [that $u(\alpha x + (1 - \alpha)y) \geq \alpha u(x) + (1 - \alpha)u(y)$ for any $x$, $y$ and all $\alpha \in [0, 1]$]. In fact, although this is a somewhat fine point, there may not be *any* concave utility function representing a particular convex preference relation $\succsim$.

In Exercise 3.C.5, you are asked to prove two other results relating utility representations and underlying preference relations:

(i) A continuous $\succsim$ on $X = \mathbb{R}^L_+$ is homothetic if and only if it admits a utility function $u(x)$ that is homogeneous of degree one [i.e., such that $u(\alpha x) = \alpha u(x)$ for all $\alpha > 0$].

(ii) A continuous $\succsim$ on $(-\infty, \infty) \times \mathbb{R}^{L-1}_+$ is quasilinear with respect to the first commodity if and only if it admits a utility function $u(x)$ of the form $u(x) = x_1 + \phi(x_2, \ldots, x_L)$.

It is important to realize that although monotonicity and convexity of $\succsim$ imply that *all* utility functions representing $\succsim$ are increasing and quasiconcave, (i) and (ii) merely say that there is at *least one* utility function that has the specified form. Increasingness and quasiconcavity are *ordinal* properties of $u(\cdot)$; they are preserved for any arbitrary increasing transformation of the utility index. In contrast, the special forms of the utility representations in (i) and (ii) are not preserved; they are *cardinal* properties that are simply convenient choices for a utility representation.[6]

## 3.D    The Utility Maximization Problem

We now turn to the study of the consumer's decision problem. We assume throughout that the consumer has a rational, continuous, and locally nonsatiated preference relation, and we take $u(x)$ to be a continuous utility function representing these preferences. For the sake of concreteness, we also assume throughout the remainder of the chapter that the consumption set is $X = \mathbb{R}^L_+$.

The consumer's problem of choosing her most preferred consumption bundle given prices $p \gg 0$ and wealth level $w > 0$ can now be stated as the following *utility maximization problem* (*UMP*):

$$\underset{x \geq 0}{\text{Max}} \quad u(x)$$
$$\text{s.t. } p \cdot x \leq w.$$

In the UMP, the consumer chooses a consumption bundle in the Walrasian budget set $B_{p,w} = \{x \in \mathbb{R}^L_+ : p \cdot x \leq w\}$ to maximize her utility level. We begin with the results stated in Proposition 3.D.1.

**Proposition 3.D.1:** If $p \gg 0$ and $u(\cdot)$ is continuous, then the utility maximization problem has a solution.

---

6. Thus, in this sense, continuity is also a cardinal property of utility functions. See also the discussion of ordinal and cardinal properties of utility representations in Section 1.B.

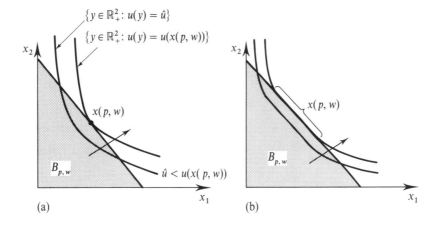

$\{y \in \mathbb{R}^2_+ : u(y) = \hat{u}\}$

$\{y \in \mathbb{R}^2_+ : u(y) = u(x(p, w))\}$

$x_2$

$x(p, w)$

$B_{p, w}$

$\hat{u} < u(x(p, w))$

$x_1$

(a)

$x_2$

$x(p, w)$

$B_{p, w}$

$x_1$

(b)

**Figure 3.D.1**

The utility maximization problem (UMP).
(a) Single solution.
(b) Multiple solutions.

**Proof:** If $p \gg 0$, then the budget set $B_{p, w} = \{x \in \mathbb{R}^L_+ : p \cdot x \leq w\}$ is a compact set because it is both bounded [for any $\ell = 1, \ldots, L$, we have $x_\ell \leq (w/p_\ell)$ for all $x \in B_{p, w}$] and closed. The result follows from the fact that a continuous function always has a maximum value on any compact set (set Section M.F. of the Mathematical Appendix). ∎

With this result, we now focus our attention on the properties of two objects that emerge from the UMP: the consumer's set of optimal consumption bundles (the solution set of the UMP) and the consumer's maximal utility value (the value function of the UMP).

### The Walrasian Demand Correspondence/Function

The rule that assigns the set of optimal consumption vectors in the UMP to each price–wealth situation $(p, w) \gg 0$ is denoted by $x(p, w) \in \mathbb{R}^L_+$ and is known as the *Walrasian* (or *ordinary* or *market*) *demand correspondence*. An example for $L = 2$ is depicted in Figure 3.D.1(a), where the point $x(p, w)$ lies in the indifference set with the highest utility level of any point in $B_{p, w}$. Note that, as a general matter, for a given $(p, w) \gg 0$ the optimal set $x(p, w)$ may have more than one element, as shown in Figure 3.D.1(b). When $x(p, w)$ is single-valued for all $(p, w)$, we refer to it as the *Walrasian* (or *ordinary* or *market*) *demand function*.[7]

The properties of $x(p, w)$ stated in Proposition 3.D.2 follow from direct examination of the UMP.

**Proposition 3.D.2:** Suppose that $u(\cdot)$ is a continuous utility function representing a locally nonsatiated preference relation $\succsim$ defined on the consumption set $X = \mathbb{R}^L_+$. Then the Walrasian demand correspondence $x(p, w)$ possesses the following properties:

---

7. This demand function has also been called the *Marshallian demand function*. However, this terminology can create confusion, and so we do not use it here. In Marshallian partial equilibrium analysis (where wealth effects are absent), all the different kinds of demand functions studied in this chapter coincide, and so it is not clear which of these demand functions would deserve the Marshall name in the more general setting.

  (i) *Homogeneity of degree zero in* $(p, w)$: $x(\alpha p, \alpha w) = x(p, w)$ for any $p$, $w$ and scalar $\alpha > 0$.

  (ii) *Walras' law:* $p \cdot x = w$ for all $x \in x(p, w)$.

  (iii) *Convexity/uniqueness:* If $\succsim$ is convex, so that $u(\cdot)$ is quasiconcave, then $x(p, w)$ is a convex set. Moreover, if $\succsim$ is *strictly convex*, so that $u(\cdot)$ is strictly quasiconcave, then $x(p, w)$ consists of a single element.

**Proof:** We establish each of these properties in turn.

  (i) For homogeneity, note that for any scalar $\alpha > 0$,

$$\{x \in \mathbb{R}^L_+ : \alpha p \cdot x \le \alpha w\} = \{x \in \mathbb{R}^L_+ : p \cdot x \le w\};$$

that is, the set of feasible consumption bundles in the UMP does not change when all prices and wealth are multiplied by a constant $\alpha > 0$. The set of utility-maximizing consumption bundles must therefore be the same in these two circumstances, and so $x(p, w) = x(\alpha p, \alpha w)$. Note that this property does not require any assumptions on $u(\cdot)$.

  (ii) Walras' law follows from local nonsatiation. If $p \cdot x < w$ for some $x \in x(p, w)$, then there must exist another consumption bundle $y$ sufficiently close to $x$ with both $p \cdot y < w$ and $y \succ x$ (see Figure 3.D.2). But this would contradict $x$ being optimal in the UMP.

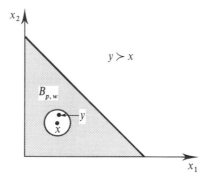

**Figure 3.D.2**

Local nonsatiation implies Walras' law.

  (iii) Suppose that $u(\cdot)$ is quasiconcave and that there are two bundles $x$ and $x'$, with $x \ne x'$, both of which are elements of $x(p, w)$. To establish the result, we show that $x'' = \alpha x + (1 - \alpha)x'$ is an element of $x(p, w)$ for any $\alpha \in [0,1]$. To start, we know that $u(x) = u(x')$. Denote this utility level by $u^*$. By quasiconcavity, $u(x'') \ge u^*$ [see Figure 3.D.3(a)]. In addition, since $p \cdot x \le w$ and $p \cdot x' \le w$, we also have

$$p \cdot x'' = p \cdot [\alpha x + (1 - \alpha)x'] \le w.$$

Therefore, $x''$ is a feasible choice in the UMP (put simply, $x''$ is feasible because $B_{p,w}$ is a convex set). Thus, since $u(x'') \ge u^*$ and $x''$ is feasible, we have $x'' \in x(p, w)$. This establishes that $x(p, w)$ is a convex set if $u(\cdot)$ is quasiconcave.

  Suppose now that $u(\cdot)$ is *strictly* quasiconcave. Following the same argument but using strict quasiconcavity, we can establish that $x''$ is a feasible choice and that $u(x'') > u^*$ for all $\alpha \in (0,1)$. Because this contradicts the assumption that $x$ and $x'$ are elements of $x(p, w)$, we conclude that there can be at most one element in $x(p, w)$. Figure 3.D.3(b) illustrates this argument. Note the difference from Figure 3.D.3(a) arising from the strict quasiconcavity of $u(x)$. ∎

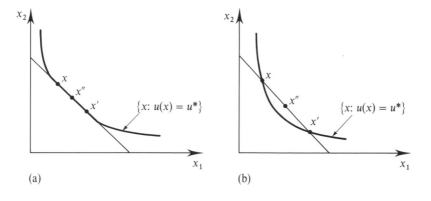

**Figure 3.D.3**

(a) Convexity of preferences implies convexity of $x(p, w)$. (b) Strict convexity of preferences implies that $x(p, w)$ is single-valued.

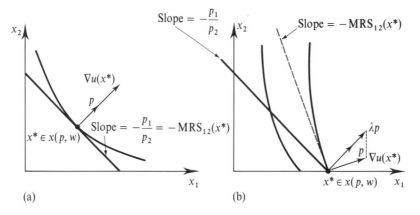

**Figure 3.D.4**

(a) Interior solution. (b) Boundary solution.

If $u(\cdot)$ is continuously differentiable, an optimal consumption bundle $x^* \in x(p, w)$ can be characterized in a very useful manner by means of first-order conditions. The *Kuhn–Tucker* (*necessary*) *conditions* (see Section M.K of the Mathematical Appendix) say that if $x^* \in x(p, w)$ is a solution to the UMP, then there exists a *Lagrange multiplier* $\lambda \geq 0$ such that for all $\ell = 1, \dots, L$:[8]

$$\frac{\partial u(x^*)}{\partial c_\ell} \leq \lambda p_\ell, \quad \text{with equality if } x_\ell^* > 0. \tag{3.D.1}$$

Equivalently, if we let $\nabla u(x) = [\partial u(x)/\partial x_1, \dots, \partial u(x)/\partial x_L]$ denote the gradient vector of $u(\cdot)$ at $x$, we can write (3.D.1) in matrix notation as

$$\nabla u(x^*) \leq \lambda p \tag{3.D.2}$$

and

$$x^* \cdot [\nabla u(x^*) - \lambda p] = 0. \tag{3.D.3}$$

Thus, if we are at an interior optimum (i.e., if $x^* \gg 0$), we must have

$$\nabla u(x^*) = \lambda p. \tag{3.D.4}$$

Figure 3.D.4(a) depicts the first-order conditions for the case of an interior optimum when $L = 2$. Condition (3.D.4) tells us that at an interior optimum, the

---

8. To be fully rigorous, these Kuhn–Tucker necessary conditions are valid only if the constraint qualification condition holds (see Section M.K of the Mathematical Appendix). In the UMP, this is always so. Whenever we use Kuhn–Tucker necessary conditions without mentioning the constraint qualification condition, this requirement is met.

gradient vector of the consumer's utility function $\nabla u(x^*)$ must be proportional to the price vector $p$, as is shown in Figure 3.D.4(a). If $\nabla u(x^*) \gg 0$, this is equivalent to the requirement that for any two goods $\ell$ and $k$, we have

$$\frac{\partial u(x^*)/\partial x_\ell}{\partial u(x^*)/\partial x_k} = \frac{p_\ell}{p_k}. \tag{3.D.5}$$

The expression on the left of (3.D.5) is the *marginal rate of substitution of good $\ell$ for good $k$ at $x^*$*, $MRS_{\ell k}(x^*)$; it tells us the amount of good $k$ that the consumer must be given to compensate her for a one-unit marginal reduction in her consumption of good $\ell$.[9] In the case where $L = 2$, the slope of the consumer's indifference set at $x^*$ is precisely $-MRS_{12}(x^*)$. Condition (3.D.5) tells us that at an interior optimum, the consumer's marginal rate of substitution between any two goods must be equal to their price ratio, the marginal rate of exchange between them, as depicted in Figure 3.D.4(a). Were this not the case, the consumer could do better by marginally changing her consumption. For example, if $[\partial u(x^*)/\partial x_\ell]/[\partial u(x^*)/\partial x_k] > (p_\ell/p_k)$, then an increase in the consumption of good $\ell$ of $dx_\ell$, combined with a decrease in good $k$'s consumption equal to $(p_\ell/p_k)\,dx_\ell$, would be feasible and would yield a utility change of $[\partial u(x^*)/\partial x_\ell]\,dx_\ell - [\partial u(x^*)/\partial x_k](p_\ell/p_k)\,dx_\ell > 0$.

Figure 3.D.4(b) depicts the first-order conditions for the case of $L = 2$ when the consumer's optimal bundle $x^*$ lies on the boundary of the consumption set (we have $x_2^* = 0$ there). In this case, the gradient vector need not be proportional to the price vector. In particular, the first-order conditions tell us that $\partial u_\ell(x^*)/\partial x_\ell \leq \lambda p_\ell$ for those $\ell$ with $x_\ell^* = 0$ and $\partial u_\ell(x^*)/\partial x_\ell = \lambda p_\ell$ for those $\ell$ with $x_\ell^* > 0$. Thus, in the figure, we see that $MRS_{12}(x^*) > p_1/p_2$. In contrast with the case of an interior optimum, an inequality between the marginal rate of substitution and the price ratio can arise at a boundary optimum because the consumer is unable to reduce her consumption of good 2 (and correspondingly increase her consumption of good 1) any further.

The Lagrange multiplier $\lambda$ in the first-order conditions (3.D.2) and (3.D.3) gives the marginal, or shadow, value of relaxing the constraint in the UMP (this is a general property of Lagrange multipliers; see Sections M.K and M.L of the Mathematical Appendix). It therefore equals the consumer's marginal utility value of wealth at the optimum. To see this directly, consider for simplicity the case where $x(p, w)$ is a differentiable function and $x(p, w) \gg 0$. By the chain rule, the change in utility from a marginal increase in $w$ is given by $\nabla u(x(p, w)) \cdot D_w x(p, w)$, where $D_w x(p, w) = [\partial x_1(p, w)/\partial w, \ldots, \partial x_L(p, w)/\partial w]$. Substituting for $\nabla u(x(p, w))$ from condition (3.D.4), we get

$$\nabla u(x(p, w)) \cdot D_w x(p, w) = \lambda p \cdot D_w x(p, w) = \lambda,$$

where the last equality follows because $p \cdot x(p, w) = w$ holds for all $w$ (Walras' law) and therefore $p \cdot D_w x(p, w) = 1$. Thus, the marginal change in utility arising from

---

9. Note that if utility is unchanged with differential changes in $x_\ell$ and $x_k$, $dx_\ell$ and $dx_k$, then $[\partial u(x)/\partial x_\ell]\,dx_\ell + [\partial u(x)/\partial x_k]\,dx_k = 0$. Thus, when $x_\ell$ falls by amount $dx_\ell < 0$, the increase required in $x_k$ to keep utility unchanged is precisely $dx_k = MRS_{\ell k}(x^*)(-dx_\ell)$.

a marginal increase in wealth—the consumer's *marginal utility of wealth*—is precisely $\lambda$.[10]

We have seen that conditions (3.D.2) and (3.D.3) must necessarily be satisfied by any $x^* \in x(p, w)$. When, on the other hand, does satisfaction of these first-order conditions by some bundle $x$ imply that $x$ is a solution to the UMP? That is, when are the first-order conditions *sufficient* to establish that $x$ is a solution? If $u(\cdot)$ is quasiconcave and monotone and has $\nabla u(x) \neq 0$ for all $x \in \mathbb{R}_+^L$, then the Kuhn–Tucker first-order conditions are indeed sufficient (see Section M.K of the Mathematical Appendix). What if $u(\cdot)$ is not quasiconcave? In that case, if $u(\cdot)$ is locally quasiconcave at $x^*$, and if $x^*$ satisfies the first-order conditions, then $x^*$ is a local maximum. Local quasiconcavity can be verified by means of a determinant test on the *bordered Hessian matrix* of $u(\cdot)$ at $x^*$. (For more on this, see Sections M.C and M.D of the Mathematical Appendix.)

Example 3.D.1 illustrates the use of the first-order conditions in deriving the consumer's optimal consumption bundle.

**Example 3.D.1:** *The Demand Function Derived from the Cobb–Douglas Utility Function.* A *Cobb–Douglas* utility function for $L = 2$ is given by $u(x_1, x_2) = k x_1^\alpha x_2^{1-\alpha}$ for some $\alpha \in (0, 1)$ and $k > 0$. It is increasing at all $(x_1, x_2) \gg 0$ and is homogeneous of degree one. For our analysis, it turns out to be easier to use the increasing transformation $\alpha \ln x_1 + (1 - \alpha) \ln x_2$, a strictly concave function, as our utility function. With this choice, the UMP can be stated as

$$\underset{x_1, x_2}{\text{Max}} \quad \alpha \ln x_1 + (1 - \alpha) \ln x_2 \qquad (3.D.6)$$

$$\text{s.t. } p_1 x_1 + p_2 x_2 = w.$$

[Note that since $u(\cdot)$ is increasing, the budget constraint will hold with strict equality at any solution.]

Since $\ln 0 = -\infty$, the optimal choice $(x_1(p, w), x_2(p, w))$ is strictly positive and must satisfy the first-order conditions (we write the consumption levels simply as $x_1$ and $x_2$ for notational convenience)

$$\frac{\alpha}{x_1} = \lambda p_1 \qquad (3.D.7)$$

and

$$\frac{1 - \alpha}{x_2} = \lambda p_2 \qquad (3.D.8)$$

for some $\lambda \geq 0$, and the budget constraint $p \cdot x(p, w) = w$. Conditions (3.D.7) and (3.D.8) imply that

$$p_1 x_1 = \frac{\alpha}{1 - \alpha} p_2 x_2$$

or, using the budget constraint,

$$p_1 x_1 = \frac{\alpha}{1 - \alpha} (w - p_1 x_1).$$

---

10. Note that if monotonicity of $u(\cdot)$ is strengthened slightly by requiring that $\nabla u(x) \geq 0$ *and* $\nabla u(x) \neq 0$ for all $x$, then condition (3.D.4) and $p \gg 0$ also imply that $\lambda$ is strictly positive at any solution of the UMP.

Hence (including the arguments of $x_1$ and $x_2$ once again)

$$x_1(p,w) = \frac{\alpha w}{p_1},$$

and (using the budget constraint)

$$x_2(p,w) = \frac{(1-\alpha)w}{p_2}.$$

Note that with the Cobb–Douglas utility function, the expenditure on each commodity is a constant fraction of wealth for any price vector $p$ [a share of $\alpha$ goes for the first commodity and a share of $(1-\alpha)$ goes for the second]. ∎

**Exercise 3.D.1:** Verify the three properties of Proposition 3.D.2 for the Walrasian demand function generated by the Cobb–Douglas utility function.

For the analysis of demand responses to changes in prices and wealth, it is also very helpful if the consumer's Walrasian demand is suitably continuous and differentiable. Because the issues are somewhat more technical, we will discuss the conditions under which demand satisfies these properties in Appendix A to this chapter. We conclude there that both properties hold under fairly general conditions. Indeed, if preferences are continuous, strictly convex, and locally nonsatiated on the consumption set $\mathbb{R}_+^L$, then $x(p, w)$ (which is then a function) is *always* continuous at all $(p, w) \gg 0$.

*The Indirect Utility Function*

For each $(p, w) \gg 0$, the utility value of the UMP is denoted $v(p, w) \in \mathbb{R}$. It is equal to $u(x^*)$ for any $x^* \in x(p, w)$. The function $v(p, w)$ is called the *indirect utility function* and often proves to be a very useful analytic tool. Proposition 3.D.3 identifies its basic properties.

**Proposition 3.D.3:** Suppose that $u(\cdot)$ is a continuous utility function representing a locally nonsatiated preference relation $\succsim$ defined on the consumption set $X = \mathbb{R}_+^L$. The indirect utility function $v(p, w)$ is

   (i) Homogeneous of degree zero.
   (ii) Strictly increasing in $w$ and nonincreasing in $p_\ell$ for any $\ell$.
   (iii) Quasiconvex; that is, the set $\{(p, w): v(p, w) \leq \bar{v}\}$ is convex for any $\bar{v}$.[11]
   (iv) Continuous in $p$ and $w$.

**Proof:** Except for quasiconvexity and continuity all the properties follow readily from our previous discussion. We forgo the proof of continuity here but note that, when preferences are strictly convex, it follows from the fact that $x(p, w)$ and $u(x)$ are continuous functions because $v(p, w) = u(x(p, w))$ [recall that the continuity of $x(p, w)$ is established in Appendix A of this chapter].

To see that $v(p,w)$ is quasiconvex, suppose that $v(p, w) \leq \bar{v}$ and $v(p', w') \leq \bar{v}$. For any $\alpha \in [0, 1]$, consider then the price–wealth pair $(p'', w'') = (\alpha p + (1 - \alpha)p', \alpha w + (1 - \alpha)w')$.

----

11. Note that property (iii) says that $v(p, w)$ is quasi*convex*, *not* quasi*concave*. Observe also that property (iii) does not require for its validity that $u(\cdot)$ be quasiconcave.

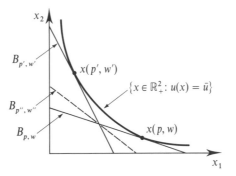

**Figure 3.D.5**

The indirect utility function $v(p, w)$ is quasiconvex.

To establish quasiconvexity, we want to show that $v(p'', w'') \leq \bar{v}$. Thus, we show that for any $x$ with $p'' \cdot x \leq w''$, we must have $u(x) \leq \bar{v}$. Note, first, that if $p'' \cdot x \leq w''$, then,

$$\alpha p \cdot x + (1 - \alpha) p' \cdot x \leq \alpha w + (1 - \alpha) w'.$$

Hence, either $p \cdot x \leq w$ or $p' \cdot x \leq w'$ (or both). If the former inequality holds, then $u(x) \leq v(p, w) \leq \bar{v}$, and we have established the result. If the latter holds, then $u(x) \leq v(p', w') \leq \bar{v}$, and the same conclusion follows. ∎

The quasiconvexity of $v(p, w)$ can be verified graphically in Figure 3.D.5 for the case where $L = 2$. There, the budget sets for price–wealth pairs $(p, w)$ and $(p', w')$ generate the same maximized utility value $\bar{u}$. The budget line corresponding to $(p'', w'') = (\alpha p + (1 - \alpha) p', \alpha w + (1 - \alpha) w')$ is depicted as a dashed line in Figure 3.D.5. Because $(p'', w'')$ is a convex combination of $(p, w)$ and $(p', w')$, its budget line lies between the budget lines for these two price–wealth pairs. As can be seen in the figure, the attainable utility under $(p'', w'')$ is necessarily no greater than $\bar{u}$.

Note that the indirect utility function depends on the utility representation chosen. In particular, if $v(p, w)$ is the indirect utility function when the consumer's utility function is $u(\cdot)$, then the indirect utility function corresponding to utility representation $\tilde{u}(x) = f(u(x))$ is $\tilde{v}(p, w) = f(v(p, w))$.

**Example 3.D.2:** Suppose that we have the utility function $u(x_1, x_2) = \alpha \ln x_1 + (1 - \alpha) \ln x_2$. Then, substituting $x_1(p, w)$ and $x_2(p, w)$ from Example 3.D.1, into $u(x)$ we have

$$v(p, w) = u(x(p, w))$$
$$= [\alpha \ln \alpha + (1 - \alpha) \ln (1 - \alpha)] + \ln w - \alpha \ln p_1 - (1 - \alpha) \ln p_2.$$

**Exercise 3.D.2:** Verify the four properties of Proposition 3.D.3 for the indirect utility function derived in Example 3.D.2.

# 3.E The Expenditure Minimization Problem

In this section, we study the following *expenditure minimization problem* (EMP) for $p \gg 0$ and $u > u(0)$:[12]

---

12. Utility $u(0)$ is the utility from consuming the consumption bundle $x = (0, 0, \ldots, 0)$. The restriction to $u > u(0)$ rules out only uninteresting situations.

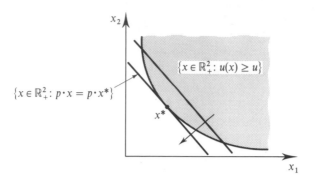

**Figure 3.E.1**

The expenditure minimization problem (EMP).

$$\underset{x \geq 0}{\text{Min}} \quad p \cdot x \qquad\qquad \text{(EMP)}$$
$$\text{s.t. } u(x) \geq u.$$

Whereas the UMP computes the maximal level of utility that can be obtained given wealth $w$, the EMP computes the minimal level of wealth required to reach utility level $u$. The EMP is the "dual" problem to the UMP. It captures the same aim of efficient use of the consumer's purchasing power while reversing the roles of objective function and constraint.[13]

Throughout this section, we assume that $u(\cdot)$ is a continuous utility function representing a locally nonsatiated preference relation $\succsim$ defined on the consumption set $\mathbb{R}^L_+$.

The EMP is illustrated in Figure 3.E.1. The optimal consumption bundle $x^*$ is the least costly bundle that still allows the consumer to achieve the utility level $u$. Geometrically, it is the point in the set $\{x \in \mathbb{R}^L_+ : u(x) \geq u\}$ that lies on the lowest possible budget line associated with the price vector $p$.

Proposition 3.E.1 describes the formal relationship between EMP and the UMP.

**Proposition 3.E.1:** Suppose that $u(\cdot)$ is a continuous utility function representing a locally nonsatiated preference relation $\succsim$ defined on the consumption set $X = \mathbb{R}^L_+$ and that the price vector is $p \gg 0$. We have

(i) If $x^*$ is optimal in the UMP when wealth is $w > 0$, then $x^*$ is optimal in the EMP when the required utility level is $u(x^*)$. Moreover, the minimized expenditure level in this EMP is exactly $w$.

(ii) If $x^*$ is optimal in the EMP when the required utility level is $u > u(0)$, then $x^*$ is optimal in the UMP when wealth is $p \cdot x^*$. Moreover, the maximized utility level in this UMP is exactly $u$.

**Proof:** (i) Suppose that $x^*$ is not optimal in the EMP with required utility level $u(x^*)$. Then there exists an $x'$ such that $u(x') \geq u(x^*)$ and $p \cdot x' < p \cdot x^* \leq w$. By local nonsatiation, we can find an $x''$ very close to $x'$ such that $u(x'') > u(x')$ and $p \cdot x'' < w$. But this implies that $x'' \in B_{p,w}$ and $u(x'') > u(x^*)$, contradicting the optimality of $x^*$ in the UMP. Thus, $x^*$ must be optimal in the EMP when the required utility level

---

13. The term "dual" is meant to be suggestive. It is usually applied to pairs of problems and concepts that are formally similar except that the role of quantities and prices, and/or maximization and minimization, and/or objective function and constraint, have been reversed.

is $u(x^*)$, and the minimized expenditure level is therefore $p \cdot x^*$. Finally, since $x^*$ solves the UMP when wealth is $w$, by Walras' law we have $p \cdot x^* = w$.

(ii) Since $u > u(0)$, we must have $x^* \neq 0$. Hence, $p \cdot x^* > 0$. Suppose that $x^*$ is not optimal in the UMP when wealth is $p \cdot x^*$. Then there exists an $x'$ such that $u(x') > u(x^*)$ and $p \cdot x' \leq p \cdot x^*$. Consider a bundle $x'' = \alpha x'$ where $\alpha \in (0,1)$ ($x''$ is a "scaled-down" version of $x'$). By continuity of $u(\cdot)$, if $\alpha$ is close enough to 1, then we will have $u(x'') > u(x^*)$ and $p \cdot x'' < p \cdot x^*$. But this contradicts the optimality of $x^*$ in the EMP. Thus, $x^*$ must be optimal in the UMP when wealth is $p \cdot x^*$, and the maximized utility level is therefore $u(x^*)$. In Proposition 3.E.3(ii), we will show that if $x^*$ solves the EMP when the required utility level is $u$, then $u(x^*) = u$. ∎

As with the UMP, when $p \gg 0$ a solution to the EMP exists under very general conditions. The constraint set merely needs to be nonempty; that is, $u(\cdot)$ must attain values at least as large as $u$ for *some* $x$ (see Exercise 3.E.3). From now on, we assume that this is so; for example, this condition will be satisfied for any $u > u(0)$ if $u(\cdot)$ is unbounded above.

We now proceed to study the optimal consumption vector and the value function of the EMP. We consider the value function first.

## The Expenditure Function

Given prices $p \gg 0$ and required utility level $u > u(0)$, the value of the EMP is denoted $e(p, u)$. The function $e(p, u)$ is called the *expenditure function*. Its value for any $(p, u)$ is simply $p \cdot x^*$, where $x^*$ is any solution to the EMP. The result in Proposition 3.E.2 describes the basic properties of the expenditure function. It parallels Proposition 3.D.3's characterization of the properties of the indirect utility function for the UMP.

**Proposition 3.E.2:** Suppose that $u(\cdot)$ is a continuous utility function representing a locally nonsatiated preference relation $\succsim$ defined on the consumption set $X = \mathbb{R}_+^L$. The expenditure function $e(p, u)$ is

    (i) Homogeneous of degree one in $p$.
    (ii) Strictly increasing in $u$ and nondecreasing in $p_\ell$ for any $\ell$.
    (iii) Concave in $p$.
    (iv) Continuous in $p$ and $u$.

**Proof:** We prove only properties (i), (ii), and (iii).

(i) The constraint set of the EMP is unchanged when prices change. Thus, for any scalar $\alpha > 0$, minimizing $(\alpha p) \cdot x$ on this set leads to the same optimal consumption bundles as minimizing $p \cdot x$. Letting $x^*$ be optimal in both circumstances, we have $e(\alpha p, u) = \alpha p \cdot x^* = \alpha e(p, u)$.

(ii) Suppose that $e(p, u)$ were not strictly increasing in $u$, and let $x'$ and $x''$ denote optimal consumption bundles for required utility levels $u'$ and $u''$, respectively, where $u'' > u'$ and $p \cdot x' \geq p \cdot x'' > 0$. Consider a bundle $\tilde{x} = \alpha x''$, where $\alpha \in (0, 1)$. By continuity of $u(\cdot)$, there exists an $\alpha$ close enough to 1 such that $u(\tilde{x}) > u'$ and $p \cdot x' > p \cdot \tilde{x}$. But this contradicts $x'$ being optimal in the EMP with required utility level $u'$.

To show that $e(p, u)$ is nondecreasing in $p_\ell$, suppose that price vectors $p''$ and $p'$ have $p_\ell'' \geq p_\ell'$ and $p_k'' = p_k'$ for all $k \neq \ell$. Let $x''$ be an optimizing vector in the EMP for prices $p''$. Then $e(p'', u) = p'' \cdot x'' \geq p' \cdot x'' \geq e(p', u)$, where the latter inequality follows from the definition of $e(p', u)$.

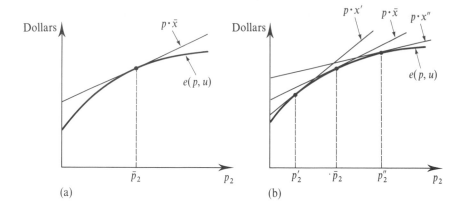

**Figure 3.E.2**
The concavity in $p$ of the expenditure function.

(iii) For concavity, fix a required utility level $\bar{u}$, and let $p'' = \alpha p + (1 - \alpha)p'$ for $\alpha \in [0, 1]$. Suppose that $x''$ is an optimal bundle in the EMP when prices are $p''$. If so,

$$e(p'', \bar{u}) = p'' \cdot x''$$
$$= \alpha p \cdot x'' + (1 - \alpha)p' \cdot x''$$
$$\geq \alpha e(p, \bar{u}) + (1 - \alpha)e(p', \bar{u}),$$

where the last inequality follows because $u(x'') \geq \bar{u}$ and the definition of the expenditure function imply that $p \cdot x'' \geq e(p, \bar{u})$ and $p' \cdot x'' \geq e(p', \bar{u})$. ∎

The concavity of $e(p, \bar{u})$ in $p$ for given $\bar{u}$, which is a very important property, is actually fairly intuitive. Suppose that we initially have prices $\bar{p}$ and that $\bar{x}$ is an optimal consumption vector at these prices in the EMP. If prices change but we do not let the consumer change her consumption levels from $\bar{x}$, then the resulting expenditure will be $p \cdot \bar{x}$, which is a *linear* expression in $p$. But when the consumer can adjust her consumption, as in the EMP, her minimized expenditure level can be no greater than this amount. Hence, as illustrated in Figure 3.E.2(a), where we keep $p_1$ fixed and vary $p_2$, the graph of $e(p, \bar{u})$ lies below the graph of the linear function $p \cdot \bar{x}$ at all $p \neq \bar{p}$ and touches it at $\bar{p}$. This amounts to concavity because a similar relation to a linear function must hold at each point of the graph of $e(\cdot, u)$; see Figure 3.E.2(b).

Proposition 3.E.1 allows us to make an important connection between the expenditure function and the indirect utility function developed in Section 3.D. In particular, for any $p \gg 0$, $w > 0$, and $u > u(0)$ we have

$$e(p, v(p, w)) = w \qquad \text{and} \qquad v(p, e(p, u)) = u. \qquad (3.E.1)$$

These conditions imply that for a fixed price vector $\bar{p}$, $e(\bar{p}, \cdot)$ and $v(\bar{p}, \cdot)$ are inverses to one another (see Exercise 3.E.8). In fact, in Exercise 3.E.9, you are asked to show that by using the relations in (3.E.1), Proposition 3.E.2 can be directly derived from Proposition 3.D.3, and vice versa. That is, there is a direct correspondence between the properties of the expenditure function and the indirect utility function. They both capture the same underlying features of the consumer's choice problem.

*The Hicksian (or Compensated) Demand Function*

The set of optimal commodity vectors in the EMP is denoted $h(p, u) \subset \mathbb{R}_+^L$ and is known as the *Hicksian*, or *compensated*, *demand correspondence*, or *function* if

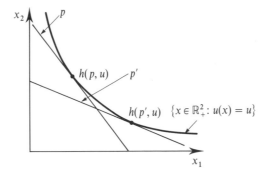

**Figure 3.E.3**

The Hicksian (or compensated) demand function.

single-valued. (The reason for the term "compensated demand" will be explained below.) Figure 3.E.3 depicts the solution set $h(p, u)$ for two different price vectors $p$ and $p'$.

Three basic properties of Hicksian demand are given in Proposition 3.E.3, which parallels Proposition 3.D.2 for Walrasian demand.

**Proposition 3.E.3:** Suppose that $u(\cdot)$ is a continuous utility function representing a locally nonsatiated preference relation $\succsim$ defined on the consumption set $X = \mathbb{R}_+^L$. Then for any $p \gg 0$, the Hicksian demand correspondence $h(p, u)$ possesses the following properties:

    (i) *Homogeneity of degree zero in $p$*: $h(\alpha p, u) = h(p, u)$ for any $p$, $u$ and $\alpha > 0$.

    (ii) *No excess utility:* For any $x \in h(p, u)$, $u(x) = u$.

    (iii) *Convexity/uniqueness:* If $\succsim$ is convex, then $h(p, u)$ is a convex set; and if $\succsim$ is *strictly* convex, so that $u(\cdot)$ is strictly quasiconcave, then there is a unique element in $h(p, u)$.

**Proof:** (i) Homogeneity of degree zero in $p$ follows because the optimal vector when minimizing $p \cdot x$ subject to $u(x) \geq u$ is the same as that for minimizing $\alpha p \cdot x$ subject to this same constraint, for any scalar $\alpha > 0$.

    (ii) This property follows from continuity of $u(\cdot)$. Suppose there exists an $x \in h(p, u)$ such that $u(x) > u$. Consider a bundle $x' = \alpha x$, where $\alpha \in (0, 1)$. By continuity, for $\alpha$ close enough to 1, $u(x') \geq u$ and $p \cdot x' < p \cdot x$, contradicting $x$ being optimal in the EMP with required utility level $u$.

    (iii) The proof of property (iii) parallels that for property (iii) of Proposition 3.D.2 and is left as an exercise (Exercise 3.E.4). ∎

As in the UMP, when $u(\cdot)$ is differentiable, the optimal consumption bundle in the EMP can be characterized using first-order conditions. As would be expected given Proposition 3.E.1, these first-order conditions bear a close similarity to those of the UMP. Exercise 3.E.1 asks you to explore this relationship.

**Exercise 3.E.1:** Assume that $u(\cdot)$ is differentiable. Show that the first-order conditions for the EMP are

$$p \geq \lambda \, \nabla u(x^*) \tag{3.E.2}$$

and

$$x^* \cdot [p - \lambda \, \nabla u(x^*)] = 0, \tag{3.E.3}$$

for some $\lambda \geq 0$. Compare this with the first-order conditions of the UMP.

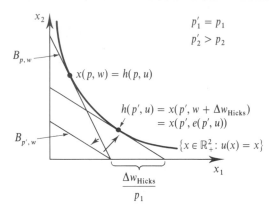

**Figure 3.E.4**
Hicksian wealth
compensation.

---

We will not discuss the continuity and differentiability properties of the Hicksian demand correspondence. With minimal qualifications, they are the same as for the Walrasian demand correspondence, which we discuss in some detail in Appendix A.

---

Using Proposition 3.E.1, we can relate the Hicksian and Walrasian demand correspondences as follows:

$$h(p, u) = x(p, e(p, u)) \qquad \text{and} \qquad x(p, w) = h(p, v(p, w)). \qquad (3.E.4)$$

The first of these relations explains the use of the term *compensated demand correspondence* to describe $h(p, u)$: As prices vary, $h(p, u)$ gives precisely the level of demand that would arise if the consumer's wealth were simultaneously adjusted to keep her utility level at $u$. This type of wealth compensation, which is depicted in Figure 3.E.4, is known as *Hicksian wealth compensation*. In Figure 3.E.4, the consumer's initial situation is the price–wealth pair $(p, w)$, and prices then change to $p'$, where $p'_1 = p_1$ and $p'_2 > p_2$. The Hicksian wealth compensation is the amount $\Delta w_{\text{Hicks}} = e(p', u) - w$. Thus, the demand function $h(p, u)$ keeps the consumer's utility level fixed as prices change, in contrast with the Walrasian demand function, which keeps money wealth fixed but allows utility to vary.

As with the value functions of the EMP and UMP, the relations in (3.E.4) allow us to develop a tight linkage between the properties of the Hicksian demand correspondence $h(p, u)$ and the Walrasian demand correspondence $x(p, w)$. In particular, in Exercise 3.E.10, you are asked to use the relations in (3.E.4) to derive the properties of each correspondence as a direct consequence of those of the other.

### Hicksian Demand and the Compensated Law of Demand

An important property of Hicksian demand is that it satisfies the *compensated law of demand*: Demand and price move in opposite directions for price changes that are accompanied by Hicksian wealth compensation. In Proposition 3.E.4, we prove this fact for the case of single-valued Hicksian demand.

**Proposition 3.E.4:** Suppose that $u(\cdot)$ is a continuous utility function representing a locally nonsatiated preference relation $\succsim$ and that $h(p, u)$ consists of a single element for all $p \gg 0$. Then the Hicksian demand function $h(p, u)$ satisfies the compensated law of demand: For all $p'$ and $p''$,

$$(p'' - p') \cdot [h(p'', u) - h(p', u)] \le 0. \qquad (3.E.5)$$

**Proof:** For any $p \gg 0$, consumption bundle $h(p, u)$ is optimal in the EMP, and so it achieves a lower expenditure at prices $p$ than any other bundle that offers a utility level of at least $u$. Therefore, we have

$$p'' \cdot h(p'', u) \leq p'' \cdot h(p', u)$$

and

$$p' \cdot h(p'', u) \geq p' \cdot h(p', u).$$

Subtracting these two inequalities yields the results. ∎

One immediate implication of Proposition 3.E.4 is that for compensated demand, own-price effects are nonpositive. In particular, if only $p_\ell$ changes, Proposition 3.E.4 implies that $(p''_\ell - p'_\ell)[h_\ell(p'', u) - h_\ell(p', u)] \leq 0$. The comparable statement is *not* true for Walrasian demand. Walrasian demand need not satisfy the law of demand. For example, the demand for a good can decrease when its price falls. See Section 2.E for a discussion of Giffen goods and Figure 2.F.5 (along with the discussion of that figure in Section 2.F) for a diagrammatic example.

**Example 3.E.1:** *Hicksian Demand and Expenditure Functions for the Cobb–Douglas Utility Function.* Suppose that the consumer has the Cobb–Douglas utility function over the two goods given in Example 3.D.1. That is, $u(x_1, x_2) = x_1^\alpha x_2^{1-\alpha}$. By deriving the first-order conditions for the EMP (see Exercise 3.E.1), and substituting from the constraint $u(h_1(p, u), h_2(p, u)) = u$, we obtain the Hicksian demand functions

$$h_1(p, u) = \left[ \frac{\alpha p_2}{(1 - \alpha) p_1} \right]^{1 - \alpha} u$$

and

$$h_2(p, u) = \left[ \frac{(1 - \alpha) p_1}{\alpha p_2} \right]^\alpha u.$$

Calculating $e(p, u) = p \cdot h(p, u)$ yields

$$e(p, u) = [\alpha^{-\alpha}(1 - \alpha)^{\alpha - 1}] p_1^\alpha p_2^{1 - \alpha} u. \quad ∎$$

**Exercise 3.E.2:** Verify the properties listed in Propositions 3.E.2 and 3.E.3 for the Hicksian demand and expenditure functions of the Cobb–Douglas utility function.

Here and in the preceding section, we have derived several basic properties of the Walrasian and Hicksian demand functions, the indirect utility function, and the expenditure function. We investigate these concepts further in Section 3.G. First, however, in Section 3.F, which is meant as optional, we offer an introductory discussion of the mathematics underlying the theory of duality. The material covered in Section 3.F provides a better understanding of the essential connections between the UMP and the EMP. We emphasize, however, that this section is not a prerequisite for the study of the remaining sections of this chapter.

# 3.F  Duality: A Mathematical Introduction

This section constitutes a mathematical detour. It focuses on some aspects of the theory of convex sets and functions.

Recall that a set $K \subset \mathbb{R}^L$ is convex if $\alpha x + (1 - \alpha)z \in K$ whenever $x, z \in K$ and $\alpha \in [0, 1]$. Note that the intersection of two convex sets is a convex set.

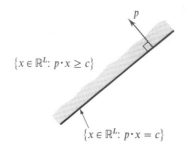

**Figure 3.F.1**

A half-space and a hyperplane.

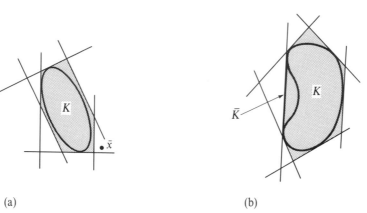

(a)                                         (b)

**Figure 3.F.2**

A closed set is convex if and only if it equals the intersection of the half-spaces that contain it.
(a) Convex $K$.
(b) Nonconvex $K$.

A *half-space* is a set of the form $\{x \in \mathbb{R}^L : p \cdot x \geq c\}$ for some $p \in \mathbb{R}^L$, $p \neq 0$, called the *normal vector* to the half-space, and some $c \in \mathbb{R}$. Its boundary $\{x \in \mathbb{R}^L : p \cdot x = c\}$ is called a *hyperplane*. The term *normal* comes from the fact that whenever $p \cdot x = p \cdot x' = c$, we have $p \cdot (x - x') = 0$, and so $p$ is orthogonal (i.e., perpendicular, or normal) to the hyperplane (see Figure 3.F.1). Note that both half-spaces and hyperplanes are convex sets.

Suppose now that $K \subset \mathbb{R}^L$ is a convex set that is also closed (i.e., it includes its boundary points), and consider any point $\bar{x} \notin K$ outside of this set. A fundamental theorem of convexity theory, the *separating hyperplane theorem*, tells us that there is a half-space containing $K$ and excluding $\bar{x}$ (see Section M.G of the Mathematical Appendix). That is, there is a $p \in \mathbb{R}^L$ and a $c \in \mathbb{R}$ such that $p \cdot \bar{x} < c \leq p \cdot x$ for all $x \in K$. The basic idea behind duality theory is the fact that a closed, convex set can equivalently ("dually") be described as the intersection of the half-spaces that contain it; this is illustrated in Figure 3.F.2(a). Because any $\bar{x} \notin K$ is excluded by some half-space that contains $K$, as we draw such half-spaces for more and more points $\bar{x} \notin K$, their intersection (the shaded area in the figure) becomes equal to $K$.

More generally, if the set $K$ is not convex, the intersection of the half-spaces that contain $K$ is the smallest closed, convex set that contains $K$, known as the *closed, convex hull* of $K$. Figure 3.F.2(b) illustrates a case where the set $K$ is nonconvex; in the figure, the closed convex hull of $K$ is $\bar{K}$.

Given any closed (but not necessarily convex) set $K \subset \mathbb{R}^L$ and a vector $p \in \mathbb{R}^L$, we can define the *support function* of $K$.

**Definition 3.F.1:** For any nonempty closed set $K \subset \mathbb{R}^L$, the *support function* of $K$ is defined for any $p \in \mathbb{R}^L$ to be

$$\mu_K(p) = \text{Infimum } \{p \cdot x : x \in K\}.$$

The *infimum* of a set of numbers, as used in Definition 3.F.1, is a generalized version of the set's minimum value. In particular, it allows for situations in which no minimum exists because although points in the set can be found that come arbitrarily close to some lower bound value, no point in the set actually attains that value. For example, consider a strictly positive function $f(x)$ that approaches zero asymptotically as $x$ increases. The minimum of this function does not exist, but its infimum is zero. The formulation also allows $\mu_K(p)$ to take the value $-\infty$ when points in $K$ can be found that make the value of $p \cdot x$ unboundedly negative.

When $K$ is convex, the function $\mu_K(\cdot)$ provides an alternative ("dual") description of $K$ because we can reconstruct $K$ from knowledge of $\mu_K(\cdot)$. In particular, for every $p$, $\{x \in \mathbb{R}^L : p \cdot x \geq \mu_K(p)\}$ is a half-space that contains $K$. In addition, as we discussed above, if $x \notin K$, then $p \cdot x < \mu_K(p)$ for some $p$. Thus, the intersection of the half-spaces generated by all possible values of $p$ is precisely $K$; that is,

$$K = \{x \in \mathbb{R}^L : p \cdot x \geq \mu_K(p) \text{ for every } p\}.$$

By the same logic, if $K$ is not convex, then $\{x \in \mathbb{R}^L : p \cdot x \geq \mu_K(p) \text{ for every } p\}$ is the smallest closed, convex set containing $K$.

The function $\mu_K(\cdot)$ is homogeneous of degree one. More interestingly, *it is concave.* To see this, consider $p'' = \alpha p + (1 - \alpha)p'$ for $\alpha \in [0,1]$. To make things simple, suppose that the infimum is in fact attained, so that there is a $z \in K$ such that $\mu_K(p'') = p'' \cdot z$. Then, because

$$\mu_K(p'') = \alpha p \cdot z + (1 - \alpha)p' \cdot z$$
$$\geq \alpha \mu_K(p) + (1 - \alpha)\mu_K(p').$$

we conclude that $\mu_K(\cdot)$ is concave.

The concavity of $\mu_K(\cdot)$ can also be seen geometrically. Figure 3.F.3 depicts the value of the function $\phi_x(p) = p \cdot x$, for various choices of $x \in K$, as a function of $p_2$ (with $p_1$ fixed at $\bar{p}_1$). For each $x$, the function $\phi_x(\cdot)$ is a linear function of $p_2$. Also shown in the figure is $\mu_K(\cdot)$. For each level of $p_2$, $\mu_K(\bar{p}_1, p_2)$ is equal to the minimum value (technically, the infimum) of the various linear functions $\phi_x(\cdot)$ at $p = (\bar{p}_1, p_2)$; that is, $\mu_K(\bar{p}_1, p_2) = \text{Min}\{\phi_x(\bar{p}_1, p_2) : x \in K\}$. For example, when $p_2 = \bar{p}_2$, $\mu_K(\bar{p}_1, \bar{p}_2) = \phi_{\bar{x}}(\bar{p}_1, \bar{p}_2) \leq \phi_x(\bar{p}_1, \bar{p}_2)$ for all $x \in K$. As can be seen in the figure, $\mu_K(\cdot)$ is therefore the "lower envelope" of the functions $\phi_x(\cdot)$. As the infimum of a family of linear functions, $\mu_K(\cdot)$ is concave.

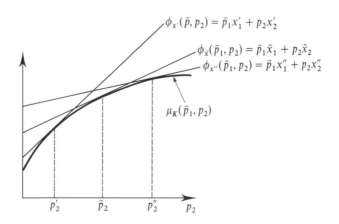

$$\phi_{x'}(\bar{p}, p_2) = \bar{p}_1 x_1' + p_2 x_2'$$

$$\phi_{\bar{x}}(\bar{p}_1, p_2) = \bar{p}_1 \bar{x}_1 + p_2 \bar{x}_2$$

$$\phi_{x''}(\bar{p}_1, p_2) = \bar{p}_1 x_1'' + p_2 x_2''$$

$$\mu_K(\bar{p}_1, p_2)$$

**Figure 3.F.3**

The support function $\mu_K(p)$ is concave.

Proposition 3.F.1, the *duality theorem*, gives the central result of the mathematical theory. Its use is pervasive in economics.

**Proposition 3.F.1:** (*The Duality Theorem*). Let $K$ be a nonempty closed set, and let $\mu_K(\cdot)$ be its support function. Then there is a unique $\bar{x} \in K$ such that $\bar{p} \cdot \bar{x} = \mu_K(\bar{p})$ if and only if $\mu_K(\cdot)$ is differentiable at $\bar{p}$. Moreover, in this case,

$$\nabla \mu_K(\bar{p}) = \bar{x}.$$

We will not give a complete proof of the theorem. Its most important conclusion is that if the minimizing vector $\bar{x}$ for the vector $\bar{p}$ is unique, then the gradient of the support function at $\bar{p}$ is equal to $\bar{x}$. To understand this result, consider the linear function $\phi_{\bar{x}}(p) = p \cdot \bar{x}$. By the definition of $\bar{x}$, we know that $\mu_K(\bar{p}) = \phi_{\bar{x}}(\bar{p})$. Moreover, the derivatives of $\phi_{\bar{x}}(\cdot)$ at $\bar{p}$ satisfy $\nabla \phi_{\bar{x}}(p) = \bar{x}$. Therefore, the duality theorem tells us that as far as the first derivatives of $\mu_K(\cdot)$ are concerned, it is as if $\mu_K(\cdot)$ is linear in $p$; that is, the first derivatives of $\mu_K(\cdot)$ at $\bar{p}$ are exactly the same as those of the function $\phi_{\bar{x}}(p) = p \cdot \bar{x}$.

The logic behind this fact is relatively straightforward. Suppose that $\mu_K(\cdot)$ is differentiable at $\bar{p}$, and consider the function $\xi(p) = p \cdot \bar{x} - \mu_K(p)$, where $\bar{x} \in K$ and $\mu_K(\bar{p}) = \bar{p} \cdot \bar{x}$. By the definition of $\mu_K(\cdot)$, $\xi(p) = p \cdot \bar{x} - \mu_K(p) \geq 0$ for all $p$. We also know that $\xi(\bar{p}) = \bar{p} \cdot \bar{x} - \mu_K(\bar{p}) = 0$. So the function $\xi(\cdot)$ reaches a minimum at $p = \bar{p}$. As a result, its partial derivatives at $\bar{p}$ must all be zero. This implies the result: $\nabla \xi(\bar{p}) = \bar{x} - \nabla \mu_K(\bar{p}) = 0$.[14]

Recalling our discussion of the EMP in Section 3.E, we see that the expenditure function is precisely the support function of the set $\{x \in \mathbb{R}_+^L : u(x) \geq u\}$. From our discussion of the support function, several of the properties of the expenditure function previously derived in Proposition 3.E.2, such as homogeneity of degree zero and concavity, immediately follow. In Section 3.G, we study the implications of the duality theorem for the theory of demand.

For a further discussion of duality theory and its applications, see Green and Heller (1981) and, for an advanced treatment, Diewert (1982). For an early application of duality to consumer theory, see McKenzie (1956–57).

---

The first part of the duality theorem says that $\mu_K(\cdot)$ is differentiable at $\bar{p}$ if and only if the minimizing vector at $\bar{p}$ is unique. If $K$ is not strictly convex, then at some $\bar{p}$, the minimizing vector will not be unique and therefore $\mu_K(\cdot)$ will exhibit a kink at $\bar{p}$. Nevertheless, in a sense that can be made precise by means of the concept of directional derivatives, the gradient $\mu_K(\cdot)$ at this $\bar{p}$ is still equal to the minimizing set, which in this case is multivalued.

This is illustrated in Figure 3.F.4 for $L = 2$. In panel (a) of Figure 3.F.4, a strictly convex set $K$ is depicted. For all $p$, its minimizing vector is unique. At $\bar{p} = (\frac{1}{2}, \frac{1}{2})$, it is $\bar{x} = (1, 1)$. Panel (b) of Figure 3.F.4 graphs $\mu_K(\frac{1}{2}, p_2)$ as a function of $p_2$. As can be seen, the function is concave and differentiable in $p_2$, with a slope of 1 (the value of $\bar{x}_2$) at $p_2 = \frac{1}{2}$.

In panel (a) of Figure 3.F.5, a convex but not strictly convex set $K$ is depicted. At $\bar{p} = (\frac{1}{2}, \frac{1}{2})$, the entire segment $[x', x'']$ is the minimizing set. If $p_1 > p_2$, then $x'$ is the minimizing vector and the value of the support function is $p_1 x_1' + p_2 x_2'$, whereas if $p_1 < p_2$, then $x''$ is optimal and the value of the support function is $p_1 x_1'' + p_2 x_2''$. Panel (b) of Figure 3.F.5

---

14. Because $\bar{x} = \nabla \mu_K(\bar{p})$ for any minimizer $\bar{x}$ at $\bar{p}$, either $\bar{x}$ is unique or if it is not unique, then $\mu_K(\cdot)$ could not be differentiable at $\bar{p}$. Thus, $\mu_K(\cdot)$ is differentiable at $\bar{p}$ only if there is a unique minimizer at $\bar{p}$.

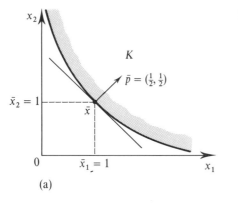

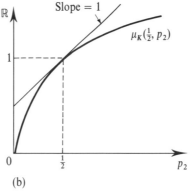

**Figure 3.F.4**

The duality theorem with a unique minimizing vector at $\bar{p}$.
(a) The minimum vector.
(b) The support function.

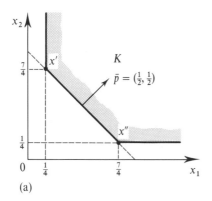

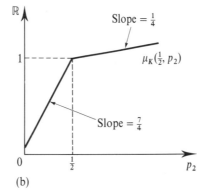

**Figure 3.F.5**

The duality theorem with a multivalued minimizing set at $\bar{p}$.
(a) The minimum set.
(b) The support function.

graphs $\mu_K(\frac{1}{2}, p_2)$ as a function of $p_2$. For $p_2 < \frac{1}{2}$, its slope is equal to $\frac{7}{4}$, the value of $x'_2$. For $p_2 > \frac{1}{2}$, its slope is $\frac{1}{4}$, the value of $x''_2$. There is a kink in the function at $\bar{p} = (\frac{1}{2}, \frac{1}{2})$, the price vector that has multiple minimizing vectors, with its left derivative with respect to $p_2$ equal to $\frac{7}{4}$ and its right derivative equal to $\frac{1}{4}$. Thus, the range of these directional derivatives at $\bar{p} = (\frac{1}{2}, \frac{1}{2})$ is equal to the range of $x_2$ in the minimizing vectors at that point.

# 3.G Relationships between Demand, Indirect Utility, and Expenditure Functions

We now continue our exploration of results flowing from the UMP and the EMP. The investigation in this section concerns three relationships: that between the Hicksian demand function and the expenditure function, that between the Hicksian and Walrasian demand functions, and that between the Walrasian demand function and the indirect utility function.

As before, we assume that $u(\cdot)$ is a continuous utility function representing the locally nonsatiated preferences $\succsim$ (defined on the consumption set $X = \mathbb{R}^L_+$), and we restrict attention to cases where $p \gg 0$. In addition, to keep matters simple, we assume throughout that $\succsim$ is strictly convex, so that the Walrasian and Hicksian demands, $x(p, w)$ and $h(p, u)$, are single-valued.[15]

*Hicksian Demand and the Expenditure Function*

From knowledge of the Hicksian demand function, the expenditure function can readily be calculated as $e(p, u) = p \cdot h(p, u)$. The important result shown in Proposition 3.G.1 establishes a more significant link between the two concepts that runs in the opposite direction.

**Proposition 3.G.1:** Suppose that $u(\cdot)$ is a continuous utility function representing a locally nonsatiated and strictly convex preference relation $\succsim$ defined on the consumption set $X = \mathbb{R}_+^L$. For all $p$ and $u$, the Hicksian demand $h(p, u)$ is the derivative vector of the expenditure function with respect to prices:

$$h(p, u) = \nabla_p e(p, u). \tag{3.G.1}$$

That is, $h_\ell(p, u) = \partial e(p, u) / \partial p_\ell$ for all $\ell = 1, \dots, L$.

Thus, given the expenditure function, we can calculate the consumer's Hicksian demand function simply by differentiating.

We provide three proofs of this important result.

**Proof 1:** (*Duality Theorem Argument*). The result is an immediate consequence of the duality theorem (Proposition 3.F.1). Since the expenditure function is precisely the support function for the set $K = \{x \in \mathbb{R}_+^L : u(x) \geq u\}$, and since the optimizing vector associated with this support function is $h(p, u)$, Proposition 3.F.1 implies that $h(p, u) = \nabla_p e(p, u)$. Note that (3.G.1) helps us understand the use of the term "dual" in this context. In particular, just as the derivatives of the utility function $u(\cdot)$ with respect to quantities have a price interpretation (we have seen in Section 3.D that at an optimum they are equal to prices multiplied by a constant factor of proportionality), (3.G.1) tells us that the derivatives of the expenditure function $e(\cdot, u)$ with respect to prices have a quantity interpretation (they are equal to the Hicksian demands). ∎

**Proof 2:** (*First-Order Conditions Argument*). For this argument, we focus for simplicity on the case where $h(p, u) \gg 0$, and we assume that $h(p, u)$ is differentiable at $(p, u)$.

Using the chain rule, the change in expenditure can be written as

$$\nabla_p e(p, u) = \nabla_p [p \cdot h(p, u)]$$
$$= h(p, u) + [p \cdot D_p h(p, u)]^{\mathsf{T}}. \tag{3.G.2}$$

Substituting from the first-order conditions for an interior solution to the EMP, $p = \lambda \nabla u(h(p, u))$, yields

$$\nabla_p e(p, u) = h(p, u) + \lambda [\nabla u(h(p, u)) \cdot D_p h(p, u)]^{\mathsf{T}}.$$

But since the constraint $u(h(p, u)) = u$ holds for all $p$ in the EMP, we know that $\nabla u(h(p, u)) \cdot D_p h(p, u) = 0$, and so we have the result. ∎

---

15. In fact, all the results of this section are local results that hold at all price vectors $\bar{p}$ with the property that for all $p$ near $\bar{p}$, the optimal consumption vector in the UMP or EMP with price vector $p$ is unique.

**Proof 3:** (*Envelope Theorem Argument*). Under the same simplifying assumptions used in Proof 2, we can directly appeal to the *envelope theorem*. Consider the value function $\phi(\alpha)$ of the constrained minimization problem

$$\underset{x}{\text{Min}} \quad f(x, \alpha)$$

$$\text{s.t.} \ g(x, \alpha) = 0.$$

If $x^*(\alpha)$ is the (differentiable) solution to this problem as a function of the parameters $\alpha = (\alpha_1, \ldots, \alpha_M)$, then the envelope theorem tells us that at any $\bar{\alpha} = (\bar{\alpha}_1, \ldots, \bar{\alpha}_M)$ we have

$$\frac{\partial \phi(\bar{\alpha})}{\partial \alpha_m} = \frac{\partial f(x^*(\bar{\alpha}), \bar{\alpha})}{\partial \alpha_m} - \lambda \frac{\partial g(x^*(\bar{\alpha}), \bar{\alpha})}{\partial \alpha_m}$$

for $m = 1, \ldots, M$, or in matrix notation,

$$\nabla_\alpha \phi(\bar{\alpha}) = \nabla_\alpha f(x^*(\bar{\alpha}), \bar{\alpha}) - \lambda \, \nabla_\alpha g(x^*(\bar{\alpha}), \bar{\alpha}).$$

See Section M.L of the Mathematical Appendix for a further discussion of this result.[16]

Because prices are parameters in the EMP that enter only the objective function $p \cdot x$, the change in the value function of the EMP with respect to a price change at $\bar{p}$, $\nabla_p e(\bar{p}, u)$, is just the vector of partial derivatives with respect to $p$ of the objective function evaluated at the optimizing vector, $h(\bar{p}, u)$. Hence $\nabla_p e(p, u) = h(p, u)$. ∎

The idea behind all three proofs is the same: If we are at an optimum in the EMP, the changes in demand caused by price changes have no first-order effect on the consumer's expenditure. This can be most clearly seen in Proof 2; condition (3.G.2) uses the chain rule to break the total effect of the price change into two effects: a direct effect on expenditure from the change in prices holding demand fixed (the first term) and an indirect effect on expenditure caused by the induced change in demand holding prices fixed (the second term). However, because we are at an expenditure minimizing bundle, the first-order conditions for the EMP imply that this latter effect is zero.

Proposition 3.G.2 summarizes several properties of the price derivatives of the Hicksian demand function $D_p h(p, u)$ that are implied by Proposition 3.G.1 [properties (i) to (iii)]. It also records one additional fact about these derivatives [property (iv)].

**Proposition 3.G.2:** Suppose that $u(\cdot)$ is a continuous utility function representing a locally nonsatiated and strictly convex preference relation $\succsim$ defined on the consumption set $X = \mathbb{R}_+^L$. Suppose also that $h(\cdot, u)$ is continuously differentiable at $(p, u)$, and denote its $L \times L$ derivative matrix by $D_p h(p, u)$. Then

    (i) $D_p h(p, u) = D_p^2 e(p, u)$.
    (ii) $D_p h(p, u)$ is a negative semidefinite matrix.
    (iii) $D_p h(p, u)$ is a symmetric matrix.
    (iv) $D_p h(p, u) p = 0$.

**Proof:** Property (i) follows immediately from Proposition 3.G.1 by differentiation. Properties (ii) and (iii) follow from property (i) and the fact that since $e(p, u)$ is a

---

16. Proof 2 is essentially a proof of the envelope theorem for the special case where the parameters being changed (in this case, prices) affect only the objective function of the problem.

twice continuously differentiable concave function, it has a symmetric and negative semidefinite Hessian (i.e., second derivative) matrix (see Section M.C of the Mathematical Appendix). Finally, for property (iv), note that because $h(p, u)$ is homogeneous of degree zero in $p$, $h(\alpha p, u) - h(p, u) = 0$ for all $\alpha$; differentiating this expression with respect to $\alpha$ yields $D_p h(p, u)p = 0$. [Note that because $h(p, u)$ is homogeneous of degree zero, $D_p h(p, u)p = 0$ also follows directly from Euler's formula; see Section M.B of the Mathematical Appendix.] ■

The negative semidefiniteness of $D_p h(p, u)$ is the differential analog of the compensated law of demand, condition (3.E.5). In particular, the differential version of (3.E.5) is $dp \cdot dh(p, u) \le 0$. Since $dh(p, u) = D_p h(p, u)\,dp$, substituting gives $dp \cdot D_p h(p, u)\,dp \le 0$ for all $dp$; therefore, $D_p h(p, u)$ is negative semidefinite. Note that negative semidefiniteness implies that $\partial h_\ell(p, u)/\partial p_\ell \le 0$ for all $\ell$; that is, compensated own-price effects are nonpositive, a conclusion that we have also derived directly from condition (3.E.5).

The symmetry of $D_p h(p, u)$ is an unexpected property. It implies that compensated price cross-derivatives between any two goods $\ell$ and $k$ must satisfy $\partial h_\ell(p, u)/\partial p_k = \partial h_k(p, u)/\partial p_\ell$. Symmetry is not easy to interpret in plain economic terms. As emphasized by Samuelson (1947), it is a property just beyond what one would derive without the help of mathematics. Once we know that $D_p h(p, u) = \nabla_p^2 e(p, u)$, the symmetry property reflects the fact that the cross derivatives of a (twice continuously differentiable) function are equal. In intuitive terms, this says that when you climb a mountain, you will cover the same net height regardless of the route.[17] As we discuss in Sections 13.H and 13.J, this path-independence feature is closely linked to the transitivity, or "no-cycling", aspect of rational preferences.

We define two goods $\ell$ and $k$ to be *substitutes* at $(p, u)$ if $\partial h_\ell(p, u)/\partial p_k \ge 0$ and *complements* if this derivative is nonpositive [when Walrasian demands have these relationships at $(p, w)$, the goods are referred to as *gross* substitutes and *gross* complements at $(p, w)$, respectively]. Because $\partial h_\ell(p, u)/\partial p_\ell \le 0$, property (iv) of Proposition 3.G.2 implies that there must be a good $k$ for which $\partial h_\ell(p, u)/\partial p_k \ge 0$. Hence, Proposition 3.G.2 implies that every good has at least one substitute.

---

17. To see why this is so, consider the twice continuously differentiable function $f(x, y)$. We can express the change in this function's value from $(x', y')$ to $(x'', y'')$ as the summation (technically, the integral) of two different paths of incremental change: $f(x'', y'') - f(x', y') = \int_{y'}^{y''} [\partial f(x', t)/\partial y]\,dt + \int_{x'}^{x''} [\partial f(s, y'')/\partial x]\,ds$ and $f(x'', y'') - f(x', y') = \int_{x'}^{x''} [\partial f(s, y')/\partial x]\,ds + \int_{y'}^{y''} [\partial f(x'', t)/\partial y]\,dt$. For these two to be equal (as they must be), we should have

$$\int_{y'}^{y''} \left[ \frac{\partial f(x'', t)}{\partial y} - \frac{\partial f(x'', t)}{\partial y} \right] dt = \int_{x'}^{x''} \left[ \frac{\partial f(s, y'')}{\partial x} - \frac{\partial f(s, y')}{\partial x} \right] ds$$

or

$$\int_{y'}^{y''} \left\{ \int_{x'}^{x''} \left[ \frac{\partial^2 f(s, t)}{\partial y\,\partial x} \right] ds \right\} dt = \int_{x'}^{x''} \left\{ \int_{y'}^{y''} \left[ \frac{\partial^2 f(s, t)}{\partial x\,\partial y} \right] dt \right\} ds.$$

So equality of cross-derivatives implies that these two different ways of "climbing the function" yield the same result. Likewise, if the cross-partials were not equal to $(x'', y'')$, then for $(x', y')$ close enough to $(x'', y'')$, the last equality would be violated.

*The Hicksian and Walrasian Demand Functions*

Although the Hicksian demand function is not directly observable (it has the consumer's utility level as an argument), we now show that $D_p h(p, u)$ can nevertheless be computed from the observable Walrasian demand function $x(p, w)$ (its arguments are all observable in principle). This important result, known as the *Slutsky equation*, means that the properties listed in Proposition 3.G.2 translate into restrictions on the observable Walrasian demand function $x(p, w)$.

**Proposition 3.G.3:** (*The Slutsky Equation*) Suppose that $u(\cdot)$ is a continuous utility function representing a locally nonsatiated and strictly convex preference relation $\succsim$ defined on the consumption set $X = \mathbb{R}^L_+$. Then for all $(p, w)$, and $u = v(p, w)$, we have

$$\frac{\partial h_\ell(p, u)}{\partial p_k} = \frac{\partial x_\ell(p, w)}{\partial p_k} + \frac{\partial x_\ell(p, w)}{\partial w} x_k(p, w) \quad \text{for all } \ell, k \qquad (3.G.3)$$

or equivalently, in matrix notation,

$$D_p h(p, u) = D_p x(p, w) + D_w x(p, w) x(p, w)^\mathsf{T}. \qquad (3.G.4)$$

**Proof:** Consider a consumer facing the price–wealth pair $(\bar{p}, \bar{w})$ and attaining utility level $\bar{u}$. Note that her wealth level $\bar{w}$ must satisfy $\bar{w} = e(\bar{p}, \bar{u})$. From condition (3.E.4), we know that for all $(p, u)$, $h_\ell(p, u) = x_\ell(p, e(p, u))$. Differentiating this expression with respect to $p_k$ and evaluating it at $(\bar{p}, \bar{u})$, we get

$$\frac{\partial h_\ell(\bar{p}, \bar{u})}{\partial p_k} = \frac{\partial x_\ell(\bar{p}, e(\bar{p}, \bar{u}))}{\partial p_k} + \frac{\partial x_\ell(\bar{p}, e(\bar{p}, \bar{u}))}{\partial w} \frac{\partial e(\bar{p}, \bar{u})}{\partial p_k}.$$

Using Proposition 3.G.1, this yields

$$\frac{\partial h_\ell(\bar{p}, \bar{u})}{\partial p_k} = \frac{\partial x_\ell(\bar{p}, e(\bar{p}, \bar{u}))}{\partial p_k} + \frac{\partial x_\ell(\bar{p}, e(\bar{p}, \bar{u}))}{\partial w} h_k(\bar{p}, \bar{u}).$$

Finally, since $\bar{w} = e(\bar{p}, \bar{u})$ and $h_k(\bar{p}, \bar{u}) = x_k(\bar{p}, e(\bar{p}, \bar{u})) = x_k(\bar{p}, \bar{w})$, we have

$$\frac{\partial h_\ell(\bar{p}, \bar{u})}{\partial p_k} = \frac{\partial x_\ell(\bar{p}, \bar{w})}{\partial p_k} + \frac{\partial x_\ell(\bar{p}, \bar{w})}{\partial w} x_k(\bar{p}, \bar{w}). \quad \blacksquare$$

Figure 3.G.1(a) depicts the Walrasian and Hicksian demand curves for good $\ell$ as a function of $p_\ell$, holding other prices fixed at $\bar{p}_{-\ell}$ [we use $\bar{p}_{-\ell}$ to denote a vector

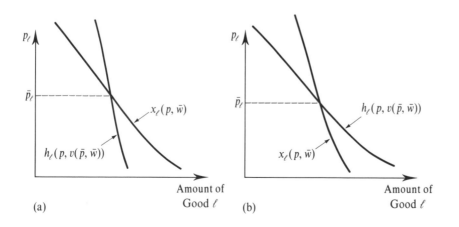

(a)                                         (b)

**Figure 3.G.1**

The Walrasian and Hicksian demand functions for good $\ell$.
(a) Normal good.
(b) Inferior good.

including all prices other than $p_\ell$ and abuse notation by writing the price vector as $p = (p_\ell, \bar{p}_{-\ell})$]. The figure shows the Walrasian demand function $x(p, \bar{w})$ and the Hicksian demand function $h(p, \bar{u})$ with required utility level $\bar{u} = v((\bar{p}_\ell, \bar{p}_{-\ell}), \bar{w})$. Note that the two demand functions are equal when $p_\ell = \bar{p}_\ell$. The Slutsky equation describes the relationship between the slopes of these two functions at price $\bar{p}_\ell$. In Figure 3.G.1(a), the slope of the Walrasian demand curve at $\bar{p}_\ell$ is less negative than the slope of the Hicksian demand curve at that price. From inspection of the Slutsky equation, this corresponds to a situation where good $\ell$ is a normal good at $(\bar{p}, \bar{w})$. When $p_\ell$ increases above $\bar{p}_\ell$, we must increase the consumer's wealth if we are to keep her at the same level of utility. Therefore, if good $\ell$ is normal, its demand falls by more in the absence of this compensation. Figure 3.G.1(b) illustrates a case in which good $\ell$ is an inferior good. In this case, the Walrasian demand curve has a more negative slope than the Hicksian curve.

Proposition 3.G.3 implies that the matrix of price derivatives $D_p h(p, u)$ of the Hicksian demand function is equal to the matrix

$$
S(p, w) = \begin{bmatrix} s_{11}(p, w) & \cdots & s_{1L}(p, w) \\ \vdots & \ddots & \vdots \\ s_{L1}(p, w) & \cdots & s_{LL}(p, w) \end{bmatrix},
$$

with $s_{\ell k}(p, w) = \partial x_\ell(p, w)/\partial p_k + [\partial x_\ell(p, w)/\partial w] x_k(p, w)$. This matrix is known as the *Slutsky substitution matrix*. Note, in particular, that $S(p, w)$ is directly computable from knowledge of the (observable) Walrasian demand function $x(p, w)$. Because $S(p, w) = D_p h(p, u)$, Proposition 3.G.2 implies that when demand is generated from preference maximization, $S(p, w)$ must possess the following three properties: it must be *negative semidefinite, symmetric, and satisfy* $S(p, w)p = 0$.

---

In Section 2.F, the Slutsky substitution matrix $S(p, w)$ was shown to be the matrix of compensated demand derivatives arising from a different form of wealth compensation, the so-called *Slutsky wealth compensation*. Instead of varying wealth to keep utility fixed, as we do here, Slutsky compensation adjusts wealth so that the initial consumption bundle $\bar{x}$ is just affordable at the new prices. Thus, we have the remarkable conclusion that the *derivative of the Hicksian demand function is equal to the derivative of this alternative Slutsky compensated demand.*

We can understand this result as follows: Suppose we have a utility function $u(\cdot)$ and are at initial position $(\bar{p}, \bar{w})$ with $\bar{x} = x(\bar{p}, \bar{w})$ and $\bar{u} = u(\bar{x})$. As we change prices to $p'$, we want to change wealth in order to compensate for the wealth effect arising from this price change. In principle, the compensation can be done in two ways. By changing wealth by amount $\Delta w_{\text{Slutsky}} = p' \cdot x(\bar{p}, \bar{w}) - \bar{w}$, we leave the consumer just able to afford her initial bundle $\bar{x}$. Alternatively, we can change wealth by amount $\Delta w_{\text{Hicks}} = e(p', \bar{u}) - \bar{w}$ to keep her utility level unchanged. We have $\Delta w_{\text{Hicks}} \le \Delta w_{\text{Slutsky}}$, and the inequality will, in general, be strict for any discrete change (see Figure 3.G.2). But because $\nabla_p e(\bar{p}, \bar{u}) = h(\bar{p}, \bar{u}) = x(\bar{p}, \bar{w})$, these two compensations are *identical* for a differential price change starting at $\bar{p}$. Intuitively, this is due to the same fact that led to Proposition 3.G.1: For a differential change in prices, the total effect on the expenditure required to achieve utility level $\bar{u}$ (the Hicksian compensation level) is simply the direct effect of the price change, assuming that the consumption bundle $\bar{x}$ does not change. But this is precisely the calculation done for Slutsky compensation. Hence, the derivatives of the compensated demand functions that arise from these two compensation mechanisms are the same.

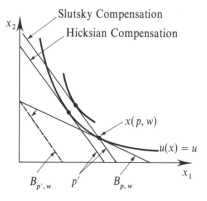

**Figure 3.G.2**

Hicksian versus Slutsky wealth compensation.

The fact that $D_p h(p, u) = S(p, w)$ allows us to compare the implications of the preference-based approach to consumer demand with those derived in Section 2.F using a choice-based approach built on the weak axiom. Our discussion in Section 2.F concluded that if $x(p, w)$ satisfies the weak axiom (plus homogeneity of degree zero and Walras' law), then $S(p, w)$ is negative semidefinite with $S(p, w)p = 0$. Moreover, we argued that except when $L = 2$, demand satisfying the weak axiom need not have a symmetric Slutsky substitution matrix. Therefore, the results here tell us that the restrictions imposed on demand in the preference-based approach are stronger than those arising in the choice-based theory built on the weak axiom. In fact, it is impossible to find preferences that rationalize demand when the substitution matrix is not symmetric. In Section 3.I, we explore further the role that this symmetry property plays in the relation between the preference and choice-based approaches to demand.

### Walrasian Demand and the Indirect Utility Function

We have seen that the minimizing vector of the EMP, $h(p, u)$, is the derivative with respect to $p$ of the EMP's value function $e(p, u)$. The exactly analogous statement for the UMP does not hold. The Walrasian demand, an ordinal concept, cannot equal the price derivative of the indirect utility function, which is not invariant to increasing transformations of utility. But with a small correction in which we normalize the derivatives of $v(p, w)$ with respect to $p$ by the marginal utility of wealth, it holds true. This proposition, called *Roy's identity* (after René Roy), is the parallel result to Proposition 3.G.1 for the demand and value functions of the UMP. As with Proposition 3.G.1, we offer several proofs.

**Proposition 3.G.4:** (*Roy's Identity*). Suppose that $u(\cdot)$ is a continuous utility function representing a locally nonsatiated and strictly convex preference relation $\succsim$ defined on the consumption set $X = \mathbb{R}^L_+$. Suppose also that the indirect utility function is differentiable at $(\bar{p}, \bar{w}) \gg 0$. Then

$$x(\bar{p}, \bar{w}) = -\frac{1}{\nabla_w v(\bar{p}, \bar{w})} \nabla_p v(\bar{p}, \bar{w}).$$

That is, for every $\ell = 1, \ldots, L$:

$$x_\ell(\bar{p}, \bar{w}) = -\frac{\partial v(\bar{p}, \bar{w})/\partial p_\ell}{\partial v(\bar{p}, \bar{w})/\partial w}.$$

**Proof 1:** Let $\bar{u} = v(\bar{p}, \bar{w})$. Because the identity $v(p, e(p, \bar{u})) = \bar{u}$ holds for all $p$, differentiating with respect to $p$ and evaluating at $p = \bar{p}$ yields

$$\nabla_p v(\bar{p}, e(\bar{p}, \bar{u})) + \frac{\partial v(\bar{p}, e(\bar{p}, \bar{u}))}{\partial w} \nabla_p e(\bar{p}, \bar{u}) = 0.$$

But $\nabla_p e(\bar{p}, \bar{u}) = h(\bar{p}, \bar{u})$ by Proposition 3.G.1, and and so we can substitute and get

$$\nabla_p v(\bar{p}, e(\bar{p}, \bar{u})) + \frac{\partial v(\bar{p}, e(\bar{p}, \bar{u}))}{\partial w} h(\bar{p}, \bar{u}) = 0.$$

Finally, since $\bar{w} = e(\bar{p}, \bar{u})$, we can write

$$\nabla_p v(\bar{p}, \bar{w}) + \frac{\partial v(\bar{p}, \bar{w})}{\partial w} x(\bar{p}, \bar{w}) = 0.$$

Rearranging, this yields the result. ∎

Proof 1 of Roy's identity derives the result using Proposition 3.G.1. Proofs 2 and 3 highlight the fact that both results actually follow from the same idea: Because we are at an optimum, the demand response to a price change can be ignored in calculating the effect of a differential price change on the value function. Thus, Roy's identity and Proposition 3.G.1 should be viewed as parallel results for the UMP and EMP. (Indeed, Exercise 3.G.1 asks you to derive Proposition 3.G.1 as a consequence of Roy's identity, thereby showing that the direction of the argument in Proof 1 can be reversed.)

**Proof 2:** (*First-Order Conditions Argument*). Assume that $x(p, w)$ is differentiable and $x(\bar{p}, \bar{w}) \gg 0$. By the chain rule, we can write

$$\frac{\partial v(\bar{p}, \bar{w})}{\partial p_\ell} = \sum_{k=1}^{L} \frac{\partial u(x(\bar{p}, \bar{w}))}{\partial x_k} \frac{\partial x_k(\bar{p}, \bar{w})}{\partial p_\ell}.$$

Substituting for $\partial u(x(\bar{p}, \bar{w}))/\partial x_k$ using the first-order conditions for the UMP, we have

$$\frac{\partial v(\bar{p}, \bar{w})}{\partial p_\ell} = \sum_{k=1}^{L} \lambda p_k \frac{\partial x_k(\bar{p}, \bar{w})}{\partial p_\ell}$$

$$= -\lambda x_\ell(\bar{p}, \bar{w}),$$

since $\sum_k p_k(\partial x_k(\bar{p}, \bar{w})/\partial p_\ell) = -x_\ell(\bar{p}, \bar{w})$ (Proposition 2.E.2). Finally, we have already argued that $\lambda = \partial v(\bar{p}, \bar{w})/\partial w$ (see Section 3.D); use of this fact yields the result. ∎

Proof 2 is again essentially a proof of the envelope theorem, this time for the case where the parameter that varies enters only the constraint. The next result uses the envelope theorem directly.

**Proof 3:** (*Envelope Theorem Argument*) Applied to the UMP, the envelope theorem tells us directly that the utility effect of a marginal change in $p_\ell$ is equal to its effect on the consumer's budget constraint weighted by the Lagrange multiplier $\lambda$ of the consumer's wealth constraint. That is, $\partial v(\bar{p}, \bar{w})/\partial p_\ell = -\lambda x_\ell(\bar{p}, \bar{w})$. Similarly, the utility effect of a differential change in wealth $\partial v(p, w)/\partial w$ is just $\lambda$. Combining these two facts yields the result. ∎

Proposition 3.G.4 provides a substantial payoff. Walrasian demand is much easier to compute from indirect than from direct utility. To derive $x(p, w)$ from the indirect

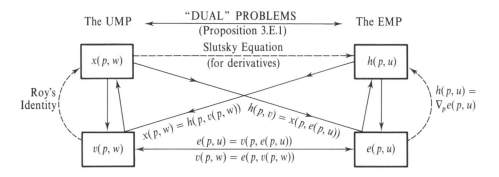

**Figure 3.G.3**

Relationships between the UMP and the EMP.

utility function, no more than the calculation of derivatives is involved; no system of first-order condition equations needs to be solved. Thus, it may often be more convenient to express tastes in indirect utility form. In Chapter 4, for example, we will be interested in preferences with the property that wealth expansion paths are linear over some range of wealth. It is simple to verify using Roy's identity that indirect utilities of the *Gorman* form $v(p, w) = a(p) + b(p)w$ have this property (see Exercise 3.G.11).

Figure 3.G.3 summarizes the connection between the demand and value functions arising from the UMP and the EMP; a similar figure appears in Deaton and Muellbauer (1980). The solid arrows indicate the derivations discussed in Sections 3.D and 3.E. Starting from a given utility function in the UMP or the EMP, we can derive the optimal consumption bundles $x(p, w)$ and $h(p, u)$ and the value functions $v(p, w)$ and $e(p, u)$. In addition, we can go back and forth between the value functions and demand functions of the two problems using relationships (3.E.1) and (3.E.4).

The relationships developed in this section are represented in Figure 3.G.3 by dashed arrows. We have seen here that the demand vector for each problem can be calculated from its value function and that the derivatives of the Hicksian demand function can be calculated from the observable Walrasian demand using Slutsky's equation.

## 3.H Integrability

If a continuously differentiable demand function $x(p, w)$ is generated by rational preferences, then we have seen that it must be homogeneous of degree zero, satisfy Walras' law, and have a substitution matrix $S(p, w)$ that is symmetric and negative semidefinite (n.s.d.) at all $(p, w)$. We now pose the reverse question: *If we observe a demand function $x(p, w)$ that has these properties, can we find preferences that rationalize $x(\cdot)$?* As we show in this section (albeit somewhat unrigorously), the answer is yes; these conditions are sufficient for the existence of rational generating preferences. This problem, known as the *integrability problem*, has a long tradition in economic theory, beginning with Antonelli (1886); we follow the approach of Hurwicz and Uzawa (1971).

There are several theoretical and practical reasons why this question and result are of interest.

On a theoretical level, the result tells us two things. First, it tells us that not only are the properties of homogeneity of degree zero, satisfaction of Walras' law, and a symmetric and negative semidefinite substitution matrix necessary consequences of the preference-based demand theory, but these are also *all* of its consequences. As long as consumer demand satisfies these properties, there is *some* rational preference relation that could have generated this demand.

Second, the result completes our study of the relation between the preference-based theory of demand and the choice-based theory of demand built on the weak axiom. We have already seen, in Section 2.F, that although a rational preference relation always generates demand possessing a symmetric substitution matrix, the weak axiom need not do so. Therefore, we already know that when $S(p, w)$ is not symmetric, demand satisfying the weak axiom cannot be rationalized by preferences. The result studied here tightens this relationship by showing that demand satisfying the weak axiom (plus homogeneity of degree zero and Walras' law) can be rationalized by preferences *if and only if* it has a symmetric substitution matrix $S(p, w)$. Hence, the *only* thing added to the properties of demand by the rational preference hypothesis, beyond what is implied by the weak axiom, homogeneity of degree zero, and Walras' law, is symmetry of the substitution matrix.

On a practical level, the result is of interest for at least two reasons. First, as we shall discuss in Section 3.J, to draw conclusions about welfare effects we need to know the consumer's preferences (or, at the least, her expenditure function). The result tells how and when we can recover this information from observation of the consumer's demand behavior.

Second, when conducting empirical analyses of demand, we often wish to estimate demand functions of a relatively simple form. If we want to allow only functions that can be tied back to an underlying preference relation, there are two ways to do this. One is to specify various utility functions and derive the demand functions that they lead to until we find one that seems statistically tractable. However, the result studied here gives us an easier way; it allows us instead to begin by specifying a tractable demand function and then simply check whether it satisfies the necessary and sufficient conditions that we identify in this section. We do not need to actually derive the utility function; the result allows us to check whether it is, in principle, possible to do so.

The problem of recovering preferences $\succsim$ from $x(p, w)$ can be subdivided into two parts: (i) recovering an expenditure function $e(p, u)$ from $x(p, w)$, and (ii) recovering preferences from the expenditure function $e(p, u)$. Because it is the more straightforward of the two tasks, we discuss (ii) first.

### Recovering Preferences from the Expenditure Function

Suppose that $e(p, u)$ is the consumer's expenditure function. By Proposition 3.E.2, it is strictly increasing in $u$ and is continuous, nondecreasing, homogeneous of degree one, and concave in $p$. In addition, because we are assuming that demand is single-valued, we know that $e(p, u)$ must be differentiable (by Propositions 3.F.1 and 3.G.1).

Given this function $e(p, u)$, how can we recover a preference relation that generates it? Doing so requires finding, for each utility level $u$, an at-least-as-good-as set $V_u \subset \mathbb{R}^L$ such that $e(p, u)$ is the minimal expenditure required for the consumer to purchase a bundle in $V_u$ at prices $p \gg 0$. That is, we want to identify a set $V_u$ such that, for all

$p \gg 0$, we have

$$e(p, u) = \underset{x \geq 0}{\text{Min}} \quad p \cdot x$$
$$\text{s.t. } x \in V_u.$$

In the framework of Section 3.F, $V_u$ is a set whose support function is precisely $e(p, u)$.

The result in Proposition 3.H.1 shows that the set $V_u = \{x \in \mathbb{R}_+^L : p \cdot x \geq e(p, u)$ for all $p \gg 0\}$ accomplishes this objective.

**Proposition 3.H.1:** Suppose that $e(p, u)$ is strictly increasing in $u$ and is continuous, increasing, homogeneous of degree one, concave, and differentiable in $p$. Then, for every utility level $u$, $e(p, u)$ is the expenditure function associated with the at-least-as-good-as set

$$V_u = \{x \in \mathbb{R}_+^L : p \cdot x \geq e(p, u) \text{ for all } p \gg 0\}.$$

That is, $e(p, u) = \text{Min } \{p \cdot x : x \in V_u\}$ for all $p \gg 0$.

---

**Proof:** The properties of $e(p, u)$ and the definition of $V_u$ imply that $V_u$ is nonempty, closed, and bounded below. Given $p \gg 0$, it can be shown that these conditions insure that $\text{Min } \{p \cdot x : x \in V_u\}$. exists. It is immediate from the definition of $V_u$ that $e(p, u) \leq \text{Min } \{p \cdot x : x \in V_u\}$. What remains in order to establish the result is to show equality. We do this by showing that $e(p, u) \geq \text{Min } \{p \cdot x : x \in V_u\}$.

For any $p$ and $p'$, the concavity of $e(p, u)$ in $p$ implies that (see Section M.C of the Mathematical Appendix)

$$e(p', u) \leq e(p, u) + \nabla_p e(p, u) \cdot (p' - p).$$

Because $e(p, u)$ is homogeneous of degree one in $p$, Euler's formula tells us that $e(p, u) = p \cdot \nabla_p e(p, u)$. Thus, $e(p', u) \leq p' \cdot \nabla_p e(p, u)$ for all $p'$. But since $\nabla_p e(p, u) \geq 0$, this means that $\nabla_p e(p, u) \in V_u$. It follows that $\text{Min } \{p \cdot x : x \in V_u\} \leq p \cdot \nabla_p e(p, u) = e(p, u)$, as we wanted (the last equality uses Euler's formula once more). This establishes the result. ∎

---

Given Proposition 3.H.1, we can construct a set $V_u$ for each level of $u$. Because $e(p, u)$ is strictly increasing in $u$, it follows that if $u' > u$, then $V_u$ strictly contains $V_{u'}$. In addition, as noted in the proof of Proposition 3.H.1, each $V_u$ is closed, convex, and bounded below. These various at-least-as-good-as sets then define a preference relation $\succsim$ that has $e(p, u)$ as its expenditure function (see Figure 3.H.1).

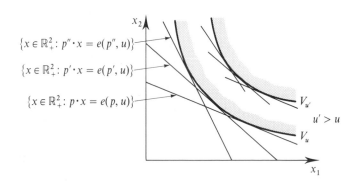

$\{x \in \mathbb{R}_+^2 : p'' \cdot x = e(p'', u)\}$

$\{x \in \mathbb{R}_+^2 : p' \cdot x = e(p', u)\}$

$\{x \in \mathbb{R}_+^2 : p \cdot x = e(p, u)\}$

**Figure 3.H.1**

Recovering preferences from the expenditure function.

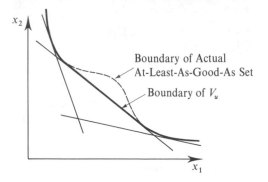

**Figure 3.H.2**

Recovering preferences from the expenditure function when the consumers' preferences are nonconvex.

Proposition 3.H.1 remains valid, with substantially the same proof, when $e(p, u)$ is not differentiable in $p$. The preference relation constructed as in the proof of the proposition provides a convex preference relation that generates $e(p, u)$. However, it could happen that there are also nonconvex preferences that generate $e(p, u)$. Figure 3.H.2 illustrates a case where the consumer's actual at-least-as-good-as set is nonconvex. The boundary of this set is depicted with a dashed curve. The solid curve shows the boundary of the set $V_u = \{x \in \mathbb{R}^L_+ : p \cdot x \geq e(p, u)$ for all $p \gg 0\}$. Formally, this set is the convex hull of the consumer's actual at-least-as-good-as set, and it also generates the expenditure function $e(p, u)$.

If $e(p, u)$ is differentiable, then any preference relation that generates $e(p, u)$ must be convex. If it were not, then there would be some utility level $u$ and price vector $p \gg 0$ with several expenditure minimizers (see Figure 3.H.2). At this price–utility pair, the expenditure function would not be differentiable in $p$.

*Recovering the Expenditure Function from Demand*

It remains to recover $e(p, u)$ from observable consumer behavior summarized in the Walrasian demand $x(p, w)$. We now discuss how this task (which is, more properly, the actual "integrability problem") can be done. We assume throughout that $x(p, w)$ satisfies Walras' law and homogeneity of degree zero and that it is single-valued.

Let us first consider the case of two commodities ($L = 2$). We normalize $p_2 = 1$. Pick an arbitrary price–wealth point $(p_1^0, 1, w^0)$ and assign a utility value of $u^0$ to bundle $x(p_1^0, 1, w^0)$. We will now recover the value of the expenditure function $e(p_1, 1, u^0)$ at all prices $p_1 > 0$. Because compensated demand is the derivative of the expenditure function with respect to prices (Proposition 3.G.1), recovering $e(\cdot)$ is equivalent to being able to solve (to "integrate") a differential equation with the independent variable $p_1$ and the dependent variable $e$. Writing $e(p_1) = e(p_1, 1, u^0)$ and $x_1(p_1, w) = x_1(p_1, 1, w)$ for simplicity, we need to solve the differential equation,

$$\frac{de(p_1)}{dp_1} = x_1(p_1, e(p_1)), \tag{3.H.1}$$

with the initial condition[18] $e(p_1^0) = w^0$.

If $e(p_1)$ solves (3.H.1) for $e(p_1^0) = w^0$, then $e(p_1)$ is the expenditure function associated with the level of utility $u^0$. Note, in particular, that if the substitution

---

18. Technically, (3.H.1) is a nonautonomous system in the $(p_1, e)$ plane. Note that $p_1$ plays the role of the "$t$" variable.

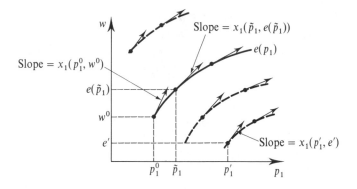

**Figure 3.H.3**
Recovering the expenditure functions from $x(p, w)$.

matrix is negative semidefinite then $e(p_1)$ will have all the properties of an expenditure function (with the price of good 2 normalized to equal 1). First, because it is the solution to a differential equation, it is by construction continuous in $p_1$. Second, since $x_1(p, w) \geq 0$, equation (3.H.1) implies that $e(p_1)$ is nondecreasing in $p_1$. Third, differentiating equation (3.H.1) tells us that

$$\frac{d^2 e(p_1)}{dp_1^2} = \frac{\partial x_1(p_1, 1, e(p_1))}{\partial p_1} + \frac{\partial x_1(p_1, 1, e(p_1))}{\partial w} x_1(p_1, 1, e(p_1))$$

$$= s_{11}(p_1, 1, e(p_1)) \leq 0,$$

so that the solution $e(p_1)$ is concave in $p_1$.

Solving equation (3.H.1) is a straightforward problem in ordinary differential equations that, nonetheless, we will not go into. A few weak regularity assumptions guarantee that a solution to (3.H.1) exists for any initial condition $(p_1^0, w^0)$. Figure 3.H.3 describes the essence of what is involved: At each price level $p_1$ and expenditure level $e$, we are given a direction of movement with slope $x_1(p_1, e)$. For the initial condition $(p_1^0, w^0)$, the graph of $e(p_1)$ is the curve that starts at $(p_1^0, w^0)$ and follows the prescribed directions of movement.

For the general case of $L$ commodities, the situation becomes more complicated. The (ordinary) differential equation (3.H.1) must be replaced by the system of partial differential equations:

$$\frac{\partial e(p)}{\partial p_1} = x_1(p, e(p))$$

$$\vdots \qquad\qquad\qquad (3.H.2)$$

$$\frac{\partial e(p)}{\partial p_L} = x_L(p, e(p))$$

for initial conditions $p^0$ and $e(p^0) = w^0$. The existence of a solution to (3.H.2) is *not* automatically guaranteed when $L > 2$. Indeed, if there is a solution $e(p)$, then its Hessian matrix $D_p^2 e(p)$ must be symmetric because the Hessian matrix of any twice continuously differentiable function is symmetric. Differentiating equations (3.H.2), which can be written as $\nabla_p e(p) = x(p, e(p))$, tells us that

$$D_p^2 e(p) = D_p x(p, e(p)) + D_w x(p, e(p)) x(p, e(p))^{\mathsf{T}}$$

$$= S(p, e(p)).$$

Therefore, a necessary condition for the existence of a solution is the symmetry of the Slutsky matrix of $x(p, w)$. This is a comforting fact because we know from previous sections that if market demand is generated from preferences, then the Slutsky matrix is indeed symmetric. It turns out that symmetry of $S(p, w)$ is also sufficient for recovery of the consumer's expenditure function. A basic result of the theory of partial differential equations (called *Frobenius' theorem*) tells us that the symmetry of the $L \times L$ derivative matrix of (3.H.2) at all points of its domain is the necessary and sufficient condition for the existence of a solution to (3.H.2). In addition, if a solution $e(p_1, u_0)$ does exist, then, as long as $S(p, w)$ is negative semidefinite, it will possess the properties of an expenditure function.

We therefore conclude that *the necessary and sufficient condition for the recovery of an underlying expenditure function is the symmetry and negative semidefiniteness of the Slutsky matrix.*[19] Recall from Section 2.F that a differentiable demand function satisfying the weak axiom, homogeneity of degree zero, and Walras' law necessarily has a negative semidefinite Slutsky matrix. Moreover, when $L = 2$, the Slutsky matrix is necessarily symmetric (recall Exercise 2.F.12). Thus, for the case where $L = 2$, we can always find preferences that rationalize any differentiable demand function satisfying these three properties. When $L > 2$, however, the Slutsky matrix of a demand function satisfying the weak axiom (along with homogeneity of degree zero and Walras' law) need not be symmetric; preferences that rationalize a demand function satisfying the weak axiom exist only when it is.

---

Observe that once we know that $S(p, w)$ is symmetric at all $(p, w)$, we can in fact use (3.H.1) to solve (3.H.2). Suppose that with initial conditions $p^0$ and $e(p^0) = w^0$, we want to recover $e(\bar{p})$. By changing prices one at a time, we can decompose this problem into $L$ subproblems where only one price changes at each step. Say it is price $\ell$. Then with $p_k$ fixed for $k \neq \ell$, the $\ell$th equation of (3.H.2) is an equation of the form (3.H.1), with the subscript 1 replaced by $\ell$. It can be solved by the methods appropriate to (3.H.1). Iterating for different goods, we eventually get to $e(\bar{p})$. It is worthwhile to point out that this method makes mechanical sense even if $S(p, w)$ is not symmetric. However, if $S(p, w)$ is not symmetric (and therefore *cannot* be associated with an underlying preference relation and expenditure function), then the value of $e(\bar{p})$ will *depend on the particular path followed from $p^0$ to $\bar{p}$* (i.e., on which price is raised first). By this absurdity, the mathematics manage to keep us honest!

---

# 3.I  Welfare Evaluation of Economic Changes

Up to this point, we have studied the preference-based theory of consumer demand from a positive (behavioral) perspective. In this section, we investigate the normative side of consumer theory, called *welfare analysis*. Welfare analysis concerns itself with the evaluation of the effects of changes in the consumer's environment on her well-being.

Although many of the positive results in consumer theory could also be deduced using an approach based on the weak axiom (as we did in Section 2.F), the preference-based approach to consumer demand is of critical importance for welfare

---

19. This is subject to minor technical requirements.

analysis. Without it, we would have no means of evaluating the consumer's level of well-being.

In this section, we consider a consumer with a rational, continuous, and locally nonsatiated preference relation $\succsim$. We assume, whenever convenient, that the consumer's expenditure and indirect utility functions are differentiable.

We focus here on the welfare effect of a price change. This is only an example, albeit a historically important one, in a broad range of possible welfare questions one might want to address. We assume that the consumer has a fixed wealth level $w > 0$ and that the price vector is initially $p^0$. We wish to evaluate the impact on the consumer's welfare of a change from $p^0$ to a new price vector $p^1$. For example, some government policy that is under consideration, such as a tax, might result in this change in market prices.[20]

Suppose, to start, that we know the consumer's preferences $\succsim$. For example, we may have derived $\succsim$ from knowledge of her (observable) Walrasian demand function $x(p, w)$, as discussed in Section 3.H. If so, it is a simple matter to determine whether the price change makes the consumer better or worse off: if $v(p, w)$ is any indirect utility function derived from $\succsim$, the consumer is worse off if and only if $v(p^1, w) - v(p^0, w) < 0$.

Although any indirect utility function derived from $\succsim$ suffices for making this comparison, one class of indirect utility functions deserves special mention because it leads to measurement of the welfare change expressed in dollar units. These are called *money metric* indirect utility functions and are constructed by means of the expenditure function. In particular, starting from any indirect utility function $v(\cdot, \cdot)$, choose an arbitrary price vector $\bar{p} \gg 0$, and consider the function $e(\bar{p}, v(p, w))$. This function gives the wealth required to reach the utility level $v(p, w)$ when prices are $\bar{p}$. Note that this expenditure is strictly increasing as a function of the level $v(p, w)$, as shown in Figure 3.I.1. Thus, viewed as a function of $(p, w)$, $e(\bar{p}, v(p, w))$ is itself an indirect utility function for $\succsim$, and

$$e(\bar{p}, v(p^1, w)) - e(\bar{p}, v(p^0, w))$$

provides a measure of the welfare change expressed in dollars.[21]

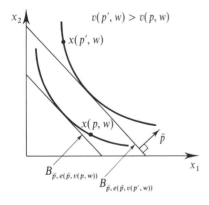

$v(p', w) > v(p, w)$

**Figure 3.I.1**

A money metric indirect utility function.

---

20. For the sake of expositional simplicity, we do not consider changes that affect wealth here. However, the analysis readily extends to that case (see Exercise 3.I.12).

21. Note that this measure is unaffected by the choice of the initial indirect utility function $v(p, w)$; it depends only on the consumer's preferences $\succsim$ (see Figure 3.I.1).

A money metric indirect utility function can be constructed in this manner for any price vector $\bar{p} \gg 0$. Two particularly natural choices for the price vector $\bar{p}$ are the initial price vector $p^0$ and the new price vector $p^1$. These choices lead to two well-known measures of welfare change originating in Hicks (1939), the *equivalent variation* ($EV$) and the *compensating variation* ($CV$). Formally, letting $u^0 = v(p^0, w)$ and $u^1 = v(p^1, w)$, and noting that $e(p^0, u^0) = e(p^1, u^1) = w$, we define

$$EV(p^0, p^1, w) = e(p^0, u^1) - e(p^0, u^0) = e(p^0, u^1) - w \qquad (3.I.1)$$

and

$$CV(p^0, p^1, w) = e(p^1, u^1) - e(p^1, u^0) = w - e(p^1, u^0). \qquad (3.I.2)$$

The equivalent variation can be thought of as the dollar amount that the consumer would be indifferent about accepting in lieu of the price change; that is, it is the change in her wealth that would be *equivalent* to the price change in terms of its welfare impact (so it is negative if the price change would make the consumer worse off). In particular, note that $e(p^0, u^1)$ is the wealth level at which the consumer achieves exactly utility level $u^1$, the level generated by the price change, at prices $p^0$. Hence, $e(p^0, u^1) - w$ is the net change in wealth that causes the consumer to get utility level $u^1$ at prices $p^0$. We can also express the equivalent variation using the indirect utility function $v(\cdot, \cdot)$ in the following way: $v(p^0, w + EV) = u^1$.[22]

The compensating variation, on the other hand, measures the net revenue of a planner who must *compensate* the consumer for the price change after it occurs, bringing her back to her original utility level $u^0$. (Hence, the compensating variation is negative if the planner would have to pay the consumer a positive level of compensation because the price change makes her worse off.) It can be thought of as the negative of the amount that the consumer would be just willing to accept from the planner to allow the price change to happen. The compensating variation can also be expressed in the following way: $v(p^1, w - CV) = u^0$.

Figure 3.I.2 depicts the equivalent and compensating variation measures of welfare change. Because both the $EV$ and the $CV$ correspond to measurements of the changes in a money metric indirect utility function, both provide a correct welfare ranking of the alternatives $p^0$ and $p^1$; that is, the consumer is better off under $p^1$ if and only if these measures are positive. In general, however, the specific dollar

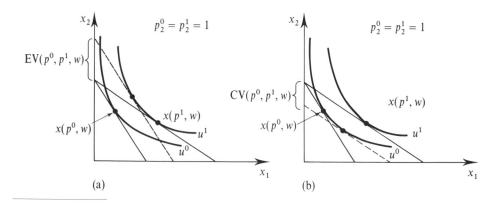

(a)                                    (b)

**Figure 3.I.2**

The equivalent (a) and compensating (b) variation measures of welfare change.

22. Note that if $u^1 = v(p^0, w + EV)$, then $e(p^0, u^1) = e(p^0, v(p^0, w + EV)) = w + EV$. This leads to (3.I.1).

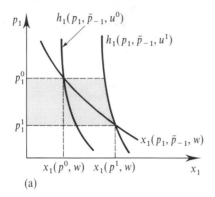
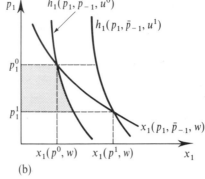

**Figure 3.I.3**

(a) The equivalent variation.

(b) The compensating variation.

amounts calculated using the $EV$ and $CV$ measures will differ because of the differing price vectors at which compensation is assumed to occur in these two measures of welfare change.

The equivalent and compensating variations have interesting representations in terms of the Hicksian demand curve. Suppose, for simplicity, that only the price of good 1 changes, so that $p_1^0 \neq p_1^1$ and $p_\ell^0 = p_\ell^1 = \bar{p}_\ell$ for all $\ell \neq 1$. Because $w = e(p^0, u^0) = e(p^1, u^1)$ and $h_1(p, u) = \partial e(p, u)/\partial p_1$, we can write

$$EV(p^0, p^1, w) = e(p^0, u^1) - w$$
$$= e(p^0, u^1) - e(p^1, u^1)$$
$$= \int_{p_1^1}^{p_1^0} h_1(p_1, \bar{p}_{-1}, u^1) \, dp_1, \qquad (3.I.3)$$

where $\bar{p}_{-1} = (\bar{p}_2, \ldots, \bar{p}_L)$. Thus, the change in consumer welfare as measured by the equivalent variation can be represented by the area lying between $p_1^0$ and $p_1^1$ and to the left of the Hicksian demand curve for good 1 associated with utility level $u^1$ (it is equal to this area if $p_1^1 < p_1^0$ and is equal to its negative if $p_1^1 > p_1^0$). The area is depicted as the shaded region in Figure 3.I.3(a).

Similarly, the compensating variation can be written as

$$CV(p^0, p^1, w) = \int_{p_1^1}^{p_1^0} h_1(p_1, \bar{p}_{-1}, u^0) \, dp_1. \qquad (3.I.4)$$

Note that we now use the initial utility level $u^0$. See Figures 3.I.3(b) for its graphic representation.

Figure 3.I.3 depicts a case where good 1 is a normal good. As can be seen in the figure, when this is so, we have $EV(p^0, p^1, w) > CV(p^0, p^1, w)$ (you should check that the same is true when $p_1^1 > p_1^0$). This relation between the $EV$ and the $CV$ reverses when good 1 is inferior (see Exercise 3.I.3). However, if there is no wealth effect for good 1 (e.g., if the underlying preferences are quasilinear with respect to some good $\ell \neq 1$), the $CV$ and $EV$ measures are the *same* because we then have

$$h_1(p_1, \bar{p}_{-1}, u^0) = x_1(p_1, \bar{p}_{-1}, w) = h_1(p_1, \bar{p}_{-1}, u^1).$$

In this case of no wealth effects, we call the common value of $CV$ and $EV$, which is also the value of the area lying between $p_1^0$ and $p_1^1$ and to the left of the market (i.e., Walrasian) demand curve for good 1, the change in *Marshallian consumer surplus*.[23]

---

23. The term originates from Marshall (1920), who used the area to the left of the market demand curve as a welfare measure in the special case where wealth effects are absent.

**Exercise 3.I.1:** Suppose that the change from price vector $p^0$ to price vector $p^1$ involves a change in the prices of both good 1 (from $p_1^0$ to $p_1^1$) and good 2 (from $p_2^0$ to $p_2^1$). Express the equivalent variation in terms of the sum of integrals under appropriate Hicksian demand curves for goods 1 and 2. Do the same for the compensating variation measure. Show also that if there are no wealth effects for either good, the compensating and equivalent variations are equal.

**Example 3.I.1:** *The Deadweight Loss from Commodity Taxation.* Consider a situation where the new price vector $p^1$ arises because the government puts a tax on some commodity. To be specific, suppose that the government taxes commodity 1, setting a tax on the consumer's purchases of good 1 of $t$ per unit. This tax changes the effective price of good 1 to $p_1^1 = p_1^0 + t$ while prices for all other commodities $\ell \neq 1$ remain fixed at $p_\ell^0$ (so we have $p_\ell^1 = p_\ell^0$ for all $\ell \neq 1$). The total revenue raised by the tax is therefore $T = tx_1(p^1, w)$.

An alternative to this commodity tax that raises the same amount of revenue for the government without changing prices is imposition of a "lump-sum" tax of $T$ directly on the consumer's wealth. Is the consumer better or worse off facing this lump-sum wealth tax rather than the commodity tax? She is worse off under the commodity tax if the equivalent variation of the commodity tax $EV(p^0, p^1, w)$, which is negative, is less than $-T$, the amount of wealth she will lose under the lump-sum tax. Put in terms of the expenditure function, this says that she is worse off under commodity taxation if $w - T > e(p^0, u^1)$, so that her wealth after the lump-sum tax is greater than the wealth level that is required at prices $p^0$ to generate the utility level that she gets under the commodity tax, $u^1$. The difference $(-T) - EV(p^0, p^1, w) = w - T - e(p^0, u^1)$ is known as the *deadweight loss of commodity taxation*. It measures the extra amount by which the consumer is made worse off by commodity taxation above what is necessary to raise the same revenue through a lump-sum tax.

The deadweight loss measure can be represented in terms of the Hicksian demand curve at utility level $u^1$. Since $T = tx_1(p^1, w) = th_1(p^1, u^1)$, we can write the deadweight loss as follows [we again let $\bar{p}_{-1} = (\bar{p}_2, \ldots, \bar{p}_L)$, where $p_\ell^0 = p_\ell^1 = \bar{p}_\ell$ for all $\ell \neq 1$]:

$$(-T) - EV(p^0, p^1, w) = e(p^1, u^1) - e(p^0, u^1) - T$$

$$= \int_{p_1^0}^{p_1^0+t} h_1(p_1, \bar{p}_{-1}, u^1)\, dp_1 - th_1(p_1^0 + t, \bar{p}_{-1}, u^1)$$

$$= \int_{p_1^0}^{p_1^0+t} [h_1(p_1, \bar{p}_{-1}, u^1) - h_1(p_1^0 + t, \bar{p}_{-1}, u^1)]\, dp_1. \quad (3.I.5)$$

Because $h_1(p, u)$ is nonincreasing in $p_1$, this expression (and therefore the deadweight loss of taxation) is nonnegative, and it is strictly positive if $h_1(p, u)$ is strictly decreasing in $p_1$. In Figure 3.I.4(a), the deadweight loss is depicted as the area of the crosshatched triangular region. This region is sometimes called the *deadweight loss triangle*.

---

This deadweight loss measure can also be represented in the commodity space. For example, suppose that $L = 2$, and normalize $p_2^0 = 1$. Consider Figure 3.I.5. Since $(p_1^0 + t)x_1(p^1, w) + p_2^0 x_2(p^1, w) = w$, the bundle $x(p^1, w)$ lies not only on the budget line associated with budget set $B_{p^1, w}$ but also on the budget line associated with budget set $B_{p^0, w-T}$. In contrast, the budget set that generates a utility of $u^1$ for the consumer at prices $p^0$ is $B_{p^0, e(p^0, u^1)}$ (or, equivalently,

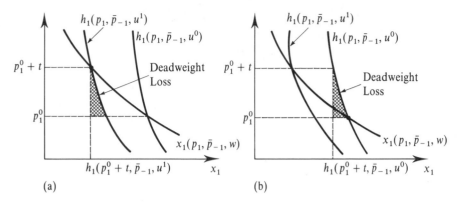

**Figure 3.1.4**

The deadweight loss from commodity taxation.
(a) Measure based at $u^1$.
(b) Measure based at $u^0$.

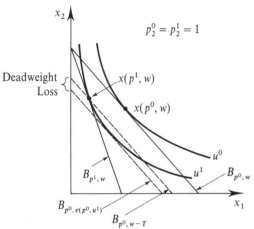

**Figure 3.1.5**

An alternative depiction of the deadweight loss from commodity taxation.

$B_{p^0, w+EV}$). The deadweight loss is the vertical distance between the budget lines associated with budget sets $B_{p^0, w-T}$ and $B_{p^0, e(p^0, u^1)}$ (recall that $p_2^0 = 1$).

---

A similar deadweight loss triangle can be calculated using the Hicksian demand curve $h_1(p, u^0)$. It also measures the loss from commodity taxation, but in a different way. In particular, suppose that we examine the surplus or deficit that would arise if the government were to compensate the consumer to keep her welfare under the tax equal to her pretax welfare $u^0$. The government would run a deficit if the tax collected $th_1(p^1, u^0)$ is less than $-CV(p^0, p^1, w)$ or, equivalently, if $th_1(p^1, u^0) < e(p^1, u^0) - w$. Thus, the deficit can be written as

$$-CV(p^0, p^1, w) - th_1(p^1, u) = e(p^1, u^0) - e(p^0, u^0) - th_1(p^1, u^0)$$
$$= \int_{p_1^0}^{p_1^0 + t} h_1(p_1, \bar{p}_{-1}, u^0)\, dp_1 - th_1(p_1^0 + t, \bar{p}_{-1}, u^0)$$
$$= \int_{p_1^0}^{p_1^0 + t} [h_1(p_1, \bar{p}_{-1}, u^0) - h_1(p_1^0 + t, \bar{p}_{-1}, u^0)]\, dp_1.$$

$$(3.1.6)$$

which is again strictly positive as long as $h_1(p, u)$ is strictly decreasing in $p_1$. This deadweight loss measure is equal to the area of the crosshatched triangular region in Figure 3.1.4(b). ∎

**Exercise 3.I.2:** Calculate the derivative of the deadweight loss measures (3.I.5) and (3.I.6) with respect to $t$. Show that, evaluated at $t = 0$, these derivatives are equal to zero but that if $h_1(p, u^0)$ is strictly decreasing in $p_1$, they are strictly positive at all $t > 0$. Interpret.

Up to now, we have considered only the question of whether the consumer was better off at $p^1$ than at the initial price vector $p^0$. We saw that both $EV$ and $CV$ provide a correct welfare ranking of $p^0$ and $p^1$. Suppose, however, that $p^0$ is being compared with two possible price vectors $p^1$ and $p^2$. In this case, $p^1$ is better than $p^2$ if and only if $EV(p^0, p^1, w) > EV(p^0, p^2, w)$, since

$$EV(p^0, p^1, w) - EV(p^0, p^2, w) = e(p^0, u^1) - e(p^0, u^2).$$

Thus, the $EV$ measures $EV(p^0, p^1, w)$ and $EV(p^0, p^2, w)$ can be used not only to compare these two price vectors with $p^0$ but also to determine which of them is better for the consumer. A comparison of the compensating variations $CV(p^0, p^1, w)$ and $CV(p^0, p^2, w)$, however, will not necessarily rank $p^1$ and $p^2$ correctly. The problem is that the $CV$ measure uses the new prices as the base prices in the money metric indirect utility function, using $p^1$ to calculate $CV(p^0, p^1, w)$ and $p^2$ to calculate $CV(p^0, p^2, w)$. So

$$CV(p^0, p^1, w) - CV(p^0, p^2, w) = e(p^2, u^0) - e(p^1, u^0),$$

which need not correctly rank $p^1$ and $p^2$ [see Exercise 3.I.4 and Chipman and Moore (1980)]. In other words, fixing $p^0$, $EV(p^0, \cdot, w)$ is a valid indirect utility function (in fact, a money metric one), but $CV(p^0, \cdot, w)$ is not.[24]

An interesting example of the comparison of several possible new price vectors arises when a government is considering which goods to tax. Suppose, for example, that two different taxes are being considered that could raise tax revenue of $T$: a tax on good 1 of $t_1$ (creating new price vector $p^1$) and a tax on good 2 of $t_2$ (creating new price vector $p^2$). Note that since they raise the same tax revenue, we have $t_1 x_1(p^1, w) = t_2 x_2(p^2, w) = T$ (see Figure 3.I.6). Because tax $t_1$

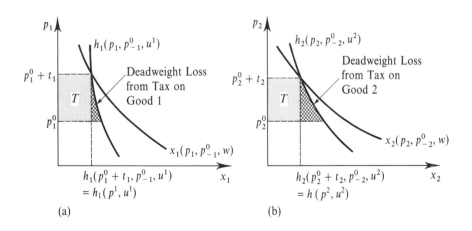

(a)                    (b)

**Figure 3.I.6**

Comparing two taxes that raise revenue T. (a) Tax on good 1. (b) Tax on good 2.

is better than tax $t_2$ if and only if $EV(p^0, p^1, w) > EV(p^0, p^2, w)$, $t_1$ is better than $t_2$ if and only if $[(-T) - EV(p^0, p^1, w)] < [(-T) - EV(p^0, p^2, w)]$, that is, if and only if the deadweight loss arising under tax $t_1$ is less than that arising under tax $t_2$.

24. Of course, we can rank $p^1$ and $p^2$ correctly by seeing whether $CV(p^1, p^2, w)$ is positive or negative.

In summary, if we know the consumer's expenditure function, we can precisely measure the welfare impact of a price change; moreover, we can do it in a convenient way (in dollars). In principle, this might well be the end of the story because, as we saw in Section 3.H, we can recover the consumer's preferences and expenditure function from the observable Walrasian demand function $x(p, w)$.[25] Before concluding, however, we consider two further issues. We first ask whether we may be able to say anything about the welfare effect of a price change when we *do not* have enough information to recover the consumer's expenditure function. We describe a test that provides a sufficient condition for the consumer's welfare to increase from the price change and that uses information only about the two price vectors $p^0$, $p^1$ and the initial consumption bundle $x(p^0, w)$. We then conclude by discussing in detail the extent to which the welfare change can be approximated by means of the area to the left of the market (Walrasian) demand curve, a topic of significant historical importance.

## Welfare Analysis with Partial Information

In some circumstances, we may not be able to derive the consumer's expenditure function because we may have only limited information about her Walrasian demand function. Here we consider what can be said when the *only* information we possess is knowledge of the two price vectors $p^0$, $p^1$ and the consumer's initial consumption bundle $x^0 = x(p^0, w)$. We begin, in Proposition 3.I.1, by developing a simple sufficiency test for whether the consumer's welfare improves as a result of the price change.

**Proposition 3.I.1:** Suppose that the consumer has a locally nonsatiated rational preference relation $\succsim$. If $(p^1 - p^0) \cdot x^0 < 0$, then the consumer is strictly better off under price–wealth situation $(p^1, w)$ than under $(p^0, w)$.

**Proof:** The result follows simply from revealed preference. Since $p^0 \cdot x^0 = w$ by Walras' law, if $(p^1 - p^0) \cdot x^0 < 0$, then $p^1 \cdot x^0 < w$. But if so, $x^0$ is still affordable under prices $p^1$ and is, moreover, in the interior of budget set $B_{p^1, w}$. By local nonsatiation, there must therefore be a consumption bundle in $B_{p^1, w}$ that the consumer strictly prefers to $x^0$. ∎

The test in Proposition 3.I.1 can be viewed as a first-order approximation to the true welfare change. To see this, take a first-order Taylor expansion of $e(p, u)$ around the initial prices $p^0$:

$$e(p^1, u^0) = e(p^0, u^0) + (p^1 - p^0) \cdot \nabla_p e(p^0, u^0) + o(\|p^1 - p^0\|). \qquad (3.I.7)$$

If $(p^1 - p^0) \cdot \nabla_p e(p^0, u^0) < 0$ and the second-order remainder term could be ignored, we would have $e(p^1, u^0) < e(p^0, u^0) = w$, and so we could conclude that the consumer's welfare is greater after the price change. But the concavity of $e(\cdot, u^0)$ in $p$ implies that the remainder term is nonpositive. Therefore, ignoring the remainder term leads to no error here; we do have $e(p^1, u^0) < w$ if $(p^1 - p^0) \cdot \nabla_p e(p^0, u^0) < 0$. Using Proposition 3.G.1 then tells us that $(p^1 - p^0) \cdot \nabla_p e(p^0, u^0) = (p^1 - p^0) \cdot h(p^0, u^0) = (p^1 - p^0) \cdot x^0$, and so we get exactly the test in Proposition 3.I.1.

---

25. As a practical matter, in applications you should use whatever are the state-of-the-art techniques for performing this recovery.

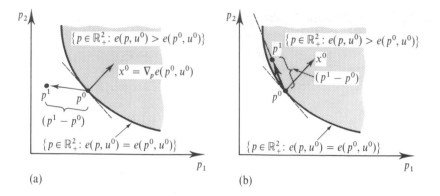

**Figure 3.I.7**

The welfare test of Propositions 3.I.1 and 3.I.2.
(a) $(p^1 - p^0) \cdot x^0 < 0$.
(b) $(p^1 - p^0) \cdot x^0 > 0$.

What if $(p^1 - p^0) \cdot x^0 > 0$? Can we then say anything about the direction of change in welfare? As a general matter, no. However, examination of the first-order Taylor expansion (3.I.7) tells us that we get a definite conclusion if the price change is, in an appropriate sense, small enough because the remainder term then becomes insignificant relative to the first-order term and can be neglected. This gives the result shown in Proposition 3.I.2.

**Proposition 3.I.2:** Suppose that the consumer has a differentiable expenditure function. Then if $(p^1 - p^0) \cdot x^0 > 0$, there is a sufficiently small $\bar{\alpha} \in (0, 1)$ such that for all $\alpha < \bar{\alpha}$, we have $e((1 - \alpha)p^0 + \alpha p^1, u^0) > w$, and so the consumer is strictly better off under price–wealth situation $(p^0, w)$ than under $((1 - \alpha)p^0 + \alpha p^1, w)$.

Figure 3.I.7 illustrates these results for the cases where $p^1$ is such that $(p^1 - p^0) \cdot x^0 < 0$ [panel (a)] and $(p^1 - p^0) \cdot x^0 > 0$ [panel (b)]. In the figure the set of prices $\{p \in \mathbb{R}^2_+ : e(p, u^0) \geq e(p^0, u^0)\}$ is drawn in price space. The concavity of $e(\cdot, u)$ gives it the shape depicted. The initial price vector $p^0$ lies in this set. By Proposition 3.G.1, the gradient of the expenditure function at this point, $\nabla_p e(p^0, u^0)$, is equal to $x^0$, the initial consumption bundle. The vector $(p^1 - p^0)$ is the vector connecting point $p^0$ to the new price point $p^1$. Figure 3.I.7(a) shows a case where $(p^1 - p^0) \cdot x^0 < 0$. As can be seen there, $p^1$ lies outside of the set $\{p \in \mathbb{R}^2_+ : e(p, u^0) \geq e(p^0, u^0)\}$, and so we must have $e(p^0, u^0) > e(p^1, u^0)$. In Figure 3.I.7(b), on the other hand, we show a case where $(p^1 - p^0) \cdot x^0 > 0$. Proposition 3.I.2 can be interpreted as asserting that in this case if $(p^1 - p^0)$ is small enough, then $e(p^0, u^0) < e(p^1, u^0)$. This can be seen in Figure 3.I.7(b), because if $(p^1 - p^0) \cdot x^0 > 0$ and $p^1$ is close enough to $p^0$ [in the ray with direction $p^1 - p^0$], then price vector $p^1$ lies in the set $\{p \in \mathbb{R}^2_+ : e(p, u^0) > e(p^0, u^0)\}$.

### Using the Area to the Left of the Walrasian (Market) Demand Curve as an Approximate Welfare Measure

Improvements in computational abilities have made the recovery of the consumer's preferences/expenditure function from observed demand behavior, along the lines discussed in Section 3.I, far easier than was previously the case.[26] Traditionally,

---

26. They have also made it much easier to estimate complicated demand systems that are explicitly derived from utility maximization and from which the parameters of the expenditure function can be derived directly.

however, it has been common practice in applied analyses to rely on approximations of the true welfare change.

We have already seen in (3.I.3) and (3.I.4) that the welfare change induced by a change in the price of good 1 can be exactly computed by using the area to the left of an appropriate Hicksian demand curve. However, these measures present the problem of not being directly observable. A simpler procedure that has seen extensive use appeals to the Walrasian (market) demand curve instead. We call this estimate of welfare change the *area variation* measure (or *AV*):

$$AV(p^0, p^1, w) = \int_{p_1^1}^{p_1^0} x_1(p_1, \bar{p}_{-1}, w) \, dp_1. \tag{3.I.8}$$

If there are no wealth effects for good 1, then, as we have discussed, $x_1(p, w) = h_1(p, u^0) = h_1(p, u^1)$ for all $p$ and the area variation measure is exactly equal to the equivalent and compensating variation measures. This corresponds to the case studied by Marshall (1920) in which the marginal utility of numeraire is constant. In this circumstance, where the *AV* measure gives an exact measure of welfare change, the measure is known as the change in *Marshallian consumer surplus*.

More generally, as Figures 3.I.3(a) and 3.I.3(b) make clear, when good 1 is a normal good, the area variation measure overstates the compensating variation and understates the equivalent variation (convince yourself that this is true both when $p_1$ falls and when $p_1$ rises). When good 1 is inferior, the reverse relations hold. Thus, when evaluating the welfare change from a change in prices of several goods, or when comparing two different possible price changes, the area variation measure need not give a correct evaluation of welfare change (e.g., see Exercise 3.I.10).

Naturally enough, however, if the wealth effects for the goods under consideration are small, the approximation errors are also small and the area variation measure is almost correct. Marshall argued that if a good is just one commodity among many, then because one extra unit of wealth will spread itself around, the wealth effect for the commodity is bound to be small; therefore, no significant errors will be made by evaluating the welfare effects of price changes for that good using the area measure. This idea can be made precise; for an advanced treatment, see Vives (1987). It is important, however, not to fall into the fallacy of composition; if we deal with a large number of commodities, then while the approximating error may be small for each individually, it may nevertheless not be small in the aggregate.

If $(p_1^1 - p_1^0)$ is small, then the error involved using the area variation measure becomes small as a fraction of the true welfare change. Consider, for example, the compensating variation.[27] In Figure 3.I.8, we see that the area $B + D$, which measures the difference between the area variation and the true compensating variation, becomes small as a fraction of the true compensating variation when $(p_1^1 - p_1^0)$ is small. This might seem to suggest that the area variation measure is a good approximation of the compensating variation measure for small price changes. Note, however, that the same property would hold if instead of the Walrasian demand

---

27. All the points that follow apply to the equivalent variation as well.

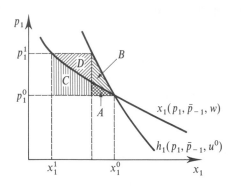

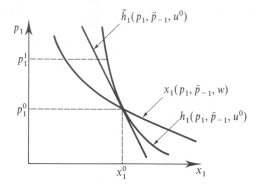

**Figure 3.I.8 (left)**

The error in using the area variation measure of welfare change.

**Figure 3.I.9 (right)**

A first-order approximation of $h(p, u^0)$ at $p^0$.

function we were to use *any* function that takes the value $x_1(p_1^0, p_{-1}^0, w)$ at $p_1^0$.[28] In fact, the approximation error may be quite large *as a fraction of the deadweight loss* [this point is emphasized by Hausman (1981)]. In Figure 3.I.8, for example, the deadweight loss calculated using the Walrasian demand curve is the area $A + C$, whereas the real one is the area $A + B$. The percentage difference between these two areas need not grow small as the price change grows small.[29]

When $(p_1^1 - p_1^0)$ is small, there is a superior approximation procedure available In particular, suppose we take a first-order Taylor approximation of $h(p, u^0)$ at $p^0$

$$\tilde{h}(p, u^0) = h(p^0, u^0) + D_p h(p^0, u^0)(p - p^0)$$

and we calculate

$$\int_{p_1^1}^{p_1^0} \tilde{h}_1(p_1, \bar{p}_{-1}, u^0)\, dp_1 \tag{3.I.9}$$

as our approximation of the welfare change. The function $\tilde{h}_1(p_1, \bar{p}_{-1}, u^0)$ is depicted in Figure 3.I.9. As can be seen in the figure, because $\tilde{h}_1(p_1, \bar{p}_{-1}, u^0)$ has the same slope as the true Hicksian demand function $h_1(p, u^0)$ at $p^0$, for small price changes this approximation comes closer than expression (3.I.8) to the true welfare change (and in contrast with the area variation measure, it provides an adequate approximation to the deadweight loss). Because the Hicksian demand curve is the first derivative of the expenditure function, this first-order expansion of the Hicksian demand function at $p^0$ is, in essence, a second-order expansion of the expenditure function around $p^0$. Thus, this approximation can be viewed as the natural extension of the first-order test discussed above; see expression (3.I.7).

The approximation in (3.I.9) is directly computable from knowledge of the observable Walrasian demand function $x_1(p, w)$. To see this, note that because $h(p^0, u^0) = x(p^0, w)$ and $D_p h(p^0, u^0) = S(p^0, w)$, $\tilde{h}(p, u^0)$ can be expressed solely in terms that involve the Walrasian demand function and its derivatives at the point

---

28. In effect, the property identified here amounts to saying that the Walrasian demand function provides a first-order approximation to the compensating variation. Indeed, note that the derivatives of $CV(p^1, p^0, w)$, $EV(p^1, p^0, w)$, and $AV(p^1, p^0, w)$ with respect to $p_1^1$ evaluated at $p_1^0$ are all precisely $x_1(p_1^0, p_{-1}^0, w)$.

29. Thus, for example, in the problem discussed above where we compare the deadweight losses induced by taxes on two different commodities that both raise revenue $T$, the area variation measure need not give the correct ranking even for small taxes.

$(p^0, w)$:

$$\tilde{h}(p, u^0) = x(p^0, w) + S(p^0, w)(p - p^0).$$

In particular, since only the price of good 1 is changing, we have

$$\tilde{h}_1(p_1, \bar{p}_{-1}, u^0) = x_1(p_1^0, \bar{p}_{-1}, w) + s_{11}(p_1^0, \bar{p}_{-1}, w)(p_1 - p_1^0),$$

where

$$s_{11}(p_1^0, \bar{p}_{-1}, w) = \frac{\partial x_1(p^0, w)}{\partial p_1} + \frac{\partial x_1(p^0, w)}{\partial w} x_1(p^0, w).$$

When $(p^1 - p^0)$ is small, this procedure provides a better approximation to the true compensating variation than does the area variation measure. However, if $(p^1 - p^0)$ is large, we cannot tell which is the better approximation. It is entirely possible for the area variation measure to be superior. After all, its use guarantees some sensitivity of the approximation to demand behavior away from $p^0$, whereas the use of $\tilde{h}(p, u^0)$ does not.

# 3.J The Strong Axiom of Revealed Preference

We have seen that in the context of consumer demand theory, consumer choice may satisfy the weak axiom but not be capable of being generated by a rational preference relation (see Sections 2.F and 3.G). We could therefore ask: Can we find a necessary and sufficient consistency condition on consumer demand behavior that is in the same style as the WA but that does imply that demand behavior can be rationalized by preferences? The answer is "yes", and it was provided by Houthakker (1950) in the form of the *strong axiom of revealed preference (SA)*, a kind of recursive closure of the weak axiom.[30]

**Definition 3.J.1:** The market demand function $x(p, w)$ satisfies the *strong axiom of revealed preference* (the SA) if for any list

$$(p^1, w^1), \ldots, (p^N, w^N)$$

with $x(p^{n+1}, w^{n+1}) \neq x(p^n, w^n)$ for all $n \leq N - 1$, we have $p^N \cdot x(p^1, w^1) > w^N$ whenever $p^n \cdot x(p^{n+1}, w^{n+1}) \leq w^n$ for all $n \leq N - 1$.

In words, if $x(p^1, w^1)$ is *directly or indirectly revealed preferred* to $x(p^N, w^N)$, then $x(p^N, w^N)$ cannot be (directly) revealed preferred to $x(p^1, w^1)$ [so $x(p^1, w^1)$ cannot be affordable at $(p^N, w^N)$]. For example, the SA was violated in Example 2.F.1. It is clear that the SA is satisfied if demand originates in rational preferences. The converse is a deeper result. It is stated in Proposition 3.J.1; the proof, which is advanced, is presented in small type.

**Proposition 3.J.1:** If the Walrasian demand function $x(p, w)$ satisfies the strong axiom of revealed preference then there is a rational preference relation $\succsim$ that rationalizes $x(p, w)$, that is, such that for all $(p, w)$, $x(p, w) \succ y$ for every $y \neq x(p, w)$ with $y \in B_{p,w}$.

---

30. For an informal account of revealed preference theory after Samuelson, see Mas-Colell (1982).

**Proof:** We follow Richter (1966). His proof is based on set theory and differs markedly from the differential equations techniques used originally by Houthakker.[31]

Define a relation $\succ^1$ on commodity vectors by letting $x \succ^1 y$ whenever $x \neq y$ and we have $x = x(p, w)$ and $p \cdot y \leq w$ for some $(p, w)$. The relation $\succ^1$ can be read as "directly revealed preferred to." From $\succ^1$ define a new relation $\succ^2$, to be read as "directly or indirectly revealed preferred to," by letting $x \succ^2 y$ whenever there is a chain $x^1 \succ^1 x^2 \succ^1, \ldots, \succ^1 x^N$ with $x^1 = x$ and $x^N = y$. Observe that, by construction, $\succ^2$ is transitive. According to the SA, $\succ^2$ is also irreflexive (i.e., $x \succ^2 x$ is impossible). A certain axiom of set theory (known as Zorn's lemma) tells us the following: *Every relation $\succ^2$ that is transitive and irreflexive* (called a *partial order*) *has a total extension $\succ^3$*, an irreflexive and transitive relation such that, first, $x \succ^2 y$ implies $x \succ^3 y$ and, second, whenever $x \neq y$, we have either $x \succ^3 y$ or $y \succ^3 x$. Finally, we can define $\succsim$ by letting $x \succsim y$ whenever $x = y$ or $x \succ^3 y$. It is not difficult now to verify that $\succsim$ is complete and transitive and that $x(p, w) \succ y$ whenever $p \cdot y \leq w$ and $y \neq x(p, w)$. ∎

The proof of Proposition 3.J.1 uses only the single-valuedness of $x(p, w)$. Provided choice is single-valued, the same result applies to the abstract theory of choice of Chapter 1. The fact that the budgets are competitive is immaterial.

In Exercise 3.J.1, you are asked to show that the WA is equivalent to the SA when $L = 2$. Hence, by Proposition 3.J.1, when $L = 2$ and demand satisfies the WA, we can always find a rationalizing preference relation, a result that we have already seen in Section 3.H. When $L > 2$, however, the SA is stronger than the WA. In fact, Proposition 3.J.1 tells us that a choice-based theory of demand founded on the strong axiom is essentially equivalent to the preference-based theory of demand presented in this chapter.

The strong axiom is therefore essentially equivalent both to the rational preference hypothesis and to the symmetry and negative semidefiniteness of the Slutsky matrix. We have seen that the weak axiom is essentially equivalent to the negative semidefiniteness of the Slutsky matrix. It is therefore natural to ask whether there is an assumption on preferences that is weaker than rationality and that leads to a theory of consumer demand equivalent to that based on the WA. Violations of the SA mean cycling choice, and violations of the symmetry of the Slutsky matrix generate path dependence in attempts to "integrate back" to preferences. This suggests preferences that may violate the transitivity axiom. See the appendix with W. Shafer in Kihlstrom, Mas-Colell, and Sonnenschein (1976) for further discussion of this point.

## APPENDIX A: CONTINUITY AND DIFFERENTIABILITY PROPERTIES OF WALRASIAN DEMAND

In this appendix, we investigate the continuity and differentiability properties of the Walrasian demand correspondence $x(p, w)$. We assume that $x \gg 0$ for all $(p, w) \gg 0$ and $x \in x(p, w)$.

---

31. Yet a third approach, based on linear programming techniques, was provided by Afriat (1967).

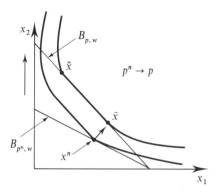

**Figure 3.AA.1**

An upper hemicontinuous Walrasian demand correspondence.

*Continuity*

Because $x(p, w)$ is, in general, a correspondence, we begin by introducing a generalization of the more familiar continuity property for functions, called *upper hemicontinuity*.

**Definition 3.AA.1:** The Walrasian demand correspondence $x(p, w)$ is *upper hemicontinuous* at $(\bar{p}, \bar{w})$ if whenever $(p^n, w^n) \to (\bar{p}, \bar{w})$, $x^n \in x(p^n, w^n)$ for all $n$, and $x = \lim_{n \to \infty} x^n$, we have $x \in x(p, w)$.[32]

In words, a demand correspondence is upper hemicontinuous at $(\bar{p}, \bar{w})$ if for any sequence of price–wealth pairs the limit of any sequence of optimal demand bundles is optimal (although not necessarily uniquely so) at the limiting price–wealth pair. If $x(p, w)$ is single-valued at all $(p, w) \gg 0$, this notion is equivalent to the usual continuity property for functions.

Figure 3.AA.1 depicts an upper hemicontinuous demand correspondence: When $p^n \to p$, $x(\cdot, w)$ exhibits a jump in demand behavior at the price vector $p$, being $x^n$ for all $p^n$ but suddenly becoming the interval of consumption bundles $[\bar{x}, \bar{\bar{x}}]$ at $p$. It is upper hemicontinuous because $\bar{x}$ (the limiting optimum for $p^n$ along the sequence) is an element of segment $[\bar{x}, \bar{\bar{x}}]$ (the set of optima at price vector $p$). See Section M.H of the Mathematical Appendix for further details on upper hemicontinuity.

**Proposition 3.AA.1:** Suppose that $u(\cdot)$ is a continuous utility function representing locally nonsatiated preferences $\succsim$ on the consumption set $X = \mathbb{R}_+^L$. Then the derived demand correspondence $x(p, w)$ is upper hemicontinuous at all $(p, w) \gg 0$. Moreover, if $x(p, w)$ is a function [i.e., if $x(p, w)$ has a single element for all $(p, w)$], then it is continuous at all $(p, w) \gg 0$.

---

**Proof:** To verify upper hemicontinuity, suppose that we had a sequence $\{(p^n, w^n)\}_{n=1}^{\infty} \to (\bar{p}, \bar{w}) \gg 0$ and a sequence $\{x^n\}_{n=1}^{\infty}$ with $x^n \in x(p^n, w^n)$ for all $n$, such that $x^n \to \tilde{x}$ and $\tilde{x} \notin x(\bar{p}, \bar{w})$. Because $p^n \cdot x^n \leq w^n$ for all $n$, taking limits as $n \to \infty$, we conclude that $\bar{p} \cdot \tilde{x} \leq \bar{w}$. Thus, $\tilde{x}$ is a feasible consumption bundle when the budget set is $B_{\bar{p}, \bar{w}}$. However, since it is not optimal in this set, it must be that $u(\bar{x}) > u(\tilde{x})$ for some $\bar{x} \in B_{\bar{p}, \bar{w}}$.

---

32. We use the notation $z^n \to z$ as synonymous with $z = \lim_{n \to \infty} z^n$. This definition of upper hemicontinuity applies only to correspondences that are "locally bounded" (see Section M.H of the Mathematical Appendix). Under our assumptions, the Walrasian demand correspondence satisfies this property at all $(p, w) \gg 0$.

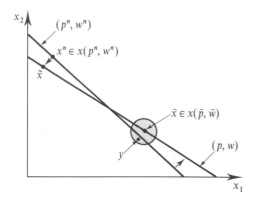

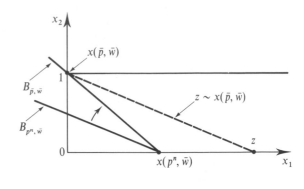

By the continuity of $u(\cdot)$, there is a $y$ arbitrarily close to $\tilde{x}$ such that $p \cdot y < w$ and $u(y) > u(\tilde{x})$. This bundle $y$ is illustrated in Figure 3.AA.2.

Note that if $n$ is large enough, we will have $p^n \cdot y < w^n$ [since $(p^n, w^n) \to (p, w)$]. Hence, $y$ is an element of the budget set $B_{p^n, w^n}$, and we must have $u(x^n) \geq u(y)$ because $x^n \in x(p^n, w^n)$. Taking limits as $n \to \infty$, the continuity of $u(\cdot)$ then implies that $u(\tilde{x}) \geq u(y)$, which gives us a contradiction. We must therefore have $\tilde{x} \in x(p, w)$, establishing upper hemicontinuity of $x(p, w)$.

The same argument also establishes continuity if $x(p, w)$ is in fact a function. ∎

**Figure 3.AA.2 (left)**

Finding a bundle $y$ such that $p \cdot y < w$ and $u(y) > u(\tilde{x})$.

**Figure 3.AA.3 (right)**

The locally cheaper test fails at price–wealth pair $(\bar{p}, \bar{w}) = (1, \bar{w}, \bar{w})$.

Suppose that the consumption set is an arbitrary closed set $X \subset \mathbb{R}^L_+$. Then the continuity (or upper hemicontinuity) property still follows at any $(\bar{p}, \bar{w})$ that passes the following (*locally cheaper consumption*) test: "Suppose that $x \in X$ is affordable (i.e., $\bar{p} \cdot x \leq \bar{w}$). Then there is a $y \in X$ arbitrarily close to $x$ and that costs less than $\bar{w}$ (i.e., $\bar{p} \cdot y < \bar{w}$)." For example, in Figure 3.AA.3, commodity 2 is available only in indivisible unit amounts. The locally cheaper test then fails at the price–wealth point $(\bar{p}, \bar{w}) = (1, \bar{w}, \bar{w})$, where a unit of good 2 becomes just affordable. You can easily verify by examining the figure [in which the dashed line indicates indifference between the points $(0, 1)$ and $z$] that demand will fail to be upper hemicontinuous when $p_2 = \bar{w}$. In particular, for price–wealth points $(p^n, \bar{w})$ such that $p^n_1 = 1$ and $p^n_2 > \bar{w}$, $x(p^n, \bar{w})$ involves only the consumption of good 1; whereas at $(\bar{p}, \bar{w}) = (1, \bar{w}, \bar{w})$, we have $x(\bar{p}, \bar{w}) = (0, 1)$. Note that the proof of Proposition 3.AA.1 fails when the locally cheaper consumption condition does not hold because we cannot find a consumption bundle $y$ with the properties described there.

## Differentiability

Proposition 3.AA.1 has established that if $x(p, w)$ is a function, then it is continuous. Often it is convenient that it be differentiable as well. We now discuss when this is so. We assume for the remaining paragraphs that $u(\cdot)$ is strictly quasiconcave and twice continuously differentiable and that $\nabla u(x) \neq 0$ for all $x$.

As we have shown in Section 3.D, the first-order conditions for the UMP imply that $x(p, w) \gg 0$ is, for some $\lambda > 0$, the unique solution of the system of $L + 1$ equations in $L + 1$ unknowns:

$$\nabla u(x) - \lambda p = 0$$
$$p \cdot x - w = 0.$$

Therefore, the *implicit function theorem* (see Section M.E of the Mathematical Appendix) tells us that the differentiability of the solution $x(p, w)$ as a function of the parameters $(p, w)$ of the system depends on the Jacobian matrix of this system having a nonzero determinant. The Jacobian matrix [i.e., the derivative matrix of the $L + 1$ component functions with respect to the $L + 1$ variables $(x, \lambda)$] is

$$\begin{bmatrix} D^2 u(x) & -p \\ p^T & 0 \end{bmatrix}.$$

Since $\nabla u(x) = \lambda p$ and $\lambda > 0$, the determinant of this matrix is nonzero if and only if the determinant of the *bordered Hessian* of $u(x)$ at $x$ is nonzero:

$$\begin{vmatrix} D^2 u(x) & \nabla u(x) \\ [\nabla u(x)]^T & 0 \end{vmatrix} \neq 0.$$

This condition has a straightforward geometric interpretation. It means that the indifference set through $x$ has a nonzero curvature at $x$; it is not (even infinitesimally) flat. This condition is a slight technical strengthening of strict quasiconcavity [just as the strictly concave function $f(x) = -(x^4)$ has $f''(0) = 0$, a strictly quasiconcave function could have a bordered Hessian determinant that is zero at a point].

We conclude, therefore, that $x(p, w)$ is differentiable *if and only if* the determinant of the bordered Hessian of $u(\cdot)$ is nonzero at $x(p, w)$. It is worth noting the following interesting fact (which we shall not prove here): If $x(p, w)$ is differentiable at $(p, w)$, then the Slutsky matrix $S(p, w)$ has maximal possible rank; that is, the rank of $S(p, w)$ equals $L - 1$.[33]

## REFERENCES

Afriat, S. (1967). The construction of utility functions from expenditure data. *International Economic Review* **8**: 67–77.

Antonelli, G. B. (1886). *Sulla Teoria Matematica della Economia Politica*. Pisa: Nella tipografia del Folchetto. [English translation: On the mathematical theory of political economy.] In *Preferences, Utility and Demand*, edited by J. Chipman, L. Hurwicz, and H. Sonnenschein. New York: Harcourt Brace Jovanovich, 1971.]

Chipman, J., and J. Moore. (1980). Compensating variation, consumer's surplus, and welfare. *American Economic Review* **70**: 933–48.

Deaton, A., and J. Muellbauer (1980). *Economics and Consumer Behavior*. Cambridge, U.K.: Cambridge University Press.

Debreu, G. (1960). Topological methods in cardinal utility. In *Mathematical Methods in the Social Studies, 1959*, edited by K. Arrow, S. Karlin, and P. Suppes. Stanford, Calif.: Stanford University Press.

Diewert, W. E. (1982). Duality approaches to microeconomic theory. Chap. 12 in *Handbook of Mathematical Economics*. Vol. 2, edited by K. Arrow and M. Intriligator. Amsterdam: North-Holland.

Green, J. R., and W. Heller. (1981). Mathematical analysis and convexity with applications to economics. Chap. 1 in *Handbook of Mathematical Economics*, Vol. 1, edited by K. Arrow and M. Intriligator. Amsterdam. North-Holland.

---

33. This statement applies only to demand generated from a twice continuously differentiable utility function. It need not be true when this condition is not met. For example, the demand function $x(p, w) = (w/(p_1 + p_2), w/(p_1 + p_2))$ is differentiable, and it is generated by the utility function $u(x) = \text{Min} \{x_1, x_2\}$, which is not twice continuously differentiable at all $x$. The substitution matrix for this demand function has all its entries equal to zero and therefore has rank equal to zero.

Hausman, J. (1981). Exact consumer surplus and deadweight loss. *American Economic Review* **71**: 662–76.

Hicks, J. (1939). *Value and Capital*. Oxford: Clarendon Press.

Houthakker, H. S. (1950). Revealed preference and the utility function. *Economica* **17**: 159–74.

Hurwicz, L., and Uzawa. (1971). On the integrability of demand functions. Chap. 6 in *Preferences, Utility and Demand*, edited by J. Chipman, L. Hurwicz, and H. Sonnenschein. New York: Harcourt Brace, Jovanovich.

Kihlstrom, R., A. Mas-Colell, and H. Sonnenschein. (1976). The demand theory of the weak axiom of revealed preference. *Econometrica* **44**: 971–78.

McKenzie, L. (1956–57). Demand theory without a utility index. *Review of Economic Studies* **24**: 185–89.

Marshall, A. (1920). *Principles of Economics*. London: Macmillan.

Mas-Colell, A. (1982). Revealed preference after Samuelson, in *Samuelson and Neoclassical Economics*, edited by G. Feiwel. Boston: Kluwer-Nijhoff.

Richter, M. (1966). Revealed preference theory. *Econometrica* **34**: 635–45.

Samuelson, P. (1947). *Foundations of Economics Analysis*. Cambridge, Mass.: Harvard University Press.

Slutsky, E. (1915). Sulla teoria del bilancio del consumatore. *Giornali degli Economisti* **51**: 1–26. [English translation: On the theory of the budget of the consumer, in *Readings in Price Theory*, edited by G. Stigler and K. Boulding. Chicago: Richard Irwin, 1952.]

Stone, J. E. (1954). Linear expenditure systems and demand analysis: An application to the pattern of British demand. *Economic Journal* **64**: 511–27.

Vives, X. (1987). Small income effects: A Marshallian theory of consumer surplus and downward sloping demand. *Review of Economic Studies* **54**: 87–103.

## EXERCISES

**3.B.1**[A] In text.

**3.B.2**[B] The preference relation $\succsim$ defined on the consumption set $X = \mathbb{R}_+^L$ is said to be *weakly monotone* if and only if $x \geq y$ implies that $x \succsim y$. Show that if $\succsim$ is transitive, locally nonsatiated, and weakly monotone, then it is monotone.

**3.B.3**[A] Draw a convex preference relation that is locally nonsatiated but is not monotone.

**3.C.1**[B] Verify that the lexicographic ordering is complete, transitive, strongly monotone, and strictly convex.

**3.C.2**[B] Show that if $u(\cdot)$ is a continuous utility function representing $\succsim$, then $\succsim$ is continuous.

**3.C.3**[C] Show that if for every $x$ the upper and lower contour sets $\{y \in \mathbb{R}_+^L : y \succsim x\}$ and $\{y \in \mathbb{R}_+^L : x \succsim y\}$ are closed, then $\succsim$ is continuous according to Definition 3.C.1.

**3.C.4**[B] Exhibit an example of a preference relation that is not continuous but is representable by a utility function.

**3.C.5**[C] Establish the following two results:

(a) A continuous $\succsim$ is homothetic if and only if it admits a utility function $u(x)$ that is homogeneous of degree one; i.e., $u(\alpha x) = \alpha u(x)$ for all $\alpha > 0$.

(b) A continuous $\succsim$ on $(-\infty, \infty) \times \mathbb{R}_+^{L-1}$ is quasilinear with respect to the first commodity if and only if it admits a utility function $u(x)$ of the form $u(x) = x_1 + \phi(x_2, \cdots, x_L)$. [*Hint:* The existence of some continuous utility representation is guaranteed by Proposition 3.G.1.]

After answering (a) and (b), argue that these properties of $u(\cdot)$ are cardinal.

**3.C.6$^{\text{B}}$** Suppose that in a two-commodity world, the consumer's utility function takes the form $u(x) = [\alpha_1 x_1^\rho + \alpha_2 x_2^\rho]^{1/\rho}$. This utility function is known as the *constant elasticity of substitution* (or *CES*) utility function.

(a) Show that when $\rho = 1$, indifference curves become linear.

(b) Show that as $\rho \to 0$, this utility function comes to represent the same preferences as the (generalized) Cobb–Douglas utility function $u(x) = x_1^{\alpha_1} x_2^{\alpha_2}$.

(c) Show that as $\rho \to -\infty$, indifference curves become "right angles"; that is, this utility function has in the limit the indifference map of the Leontief utility function $u(x_1, x_2) = \text{Min} \{x_1, x_2\}$.

**3.D.1$^{\text{A}}$** In text.

**3.D.2$^{\text{A}}$** In text.

**3.D.3$^{\text{B}}$** Suppose that $u(x)$ is differentiable and strictly quasiconcave and that the Walrasian demand function $x(p, w)$ is differentiable. Show the following:

(a) If $u(x)$ is homogeneous of degree one, then the Walrasian demand function $x(p, w)$ and the indirect utility function $v(p, w)$ are homogeneous of degree one [and hence can be written in the form $x(p, w) = w\tilde{x}(p)$ and $v(p, w) = w\tilde{v}(p)$] and the wealth expansion path (see Section 2.E) is a straight line through the origin. What does this imply about the wealth elasticities of demand?

(b) If $u(x)$ is strictly quasiconcave and $v(p, w)$ is homogeneous of degee one in $w$, then $u(x)$ must be homogeneous of degree one.

**3.D.4$^{\text{B}}$** Let $(-\infty, \infty) \times \mathbb{R}_+^{L-1}$ denote the consumption set, and assume that preferences are strictly convex and quasilinear. Normalize $p_1 = 1$.

(a) Show that the Walrasian demand functions for goods $2, \ldots, L$ are independent of wealth. What does this imply about the wealth effect (see Section 2.E) of demand for good 1?

(b) Argue that the indirect utility function can be written in the form $v(p, w) = w + \phi(p)$ for some function $\phi(\cdot)$.

(c) Suppose, for simplicity, that $L = 2$, and write the consumer's utility function as $u(x_1, x_2) = x_1 + \eta(x_2)$. Now, however, let the consumption set be $\mathbb{R}_+^2$ so that there is a nonnegativity constraint on consumption of the numeraire $x_1$. Fix prices $p$, and examine how the consumer's Walrasian demand changes as wealth $w$ varies. When is the nonnegativity constraint on the numeraire irrelevant?

**3.D.5$^{\text{B}}$** Consider again the CES utility function of Exercise 3.C.6, and assume that $\alpha_1 = \alpha_2 = 1$.

(a) Compute the Walrasian demand and indirect utility functions for this utility function.

(b) Verify that these two functions satisfy all the properties of Propositions 3.D.2 and 3.D.3.

(c) Derive the Walrasian demand correspondence and indirect utility function for the case of linear utility and the case of Leontief utility (see Exercise 3.C.6). Show that the CES Walrasian demand and indirect utility functions approach these as $\rho$ approaches 1 and $-\infty$, respectively.

(d) The *elasticity of substitution between goods* 1 and 2 is defined as

$$\xi_{12}(p, w) = -\frac{\partial[x_1(p, w)/x_2(p, w)]}{\partial[p_1/p_2]} \frac{p_1/p_2}{x_1(p, w)/x_2(p, w)}.$$

Show that for the CES utility function, $\xi_{12}(p, w) = 1/(1 - \rho)$, thus justifying its name. What is $\xi_{12}(p, w)$ for the linear, Leontief, and Cobb–Douglas utility functions?

**3.D.6$^B$** Consider the three-good setting in which the consumer has utility function $u(x) = (x_1 - b_1)^\alpha (x_2 - b_2)^\beta (x_3 - b_3)^\gamma$.

**(a)** Why can you assume that $\alpha + \beta + \gamma = 1$ without loss of generality? Do so for the rest of the problem.

**(b)** Write down the first-order conditions for the UMP, and derive the consumer's Walrasian demand and indirect utility functions. This system of demands is known as the *linear expenditure system* and is due to Stone (1954).

**(c)** Verify that these demand functions satisfy the properties listed in Propositions 3.D.2 and 3.D.3.

**3.D.7$^B$** There are two commodities. We are given two budget sets $B_{p^0, w^0}$ and $B_{p^1, w^1}$ described, respectively, by $p^0 = (1, 1)$, $w^0 = 8$ and $p^1 = (1, 4)$, $w^1 = 26$. The observed choice at $(p^0, w^0)$ is $x^0 = (4, 4)$. At $(p^1, w^1)$, we have a choice $x^1$ such that $p \cdot x^1 = w^1$.

**(a)** Determine the region of permissible choices $x^1$ if the choices $x^0$ and $x^1$ are consistent with maximization of preferences.

**(b)** Determine the region of permissible choices $x^1$ if the choices $x^0$ and $x^1$ are consistent with maximization of preferences that are quasilinear with respect to the *first* good.

**(c)** Determine the region of permissible choices $x^1$ if the choices $x^0$ and $x^1$ are consistent with maximization of preferences that are quasilinear with respect to the *second* good.

**(d)** Determine the region of permissible choices $x^1$ if the choices $x^0$ and $x^1$ are consistent with maximization of preferences for which both goods are normal.

**(e)** Determine the region of permissible choices $x^1$ if the choices $x^0$ and $x^1$ are consistent with maximization of homothetic preferences.

[*Hint*: The ideal way to answer this exercise relies on (good) pictures as much as possible.]

**3.D.8$^A$** Show that for all $(p, w)$, $w \, \partial v(p, w)/\partial w = -p \cdot \nabla_p v(p, w)$.

**3.E.1$^A$** In text.

**3.E.2$^A$** In text.

**3.E.3$^B$** Prove that a solution to the EMP exists if $p \gg 0$ and there is some $x \in \mathbb{R}_+^L$ satisfying $u(x) \geq u$.

**3.E.4$^B$** Show that if the consumer's preferences $\succsim$ are convex, then $h(p, u)$ is a convex set. Also show that if $u(x)$ is strictly convex, then $h(p, u)$ is single-valued.

**3.E.5$^B$** Show that if $u(\cdot)$ is homogeneous of degree one, then $h(p, u)$ and $e(p, u)$ are homogeneous of degree one in $u$ [i.e., they can be written as $h(p, u) = \tilde{h}(p)u$ and $e(p, u) = \tilde{e}(p)u$].

**3.E.6$^B$** Consider the constant elasticity of substitution utility function studied in Exercises 3.C.6 and 3.D.5 with $\alpha_1 = \alpha_2 = 1$. Derive its Hicksian demand function and expenditure function. Verify the properties of Propositions 3.E.2 and 3.E.3.

**3.E.7$^B$** Show that if $\succsim$ is quasilinear with respect to good 1, the Hicksian demand functions for goods $2, \ldots, L$ do not depend on $u$. What is the form of the expenditure function in this case?

**3.E.8$^A$** For the Cobb–Douglas utility function, verify that the relationships in (3.E.1) and (3.E.4) hold. Note that the expenditure function can be derived by simply inverting the indirect utility function, and vice versa.

**3.E.9^B** Use the relations in (3.E.1) to show that the properties of the indirect utility function identified in Proposition 3.D.3 imply Proposition 3.E.2. Likewise, use the relations in (3.E.1) to prove that Proposition 3.E.2 implies Proposition 3.D.3.

**3.E.10^B** Use the relations in (3.E.1) and (3.E.4) and the properties of the indirect utility and expenditure functions to show that Proposition 3.D.2 implies Proposition 3.E.4. Then use these facts to prove that Proposition 3.E.3 implies Proposition 3.D.2.

**3.F.1^B** Prove formally that a closed, convex set $K \subset \mathbb{R}^L$ equals the intersection of the half-spaces that contain it (use the separating hyperplane theorem).

**3.F.2^A** Show by means of a graphic example that the separating hyperplane theorem does not hold for nonconvex sets. Then argue that if $K$ is closed and not convex, there is always some $x \notin K$ that cannot be separated from $K$.

**3.G.1^B** Prove that Proposition 3.G.1 is implied by Roy's identity (Proposition 3.G.4).

**3.G.2^B** Verify for the case of a Cobb–Douglas utility function that all of the propositions in Section 3.G hold.

**3.G.3^B** Consider the (linear expenditure system) utility function given in Exercise 3.D.6.

(a) Derive the Hicksian demand and expenditure functions. Check the properties listed in Propositions 3.E.2 and 3.E.3.

(b) Show that the derivatives of the expenditure function are the Hicksian demand function you derived in (a).

(c) Verify that the Slutsky equation holds.

(d) Verify that the own-substitution terms are negative and that compensated cross-price effects are symmetric.

(e) Show that $S(p, w)$ is negative semidefinite and has rank 2.

**3.G.4^B** A utility function $u(x)$ is *additively separable* if it has the form $u(x) = \sum_\ell u_\ell(x_\ell)$.

(a) Show that additive separability is a cardinal property that is preserved only under linear transformations of the utility function.

(b) Show that the induced ordering on any group of commodities is independent of whatever fixed values we attach to the remaining ones. It turns out that this ordinal property is not only necessary but also sufficient for the existence of an additive separable representation. [You should *not* attempt a proof. This is very hard. See Debreu (1960)].

(c) Show that the Walrasian and Hicksian demand functions generated by an additively separable utility function admit no inferior goods if the functions $u_\ell(\cdot)$ are strictly concave. (You can assume differentiability and interiority to answer this question.)

(d) (Harder) Suppose that all $u_\ell(\cdot)$ are identical and twice differentiable. Let $\hat{u}(\cdot) = u_\ell(\cdot)$. Show that if $-[t\hat{u}''(t)/\hat{u}'(t)] < 1$ for all $t$, then the Walrasian demand $x(p, w)$ has the so-called *gross substitute property*, i.e., $\partial x_\ell(p, w)/\partial p_k > 0$ for all $\ell$ and $k \neq \ell$.

**3.G.5^C** (*Hicksian composite commodities.*) Suppose there are two groups of desirable commodities, $x$ and $y$, with corresponding prices $p$ and $q$. The consumer's utility function is $u(x, y)$, and her wealth is $w > 0$. Suppose that prices for goods $y$ always vary in proportion to one another, so that we can write $q = \alpha q_0$. For any number $z \geq 0$, define the function

$$\tilde{u}(x, z) = \underset{y}{\text{Max}} \quad u(x, y)$$

$$\text{s.t. } q_0 \cdot y \leq z.$$

**(a)** Show that if we imagine that the goods in the economy are $x$ and a single composite commodity $z$, that $\tilde{u}(x, z)$ is the consumer's utility function, and that $\alpha$ is the price of the composite commodity, then the solution to $\text{Max}_{x,z}\, \tilde{u}(x, z)$ s.t. $p \cdot x + \alpha z \leq w$ will give the consumer's actual levels of $x$ and $z = q_0 \cdot y$.

**(b)** Show that properties of Walrasian demand functions identified in Propositions 3.D.2 and 3.G.4 hold for $x(p, \alpha, w)$ and $z(p, \alpha, w)$.

**(c)** Show that the properties in Propositions 3.E.3, and 3.G.1 to 3.G.3 hold for the Hicksian demand functions derived using $\tilde{u}(x, z)$.

**3.G.6$^B$** (F. M. Fisher)   A consumer in a three-good economy (goods denoted $x_1, x_2$, and $x_3$; prices denoted $p_1, p_2, p_3$) with wealth level $w > 0$ has demand functions for commodities 1 and 2 given by

$$x_1 = 100 - 5\frac{p_1}{p_3} + \beta\frac{p_2}{p_3} + \delta\frac{w}{p_3}$$

$$x_2 = \alpha + \beta\frac{p_1}{p_3} + \gamma\frac{p_2}{p_3} + \delta\frac{w}{p_3}$$

where Greek letters are nonzero constants.

**(a)** Indicate how to calculate the demand for good 3 (but do not actually do it).

**(b)** Are the demand functions for $x_1$ and $x_2$ appropriately homogeneous?

**(c)** Calculate the restrictions on the numerical values of $\alpha$, $\beta$, $\gamma$ and $\delta$ implied by utility maximization.

**(d)** Given your results in part (c), for a fixed level of $x_3$ draw the consumer's indifference curve in the $x_1, x_2$ plane.

**(e)** What does your answer to (d) imply about the form of the consumer's utility function $u(x_1, x_2, x_3)$?

**3.G.7$^A$** A striking duality is obtained by using the concept of *indirect demand function*. Fix $w$ at some level, say $w = 1$; from now on, we write $x(p, 1) = x(p)$, $v(p, 1) = v(p)$. The *indirect demand function* $g(x)$ is the inverse of $x(p)$; that is, it is the rule that assigns to every commodity bundle $x \gg 0$ the price vector $g(x)$ such that $x = x(g(x), 1)$. Show that

$$g(x) = \frac{1}{x \cdot \nabla u(x)}\, \nabla u(x).$$

Deduce from Proposition 3.G.4 that

$$x(p) = \frac{1}{p \cdot \nabla v(p)}\, \nabla v(p).$$

Note that this is a completely symmetric expression. Thus, direct (Walrasian) demand is the normalized derivative of indirect utility, and indirect demand is the normalized derivative of direct utility.

**3.G.8$^B$** The indirect utility function $v(p, w)$ is logarithmically homogeneous if $v(p, \alpha w) = v(p, w) + \ln \alpha$ for $\alpha > 0$ [in other words, $v(p, w) = \ln (v^*(p, w))$, where $v^*(p, w)$ is homogeneous of degree one]. Show that if $v(\cdot, \cdot)$ is logarithmically homogeneous, then $x(p, 1) = -\nabla_p v(p, 1)$.

**3.G.9$^C$** Compute the Slutsky matrix from the indirect utility function.

**3.G.10$^B$** For a function of the Gorman form $v(p, w) = a(p) + b(p)w$, which properties will the functions $a(\cdot)$ and $b(\cdot)$ have to satisfy for $v(p, w)$ to qualify as an indirect utility function?

**3.G.11**[B] Verify that an indirect utility function in Gorman form exhibits linear wealth-expansion curves.

**3.G.12**[B] What restrictions on the Gorman form correspond to the cases of homothetic and quasilinear preferences?

**3.G.13**[C] Suppose that the indirect utility function $v(p, w)$ is a polynomial of degree $n$ on $w$ (with coefficients that may depend on $p$). Show that any individual wealth-expansion path is contained in a linear subspace of at most dimension $n + 1$. Interpret.

**3.G.14**[A] The matrix below records the (Walrasian) demand substitution effects for a consumer endowed with rational preferences and consuming three goods at the prices $p_1 = 1$, $p_2 = 2$, and $p_3 = 6$:

$$\begin{bmatrix} -10 & ? & ? \\ ? & -4 & ? \\ 3 & ? & ? \end{bmatrix}.$$

Supply the missing numbers. Does the resulting matrix possess all the properties of a substitution matrix?

**3.G.15**[B] Consider the utility function

$$u = 2x_1^{1/2} + 4x_2^{1/2}.$$

(a) Find the demand functions for goods 1 and 2 as they depend on prices and wealth.

(b) Find the compensated demand function $h(\cdot)$.

(c) Find the expenditure function, and verify that $h(p, u) = \nabla_p e(p, u)$.

(d) Find the indirect utility function, and verify Roy's identity.

**3.G.16**[C] Consider the expenditure function

$$e(p, u) = \exp \left\{ \sum_\ell \alpha_\ell \log p_\ell + \left( \prod_\ell p_\ell^{\beta_\ell} \right) u \right\}.$$

(a) What restrictions on $\alpha_1, \ldots, \alpha_n, \beta_1, \ldots, \beta_n$ are necessary for this to be derivable from utility maximization?

(b) Find the indirect utility that corresponds to it.

(c) Verify Roy's identity and the Slutsky equation.

**3.G.17**[B] [From Hausman (1981)]   Suppose $L = 2$. Consider a "local" indirect utility function defined in some neighborhood of price–wealth pair $(\bar{p}, \bar{w})$ by

$$v(p, w) = -\exp\left(-bp_1/p_2\right) \left[ \frac{w}{p_2} + \frac{1}{b}\left( a\frac{p_1}{p_2} + \frac{a}{b} + c \right) \right].$$

(a) Verify that the local demand function for the first good is

$$x_1(p, w) = a\frac{p_1}{p_2} + b\frac{w}{p_2} + c.$$

(b) Verify that the local expenditure function is

$$e(p, u) = -p_2 u \exp\left(bp_1/p_2\right) - \frac{1}{b}\left( ap_1 + \frac{a}{b}p_2 + cp_2 \right).$$

(c) Verify that the local Hicksian demand function for the first commodity is

$$h_1(p, u) = -ub \exp (bp_1/p_2) - \frac{a}{b}.$$

**3.G.18$^C$** Show that every good is related to every other good by a chain of (weak) substitutes; that is, for any goods $\ell$ and $k$, either $\partial h_\ell(p, u)/\partial p_k \geq 0$, or there exists a good $r$ such that $\partial h_\ell(p, u)/\partial p_r \geq 0$ and $\partial h_r(p, u)/\partial p_k \geq 0$, or there is $\ldots$, and so on. [*Hint:* Argue first the case of two commodities. Use next the insights on composite commodities gained in Exercise 3.G.5 to handle the case of three, and then $L$, commodities.]

**3.H.1$^C$** Show that if $e(p, u)$ is continuous, increasing in $u$, homogeneous of degree one, nondecreasing, and concave in $p$, then the utility function $u(x) = \text{Sup}\, \{u: x \in V_u\}$, where $V_u = \{y: p \cdot y \geq e(p, u) \text{ for all } p \gg 0\}$, defined for $x \gg 0$, satisfies $e(p, u) = \text{Min}\, \{p \cdot x: u(x) \geq u\}$ for any $p \gg 0$.

**3.H.2$^B$** Use Proposition 3.F.1 to argue that if $e(p, u)$ is differentiable in $p$, then there are no (strongly monotone) nonconvex preferences generating $e(\cdot)$.

**3.H.3$^A$** How would you recover $v(p, w)$ from $e(p, u)$?

**3.H.4$^B$** Suppose that we are given as primitive, not the Walrasian demand but the indirect demand function $g(x)$ introduced in Exercise 3.G.7. How would you go about recovering $\succsim$? Restrict yourself to the case $L = 2$.

**3.H.5$^B$** Suppose you know the indirect utility function. How would you recover from it the expenditure function and the direct utility function?

**3.H.6$^B$** Suppose that you observe the Walrasian demand functions $x_\ell(p, w) = \alpha_\ell w/p_\ell$ for all $\ell = 1, \ldots, L$ with $\sum_\ell \alpha_\ell = 1$. Derive the expenditure function of this demand system. What is the consumer's utility function?

**3.H.7$^B$** Answer the following questions with reference to the demand function in Exercise 2.F.17.

(a) Let the utility associated with consumption bundle $x = (1, 1, \ldots, 1)$ be 1. What is the expenditure function $e(p, 1)$ associated with utility level $u = 1$? [*Hint:* Use the answer to (d) in Exercise 2.F.17.]

(b) What is the upper contour set of consumption bundle $x = (1, 1, \ldots, 1)$?

**3.I.1$^B$** In text.

**3.I.2$^B$** In text.

**3.I.3$^B$** Consider a price change from initial price vector $p^0$ to new price vector $p^1 \leq p^0$ in which only the price of good $\ell$ changes. Show that $CV(p^0, p^1, w) > EV(p^0, p^1, w)$ if good $\ell$ is inferior.

**3.I.4$^B$** Construct an example in which a comparison of $CV(p^0, p^1, w)$ and $CV(p^0, p^2, w)$ does not give the correct welfare ranking of $p^1$ versus $p^2$.

**3.I.5$^B$** Show that if $u(x)$ is quasilinear with respect to the first good (and we fix $p_1 = 1$), then $CV(p^0, p^1, w) = EV(p^0, p^1, w)$ for any $(p^0, p^1, w)$.

**3.I.6$^A$** Suppose there are $i = 1, \ldots, I$ consumers with utility functions $u_i(x)$ and wealth $w_i$. We consider a change from $p^0$ to $p^1$. Show that if $\sum_i CV_i(p^0, p^1, w_i) > 0$ then we can find $\{w_i'\}_{i=1}^I$ such that $\sum_i w_i' \leq \sum_i w_i$ and $v_i(p^1, w_i') \geq v_i(p^0, w_i)$ for all $i$. That is, it is in principle possible to compensate everybody for the change in prices.

**3.I.7$^B$** There are three commodities (i.e., $L = 3$), of which the third is a numeraire (let $p_3 = 1$). The market demand function $x(p, w)$ has

$$x_1(p, w) = a + bp_1 + cp_2$$
$$x_2(p, w) = d + ep_1 + gp_2.$$

**(a)** Give the parameter restrictions implied by utility maximization.

**(b)** Estimate the equivalent variation for a change of prices from $(p_1, p_2) = (1, 1)$ to $(\bar{p}_1, \bar{p}_2) = (2, 2)$. Verify that without appropriate symmetry, there is no path independence. Assume symmetry for the rest of the exercise.

**(c)** Let $EV_1$, $EV_2$, and $EV$ be the equivalent variations for a change of prices from $(p_1, p_2) = (1, 1)$ to, respectively, $(2, 1)$, $(1, 2)$, and $(2, 2)$. Compare $EV$ with $EV_1 + EV_2$ as a function of the parameters of the problem. Interpret.

**(d)** Suppose that the price increases in (c) are due to taxes. Denote the deadweight losses for each of the three experiments by $DW_1$, $DW_2$, and $DW$. Compare $DW$ with $DW_1 + DW_2$ as a function of the parameters of the problem.

**(e)** Suppose the initial tax situation has prices $(p_1, p_2) = (1, 1)$. The government wants to raise a fixed (small) amount of revenue $R$ through commodity taxes. Call $t_1$ and $t_2$ the tax rates for the two commodities. Determine the optimal tax rates as a function of the parameters of demand if the optimality criterion is the minimization of deadweight loss.

**3.I.8$^B$** Suppose we are in a three-commodity market (i.e. $L = 3$). Letting $p_3 = 1$, the demand functions for goods 1 and 2 are

$$x_1(p, w) = a_1 + b_1 p_1 + c_1 p_2 + d_1 p_1 p_2$$
$$x_2(p, w) = a_2 + b_2 p_1 + c_2 p_2 + d_2 p_1 p_2.$$

**(a)** Note that the demand for goods 1 and 2 does not depend on wealth. Write down the most general class of utility functions whose demand has this property.

**(b)** Argue that if the demand functions in (a) are generated from utility maximization, then the values of the parameters cannot be arbitrary. Write down as exhaustive a list as you can of the restrictions implied by utility maximization. Justify your answer.

**(c)** Suppose that the conditions in (b) hold. The initial price situation is $p = (p_1, p_2)$, and we consider a change to $p' = (p'_1, p'_2)$. Derive a measure of welfare change generated in going from $p$ to $p'$.

**(d)** Let the values of the parameters be $a_1 = a_2 = 3/2$, $b_1 = c_2 = 1$, $c_1 = b_2 = 1/2$, and $d_1 = d_2 = 0$. Suppose the initial price situation is $p = (1, 1)$. Compute the equivalent variation for a move to $p'$ for each of the following three cases: (i) $p' = (2, 1)$, (ii) $p' = (1, 2)$, and (iii) $p' = (2, 2)$. Denote the respective answers by $EV_1$, $EV_2$, $EV_3$. Under which condition will you have $EV_3 = EV_1 + EV_2$? Discuss.

**3.I.9$^B$** In a one-consumer economy, the government is considering putting a tax of $t$ per unit on good $\ell$ and rebating the proceeds to the consumer (who nonetheless does not consider the effect of her purchases on the size of the rebate). Suppose that $s_{\ell\ell}(p, w) < 0$ for all $(p, w)$. Show that the optimal tax (in the sense of maximizing the consumer's utility) is zero.

**3.I.10$^B$** Construct an example in which the area variation measure approach incorrectly ranks $p^0$ and $p^1$. [*Hint*: Let the change from $p^0$ to $p^1$ involve a change in the price of more than one good.]

**3.I.11$^B$** Suppose that we know not only $p^0$, $p^1$, and $x^0$ but also $x^1 = x(p^1, w)$. Show that if $(p^1 - p^0) \cdot x^1 > 0$, then the consumer must be worse off at price–wealth situation $(p^1, w)$ than at $(p^0, w)$. Interpret this test as a first-order approximation to the expenditure function at $p^1$.

Also show that an alternative way to write this test is $p^0 \cdot (x^1 - x^0) < 0$, and depict the test for the case where $L = 2$ in $(x_1, x_2)$ space. [*Hint*: Locate the point $x^0$ on the set $\{x \in \mathbb{R}^L_+ : u(x) = u^0\}$.]

**3.I.12**[B] Extend the compensating and equivalent variation measures of welfare change to the case of changes in both prices and wealth, so that we change from $(p^0, w^0)$ to $(p^1, w^1)$. Also extend the "partial information" test developed in Section 3.I to this case.

**3.J.1**[C] Show that when $L = 2$, $x(p, w)$ satisfies the strong axiom if and only if it satisfies the weak axiom.

**3.AA.1**[B] Suppose that the consumption set is $X = \{x \in \mathbb{R}^2_+ : x_1 + x_2 \geq 1\}$ and the utility function is $u(x) = x_2$. Represent graphically, and show (a) that the locally cheaper consumption test fails at $(p, w) = (1, 1, 1)$ and (b) that market demand is not continuous at this point. Interpet economically.

**3.AA.2**[C] Under the conditions of Proposition 3.AA.1, show that $h(p, u)$ is upper hemicontinuous and that $e(p, u)$ is continuous (even if we replace minimum by infimum and allow $p \geq 0$). Also, assuming that $h(p, u)$ is a function, give conditions for its differentiability.

# Aggregate Demand

## 4.A Introduction

For most questions in economics, the aggregate behavior of consumers is more important than the behavior of any single consumer. In this chapter, we investigate the extent to which the theory presented in Chapters 1 to 3 can be applied to *aggregate demand*, a suitably defined sum of the demands arising from all the economy's consumers. There are, in fact, a number of different properties of individual demand that we might hope would also hold in the aggregate. Which ones we are interested in at any given moment depend on the particular application at hand.

In this chapter, we ask three questions about aggregate demand:

(i) Individual demand can be expressed as a function of prices and the individual's wealth level. *When can aggregate demand be expressed as a function of prices and aggregate wealth?*

(ii) Individual demand derived from rational preferences necessarily satisfies the weak axiom of revealed preference. *When does aggregate demand satisfy the weak axiom?* More generally, when can we apply in the aggregate the demand theory developed in Chapter 2 (especially Section 2.F)?

(iii) Individual demand has welfare significance; from it, we can derive measures of welfare change for the consumer, as discussed in Section 3.I. *When does aggregate demand have welfare significance?* In particular, when do the welfare measures discussed in Section 3.I have meaning when they are computed from the aggregate demand function?

These three questions could, with a grain of salt, be called the *aggregation theories of*, respectively, *the econometrician, the positive theorist*, and *the welfare theorist*.

The econometrician is interested in the degree to which he can impose a simple structure on aggregate demand functions in estimation procedures. One aspect of these concerns, which we address here, is the extent to which aggregate demand can be accurately modeled as a function of only *aggregate* variables, such as aggregate (or, equivalently, average) consumer wealth. This question is important because the econometrician's data may be available only in an aggregate form.

The positive (behavioral) theorist, on the other hand, is interested in the degree to which the positive restrictions of individual demand theory apply in the aggregate. This can be significant for deriving predictions from models of market equilibrium in which aggregate demand plays a central role.[1]

The welfare theorist is interested in the normative implications of aggregate demand. He wants to use the measures of welfare change derived in Section 3.I to evaluate the welfare significance of changes in the economic environment. Ideally, he would like to treat aggregate demand as if it were generated by a "representative consumer" and use the changes in this fictional individual's welfare as a measure of aggregate welfare.

Although the conditions we identify as important for each of these aggregation questions are closely related, the questions being asked in the three cases are conceptually quite distinct. Overall, we shall see that, in all three cases, very strong restrictions will need to hold for the desired aggregation properties to obtain. We discuss these three questions, in turn, in Sections 4.B to 4.D.

Finally, Appendix A discusses the regularizing (i.e., "smoothing") effects arising from aggregation over a large number of consumers.

# 4.B Aggregate Demand and Aggregate Wealth

Suppose that there are $I$ consumers with rational preference relations $\succsim_i$ and corresponding Walrasian demand functions $x_i(p, w_i)$. In general, given prices $p \in \mathbb{R}^L$ and wealth levels $(w_1, \ldots, w_I)$ for the $I$ consumers, aggregate demand can be written as

$$x(p, w_1, \ldots, w_I) = \sum_{i=1}^{I} x_i(p, w_i).$$

Thus, aggregate demand depends not only on prices but also on the specific wealth levels of the various consumers. In this section, we ask when we are justified in writing aggregate demand in the simpler form $x(p, \sum_i w_i)$, where aggregate demand depends only on aggregate wealth $\sum_i w_i$.

For this property to hold in all generality, aggregate demand must be identical for any two distributions of the same total amount of wealth across consumers. That is, for any $(w_1, \ldots, w_I)$ and $(w'_1, \ldots, w'_I)$ such that $\sum_i w_i = \sum_i w'_i$, we must have $\sum_i x_i(p, w_i) = \sum_i x_i(p, w'_i)$.

To examine when this condition is satisfied, consider, starting from some initial distribution $(w_1, \ldots, w_I)$, a differential change in wealth $(dw_1, \ldots, dw_I) \in \mathbb{R}^I$ satisfying $\sum_i dw_i = 0$. If aggregate demand can be written as a function of aggregate wealth, then assuming differentiability of the demand functions, we must have

$$\sum_i \frac{\partial x_{\ell i}(p, w_i)}{\partial w_i} dw_i = 0 \quad \text{for every } \ell.$$

This can be true for all redistributions $(dw_1, \ldots, dw_I)$ satisfying $\sum_i dw_i = 0$ and from any initial wealth distribution $(w_1, \ldots, w_I)$ if and only if the coefficients of the different

---

1. The econometrician may also be interested in these questions because a priori restrictions on the properties of aggregate demand can be incorporated into his estimation procedures.

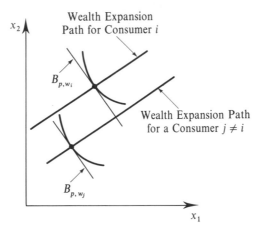

**Figure 4.B.1**

Invariance of
aggregate demand to
redistribution of
wealth implies wealth
expansion paths that
are straight and
parallel across
consumers.

$dw_i$ are equal; that is,

$$\frac{\partial x_{\ell i}(p, w_i)}{\partial w_i} = \frac{\partial x_{\ell j}(p, w_j)}{\partial w_j} \tag{4.B.1}$$

for every $\ell$, any two individuals $i$ and $j$, and all $(w_1, \ldots, w_I)$.[2]

In short, for any fixed price vector $p$, and any commodity $\ell$, the wealth effect at $p$ must be the same whatever consumer we look at and whatever his level of wealth.[3] It is indeed fairly intuitive that in this case, the individual demand changes arising from any wealth redistribution across consumers will cancel out. Geometrically, the condition is equivalent to the statement that all consumers' wealth expansion paths are parallel, straight lines. Figure 4.B.1 depicts parallel, straight wealth expansion paths.

One special case in which this property holds arises when all consumers have identical preferences that are homothetic. Another is when all consumers have preferences that are quasilinear with respect to the same good. Both cases are examples of a more general result shown in Proposition 4.B.1.

**Proposition 4.B.1:** A necessary and sufficient condition for the set of consumers to exhibit parallel, straight wealth expansion paths at any price vector $p$ is that preferences admit indirect utility functions of the Gorman form with the coefficients on $w_i$ the same for every consumer $i$. That is:

$$v_i(p, w_i) = a_i(p) + b(p)w_i.$$

**Proof:** You are asked to establish sufficiency in Exercise 4.B.1 (this is not too difficult; use Roy's identity). Keep in mind that we are neglecting boundaries (alternatively, the significance of a result such as this is only local). You should not attempt to prove necessity. For a discussion of this result, see Deaton and Muellbauer (1980). ∎

---

2. As usual, we are neglecting boundary constraints; hence, strictly speaking, the validity of our claims in this section is only local.

3. Note that $\partial x_{\ell i}(p, w_i)/\partial w_i = \partial x_{\ell i}(p, w_i')/\partial w_i$ for all $w_i \neq w_i'$ because for any values of $w_j, j \neq i$, (4.B.1) must hold for the wealth distributions $(w_1, \ldots, w_{i-1}, w_i, w_{i+1}, \ldots, w_I)$ and $(w_1, \ldots, w_{i-1}, w_i',$ $w_{i+1}, \ldots, w_I)$. Hence, $\partial x_{\ell i}(p, w_i)/\partial w_i = \partial x_{\ell j}(p, w_j)/\partial w_j = \partial x_{\ell i}(p, w_i')/\partial w_i$ for any $j \neq i$.

Thus, aggregate demand can be written as a function of aggregate wealth if and only if all consumers have preferences that admit indirect utility functions of the Gorman form with equal wealth coefficients $b(p)$. Needless to say, this is a very restrictive condition on preferences.[4]

Given this conclusion, we might ask whether less restrictive conditions can be obtained if we consider aggregate demand functions that depend on a wider set of aggregate variables than just the total (or, equivalently, the mean) wealth level. For example, aggregate demand might be allowed to depend on both the mean and the variance of the statistical distribution of wealth or even on the whole statistical distribution itself. Note that the latter condition is still restrictive. It implies that aggregate demand depends only on how many rich and poor there are, not on who in particular is rich or poor.

These more general forms of dependence on the distribution of wealth are indeed valid under weaker conditions than those required for aggregate demand to depend only on aggregate wealth. For a trivial example, note that aggregate demand depends only on the statistical distribution of wealth whenever all consumers possess identical but otherwise arbitrary preferences and differ only in their wealth levels. We shall not pursue this topic further here; good references are Deaton and Muellbauer (1980), Lau (1982) and Jorgenson (1990).

There is another way in which we might be able to get a more positive answer to our question. So far, the test that we have applied is whether the aggregate demand function can be written as a function of aggregate wealth for *any* distribution of wealth across consumers. The requirement that this be true for every conceivable wealth distribution is a strong one. Indeed, in many situations, individual wealth levels may be generated by some underlying process that restricts the set of individual wealth levels which can arise. If so, it may still be possible to write aggregate demand as a function of prices and aggregate wealth.

For example, when we consider general equilibrium models in Part IV, individual wealth is generated by individuals' shareholdings of firms and by their ownership of given, fixed stocks of commodities. Thus, the individual levels of real wealth are determined as a function of the prevailing price vector.

Alternatively, individual wealth levels may be determined in part by various government programs that redistribute wealth across consumers (see Section 4.D). Again, these programs may limit the set of possible wealth distributions that may arise.

To see how this can help, consider an extreme case. Suppose that individual $i$'s wealth level is generated by some process that can be described as a function of prices $p$ and aggregate wealth $w$, $w_i(p, w)$. This was true, for example, in the general equilibrium illustration above. Similarly, the government program may base an individual's taxes (and hence his final wealth position) on his wage rate and the total (real) wealth of the society. We call a family of functions $(w_1(p, w), \ldots, w_I(p, w))$ with $\sum_i w_i(p, w) = w$ for all $(p, w)$ a *wealth distribution rule*. When individual wealth levels

---

4. Recall, however, that it includes some interesting and important classes of preferences. For example, if preferences are quasilinear with respect to good $\ell$, then there is an indirect utility of the form $a_i(p) + w_i/p_\ell$, which, letting $b(p) = 1/p_\ell$, we can see is of the Gorman type with identical $b(p)$.

are generated by a wealth distribution rule, we can indeed *always* write aggregate demand as a function $x(p, w) = \sum_i x_i(p, w_i(p, w))$, and so aggregate demand depends only on prices and aggregate wealth.

# 4.C Aggregate Demand and the Weak Axiom

To what extent do the positive properties of individual demand carry over to the aggregate demand function $x(p, w_1, \ldots, w_I) = \sum_i x_i(p, w_i)$? We can note immediately three properties that do: continuity, homogeneity of degree zero, and Walras' law [that is, $p \cdot x(p, w_1, \ldots, w_I) = \sum_I w_i$ for all $(p, w_1, \ldots, w_I)$]. In this section, we focus on the conditions under which aggregate demand also satisfies the weak axiom, arguably the most central positive property of the individual Walrasian demand function.

To study this question, we would like to operate on an aggregate demand written in the form $x(p, w)$, where $w$ is aggregate wealth. This is the form for which we gave the definition of the weak axiom in Chapter 2. We accomplish this by supposing that there is a wealth distribution rule $(w_1(p, w), \ldots, w_I(p, w))$ determining individual wealths from the price vector and total wealth. We refer to the end of Section 4.B for a discussion of wealth distribution rules.[5] With the wealth distribution rule at our disposal, aggregate demand can automatically be written as

$$x(p, w) = \sum_i x_i(p, w_i(p, w)).$$

Formally, therefore, the aggregate demand function $x(p, w)$ depends then only on aggregate wealth and is therefore a market demand function in the sense discussed in Chapter 2.[6] We now investigate the fulfillment of the weak axiom by $x(\cdot, \cdot)$.

In point of fact, and merely for the sake of concreteness, we shall be even more specific and focus on a particularly simple example of a distribution rule. Namely, we restrict ourselves to the case in which relative wealths of the consumers remain fixed, that is, are independent of prices. Thus, we assume that we are given wealth shares $\alpha_i \geq 0$, $\sum_i \alpha_i = 1$, so that $w_i(p, w) = \alpha_i w$ for every level $w \in \mathbb{R}$ of aggregate wealth.[7] We have then

$$x(p, w) = \sum_i x_i(p, \alpha_i w).$$

We begin by recalling from Chapter 2 the definition of the weak axiom.

**Definition 4.C.1:** The aggregate demand function $x(p, w)$ satisfies the weak axiom (WA) if $p \cdot x(p', w') \leq w$ and $x(p, w) \neq x(p', w')$ imply $p' \cdot x(p, w) > w'$ for any $(p, w)$ and $(p', w')$.

---

5. There is also a methodological advantage to assuming the presence of a wealth distribution rule. It avoids confounding different aggregation issues because the aggregation problem studied in Section 4.B (invariance of demand to redistributions) is then entirely assumed away.

6. Note that it assigns commodity bundles to price–wealth combinations, and, provided every $w_i(\cdot, \cdot)$ is continuous and homogeneous of degree one, that it is continuous, homogeneous of degree zero, and satisfies Walras's law.

7. Observe that this distribution rule amounts to leaving the wealth levels $(w_1, \ldots, w_I)$ unaltered and considering only changes in the price vector $p$. This is because the homogeneity of degree zero of $x(p, w_1, \ldots, w_I)$ implies that any proportional change in wealths can also be captured by a proportional change in prices. The description by means of shares is, however, analytically more convenient.

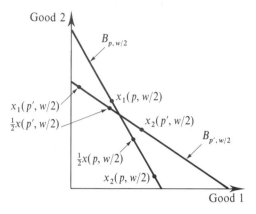

**Figure 4.C.1**

Failure of aggregate demand to satisfy the weak axiom.

We next provide an example illustrating that aggregate demand may not satisfy the weak axiom.

**Example 4.C.1:** *Failure of Aggregate Demand to Satisfy the WA.* Suppose that there are two commodities and two consumers. Wealth is distributed equally so that $w_1 = w_2 = w/2$, where $w$ is aggregate wealth. Two price vectors $p$ and $p'$ with corresponding individual demands $x_1(p, w/2)$ and $x_2(p, w/2)$ under $p$, and $x_1(p', w/2)$ and $x_2(p', w/2)$ under $p'$, are depicted in Figure 4.C.1.

These individual demands satisfy the weak axiom, but the aggregate demands do not. Figure 4.C.1 shows the vectors $\frac{1}{2}x(p, w)$ and $\frac{1}{2}x(p', w)$, which are equal to the average of the two consumers' demands; (and so for each price vector, they must lie at the midpoint of the line segment connecting the two individuals' consumption vectors). As illustrated in the figure, we have

$$\tfrac{1}{2}p \cdot x(p', w) < w/2 \qquad \text{and} \qquad \tfrac{1}{2}p' \cdot x(p, w) < w/2,$$

which (multiply both sides by 2) constitutes a violation of the weak axiom at the price-wealth pairs considered.  ∎

The reason for the failure illustrated in Example 4.C.1 can be traced to wealth effects. Recall from Chapter 2 (Proposition 2.F.1) that $x(p, w)$ satisfies the weak axiom if and only if it satisfies the law of demand for *compensated* price changes. Precisely, if and only if for any $(p, w)$ and any price change $p'$ that is compensated [so that $w' = p' \cdot x(p, w)$], we have

$$(p' - p) \cdot [x(p', w') - x(p, w)] \leq 0, \tag{4.C.1}$$

with strict inequality if $x(p, w) \neq x(p', w')$.[8]

If the price–wealth change under consideration, say from $(p, w)$ to $(p', w')$, happened to be a compensated price change for *every* consumer $i$—that is, if $\alpha_i w' = p' \cdot x_i(p, \alpha_i w)$ for all $i$—then because individual demand satisfies the weak axiom, we would know (again by Proposition 2.F.1) that for all $i = 1, \ldots, I$:

$$(p' - p) \cdot [x_i(p', \alpha_i w') - x_i(p, \alpha_i w)] \leq 0, \tag{4.C.2}$$

---

8. Note that if $p \cdot x(p', w') \leq w$ and $x(p', w') \neq x(p, w)$, then we must have $p' \cdot x(p, w) > w'$, in agreement with the weak axiom.

with strict inequality if $x_i(p', \alpha_i w) \neq x_i(p, \alpha_i w')$. Adding (4.C.2) over $i$ gives us precisely (4.C.1). Thus, we conclude that aggregate demand must satisfy the WA for any price–wealth change that is compensated for every consumer.

The difficulty arises because a price–wealth change that is compensated in the aggregate, so that $w' = p' \cdot x(p, w)$, need not be compensated for each individual; we may well have $\alpha_i w' \neq p' \cdot x_i(p, \alpha_i w)$ for some or all $i$. If so, the individual wealth effects [which, except for the condition $p \cdot D_{w_i} x(p, \alpha_i w) = 1$, are essentially unrestricted] can play havoc with the well-behaved but possibly small individual substitution effects. The result may be that (4.C.2) fails to hold for some $i$, thus making possible the failure of the similar expression (4.C.1) in the aggregate.

Given that a property of individual demand as basic as the WA cannot be expected to hold generally for aggregate demand, we might wish to know whether there are any restrictions on individual preferences under which it must be satisfied. The preceding discussion suggests that it may be worth exploring the implications of assuming that the law of demand, expression (4.C.2), holds at the individual level for price changes that are left uncompensated. Suppose, indeed, that given an initial position $(p, w_i)$, we consider a price change $p'$ that is not compensated, namely, we leave $w'_i = w_i$. If (4.C.2) nonetheless holds, then by addition so does (4.C.1). More formally, we begin with a definition.

**Definition 4.C.2:** The individual demand function $x_i(p, w_i)$ satisfies the *uncompensated law of demand (ULD)* property if

$$(p' - p) \cdot [x_i(p', w_i) - x_i(p, w_i)] \leq 0 \qquad (4.C.3)$$

for any $p$, $p'$, and $w_i$, with strict inequality if $x_i(p', w_i) \neq x_i(p, w_i)$.
The analogous definition applies to the aggregate demand function $x(p, w)$.

In view of our discussion of the weak axiom in Section 2.F, the following differential version of the ULD property should come as no surprise (you are asked to prove it in Exercise 4.C.1):

> If $x_i(p, w_i)$ satisfies the ULD property, then $D_p x_i(p, w_i)$ is negative semidefinite; that is, $dp \cdot D_p x_i(p, w_i)\, dp \leq 0$ for all $dp$.

As with the weak axiom, there is a converse to this:

> If $D_p x_i(p, w_i)$ is negative definite for all $p$, then $x_i(p, w_i)$ satisfies the ULD property.

The analogous differential version holds for the aggregate demand function $x(p, w)$.

The great virtue of the ULD property is that, in contrast with the WA, it does, in fact, aggregate. Adding the individual condition (4.C.3) for $w_i = \alpha_i w$ gives us $(p' - p) \cdot [x(p', w) - x(p, w)] \leq 0$, with strict inequality if $x(p, w) \neq x'(p, w)$. This leads us to Proposition 4.C.1.

**Proposition 4.C.1:** If every consumer's Walrasian demand function $x_i(p, w_i)$ satisfies the uncompensated law of demand (ULD) property, so does the aggregate demand $x(p, w) = \sum_i x_i(p, \alpha_i w)$. As a consequence, the aggregate demand $x(p, w)$ satisfies the weak axiom.

**Proof:** Consider any $(p, w)$, $(p', w)$ with $x(p, w) \neq x(p', w)$. We must have

$$x_i(p, \alpha_i w) \neq x_i(p', \alpha_i w)$$

for some $i$. Therefore, adding (4.C.3) over $i$, we get

$$(p' - p) \cdot [x(p, w) - x(p', w)] < 0.$$

This holds for all $p$, $p'$, and $w$.

To verify the WA, take any $(p, w)$, $(p', w')$ with $x(p, w) \neq x(p', w')$ and $p \cdot x(p', w') \leq w$.[9] Define $p'' = (w/w')p'$. By homogeneity of degree zero, we have $x(p'', w) = x(p', w')$. From $(p'' - p) \cdot [x(p'', w) - x(p, w)] < 0$, $p \cdot x(p'', w) \leq w$, and Walras' law, it follows that $p'' \cdot x(p, w) > w$. That is, $p' \cdot x(p, w) > w'$. ∎

How restrictive is the ULD property as an axiom of individual behavior? It is clearly not implied by preference maximization (see Exercise 4.C.3). Propositions 4.C.2 and 4.C.3 provide sufficient conditions for individual demands to satisfy the ULD property.

**Proposition 4.C.2:** If $\succsim_i$ is homothetic, then $x_i(p, w_i)$ satisfies the uncompensated law of demand (ULD) property.

**Proof:** We consider the differentiable case [i.e., we assume that $x_i(p, w_i)$ is differentiable and that $\succsim_i$ is representable by a differentiable utility function]. The matrix $D_p x_i(p, w_i)$ is

$$D_p x_i(p, w_i) = S_i(p, w_i) - \frac{1}{w_i} x_i(p, w_i) \, x_i(p, w_i)^T,$$

where $S_i(p, w_i)$ is consumer $i$'s Slutsky matrix. Because $[dp \cdot x_i(p, w_i)]^2 > 0$ except when $dp \cdot x_i(p, w_i) = 0$ and $dp \cdot S_i(p, w_i) \, dp < 0$ except when $dp$ is proportional to $p$, we can conclude that $D_p x_i(p, w_i)$ is negative definite, and so the ULD condition holds. ∎

In Proposition 4.C.2, the conclusion is obtained with minimal help from the substitution effects. Those could all be arbitrarily small. The wealth effects by themselves turn out to be sufficiently well behaved. Unfortunately, the homothetic case is the only one in which this is so (see Exercise 4.C.4). More generally, for the ULD property to hold, the substitution effects (which are always well behaved) must be large enough to overcome possible "perversities" coming from the wealth effects. The intriguing result in Proposition 4.3.C [due to Mitiushin and Polterovich (1978) and Milleron (1974); see Mas-Colell (1991) for an account and discussion of this result] gives a concrete expression to this relative dominance of the substitution effects.

**Proposition 4.C.3:** Suppose that $\succsim_i$ is defined on the consumption set $X = \mathbb{R}^L_+$ and is representable by a twice continuously differentiable concave function $u_i(\cdot)$. If

$$-\frac{x_i \cdot D^2 u_i(x_i) x_i}{x_i \cdot \nabla u_i(x_i)} < 4 \quad \text{for all } x_i,$$

then $x_i(p, w_i)$ satisfies the unrestricted law of demand (ULD) property.

---

9. Strictly speaking, this proof is required because although we know that the WA is equivalent to the law of demand for compensated price changes, we are now dealing with uncompensated price changes.

The proof of Proposition 4.C.3 will not be given. The courageous reader can attempt it in Exercise 4.C.5.

The condition in Proposition 4.C.3 is not an extremely stringent one. In particular, notice how amply the homothetic case fits into it (Exercise 4.C.6). So, to the question "How restrictive is the ULD property as an axiom of individual behavior?" perhaps we can answer: "restrictive, but not extremely so."[10]

Note, in addition, that for the ULD property to hold for aggregate demand, it is not necessary that the ULD be satisfied at the individual level. It may arise out of aggregation itself. The example in Proposition 4.C.4, due to Hildenbrand (1983), is not very realistic, but it is nonetheless highly suggestive.

**Proposition 4.C.4:** Suppose that all consumers have identical preferences $\succsim$ defined on $\mathbb{R}_+^\ell$ [with individual demand functions denoted $\tilde{x}(p, w)$] and that individual wealth is uniformly distributed on an interval $[0, \bar{w}]$ (strictly speaking, this requires a continuum of consumers). Then the aggregate (rigorously, the average) demand function

$$x(p) = \int_0^{\bar{w}} \tilde{x}(p, w)\, dw$$

satisfies the unrestricted law of demand (ULD) property.

---

**Proof:** Consider the differentiable case. Take $v \neq 0$. Then

$$v \cdot Dx(p)v = \int_0^{\bar{w}} v \cdot D_p \tilde{x}(p, w)v\, dw.$$

Also

$$D_p \tilde{x}(p, w) = S(p, w) - D_w \tilde{x}(p, w)\tilde{x}(p, w)^T,$$

where $S(p, w)$ is the Slutsky matrix of the individual demand function $x(\cdot, \cdot)$ at $(p, w)$. Hence,

$$v \cdot Dx(p)v = \int_0^{\bar{w}} v \cdot S(p, w)v\, dw - \int_0^{\bar{w}} (v \cdot D_w \tilde{x}(p, w))(v \cdot \tilde{x}(p, w))\, dw.$$

The first term of this sum is negative, unless $v$ is proportional to $p$. For the second, note that

$$2(v \cdot D_w \tilde{x}(p, w))(v \cdot \tilde{x}(p, w)) = \frac{d(v \cdot \tilde{x}(p, w))^2}{dw}.$$

So

$$-\int_0^{\bar{w}} (v \cdot D_w \tilde{x}(p, w))(v \cdot \tilde{x}(p, w))\, dw = -\frac{1}{2}\int_0^{\bar{w}} \frac{d(v \cdot \tilde{x}(p, w))^2}{dw}\, dw = -\frac{1}{2}(v \cdot \tilde{x}(p, \bar{w}))^2 \leq 0,$$

where we have used $\tilde{x}(p, 0) = 0$. Observe that the sign is negative when $v$ is proportional to $p$. ∎

Recall that the ULD property is additive across groups of consumers. Therefore, what we need in order to apply Proposition 4.C.4 is, not that preferences be identical, but that for every preference relation, the distribution of wealth conditional on that preference be uniform over

---

10. Not to misrepresent the import of this claim, we should emphasize that Proposition 4.C.1, which asserts that the ULD property is preserved under addition, holds for the price-independent distribution rules that we are considering in this section. When the distribution of real wealth may depend on prices (as it typically will in the general equilibrium applications of Part IV), then aggregate demand may violate the WA even if individual demand satisfies the ULD property (see Exercise 4.C.13). We discuss this point further in Section 17.F.

some interval that includes the level 0 (in fact, a nonincreasing density function is enough; see Exercise 4.C.7).

One lesson of Proposition 4.C.4 is that the properties of aggregate demand will depend on how preferences and wealth are distributed. We could therefore pose the problem quite generally and ask which distributional conditions on preferences and wealth will lead to satisfaction of the weak axiom by aggregate demand.[11]

As mentioned in Section 2.F, a market demand function $x(p, w)$ can be shown to satisfy the WA if for all $(p, w)$, the Slutsky matrix $S(p, w)$ derived from the function $x(p, w)$ satisfies $dp \cdot S(p, w) \, dp < 0$ for every $dp \neq 0$ not proportional to $p$. We now examine when this property might hold for the aggregate demand function.

The Slutsky equation for the aggregate demand function is

$$S(p, w) = D_p x(p, w) + D_w x(p, w) \, x(p, w)^{\mathrm{T}}. \tag{4.C.4}$$

Or, since $x(p, w) = \sum_i x_i(p, \alpha_i w)$,

$$S(p, w) = D_p x(p, w) + \left[\sum_i \alpha_i D_{w_i} x_i(p, \alpha_i w)\right] x(p, w)^{\mathrm{T}} \tag{4.C.5}$$

Next, let $S_i(p, w_i)$ denote the individual Slutsky matrices. Adding the individual Slutsky equations gives

$$\sum_i S_i(p, \alpha_i w) = \sum_i D_p x_i(p, \alpha_i w) + \sum_i D_{w_i} x_i(p, \alpha_i w) \, x_i(p, \alpha_i w)^{\mathrm{T}} \tag{4.C.6}$$

Since $D_p x(p, w) = \sum_i D_p x_i(p, \alpha_i w)$, we can substitute (4.C.6) into (4.C.5) to get

$$S(p, w) = \sum_i S_i(p, w_i) - \sum_i \alpha_i [D_{w_i} x_i(p, \alpha_i w) - D_w x(p, w)] \left[\frac{1}{\alpha_i} x_i(p, \alpha_i w) - x(p, w)\right]^{\mathrm{T}}. \tag{4.C.7}$$

Note that because of wealth effects, the Slutsky matrix of aggregate demand is *not* the sum of the individual Slutsky matrices. The difference

$$C(p, w) = \sum_i S_i(p, \alpha w) - S(p, w)$$

$$= \sum_i \alpha_i [D_{w_i} x_i(p, \alpha_i w) - D_w x(p, w)] \left[\frac{1}{\alpha_i} x_i(p, \alpha_i w) - x(p, w)\right]^{\mathrm{T}} \tag{4.C.8}$$

is a covariance matrix between wealth effect vectors $D_{w_i} x_i(p, \alpha_i w)$ and proportionately adjusted consumption vectors $(1/\alpha_i) x_i(p, \alpha_i w)$. The former measures how the marginal dollar is spent across commodities; the latter measures the same thing for the average dollar [e.g., $(1/\alpha_i w) x_{\ell i}(p, \alpha_i w)$ is the per-unit-of-wealth consumption of good $\ell$ by consumer $i$]. Every "observation" receives weight $\alpha_i$. Note also that, as it should be, we have

$$\sum_i \alpha_i [D_{w_i} x_i(p, \alpha_i w) - D_w x(p, w)] = 0 \quad \text{and} \quad \sum_i \alpha_i [(1/\alpha_i) x_i(p, \alpha_i w) - x(p, w)] = 0.$$

For an individual Slutsky matrix $S_i(\cdot, \cdot)$ we always have $dp \cdot S_i(p, \alpha_i w) \, dp < 0$ for $dp \neq 0$ not proportional to $p$. Hence, a *sufficient* condition for the Slutsky matrix of aggregate demand to have the desired property is that $C(p, w)$ be positive semidefinite. Speaking loosely, this will be the case if, on average, there is a *positive association* across consumers between consumption (per unit of wealth) in one commodity and the wealth effect for that commodity. Figure 4.C.2(a) depicts a case for $L = 2$ in which, assuming a uniform distribution of wealth across consumers, this association is positive: Consumers with higher-than-average

---

11. In the next few paragraphs, we follow Jerison (1982) and Freixas and Mas-Colell (1987).

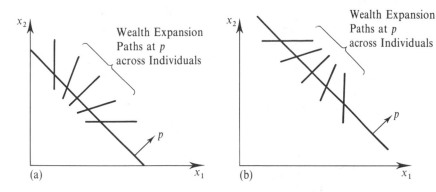

**Figure 4.C.2**

The relation across consumers between expenditure per unit of wealth on a commodity and its wealth effect when all consumers have the same wealth.
(a) Positive relation.
(b) Negative relation.

consumption of one good spend a higher-than-average fraction of their last unit of wealth on that good. The association is negative in Figure 4.C.2(b).[12,13]

From the preceding derivation, we can see that aggregate demand satisfies the WA in two cases of interest: (i) All the $D_{w_i} x_i(p, \alpha_i w)$ are equal (there are equal wealth effects), and (ii) all the $(1/\alpha_i) x_i(p, \alpha_i w)$ are equal (there is proportional consumption). In both cases, we have $C(p, w) = 0$, and so $dp \cdot S(p, w) dp < 0$ whenever $dp \neq 0$ is not proportional to $p$.

Case (i) has important implications. In particular, if every consumer has indirect utility functions of the Gorman form $v_i(p, w_i) = a_i(p) + b(p)w$, with the coefficient $b(p)$ identical across consumers, then (as we saw in Section 4.B) the wealth effects are the same for all consumers and we can therefore conclude that the WA is satisfied. We know from Section 4.B that one is led to this family of indirect utility functions by the requirement that aggregate demand be invariant to redistribution of wealth. Thus, aggregate demand satisfying the weak axiom for a fixed distribution of wealth is a less demanding property than the invariance to redistribution property considered in Section 4.B. In particular, if the second property holds, then the first also holds, but aggregate demand (for a fixed distribution of wealth) may satisfy the weak axiom even though aggregate demand may not be invariant to redistribution of wealth (e.g., individual preferences may be homothetic but not identical).

Having spent all this time investigating the weak axiom (WA), you might ask: "What about the strong axiom (SA)?" We have not focused on the Strong Axiom for three reasons.

First, the WA is a robust property, whereas the SA (which, remember, yields the symmetry of the Slutsky matrix) is not; a priori, the chances of it being satisfied by a real economy are essentially zero. For example, if we start with a group of consumers with identical preferences and wealth, then aggregate demand obviously satisfies the SA. However, if we now perturb every preference slightly and independently across consumers, the negative semidefiniteness of the Slutsky matrices (and therefore the WA) may well be preserved but the symmetry (and therefore the SA) will almost certainly not be.

12. You may want to verify that the wealth expansion paths of Example 4.C.1 must indeed look like Figure 4.C.2(b).

13. A priori, we cannot say which form is more likely. Because the demand at zero wealth is zero, it is true that for a consumer, *some* dollar must be spent among the two goods according to shares similar to the shares of the average dollar. But if the levels of wealth are not close to zero, it does not follow that this is the case for the *marginal* dollar. It may even happen that because of incipient satiation, the shares of the marginal dollar display consumption propensities that are the reverse of the ones exhibited by the average dollar. See Hildenbrand (1994) for an account of empirical research on this matter.

Second, many of the strong positive results of general equilibrium (to be reviewed in Part IV, especially Chapters 15 and 17) to which one wishes to apply the aggregation theory discussed in this chapter depend on the weak axiom, not on the strong axiom, holding in the aggregate.

Third, while one might initially think that the existence of a preference relation explaining aggregate behavior (which is what we get from the SA) would be the condition required to use aggregate demand measures (such as aggregate consumer surplus) as welfare indicators, we will see in Section 4.D that, in fact, more than this condition is required anyway.

---

# 4.D   Aggregate Demand and the Existence of a Representative Consumer

The aggregation question we pose in this section is: When can we compute meaningful measures of aggregate welfare using the aggregate demand function and the welfare measurement techniques discussed in Section 3.I for individual consumers? More specifically, when can we treat the aggregate demand function as if it were generated by a fictional *representative consumer* whose preferences can be used as a measure of aggregate societal (or *social*) welfare?

We take as our starting point a distribution rule $(w_1(p, w), \ldots, w_I(p, w))$ that to every level of aggregate wealth $w \in \mathbb{R}$ assigns individual wealths. We assume that $\sum_i w_i(p, w) = w$ for all $(p, w)$ and that every $w_i(\cdot, \cdot)$ is continuous and homogeneous of degree one. As discussed in Sections 4.B and 4.C, aggregate demand then takes the form of a conventional market demand function $x(p, w) = \sum_i x_i(p, w_i(p, w))$. In particular, $x(p, w)$ is continuous, is homogeneous of degree zero, and satisfies Walras' law. It is important to keep in mind that the aggregate demand function $x(p, w)$ depends on the wealth distribution rule (except under the special conditions identified in Section 4.B).

It is useful to begin by distinguishing two senses in which we could say that there is a representative consumer. The first is a positive, or behavioral, sense.

**Definition 4.D.1:** A *positive representative consumer* exists if there is a rational preference relation $\succsim$ on $\mathbb{R}_+^L$ such that the aggregate demand function $x(p, w)$ is precisely the Walrasian demand function generated by this preference relation. That is, $x(p, w) \succ x$ whenever $x \neq x(p, w)$ and $p \cdot x \leq w$.

A positive representative consumer can thus be thought of as a fictional individual whose utility maximization problem when facing society's budget set $\{x \in \mathbb{R}_+^L : p \cdot x \leq w\}$ would generate the economy's aggregate demand function.

For it to be correct to treat aggregate demand as we did individual demand functions in Section 3.I, there must be a positive representative consumer.[14] However, although this is a necessary condition for the property of aggregate demand that we seek, it is not sufficient. We also need to be able to assign welfare significance to this

---

14. Note that if there is a positive representative consumer, then aggregate demand satisfies the positive properties sought in Section 4.C. Indeed, not only will aggregate demand satisfy the weak axiom, but it will also satisfy the strong axiom. Thus, the aggregation property we are after in this section is stronger than the one discussed in Section 4.C.

fictional individual's demand function. This will lead to the definition of a *normative* representative consumer. To do so, however, we first have to be more specific about what we mean by the term *social welfare*. We accomplish this by introducing the concept of a *social welfare function*, a function that provides a summary (social) utility index for any collection of individual utilities.

**Definition 4.D.2:** A *(Bergson-Samuelson)* *social welfare function* is a function $W: \mathbb{R}^I \to \mathbb{R}$ that assigns a utility value to each possible vector $(u_1, \dots, u_I) \in \mathbb{R}^I$ of utility levels for the $I$ consumers in the economy.

The idea behind a social welfare function $W(u_1, \dots, u_I)$ is that it accurately expresses society's judgments on how individual utilities have to be compared to produce an ordering of possible social outcomes. (We do not discuss in this section the issue of where this social preference ranking comes from. Chapters 21 and 22 cover this point in much more detail.) We also assume that social welfare functions are increasing, concave, and whenever convenient, differentiable.

Let us now hypothesize that there is a process, a benevolent central authority perhaps, that, for any given prices $p$ and aggregate wealth level $w$, redistributes wealth in order to maximize social welfare. That is, for any $(p, w)$, the wealth distribution $(w_1(p, w), \dots, w_I(p, w))$ solves

$$\underset{w_1, \dots, w_I}{\text{Max}} \quad W(v_1(p, w_1), \dots, v_I(p, w_I)) \qquad (4.D.1)$$
$$\text{s.t. } \sum_{i=1}^{I} w_i \leq w,$$

where $v_i(p, w)$ is consumer $i$'s indirect utility function.[15,16] The optimum value of problem (4.D.1) defines a social indirect utility function $v(p, w)$. Proposition 4.D.1 shows that this indirect utility function provides a positive representative consumer for the aggregate demand function $x(p, w) = \sum_i x_i(p, w_i(p, w))$.

**Proposition 4.D.1:** Suppose that for each level of prices $p$ and aggregate wealth $w$, the wealth distribution $(w_1(p, w), \dots, w_I(p, w))$ solves problem (4.D.1). Then the value function $v(p, w)$ of problem (4.D.1) is an indirect utility function of a positive representative consumer for the aggregate demand function $x(p, w) = \sum_i x_i(p, w_i(p, w))$.

**Proof:** In Exercise 4.D.2, you are asked to establish that $v(p, w)$ does indeed have the properties of an indirect utility function. The argument for the proof then consists of using Roy's identity to derive a Walrasian demand function from $v(p, w)$, which we denote by $x_R(p, w)$, and then establishing that it actually equals $x(p, w)$.

We begin by recording the first-order conditions of problem (4.D.1) for a

---

15. We assume in this section that our direct utility functions $u_i(\cdot)$ are concave. This is a weak hypothesis (once quasiconcavity has been assumed) which makes sure that in all the optimization problems to be considered, the first-order conditions are sufficient for the determination of global optima. In particular, $v_i(p, \cdot)$ is then a concave function of $w_i$.

16. In Exercise 4.D.1, you are asked to show that if so desired, problem (4.D.1) can be equivalently formulated as one where social utility is maximized, not by distributing wealth, but by distributing bundles of goods with aggregate value at prices $p$ not larger than $w$. The fact that in optimally redistributing goods, we can also restrict ourselves to redistributing wealth is, in essence, a version of the second fundamental theorem of welfare economics, which will be covered extensively in Chapter 16.

given value of $(p, w)$. Neglecting boundary solutions, these require that for some $\lambda \geq 0$, we have

$$\lambda = \frac{\partial W}{\partial v_1} \frac{\partial v_1}{\partial w_1} = \cdots = \frac{\partial W}{\partial v_I} \frac{\partial v_I}{\partial w_I} \tag{4.D.2}$$

(For notational convenience, we have omitted the points at which the derivatives are evaluated.) Condition (4.D.2) simply says that at a socially optimal wealth distribution, the social utility of an extra unit of wealth is the same irrespective of who gets it.

By Roy's identity, we have $x_R(p, w) = -[1/(\partial v(p, w)/\partial w)] \nabla_p v(p, w)$. Since $v(p, w)$ is the value function of problem (4.D.1), we know that $\partial v/\partial w = \lambda$. (See Section M.K of the Mathematical Appendix) In addition, for any commodity $\ell$, the chain rule and (4.D.2)—or, equivalently, the envelope theorem—give us

$$\frac{\partial v}{\partial p_\ell} = \sum_i \frac{\partial W}{\partial v_i} \frac{\partial v_i}{\partial p_\ell} + \lambda \sum_i \frac{\partial w_i}{\partial p_\ell} = \sum_i \frac{\partial W}{\partial v_i} \frac{\partial v_i}{\partial p_\ell},$$

where the second equality follows because $\sum_i w_i(p, w) = w$ for all $(p, w)$ implies that $\sum_i (\partial w_i/\partial p_\ell) = 0$. Hence, in matrix notation, we have

$$\nabla_p v(p, w) = \sum_i (\partial W/\partial v_i) \nabla_p v_i(p, w_i(p, w)).$$

Finally, using Roy's identity and the first-order condition (4.D.2), we get

$$\begin{aligned}
x_R(p, w) &= -\frac{1}{\lambda} \sum_i \left[ \frac{\lambda}{\partial v_i/\partial w_i} \right] \nabla_p v_i(p, w_i(p, w)) \\
&= -\sum_i \left[ \frac{1}{\partial v_i/\partial w_i} \right] \nabla_p v_i(p, w_i(p, w)) \\
&= \sum_i x_i(p, w_i(p, w)) = x(p, w),
\end{aligned}$$

as we wanted to show. ∎

Equipped with Proposition 4.D.1, we can now define a *normative representative consumer*.

**Definition 4.D.3:** The positive representative consumer $\succsim$ for the aggregate demand $x(p, w) = \sum_i x_i(p, w_i(p, w))$ is a *normative representative consumer* relative to the social welfare function $W(\cdot)$ if for every $(p, w)$, the distribution of wealth $(w_1(p, w), \ldots, w_I(p, w))$ solves problems (4.D.1) and, therefore, the value function of problem (4.D.1) is an indirect utility function for $\succsim$.

If there is a normative representative consumer, the preferences of this consumer have welfare significance and the aggregate demand function $x(p, w)$ can be used to make welfare judgments by means of the techniques described in Section 3.I. In doing so, however, it should never be forgotten that a given wealth distribution rule [the one that solves (4.D.1) for the given social welfare function] is being adhered to and that the "level of wealth" should always be understood as the "optimally distributed level of wealth." For further discussion, see Samuelson (1956) and Chipman and Moore (1979).

**Example 4.D.1:** Suppose that consumers all have homothetic preferences represented by utility functions homogeneous of degree one. Consider now the social welfare function $W(u_1, \ldots, u_I) = \sum_i \alpha_i \ln u_i$ with $\alpha_i > 0$ and $\sum_i \alpha_i = 1$. Then the optimal wealth distribution function [for problem (4.D.1)] is the price-independent rule that we adopted in Section 4.C: $w_i(p, w) = \alpha_i w$. (You are asked to demonstrate this fact in Exercise 4.D.6.) Therefore, in the homothetic case, the aggregate demand $x(p, w) = \sum_i x_i(p, \alpha_i w)$ can be viewed as originating from the normative representative consumer generated by this social welfare function. ∎

**Example 4.D.2:** Suppose that all consumers' preferences have indirect utilities of the Gorman form $v_i(p, w_i) = a_i(p) + b(p)w_i$. Note that $b(p)$ does not depend on $i$, and recall that this includes as a particular case the situation in which preferences are quasilinear with respect to a common numeraire. From Section 4.B, we also know that aggregate demand $x(p, w)$ is independent of the distribution of wealth.[17]

Consider now the *utilitarian* social welfare function $\sum_i u_i$. Then *any* wealth distribution rule $(w_1(p, w), \dots, w_I(p, w))$ solves the optimization problem (4.D.1), and the indirect utility function that this problem generates is simply $v(p, w) = \sum_i a_i(p) + b(p)w$. (You are asked to show these facts in Exercise 4.D.7.) One conclusion is, therefore, that when indirect utility functions have the Gorman form [with common $b(p)$] and the social welfare function is utilitarian, then aggregate demand can *always* by viewed as being generated by a normative representative consumer.

When consumers have Gorman-form indirect utility functions [with common $b(p)$], the theory of the normative representative consumer admits an important strengthening. In general, the preferences of the representative consumer depend on the form of the social welfare function. *But not in this case.* We now verify that if the indirect utility functions of the consumers have the Gorman form [with common $b(p)$], then the preferences of the representative consumer are independent of the particular social welfare function used.[18] In fact, we show that $v(p, w) = \sum_i a_i(p) + b(p)w$ is an admissible indirect utility function for the normative representative consumer relative to *any* social welfare function $W(u_1, \dots, u_I)$.

To verify this claim, consider a particular social welfare function $W(\cdot)$, and denote the value function of problem (4.D.1), relative to $W(\cdot)$, by $v^*(p, w)$. We must show that the ordering induced by $v(\cdot)$ and $v^*(\cdot)$ is the same, that is, that for any pair $(p, w)$ and $(p', w')$ with $v(p, w) < v(p', w')$, we have $v^*(p, w) < v^*(p', w')$. Take the vectors of individual wealths $(w_1, \dots, w_I)$ and $(w'_1, \dots, w'_I)$ reached as optima of (4.D.1), relative to $W(\cdot)$, for $(p, w)$ and $(p', w')$, respectively. Denote $u_i = a_i(p) + b(p)w_i$, $u'_i = a_i(p) + b(p)w'_i$, $u = (u_1, \dots, u_I)$, and $u' = (u'_1, \dots, u'_I)$. Then $v^*(p, w) = W(u)$ and $v^*(p', w') = W(u')$. Also $v(p, w) = \sum_i a_i(p) + b(p)w = \sum_i u_i$, and similarly, $v(p', w') = \sum_i u'_i$. Therefore, $v(p, w) < v(p', w')$ implies $\sum_i u_i < \sum_i u'_i$. We argue that $\nabla W(u') \cdot (u - u') < 0$, which, $W(\cdot)$ being concave, implies the desired result, namely $W(u) < W(u')$.[19] By expression (4.D.2), at an optimum we have $(\partial W/\partial v_i)(\partial v_i/\partial w_i) = \lambda$ for all $i$. But in our case, $\partial v_i/\partial w_i = b(p)$ for all $i$. Therefore, $\partial W/\partial v_i = \partial W/\partial v_j > 0$ for any $i, j$. Hence, $\sum_i u_i < \sum_i u'_i$ implies $\nabla W(u') \cdot (u - u') < 0$.

The previous point can perhaps be better understood if we observe that when

---

17. As usual, we neglect the nonnegativity constraints on consumption.

18. But, of course, the optimal distribution rules will typically depend on the social welfare function. Only for the utilitarian social welfare function will it not matter how wealth is distributed.

19. Indeed, concavity of $W(\cdot)$ implies $W(u') + \nabla W(u') \cdot (u - u') \geq W(u)$; see Section M.C of the Mathematical Appendix.

preferences have the Gorman form [with common $b(p)$], then $(p', w')$ is socially better than $(p, w)$ for the utilitarian social welfare function $\sum_i u_i$ *if and only if* when compared with $(p, w)$, $(p', w')$ passes the following *potential compensation test*: For any distribution $(w_1, \ldots, w_I)$ of $w$, there is a distribution $(w'_1, \ldots, w'_I)$ of $w'$ such that $v_i(p', w'_i) > v_i(p, w_i)$ for all $i$. To verify this is straightforward. Suppose that

$$\left(\sum_i a_i(p') + b(p')w'\right) - \left(\sum_i a_i(p) + b(p)w\right) = c > 0.$$

Then the wealth levels $w'_i$ implicitly defined by $a_i(p') + b(p')w'_i = a_i(p) + b(p)w_i + c/I$ will be as desired.[20] Once we know that $(p', w')$ when compared with $(p, w)$ passes the potential compensation test, it follows merely from the definition of the optimization problem (4.D.1) that $(p', w')$ is better than $(p, w)$ for any normative consumer, that is, for any social welfare function that we may wish to employ (see Exercise 4.D.8).

The two properties just presented—independence of the representative consumer's preferences from the social welfare function and the potential compensation criterion—will be discussed further in Sections 10.F and 22.C. For the moment, we simply emphasize that they are not general properties of normative representative consumers. By choosing the distribution rules that solve (4.D.1), we can generate a normative representative consumer for any set of individual utilities and any social welfare function. For the properties just reviewed to hold, the individual preferences have been required to have the Gorman form [with common $b(p)$]. ∎

It is important to stress the distinction between the concepts of a positive and a normative representative consumer. It is *not* true that whenever aggregate demand can be generated by a positive representative consumer, this representative consumer's preferences have normative content. It may even be the case that a positive representative consumer exists but that there is *no* social welfare function that leads to a normative representative consumer. We expand on this point in the next few paragraphs [see also Dow and Werlang (1988) and Jerison (1994)].

---

We are given a distribution rule $(w_1(p, w), \ldots, w_I(p, w))$ and assume that a positive representative consumer with utility function $u(x)$ exists for the aggregate demand $x(p, w) = \sum_i x_i(p, w_i(p, w))$. In principle, using the integrability techniques presented in Section 3.H, it should be possible to determine the preferences of the representative consumer from the knowledge of $x(p, w)$. Now fix any $(\bar{p}, \bar{w})$, and let $\bar{x} = x(\bar{p}, \bar{w})$. Relative to the aggregate consumption vector $\bar{x}$, we can define an at-least-as-good-as set for the representative consumer:

$$B = \{x \in \mathbb{R}^L_+ : u(x) \geq (\bar{x})\} \subset \mathbb{R}^L_+.$$

Next, let $\bar{w}_i = w_i(\bar{p}, \bar{w})$ and $\bar{x}_i = x_i(\bar{p}, \bar{w}_i)$, and consider the set

$$A = \{x = \textstyle\sum_i x_i : x_i \succsim_i \bar{x}_i \text{ for all } i\} \subset \mathbb{R}^L_+.$$

In words, $A$ is the set of aggregate consumption vectors for which there is a distribution of commodities among consumers that makes every consumer as well off as under $(\bar{x}_1, \ldots, \bar{x}_I)$. The boundary of this set is sometimes called a *Scitovsky contour*. Note that both set $A$ and set $B$ are supported by the price vector $\bar{p}$ at $\bar{x}$ (see Figure 4.D.1).

If the given wealth distribution comes from the solution to a social welfare optimization problem of the type (4.D.1) (i.e., if the positive representative consumer is in fact a normative

---

20. We continue to neglect nonnegativity constraints on wealth.

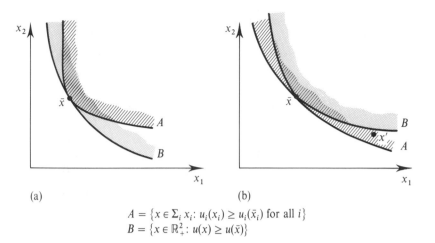

**Figure 4.D.1**

Comparing the at-least-as-good-as set of the positive representative consumer with the sum of the at-least-as-good-as sets of the individual consumers.
(a) The positive representative consumer could be a normative representative consumer.
(b) The positive representative consumer cannot be a normative representative consumer.

$$A = \{x \in \Sigma_i \, x_i : u_i(x_i) \geq u_i(\bar{x}_i) \text{ for all } i\}$$
$$B = \{x \in \mathbb{R}^2_+ : u(x) \geq u(\bar{x})\}$$

representative consumer), then this places an important restriction on how sets $A$ and $B$ relate to each other: Every element of set $A$ must be an element of set $B$. This is so because the social welfare function underlying the normative representative consumer is increasing in the utility level of every consumer (and thus any aggregate consumption bundle that could be distributed in a manner that guarantees to every consumer a level of utility as high as the levels corresponding to the optimal distribution of $\bar{x}$ must receive a social utility higher than the latter; see Exercise 4.D.4). That is, a *necessary* condition for the existence of a normative representative consumer is that $A \subset B$. A case that satisfies this necessary condition is depicted in Figure 4.D.1(a).

However, there is nothing to prevent the existence, in a particular setting, of a positive representative consumer with a utility function $u(x)$ that fails to satisfy this condition, as in Figure 4.D.1(b). To provide some further understanding of this point, Exercise 4.D.9 asks you to show that $A \subset B$ implies that $\sum_i S_i(\bar{p}, \bar{w}_i) - S(\bar{p}, \bar{w})$ is positive semidefinite, where $S(p, w)$ and $S_i(p, w_i)$ are the Slutsky matrices of aggregate and individual demand, respectively. Informally, we could say that the substitution effects of aggregate demand must be larger in absolute value than the sum of individual substitution effects (geometrically, this corresponds to the boundary of $B$ being flatter at $\bar{x}$ than the boundary of $A$). This observation allows us to generate in a simple manner examples in which aggregate demand can be rationalized by preferences but, nonetheless, there is no normative representative consumer.

Suppose, for example, that the wealth distribution rule is of the form $w_i(p, w) = \alpha_i w$. Suppose also that $S(p, w)$ happens to be symmetric for all $(p, w)$; if $L = 2$, this is automatically satisfied. Then, from integrability theory (see Section 3.H), we know that a sufficient condition for the existence of underlying preferences is that, for all $(p, w)$, we have $dp \cdot S(p, w) \, dp < 0$ for all $dp \neq 0$ not proportional to $p$ (we abbreviate this as the *n.d. property*). On the other hand, as we have just seen, a necessary condition for the existence of a normative representative consumer is that $C(\bar{p}, \bar{w}) = \sum_i S_i(\bar{p}, \bar{w}_i) - S(\bar{p}, \bar{w})$ be positive semidefinite [this is the same matrix discussed in Section 4.C; see expression (4.C.8)]. Thus, if $S(p, w)$ has the n.d. property for all $(p, w)$ but $C(\bar{p}, \bar{w})$ is not positive semidefinite [i.e., wealth effects are such that $S(\bar{p}, \bar{w})$ is "less negative" than $\sum_i S_i(\bar{p}, \bar{w}_i)$], then a positive representative consumer exists that, nonetheless, cannot be made normative for any social welfare function. (Exercise 4.D.10 provides an instance where this is indeed the case.) In any example of this nature we have moves in aggregate consumption that would pass a potential compensation test (each consumer's welfare could be made better off by an appropriate distribution of the move) but are regarded as socially inferior under the utility function that rationalizes aggregate demand. [In Figure 4.D.1(b), this could be the move from $\bar{x}$ to $x'$.]

The moral of all this is clear: The existence of preferences that explain behavior is not enough to attach to them any welfare significance. For the latter, it is also necessary that these preferences exist for the right reasons. ∎

---

### APPENDIX A: REGULARIZING EFFECTS OF AGGREGATION

This appendix is devoted to making the point that although aggregation can be deleterious to the preservation of the good properties of individual demand, it can also have helpful *regularizing* effects. By regularizing, we mean that the average (per-consumer) demand will tend to be more continuous or smooth, as a function of prices, than the individual components of the sum.

Recall that if preferences are strictly convex, individual demand functions are continuous. As we noted, aggregate demand will then be continuous as well. But average demand can be (nearly) continuous even when individual demands are not. The key requirement is one of *dispersion* of individual preferences.

**Example 4.AA.1:** Suppose that there are two commodities. Consumers have quasi-linear preferences with the second good as numeraire. The first good, on the other hand, is available only in integer amounts, and consumers have no wish for more than one unit of it. Thus, normalizing the utility of zero units of the first good to be zero, the preferences of consumer $i$ are completely described by a number $v_{1i}$, the utility in terms of numeraire of holding one unit of the first good. It is then clear that the demand for the first good by consumer $i$ is given by the correspondence

$$x_{1i}(p_1) = 1 \qquad \text{if } p_1 < v_{1i},$$
$$= \{0, 1\} \quad \text{if } p_1 = v_{1i},$$
$$= 0 \qquad \text{if } p_1 > v_{1i},$$

which is depicted in Figure 4.AA.1(a). Thus, individual demand exhibits a sudden, discontinuous jump in demand from 0 to 1 as the price crosses the value $p_1 = v_{1i}$.

Suppose now that there are many consumers. In fact, consider the limit situation where there is an actual continuum of consumers. We could then say that individual preferences are *dispersed* if there is no concentrated group of consumers having any particular value of $v_1$ or, more precisely, if the statistical distribution function of the $v_1$'s, $G(v_1)$, is continuous. Then, denoting by $x_1(p_1)$ the average demand for the first good, we have $x_1(p_1) = $ "mass of consumers with $v_1 > p_1$" $= 1 - G(p_1)$.

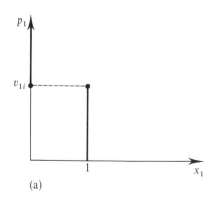

(a)

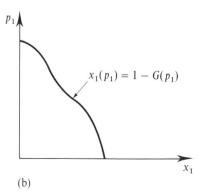

(b)

**Figure 4.AA.1**

The regularizing effect of aggregation.
(a) Individual demand.
(b) Aggregate demand when the distribution of the $v_1$'s is $G(\cdot)$.

Hence, the aggregate demand $x_1(\cdot)$, shown in Figure 4.AA.1(b), is a nice continuous function even though none of the individual demand correspondences are so. Note that with only a finite number of consumers, the distribution function $G(\cdot)$ cannot quite be a continuous function; but if the consumers are many, then it can be nearly continuous. ∎

The regularizing effects of aggregation are studied again in Section 17.I. We show there that in general (i.e., without dispersedness requirements), the aggregation of numerous individual demand correspondences will generate a (nearly) *convex-valued* average demand correspondence.

## REFERENCES

Chipman, J. S., and J. Moore. (1979). On social welfare functions and the aggregation of preferences. *Journal of Economic Theory* **21**: 111–39.

Deaton, A., and J. Muellbauer. (1980). *Economics and Consumer Behavior*. Cambridge, UK: Cambridge University Press.

Dow, J., and S. Werlang. (1988). The consistency of welfare judgments with a representative consumer. *Journal of Economic Theory* **44**: 265–80.

Freixas, X., and A. Mas-Colell. (1987). Engel curves leading to the weak axiom in the aggregate. *Econometrica* **21**: 63–80.

Hildenbrand, W. (1983). On the "law of demand." *Econometrica* **51**: 997–1020.

Hildenbrand, W. (1994). *Market Demand: Theory and Empirical Evidence*. Princeton: Princeton University Press.

Jerison, M. (1982). The representative consumer and the weak axiom when the distribution of income is fixed. Working paper, Department of Economics, SUNY Albany.

Jerison, M. (1994). Optimal income distribution rules and representative consumers. *Review of Economic Studies* **61**: 739–71.

Jorgenson, D. (1990). Aggregate consumer behavior and the measurement of social welfare *Econometrica* **58**: 1007–1030.

Lau, L. (1982). A note on the fundamental theorem of exact aggregation, *Economic letters* **9**: 119–26.

Mas-Colell, A. (1991). On the uniqueness of equilibrium once again. Chap. 12 in *Equilibrium Theory and Applications*, edited by W. Barnett, B. Cornet, C. d'Aspremont, J. Gabszewicz, A. Mas-Colell. Cambridge, U.K.: Cambridge University Press.

Milleron, J. C. (1974). Unicité et stabilité de l'équilibre en économie de distribution. Seminaire d'Econométrie Roy-Malinvaud, preprint.

Mitiushin, L. G., and W. M. Polterovich (1978). Criteria for monotonicity of demand functions [in Russian]. *Ekonomika i Matematichskie Metody* **14**: 122–28.

Samuelson, P. (1956). Social indifference curves. *Quarterly Journal of Economics* **70**: 1–22.

## EXERCISES

**4.B.1<sup>B</sup>** Prove the sufficiency part of Proposition 4.B.1. Show also that if preferences admit Gorman-form indirect utility functions with the same $b(p)$, then preferences admit expenditure functions of the form $e_i(p, u_i) = c(p)u_i + d_i(p)$.

**4.B.2<sup>B</sup>** Suppose that there are $I$ consumers and $L$ commodities. Consumers differ only by their wealth levels $w_i$ and by a taste parameter $s_i$, which we could call *family size*. Thus, denote the indirect utility function of consumer $i$ by $v(p, w_i, s_i)$. The corresponding Walrasian demand function for consumer $i$ is $x(p, w_i, s_i)$.

**(a)** Fix $(s_1, \ldots, s_I)$. Show that if for any $(w_1, \ldots, w_I)$ aggregate demand can be written as a function of only $p$ and aggregate wealth $w = \sum_i w_i$ (or, equivalently, average wealth), and if every consumer's preference relationship $\succsim_i$ is homothetic, then all these preferences must be identical [and so $x(p, w_i, s_i)$ must be independent of $s_i$].

**(b)** Give a sufficient condition for aggregate demand to depend only on aggregate wealth $w$ and $\sum_i s_i$ (or, equivalently, average wealth and average family size).

**4.C.1$^C$** Prove that if $x_i(p, w_i)$ satisfies the ULD, then $D_p x_i(p, w_i)$ is negative semidefinite [i.e., $dp \cdot D_p x_i(p, w_i)\, dp \leq 0$ for all $dp$]. Also show that if $D_p x_i(p, w_i)$ is negative definite for all $p$, then $x_i(p, w_i)$ satisfies the ULD (this second part is harder).

**4.C.2$^A$** Prove a version of Proposition 4.C.1 by using the (sufficient) differential versions of the ULD and the WA. (Recall from the small type part of Section 2.F that a sufficient condition for the WA is that $v \cdot S(p, w)v < 0$ whenever $v$ is not proportional to $p$.)

**4.C.3$^A$** Give a graphical two-commodity example of a preference relation generating a Walrasian demand that does not satisfy the ULD property. Interpret.

**4.C.4$^C$** Show that if the preference relation $\succsim_i$ on $\mathbb{R}^2_+$ has L-shaped indifference curves and the demand function $x_i(p, w_i)$ has the ULD property, then $\succsim_i$ must be homothetic. [*Hint*: The L shape of indifference curves implies $S_i(p, w_i) = 0$ for all $(p, w_i)$; show that if $D_{w_i} x_i(\bar{p}, \bar{w}_i) \neq (1/\bar{w}_i) x_i(\bar{p}, \bar{w}_i)$, then there is $v \in \mathbb{R}^L$ such that $v \cdot D_p x_i(\bar{p}, \bar{w}_i)v > 0$.]

**4.C.5$^C$** Prove Proposition 4.C.3. To that effect, you can fix $w = 1$. The proof is best done in terms of the indirect demand function $g_i(x) = (1/x \cdot \nabla u_i(x)) \nabla u_i(x)$ [note that $x = x_i(g_i(x), 1)$]. For an individual consumer, the ULD is self-dual; that is, it is equivalent to $(g_i(x) - g_i(y)) \cdot (x - y) < 0$ for all $x \neq y$. In turn, this property is implied by the negative definiteness of $Dg_i(x)$ for all $x$. Hence, concentrate on proving this last property. More specifically, let $v \neq 0$, and denote $q = \nabla u_i(x)$ and $C = D^2 u_i(x)$. You want to prove $v \cdot Dg_i(x)v < 0$. [*Hint*: You can first assume $q \cdot v = q \cdot x$; then differentiate $g_i(x)$, and make use of the equality $v \cdot Cv - x \cdot Cv = (v - \frac{1}{2}x) \cdot C(v - \frac{1}{2}x) - \frac{1}{4}x \cdot Cx$.]

**4.C.6$^A$** Show that if $u_i(x_i)$ is homogeneous of degree one, so that $\succsim_i$ is homothetic, then $\sigma_i(x_i) = 0$ for all $x_i$ [$\sigma_i(x_i)$ is the quotient defined in Proposition 4.C.3].

**4.C.7$^B$** Show that Proposition 4.C.4 still holds if the distribution of wealth has a nonincreasing density function on $[0, \bar{w}]$. A more realistic distribution of wealth would be *unimodal* (i.e., an increasing and then decreasing density function with a single peak). Argue that there are unimodal distributions for which the conclusions of the proposition do not hold.

**4.C.8$^A$** Derive expression (4.C.7), the aggregate version of the Slutsky matrix.

**4.C.9$^A$** Verify that if individual preferences $\succsim_i$ are homothetic, then the matrix $C(p, w)$ defined in expression (4.C.8) is positive semidefinite.

**4.C.10$^C$** Argue that for the Hildenbrand example studied in Proposition 4.C.4, $C(p, w)$ is positive semidefinite. Conclude that aggregate demand satisfies the WA for that wealth distribution. [Note: You must first adapt the definition of $C(p, w)$ to the continuum-of-consumers situation of the example.]

**4.C.11$^B$** Suppose there are two consumers, 1 and 2, with utility functions over two goods, 1 and 2, of $u_1(x_{11}, x_{21}) = x_{11} + 4\sqrt{x_{21}}$ and $u_2(x_{12}, x_{22}) = 4\sqrt{x_{12}} + x_{22}$. The two consumers have identical wealth levels $w_1 = w_2 = w/2$.

**(a)** Calculate the individual demand functions and the aggregate demand function.

**(b)** Compute the individual Slutsky matrices $S_i(p, w/2)$ (for $i = 1, 2$) and the aggregate

Slutsky matrix $S(p, w)$. [*Hint*: Note that for this two-good example, only one element of each matrix must be computed to determine the entire matrix.] Show that $dp \cdot S(p, w)\, dp < 0$ for all $dp \neq 0$ not proportional to $p$. Conclude that aggregate demand satisfies the *WA*.

**(c)** Compute the matrix $C(p, w) = \sum_i S_i(p, w/2) - S(p, w)$ for prices $p_1 = p_2 = 1$. Show that it is positive semidefinite if $w > 16$ and that it is negative semidefinite if $8 < w < 16$. In fact, argue that in the latter case, $dp \cdot C(p, w)\, dp < 0$ for some $dp$ [so that $C(p, w)$ is *not* positive semidefinite]. Conclude that $C(p, w)$ positive semidefinite is not necessary for the WA to be satisfied.

**(d)** For each of the two cases $w > 16$ and $8 < w < 16$, draw a picture in the $(x_1, x_2)$ plane depicting each consumer's consumption bundle and his wealth expansion path for the prices $p_1 = p_2 = 1$. Compare your picture with Figure 4.C.2.

**4.C.12$^B$** The results presented in Sections 4.B and 4.C indicate that if for any $(w_1, \ldots, w_I)$ aggregate demand can be written as a function of only aggregate wealth [i.e., as $x(p, \sum_i w_i)$], then aggregate demand must satisfy the WA. The *distribution function* $F: [0, \infty) \to [0, 1]$ of $(w_1, \ldots, w_I)$ is defined as $F(w) = (1/I)(\textit{number of } i\text{'s with } w_i \leq w)$ for any $w$. Suppose now that for any $(w_1, \ldots, w_I)$, aggregate demand can be written as a function of the corresponding aggregate *distribution* $F(\cdot)$ of wealth. Show that aggregate demand does not necessarily satisfy the WA. [*Hint*: It suffices to give a two-commodity, two-consumer example where preferences are identical, wealths are $w_1 = 1$ and $w_2 = 3$, and the WA fails. Try to construct the example graphically. It is a matter of making sure that four suitably positioned indifference curves can be fitted together without crossing.]

**4.C.13$^C$** Consider a two-good environment with two consumers. Let the wealth distribution rule be $w_1(p, w) = wp_1/(p_1 + p_2)$, $w_2(p, w) = wp_2/(p_1 + p_2)$. Exhibit an example in which the two consumers have homothetic preferences but, nonetheless, the aggregate demand fails to satisfy the weak axiom. A good picture will suffice. Why does not Proposition 4.C.1 apply?

**4.D.1$^B$** In this question we are concerned with a normative representative consumer. Denote by $v(p, w)$ the optimal value of problem (4.D.1), and by $(w_1(p, w), \ldots, w_I(p, w))$ the corresponding optimal wealth distribution rules. Verify that $v(p, w)$ is also the optimal value of

$$\underset{x_1, \ldots, x_I}{\text{Max}} \quad W(u_1(x_1), \ldots, u_I(x_I))$$
$$\text{s.t. } p \cdot \left(\sum_i x_i\right) \leq w$$

and that $[x_1(p, w_1(p, w)), \ldots, x_I(p, w_I(p, w))]$ is a solution to this latter problem. Note the implication that to maximize social welfare given prices $p$ and wealth $w$, the planner need not control consumption directly, but rather need only distribute wealth optimally and allow consumers to make consumption decisions independently given prices $p$.

**4.D.2$^B$** Verify that $v(p, w)$, defined as the optimal value of problem (4.D.1), has the properties of an indirect utility function (i.e., that it is homogeneous of degree zero, increasing in $w$ and decreasing in $p$, and quasiconvex).

**4.D.3$^B$** It is good to train one's hand in the use of inequalities and the Kuhn–Tucker conditions. Prove Proposition 4.D.1 again, this time allowing for corner solutions.

**4.D.4$^C$** Suppose that there is a normative representative consumer with wealth distribution rule $(w_1(p, w), \ldots, w_I(p, w))$. For any $x \in \mathbb{R}_+^L$, define

$$u(x) = \underset{(x_1, \ldots, x_I)}{\text{Max}} \quad W(u_1(x_1), \ldots, u_I(x_I))$$
$$\text{s.t. } \sum_i x_i \leq x.$$

**(a)** Give conditions implying that $u(\cdot)$ has the properties of a utility function; that is, it is monotone, continuous, and quasiconcave (and even concave).

**(b)** Show that for any $(p, w)$, the Walrasian demand generated from the problem $\text{Max}_x \, u(x)$ s.t. $p \cdot x \leq w$ is equal to the aggregate demand function.

**4.D.5**[A] Suppose that there are $I$ consumers and that consumer $i$'s utility function is $u_i(x_i)$, with demand function $x_i(p, w_i)$. Consumer $i$'s wealth $w_i$ is generated according to a wealth distribution rule $w_i = \alpha_i w$, where $\alpha_i \geq 0$ and $\sum_i \alpha_i = 1$. Provide an example (i.e., a set of utility functions) in which this economy does *not* admit a positive representative consumer.

**4.D.6**[B] Establish the claims made in Example 4.D.1.

**4.D.7**[B] Establish the claims made in the second paragraph of Example 4.D.2.

**4.D.8**[A] Say that $(p', w')$ passes the *potential compensation test* over $(p, w)$ if for any distribution $(w_1, \ldots, w_I)$ of $w$ there is a distribution $(w'_1, \ldots, w'_I)$ of $w'$ such that $v_i(p', w'_i) > v_i(p, w_i)$ for all $i$. Show that if $(p'w')$ passes the potential compensation test over $(p, w)$, any normative representative consumer must prefer $(p', w')$ over $(p, w)$.

**4.D.9**[B] Show that $A \subset B$ (notation as in Section 4.D) implies that $S(\bar{p}, \bar{w}) - \sum_i S_i(\bar{p}, \bar{w}_i)$ is negative semidefinite. [*Hint*: Consider $g(p) = e(p, u(\bar{x})) - \sum_i e_i(p, u_i(\bar{x}_i))$, where $e(\cdot)$ is the expenditure function for $u(\cdot)$ and $e_i(\cdot)$ is the expenditure function for $u_i(\cdot)$. Note that $A = \sum_i \{x_i : u_i(x_i) \geq u_i(\bar{x}_i)\}$ implies that $\sum_i e_i(p, u_i(\bar{x}_i))$ is the optimal value of the problem $\text{Min}_{x \in A} \, p \cdot x$. From this and $A \subset B$, you get $g(p) \leq 0$ for all $p$ and $g(\bar{p}) = 0$. Therefore, $D^2 g(\bar{p})$ is negative semidefinite. Show then that $D^2 g(\bar{p}) = S(\bar{p}, \bar{w}) - \sum_i S_i(\bar{p}, \bar{w}_i)$.]

**4.D.10**[A] Argue that in the example considered in Exercise 4.C.11, there is a positive representative consumer rationalizing aggregate demand but that there cannot be a normative representative consumer.

**4.D.11**[C] Argue that for $L > 2$, the Hildenbrand case of Proposition 4.C.4 need not admit a positive representative consumer. [*Hint*: Argue that the Slutsky matrix may fail to be symmetric.]

# 5

# Production

## 5.A Introduction

In this chapter, we move to the supply side of the economy, studying the process by which the goods and services consumed by individuals are produced. We view the supply side as composed of a number of productive units, or, as we shall call them, "firms." Firms may be corporations or other legally recognized businesses. But they must also represent the productive possibilities of individuals or households. Moreover, the set of all firms may include some potential productive units that are never actually organized. Thus, the theory will be able to accommodate both active production processes and potential but inactive ones.

Many aspects enter a full description of a firm: Who owns it? Who manages it? How is it managed? How is it organized? What can it do? Of all these questions, we concentrate on the last one. Our justification is not that the other questions are not interesting (indeed, they are), but that we want to arrive as quickly as possible at a minimal conceptual apparatus that allows us to analyze market behavior. Thus, our model of production possibilities is going to be very parsimonious: The firm is viewed merely as a "black box", able to transform inputs into outputs.

In Section 5.B, we begin by introducing the firm's *production set*, a set that represents the production *activities*, or *production plans*, that are technologically feasible for the firm. We then enumerate and discuss some commonly assumed properties of production sets, introducing concepts such as *returns to scale*, *free disposal*, and *free entry*.

After studying the firm's technological possibilities in Section 5.B, we introduce its objective, the goal of *profit maximization*, in Section 5.C. We then formulate and study the firm's profit maximization problem and two associated objects, the firm's *profit function* and its *supply correspondence*. These are, respectively, the value function and the optimizing vectors of the firm's profit maximization problem. Related to the firm's goal of profit maximization is the task of achieving cost-minimizing production. We also study the firm's cost minimization problem and two objects associated with it: The firm's *cost function* and its *conditional factor demand correspondence*. As with the utility maximization and expenditure minimization problems in the theory of demand, there is a rich duality theory associated with the profit maximization and cost minimization problems.

Section 5.D analyzes in detail the geometry associated with cost and production relationships for the special but theoretically important case of a technology that produces a single output.

Aggregation theory is studied in Section 5.E. We show that aggregation on the supply side is simpler and more powerful than the corresponding theory for demand covered in Chapter 4.

Section 5.F constitutes an excursion into welfare economics. We define the concept of *efficient production* and study its relation to profit maximization. With some minor qualifications, we see that profit-maximizing production plans are efficient and that when suitable convexity properties hold, the converse is also true: An efficient plan is profit maximizing for an appropriately chosen vector of prices. This constitutes our first look at the important ideas of the *fundamental theorems of welfare economics.*

In Section 5.G, we point out that profit maximization does not have the same primitive status as preference maximization. Rigorously, it should be derived from the latter. We discuss this point and related issues.

In Appendix A, we study in more detail a particular, important case of production technologies: Those describable by means of linear constraints. It is known as the *linear activity model.*

# 5.B  Production Sets

As in the previous chapters, we consider an economy with $L$ commodities. A *production vector* (also known as an *input–output*, or *netput*, vector, or as a *production plan*) is a vector $y = (y_1, \ldots, y_L) \in \mathbb{R}^L$ that describes the (net) outputs of the $L$ commodities from a production process. We adopt the convention that positive numbers denote outputs and negative numbers denote inputs. Some elements of a production vector may be zero; this just means that the process has no net output of that commodity.

**Example 5.B.1:** Suppose that $L = 5$. Then $y = (-5, 2, -6, 3, 0)$ means that 2 and 3 units of goods 2 and 4, respectively, are produced, while 5 and 6 units of goods 1 and 3, respectively, are used. Good 5 is neither produced nor used as an input in this production vector.  ∎

To analyze the behavior of the firm, we need to start by identifying those production vectors that are technologically possible. The set of all production vectors that constitute feasible plans for the firm is known as the *production set* and is denoted by $Y \subset \mathbb{R}^L$. Any $y \in Y$ is possible; any $y \notin Y$ is not. The production set is taken as a primitive datum of the theory.

The set of feasible production plans is limited first and foremost by technological constraints. However, in any particular model, legal restrictions or prior contractual commitments may also contribute to the determination of the production set.

It is sometimes convenient to describe the production set $Y$ using a function $F(\cdot)$, called the *transformation function*. The transformation function $F(\cdot)$ has the property that $Y = \{ y \in \mathbb{R}^L : F(y) \leq 0 \}$ and $F(y) = 0$ if and only if $y$ is an element of the boundary of $Y$. The set of boundary points of $Y$, $\{ y \in \mathbb{R}^L : F(y) = 0 \}$, is known as the *transformation frontier*. Figure 5.B.1 presents a two-good example.

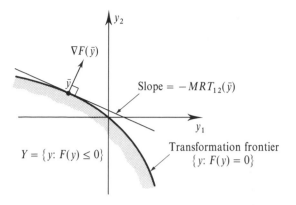

**Figure 5.B.1**

The production set
and transformation
frontier.

If $F(\cdot)$ is differentiable, and if the production vector $\bar{y}$ satisfies $F(\bar{y}) = 0$, then for any commodities $\ell$ and $k$, the ratio

$$MRT_{\ell k}(\bar{y}) = \frac{\partial F(\bar{y})/\partial y_\ell}{\partial F(\bar{y})/\partial y_k}$$

is called the *marginal rate of transformation (MRT) of good $\ell$ for good $k$ at $\bar{y}$.*[1] The marginal rate of transformation is a measure of how much the (net) output of good $k$ can increase if the firm decreases the (net) output of good $\ell$ by one marginal unit. Indeed, from $F(\bar{y}) = 0$, we get

$$\frac{\partial F(\bar{y})}{\partial y_k} dy_k + \frac{\partial F(\bar{y})}{\partial y_\ell} dy_\ell = 0,$$

and therefore the slope of the transformation frontier at $\bar{y}$ in Figure 5.B.1 is precisely $-MRT_{12}(\bar{y})$.

### Technologies with Distinct Inputs and Outputs

In many actual production processes, the set of goods that can be outputs is distinct from the set that can be inputs. In this case, it is sometimes convenient to notationally distinguish the firm's inputs and outputs. We could, for example, let $q = (q_1, \ldots, q_M) \geq 0$ denote the production levels of the firm's $M$ outputs and $z = (z_1, \ldots, z_{L-M}) \geq 0$ denote the amounts of the firm's $L - M$ inputs, with the convention that the amount of input $z_\ell$ used is now measured as a *nonnegative* number (as a matter of notation, we count all goods not actually used in the process as inputs).

One of the most frequently encountered production models is that in which there is a single output. A single-output technology is commonly described by means of a *production function* $f(z)$ that gives the maximum amount $q$ of output that can be produced using input amounts $(z_1, \ldots, z_{L-1}) \geq 0$. For example, if the output is good $L$, then (assuming that output can be disposed of at no cost) the production function $f(\cdot)$ gives rise to the production set:

$$Y = \{(-z_1, \ldots, -z_{L-1}, q) : q - f(z_1, \ldots, z_{L-1}) \leq 0 \quad \text{and} \quad (z_1, \ldots, z_{L-1}) \geq 0\}.$$

Holding the level of output fixed, we can define the *marginal rate of technical*

---

1. As in Chapter 3, in computing ratios such as this, we always assume that $\partial F(\bar{y})/\partial y_k \neq 0$.

substitution (MRTS) of input $\ell$ *for input k at* $\bar{z}$ as

$$MRTS_{\ell k}(\bar{z}) = \frac{\partial f(\bar{z})/\partial z_\ell}{\partial f(\bar{z})/\partial z_k}.$$

The number $MRTS_{\ell k}(\bar{z})$ measures the additional amount of input $k$ that must be used to keep output at level $\bar{q} = f(\bar{z})$ when the amount of input $\ell$ is decreased marginally. It is the production theory analog to the consumer's marginal rate of substitution. In consumer theory, we look at the trade-off between commodities that keeps utility constant, here, we examine the trade-off between inputs that keeps the amount of output constant. Note that $MRTS_{\ell k}$ is simply a renaming of the marginal rate of transformation of input $\ell$ for input $k$ in the special case of a single-output, many-input technology.

**Example 5.B.2:** *The Cobb–Douglas Production Function* The *Cobb–Douglas* production function with two inputs is given by $f(z_1, z_2) = z_1^\alpha z_2^\beta$, where $\alpha \geq 0$ and $\beta \geq 0$. The marginal rate of technical substitution between the two inputs at $z = (z_1, z_2)$ is $MRTS_{12}(z) = \alpha z_2 / \beta z_1$. ∎

## Properties of Production Sets

We now introduce and discuss a fairly exhaustive list of commonly assumed properties of production sets. The appropriateness of each of these assumptions depends on the particular circumstances (indeed, some of them are mutually exclusive).[2]

(i) *Y is nonempty.* This assumption simply says that the firm has something it can plan to do. Otherwise, there is no need to study the behavior of the firm in question.

(ii) *Y is closed.* The set $Y$ includes its boundary. Thus, the limit of a sequence of technologically feasible input–output vectors is also feasible; in symbols, $y^n \to y$ and $y^n \in Y$ imply $y \in Y$. This condition should be thought of as primarily technical.[3]

(iii) *No free lunch.* Suppose that $y \in Y$ and $y \geq 0$, so that the vector $y$ does not use any inputs. The no-free-lunch property is satisfied if this production vector cannot produce output either. That is, whenever $y \in Y$ and $y \geq 0$, then $y = 0$; it is not possible to produce something from nothing. Geometrically, $Y \cap \mathbb{R}^L_+ \subset \{0\}$. For $L = 2$, Figure 5.B.2(a) depicts a set that violates the no-free-lunch property, the set in Figure 5.B.2(b) satisfies it.

(iv) *Possibility of inaction* This property says that $0 \in Y$: Complete shutdown is possible. Both sets in Figure 5.B.2, for example, satisfy this property. The point in time at which production possibilities are being analyzed is often important for the validity of this assumption. If we are contemplating a firm that could access a set of technological possibilities but that has not yet been organized, then inaction is clearly

---

2. For further discussion of these properties, see Koopmans (1957) and Chapter 3 of Debreu (1959).

3. Nonetheless, we show in Exercise 5.B.4 that there is an important case of economic interest when it raises difficulties.

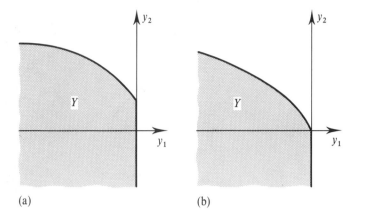

**Figure 5.B.2**

The no free lunch property.
(a) Violates no free lunch.
(b) Satisfies no free lunch.

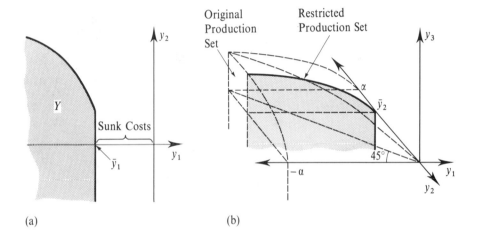

**Figure 5.B.3**

Two production sets with sunk costs.
(a) A minimal level of expenditure committed.
(b) One kind of input fixed.

possible. But if some production decisions have already been made, or if irrevocable contracts for the delivery of some inputs have been signed, inaction is not possible. In that case, we say that some costs are *sunk*. Figure 5.B.3 depicts two examples. The production set in Figure 5.B.3(a) represents the *interim* production possibilities arising when the firm is already committed to use at least $-\bar{y}_1$ units of good 1 (perhaps because it has already signed a contract for the purchase of this amount); that is, the set is a *restricted production set* that reflects the firm's remaining choices from some original production set $Y$ like the ones in Figure 5.B.2. In Figure 5.B.3(b), we have a second example of sunk costs. For a case with one output (good 3) and two inputs (goods 1 and 2), the figure illustrates the restricted production set arising when the level of the second input has been irrevocably set at $\bar{y}_2 < 0$ [here, in contrast with Figure 5.B.3(a), increases in the use of the input are impossible].

(v) *Free disposal.* The property of free disposal holds if the absorption of any additional amounts of inputs without any reduction in output is always possible. That is, if $y \in Y$ and $y' \le y$ (so that $y'$ produces at most the same amount of outputs using at least the same amount of inputs), then $y' \in Y$. More succinctly, $Y - \mathbb{R}_+^L \subset Y$ (see Figure 5.B.4). The interpretation is that the extra amount of inputs (or outputs) can be disposed of or eliminated at no cost.

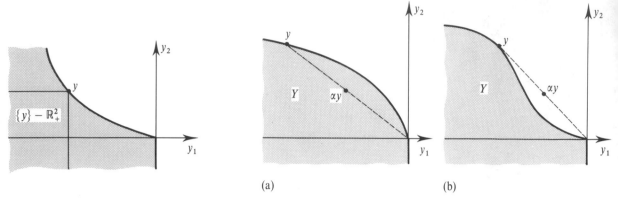

(a)                          (b)

(vi) *Irreversibility.* Suppose that $y \in Y$ and $y \neq 0$. Then irreversiblity says that $-y \notin Y$. In words, it is impossible to reverse a technologically possible production vector to transform an amount of output into the same amount of input that was used to generate it. If, for example, the description of a commodity includes the time of its availability, then irreversibility follows from the requirement that inputs be used before outputs emerge.

**Figure 5.B.4 (left)**
The free disposal property.

**Exercise 5.B.1:** Draw two production sets: one that violates irreversibility and one that satisfies this property.

**Figure 5.B.5 (right)**
The nonincreasing returns to scale property.
(a) Nonincreasing returns satisfied.
(b) Nonincreasing returns violated.

(vii) *Nonincreasing returns to scale.* The production technology $Y$ exhibits nonincreasing returns to scale if for any $y \in Y$, we have $\alpha y \in Y$ for all scalars $\alpha \in [0, 1]$. In words, any feasible input–output vector can be scaled down (see Figure 5.B.5). Note that nonincreasing returns to scale imply that inaction is possible [property (iv)].

(viii) *Nondecreasing returns to scale.* In contrast with the previous case, the production process exhibits nondecreasing returns to scale if for any $y \in Y$, we have $\alpha y \in Y$ for any scale $\alpha \geq 1$. In words, any feasible input–output vector can be scaled up. Figure 5.B.6(a) presents a typical example; in the figure, units of output (good 2) can be produced at a constant cost of input (good 1) except that in order to produce at all, a fixed setup cost is required. It does not matter for the existence of nondecreasing returns if this fixed cost is sunk [as in Figure 5.B.6(b)] or not [as in Figure 5.B.6(a), where inaction is possible].

(ix) *Constant returns to scale.* This property is the conjunction of properties (vii) and (viii). The production set $Y$ exhibits constant returns to scale if $y \in Y$ implies $\alpha y \in Y$ for any scalar $\alpha \geq 0$. Geometrically, $Y$ is a *cone* (see Figure 5.B.7).

For single-output technologies, properties of the production set translate readily into properties of the production function $f(\cdot)$. Consider Exercise 5.B.2 and Example 5.B.3.

**Exercise 5.B.2:** Suppose that $f(\cdot)$ is the production function associated with a single-output technology, and let $Y$ be the production set of this technology. Show that $Y$ satisfies constant returns to scale if and only if $f(\cdot)$ is homogeneous of degree one.

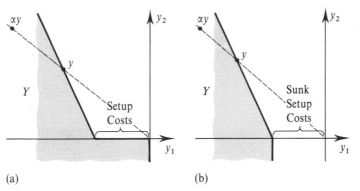

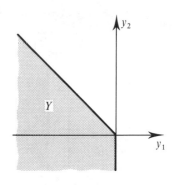

(a)                                    (b)

**Example 5.B.3:** *Returns to Scale with the Cobb–Douglas Production Function*: For the Cobb–Douglas production function introduced in Example 5.B.2, $f(2z_1, 2z_2) = 2^{\alpha+\beta}z_1^{\alpha}z_2^{\beta} = 2^{\alpha+\beta}f(z_1, z_2)$. Thus, when $\alpha + \beta = 1$, we have constant returns to scale; when $\alpha + \beta < 1$, we have decreasing returns to scale; and when $\alpha + \beta > 1$, we have increasing returns to scale. ∎

**Figure 5.B.6 (left)**

The nondecreasing returns to scale property.

**Figure 5.B.7 (right)**

A technology satisfying the constant returns to scale property.

(x) *Additivity (or free entry)*. Suppose that $y \in Y$ and $y' \in Y$. The additivity property requires that $y + y' \in Y$. More succinctly, $Y + Y \subset Y$. This implies, for example, that $ky \in Y$ for any positive *integer* $k$. In Figure 5.B.8, we see an example where $Y$ is additive. Note that in this example, output is available only in integer amounts (perhaps because of indivisibilities). The economic interpretation of the additivity condition is that if $y$ and $y'$ are both possible, then one can set up two plants that do not interfere with each other and carry out production plans $y$ and $y'$ independently. The result is then the production vector $y + y'$.

Additivity is also related to the idea of entry. If $y \in Y$ is being produced by a firm and another firm enters and produces $y' \in Y$, then the net result is the vector $y + y'$. Hence, the *aggregate production set* (the production set describing feasible production plans for the economy as a whole) must satisfy additivity whenever unrestricted entry, or (as it is called in the literature) *free entry*, is possible.

(xi) *Convexity*. This is one of the fundamental assumptions of microeconomics. It postulates that the production set $Y$ is convex. That is, if $y, y' \in Y$ and $\alpha \in [0, 1]$, then $\alpha y + (1 - \alpha)y' \in Y$. For example, $Y$ is convex in Figure 5.B.5(a) but is not convex in Figure 5.B.5(b).

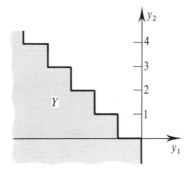

**Figure 5.B.8**

A production set satisfying the additivity property.

The convexity assumption can be interpreted as incorporating two ideas about production possibilities. The first is nonincreasing returns. In particular, if inaction is possible (i.e., if $0 \in Y$), then convexity implies that $Y$ has nonincreasing returns to scale. To see this, note that for any $\alpha \in [0, 1]$, we can write $\alpha y = \alpha y + (1 - \alpha)0$. Hence, if $y \in Y$ and $0 \in Y$, convexity implies that $\alpha y \in Y$. Second, convexity captures the idea that "unbalanced" input combinations are not more productive than balanced ones (or, symmetrically, that "unbalanced" output combinations are not least costly to produce than balanced ones). In particular, if production plans $y$ and $y'$ produce exactly the same amount of output but use different input combinations, then a production vector that uses a level of each input that is the average of the levels used in these two plans can do at least as well as either $y$ or $y'$.

Exercise 5.B.3 illustrates these two ideas for the case of a single-output technology.

**Exercise 5.B.3:** Show that for a single-output technology, $Y$ is convex if and only if the production function $f(z)$ is concave.

(xii) *Y is a convex cone.* This is the conjunction of the convexity (xi) and constant returns to scale (ix) properties. Formally, $Y$ is a convex cone if for any production vector $y, y' \in Y$ and constants $\alpha \geq 0$ and $\beta \geq 0$, we have $\alpha y + \beta y' \in Y$. The production set depicted in Figure 5.B.7 is a convex cone.

An important fact is given in Proposition 5.B.1.

**Proposition 5.B.1:** The production set $Y$ is additive and satisfies the nonincreasing returns condition if and only if it is a convex cone.

**Proof:** The definition of a convex cone directly implies the nonincreasing returns and additivity properties. Conversely, we want to show that if nonincreasing returns and additivity hold, then for any $y, y' \in Y$ and any $\alpha > 0$, and $\beta > 0$, we have $\alpha y + \beta y' \in Y$. To this effect, let $k$ be any integer such that $k > \text{Max} \{\alpha, \beta\}$. By additivity, $ky \in Y$ and $ky' \in Y$. Since $(\alpha/k) < 1$ and $\alpha y = (\alpha/k)ky$, the nonincreasing returns condition implies that $\alpha y \in Y$. Similarly, $\beta y' \in Y$. Finally, again by additivity, $\alpha y + \beta y' \in Y$. ∎

Proposition 5.B.1 provides a justification for the convexity assumption in production. Informally, we could say that if feasible input–output combinations can always be scaled down, and if the simultaneous operation of several technologies without mutual interference is always possible, then, in particular, convexity obtains. (See Appendix A of Chapter 11 for several examples in which there is mutual interference and, as a consequence, convexity does not arise.)

---

It is important not to lose sight of the fact that the production set describes technology, not limits on resources. It can be argued that if all inputs (including, say, entrepreneurial inputs) are explicitly accounted for, then it should always be possible to replicate production. After all, we are not saying that doubling output is actually feasible, only that in principle it would be possible if *all* inputs (however esoteric, be they marketed or not) were doubled. In this view, which originated with Marshall and has been much emphasized by McKenzie (1959), decreasing returns must reflect the scarcity of an underlying, unlisted input of production. For this reason, some economists believe that among models with convex technologies the constant returns model is the most fundamental. Proposition 5.B.2 makes this idea precise.

**Proposition 5.B.2:** For any convex production set $Y \subset \mathbb{R}^L$ with $0 \in Y$, there is a constant returns, convex production set $Y' \subset \mathbb{R}^{L+1}$ such that $Y = \{y \in \mathbb{R}^L : (y, -1) \in Y'\}$.

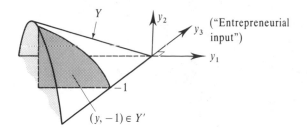

**Figure 5.B.9**

A constant returns
production set with an
"entrepreneurial
factor."

**Proof:** Simply let $Y' = \{y' \in \mathbb{R}^{L+1} : y' = \alpha(y, -1)$ for some $y \in Y$ and $\alpha \geq 0\}$. (See Figure 5.B.9.) ∎

The additional input included in the extended production set (good $L + 1$) can be called the "entrepreneurial factor." (The justification for this can be seen in Exercise 5.C.12; in a competitive environment, the return to this entrepreneurial factor is precisely the firm's profit.) In essence, the implication of Proposition 5.B.2 is that in a competitive, convex setting, there may be little loss of conceptual generality in limiting ourselves to constant returns technologies.

# 5.C  Profit Maximization and Cost Minimization

In this section, we begin our study of the market behavior of the firm. In parallel to our study of consumer demand, we assume that there is a vector of prices quoted for the $L$ goods, denoted by $p = (p_1, \ldots, p_L) \gg 0$, and that these prices are independent of the production plans of the firm (the *price-taking assumption*).

We assume throughout this chapter that the firm's objective is to maximize its profit. (It is quite legitimate to ask why this should be so, and we will offer a brief discussion of the issue in Section 5.G.) Moreover, we always assume that the firm's production set $Y$ satisfies the properties of *nonemptiness*, *closedness*, and *free disposal* (see Section 5.B).

*The Profit Maximization Problem*

Given a price vector $p \gg 0$ and a production vector $y \in \mathbb{R}^L$, the profit generated by implementing $y$ is $p \cdot y = \sum_{\ell=1}^{L} p_\ell y_\ell$. By the sign convention, this is precisely the total revenue minus the total cost. Given the technological constraints represented by its production set $Y$, the firm's *profit maximization problem (PMP)* is then

$$\text{Max}_{y} \quad p \cdot y$$
$$\text{s.t. } y \in Y. \tag{PMP}$$

Using a transformation function to describe $Y$, $F(\cdot)$, we can equivalently state the PMP as

$$\text{Max}_{y} \quad p \cdot y$$
$$\text{s.t. } F(y) \leq 0.$$

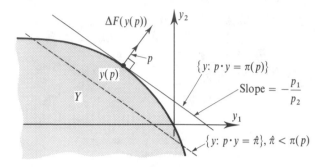

**Figure 5.C.1**

The profit maximization problem.

Given a production set $Y$, the firm's *profit function* $\pi(p)$ associates to every $p$ the amount $\pi(p) = \text{Max } \{p \cdot y : y \in Y\}$, the value of the solution to the PMP. Correspondingly, we define the firm's *supply correspondence* at $p$, denoted $y(p)$, as the set of profit-maximizing vectors $y(p) = \{y \in Y : p \cdot y = \pi(p)\}$.[4] Figure 5.C.1 depicts the supply to the PMP for a strictly convex production set $Y$. The optimizing vector $y(p)$ lies at the point in $Y$ associated with the highest level of profit. In the figure, $y(p)$ therefore lies on the *iso-profit line* (a line in $\mathbb{R}^2$ along which all points generate equal profits) that intersects the production set farthest to the northeast and is, therefore, tangent to the boundary of $Y$ at $y(p)$.

In general, $y(p)$ may be a set rather than a single vector. Also, it is possible that no profit-maximizing production plan exists. For example, the price system may be such that there is no bound on how high profits may be. In this case, we say that $\pi(p) = +\infty$.[5] To take a concrete example, suppose that $L = 2$ and that a firm with a constant returns technology produces one unit of good 2 for every unit of good 1 used as an input. Then $\pi(p) = 0$ whenever $p_2 \leq p_1$. But if $p_2 > p_1$, then the firm's profit is $(p_2 - p_1)y_2$, where $y_2$ is the production of good 2. Clearly, by choosing $y_2$ appropriately, we can make profits arbitrarily large. Hence, $\pi(p) = +\infty$ if $p_2 > p_1$.

**Exercise 5.C.1:** Prove that, in general, if the production set $Y$ exhibits nondecreasing returns to scale, then either $\pi(p) \leq 0$ or $\pi(p) = +\infty$.

If the transformation function $F(\cdot)$ is differentiable, then first-order conditions can be used to characterize the solution to the PMP. If $y^* \in y(p)$, then, for some $\lambda \geq 0$, $y^*$ must satisfy the first-order conditions

$$p_\ell = \lambda \frac{\partial F(y^*)}{\partial y_\ell} \quad \text{for } \ell = 1, \ldots, L$$

or, equivalently, in matrix notation,

$$p = \lambda \nabla F(y^*). \tag{5.C.1}$$

---

4. We use the term *supply correspondence* to keep the parallel with the *demand* terminology of the consumption side. Recall however that $y(p)$ is more properly thought of as the firm's *net* supply to the market. In particular, the negative entries of a supply vector should be interpreted as demand for inputs.

5. Rigorously, to allow for the possibility that $\pi(p) = +\infty$ (as well as for other cases where no profit-maximizing production plan exists), the profit function should be defined by $\pi(p) = \text{Sup } \{p \cdot y : y \in Y\}$. We will be somewhat loose, however, and continue to use *Max* while allowing for this possiblity.

In words, the *price vector p and the gradient* $\nabla F(y^*)$ *are proportional* (Figure 5.C.1 depicts this fact). Condition (5.C.1) also yields the following ratio equality: $p_\ell/p_k = MRT_{\ell k}(y^*)$ for all $\ell, k$. For $L = 2$, this says that the slope of the transformation frontier at the profit-maximizing production plan must be equal to the negative of the price ratio, as shown in Figure 5.C.1. Were this not so, a small change in the firm's production plan could be found that increases the firm's profits.

When $Y$ corresponds to a single-output technology with differentiable production function $f(z)$, we can view the firm's decision as simply a choice over its input levels $z$. In this special case, we shall let the scalar $p > 0$ denote the price of the firm's output and the vector $w \gg 0$ denote its input prices.[6] The input vector $z^*$ maximizes profit given $(p, w)$ if it solves

$$\underset{z \geq 0}{\text{Max}}\ pf(z) - w \cdot z.$$

If $z^*$ is optimal, then the following first-order conditions must be satisfied for $\ell = 1, \ldots, L - 1$:

$$p \frac{\partial f(z^*)}{\partial z_\ell} \leq w_\ell, \quad \text{with equality if } z_\ell^* > 0,$$

or, in matrix notation,

$$p \nabla f(z^*) \leq w \quad \text{and} \quad [p \nabla f(z^*) - w] \cdot z^* = 0.^7 \tag{5.C.2}$$

Thus, the marginal product of every input $\ell$ actually used (i.e., with $z_\ell^* > 0$) must equal its price in terms of output, $w_\ell/p$. Note also that for any two inputs $\ell$ and $k$ with $(z_\ell^*, z_k^*) \gg 0$, condition (5.C.2) implies that $MRTS_{\ell k} = w_\ell/w_k$; that is, the marginal rate of technical substitution between the two inputs is equal to their price ratio, the economic rate of substitution between them. This ratio condition is merely a special case of the more general condition derived in (5.C.1).

If the production set $Y$ is convex, then the first-order conditions in (5.C.1) and (5.C.2) are not only necessary but also sufficient for the determination of a solution to the PMP.

Proposition 5.C.1, which lists the properties of the profit function and supply correspondence, can be established using methods similar to those we employed in Chapter 3 when studying consumer demand. Observe, for example, that mathematically the concept of the profit function should be familiar from the discussion of duality in Chapter 3. In fact, $\pi(p) = -\mu_{-Y}(p)$, where $\mu_{-Y}(p) = \text{Min}\ \{p \cdot (-y): y \in Y\}$ is the support function of the set $-Y$. Thus, the list of important properties in Proposition 5.C.1 can be seen to follow from the general properties of support functions discussed in Section 3.F.

---

6. Up to now, we have always used the symbol $p$ for an overall vector of prices; here we use it only for the output price and we denote the vector of input prices by $w$. This notation is fairly standard. As a rule of thumb, unless we are in a context of explicit classification of commodities as inputs or outputs (as in the single-output case), we will continue to use $p$ to denote an overall vector of prices $p = (p_1, \ldots, p_L)$.

7. The concern over boundary conditions arises here, but not in condition (5.C.1), because the assumption of distinct inputs and outputs requires that $z \geq 0$, whereas the formulation leading to (5.C.1) allows the net output of every good to be either positive or negative. Nonetheless, when using the first-order conditions (5.C.2), we will typically assume that $z^* \gg 0$.

**Proposition 5.C.1:** Suppose that $\pi(\cdot)$ is the profit function of the production set $Y$ and that $y(\cdot)$ is the associated supply correspondence. Assume also that $Y$ is closed and satisfies the free disposal property. Then

(i) $\pi(\cdot)$ is homogeneous of degree one.

(ii) $\pi(\cdot)$ is convex.

(iii) If $Y$ is convex, then $Y = \{y \in \mathbb{R}^L : p \cdot y \leq \pi(p) \text{ for all } p \gg 0\}$.

(iv) $y(\cdot)$ is homogeneous of degree zero.

(v) If $Y$ is convex, then $y(p)$ is a convex set for all $p$. Moreover, if $Y$ is strictly convex, then $y(p)$ is single-valued (if nonempty).

(vi) (*Hotelling's lemma*) If $y(\bar{p})$ consists of a single point, then $\pi(\cdot)$ is differentiable at $\bar{p}$ and $\nabla \pi(\bar{p}) = y(\bar{p})$.

(vii) If $y(\cdot)$ is a function differentiable at $\bar{p}$, then $Dy(\bar{p}) = D^2\pi(\bar{p})$ is a symmetric and positive semidefinite matrix with $Dy(\bar{p})\bar{p} = 0$.

Properties (ii), (iii), (vi), and (vii) are the nontrivial ones.

**Exercise 5.C.2:** Prove that $\pi(\cdot)$ is a convex function [Property (ii) of Proposition 5.C.1]. [*Hint*: Suppose that $y \in y(\alpha p + (1 - \alpha)p')$. Then

$$\pi(\alpha p + (1 - \alpha)p') = \alpha p \cdot y + (1 - \alpha)p' \cdot y \leq \alpha\pi(p) + (1 - \alpha)\pi(p').]$$

Property (iii) tells us that if $Y$ is closed, convex, and satisfies free disposal, then $\pi(p)$ provides an alternative ("dual") description of the technology. As for the indirect utility function's (or expenditure function's) representation of preferences (discussed in Chapter 3), it is a less primitive description than $Y$ itself because it depends on the notions of prices and of price-taking behavior. But thanks to property (vi), it has the great virtue in applications of often allowing for an immediate computation of supply.

Property (vi) relates supply behavior to the derivatives of the profit function. It is a direct consequence of the duality theorem (Proposition 3.F.1). As in Proposition 3.G.1, the fact that $\nabla\pi(\bar{p}) = y(\bar{p})$ can also be established by the related arguments of the envelope theorem and of first-order conditions.

The positive semidefiniteness of the matrix $Dy(p)$ in property (vii), which in view of property (vi) is a consequence of the convexity of $\pi(\cdot)$, is the general mathematical expression of the *law of supply*: *Quantities respond in the same direction as price changes*. By the sign convention, this means that *if the price of an output increases* (all other prices remaining the same), then *the supply of the output increases*; and *if the price of an input increases*, then *the demand for the input decreases*.

Note that the law of supply holds for *any* price change. Because, in contrast with demand theory, there is no budget constraint, there is no compensation requirement of any sort. In essence, we have no wealth effects here, only substitution effects.

In nondifferentiable terms, the law of supply can be expressed as

$$(p - p') \cdot (y - y') \geq 0 \tag{5.C.3}$$

for all $p, p', y \in y(p)$, and $y' \in y(p')$. In this form, it can also be established by a straightforward revealed preference argument. In particular,

$$(p - p') \cdot (y - y') = (p \cdot y - p \cdot y') + (p' \cdot y' - p' \cdot y) \geq 0,$$

where the inequality follows from the fact that $y \in y(p)$ and $y' \in y(p')$ (i.e., from the fact that $y$ is profit maximizing given prices $p$ and $y'$ is profit maximizing for prices $p'$).

Property (vii) of Proposition 5.C.1 implies that the matrix $Dy(p)$, the *supply substitution matrix*, has properties that parallel (although with the reverse sign) those for the substitution matrix of demand theory. Thus, own-substitution effects are nonnegative as noted above [$\partial y_\ell(p)/\partial p_\ell \geq 0$ for all $\ell$], and substitution effects are symmetric [$\partial y_\ell(p)/\partial p_k = \partial y_k(p)/\partial p_\ell$ for all $\ell, k$]. The fact that $Dy(p)p = 0$ follows from the homogeneity of $y(\cdot)$ [property (iv)] in a manner similar to the parallel property of the demand substitution matrix discussed in Chapter 3.

## Cost Minimization

An important implication of the firm choosing a profit-maximizing production plan is that there is no way to produce the same amounts of outputs at a lower total input cost. Thus, cost minimization is a necessary condition for profit maximization. This observation motivates us to an independent study of the firm's *cost minimization problem*. The problem is of interest for several reasons. First, it leads us to a number of results and constructions that are technically very useful. Second, as we shall see in Chapter 12, when a firm is not a price taker in its output market, we can no longer use the profit function for analysis. Nevertheless, as long as the firm is a price taker in its input market, the results flowing from the cost minimization problem continue to be valid. Third, when the production set exhibits nondecreasing returns to scale, the value function and optimizing vectors of the cost minimization problem, which keep the levels of outputs fixed, are better behaved than the profit function and supply correspondence of the PMP (e.g., recall from Exercise 5.C.1 that the profit function can take only the values 0 and $+\infty$).

To be concrete, we focus our analysis on the single-output case. As usual, we let $z$ be a nonnegative vector of inputs, $f(z)$ the production function, $q$ the amounts of output, and $w \gg 0$ the vector of input prices. The *cost minimization problem* (CMP) can then be stated as follows (we assume free disposal of output):

$$\underset{z \geq 0}{\text{Min}} \quad w \cdot z$$
$$\text{s.t. } f(z) \geq q. \qquad \text{(CMP)}$$

The optimized value of the CMP is given by the *cost function* $c(w, q)$. The corresponding optimizing set of input (or factor) choices, denoted by $z(w, q)$, is known as the *conditional factor demand correspondence* (or *function* if it is always single-valued). The term *conditional* arises because these factor demands are conditional on the requirement that the output level $q$ be produced.

The solution to the CMP is depicted in Figure 5.C.2(a) for a case with two inputs. The shaded region represents the set of input vectors $z$ that can produce at least the amount $q$ of output. It is the projection (into the positive orthant of the input space) of the part of the production set $Y$ than generates output of at least $q$, as shown in Figure 5.C.2(b). In Figure 5.C.2(a), the solution $z(w, q)$ lies on the iso-cost line (a line in $\mathbb{R}^2$ on which all input combinations generate equal cost) that intersects the set $\{z \in \mathbb{R}_+^L : f(z) \geq q\}$ closest to the origin.

If $z^*$ is optimal in the CMP, and if the production function $f(\cdot)$ is differentiable,

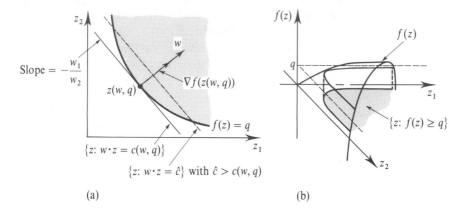

**Figure 5.C.2**
The cost minimization problem.
(a) Two inputs.
(b) The isoquant as a section of the production set.

then for some $\lambda \geq 0$, the following first-order conditions must hold for every input $\ell = 1, \ldots, L - 1$:

$$w_\ell \geq \lambda \frac{\partial f(z^*)}{\partial z_\ell}, \quad \text{with equality if } z_\ell^* > 0,$$

or, in matrix notation,

$$w \geq \lambda \nabla f(z^*) \quad \text{and} \quad [w - \lambda \nabla f(z^*)] \cdot z^* = 0. \tag{5.C.4}$$

As with the PMP, if the production set $Y$ is convex [i.e., if $f(\cdot)$ is concave], then condition (5.C.4) is not only necessary but also sufficient for $z^*$ to be an optimum in the CMP.[8]

Condition (5.C.4), like condition (5.C.2) of the PMP, implies that for any two inputs $\ell$ and $k$ with $(z_\ell, z_k) \gg 0$, we have $MRTS_{\ell k} = w_\ell / w_k$. This correspondence is to be expected because, as we have noted, profit maximization implies that input choices are cost minimizing for the chosen output level $q$. For $L = 2$, condition (5.C.4) entails that the slope at $z^*$ of the *isoquant* associated with production level $q$ is exactly equal to the negative of the ratio of the input prices $-w_1/w_2$. Figure 5.C.2(a) depicts this fact as well.

As usual, the Lagrange multiplier $\lambda$ can be interpreted as the marginal value of relaxing the constraint $f(z^*) \geq q$. Thus, $\lambda$ equals $\partial c(w, q)/\partial q$, the *marginal cost of production*.

Note the close formal analogy with consumption theory here. Replace $f(\cdot)$ *by* $u(\cdot)$, $q$ by $u$, and $z$ by $x$ (i.e., interpret the production function as a utility function), and the CMP becomes the expenditure minimization problem (EMP) discussed in Section 3.E. Therefore, in Proposition 5.C.2, properties (i) to (vii) of the cost function and conditional factor demand correspondence follow from the analysis in Sections 3.E to 3.G by this reinterpretation. [You are asked to prove properties (viii) and (ix) in Exercise 5.C.3.]

**Proposition 5.C.2:** Suppose that $c(w, q)$ is the cost function of a single-output technology $Y$ with production function $f(\cdot)$ and that $z(w, q)$ is the associated

---

8. Note, however, that the first-order conditions are sufficient for a solution to the CMP as long as the set $\{z : f(z) \geq q\}$ is convex. Thus, the key condition for the sufficiency of the first-order conditions of the CMP is the *quasiconcavity* of $f(\cdot)$. This is an important fact because the quasiconcavity of $f(\cdot)$ is compatible with increasing returns to scale (see Example 5.C.1).

conditional factor demand correspondence. Assume also that $Y$ is closed and satisfies the free disposal property. Then

(i) $c(\cdot)$ is homogeneous of degree one in $w$ and nondecreasing in $q$.

(ii) $c(\cdot)$ is a concave function of $w$.

(iii) If the sets $\{z \geq 0 : f(z) \geq q\}$ are convex for every $q$, then $Y = \{(-z, q) : w \cdot z \geq c(w, q) \text{ for all } w \gg 0\}$.

(iv) $z(\cdot)$ is homogeneous of degree zero in $w$.

(v) If the set $\{z \geq 0 : f(z) \geq q\}$ is convex, then $z(w, q)$ is a convex set. Moreover, if $\{z \geq 0 : f(z) \geq q\}$ is a strictly convex set, then $z(w, q)$ is single-valued.

(vi) (*Shepard's lemma*) If $z(\bar{w}, q)$ consists of a single point, then $c(\cdot)$ is differentiable with respect to $w$ at $\bar{w}$ and $\nabla_w c(\bar{w}, q) = z(\bar{w}, q)$.

(vii) If $z(\cdot)$ is differentiable at $\bar{w}$, then $D_w z(\bar{w}, q) = D^2_w c(\bar{w}, q)$ is a symmetric and negative semidefinite matrix with $D_w z(\bar{w}, q) \bar{w} = 0$.

(viii) If $f(\cdot)$ is homogeneous of degree one (i.e., exhibits constant returns to scale), then $c(\cdot)$ and $z(\cdot)$ are homogeneous of degree one in $q$.

(ix) If $f(\cdot)$ is concave, then $c(\cdot)$ is a convex function of $q$ (in particular, marginal costs are nondecreasing in $q$).

In Exercise 5.C.4 we are asked to show that properties (i) to (vii) of Proposition 5.C.2 also hold for technologies with multiple outputs.

The cost function can be particularly useful when the production set is of the constant returns type. In this case, $y(\cdot)$ is not single-valued at any price vector allowing for nonzero production, making Hotelling's lemma [Proposition 5.C.1(vi)] inapplicable at these prices. Yet, the conditional input demand $z(w, q)$ may nevertheless be single-valued, allowing us to use Shepard's lemma. Keep in mind, however, that the cost function does not contain more information than the profit function. In fact, we know from property (iii) of Propositions 5.C.1 and 5.C.2 that under convexity restrictions there is a one-to-one correspondence between profit and cost functions; that is, from either function, the production set can be recovered, and the other function can then be derived.

Using the cost function, we can restate the firm's problem of determining its profit-maximizing production level as

$$\operatorname*{Max}_{q \geq 0} pq - c(w, q). \tag{5.C.5}$$

The necessary first-order condition for $q^*$ to be profit maximizing is then

$$p - \frac{\partial c(w, q^*)}{\partial q} \leq 0, \quad \text{with equality if } q^* > 0. \tag{5.C.6}$$

In words, at an interior optimum (i.e., if $q^* > 0$), *price equals marginal cost*.[9] If $c(w, q)$ is convex in $q$, then the first-order condition (5.C.6) is also sufficient for $q^*$ to be the firm's optimal output level. (We study the relationship between the firm's supply behavior and the properties of its technology and cost function in detail in Section 5.D.)

---

9. This can also be seen by noting that the first-order condition (5.C.4) of the CMP coincides with first-order condition (5.C.2) of the PMP if and only if $\lambda = p$. Recall that $\lambda$, the multiplier on the constraint in the CMP, is equal to $\partial c(w, q)/\partial q$.

We could go on for many pages analyzing profit and cost functions. Some examples and further properties are contained in the exercises. See McFadden (1978) for an extensive treatment of this topic.

**Example 5.C.1:** *Profit and Cost Functions for the Cobb–Douglas Production Function.* Here we derive the profit and cost functions for the Cobb–Douglas production function of Example 5.B.2, $f(z_1, z_2) = z_1^\alpha z_2^\beta$. Recall from Example 5.B.3 that $\alpha + \beta = 1$ corresponds to the case of constant returns to scale, $\alpha + \beta < 1$ corresponds to decreasing returns, and $\alpha + \beta > 1$ corresponds to increasing returns.

The conditional factor demand equations and cost function have exactly the same form, and are derived in exactly the same way, as the expenditure function in Section 3.E (see Example 3.E.1; the only difference in the computations is that we now do not impose $\alpha + \beta = 1$):

$$z_1(w_1, w_2, q) = q^{1/(\alpha + \beta)}(\alpha w_2/\beta w_1)^{\beta/(\alpha + \beta)},$$

$$z_2(w_1, w_2, q) = q^{1/(\alpha + \beta)}(\beta w_1/\alpha w_2)^{\alpha/(\alpha + \beta)},$$

and

$$c(w_1, w_2, q) = q^{1/(\alpha + \beta)}[(\alpha/\beta)^{\beta/(\alpha + \beta)} + (\alpha/\beta)^{-\alpha/(\alpha + \beta)}]w_1^{\alpha/(\alpha + \beta)}w_2^{\beta/(\alpha + \beta)}.$$

This cost function has the form $c(w_1, w_2, q) = q^{1/(\alpha + \beta)}\theta\phi(w_1, w_2)$, where

$$\theta = [(\alpha/\beta)^{\beta/(\alpha + \beta)} + (\alpha/\beta)^{-\alpha/(\alpha + \beta)}]$$

is a constant and $\phi(w_1, w_2) = w_1^{\alpha/(\alpha + \beta)}w_2^{\beta/(\alpha + \beta)}$ is a function that does not depend on the output level $q$. When we have constant returns, $\theta\phi(w_1, w_2)$ is the per-unit cost of production.

One way to derive the firm's supply function and profit function is to use this cost function and solve problem (5.C.5). Applying (5.C.6), the first-order condition for this problem is

$$p \le \theta\phi(w_1, w_2)\left(\frac{1}{\alpha + \beta}\right)q^{(1/(\alpha + \beta)) - 1}, \quad \text{with equality if } q > 0 \qquad (5.C.7)$$

The first-order condition (5.C.7) is sufficient for a maximum when $\alpha + \beta \le 1$ because the firm's cost function is then convex in $q$.

When $\alpha + \beta < 1$, (5.C.7) can be solved for a unique optimal output level:

$$q(w_1, w_2, p) = (\alpha + \beta)[p/\theta\phi(w_1, w_2)]^{(\alpha + \beta)/(1 - \alpha - \beta)}.$$

The factor demands can then be obtained through substitution,

$$z_\ell(w_1, w_2, p) = z_\ell(w_1, w_2, q(w_1, w_2, p)) \quad \text{for } \ell = 1, 2,$$

as can the profit function,

$$\pi(w_1, w_2, p) = pq(w_1, w_2, p) - w \cdot z(w_1, w_2, q(w_1, w_2, p)).$$

When $\alpha + \beta = 1$, the right-hand side of the first-order condition (5.C.7) becomes $\theta\phi(w_1, w_2)$, the unit cost of production (which is independent of $q$). If $\theta\phi(w_1, w_2)$ is greater than $p$, then $q = 0$ is optimal; if it is smaller than $p$, then no solution exists (again, unbounded profits can be obtained by increasing $q$); and when $\theta\phi(w_1, w_2) = p$, any non-negative output level is a solution to the PMP and generates zero profits.

Finally, when $\alpha + \beta > 1$ (so that we have increasing returns to scale), a quantity $q$ satisfying the first-order condition (5.C.7) does not yield a profit-maximizing production. [Actually, in this case, the cost function is strictly concave in $q$, so that any solution to the first-order condition (5.C.7) yields a local *minimum* of profits, subject to output being always produced at minimum cost]. Indeed, since $p > 0$, a doubling of the output level starting from any $q$ doubles the firm's revenue but increases input costs only by a factor of $2^{1/(\alpha+\beta)} > 2$. With enough doublings, the firm's profits can therefore be made arbitrarily large. Hence, with increasing returns to scale, there is no solution to the PMP. ∎

## 5.D  The Geometry of Cost and Supply in the Single-Output Case

In this section, we continue our analysis of the relationships among a firm's technology, its cost function, and its supply behavior for the special but commonly used case in which there is a single output. A significant advantage of considering the single-output case is that it lends itself to extensive graphical illustration.

Throughout, we denote the amount of output by $q$ and hold the vector of factor prices constant at $\bar{w} \gg 0$. For notational convenience, we write the firm's cost function as $C(q) = c(\bar{w}, q)$. For $q > 0$, we can denote the firm's average cost by $AC(q) = C(q)/q$ and assuming that the derivative exists, we denote its *marginal cost* by $C'(q) = dC(q)/dq$.

Recall from expression (5.C.6) that for a given output price $p$, all profit-maximizing output levels $q \in q(p)$ must satisfy the first-order condition [assuming that $C'(q)$ exists]:

$$p \leq C'(q) \quad \text{with equality if } q > 0. \tag{5.D.1}$$

If the production set $Y$ is convex, $C(\cdot)$ is a convex function [see property (ix) of Proposition 5.C.2], and therefore marginal cost is nondecreasing. In this case, as we noted in Section 5.C, satisfaction of this first-order condition is also sufficient to establish that $q$ is a profit-maximizing output level at price $p$.

Two examples of convex production sets are given in Figures 5.D.1 and 5.D.2. In the figures, we assume that there is only one input, and we normalize its price to equal 1 (you can think of this input as the total expense of factor use).[10] Figure 5.D.1 depicts the production set (a), cost function (b), and average and marginal cost functions (c) for a case with decreasing returns to scale. Observe that the cost function is obtained from the production set by a 90-degree rotation. The determination of average cost and marginal cost from the cost function is shown in Figure 5.D.1(b) (for an output level $\hat{q}$). Figure 5.D.2 depicts the same objects for a case with constant returns to scale.

In Figures 5.D.1(c) and 5.D.2(c), we use a heavier trace to indicate the firm's profit-maximizing supply locus, the graph of $q(\cdot)$. (*Note: In this and subsequent figures, the supply locus is always indicated by a heavier trace.*) Because the technologies in these two examples are convex, the supply locus in each case coincides exactly with the $(q, p)$ combinations that satisfy the first-order condition (5.D.1).

If the technology is not convex, perhaps because of the presence of some underlying indivisibility, then satisfaction of the first-order necessary condition

---

10. Thus, the single input can be thought of as a Hicksian composite commodity in a sense analogous to that in Exercise 3.G.5.

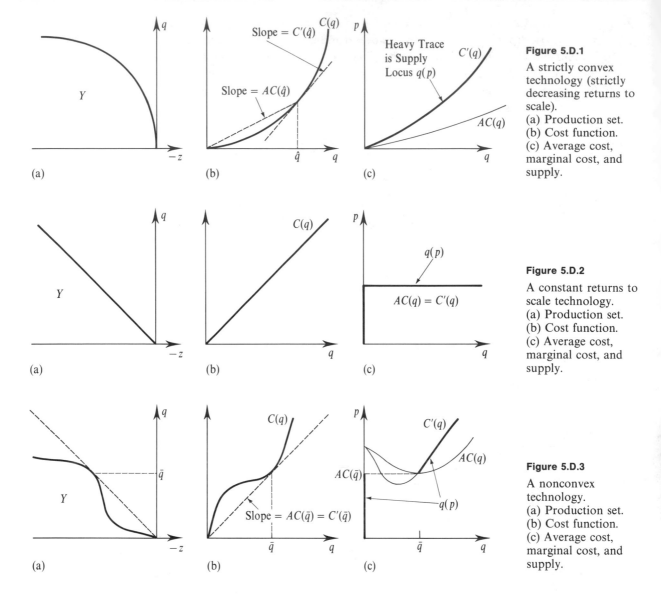

**Figure 5.D.1**

A strictly convex technology (strictly decreasing returns to scale).
(a) Production set.
(b) Cost function.
(c) Average cost, marginal cost, and supply.

**Figure 5.D.2**

A constant returns to scale technology.
(a) Production set.
(b) Cost function.
(c) Average cost, marginal cost, and supply.

**Figure 5.D.3**

A nonconvex technology.
(a) Production set.
(b) Cost function.
(c) Average cost, marginal cost, and supply.

(5.D.1) no longer implies that $q$ is profit maximizing. The supply locus will then be only a subset of the set of $(q, p)$ combinations that satisfy (5.D.1).

Figure 5.D.3 depicts a situation with a nonconvex technology. In the figure, we have an initial segment of increasing returns over which the average cost decreases and then a region of decreasing returns over which the average cost increases. The level (or levels) of production corresponding to the minimum average cost is called the *efficient scale*, which, if unique, we denote by $\bar{q}$. Looking at the cost functions in Figure 5.D.3(a) and (b), we see that at $\bar{q}$ we have $AC(\bar{q}) = C'(\bar{q})$. In Exercise 5.D.1, you are asked to establish this fact as a general result.

**Exercise 5.D.1:** Show that $AC(\bar{q}) = C'(\bar{q})$ at any $\bar{q}$ satisfying $AC(\bar{q}) \leq AC(q)$ for all $q$. Does this result depend on the differentiability of $C(\cdot)$ everywhere?

The supply locus for this nonconvex example is depicted by the heavy trace in

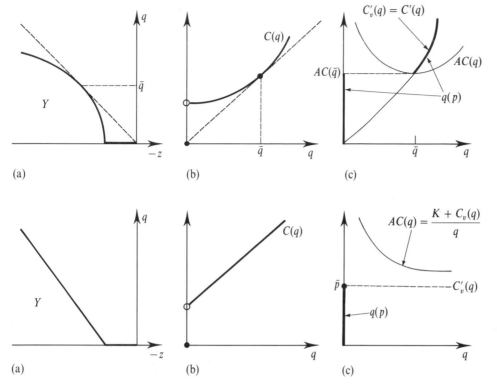

**Figure 5.D.4**

Strictly convex variable costs with a nonsunk setup cost.
(a) Production set.
(b) Cost function.
(c) Average cost, marginal cost, and supply.

**Figure 5.D.5**

Constant returns variable costs with a nonsunk setup cost.
(a) Production set.
(b) Cost function.
(c) Average cost, marginal cost, and supply.

Figure 5.D.3(c). When $p > AC(\bar{q})$, the firm maximizes its profit by producing at the unique level of $q$ satisfying $p = C'(q) > AC(q)$. [Note that the firm earns strictly positive profits doing so, exceeding the zero profits earned by setting $q = 0$, which in turn exceed the strictly negative profits earned by choosing any $q > 0$ with $p = C'(q) < AC(q)$.] On the other hand, when $p < AC(\bar{q})$, any $q > 0$ earns strictly negative profits, and so the firm's optimal supply is $q = 0$ [note that $q = 0$ satisfies the necessary first-order condition (5.D.1) because $p < C'(0)$]. When $p = AC(\bar{q})$, the profit-maximizing set of output levels is $\{0, \bar{q}\}$. The supply locus is therefore as shown in Figure 5.D.3(c).

An important source of nonconvexities is fixed setup costs. These may or may not be sunk. Figures 5.D.4 and 5.D.5 (which parallel 5.D.1 and 5.D.2) depict two cases with nonsunk fixed setup costs (so inaction is possible). In these figures, we consider a case in which the firm incurs a fixed cost $K$ if and only if it produces a positive amount of output and otherwise has convex costs. In particular, total cost is of the form $C(0) = 0$, and $C(q) = C_v(q) + K$ for $q > 0$, where $K > 0$ and $C_v(q)$, the *variable cost function*, is convex [and has $C_v(0) = 0$]. Figure 5.D.4 depicts the case in which $C_v(\cdot)$ is strictly convex, whereas $C_v(\cdot)$ is linear in Figure 5.D.5. The supply loci are indicated in the figures. In both illustrations, the firm will produce a positive amount of output only if its profit is sufficient to cover not only its variable costs but also the fixed cost $K$. You should read the supply locus in Figure 5.D.5(c) as saying that for $p > \bar{p}$, the supply is "infinite," and that $q = 0$ is optimal for $p \leq \bar{p}$.

In Figure 5.D.6, we alter the case studied in Figure 5.D.4 by making the fixed costs sunk, so that $C(0) > 0$. In particular, we now have $C(q) = C_v(q) + K$ for all $q \geq 0$; therefore, the firm must pay $K$ whether or not it produces a positive quantity.

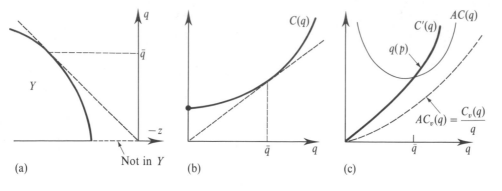

**Figure 5.D.6**

Strictly convex
variable costs with
sunk costs.
(a) Production set.
(b) Cost function.
(c) Average cost,
marginal cost, and
supply.

Although inaction is not possible here, the firm's cost function is convex, and so we are back to the case in which the first-order condition (5.D.1) is sufficient. Because the firm must pay $K$ regardless of whether it produces a positive output level, it will not shut down simply because profits are negative. Note that because $C_v(\cdot)$ is convex and $C_v(0) = 0$, $p = C'_v(q)$ implies that $pq > C_v(q)$; hence, the firm covers its variable costs when it sets output to satisfy its first-order condition. The firm's supply locus is therefore that depicted in Figure 5.D.6(c). Note that its supply behavior is exactly the same as if it did not have to pay the sunk cost $K$ at all [compare with Figure 5.D.1(c)].

**Exercise 5.D.2:** Depict the supply locus for a case with partially sunk costs, that is, where $C(q) = K + C_v(q)$ if $q > 0$ and $0 < C(0) < K$.

As we noted in Section 5.B, one source of sunk costs, at least in the short run, is input choices irrevocably set by prior decisions. Suppose, for example, that we have two inputs and a production function $f(z_1, z_2)$. Recall that we keep the prices of the two inputs fixed at $(\bar{w}_1, \bar{w}_2)$. In Figure 5.D.7(a), the cost function excluding any prior input commitments is depicted by $C(\cdot)$. We call it the *long-run cost function*. If one input, say $z_2$, is fixed at level $\bar{z}_2$ in the short-run, then the *short-run cost function* of the firm becomes $C(q|\bar{z}_2) = \bar{w}_1 z_1 + \bar{w}_2 \bar{z}_2$, where $z_1$ is chosen so that $f(z_1, \bar{z}_2) = q$. Several such short-run cost functions corresponding to different levels of $z_2$ are illustrated in Figure 5.D.7(a). Because restrictions on the firm's input decisions can only increase its costs of production, $C(q|\bar{z}_2)$ lies above $C(q)$ at all $q$ except the $q$ for

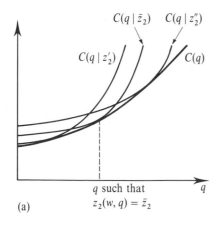

(a)

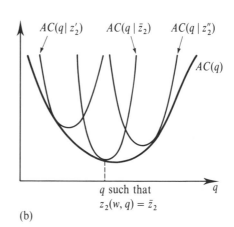

(b)

**Figure 5.D.7**

Costs when an input
level is fixed in the
short run but is free to
vary in the long run.
(a) Long-run and
short-run cost
functions.
(b) Long-run and
short-run average
cost.

which $\bar{z}_2$ is the optimal long-run input level [i.e., the $q$ such that $z_2(\bar{w}, q) = \bar{z}_2$]. Thus, $C(q|z_2(\bar{w},q)) = C(q)$ for all $q$. It follows from this and from the fact that $C(q'|z_2(\bar{w}, q)) \geq C(q')$ for all $q'$, that $C'(q) = C'(q|z_2(\bar{w}, q))$ for all $q$; that is, if the level of $z_2$ is at its long-run value, then the short-run marginal cost equals the long-run marginal cost. Geometrically, $C(\cdot)$ is the lower envelope of the family of short-run functions $C(q|z_2)$ generated by letting $z_2$ take all possible values.

Observe finally that given the long-run and short-run cost functions, the long-run and short-run average cost functions and long-run and short-run supply functions of the firm can be derived in the manner discussed earlier in the section. The average-cost version of Figure 5.D.7(a) is given in Figure 5.D.7(b). (Exercise 5.D.3 asks you to investigate the short-run and long-run supply behavior of the firm in more detail.)

# 5.E Aggregation

In this section, we study the theory of aggregate (net) supply. As we saw in Section 5.C, the absence of a budget constraint implies that individual supply is not subject to wealth effects. As prices change, there are only substitution effects along the production frontier. In contrast with the theory of aggregate demand, this fact makes for an aggregation theory that is simple and powerful.[11]

Suppose there are $J$ production units (firms or, perhaps, plants) in the economy, each specified by a production set $Y_1, \ldots, Y_J$. We assume that each $Y_j$ is nonempty, closed, and satisfies the free disposal property. Denote the profit function and supply correspondences of $Y_j$ by $\pi_j(p)$ and $y_j(p)$, respectively. The *aggregate supply correspondence* is the sum of the individual supply correspondences:

$$y(p) = \sum_{j=1}^{J} y_j(p) = \{y \in \mathbb{R}^L : y = \sum_j y_j \text{ for some } y_j \in y_j(p), j = 1, \ldots, J\}.$$

Assume, for a moment, that every $y_j(\cdot)$ is a single-valued, differentiable function at a price vector $p$. From Proposition 5.C.1, we know that every $Dy_j(p)$ is a symmetric, positive semidefinite matrix. Because these two properties are preserved under addition, we can conclude that the matrix $Dy(p)$ is *symmetric and positive semidefinite*.

As in the theory of individual production, the positive semidefiniteness of $Dy(p)$ implies the *law of supply* in the aggregate: If a price increases, then so does the corresponding *aggregate* supply. As with the law of supply at the firm level, this property of aggregate supply holds for *all* price changes. We can also prove this aggregate law of supply directly because we know from (5.C.3) that $(p - p') \cdot [y_j(p) - y_j(p')] \geq 0$ for every $j$; therefore, adding over $j$, we get

$$(p - p') \cdot [y(p) - y(p')] \geq 0.$$

The symmetry of $Dy(p)$ suggests that underlying $y(p)$ there is a "representative producer." As we now show, this is true in a particularly strong manner.

Given $Y_1, \ldots, Y_J$, we can define the *aggregate production set* by

$$Y = Y_1 + \cdots + Y_J = \{y \in \mathbb{R}^L : y = \sum_j y_j \text{ for some } y_j \in Y_J, j = 1, \ldots, J\}.$$

---

11. A classical and very readable account for the material in this section and in Section 5.F is Koopmans (1957).

The aggregate production set $Y$ describes the production vectors that are feasible in the aggregate if all the production sets are used together. Let $\pi^*(p)$ and $y^*(p)$ be the profit function and the supply correspondence of the aggregate production set $Y$. They are the profit function and supply correspondence that would arise if a single price-taking firm were to operate, under the same management so to speak, all the individual production sets.

Proposition 5.E.1 establishes a strong aggregation result for the supply side: *The aggregate profit obtained by each production unit maximizing profit separately taking prices as given is the same as that which would be obtained if they were to coordinate their actions* (i.e., *their $y_j$s) in a joint profit maximizing decision.*

**Proposition 5.E.1:** For all $p \gg 0$, we have

(i)  $\pi^*(p) = \sum_j \pi_j(p)$

(ii)  $y^*(p) = \sum_j y_j(p)$ $\left( = \{ \sum_j y_j : y_j \in y_j(p) \text{ for every } j \} \right)$.

**Proof:** (i)   For the first equality, note that if we take any collection of production plans $y_j \in Y_j$, $j = 1, \ldots, J$, then $\sum_j y_j \in Y$. Because $\pi^*(\cdot)$ is the profit function associated with $Y$, we therefore have $\pi^*(p) \geq p \cdot (\sum_j y_j) = \sum_j p \cdot y_j$. Hence, it follows that $\pi^*(p) \geq \sum_j \pi_j(p)$. In the other direction, consider any $y \in Y$. By the definition of the set $Y$, there are $y_j \in Y_j, j = 1, \ldots, J$, such that $\sum_j y_j = y$. So $p \cdot y = p \cdot (\sum_j y_j) = \sum_j p \cdot y_j \leq \sum_j \pi_j(p)$ for all $y \in Y$. Thus, $\pi^*(p) \leq \sum_j \pi_j(p)$. Together, these two inequalities imply that $\pi^*(p) = \sum_j \pi(p)$.

(ii) For the second equality, we must show that $\sum_j y_j(p) \subset y^*(p)$ and that $y^*(p) \subset \sum_j y_j(p)$. For the former relation, consider any set of individual production plans $y_j \in y_j(p), j = 1, \ldots, J$. Then $p \cdot (\sum_j y_j) = \sum_j p \cdot y_j = \sum_j \pi_j(p) = \pi^*(p)$, where the last equality follows from part (i) of the proposition. Hence, $\sum_j y_j \in y^*(p)$, and therefore, $\sum_j y_j(p) \subset y^*(p)$. In the other direction, take any $y \in y^*(p)$. Then $y = \sum_j y_j$ for some $y_j \in Y_j, j = 1, \ldots, J$. Since $p \cdot (\sum_j y_j) = \pi^*(p) = \sum_j \pi_j(p)$ and, for every $j$, we have $p \cdot y_j \leq \pi_j(p)$, it must be that $p \cdot y_j = \pi_j(p)$ for every $j$. Thus, $y_j \in y_j(p)$ for all $j$, and so $y \in \sum_j y_j(p)$. Thus, we have shown that $y^*(p) \subset \sum_j y_j(p)$. ∎

The content of Proposition 5.E.1 is illustrated in Figure 5.E.1. The proposition can be interpreted as a decentralization result: To find the solution of the aggregate profit maximization problem for given prices $p$, it is enough to add the solutions of the corresponding individual problems.

Simple as this result may seem, it nevertheless has many important implications. Consider, for example, the single-output case. The result tells us that if firms are maximizing profit facing output price $p$ and factor prices $w$, then their supply behavior maximizes aggregate profits. But this must mean that if $q = \sum_j q_j$ is the aggregate output produced by the firms, then the total cost of production is exactly equal to $c(w, q)$, the value of the *aggregate cost function* (the cost function corresponding to the aggregate production set $Y$). *Thus, the allocation of the production of output level $q$ among the firms is cost minimizing.* In addition, this allows us to relate the firms' aggregate supply function for output $q(p)$ to the aggregate cost function in the same manner as done in Section 5.D for an individual firm. (This fact will prove useful when we study partial equilibrium models of competitive markets in Chapter 10.)

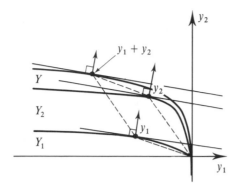

**Figure 5.E.1**

Joint profit
maximization as a
result of individual
profit maximization.

In summary: If firms maximize profits taking prices as given, then the production side of the economy aggregates beautifully.

As in the consumption case (see Appendix A of Chapter 4), aggregation can also have helpful regularizing effects in the production context. An interesting and important fact is that the existence of many firms or plants with technologies that are not too dissimilar can make the *average* production set almost convex, even if the individual production sets are not so. This is illustrated in Figure 5.E.2, where there are $J$ firms with identical production sets equal to

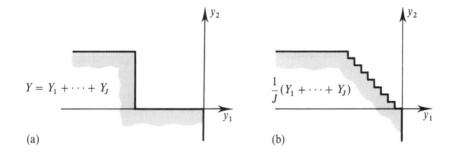

(a)                                          (b)

**Figure 5.E.2**

An example of the
convexifying effects of
aggregation.
(a) The individual
production
set.
(b) The average
production set.

that displayed in 5.E.2(a). Defining the average production set as $(1/J)(Y_1 + \cdots + Y_J) = \{y: y = (1/J)(y_1 + \cdots + y_J)$ for some $y_j \in Y_j, j = 1, \ldots, J\}$, we see that for large $J$, this set is nearly convex, as depicted in Figure 5.E.2(b).[12]

# 5.F  Efficient Production

Because much of welfare economics focuses on efficiency (see, for example, Chapters 10 and 16), it is useful to have algebraic and geometric characterizations of productions plans that can unambiguously be regarded as nonwasteful. This motivates Definition 5.F.1.

---

12. Note that this production set is bounded above. This is important because it insures that the individual nonconvexity is of finite size. If the individual production set was like that shown in, say, Figure 5.B.4, where neither the set nor the nonconvexity is bounded, then the average set would display a large nonconvexity (for any $J$). In Figure 5.B.5, we have a case of an unbounded production set but with a bounded nonconvexity; as for Figure 5.E.2, the average set will in this case be almost convex.

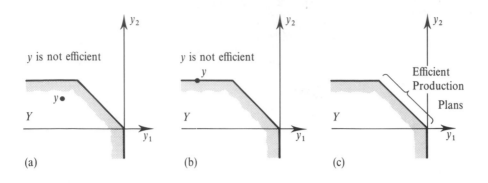

**Figure 5.F.1**

An efficient production
plan must be on the
boundary of $Y$, but
not all points on the
boundary of $Y$ are
efficient.
(a) An inefficient
production plan in the
interior of $Y$.
(b) An inefficient
production plan at the
boundary of $Y$.
(c) The set of efficient
production plans.

**Definition 5.F.1:** A production vector $y \in Y$ is *efficient* if there is no $y' \in Y$ such that $y' \geq y$ and $y' \neq y$.

In words, a production vector is efficient if there is no other feasible production vector that generates as much output as $y$ using no additional inputs, and that actually produces more of some output or uses less of some input.

As we see in Figure 5.F.1, every efficient $y$ must be on the boundary of $Y$, but the converse is not necessarily the case: There may be boundary points of $Y$ that are not efficient.

We now show that the concept of efficiency is intimately related to that of supportability by profit maximization. This constitutes our first look at a topic that we explore in much more depth in Chapter 10 and especially in Chapter 16

Proposition 5.F.1 provides an elementary but important result. It is a version of the *first fundamental theorem of welfare economics*.

**Proposition 5.F.1:** If $y \in Y$ is profit maximizing for some $p \gg 0$, then $y$ is efficient.

**Proof:** Suppose otherwise: That there is a $y' \in Y$ such that $y' \neq y$ and $y' \geq y$. Because $p \gg 0$, this implies that $p \cdot y' > p \cdot y$, contradicting the assumption that $y$ is profit maximizing. ∎

It is worth emphasizing that Proposition 5.F.1 is valid even if the production set is nonconvex. This is illustrated in Figure 5.F.2.

When combined with the aggregation results discussed in Section 5.E, Proposition 5.F.1 tells us that *if a collection of firms each independently maximizes profits with respect to the same fixed price vector $p \gg 0$, then the aggregate production is*

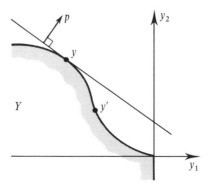

**Figure 5.F.2**

A profit-maximizing
production plan (for
$p \gg 0$) is efficient.

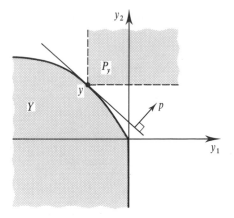

**Figure 5.F.3**

The use of the separating hyperplane theorem to prove Proposition 5.F.2: If $Y$ is convex, every efficient $y \in Y$ is profit maximizing for some $p \geq 0$.

*socially efficient.* That is, there is no other production plan for the economy as a whole that could produce more output using no additional inputs. This is in line with our conclusion in Section 5.E that, in the single-output case, the aggregate output level is produced at the lowest-possible cost when all firms maximize profits facing the same prices.

The need for strictly positive prices in Proposition 5.F.1 is unpleasant, but it cannot be dispensed with, as Exercise 5.F.1 asks you to demonstrate.

**Exercise 5.F.1:** Give an example of a $y \in Y$ that is profit maximizing for some $p \geq 0$ with $p \neq 0$ but that is also inefficient (i.e. not efficient).

A converse of Proposition 5.F.1 would assert that any efficient production vector is profit maximizing for *some* price system. However, a glance at the efficient production $y'$ in Figure 5.F.2 shows that this cannot be true in general. Nevertheless, this converse does hold with the added assumption of convexity. Proposition 5.F.2, which is less elementary than Proposition 5.F.1, is a version of the so-called *second fundamental theorem of welfare economics.*

**Proposition 5.F.2:** Suppose that $Y$ is convex. Then every efficient production $y \in Y$ is a profit-maximizing production for some nonzero price vector $p \geq 0$.[13]

**Proof:** This proof is an application of the separating hyperplane theorem for convex sets (see Section M.G of the Mathematical Appendix). Suppose that $y \in Y$ is efficient, and define the set $P_y = \{y' \in \mathbb{R}^L : y' \gg y\}$. The set $P_y$ is depicted in Figure 5.F.3. It is convex, and because $y$ is efficient, we have $Y \cap P_y = \varnothing$. We can therefore invoke the separating hyperplane theorem to establish that there is *some* $p \neq 0$ such that $p \cdot y' \geq p \cdot y''$ for every $y' \in P_y$ and $y'' \in Y$ (see Figure 5.F.3). Note, in particular, that this implies $p \cdot y' \geq p \cdot y$ for every $y' \gg y$. Therefore, we must have $p \geq 0$ because if $p_\ell < 0$ for some $\ell$, then we would have $p \cdot y' < p \cdot y$ for some $y' \gg y$ with $y'_\ell - y_\ell$ sufficiently large.

Now take any $y'' \in Y$. Then $p \cdot y' \geq p \cdot y''$ for every $y' \in P_y$. Because $y'$ can be chosen to be arbitrarily close to $y$, we conclude that $p \cdot y \geq p \cdot y''$ for any $y'' \in Y$; that is, $y$ is profit maximizing for $p$. ∎

---

13. As the proof makes clear, the result also applies to *weakly efficient* productions, that is, to productions such as $y$ in Figure 5.F.1(b) where there is no $y' \in Y$ such that $y' \gg y$.

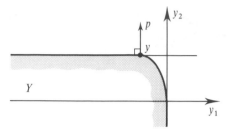

**Figure 5.F.4**

Proposition 5.C.2 cannot be extended to require $p \gg 0$.

The second part of Proposition 5.F.2 cannot be strengthened to read "$p \gg 0$." In Figure 5.F.4, for example, the production vector $y$ is efficient, but it cannot be supported by any strictly positive price vector.

As an illustration of Proposition 5.F.2, consider a single-output, concave production function $f(z)$. Fix an input vector $\bar{z}$, and suppose that $f(\cdot)$ is differentiable at $\bar{z}$ and $\nabla f(\bar{z}) \gg 0$. Then the production plan that uses input vector $\bar{z}$ to produce output level $f(\bar{z})$ is efficient. Letting the price of output be 1, condition (5.C.2) tells us that the input price vector that makes this efficient production profit maximizing is precisely $w = \nabla f(\bar{z})$, the vector of marginal productivities.

# 5.G   Remarks on the Objectives of the Firm

Although it is logical to take the assumption of preference maximization as a primitive concept for the theory of the consumer, the same cannot be said for the assumption of profit maximization by the firm. Why this objective rather than, say, the maximization of sales revenues or the size of the firm's labor force? The objectives of the firm assumed in our economic analysis should emerge from the objectives of those individuals who control it. Firms in the type of economies we consider are owned by individuals who, wearing another hat, are also consumers. A firm owned by a single individual has well-defined objectives: those of the owner. In this case, the only issue is whether this objective coincides with profit maximization. Whenever there is more than one owner, however, we have an added level of complexity. Indeed, we must either reconcile any conflicting objectives the owners may have or show that no conflict exists.

Fortunately, it is possible to resolve these issues and give a sound theoretical grounding to the objective of profit maximization. We shall now show that under reasonable assumptions this is the goal that all owners would agree upon.

Suppose that a firm with production set $Y$ is owned by consumers. Ownership here simply means that each consumer $i = 1, \ldots, I$ is entitled to a share $\theta_i \geq 0$ of profits, where $\sum_i \theta_i = 1$ (some of the $\theta_i$'s may equal zero). Thus, if the production decision is $y \in Y$, then a consumer $i$ with utility function $u_i(\cdot)$ achieves the utility level

$$\underset{x_i \geq 0}{\text{Max}} \quad u_i(x_i)$$
$$\text{s.t.} \ \ p \cdot x_i \leq w_i + \theta_i p \cdot y,$$

where $w_i$ is consumer $i$'s nonprofit wealth. Hence at fixed prices, higher profit increases consumer–owner $i$'s overall wealth and expands her budget set, a desirable outcome. It follows that at any fixed price vector $p$, the consumer–owners *unanimously* prefer that the firm implement a production plan $y' \in Y$ instead of $y \in Y$ whenever $p \cdot y' > p \cdot y$. Hence, we conclude that if we maintain the assumption of price-taking behavior, all owners would agree, whatever their utility functions, to instruct the manager of the firm to maximize profits.[14]

It is worth emphasizing three of the implicit assumptions in the previous reasoning: (i) prices are fixed and do not depend on the actions of the firm, (ii) profits are not uncertain, and (iii) managers can be controlled by owners. We comment on these assumptions very informally.

(i) If prices may depend on the production of the firm, the objective of the owners may depend on their tastes as consumers. Suppose, for example, that each consumer has no wealth from sources other than the firm ($w_i = 0$), that $L = 2$, and that the firm produces good 1 from good 2 with production function $f(\cdot)$. Also, normalize the price of good 2 to be 1, and suppose that the price of good 1, in terms of good 2, is $p(q)$ if output is $q$. If, for example, the preferences of the owners are such that they care only about the consumption of good 2, then they will unanimously want to solve $\text{Max}_{z \geq 0}\, p(f(z))f(z) - z$. This maximizes the amount of good 2 that they get to consume. On the other hand, if they want to consume only good 1, then they will wish to solve $\text{Max}_{z \geq 0}\, f(z) - [z/p(f(z))]$ because if they earn $p(f(z))f(z) - z$ units of good 2, then end up with $[p(f(z))f(z) - z]/p(f(z))$ units of good 1. But these two problems have different solutions. (Check the first-order conditions.) Moreover, as this suggests, if the owners differ in their tastes as consumers, then they will not agree about what they want the firm to do (Exercise 5.G.1 elaborates on this point.)

(ii) If the output of the firm is random, then it is crucial to distinguish whether the output is sold before or after the uncertainty is resolved. If the output is sold after the uncertainty is resolved (as in the case of agricultural products sold in spot markets after harvesting), then the argument for a unanimous desire for profit maximization breaks down. Because profit, and therefore derived wealth, are now uncertain, the risk attitudes and expectations of owners will influence their preferences with regard to production plans. For example, strong risk averters will prefer relatively less risky production plans than moderate risk averters.

On the other hand, if the output is sold before uncertainty is resolved (as in the case of agricultural products sold in futures markets before harvesting), then the risk is fully carried by the buyer. The profit of the firm is not uncertain, and the argument for unanimity in favor of profit maximization still holds. In effect, the firm can be thought of as producing a commodity that is sold before uncertainty is resolved in a market of the usual kind. (Further analysis of this issue would take us too far afield. We come back to it in Section 19.G after covering the foundations of decision theory under uncertainty in Chapter 6.)

(iii) It is plain that shareholders cannot usually exercise control directly. They need managers, who, naturally enough, have their own objectives. Especially if ownership is very diffuse, it is an important theoretical challenge to understand how and to what extent managers are, or can be, controlled by owners. Some relevant considerations are factors such as the degree of observability of managerial actions

---

14. In actuality, there are public firms and quasipublic organizations such as universities that do not have *owners* in the sense that private firms have shareholders. Their objectives may be different, and the current discussion does not apply to them.

and the stake of individual owners. [These issues will be touched on in Section 14.C (agency contracts as a mechanism of internal control) and in Section 19.G (stock markets as a mechanism of external control).]

## APPENDIX A: THE LINEAR ACTIVITY MODEL

The saliency of the model of production with convexity and constant returns to scale technologies recommends that we examine it in some further detail.

Given a constant returns to scale technology $Y$, the *ray* generated (or spanned) by a vector $\bar{y} \in Y$ is the set $\{y \in Y : y = \alpha \bar{y} \text{ for some scalar } \alpha \geq 0\}$. We can think of a ray as representing a production *activity* that can be run at any *scale of operation*. That is, the production plan $\bar{y}$ can be scaled up or down by any factor $\alpha \geq 0$, generating, in this way, other possible production plans.

We focus here on a particular case of constant returns to scale technologies that lends itself to explicit computation and is therefore very important in applications. We assume that we are given as a primitive of our theory a list of *finitely many activities* (say $M$), each of which can be run at any scale of operation and any number of which can be run simultaneously. Denote the $M$ activities, to be called the *elementary activities*, by $a_1 \in \mathbb{R}^L, \ldots, a_M \in \mathbb{R}^L$. Then, the production set is

$$Y = \{y \in \mathbb{R}^L : y = \sum_{m=1}^{M} \alpha_m a_m \text{ for some scalars } (\alpha_1, \ldots, \alpha_M) \geq 0\}.$$

The scalar $\alpha_m$ is called the *level of elementary activity m*; it measures the scale of operation of the $m$th activity. Geometrically, $Y$ is a *polyhedral cone*, a set generated as the convex hull of a finite number of rays.

An activity of the form $(0, \ldots, 0, -1, 0, \ldots, 0)$, where $-1$ is in the $\ell$th place, is known as the *disposal activity* for good $\ell$. Henceforth, we shall always assume that, in addition to the $M$ listed elementary activities, the $L$ disposal activities are also available. Figure 5.AA.1 illustrates a production set arising in the case where $L = 2$ and $M = 2$.

Given a price vector $p \in \mathbb{R}_{++}^L$, a profit-maximizing plan exists in $Y$ if and only if $p \cdot a_m \leq 0$ for every $m$. To see this, note that if $p \cdot a_m < 0$, then the profit-maximizing level of activity $m$ is $\alpha_m = 0$. If $p \cdot a_m = 0$, then any level of activity $m$ generates zero profits. Finally, if $p \cdot a_m > 0$ for some $m$, then by making $\alpha_m$ arbitrarily large, we could generate arbitrarily large profits. Note that the presence of the disposal activities implies that we must have $p \in \mathbb{R}_+^L$ for a profit-maximizing plan to exist. If $p_\ell < 0$, then the $\ell$th disposal activity would generate strictly positive (hence, arbitrarily large) profits.

For any price vector $p$ generating zero profits, let $A(p)$ denote the set of activities that generate exactly zero profits: $A(p) = \{a_m : p \cdot a_m = 0\}$. If $a_m \notin A(p)$, then $p \cdot a_m < 0$, and so activity $m$ is not used at prices $p$. The profit-maximizing supply set $y(p)$ is therefore the convex cone generated by the activities in $A(p)$; that is, $y(p) = \{\sum_{a_m \in A(p)} \alpha_m a_m : \alpha_m \geq 0\}$. The set $y(p)$ is also illustrated in Figure 5.AA.1. In the figure, at price vector $p$, activity $a_1$ makes exactly zero profits, and activity $a_2$

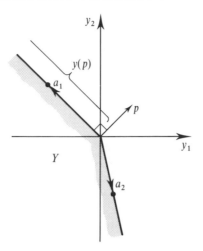

**Figure 5.AA.1**

A production set generated by two activities.

incurs a loss (if operated at all). Therefore, $A(p) = \{a_1\}$ and $y(p) = \{y: y = \alpha_1 a_1$ for any scalar $\alpha_1 \geq 0\}$, the ray spanned by activity $a_1$.

A significant result that we shall not prove is that for the linear activity model the converse of the efficiency Proposition 5.F.1 holds exactly; that is, we can strengthen Proposition 5.F.2 to say: *Every efficient $y \in Y$ is a profit-maximizing production for some $p \gg 0$.*

An important special case of the linear activity model is *Leontief's input–output model*. It is characterized by two additional features:

(i) There is one commodity, say the $L$th, which is not produced by any activity. For this reason, we will call it the *primary factor*. In most applications of the Leontief model, the primary factor is labor.
(ii) Every elementary activity has at most a single positive entry. This is called the assumption of *no joint production*. Thus, it is as if every good except the primary factor is produced from a certain type of constant returns production function using the other goods and the primary factor as inputs.

### The Leontief Input–Output Model with No Substitution Possibilities

The simplest Leontief model is one in which each producible good is produced by only one activity. In this case, it is natural to label the activity that produces good $\ell = 1, \ldots, L - 1$ as $a_\ell = (a_{1\ell}, \ldots, a_{L\ell}) \in \mathbb{R}^L$. So the number of elementary activities $M$ is equal to $L - 1$. As an example, in Figure 5.AA.2, for a case where $L = 3$, we represent the unit production isoquant [the set $\{(z_2, z_3): f(z_2, z_3) = 1\}$] for the implied production function of good 1. In the figure, the disposal activities for goods 2 and 3 are used to get rid of any excess of inputs. Because inputs must be used in fixed proportions (disposal aside), this special case is called a *Leontief model with no substitution possibilities*.

If we normalize the activity vectors so that $a_{\ell\ell} = 1$ for all $\ell = 1, \ldots, L - 1$, then the vector $\alpha = (\alpha_1, \ldots, \alpha_{L-1}) \in \mathbb{R}^{L-1}$ of activity levels equals the vector of *gross* production of goods 1 through $L - 1$. To determine the levels of *net* production, it is convenient to denote by $A$ the $(L - 1) \times (L - 1)$ matrix in which the $\ell$th column is

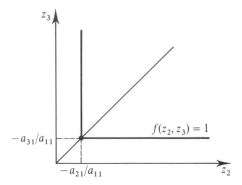

**Figure 5.AA.2**

Unit isoquant of production function for good 1 in the Leontief model with no substitution.

the negative of the activity vector $a_\ell$ except that its last entry has been deleted and entry $a_{\ell\ell}$ has been replaced by a zero (recall that entries $a_{k\ell}$ with $k \neq \ell$ are nonpositive):

$$
A = \begin{bmatrix}
0 & -a_{12} & \cdots & -a_{1,L-1} \\
-a_{21} & 0 & \cdots & -a_{2,L-1} \\
\vdots & & \ddots & \\
-a_{L-1,1} & -a_{L-1,2} & \cdots & 0
\end{bmatrix}.
$$

The matrix $A$ is known as the *Leontief input–output matrix*. Its $k\ell$th entry, $-a_{k\ell} \geq 0$, measures how much of good $k$ is needed to produce one unit of good $\ell$. We also denote by $b \in \mathbb{R}^{L-1}$ the vector of primary factor requirements, $b = (-a_{L1}, \ldots, -a_{L,L-1})$. The vector $(I - A)\alpha$ then gives the *net* production levels of the $L - 1$ outputs when the activities are run at levels $\alpha = (\alpha_1, \ldots, \alpha_{L-1})$. To see this, recall that the activities are normalized so that the gross production levels of the $L - 1$ produced goods are exactly $\alpha = (\alpha_1, \ldots, \alpha_{L-1})$. On the other hand, $A\alpha$ gives the amounts of each of these goods that are used as inputs for other produced goods. The difference, $(I - A)\alpha$, is therefore the net production of goods $1, \ldots, L - 1$. In addition, the scalar $b \cdot \alpha$ gives the total use of the primary factor. In summary, with this notation, we can write the set of technologically feasible production vectors (assuming free disposal) as

$$
Y = \left\{ y : y \leq \begin{bmatrix} I - A \\ -b \end{bmatrix} \alpha \text{ for some } \alpha \in \mathbb{R}_+^L \right\}.
$$

If $(I - A)\bar{\alpha} \gg 0$ for some $\bar{\alpha} \geq 0$, the input–output matrix $A$ is said to be *productive*. That is, the input–output matrix $A$ is productive if there is *some* production plan that can produce positive net amounts of the $L - 1$ outputs, provided only that there is a sufficient amount of primary input available.

A remarkable fact of Leontief input–output theory is the all-or-nothing property stated in Proposition 5.AA.1.

**Proposition 5.AA.1:** If $A$ is productive, then for any nonnegative amounts of the $L - 1$ producible commodities $c \in \mathbb{R}_+^{L-1}$, there is a vector of activity levels $\alpha \geq 0$ such that $(I - A)\alpha = c$. That is, if $A$ is productive, then it is possible to produce *any* nonnegative net amount of outputs (perhaps for purposes of final consumption), provided only that there is enough primary factor available.

**Proof:** We will show that if $A$ is productive, then the inverse of the matrix $(I - A)$ exists and is nonnegative. This will give the result because we can then achieve net output levels $c \in \mathbb{R}_+^{L-1}$ by setting the (nonnegative) activity levels $\alpha = (I - A)^{-1}c$.

To prove the claim, we begin by establishing a matrix-algebra fact. We show that if $A$ is productive, then the matrix $\sum_{n=0}^{N} A^n$, where $A^n$ is the $n$th power of $A$, approaches a limit as $N \to \infty$. Because $A$ has only nonnegative entries, every entry of $\sum_{n=0}^{N} A^n$ is *nonde*creasing with $N$. Therefore, to establish that $\sum_{n=0}^{N} A^n$ has a limit, it suffices to show that there is an upper bound for its entries. Since $A$ is productive, there is an $\bar{\alpha}$ and $\bar{c} \gg 0$ such that $\bar{c} = (I - A)\bar{\alpha}$. If we premultiply both sides of this equality by $\sum_{n=0}^{N} A^n$, we get $(\sum_{n=0}^{N} A^n)\bar{c} = (I - A^{N+1})\bar{\alpha}$ (recall that $A^0 = I$). But $(I - A^{N+1})\bar{\alpha} \le \bar{\alpha}$ because all elements of the matrix $A^{N+1}$ are nonnegative. Therefore, $(\sum_{n=0}^{N} A^n)\bar{c} \le \bar{\alpha}$. With $\bar{c} \gg 0$, this implies that no entry of $\sum_{n=0}^{N} A^n$ can exceed $\{\mathrm{Max}\,\{\bar{\alpha}_1, \ldots, \bar{\alpha}_{L-1}\}/\mathrm{Min}\,\{\bar{c}_1, \ldots, \bar{c}_{L-1}\}\}$, and so we have established the desired upper bound. We conclude, therefore, that $\sum_{n=0}^{\infty} A^n$ exists.

The fact that $\sum_{n=0}^{\infty} A^n$ exists must imply that $\lim_{N \to \infty} A^N = 0$. Thus, since $(\sum_{n=0}^{N} A^n)(I - A) = (I - A^{N+1})$ and $\lim_{N \to \infty}(I - A^{N+1}) = I$, it must be that $\sum_{n=0}^{\infty} A^n = (I - A)^{-1}$. (If $A$ is a single number, this is precisely the high-school formula for adding up the terms of a geometric series.) The conclusion is that $(I - A)^{-1}$ exists and that all its entries are nonnegative. This establishes the result. ∎

The focus on $\sum_{n=0}^{N} A^n$ in the proof of Proposition 5.AA.1 makes economic sense. Suppose we want to produce the vector of final consumptions $c \in \mathbb{R}_+^{L-1}$. How much total production will be needed? To produce final outputs $c = A^0c$, we need to use as inputs the amounts $A(A^0c) = Ac$ of produced goods. In turn, to produce these amounts requires that $A(Ac) = A^2c$ of additional produced goods be used, and so on ad infinitum. The *total* amounts of goods required to be produced is therefore the limit of $(\sum_{n=0}^{N} A^n)c$ as $N \to \infty$. Thus, we can conclude that the vector $c \ge 0$ will be producible if and only if $\sum_{n=0}^{\infty} A^n$ is well defined (i.e., all its entries are finite).

---

**Example 5.AA.1:** Suppose that $L = 3$, and let $a_1 = (1, -1, -2)$ and $a_2 = (-\beta, 1, -4)$ for some constant $\beta \ge 0$. Activity levels $\alpha = (\alpha_1, \alpha_2)$ generate a positive net output of good 2 if $\alpha_2 > \alpha_1$; they generate a positive net output of good 1 if $\alpha_1 - \beta\alpha_2 > 0$. The input–output matrix $A$ and the matrix $(I - A)^{-1}$ are

$$A = \begin{bmatrix} 0 & \beta \\ 1 & 0 \end{bmatrix} \quad \text{and} \quad (I - A)^{-1} = \frac{1}{1 - \beta}\begin{bmatrix} 1 & \beta \\ 1 & 1 \end{bmatrix}.$$

Hence, matrix $A$ is productive if and only if $\beta < 1$. Figure 5.AA.3(a) depicts a case where $A$ is productive. The shaded region represents the vectors of net outputs that can be generated using the two activity vectors; note how the two activity vectors can span all of $\mathbb{R}_+^2$. In contrast, in Figure 5.AA.3(b), the matrix $A$ is not productive: No strictly positive vector of net outputs can be achieved by running the two activities at nonnegative scales. [Again, the shaded region represents those vectors that can be generated using the two activity vectors, here a set whose only intersection with $\mathbb{R}_+^2$ is the point $(0, 0)$]. Note also that the closer $\beta$ is to the value 1, the larger the levels of activity required to produce any final vector of consumptions. ∎

## The Leontief Model with Substitution Possibilities

We now move to the consideration of the general Leontief model in which each good may have more than one activity capable of producing it. We shall see that the

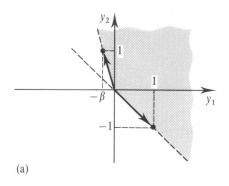

(a)

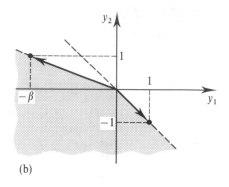

(b)

**Figure 5.AA.3**
Leontief model of
Example 5.AA.1.
(a) Productive ($\beta < 1$).
(b) Unproductive
($\beta \geq 1$).

properties of the nonsubstitution model remain very relevant for the more general case where substitution is possible.

The first thing to observe is that the computation of the production function of a good, say good 1, now becomes a linear programming problem (see Section M.M of the Mathematical Appendix). Indeed, suppose that $a_1 \in \mathbb{R}^L, \ldots, a_{M_1} \in \mathbb{R}^L$ is a list of $M_1$ elementary activities capable of producing good 1 and that we are given initial levels of goods $2, \ldots, L$ equal to $z_2, \ldots, z_L$. Then the maximal possible production of good 1 given these available inputs $f(z_2, \ldots, z_L)$ is the solution to the problem

$$\underset{\alpha_1 \geq 0, \ldots, \alpha_{M_1} \geq 0}{\text{Max}} \quad \alpha_1 a_{11} + \cdots + \alpha_{M_1} a_{1M_1}$$

$$\text{s.t.} \quad \sum_{m=1}^{M_1} \alpha_m a_{\ell m} \geq -z_\ell \quad \text{for all } \ell = 2, \ldots, L.$$

We also know from linear programming theory that the $L - 1$ dual variables $(\lambda_2, \ldots, \lambda_L)$ of this problem (i.e., the multipliers associated with the $L - 1$ constraints) can be interpreted as the marginal productivities of the $L - 1$ inputs. More precisely, for any $\ell = 2, \ldots, L$, we have $(\partial f/\partial z_\ell)^+ \leq \lambda_\ell \leq (\partial f/\partial z_\ell)^-$, where $(\partial f/\partial z_\ell)^+$ and $(\partial f/\partial z_\ell)^-$ are, respectively, the left-hand and right-hand $\ell$th partial derivatives of $f(\cdot)$ at $(z_2, \ldots, z_L)$.

Figure 5.AA.4 illustrates the unit isoquant for the case in which good 1 can be produced using two other goods (goods 2 and 3) as inputs with two possible activities $a_1 = (1, -2, -1)$ and $a_2 = (1, -1, -2)$. If the ratio of inputs is either higher than 2 or lower than $\frac{1}{2}$, one of the disposal activities is used to eliminate any excess inputs.

For any vector $y \in \mathbb{R}^L$, it will be convenient to write $y = (y_{-L}, y_L)$, where $y_{-L} = (y_1, \ldots, y_{L-1})$. We shall assume that our Leontief model is *productive* in the sense that there is a technologically feasible vector $y \in Y$ such that $y_{-L} \gg 0$.

A striking implication of the Leontief structure (constant returns, no joint products, single primary factor) is that we can associate with each good a *single optimal technique* (which could be a mixture of several of the elementary techniques corresponding to that good). What this means is that optimal techniques (one for each output) supporting efficient production vectors can be chosen independently of the particular output vector that is being produced (as long as the net output of every producible good is positive). Thus, although substitution is possible in principle, efficient production requires no substitution of techniques as desired final consumption levels change. This is the content of the celebrated *non-substitution theorem* (due to Samuelson [1951]).

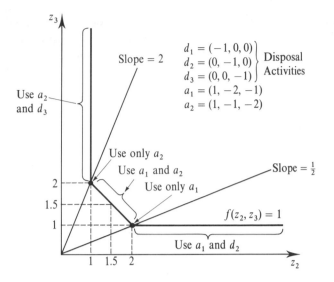

$$d_1 = (-1, 0, 0)$$
$$d_2 = (0, -1, 0)$$ Disposal Activities
$$d_3 = (0, 0, -1)$$
$$a_1 = (1, -2, -1)$$
$$a_2 = (1, -1, -2)$$

**Figure 5.AA.4**

Unit isoquant of production function of good 1, in the Leontief model with substitution.

**Proposition 5.AA.2:** (*The Nonsubstitution Theorem*) Consider a productive Leontief input–output model with $L - 1$ producible goods and $M_\ell \geq 1$ elementary activities for the producible good $\ell = 1, \ldots, L - 1$. Then there exist $L - 1$ activities $(a_1, \ldots, a_{L-1})$, with $a_\ell$ possibly a nonnegative linear combination of the $M_\ell$ elementary activities for producing good $\ell$, such that *all* efficient production vectors with $y_{-L} \gg 0$ can be generated with these $L - 1$ activities.

**Proof:** Let $y \in Y$ be an efficient production vector with $y_{-L} \gg 0$. As a general matter, the vector $y$ must be generated by a collection of $L - 1$ activities $(a_1, \ldots, a_{L-1})$ (some of these may be "mixtures" of the original activities) run at activity levels $(\alpha_1, \ldots, \alpha_{L-1}) \gg 0$; that is, $y = \sum_{\ell=1}^{L-1} \alpha_\ell a_\ell$. We show that any efficient production plan $y'$ with $y'_{-L} \gg 0$ can be achieved using the activities $(a_1, \ldots, a_{L-1})$.

Since $y \in Y$ is efficient, there exists a $p \gg 0$ such that $y$ is profit maximizing with respect to $p$ (this is from Proposition 5.F.2, as strengthened for the linear activity model). From $p \cdot a_\ell \leq 0$ for all $\ell = 1, \ldots, L - 1$, $\alpha_\ell > 0$, and

$$0 = p \cdot y = p \cdot \left( \sum_{\ell=1}^{L-1} \alpha_\ell a_\ell \right) = \sum_{\ell=1}^{L-1} \alpha_\ell \, p \cdot a_\ell,$$

it follows that $p \cdot a_\ell = 0$ for all $\ell = 1, \ldots, L - 1$.

Consider now any other efficient production $y' \in Y$ with $y'_{-L} \gg 0$. We want to show that $y'$ can be generated from the activities $(a_1, \ldots, a_{L-1})$. Denote by $A$ the input–output matrix associated with $(a_1, \ldots, a_{L-1})$. Because $y_{-L} \gg 0$, it follows by definition that $A$ is productive. Therefore, by Proposition 5.AA.1, we know that there are activity levels $(\alpha''_1, \ldots, \alpha''_{L-1})$ such that the production vector $y'' = \sum_{\ell=1}^{L-1} \alpha''_\ell a_\ell$ has $y''_{-L} = y'_{-L}$. Note that since $p \cdot a_\ell = 0$ for all $\ell = 1, \ldots, L - 1$, we must have $p \cdot y'' = 0$. Thus, $y''$ is profit maximizing for $p \gg 0$ (recall that the maximum profits for $p$ are zero), and so it follows that $y''$ is efficient by Proposition 5.F.1. But then we have two production vectors, $y'$ and $y''$, with $y'_{-L} = y''_{-L}$, and both are efficient. It must therefore be that $y''_L = y'_L$. Hence, we conclude that $y'$ can be produced using only the activities $(a_1, \ldots, a_{L-1})$, which is the desired result. ∎

The nonsubstitution theorem depends critically on the presence of only one primary factor. This makes sense. With more than one primary factor, the optimal choice of techniques should depend on the relative prices of these factors. In turn, it is logical to expect that these relative prices will not be independent of the composition of final demand (e.g., if demand moves from land-intensive goods toward labour-intensive goods, we would expect the price of labor relative to the price of land to increase). Nonetheless, it is worth mentioning that the nonsubstitution result remains valid as long as the prices of the primary factors do not change.

For further reading on the material discussed in this appendix see Gale (1960).

## REFERENCES

Champsaur, P., and J.-C. Milleron (1983). *Advanced Exercises in Microeconomics*. Cambridge, Mass.: Harvard University Press.

Debreu, G. (1959). *Theory of Value*. New York: Wiley.

Gale, D. (1960). *The Theory of Linear Economic Models*. New York: McGraw-Hill.

Koopmans, T. (1957). *Three Essays on the State of Economic Science*. Essay 1. New York: McGraw-Hill.

McFadden, D. (1978). Cost, revenue and profit functions. In *Production economics: A dual approach to theory and applications*, edited by M. Fuss and D. McFadden. Amsterdam: North-Holland.

McKenzie, L. (1959). On the existence of a general equilibrium for a competitive market. *Econometrica* **27**: 54–71.

Samuelson, P. (1951). Abstract of a theorem concerning substitutability in open Leontief models. In *Activity analysis of production and allocation*, edited by T. Koopmans. New York: Wiley.

## EXERCISES

**5.B.1[A]**  In text

**5.B.2[A]**  In text.

**5.B.3[A]**  In text.

**5.B.4[B]**  Suppose that $Y$ is a production set, interpreted now as the technology of a single production unit. Denote by $Y^+$ the additive closure of $Y$, that is, the smallest production set that is additive and contains $Y$ (in other words, $Y^+$ is the total production set if technology $Y$ can be replicated an arbitrary number of times). Represent $Y^+$ for each of the examples of production sets depicted graphically in Section 5.B. In particular, note that for the typical decreasing returns technology of Figure 5.B.5(a), the additive closure $Y^+$ violates the closedness condition (ii). Discuss and compare with the case corresponding to Figure 5.B.5(b), where $Y^+$ is closed.

**5.B.5[C]**  Show that if $Y$ is closed and convex, and $-\mathbb{R}_+^L \subset Y$, then free disposal holds.

**5.B.6[B]**  There are three goods. Goods 1 and 2 are inputs. The third, with amounts denoted by $q$, is an output. Output can be produced by two techniques that can be operated simultaneously or separately. The techniques are not necessarily linear. The first (respectively, the second) technique uses only the first (respectively, the second) input. Thus, the first (respectively, the second) technique is completely specified by $\phi_1(q_1)$ [respectively, $\phi_2(q_2)$], the minimal amount of input one (respectively, two) *sufficient* to produce the amount of output $q_1$ (respectively, $q_2$). The two functions $\phi_1(\cdot)$ and $\phi_2(\cdot)$ are increasing and $\phi_1(0) = \phi_2(0) = 0$.

**(a)** Describe the three-dimensional production set associated with these two techniques. Assume free disposal.

**(b)** Give sufficient conditions on $\phi_1(\cdot), \phi_2(\cdot)$ for the production set to display additivity.

**(c)** Suppose that the input prices are $w_1$ and $w_2$. Write the first-order necessary conditions for profit maximization and interpret. Under which conditions on $\phi_1(\cdot), \phi_2(\cdot)$ will the necessary conditions be sufficient?

**(d)** Show that if $\phi_1(\cdot)$ and $\phi_2(\cdot)$ are strictly concave, then a cost-minimizing plan cannot involve the simultaneous use of the two techniques. Interpret the meaning of the concavity requirement, and draw isoquants in the two-dimensional space of input uses.

**5.C.1$^A$** In text.

**5.C.2$^A$** In text.

**5.C.3$^B$** Establish properties (viii) and (ix) of Proposition 5.C.2. [*Hint:* Property (viii) is easy; (ix) is more difficult. Try the one-input case first.]

**5.C.4$^A$** Establish properties (i) to (vii) of Proposition 5.C.2 for the case in which there are multiple outputs.

**5.C.5$^A$** Argue that for property (iii) of Proposition 5.C.2 to hold, it suffices that $f(\cdot)$ be quasiconcave. Show that quasiconcavity of $f(\cdot)$ is compatible with increasing returns.

**5.C.6$^C$** Suppose $f(z)$ is a concave production function with $L - 1$ inputs $(z_1, \ldots, z_{L-1})$. Suppose also that $\partial f(z)/\partial z_\ell \geq 0$ for all $\ell$ and $z \geq 0$ and that the matrix $D^2 f(z)$ is negative definite at all $z$. Use the firm's first-order conditions and the implicit function theorem to prove the following statements:

**(a)** An increase in the output price always increases the profit-maximizing level of output.

**(b)** An increase in output price increases the demand for *some* input.

**(c)** An increase in the price of an input leads to a reduction in the demand for the input.

**5.C.7$^C$** A price-taking firm producing a single product according to the technology $q = f(z_1, \ldots, z_{L-1})$ faces prices $p$ for its output and $w_1, \ldots, w_{L-1}$ for each of its inputs. Assume that $f(\cdot)$ is strictly concave and increasing, and that $\partial^2 f(z)/\partial z_\ell \, \partial z_k < 0$ for all $\ell \neq k$. Show that for all $\ell = 1, \ldots, L - 1$, the factor demand functions $z_\ell(p, w)$ satisfy $\partial z_\ell(p, w)/\partial p > 0$ and $\partial z_\ell(p, w)/\partial w_k < 0$ for all $k \neq \ell$.

**5.C.8$^B$** Alpha Incorporated (AI) produces a single output $q$ from two inputs $z_1$ and $z_2$. You are assigned to determine AI's technology. You are given 100 monthly observations. Two of these monthly observations are shown in the following table:

| | Input prices | | Input levels | | Output price | Output level |
|---|---|---|---|---|---|---|
| *Month* | $w_1$ | $w_2$ | $z_1$ | $z_2$ | $p$ | $q$ |
| 3 | 3 | 1 | 40 | 50 | 4 | 60 |
| 95 | 2 | 2 | 55 | 40 | 4 | 60 |

In light of these two monthly observations, what problem will you encounter in trying to accomplish your task?

**5.C.9$^A$** Derive the profit function $\pi(p)$ and supply function (or correspondence) $y(p)$ for the single-output technologies whose production functions $f(z)$ are given by

**(a)** $f(z) = \sqrt{z_1 + z_2}$.

**(b)** $f(z) = \sqrt{\text{Min}\{z_1, z_2\}}$.

**(c)** $f(z) = (z_1^\rho + z_2^\rho)^{1/\rho}$,   for $\rho \le 1$.

**5.C.10$^A$** Derive the cost function $c(w, q)$ and conditional factor demand functions (or correspondences) $z(w, q)$ for each of the following single-output constant return technologies with production functions given by

**(a)** $f(z) = z_1 + z_2$          (perfect substitutable inputs)

**(b)** $f(z) = \text{Min}\{z_1, z_2\}$          (Leontief technology)

**(c)** $f(z) = (z_1^\rho + z_2^\rho)^{1/\rho}$,   $\rho \le 1$   (constant elasticity of substitution technology)

**5.C.11$^A$** Show that $\partial z_\ell(w, q)/\partial q > 0$ if and only if marginal cost at $q$ is increasing in $w_\ell$.

**5.C.12$^A$** We saw at the end of Section 5.B that any convex $Y$ can be viewed as the section of a constant returns technology $Y' \subset \mathbb{R}^{L+1}$, where the $L + 1$ coordinate is fixed at the level $-1$. Show that if $y \in Y$ is profit maximizing at prices $p$ then $(y, -1) \in Y'$ is profit maximizing at $(p, \pi(p))$, that is, profits emerge as the price of the implicit fixed input. The converse is also true: If $(y, -1) \in Y'$ is profit maximizing at prices $(p, p_{L+1})$, then $y \in Y$ is profit maximizing at $p$ and the profit is $p_{L+1}$.

**5.C.13$^B$** A price-taking firm produces output $q$ from inputs $z_1$ and $z_2$ according to a differentiable concave production function $f(z_1, z_2)$. The price of its output is $p > 0$, and the prices of its inputs are $(w_1, w_2) \gg 0$. However, there are two unusual things about this firm. First, rather than maximizing profit, the firm maximizes revenue (the manager wants her firm to have bigger dollar sales than any other). Second, the firm is cash constrained. In particular, it has only $C$ dollars on hand before production and, as a result, its total expenditures on inputs cannot exceed $C$.

Suppose one of your econometrician friends tells you that she has used repeated observations of the firm's revenues under various output prices, input prices, and levels of the financial constraint and has determined that the firm's revenue level $R$ can be expressed as the following function of the variables $(p, w_1, w_2, C)$:

$$R(p, w_1, w_2, C) = p[\gamma + \ln C - \alpha \ln w_1 - (1 - \alpha) \ln w_2].$$

($\gamma$ and $\alpha$ are scalars whose values she tells you.) What is the firm's use of input $z_1$ when prices are $(p, w_1, w_2)$ and it has $C$ dollars of cash on hand?

**5.D.1$^A$** In text.

**5.D.2$^A$** In text.

**5.D.3$^B$** Suppose that a firm can produce good $L$ from $L - 1$ factor inputs ($L > 2$). Factor prices are $w \in \mathbb{R}^{L-1}$ and the price of output is $p$. The firm's differentiable cost function is $c(w, q)$. Assume that this function is strictly convex in $q$. However, although $c(w, q)$ is the cost function when all factors can be freely adjusted, factor 1 cannot be adjusted in the short run.

Suppose that the firm is initially at a point where it is producing its long-run profit-maximizing output level of good $L$ given prices $w$ and $p$, $q(w, p)$ [i.e., the level that is optimal under the long-run cost conditions described by $c(w, q)$], and that all inputs are optimally adjusted [i.e., $z_\ell = z_\ell(w, q(w, p))$ for all $\ell = 1, \ldots, L - 1$, where $z_\ell(\cdot, \cdot)$ is the long-run input demand function]. Show that the firm's profit-maximizing output response to a marginal increase in the price of good $L$ is larger in the long run than in the short run. [*Hint*: Define a short-run cost function $c_s(w, q \,|\, z_1)$ that gives the minimized costs of producing output level $q$ given that input 1 is fixed at level $z_1$.]

**5.D.4$^B$** Consider a firm that has a distinct set of inputs and outputs. The firm produces $M$ outputs; let $q = (q_1, \ldots, q_M)$ denote a vector of its output levels. Holding factor prices fixed, $C(q_1, \ldots, q_M)$ is the firm's cost function. We say that $C(\cdot)$ is *subadditive* if for all $(q_1, \ldots, q_M)$, there is no way to break up the production of amounts $(q_1, \ldots, q_M)$ among several firms, each with cost function $C(\cdot)$, and lower the costs of production. That is, there is no set of, say, $J$ firms and collection of production vectors $\{q_j = (q_{1j}, \ldots, q_{Mj})\}_{j=1}^{J}$ such that $\sum_j q_j = q$ and $\sum_j C(q_j) < C(q)$. When $C(\cdot)$ is subadditive, it is usual to say that the industry is a *natural monopoly* because production is cheapest when it is done by only one firm.

**(a)** Consider the single-output case, $M = 1$. Show that if $C(\cdot)$ exhibits decreasing average costs, then $C(\cdot)$ is subadditive.

**(b)** Now consider the multiple-output case, $M > 1$. Show by example that the following multiple-output extension of the decreasing average cost assumption is *not* sufficient for $C(\cdot)$ to be subadditive:

$$C(\cdot) \text{ exhibits } \textit{decreasing ray average cost } \text{if for any } q \in \mathbb{R}^M_+,$$

$$C(q) > C(kq)/k \text{ for all } k > 1.$$

**(c)** (Harder) Prove that, if $C(\cdot)$ exhibits decreasing ray average cost *and* is quasiconvex, then $C(\cdot)$ is subadditive. [Assume that $C(\cdot)$ is continuous, increasing, and satisfies $C(0) = 0$.]

**5.D.5$^B$** Suppose there are two goods: an input $z$ and an output $q$. The production function is $q = f(z)$. We assume that $f(\cdot)$ exhibits increasing returns to scale.

**(a)** Assume that $f(\cdot)$ is differentiable. Do the increasing returns of $f(\cdot)$ imply that the average product is necessarily nondecreasing in input? What about the marginal product?

**(b)** Suppose there is a representative consumer with the utility function $u(q) - z$ (the negative sign indicates that the input is taken away from the consumer). Suppose that $\bar{q} = f(\bar{z})$ is a production plan that maximizes the representative consumer utility. Argue, either mathematically or economically (disregard boundary solutions), that the equality of marginal utility and marginal cost is a necessary condition for this maximization problem.

**(c)** Assume the existence of a representative consumer as in (b). "The equality of marginal cost and marginal utility is a sufficient condition for the optimality of a production plan." Right or wrong? Discuss.

**5.E.1$^A$** Assuming that every $\pi_j(\cdot)$ is differentiable and that you already know that $\pi^*(p) = \sum_{j=1}^{J} \pi_j(p)$, give a proof of $y^*(p) = \sum_{j=1}^{J} y_j(p)$ using differentiability techniques.

**5.E.2$^A$** Verify that Proposition 5.E.1 and its interpretation do not depend on any convexity hypothesis on the sets $Y_1, \ldots, Y_J$.

**5.E.3$^B$** Assuming that the sets $Y_1, \ldots, Y_J$ are convex and satisfy the free disposal property, and that $\sum_{j=1}^{J} Y_j$ is closed, show that the latter set equals $\{y : p \cdot y \leq \sum_{j=1}^{J} \pi_j(p) \text{ for all } p \gg 0\}$.

**5.E.4$^B$** One output is produced from two inputs. There are many technologies. Every technology can produce up to one unit of output (but no more) with fixed and proportional input requirements $z_1$ and $z_2$. So a technology is characterized by $z = (z_1, z_2)$, and we can describe the population of technologies by a density function $g(z_1, z_2)$. Take this density to be uniform on the square $[0, 10] \times [0, 10]$.

**(a)** Given the input prices $w = (w_1, w_2)$, solve the profit maximization problem of a firm with characteristics $z$. The output price is 1.

**(b)** More generally, find the profit function $\pi(w_1, w_2, 1)$ for

$$w_1 \geq \frac{1}{10} \quad \text{and} \quad w_2 \geq \frac{1}{10}.$$

**(c)** Compute the aggregate input demand function. Ideally, do that directly, and check that the answer is correct by using your finding in (b); this way you also verify (b).

**(d)** What can you say about the aggregate production function? If you were to assume that the profit function derived in (b) is valid for $w_1 \geq 0$ and $w_2 \geq 0$, what would the underlying aggregate production function be?

**5.E.5[A]** (M. Weitzman) Suppose that there are $J$ single-output plants. Plant $j$'s average cost is $AC_j(q_j) = \alpha + \beta_j q_j$ for $q_j \geq 0$. Note that the coefficient $\alpha$ is the same for all plants but that the coefficient $\beta_j$ may differ from plant to plant. Consider the problem of determining the cost-minimizing aggregate production plan for producing a total output of $q$, where $q < (\alpha/\text{Max}_j |\beta_j|)$.

**(a)** If $\beta_j > 0$ for all $j$, how should output be allocated among the $J$ plants?

**(b)** If $\beta_j < 0$ for all $j$, how should output be allocated among the $J$ plants?

**(c)** What if $\beta_j > 0$ for some plants and $\beta_j < 0$ for others?

**5.F.1[A]** In text.

**5.G.1[B]** Let $f(z)$ be a single-input, single-output production function. Suppose that owners have quasilinear utilities with the firm's input as the numeraire.

**(a)** Show that a necessary condition for consumer–owners to unanimously agree to a production plan $z$ is that consumption shares among owners at prices $p(z)$ coincide with ownership shares.

**(b)** Suppose that ownership shares are identical. Comment on the conflicting instructions to managers and how they depend on the consumer–owners' tastes for output.

**(c)** With identical preferences and ownership shares, argue that owners will unanimously agree to maximize profits in terms of input. (Recall that we are assuming preferences are quasilinear with respect to input; hence, the numeraire is intrinsically determined.)

**5.AA.1[A]** Compute the cost function $c(w, 1)$ and the input demand $z(w, 1)$ for the production function in Figure 5.AA.4. Verify that whenever $z(w, 1)$ is single-valued, we have $z(w, 1) = \nabla_w c(w, 1)$.

**5.AA.2[B]** Consider a Leontief input–output model with no substitution. Assume that the input matrix $A$ is productive and that the vector of primary factor requirements $b$ is strictly positive.

**(a)** Show that for any $\alpha \geq 0$, the production plan

$$y = \begin{bmatrix} I - A \\ -b \end{bmatrix} \alpha.$$

is efficient.

**(b)** Fixing the price of the primary factor to equal 1, show that any production plan with $\alpha \gg 0$ is profit maximizing at a unique vector of prices.

**(c)** Show that the prices obtained in (b) have the interpretation of amounts of the primary factor directly or indirectly embodied in the production of one unit of the different goods.

**(d)** (Harder) Suppose that $A$ corresponds to the techniques singled out by the nonsubstitution theorem for a model that, in principle, admits substitution. Show that every component of the price vector obtained from $A$ in (c) is less than or equal to the corresponding component of the price vector obtained from any other selection of techniques.

**5.AA.3**[B] There are two produced goods and labor. The input–output matrix is

$$A = \begin{bmatrix} 0 & 1 \\ \alpha & 0 \end{bmatrix}.$$

Here $a_{\ell k}$ is the amount of good $\ell$ required to produce one unit of good $k$.

**(a)** Let $\alpha = \frac{1}{2}$, and suppose that the labor coefficients vector is

$$b = \begin{bmatrix} 1 \\ 2 \end{bmatrix},$$

where $b_1$ (respectively, $b_2$) is the amount of labor required to produce one unit of good 1 (respectively, good 2). Represent graphically the production possibility set (i.e., the locus of possible productions) for the two goods if the total availability of labor is 10.

**(b)** For the values of $\alpha$ and $b$ in (a), compute equilibrium prices $p_1, p_2$ (normalize the wage to equal 1) from the profit maximization conditions (assume positive production of the two goods).

**(c)** For the values of $\alpha$ and $b$ in (a), compute the amount of labor directly or indirectly incorporated into the production of one net (i.e., available for consumption) unit of good 1. How does this amount relate to your answer in **(b)**?

**(d)** Suppose there is a second technique to produce good 2. To

$$\begin{bmatrix} a_{12} \\ a_{22} \end{bmatrix} = \begin{bmatrix} 1 \\ 0 \end{bmatrix}, \qquad b_2 = 2$$

we now add

$$\begin{bmatrix} a'_{12} \\ a'_{22} \end{bmatrix} = \begin{bmatrix} \frac{1}{2} \\ 0 \end{bmatrix}, \qquad b'_2 = \beta.$$

Taking the two techniques into account, represent graphically the locus of amounts of good 1 and of labor necessary to produce one unit of good 2. (Assume free disposal.)

**(e)** In the context of **(d)**, what does the nonsubstitution theorem say? Determine the value of $\beta$ at which there is a switch of optimal techniques.

**5.AA.4**[B] Consider the following linear activity model:

$$a_1 = (1, -1, \quad 0, \quad 0)$$
$$a_2 = (0, -1, \quad 1, \quad 0)$$
$$a_3 = (0, \quad 0, -1, \quad 1)$$
$$a_4 = (2, \quad 0, \quad 0, -1)$$

**(a)** For each of the following input–output vectors, check whether they belong or do not belong to the aggregate production set. Justify your answers:

$$y_1 = (6, \quad 0, \quad 0, -2)$$
$$y_2 = (5, -3, \quad 0, -1)$$
$$y_3 = (6, -3, \quad 0, \quad 0)$$
$$y_4 = (0, -4, \quad 0, \quad 4)$$
$$y_5 = (0, -3, \quad 4, \quad 0)$$

**(b)** The input–output vector $y = (0, -5, 5, 0)$ is efficient. Prove this by finding a $p \gg 0$ for which $y$ is profit-maximizing.

**(c)** The input–output vector $y = (1, -1, 0, 0)$ is feasible, but it is not efficient. Why?

**5.AA.5**[B] [This exercise was inspired by an exercise of Champsaur and Milleron (1983).] There are four commodities indexed by $\ell = 1, 2, 3, 4$. The technology of a firm is described by eight elementary activities $a_m$, $m = 1, \ldots, 8$. With the usual sign convention, the numerical values of these activities are

$$a_1 = (\ -3,\ -6,\ 4,\ 0)$$
$$a_2 = (\ -7,\ -9,\ 3,\ 2)$$
$$a_3 = (\ -1,\ -2,\ 3, -1)$$
$$a_4 = (\ -8, -13,\ 3,\ 1)$$
$$a_5 = (-11, -19,\ 12,\ 0)$$
$$a_6 = (\ -4,\ -3, -2,\ 5)$$
$$a_7 = (\ -8,\ -5,\ 0,\ 10)$$
$$a_8 = (\ -2,\ -4,\ 5,\ 2)$$

It is assumed that any activity can be operated at any nonnegative level $\alpha_m \geq 0$ and that all activities can operate simultaneously at any scale (i.e., for any $\alpha_m \geq 0$, $m = 1, \ldots, 8$, the production $\sum_m \alpha_m a_m$ is feasible).

(a) Define the corresponding production set $Y$, and show that it is convex.

(b) Verify the no-free-lunch property.

(c) Verify that $Y$ does *not* satisfy the free-disposal property. The free-disposal property would be satisfied if we added new elementary activities to our list. How would you choose them (given specific numerical values)?

(d) Show by direct comparison of $a_1$ with $a_5$, $a_2$ with $a_4$, $a_3$ with $a_8$, and $a_6$ with $a_7$ that four of the elementary activities are not efficient.

(e) Show that $a_1$ and $a_2$ are inefficient be exhibiting two positive linear combinations of $a_3$ and $a_7$ that dominate $a_1$ and $a_2$, respectively.

(f) Could you venture a complete description of the set of efficient production vectors?

(g) Suppose that the amounts of the four goods available as initial resources to the firm are

$$s_1 = 480, \qquad s_2 = 300, \qquad s_3 = 0, \qquad s_4 = 0.$$

Subject to those limitations on the net use of resources, the firm is interested in maximizing the net production of the third good. How would you set up the problem as a linear program?

(h) By using all the insights you have gained on the set of efficient production vectors, can you solve the optimization problem in (g)? [*Hint*: It can be done graphically.]

# 6
# Choice Under Uncertainty

## 6.A Introduction

In previous chapters, we studied choices that result in perfectly certain outcomes. In reality, however, many important economic decisions involve an element of risk. Although it is formally possible to analyze these situations using the general theory of choice developed in Chapter 1, there is good reason to develop a more specialized theory: Uncertain alternatives have a structure that we can use to restrict the preferences that "rational" individuals may hold. Taking advantage of this structure allows us to derive stronger implications than those based solely on the framework of Chapter 1.

In Section 6.B, we begin our study of choice under uncertainty by considering a setting in which alternatives with uncertain outcomes are describable by means of objectively known probabilities defined on an abstract set of possible outcomes. These representations of risky alternatives are called *lotteries*. In the spirit of Chapter 1, we assume that the decision maker has a rational preference relation over these lotteries. We then proceed to derive the *expected utility theorem*, a result of central importance. This theorem says that under certain conditions, we can represent preferences by an extremely convenient type of utility function, one that possesses what is called the *expected utility form*. The key assumption leading to this result is the *independence axiom*, which we discuss extensively.

In the remaining sections, we focus on the special case in which the outcome of a risky choice is an amount of money (or any other one-dimensional measure of consumption). This case underlies much of finance and portfolio theory, as well as substantial areas of applied economics.

In Section 6.C, we present the concept of *risk aversion* and discuss its measurement. We then study the comparison of risk aversions both across different individuals and across different levels of an individual's wealth.

Section 6.D is concerned with the comparison of alternative distributions of monetary returns. We ask when one distribution of monetary returns can unambiguously be said to be "better" than another, and also when one distribution can be said to be "more risky than" another. These comparisons lead, respectively, to the concepts of *first-order* and *second-order stochastic dominance*.

In Section 6.E, we extend the basic theory by allowing utility to depend on *states of nature* underlying the uncertainty as well as on the monetary payoffs. In the process, we develop a framework for modeling uncertainty in terms of these underlying states. This framework is often of great analytical convenience, and we use it extensively later in this book.

In Section 6.F, we consider briefly the theory of *subjective probability*. The assumption that uncertain prospects are offered to us with known objective probabilities, which we use in Section 6.B to derive the expected utility theorem, is rarely descriptive of reality. The subjective probability framework offers a way of modeling choice under uncertainty in which the probabilities of different risky alternatives are not given to the decision maker in any objective fashion. Yet, as we shall see, the theory of subjective probability offers something of a rescue for our earlier objective probability approach.

For further reading on these topics, see Kreps (1988) and Machina (1987). Diamond and Rothschild (1978) is an excellent sourcebook for original articles.

# 6.B  Expected Utility Theory

We begin this section by developing a formal apparatus for modeling risk. We then apply this framework to the study of preferences over risky alternatives and to establish the important expected utility theorem.

### Description of Risky Alternatives

Let us imagine that a decision maker faces a choice among a number of risky alternatives. Each risky alternative may result in one of a number of possible *outcomes*, but which outcome will actually occur is uncertain at the time that he must make his choice.

Formally, we denote the set of all possible outcomes by $C$.[1] These outcomes could take many forms. They could, for example, be consumption bundles. In this case, $C = X$, the decision maker's consumption set. Alternatively, the outcomes might take the simpler form of monetary payoffs. This case will, in fact, be our leading example later in this chapter. Here, however, we treat $C$ as an abstract set and therefore allow for very general outcomes.

To avoid some technicalities, we assume in this section that the number of possible outcomes in $C$ is finite, and we index these outcomes by $n = 1, \ldots, N$.

Throughout this and the next several sections, we assume that the probabilities of the various outcomes arising from any chosen alternative are *objectively known*. For example, the risky alternatives might be monetary gambles on the spin of an unbiased roulette wheel.

The basic building block of the theory is the concept of a *lottery*, a formal device that is used to represent risky alternatives.

**Definition 6.B.1:** A *simple lottery* $L$ is a list $L = (p_1, \ldots, p_N)$ with $p_n \geq 0$ for all $n$ and $\sum_n p_n = 1$, where $p_n$ is interpreted as the probability of outcome $n$ occurring.

---

1. It is also common, following Savage (1954), to refer to the elements of $C$ as *consequences*.

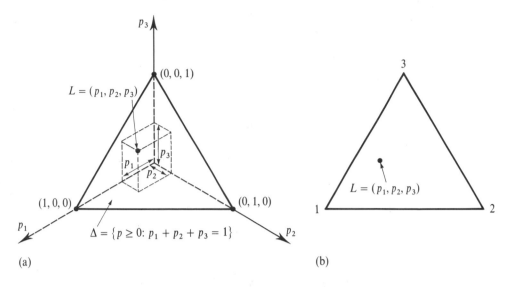

**Figure 6.B.1**

Representations of the simplex when $N = 3$. (a) Three-dimensional representation. (b) Two-dimensional representation.

A simple lottery can be represented geometrically as a point in the $(N-1)$ *dimensional simplex*, $\Delta = \{p \in \mathbb{R}_+^N : p_1 + \cdots + p_N = 1\}$. Figure 6.B.1(a) depicts this simplex for the case in which $N = 3$. Each vertex of the simplex stands for the degenerate lottery where one outcome is certain and the other two outcomes have probability zero. Each point in the simplex represents a lottery over the three outcomes. When $N = 3$, it is convenient to depict the simplex in two dimensions, as in Figure 6.B.1(b), where it takes the form of an equilateral triangle.[2]

In a simple lottery, the outcomes that may result are certain. A more general variant of a lottery, known as a *compound lottery*, allows the outcomes of a lottery themselves to be simple lotteries.[3]

**Definition 6.B.2:** Given $K$ simple lotteries $L_k = (p_1^k, \ldots, p_N^k)$, $k = 1, \ldots, K$, and probabilities $\alpha_k \geq 0$ with $\sum_k \alpha_k = 1$, the *compound lottery* $(L_1, \ldots, L_K; \alpha_1, \ldots, \alpha_K)$ is the risky alternative that yields the simple lottery $L_k$ with probability $\alpha_k$ for $k = 1, \ldots, K$.

For any compound lottery $(L_1, \ldots, L_K; \alpha_1, \ldots, \alpha_K)$, we can calculate a corresponding *reduced lottery* as the simple lottery $L = (p_1, \ldots, p_N)$ that generates the same ultimate distribution over outcomes. The value of each $p_n$ is obtained by multiplying the probability that each lottery $L_k$ arises, $\alpha_k$, by the probability $p_n^k$ that outcome $n$ arises in lottery $L_k$, and then adding over $k$. That is, the probability of outcome $n$ in the reduced lottery is

$$p_n = \alpha_1 p_n^1 + \cdots + \alpha_K p_n^K$$

---

2. Recall that equilateral triangles have the property that the sum of the perpendiculars from any point to the three sides is equal to the altitude of the triangle. It is therefore common to depict the simplex when $N = 3$ as an equilateral triangle with altitude equal to 1 because by doing so, we have the convenient geometric property that the probability $p_n$ of outcome $n$ in the lottery associated with some point in this simplex is equal to the length of the perpendicular from this point to the side opposite the vertex labeled $n$.

3. We could also define compound lotteries with more than two stages. We do not do so because we will not need them in this chapter. The principles involved, however, are the same.

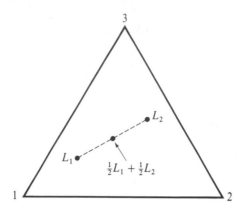

**Figure 6.B.2**

The reduced lottery of a compound lottery.

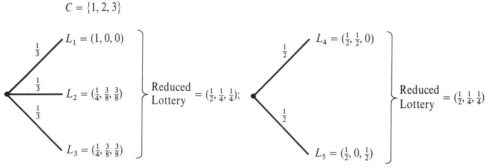

**Figure 6.B.3**

Two compound lotteries with the same reduced lottery.

for $n = 1, \ldots, N.$[4] Therefore, the reduced lottery $L$ of any compound lottery $(L_1, \ldots, L_K; \alpha_1, \ldots, \alpha_K)$ can be obtained by vector addition:

$$L = \alpha_1 L_1 + \cdots + \alpha_K L_K \in \Delta.$$

In Figure 6.B.2, two simple lotteries $L_1$ and $L_2$ are depicted in the simplex $\Delta$. Also depicted is the reduced lottery $\frac{1}{2}L_1 + \frac{1}{2}L_2$ for the compound lottery $(L_1, L_2; \frac{1}{2}, \frac{1}{2})$ that yields either $L_1$ or $L_2$ with a probability of $\frac{1}{2}$ each. This reduced lottery lies at the midpoint of the line segment connecting $L_1$ and $L_2$. The linear structure of the space of lotteries is central to the theory of choice under uncertainty, and we exploit it extensively in what follows.

### Preferences over Lotteries

Having developed a way to model risky alternatives, we now study the decision maker's preferences over them. The theoretical analysis to follow rest on a basic *consequentialist* premise: We assume that for any risky alternative, only the reduced lottery over final outcomes is of relevance to the decision maker. Whether the probabilities of various outcomes arise as a result of a simple lottery or of a more complex compound lottery has no significance. Figure 6.B.3 exhibits two different compound lotteries that yield the same reduced lottery. Our consequentialist hypothesis requires that the decision maker view these two lotteries as equivalent.

---

4. Note that $\sum_n p_n = \sum_k \alpha_k (\sum_n p_n^k) = \sum_k \alpha_k = 1$.

We now pose the decision maker's choice problem in the general framework developed in Chapter 1 (see Section 1.B). In accordance with our consequentialist premise, we take the set of alternatives, denoted here by $\mathscr{L}$, to be *the set of all simple lotteries over the set of outcomes C*. We next assume that the decision maker has a rational preference relation $\succsim$ on $\mathscr{L}$, a complete and transitive relation allowing comparison of any pair of simple lotteries. It should be emphasized that, if anything, the rationality assumption is stronger here than in the theory of choice under certainty discussed in Chapter 1. The more complex the alternatives, the heavier the burden carried by the rationality postulates. In fact, their realism in an uncertainty context has been much debated. However, because we want to concentrate on the properties that are specific to uncertainty, we do not question the rationality assumption further here.

We next introduce two additional assumptions about the decision maker's preferences over lotteries. The most important and controversial is the *independence axiom*. The first, however, is a continuity axiom similar to the one discussed in Section 3.C.

**Definition 6.B.3:** The preference relation $\succsim$ on the space of simple lotteries $\mathscr{L}$ is *continuous* if for any $L, L', L'' \in \mathscr{L}$, the sets

$$\{\alpha \in [0, 1]: \alpha L + (1 - \alpha)L' \succsim L''\} \subset [0, 1]$$

and

$$\{\alpha \in [0, 1]: L'' \succsim \alpha L + (1 - \alpha)L'\} \subset [0, 1]$$

are closed.

In words, continuity means that small changes in probabilities do not change the nature of the ordering between two lotteries. For example, if a "beautiful and uneventful trip by car" is preferred to "staying home," then a mixture of the outcome "beautiful and uneventful trip by car" with a sufficiently small but positive probability of "death by car accident" is still preferred to "staying home." Continuity therefore rules out the case where the decision maker has lexicographic ("safety first") preferences for alternatives with a zero probability of some outcome (in this case, "death by car accident").

As in Chapter 3, the continuity axiom implies the existence of a utility function representing $\succsim$, a function $U: \mathscr{L} \to \mathbb{R}$ such that $L \succsim L'$ if and only if $U(L) \geq U(L')$. Our second assumption, the independence axiom, will allow us to impose considerably more structure on $U(\cdot)$.[5]

**Definition 6.B.4:** The preference relation $\succsim$ on the space of simple lotteries $\mathscr{L}$ satisfies the *independence axiom* if for all $L, L', L'' \in \mathscr{L}$ and $\alpha \in (0, 1)$ we have

$$L \succsim L' \quad \text{if and only if} \quad \alpha L + (1 - \alpha)L'' \succsim \alpha L' + (1 - \alpha)L''.$$

In other words, if we mix each of two lotteries with a third one, then the preference ordering of the two resulting mixtures does not depend on (is *independent* of) the particular third lottery used.

---

5. The independence axiom was first proposed by von Neumann and Morgenstern (1944) as an incidental result in the theory of games.

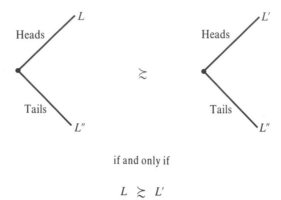

if and only if

$$L \succsim L'$$

**Figure 6.B.4**

The independence
axiom.

Suppose, for example, that $L \succsim L'$ and $\alpha = \frac{1}{2}$. Then $\frac{1}{2}L + \frac{1}{2}L''$ can be thought of as the compound lottery arising from a coin toss in which the decision maker gets $L$ if heads comes up and $L''$ if tails does. Similarly, $\frac{1}{2}L' + \frac{1}{2}L''$ would be the coin toss where heads results in $L'$ and tails results in $L''$ (see Figure 6.B.4). Note that conditional on heads, lottery $\frac{1}{2}L + \frac{1}{2}L''$ is at least as good as lottery $\frac{1}{2}L' + \frac{1}{2}L''$; but conditional on tails, the two compound lotteries give identical results. The independence axiom requires the sensible conclusion that $\frac{1}{2}L + \frac{1}{2}L''$ be at least as good as $\frac{1}{2}L' + \frac{1}{2}L''$.

The independence axiom is at the heart of the theory of choice under uncertainty. It is unlike anything encountered in the formal theory of preference-based choice discussed in Chapter 1 or its applications in Chapters 3 to 5. This is so precisely because it exploits, in a fundamental manner, the structure of uncertainty present in the model. In the theory of consumer demand, for example, there is no reason to believe that a consumer's preferences over various bundles of goods 1 and 2 should be independent of the quantities of the other goods that he will consume. In the present context, however, it *is* natural to think that a decision maker's preference between two lotteries, say $L$ and $L'$, should determine which of the two he prefers to have as part of a compound lottery *regardless* of the other possible outcome of this compound lottery, say $L''$. This other outcome $L''$ should be irrelevant to his choice because, in contrast with the consumer context, he does not consume $L$ or $L'$ together with $L''$ but, rather, only *instead* of it (if $L$ or $L'$ is the realized outcome).

**Exercise 6.B.1:** Show that if the preferences $\succsim$ over $\mathscr{L}$ satisfy the independence axiom, then for all $\alpha \in (0, 1)$ and $L, L', L'' \in \mathscr{L}$ we have

$$L \succ L' \quad \text{if and only if} \quad \alpha L + (1 - \alpha)L'' \succ \alpha L' + (1 - \alpha)L''$$

and

$$L \sim L' \quad \text{if and only if} \quad \alpha L + (1 - \alpha)L'' \sim \alpha L' + (1 - \alpha)L''.$$

Show also that if $L \succ L'$ and $L'' \succ L'''$, then $\alpha L + (1 - \alpha)L'' \succ \alpha L' + (1 - \alpha)L'''$.

As we will see shortly, the independence axiom is intimately linked to the representability of preferences over lotteries by a utility function that has an *expected utility form*. Before obtaining that result, we define this property and study some of its features.

**Definition 6.B.5:** The utility function $U: \mathcal{L} \to \mathbb{R}$ has an *expected utility form* if there is an assignment of numbers $(u_1, \ldots, u_N)$ to the $N$ outcomes such that for every simple lottery $L = (p_1, \ldots, p_N) \in \mathcal{L}$ we have

$$U(L) = u_1 p_1 + \cdots + u_N p_N.$$

A utility function $U: \mathcal{L} \to \mathbb{R}$ with the expected utility form is called a *von Neumann–Morgenstern (v.N–M) expected utility function*.

Observe that if we let $L^n$ denote the lottery that yields outcome $n$ with probability one, then $U(L^n) = u_n$. Thus, the term *expected utility* is appropriate because with the v.N–M expected utility form, the utility of a lottery can be thought of as the expected value of the utilities $u_n$ of the $N$ outcomes.

The expression $U(L) = \sum_n u_n p_n$ is a general form for a *linear function in the probabilities* $(p_1, \ldots, p_N)$. This linearity property suggests a useful way to think about the expected utility form.

**Proposition 6.B.1:** A utility function $U: \mathcal{L} \to \mathbb{R}$ has an expected utility form if and only if it is *linear*, that is, if and only if it satisfies the property that

$$U\left( \sum_{k=1}^{K} \alpha_K L_k \right) = \sum_{k=1}^{K} \alpha_k U(L_k) \tag{6.B.1}$$

for any $K$ lotteries $L_k \in \mathcal{L}$, $k = 1, \ldots, K$, and probabilities $(\alpha_1, \ldots, \alpha_K) \geq 0$, $\sum_k \alpha_k = 1$.

**Proof:** Suppose that $U(\cdot)$ satisfies property (6.B.1). We can write any $L = (p_1, \ldots, p_N)$ as a convex combination of the degenerate lotteries $(L^1, \ldots, L^N)$, that is, $L = \sum_n p_n L^n$. We have then $U(L) = U(\sum_n p_n L^n) = \sum_n p_n U(L^n) = \sum_n p_n u_n$. Thus, $U(\cdot)$ has the expected utility form.

In the other direction, suppose that $U(\cdot)$ has the expected utility form, and consider any compound lottery $(L_1, \ldots, L_K; \alpha_1, \ldots, \alpha_K)$, where $L_k = (p_1^k, \ldots, p_N^k)$. Its reduced lottery is $L' = \sum_k \alpha_k L_k$. Hence,

$$U\left( \sum_k \alpha_k L_k \right) = \sum_n u_n \left( \sum_k \alpha_k p_n^k \right) = \sum_k \alpha_k \left( \sum_n u_n p_n^k \right) = \sum_k \alpha_k U(L_k).$$

Thus, property (6.B.1) is satisfied. ∎

The expected utility property is a *cardinal* property of utility functions defined on the space of lotteries. In particular, the result in Proposition 6.B.2 shows that the expected utility form is preserved only by increasing *linear* transformations.

**Proposition 6.B.2:** Suppose that $U: \mathcal{L} \to \mathbb{R}$ is a v.N–M expected utility function for the preference relation $\succsim$ on $\mathcal{L}$. Then $\tilde{U}: \mathcal{L} \to \mathbb{R}$ is another v.N–M utility function for $\succsim$ if and only if there are scalars $\beta > 0$ and $\gamma$ such that $\tilde{U}(L) = \beta U(L) + \gamma$ for every $L \in \mathcal{L}$.

**Proof:** Begin by choosing two lotteries $\bar{L}$ and $\underline{L}$ with the property that $\bar{L} \succsim L \succsim \underline{L}$ for all $L \in \mathcal{L}$.[6] If $\bar{L} \sim \underline{L}$, then every utility function is a constant and the result follows immediately. Therefore, we assume from now on that $\bar{L} \succ \underline{L}$.

---

6. These best and worst lotteries can be shown to exist. We could, for example, choose a maximizer and a minimizer of the linear, hence continuous, function $U(\cdot)$ on the simplex of probabilities, a compact set.

Note first that if $U(\cdot)$ is a v.N–M expected utility function and $\tilde{U}(L) = \beta U(L) + \gamma$, then

$$\tilde{U}\left(\sum_{k=1}^{K} \alpha_k L_k\right) = \beta U\left(\sum_{k=1}^{K} \alpha_k L_k\right) + \gamma$$

$$= \beta\left[\sum_{k=1}^{K} \alpha_k U(L_k)\right] + \gamma$$

$$= \sum_{k=1}^{K} \alpha_k [\beta U(L_k) + \gamma]$$

$$= \sum_{k=1}^{K} \alpha_k \tilde{U}(L_k).$$

Since $\tilde{U}(\cdot)$ satisfies property (6.B.1), it has the expected utility form.

For the reverse direction, we want to show that if both $\tilde{U}(\cdot)$ and $U(\cdot)$ have the expected utility form, then constants $\beta > 0$ and $\gamma$ exist such that $\tilde{U}(L) = \beta U(L) + \gamma$ for all $L \in \mathcal{L}$. To do so, consider any lottery $L \in \mathcal{L}$, and define $\lambda_L \in [0,1]$ by

$$U(L) = \lambda_L U(\bar{L}) + (1 - \lambda_L) U(\underline{L}).$$

Thus

$$\lambda_L = \frac{U(L) - U(\underline{L})}{U(\bar{L}) - U(\underline{L})} \tag{6.B.2}$$

Since $\lambda_L U(\bar{L}) + (1 - \lambda_L) U(\underline{L}) = U(\lambda_L \bar{L} + (1 - \lambda_L)\underline{L})$ and $U(\cdot)$ represents the preferences $\succsim$, it must be that $L \sim \lambda_L \bar{L} + (1 - \lambda_L)\underline{L}$. But if so, then since $\tilde{U}(\cdot)$ is also linear and represents these same preferences, we have

$$\tilde{U}(L) = \tilde{U}(\lambda_L \bar{L} + (1 - \lambda_L)\underline{L})$$

$$= \lambda_L \tilde{U}(\bar{L}) + (1 - \lambda_L)\tilde{U}(\underline{L})$$

$$= \lambda_L(\tilde{U}(\bar{L}) - \tilde{U}(\underline{L})) + \tilde{U}(\underline{L}).$$

Substituting for $\lambda_L$ from (6.B.2) and rearranging terms yields the conclusion that $\tilde{U}(L) = \beta U(L) + \gamma$, where

$$\beta = \frac{\tilde{U}(\bar{L}) - \tilde{U}(\underline{L})}{U(\bar{L}) - U(\underline{L})}$$

and

$$\gamma = \tilde{U}(\underline{L}) - U(\underline{L})\frac{\tilde{U}(\bar{L}) - \tilde{U}(\underline{L})}{U(\bar{L}) - U(\underline{L})}.$$

This completes the proof ∎

A consequence of Proposition 6.B.2 is that for a utility function with the expected utility form, differences of utilities have meaning. For example, if there are four outcomes, the statement "the difference in utility between outcomes 1 and 2 is greater than the difference between outcomes 3 and 4," $u_1 - u_2 > u_3 - u_4$, is equivalent to

$$\tfrac{1}{2}u_1 + \tfrac{1}{2}u_4 > \tfrac{1}{2}u_2 + \tfrac{1}{2}u_3.$$

Therefore, the statement means that the lottery $L = (\tfrac{1}{2}, 0, 0, \tfrac{1}{2})$ is preferred to the lottery $L' = (0, \tfrac{1}{2}, \tfrac{1}{2}, 0)$. This ranking of utility differences is preserved by all linear transformations of the v.N–M expected utility function.

Note that if a preference relation $\succsim$ on $\mathscr{L}$ is representable by a utility function $U(\cdot)$ that has the expected utility form, then since a linear utility function is continuous, it follows that $\succsim$ is continuous on $\mathscr{L}$. More importantly, the preference relation $\succsim$ must also satisfy the independence axiom. You are asked to show this in Exercise 6.B.2.

**Exercise 6.B.2:** Show that if the preference relation $\succsim$ on $\mathscr{L}$ is represented by a utility function $U(\cdot)$ that has the expected utility form, then $\succsim$ satisfies the independence axiom.

The expected utility theorem, the central result of this section, tells us that the converse is also true.

### The Expected Utility Theorem

The *expected utility theorem* says that if the decision maker's preferences over lotteries satisfy the continuity and independence axioms, then his preferences are representable by a utility function with the expected utility form. It is the most important result in the theory of choice under uncertainty, and the rest of the book bears witness to its usefulness.

Before stating and proving the result formally, however, it may be helpful to attempt an intuitive understanding of why it is true.

Consider the case where there are only three outcomes. As we have already observed, the continuity axiom insures that preferences on lotteries can be represented by some utility function. Suppose that we represent the indifference map in the simplex, as in Figure 6.B.5. Assume, for simplicity, that we have a conventional map with one-dimensional indifference curves. Because the expected utility form is linear in the probabilities, representability by the expected utility form is equivalent to these indifference curves being straight, parallel lines (you should check this). Figure 6.B.5(a) exhibits an indifference map satisfying these properties. We now argue that these properties are, in fact, consequences of the independence axiom.

Indifference curves are straight lines if, for every pair of lotteries $L, L'$, we have that $L \sim L'$ implies $\alpha L + (1 - \alpha)L' \sim L$ for all $\alpha \in [0,1]$. Figure 6.B.5(b) depicts a situation where the indifference curve is not a straight line; we have $L' \sim L$ but

**Figure 6.B.5** Geometric explanation of the expected utility theorem. (a) $\succsim$ is representable by a utility function with the expected utility form. (b) Contradiction of the independence axiom. (c) Contradiction of the independence axiom.

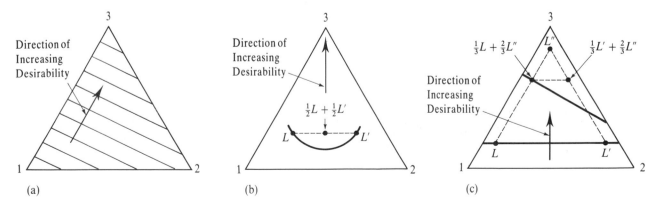

$\frac{1}{2}L' + \frac{1}{2}L \succ L$. This is equivalent to saying that

$$\frac{1}{2}L' + \frac{1}{2}L \succ \frac{1}{2}L + \frac{1}{2}L. \tag{6.B.3}$$

But since $L \sim L'$, the independence axiom implies that we must have $\frac{1}{2}L' + \frac{1}{2}L \sim \frac{1}{2}L + \frac{1}{2}L$ (see Exercise 6.B.1). This contradicts (6.B.3), and so we must conclude that indifference curves are straight lines.

Figure 6.B.5(c) depicts two straight but nonparallel indifference lines. A violation of the independence axiom can be constructed in this case, as indicated in the figure. There we have $L \succsim L'$ (in fact, $L \sim L'$), but $\frac{1}{3}L + \frac{2}{3}L'' \succsim \frac{1}{3}L' + \frac{2}{3}L''$ does not hold for the lottery $L''$ shown in the figure. Thus, indifference curves must be parallel, straight lines if preferences satisfy the independence axiom.

In Proposition 6.B.3, we formally state and prove the expected utility theorem.

**Proposition 6.B.3:** *(Expected Utility Theorem)* Suppose that the rational preference relation $\succsim$ on the space of lotteries $\mathscr{L}$ satisfies the continuity and independence axioms. Then $\succsim$ admits a utility representation of the expected utility form. That is, we can assign a number $u_n$ to each outcome $n = 1, \ldots, N$ in such a manner that for any two lotteries $L = (p_1, \ldots, p_N)$ and $L' = (p'_1, \ldots, p'_N)$, we have

$$L \succsim L' \quad \text{if and only if} \quad \sum_{n=1}^{N} u_n p_n \geq \sum_{n=1}^{N} u_n p'_n. \tag{6.B.4}$$

**Proof:** We organize the proof in a succession of steps. For simplicity, we assume that there are best and worst lotteries in $\mathscr{L}$, $\bar{L}$ and $\underline{L}$ (so, $\bar{L} \succsim L \succsim \underline{L}$ for any $L \in \mathscr{L}$).[7] If $\bar{L} \sim \underline{L}$, then all lotteries in $\mathscr{L}$ are indifferent and the conclusion of the proposition holds trivially. Hence, from now on, we assume that $\bar{L} \succ \underline{L}$.

*Step 1.   If $L \succ L'$ and $\alpha \in (0, 1)$, then $L \succ \alpha L + (1 - \alpha)L' \succ L'$.*

This claim makes sense. A nondegenerate mixture of two lotteries will hold a preference position strictly intermediate between the positions of the two lotteries. Formally, the claim follows from the independence axiom. In particular, since $L \succ L'$, the independence axiom implies that (recall Exercise 6.B.1)

$$L = \alpha L + (1 - \alpha)L \succ \alpha L + (1 - \alpha)L' \succ \alpha L' + (1 - \alpha)L' = L'.$$

*Step 2.   Let $\alpha, \beta \in [0, 1]$. Then $\beta \bar{L} + (1 - \beta)\underline{L} \succ \alpha \bar{L} + (1 - \alpha)\underline{L}$ if and only if $\beta > \alpha$.*

Suppose that $\beta > \alpha$. Note first that we can write

$$\beta \bar{L} + (1 - \beta)\underline{L} = \gamma \bar{L} + (1 - \gamma)[\alpha \bar{L} + (1 - \alpha)\underline{L}],$$

where $\gamma = [(\beta - \alpha)/(1 - \alpha)] \in (0, 1]$. By Step 1, we know that $\bar{L} \succ \alpha \bar{L} + (1 - \alpha)\underline{L}$. Applying Step 1 again, this implies that $\gamma \bar{L} + (1 - \gamma)(\alpha \bar{L} + (1 - \alpha)\underline{L}) \succ \alpha \bar{L} + (1 - \alpha)\underline{L}$, and so we conclude that $\beta \bar{L} + (1 - \beta)\underline{L} \succ \alpha \bar{L} + (1 - \alpha)\underline{L}$.

For the converse, suppose that $\beta \leq \alpha$. If $\beta = \alpha$, we must have $\beta \bar{L} + (1 - \beta)\underline{L} \sim \alpha \bar{L} + (1 - \alpha)\underline{L}$. So suppose that $\beta < \alpha$. By the argument proved in the previous

---

7. In fact, with our assumption of a finite set of outcomes, this can be established as a consequence of the independence axiom (see Exercise 6.B.3).

paragraph (reversing the roles of $\alpha$ and $\beta$), we must then have $\alpha \bar{L} + (1 - \alpha)\underline{L} \succ \beta \bar{L} + (1 - \beta)\underline{L}$.

*Step 3.  For any $L \in \mathscr{L}$, there is a unique $\alpha_L$ such that $[\alpha_L \bar{L} + (1 - \alpha_L)\underline{L}] \sim L$.*

Existence of such an $\alpha_L$ is implied by the continuity of $\succsim$ and the fact that $\bar{L}$ and $\underline{L}$ are, respectively, the best and the worst lottery. Uniqueness follows from the result of Step 2.

---

The existence of $\alpha_L$ is established in a manner similar to that used in the proof of Proposition 3.C.1. Specifically, define the sets

$$\{\alpha \in [0, 1] : \alpha \bar{L} + (1 - \alpha)\underline{L} \succsim L\} \quad \text{and} \quad \{\alpha \in [0, 1] : L \succsim \alpha \bar{L} + (1 - \alpha)\underline{L}\}.$$

By the continuity and completeness of $\succsim$, both sets are closed, and any $\alpha \in [0, 1]$ belongs to at least one of the two sets. Since both sets are nonempty and $[0, 1]$ is connected, it follows that there is some $\alpha$ belonging to both. This establishes the existence of an $\alpha_L$ such that $\alpha_L \bar{L} + (1 - \alpha_L)\underline{L} \sim L$.

---

*Step 4.  The function $U : \mathscr{L} \to \mathbb{R}$ that assigns $U(L) = \alpha_L$ for all $L \in \mathscr{L}$ represents the preference relation $\succsim$.*

Observe that, by Step 3, for any two lotteries $L, L' \in \mathscr{L}$, we have

$$L \succsim L' \quad \text{if and only if} \quad \alpha_L \bar{L} + (1 - \alpha_L)\underline{L} \succsim \alpha_{L'} \bar{L} + (1 - \alpha_{L'})\underline{L}.$$

Thus, by Step 2, $L \succsim L'$ if and only if $\alpha_L \geq \alpha_{L'}$.

*Step 5.  The utility function $U(\cdot)$ that assigns $U(L) = \alpha_L$ for all $L \in \mathscr{L}$ is linear and therefore has the expected utility form.*

We want to show that for any $L, L' \in \mathscr{L}$, and $\beta \in [0, 1]$, we have $U(\beta L + (1 - \beta)L') = \beta U(L) + (1 - \beta)U(L')$. By definition, we have

$$L \sim U(L)\bar{L} + (1 - U(L))\underline{L}$$

and

$$L' \sim U(L')\bar{L} + (1 - U(L'))\underline{L}.$$

Therefore, by the independence axiom (applied twice),

$$\beta L + (1 - \beta)L' \sim \beta[U(L)\bar{L} + (1 - U(L))\underline{L}] + (1 - \beta)L'$$

$$\sim \beta[U(L)\bar{L} + (1 - U(L))\underline{L}] + (1 - \beta)[U(L')\bar{L} + (1 - U(L'))\underline{L}].$$

Rearranging terms, we see that the last lottery is algebraically identical to the lottery

$$[\beta U(L) + (1 - \beta)U(L')]\bar{L} + [1 - \beta U(L) - (1 - \beta)U(L')]\underline{L}.$$

In other words, the compound lottery that gives lottery $[U(L)\bar{L} + (1 - U(L))\underline{L}]$ with probability $\beta$ and lottery $[U(L')\bar{L} + (1 - U(L'))\underline{L}]$ with probability $(1 - \beta)$ has the same reduced lottery as the compound lottery that gives lottery $\bar{L}$ with probability $[\beta U(L) + (1 - \beta)U(L')]$ and lottery $\underline{L}$ with probability $[1 - \beta U(L) - (1 - \beta)U(L')]$. Thus

$$\beta L + (1 - \beta)L' \sim [\beta U(L) + (1 - \beta)U(L')]\bar{L} + [1 - \beta U(L) - (1 - \beta)U(L')]\underline{L}.$$

By the construction of $U(\cdot)$ in Step 4, we therefore have

$$U(\beta L + (1 - \beta)L') = \beta U(L) + (1 - \beta)U(L'),$$

as we wanted.

Together, Steps 1 to 5 establish the existence of a utility function representing $\succsim$ that has the expected utility form. ∎

### Discussion of the Theory of Expected Utility

A first advantage of the expected utility theorem is technical: It is extremely convenient analytically. This, more than anything else, probably accounts for its pervasive use in economics. It is very easy to work with expected utility and very difficult to do without it. As we have already noted, the rest of the book attests to the importance of the result. Later in this chapter, we will explore some of the analytical uses of expected utility.

A second advantage of the theorem is normative: Expected utility may provide a valuable guide to action. People often find it hard to think systematically about risky alternatives. But if an individual believes that his choices should satisfy the axioms on which the theorem is based (notably, the independence axiom), then the theorem can be used as a guide in his decision process. This point is illustrated in Example 6.B.1.

**Example 6.B.1:** *Expected Utility as a Guide to Introspection.* A decision maker may not be able to assess his preference ordering between the lotteries $L$ and $L'$ depicted in Figure 6.B.6. The lotteries are too close together, and the differences in the probabilities involved are too small to be understood. Yet, if the decision maker believes that his preferences should satisfy the assumptions of the expected utility theorem, then he may consider $L''$ instead, which is on the straight line spanned by $L$ and $L'$ but at a significant distance from $L$. The lottery $L''$ may not be a feasible choice, but if he determines that $L'' \succ L$, then he can conclude that $L' \succ L$. Indeed, if $L'' \succ L$, then there is an indifference curve separating these two lotteries, as shown in the figure, and it follows from the fact that indifference curves are a family of parallel straight lines that there is also an indifference curve separating $L'$ and $L$, so that $L' \succ L$. Note that this type of inference is not possible using only the general

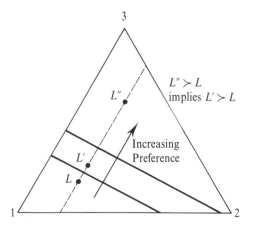

**Figure 6.B.6**

Expected utility as a guide to introspection.

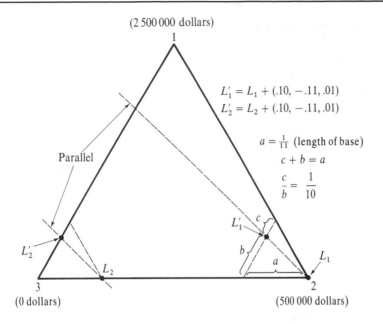

**Figure 6.B.7**

Depiction of the Allais paradox in the simplex.

choice theory of Chapter 1 because, without the hypotheses of the expected utility theorem, the indifference curves need not be straight lines (with a general indifference map, we could perfectly well have $L'' \succ L$ and $L \succ L'$).

A concrete example of this use of the expected utility theorem is developed in Exercise 6.B.4. ∎

As a descriptive theory, however, the expected utility theorem (and, by implication, its central assumption, the independence axiom), is not without difficulties. Examples 6.B.2 and 6.B.3 are designed to test its plausibility.

**Example 6.B.2:** *The Allais Paradox.*  This example, known as the Allais paradox [from Allais (1953)], constitutes the oldest and most famous challenge to the expected utility theorem. It is a thought experiment. There are three possible monetary prizes (so the number of outcomes is $N = 3$):

| *First Prize* | *Second Prize* | *Third Prize* |
|:---:|:---:|:---:|
| 2 500 000 dollars | 500 000 dollars | 0 dollars |

The decision maker is subjected to two choice tests. The first consists of a choice between the lotteries $L_1$ and $L_1'$:

$$L_1 = (0, 1, 0) \qquad L_1' = (.10, .89, .01).$$

The second consists of a choice between the lotteries $L_2$ and $L_2'$:

$$L_2 = (0, .11, .89) \qquad L_2' = (.10, 0, .90).$$

The four lotteries involved are represented in the simplex diagram of Figure 6.B.7. It is common for individuals to express the preferences $L_1 \succ L_1'$ and $L_2' \succ L_2$.[8]

---

8. In our classroom experience, roughly half the students choose this way.

The first choice means that one prefers the certainty of receiving 500 000 dollars over a lottery offering a 1/10 probability of getting five times more but bringing with it a tiny risk of getting nothing. The second choice means that, all things considered, a 1/10 probability of getting 2 500 000 dollars is preferred to getting only 500 000 dollars with the slightly better odds of 11/100.

However, these choices are not consistent with expected utility. This can be seen in Figure 6.B.7: The straight lines connecting $L_1$ to $L_1'$ and $L_2$ to $L_2'$ are parallel. Therefore, if an individual has a linear indifference curve that lies in such a way that $L_1$ is preferred to $L_1'$, then a parallel linear indifference curve must make $L_2$ preferred to $L_2'$, and vice versa. Hence, choosing $L_1$ and $L_2'$ is inconsistent with preferences satisfying the assumptions of the expected utility theorem.

More formally, suppose that there was a v.N–M expected utility function. Denote by $u_{25}$, $u_{05}$, and $u_0$ the utility values of the three outcomes. Then the choice $L_1 \succ L_1'$ implies

$$u_{05} > (.10)u_{25} + (.89)u_{05} + (.01)u_0.$$

Adding $(.89)u_0 - (.89)u_{05}$ to both sides, we get

$$(.11)u_{05} + (.89)u_0 > (.10)u_{25} + (.90)u_0,$$

and therefore any individual with a v.N–M utility function must have $L_2 \succ L_2'$.  ∎

There are four common reactions to the Allais paradox. The first, propounded by J. Marshack and L. Savage, goes back to the normative interpretation of the theory. It argues that choosing under uncertainty is a reflective activity in which one should be ready to correct mistakes if they are proven inconsistent with the basic principles of choice embodied in the independence axiom (much as one corrects arithmetic mistakes).

The second reaction maintains that the Allais paradox is of limited significance for economics as a whole because it involves payoffs that are out of the ordinary and probabilities close to 0 and 1.

A third reaction seeks to accommodate the paradox with a theory that defines preferences over somewhat larger and more complex objects than simply the ultimate lottery over outcomes. For example, the decision maker may value not only what he receives but also what he receives compared with what he might have received by choosing differently. This leads to *regret theory*. In the example, we could have $L_1 \succ L_1'$ because the expected regret caused by the possibility of getting zero in lottery $L_1'$, when choosing $L_1$ would have assured 500 000 dollars, is too great. On the other hand, with the choice between $L_2$ and $L_2'$, no such clear-cut regret potential exists; the decision maker was very likely to get nothing anyway.

The fourth reaction is to stick with the original choice domain of lotteries but to give up the independence axiom in favor of something weaker. Exercise 6.B.5 develops this point further.

**Example 6.B.3:** *Machina's paradox.* Consider the following three outcomes: "a trip to Venice," "watching an excellent movie about Venice," and "staying home." Suppose that you prefer the first to the second and the second to the third.

Now you are given the opportunity to choose between two lotteries. The first lottery gives "a trip to Venice" with probability 99.9% and "watching an excellent movie about Venice" with probability 0.1%. The second lottery gives "a trip to

Venice," again with probability 99.9% and "staying home" with probability 0.1%. The independence axiom forces you to prefer the first lottery to the second. Yet, it would be understandable if you did otherwise. Choosing the second lottery is the rational thing to do if you anticipate that in the event of not getting the trip to Venice, your tastes over the other two outcomes will change: You will be severely *disappointed* and will feel miserable watching a movie about Venice.

The idea of disappointment has parallels with the idea of regret that we discussed in connection with the Allais paradox, but it is not quite the same. Both ideas refer to the influence of "what might have been" on the level of well-being experienced, and it is because of this that they are in conflict with the independence axiom. But disappointment is more directly concerned with what might have been if another outcome of a given lottery had come up, whereas regret should be thought of as regret over a choice not made. ∎

Because of the phenomena illustrated in the previous two examples, the search for a useful theory of choice under uncertainty that does not rely on the independence axiom has been an active area of research [see Machina (1987) and also Hey and Orme (1994)]. Nevertheless, the use of the expected utility theorem is pervasive in economics.

---

An argument sometimes made against the practical significance of violations of the independence axiom is that individuals with such preferences would be weeded out of the marketplace because they would be open to the acceptance of so-called "Dutch books," that is, deals leading to a sure loss of money. Suppose, for example, that there are three lotteries such that $L \succ L'$ and $L \succ L''$ but, in violation of the independence axiom, $\alpha L' + (1 - \alpha)L'' \succ L$ for some $\alpha \in (0, 1)$. Then, when the decision maker is in the initial position of owning the right to lottery $L$, he would be willing to pay a small fee to trade $L$ for a compound lottery yielding lottery $L'$ with probability $\alpha$ and lottery $L''$ with probability $(1 - \alpha)$. But as soon as the first stage of this lottery is over, giving him either $L'$ or $L''$ we could get him to pay a fee to trade this lottery for $L$. Hence, at that point, he would have paid the two fees but would otherwise be back to his original position.

This may well be a good argument for convexity of the not-better-than sets of $\succsim$, that is, for it to be the case that $L \succsim \alpha L' + (1 - \alpha)L''$ whenever $L \succsim L'$ and $L \succsim L''$. This property is implied by the independence axiom but is weaker than it. Dutch book arguments for the full independence axiom are possible, but they are more contrived [see Green (1987)].

---

Finally, one must use some caution in applying the expected utility theorem because in many practical situations the final outcomes of uncertainty are influenced by actions taken by individuals. Often, these actions should be explicitly modeled but are not. Example 6.B.4 illustrates the difficulty involved.

**Example 6.B.4:** *Induced preferences.* You are invited to a dinner where you may be offered fish (F) or meat (M). You would like to do the proper thing by showing up with white wine if F is served and red wine if M is served. The action of buying the wine must be taken *before* the uncertainty is resolved.

Suppose now that the cost of the bottle of red or white wine is the same and that you are also indifferent between F and M. If you think of the possible outcomes as F and M, then you are apparently indifferent between the lottery that gives F with certainty and the lottery that gives M with certainty. The independence axiom would then seem to require that you also be indifferent to a lottery that gives F or M with probability $\frac{1}{2}$ each. But you would clearly not be indifferent, since knowing that either F or M will be served with certainty allows you to buy the right wine, whereas, if you are not certain, you will either have to buy both wines or else bring the wrong wine with probability $\frac{1}{2}$.

Yet this example does not contradict the independence axiom. To appeal to the axiom, the decision framework must be set up so that the satisfaction derived from an outcome does not depend on any action taken by the decision maker before the uncertainty is resolved. *Thus, preferences should not be induced or derived from ex ante actions.*[9] Here, the action "acquisition of a bottle of wine" is taken before the uncertainty about the meal is resolved.

To put this situation into the framework required, we must include the ex ante action as part of the description of outcomes. For example, here there would be four outcomes: "bringing red wine when served M," "bringing white wine when served M," "bringing red wine when served F," and "bringing white wine when served F." For any underlying uncertainty about what will be served, you induce a lottery over these outcomes by your choice of action. In this setup, it is quite plausible to be indifferent among "having meat and bringing red wine," "having fish and bringing white wine," or any lottery between these two outcomes, as the independence axiom requires. ∎

Although it is not a contradiction to the postulates of expected utility theory, and therefore it is not a serious conceptual difficulty, the induced preferences example nonetheless raises a practical difficulty in the use of the theory. The example illustrates the fact that, in applications, many economic situations do not fit the pure framework of expected utility theory. Preferences are almost always, to some extent, induced.[10]

---

The expected utility theorem does impose some structure on induced preferences. For example, suppose the complete set of outcomes is $B \times A$, where $B = \{b_1, \ldots, b_N\}$ is the set of possible realizations of an exogenous randomness and $A$ is the decision maker's set of possible (ex ante) actions. Under the conditions of the expected utility theorem, for every $a \in A$ and $b_n \in B$, we can assign some utility value $u_n(a)$ to the outcome $(b_n, a)$. Then, for every exogenous lottery $L = (p_1, \ldots, p_N)$ on $B$, we can define a derived utility function by maximizing expected utility:

$$U(L) = \underset{a \in A}{\text{Max}} \sum_n p_n u_n(a).$$

In Exercise 6.B.6, you are asked to show that while $U(L)$, a function on $\mathscr{L}$, need not be linear,

---

9. Actions taken ex post do not create problems. For example, suppose that $u_n(a_n)$ is the utility derived from outcome $n$ when action $a_n$ is taken after the realization of uncertainty. The decision maker therefore chooses $a_n$ to solve $\text{Max}_{a_n \in A_n} u_n(a_n)$, where $A_n$ is the set of possible actions when outcome $n$ occurs. We can then let $u_n = \text{Max}_{a_n \in A_n} u_n(a_n)$ and evaluate lotteries over the $N$ outcomes as in expected utility theory.

10. Consider, for example, preferences for lotteries over amounts of money available tomorrow. Unless the individual's preferences over consumption today and tomorrow are additively separable, his decision of how much to consume today—a decision that must be made before the resolution of the uncertainty concerning tomorrow's wealth—affects his preferences over these lotteries in a manner that conflicts with the fulfillment of the independence axiom.

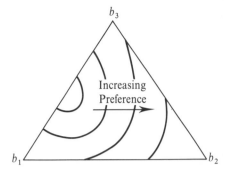

**Figure 6.B.8**

An indifference map
for induced preferences
over lotteries on
$B = \{b_1, b_2, b_3\}$.

it is nonetheless always *convex*; that is,

$$U(\alpha L + (1 - \alpha)L') \leq \alpha U(L) + (1 - \alpha)U(L').$$

Figure 6.B.8 represents an indifference map for induced preferences in the probability simplex for a case where $N = 3$.

# 6.C  Money Lotteries and Risk Aversion

In many economic settings, individuals seem to display aversion to risk. In this section, we formalize the notion of *risk aversion* and study some of its properties.

From this section through the end of the chapter, we concentrate on risky alternatives whose outcomes are amounts of money. It is convenient, however, when dealing with monetary outcomes, to treat money as a continuous variable. Strictly speaking, the derivation of the expected utility representation given in Section 6.B assumed a finite number of outcomes. However, the theory can be extended, with some minor technical complications, to the case of an infinite domain. We begin by briefly discussing this extension.

*Lotteries over Monetary Outcomes and the Expected Utility Framework*

Suppose that we denote amounts of money by the continuous variable $x$. We can describe a monetary lottery by means of a *cumulative distribution function* $F: \mathbb{R} \to [0, 1]$. That is, for any $x$, $F(x)$ is the probability that the realized payoff is less than or equal to $x$. Note that if the distribution function of a lottery has a density function $f(\cdot)$ associated with it, then $F(x) = \int_{-\infty}^{x} f(t) \, dt$ for all $x$. The advantage of a formalism based on distribution functions over one based on density functions, however, is that the first is completely general. It does not exclude a priori the possibility of a discrete set of outcomes. For example, the distribution function of a lottery with only three monetary outcomes receiving positive probability is illustrated in Figure 6.C.1.

Note that distribution functions preserve the linear structure of lotteries (as do density functions). For example, the final distribution of money, $F(\cdot)$, induced by a compound lottery $(L_1, \ldots, L_K; \alpha_1, \ldots, \alpha_K)$ is just the weighted average of the distributions induced by each of the lotteries that constitute it: $F(x) = \sum_k \alpha_k F_k(x)$, where $F_k(\cdot)$ is the distribution of the payoff under lottery $L_k$.

From this point on, we shall work with distribution functions to describe lotteries over monetary outcomes. We therefore take the lottery space $\mathscr{L}$ to be the *set of all*

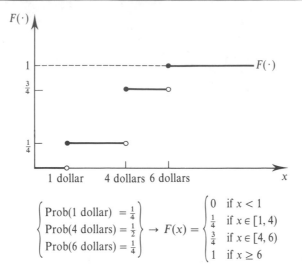

$$\left\{\begin{array}{l} \text{Prob(1 dollar)} = \frac{1}{4} \\ \text{Prob(4 dollars)} = \frac{1}{2} \\ \text{Prob(6 dollars)} = \frac{1}{4} \end{array}\right\} \rightarrow F(x) = \left\{\begin{array}{ll} 0 & \text{if } x < 1 \\ \frac{1}{4} & \text{if } x \in [1, 4) \\ \frac{3}{4} & \text{if } x \in [4, 6) \\ 1 & \text{if } x \geq 6 \end{array}\right.$$

**Figure 6.C.1**

A distribution function.

*distribution functions over nonnegative amounts of money,* or, more generally, over an interval $[a, +\infty)$.

As in Section 6.B, we begin with a decision maker who has rational preferences $\succsim$ defined over $\mathcal{L}$. The application of the expected utility theorem to outcomes defined by a continuous variable tells us that under the assumptions of the theorem, there is an assignment of utility values $u(x)$ to nonnegative amounts of money with the property that any $F(\cdot)$ can be evaluated by a utility function $U(\cdot)$ of the form

$$U(F) = \int u(x) \, dF(x). \tag{6.C.1}$$

Expression (6.C.1) is the exact extension of the expected utility form to the current setting. The v.N–M utility function $U(\cdot)$ is the mathematical expectation, over the realizations of $x$, of the values $u(x)$. The latter takes the place of the values $(u_1, \ldots, u_N)$ used in the discrete treatment of Section 6.B.[11] Note that, as before, $U(\cdot)$ is linear in $F(\cdot)$.

The strength of the expected utility representation is that it preserves the very useful expectation form while making the utility of monetary lotteries sensitive not only to the mean but also to the higher moments of the distribution of the monetary payoffs. (See Exercise 6.C.2 for an illuminating quadratic example.)

It is important to distinguish between the utility function $U(\cdot)$, defined on lotteries, and the utility function $u(\cdot)$ defined on sure amounts of money. For this reason, we call $U(\cdot)$ the *von-Neumann–Morgenstern (v.N–M) expected utility function* and $u(\cdot)$ the *Bernoulli utility function.*[12]

---

11. Given a distribution function $F(x)$, the expected value of a function $\phi(x)$ is given by $\int \phi(x) \, dF(x)$. When $F(\cdot)$ has an associated density function $f(x)$, this expression is exactly equal to $\int \phi(x)f(x) \, dx$. Note also that for notational simplicity, we do not explicitly write the limits of integration when the integral is over the full range of possible realizations of $x$.

12. The terminology is not standardized. It is common to call $u(\cdot)$ the v.N–M utility function or the expected utility function. We prefer to have a name that is specific to the $u(\cdot)$ function, and so we call it the Bernoulli function for Daniel Bernoulli, who first used an instance of it.

Although the general axioms of Section 6.B yield the expected utility representation, they place no restrictions whatsoever on the Bernoulli utility function $u(\cdot)$. In large part, the analytical power of the expected utility formulation hinges on specifying the Bernoulli utility function $u(\cdot)$ in such a manner that it captures interesting economic attributes of choice behavior. At the simplest level, it makes sense in the current monetary context to postulate that $u(\cdot)$ is *increasing* and *continuous*.[13] We maintain both of these assumptions from now on.

Another restriction, based on a subtler argument, is the *boundedness* (above and below) of $u(\cdot)$. To argue the plausibility of boundedness above (a similar argument applies for boundedness below), we refer to the famous *St. Petersburg–Menger paradox*. Suppose that $u(\cdot)$ is unbounded, so that for every integer $m$ there is an amount of money $x_m$ with $u(x_m) > 2^m$. Consider the following lottery: we toss a coin repeatedly until tails comes up. If this happens in the $m$th toss, the lottery gives a monetary payoff of $x_m$. Since the probability of this outcome is $1/2^m$, the expected utility of this lottery is $\sum_{m=1}^{\infty} u(x_m)(1/2^m) \geq \sum_{m=1}^{\infty} (2^m)(1/2^m) = +\infty$. But this means that an individual should be willing to give up all his wealth for the opportunity to play this lottery, a patently absurd conclusion (how much would you pay?).[14]

The rest of this section concentrates on the important property of *risk aversion*, its formulation in terms of the Bernoulli utility function $u(\cdot)$, and its measurement.[15]

## Risk Aversion and Its Measurement

The concept of risk aversion provides one of the central analytical techniques of economic analysis, and it is assumed in this book whenever we handle uncertain situations. We begin our discussion of risk aversion with a general definition that does not presume an expected utility formulation.

**Definition 6.C.1:** A decision maker is a *risk averter* (or exhibits *risk aversion*) if for any lottery $F(\cdot)$, the degenerate lottery that yields the amount $\int x \, dF(x)$ with certainty is at least as good as the lottery $F(\cdot)$ itself. If the decision maker is always [i.e., for any $F(\cdot)$] indifferent between these two lotteries, we say that he is *risk neutral*. Finally, we say that he is *strictly risk averse* if indifference holds only when the two lotteries are the same [i.e., when $F(\cdot)$ is degenerate].

If preferences admit an expected utility representation with Bernoulli utility function $u(x)$, it follows directly from the definition of risk aversion that the decision maker is risk averse if and only if

$$\int u(x) \, dF(x) \leq u\left( \int x \, dF(x) \right) \quad \text{for all } F(\cdot). \tag{6.C.2}$$

Inequality (6.C.2) is called *Jensen's inequality*, and it is the defining property of a concave function (see Section M.C of the Mathematical Appendix). Hence, in the

---

13. In applications, an exception to continuity is sometimes made at $x = 0$ by setting $u(0) = -\infty$.

14. In practice, most utility functions commonly used are not bounded. Paradoxes are avoided because the class of distributions allowed by the modeler in each particular application is a limited one. Note also that if we insisted on $u(\cdot)$ being defined on $(-\infty, \infty)$ then any nonconstant $u(\cdot)$ could not be both concave and bounded (above and below).

15. Arrow (1971) and Pratt (1964) are the classical references in this area.

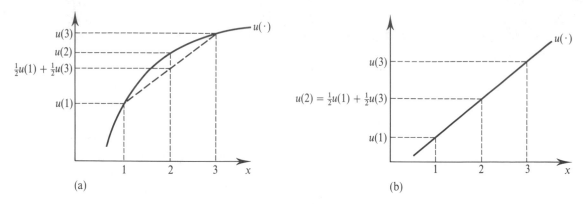

**Figure 6.C.2**  Risk aversion (a) and risk neutrality (b).

context of expected utility theory, we see that *risk aversion is equivalent to the concavity of* $u(\cdot)$ and that strict risk aversion is equivalent to the strict concavity of $u(\cdot)$. This makes sense. Strict concavity means that the marginal utility of money is decreasing. Hence, at any level of wealth $x$, the utility gain from an extra dollar is smaller than (the absolute value of) the utility loss of having a dollar less. It follows that a risk of gaining or losing a dollar with even probability is not worth taking. This is illustrated in Figure 6.C.2(a); in the figure we consider a gamble involving the gain or loss of 1 dollar from an initial position of 2 dollars. The (v.N–M )utility of this gamble, $\frac{1}{2}u(1) + \frac{1}{2}u(3)$, is strictly less than that of the initial certain position $u(2)$.

For a risk-neutral expected utility maximizer, (6.C.2) must hold with *equality* for all $F(\cdot)$. Hence, the decision maker is risk neutral if and only if the Bernoulli utility function of money $u(\cdot)$ is linear. Figure 6.C.2(b) depicts the (v.N–M) utility associated with the previous gamble for a risk neutral individual. Here the individual is indifferent between the gambles that yield a mean wealth level of 2 dollars and a certain wealth of 2 dollars. Definition 6.C.2 introduces two useful concepts for the analysis of risk aversion.

**Definition 6.C.2:** Given a Bernoulli utility function $u(\cdot)$ we define the following concepts:

(i) The *certainty equivalent of* $F(\cdot)$, denoted $c(F, u)$, is the amount of money for which the individual is indifferent between the gamble $F(\cdot)$ and the certain amount $c(F, u)$; that is,

$$u(c(F, u)) = \int u(x)\, dF(x). \qquad (6.C.3)$$

(ii) For any fixed amount of money $x$ and positive number $\varepsilon$, the *probability premium* denoted by $\pi(x, \varepsilon, u)$, is the excess in winning probability over fair odds that makes the individual indifferent between the certain outcome $x$ and a gamble between the two outcomes $x + \varepsilon$ and $x - \varepsilon$. That is

$$u(x) = (\tfrac{1}{2} + \pi(x, \varepsilon, u))\,u(x + \varepsilon) + (\tfrac{1}{2} - \pi(x, \varepsilon, u))\,u(x - \varepsilon). \qquad (6.C.4)$$

These two concepts are illustrated in Figure 6.C.3. In Figure 6.C.3(a), we exhibit the geometric construction of $c(F, u)$ for an even probability gamble between 1 and 3 dollars. Note that $c(F, u) < 2$, implying that some expected return is traded for certainty. The satisfaction of the inequality $c(F, u) \le \int x\, dF(x)$ for all $F(\cdot)$ is, in fact,

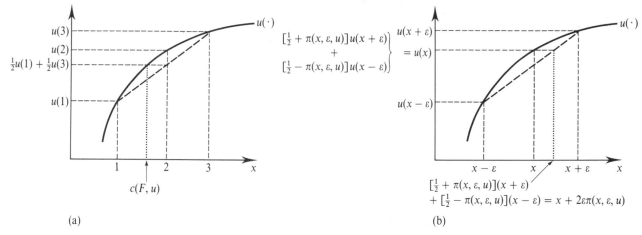

**Figure 6.C.3**  The certainty equivalent (a) and the probability premium (b).

equivalent to the decision maker being a risk averter. To see this, observe that since $u(\cdot)$ is nondecreasing, we have

$$c(F, u) \le \int x \, dF(x) \;\Leftrightarrow\; u(c(F, u)) \le u\!\left(\int x \, dF(x)\right) \;\Leftrightarrow\; \int u(x) \, dF(x) \le u\!\left(\int x \, dF(x)\right),$$

where the last $\Leftrightarrow$ follows from the definition of $c(F, u)$.

In Figure 6.C.3(b), we exhibit the geometric construction of $\pi(x, \varepsilon, u)$. We see that $\pi(x, \varepsilon, u) > 0$; that is, better than fair odds must be given for the individual to accept the risk. In fact, the satisfaction of the inequality $\pi(x, \varepsilon, u) \ge 0$ for all $x$ and $\varepsilon > 0$ is also equivalent to risk aversion (see Exercise 6.C.3).

These points are formally summarized in Proposition 6.C.1.

**Proposition 6.C.1:** Suppose a decision maker is an expected utility maximizer with a Bernoulli utility function $u(\cdot)$ on amounts of money. Then the following properties are equivalent:

(i) The decision maker is risk averse.
(ii) $u(\cdot)$ is concave.[16]
(iii) $c(F, u) \le \int x \, dF(x)$ for all $F(\cdot)$.
(iv) $\pi(x, \varepsilon, u) \ge 0$ for all $x, \varepsilon$.

Examples 6.C.1 to 6.C.3 illustrate the use of the risk aversion concept.

**Example 6.C.1:** *Insurance.*  Consider a strictly risk-averse decision maker who has an initial wealth of $w$ but who runs a risk of a loss of $D$ dollars. The probability of the loss is $\pi$. It is possible, however, for the decision maker to buy insurance. One unit of insurance costs $q$ dollars and pays 1 dollar if the loss occurs. Thus, if $\alpha$ units of insurance are bought, the wealth of the individual will be $w - \alpha q$ if there is no loss and $w - \alpha q - D + \alpha$ if the loss occurs. Note, for purposes of later discussion, that the decision maker's expected wealth is then $w - \pi D + \alpha(\pi - q)$. The decision maker's problem is to choose the optimal level of $\alpha$. His utility maximization problem is

---

16. Recall that if $u(\cdot)$ is twice differentiable then concavity is equivalent to $u''(x) \le 0$ for all $x$.

therefore

$$\operatorname*{Max}_{\alpha \geq 0} \ (1 - \pi)u(w - \alpha q) + \pi u(w - \alpha q - D + \alpha).$$

If $\alpha^*$ is an optimum, it must satisfy the first-order condition:

$$-q(1 - \pi)u'(w - \alpha^* q) + \pi(1 - q)u'(w - D + \alpha^*(1 - q)) \leq 0,$$

with equality if $\alpha^* > 0$.

Suppose now that the price $q$ of one unit of insurance is *actuarially fair* in the sense of it being equal to the expected cost of insurance. That is, $q = \pi$. Then the first-order condition requires that

$$u'(w - D + \alpha^*(1 - \pi)) - u'(w - \alpha^* \pi) \leq 0,$$

with equality if $\alpha^* > 0$.

Since $u'(w - D) > u'(w)$, we must have $\alpha^* > 0$, and therefore

$$u'(w - D + \alpha^*(1 - \pi)) = u'(w - \alpha^* \pi).$$

Because $u'(\cdot)$ is strictly decreasing, this implies

$$w - D + \alpha^*(1 - \pi) = w - \alpha^* \pi,$$

or, equivalently,

$$\alpha^* = D.$$

Thus, *if insurance is actuarially fair, the decision maker insures completely.* The individual's final wealth is then $w - \pi D$, regardless of the occurrence of the loss.

This proof of the complete insurance result uses first-order conditions, which is instructive but not really necessary. Note that if $q = \pi$, then the decision maker's expected wealth is $w - \pi D$ for any $\alpha$. Since setting $\alpha = D$ allows him to reach $w - \pi D$ with certainty, the definition of risk aversion directly implies that this is the optimal level of $\alpha$. ∎

**Example 6.C.2:** *Demand for a Risky Asset.* An *asset* is a divisible claim to a financial return in the future. Suppose that there are two assets, a safe asset with a return of 1 dollar per dollar invested and a risky asset with a random return of $z$ dollars per dollar invested. The random return $z$ has a distribution function $F(z)$ that we assume satisfies $\int z \, dF(z) > 1$; that is, its mean return exceeds that of the safe asset.

An individual has initial wealth $w$ to invest, which can be divided in any way between the two assets. Let $\alpha$ and $\beta$ denote the amounts of wealth invested in the risky and the safe asset, respectively. Thus, for any realization $z$ of the random return, the individual's *portfolio* $(\alpha, \beta)$ pays $\alpha z + \beta$. Of course, we must also have $\alpha + \beta = w$.

The question is how to choose $\alpha$ and $\beta$. The answer will depend on $F(\cdot)$, $w$, and the Bernoulli utility function $u(\cdot)$. The utility maximization problem of the individual is

$$\operatorname*{Max}_{\alpha, \beta \geq 0} \ \int u(\alpha z + \beta) \, dF(z)$$

$$\text{s.t. } \alpha + \beta = w.$$

Equivalently, we want to maximize $\int u(w + \alpha(z - 1)) \, dF(z)$ subject to $0 \leq \alpha \leq w$. If

$\alpha^*$ is optimal, it must satisfy the Kuhn–Tucker first-order conditions:[17]

$$\phi(\alpha^*) = \int u'(w + \alpha^*[z - 1])(z - 1)\, dF(z) \begin{cases} \leq 0 & \text{if } \alpha^* < w, \\ \geq 0 & \text{if } \alpha^* > 0. \end{cases}$$

Note that $\int z\, dF(z) > 1$ implies $\phi(0) > 0$. Hence, $\alpha^* = 0$ cannot satisfy this first-order condition. We conclude that the optimal portfolio has $\alpha^* > 0$. The general principle illustrated in this example, is that *if a risk is actuarially favorable,* then a risk averter *will always accept at least a small amount of it.*

This same principle emerges in Example 6.C.1 if insurance is not actuarially fair. In Exercise 6.C.1, you are asked to show that if $q > \pi$, then the decision maker will not fully insure (i.e., will accept some risk). ∎

**Example 6.C.3:** *General Asset Problem.* In the previous example, we could define the utility $U(\alpha, \beta)$ of the portfolio $(\alpha, \beta)$ as $U(\alpha, \beta) = \int u(\alpha z + \beta)\, dF(z)$. Note that $U(\cdot)$ is then an increasing, continuous, and concave utility function. We now discuss an important generalization. We assume that we have $N$ assets (one of which may be the safe asset) with asset $n$ giving a return of $z_n$ per unit of money invested. These returns are jointly distributed according to a distribution function $F(z_1, \ldots, z_N)$. The utility of holding a *portfolio* of assets $(\alpha_1, \ldots, \alpha_N)$ is then

$$U(\alpha_1, \ldots, \alpha_N) = \int u(\alpha_1 z_1 + \cdots + \alpha_N z_N)\, dF(z_1, \ldots, z_N).$$

This utility function for portfolios, defined on $\mathbb{R}_+^N$, is also increasing, continuous, and concave (see Exercise 6.C.4). This means that, formally, we can treat assets as the usual type of commodities and apply to them the demand theory developed in Chapters 2 and 3. Observe, in particular, how risk aversion leads to a convex indifference map for portfolios. ∎

---

Suppose that the lotteries pay in vectors of physical goods rather than in money. Formally, the space of outcomes is then the consumption set $\mathbb{R}_+^L$ (all the previous discussion can be viewed as the special case in which there is a single good). In this more general setting, the concept of risk aversion given by Definition 6.C.1 is perfectly well defined. Furthermore, if there is a Bernoulli utility function $u: \mathbb{R}_+^L \to \mathbb{R}$, then risk aversion is still equivalent to the concavity of $u(\cdot)$. Hence, we have here another justification for the convexity assumption of Chapter 3: Under the assumptions of the expected utility theorem, the convexity of preferences for perfectly certain amounts of the physical commodities must hold if for any lottery with commodity payoffs the individual always prefers the certainty of the mean commodity bundle to the lottery itself.

In Exercise 6.C.5, you are asked to show that if preferences over lotteries with commodity payoffs exhibit risk aversion, then, at given commodity prices, the induced preferences on money lotteries (where consumption decisions are made after the realization of wealth) are also risk averse. Thus, in principle, it is possible to build the theory of risk aversion on the more primitive notion of lotteries over the final consumption of goods.

---

17. The objective function is concave in $\alpha$ because the concavity of $u(\cdot)$ implies that $\int u''(w + \alpha(z - 1))(z - 1)^2\, dF(x) \leq 0$.

*The Measurement of Risk Aversion*

Now that we know what it means to be risk averse, we can try to measure the extent of risk aversion. We begin by defining one particularly useful measure and discussing some of its properties.

**Definition 6.C.3:** Given a (twice-differentiable) Bernoulli utility function $u(\cdot)$ for money, the *Arrow–Pratt coefficient of absolute risk aversion* at $x$ is defined as $r_A(x) = -u''(x)/u'(x)$.

The Arrow–Pratt measure can be motivated as follows: We know that risk neutrality is equivalent to the linearity of $u(\cdot)$, that is, to $u''(x) = 0$ for all $x$. Therefore, it seems logical that the degree of risk aversion be related to the *curvature* of $u(\cdot)$. In Figure 6.C.4, for example, we represent two Bernoulli utility functions $u_1(\cdot)$ and $u_2(\cdot)$ normalized (by choice of origin and units) to have the same utility and marginal utility values at wealth level $x$. The certainty equivalent for a small risk with mean $x$ is smaller for $u_2(\cdot)$ than for $u_1(\cdot)$, suggesting that risk aversion increases with the curvature of the Bernoulli utility function at $x$. One possible measure of curvature of the Bernoulli utility function $u(\cdot)$ at $x$ is $u''(x)$. However, this is not an adequate measure because it is not invariant to positive linear transformations of the utility function. To make it invariant, the simplest modification is to use $u''(x)/u'(x)$. If we change sign so as to have a positive number for an increasing and concave $u(\cdot)$, we get the Arrow–Pratt measure.

A more precise motivation for $r_A(x)$ as a measure of the degree of risk aversion can be obtained by considering a fixed wealth $x$ and studying the behavior of the probability premium $\pi(x, \varepsilon, u)$ as $\varepsilon \to 0$ [for simplicity, we write it as $\pi(\varepsilon)$]. Differentiating the identity (6.C.4) that defines $\pi(\cdot)$ twice with respect to $\varepsilon$ (assume that $\pi(\cdot)$ is differentiable), and evaluating at $\varepsilon = 0$, we get $4\pi'(0)u'(x) + u''(x) = 0$. Hence

$$r_A(x) = 4\pi'(0).$$

Thus, $r_A(x)$ measures the rate at which the probability premium increases at certainty with the small risk measured by $\varepsilon$.[18] As we go along, we will find additional related interpretations of the Arrow–Pratt measure.

---

18. For a similar derivation relating $r_A(\cdot)$ to the rate of change of the certainty equivalent with respect to a small increase in a small risk around certainty, see Exercise 6.C.20.

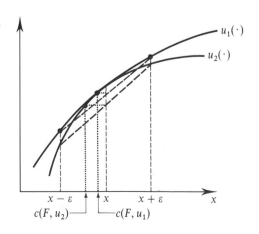

**Figure 6.C.4**

Differing degrees of risk aversion.

Note that, up to two integration constants, the utility function $u(\cdot)$ can be recovered from $r_A(\cdot)$ by integrating twice. The integration constants are irrelevant because the Bernoulli utility is identified only up to two constants (origin and units). Thus, the Arrow–Pratt risk aversion measure $r_A(\cdot)$ fully characterizes behavior under uncertainty.

**Example 6.C.4:** Consider the utility function $u(x) = -e^{-ax}$ for $a > 0$. Then $u'(x) = ae^{-ax}$ and $u''(x) = -a^2 e^{-ax}$. Therefore, $r_A(x, u) = a$ for all $x$. It follows from the observation just made that the general form of a Bernoulli utility function with an Arrow–Pratt measure of absolute risk aversion equal to the constant $a > 0$ at all $x$ is $u(x) = -\alpha e^{-ax} + \beta$ for some $\alpha > 0$ and $\beta$. ∎

Once we are equipped with a measure of risk aversion, we can put it to use in comparative statics exercises. Two common situations are the comparisons of risk attitudes across individuals with different utility functions and the comparison of risk attitudes for one individual at different levels of wealth.

*Comparisons across individuals*
Given two Bernoulli utility functions $u_1(\cdot)$ and $u_2(\cdot)$, when can we say that $u_2(\cdot)$ is unambiguously *more risk averse than* $u_1(\cdot)$? Several possible approaches to a definition seem plausible:

    (i) $r_A(x, u_2) \geq r_A(x, u_1)$ for every $x$.
    (ii) There exists an increasing concave function $\psi(\cdot)$ such that $u_2(x) = \psi(u_1(x))$ at all $x$; that is, $u_2(\cdot)$ is a concave transformation of $u_1(\cdot)$. [In other words, $u_2(\cdot)$ is "more concave" than $u_1(\cdot)$.]
    (iii) $c(F, u_2) \leq c(F, u_1)$ for any $F(\cdot)$.
    (iv) $\pi(x, \varepsilon, u_2) \geq \pi(x, \varepsilon, u_1)$ for any $x$ and $\varepsilon$.
    (v) Whenever $u_2(\cdot)$ finds a lottery $F(\cdot)$ at least as good as a riskless outcome $\bar{x}$, then $u_1(\cdot)$ also finds $F(\cdot)$ at least as good as $\bar{x}$. That is, $\int u_2(x)\, dF(x) \geq u_2(\bar{x})$ implies $\int u_1(x)\, dF(x) \geq u_1(\bar{x})$ for any $F(\cdot)$ and $\bar{x}$.[19]

In fact, these five definitions are equivalent.

**Proposition 6.C.2:** Definitions (i) to (v) of the *more-risk-averse-than* relation are equivalent.

**Proof:** We will not give a complete proof. (You are asked to establish some of the implications in Exercises 6.C.6 and 6.C.7.) Here we will show the equivalence of (i) and (ii) under differentiability assumptions.

Note, first that we always have $u_2(x) = \psi(u_1(x))$ for some increasing function $\psi(\cdot)$; this is true simply because $u_1(\cdot)$ and $u_2(\cdot)$ are ordinally identical (more money is preferred to less). Differentiating, we get

$$u_2'(x) = \psi'(u_1(x))u_1'(x)$$

and

$$u_2''(x) = \psi'(u_1(x))u_1''(x) + \psi''(u_1(x))(u_1'(x))^2.$$

Dividing both sides of the second expression by $u_2'(x) > 0$, and using the first

---

    19. In other words, any risk that $u_2(\cdot)$ would accept starting from a position of certainty would also be accepted by $u_1(\cdot)$.

expression, we get

$$r_A(x, u_2) = r_A(x, u_1) - \frac{\psi''(u_1(x))}{\psi'(u_1(x))} u_1'(x).$$

Thus, $r_A(x, u_2) \geq r_A(x, u_1)$ for all $x$ if and only if $\psi''(u_1) \leq 0$ for all $u_1$ in the range of $u_1(\cdot)$. ∎

The more-risk-averse-than relation is a *partial ordering* of Bernoulli utility functions; it is transitive but far from complete. Typically, two Bernoulli utility functions $u_1(\cdot)$ and $u_2(\cdot)$ will not be comparable; that is, we will have $r_A(x, u_1) > r_A(x, u_2)$ at some $x$ but $r_A(x', u_1) < r_A(x', u_2)$ at some other $x' \neq x$.

**Example 6.C.2 continued:** We take up again the asset portfolio problem between a safe and a risky asset discussed in Example 6.C.2. Suppose that we now have two individuals with Bernoulli utility functions $u_1(\cdot)$ and $u_2(\cdot)$, and denote by $\alpha_1^*$ and $\alpha_2^*$ their respective optimal investments in the risky asset. We will show that *if $u_2(\cdot)$ is more risk averse than $u_1(\cdot)$, then $\alpha_2^* < \alpha_1^*$*; that is, the second decision maker invests less in the risky asset than the first.

To repeat from our earlier discussion, the asset allocation problem for $u_1(\cdot)$ is

$$\underset{0 \leq \alpha \leq w}{\text{Max}} \int u_1(w - \alpha + \alpha z) \, dF(z).$$

Assuming an interior solution, the first-order condition is

$$\int (z - 1) u_1'(w + \alpha_1^*[z - 1]) \, dF(z) = 0. \tag{6.C.5}$$

The analogous expression for the utility function $u_2(\cdot)$ is

$$\phi_2(\alpha_2^*) = \int (z - 1) u_2'(w + \alpha_2^*[z - 1]) \, dF(z) = 0. \tag{6.C.6}$$

As we know, the concavity of $u_2(\cdot)$ implies that $\phi_2(\cdot)$ is decreasing. Therefore, if we show that $\phi_2(\alpha_1^*) < 0$, it must follow that $\alpha_2^* < \alpha_1^*$, which is the result we want. Now, $u_2(x) = \psi(u_1(x))$ allows us to write

$$\phi_2(\alpha_1^*) = \int (z - 1) \psi'(u_1(w + \alpha_1^*[z - 1])) u_1'(w + \alpha_1^*[z - 1]) \, dF(z) < 0. \tag{6.C.7}$$

To understand the final inequality, note that the integrand of expression (6.C.7) is the same as that in (6.C.5) except that it is multiplied by $\psi'(\cdot)$, a positive decreasing function of $z$ [recall that $u_2(\cdot)$ more risk averse than $u_1(\cdot)$ means that the increasing function $\psi(\cdot)$ is concave; that is, $\psi'(\cdot)$ is positive and decreasing]. Hence, the integral (6.C.7) underweights the positive values of $(z - 1) u_1'(w + \alpha_1^*[z - 1])$, which obtain for $z > 1$, relative to the negative values, which obtain for $z < 1$. Since, in (6.C.5), the integral of the positive and the negative parts of the integrand added to zero, they now must add to a negative number. This establishes the desired inequality. ∎

*Comparisons across wealth levels*

It is a common contention that wealthier people are willing to bear more risk than poorer people. Although this might be due to differences in utility functions across people, it is more likely that the source of the difference lies in the possibility that richer people "can afford to take a chance." Hence, we shall explore the implications of the condition stated in Definition 6.C.4.

**Definition 6.C.4:** The Bernoulli utility function $u(\cdot)$ for money exhibits *decreasing absolute risk aversion* if $r_A(x, u)$ is a decreasing function of $x$.

Individuals whose preferences satisfy the decreasing absolute risk aversion property take more risk as they become wealthier. Consider two levels of initial wealth $x_1 > x_2$. Denote the increments or decrements to wealth by $z$. Then the individual evaluates risk at $x_1$ and $x_2$ by, respectively, the induced Bernoulli utility functions $u_1(z) = u(x_1 + z)$ and $u_2(z) = u(x_2 + z)$. Comparing an individual's attitudes toward risk as his level of wealth changes is like comparing the utility functions $u_1(\cdot)$ and $u_2(\cdot)$, a problem we have just studied. If $u(\cdot)$ displays decreasing absolute risk aversion, then $r_A(z, u_2) \geq r_A(z, u_1)$ for all $z$. This is condition (i) of Proposition 6.C.2. Hence, the result in Proposition 6.C.3 follows directly from Proposition 6.C.2.

**Proposition 6.C.3:** The following properties are equivalent:
   (i) The Bernoulli utility function $(\cdot)$ exhibits decreasing absolute risk aversion.
   (ii) Whenever $x_2 < x_1$, $u_2(z) = u(x_2 + z)$ is a concave transformation of $u_1(z) = u(x_1 + z)$.
   (iii) For any risk $F(z)$, the certainty equivalent of the lottery formed by adding risk $z$ to wealth level $x$, given by the amount $c_x$ at which $u(c_x) = \int u(x + z)\, dF(z)$, is such that $(x - c_x)$ is decreasing in $x$. That is, the higher $x$ is, the less is the individual willing to pay to get rid of the risk.
   (iv) The probability premium $\pi(x, \varepsilon, u)$ is decreasing in $x$.
   (v) For any $F(z)$, if $\int u(x_2 + z)\, dF(z) \geq u(x_2)$ and $x_2 < x_1$, then $\int u(x_1 + z)\, dF(z) \geq u(x_1)$.

**Exercise 6.C.8:** Assume that the Bernoulli utility function $u(\cdot)$ exhibits decreasing absolute risk aversion. Show that for the asset demand model of Example 6.C.2 (and Example 6.C.2 continued), the optimal allocation between the safe and the risky assets places an increasing amount of wealth in the risky asset as $w$ rises (i.e., the risky asset is a normal good).

The assumption of decreasing absolute risk aversion yields many other economically reasonable results concerning risk-bearing behavior. However, in applications, it is often too weak and, because of its analytical convenience, it is sometimes complemented by a stronger assumption: *nonincreasing relative risk aversion*.

To understand the concept of relative risk aversion, note that the concept of absolute risk aversion is suited to the comparison of attitudes toward risky projects whose outcomes are *absolute gains or losses* from current wealth. But it is also of interest to evaluate risky projects whose outcomes are *percentage* gains or losses of current wealth. The concept of relative risk aversion does just this.

Let $t > 0$ stand for *proportional* increments or decrements of wealth. Then, an individual with Bernoulli utility function $u(\cdot)$ and initial wealth $x$ can evaluate a random percentage risk by means of the utility function $\tilde{u}(t) = u(tx)$. The initial wealth position corresponds to $t = 1$. We already know that for a small risk around $t = 1$, the degree of risk aversion is well captured by $\tilde{u}''(1)/\tilde{u}'(1)$. Noting that $\tilde{u}''(1)/\tilde{u}'(1) = xu''(x)/u'(x)$, we are led to the concept stated in Definition 6.C.5.

**Definition 6.C.5:** Given a Bernoulli utility function $u(\cdot)$, the *coefficient of relative risk aversion at $x$* is $r_R(x, u) = -xu''(x)/u'(x)$.

Consider now how this measure varies with wealth. The property of *nonincreasing relative risk aversion* says that the individual becomes less risk averse with regard to gambles that are proportional to his wealth as his wealth increases. This is a stronger assumption than decreasing absolute risk aversion: Since $r_R(x, u) = xr_A(x, u)$, a risk-averse individual with decreasing relative risk aversion will exhibit decreasing absolute risk aversion, but the converse is not necessarily the case.

As before, we can examine various implications of this concept. Proposition 6.C.4 is an abbreviated parallel to Proposition 6.C.3.

**Proposition 6.C.4:** The following conditions for a Bernoulli utility function $u(\cdot)$ on amounts of money are equivalent:

(i) $r_R(x, u)$ is decreasing in $x$.
(ii) Whenever $x_2 < x_1$, $\tilde{u}_2(t) = u(tx_2)$ is a concave transformation of $\tilde{u}_1(t) = u(tx_1)$.
(iii) Given any risk $F(t)$ on $t > 0$, the certainty equivalent $\bar{c}_x$ defined by $u(\bar{c}_x) = \int u(tx)\, dF(t)$ is such that $x/\bar{c}_x$ is decreasing in $x$.

**Proof:** Here we show only that (i) implies (iii). To this effect, fix a distribution $F(t)$ on $t > 0$, and, for any $x$, define $u_x(t) = u(tx)$. Let $c(x)$ be the usual certainty equivalent (from Definition 6.C.2): $u_x(c(x)) = \int u_x(t)\, dF(t)$. Note that $-u_x''(t)/u_x'(t) = -(1/t)tx[u''(tx)/u'(tx)]$ for any $x$. Hence if (i) holds, then $u_{x'}(\cdot)$ is less risk averse than $u_x(\cdot)$ whenever $x' > x$. Therefore, by Proposition 6.C.2, $c(x') > c(x)$ and we conclude that $c(\cdot)$ is increasing. Now, by the definition of $u_x(\cdot)$, $u_x(c(x)) = u(xc(x))$. Also

$$u_x(c(x)) = \int u_x(t)\, dF(t) = \int u(tx)\, dF(t) = u(\bar{c}_x).$$

Hence, $\bar{c}_x/x = c(x)$, and so $x/\bar{c}_x$ is decreasing. This concludes the proof. ∎

**Example 6.C.2 continued:** In Exercise 6.C.11, you are asked to show that if $r_R(x, u)$ is decreasing in $x$, then the proportion of wealth invested in the risky asset $\gamma = \alpha/w$ is increasing with the individual's wealth level $w$. The opposite conclusion holds if $r_R(x, u)$ is increasing in $x$. If $r_R(x, u)$ is a constant independent of $x$, then the fraction of wealth invested in the risky asset is independent of $w$ [see Exercise 6.C.12 for the specific analytical form that $u(\cdot)$ must have]. Models with constant relative risk aversion are encountered often in finance theory, where they lead to considerable analytical simplicity. Under this assumption, no matter how the wealth of the economy and its distribution across individuals evolves over time, the portfolio decisions of individuals in terms of budget shares do not vary (as long as the safe return and the distribution of random returns remain unchanged). ∎

# 6.D Comparison of Payoff Distributions in Terms of Return and Risk

In this section, we continue our study of lotteries with monetary payoffs. In contrast with Section 6.C, where we compared utility functions, our aim here is to compare payoff distributions. There are two natural ways that random outcomes can be compared: according to the level of returns and according to the dispersion of returns. We will therefore attempt to give meaning to two ideas: that of a distribution $F(\cdot)$ yielding unambiguously higher returns than $G(\cdot)$ and that of $F(\cdot)$ being unambiguously less risky than $G(\cdot)$. These ideas are known, respectively, by the technical terms of *first-order stochastic dominance* and *second-order stochastic dominance*.[20]

In all subsequent developments, we restrict ourselves to distributions $F(\cdot)$ such that $F(0) = 0$ and $F(x) = 1$ for some $x$.

### First-Order Stochastic Dominance

We want to attach meaning to the expression: "The distribution $F(\cdot)$ yields unambiguously higher returns than the distribution $G(\cdot)$." At least two sensible criteria suggest themselves. First, we could test whether every expected utility maximizer who values more over less prefers $F(\cdot)$ to $G(\cdot)$. Alternatively, we could verify whether, for every amount of money $x$, the probability of getting at least $x$ is higher under $F(\cdot)$ than under $G(\cdot)$. Fortunately, these two criteria lead to the same concept.

**Definition 6.D.1:** The distribution $F(\cdot)$ *first-order stochastically dominates* $G(\cdot)$ if, for every nondecreasing function $u: \mathbb{R} \to \mathbb{R}$, we have

$$\int u(x)\, dF(x) \geq \int u(x)\, dG(x).$$

**Proposition 6.D.1:** The distribution of monetary payoffs $F(\cdot)$ first-order stochastically dominates the distribution $G(\cdot)$ if and only if $F(x) \leq G(x)$ for every $x$.

**Proof:** Given $F(\cdot)$ and $G(\cdot)$ denote $H(x) = F(x) - G(x)$. Suppose that $H(\bar{x}) > 0$ for some $\bar{x}$. Then we can define a nondecreasing function $u(\cdot)$ by $u(x) = 1$ for $x > \bar{x}$ and $u(x) = 0$ for $x \leq \bar{x}$. This function has the property that $\int u(x)\, dH(x) = -H(\bar{x}) < 0$, and so the "only if" part of the proposition follows.

For the "if" part of the proposition we first put on record, without proof, that it suffices to establish the equivalence for differentiable utility functions $u(\cdot)$. Given $F(\cdot)$ and $G(\cdot)$, denote $H(x) = F(x) - G(x)$. Integrating by parts, we have

$$\int u(x)\, dH(x) = [u(x)H(x)]_0^\infty - \int u'(x)H(x)\, dx.$$

Since $H(0) = 0$ and $H(x) = 0$ for large $x$, the first term of this expression is zero. It follows that $\int u(x)\, dH(x) \geq 0$ [or, equivalently, $\int u(x)\, dF(x) - \int u(x)\, dG(x) \geq 0$] if and only if $\int u'(x)H(x)\, dx \leq 0$. Thus, if $H(x) \leq 0$ for all $x$ and $u(\cdot)$ is increasing, then $\int u'(x)H(x)\, dx \leq 0$ and the "if" part of the proposition follows. ∎

In Exercise 6.D.1 you are asked to verify Proposition 6.D.1 for the case of lotteries over three possible outcomes. In Figure 6.D.1, we represent two distributions $F(\cdot)$ and $G(\cdot)$. Distribution $F(\cdot)$ first-order stochastically dominates $G(\cdot)$ because the graph of $F(\cdot)$ is uniformly below the graph of $G(\cdot)$. Note two important points: First, first-order stochastic dominance does *not* imply that every possible return of the

---

20. They were introduced into economics in Rothschild and Stiglitz (1970).

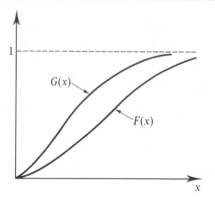

**Figure 6.D.1**

$F(\cdot)$ first-order stochastically dominates $G(\cdot)$.

superior distribution is larger than every possible return of the inferior one. In the figure, the set of possible outcomes is the same for the two distributions. Second, although $F(\cdot)$ first-order stochastically dominating $G(\cdot)$ implies that the mean of $x$ under $F(\cdot)$, $\int x\, dF(x)$, is greater than its mean under $G(\cdot)$, a ranking of the means of two distributions does *not* imply that one first-order stochastically dominates the other; rather, the entire distribution matters (see Exercise 6.D.3).

**Example 6.D.1:** Consider a compound lottery that has as its first stage a realization of $x$ distributed according to $G(\cdot)$ and in its second stage applies to the outcome $x$ of the first stage an "upward probabilistic shift." That is, if outcome $x$ is realized in the first stage, then the second stage pays a final amount of money $x + z$, where $z$ is distributed according to a distribution $H_x(z)$ with $H_x(0) = 0$. Thus, $H_x(\cdot)$ generates a *final* return of at least $x$ with probability one. (Note that the distributions applied to different $x$'s may differ.)

Denote the resulting reduced distribution by $F(\cdot)$. Then for any nondecreasing function $u: \mathbb{R} \to \mathbb{R}$, we have

$$\int u(x)\, dF(x) = \int \left[ \int u(x + z)\, dH_x(z) \right] dG(x) \geq \int u(x)\, dG(x).$$

So $F(\cdot)$ first-order stochastically dominates $G(\cdot)$.

A specific example is illustrated in Figure 6.D.2. As Figure 6.D.2(a) shows, $G(\cdot)$ is an even randomization between 1 and 4 dollars. The outcome "1 dollar" is then

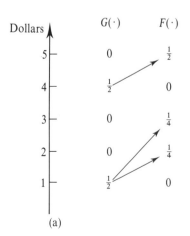

(a)

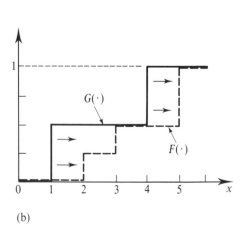

(b)

**Figure 6.D.2**

$F(\cdot)$ first-order stochastically dominates $G(\cdot)$.

shifted up to an even probability between 2 and 3 dollars, and the outcome "4 dollars" is shifted up to 5 dollars with probability one. Figure 6.D.2(b) shows that $F(x) \leq G(x)$ at all $x$.

It can be shown that the reverse direction also holds. Whenever $F(\cdot)$ first-order stochastically dominates $G(\cdot)$, it is possible to generate $F(\cdot)$ from $G(\cdot)$ in the manner suggested in this example. Thus, this provides yet another approach to the characterization of the first-order stochastic dominance relation. ∎

### Second-Order Stochastic Dominance

First-order stochastic dominance involves the idea of "higher/better" vs. "lower/worse." We want next to introduce a comparison based on relative *riskiness* or *dispersion*. To avoid confusing this issue with the trade-off between returns and risk, *we will restrict ourselves for the rest of this section to comparing distributions with the same mean.*

Once again, a definition suggests itself: Given two distributions $F(\cdot)$ and $G(\cdot)$ with the same mean [that is, with $\int x \, dF(x) = \int x \, dG(x)$], we say that $G(\cdot)$ is riskier than $F(\cdot)$ if every risk averter prefers $F(\cdot)$ and $G(\cdot)$. This is stated formally in Definition 6.D.2.

**Definition 6.D.2:** For any two distributions $F(x)$ and $G(\cdot)$ with the same mean, $F(\cdot)$ *second-order stochastically dominates* (or *is less risky than*) $G(\cdot)$ if for every nondecreasing concave function $u: \mathbb{R}_+ \to \mathbb{R}$, we have

$$\int u(x) \, dF(x) \geq \int u(x) \, dG(x).$$

Example 6.D.2 introduces an alternative way to characterize the second-order stochastic dominance relation.

**Example 6.D.2:** *Mean-Preserving Spreads.* Consider the following compound lottery: In the first stage, we have a lottery over $x$ distributed according to $F(\cdot)$. In the second stage, we randomize each possible outcome $x$ further so that the final payoff is $x + z$, where $z$ has a distribution function $H_x(z)$ with a mean of zero [i.e., $\int z \, dH_x(z) = 0$]. Thus, the mean of $x + z$ is $x$. Let the resulting reduced lottery be denoted by $G(\cdot)$. When lottery $G(\cdot)$ can be obtained from lottery $F(\cdot)$ in this manner for some distribution $H_x(\cdot)$, we say that $G(\cdot)$ is a *mean-preserving spread* of $F(\cdot)$.

For example, $F(\cdot)$ may be an even probability distribution between 2 and 3 dollars. In the second step we may spread the 2 dollars outcome to an even probability between 1 and 3 dollars, and the 3 dollars outcome to an even probability between 2 and 4 dollars. Then $G(\cdot)$ is the distribution that assigns probability $\frac{1}{4}$ to the four outcomes: 1, 2, 3, 4 dollars. These two distributions $F(\cdot)$ and $G(\cdot)$ are depicted in Figure 6.D.3.

The type of two-stage operation just described keeps the mean of $G(\cdot)$ equal to that of $F(\cdot)$. In addition, if $u(\cdot)$ is concave, we can conclude that

$$\int u(x) \, dG(x) = \int \left( \int u(x + z) \, dH_x(z) \right) dF(x) \leq \int u\left( \int (x + z) \, dH_x(z) \right) dF(x)$$

$$= \int u(x) \, dF(x),$$

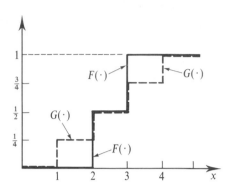

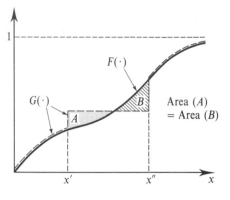

**Figure 6.D.3 (left)**

$G(\cdot)$ is a mean-preserving spread of $F(\cdot)$.

**Figure 6.D.4 (right)**

$G(\cdot)$ is an elementary increase in risk from $F(\cdot)$.

and so $F(\cdot)$ second-order stochastically dominates $G(\cdot)$. It turns out that the converse is also true: If $F(\cdot)$ second-order stochastically dominates $G(\cdot)$, then $G(\cdot)$ is a mean-preserving spread of $F(\cdot)$. Hence, *saying that $G(\cdot)$ is a mean-preserving spread of $F(\cdot)$ is equivalent to saying that $F(\cdot)$ second-order stochastically dominates $G(\cdot)$.* ∎

Example 6.D.3 provides another illustration of a mean-preserving spread.

**Example 6.D.3:** *An Elementary Increase in Risk.* We say that $G(\cdot)$ constitutes an *elementary increase in risk* from $F(\cdot)$ if $G(\cdot)$ is generated from $F(\cdot)$ by taking all the mass that $F(\cdot)$ assigns to an interval $[x', x'']$ and transferring it to the endpoints $x'$ and $x''$ in such a manner that the mean is preserved. This is illustrated in Figure 6.D.4. An elementary increase in risk is a mean-preserving spread. [In Exercise 6.D.3, you are asked to verify directly that if $G(\cdot)$ is an elementary increase in risk from $F(\cdot)$, then $F(\cdot)$ second-order stochastically dominates $G(\cdot)$.] ∎

We can develop still another way to capture the second-order stochastic dominance idea. Suppose that we have two distributions $F(\cdot)$ and $G(\cdot)$ with the same mean. Recall that, for simplicity, we assume that $F(\bar{x}) = G(\bar{x}) = 1$ for some $\bar{x}$. Integrating by parts (and recalling the equality of the means) yields

$$\int_0^{\bar{x}} (F(x) - G(x))\,dx = -\int_0^{\bar{x}} x\,d(F(x) - G(x)) + (F(\bar{x}) - G(\bar{x}))\bar{x} = 0. \quad (6.D.1)$$

That is, the areas below the two distribution functions are the same over the interval $[0, \bar{x}]$. Because of this fact, the regions marked $A$ and $B$ in Figure 6.D.4 must have the same area. Note that for the two distributions in the figure, this implies that

$$\int_0^x G(t)\,dt \geq \int_0^x F(t)\,dt \quad \text{for all } x. \quad (6.D.2)$$

It turns out that property (6.D.2) is equivalent to $F(\cdot)$ second-order stochastically dominating $G(\cdot)$.[21] As an application, suppose that $F(\cdot)$ and $G(\cdot)$ have the same mean and that the graph of $G(\cdot)$ is initially above the graph of $F(\cdot)$ and then moves

21. We will not prove this. The claim can be established along the same lines used to prove Proposition 6.D.1 except that we must integrate by parts twice and take into account expression (6.D.1).

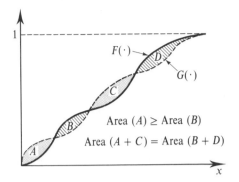

Area $(A) \geq$ Area $(B)$

Area $(A + C) =$ Area $(B + D)$

**Figure 6.D.5**

$F(\cdot)$ second-order stochastically dominates $G(\cdot)$.

permanently below it (as in Figures 6.D.3 and 6.D.4). Then because of (6.D.1), condition (6.D.2) must be satisfied, and we can conclude that $G(\cdot)$ is riskier than $F(\cdot)$. As a more elaborate example, consider Figure 6.D.5, which shows two distributions having the same mean and satisfying (6.D.2). To verify that (6.D.2) is satisfied, note that area $A$ has been drawn to be at least as large as area $B$ and that the equality of the means [i.e., (6.D.1)] implies that the areas $B + D$ and $A + C$ must be equal.

We state Proposition 6.D.2 without proof.

**Proposition 6.D.2:** Consider two distributions $F(\cdot)$ and $G(\cdot)$ with the same mean. Then the following statements are equivalent:

    (i) $F(\cdot)$ second-order stochastically dominates $G(\cdot)$.

    (ii) $G(\cdot)$ is a mean-preserving spread of $F(\cdot)$.

    (iii) Property (6.D.2) holds.

In Exercise 6.D.4, you are asked to verify the equivalence of these three properties in the probability simplex diagram.

# 6.E State-dependent Utility

In this section, we consider an extension of the analysis presented in the preceding two sections. In Sections 6.C and 6.D, we assumed that the decision maker cares solely about the distribution of monetary payoffs he receives. This says, in essence, that the underlying cause of the payoff is of no importance. If the cause is one's state of health, however, this assumption is unlikely to be fulfilled.[22] The distribution function of monetary payoffs is then not the appropriate object of individual choice. Here we consider the possibility that the decision maker may care not only about his monetary returns but also about the underlying events, or *states of nature*, that cause them.

We begin by discussing a convenient framework for modeling uncertain alternatives that, in contrast to the lottery apparatus, recognizes underlying states of nature. (We will encounter it repeatedly throughout the book, especially in Chapter 19.)

---

22. On the other hand, if it is an event such as the price of some security in a portfolio, the assumption is more likely to be a good representation of reality.

*State-of-Nature Representations of Uncertainty*

In Sections 6.C and 6.D, we modeled a risky alternative by means of a distribution function over monetary outcomes. Often, however, we know that the random outcome is generated by some underlying causes. A more detailed description of uncertain alternatives is then possible. For example, the monetary payoff of an insurance policy might depend on whether or not a certain accident has happened, the payoff on a corporate stock on whether the economy is in a recession, and the payoff of a casino gamble on the number selected by the roulette wheel.

We call these underlying causes *states*, or *states of nature*. We denote the set of states by $S$ and an individual state by $s \in S$. For simplicity, we assume here that the set of states is finite and that each state $s$ has a well-defined, objective probability $\pi_s > 0$ that it occurs. We abuse notation slightly by also denoting the total number of states by $S$.

An uncertain alternative with (nonnegative) monetary returns can then be described as a function that maps realizations of the underlying state of nature into the set of possible money payoffs $\mathbb{R}_+$. Formally, such a function is known as a *random variable*.

**Definition 6.E.1:** A *random variable* is a function $g: S \to \mathbb{R}_+$ that maps states into monetary outcomes.[23]

Every random variable $g(\cdot)$ gives rise to a money lottery describable by the distribution function $F(\cdot)$ with $F(x) = \sum_{\{s: g(s) \le x\}} \pi_s$ for all $x$. Note that there is a loss in information in going from the random variable representation of uncertainty to the lottery representation; we do not keep track of which states give rise to a given monetary outcome, and only the aggregate probability of every monetary outcome is retained.

Because we take $S$ to be finite, we can represent a random variable with monetary payoffs by the vector $(x_1, \ldots, x_S)$, where $x_s$ is the nonnegative monetary payoff in state $s$. The set of all nonnegative random variables is then $\mathbb{R}_+^S$.

*State-Dependent Preferences and the Extended Expected Utility Representation*

The primitive datum of our theory is now a rational preference relation $\succsim$ on the set $\mathbb{R}_+^S$ of nonnegative random variables. Note that this formal setting is parallel to the one developed in Chapters 2 to 4 for consumer choice. The similarity is not merely superficial. If we define commodity $s$ as the random variable that pays one dollar if and only if state $s$ occurs (this is called a *contingent commodity* in Chapter 19), then the set of nonnegative random variables $\mathbb{R}_+^S$ is precisely the set of nonnegative bundles of these $S$ contingent commodities.

As we shall see, it is very convenient if, in the spirit of the previous sections of this chapter, we can represent the individual's preferences over monetary outcomes by a utility function that possesses an *extended expected utility form*.

---

23. For concreteness, we restrict the outcomes to be nonnegative amounts of money. As we did in Section 6.B, we could equally well use an abstract outcome set $C$ instead of $\mathbb{R}_+$.

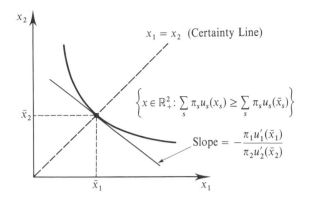

$x_1 = x_2$ (Certainty Line)

$$\left\{ x \in \mathbb{R}_+^2 : \sum_s \pi_s u_s(x_s) \geq \sum_s \pi_s u_s(\bar{x}_s) \right\}$$

$$\text{Slope} = -\frac{\pi_1 u_1'(\bar{x}_1)}{\pi_2 u_2'(\bar{x}_2)}$$

**Figure 6.E.1**

State-dependent preferences.

**Definition 6.E.2:** The preference relation $\succsim$ has an *extended expected utility representation* if for every $s \in S$, there is a function $u_s : \mathbb{R}_+ \to \mathbb{R}$ such that for any $(x_1, \ldots, x_S) \in \mathbb{R}_+^S$ and $(x_1', \ldots, x_S') \in \mathbb{R}_+^S$,

$$(x_1, \ldots, x_S) \succsim (x_1', \ldots, x_S') \quad \text{if and only if} \quad \sum_s \pi_s u_s(x_s) \geq \sum_s \pi_s u_s(x_s').$$

To understand Definition 6.E.2, recall the analysis in Section 6.B. If only the distribution of money payoffs mattered, and if preferences on money distributions satisfied the expected utility axioms, then the expected utility theorem leads to a *state-independent* (we will also say *state-uniform*) expected utility representation $\sum_s \pi_s u(x_s)$, where $u(\cdot)$ is the Bernoulli utility function on amounts of money.[24] The generalization in Definition 6.E.2 allows for a different function $u_s(\cdot)$ in every state.

Before discussing the conditions under which an extended utility representation exists, we comment on its usefulness as a tool in the analysis of choice under uncertainty. This usefulness is primarily a result of the behavior of the indifference sets around the *money certainty line*, the set of random variables that pay the same amount in every state. Figure 6.E.1 depicts state-dependent preferences in the space $\mathbb{R}_+^S$ for a case where $S = 2$ and the $u_s(\cdot)$ functions are concave (as we shall see later, concavity of these functions follows from risk aversion considerations). The certainty line in Figure 6.E.1 is the set of points with $x_1 = x_2$. The marginal rate of substitution at a point $(\bar{x}, \bar{x})$ is $\pi_1 u_1'(\bar{x})/\pi_2 u_2'(\bar{x})$. Thus, the slope of the indifference curves on the certainty line reflects the nature of state dependence as well as the probabilities of the different states. In contrast, with state-uniform (i.e., identical across states) utility functions, the marginal rate of substitution at any point on the certainty line equals the ratio of the probabilities of the states (implying that this slope is the same at all points on the certainty line).

**Example 6.E.1:** *Insurance with State-dependent Utility.* One interesting implication of state dependency arises when actuarially fair insurance is available. Suppose there are two states: State 1 is the state where no loss occurs, and state 2 is the state where a loss occurs. (This economic situation parallels that in Example 6.C.1.) The individual's initial situation (i.e., in the absence of any insurance purchase) is a

---

24. Note that the random variable $(x_1, \ldots, x_S)$ induces a money lottery that pays $x_s$ with probability $\pi_s$. Hence, $\sum_s \pi_s u(x_s)$ is its expected utility.

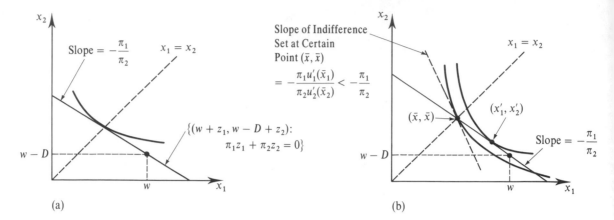

**Figure 6.E.2**  Insurance purchase with state-dependent utility. (a) State-uniform utility. (b) State-dependent utility.

random variable $(w, w - D)$ that gives the individual's wealth in the two states. This is depicted in Figure 6.E.2(a). We can represent an insurance contract by a random variable $(z_1, z_2) \in \mathbb{R}^2$ specifying the net change in wealth in the two states (the insurance payoff in the state less any premiums paid). Thus, if the individual purchases insurance contract $(z_1, z_2)$, his final wealth position will be $(w + z_1, w - D + z_2)$. The insurance policy $(z_1, z_2)$ is actuarially fair if its expected payoff is zero, that is, if $\pi_1 z_1 + \pi_2 z_2 = 0$.

Figure 6.E.2(a) shows the optimal insurance purchase when a risk-averse expected utility maximizer with state-uniform preferences can purchase any actuarially fair insurance policy he desires. His budget set is the straight line drawn in the figure. We saw in Example 6.C.2 that under these conditions, a decision maker with state-uniform utility would insure completely. This is confirmed here because if there is no state dependency, the budget line is tangent to an indifference curve at the certainty line.

Figure 6.E.2(b) depicts the situation with state-dependent preferences. The decision maker will now prefer a point such as $(x'_1, x'_2)$ to the certain outcome $(\bar{x}, \bar{x})$. This creates a desire to have a higher payoff in state 1, where $u'_1(\cdot)$ is relatively higher, in exchange for a lower payoff in state 2.  ∎

*Existence of an Extended Expected Utility Representation*

We now investigate conditions for the existence of an extended expected utility representation.

Observe first that since $\pi_s > 0$ for every $s$, we can formally include $\pi_s$ in the definition of the utility function at state $s$. That is, to find an extended expected utility representation, it suffices that there be functions $u_s(\cdot)$ such that

$$(x_1, \ldots, x_S) \succsim (x'_1, \ldots, x'_S) \quad \text{if and only if} \quad \sum_s u_s(x_s) \geq \sum_s u_s(x'_s).$$

This is because if such functions $u_s(\cdot)$ exist, then we can define $\tilde{u}_s(\cdot) = (1/\pi_s)u_s(\cdot)$ for each $s \in S$, and we will have $\sum_s u_s(x_s) \geq \sum_s u_s(x'_s)$ if and only if $\sum_s \pi_s \tilde{u}_s(x_s) \geq \sum_s \pi_s \tilde{u}_s(x'_s)$. Thus, from now on, we focus on the existence of an additively separable form $\sum_s u_s(\cdot)$, and the $\pi_s$'s cease to play any role in the analysis.

It turns out that the extended expected utility representation can be derived *in exactly the same way* as the expected utility representation of Section 6.B if we appropriately enlarge the domain over which preferences are defined.[25] Accordingly, we now allow for the possibility that within each state $s$, the monetary payoff is not a certain amount of money $x_s$ but a random amount with distribution function $F_s(\cdot)$. We denote these uncertain alternatives by $L = (F_1, \ldots, F_S)$. Thus, $L$ is a kind of compound lottery that assigns well-defined monetary gambles as prizes contingent on the realization of the state of the world $s$. We denote by $\mathscr{L}$ the set of all such possible lotteries.

Our starting point is now a rational preference relation $\succsim$ on $\mathscr{L}$. Note that $\alpha L + (1 - \alpha)L' = (\alpha F_1 + (1 - \alpha)F_1', \ldots, \alpha F_S + (1 - \alpha)F_S')$ has the usual interpretation as the reduced lottery arising from a randomization between $L$ and $L'$, although here we are dealing with a reduced lottery within each state $s$. Hence, we can appeal to the same logic as in Section 6.B and impose an independence axiom on preferences.

**Definition 6.E.3:** The preference relation $\succsim$ on $\mathscr{L}$ satisfies the *extended independence axiom* if for all $L, L', L'' \in \mathscr{L}$ and $\alpha \in (0, 1)$, we have

$$L \succsim L' \quad \text{if and only if} \quad \alpha L + (1 - \alpha)L'' \succsim \alpha L' + (1 - \alpha)L''.$$

We also make a continuity assumption: Except for the reinterpretation of $\mathscr{L}$, this *continuity axiom* is exactly the same as that in Section 6.B; we refer to Definition 6.B.3 for its statement.

**Proposition 6.E.1:** (*Extended Expected Utility Theorem*) Suppose that the preference relation $\succsim$ on the space of lotteries $\mathscr{L}$ satisfies the continuity and extended independence axioms. Then we can assign a utility function $u_s(\cdot)$ for money in every state $s$ such that for any $L = (F_1, \ldots, F_S)$ and $L' = (F_1', \ldots, F_S')$, we have

$$L \succsim L' \quad \text{if and only if} \quad \sum_s \left( \int u_s(x_s) \, dF_s(x_s) \right) \geq \sum_s \left( \int u_s(x_s) \, dF_s'(x_s) \right).$$

**Proof:** The proof is identical, almost word for word, to the proof of the expected utility theorem (Proposition 6.B.2).

Suppose, for simplicity, that we restrict ourselves to a finite number $\{x_1, \ldots, x_N\}$ of monetary outcomes. Then we can identify the set $\mathscr{L}$ with $\Delta^S$, where $\Delta$ is the $(N - 1)$-dimensional simplex. Our aim is to show that $\succsim$ can be represented by a linear utility function $U(L)$ on $\Delta^S$. To see this, note that, up to an additive constant that can be neglected, $U(p_1^1, \ldots, p_N^1, \ldots, p_1^S, \ldots, p_N^S)$ is a linear function of its arguments if it can be written as $U(L) = \sum_{n,s} u_{n,s} p_n^s$ for some values $u_{n,s}$. In this case, we can write $U(L) = \sum_s (\sum_n u_{n,s} p_n^s)$, which, letting $u_s(x_n) = u_{n,s}$, is precisely the form of a utility function on $\mathscr{L}$ that we want.

Choose $\bar{L}$ and $\underline{L}$ such that $\bar{L} \succsim L \succsim \underline{L}$ for all $L \in \mathscr{L}$. As in the proof of Proposition 6.B.2, we can then define $U(L)$ by the condition

$$L \sim U(L)\bar{L} + (1 - U(L))\underline{L}.$$

Applying the extended independence axiom in exactly the same way as we applied the independence axiom in the proof of Proposition 6.B.2 yields the result that $U(L)$ is indeed a linear utility function on $\mathscr{L}$. ∎

---

25. By pushing the enlargement further than we do here, it would even be possible to view the existence of an extended utility representation as a corollary of the expected utility theorem.

Proposition 6.F.1 gives us a utility representation $\sum_s u_s(x_s)$ for the preferences on state-by-state sure outcomes $(x_1, \ldots, x_S) \in \mathbb{R}_+^S$ that has two properties. First, it is additively separable across states. Second, every $u_s(\cdot)$ is a Bernoulli utility function that can be used to evaluate lotteries over money payoffs in state $s$ by means of expected utility. It is because of the second property that risk aversion (defined in exactly the same manner as in Section 6.C) is equivalent to the concavity of each $u_s(\cdot)$.

There is another approach to the extended expected utility representation that rests with the preferences $\succsim$ defined on $\mathbb{R}_+^S$ and does not appeal to preferences defined on a larger space. It is based on the so-called *sure-thing axiom*.

**Definition 6.E.4:** The preference relation $\succsim$ satisfies the *sure-thing axiom* if, for any subset of states $E \subset S$ ($E$ is called an *event*), whenever $(x_1, \ldots, x_S)$ and $(x_1', \ldots, x_S')$ differ only in the entries corresponding to $E$ (so that $x_s' = x_s$ for $s \notin E$), the preference ordering between $(x_1, \ldots, x_S)$ and $(x_1', \ldots, x_S')$ is independent of the particular (common) payoffs for states not in $E$. Formally, suppose that $(x_1, \ldots, x_S)$, $(x_1', \ldots, x_S')$, $(\bar{x}_1, \ldots, \bar{x}_S)$, and $(\bar{x}_1', \ldots, \bar{x}_S')$ are such that

$$\text{For all } s \notin E: \quad x_s = x_s' \quad \text{and} \quad \bar{x}_s = \bar{x}_s'.$$
$$\text{For all } s \in E: \quad x_s = \bar{x}_s \quad \text{and} \quad x_s' = \bar{x}_s'.$$

Then $(\bar{x}_1, \ldots, \bar{x}_S) \succsim (\bar{x}_1', \ldots, \bar{x}_S')$ if and only if $(x_1, \ldots, x_S) \succsim (x_1', \ldots, x_S')$.

The intuitive content of this axiom is similar to that of the independence axiom. It simply says that if two random variables cannot be distinguished in the complement of $E$, then the ordering among them can depend only on the values they take on $E$. In other words, tastes conditional on an event should not depend on what the payoffs would have been in states that have not occurred.

If $\succsim$ admits an extended expected utility representation, the sure-thing axiom holds because then $(x_1, \ldots, x_S) \succsim (x_1', \ldots, x_S')$ if and only if $\sum_s (u_s(x_s) - u_s(x_s')) \geq 0$, and any term of the sum with $x_s = x_s'$ will cancel. In the other direction we have Proposition 6.E.2.

**Proposition 6.E.2:** Suppose that there are at least three states and that the preferences $\succsim$ on $\mathbb{R}_+^S$ are continuous and satisfy the sure-thing axiom. Then $\succsim$ admits an extended expected utility representation.

**Idea of Proof:** A complete proof is too advanced to be given in any detail. One wants to show that under the assumptions, preferences admit an additively separable utility representation $\sum_s u_s(x_s)$. This is not easy to show, and it is not a result particularly related to uncertainty. The conditions for the existence of an additively separable utility function for continuous preferences on the positive orthant of a Euclidean space (i.e., the context of Chapter 3) are well understood; as it turns out, they are *formally identical* to the sure-thing axiom (see Exercise 3.G.4). ∎

Although the sure-thing axiom yields an extended expected utility representation $\sum_s \pi_s u_s(x_s)$, we would emphasize that randomizations over monetary payoffs in a state $s$ have not been considered in this approach, and therefore we cannot bring the idea of risk aversion to bear on the determination of the properties of $u_s(\cdot)$. Thus, the approach via the extended independence axiom assumes a stronger basic framework (preferences are defined on the set $\mathscr{L}$ rather than on the smaller $\mathbb{R}_+^S$), but it also yields stronger conclusions.

# 6.F  Subjective Probability Theory

Up to this point in the development of the theory, we have been assuming that risk, summarized by means of numerical probabilities, is regarded as an objective fact by the decision maker. But this is rarely true in reality. Individuals make judgments about the chances of uncertain events that are not necessarily expressible in quantitative form. Even when probabilities are mentioned, as sometimes happens when a doctor discusses the likelihood of various outcomes of medical treatment, they are often acknowledged as imprecise *subjective* estimates.

It would be very helpful, both theoretically and practically, if we could assert that choices are made *as if* individuals held probabilistic beliefs. Even better, we would like that well-defined probabilistic beliefs be revealed by choice behavior. This is the intent of *subjective probability theory*. The theory argues that even if states of the world are not associated with recognizable, objective probabilities, consistency-like restrictions on preferences among gambles still imply that decision makers behave *as if* utilities were assigned to outcomes, probabilities were attached to states of nature, and decisions were made by taking expected utilities. Moreover, this rationalization of the decision maker's behavior with an expected utility function can be done uniquely (up to a positive linear transformation for the utility functions). The theory is therefore a far-reaching generalization of expected utility theory. The classical reference for subjective probability theory is Savage (1954), which is very readable but also advanced. It is, however, possible to gain considerable insight into the theory if one is willing to let the analysis be aided by the use of lotteries with objective random outcomes. This is the approach suggested by Anscombe and Aumann (1963), and we will follow it here.

We begin, as in Section 6.E, with a set of states $\{1, \ldots, S\}$. The probabilities on $\{1, \ldots, S\}$ are not given. In effect, we aim to *deduce* them. As before, a random variable with monetary payoffs is a vector $x = (x_1, \ldots, x_S) \in \mathbb{R}_+^S$.[26] We also want to allow for the possibility that the monetary payoffs in a state are not certain but are themselves money lotteries with objective distributions $F_s$. Thus, our set of risky alternatives, denoted $\mathcal{L}$, is the set of all $S$-tuples $(F_1, \ldots, F_S)$ of distribution functions.

Suppose now that we are given a rational preference relation $\succsim$ on $\mathcal{L}$. We assume that $\succsim$ satisfies the continuity and the extended independence axioms introduced in Section 6.E. Then, by Proposition 6.E.1, we conclude that there are $u_s(\cdot)$ such that any $(x_1, \ldots, x_S) \in \mathbb{R}_+^S$ can be evaluated by $\sum_s u_s(x_s)$. In addition, $u_s(\cdot)$ is a Bernoulli utility function for money lotteries in state $s$.

The existence of the $u_s(\cdot)$ functions does not yet allow us to identify subjective probabilities. Indeed, for *any* $(\pi_1, \ldots, \pi_S) \gg 0$, we could define $\tilde{u}_s(\cdot) = (1/\pi_s)u_s(\cdot)$, and we could then evaluate $(x_1, \ldots, x_S)$ by $\sum_s \pi_s \tilde{u}_s(x_s)$. What is needed is some way to disentangle utilities from probabilities.

Consider an example. Suppose that a gamble that gives one dollar in state 1 and none in state 2 is preferred to a gamble that gives one dollar in state 2 and none in state 1. Provided *there is no reason to think that the labels of the states have any*

---

26. To be specific, we consider monetary payoffs here. All the subsequent arguments, however, work with arbitrary sets of outcomes.

*particular influence on the value of money*, it is then natural to conclude that the decision maker regards state 2 as less likely than state 1.

This example suggests an additional postulate. Preferences over money lotteries within state $s$ should be the same as those within any other state $s'$; that is, risk attitudes towards money gambles should be the same across states. To formulate such a property, we define the state $s$ preferences $\succsim_s$ on state $s$ lotteries by

$$F_s \succsim_s F_s' \quad \text{if} \quad \int u_s(x_s)\, dF_s(x_s) \geq \int u_s(x_s)\, dF_s'(x_s).$$

**Definition 6.F.1:** The state preferences $(\succsim_1, \ldots, \succsim_S)$ on state lotteries are *state uniform* if $\succsim_s = \succsim_{s'}$ for any $s$ and $s'$.

With state uniformity, $u_s(\cdot)$ and $u_{s'}(\cdot)$ can differ only by an increasing linear transformation. Therefore, there is $u(\cdot)$ such that, for all $s = 1, \ldots, S$,

$$u_s(\cdot) = \pi_s u(\cdot) + \beta_s$$

for some $\pi_s > 0$ and $\beta_s$. Moreover, because we still represent the same preferences if we divide all $\pi_s$ and $\beta_s$ by a common constant, we can normalize the $\pi_s$ so that $\sum_s \pi_s = 1$. These $\pi_s$ are going to be our subjective probabilities.

**Proposition 6.F.1:** (*Subjective Expected Utility Theorem*) Suppose that the preference relation $\succsim$ on $\mathscr{L}$ satisfies the continuity and extended independence axioms. Suppose, in addition, that the derived state preferences are state uniform. Then there are probabilities $(\pi_1, \ldots, \pi_S) \gg 0$ and a utility function $u(\cdot)$ on amounts of money such that for any $(x_1, \ldots, x_S)$ and $(x_1', \ldots, x_S')$ we have

$$(x_1, \ldots, x_S) \succsim (x_1', \ldots, x_S') \quad \text{if and only if} \quad \sum_s \pi_s u(x_s) \geq \sum_s \pi_s u(x_s').$$

Moreover, the probabilities are uniquely determined, and the utility function is unique up to origin and scale.

**Proof:** Existence has already been proven. You are asked to establish uniqueness in Exercise 6.F.1. ∎

The practical advantages of the subjective expected utility representation are similar to those of the objective version, which we discussed in Section 6.B, and we will not repeat them here. A major virtue of the theory is that it gives a precise, quantifiable, and operational meaning to uncertainty. It is, indeed, most pleasant to be able to remain in the familiar realm of the probability calculus.

But there are also problems. The plausibility of the axioms cannot be completely dissociated from the complexity of the choice situations. The more complex these become, the more strained even seemingly innocent axioms are, For example, is the completeness axiom reasonable for preferences defined on huge sets of random variables? Or consider the implicit axiom (often those are the most treacherous) that the situation can actually be formalized as indicated by the model. This posits the ability to list all conceivable states of the world (or, at least, a sufficiently disaggregated version of this list). In summary, every difficulty so far raised against our model of the rational consumer (i.e., to transitivity, to completeness, to independence) will apply with increased force to the current model.

There are also difficulties specific to the nonobjective nature of probabilities. We devote Example 6.F.1 to this point.

**Example 6.F.1:** This example is a variation of the *Ellsberg paradox.*[27] There are two urns, denoted R and H. Each urn contains 100 balls. The balls are either white or black. Urn R contains 49 white balls and 51 black balls. Urn H contains an unspecified assortment of balls. A ball has been randomly picked from each urn. Call them the *R-ball* and the *H-ball*, respectively. The color of these balls has not been disclosed. Now we consider two choice situations. In both experiments, the decision maker must choose either the R-ball or the H-ball. After the choices have been made, the color will be disclosed. In the first choice situation, a prize of 1000 dollars is won if the chosen ball is black. In the second choice situation, the same prize is won if the ball is white. With the information given, most people will choose the R-ball in the first experiment. If the decision is made using subjective probabilities, this should mean that the subjective probability that the H-ball is white is larger than .49. Hence, most people should choose the H-ball in the second experiment. However, it turns out that this does not happen overwhelmingly in actual experiments. The decision maker understands that by choosing the R-ball, he has only a 49% chance of winning. However, this chance is "safe" and well understood. The uncertainties incurred are much less clear if he chooses the H-ball. ∎

Knight (1921) proposed distinguishing between *risk* and *uncertainty* according to whether the probabilities are given to us objectively or not. In a sense, the theory of subjective probability nullifies this distinction by reducing all uncertainty to risk through the use of beliefs expressible as probabilities. The Example 6.F.1 suggests that there may be something to the distinction. This is an active area of research [e.g., Bewley (1986) and Gilboa and Schmeidler (1989)].

---

27. From Ellsberg (1961).

## REFERENCES

Allais, M. (1953). Le comportement de l'homme rationnel devant le risque, critique des postulats et axiomes de l'école Américaine. *Econometrica* **21**: 503–46.

Anscombe, F., and R. Aumann. (1963). A definition of subjective probability. *Annals of Mathematical Statistics* **34**: 199–205.

Arrow, K. J. (1971). *Essays in the Theory of Risk Bearing.* Chicago: Markham.

Bewley, T. (1986). Knightian Decision Theory: Part 1. New Haven: Cowles Foundation Discussion Paper No. 807.

Dekel, E. (1986). An axiomatic characterization of preferences under uncertainty: Weakening the independence axiom. *Journal of Economic Theory* **40**: 304–18.

Diamond, P., and M. Rothschild. (1978). *Uncertainty in Economics: Readings and Exercises.* New York: Academic Press.

Ellsberg, D. (1961). Risk, ambiguity, and the Savage axioms. *Quarterly Journal of Economics* **75**: 643–69.

Gilboa, I., and D. Schmeidler. (1989). Maximin expected utility with a unique prior. *Journal of Mathematical Economics* **18**: 141–53.

Grether, D., and C. H. Plott. (1979). Economic theory of choice and the preference reversal phenomenon. *American Economic Review* **69**: 623–38.

Green, J. (1987). 'Making book against oneself,' the independence axiom, and nonlinear utility theory. *Quarterly Journal of Economics* **98**: 785–96.

Hey, J. D. and C. Orme. (1994). Investigating generalizations of expected utility theory using experimental data. *Econometrica* **62**: 1291–326.

Knight, F. (1921). *Risk, Uncertainty and Profit*. Boston, Mass.: Houghton Mifflin. Reprint, London: London School of Economics 1946.

Kreps, D. (1988). *Notes on the Theory of Choice*. Boulder, Colo.: Westview Press.

Machina, M. (1987). Choice under uncertainty: Problems solved and unsolved. *The Journal of Perspectives* **1**: 121–54.

Pratt, J. (1964). Risk aversion in the small and in the large. *Econometrica* **32**: 122–36. Reprinted in Diamond and Rothschild.

Rothschild, M. and J. Stiglitz. (1970). Increasing risk I: A definition. *Journal of Economic Theory* **2**: 225–43. Reprinted in Diamond and Rothschild.

Savage, L. (1954). *The Foundations of Statistics*. New York: Wiley.

Von Neumann, J., and O. Morgenstern. (1944). *Theory of Games and Economic Behavior*. Princeton, N.J.: Princeton University Press.

## EXERCISES

**6.B.1$^A$** In text.

**6.B.2$^A$** In text.

**6.B.3$^B$** Show that if the set of outcomes $C$ is finite and the rational preference relation $\succsim$ on the set of lotteries $\mathscr{L}$ satisfies the independence axiom, then there are best and worst lotteries in $\mathscr{L}$. That is, we can find lotteries $\bar{L}$ and $\underline{L}$ such that $\bar{L} \succsim L \succsim \underline{L}$ for all $L \in \mathscr{L}$.

**6.B.4$^B$** The purpose of this exercise is to illustrate how expected utility theory allows us to make consistent decisions when dealing with extremely small probabilities by considering relatively large ones. Suppose that a safety agency is thinking of establishing a criterion under which an area prone to flooding should be evacuated. The probability of flooding is 1%. There are four possible outcomes:

(A) No evacuation is necessary, and none is performed.
(B) An evacuation is performed that is unnecessary.
(C) An evacuation is performed that is necessary.
(D) No evacuation is performed, and a flood causes a disaster.

Suppose that the agency is indifferent between the sure outcome B and the lottery of A with probability $p$ and D with probability $1 - p$, and between the sure outcome C and the lottery of B with probability $q$ and D with probability $1 - q$. Suppose also that it prefers A to D and that $p \in (0, 1)$ and $q \in (0, 1)$. Assume that the conditions of the expected utility theorem are satisfied.

(a) Construct a utility function of the expected utility form for the agency.

(b) Consider two different policy criteria:

   *Criterion 1:* This criterion will result in an evacuation in 90% of the cases in which flooding will occur and an unnecessary evacuation in 10% of the cases in which no flooding occurs.

   *Criterion 2:* This criterion is more conservative. It results in an evacuation in 95% of the cases in which flooding will occur and an unnecessary evacuation in 5% of the cases in which no flooding occurs.

First, derive the probability distributions over the four outcomes under these two criteria. Then, by using the utility function in (a), decide which criterion the agency would prefer.

**6.B.5$^B$** The purpose of this exercise is to show that the Allais paradox is compatible with a weaker version of the independence axiom. We consider the following axiom, known as the *betweenness axiom* [see Dekel (1986)]:

For all $L$, $L'$ and $\lambda \in (0, 1)$, if $L \sim L'$, then $\lambda L + (1 - \lambda)L' \sim L$.

Suppose that there are three possible outcomes.

**(a)** Show that a preference relation on lotteries satisfying the independence axiom also satisfies the betweenness axiom.

**(b)** Using a simplex representation for lotteries similar to the one in Figure 6.B.1(b), show that if the continuity and betweenness axioms are satisfied, then the indifference curves of a preference relation on lotteries are straight lines. Conversely, show that if the indifference curves are straight lines, then the betweenness axiom is satisfied. Do these straight lines need to be parallel?

**(c)** Using **(b)**, show that the betweenness axiom is weaker (less restrictive) than the independence axiom.

**(d)** Using Figure 6.B.7, show that the choices of the Allais paradox are compatible with the betweeness axiom by exhibiting an indifference map satisfying the betweenness axiom that yields the choices of the Allais paradox.

**6.B.6**[B] Prove that the induced utility function $U(\cdot)$ defined in the last paragraph of Section 6.B is convex. Give an example of a set of outcomes and a Bernoulli utility function for which the induced utility function is not linear.

**6.B.7**[A] Consider the following two lotteries:

$$L: \begin{cases} 200 \text{ dollars with probability } .7. \\ \phantom{200} 0 \text{ dollars with probability } .3. \end{cases}$$

$$L': \begin{cases} 1200 \text{ dollars with probability } .1. \\ \phantom{120} 0 \text{ dollars with probability } .9. \end{cases}$$

Let $x_L$ and $x_{L'}$ be the sure amounts of money that an individual finds indifferent to $L$ and $L'$. Show that if his preferences are transitive and monotone, the individual must prefer $L$ to $L'$ if and only if $x_L > x_{L'}$. [*Note*: In actual experiments, however, a preference reversal is often observed in which $L$ is preferred to $L'$ but $x_L < x_{L'}$. See Grether and Plott (1979) for details.]

**6.C.1**[B] Consider the insurance problem studied in Example 6.C.1. Show that if insurance is not actuarially fair (so that $q > \pi$), then the individual will not insure completely.

**6.C.2**[B]

**(a)** Show that if an individual has a Bernoulli utility function $u(\cdot)$ with the quadratic form

$$u(x) = \beta x^2 + \gamma x,$$

then his utility from a distribution is determined by the mean and variance of the distribution and, in fact, by these moments alone. [*Note*: The number $\beta$ should be taken to be negative in order to get the concavity of $u(\cdot)$. Since $u(\cdot)$ is then decreasing at $x > -\gamma/2\beta$, $u(\cdot)$ is useful only when the distribution cannot take values larger than $-\gamma/2\beta$.]

**(b)** Suppose that a utility function $U(\cdot)$ over distributions is given by

$$U(F) = (\text{mean of } F) - r(\text{variance of } F),$$

where $r > 0$. Argue that unless the set of possible distributions is further restricted (see, e.g., Exercise 6.C.19), $U(\cdot)$ cannot be compatible with any Bernoulli utility function. Give an example of two lotteries $L$ and $L'$ over the same two amounts of money, say $x'$ and $x'' > x'$, such that $L$ gives a higher probability to $x''$ than does $L'$ and yet according to $U(\cdot)$, $L'$ is preferred to $L$.

**6.C.3$^B$** Prove that the four conditions of Proposition 6.C.1 are equivalent. [*Hint*: The equivalence of (i), (ii), and (iii) has already been shown. As for (iv), prove that (i) implies (iv) and that (iv) implies $u(\frac{1}{2}x + \frac{1}{2}y) \geq \frac{1}{2}u(x) + \frac{1}{2}u(y)$ for any $x$ and $y$, which is, in fact, sufficient for (ii).]

**6.C.4$^B$** Suppose that there are $N$ risky assets whose returns $z_n$ $(n = 1, \ldots, N)$ per dollar invested are jointly distributed according to the distribution function $F(z_1, \ldots, z_N)$. Assume also that all the returns are nonnegative with probability one. Consider an individual who has a continuous, increasing, and concave Bernoulli utility function $u(\cdot)$ over $\mathbb{R}_+$. Define the utility function $U(\cdot)$ of this investor over $\mathbb{R}_+^N$, the set of all nonnegative portfolios, by

$$U(\alpha_1, \ldots, \alpha_N) = \int u(\alpha_1 z_1 + \cdots + \alpha_N z_N)\, dF(z_1, \ldots, z_N).$$

Prove that $U(\cdot)$ is (a) increasing, (b) concave, and (c) continuous (this is harder).

**6.C.5$^A$** Consider a decision maker with utility function $u(\cdot)$ defined over $\mathbb{R}_+^L$, just as in Chapter 3.

**(a)** Argue that concavity of $u(\cdot)$ can be interpreted as the decision maker exhibiting risk aversion with respect to lotteries whose outcomes are bundles of the $L$ commodities.

**(b)** Suppose now that a Bernoulli utility function $u(\cdot)$ for wealth is derived from the maximization of a utility function defined over bundles of commodities for each given wealth level $w$, while prices for those commodities are fixed. Show that, if the utility function for the commodities exhibits risk aversion, then so does the derived Bernoulli utility function for wealth. Interpret.

**(c)** Argue that the converse of part **(b)** does not need to hold: There are nonconcave functions $u: \mathbb{R}_+^L \to \mathbb{R}$ such that for any price vector the derived Bernoulli utility function on wealth exhibits risk aversion.

**6.C.6$^B$** For Proposition 6.C.2:

**(a)** Prove the equivalence of conditions (ii) and (iii).

**(b)** Prove the equivalence of conditions (iii) and (v).

**6.C.7$^A$** Prove that, in Proposition 6.C.2, condition (iii) implies condition (iv), and (iv) implies (i).

**6.C.8$^A$** In text.

**6.C.9$^B$** (M. Kimball) The purpose of this problem is to examine the implications of uncertainty and precaution in a simple consumption–savings decision problem.

In a two-period economy, a consumer has first-period initial wealth $w$. The consumer's utility level is given by

$$u(c_1, c_2) = u(c_1) + v(c_2),$$

where $u(\cdot)$ and $v(\cdot)$ are concave functions and $c_1$ and $c_2$ denote consumption levels in the first and the second period, respectively. Denote by $x$ the amount saved by the consumer in the first period (so that $c_1 = w - x$ and $c_2 = x$), and let $x_0$ be the optimal value of $x$ in this problem.

We now introduce uncertainty in this economy. If the consumer saves an amount $x$ in the first period, his wealth in the second period is given by $x + y$, where $y$ is distributed according to $F(\cdot)$. In what follows, $E[\cdot]$ always denotes the expectation with respect to $F(\cdot)$. Assume that the Bernoulli utility function over realized wealth levels in the two periods $(w_1, w_2)$ is $u(w_1) + v(w_2)$. Hence, the consumer now solves

$$\operatorname*{Max}_x u(w - x) + E[v(x + y)].$$

Denote the solution to this problem by $x^*$.

**(a)** Show that if $E[v'(x_0 + y)] > v'(x_0)$, then $x^* > x_0$.

**(b)** Define the *coefficient of absolute prudence* of a utility function $v(\cdot)$ at wealth level $x$ to be $-v'''(x)/v''(x)$. Show that if the coefficient of absolute prudence of a utility function $v_1(\cdot)$ is not larger than the coefficient of absolute prudence of utility function $v_2(\cdot)$ for all levels of wealth, then $E[v_1'(x_0 + y)] > v_1'(x_0)$ implies $E[v_2'(x_0 + y)] > v_2'(x_0)$. What are the implications of this fact in the context of part **(a)**?

**(c)** Show that if $v'''(\cdot) > 0$, and $E[y] = 0$, then $E[v'(x + y)] > v'(x)$ for all values of $x$.

**(d)** Show that if the coefficient of absolute risk aversion of $v(\cdot)$ is decreasing with wealth, then $-v'''(x)/v''(x) > -v''(x)/v'(x)$ for all $x$, and hence $v'''(\cdot) > 0$.

**6.C.10$^A$** Prove the equivalence of conditions (i) through (v) in Proposition 6.C.3. [*Hint*: By letting $u_1(z) = u(w_1 + z)$ and $u_2(z) = u(w_2 + z)$, show that each of the five conditions in Proposition 6.C.3 is equivalent to the counterpart in Proposition 6.C.2.]

**6.C.11$^B$** For the model in Example 6.C.2, show that if $r_R(x, u)$ is increasing in $x$ then the proportion of wealth invested in the risky asset $\gamma = \alpha/x$ is decreasing with $x$. Similarly, if $r_R(x, u)$ is decreasing in $x$, then $\gamma = \alpha/x$ is increasing in $x$. [*Hint*: Let $u_1(t) = u(tw_1)$ and $u_2(t) = u(tw_2)$, and use the fact, stated in the analysis of Example 6.C.2, that if one Bernoulli utility function is more risk averse than another, then the optimal level of investment in the risky asset for the first function is smaller than that for the second function. You could also attempt a direct proof using first-order conditions.]

**6.C.12$^B$** Let $u: \mathbb{R}_+ \to \mathbb{R}$ be a strictly increasing Bernoulli utility function. Show that

**(a)** $u(\cdot)$ exhibits constant relative risk aversion equal to $\rho \neq 1$ if and only if $u(x) = \beta x^{1-\rho} + \gamma$, where $\beta > 0$ and $\gamma \in \mathbb{R}$.

**(b)** $u(\cdot)$ exhibits constant relative risk aversion equal to 1 if and only if $u(x) = \beta \ln x + \gamma$, where $\beta > 0$ and $\gamma \in \mathbb{R}$.

**(c)** $\lim_{\rho \to 1} (x^{1-\rho}/(1 - \rho)) = \ln x$ for all $x > 0$.

**6.C.13$^B$** Assume that a firm is risk neutral with respect to profits and that if there is any uncertainty in prices, production decisions are made after the resolution of such uncertainty. Suppose that the firm faces a choice between two alternatives. In the first, prices are uncertain. In the second, prices are nonrandom and equal to the expected price vector in the first alternative. Show that a firm that maximizes expected profits will prefer the first alternative over the second.

**6.C.14$^B$** Consider two risk-averse decision makers (i.e., two decision makers with concave Bernoulli utility functions) choosing among monetary lotteries. Define the utility function $u^*(\cdot)$ to be strongly more risk averse than $u(\cdot)$ if and only if there is a positive constant $k$ and a nonincreasing and concave function $v(\cdot)$ such that $u^*(x) = ku(x) + v(x)$ for all $x$. The monetary amounts are restricted to lie in the interval $[0, r]$.

**(a)** Show that if $u^*(\cdot)$ is strongly more risk averse than $u(\cdot)$, then $u^*(\cdot)$ is more risk averse than $u(\cdot)$ in the usual Arrow–Pratt sense.

**(b)** Show that if $u(\cdot)$ is bounded, then there is no $u^*(\cdot)$ other than $u^*(\cdot) = ku(\cdot) + c$, where $c$ is a constant, that is strongly more risk averse than $u(\cdot)$ on the entire interval $[0, +\infty]$. [*Hint*: in this part, disregard the assumption that the monetary amounts are restricted to lie in the interval $[0, r]$.]

**(c)** Using **(b)**, argue that the concept of a strongly more risk-averse utility function is stronger (i.e., more restrictive) than the Arrow–Pratt concept of a more risk-averse utility function.

**6.C.15$^A$** Assume that, in a world with uncertainty, there are two assets. The first is a riskless asset that pays 1 dollar. The second pays amounts $a$ and $b$ with probabilities of $\pi$ and $1 - \pi$, respectively. Denote the demand for the two assets by $(x_1, x_2)$.

Suppose that a decision maker's preferences satisfy the axioms of expected utility theory and that he is a risk averter. The decision maker's wealth is 1, and so are the prices of the assets. Therefore, the decision maker's budget constraint is given by

$$x_1 + x_2 = 1, \quad x_1, x_2 \in [0, 1].$$

**(a)** Give a simple *necessary* condition (involving $a$ and $b$ only) for the demand for the riskless asset to be strictly positive.

**(b)** Give a simple *necessary* condition (involving $a$, $b$, and $\pi$ only) for the demand for the risky asset to be strictly positive.

In the next three parts, assume that the conditions obtained in **(a)** and **(b)** are satisfied.

**(c)** Write down the first-order conditions for utility maximization in this asset demand problem.

**(d)** Assume that $a < 1$. Show by analyzing the first-order conditions that $dx_1/da \leq 0$.

**(e)** Which sign do you conjecture for $dx_1/d\pi$? Give an economic interpretation.

**(f)** Can you prove your conjecture in **(e)** by analyzing the first-order conditions?

**6.C.16$^A$** An individual has Bernoulli utility function $u(\cdot)$ and initial wealth $w$. Let lottery $L$ offer a payoff of $G$ with probability $p$ and a payoff of $B$ with probability $1 - p$.

**(a)** If the individual owns the lottery, what is the minimum price he would sell it for?

**(b)** If he does not own it, what is the maximum price he would be willing to pay for it?

**(c)** Are buying and selling prices equal? Give an economic interpretation for your answer. Find conditions on the parameters of the problem under which buying and selling prices are equal.

**(d)** Let $G = 10$, $B = 5$, $w = 10$, and $u(x) = \sqrt{x}$. Compute the buying and selling prices for this lottery and this utility function.

**6.C.17$^B$** Assume that an individual faces a two-period portfolio allocation problem. In period $t = 0, 1$, his wealth $w_t$ is to be divided between a safe asset with return $R$ and a risky asset with return $x$. The initial wealth at period 0 is $w_0$. Wealth at period $t = 1, 2$ depends on the portfolio $\alpha_{t-1}$ chosen at period $t - 1$ and on the return $x_t$ realized at period $t$, according to

$$w_t = ((1 - \alpha_{t-1})R + \alpha_{t-1}x_t)w_{t-1}.$$

The objective of this individual is to maximize the expected utility of terminal wealth $w_2$. Assume that $x_1$ and $x_2$ are independently and identically distributed. Prove that the individual optimally sets $\alpha_0 = \alpha_1$ if his utility function exhibits constant relative risk aversion. Show also that this fails to hold if his utility function exhibits constant absolute risk aversion.

**6.C.18$^B$** Suppose that an individual has a Bernoulli utility function $u(x) = \sqrt{x}$.

**(a)** Calculate the Arrow–Pratt coefficients of absolute and relative risk aversion at the level of wealth $w = 5$.

**(b)** Calculate the certainty equivalent and the probability premium for a gamble $(16, 4; \frac{1}{2}, \frac{1}{2})$.

**(c)** Calculate the certainty equivalent and the probability premium for a gamble $(36, 16; \frac{1}{2}, \frac{1}{2})$. Compare this result with the one in **(b)** and interpret.

**6.C.19$^C$** Suppose that an individual has a Bernoulli utility function $u(x) = -e^{-\alpha x}$ where $\alpha > 0$. His (nonstochastic) initial wealth is given by $w$. There is one riskless asset and there are $N$

risky assets. The return per unit invested on the riskless asset is $r$. The returns of the risky assets are jointly normally distributed random variables with means $\mu = (\mu_1, \ldots, \mu_N)$ and variance–covariance matrix $V$. Assume that there is no redundancy in the risky assets, so that $V$ is of full rank. Derive the demand function for these $N + 1$ assets.

**6.C.20**[A] Consider a lottery over monetary outcomes that pays $x + \varepsilon$ with probability $\frac{1}{2}$ and $x - \varepsilon$ with probability $\frac{1}{2}$. Compute the second derivative of this lottery's certainty equivalent with respect to $\varepsilon$. Show that the limit of this derivative as $\varepsilon \to 0$ is exactly $-r_A(x)$.

**6.D.1**[A] The purpose of this exercise is to prove Proposition 6.D.1 in a two-dimensional probability simplex. Suppose that there are three monetary outcomes: 1 dollar, 2 dollars, and 3 dollars. Consider the probability simplex of Figure 6.B.1(b).

(a) For a given lottery $L$ over these outcomes, determine the region of the probability simplex in which lie the lotteries whose distributions first-order stochastically dominate the distribution of $L$.

(b) Given a lottery $L$, determine the region of the probability simplex in which lie the lotteries $L'$ such that $F(x) \leq G(x)$ for every $x$, where $F(\cdot)$ is the distribution of $L'$ and $G(\cdot)$ is the distribution of $L$. [Notice that we get the same region as in (a).]

**6.D.2**[A] Prove that if $F(\cdot)$ first-order stochastically dominates $G(\cdot)$, then the mean of $x$ under $F(\cdot)$, $\int x\, dF(x)$, exceeds that under $G(\cdot)$, $\int x\, dG(x)$. Also provide an example where $\int x\, dF(x) > \int x\, dG(x)$ but $F(\cdot)$ does not first-order stochastically dominate $G(\cdot)$.

**6.D.3**[A] Verify that if a distribution $G(\cdot)$ is an elementary increase in risk from a distribution $F(\cdot)$, then $F(\cdot)$ second-order stochastically dominates $G(\cdot)$.

**6.D.4**[A] The purpose of this exercise is to verify the equivalence of the three statements of Proposition 6.D.2 in a two-dimensional probability simplex. Suppose that there are three monetary outcomes: 1, 2, and 3 dollars. Consider the probability simplex in Figure 6.B.1(b).

(a) If two lotteries have the same mean, what are their positions relative to each other in the probability simplex.

(b) Given a lottery $L$, determine the region of the simplex in which lie the lotteries $L'$ whose distributions are second-order stochastically dominated by the distribution of $L$.

(c) Given a lottery $L$, determine the region of the simplex in which lie the lotteries $L'$ whose distributions are mean preserving spreads of $L$.

(d) Given a lottery $L$, determine the region of the simplex in which lie the lotteries $L'$ for which condition (6.D.2) holds, where $F(\cdot)$ and $G(\cdot)$ are, respectively, the distributions of $L$ and $L'$.

Notice that in (b), (c), and (d), you always have the same region.

**6.E.1**[B] The purpose of this exercise is to show that preferences may not be transitive in the presence of regret. Let there be $S$ states of the world, indexed by $s = 1, \ldots, S$. Assume that state $s$ occurs with probability $\pi_s$. Define the expected regret associated with lottery $x = (x_1, \ldots, x_S)$ relative to lottery $x' = (x'_1, \ldots, x'_S)$ by

$$\sum_{s=1}^{S} \pi_s h(\text{Max}\{0, x'_s - x_s\}),$$

where $h(\cdot)$ is a given increasing function. [We call $h(\cdot)$ the *regret valuation function*; it measures the regret the individual has after the state of nature is known.] We define $x$ to be at least as good as $x'$ in the presence of regret if and only if the expected regret associated with $x$ relative to $x'$ is not greater than the expected regret associated with $x'$ relative to $x$.

Suppose that $S = 3$, $\pi_1 = \pi_2 = \pi_3 = \frac{1}{3}$, and $h(x) = \sqrt{x}$. Consider the following three lotteries:

$$x = (0, -2, \quad 1),$$
$$x' = (0, \quad 2, -2),$$
$$x'' = (2, -3, -1).$$

Show that the preference ordering over these three lotteries is not transitive.

**6.E.2$^A$** Assume that in a world with uncertainty there are two possible states of nature ($s = 1, 2$) and a single consumption good. There is a single decision maker whose preferences over lotteries satisfy the axioms of expected utility theory and who is a risk averter. For simplicity, we assume that utility is state-independent.

Two contingent commodities are available to the decision maker. The first (respectively, the second) pays one unit of the consumption good in state $s = 1$ (respectively $s = 2$) and zero otherwise. Denote the vector quantities of the two contingent commodities by $(x_1, x_2)$.

**(a)** Show that the preference relation of the decision maker on $(x_1, x_2)$ is convex.

**(b)** Argue that the decision maker is also a risk averter when choosing between lotteries whose outcomes are vectors $(x_1, x_2)$.

**(c)** Show that the Walrasian demand functions for $x_1$ and $x_2$ are normal.

**6.E.3$^B$** Let $g: S \rightarrow \mathbb{R}_+$ be a random variable with mean $E(g) = 1$. For $\alpha \in (0, 1)$, define a new random variable $g^*: S \rightarrow \mathbb{R}_+$ by $g^*(s) = \alpha g(s) + (1 - \alpha)$. Note that $E(g^*) = 1$. Denote by $G(\cdot)$ and $G^*(\cdot)$ the distribution functions of $g(\cdot)$ and $g^*(\cdot)$, respectively. Show that $G^*(\cdot)$ second-order stochastically dominates $G(\cdot)$. Interpret.

**6.F.1$^B$** Prove that in the subjective expected utility theorem (Proposition 6.F.2), the obtained utility function $u(\cdot)$ on money is uniquely determined up to origin and scale. That is, if both $u(\cdot)$ and $\hat{u}(\cdot)$ satisfy the condition of the theorem, then there exist $\beta > 0$ and $\gamma \in \mathbb{R}$ such that $\hat{u}(x) = \beta u(x) + \gamma$ for all $x$. Prove also that the subjective probabilities are uniquely determined.

**6.F.2$^A$** The purpose of this exercise is to explain the outcomes of the experiments described in Example 6.F.1 by means of the theory of *nonunique prior beliefs* of Gilboa and Schmeidler (1989).

We consider a decision maker with a Bernoulli utility function $u(\cdot)$ defined on $\{0, 1000\}$. We normalize $u(\cdot)$ so that $u(0) = 0$ and $u(1000) = 1$.

The probabilistic belief that the decision maker might have on the color of the H-ball being white is a number $\pi \in [0, 1]$. We assume that the decision maker has, not a single belief but a *set* of beliefs given by a subset $P$ of $[0, 1]$. The actions that he may take are denoted R or H with R meaning that he chooses the R-ball and H meaning that he chooses the H-ball.

As in Example 6.F.1, the decision maker is faced with two different choice situations. In choice situation $W$, he receives 1000 dollars if the ball chosen is white and 0 dollars otherwise. In choice situation $B$, he receives 1000 dollars if the ball chosen is black and 0 dollars otherwise.

For each of the two choice situations, define his utility function over the actions R and H in the following way:

For situation $W$, $U_W: \{R, H\} \rightarrow \mathbb{R}$ is defined by

$$U_W(R) = .49 \quad \text{and} \quad U_W(H) = \text{Min}\,\{\pi: \pi \in P\}.$$

For situation $B$, $U_B: \{R, H\} \rightarrow \mathbb{R}$ is defined by

$$U_B(R) = .51 \quad \text{and} \quad U_B(H) = \text{Min}\,\{(1 - \pi): \pi \in P\}.$$

Namely, his utility from choice R is the expected utility of 1000 dollars with the (objective) probability calculated from the number of white and black balls in urn R. However, his utility from choice H is the expected utility of 1000 dollars with the probability associated with the most pessimistic belief in $P$.

**(a)** Prove that if $P$ consists of only one belief, then $U_W$ and $U_B$ are derived from a von Neumann–Morgenstern utility function and that $U_W(R) > U_W(H)$ if and only if $U_B(R) < U_B(H)$.

**(b)** Find a set $P$ for which $U_W(R) > U_W(H)$ and $U_B(R) > U_B(H)$.

# Game Theory

In Part I, we analyzed individual decision making, both in abstract decision problems and in more specific economic settings. Our primary aim was to lay the groundwork for the study of how the simultaneous behavior of many self-interested individuals (including firms) generates economic outcomes in market economies. Most of the remainder of the book is devoted to this task. In Part II, however, we study in a more general way how multiperson interactions can be modeled.

A central feature of multiperson interaction is the potential for the presence of *strategic interdependence*. In our study of individual decision making in Part I, the decision maker faced situations in which her well-being depended only on the choices she made (possibly with some randomness). In contrast, in multiperson situations with strategic interdependence, each agent recognizes that the payoff she receives (in utility or profits) depends not only on her own actions but also on the actions of *other* individuals. The actions that are best for her to take may depend on actions these other individuals have already taken, on those she expects them to be taking at the same time, and even on future actions that they may take, or decide not to take, as a result of her current actions.

The tool that we use for analyzing settings with strategic interdependence is *noncooperative game theory*. Although the term "game" may seem to undersell the theory's importance, it correctly highlights the theory's central feature: The agents under study are concerned with strategy and winning (in the general sense of utility or profit maximization) in much the same way that players of most parlor games are.

Multiperson economic situations vary greatly in the degree to which strategic interaction is present. In settings of monopoly (where a good is sold by only a single firm; see Section 12.B) or of perfect competition (where all agents act as price takers; see Chapter 10 and Part IV), the nature of strategic interaction is minimal enough that our analysis need not make any formal use of game theory.[1] In other settings, however, such as the analysis of oligopolistic markets (where there is more than one

---

1. However, we could well do so in both cases; see, for example, the proof of existence of competitive equilibrium in Chapter 17, Appendix B. Moreover, we shall stress how perfect competition can be viewed usefully as a limiting case of oligopolistic strategic interaction; see, for example, Section 12.F.

but still not many sellers of a good; see Sections 12.C to 12.G), the central role of strategic interaction makes game theory indispensable for our analysis.

Part II is divided into three chapters. Chapter 7 provides a short introduction to the basic elements of noncooperative game theory, including a discussion of exactly what a game is, some ways of representing games, and an introduction to a central concept of the theory, a player's *strategy*. Chapter 8 addresses how we can predict outcomes in the special class of games in which all the players move simultaneously, known as *simultaneous-move games*. This restricted focus helps us isolate some central issues while deferring a number of more difficult ones. Chapter 9 studies *dynamic games* in which players' moves may precede one another, and in which some of these more difficult (but also interesting) issues arise.

Note that we have used the modifier *noncooperative* to describe the type of game theory we discuss in Part II. There is another branch of game theory, known as *cooperative game theory*, that we do not discuss here. In contrast with noncooperative game theory, the fundamental units of analysis in cooperative theory are groups and subgroups of individuals that are assumed, as a primitive of the theory, to be able to attain particular outcomes for themselves through binding cooperative agreements. Cooperative game theory has played an important role in general equilibrium theory, and we provide a brief introduction to it in Appendix A of Chapter 18. We should emphasize that the term *noncooperative game theory* does *not* mean that noncooperative theory is incapable of explaining cooperation within groups of individuals. Rather, it focuses on how cooperation may emerge as rational behavior in the absence of an ability to make binding agreements (e.g., see the discussion of repeated interaction among oligopolists in Chapter 12).

Some excellent recent references for further study of noncooperative game theory are Fudenberg and Tirole (1991), Myerson (1992), and Osborne and Rubinstein (1994), and at a more introductory level Gibbons (1992) and Binmore (1992). Kreps (1990) provides a very interesting discussion of some of the strengths and weaknesses of the theory. Von Neumann and Morgenstern (1944), Luce and Raiffa (1957), and Schelling (1960) remain classic references.

## REFERENCES

Binmore, K. (1992). *Fun and Games: A Text on Game Theory*. Lexington, Mass.: D. C. Heath.

Fudenberg, D., and J. Tirole. (1991). *Game Theory*. Cambridge, Mass.: MIT Press.

Gibbons, R. (1992). *Game Theory for Applied Economists*. Princeton, N.J.: Princeton University Press.

Kreps, D. M. (1990). *Game Theory and Economic Modeling*. New York: Oxford University Press.

Luce, R. D., and H. Raiffa. (1957). *Games and Decisions: Introduction and Critical Survey*. New York: Wiley.

Myerson, R. B. (1992). *Game Theory: Analysis of Conflict*. Cambridge, Mass.: Harvard University Press.

Osborne, M. J., and A. Rubinstein. (1994). *A Course in Game Theory*, Cambridge, Mass.: MIT Press.

Schelling, T. (1960). *The Strategy of Conflict*. Cambridge, Mass.: Harvard University Press.

Von Neumann, J., and O. Morgenstern. (1944). *The Theory of Games and Economic Behavior*. Princeton, N.J.: Princeton University Press.

# Basic Elements of

# Noncooperative Games

## 7.A Introduction

In this chapter, we begin our study of noncooperative game theory by introducing some of its basic building blocks. This material serves as a prelude to our analysis of games in Chapters 8 and 9.

Section 7.B begins with an informal introduction to the concept of a *game*. It describes the four basic elements of any setting of strategic interaction that we must know to specify a game.

In Section 7.C, we show how a game can be described by means of what is called its *extensive form representation*. The extensive form representation provides a very rich description of a game, capturing who moves when, what they can do, what they know when it is their turn to move, and the outcomes associated with any collection of actions taken by the individuals playing the game.

In Section 7.D, we introduce a central concept of game theory, a player's *strategy*. A player's strategy is a complete contingent plan describing the actions she will take in each conceivable evolution of the game. We then show how the notion of a strategy can be used to derive a much more compact representation of a game, known as its *normal* (or *strategic*) *form representation*.

In Section 7.E, we consider the possibility that a player might randomize her choices. This gives rise to the notion of a *mixed strategy*.

## 7.B What Is a Game?

A *game* is a formal representation of a situation in which a number of individuals interact in a setting of *strategic interdependence*. By that, we mean that each individual's welfare depends not only on her own actions but also on the actions of the other individuals. Moreover, the actions that are best for her to take may depend on what she expects the other players to do.

To describe a situation of strategic interaction, we need to know four things:

   (i) *The players:*   Who is involved?

  (ii) *The rules:*    Who moves when? What do they know when they move? What can they do?

(iii) *The outcomes:*   For each possible set of actions by the players, what is the outcome of the game?

(iv) *The payoffs:*   What are the players' preferences (i.e., utility functions) over the possible outcomes?

We begin by considering items (i) to (iii). A simple example is provided by the school-yard game of *Matching Pennies*.

**Example 7.B.1:** *Matching Pennies.* Items (i) to (iii) are as follows:

*Players:*   There are two players, denoted 1 and 2.

*Rules:*   Each player simultaneously puts a penny down, either heads up or tails up.

*Outcomes:*   If the two pennies match (either both heads up or both tails up), player 1 pays 1 dollar to player 2; otherwise, player 2 pays 1 dollar to player 1.  ∎

Consider another example, the game of *Tick-Tack-Toe*.

**Example 7.B.2:** *Tick-Tack-Toe.* Items (i) to (iii) are as follows:

*Players:*   There are two players, X and O.

*Rules:*   The players are faced with a board that consists of nine squares arrayed with three rows of three squares each stacked on one another (see Figure 7.B.1). The players take turns putting their marks (an X or an O) into an as-yet-unmarked square. Player X moves first. Both players observe all choices previously made.

*Outcomes:*   The first player to have three of her marks in a row (horizontally, vertically, or diagonally) wins and receives 1 dollar from the other player. If no one succeeds in doing so after all nine boxes are marked, the game is a tie and no payments are made or received by either player.  ∎

To complete our description of these two games, we need to say what the players' preferences are over the possible outcomes [item (iv) in our list]. As a general matter, we describe a player's preferences by a utility function that assigns a utility level for each possible outcome. It is common to refer to the player's utility function as her *payoff function* and the utility level as her *payoff*. Throughout, we assume that these utility functions take an expected utility form (see Chapter 6) so that when we consider situations in which outcomes are random, we can evaluate the random prospect by means of the player's expected utility.

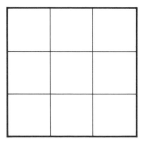

**Figure 7.B.1**

A Tick-Tack-Toe board.

In later references to Matching Pennies and Tick-Tack-Toe, we assume that each player's payoff is simply equal to the amount of money she gains or loses. Note that in both examples, the actions that maximize a player's payoff depend on what she expects her opponent to do.

Examples 7.B.1 and 7.B.2 involve situations of pure conflict: What one player wins, the other player loses. Such games are called *zero-sum games*. But strategic interaction and game theory are not limited to situations of pure or even partial conflict. Consider the situation in Example 7.B.3.

**Example 7.B.3:** *Meeting in New York.* Items (i) to (iv) are as follows:

*Players:*   Two players, Mr. Thomas and Mr. Schelling.
*Rules:*     The two players are separated and cannot communicate. They are supposed to meet in New York City at noon for lunch but have forgotten to specify where. Each must decide where to go (each can make only one choice).
*Outcomes:*  If they meet each other, they get to enjoy each other's company at lunch. Otherwise, they must eat alone.
*Payoffs:*   They each attach a monetary value of 100 dollars to the other's company (their payoffs are each 100 dollars if they meet, 0 dollars if they do not).

In this example, the two players' interests are completely aligned. Their problem is simply one of coordination. Nevertheless, each player's payoff depends on what the other player does; and more importantly, *each player's optimal action depends on what he thinks the other will do.* Thus, even the task of coordination can have a strategic nature. ∎

Although the information given in items (i) to (iv) fully describe a game, it is useful for purposes of analysis to represent this information in particular ways. We examine one of these ways in Section 7.C.

# 7.C  The Extensive Form Representation of a Game

If we know the items (i) to (iv) described in Section 7.B (the players, the rules, the outcomes, and the payoffs), then we can formally represent the game in what is called its *extensive form*. The extensive form captures who moves when, what actions each player can take, what players know when they move, what the outcome is as a function of the actions taken by the players, and the players' payoffs from each possible outcome.

We begin by informally introducing the elements of the extensive form representation through a series of examples. After doing so, we then provide a formal specification of the extensive form (some readers may want to begin with this and then return to the examples).

The extensive form relies on the conceptual apparatus known as a *game tree*. As our starting point, it is useful to begin with a very simple variation of Matching Pennies, which we call *Matching Pennies Version B*.

**Example 7.C.1:** *Matching Pennies Version B and Its Extensive Form.* Matching Pennies Version B is identical to Matching Pennies (see Example 7.B.1) except

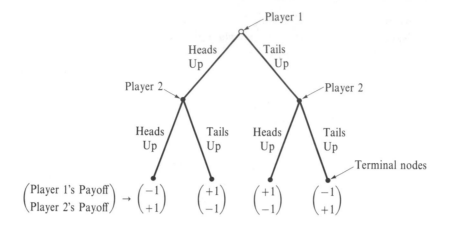

**Figure 7.C.1**

Extensive form for Matching Pennies Version B.

that the two players move sequentially, rather than simultaneously. In particular, player 1 puts her penny down (heads up or tails up) first. Then, after seeing player 1's choice, player 2 puts her penny down. (This is a very nice game for player 2!)

The extensive form representation of this game is depicted in Figure 7.C.1. The game starts at an *initial decision node* (represented by an open circle), where player 1 makes her move, deciding whether to place her penny heads up or tails up. Each of the two possible choices for player 1 is represented by a *branch* from this initial decision node. At the end of each branch is another decision node (represented by a solid dot), at which player 2 can choose between two actions, heads up or tails up, after seeing player 1's choice. The initial decision node is referred to as *player 1's decision node*; the latter two as *player 2's decision nodes*. After player 2's move, we reach the end of the game, represented by *terminal nodes*. At each terminal node, we list the players' payoffs arising from the sequence of moves leading to that terminal node.

Note the treelike structure of Figure 7.C.1: Like an actual tree, it has a unique connected path of branches from the initial node (sometimes also called the *root*) to each point in the tree. This type of figure is known as a *game tree*. ∎

**Example 7.C.2:** *The Extensive Form of Tick-Tack-Toe.* The more elaborate game tree shown in Figure 7.C.2 depicts the extensive form for Tick-Tack-Toe (to conserve space, many parts are omitted). Note that every path through the tree represents a unique sequence of moves by the players. In particular, when a given board position (such as the two left corners filled by X and the two right corners filled by O) can be reached through several different sequences of moves, each of these sequences is depicted separately in the game tree. Nodes represent not only the current position but also *how it was reached.* ∎

In both Matching Pennies Version B and Tick-Tack-Toe, when it is a player's turn to move, she is able to observe all her rival's previous moves. They are games of *perfect information* (we give a precise definition of this term in Definition 7.C.1). The concept of an *information set* allows us to accommodate the possibility that this is not so. Formally, the elements of an information set are a subset of a particular player's decision nodes. The interpretation is that when play has reached one of the decision nodes in the information set and it is that player's turn to move, she does

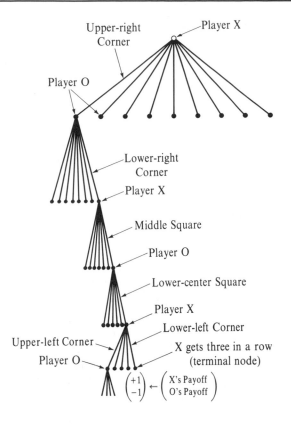

**Figure 7.C.2**

Part of the extensive form for Tick-Tack-Toe.

not know which of these nodes she is actually at. The reason for this ignorance is that the player does not observe something about what has previously transpired in the game. A further variation of Matching Pennies, which we call *Matching Pennies Version C*, helps make this concept clearer.

**Example 7.C.3:** *Matching Pennies Version C and Its Extensive Form.* This version of Matching Pennies is just like Matching Pennies Version B (in Example 7.C.1) except that when player 1 puts her penny down, she keeps it covered with her hand. Hence, player 2 cannot see player 1's choice until after player 2 has moved.

The extensive form for this game is represented in Figure 7.C.3. It is identical to Figure 7.C.1 except that we have drawn a circle around player 2's two decision nodes to indicate that these two nodes are in a single information set. The meaning of this information set is that when it is player 2's turn to move, she cannot tell which of these two nodes she is at because she has not observed player 1's previous move. Note that player 2 has the same two possible actions at each of the two nodes in her information set. This must be the case if player 2 is unable to distinguish the two nodes; otherwise, she could figure out which move player 1 had taken simply by what her own possible actions are.

In principle, we could also associate player 1's decision node with an information set. Because player 1 knows that nothing has happened before it is her turn to move, this information set has only one member (player 1 knows exactly which node she is at when she moves). To be fully rigorous, we should therefore also draw an information set circle around player 1's decision node in Figure 7.C.3. It is common, however, to

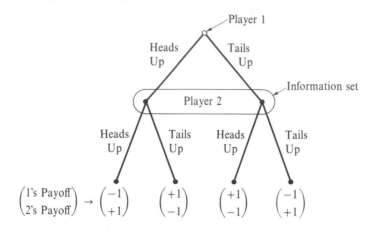

**Figure 7.C.3**

Extensive form for Matching Pennies Version C.

simplify the diagrammatic depiction of a game in extensive form by not drawing the information sets that contain a single node. Thus, any uncircled decision nodes are understood to be elements of *singleton* information sets. In Figures 7.C.1 and 7.C.2, for example, every decision node belongs to a singleton information set. ■

A listing of all of a player's information sets gives a listing, from the player's perspective, of all of the possible distinguishable "events" or "circumstances" in which she might be called upon to move. For example, in Example 7.C.1, from player 2's perspective there are two distinguishable events that might arise in which she would be called upon to move, each one corresponding to play having reached one of her two (singleton) information sets. By way of contrast, player 2 foresees only one possible circumstance in which she would need to move in Example 7.C.3 (this circumstance is, however, certain to arise).

In Example 7.C.3, we noted a natural restriction on information sets: At every node within a given information set, a player must have the same set of possible actions. Another restriction we impose is that players possess what is known as *perfect recall*. Loosely speaking, perfect recall means that a player does not forget what she once knew, including her own actions. Figure 7.C.4 depicts two games in which this condition is not met. In Figure 7.C.4(a), as the game progresses, player 2 forgets a move by player 1 that she once knew (namely, whether player 1 chose $\ell$ or $r$). In Figure 7.C.4(b), player 1 forgets her own previous move.[1] All the games we consider in this book satisfy the property of perfect recall.

The use of information sets also allows us to capture play that is simultaneous rather than sequential. This is illustrated in Example 7.C.4 for the game of (standard) Matching Pennies introduced in Example 7.B.1.

---

1. In terms of the formal specification of the extensive form given later in this section, if we denote the information set containing decision node $x$ by $H(x)$, a game is formally characterized as one of perfect recall if the following two conditions hold: (i) If $H(x) = H(x')$, $x$ is neither a predecessor nor a successor of $x'$; and (ii) if $x$ and $x'$ are two decision nodes for player $i$ with $H(x) = H(x')$, and if $x''$ is a predecessor of $x$ (not necessarily an immediate one) that is also in one of player $i$'s information sets, with $a''$ being the action at $H(x'')$ on the path to $x$, then there must be a predecessor node to $x'$ that is an element of $H(x'')$ and the action at this predecessor node that is on the path to $x'$ must also be $a''$.

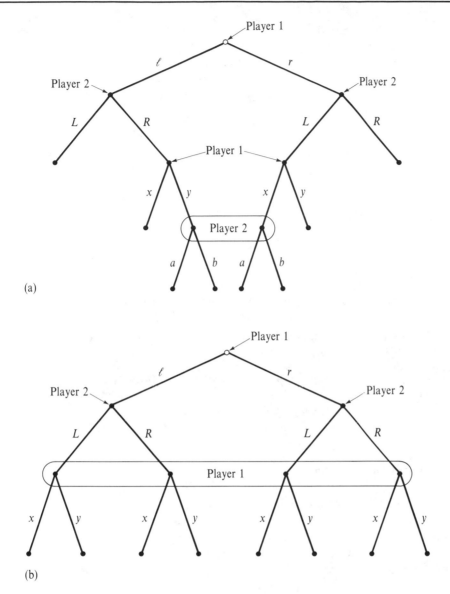

(a)

(b)

**Figure 7.C.4**
Two games not satisfying perfect recall.

**Example 7.C.4:** *The Extensive Form for Matching Pennies.* Suppose now that the players put their pennies down simultaneously. For each player, this game is strategically equivalent to the Version C game. In Version C, player 1 was unable to observe player 2's choice because player 1 moved first, and player 2 was unable to observe player 1's choice because player 1 kept it covered; here each player is unable to observe the other's choice because they move simultaneously. As long as they cannot observe each other's choices, the timing of moves is irrelevant. Thus, we can use the game tree in Figure 7.C.3 to describe the game of (standard) Matching Pennies. Note that by this logic we can also describe this game with a game tree that reverses the decision nodes of players 1 and 2 in Figure 7.C.3. ∎

We can now return to the notion of a game of perfect information and offer a formal definition.

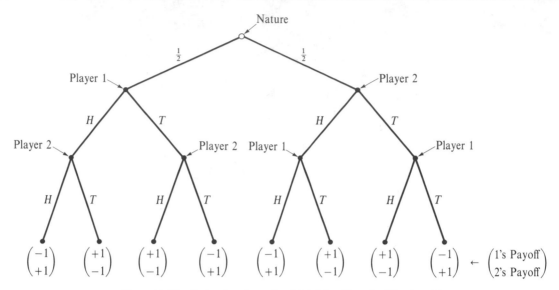

**Figure 7.C.5**  Extensive form for Matching Pennies Version D.

**Definition 7.C.1:** A game is one of *perfect information* if each information set contains a single decision node. Otherwise, it is a game of *imperfect information*.

Up to this point, the outcome of a game has been a deterministic function of the players' choices. In many games, however, there is an element of chance. This, too, can be captured in the extensive form representation by including *random moves of nature*. We illustrate this point with still another variation, *Matching Pennies Version D*.

**Example 7.C.5:** *Matching Pennies Version D and Its Extensive Form.* Suppose that prior to playing Matching Pennies Version B, the two players flip a coin to see who will move first. Thus, with equal probability either player 1 will put her penny down first, or player 2 will. In Figure 7.C.5, this game is depicted as beginning with a *move of nature* at the initial node that has two branches, each with probability $\frac{1}{2}$. Note that this is drawn as if nature were an additional player who must play its two actions with fixed probabilities. (In the figure, H stands for "heads up" and T stands for "tails up".) ■

It is a basic postulate of game theory that all players know the structure of the game, know that their rivals know it, know that their rivals know that they know it, and so on. In theoretical parlance, we say that the structure of the game is *common knowledge* [see Aumann (1976) and Milgrom (1981) for discussions of this concept].

In addition to being depicted graphically, the extensive form can be described mathematically. The basic components are fairly easily explained and can help you keep in mind the fundamental building blocks of a game. Formally, a game represented in extensive form consists of the following items:[2]

---

2. To be a bit more precise about terminology: A collection of items (i) to (vi) is formally known as an extensive *game form*; adding item (vii), the players' preferences over the outcomes, leads to a *game* represented in extensive form. We will not make anything of this distinction here. See Kuhn (1953) or Section 2 of Kreps and Wilson (1982) for additional discussion of this and other points regarding the extensive form.

(i) A finite set of nodes $\mathscr{X}$, a finite set of possible actions $\mathscr{A}$, and a finite set of players $\{1, \ldots, I\}$.

(ii) A function $p: \mathscr{X} \to \{\mathscr{X} \cup \varnothing\}$ specifying a single immediate predecessor of each node $x$; $p(x)$ is nonempty for all $x \in \mathscr{X}$ but one, designated as the *initial node* $x_0$. The immediate successor nodes of $x$ are then $s(x) = p^{-1}(x)$, and the set of *all* predecessors and *all* successors of node $x$ can be found by iterating $p(x)$ and $s(x)$. To have a tree structure, we require that these sets be disjoint (a predecessor of node $x$ cannot also be a successor to it). The set of *terminal nodes* is $T = \{x \in \mathscr{X}: s(x) = \varnothing\}$. All other nodes $\mathscr{X} \setminus T$ are known as *decision nodes*.

(iii) A function $\alpha: \mathscr{X} \setminus \{x_0\} \to \mathscr{A}$ giving the action that leads to any noninitial node $x$ from its immediate predecessor $p(x)$ and satisfying the property that if $x', x'' \in s(x)$ and $x' \neq x''$, then $\alpha(x') \neq \alpha(x'')$. The set of choices available at decision node $x$ is $c(x) = \{a \in \mathscr{A}: a = \alpha(x') \text{ for some } x' \in s(x)\}$.

(iv) A collection of information sets $\mathscr{H}$, and a function $H: \mathscr{X} \to \mathscr{H}$ assigning each decision node $x$ to an information set $H(x) \in \mathscr{H}$. Thus, the information sets in $\mathscr{H}$ form a partition of $\mathscr{X}$. We require that all decision nodes assigned to a single information set have the same choices available; formally, $c(x) = c(x')$ if $H(x) = H(x')$. We can therefore write the choices available at information set $H$ as $C(H) = \{a \in \mathscr{A}: a \in c(x) \text{ for } x \in H\}$.

(v) A function $\iota: \mathscr{H} \to \{0, 1, \ldots, I\}$ assigning each information set in $\mathscr{H}$ to the player (or to nature: formally, player 0) who moves at the decision nodes in that set. We can denote the collection of player $i$'s information sets by $\mathscr{H}_i = \{H \in \mathscr{H}: i = \iota(H)\}$.

(vi) A function $\rho: \mathscr{H}_0 \times \mathscr{A} \to [0, 1]$ assigning probabilities to actions at information sets where nature moves and satisfying $\rho(H, a) = 0$ if $a \notin C(H)$ and $\sum_{a \in C(H)} \rho(H, a) = 1$ for all $H \in \mathscr{H}_0$.

(vii) A collection of payoff functions $u = \{u_1(\cdot), \ldots, u_I(\cdot)\}$ assigning utilities to the players for each terminal node that can be reached, $u_i: T \to \mathbb{R}$. As we noted in Section 7.B, because we want to allow for a random realization of outcomes we take each $u_i(\cdot)$ to be a Bernoulli utility function.

Thus, formally, a game in extensive form is specified by the collection $\Gamma_E = \{\mathscr{X}, \mathscr{A}, I, p(\cdot), \alpha(\cdot), \mathscr{H}, H(\cdot), \iota(\cdot), \rho(\cdot), u\}$.

---

We should note that there are three implicit types of finiteness hidden in the formulation just presented. Because we will often encounter games not sharing these features in the economic applications discussed in later chapters, we briefly identify them here, although without any formal treatment. The formal definition of an extensive form representation of a game can be extended to these infinite cases without much difficulty, although there can be important differences in the predicted outcomes of finite and infinite economic models, as we shall see later (e.g., in Chapters 12 and 20).

First, we have assumed that players have a finite number of actions available at each decision node. This would rule out a game in which, say, a player can choose any number from some interval $[a, b] \subset \mathbb{R}$. In fact, allowing for an infinite set of actions requires that we allow for an infinite set of nodes as well. But with this change, items (i) to (vii) remain the basic elements of an extensive form representation (e.g., decision nodes and terminal nodes are still associated with a unique path through the tree).

Second, we have described the extensive form of a game that must end after a finite number of moves (because the set of decision nodes is finite). Indeed, all the examples we have considered so far fall into this category. There are, however, other types of games. For example, suppose that two players with infinite life spans (perhaps two firms) play Matching Pennies repeatedly every January 1. The players discount the money gained or lost at future dates with interest rate $r$ and seek to maximize their discounted net gains. In this game, there are no terminal nodes. Even so, we can still associate discounted payoffs for the two players with every (infinite) sequence of moves the players make. Of course, actually drawing a complete game tree would be impossible, but the basic elements of the extensive form can nonetheless be captured as before (with payoffs being associated with paths through the tree rather than with terminal nodes).

Third, we may at times also imagine that there are an infinite number of players who take actions in a game. For example, models involving overlapping generations of players (as in various macroeconomic models) have this feature, as do models of entry in which we want to allow for an infinite number of potential firms. In the games of this type that we consider, this issue can be handled in a simple and natural manner.

Note that all three of these extensions require that we relax the assumption that there is a finite set of nodes. Games with a finite number of nodes, such as those we have been considering, are known as *finite games*.

For pedagogical purposes, we restrict our attention in Part II to finite games except where specifically indicated otherwise. The extension of the formal concepts we discuss here to the economic games studied later in the book that do not share these finiteness properties is straightforward.

# 7.D  Strategies and the Normal Form Representation of a Game

A central concept of game theory is the notion of a player's *strategy*. A strategy is a *complete contingent plan*, or *decision rule*, that specifies how the player will act in *every possible distinguishable circumstance* in which she might be called upon to move. Recall that, from a player's perspective, the set of such circumstances is represented by her collection of information sets, with each information set representing a different distinguishable circumstance in which she may need to move (see Section 7.C). Thus, a player's strategy amounts to a specification of how she plans to move at each one of her information sets, should it be reached during play of the game. This is stated formally in Definition 7.D.1.

**Definition 7.D.1:** Let $\mathscr{H}_i$ denote the collection of player $i$'s information sets, $\mathscr{A}$ the set of possible actions in the game, and $C(H) \subset \mathscr{A}$ the set of actions possible at information set $H$. A *strategy* for player $i$ is a function $s_i: \mathscr{H}_i \to \mathscr{A}$ such that $s_i(H) \in C(H)$ for all $H \in \mathscr{H}_i$.

The fact that a strategy is a complete contingent plan cannot be overemphasized, and it is often a source of confusion to those new to game theory. When a player specifies her strategy, it is as if she had to write down an instruction book prior to play so that a representative could act on her behalf merely by consulting that book.

As a complete contingent plan, a strategy often specifies actions for a player at information sets that may not be reached during the actual play of the game.

For example, in Tick-Tack-Toe, player O's strategy describes what she will do on her first move if player X starts the game by marking the center square. But in the actual play of the game, player X might not begin in the center; she may instead mark the lower-right corner first, making this part of player O's plan no longer relevant.

In fact, there is an even subtler point: A player's strategy may include plans for actions that her *own* strategy makes irrelevant. For example, a complete contingent plan for player X in Tick-Tack-Toe includes a description of what she will do after she plays "center" and player O then plays "lower-right corner," even though her own strategy may call for her first move to be "upper-left corner." This probably seems strange; its importance will become apparent only when we talk about dynamic games in Chapter 9. Nevertheless, remember: *A strategy is a complete contingent plan that says what a player will do at each of her information sets if she is called on to play there.*

It is worthwhile to consider what the players' possible strategies are for some of the simple Matching Pennies games.

**Example 7.D.1:** *Strategies in Matching Pennies Version B.* In Matching Pennies Version B, a strategy for player 1 simply specifies her move at the game's initial node. She has two possible strategies: She can play heads (H) or tails (T). A strategy for player 2, on the other hand, specifies how she will play (H or T) at each of her two information sets, that is, how she will play if player 1 picks H *and* how she will play if player 1 picks T. Thus, player 2 has *four* possible strategies.

*Strategy 1 ($s_1$):* Play H if player 1 plays H; play H if player 1 plays T.
*Strategy 2 ($s_2$):* Play H if player 1 plays H; play T if player 1 plays T.
*Strategy 3 ($s_3$):* Play T if player 1 plays H; play H if player 1 plays T.
*Strategy 4 ($s_4$):* Play T if player 1 plays H; play T if player 1 plays T. ∎

**Example 7.D.2:** *Strategies in Matching Pennies Version C.* In Matching Pennies Version C, player 1's strategies are exactly the same as in Version B; but player 2 now only has two possible strategies, "play H" and "play T", because she now has only one information set. She can no longer condition her action on player 1's previous action. ∎

We will often find it convenient to represent a profile of players' strategy choices in an $I$-player game by a vector $s = (s_1, \ldots, s_I)$, where $s_i$ is the strategy chosen by player $i$. We will also sometimes write the strategy profile $s$ as $(s_i, s_{-i})$, where $s_{-i}$ is the $(I - 1)$ vector of strategies for players other than $i$.

## The Normal Form Representation of a Game

Every profile of strategies for the players $s = (s_1, \ldots, s_I)$ induces an outcome of the game: a sequence of moves actually taken and a probability distribution over the terminal nodes of the game. Thus, for any profile of strategies $(s_1, \ldots, s_I)$, we can deduce the payoffs received by each player. We might think, therefore, of specifying the game directly in terms of strategies and their associated payoffs. This second way to represent a game is known as the *normal* (or *strategic*) *form*. It is, in essence, a condensed version of the extensive form.

Player 2

|  |  | $s_1$ | $s_2$ | $s_3$ | $s_4$ |
|---|---|---|---|---|---|
| Player 1 | H | $-1, +1$ | $-1, +1$ | $+1, -1$ | $+1, -1$ |
|  | T | $+1, -1$ | $-1, +1$ | $+1, -1$ | $-1, +1$ |

**Figure 7.D.1**

The normal form of Matching Pennies Version B.

**Definition 7.D.2:** For a game with $I$ players, the *normal form representation* $\Gamma_N$ specifies for each player $i$ a set of strategies $S_i$ (with $s_i \in S_i$) and a payoff function $u_i(s_1, \ldots, s_I)$ giving the von Neumann–Morgenstern utility levels associated with the (possibly random) outcome arising from strategies $(s_1, \ldots, s_I)$. Formally, we write $\Gamma_N = [I, \{S_i\}, \{u_i(\cdot)\}]$.

In fact, when describing a game in its normal form, there is no need to keep track of the specific moves associated with each strategy. Instead, we can simply number the various possible strategies of a player, writing player $i$'s strategy set as $S_i = \{s_{1i}, s_{2i}, \ldots\}$ and then referring to each strategy by its number.

A concrete example of a game in normal form is presented in Example 7.D.3 for Matching Pennies Version B.

**Example 7.D.3:** *The Normal Form of Matching Pennies Version B.* We have already described the strategy sets of the two players in Example 7.D.1. The payoff functions are

$$u_1(s_1, s_2) = \begin{cases} +1 \text{ if } (s_1, s_2) = (\text{H, strategies 3 or 4}) \text{ or (T, strategies 1 or 3)}, \\ -1 \text{ if } (s_1, s_2) = (\text{H, strategies 1 or 2}) \text{ or (T, strategies 2 or 4)}, \end{cases}$$

and $u_2(s_1, s_2) = -u_1(s_1, s_2)$. A convenient way to summarize this information is in the "game box" depicted in Figure 7.D.1. The different rows correspond to the strategies of player 1, and the columns to those of player 2. Within each cell, the payoffs of the two players are depicted as $(u_1(s_1, s_2), u_2(s_1, s_2))$. ∎

**Exercise 7.D.2:** Depict the normal forms for Matching Pennies Version C and the standard version of Matching Pennies.

The idea behind using the normal form representation to study behavior in a game is that a player's decision problem can be thought of as one of choosing her strategy (her contingent plan of action) given the strategies that she thinks her rivals will be adopting. Because each player is faced with this problem, we can think of the players as simultaneously choosing their strategies from the sets $\{S_i\}$. It is as if the players each simultaneously write down their strategies on slips of paper and hand them to a referee, who then computes the outcome of the game from the players' submitted strategies.

From the previous discussion, it is clear that for any extensive form representation of a game, there is a unique normal form representation (more precisely, it is unique up to any renaming or renumbering of the strategies). The converse is not true, however. Many different extensive forms may be represented by the same normal form. For example, the normal form shown in Figure 7.D.1 represents not only the extensive form in Figure 7.C.1 but also the

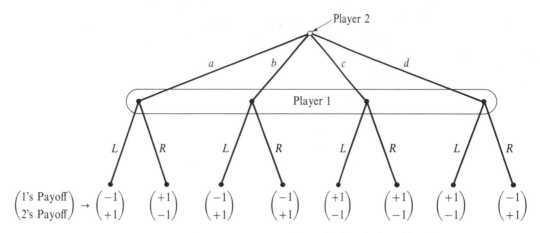

**Figure 7.D.2**  An extensive form whose normal form is that depicted in Figure 7.D.1.

extensive form in Figure 7.D.2. In the latter game, players move simultaneously, player 1 choosing between two strategies, $L$ and $R$, and player 2 choosing among four strategies: $a$, $b$, $c$, and $d$. In terms of their representations in a game box, the only difference between the normal forms for these games lies in the "labels" given to the rows and columns.

Because the condensed representation of the game in the normal form generally omits some of the details present in the extensive form, we may wonder whether this omission is important or whether the normal form summarizes all of the strategically relevant information (as the last paragraph in regular type seems to suggest). The question can be put a little differently: Is the scenario in which players simultaneously write down their strategies and submit them to a referee really equivalent to their playing the game over time as described in the extensive form? This question is currently a subject of some controversy among game theorists. The debate centers on issues arising in dynamic games such as those studied in Chapter 9.

For the simultaneous-move games that we study in Chapter 8, in which all players choose their actions at the same time, the normal form captures *all* the strategically relevant information. In simultaneous-move games, a player's strategy is a simple non-contingent choice of an action. In this case, players' simultaneous choice of strategies in the normal form is clearly equivalent to their simultaneous choice of actions in the extensive form (captured there by having players not observing each other's choices).

## 7.E  Randomized Choices

Up to this point, we have assumed that players make their choices with certainty. However, there is no a priori reason to exclude the possibility that a player could randomize when faced with a choice. Indeed, we will see in Chapters 8 and 9 that in certain circumstances the possibility of randomization can play an important role in the analysis of games.

As stated in Definition 7.D.1, a deterministic strategy for player $i$, which we now call a *pure strategy*, specifies a deterministic choice $s_i(H)$ at each of her information sets $H \in \mathscr{H}_i$. Suppose that player $i$'s (finite) set of pure strategies is $S_i$. One way for the player to randomize is to choose randomly one element of this set. This kind of randomization gives rise to what is called a *mixed strategy*.

**Definition 7.E.1:** Given player $i$'s (finite) pure strategy set $S_i$, a *mixed strategy* for player $i$, $\sigma_i\colon S_i \to [0, 1]$, assigns to each pure strategy $s_i \in S_i$ a probability $\sigma_i(s_i) \geq 0$ that it will be played, where $\sum_{s_i \in S_i} \sigma_i(s_i) = 1$.

Suppose that player $i$ has $M$ pure strategies in set $S_i = \{s_{1i}, \ldots, s_{Mi}\}$. Player $i$'s set of possible mixed strategies can therefore be associated with the points of the following simplex (recall our use of a simplex to represent lotteries in Chapter 6):

$$\Delta(S_i) = \{(\sigma_{1i}, \ldots, \sigma_{Mi}) \in \mathbb{R}^M \colon \sigma_{mi} \geq 0 \text{ for all } m = 1, \ldots, M \text{ and } \sum_{m=1}^{M} \sigma_{mi} = 1\}.$$

This simplex is called the *mixed extension* of $S_i$. Note that a pure strategy can be viewed as a special case of a mixed strategy in which the probability distribution over the elements of $S_i$ is degenerate.

When players randomize over their pure strategies, the induced outcome is itself random, leading to a probability distribution over the terminal nodes of the game. Since each player $i$'s normal form payoff function $u_i(s)$ is of the von Neumann–Morgenstern type, player $i$'s payoff given a profile of mixed strategies $\sigma = (\sigma_1, \ldots, \sigma_I)$ for the $I$ players is her expected utility $E_\sigma[u_i(s)]$, the expectation being taken with respect to the probabilities induced by $\sigma$ on pure strategy profiles $s = (s_1, \ldots, s_I)$. That is, letting $S = S_1 \times \cdots \times S_I$, player $i$'s von Neumann–Morgenstern utility from mixed strategy profile $\sigma$ is

$$\sum_{s \in S} [\sigma_1(s_1)\, \sigma_2(s_2) \cdots \sigma_I(s_I)] u_i(s),$$

which, with a slight abuse of notation, we denote by $u_i(\sigma)$. Note that because we assume that each player randomizes on her own, we take the realizations of players' randomizations to be independent of one another.[3]

The basic definition of the normal form representation need not be changed to accommodate the possibility that players might choose to play mixed strategies. We can simply consider the normal form game $\Gamma_N = [I, \{\Delta(S_i)\}, \{u_i(\cdot)\}]$ in which players' strategy sets are extended to include both pure and mixed strategies.

---

Note that we can equivalently think of a player forming her mixed strategy as follows: Player $i$ has access to a private signal $\theta_i$ that is uniformly distributed on the interval $[0, 1]$ and is independent of other players' signals, and she forms her mixed strategy by making her plan of action contingent on the realization of the signal. That is, she specifies a pure strategy $s_i(\theta_i) \in S_i$ for each realization of $\theta_i$. We shall return to this alternative interpretation of mixed strategies in Chapter 8.

---

If we use the extensive form description of a game, there is another way that player $i$ could randomize. Rather than randomizing over the potentially very

---

3. In Chapter 8, however, we discuss the possibility that players' randomizations could be correlated.

large set of pure strategies in $S_i$, she could randomize separately over the possible actions at each of her information sets $H \in \mathscr{H}_i$. This way of randomizing is called a *behavior strategy*.

**Definition 7.E.2:** Given an extensive form game $\Gamma_E$, a *behavior strategy* for player $i$ specifies, for every information set $H \in \mathscr{H}_i$ and action $a \in C(H)$, a probability $\lambda_i(a, H) \geq 0$, with $\sum_{a \in C(H)} \lambda_i(a, H) = 1$ for all $H \in \mathscr{H}_i$.

As might seem intuitive, for games of perfect recall (and we deal only with these), the two types of randomization are equivalent. For any behavior strategy of player $i$, there is a mixed strategy for that player that yields exactly the same distribution over outcomes for any strategies, mixed or behavior, that might be played by $i$'s rivals, and vice versa [this result is due to Kuhn (1953); see Exercise 7.E.1]. Which form of randomized strategy we consider is therefore a matter of analytical convenience; we typically use behavior strategies when analyzing the extensive form representation of a game and mixed strategies when analyzing the normal form.

Because the way we introduce randomization is solely a matter of analytical convenience, we shall be a bit loose in our terminology and refer to all randomized strategies as *mixed strategies*.

## REFERENCES

Aumann, R. (1976). Agreeing to disagree. *Annals of Statistics* **4**: 1236–39.

Kreps, D. M., and R. Wilson. (1982). Sequential equilibrium. *Econometrica* **50**: 863–94.

Kuhn, H. W. (1953). Extensive games and the problem of information. In *Contributions to the Theory of Games*. vol. 2, edited by H. W. Kuhn and A. W. Tucker. Princeton, N.J.: Princeton University Press, 193–216.

Milgrom, P. (1981). An axiomatic characterization of common knowledge. *Econometrica* **49**: 219–22.

## EXERCISES

**7.C.1**[A] Suppose that in the Meeting in New York game (Example 7.B.3), there are two possible places where the two players can meet: Grand Central Station and the Empire State Building. Draw an extensive form representation (game tree) for this game.

**7.D.1**[B] In a game where player $i$ has $N$ information sets indexed $n = 1, \ldots, N$ and $M_n$ possible actions at information set $n$, how many strategies does player $i$ have?

**7.D.2**[A] In text.

**7.E.1**[B] Consider the two-player game whose extensive form representation (excluding payoffs) is depicted in Figure 7.Ex.1.

(a) What are player 1's possible strategies? Player 2's?

(b) Show that for any behavior strategy that player 1 might play, there is a realization equivalent mixed strategy; that is, a mixed strategy that generates the same probability distribution over the terminal nodes for *any* mixed strategy choice by player 2.

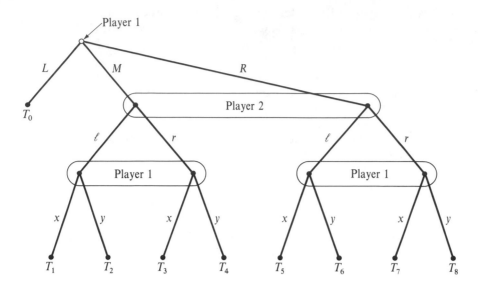

**Figure 7.Ex.1**

(c) Show that the converse is also true: For any mixed strategy that player 1 might play, there is a realization equivalent behavior strategy.

(d) Suppose that we change the game by merging the information sets at player 1's second round of moves (so that all four nodes are now in a single information set). Argue that the game is no longer one of perfect recall. Which of the two results in (b) and (c) still holds?

# Simultaneous-Move Games

## 8.A Introduction

We now turn to the central question of game theory: What should we expect to observe in a game played by rational players who are fully knowledgeable about the structure of the game and each others' rationality? In this chapter, we study *simultaneous-move* games, in which all players move only once and at the same time. Our motivation for beginning with these games is primarily pedagogic; they allow us to concentrate on the study of strategic interaction in the simplest possible setting and to defer until Chapter 9 some difficult issues that arise in more general, dynamic games.

In Section 8.B, we introduce the concepts of *dominant* and *dominated* strategies. These notions and their extension in the concept of *iterated dominance* provide a first and compelling restriction on the strategies rational players should choose to play.

In Section 8.C, we extend these ideas by defining the notion of a *rationalizable strategy*. We argue that the implication of players' common knowledge of each others' rationality and of the structure of the game is precisely that they will play rationalizable strategies.

Unfortunately, in many games, the set of rationalizable strategies does not yield a very precise prediction of the play that will occur. In the remaining sections of the chapter, we therefore study solution concepts that yield more precise predictions by adding "equilibrium" requirements regarding players' behavior.

Section 8.D begins our study of equilibrium-based solution concepts by introducing the important and widely applied concept of *Nash equilibrium*. This concept adds to the assumption of common knowledge of players' rationality a requirement of *mutually correct expectations*. By doing so, it often greatly narrows the set of predicted outcomes of a game. We discuss in some detail the reasonableness of this requirement, as well as the conditions under which we can be assured that a Nash equilibrium exists.

In Sections 8.E and 8.F, we examine two extensions of the Nash equilibrium concept. In Section 8.E, we broaden the notion of a Nash equilibrium to cover situations with *incomplete information*, where each player's payoffs may, to some extent, be known only by the player. This yields the concept of *Bayesian Nash equilibrium.* In Section 8.F, we explore the implications of players entertaining the possibility that, with some small but positive probability, their opponents might make a mistake in choosing their strategies. We define the notion of a (*normal form*) *trembling-hand perfect Nash equilibrium*, an extension of the Nash equilibrium concept that requires that equilibria be robust to the possibility of small mistakes.

Throughout the chapter, we study simultaneous-move games using their normal form representations (see Section 7.D). Thus, we use $\Gamma_N = [I, \{S_i\}, \{u_i(\cdot)\}]$ when we consider only pure (nonrandom) strategy choices and $\Gamma_N = [I, \{\Delta(S_i)\}, \{u_i(\cdot)\}]$ when we allow for the possibility of randomized choices by the players (see Section 7.E for a discussion of randomized choices). We often denote a profile of pure strategies for player $i$'s opponents by $s_{-i} = (s_1, \ldots, s_{i-1}, s_{i+1}, \ldots, s_I)$, with a similar meaning applying to the profile of mixed strategies $\sigma_{-i}$. We then write $s = (s_i, s_{-i})$ and $\sigma = (\sigma_i, \sigma_{-i})$. We also let $S = S_1 \times \cdots \times S_I$ and $S_{-i} = S_1 \times \cdots \times S_{i-1} \times S_{i+1} \times \cdots \times S_I$.

## 8.B  Dominant and Dominated Strategies

We begin our study of simultaneous-move games by considering the predictions that can be made based on a relatively simple means of comparing a player's possible strategies: that of *dominance*.

To keep matters as simple as possible, we initially ignore the possibility that players might randomize in their strategy choices. Hence, our focus is on games $\Gamma_N = [I, \{S_i\}, \{u_i(\cdot)\}]$ whose strategy sets allow for only pure strategies.

Consider the game depicted in Figure 8.B.1, the famous *Prisoner's Dilemma*. The story behind this game is as follows: Two individuals are arrested for allegedly engaging in a serious crime and are held in separate cells. The district attorney (the DA) tries to extract a confession from each prisoner. Each is privately told that if he is the only one to confess, then he will be rewarded with a light sentence of 1 year while the recalcitrant prisoner will go to jail for 10 years. However, if he is the only one not to confess, then it is he who will serve the 10-year sentence. If both confess, they will both be shown some mercy: they will each get 5 years. Finally, if neither confesses, it will still be possible to convict both of a lesser crime that carries a sentence of 2 years. Each player wishes to minimize the time he spends in jail (or maximize the negative of this, the payoffs that are depicted in Figure 8.B.1).

What will the outcome of this game be? There is only one plausible answer: (confess, confess). To see why, note that playing "confess" is each player's best strategy *regardless of what the other player does*. This type of strategy is known as a *strictly dominant strategy*.

|  |  | Prisoner 2 | |
|---|---|---|---|
|  |  | Don't Confess | Confess |
| Prisoner 1 | Don't Confess | $-2, -2$ | $-10, -1$ |
|  | Confess | $-1, -10$ | $-5, -5$ |

**Figure 8.B.1**

The Prisoner's Dilemma.

**Definition 8.B.1:** A strategy $s_i \in S_i$ is a *strictly dominant strategy* for player $i$ in game $\Gamma_N = [I, \{S_i\}, \{u_i(\cdot)\}]$ if for all $s_i' \neq s_i$, we have

$$u_i(s_i, s_{-i}) > u_i(s_i', s_{-i})$$

for all $s_{-i} \in S_{-i}$.

In words, a strategy $s_i$ is a strictly dominant strategy for player $i$ if it maximizes uniquely player $i$'s payoff for any strategy that player $i$'s rivals might play. (The reason for the modifier *strictly* in Definition 8.B.1 will be made clear in Definition 8.B.3.) If a player has a strictly dominant strategy, as in the Prisoner's Dilemma, we should expect him to play it.

The striking aspect of the (confess, confess) outcome in the Prisoner's Dilemma is that although it is the one we expect to arise, it is not the best outcome for the players *jointly*; both players would prefer that neither of them confess. For this reason, the Prisoner's Dilemma is the paradigmatic example of self-interested, rational behavior *not* leading to a socially optimal result.

One way of viewing the outcome of the Prisoner's Dilemma is that, in seeking to maximize his own payoff, each prisoner has a negative effect on his partner; by moving away from the (don't confess, don't confess) outcome, a player reduces his jail time by 1 year but increases that of his partner by 8 (in Chapter 11, we shall see this as an example of an *externality*).

### Dominated Strategies

Although it is compelling that players should play strictly dominant strategies if they have them, it is rare for such strategies to exist. Often, one strategy of player $i$'s may be best when his rivals play $s_{-i}$ and another when they play some other strategies $s_{-i}'$ (think of the standard Matching Pennies game in Chapter 7). Even so, we might still be able to use the idea of dominance to eliminate some strategies as possible choices. In particular, we should expect that player $i$ will not play *dominated* strategies, those for which there is some alternative strategy that yields him a greater payoff regardless of what the other players do.

**Definition 8.B.2:** A strategy $s_i \in S_i$ is *strictly dominated* for player $i$ in game $\Gamma_N = [I, \{S_i\}, \{u_i(\cdot)\}]$ if there exists another strategy $s_i' \in S_i$ such that for all $s_{-i} \in S_{-i}$,

$$u_i(s_i', s_{-i}) > u_i(s_i, s_{-i}).$$

In this case, we say that strategy $s_i'$ *strictly dominates* strategy $s_i$.

With this definition, we can restate our definition of a strictly dominant strategy (Definition 8.B.1) as follows: Strategy $s_i$ is a strictly dominant strategy for player $i$ in game $\Gamma_N = [I, \{S_i\}, \{u_i(\cdot)\}]$ if it strictly dominates every other strategy in $S_i$.

**Example 8.B.1:** Consider the game shown in Figure 8.B.2. There is no strictly dominant strategy, but strategy $D$ for player 1 is strictly dominated by strategy $M$ (and also by strategy $U$).  ∎

Definition 8.D.3 presents a related, weaker notion of a dominated strategy that is of some importance.

Player 2

|   |   | L | R |
|---|---|---|---|
|   |   | L | R |
| U |   | 1, −1 | −1, 1 |
| Player 1 | M | −1, 1 | 1, −1 |
|   | D | −2, 5 | −3, 2 |

Player 2

|   |   | L | R |
|---|---|---|---|
| U |   | 5, 1 | 4, 0 |
| Player 1 | M | 6, 0 | 3, 1 |
|   | D | 6, 4 | 4, 4 |

**Figure 8.B.2 (left)**
Strategy $D$ is strictly dominated.

**Figure 8.B.3 (right)**
Strategies $U$ and $M$ are weakly dominated.

**Definition 8.B.3:** A strategy $s_i \in S_i$ is *weakly dominated* in game $\Gamma_N = [I, \{S_i\}, \{u_i(\cdot)\}]$ if there exists another strategy $s_i' \in S_i$ such that for all $s_{-i} \in S_{-i}$,

$$u_i(s_i', s_{-i}) \geq u_i(s_i, s_{-i}),$$

with strict inequality for *some* $s_{-i}$. In this case, we say that strategy $s_i'$ *weakly dominates* strategy $s_i$. A strategy is a *weakly dominant strategy* for player $i$ in game $\Gamma_N = [I, \{S_i\}, \{u_i(\cdot)\}]$ if it weakly dominates every other strategy in $S_i$.

Thus, a strategy is weakly dominated if another strategy does at least as well for all $s_{-i}$ and strictly better for some $s_{-i}$.

**Example 8.B.2:** Figure 8.B.3 depicts a game in which player 1 has two weakly dominated strategies, $U$ and $M$. Both are weakly dominated by strategy $D$. ∎

Unlike a strictly dominated strategy, a strategy that is only weakly dominated cannot be ruled out based solely on principles of rationality. For any alternative strategy that player $i$ might pick, there is at least one profile of strategies for his rivals for which the weakly dominated strategy does as well. In Figure 8.B.3, for example, player 1 could rationally pick $M$ if he was *absolutely sure* that player 2 would play $L$. Yet, if the probability of player 2 choosing strategy $R$ was perceived by player 1 as positive (no matter how small), then $M$ would not be a rational choice for player 1. *Caution* might therefore rule out $M$. More generally, weakly dominated strategies could be dismissed if players always believed that there was at least some positive probability that any strategies of their rivals could be chosen. We do not pursue this idea here, although we return to it in Section 8.F. For now, we continue to allow a player to entertain any conjecture about what an opponent might play, even a perfectly certain one.

*Iterated Deletion of Strictly Dominated Strategies*

As we have noted, it is unusual for elimination of strictly dominated strategies to lead to a unique prediction for a game (e.g., recall the game in Figure 8.B.2). However, the logic of eliminating strictly dominated strategies can be pushed further, as demonstrated in Example 8.B.3.

**Example 8.B.3:** In Figure 8.B.4, we depict a modification of the Prisoner's Dilemma, which we call the *DA's Brother*.

The story (a somewhat far-fetched one!) is now as follows: One of the prisoners, prisoner 1, is the DA's brother. The DA has some discretion in the fervor with which

Prisoner 2

|  | Don't Confess | Confess |
|---|---|---|
| **Don't Confess** | 0, −2 | −10, −1 |
| **Confess** | −1, −10 | −5, −5 |

Prisoner 1

**Figure 8.B.4**
The DA's Brother.

he prosecutes and, in particular, can allow prisoner 1 to go free if neither of the prisoners confesses. With this change, if prisoner 2 confesses, then prisoner 1 should also confess; but "don't confess" has become prisoner 1's best strategy if prisoner 2 plays "don't confess." Thus, we are unable to rule out either of prisoner 1's strategies as being dominated, and so elimination of strictly dominated (or, for that matter, weakly dominated) strategies does not lead to a unique prediction.

However, we can still derive a unique prediction in this game if we push the logic of eliminating strictly dominated strategies further. Note that "don't confess" is still strictly dominated for prisoner 2. Furthermore, once prisoner 1 eliminates "don't confess" as a possible action by prisoner 2, "confess" is prisoner 1's unambiguously optimal action; that is, it is his strictly dominant strategy once the strictly dominated strategy of prisoner 2 has been deleted. Thus, the unique predicted outcome in the DA's Brother game should still be (confess, confess). ∎

Note the way players' common knowledge of each other's payoffs and rationality is used to solve the game in Example 8.B.3. Elimination of strictly dominated strategies requires only that each player be rational. What we have just done, however, requires not only that prisoner 2 be rational but also that prisoner 1 *know* that prisoner 2 is rational. Put somewhat differently, a player need not know anything about his opponents' payoffs or be sure of their rationality to eliminate a strictly dominated strategy from consideration as his own strategy choice; but for the player to eliminate one of his strategies from consideration because it is dominated if his opponents never play *their* dominated strategies *does* require this knowledge.

As a general matter, if we are willing to assume that all players are rational *and* that this fact and the players' payoffs are common knowledge (so everybody knows that everybody knows that . . . everybody is rational), then we do not need to stop after only two iterations. We can eliminate not only strictly dominated strategies and strategies that are strictly dominated after the first deletion of strategies but also strategies that are strictly dominated after this *next* deletion of strategies, and so on. Note that with each elimination of strategies, it becomes possible for additional strategies to become dominated because the fewer strategies that a player's opponents might play, the more likely that a particular strategy of his is dominated. However, each additional iteration requires that players' knowledge of each others' rationality be one level deeper. A player must now know not only that his rivals are rational but also that they know that he is, and so on.

One feature of the process of iteratively eliminating strictly dominated strategies is that the order of deletion does not affect the set of strategies that remain in the end (see Exercise 8.B.4), That is, if at any given point several strategies (of one or several players) are strictly dominated, then we can eliminate them all at once or in any sequence without changing the set of strategies that we ultimately end up with. This is fortunate, since we would worry if our prediction depended on the arbitrarily chosen order of deletion.

Exercise 8.B.5 presents an interesting example of a game for which the iterated removal of strictly dominated strategies yields a unique prediction: the *Cournot duopoly game* (which we will discuss in detail in Chapter 12).

---

The iterated deletion of *weakly* dominated strategies is harder to justify. As we have already indicated, the argument for deletion of a weakly dominated strategy for player $i$ is that he contemplates the possibility that every strategy combination of his rivals occurs with positive probability. However, this hypothesis clashes with the logic of iterated deletion, which assumes, precisely, that eliminated strategies are not expected to occur. This inconsistency leads the iterative elimination of weakly dominated strategies to have the undesirable feature that it *can* depend on the order of deletion. The game in Figure 8.B.3 provides an example. If we first eliminate strategy $U$, we next eliminate strategy $L$, and we can then eliminate strategy $M$; $(D, R)$ is therefore our prediction. If, instead, we eliminate strategy $M$ first, we next eliminate strategy $R$, and we can then eliminate strategy $U$; now $(D, L)$ is our prediction.

---

## Allowing for Mixed Strategies

When we recognize that players may randomize over their pure strategies, the basic definitions of strictly dominated and dominant strategies can be generalized in a straightforward way.

**Definition 8.B.4:** A strategy $\sigma_i \in \Delta(S_i)$ is *strictly dominated* for player $i$ in game $\Gamma_N = [I, \{\Delta(S_i)\}, \{u_i(\cdot)\}]$ if there exists another strategy $\sigma_i' \in \Delta(S_i)$ such that for all $\sigma_{-i} \in \prod_{j \neq i} \Delta(S_j)$,

$$u_i(\sigma_i', \sigma_{-i}) > u_i(\sigma_i, \sigma_{-i}).$$

In this case, we say that strategy $\sigma_i'$ *strictly dominates* strategy $\sigma_i$. A strategy $\sigma_i$ is a *strictly dominant strategy* for player $i$ in game $\Gamma_N = [I, \{\Delta(S_i)\}, \{u_i(\cdot)\}]$ if it strictly dominates every other strategy in $\Delta(S_i)$.

---

Using this definition and the structure of mixed strategies, we can say a bit more about the set of strictly dominated strategies in game $\Gamma_N = [I, \{\Delta(S_i)\}, \{u_i(\cdot)\}]$.

Note first that when we test whether a strategy $\sigma_i$ is strictly dominated by strategy $\sigma_i'$ for player $i$, we need only consider these two strategies' payoffs against the *pure* strategies of $i$'s opponents. That is,

$$u_i(\sigma_i', \sigma_{-i}) > u_i(\sigma_i, \sigma_{-i}) \quad \text{for all } \sigma_{-i}$$

if and only if

$$u_i(\sigma_i', s_{-i}) > u_i(\sigma_i, s_{-i}) \quad \text{for all } s_{-i}.$$

This follows because we can write

$$u_i(\sigma_i', \sigma_{-i}) - u_i(\sigma_i, \sigma_{-i}) = \sum_{s_{-i} \in S_{-i}} \left[ \prod_{k \neq i} \sigma_k(s_k) \right] [u_i(\sigma_i', s_{-i}) - u_i(\sigma_i, s_{-i})].$$

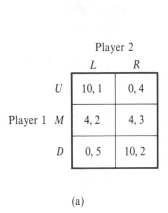

(a)

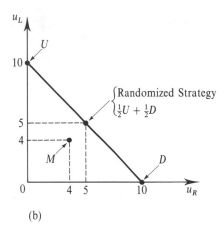

(b)

**Figure 8.B.5**

Domination of a pure strategy by a randomized strategy.

This expression is positive for all $\sigma_{-i}$ if and only if $[u_i(\sigma'_i, s_{-i}) - u_i(\sigma_i, s_{-i})]$ is positive for all $s_{-i}$. One implication of this point is presented in Proposition 8.B.1.

**Proposition 8.B.1:** Player $i$'s pure strategy $s_i \in S_i$ is strictly dominated in game $\Gamma_N = [I, \{\Delta(S_i)\}, \{u_i(\cdot)\}]$ if and only if there exists another strategy $\sigma'_i \in \Delta(S_i)$ such that

$$u_i(\sigma'_i, s_{-i}) > u_i(s_i, s_{-i})$$

for all $s_{-i} \in S_{-i}$.

Proposition 8.B.1 tells us that to test whether a pure strategy $s_i$ is dominated when randomized play is possible, the test given in Definition 8.B.2 need only be augmented by checking whether any of player $i$'s mixed strategies does better than $s_i$ against every possible profile of pure strategies by $i$'s rivals.

In fact, this extra requirement can eliminate additional pure strategies because a pure strategy $s_i$ may be dominated only by a randomized combination of other pure strategies; that is, to dominate a strategy, even a pure one, it may be necessary to consider alternative strategies that involve randomization. To see this, consider the two-player game depicted in Figure 8.B.5(a). Player 1 has three strategies: $U$, $M$, and $D$. We can see that $U$ is an excellent strategy when player 2 plays $L$ but a poor one against $R$ and that $D$ is excellent against $R$ and poor against $L$. Strategy $M$, on the other hand, is a good but not great strategy against both $L$ and $R$. None of these three pure strategies is strictly dominated by any of the others. But if we allow player 1 to randomize, then playing $U$ and $D$ each with probability $\frac{1}{2}$ yields player 1 an expected payoff of 5 regardless of player 2's strategy, strictly dominating $M$ (remember, payoffs are levels of von Neumann–Morgenstern utilities). This is shown in Figure 8.B.5(b), where player 1's expected payoffs from playing $U$, $D$, $M$, and the randomized strategy $\frac{1}{2}U + \frac{1}{2}D$ are plotted as points in $\mathbb{R}^2$ (the two dimensions correspond to a strategy's expected payoff for player 1 when player 2 plays $R$, denoted by $u_R$, and $L$, denoted by $u_L$). In the figure, the payoff vectors achievable by randomizing over $U$ and $D$, and that from the randomized strategy $\frac{1}{2}U + \frac{1}{2}D$ in particular, lie on the line connecting points $(0, 10)$ and $(10, 0)$. As can be seen, the payoffs from $\frac{1}{2}U + \frac{1}{2}D$ strictly dominate those from strategy $M$.

Once we have determined the set of undominated pure strategies for player $i$, we need to consider which mixed strategies are undominated. We can immediately eliminate any mixed strategy that uses a dominated pure strategy; if pure strategy $s_i$ is strictly dominated for player $i$, then so is every mixed strategy that assigns a positive probability to this strategy.

**Exercise 8.B.6:** Prove that if pure strategy $s_i$ is a strictly dominated strategy in game $\Gamma_N = [I, \{\Delta(S_i)\}, \{u_i(\cdot)\}]$, then so is any strategy that plays $s_i$ with positive probability.

But these are not the only mixed strategies that may be dominated. A mixed strategy that randomizes over undominated pure strategies may itself be dominated. For example, if strategy $M$ in Figure 8.B.5(a) instead gave player 1 a payoff of 6 for either strategy chosen by player 2, then although neither strategy $U$ nor strategy $D$ would be strictly dominated, the randomized strategy $\frac{1}{2}U + \frac{1}{2}D$ would be strictly dominated by strategy $M$ [look where the point $(6, 6)$ would lie in Figure 8.B.5(b)].

In summary, to find the set of strictly dominated strategies for player $i$ in $\Gamma_N = [I, \{\Delta(S_i)\}, \{u_i(\cdot)\}]$, we can first eliminate those pure strategies that are strictly dominated by applying the test in Proposition 8.B.1. Call player $i$'s set of undominated pure strategies $S_i^u \subset S_i$. Next, eliminate any mixed strategies in set $\Delta(S_i^u)$ that are dominated. Player $i$'s set of undominated strategies (pure and mixed) is exactly the remaining strategies in set $\Delta(S_i^u)$.

As when we considered only pure strategies, we can push the logic of removal of strictly dominated strategies in game $\Gamma_N = [I, \{\Delta(S_i)\}, \{u_i(\cdot)\}]$ further through iterative elimination. The preceding discussion implies that this iterative procedure can be accomplished with the following two-stage procedure: First iteratively eliminate dominated pure strategies using the test in Proposition 8.B.1, applied at each stage using the remaining set of pure strategies. Call the remaining sets of pure strategies $\{\bar{S}_1^u, \ldots, \bar{S}_I^u\}$. Then, eliminate any mixed strategies in sets $\{\Delta(\bar{S}_1^u), \ldots, \Delta(\bar{S}_I^u)\}$ that are dominated.

# 8.C   Rationalizable Strategies

In Section 8.B, we eliminated strictly dominated strategies based on the argument that a rational player would never choose such a strategy regardless of the strategies that he anticipates his rivals will play. We then used players' common knowledge of each others' rationality and the structure of the game to justify iterative removal of strictly dominated strategies.

In general, however, players' common knowledge of each others' rationality and the game's structure allows us to eliminate more than just those strategies that are iteratively strictly dominated. Here, we develop this point, leading to the concept of a *rationalizable strategy*. The set of rationalizable strategies consists precisely of those strategies that may be played in a game where the structure of the game and the players' rationality are common knowledge among the players. Throughout this section, we focus on games of the form $\Gamma_N = [I, \{\Delta(S_i)\}, \{u_i(\cdot)\}]$ (mixed strategies are permitted).

We begin with Definition 8.C.1.

**Definition 8.C.1:** In game $\Gamma_N = [I, \{\Delta(S_i)\}, \{u_i(\cdot)\}]$, strategy $\sigma_i$ is a *best response* for player $i$ to his rivals' strategies $\sigma_{-i}$ if

$$u_i(\sigma_i, \sigma_{-i}) \geq u_i(\sigma_i', \sigma_{-i})$$

for all $\sigma_i' \in \Delta(S_i)$. Strategy $\sigma_i$ is *never a best response* if there is no $\sigma_{-i}$ for which $\sigma_i$ is a best response.

Strategy $\sigma_i$ is a best response to $\sigma_{-i}$ if it is an optimal choice when player $i$ conjectures that his opponents will play $\sigma_{-i}$. Player $i$'s strategy $\sigma_i$ is never a best response if there is no belief that player $i$ may hold about his opponents' strategy choices $\sigma_{-i}$ that justifies choosing strategy $\sigma_i$.[1] Clearly, a player should not play a strategy that is never a best response.

Note that a strategy that is strictly dominated is never a best response. However, as a general matter, a strategy might never be a best response even though it is not strictly dominated (we say more about this relation at the end of this section in small type). Thus, eliminating strategies that are never a best response must eliminate at least as many strategies as eliminating just strictly dominated strategies and may eliminate more.

Moreover, as in the case of strictly dominated strategies, common knowledge of rationality and the game's structure implies that we can iterate the deletion of strategies that are never a best response. In particular, a rational player should not play a strategy that is never a best response once he eliminates the possibility that any of his rivals might play a strategy that is never a best response for them, and so on.

Equally important, the strategies that remain after this iterative deletion are the strategies that a rational player can *justify*, or *rationalize*, affirmatively with some reasonable conjecture about the choices of his rivals; that is, with a conjecture that does not assume that any player will play a strategy that is never a best response or one that is only a best response to a conjecture that someone else will play such a strategy, and so on. (Example 8.C.1 provides an illustration of this point.) As a result, the set of strategies surviving this iterative deletion process can be said to be precisely the set of strategies that can be played by rational players in a game in which the players' rationality and the structure of the game are common knowledge. They are known as *rationalizable strategies* [a concept developed independently by Bernheim (1984) and Pearce (1984)].

**Definition 8.C.2:** In game $\Gamma_N = [I, \{\Delta(S_i)\}, \{u_i(\cdot)\}]$, the strategies in $\Delta(S_i)$ that survive the iterated removal of strategies that are never a best response are known as player $i$'s *rationalizable strategies*.

Note that the set of rationalizable strategies can be no larger than the set of strategies surviving iterative removal of strictly dominated strategies because, at each stage of the iterative process in Definition 8.C.2, all strategies that are strictly dominated at that stage are eliminated. As in the case of iterated deletion of strictly dominated strategies, the order of removal of strategies that are never a best response can be shown not to affect the set of strategies that remain in the end (see Exercise 8.C.2).

---

1. We speak here as if a player's conjecture is necessarily deterministic in the sense that the player believes it is certain that his rivals will play a particular profile of mixed strategies $\sigma_{-i}$. One might wonder about conjectures that are probabilistic, that is, that take the form of a nondegenerate probability distribution over possible profiles of mixed strategy choices by his rivals. In fact, a strategy $\sigma_i$ is an optimal choice for player $i$ given some probabilistic conjecture (that treats his opponents' choices as independent random variables) only if it is an optimal choice given some deterministic conjecture. The reason is that if $\sigma_i$ is an optimal choice given some probabilistic conjecture, then it must be a best response to the profile of mixed strategies $\sigma_{-i}$ that plays each possible pure strategy profile $s_{-i} \in S_{-i}$ with exactly the compound probability implied by the probabilistic conjecture.

Player 2

|       | $b_1$ | $b_2$ | $b_3$ | $b_4$ |
|-------|-------|-------|-------|-------|
| $a_1$ | 0, 7  | 2, 5  | 7, 0  | 0, 1  |
| $a_2$ | 5, 2  | 3, 3  | 5, 2  | 0, 1  |
| $a_3$ | 7, 0  | 2, 5  | 0, 7  | 0, 1  |
| $a_4$ | 0, 0  | 0, −2 | 0, 0  | 10, −1 |

Player 1

**Figure 8.C.1**

$\{a_1, a_2, a_3\}$ are rationalizable strategies for player 1; $\{b_1, b_2, b_3\}$ are rationalizable strategies for player 2.

**Example 8.C.1:** Consider the game depicted in Figure 8.C.1, which is taken from Bernheim (1984). What is the set of rationalizable pure strategies for the two players? In the first round of deletion, we can eliminate strategy $b_4$, which is never a best response because it is strictly dominated by a strategy that plays strategies $b_1$ and $b_3$ each with probability $\frac{1}{2}$. Once strategy $b_4$ is eliminated, strategy $a_4$ can be eliminated because it is strictly dominated by $a_2$ once $b_4$ is deleted. At this point, no further strategies can be ruled out: $a_1$ is a best response to $b_3$, $a_2$ is a best response to $b_2$, and $a_3$ is a best response to $b_1$. Similarly, you can check that $b_1$, $b_2$, and $b_3$ are each best responses to one of $a_1$, $a_2$, and $a_3$. Thus, the set of rationalizable pure strategies for player 1 is $\{a_1, a_2, a_3\}$, and the set $\{b_1, b_2, b_3\}$ is rationalizable for player 2.

Note that for each of these rationalizable strategies, a player can construct a *chain of justification* for his choice that never relies on any player believing that another player will play a strategy that is never a best response.[2] For example, in the game in Figure 8.C.1, player 1 can justify choosing $a_2$ by the belief that player 2 will play $b_2$, which player 1 can justify to himself by believing that player 2 will think that he is going to play $a_2$, which is reasonable if player 1 believes that player 2 is thinking that he, player 1, thinks player 2 will play $b_2$, and so on. Thus, player 1 can construct an (infinite) chain of justification for playing strategy $a_2$, $(a_2, b_2, a_2, b_2, \ldots)$, where each element is justified using the next element in the sequence.

Similarly, player 1 can rationalize playing strategy $a_1$ with the chain of justification $(a_1, b_3, a_3, b_1, a_1, b_3, a_3, b_1, a_1, \ldots)$. Here player 1 justifies playing $a_1$ by believing that player 2 will play $b_3$. He justifies the belief that player 2 will play $b_3$ by thinking that player 2 believes that he, player 1, will play $a_3$. He justifies this belief by thinking that player 2 thinks that he, player 1, believes that player 2 will play $b_1$. And so on.

Suppose, however, that player 1 tried to justify $a_4$. He could do so only by a belief that player 2 would play $b_4$, but there is *no* belief that player 2 could have that would justify $b_4$. Hence, player 1 cannot justify playing the nonrationalizable strategy $a_4$. ∎

---

2. In fact, this chain-of-justification approach to the set of rationalizable strategies is used in the original definition of the concept [for a formal treatment, consult Bernheim (1984) and Pearce (1984)].

It can be shown that under fairly weak conditions a player always has at least one rationalizable strategy.[3] Unfortunately, players may have many rationalizable strategies, as in Example 8.C.1. If we want to narrow our predictions further, we need to make additional assumptions beyond common knowledge of rationality. The solution concepts studied in the remainder of this chapter do so by imposing "equilibrium" requirements on players' strategy choices.

We have said that the set of rationalizable strategies is no larger than the set remaining after iterative deletion of strictly dominated strategies. It turns out, however, that for the case of two-player games ($I = 2$), these two sets are identical because in two-player games a (mixed) strategy $\sigma_i$ is a best response to some strategy choice of a player's rival whenever $\sigma_i$ is not strictly dominated.

To see that this is plausible, reconsider the game in Figure 8.B.5 (Exercise 8.C.3 asks you for a general proof). Suppose that the payoffs from strategy $M$ are altered so that $M$ is not strictly dominated. Then, as depicted in Figure 8.C.2, the payoffs from $M$ lie somewhere above

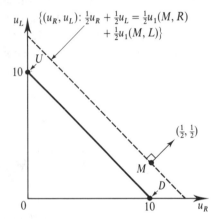

**Figure 8.C.2**

In a two-player game, a strategy is a best response if it is not strictly dominated.

the line connecting the points for strategies $U$ and $D$. Is $M$ a best response here? Yes. To see this, note that if player 2 plays strategy $R$ with probability $\sigma_2(R)$, then player 1's expected payoff from choosing a strategy with payoffs $(u_R, u_L)$ is $\sigma_2(R)u_R + (1 - \sigma_2(R))u_L$. Points yielding the same expected payoff as strategy $M$ therefore lie on a hyperplane with normal vector $(1 - \sigma_2(R), \sigma_2(R))$. As can be seen, strategy $M$ is a best response to $\sigma_2(R) = \frac{1}{2}$; it yields an expected payoff strictly larger than any expected payoff achievable by playing strategies $U$ and/or $D$.

With more than two players, however, there can be strategies that are never a best response and yet are not strictly dominated. The reason can be traced to the fact that players' randomizations are independent. If the randomizations by $i$'s rivals can be correlated (we discuss how this might happen at the end of Sections 8.D and 8.E), the equivalence reemerges. Exercise 8.C.4 illustrates these points.

3. This will be true, for example, whenever a Nash equilibrium (introduced in Section 8.D) exists.

## 8.D Nash Equilibrium

In this section, we present and discuss the most widely used solution concept in applications of game theory to economics, that of *Nash equilibrium* [due to Nash (1951)]. Throughout the rest of the book, we rely on it extensively.

For ease of exposition, we initially ignore the possibility that players might randomize over their pure strategies, restricting our attention to game $\Gamma_N = [I, \{S_i\}, \{u_i(\cdot)\}]$. Mixed strategies are introduced later in the section.

We begin with Definition 8.D.1.

**Definition 8.D.1:** A strategy profile $s = (s_1, \ldots, s_I)$ constitutes a *Nash equilibrium* of game $\Gamma_N = [I, \{S_i\}, \{u_i(\cdot)\}]$ if for every $i = 1, \ldots, I$,

$$u_i(s_i, s_{-i}) \geq u_i(s_i', s_{-i})$$

for all $s_i' \in S_i$.

In a Nash equilibrium, each player's strategy choice is a best response (see Definition 8.C.1) to the strategies *actually played* by his rivals. The italicized words distinguish the concept of Nash equilibrium from the concept of rationalizability studied in Section 8.C. Rationalizability, which captures the implications of the players' common knowledge of each others' rationality and the structure of the game, requires only that a player's strategy be a best response to some reasonable conjecture about what his rivals will be playing, where *reasonable* means that the conjectured play of his rivals can also be so justified. Nash equilibrium adds to this the requirement that players be *correct* in their conjectures.

Examples 8.D.1 and 8.D.2 illustrate the use of the concept.

**Example 8.D.1:** Consider the two-player simultaneous-move game shown in Figure 8.D.1. We can see that $(M, m)$ is a Nash equilibrium. If player 1 chooses $M$, then the best response of player 2 is to choose $m$; the reverse is true for player 2. Moreover, $(M, m)$ is the only combination of (pure) strategies that is a Nash equilibrium. For example, strategy profile $(U, r)$ cannot be a Nash equilibrium because player 1 would prefer to deviate to strategy $D$ given that player 2 is playing $r$. (Check the other possibilities for yourself.) ∎

**Example 8.D.2:** *Nash Equilibrium in the Game of Figure 8.C.1.* In this game, the unique Nash equilibrium profile of (pure) strategies is $(a_2, b_2)$. Player 1's best response to $b_2$ is $a_2$, and player 2's best response to $a_2$ is $b_2$, so $(a_2, b_2)$ is a Nash equilibrium.

Player 2

|          |   | $\ell$ | $m$ | $r$ |
|----------|---|--------|-----|-----|
|          | $U$ | 5, 3 | 0, 4 | 3, 5 |
| Player 1 | $M$ | 4, 0 | (5, 5) | 4, 0 |
|          | $D$ | 3, 5 | 0, 4 | 5, 3 |

**Figure 8.D.1**

A Nash equilibrium.

Mr. Schelling

|  | Empire State | Grand Central |
|---|---|---|
| **Empire State** | 100, 100 | 0, 0 |
| **Grand Central** | 0, 0 | 100, 100 |

Mr. Thomas

**Figure 8.D.2**

Nash equilibria in the Meeting in New York game.

At any other strategy profile, one of the players has an incentive to deviate. [In fact, $(a_2, b_2)$ is the unique Nash equilibrium even when randomization is permitted; see Exercise 8.D.1.]

This example illustrates a general relationship between the concept of Nash equilibrium and that of rationalizable strategies: *Every strategy that is part of a Nash equilibrium profile is rationalizable* because each player's strategy in a Nash equilibrium can be justified by the Nash equilibrium strategies of the other players. Thus, as a general matter, the Nash equilibrium concept offers at least as sharp a prediction as does the rationalizability concept. In fact, it often offers a *much* sharper prediction. In the game of Figure 8.C.1, for example, the rationalizable strategies $a_1$, $a_3$, $b_1$, and $b_3$ are eliminated as predictions because they cannot be sustained when players' beliefs about each other's play are required to be correct. ∎

In the previous two examples, the Nash equilibrium concept yields a unique prediction. However, this is not always the case. Consider the Meeting in New York game.

**Example 8.D.3:** *Nash Equilibria in the Meeting in New York Game.* Figure 8.D.2 depicts a simple version of the Meeting in New York game. Mr. Thomas and Mr. Schelling each have two choices: They can meet either at noon at the top of the Empire State Building or at noon at the clock in Grand Central Station. There are two Nash equilibria (ignoring the possibility of randomization): (Empire State, Empire State) and (Grand Central, Grand Central). ∎

Example 8.D.3 emphasizes how strongly the Nash equilibrium concept uses the assumption of mutually correct expectations. The theory of Nash equilibrium is silent on *which* equilibrium we should expect to see when there are many. Yet, the players are assumed to correctly forecast which one it will be.

A compact restatement of the definition of a Nash equilibrium can be obtained through the introduction of the concept of a player's *best-response correspondence.* Formally, we say that player $i$'s best-response correspondence $b_i: S_{-i} \to S_i$ in the game $\Gamma_N = [I, \{S_i\} \{u_i(\cdot)\}]$, is the correspondence that assigns to each $s_{-i} \in S_{-i}$ the set

$$b_i(s_{-i}) = \{s_i \in S_i : u_i(s_i, s_{-i}) \geq u_i(s_i', s_{-i}) \text{ for all } s_i' \in S_i\}.$$

With this notion, we can restate the definition of a Nash equilibrium as follows: The strategy profile $(s_1, \ldots, s_I)$ is a Nash equilibrium of game $\Gamma_N = [I, \{S_i\}, \{u_i(\cdot)\}]$ if and only if $s_i \in b_i(s_{-i})$ for $i = 1, \ldots, I$.

### Discussion of the Concept of Nash Equilibrium

Why might it be reasonable to expect players' conjectures about each other's play to be correct? Or, in sharper terms, why should we concern ourselves with the concept of Nash equilibrium?

A number of arguments have been put forward for the Nash equilibrium concept and you will undoubtedly react to them with varying degrees of satisfaction. Moreover, one argument might seem compelling in one application but not at all convincing in another. Until very recently, all these arguments have been informal, as will be our discussion. The issue is one of the more important open questions in game theory, particularly given the Nash equilibrium concept's widespread use in applied problems, and it is currently getting some formal attention.

(i) *Nash equilibrium as a consequence of rational inference.* It is sometimes argued that because each player can think through the strategic considerations faced by his opponents, rationality alone implies that players must be able to correctly forecast what their rivals will play. Although this argument may seem appealing, it is faulty. As we saw in Section 8.C, the implication of common knowledge of the players' rationality (and of the game's structure) is precisely that each player must play a rationalizable strategy. Rationality need not lead players' forecasts to be correct.

(ii) *Nash equilibrium as a necessary condition if there is a unique predicted outcome to a game.* A more satisfying version of the previous idea argues that if there is a unique predicted outcome for a game, then rational players will understand this. Therefore, for no player to wish to deviate, this predicted outcome must be a Nash equilibrium. Put somewhat differently [as in Kreps (1990)], if players think and share the belief that there is an *obvious* (in particular, a unique) way to play a game, then it must be a Nash equilibrium.

Of course, this argument is only relevant if there is a unique prediction for how players will play a game. The discussion of rationalizability in Section 8.C, however, shows that common knowledge of rationality alone does not imply this. Therefore, this argument is really useful only in conjunction with some reason why a particular profile of strategies might be the obvious way to play a particular game. The other arguments for Nash equilibrium that we discuss can be viewed as combining this argument with a reason why there might be an "obvious" way to play a game.

(iii) *Focal points.* It sometimes happens that certain outcomes are what Schelling (1960) calls *focal*. For example, take the Meeting in New York game depicted in Figure 8.D.2, and suppose that restaurants in the Grand Central area are so much better then those around the Empire State Building that the payoffs to meeting at Grand Central are (1000, 1000) rather than (100, 100). Suddenly, going to Grand Central seems like the obvious thing to do. Focal outcomes could also be culturally determined. As Schelling pointed out in his original discussion, two people who do not live in New York will tend to find meeting at the top of the Empire State building (a famous tourist site) to be focal, whereas two native New Yorkers will find Grand

Central Station (the central railroad station) a more compelling choice. In both examples, one of the outcomes has a natural appeal. The implication of argument (ii) is that this kind of appeal can lead an outcome to be the clear prediction in a game only if the outcome is a Nash equilibrium.

(iv) *Nash equilibrium as a self-enforcing agreement.* Another argument for Nash equilibrium comes from imagining that the players can engage in nonbinding communication prior to playing the game. If players agree to an outcome to be played, this naturally becomes the obvious candidate for play. However, because players cannot bind themselves to their agreed-upon strategies, any agreement that the players reach must be self-enforcing if it is to be meaningful. Hence, any meaningful agreement must involve the play of a Nash equilibrium strategy profile. Of course, even though players have reached an agreement to play a Nash equilibrium, they could still deviate from it if they expect others to do so. In essence, this justification assumes that once the players have agreed to a choice of strategies, this agreement becomes focal.

(v) *Nash equilibrium as a stable social convention.* A particular way to play a game might arise over time if the game is played repeatedly and some stable social convention emerges. If it does, it may be "obvious" to all players that the convention will be maintained. The convention, so to speak, becomes focal.

A good example is the game played by New Yorkers every day: Walking in Downtown Manhattan. Every day, people who walk to work need to decide which side of the sidewalk they will walk on. Over time, the stable social convention is that everyone walks on the right side, a convention that is enforced by the fact that any individual who unilaterally deviates from it is sure to be severely trampled. Of course, on any given day, it is *possible* that an individual might decide to walk on the left by conjecturing that everyone else suddenly expects the convention to change. Nevertheless, the prediction that we will remain at the Nash equilibrium "everyone walks on the right" seems reasonable in this case. Note that if an outcome is to become a stable social convention, it must be a Nash equilibrium. If it were not, then individuals would deviate from it as soon as it began to emerge.

The notion of an equilibrium as a rest point for some dynamic adjustment process underlies the use and the traditional appeal of equilibrium notions in economics. In this sense, the stable social convention justification of Nash equilibrium is closest to the tradition of economic theory.

---

To formally model the emergence of stable social conventions is not easy. One difficulty is that the repeated one-day game may itself be viewed as a larger dynamic game. Thus, when we consider rational players choosing their strategies in this overall game, we are merely led back to our original conundrum: Why should we expect a Nash equilibrium in this larger game? One response to this difficulty currently getting some formal attention imagines that players follow simple rules of thumb concerning their opponents' likely play in situations where play is repeated (note that this implies a certain withdrawal from the assumption of complete rationality). For example, a player could conjecture that whatever his opponents did yesterday will be repeated today. If so, then each day players will play a best response to yesterday's play. If a combination of strategies arises that is a stationary point of this process (i.e., the

Player 2

|          |       | Heads   | Tails   |
|----------|-------|---------|---------|
|          | Heads | −1, +1  | +1, −1  |
| Player 1 | Tails | +1, −1  | −1, +1  |

**Figure 8.D.3**
Matching Pennies.

play today is the same as it was yesterday), it must be a Nash equilibrium. However, it is less clear that from any initial position, the process will converge to a stationary outcome; convergence turns out to depend on the game.[4]

### Mixed Strategy Nash Equilibria

It is straightforward to extend the definition of Nash equilibrium to games in which we allow the players to randomize over their pure strategies.

**Definition 8.D.2:** A mixed strategy profile $\sigma = (\sigma_1, \ldots, \sigma_I)$ constitutes a *Nash equilibrium* of game $\Gamma_N = [I, \{\Delta(S_i)\}, \{u_i(\cdot)\}]$ if for every $i = 1, \ldots, I$,

$$u_i(\sigma_i, \sigma_{-i}) \geq u_i(\sigma_i', \sigma_{-i})$$

for all $\sigma_i' \in \Delta(S_i)$.

**Example 8.D.4:** As a very simple example, consider the standard version of Matching Pennies depicted in Figure 8.D.3. This is a game with no pure strategy equilibrium. On the other hand, it is fairly intuitive that there is a mixed strategy equilibrium in which each player chooses H or T with equal probability. When a player randomizes in this way, it makes his rival indifferent between playing heads or tails, and so his rival is also willing to randomize between heads and tails with equal probability. ∎

It is not an accident that a player who is randomizing in a Nash equilibrium of Matching Pennies is indifferent between playing heads and tails. As Proposition 8.D.1 confirms, this indifference among strategies played with positive probability is a general feature of mixed strategy equilibria.

**Proposition 8.D.1:** Let $S_i^+ \subset S_i$ denote the set of pure strategies that player $i$ plays with positive probability in mixed strategy profile $\sigma = (\sigma_1, \ldots, \sigma_I)$. Strategy profile $\sigma$ is a Nash equilibrium in game $\Gamma_N = [I, \{\Delta(S_i)\}, \{u_i(\cdot)\}]$ if and only if for all $i = 1, \ldots, I$,

(i) $u_i(s_i, \sigma_{-i}) = u_i(s_i', \sigma_{-i})$   for all $s_i, s_i' \in S_i^+$;
(ii) $u_i(s_i, \sigma_{-i}) \geq u_i(s_i', \sigma_{-i})$   for all $s_i \in S_i^+$ and all $s_i' \notin S_i^+$.

**Proof:** For necessity, note that if either of conditions (i) or (ii) does not hold for some player $i$, then there are strategies $s_i \in S_i^+$ and $s_i' \in S_i$ such that $u_i(s_i', \sigma_{-i}) > u_i(s_i, \sigma_{-i})$. If so, player $i$ can strictly increase his payoff by playing strategy $s_i'$ whenever he would have played strategy $s_i$.

---

4. This approach actually dates to Cournot's (1838) myopic adjustment procedure. A recent example can be found in Milgrom and Roberts (1990). Interestingly, this work explains the "ultrarational" Nash outcome by *relaxing* the assumption of rationality. It also can be used to try to identify the likelihood of various Nash equilibria arising when multiple Nash equilibria exist.

For sufficiency, suppose that conditions (i) and (ii) hold but that $\sigma$ is not a Nash equilibrium. Then there is some player $i$ who has a strategy $\sigma_i'$ with $u_i(\sigma_i', \sigma_{-i}) > u_i(\sigma_i, \sigma_{-i})$. But if so, then there must be some pure strategy $s_i'$ that is played with positive probability under $\sigma_i'$ for which $u_i(s_i', \sigma_{-i}) > u_i(\sigma_i, \sigma_{-i})$. Since $u_i(\sigma_i, \sigma_{-i}) = u_i(s_i, \sigma_{-i})$ for all $s_i \in S_i^+$, this contradicts conditions (i) and (ii) being satisfied. $\blacksquare$

Hence, a necessary and sufficient condition for mixed strategy profile $\sigma$ to be a Nash equilibrium of game $\Gamma_N = [I, \{\Delta(S_i)\}, \{u_i(\cdot)\}]$ is that each player, given the distribution of strategies played by his opponents, is indifferent among all the pure strategies that he plays with positive probability and that these pure strategies are at least as good as any pure strategy he plays with zero probability.

An implication of Proposition 8.D.1 is that to test whether a strategy profile $\sigma$ is a Nash equilibrium it suffices to consider only pure strategy deviations (i.e., changes in a player's strategy $\sigma_i$ to some pure strategy $s_i'$). As long as no player can improve his payoff by switching to any pure strategy, $\sigma$ is a Nash equilibrium. We therefore get the comforting result given in Corollary 8.D.1.

**Corollary 8.D.1:** Pure strategy profile $s = (s_1, \ldots, s_I)$ is a Nash equilibrium of game $\Gamma_N = [I, \{S_i\}, \{u_i(\cdot)\}]$ if and only if it is a (degenerate) mixed strategy Nash equilibrium of game $\Gamma_N' = [I, \{\Delta(S_i)\}, \{u_i(\cdot)\}]$.

Corollary 8.D.1 tells us that to identify the pure strategy equilibria of game $\Gamma_N' = [I, \{\Delta(S_i)\}, \{u_i(\cdot)\}]$, it suffices to restrict attention to the game $\Gamma_N = [I, \{S_i\}, \{u_i(\cdot)\}]$ in which randomization is not permitted.

Proposition 8.D.1 can also be of great help in the computation of mixed strategy equilibria as Example 8.D.5 illustrates.

**Example 8.D.5:** *Mixed Strategy Equilibria in the Meeting in New York Game.* Let us try to find a mixed strategy equilibrium in the variation of the Meeting in New York game where the payoffs of meeting at Grand Central are (1000, 1000). By Proposition 8.D.1, if Mr. Thomas is going to randomize between Empire State and Grand Central, he must be indifferent between them. Suppose that Mr. Schelling plays Grand Central with probability $\sigma_s$. Then Mr. Thomas' expected payoff from playing Grand Central is $1000\sigma_s + 0(1 - \sigma_s)$, and his expected payoff from playing Empire State is $100(1 - \sigma_s) + 0\sigma_s$. These two expected payoffs are equal only when $\sigma_s = 1/11$. Now, for Mr. Schelling to set $\sigma_s = 1/11$, he must also be indifferent between his two pure strategies. By a similar argument, we find that Mr. Thomas' probability of playing Grand Central must also be $1/11$. We conclude that each player going to Grand Central with a probability of $1/11$ is a Nash equilibrium. $\blacksquare$

Note that in accordance with Proposition 8.D.1, the players in Example 8.D.5 have no real preference over the probabilities that they assign to the pure strategies they play with positive probability. What determines the probabilities that each player uses is an equilibrium consideration: the need to make the *other* player indifferent over *his* strategies.

This fact has led some economists and game theorists to question the usefulness of mixed strategy Nash equilibria as predictions of play. They raise two concerns: First, if players always have a pure strategy that gives them the same expected payoff as their equilibrium mixed strategy, it is not clear why they will bother to randomize.

One answer to this objection is that players may not actually randomize. Rather, they may make definite choices that are affected by seemingly inconsequential variables ("signals") that only they observe. For example, consider how a pitcher for a major league baseball team "mixes his pitches" to keep batters guessing. He may have a completely deterministic plan for what he will do, but it may depend on which side of the bed he woke up on that day or on the number of red traffic lights he came to on his drive to the stadium. As a result, batters view the behavior of the pitcher as random even though it is not. We touched briefly on this interpretation of mixed strategies as behavior contingent on realizations of a signal in Section 7.E, and we will examine it in more detail in Section 8.E.

The second concern is that the stability of mixed strategy equilibria seems tenuous. Players must randomize with exactly the correct probabilities, but they have no positive incentive to do so. One's reaction to this problem may depend on why one expects a Nash equilibrium to arise in the first place. For example, the use of the correct probabilities may be unlikely to arise as a stable social convention, but may seem more plausible when the equilibrium arises as a self-enforcing agreement.

---

Up to this point, we have assumed that players' randomizations are independent. In the Meeting in New York game in Example 8.D.5, for instance, we could describe a mixed strategy equilibrium as follows: Nature provides *private and independently distributed* signals $(\theta_1, \theta_2) \in [0, 1] \times [0, 1]$ to the two players, and each player $i$ assigns decisions to the various possible realizations of his signal $\theta_i$.

However, suppose that there are also *public* signals available that both players observe. Let $\theta \in [0, 1]$ be such a signal. Then many new possibilities arise. For example, the two players could both decide to go to Grand Central if $\theta < \frac{1}{2}$ and to Empire State if $\theta \geq \frac{1}{2}$. Each player's strategy choice is still random, but the coordination of their actions is now perfect and they always meet. More importantly, the decisions have an equilibrium character. If one player decides to follow this decision rule, then it is also optimal for the other player to do so. This is an example of a *correlated equilibrium* [due to Aumann (1974)]. More generally, we could allow for correlated equilibria in which nature's signals are partly private and partly public.

Allowing for such correlation may be important because economic agents observe many public signals. Formally, a correlated equilibrium is a special case of a Bayesian Nash equilibrium, a concept that we introduce in Section 8.E; hence, we defer further discussion to the end of that section.

---

### Existence of Nash Equilibria

Does a Nash equilibrium necessarily exist in a game? Fortunately, the answer turns out to be "yes" under fairly broad circumstances. Here we describe two of the more important existence results; their proofs, based on mathematical fixed point theorems, are given in Appendix A of this chapter. (Proposition 9.B.1 of Section 9.B provides another existence result.)

**Proposition 8.D.2:** Every game $\Gamma_N = [I, \{\Delta(S_i)\}, \{u_i(\cdot)\}]$ in which the sets $S_1, \ldots, S_I$ have a finite number of elements has a mixed strategy Nash equilibrium.

Thus, for the class of games we have been considering, a Nash equilibrium always exists as long as we are willing to accept equilibria in which players randomize. (If you want to be convinced without going through the proof, try Exercise 8.D.6.) Allowing for randomization is essential for this result. We have already seen in (standard) Matching Pennies, for example, that a pure strategy equilibrium may not exist in a game with a finite number of pure strategies.

Up to this point, we have focused on games with finite strategy sets. However, in economic applications, we frequently encounter games in which players have strategies naturally modeled as continuous variables. This can be helpful for the existence of a pure strategy equilibrium. In particular, we have the result given in Proposition 8.D.3.

**Proposition 8.D.3:** A Nash equilibrium exists in game $\Gamma_N = [I, \{S_i\}, \{u_i(\cdot)\}]$ if for all $i = 1, \dots, I$,

(i) $S_i$ is a nonempty, convex, and compact subset of some Euclidean space $\mathbb{R}^M$.

(ii) $u_i(s_1, \dots, s_I)$ is continuous in $(s_1, \dots, s_I)$ and quasiconcave in $s_i$.

Proposition 8.D.3 provides a significant result whose requirements are satisfied in a wide range of economic applications. The convexity of strategy sets and the nature of the payoff functions help to smooth out the structure of the model, allowing us to achieve a pure strategy equilibrium.[5]

Further existence results can also be established. In situations where quasi-concavity of the payoff functions $u_i(\cdot)$ fails but they are still continuous, existence of a mixed strategy equilibrium can still be demonstrated. In fact, even if continuity of the payoff functions fails to hold, a mixed strategy equilibrium can be shown to exist in a variety of cases [see Dasgupta and Maskin (1986)].

Of course, these results do not mean that we *cannot* have an equilibrium if the conditions of these existence results do not hold. Rather, we just cannot be *assured* that there is one.

# 8.E Games of Incomplete Information: Bayesian Nash Equilibrium

Up to this point, we have assumed that players know all relevant information about each other, including the payoffs that each receives from the various outcomes of the game. Such games are known as games of *complete information*. A moment of thought, however, should convince you that this is a very strong assumption. Do two firms in an industry necessarily know each other's costs? Does a firm bargaining with a union necessarily know the disutility that union members will feel if they go out on strike for a month? Clearly, the answer is "no." Rather, in many circumstances, players have what is known as *incomplete information*.

The presence of incomplete information raises the possibility that we may need to consider a player's beliefs about other players' preferences, his beliefs about their beliefs about his preferences, and so on, much in the spirit of rationalizability.[6]

---

5. Note that a finite strategy set $S_i$ cannot be convex. In fact, the use of mixed strategies in Proposition 8.D.2 helps us to obtain existence of equilibrium in much the same way that Proposition 8.D.3's assumptions assure existence of a pure strategy Nash equilibrium: It convexifies players' strategy sets and yields well-behaved payoff functions. (See Appendix A for details.)

6. For more on this problem, see Mertens and Zamir (1985).

Fortunately, there is a widely used approach to this problem, originated by Harsanyi (1967–68), that makes this unnecessary. In this approach, one imagines that each player's preferences are determined by the realization of a random variable. Although the random variable's actual realization is observed only by the player, its ex ante probability distribution is assumed to be common knowledge among all the players. Through this formulation, the situation of incomplete information is reinterpreted as a game of imperfect information: Nature makes the first move, choosing realizations of the random variables that determine each player's preference *type*, and each player observes the realization of only his own random variable. A game of this sort is known as a *Bayesian game*.

**Example 8.E.1:** Consider a modification of the DA's Brother game discussed in Example 8.B.3. With probability $\mu$, prisoner 2 has the preferences in Figure 8.B.4 (we call these *type I preferences*), while with probability $(1 - \mu)$, prisoner 2 hates to rat on his accomplice (this is *type II*). In this case, he pays a psychic penalty equal to 6 years in prison for confessing. Prisoner 1, on the other hand, always has the preferences depicted in Figure 8.B.4. The extensive form of this Bayesian game is represented in Figure 8.E.1 (in the figure, "C" and "DC" stand for "confess" and "don't confess" respectively).

In this game, a pure strategy (a complete contingent plan) for player 2 can be viewed as a function that for each possible realization of his preference type

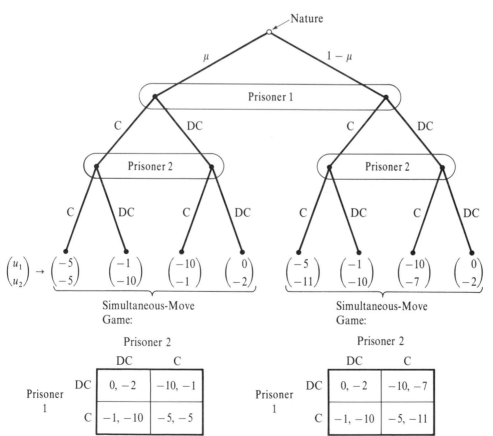

**Figure 8.E.1**

The DA's Brother game with incomplete information.

indicates what action he will take. Hence, prisoner 2 now has four possible pure strategies:

(confess if type I, confess if type II);
(confess if type I, don't confess if type II);
(don't confess if type I, confess if type II);
(don't confess if type I, don't confess if type II).

Notice, however, that player 1 does not observe player 2's type, and so a pure strategy for player 1 in this game is simply a (noncontingent) choice of either "confess" or "don't confess." ∎

Formally, in a Bayesian game, each player $i$ has a payoff function $u_i(s_i, s_{-i}, \theta_i)$, where $\theta_i \in \Theta_i$ is a random variable chosen by nature that is observed only by player $i$. The joint probability distribution of the $\theta_i$'s is given by $F(\theta_1, \ldots, \theta_I)$, which is assumed to be common knowledge among the players. Letting $\Theta = \Theta_1 \times \cdots \times \Theta_I$, a Bayesian game is summarized by the data $[I, \{S_i\}, \{u_i(\cdot)\}, \Theta, F(\cdot)]$.

A pure strategy for player $i$ in a Bayesian game is a function $s_i(\theta_i)$, or *decision rule*, that gives the player's strategy choice for each realization of his type $\theta_i$. Player $i$'s pure strategy set $\mathscr{S}_i$ is therefore the set of all such functions. Player $i$'s expected payoff given a profile of pure strategies for the $I$ players $(s_1(\cdot), \ldots, s_I(\cdot))$ is then given by

$$\tilde{u}_i(s_1(\cdot), \ldots, s_I(\cdot)) = E_\theta[u_i(s_1(\theta_1), \ldots, s_I(\theta_I), \theta_i)]. \qquad (8.E.1)$$

We can now look for an ordinary (pure strategy) Nash equilibrium of this game of imperfect information, which is known in this context as a *Bayesian Nash equilibrium*.[7]

**Definition 8.E.1:** A (pure strategy) *Bayesian Nash equilibrium* for the Bayesian game $[I, \{S_i\}, \{u_i(\cdot)\}, \Theta, F(\cdot)]$ is a profile of decision rules $(s_1(\cdot), \ldots, s_I(\cdot))$ that constitutes a Nash equilibrium of game $\Gamma_N = [I, \{\mathscr{S}_i\}, \{\tilde{u}_i(\cdot)\}]$. That is, for every $i = 1, \ldots, I$,

$$\tilde{u}_i(s_i(\cdot), s_{-i}(\cdot)) \geq \tilde{u}_i(s_i'(\cdot), s_{-i}(\cdot))$$

for all $s_i'(\cdot) \in \mathscr{S}_i$, where $\tilde{u}_i(s_i(\cdot), s_{-i}(\cdot))$ is defined as in (8.E.1).

A very useful point to note is that in a (pure strategy) Bayesian Nash equilibrium each player must be playing a best response to the conditional distribution of his opponents' strategies *for each type that he might end up having*. Proposition 8.E.1 provides a more formal statement of this point.

**Proposition 8.E.1:** A profile of decision rules $(s_1(\cdot), \ldots, s_I(\cdot))$ is a Bayesian Nash equilibrium in Bayesian game $[I, \{S_i\}, \{u_i(\cdot)\}, \Theta, F(\cdot)]$ if and only if, for all $i$ and

---

7. We shall restrict our attention to pure strategies here; mixed strategies involve randomization over the strategies in $\mathscr{S}_i$. Note also that we have not been very explicit about whether the $\Theta_i$'s are finite sets. If they are, then the strategy sets $\mathscr{S}_i$ are finite; if they are not, then the sets $\mathscr{S}_i$ include an infinite number of possible functions $s_i(\cdot)$. Either way, however, the basic definition of a Bayesian Nash equilibrium is the same.

all $\bar{\theta}_i \in \Theta_i$ occurring with positive probability[8]

$$E_{\theta_{-i}}[u_i(s_i(\bar{\theta}_i), s_{-i}(\theta_{-i}), \bar{\theta}_i)|\bar{\theta}_i] \geq E_{\theta_{-i}}[u_i(s_i', s_{-i}(\theta_{-i}), \bar{\theta}_i)|\bar{\theta}_i] \qquad (8.E.2)$$

for all $s_i' \in S_i$, where the expectation is taken over realizations of the other players' random variables conditional on player $i$'s realization of his signal $\bar{\theta}_i$.

**Proof:** For necessity, note that if (8.E.2) did not hold for some player $i$ for some $\bar{\theta}_i \in \Theta_i$ that occurs with positive probability, then player $i$ could do better by changing his strategy choice in the event he gets realization $\bar{\theta}_i$, contradicting $(s_1(\cdot), \ldots, s_I(\cdot))$ being a Bayesian Nash equilibrium. In the other direction, if condition (8.E.2) holds for all $\bar{\theta}_i \in \Theta_i$ occurring with positive probability, then player $i$ cannot improve on the payoff he receives by playing strategy $s_i(\cdot)$. ∎

Proposition 8.E.1 tells us that, in essence, we can think of each type of player $i$ as being a separate player who maximizes his payoff given his conditional probability distribution over the strategy choices of his rivals.

**Example 8.E.1 Continued:** To solve for the (pure strategy) Bayesian Nash equilibrium of this game, note first that type I of prisoner 2 must play "confess" with probability 1 because this is that type's dominant strategy. Likewise, type II of prisoner 2 also has a dominant strategy: "don't confess." Given this behavior by prisoner 2, prisoner 1's best response is to play "don't confess" if $[-10\mu + 0(1 - \mu)] > [-5\mu - 1(1 - \mu)]$, or equivalently, if $\mu < \frac{1}{6}$, and is to play "confess" if $\mu > \frac{1}{6}$. (He is indifferent if $\mu = \frac{1}{6}$.) ∎

**Example 8.E.2:** The Alphabeta research and development consortium has two (noncompeting) members, firms 1 and 2. The rules of the consortium are that any independent invention by one of the firms is shared fully with the other. Suppose that there is a new invention, the "Zigger," that either of the two firms could potentially develop. To develop this new product costs a firm $c \in (0, 1)$. The benefit of the Zigger to each firm $i$ is known only by that firm. Formally, each firm $i$ has a type $\theta_i$ that is independently drawn from a uniform distribution on $[0, 1]$, and its benefit from the Zigger when its type is $\theta_i$ is $(\theta_i)^2$. The timing is as follows: The two firms each privately observe their own type. Then they each simultaneously choose either to develop the Zigger or not.

Let us now solve for the Bayesian Nash equilibrium of this game. We shall write $s_i(\theta_i) = 1$ if type $\theta_i$ of firm $i$ develops the Zigger and $s_i(\theta_i) = 0$ if it does not. If firm $i$ develops the Zigger when its type is $\theta_i$, its payoff is $(\theta_i)^2 - c$ regardless of whether firm $j$ does so. If firm $i$ decides not to develop the Zigger when its type is $\theta_i$, it will have an expected payoff equal to $(\theta_i)^2 \text{ Prob}(s_j(\theta_j) = 1)$. Hence, firm $i$'s best response is to develop the Zigger if and only if its type $\theta_i$ is such that (we assume firm $i$ develops the Zigger if it is indifferent):

$$\theta_i \geq \left[\frac{c}{1 - \text{Prob}(s_j(\theta_j) = 1)}\right]^{1/2}. \qquad (8.E.3)$$

---

8. The formulation given here (and the proof) is for the case in which the sets $\Theta_i$ are finite. When a player $i$ has an infinite number of possible types, condition (8.E.2) must hold on a subset of $\Theta_i$ that is of full measure (i.e., that occurs with probability equal to one). It is then said that (8.E.2) holds for *almost every* $\bar{\theta}_i \in \Theta_i$.

Note that for any given strategy of firm $j$, firm $i$'s best response takes the form of a *cutoff rule*: It optimally develops the Zigger for all $\theta_i$ above the value on the right-hand side of (8.E.3) and does not for all $\theta_i$ below it. [Note that if firm $i$ existed in isolation, it would be indifferent about developing the Zigger when $\theta_i = \sqrt{c}$. But (8.E.3) tells us that when firm $i$ is part of the consortium, its cutoff is always (weakly) above this. This is true because each firm hopes to *free-ride* on the other firm's development effort; see Chapter 11 for more on this.]

Suppose then that $\hat{\theta}_1, \hat{\theta}_2 \in (0, 1)$ are the cutoff values for firms 1 and 2 respectively in a Bayesian Nash equilibrium (it can be shown that $0 < \hat{\theta}_i < 1$ for $i = 1, 2$ in any Bayesian Nash equilibrium of this game). If so, then using the fact that $\text{Prob}(s_j(\theta_j) = 1) = 1 - \hat{\theta}_j$, condition (8.E.3) applied first for $i = 1$ and then for $i = 2$ tells us that we must have

$$(\hat{\theta}_1)^2 \hat{\theta}_2 = c$$

and

$$(\hat{\theta}_2)^2 \hat{\theta}_1 = c.$$

Because $(\hat{\theta}_1)^2 \hat{\theta}_2 = (\hat{\theta}_2)^2 \hat{\theta}_1$ implies that $\hat{\theta}_1 = \hat{\theta}_2$, we see that any Bayesian Nash equilibrium of this game involves an identical cutoff value for the two firms, $\theta^* = (c)^{1/3}$. In this equilibrium, the probability that neither firm develops the Zigger is $(\theta^*)^2$, the probability that exactly one firm develops it is $2\theta^*(1 - \theta^*)$, and the probability that both do is $(1 - \theta^*)^2$. ∎

The exercises at the end of this chapter consider several other examples of Bayesian Nash equilibria. Another important application arises in the theory of implementation with incomplete information, studied in Chapter 23.

In Section 8.D, we argued that mixed strategies could be interpreted as situations where players play deterministic strategies conditional on seemingly irrelevant signals (recall the baseball pitcher). We can now say a bit more about this. Suppose we start with a game of complete information that has a unique mixed strategy equilibrium in which players actually randomize. Now consider changing the game by introducing many different types (formally, a continuum) of each player, with the realizations of the various players' types being statistically independent of one another. Suppose, in addition, that all types of a player have *identical* preferences. A (pure strategy) Bayesian Nash equilibrium of this Bayesian game is then precisely equivalent to a mixed strategy Nash equilibrium of the original complete information game. Moreover, in many circumstances, one can show that there are also "nearby" Bayesian games in which preferences of the different types of a player differ only slightly from one another, the Bayesian Nash equilibria are close to the mixed strategy distribution, and each type has a strict preference for his strategy choice. Such results are known as *purification theorems* [see Harsanyi (1973)].

---

We can also return to the issue of *correlated equilibria* raised in Section 8.D. In particular, if we allow the realizations of the various players' types in the previous paragraph to be statistically correlated, then a (pure strategy) Bayesian Nash equilibrium of this Bayesian game is a correlated equilibrium of the original complete information game. The set of all correlated equilibria in game $[I, \{S_i\}, \{u_i(\cdot)\}]$ is identified by considering all possible Bayesian games of this sort (i.e., we allow for all possible signals that the players might observe).

---

# 8.F The Possibility of Mistakes: Trembling-Hand Perfection

In Section 8.B, we noted that although rationality per se does not rule out the choice of a weakly dominated strategy, such strategies are unappealing because they are dominated unless a player is absolutely sure of what his rivals will play. In fact, as the game depicted in Figure 8.F.1 illustrates, the Nash equilibrium concept also does not preclude the use of such strategies. In this game, $(D, R)$ is a Nash equilibrium in which both players play a weakly dominated strategy with certainty.

Here, we elaborate on the idea, raised in Section 8.B, that *caution* might preclude the use of such strategies. The discussion leads us to define a refinement of the concept of Nash equilibrium, known as a *(normal form) trembling-hand perfect Nash equilibrium*, which identifies Nash equilibria that are robust to the possibility that, with some very small probability, players make mistakes.

Following Selten (1975), for any normal form game $\Gamma_N = [I, \{\Delta(S_i)\}, \{u_i(\cdot)\}]$, we can define a *perturbed* game $\Gamma_\varepsilon = [I, \{\Delta_\varepsilon(S_i)\}, \{u_i(\cdot)\}]$ by choosing for each player $i$ and strategy $s_i \in S_i$ a number $\varepsilon_i(s_i) \in (0, 1)$, with $\sum_{s_i \varepsilon S_i} \varepsilon_i(s_i) < 1$, and then defining player $i$'s perturbed strategy set to be

$$\Delta_\varepsilon(S_i) = \{\sigma_i : \sigma_i(s_i) \geq \varepsilon_i(s_i) \text{ for all } s_i \in S_i \text{ and } \sum_{s_i \varepsilon S_i} \sigma_i(s_i) = 1\}.$$

That is, perturbed game $\Gamma_\varepsilon$ is derived from the original game $\Gamma_N$ by requiring that each player $i$ play every one of his strategies, say $s_i$, with at least some minimal positive probability $\varepsilon_i(s_i)$; $\varepsilon_i(s_i)$ is interpreted as the unavoidable probability that strategy $s_i$ gets played by mistake.

Having defined this perturbed game, we want to consider as predictions in game $\Gamma_N$ only those Nash equilibria $\sigma$ that are robust to the possibility that players make mistakes. The robustness test we employ can be stated roughly as: To consider $\sigma$ as a robust equilibrium, we want there to be at least some slight perturbations of $\Gamma_N$ whose equilibria are close to $\sigma$. The formal definition of a *(normal form) trembling-hand perfect Nash equilibrium* (the name comes from the idea of players making mistakes because of their trembling hands) is presented in Definition 8.F.1.

**Definition 8.F.1:** A Nash equilibrium $\sigma$ of game $\Gamma_N = [I, \{\Delta(S_i)\}, \{u_i(\cdot)\}]$ is *(normal form) trembling-hand perfect* if there is *some* sequence of perturbed games $\{\Gamma_{\varepsilon^k}\}_{k=1}^\infty$ that converges to $\Gamma_N$ [in the sense that $\lim_{k \to \infty} \varepsilon_i^k(s_i) = 0$ for all $i$ and $s_i \in S_i$], for which there is *some* associated sequence of Nash equilibria $\{\sigma^k\}_{k=1}^\infty$ that converges to $\sigma$ (i.e., such that $\lim_{k \to \infty} \sigma^k = \sigma$).

We use the modifier *normal form* because Selten (1975) also proposes a slightly different form of trembling-hand perfection for dynamic games; we discuss this version of the concept in Chapter 9.[9]

Note that the concept of a (normal form) trembling-hand perfect Nash equilibrium provides a relatively mild test of robustness: We require only that *some* perturbed games exist that have equilibria arbitrarily close to $\sigma$. A stronger test would

---

9. In fact, Selten (1975) is primarily concerned with the problem of identifying desirable equilibria in dynamic games. See Chapter 9, Appendix B for more on this.

|   | L | R |
|---|---|---|
| U | 1, 1 | 0, −3 |
| D | −3, 0 | 0, 0 |

**Figure 8.F.1**

$(D, R)$ is a Nash equilibrium involving play of weakly dominated strategies.

require that the equilibrium $\sigma$ be robust to *all* perturbations close to the original game.

In general, the criterion in Definition 8.F.1 can be difficult to work with because it requires that we compute the equilibria of many possible perturbed games. The result presented in Proposition 8.F.1 provides a formulation that makes checking whether a Nash equilibrium is trembling-hand perfect much easier (in its statement, a *totally mixed* strategy is a mixed strategy in which every pure strategy receives positive probability).

**Proposition 8.F.1:** A Nash equilibrium $\sigma$ of game $\Gamma_N = [I, \{\Delta(S_i)\}, \{u_i(\cdot)\}]$ is (normal form) trembling-hand perfect if and only if there is some sequence of totally mixed strategies $\{\sigma^k\}_{k=1}^{\infty}$ such that $\lim_{k \to \infty} \sigma^k = \sigma$ and $\sigma_i$ is a best response to every element of sequence $\{\sigma_{-i}^k\}_{k=1}^{\infty}$ for all $i = 1, \ldots, I$.

You are asked to prove this result in Exercise 8.F.1 [or consult Selten (1975)]. The result presented in Proposition 8.F.2 is an immediate consequence of Definition 8.F.1 and Proposition 8.F.1.

**Proposition 8.F.2:** If $\sigma = (\sigma_1, \ldots, \sigma_I)$ is a (normal form) trembling-hand perfect Nash equilibrium, then $\sigma_i$ is not a weakly dominated strategy for any $i = 1, \ldots, I$. Hence, in any (normal form) trembling-hand perfect Nash equilibrium, no weakly dominated pure strategy can be played with positive probability.

---

The converse, that any Nash equilibrium not involving play of a weakly dominated strategy is necessarily trembling-hand perfect, turns out to be true for two-player games but not for games with more than two players. Thus, trembling-hand perfection can rule out more than just Nash equilibria involving weakly dominated strategies. The reason is tied to the fact that when a player's rivals make mistakes with small probability, this can give rise to only a limited set of probability distributions over their nonequilibrium strategies. For example, if a player's two rivals each have a small probability of making a mistake, there is a much greater probability that one will make a mistake than that both will. If the player's equilibrium strategy is a unique best response only when both of his rivals make a mistake, his strategy may not be a best response to any local perturbation of his rivals' strategies even though his strategy is not weakly dominated. (Exercise 8.F.2 provides an example.) However, if players' trembles are allowed to be correlated (e.g., as in the correlated equilibrium concept), then the converse of Proposition 8.F.2 would hold regardless of the number of players.

---

Selten (1975) also proves an existence result that parallels Proposition 8.D.2: Every game $\Gamma_N = [I, \{\Delta(S_i)\}, \{u_i(\cdot)\}]$ with finite strategy sets $S_1, \ldots, S_I$ has a trembling-hand perfect Nash equilibrium. An implication of this result is that every such game has at least one Nash equilibrium in which no player plays any weakly dominated strategy with positive probability. Hence, if we decide to accept only Nash equilibria that do not involve the play of weakly dominated strategies, with great generality there is at least one such equilibrium.[10]

Myerson (1978) proposes a refinement of Selten's idea in which players are less likely to make more costly mistakes (the idea is that they will try harder to avoid these mistakes). He establishes that the resulting solution concept, called a *proper Nash equilibrium*, exists under the conditions described in the previous paragraph for trembling-hand perfect Nash equilibria. van Damme (1983) presents a good discussion of this and other refinements of trembling-hand perfection.

## APPENDIX A: EXISTENCE OF NASH EQUILIBRIUM

In this appendix, we prove Propositions 8.D.2 and 8.D.3. We begin with Lemma 8.AA.1, which provides a key technical result.

**Lemma 8.AA.1:** If the sets $S_1, \ldots, S_I$ are nonempty, $S_i$ is compact and convex, and $u_i(\cdot)$ is continuous in $(s_1, \ldots, s_I)$ and quasiconcave in $s_i$, then player $i$'s best-response correspondence $b_i(\cdot)$ is nonempty, convex-valued, and upper hemicontinuous.[11]

**Proof:** Note first that $b_i(s_{-i})$ is the set of maximizers of the continuous function $u_i(\cdot, s_{-i})$ on the compact set $S_i$. Hence, it is nonempty (see Theorem M.F.2 of the Mathematical Appendix). The convexity of $b_i(s_{-i})$ follows because the set of maximizers of a quasiconcave function [here, the function $u_i(\cdot, s_{-i})$] on a convex set (here, $S_i$) is convex. Finally, for upper hemicontinuity, we need to show that for any sequence $(s_i^n, s_{-i}^n) \to (s_i, s_{-i})$ such that $s_i^n \in b_i(s_{-i}^n)$ for all $n$, we have $s_i \in b_i(s_{-i})$. To see this, note that for all $n$, $u_i(s_i^n, s_{-i}^n) \geq u_i(s_i', s_{-i}^n)$ for all $s_i' \in S_i$. Therefore, by the continuity of $u_i(\cdot)$, we have $u_i(s_i, s_{-i}) \geq u_i(s_i', s_{-i})$. ∎

It is convenient to prove Proposition 8.D.3 first.

**Proposition 8.D.3:** A Nash equilibrium exists in game $\Gamma_N = [I, \{S_i\}, \{u_i(\cdot)\}]$ if for all $i = 1, \ldots, I$,

    (i) $S_i$ is a nonempty, convex, and compact subset of some Euclidean space $\mathbb{R}^M$.

    (ii) $u_i(s_1, \ldots, s_I)$ *is continuous in* $(s_1, \ldots, s_I)$ *and quasiconcave in* $s_i$.

---

10. The Bertrand duopoly game discussed in Chapter 12 provides one example of a game in which this is not the case; its unique Nash equilibrium involves the play of weakly dominated strategies. The problem arises because the strategies in that game are continuous variables (and so the sets $S_i$ are not finite). Fortunately, this equilibrium can be viewed as the limit of undominated equilibria in "nearby" discrete versions of the game. (See Exercise 12.C.3 for more on this point.)

11. See Section M.H of the Mathematical Appendix for a discussion of upper hemicontinuous correspondences.

**Proof:** Define the correspondence $b: S \to S$ by

$$b(s_1, \ldots, s_I) = b_1(s_{-1}) \times \cdots \times b_I(s_{-I}).$$

Note that $b(\cdot)$ is a correspondence from the nonempty, convex, and compact set $S = S_1 \times \cdots \times S_I$ to itself. In addition, by Lemma 8.AA.1, $b(\cdot)$ is a nonempty, convex-valued, and upper hemicontinuous correspondence. Thus, all the conditions of the Kakutani fixed point theorem are satisfied (see Section M.I of the Mathematical Appendix). Hence, there exists a fixed point for this correspondence, a strategy profile $s \in S$ such that $s \in b(s)$. The strategies at this fixed point constitute a Nash equilibrium because by construction $s_i \in b_i(s_{-i})$ for all $i = 1, \ldots, I$. ∎

Now we move to the proof of Proposition 8.D.2.

**Proposition 8.D.2:** Every game $\Gamma_N = [I, \{\Delta(S_i)\}, \{u_i(\cdot)\}]$ in which the sets $S_1, \ldots, S_I$ have a finite number of elements has a mixed strategy Nash equilibrium.

**Proof:** The game $\Gamma_N = [I, \{\Delta(S_i)\}, \{u_i(\cdot)\}]$, viewed as a game with strategy sets $\{\Delta(S_i)\}$ and payoff functions $u_i(\sigma_1, \ldots, \sigma_I) = \sum_{s \in S}[\prod_{k=1}^{I} \sigma_k(s_k)]u_i(s)$ for all $i = 1, \ldots, I$, satisfies all the assumptions of Proposition 8.D.3. Hence, Proposition 8.D.2 is a direct corollary of that result. ∎

## REFERENCES

Aumann, R. (1974). Subjectivity and correlation in randomized strategies. *Journal of Mathematical Economics* **1**: 67–96.

Bernheim, B. D. (1984). Rationalizable strategic behavior. *Econometrica* **52**: 1007–28.

Bernheim, B. D. (1986). Axiomatic characterizations of rational choice in strategic environments. *Scandinavian Journal of Economics* **88**: 473–88.

Brandenberger, A., and E. Dekel. (1987). Rationalizability and correlated equilibria. *Econometrica* **55**: 1391–1402.

Cournot, A. (1838). *Recherches sur les Principes Mathématiques de la Théorie des Richesses.* [English edition: *Researches into the Mathematical Principles of the Theory of Wealth.* New York: Macmillan, 1897.]

Dasgupta, P., and E. Maskin. (1986). The existence of equilibrium in discontinuous economic games. *Review of Economic Studies* **53**: 1–41.

Harsanyi, J. (1967–68). Games with incomplete information played by Bayesian players. *Management Science* **14**: 159–82, 320–34, 486–502.

Harsanyi, J. (1973). Games with randomly disturbed payoffs: A new rationale for mixed-strategy equilibrium points. *International Journal of Game Theory* **2**: 1–23.

Kreps, D. M. (1990). *Game Theory and Economic Modelling.* Oxford: Oxford University Press.

Mertens, J. F., and S. Zamir. (1985). Formulation of Bayesian analysis for games with incomplete information. *International Journal of Game Theory* **10**: 619–32.

Milgrom, P., and J. Roberts. (1990). Rationalizability, learning, and equilibrium in games with strategic complementarities. *Econometrica* **58**: 1255–78.

Myerson, R. B. (1978). Refinements of the Nash equilibrium concept. *International Journal of Game Theory* **7**: 73–80.

Nash, J. F. (1951). Non-cooperative games. *Annals of Mathematics* **54**: 289–95.

Pearce, D. G. (1984). Rationalizable strategic behavior and the problem of perfection. *Econometrica* **52**: 1029–50.

Schelling, T. (1960). *The Strategy of Conflict.* Cambridge, Mass.: Harvard University Press.

Selten, R. (1975). Reexamination of the perfectness concept for equilibrium points in extensive games. *International Journal of Game Theory* **4**: 25–55.

van Damme, E. (1983). *Refinements of the Nash Equilibrium Concept.* Berlin: Springer-Verlag.

**EXERCISES**

**8.B.1**[A]  There are $I$ firms in an industry. Each can try to convince Congress to give the industry a subsidy. Let $h_i$ denote the number of hours of effort put in by firm $i$, and let $c_i(h_i) = w_i(h_i)^2$, where $w_i$ is a positive constant, be the cost of this effort to firm $i$. When the effort levels of the firms are $(h_1, \ldots, h_I)$, the value of the subsidy that gets approved is $\alpha \sum_i h_i + \beta(\prod_i h_i)$, where $\alpha$ and $\beta$ are constants.

Consider a game in which the firms decide simultaneously and independently how many hours they will each devote to this effort. Show that each firm has a strictly dominant strategy if and only if $\beta = 0$. What is firm $i$'s strictly dominant strategy when this is so?

**8.B.2**[B]  **(a)** Argue that if a player has two weakly dominant strategies, then for every strategy choice by his opponents, the two strategies yield him equal payoffs.

**(b)** Provide an example of a two-player game in which a player has two weakly dominant pure strategies but his opponent prefers that he play one of them rather than the other.

**8.B.3**[B]  Consider the following auction (known as a *second-price*, or *Vickrey*, auction). An object is auctioned off to $I$ bidders. Bidder $i$'s valuation of the object (in monetary terms) is $v_i$. The auction rules are that each player submit a bid (a nonnegative number) in a sealed envelope. The envelopes are then opened, and the bidder who has submitted the highest bid gets the object but pays the auctioneer the amount of the *second-highest* bid. If more than one bidder submits the highest bid, each gets the object with equal probability. Show that submitting a bid of $v_i$ with certainty is a weakly dominant strategy for bidder $i$. Also argue that this is bidder $i$'s unique weakly dominant strategy.

**8.B.4**[C]  Show that the order of deletion does not matter for the set of strategies surviving a process of iterated deletion of strictly dominated strategies.

**8.B.5**[C]  Consider the Cournot duopoly model (discussed extensively in Chapter 12) in which two firms, 1 and 2, simultaneously choose the quantities they will sell on the market, $q_1$ and $q_2$. The price each receives for each unit given these quantities is $P(q_1, q_2) = a - b(q_1 + q_2)$. Their costs are $c$ per unit sold.

**(a)** Argue that successive elimination of strictly dominated strategies yields a unique prediction in this game.

**(b)** Would this be true if there were three firms instead of two?

**8.B.6**[B]  In text.

**8.B.7**[B]  Show that any strictly dominant strategy in game $[I, \{\Delta(S_i)\}, \{u_i(\cdot)\}]$ must be a pure strategy.

**8.C.1**[A]  Argue that if elimination of strictly dominated strategies yields a unique prediction in a game, this prediction also results from eliminating strategies that are never a best response.

**8.C.2**[C]  Prove that the order of removal does not matter for the set of strategies that survives a process of iterated deletion of strategies that are never a best response.

**8.C.3**[C]  Prove that in a two-player game (with finite strategy sets), if a pure strategy $s_i$ for player $i$ is never a best response for any mixed strategy by $i$'s opponent, then $s_i$ is strictly dominated by some mixed strategy $\sigma_i \in \Delta(S_i)$. [*Hint:* Try using the supporting hyperplane theorem presented in Section M.G of the Mathematical Appendix.]

**8.C.4$^B$** Consider a game $\Gamma_N$ with players 1, 2, and 3 in which $S_1 = \{L, M, R\}$, $S_2 = \{U, D\}$, and $S_3 = \{\ell, r\}$. Player 1's payoffs from each of his three strategies conditional on the strategy choices of players 2 and 3 are depicted as $(u_L, u_M, u_R)$ in each of the four boxes shown below, where $(\pi, \varepsilon, \eta) \gg 0$. Assume that $\eta < 4\varepsilon$.

Player 3's Strategy

|  |  | $\ell$ | $r$ |
|---|---|---|---|
| Player 2's Strategy | $U$ | $\pi + 4\varepsilon,\ \pi - \eta,\ \pi - 4\varepsilon$ | $\pi - 4\varepsilon,\ \pi + \dfrac{\eta}{2},\ \pi + 4\varepsilon$ |
|  | $D$ | $\eta + 4\varepsilon,\ \pi + \dfrac{\eta}{2},\ \pi - 4\varepsilon$ | $\pi - 4\varepsilon,\ \pi - \eta,\ \pi + 4\varepsilon$ |

(a) Argue that (pure) strategy $M$ is never a best response for player 1 to any independent randomizations by players 2 and 3.

(b) Show that (pure) strategy $M$ is not strictly dominated.

(c) Show that (pure) strategy $M$ can be a best response if player 2's and player 3's randomizations are allowed to be correlated.

**8.D.1$^B$** Show that $(a_2, b_2)$ being played with certainty is the unique mixed strategy Nash equilibrium in the game depicted in Figure 8.C.1.

**8.D.2$^B$** Show that if there is a unique profile of strategies that survives iterated removal of strictly dominated strategies, this profile is a Nash equilibrium.

**8.D.3$^B$** Consider a first-price sealed-bid auction of an object with two bidders. Each bidder $i$'s valuation of the object is $v_i$, which is known to both bidders. The auction rules are that each player submits a bid in a sealed envelope. The envelopes are then opened, and the bidder who has submitted the highest bid gets the object and pays the auctioneer the amount of his bid. If the bidders submit the same bid, each gets the object with probability $\frac{1}{2}$. Bids must be in dollar multiples (assume that valuations are also).

(a) Are any strategies strictly dominated?

(b) Are any strategies weakly dominated?

(c) Is there a Nash equilibrium? What is it? Is it unique?

**8.D.4$^B$** Consider a bargaining situation in which two individuals are considering undertaking a business venture that will earn them 100 dollars in profit, but they must agree on how to split the 100 dollars. Bargaining works as follows: The two individuals each make a demand simultaneously. If their demands sum to more than 100 dollars, then they fail to agree, and each gets nothing. If their demands sum to less than 100 dollars, they do the project, each gets his demand, and the rest goes to charity.

(a) What are each player's strictly dominated strategies?

(b) What are each player's weakly dominated strategies?

(c) What are the pure strategy Nash equilibria of this game?

**8.D.5$^B$** Consumers are uniformly distributed along a boardwalk that is 1 mile long. Ice-cream prices are regulated, so consumers go to the nearest vendor because they dislike walking (assume that at the regulated prices all consumers will purchase an ice cream even if they have to walk a full mile). If more than one vendor is at the same location, they split the business evenly.

**(a)** Consider a game in which two ice-cream vendors pick their locations simultaneously. Show that there exists a unique pure strategy Nash equilibrium and that it involves both vendors locating at the midpoint of the boardwalk.

**(b)** Show that with three vendors, no pure strategy Nash equilibrium exists.

**8.D.6$^B$** Consider any two-player game of the following form (where letters indicate arbitrary payoffs):

Player 2

|            |       | $b_1$    | $b_2$     |
|------------|-------|----------|-----------|
|            | $a_1$ | $u, v$   | $\ell, m$ |
| Player 1   | $a_2$ | $w, x$   | $y, z$    |

Show that a mixed strategy Nash equilibrium always exists in this game. [*Hint:* Define player 1's strategy to be his probability of choosing action $a_1$ and player 2's to be his probability of choosing $b_1$; then examine the best-response correspondences of the two players.]

**8.D.7$^C$** (*The Minimax Theorem*) A two-player game with finite strategy sets $\Gamma_N = [I, \{S_1, S_2\}, \{u_1(\cdot), u_2(\cdot)\}]$ is a *zero-sum* game if $u_2(s_1, s_2) = -u_1(s_1, s_2)$ for all $(s_1, s_2) \in S_1 \times S_2$.

Define $i$'s *maximin* expected utility level $\underline{w}_i$ to be the level he can guarantee himself in game $[I, \{\Delta(S_1), \Delta(S_2)\}, \{u_1(\cdot), u_2(\cdot)\}]$:

$$\underline{w}_i = \underset{\sigma_i}{\text{Max}} \left[ \underset{\sigma_{-i}}{\text{Min}} \, u_i(\sigma_i, \sigma_{-i}) \right].$$

Define player $i$'s *minimax* utility level $\underline{v}_i$ to be the worst expected utility level he can be forced to receive if he gets to respond to his rival's actions:

$$\underline{v}_i = \underset{\sigma_{-i}}{\text{Min}} \left[ \underset{\sigma_i}{\text{Max}} \, u_i(\sigma_i, \sigma_{-i}) \right].$$

**(a)** Show that $\underline{v}_i \geq \underline{w}_i$ in any game.

**(b)** Prove that in any mixed strategy Nash equilibrium of the zero-sum game $\Gamma_N = [I, \{\Delta(S_1), \Delta(S_2)\}, \{u_1(\cdot), u_2(\cdot)\}]$, player $i$'s expected utility $u_i^\circ$ satisfies $u_i^\circ = \underline{v}_i = \underline{w}_i$. [*Hint:* Such an equilibrium must exist by Proposition 8.D.2.]

**(c)** Show that if $(\sigma_1', \sigma_2')$ and $(\sigma_1'', \sigma_2'')$ are both Nash equilibria of the zero-sum game $\Gamma_N = [I, \{\Delta(S_1), \Delta(S_2)\}, \{u_1(\cdot), u_2(\cdot)\}]$, then so are $(\sigma_1', \sigma_2'')$ and $(\sigma_1'', \sigma_2')$.

**8.D.8$^C$** Consider a simultaneous-move game with normal form $[I, \{\Delta(S_i)\}, \{u_i(\cdot)\}]$. Suppose that, for all $i$, $S_i$ is a convex set and $u_i(\cdot)$ is strictly quasiconvex. Argue that any mixed strategy Nash equilibrium of this game must be degenerate, with each player playing a single pure strategy with probability 1.

**8.D.9$^B$** Consider the following game [based on an example from Kreps (1990)]:

Player 2

|          |     | $LL$          | $L$          | $M$     | $R$            |
|----------|-----|---------------|--------------|---------|----------------|
|          | $U$ | $100, 2$      | $-100, 1$    | $0, 0$  | $-100, -100$   |
| Player 1 | $D$ | $-100, -100$  | $100, -49$   | $1, 0$  | $100, 2$       |

(a) If you were player 2 in this game and you were playing it once without the ability to engage in preplay communication with player 1, what strategy would you choose?

(b) What are all the Nash equilibria (pure and mixed) of this game?

(c) Is your strategy choice in (a) a component of any Nash equilibrium strategy profile? Is it a rationalizable strategy?

(d) Suppose now that preplay communication were possible. Would you expect to play something different from your choice in (a)?

**8.E.1**[B] Consider the following strategic situation. Two opposed armies are poised to seize an island. Each army's general can choose either "attack" or "not attack." In addition, each army is either "strong" or "weak" with equal probability (the draws for each army are independent), and an army's type is known only to its general. Payoffs are as follows: The island is worth M if captured. An army can capture the island either by attacking when its opponent does not or by attacking when its rival does if it is strong and its rival is weak. If two armies of equal strength both attack, neither captures the island. An army also has a "cost" of fighting, which is $s$ if it is strong and $w$ if it is weak, where $s < w$. There is no cost of attacking if its rival does not.

Identify all pure strategy Bayesian Nash equilibria of this game.

**8.E.2**[C] Consider the first-price sealed-bid auction of Exercise 8.D.3, but now suppose that each bidder $i$ observes only his own valuation $v_i$. This valuation is distributed uniformly and independently on $[0, \bar{v}]$ for each bidder.

(a) Derive a symmetric (pure strategy) Bayesian Nash equilibrium of this auction. (You should now suppose that bids can be any real number.) [*Hint:* Look for an equilibrium in which bidder $i$'s bid is a linear function of his valuation.]

(b) What if there are $I$ bidders? What happens to each bidder's equilibrium bid function $s(v_i)$ as $I$ increases?

**8.E.3**[B] Consider the linear Cournot model described in Exercise 8.B.5. Now, however, suppose that each firm has probability $\mu$ of having unit costs of $c_L$ and $(1 - \mu)$ of having unit costs of $c_H$, where $c_H > c_L$. Solve for the Bayesian Nash equilibrium.

**8.F.1**[C] Prove Proposition 8.F.1.

**8.F.2**[B] Consider the following three-player game [taken from van Damme (1983)], in which player 1 chooses rows ($S_1 = \{U, D\}$), player 2 chooses columns ($S_2 = \{L, R\}$), and player 3 chooses boxes ($S_3 = \{B_1, B_2\}$):

| | $B_1$ | | | $B_2$ | |
|---|---|---|---|---|---|
| | $L$ | $R$ | | $L$ | $R$ |
| $U$ | (1, 1, 1) | (1, 0, 1) | $U$ | (1, 1, 0) | (0, 0, 0) |
| $D$ | (1, 1, 1) | (0, 0, 1) | $D$ | (0, 1, 0) | (1, 0, 0) |

Each cell describes the payoffs to the three players ($u_1, u_2, u_3$) from that strategy combination. Both ($D, L, B_1$) and ($U, L, B_1$) are pure strategy Nash equilibria. Show that ($D, L, B_1$) is not (normal form) trembling-hand perfect even though none of these three strategies is weakly dominated.

**8.F.3**[C] Prove that every game $\Gamma_N = [I, \{\Delta(S_i)\}, \{u_i(\cdot)\}]$ in which the $S_i$ are finite sets has a (normal form) trembling-hand perfect Nash equilibrium. [*Hint:* Show that every perturbed game has an equilibrium and that for any sequence of perturbed games converging to the original game $\Gamma_N$ and corresponding sequence of equilibria, there is a subsequence that converges to an equilibrium of $\Gamma_N$.]

# Dynamic Games

## 9.A Introduction

In Chapter 8, we studied simultaneous-move games. Most economic situations, however, involve players choosing actions over time.[1] For example, a labor union and a firm might make repeated offers and counteroffers to each other in the course of negotiations over a new contract. Likewise, firms in a market may invest today in anticipation of the effects of these investments on their competitive interactions in the future. In this chapter, we therefore shift our focus to the study of *dynamic games*.

One way to approach the problem of prediction in dynamic games is to simply derive their normal form representations and then apply the solution concepts studied in Chapter 8. However, an important new issue arises in dynamic games: the *credibility* of a player's strategy. This issue is the central concern of this chapter.

Consider a vivid (although far-fetched) example: You walk into class tomorrow and your instructor, a sane but very enthusiastic game theorist, announces, "This is an important course, and I want exclusive dedication. Anyone who does not drop every other course will be barred from the final exam and will therefore flunk." After a moment of bewilderment and some mental computation, your first thought is, "Given that I indeed prefer this course to all others, I had better follow her instructions" (after all, you have studied Chapter 8 carefully and know what a best response is). But after some further reflection, you ask yourself, "Will she really bar me from the final exam if I do not obey? This is a serious institution, and she will surely lose her job if she carries out the threat." You conclude that the answer is "no" and refuse to drop the other courses, and indeed, she ultimately does not bar you from the exam. In this example, we would say that your instructor's announced strategy, "I will bar you from the exam if you do not drop every other course," is not credible. Such empty threats are what we want to rule out as equilibrium strategies in dynamic games.

In Section 9.B, we demonstrate that the Nash equilibrium concept studied in Chapter 8 does not suffice to rule out noncredible strategies. We then introduce a stronger solution concept, known as *subgame perfect Nash equilibrium*, that helps

---

1. As do most parlor games.

to do so. The central idea underlying this concept is the *principle of sequential rationality*: equilibrium strategies should specify optimal behavior from any point in the game onward, a principle that is intimately related to the procedure of *backward induction*.

In Section 9.C, we show that the concept of subgame perfection is not strong enough to fully capture the idea of sequential rationality in games of imperfect information. We then introduce the notion of a *weak perfect Bayesian equilibrium* (also known as a *weak sequential equilibrium*) to push the analysis further. The central feature of a weak perfect Bayesian equilibrium is its explicit introduction of a player's *beliefs* about what may have transpired prior to her move as a means of testing the sequential rationality of the player's strategy. The modifier *weak* refers to the fact that the weak perfect Bayesian equilibrium concept imposes a *minimal* set of consistency restrictions on players' beliefs. Because the weak perfect Bayesian equilibrium concept can be too weak, we also examine some related equilibrium notions that impose stronger consistency restrictions on beliefs, discussing briefly stronger notions of *perfect Bayesian equilibrium* and, in somewhat greater detail, the concept of *sequential equilibrium*.

In Section 9.D, we go yet further by asking whether certain beliefs can be regarded as "unreasonable" in some situations, thereby allowing us to further refine our predictions. This leads us to consider the notion of *forward induction*.

Appendix A studies finite and infinite horizon models of bilateral bargaining as an illustration of the use of subgame perfect Nash equilibrium in an important economic application. Appendix B extends the discussion in Section 9.C by examining the notion of an *extensive form trembling-hand perfect Nash equilibrium*.

We should note that—following most of the literature on this subject—all the analysis in this chapter consists of attempts to "refine" the concept of Nash equilibrium; that is, we take the position that we want our prediction to be a Nash equilibrium, and we then propose additional conditions for such an equilibrium to be a "satisfactory" prediction. However, the issues that we discuss here are not confined to this approach. We might, for example, be concerned about noncredible strategies even if we were unwilling to impose the mutually correct expectations condition of Nash equilibrium and wanted to focus instead only on rationalizable outcomes. See Bernheim (1984) and, especially, Pearce (1984) for a discussion of nonequilibrium approaches to these issues.

# 9.B   Sequential Rationality, Backward Induction, and Subgame Perfection

We begin with an example to illustrate that in dynamic games the Nash equilibrium concept may not give sensible predictions. This observation leads us to develop a strengthening of the Nash equilibrium concept known as *subgame perfect Nash equilibrium*.

**Example 9.B.1:** Consider the following *predation* game. Firm E (for entrant) is considering entering a market that currently has a single incumbent (firm I). If it does so (playing "in"), the incumbent can respond in one of two ways: It can either accommodate the entrant, giving up some of its sales but causing no change in

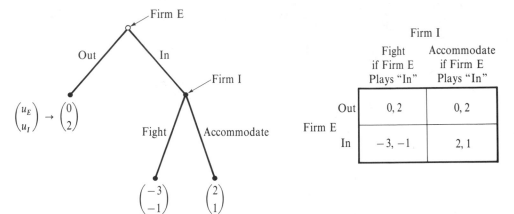

**Figure 9.B.1**

Extensive and normal forms for Example 9.B.1. The Nash equilibrium $(\sigma_E, \sigma_I) = $ (out, fight if firm E plays "in") involves a noncredible threat.

the market price, or it can fight the entrant, engaging in a costly war of predation that dramatically lowers the market price. The extensive and normal form representations of this game are depicted in Figure 9.B.1.

Examining the normal form, we see that this game has two pure strategy Nash equilibria: $(\sigma_E, \sigma_I) = $ (out, fight if firm E plays "in") and $(\sigma_E, \sigma_I) = $ (in, accommodate if firm E plays "in"). Consider the first of these strategy profiles. Firm E prefers to stay out of the market if firm I will fight after it enters. On the other hand, "fight if firm E plays 'in'" is an optimal choice for the incumbent if firm E is playing "out." Similar arguments show that the second pair of strategies is also a Nash equilibrium.

Yet, we claim that (out, fight if firm E plays "in") is not a sensible prediction for this game. As in the example of your instructor that we posed in Section 9.A, firm E can foresee that if it does enter, the incumbent will, in fact, find it optimal to accommodate (by doing so, firm I earns 1 rather than −1). Hence, the incumbent's strategy "fight if firm E plays 'in'" is not credible. ∎

Example 9.B.1 illustrates a problem with the Nash equilibrium concept in dynamic games. In this example, the concept is, in effect, permitting the incumbent to make an empty threat that the entrant nevertheless takes seriously when choosing its strategy. The problem with the Nash equilibrium concept here arises from the fact that when the entrant plays "out," actions at decision nodes that are unreached by play of the equilibrium strategies (here, firm I's action at the decision node following firm E's unchosen move "in") do not affect firm I's payoff. As a result, firm I can plan to do *absolutely anything* at this decision node: Given firm E's strategy of choosing "out," firm I's payoff is still maximized. *But*—and here is the crux of the matter—what firm I's strategy says it will do at the unreached node can actually *insure* that firm E, taking firm I's strategy as given, wants to play "out."

To rule out predictions such as (out, fight if firm E plays "in"), we want to insist that players' equilibrium strategies satisfy what might be called the *principle of sequential rationality*: A player's strategy should specify optimal actions *at every point in the game tree*. That is, given that a player finds herself at some point in the tree, her strategy should prescribe play that is optimal from that point on given her opponents' strategies. Clearly, firm I's strategy "fight if firm E plays 'in'" does not: after entry, the only optimal strategy for firm I is "accommodate."

In Example 9.B.1, there is a simple procedure that can be used to identify the

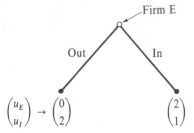

**Figure 9.B.2**

Reduced game after solving for post-entry behavior in Example 9.B.1.

desirable (i.e., sequentially rational) Nash equilibrium $(\sigma_E, \sigma_I) = $ (in, accommodate if firm E plays "in"). We first determine optimal behavior for firm I in the post-entry stage of the game; this is "accommodate." Once we have done this, we then determine firm E's optimal behavior earlier in the game given the anticipation of what will happen after entry. Note that this second step can be accomplished by considering a *reduced* extensive form game in which firm I's post-entry decision is replaced by the payoffs that will result from firm I's optimal post-entry behavior. See Figure 9.B.2. This reduced game is a very simple single-player decision problem in which firm E's optimal decision is to play "in." In this manner, we identify the sequentially rational Nash equilibrium strategy profile $(\sigma_E, \sigma_I) = $ (in, accommodate if firm E plays "in").

This type of procedure, which involves solving first for optimal behavior at the "end" of the game (here, at the post-entry decision node) and then determining what optimal behavior is earlier in the game given the anticipation of this later behavior, is known as *backward induction* (or *backward programming*). It is a procedure that is intimately linked to the idea of sequential rationality because it insures that players' strategies specify optimal behavior at every decision node of the game.

The game in Example 9.B.1 is a member of a general class of games in which the backward induction procedure can be applied to capture the idea of sequential rationality with great generality and power: *finite games of perfect information*. These are games in which every information set contains a single decision node and there is a finite number of such nodes (see Chapter 7).[2] Before introducing a formal equilibrium concept, we first discuss the general application of the backward induction procedure to this class of games.

### Backward Induction in Finite Games of Perfect Information

To apply the idea of backward induction in finite games of perfect information, we start by determining the optimal actions for moves at the final decision nodes in the tree (those for which the only successor nodes are terminal nodes). Just as in firm I's post-entry decision in Example 9.B.1, play at these nodes involves no further strategic interactions among the players, and so the determination of optimal behavior at these decision nodes involves a simple single-person decision problem. Then, given that these will be the actions taken at the final decision nodes, we can proceed to the next-to-last decision nodes and determine the optimal actions to be

---

2. The assumption of finiteness is important for some aspects of this analysis. We discuss this point further toward the end of the section.

taken there by players who correctly anticipate the actions that will follow at the final decision nodes, and so on backward through the game tree.

This procedure is readily implemented using reduced games. At each stage, after solving for the optimal actions at the current final decision nodes, we can derive a new reduced game by deleting the part of the game following these nodes and assigning to these nodes the payoffs that result from the already determined continuation play.

**Example 9.B.2:** Consider the three-player finite game of perfect information depicted in Figure 9.B.3(a). The arrows in Figure 9.B.3(a) indicate the optimal play at the final decision nodes of the game. Figure 9.B.3(b) is the reduced game formed by replacing these final decision nodes by the payoffs that result from optimal play once these nodes have been reached. Figure 9.B.3(c) represents the reduced game derived

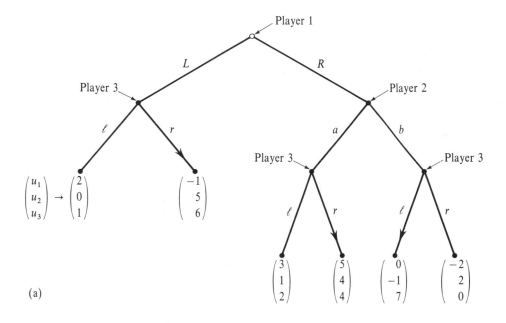

(a)

**Figure 9.B.3**

Reduced games in a backward induction procedure for a finite game of perfect information.
(a) Original game.
(b) First reduced game. (c) Second reduced game.

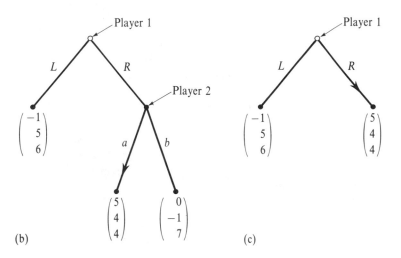

(b)

(c)

in the next stage of the backward induction procedure, when the final decision nodes of the reduced game in Figure 9.B.3(b) are replaced by the payoffs arising from optimal play at these nodes (again indicated by arrows). The backward induction procedure therefore identifies the strategy profile $(\sigma_1, \sigma_2, \sigma_3)$ in which $\sigma_1 = R$, $\sigma_2 = $ "$a$ if player 1 plays $R$," and

$$\sigma_3 = \begin{cases} r \text{ if player 1 plays } L \\ r \text{ if player 1 plays } R \text{ and player 2 plays } a \\ \ell \text{ if player 1 plays } R \text{ and player 2 plays } b. \end{cases}$$

Note that this strategy profile is a Nash equilibrium of this three-player game but that the game also has other pure strategy Nash equilibria. (Exercise 9.B.3 asks you to verify these two points and to argue that these other Nash equilibria do not satisfy the principle of sequential rationality.) ∎

In fact, for finite games of perfect information, we have the general result presented in Proposition 9.B.1.

**Proposition 9.B.1:** (*Zermelo's Theorem*) Every finite game of perfect information $\Gamma_E$ has a pure strategy Nash equilibrium that can be derived through backward induction. Moreover, if no player has the same payoffs at any two terminal nodes, then there is a unique Nash equilibrium that can be derived in this manner.

**Proof:** First, note that in finite games of perfect information, the backward induction procedure is well defined: The player who moves at each decision node has a finite number of possible choices, so optimal actions necessarily exist at each stage of the procedure (if a player is indifferent, we can choose any of her optimal actions). Moreover, the procedure fully specifies all of the players' strategies after a finite number of stages. Second, note that if no player has the same payoffs at any two terminal nodes, then the optimal actions must be *unique* at every stage of the procedure, and so in this case the backward induction procedure identifies a unique strategy profile for the game.

What remains is to show that a strategy profile identified in this way, say $\sigma = (\sigma_1, \ldots, \sigma_I)$, is necessarily a Nash equilibrium of $\Gamma_E$. Suppose that it is not. Then there is some player $i$ who has a deviation, say to strategy $\hat{\sigma}_i$, that strictly increases her payoff given that the other players continue to play strategies $\sigma_{-i}$. That is, letting $u_i(\sigma_i, \sigma_{-i})$ be player $i$'s payoff function,[3]

$$u_i(\hat{\sigma}_i, \sigma_{-i}) > u_i(\sigma_i, \sigma_{-i}). \tag{9.B.1}$$

We argue that this cannot be. The proof is inductive. We shall say that decision node $x$ has *distance* $n$ if, among the various paths that continue from it to the terminal nodes, the maximal number of decision nodes lying between it and a terminal node is $n$. We let $N$ denote the maximum distance of any decision node in the game; since $\Gamma_E$ is a finite game, $N$ is a finite number. Define $\hat{\sigma}_i(n)$ to be the strategy that plays in accordance with strategy $\sigma_i$ at all nodes with distances $0, \ldots, n$, and plays in accordance with strategy $\hat{\sigma}_i$ at all nodes with distances greater than $n$.

By the construction of $\sigma$ through the backward induction procedure, $u_i(\hat{\sigma}_i(0), \sigma_{-i}) \geq u_i(\hat{\sigma}_i, \sigma_{-i})$. That is, player $i$ can do at least as well as she does with strategy $\hat{\sigma}_i$ by instead playing the moves specified in strategy $\sigma_i$ at all nodes with distance 0 (i.e., at the final decision nodes in the game) and following strategy $\hat{\sigma}_i$ elsewhere.

---

3. To be precise, $u_i(\cdot)$ is player $i$'s payoff function in the normal form derived from extensive form game $\Gamma_E$.

We now argue that if $u_i(\hat{\sigma}_i(n-1), \sigma_{-i}) \geq u_i(\hat{\sigma}_i, \sigma_{-i})$, then $u_i(\hat{\sigma}_i(n), \sigma_{-i}) \geq u_i(\hat{\sigma}_i, \sigma_{-i})$. This is straightforward. The only difference between strategy $\hat{\sigma}_i(n)$ and strategy $\hat{\sigma}_i(n-1)$ is in player $i$'s moves at nodes with distance $n$. In both strategies, player $i$ plays according to $\sigma_i$ at all decision nodes that follow the distance-$n$ nodes and in accordance with strategy $\hat{\sigma}_i$ before them. But given that all players are playing in accordance with strategy profile $\sigma$ after the distance-$n$ nodes, the moves derived for the distance-$n$ decision nodes through backward induction, namely those in $\sigma_i$, must be optimal choices for player $i$ at these nodes. Hence, $u_i(\hat{\sigma}_i(n), \sigma_{-i}) \geq u_i(\hat{\sigma}_i(n-1), \sigma_{-i})$.

Applying induction, we therefore have $u_i(\hat{\sigma}_i(N), \sigma_{-i}) \geq u_i(\hat{\sigma}_i, \sigma_{-i})$. But $\hat{\sigma}_i(N) = \sigma_i$, and so we have a contradiction to (9.B.1). Strategy profile $\sigma$ must therefore constitute a Nash equilibrium of $\Gamma_E$. ∎

Note, incidentally, that Proposition 9.B.1 establishes the existence of a pure strategy Nash equilibrium in all finite games of perfect information.

### Subgame Perfect Nash Equilibria

It is clear enough how to apply the principle of sequential rationality in Example 9.B.1 and, more generally, in finite games of perfect information. Before distilling a general solution concept, however, it is useful to discuss another example. This example suggests how we might identify Nash equilibria that satisfy the principle of sequential rationality in more general games involving imperfect information.

**Example 9.B.3:** We consider the same situation as in Example 9.B.1 except that firms I and E now play a simultaneous-move game after entry, each choosing either "fight" or "accommodate." The extensive and normal form representations are depicted in Figure 9.B.4.

Examining the normal form, we see that in this game there are three pure strategy Nash equilibria $(\sigma_E, \sigma_I)$:[4]

((out, accommodate if in), (fight if firm E plays "in")),

((out, fight if in), (fight if firm E plays "in")),

((in, accommodate if in), (accommodate if firm E plays "in")).

Notice, however, that (accommodate, accommodate) is the sole Nash equilibrium in the simultaneous-move game that follows entry. Thus, the firms should expect that they will both play "accommodate" following firm E's entry.[5] But if this is so, firm E

---

4. The entrant's strategy in the first two equilibria may appear odd. Firm E is planning to take an action conditional on entering while at the same time planning not to enter. Recall from Section 7.D, however, that a strategy is a *complete contingent plan*. Indeed, the reason we have insisted on this requirement is precisely the need to test the sequential rationality of a player's strategy.

5. Recall that throughout this chapter we maintain the assumption that rational players always play some Nash equilibrium in any strategic situation in which they find themselves (i.e., we assume that players will have mutually correct expectations). Two points about this assumption are worth noting. First, some justifications for a Nash equilibrium may be less compelling in the context of dynamic games. For example, if players never reach certain parts of a game, the stable social convention argument given in Section 8.D may no longer provide a good reason for believing that a Nash equilibrium would be played *if* that part of the game tree were reached. Second, the idea of sequential rationality can still have force even if we do not make this assumption. For example, here we would reach the same conclusion even if we assumed only that neither player would play an iteratively strictly dominated strategy in the post-entry simultaneous-move game.

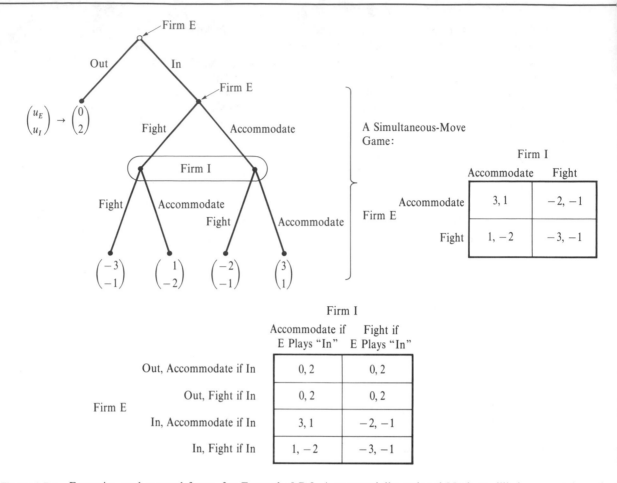

**Figure 9.B.4** Extensive and normal forms for Example 9.B.3. A sequentially rational Nash equilibrium must have both firms play "accommodate" after entry.

should enter. The logic of sequential rationality therefore suggests that only the last of the three equilibria is a reasonable prediction in this game. ∎

The requirement of sequential rationality illustrated in this and the preceding examples is captured by the notion of a *subgame perfect Nash equilibrium* [introduced by Selten (1965)]. Before formally defining this concept, however, we need to specify what a *subgame* is.

**Definition 9.B.1:** A *subgame* of an extensive form game $\Gamma_E$ is a subset of the game having the following properties:

(i) It begins with an information set containing a single decision node, contains all the decision nodes that are successors (both immediate and later) of this node, and contains *only* these nodes.

(ii) If decision node $x$ is in the subgame, then every $x' \in H(x)$ is also, where $H(x)$ is the information set that contains decision node $x$. (That is, there are no "broken" information sets.)

Note that according to Definition 9.B.1, the game as a whole is a subgame, as may be some strict subsets of the game.[6] For example, in Figure 9.B.1, there are two subgames: the game as a whole and the part of the game tree that begins with and follows firm I's decision node. The game in Figure 9.B.4 also has two subgames: the game as a whole and the part of the game beginning with firm E's post-entry decision node. In Figure 9.B.5, the dotted lines indicate three parts of the game of Figure 9.B.4 that are *not* subgames.

Finally, note that in a finite game of perfect information, every decision node initiates a subgame. (Exercise 9.B.1 asks you to verify this fact for the game of Example 9.B.2.)

The key feature of a subgame is that, contemplated in isolation, it is a game in its own right. We can therefore apply to it the idea of Nash equilibrium predictions. In the discussion that follows, we say that a strategy profile $\sigma$ in extensive form game $\Gamma_E$ *induces* a Nash equilibrium in a particular subgame of $\Gamma_E$ if the moves specified in $\sigma$ for information sets within the subgame constitute a Nash equilibrium when this subgame is considered in isolation.

**Definition 9.B.2:** A profile of strategies $\sigma = (\sigma_1, \ldots, \sigma_I)$ in an *I*-player extensive form game $\Gamma_E$ is a *subgame perfect Nash equilibrium* (SPNE) if it induces a Nash equilibrium in every subgame of $\Gamma_E$.

Note that any SPNE is a Nash equilibrium (since the game as a whole is a subgame) but that not every Nash equilibrium is subgame perfect.

**Exercise 9.B.2:** Consider a game $\Gamma_E$ in extensive form. Argue that:

(a) If the only subgame is the game as a whole, then every Nash equilibrium is subgame perfect.

(b) A subgame perfect Nash equilibrium induces a subgame perfect Nash equilibrium in every subgame of $\Gamma_E$.

The SPNE concept isolates the reasonable Nash equilibria in Examples 9.B.1 and 9.B.3. In Example 9.B.1, any subgame perfect Nash equilibrium must have firm I playing "accommodate if firm E plays 'in'" because this is firm I's strictly dominant strategy in the subgame following entry. Likewise, in Example 9.B.3, any SPNE must have the firms both playing "accommodate" after entry because this is the unique Nash equilibrium in this subgame.

Note also that in finite games of perfect information, such as the games of Examples 9.B.1 and 9.B.2, the set of SPNEs coincides with the set of Nash equilibria that can be derived through the backward induction procedure. Recall, in particular, that in finite games of perfect information every decision node initiates a subgame. Thus, in any SPNE, the strategies must specify actions at each of the final decision nodes of the game that are optimal in the single-player subgame that begins there. Given that this must be the play at the final decision nodes in any SPNE, consider play in the subgames starting at the next-to-last decision nodes. Nash equilibrium play in these subgames, which is required in any SPNE, must have the players who

---

6. In the literature, the term *proper subgame* is sometimes used with the same meaning we assign to *subgame*. We choose to use the unqualified term *subgame* here to make clear that the game itself qualifies.

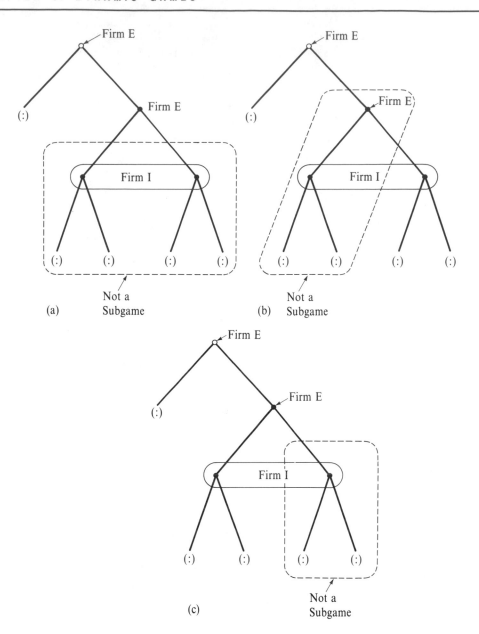

**Figure 9.B.5**

Three parts of the game in Figure 9.B.4 that are not subgames.

move at these next-to-last nodes choosing optimal strategies given the play that will occur at the last nodes. And so on. An implication of this fact and Proposition 9.B.1 is therefore the result stated in Proposition 9.B.2.

**Proposition 9.B.2:** Every finite game of perfect information $\Gamma_E$ has a pure strategy subgame perfect Nash equilibrium. Moreover, if no player has the same payoffs at any two terminal nodes, then there is a unique subgame perfect Nash equilibrium.[7]

---

7. The result can also be seen directly from Proposition 9.B.1. Just as the strategy profile derived using the backward induction procedure constitutes a Nash equilibrium in the game as a whole, it is also a Nash equilibrium in every subgame.

In fact, to identify the set of subgame perfect Nash equilibria in a general (finite) dynamic game $\Gamma_E$, we can use a generalization of the backward induction procedure. This *generalized backward induction procedure* works as follows:

1. Start at the end of the game tree, and identify the Nash equilibria for each of the *final* subgames (i.e., those that have no other subgames nested within them).
2. Select one Nash equilibrium in each of these final subgames, and derive the reduced extensive form game in which these final subgames are replaced by the payoffs that result in these subgames when players use these equilibrium strategies.
3. Repeat steps 1 and 2 for the reduced game. Continue the procedure until every move in $\Gamma_E$ is determined. This collection of moves at the various information sets of $\Gamma_E$ constitutes a profile of SPNE strategies.
4. If multiple equilibria are never encountered in any step of this process, this profile of strategies is the unique SPNE. If multiple equilibria are encountered, the full set of SPNEs is identified by repeating the procedure for each possible equilibrium that could occur for the subgames in question.

The formal justification for using this generalized backward induction procedure to identify the set of SPNEs comes from the result shown in Proposition 9.B.3.

**Proposition 9.B.3:** Consider an extensive form game $\Gamma_E$ and some subgame $S$ of $\Gamma_E$. Suppose that strategy profile $\sigma^S$ is an SPNE in subgame $S$, and let $\hat{\Gamma}_E$ be the reduced game formed by replacing subgame $S$ by a terminal node with payoffs equal to those arising from play of $\sigma^S$. Then:

(i) In any SPNE $\sigma$ of $\Gamma_E$ in which $\sigma^S$ is the play in subgame $S$, players' moves at information sets outside subgame $S$ must constitute an SPNE of reduced game $\hat{\Gamma}_E$.

(ii) If $\hat{\sigma}$ is an SPNE of $\hat{\Gamma}_E$, then the strategy profile $\sigma$ that specifies the moves in $\sigma^S$ at information sets in subgame $S$ and that specifies the moves in $\hat{\sigma}$ at information sets not in $S$ is an SPNE of $\Gamma_E$.

**Proof:** (i) Suppose that strategy profile $\sigma$ specifies play at information sets outside subgame $S$ that does not constitute an SPNE of reduced game $\hat{\Gamma}_E$. Then there exists a subgame of $\hat{\Gamma}_E$ in which $\sigma$ does not induce a Nash equilibrium. In this subgame of $\hat{\Gamma}_E$, some player has a deviation that improves her payoff, taking as given the strategies of her opponents. But then it must be that this player also has a profitable deviation in the corresponding subgame of game $\Gamma_E$. She makes the same alterations in her moves at information sets not in $S$ and leaves her moves at information sets in $S$ unchanged. Hence, $\sigma$ could not be an SPNE of the overall game $\Gamma_E$.

(ii) Suppose that $\hat{\sigma}$ is an SPNE of reduced game $\hat{\Gamma}_E$, and let $\sigma$ be the strategy in the overall game $\Gamma_E$ formed by specifying the moves in $\sigma^S$ at information sets in subgame $S$ and the moves in $\hat{\sigma}$ at information sets not in $S$. We argue that $\sigma$ induces a Nash equilibrium in every subgame of $\Gamma_E$. This follows immediately from the construction of $\sigma$ for subgames of $\Gamma_E$ that either lie entirely in subgame $S$ or never intersect with subgame $S$ (i.e., that do not have subgame $S$ nested within them). So consider any subgame that has subgame $S$ nested within it. If some player $i$ has a profitable deviation in this subgame given her opponent's strategies, then she must also have a profitable deviation that leaves her moves within subgame $S$ unchanged because, by hypothesis, a player does best within subgame $S$ by playing the moves specified in strategy profile $\sigma^S$ given that her opponents do so. But if she has such a profitable deviation, then she must have a profitable deviation in the corresponding subgame of reduced game $\hat{\Gamma}_E$, in contradiction to $\hat{\sigma}$ being an SPNE of $\hat{\Gamma}_E$. ∎

Note that for the final subgames of $\Gamma_E$, the set of Nash equilibria and SPNEs coincide, because these subgames contain no nested subgames. Identifying Nash equilibria in these final subgames therefore allows us to begin the inductive application of Proposition 9.B.3.

---

This generalized backward induction procedure reduces to our previous backward induction procedure in the case of games of perfect information. But it also applies to games of imperfect information. Example 9.B.3 provides a simple illustration. There we can identify the unique SPNE by first identifying the unique Nash equilibrium in the post-entry subgame: (accommodate, accommodate). Having done this, we can replace this subgame with the payoffs that result from equilibrium play in it. The reduced game that results is then much the same as that shown in Figure 9.B.2, the only difference being that firm E's payoff from playing "in" is now 3 instead of 2. Hence, in this manner, we can derive the unique SPNE of Example 9.B.3: $(\sigma_E, \sigma_I) =$ ((in, accommodate if in), (accommodate if firm E plays "in")).

The game in Example 9.B.3 is simple to solve in two respects. First, there is a unique equilibrium in the post-entry subgame. If this were not so, behavior earlier in the game could depend on *which* equilibrium resulted after entry. Example 9.B.4 illustrates this point:[8]

**Example 9.B.4:** *The Niche Choice Game.* Consider a modification of Example 9.B.3 in which instead of having the two firms choose whether to fight or accommodate each other, we suppose that there are actually two niches in the market, one large and one small. After entry, the two firms decide simultaneously which niche they will be in. For example, the niches might correspond to two types of customers, and the firms may be deciding to which type they are targeting their product design. Both firms lose money if they choose the same niche, with more lost if it is the small niche. If they choose different niches, the firm that targets the large niche earns a profit, and the firm with the small niche incurs a loss, but a smaller loss than if the two firms targeted the same niche. The extensive form of this game is depicted in Figure 9.B.6.

To determine the SPNE of this game, consider the post-entry subgame first. There are two pure strategy Nash equilibria of this simultaneous-move game: (large niche, small niche) and (small niche, large niche).[9] In any pure strategy SPNE, the firms' strategies must induce one of these two Nash equilibria in the post-entry subgame. Suppose, first, that the firms will play (large niche, small niche). In this case, the payoffs from reaching the post-entry subgame are $(u_E, u_I) = (1, -1)$, and the reduced game is as depicted in Figure 9.B.7(a). The entrant optimally chooses to enter in this

---

8. Similar issues can arise in games of perfect information when a player is indifferent between two actions. However, the presence of multiple equilibria in subgames involving simultaneous play is, in a sense, a more robust phenomenon. Multiple equilibria are generally robust to small changes in players' payoffs, but ties in games of perfect information are not.

9. We restrict attention here to pure strategy SPNEs. There is also a mixed strategy Nash equilibrium in the post-entry subgame. Exercise 9.B.6 asks you to investigate the implications of this mixed strategy play being the post-entry equilibrium behavior.

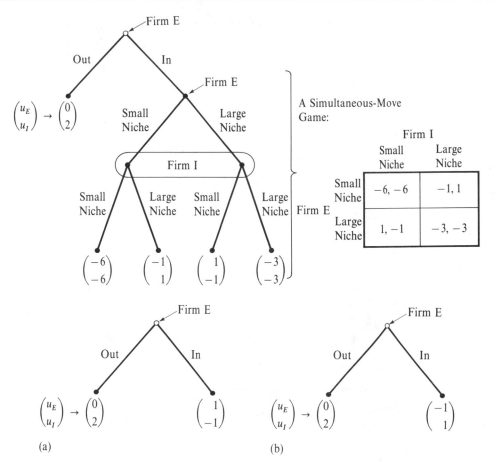

**Figure 9.B.6**

Extensive form for the Niche Choice game. The post-entry subgame has multiple Nash equilibria.

**Figure 9.B.7**

Reduced games after identifying (pure strategy) Nash equilibria in the post-entry subgame of the Niche Choice game. (a) Reduced game if (large niche, small niche) is post-entry equilibrium. (b) Reduced game if (small niche, large niche) is post-entry equilibrium.

case. Hence, one SPNE is $(\sigma_E, \sigma_I) = ((\text{in}, \text{large niche if in}), (\text{small niche if firm E plays "in"}))$.

Now suppose that the post-entry play is (small niche, large niche). Then the payoffs from reaching the post-entry game are $(u_E, u_I) = (-1, 1)$, and the reduced game is that depicted in Figure 9.B.7(b). The entrant optimally chooses not to enter in this case. Hence, there is a second pure strategy SPNE: $(\sigma_E, \sigma_I) = ((\text{out}, \text{small niche if in}), (\text{large niche if firm E plays "in"}))$. ∎

A second sense in which the game in Example 9.B.3 is simple to solve is that it involves only one subgame other than the game as a whole. Like games of perfect information, a game with imperfect information may in general have *many* subgames, with one subgame nested within another, and that larger subgame nested within a still larger one, and so on.

One interesting class of imperfect information games in which the generalized backward induction procedure gives a very clean conclusion is described in Proposition 9.B.4.

**Proposition 9.B.4:** Consider an $I$-player extensive form game $\Gamma_E$ involving successive play of $T$ simultaneous-move games, $\Gamma_N^t = [I, \{\Delta(S_i^t)\}, \{u_i^t(\cdot)\}]$ for $t = 1, \ldots, T$, with the players observing the pure strategies played in each game immediately after its play is concluded. Assume that each player's payoff is equal to the sum of her payoffs in the plays of the $T$ games. If there is a unique Nash equilibrium in each game $\Gamma_N^t$, say $\sigma^t = (\sigma_1^t, \ldots, \sigma_I^t)$, then there is a unique SPNE of $\Gamma_E$ and it consists of each player $i$ playing strategy $\sigma_i^t$ in each game $\Gamma_N^t$ regardless of what has happened previously.

---

**Proof:** The proof is by induction. The result is clearly true for $T = 1$. Now suppose it is true for all $T \leq n - 1$. We will show that it is true for $T = n$.

We know by hypothesis that in any SPNE of the overall game, after play of game $\Gamma_N^1$ the play in the remaining $n - 1$ simultaneous-move games must simply involve play of the Nash equilibrium of each game (since any SPNE of the overall game induces an SPNE in each of its subgames). Let player $i$ earn $G_i$ from this equilibrium play in these $n - 1$ games. Then in the reduced game that replaces all the subgames that follow $\Gamma_N^1$ with their equilibrium payoffs, player $i$ earns an overall payoff of $u_i(s_1^1, \ldots, s_I^1) + G_i$ if $(s_1^1, \ldots, s_I^1)$ is the profile of pure strategies played in game $\Gamma_N^1$. The unique Nash equilibrium of this reduced game is clearly $\sigma^1$. Hence, the result is also true for $T = n$. ∎

---

The basic idea behind Proposition 9.B.4 is an application of backward induction logic: Play in the last game must result in the unique Nash equilibrium of that game being played because at that point players essentially face just that game. But if play in the last game is predetermined, then when players play the next-to-last game, it is again as if they were playing just *that* game in isolation (think of the case where $T = 2$). And so on.

An interesting aspect of Proposition 9.B.4 is the way the SPNE concept rules out history dependence of strategies in the class of games considered there. In general, a player's strategy could potentially promise later rewards or punishments to other players if they take particular actions early in the game. But as long as each of the component games has a unique Nash equilibrium, SPNE strategies cannot be history dependent.[10]

Exercises 9.B.9 to 9.B.11 provide some additional examples of the use of the subgame perfect Nash equilibrium concept. In Appendix A we also study an important economic application of subgame perfection to a finite game of perfect information (albeit one with an infinite number of possible moves at some decision nodes): a finite horizon model of bilateral bargaining.

Up to this point, our analysis has assumed that the game being studied is finite. This has been important because it has allowed us to identify subgame perfect Nash equilibria by starting at the end of the game and working backward. As a general matter, in games in which there can be an infinite sequence of moves (so that some paths through the tree never reach a terminal node), the definition of a subgame perfect Nash equilibrium remains that given in Definition 9.B.2: Strategies must induce a Nash equilibrium in every subgame. Nevertheless, the lack of a definite finite point of termination of the game can reduce the power of the SPNE concept because we can no longer use the end of the game to pin down behavior. In games in which there is always a future, a wide range of behaviors can sometimes be justified as sequentially rational (i.e., as part of an SPNE). A striking example of this sort arises in

---

10. This lack of history dependence depends importantly on the uniqueness assumption of Proposition 9.B.4. With multiple Nash equilibria in the component games, we can get outcomes that are not merely the repeated play of the static Nash equilibria. (See Exercise 9.B.9 for an example.)

Chapter 12 and its Appendix A when we consider *infinitely repeated games* in the context of studying oligopolistic pricing.

Nevertheless, it is not always the case that an infinite horizon weakens the power of the subgame perfection criterion. In Appendix A of this chapter, we study an infinite horizon model of bilateral bargaining in which the SPNE concept predicts a unique outcome, and this outcome coincides with the limiting outcome of the corresponding finite horizon bargaining model as the horizon grows long.

The methods used to identify subgame perfect Nash equilibria in infinite horizon games are varied. Sometimes, the method involves showing that the game can effectively be truncated because after a certain point it is obvious what equilibrium play must be (see Exercise 9.B.11). In other situations, the game possesses a stationarity property that can be exploited; the analysis of the infinite horizon bilateral bargaining model in Appendix A is one example of this kind.

---

After the preceding analysis, the logic of sequential rationality may seem unassailable. But things are not quite so clear. For example, nowhere could the principle of sequential rationality seem on more secure footing than in finite games of perfect information. But chess is a game of this type (the game ends if 50 moves occur without a piece being taken or a pawn being moved), and so its "solution" should be simple to predict. Of course, it is exactly players' *inability* to do so that makes it an exciting game to play. The same could be said even of the much simpler game of Chinese checkers. It is clear that in practice, players may be only boundedly rational. As a result, we might feel more comfortable with our rationality hypotheses in games that are relatively simple, in games where repetition helps players learn to think through the game, or in games where large stakes encourage players to do so as much as possible. Of course, the possibility of bounded rationality is not a concern limited to dynamic games and subgame perfect Nash equilibria; it is also relevant for simultaneous-move games containing many possible strategies.

There is, however, an interesting tension present in the SPNE concept that is related to this bounded rationality issue and that does not arise in the context of simultaneous-move games. In particular, the SPNE concept insists that players should play an SPNE wherever they find themselves in the game tree, even after a sequence of events that is contrary to the predictions of the theory. To see this point starkly, consider the following example due to Rosenthal (1981), known as the *Centipede game*.

**Example 9.B.5:** *The Centipede Game.* In this finite game of perfect information, there are two players, 1 and 2. The players each start with 1 dollar in front of them. They alternate saying "stop" or "continue," starting with player 1. When a player says "continue," 1 dollar is taken by a referee from her pile and 2 dollars are put in her opponent's pile. As soon as either player says "stop," play is terminated, and each player receives the money currently in her pile. Alternatively, play stops if both players' piles reach 100 dollars. The extensive form for this game is depicted in Figure 9.B.8.

The unique SPNE in this game has both players saying "stop" whenever it is their turn, and the players each receive 1 dollar in this equilibrium. To see this, consider player 2's move at the final decision node of the game (after the players have said "continue" a total of 197 times). Her optimal move if play reaches this point is to say "stop"; by doing so, she receives 101 dollars compared with a payoff of 100 dollars if she says "continue." Now consider what happens if play reaches the next-to-last decision node. Player 1, anticipating player 2's move at the final decision node, also says "stop"; doing so, she earns 99 dollars, compared with 98 dollars if she says "continue." Continuing backward through the tree in this fashion, we identify saying "stop" as the optimal move at every decision node.

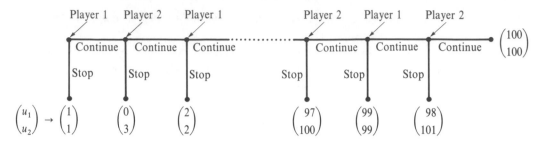

**Figure 9.B.8**  The Centipede game.

A striking aspect of the SPNE in the Centipede game is how bad it is for the players. They each get 1 dollar, whereas they might get 100 dollars by repeatedly saying "continue."

Is this (unique) SPNE in the Centipede game a reasonable prediction? Consider player 1's initial decision to say "stop." For this to be rational, player 1 must be pretty sure that if instead she says "continue," player 2 will say "stop" at her first turn. Indeed, "continue" would be better for player 1 as long as she could be sure that player 2 would say "continue" at her next move. Why might player 2 respond to player 1 saying "continue" by also saying "continue"? First, as we have pointed out, player 2 might not be fully rational, and so she might not have done the backward induction computation assumed in the SPNE concept. More interestingly, however, once she sees that player 1 has chosen "continue"—an event that should never happen according to the SPNE prediction—she might entertain the possibility that player 1 is not rational in the sense demanded by the SPNE concept. If, as a result, she thinks that player 1 would say "continue" at her next move if given the chance, then player 2 would want to say "continue" herself. The SPNE concept denies this possibility, instead assuming that at any point in the game, players will assume that the remaining play of the game will be an SPNE even if play up to that point has contradicted the theory. One way of resolving this tension is to view the SPNE theory as treating any deviation from prescribed play as the result of an extremely unlikely "mistake" that is unlikely to occur again. In Appendix B, we discuss one concept that makes this idea explicit.  ■

# 9.C  Beliefs and Sequential Rationality

Although subgame perfection is often very useful in capturing the principle of sequential rationality, sometimes it is not enough. Consider Example 9.C.1's adaptation of the entry game studied in Example 9.B.1.

**Example 9.C.1:**  We now suppose that there are two strategies firm E can use to enter, "$in_1$" and "$in_2$," and that the incumbent is unable to tell which strategy firm E has used if entry occurs. Figure 9.C.1 depicts this game and its payoffs.

As in the original entry game in Example 9.B.1, there are two pure strategy Nash equilibria here: (out, fight if entry occurs) and ($in_1$, accommodate if entry occurs). Once again, however, the first of these does not seem very reasonable; regardless of what entry strategy firm E has used, the incumbent prefers to accommodate once entry has occurred. *But the criterion of subgame perfection is of absolutely no use here*: Because the only subgame is the game as a whole, both pure strategy Nash equilibria are subgame perfect.  ■

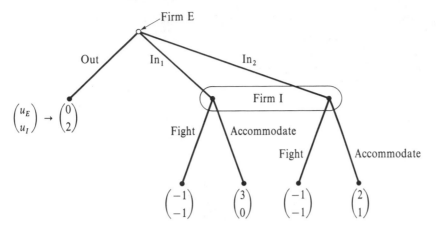

**Figure 9.C.1**

Extensive form for Example 9.C.1. The SPNE concept may fail to insure sequential rationality.

How can we eliminate the unreasonable equilibrium here? One possibility, which is in the spirit of the principle of sequential rationality, might be to insist that the incumbent's action after entry be optimal for *some belief* that she might have about which entry strategy was used by firm E. Indeed, in Example 9.C.1, "fight if entry occurs" is not an optimal choice for *any* belief that firm I might have. This suggests that we may be able to make some progress by formally considering players' beliefs and using them to test the sequential rationality of players' strategies.

We now introduce a solution concept, which we call a *weak perfect Bayesian equilibrium* [Myerson (1991) refers to this same concept as a *weak sequential equilibrium*], that extends the principle of sequential rationality by formally introducing the notion of beliefs.[11] It requires, roughly, that at any point in the game, a player's strategy prescribe optimal actions from that point on given her opponents' strategies and her beliefs about what has happened so far in the game and that her beliefs be consistent with the strategies being played.

To express this notion formally, we must first formally define the two concepts that are its critical components: the notions of a *system of beliefs* and the *sequential rationality of strategies*. Beliefs are simple.

**Definition 9.C.1:** A *system of beliefs* $\mu$ in extensive form game $\Gamma_E$ is a specification of a probability $\mu(x) \in [0, 1]$ for each decision node $x$ in $\Gamma_E$ such that

$$\sum_{x \in H} \mu(x) = 1$$

for all information sets $H$.

A system of beliefs can be thought of as specifying, for each information set, a probabilistic assessment by the player who moves at that set of the relative likelihoods of being at each of the information set's various decision nodes, conditional upon play having reached that information set.

---

11. The concept of a *perfect Bayesian equilibrium* was first developed to capture the requirements of sequential rationality in dynamic games with incomplete information, that is (using the terminology introduced in Section 8.E), in dynamic Bayesian games. The *weak perfect Bayesian equilibrium* concept is a variant that is introduced here primarily for pedagogic purposes (the reason for the modifier *weak* will be made clear later in this section). Myerson (1991) refers to this same concept as a *weak sequential equilibrium* because it may also be considered a weak variant of the *sequential equilibrium* concept introduced in Definition 9.C.4.

To define sequential rationality, it is useful to let $E[u_i \mid H, \mu, \sigma_i, \sigma_{-i}]$ denote player $i$'s expected utility starting at her information set $H$ if her beliefs regarding the conditional probabilities of being at the various nodes in $H$ are given by $\mu$, if she follows strategy $\sigma_i$, and if her rivals use strategies $\sigma_{-i}$. [We will not write out the formula for this expression explicitly, although it is conceptually straightforward: Pretend that the probability distribution $\mu(x)$ over nodes $x \in H$ is generated by nature; then player $i$'s expected payoff is determined by the probability distribution that is induced on the terminal nodes by the combination of this initial distribution plus the players' strategies from this point on.]

**Definition 9.C.2:** A strategy profile $\sigma = (\sigma_1, \ldots, \sigma_I)$ in extensive form game $\Gamma_E$ is *sequentially rational at information set H given a system of beliefs* $\mu$ if, denoting by $\iota(H)$ the player who moves at information set $H$, we have

$$E[u_{\iota(H)} \mid H, \mu, \sigma_{\iota(H)}, \sigma_{-\iota(H)}] \geq E[u_{\iota(H)} \mid H, \mu, \tilde{\sigma}_{\iota(H)}, \sigma_{-\iota(H)}]$$

for all $\tilde{\sigma}_{\iota(H)} \in \Delta(S_{\iota(H)})$. If strategy profile $\sigma$ satisfies this condition for *all* information sets $H$, then we say that $\sigma$ is *sequentially rational given belief system* $\mu$.

In words, a strategy profile $\sigma = (\sigma_1, \ldots, \sigma_I)$ is sequentially rational if no player finds it worthwhile, once one of her information sets has been reached, to revise her strategy given her beliefs about what has already occurred (as embodied in $\mu$) and her rivals' strategies.

With these two notions, we can now define a weak perfect Bayesian equilibrium. The definition involves two conditions: First, strategies must be sequentially rational given beliefs. Second, whenever possible, beliefs must be consistent with the strategies. The idea behind the consistency condition on beliefs is much the same as the idea underlying the concept of Nash equilibrium (see Section 8.D): In an equilibrium, players should have correct beliefs about their opponents' strategy choices.

To motivate the specific consistency requirement on beliefs to be made in the definition of a weak perfect Bayesian equilibrium, consider how we might define the notion of consistent beliefs in the special case in which each player's equilibrium strategy assigns a strictly positive probability to each possible action at every one of her information sets (known as a *completely mixed strategy*).[12] In this case, every information set in the game is reached with positive probability. The natural notion of beliefs being consistent with the play of the equilibrium strategy profile $\sigma$ is in this case straightforward: For each node $x$ in a given player's information set $H$, the player should compute the probability of reaching that node given play of strategies $\sigma$, Prob $(x \mid \sigma)$, and she should then assign conditional probabilities of being at each of these nodes given that play has reached this information set using *Bayes' rule*:[13]

$$\text{Prob}\,(x \mid H, \sigma) = \frac{\text{Prob}\,(x \mid \sigma)}{\sum_{x' \in H} \text{Prob}\,(x' \mid \sigma)}.$$

---

12. Equivalently, a completely mixed strategy can be thought of as a strategy that assigns a strictly positive probability to each of the player's pure strategies in the normal form derived from extensive form game $\Gamma_E$.

13. Bayes' rule is a basic principle of statistical inference. See, for example, DeGroot (1970), where it is referred to as *Bayes' theorem*.

As a concrete example, suppose that in the game in Example 9.C.1, firm E is using the completely mixed strategy that assigns a probability of $\frac{1}{4}$ to "out," $\frac{1}{2}$ to "in$_1$," and $\frac{1}{4}$ to "in$_2$." Then the probability of reaching firm I's information set given this strategy is $\frac{3}{4}$. Using Bayes' rule, the probability of being at the left node of firm I's information set conditional on this information set having been reached is $\frac{2}{3}$, and the conditional probability of being at the right node in the set is $\frac{1}{3}$. For firm I's beliefs following entry to be consistent with firm E's strategy, firm I's beliefs should assign exactly these probabilities.

The more difficult issue arises when players are not using completely mixed strategies. In this case, some information sets may no longer be reached with positive probability, and so we cannot use Bayes' rule to compute conditional probabilities for the nodes in these information sets. At an intuitive level, this problem corresponds to the idea that even if players were to play the game repeatedly, the equilibrium play would generate no experience on which they could base their beliefs at these information sets. The weak perfect Bayesian equilibrium concept takes an agnostic view toward what players should believe if play were to reach these information sets unexpectedly. In particular, it allows us to assign *any* beliefs at these information sets. It is in this sense that the modifier *weak* is appropriately attached to this concept.

We can now give a formal definition.

**Definition 9.C.3:** A profile of strategies and system of beliefs $(\sigma, \mu)$ is a *weak perfect Bayesian equilibrium* (weak PBE) in extensive form game $\Gamma_E$ if it has the following properties:

(i) The strategy profile $\sigma$ is sequentially rational given belief system $\mu$.

(ii) The system of beliefs $\mu$ is derived from strategy profile $\sigma$ through Bayes' rule whenever possible. That is, for any information set $H$ such that Prob $(H \mid \sigma) > 0$ (read as "the probability of reaching information set $H$ is positive under strategies $\sigma$"), we must have

$$\mu(x) = \frac{\text{Prob } (x \mid \sigma)}{\text{Prob } (H \mid \sigma)} \quad \text{for all } x \in H.$$

It should be noted that the definition formally incorporates beliefs as part of an equilibrium by identifying a *strategy–beliefs pair* $(\sigma, \mu)$ as a weak perfect Bayesian equilibrium. In the literature, however, it is not uncommon to see this treated a bit loosely: a set of strategies $\sigma$ will be referred to as an equilibrium with the meaning that there is at least one associated set of beliefs $\mu$ such that $(\sigma, \mu)$ satisfies Definition 9.C.3. At times, however, it can be very useful to be more explicit about what these beliefs are, such as when testing them against some of the "reasonableness" criteria that we discuss in Section 9.D.

A useful way to understand the relationship between the weak PBE concept and that of Nash equilibrium comes in the characterization of Nash equilibrium given in Proposition 9.C.1.

**Proposition 9.C.1:** A strategy profile $\sigma$ is a Nash equilibrium of extensive form game $\Gamma_E$ if and only if there exists a system of beliefs $\mu$ such that

(i) The strategy profile $\sigma$ is sequentially rational given belief system $\mu$ *at all information sets $H$ such that Prob $(H \mid \sigma) > 0$.*

(ii) The system of beliefs $\mu$ is derived from strategy profile $\sigma$ through Bayes' rule whenever possible.

Exercise 9.C.1 asks you to prove this result. The italicized portion of condition (i) is the only change from Definition 9.C.3: For a Nash equilibrium, we require sequential rationality only on the equilibrium path. Hence, a weak perfect Bayesian equilibrium of game $\Gamma_E$ is a Nash equilibrium, but not every Nash equilibrium is a weak PBE.

We now illustrate the application of the weak PBE concept in several examples. We first consider how the concept performs in Example 9.C.1.

**Example 9.C.1 Continued:** Clearly, firm I must play "accommodate if entry occurs" in any weak perfect Bayesian equilibrium because that is firm I's optimal action starting at its information set for *any* system of beliefs. Thus, the Nash equilibrium strategies (out, fight if entry occurs) cannot be part of any weak PBE.

What about the other pure strategy Nash equilibrium, (in$_1$, accommodate if entry occurs)? To show that this strategy profile *is* part of a weak PBE, we need to supplement these strategies with a system of beliefs that satisfy criterion (ii) of Definition 9.C.3 and that lead these strategies to be sequentially rational. Note first that to satisfy criterion (ii), the incumbent's beliefs must assign probability 1 to being at the left node in her information set because this information set is reached with positive probability given the strategies (in$_1$, accommodate if entry occurs) [a specification of beliefs at this information set fully describes a system of beliefs in this game because the only other information set is a singleton]. Moreover, these strategies are, indeed, sequentially rational given this system of beliefs. In fact, this strategy–beliefs pair is the unique weak PBE in this game (pure or mixed). ∎

Examples 9.C.2 and 9.C.3 provide further illustrations of the application of the weak PBE concept.

**Example 9.C.2:** Consider the following "joint venture" entry game: Now there is a second potential entrant E2. The story is as follows: Firm E1 has the essential capability to enter the market but lacks some important capability that firm E2 has. As a result, E1 is considering proposing a joint venture with E2 in which E2 shares its capability with E1 and the two firms split the profits from entry. Firm E1 has three initial choices: enter directly on its own, propose a joint venture with E2, or stay out of the market. If it proposes a joint venture, firm E2 can either accept or decline. If E2 accepts, then E1 enters with E2's assistance. If not, then E1 must decide whether to enter on its own. The incumbent can observe whether E1 has entered, but not whether it is with E2's assistance. Fighting is the best response for the incumbent if E1 is unassisted (E1 can then be wiped out quickly) but is not optimal for the incumbent if E1 is assisted (E1 is then a tougher competitor). Finally, if E1 is unassisted, it wants to enter only if the incumbent accommodates; but if E1 is assisted by E2, then because it will be such a strong competitor, its entry is profitable regardless of whether the incumbent fights. The extensive form of this game is depicted in Figure 9.C.2.

To identify the weak PBE of this game note first that, in any weak PBE, firm E2 must accept the joint venture if firm E1 proposes it because E2 is thereby assured of a positive payoff regardless of firm I's strategy. But if so, then in any weak PBE

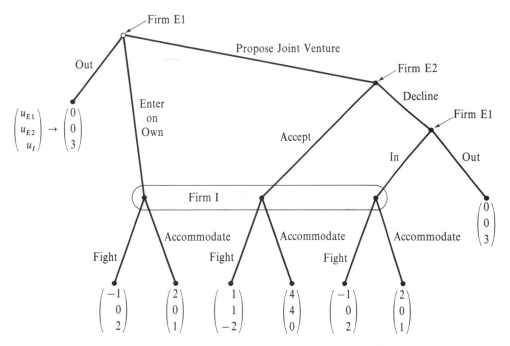

**Figure 9.C.2**

Extensive form for Example 9.C.2.

firm E1 must propose the joint venture since if firm E2 will accept its proposal, then firm E1 does better proposing the joint venture than it does by either staying out or entering on its own, regardless of firm I's post-entry strategy. Next, these two conclusions imply that firm I's information set is reached with positive probability (in fact, with certainty) in any weak PBE. Applying Bayesian updating at this information set, we conclude that the beliefs at this information set must assign a probability of 1 to being at the middle node. Given this, in any weak PBE firm I's strategy must be "accommodate if entry occurs." Finally, if firm I is playing "accommodate if entry occurs," then firm E1 must enter if it proposes a joint venture that firm E2 then rejects.

We conclude that the unique weak PBE in this game is a strategy–beliefs pair with strategies of $(\sigma_{E1}, \sigma_{E2}, \sigma_I) = ((\text{propose joint venture, in if E2 declines}), (\text{accept}), (\text{accommodate if entry occurs}))$ and a belief system of $\mu$ (middle node of incumbent's information set) $= 1$. Note that this is not the only Nash equilibrium or, for that matter, the only SPNE. For example, $(\sigma_{E1}, \sigma_{E2}, \sigma_I) = ((\text{out, out if E2 declines}), (\text{decline}), (\text{fight if entry occurs}))$ is an SPNE in this game. ∎

**Example 9.C.3:** In the games of Examples 9.C.1 and 9.C.2 the trick to identifying the weak PBEs consisted of seeing that some player had an optimal strategy that was independent of her beliefs and/or the future play of her opponents. In the game depicted in Figure 9.C.3, however, this is not so for either player. Firm I is now willing to fight if she thinks that firm E has played "$\text{in}_1$," and the optimal strategy for firm E depends on firm I's behavior (note that $\gamma > -1$).

To solve this game, we look for a *fixed point* at which the behavior generated by beliefs is consistent with these beliefs. We restrict attention to the case where $\gamma > 0$. [Exercise 9.C.2 asks you to determine the set of weak PBEs when $\gamma \in (-1, 0)$.] Let $\sigma_F$ be the probability that firm I fights after entry, let $\mu_1$ be firm I's belief that

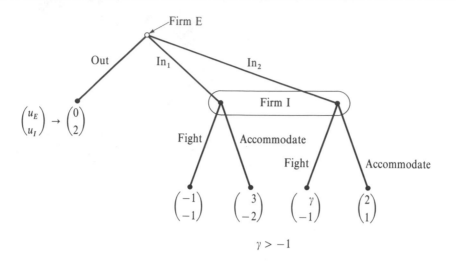

**Figure 9.C.3**

Extensive form for Example 9.C.3.

"$\text{in}_1$" was E's entry strategy if entry has occurred, and let $\sigma_0, \sigma_1, \sigma_2$ denote the probabilities with which firm E actually chooses "out," "$\text{in}_1$," and "$\text{in}_2$," respectively.

Note, first, that firm I is willing to play "fight" with positive probability if and only if $-1 \geq -2\mu_1 + 1(1 - \mu_1)$, or $\mu_1 \geq \frac{2}{3}$.

Suppose, first, that $\mu_1 > \frac{2}{3}$ in a weak PBE. Then firm I must be playing "fight" with probability 1. But then firm E must be playing "$\text{in}_2$" with probability 1 (since $\gamma > 0$), and the weak PBE concept would then require that $\mu_1 = 0$, which is a contradiction.

Suppose, instead, that $\mu_1 < \frac{2}{3}$ in a weak PBE. Then firm I must be playing "accommodate" with probability 1. But, if so, then firm E must be playing "$\text{in}_1$" with probability 1, and the weak PBE concept then requires that $\mu_1 = 1$, another contradiction.

Hence, in any weak PBE of this game, we must have $\mu_1 = \frac{2}{3}$. If so, then firm E must be randomizing in the equilibrium with positive probabilities attached to both "$\text{in}_1$" and "$\text{in}_2$" and with "$\text{in}_1$" twice as likely as "$\text{in}_2$." This means that firm I's probability of playing "fight" must make firm E indifferent between "$\text{in}_1$" and "$\text{in}_2$." Hence, we must have $-1\sigma_F + 3(1 - \sigma_F) = \gamma\sigma_F + 2(1 - \sigma_F)$, or $\sigma_F = 1/(\gamma + 2)$. Firm E's payoff from playing "$\text{in}_1$" or "$\text{in}_2$" is then $(3\gamma + 2)/(\gamma + 2) > 0$, and so firm E must play "out" with zero probability. Therefore, the unique weak PBE in this game when $\gamma > 0$ has $(\sigma_0, \sigma_1, \sigma_2) = (0, \frac{2}{3}, \frac{1}{3})$, $\sigma_F = 1/(\gamma + 2)$, and $\mu_1 = \frac{2}{3}$. ∎

### Strengthenings of the Weak Perfect Bayesian Equilibrium Concept

We have referred to the concept defined in Definition 9.C.3 as a *weak* perfect Bayesian equilibrium because the consistency requirements that it puts on beliefs are very minimal: The *only* requirement for beliefs, other than that they specify nonnegative probabilities which add to 1 within each information set, is that they are consistent with the equilibrium strategies on the equilibrium path, in the sense of being derived from them through Bayes' rule. *No restrictions at all are placed on beliefs off the equilibrium path* (i.e., at information sets not reached with positive probability with play of the equilibrium strategies). In the literature, a number of strengthenings of this concept that put additional consistency restrictions on off-the-equilibrium-path

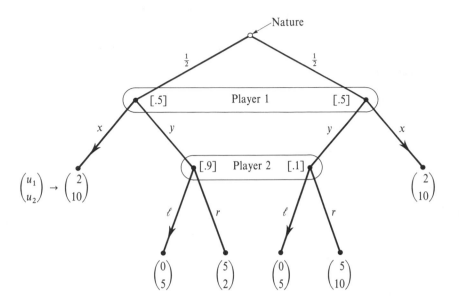

**Figure 9.C.4**

Extensive form for Example 9.C.4. Beliefs in a weak PBE may not be structurally consistent.

beliefs are used. Examples 9.C.4 and 9.C.5 illustrate why a strengthening of the weak PBE concept is often needed.

**Example 9.C.4:** Consider the game shown in Figure 9.C.4. The pure strategies and beliefs depicted in the figure constitute a weak PBE (the strategies are indicated by arrows on the chosen branches at each information set, and beliefs are indicated by numbers in brackets at the nodes in the information sets). The beliefs satisfy criterion (ii) of Definition 9.C.3; only player 1's information set is reached with positive probability, and player 1's beliefs there do reflect the probabilities assigned by nature. But the beliefs specified for player 2 in this equilibrium are not very sensible; player 2's information set can be reached only if player 1 deviates by instead choosing action $y$ with positive probability, a deviation that must be independent of nature's actual move, since player 1 is ignorant of it. Hence, player 2 could reasonably have only beliefs that assign an equal probability to the two nodes in her information set. Here we see that it is desirable to require that beliefs at least be "structurally consistent" off the equilibrium path in the sense that there is *some* subjective probability distribution over strategy profiles that could generate probabilities consistent with the beliefs. ■

**Example 9.C.5:** A second and more significant problem is that a weak perfect Bayesian equilibrium need not be subgame perfect. To see this, consider again the entry game in Example 9.B.3. One weak PBE of this game involves strategies of $(\sigma_E, \sigma_I) = ((\text{out, accommodate if in}), (\text{fight if firm E plays "in"}))$ combined with beliefs for firm I that assign probability 1 to firm E having played "fight." This weak PBE is shown in Figure 9.C.5. But note that these strategies are not subgame perfect; they do not specify a Nash equilibrium in the post-entry subgame.

The problem is that firm I's post-entry belief about firm E's post-entry play is unrestricted by the weak PBE concept because firm I's information set is off the equilibrium path. ■

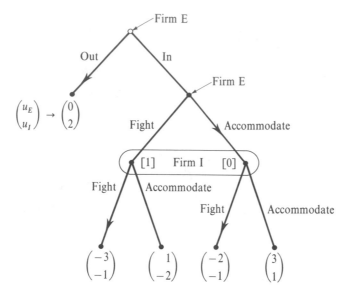

**Figure 9.C.5**

Extensive form for Example 9.C.5. A weak PBE may not be subgame perfect.

These two examples indicate that the weak PBE concept can be too weak. Thus, in applications in the literature, extra consistency restrictions on beliefs are often added to the weak PBE concept to avoid these problems, with the resulting solution concept referred to as a *perfect Bayesian equilibrium*. (As a simple example, restricting attention to equilibria that induce a weak PBE in every subgame insures subgame perfection.) We shall also do this when necessary later in the book; see, in particular, the discussion of signaling in Section 13.C. For formal definitions and discussion of some notions of perfect Bayesian equilibrium, see Fudenberg and Tirole (1991a) and (1991b).

An important closely related equilibrium notion that also strengthens the weak PBE concept by embodying additional consistency restrictions on beliefs is the *sequential equilibrium* concept developed by Kreps and Wilson (1982). In contrast to notions of perfect Bayesian equilibrium (such as the one we develop in Section 13.C), the sequential equilibrium concept introduces these consistency restrictions indirectly through the formalism of a limiting sequence of strategies. Definition 9.C.4 describes its requirements.

**Definition 9.C.4:** A strategy profile and system of beliefs $(\sigma, \mu)$ is a *sequential equilibrium* of extensive form game $\Gamma_E$ if it has the following properties:

(i) Strategy profile $\sigma$ is sequentially rational given belief system $\mu$.

(ii) There exists a sequence of completely mixed strategies $\{\sigma^k\}_{k=1}^{\infty}$, with $\lim_{k \to \infty} \sigma^k = \sigma$, such that $\mu = \lim_{k \to \infty} \mu^k$, where $\mu^k$ denotes the beliefs derived from strategy profile $\sigma^k$ using Bayes' rule.

In essence, the sequential equilibrium notion requires that beliefs be justifiable as coming from some set of totally mixed strategies that are "close to" the equilibrium strategies $\sigma$ (i.e., a small perturbation of the equilibrium strategies). This can be viewed as requiring that players can (approximately) justify their beliefs by some story in which, with some small probability, players make mistakes in choosing their strategies. Note that every sequential equilibrium is a weak perfect Bayesian equilibrium because the limiting beliefs in Definition 9.C.4 exactly coincide with the beliefs derived from the equilibrium strategies $\sigma$ via Bayes' rule on the outcome path of strategy profile $\sigma$. But, in general, the reverse is not true.

As we now show, the sequential equilibrium concept strengthens the weak perfect Bayesian equilibrium concept in a manner that avoids the problems identified in Examples 9.C.4 and 9.C.5.

**Example 9.C.4 Continued:** Consider again the game in Figure 9.C.4. In this game, all beliefs that can be derived from any sequence of totally mixed strategies assign equal probability to the two nodes in player 2's information set. Given this fact, in any sequential equilibrium player 2 must play $r$ and player 1 must therefore play $y$. In fact, strategies $(y, r)$ and beliefs giving equal probability to the two nodes in both players' information sets constitute the unique sequential equilibrium of this game. ∎

**Example 9.C.5 Continued:** The unique sequential equilibrium strategies in the game in Example 9.C.5 (see Figure 9.C.5) are those of the unique SPNE: ((in, accommodate if in), (accommodate if firm E plays "in")). To verify this point, consider any totally mixed strategy $\bar{\sigma}$ and any node $x$ in firm I's information set, which we denote by $H_I$. Letting $z$ denote firm E's decision node following entry (the initial node of the subgame following entry), the beliefs $\mu_{\bar{\sigma}}$ associated with $\bar{\sigma}$ at information set $H_I$ are equal to

$$\mu_{\bar{\sigma}}(x) = \frac{\text{Prob}(x \mid \bar{\sigma})}{\text{Prob}(H_I \mid \bar{\sigma})} = \frac{\text{Prob}(x \mid z, \bar{\sigma})\,\text{Prob}(z \mid \bar{\sigma})}{\text{Prob}(H_I \mid z, \bar{\sigma})\,\text{Prob}(z \mid \bar{\sigma})},$$

where $\text{Prob}(x \mid z, \bar{\sigma})$ is the probability of reaching node $x$ under strategies $\bar{\sigma}$ conditional on having reached node $z$. Canceling terms and noting that $\text{Prob}(H_I \mid z, \bar{\sigma}) = 1$, we then have $\mu_{\bar{\sigma}}(x) = \text{Prob}(x \mid z, \bar{\sigma})$. But this is exactly the probability that firm E plays the action that leads to node $x$ in strategy $\bar{\sigma}$. Thus, any sequence of totally mixed strategies $\{\bar{\sigma}^k\}_{k=1}^{\infty}$ that converge to $\sigma$ must generate limiting beliefs for firm I that coincide with the play at node $z$ specified in firm E's actual strategy $\sigma_E$. It is then immediate that the strategies in any sequential equilibrium must specify Nash equilibrium behavior in this post-entry subgame and thus must constitute a subgame perfect Nash equilbrium. ∎

Proposition 9.C.2 gives a general result on the relation between sequential equilibria and subgame perfect Nash equilibria.

**Proposition 9.C.2:** In every sequential equilibrium $(\sigma, \mu)$ of an extensive form game $\Gamma_E$, the equilibrium strategy profile $\sigma$ constitutes a subgame perfect Nash equilibrium of $\Gamma_E$.

Thus, the sequential equilibrium concept strengthens both the SPNE and the weak PBE concepts; every sequential equilibrium is both a weak PBE and an SPNE.

Although the concept of sequential equilibrium restricts beliefs that are off the equilibrium path enough to take care of the problems with the weak PBE concept illustrated in Examples 9.C.4 and 9.C.5, there are some ways in which the requirements on off-equilibrium-path beliefs embodied in the notion of sequential equilibrium may be too strong. For example, they imply that any two players with the same information must have exactly the same beliefs regarding the deviations by other players that have caused play to reach a given part of the game tree.

In Appendix B, we briefly describe another related (and still stronger) solution concept, an *extensive form trembling-hand perfect Nash equilibrium*, first proposed by Selten (1975).[14]

# 9.D   Reasonable Beliefs and Forward Induction

In Section 9.C, we saw the importance of beliefs at unreached information sets for testing the sequential rationality of a strategy. Although the weak perfect Bayesian equilibrium concept and the related stronger concepts discussed in Section 9.C can help rule out noncredible threats, in many games we can nonetheless justify a large range of off-equilibrium-path behavior by picking off-equilibrium-path beliefs appropriately (we shall see some examples shortly). This has led to a considerable amount of recent research aimed at specifying additional restrictions that "reasonable" beliefs should satisfy. In this section, we provide a brief introduction to these ideas. (We shall encounter them again when we study signaling models in Chapter 13, particularly in Appendix A of that chapter.)

To start, consider the two games depicted in Figure 9.D.1. The first is a variant of the entry game of Figure 9.C.1 in which firm I would now find it worthwhile to fight if it knew that the entrant chose strategy "in$_1$"; the second is a variant of the Niche Choice game of Example 9.B.4, in which firm E now targets a niche at the time of its entry. Also shown in each diagram is a weak perfect Bayesian equilibrium (arrows denote pure strategy choices, and the numbers in brackets in firm I's information set denote beliefs).

One can argue that in neither game is the equilibrium depicted very sensible.[15] Consider the game in Figure 9.D.1(a). In the weak PBE depicted, if entry occurs, firm I plays "fight" because it believes that firm E has chosen "in$_1$." But "in$_1$" is strictly dominated for firm E by "in$_2$." Hence, it seems reasonable to think that if firm E decided to enter, it must have used strategy "in$_2$." Indeed, as is commonly done in this literature, one can imagine firm E making the following speech upon entering: "I have entered, but notice that I would never have used 'in$_1$' to do so because 'in$_2$' is always a better entry strategy for me. Think about this carefully before you choose your strategy."

A similar argument holds for the weak PBE depicted in Figure 9.D.1(b). Here "small niche" is strictly dominated for firm E, not by "large niche", but by "out." Once again, firm I could not reasonably hold the beliefs that are depicted. In this case, firm I should recognize that if firm E entered rather than playing "out," it must have chosen the large niche. Now you can imagine firm E saying: "Notice that the only way I could ever do better by entering than by choosing 'out' is by targeting the large niche."

---

14. Selten actually gave it the name *trembling-hand perfect Nash equilibrium*; we add the modifier *extensive form* to help distinguish it from the normal form concept introduced in Section 8.F.

15. For simplicity, we focus on weak perfect Bayesian equilibria here. The points to be made apply as well to the stronger related notions discussed in Section 9.C. In fact, all the weak perfect Bayesian equilibria discussed here are also sequential equilibria; indeed, they are even extensive form trembling-hand perfect.

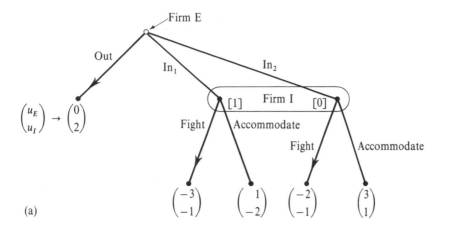

(a)

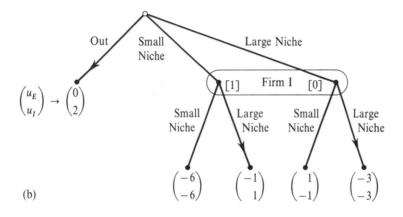

(b)

**Figure 9.D.1**
Two weak PBEs with
unreasonable beliefs.

These arguments make use of what is known as *forward induction* reasoning [see Kohlberg (1989) and Kohlberg and Mertens (1986)]. In using backward induction, a player decides what is an optimal action for her at some point in the game tree based on her calculations of the actions that her opponents will rationally play at *later* points of the game. In contrast, in using forward induction, a player reasons about what could have rationally happened *previously*. For example, here firm I decides on its optimal post-entry action by assuming that firm E must have behaved rationally in its entry decision.

This type of idea is sometimes extended to include arguments based on *equilibrium domination*. For example, suppose that we augment the game in Figure 9.D.1(b) by also giving firm I a move after firm E plays "out," as depicted in Figure 9.D.2 (perhaps "out" really involves entry into some alternative market of firm I's in which firm E has only one potential entry strategy).

The figure depicts a weak PBE of this game in which firm E plays "out" and firm I believes that firm E has chosen "small niche" whenever its post-entry information set is reached. In this game, "small niche" is no longer strictly dominated for firm E by "out," so our previous argument does not apply. Nevertheless, if firm E deviates from this equilibrium by entering, we can imagine firm I thinking that since firm E could have received a payoff of 0 by following its equilibrium strategy, it must be hoping to do better than that by entering, and so it must

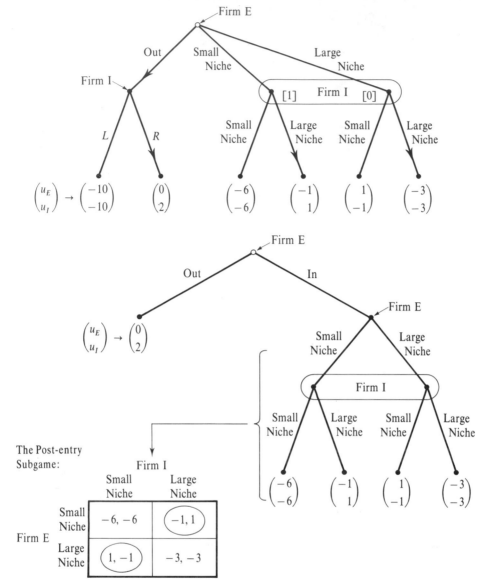

**Figure 9.D.2**

Strategy "small niche" is equilibrium dominated for firm E.

**Figure 9.D.3**

Forward induction selects equilibrium (large niche, small niche) in the post-entry subgame.

have chosen to target the large niche. In this case, we say that "small niche" is *equilibrium dominated* for firm E; that is, it is dominated if firm E treats its equilibrium payoff as something that it can achieve with certainty by following its equilibrium strategy. (This type of argument is embodied in the *intuitive criterion* refinement that we discuss in Section 13.C and Appendix A of Chapter 13 in the context of signaling models.)

Forward induction can be quite powerful. For example, reconsider the original Niche Choice game depicted in Figure 9.D.3. Recall that there are two (pure strategy) Nash equilibria in the post-entry subgame: (large niche, small niche) and (small niche, large niche). However, the force of the forward induction argument for the game in Figure 9.D.1(b) seems to apply equally well here: Strategy (in, small niche if in) is strictly dominated for firm E by playing "out." As a result, the incumbent should reason that if firm E has played "in," it intends to target the large niche in the post-entry game. If so, firm I is better off targeting the small niche. Thus, forward induction rules out one of the two Nash equilibria in the post-entry subgame.

Although these arguments may seem very appealing, there are also some potential problems. For example, suppose that we are in a world where players make mistakes with some small probability. In such a world, are the forward induction arguments just given convincing? Perhaps not. To see why, suppose that firm E enters in the game shown in Figure 9.D.1(a) when it was supposed to play "out." Now firm I can explain the deviation to itself as being the result of a mistake on firm E's part, a mistake that might equally well have led firm E to pick "in$_1$" as "in$_2$." And firm E's speech may not fall on very sympathetic ears: "Of course, firm E is telling me this," reasons the incumbent, "it has made a mistake and now is trying to make the best of it by convincing me to accommodate."

To see this in an even more striking manner, consider the game in Figure 9.D.3. Now, after firm E has entered and the two firms are about to play the simultaneous-move post-entry game, firm E makes its speech. But the incumbent retorts: "Forget it! I think you just made a mistake—and even if you did not, I'm going to target the large niche!"

Clearly, the issues here, although interesting and important, are also tricky.

---

A noticeable feature of these forward induction arguments is how they use the normal form notion of dominance to restrict predicted play in dynamic games. This stands in sharp contrast with our discussion earlier in this chapter, which relied exclusively on the extensive form to determine how players should play in dynamic games. This raises a natural question: Can we somehow use the normal form representation to predict play in dynamic games?

There are at least two reasons why we might think we can. First, as we discussed in Chapter 7, it seems appealing as a matter of logic to think that players simultaneously choosing their strategies in the normal form (e.g., submitting contingent plans to a referee) is equivalent to their actually playing out the game dynamically as represented in the extensive form. Second, in many circumstances, it seems that the notion of weak dominance can get at the idea of sequential rationality. For example, for finite games of perfect information in which no player has equal payoffs at any two terminal nodes, any strategy profile surviving a process of iterated deletion of weakly dominated strategies leads to the same predicted outcome as the SPNE concept (take a look at Example 9.B.1, and see Exercise 9.D.1).

The argument for using the normal form is also bolstered by the fact that extensive form concepts such as weak PBE can be sensitive to what may seem like irrelevant changes in the extensive form. For example, by breaking up firm E's decision in the game in Figure 9.D.1(a) into an "out" or "in" decision followed by an "in$_1$" or "in$_2$" decision [just as we did in Figure 9.D.3 for the game in Figure 9.D.1(b)], the unique SPNE (and, hence, the unique sequential equilibrium) becomes firm E entering and playing "in$_2$" and firm I accommodating. However, the reduced normal form associated with these two games (i.e., the normal form where we eliminate all but one of a player's strategies that have identical payoffs) is invariant to this change in the extensive form; therefore, any solution based on the (reduced) normal form would be unaffected by this change.

These points have led to a renewed interest in the use of the normal form as a device for predicting play in dynamic games [see, in particular, Kohlberg and Mertens (1986)]. At the same time, this issue remains controversial. Many game theorists believe that there is a loss of some information of strategic importance in going from the extensive form to the more condensed normal form. For example, are the games in Figures 9.D.3 and 9.D.1(b) really the same? If you were firm I, would you be as likely to rely on the forward induction argument in the game in Figure 9.D.3 as in that in Figure 9.D.1(b)? Does it matter for your answer whether in the game in Figure 9.D.3 a minute or a month passes between firm E's two decisions? These issues remain to be sorted out.

## APPENDIX A: FINITE AND INFINITE HORIZON BILATERAL BARGAINING

In this appendix we study two models of bilateral bargaining as an economically important example of the use of the subgame perfect Nash equilibrium concept. We begin by studying a finite horizon model of bargaining and then consider its infinite horizon counterpart.

**Example 9.AA.1:** *Finite Horizon Bilateral Bargaining.* Two players, 1 and 2, bargain to determine the split of $v$ dollars. The rules are as follows: The game begins in period 1; in period 1, player 1 makes an offer of a split (a real number between 0 and $v$) to player 2, which player 2 may then accept or reject. If she accepts, the proposed split is immediately implemented and the game ends. If she rejects, nothing happens until period 2. In period 2, the players' roles are reversed, with player 2 making an offer to player 1 and player 1 then being able to accept or reject it. Each player has a discount factor of $\delta \in (0, 1)$, so that a dollar received in period $t$ is worth $\delta^{t-1}$ in period 1 dollars. However, after some finite number of periods $T$, if an agreement has not yet been reached, the bargaining is terminated and the players each receive nothing. A portion of the extensive form of this game is depicted in Figure 9.AA.1 [this model is due to Stahl (1972)].

There is a unique subgame perfect Nash equilibrium (SPNE) in this game. To see this, suppose first that $T$ is odd, so that player 1 makes the offer in period $T$ if no previous agreement has been reached. Now, player 2 is willing to accept *any* offer in this period because she will get zero if she refuses and the game is terminated (she is indifferent about accepting an offer of zero). Given this fact, the unique SPNE in the subgame that begins in the final period when no agreement has been previously reached has player 1 offer player 2 zero and player 2 accept.[16] Therefore, the payoffs from equilibrium play in this subgame are $(\delta^{T-1}v, 0)$.

Now consider play in the subgame starting in period $T - 1$ when no previous agreement has been reached. Player 2 makes the offer in this period. In any SPNE, player 1 will accept an offer in period $T - 1$ if and only if it provides her with a payoff of at least $\delta^{T-1}v$, since otherwise she will do better rejecting it and waiting to make an offer in period $T$ (she earns $\delta^{T-1}v$ by doing so). Given this fact, in any SPNE, player 2 must make an offer in period $T - 1$ that gives player 1 a payoff of exactly $\delta^{T-1}v$, and player 1 accepts this offer (note that this is player 2's best offer

---

16. Note that if player 2 is unwilling to accept an offer of zero, then player 1 has no optimal strategy; she wants to make a strictly positive offer ever closer to zero (since player 1 will accept any strictly positive offer). If the reliance on player 1 accepting an offer over which she is indifferent bothers you, you can convince yourself that the analysis of the game in which offers must be in small increments (pennies) yields exactly the same outcome as that identified in the text as the size of these increments goes to zero.

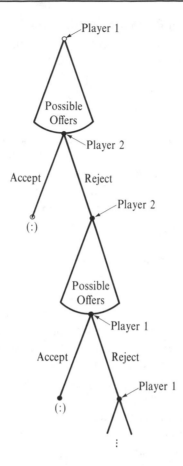

**Figure 9.AA.1**

The alternating-offer bilateral bargaining game.

among all those that would be accepted, and making an offer that will be rejected is worse for player 2 because it results in her receiving a payoff of zero). The payoffs arising if the game reaches period $T - 1$ must therefore be $(\delta^{T-1}v, \delta^{T-2}v - \delta^{T-1}v)$.

Continuing in this fashion, we can determine that the unique SPNE when $T$ is odd results in an agreement being reached in period 1, a payoff for player 1 of

$$v_1^*(T) = v[1 - \delta + \delta^2 - \cdots + \delta^{T-1}]$$
$$= v\left[(1 - \delta)\left(\frac{1 - \delta^{T-1}}{1 - \delta^2}\right) + \delta^{T-1}\right],$$

and a payoff to player 2 of $v_2^*(T) = v - v_1^*(T)$.

If $T$ is instead even, then player 1 must earn $v - \delta v_1^*(T - 1)$ because in any SPNE, player 2 (who will be the first offerer in the odd-number-of-periods subgame that begins in period 2 if she rejects player 1's period 1 offer) will accept an offer in period 1 if and only if it gives her at least $\delta v_1^*(T - 1)$, and player 1 will offer her exactly this amount.

Finally, note that as the number of periods grows large ($T \to \infty$), player 1's payoff converges to $v/(1 + \delta)$, and player 2's payoff converges to $\delta v/(1 + \delta)$. ■

In Example 9.AA.1, the application of the SPNE concept was relatively straightforward; we simply needed to start at the end of the game and work backward. We now consider the infinite horizon counterpart of this game. As we noted in Section

9.B, we can no longer solve for the SPNE in this simple manner when the game has an infinite horizon. Moreover, in many games, introduction of an infinite horizon allows a broad range of behavior to emerge as subgame perfect. Nevertheless, in the infinite horizon bargaining model, the SPNE concept is quite powerful. There is a unique SPNE in this game, and it turns out to be exactly the limiting outcome of the finite horizon model as the length of the horizon $T$ approaches $\infty$.

**Example 9.AA.2:** *Infinite Horizon Bilateral Bargaining.* Consider an extension of the finite horizon bargaining game considered in Example 9.AA.1 in which bargaining is no longer terminated after $T$ rounds but, rather, can potentially go on forever. If this happens, the players both earn zero. This model is due to Rubinstein (1982).

We claim that this game has a unique SPNE. In this equilibrium, the players reach an immediate agreement in period 1, with player 1 earning $v/(1 + \delta)$ and player 2 earning $\delta v/(1 + \delta)$.

The method of analysis we use here, following Shaked and Sutton (1984), makes heavy use of the stationarity of the game (the subgame starting in period 2 looks exactly like that in period 1, but with the players' roles reversed).

To start, let $\bar{v}_1$ denote the largest payoff that player 1 gets in *any* SPNE (i.e., there may, in principle, be multiple SPNEs in this model).[17] Given the stationarity of the model, this is also the largest amount that player 2 can expect in the subgame that begins in period 2 after her rejection of player 1's period 1 offer, a subgame in which player 2 has the role of being the first player to make an offer. As a result, player 1's payoff in any SPNE cannot be lower than the amount $\underline{v}_1 = v - \delta\bar{v}_1$ because, if it was, then player 1 could do better by making a period 1 offer that gives player 2 just slightly more than $\delta\bar{v}_1$. Player 2 is certain to accept any such offer because she will earn only $\delta\bar{v}_1$ by rejecting it (note that we are using subgame perfection here, because we are requiring that the continuation of play after rejection is an SPNE in the continuation subgame and that player 2's response will be optimal given this fact).

Next, we claim that, in any SPNE, $\bar{v}_1$ cannot be larger than $v - \delta\underline{v}_1$. To see this, note that in any SPNE, player 2 is certain to reject any offer in period 1 that gives her less than $\delta\underline{v}_1$ because she can earn at least $\delta\underline{v}_1$ by rejecting it and waiting to make an offer in period 2. Thus, player 1 can do no better than $v - \delta\underline{v}_1$ by making an offer that is accepted in period 1. What about by making an offer that is rejected in period 1? Since player 2 must earn at least $\delta\underline{v}_1$ if this happens, and since agreement cannot occur before period 2, player 1 can earn no more than $\delta v - \delta\underline{v}_1$ by doing this. Hence, we have $\bar{v}_1 \leq v - \delta\underline{v}_1$.

Next, note that these derivations imply that

$$\bar{v}_1 \leq v - \delta\underline{v}_1 = (\underline{v}_1 + \delta\bar{v}_1) - \delta\underline{v}_1,$$

so that

$$\bar{v}_1(1 - \delta) \leq \underline{v}_1(1 - \delta).$$

Given the definitions of $\underline{v}_1$ and $\bar{v}_1$, this implies that $\underline{v}_1 = \bar{v}_1$, and so player 1's SPNE payoff is uniquely determined. Denote this payoff by $v_1^\circ$. Since $v_1^\circ = v - \delta v_1^\circ$, we find that player 1 must earn $v_1^\circ = v/(1 + \delta)$ and player 2 must earn $v_2^\circ = v - v_1^\circ = \delta v/(1 + \delta)$. In addition, recalling the argument in the previous paragraph, we see

---

17. This maximum can be shown to be well defined, but we will not do so here.

that an agreement will be reached in the first period (player 1 will find it worthwhile to make an offer that player 2 accepts). The SPNE strategies are as follows: A player who has just received an offer accepts it if and only if she is offered at least $\delta v_1^\circ$, while a player whose turn it is to make an offer offers exactly $\delta v_1^\circ$ to the player receiving the offer.

Note that the equilibrium strategies, outcome, and payoffs are precisely the limit of those in the finite game in Example 9.AA.1 as $T \to \infty$. ∎

The coincidence of the infinite horizon equilibrium with the limit of the finite horizon equilibria in this model is not a general property of infinite horizon games. The discussion of infinitely repeated games in Chapter 12 provides an illustration of this point.

We should also point out that the outcomes of game-theoretic models of bargaining can be quite sensitive to the precise specification of the bargaining process and players' preferences. Exercises 9.B.7 and 9.B.13 provide an illustration.

## APPENDIX B: EXTENSIVE FORM TREMBLING-HAND PERFECT NASH EQUILIBRIUM

In this appendix we extend the analysis presented in Section 9.C by discussing another equilibrium notion that strengthens the consistency conditions on beliefs in the weak PBE concept: *extensive form trembling-hand perfect Nash equilibrium* [due to Selten (1975)]. In fact, this equilibrium concept is the strongest among those discussed in Section 9.C.

The definition of an extensive form trembling-hand perfect Nash equilibrium parallels that for the normal form (see Section 8.F) but has the trembles applied not to a player's mixed strategies, but rather to the player's choice at each of her information sets. A useful way to view this idea is with what Selten (1975) calls the *agent normal form*. This is the normal form that we would derive if we pretended that the player had a set of agents in charge of moving for her at each of her information sets (a different one for each), each acting independently to try to maximize the player's payoff.

**Definition 9.BB.1:** Strategy profile $\sigma$ in extensive form game $\Gamma_E$ is an *extensive form trembling-hand perfect Nash equilibrium* if and only if it is a normal form trembling-hand perfect Nash equilibrium of the agent normal form derived from $\Gamma_E$.

To see why it is desirable to have the trembles occurring at each information set rather than over strategies as in the normal-form concept considered in Section 8.F, consider Figure 9.BB.1, which is taken from van Damme (1983). This game has a unique subgame perfect Nash equilibrium: $(\sigma_1, \sigma_2) = ((NR, L), \ell)$. But you can check that $((NR, L), \ell)$ is not the only normal form trembling-hand perfect Nash equilibrium: so are $((R, L), r)$ and $((R, M), r)$. The reason that these two strategy profiles are normal form trembling-hand perfect is that, in the normal form, the tremble to strategy $(NR, M)$ by player 1 can be larger than that to $(NR, L)$ despite the fact that the latter is a better choice for player 1 at her second decision node.

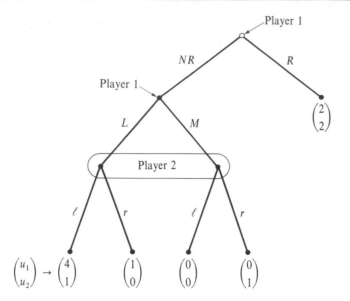

**Figure 9.BB.1**

Strategy profiles
$((R, L), r)$ and
$((R, M), r)$ are normal
form trembling-hand
perfect but are not
subgame perfect.

With such a tremble, player 2's best response to player 1's perturbed strategy is $r$. It is not difficult to see, however, that the unique extensive form trembling-hand perfect Nash equilibrium of this game is $((NR, L), \ell)$ because the agent who moves at player 1's second decision node will put as high a probability as possible on $L$.

When we compare Definitions 9.BB.1 and 9.C.4, it is apparent that every extensive form trembling-hand perfect Nash equilibrium is a sequential equilibrium. In particular, even though the trembling-hand perfection criterion is not formulated in terms of beliefs, we can use the sequence of (strictly mixed) equilibrium strategies $\{\sigma^k\}_{k=1}^\infty$ in the perturbed games of the agent normal form as our strategy sequence for deriving sequential equilibrium beliefs. Because the limiting strategies $\sigma$ in the extensive form trembling-hand perfect equilibrium are best responses to every element of this sequence, they are also best responses to each other with these derived beliefs. (Every extensive form trembling-hand perfect Nash equilibrium is therefore also subgame perfect.)

In essence, by introducing trembles, the extensive form trembling-hand perfect equilibrium notion makes every part of the tree be reached when strategies are perturbed, and because equilibrium strategies are required to be best responses to perturbed strategies, it insures that equilibrium strategies are sequentially rational. The primary difference between this notion and that of sequential equilibrium is that, like its normal form cousin, the extensive form trembling-hand perfect equilibrium concept can also eliminate some sequential equilibria in which weakly dominated strategies are played. Figure 9.BB.2 (a slight modification of the game in Figure 9.C.1) depicts a sequential equilibrium whose strategies are not extensive form trembling-hand perfect.

In general, however, the concepts are quite close [see Kreps and Wilson (1982) for a formal comparison]; and because it is much easier to check that strategies are best responses at the limiting beliefs than it is to check that they are best responses for a sequence of strategies, sequential equilibrium is much more commonly used. For an interesting further discussion of this concept, consult van Damme (1983).

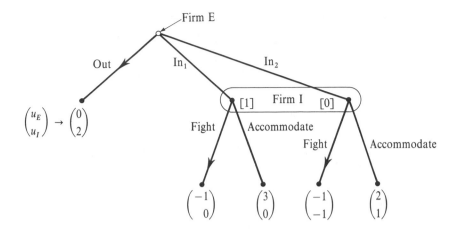

**Figure 9.BB.2**

A sequential equilibrium need not be extensive form trembling-hand perfect.

## REFERENCES

Bernheim, B. D. (1984). Rationalizable strategic behavior. *Econometrica* **52**: 1007–28.

DeGroot, M. H. (1970). *Optimal Statistical Decisions.* New York: McGraw-Hill.

Fudenberg, D., and J. Tirole. (1991a). Perfect Bayesian and sequential equilibrium. *Journal of Economic Theory* **53**: 236–60.

Fudenberg, D., and J. Tirole. (1991b). *Game Theory.* Cambridge, Mass.: MIT Press.

Kohlberg, E. (1989). Refinement of Nash equilibrium: the main ideas. Harvard Business School Working Paper No. 89-073.

Kohlberg, E., and J.-F. Mertens. (1986). On the strategic stability of equilibria. *Econometrica* **54**: 1003–38.

Kreps, D. M., and R. Wilson. (1982). Sequential equilibrium. *Econometrica* **50**: 863–94.

Moulin, H. (1981). *Game Theory for the Social Sciences.* New York: New York University Press.

Myerson, R. (1991). *Game Theory: Analysis of Conflict.* Cambridge, Mass.: Harvard University Press.

Pearce, D. G. (1984). Rationalizable strategic behavior and the problem of perfection. *Econometrica* **52**: 1029–50.

Rosenthal, R. (1981). Games of perfect information, predatory pricing, and the chain-store paradox. *Journal of Economic Theory* **25**: 92–100.

Rubinstein, A. (1982). Perfect equilibrium in a bargaining model. *Econometrica* **50**: 97–109.

Selten, R. (1965). Spieltheoretische behandlung eines oligopolmodells mit nachfragetragheit. *Zeitschrift für die gesamte Staatswissenschaft* **121**: 301–24.

Selten, R. (1975). Re-examination of the perfectness concept for equilibrium points in extensive games. *International Journal of Game Theory* **4**: 25–55.

Shaked, A., and J. Sutton. (1984). Involuntary unemployment as a perfect equilibrium in a bargaining model. *Econometrica* **52**: 1351–64.

Stahl, I. (1972). *Bargaining Theory.* Stockholm: Economics Research Unit.

van Damme, E. (1983). *Refinements of the Nash Equilibrium Concept.* Berlin: Springer-Verlag.

## EXERCISES

**9.B.1**[A] How many subgames are there in the game of Example 9.B.2 (depicted in Figure 9.B.3)?

**9.B.2**[A] In text.

**9.B.3**[B] Verify that the strategies identified through backward induction in Example 9.B.2 constitute a Nash equilibrium of the game studied there. Also, identify *all other* pure strategy Nash equilibria of this game. Argue that each of these other equilibria does not satisfy the principle of sequential rationality.

**9.B.4[B]** Prove that in a finite *zero-sum* game of perfect information, there are unique subgame perfect Nash equilibrium payoffs.

**9.B.5[B]** (E. Maskin) Consider a game with two players, player 1 and player 2, in which each player $i$ can choose an action from a finite set $M_i$ that contains $m_i$ actions. Player $i$'s payoff if the action choices are $(m_1, m_2)$ is $\phi_i(m_1, m_2)$.

**(a)** Suppose, first, that the two players move simultaneously. How many strategies does each player have?

**(b)** Now suppose that player 1 moves first and that player 2 observes player 1's move before choosing her move. How many strategies does each player have?

**(c)** Suppose that the game in **(b)** has multiple SPNEs. Show that if this is the case, then there exist two pairs of moves $(m_1, m_2)$ and $(m'_1, m'_2)$ (where either $m_1 \neq m'_1$ or $m_2 \neq m'_2$) such that either

$$\text{(i)} \quad \phi_1(m_1, m_2) = \phi_1(m'_1, m'_2)$$

or

$$\text{(ii)} \quad \phi_2(m_1, m_2) = \phi_2(m'_1, m'_2).$$

**(d)** Suppose that for any two pairs of moves $(m_1, m_2)$ and $(m'_1, m'_2)$ such that $m_1 \neq m'_1$ or $m_2 \neq m'_2$, condition (ii) is violated (i.e., player 2 is never indifferent between pairs of moves). Suppose also that there exists a pure strategy Nash equilibrium in the game in **(a)** in which $\pi_1$ is player 1's payoff. Show that in any SPNE of the game in **(b)**, player 1's payoff is at least $\pi_1$. Would this conclusion necessarily hold for any *Nash* equilibrium of the game in **(b)**?

**(e)** Show by example that the conclusion in **(d)** may fail either if condition (ii) holds for some strategy pairs $(m_1, m_2)$, $(m'_1, m'_2)$ with $m_1 \neq m'_1$ or $m_2 \neq m'_2$ or if we replace the phrase *pure strategy Nash equilibrium* with the phrase *mixed strategy Nash equilibrium*.

**9.B.6[B]** Solve for the mixed strategy equilibrium involving actual randomization in the post-entry subgame of the Niche Choice game in Example 9.B.4. Is there an SPNE that induces this behavior in the post-entry subgame? What are the SPNE strategies?

**9.B.7[B]** Consider the finite horizon bilateral bargaining game in Appendix A (Example 9.AA.1); but instead of assuming that players discount future payoffs, assume that it costs $c < v$ to make an offer. (Only the player making an offer incurs this cost, and players who have made offers incur this cost even if no agreement is ultimately reached.) What is the (unique) SPNE of this alternative model? What happens as $T$ approaches $\infty$?

**9.B.8[C]** Prove that every (finite) game $\Gamma_E$ has a mixed strategy subgame perfect Nash equilibrium.

**9.B.9[B]** Consider a game in which the following simultaneous-move game is played twice:

|  |  | Player 2 $b_1$ | $b_2$ | $b_3$ |
|---|---|---|---|---|
| | $a_1$ | 10, 10 | 2, 12 | 0, 13 |
| Player 1 | $a_2$ | 12, 2 | 5, 5 | 0, 0 |
| | $a_3$ | 13, 0 | 0, 0 | 1, 1 |

The players observe the actions chosen in the first play of the game prior to the second play. What are the pure strategy subgame perfect Nash equilibria of this game?

**9.B.10$^{\mathbf{B}}$** Reconsider the game in Example 9.B.3, but now change the post-entry game so that when both players choose "accommodate", instead of receiving the payoffs $(u_E, u_I) = (3, 1)$, the players now must play the following simultaneous-move game:

Firm $I$

|  | $\ell$ | $r$ |
|---|---|---|
| $U$ | 3, 1 | 0, 0 |
| $D$ | 0, 0 | $x$, 3 |

Firm $E$ (at rows $U$, $D$)

What are the SPNEs of this game when $x \geq 0$? When $x < 0$?

**9.B.11$^{\mathbf{B}}$** Two firms, A and B, are in a market that is declining in size. The game starts in period 0, and the firms can compete in periods 0, 1, 2, 3, . . . (i.e., indefinitely) if they so choose. Duopoly profits in period $t$ for firm A are equal to $105 - 10t$, and they are $10.5 - t$ for firm B. Monopoly profits (those if a firm is the only one left in the market) are $510 - 25t$ for firm A and $51 - 2t$ for firm B.

Suppose that at the start of each period, each firm must decide either to "stay in" or "exit" if it is still active (they do so simultaneously if both are still active). Once a firm exits, it is out of the market forever and earns zero in each period thereafter. Firms maximize their (undiscounted) sum of profits.

What is this game's subgame perfect Nash equilibrium outcome (and what are the firms' strategies in the equilibrium)?

**9.B.12$^{\mathbf{C}}$** Consider the infinite horizon bilateral bargaining model of Appendix A (Example 9.AA.2). Suppose the discount factors $\delta_1$ and $\delta_2$ of the two players differ. Now what is the (unique) subgame perfect Nash equilibrium?

**9.B.13$^{\mathbf{B}}$** What are the subgame perfect Nash equilibria of the infinite horizon version of Exercise 9.B.7?

**9.B.14$^{\mathbf{B}}$** At time 0, an incumbent firm (firm I) is already in the widget market, and a potential entrant (firm E) is considering entry. In order to enter, firm E must incur a cost of $K > 0$. Firm E's only opportunity to enter is at time 0. There are three production periods. In any period in which both firms are active in the market, the game in Figure 9.Ex.1 is played. Firm E moves first, deciding whether to stay in or exit the market. If it stays in, firm I decides whether to fight (the upper payoff is for firm E). Once firm E plays "out," it is out of

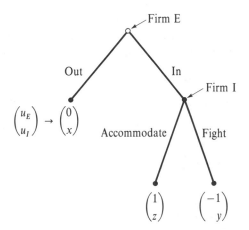

**Figure 9.Ex.1**

the market forever; firm E earns zero in any period during which it is out of the market, and firm I earns $x$. The discount factor for both firms is $\delta$.

Assume that:

(A.1)  $x > z > y$.
(A.2)  $y + \delta x > (1 + \delta)z$.
(A.3)  $1 + \delta > K$.

**(a)** What is the (unique) subgame perfect Nash equilibrium of this game?

**(b)** Suppose now that firm E faces a financial constraint. In particular, if firm I fights *once* against firm E (in any period), firm E will be forced out of the market from that point on. Now what is the (unique) subgame perfect Nash equilibrium of this game? (If the answer depends on the values of parameters beyond the three assumptions, indicate how.)

**9.C.1**[B] Prove Proposition 9.C.1.

**9.C.2**[B] What is the set of weak PBEs in the game in Example 9.C.3 when $\gamma \in (-1, 0)$?

**9.C.3**[C] A buyer and a seller are bargaining. The seller owns an object for which the buyer has value $v > 0$ (the seller's value is zero). This value is known to the buyer but not to the seller. The value's prior distribution is common knowledge. There are two periods of bargaining. The seller makes a take-it-or-leave-it offer (i.e., names a price) at the start of each period that the buyer may accept or reject. The game ends when an offer is accepted or after two periods, whichever comes first. Both players discount period 2 payoffs with a discount factor of $\delta \in (0, 1)$.

Assume throughout that the buyer always accepts the seller's offer whenever she is indifferent.

**(a)** Characterize the (pure strategy) weak perfect Bayesian equilibria for a case in which $v$ can take two values $v_L$ and $v_H$, with $v_H > v_L > 0$, and where $\lambda = \text{Prob}\,(v_H)$.

**(b)** Do the same for the case in which $v$ is uniformly distributed on $[\underline{v}, \bar{v}]$.

**9.C.4**[C] A plaintiff, Ms. P, files a suit against Ms. D (the defendant). If Ms. P wins, she will collect $\pi$ dollars in damages from Ms. D. Ms. D knows the likelihood that Ms. P will win, $\lambda \in [0, 1]$, but Ms. P does not (Ms. D might know if she was actually at fault). They both have strictly positive costs of going to trial of $c_p$ and $c_d$. The prior distribution of $\lambda$ has density $f(\lambda)$ (which is common knowledge).

Suppose pretrial settlement negotiations work as follows: Ms. P makes a take-it-or-leave-it settlement offer (a dollar amount) to Ms. D. If Ms. D accepts, she pays Ms. P and the game is over. If she does not accept, they go to trial.

**(a)** What are the (pure strategy) weak perfect Bayesian equilibria of this game?

**(b)** What effects do changes in $c_p$, $c_d$, and $\pi$ have?

**(c)** Now allow Ms. D, after having her offer rejected, to decide not to go to court after all. What are the weak perfect Bayesian equilibria? What about the effects of the changes in **(b)**?

**9.C.5**[C] Reconsider Exercise 9.C.4. Now suppose it is Ms. P who knows $\lambda$.

**9.C.6**[B] What are the sequential equilibria in the games in Exercises 9.C.3 to 9.C.5?

**9.C.7**[B] (Based on work by K. Bagwell and developed as an exercise by E. Maskin) Consider the extensive form game depicted in Figure 9.Ex.2.

**(a)** Find a subgame perfect Nash equilibrium of this game. Is it unique? Are there any other Nash equilibria?

**(b)** Now suppose that player 2 cannot observe player 1's move. Write down the new extensive form. What is the set of Nash equilibria?

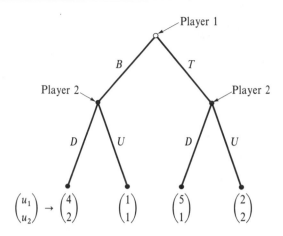

$$\begin{pmatrix} u_1 \\ u_2 \end{pmatrix} \rightarrow \begin{pmatrix} 4 \\ 2 \end{pmatrix} \qquad \begin{pmatrix} 1 \\ 1 \end{pmatrix} \qquad \begin{pmatrix} 5 \\ 1 \end{pmatrix} \qquad \begin{pmatrix} 2 \\ 2 \end{pmatrix}$$

**Figure 9.Ex.2**

**(c)**  Now suppose that player 2 observes player 1's move correctly with probability $p \in (0, 1)$ and incorrectly with probability $1 - p$ (e.g., if player 1 plays $T$, player 2 observes $T$ with probability $p$ and observes $B$ with probability $1 - p$). Suppose that player 2's propensity to observe incorrectly (i.e., given by the value of $p$) is common knowledge to the two players. What is the extensive form now? Show that there is a unique weak perfect Bayesian equilibrium. What is it?

**9.D.1**[B]  Show that under the condition given in Proposition 9.B.2 for existence of a unique subgame perfect Nash equilibrium in a finite game of perfect information, there is an order of iterated removal of weakly dominated strategies for which all surviving strategy profiles lead to the same outcome (i.e., have the same equilibrium path and payoffs) as the subgame perfect Nash equilibrium. [In fact, *any* order of deletion leads to this result; see Moulin (1981).]

# Market Equilibrium and Market Failure

In Part III, our focus shifts to the fundamental issue of economics: *the organization of production and the allocation of the resulting commodities among consumers.* This fundamental issue can be addressed from two perspectives, one *positive* and the other *normative.*

From a positive (or *descriptive*) perspective, we can investigate the determination of production and consumption under various institutional mechanisms. The institutional arrangement that is our central focus is that of a *market* (or *private ownership*) *economy.* In a market economy, individual consumers have ownership rights to various assets (such as their labor) and are free to trade these assets in the market-place for other assets or goods. Likewise, firms, which are themselves owned by consumers, decide on their production plan and trade in the market to secure necessary inputs and sell the resulting outputs. Roughly speaking, we can identify a *market equilibrium* as an outcome of a market economy in which each agent in the economy (i.e., each consumer and firm) is doing as well as he can given the actions of all other agents.

In contrast, from a normative (or *prescriptive*) perspective, we can ask what constitutes a *socially optimal* plan of production and consumption (of course, we will need to be more specific about what "socially optimal" means), and we can then examine the extent to which specific institutions, such as a market economy, perform well in this regard.

In Chapter 10, we study *competitive* (or *perfectly competitive*) *market economies* for the first time. These are market economies in which every relevant good is traded in a market at publicly known prices and all agents act as price takers (recall that much of the analysis of individual behavior in Part I was geared to this case). We begin by defining, in a general way, two key concepts: *competitive* (or *Walrasian*) *equilibrium* and *Pareto optimality* (or *Pareto efficiency*). The concept of competitive equilibrium provides us with an appropriate notion of market equilibrium for competitive market economies. The concept of Pareto optimality offers a minimal and uncontroversial test that any social optimal economic outcome should pass. An economic outcome is said to be Pareto optimal if it is impossible to make some individuals better off without making some other individuals worse off. This concept is a formalization of the idea that there is no waste in society, and it conveniently separates the issue of economic efficiency from more controversial (and political) questions regarding the ideal *distribution* of well-being across individuals.

Chapter 10 then explores these two concepts and the relationships between them in the special context of the *partial equilibrium model*. The partial equilibrium model, which forms the basis for our analysis throughout Part III, offers a considerable analytical simplification; in it, our analysis can be conducted by analyzing a single market (or a small group of related markets) at a time. In this special context, we establish two central results regarding the optimality properties of competitive equilibria, known as the *fundamental theorems of welfare economics*. These can be roughly paraphrased as follows:

> *The First Fundamental Welfare Theorem.* If every relevant good is traded in a market at publicly known prices (i.e., if there is a complete set of markets), and if households and firms act perfectly competitively (i.e., as price takers), then the market outcome is Pareto optimal. That is, when markets are complete, *any competitive equilibrium is necessarily Pareto optimal.*

> *The Second Fundamental Welfare Theorem.* If household preferences and firm production sets are convex, there is a complete set of markets with publicly known prices, and every agent acts as a price taker, then *any Pareto optimal outcome can be achieved as a competitive equilibrium if appropriate lump-sum transfers of wealth are arranged.*

The first welfare theorem provides a set of conditions under which we can be assured that a market economy will achieve a Pareto optimal result; it is, in a sense, the formal expression of Adam Smith's claim about the "invisible hand" of the market. The second welfare theorem goes even further. It states that under the same set of assumptions as the first welfare theorem plus convexity conditions, *all* Pareto optimal outcomes can in principle be implemented through the market mechanism. That is, a public authority who wishes to implement a particular Pareto optimal outcome (reflecting, say, some political consensus on proper distributional goals) may always do so by appropriately redistributing wealth and then "letting the market work."

In an important sense, the first fundamental welfare theorem establishes the perfectly competitive case as a benchmark for thinking about outcomes in market economies. In particular, any inefficiencies that arise in a market economy, and hence any role for Pareto-improving market intervention, *must* be traceable to a violation of at least one of the assumptions of this theorem.

The remainder of Part III, Chapters 11 to 14, can be viewed as a development of this theme. In these chapters, we study a number of ways in which actual markets may depart from this perfectly competitive ideal and where, as a result, market equilibria fail to be Pareto optimal, a situation known as *market failure*.

In Chapter 11, we study *externalities* and *public goods*. In both cases, the actions of one agent directly affect the utility functions or production sets of other agents in the economy. We see there that the presence of these nonmarketed "goods" or "bads" (which violates the complete markets assumption of the first welfare theorem) undermines the Pareto optimality of market equilibrium.

In Chapter 12, we turn to the study of settings in which some agents in the economy have *market power* and, as a result, fail to act as price takers. Once again, an assumption of the first fundamental welfare theorem fails to hold, and market equilibria fail to be Pareto optimal as a result.

In Chapters 13 and 14, we consider situations in which an *asymmetry of information* exists among market participants. The complete markets assumption of the first welfare theorem implicitly requires that the characteristics of traded commodities be observable by all market participants because, without this observability, distinct markets cannot exist for commodities that have different characteristics. Chapter 13 focuses on the case in which asymmetric information exists between agents at the time of contracting. Our discussion highlights several phenomena—*adverse selection*, *signaling*, and *screening*—that can arise as a result of this informational imperfection, and the welfare loss that it causes. Chapter 14 in contrast, investigates the case of postcontractual asymmetric information, a problem that leads us to the study of the *principal-agent model*. Here, too, the presence of asymmetric information prevents trade of all relevant commodities and can lead market outcomes to be Pareto inefficient.

We rely extensively in some places in Part III on the tools that we developed in Parts I and II. This is particularly true in Chapter 10, where we use material developed in Part I, and Chapters 12 and 13, where we use the game-theoretic tools developed in Part II.

A much more complete and general study of competitive market economies and the fundamental welfare theorems is reserved for Part IV.

# 10

# Competitive Markets

## 10.A Introduction

In this chapter, we consider, for the first time, an entire economy in which consumers and firms interact through markets. The chapter has two principal goals: first, to formally introduce and study two key concepts, the notions of *Pareto optimality* and *competitive equilibrium*, and second, to develop a somewhat special but analytically very tractable context for the study of market equilibrium, the *partial equilibrium model*.

We begin in Section 10.B by presenting the notions of a *Pareto optimal* (or *Pareto efficient*) *allocation* and of a *competitive* (or *Walrasian*) *equilibrium* in a general setting.

Starting in Section 10.C, we narrow our focus to the partial equilibrium context. The partial equilibrium approach, which originated in Marshall (1920), envisions the market for a single good (or group of goods) for which each consumer's expenditure constitutes only a small portion of his overall budget. When this is so, it is reasonable to assume that changes in the market for this good will leave the prices of all other commodities approximately unaffected and that there will be, in addition, negligible wealth effects in the market under study. We capture these features in the simplest possible way by considering a two-good model in which the expenditure on all commodities other than that under consideration is treated as a single composite commodity (called the *numeraire* commodity), and in which consumers' utility functions take a quasilinear form with respect to this numeraire. Our study of the competitive equilibria of this simple model lends itself to extensive demand-and-supply graphical analysis. We also discuss how to determine the comparative statics effects that arise from exogenous changes in the market environment. As an illustration, we consider the effects on market equilibrium arising from the introduction of a distortionary commodity tax.

In Section 10.D, we analyze the properties of Pareto optimal allocations in the partial equilibrium model. Most significantly, we establish for this special context the validity of the *fundamental theorems of welfare economics*: Competitive equilibrium allocations are necessarily Pareto optimal, and any Pareto optimal allocation can be achieved as a competitive equilibrium if appropriate lump-sum transfers are made.

As we noted in the introduction to Part III, these results identify an important benchmark case in which market equilibria yield desirable economic outcomes. At the same time, they provide a framework for identifying situations of market failure, such as those we study in Chapters 11 to 14.

In Section 10.E, we consider the measurement of welfare changes in the partial equilibrium context. We show that these can be represented by areas between properly defined demand and supply curves. As an application, we examine the deadweight loss of distortionary taxation.

Section 10.F contemplates settings characterized by *free entry*, that is, settings in which all potential firms have access to the most efficient technology and may enter and exit markets in response to the profit opportunities they present. We define a notion of *long-run competitive equilibrium* and then use it to distinguish between long-run and short-run comparative static effects in response to changes in market conditions.

In Section 10.G, we provide a more extended discussion of the use of partial equilibrium analysis in economic modeling.

The material covered in this chapter traces its roots far back in economic thought. An excellent source for further reading is Stigler (1987). We should emphasize that the analysis of competitive equilibrium and Pareto optimality presented here is very much a first pass. In Part IV we return to the topic for a more complete and general investigation; many additional references will be given there.

# 10.B  Pareto Optimality and Competitive Equilibria

In this section, we introduce and discuss the concepts of *Pareto optimality* (or *Pareto efficiency*) and *competitive* (or *Walrasian*) *equilibrium* in a general setting.

Consider an economy consisting of $I$ consumers (indexed by $i = 1, \ldots, I$), $J$ firms (indexed by $j = 1, \ldots, J$), and $L$ goods (indexed by $\ell = 1, \ldots, L$). Consumer $i$'s preferences over consumption bundles $x_i = (x_{1i}, \ldots, x_{Li})$ in his consumption set $X_i \subset \mathbb{R}^L$ are represented by the utility function $u_i(\cdot)$. The total amount of each good $\ell = 1, \ldots, L$ initially available in the economy, called the total *endowment* of good $\ell$, is denoted by $\omega_\ell \geq 0$ for $\ell = 1, \ldots, L$. It is also possible, using the production technologies of the firms, to transform some of the initial endowment of a good into additional amounts of other goods. Each firm $j$ has available to it the production possibilities summarized by the production set $Y_j \subset \mathbb{R}^L$. An element of $Y_j$ is a production vector $y_j = (y_{1j}, \ldots, y_{Lj}) \in \mathbb{R}^L$. Thus, if $(y_1, \ldots, y_J) \in \mathbb{R}^{LJ}$ are the production vectors of the $J$ firms, the total (net) amount of good $\ell$ available to the economy is $\omega_\ell + \sum_j y_{\ell j}$ (recall that negative entries in a production vector denote input usage; see Section 5.B).

We begin with Definition 10.B.1, which identifies the set of possible outcomes in this economy:

**Definition 10.B.1:** An *economic allocation* $(x_1, \ldots, x_I, y_1, \ldots, y_J)$ is a specification of a consumption vector $x_i \in X_i$ for each consumer $i = 1, \ldots, I$ and a production vector $y_j \in Y_j$ for each firm $j = 1, \ldots, J$. The allocation $(x_1, \ldots, x_I, y_1, \ldots, y_J)$ is *feasible* if

$$\sum_{i=1}^{I} x_{\ell i} \leq \omega_\ell + \sum_{j=1}^{J} y_{\ell j} \quad \text{for } \ell = 1, \ldots, L.$$

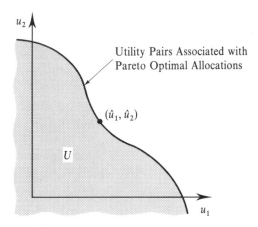

**Figure 10.B.1**
A utility possibility set.

Thus, an economic allocation is feasible if the total amount of each good consumed does not exceed the total amount available from both the initial endowment and production.

### Pareto Optimality

It is often of interest to ask whether an economic system is producing an "optimal" economic outcome. An essential requirement for any optimal economic allocation is that it possess the property of *Pareto optimality* (or *Pareto efficiency*).

**Definition 10.B.2:** A feasible allocation $(x_1, \ldots, x_I, y_1, \ldots, y_J)$ is *Pareto optimal* (or *Pareto efficient*) if there is no other feasible allocation $(x'_1, \ldots, x'_I, y'_1, \ldots, y'_J)$ such that $u_i(x'_i) \geq u_i(x_i)$ for all $i = 1, \ldots, I$ and $u_i(x'_i) > u_i(x_i)$ for some $i$.

An allocation that is Pareto optimal uses society's initial resources and technological possibilities efficiently in the sense that there is no alternative way to organize the production and distribution of goods that makes some consumer better off without making some other consumer worse off.

Figure 10.B.1 illustrates the concept of Pareto optimality. There we depict the set of attainable utility levels in a two-consumer economy. This set is known as a *utility possibility set* and is defined in this two-consumer case by

$$U = \{(u_1, u_2) \in \mathbb{R}^2 : \text{there exists a feasible allocation } (x_1, x_2, y_1, \ldots, y_J)$$
$$\text{such that } u_i \leq u_i(x_i) \text{ for } i = 1, 2\}.$$

The set of Pareto optimal allocations corresponds to those allocations that generate utility pairs lying in the utility possibility set's northeast boundary, such as point $(\hat{u}_1, \hat{u}_2)$. At any such point, it is impossible to make one consumer better off without making the other worse off.

It is important to note that the criterion of Pareto optimality does not insure that an allocation is in any sense equitable. For example, using all of society's resources and technological capabilities to make a single consumer as well off as possible, subject to all other consumers receiving a subsistence level of utility, results in an allocation that is Pareto optimal but not in one that is very desirable on distributional grounds. Nevertheless, Pareto optimality serves as an important minimal test for the desirability of an allocation; it does, at the very least, say that there is no waste in the allocation of resources in society.

*Competitive Equilibria*

Throughout this chapter, we are concerned with the analysis of competitive market economies. In such an economy, society's initial endowments and technological possibilities (i.e., the firms) are owned by consumers. We suppose that consumer $i$ initially owns $\omega_{\ell i}$ of good $\ell$, where $\sum_i \omega_{\ell i} = \omega_\ell$. We denote consumer $i$'s vector of endowments by $\omega_i = (\omega_{1i}, \ldots, \omega_{Li})$. In addition, we suppose that consumer $i$ owns a share $\theta_{ij}$ of firm $j$ (where $\sum_i \theta_{ij} = 1$), giving him a claim to fraction $\theta_{ij}$ of firm $j$'s profits.

In a competitive economy, a market exists for each of the $L$ goods, and all consumers and producers act as price takers. The idea behind the price-taking assumption is that if consumers and producers are small relative to the size of the market, they will regard market prices as unaffected by their own actions.[1]

Denote the vector of market prices for goods $1, \ldots, L$ by $p = (p_1, \ldots, p_L)$. Definition 10.B.3 introduces the notion of a competitive (or Walrasian) equilibrium.

**Definition 10.B.3:** The allocation $(x_1^*, \ldots, x_I^*, y_1^*, \ldots, y_J^*)$ and price vector $p^* \in \mathbb{R}^L$ constitute a *competitive* (or *Walrasian*) *equilibrium* if the following conditions are satisfied:

(i) *Profit maximization*: For each firm $j$, $y_j^*$ solves

$$\underset{y_j \in Y_j}{\text{Max}} \quad p^* \cdot y_j. \tag{10.B.1}$$

(ii) *Utility maximization*: For each consumer $i$, $x_i^*$ solves

$$\underset{x_i \in X_i}{\text{Max}} \quad u_i(x_i) \tag{10.B.2}$$

$$\text{s.t. } p^* \cdot x_i \leq p^* \cdot \omega_i + \sum_{j=1}^{J} \theta_{ij}(p^* \cdot y_j^*).$$

(iii) *Market clearing*: For each good $\ell = 1, \ldots, L$,

$$\sum_{i=1}^{I} x_{\ell i}^* = \omega_\ell + \sum_{j=1}^{J} y_{\ell j}^*. \tag{10.B.3}$$

Definition 10.B.3 delineates three sorts of conditions that must be met for a competitive economy to be considered to be in equilibrium. Conditions (i) and (ii) reflect the underlying assumption, common to nearly all economic models, that agents in the economy seek to do as well as they can for themselves. Condition (i) states that each firm must choose a production plan that maximizes its profits, taking as given the equilibrium vector of prices of its outputs and inputs (for the justification of the profit-maximization assumption, see Section 5.G). We studied this competitive behavior of the firm extensively in Chapter 5.

Condition (ii) requires that each consumer chooses a consumption bundle that maximizes his utility given the budget constraint imposed by the equilibrium prices and by his wealth. We studied this competitive behavior of the consumer extensively in Chapter 3. One difference here, however, is that the consumer's wealth is now a function of prices. This dependence of wealth on prices arises in

---

1. Strictly speaking, it is *equilibrium* market prices that they will regard as unaffected by their actions. For more on this point, see the small-type discussion later in this section.

two ways: First, prices determine the value of the consumer's initial endowments; for example, an individual who initially owns real estate is poorer if the price of real estate falls. Second, the equilibrium prices affect firms' profits and hence the value of the consumer's shareholdings.

Condition (iii) is somewhat different. It requires that, at the equilibrium prices, the desired consumption and production levels identified in conditions (i) and (ii) are in fact mutually compatible; that is, the aggregate supply of each commodity (its total endowment plus its net production) equals the aggregate demand for it. If excess supply or demand existed for a good at the going prices, the economy could not be at a point of equilibrium. For example, if there is excess demand for a particular commodity at the existing prices, some consumer who is not receiving as much of the commodity as he desires could do better by offering to pay just slightly more than the going market price and thereby get sellers to offer the commodity to him first. Similarly, if there is excess supply, some seller will find it worthwhile to offer his product at a slight discount from the going market price.[2]

---

Note that in justifying why an equilibrium must involve no excess demand or supply, we have actually made use of the fact that consumers and producers *might not* simply take market prices as given. How are we to reconcile this argument with the underlying price-taking assumption?

An answer to this apparent paradox comes from recognizing that consumers and producers *always* have the ability to alter their offered prices (in the absence of any institutional constraints preventing this). For the price-taking assumption to be appropriate, what we want is that they have no *incentive* to alter prices that, if taken as given, equate demand and supply (we have already seen that they *do* have an incentive to alter prices that do not equate demand and supply).

Notice that as long as consumers can make their desired trades at the going market prices, they will not wish to offer more than the market price to entice sellers to sell to them first. Similarly, if producers are able to make their desired sales, they will have no incentive to undercut the market price. Thus, at a price that equates demand and supply, consumers do not wish to raise prices, and firms do not wish to lower them.

More troublesome is the possibility that a buyer might try to lower the price he pays or that a seller might try to raise the price he charges. A seller, for example, may possess the ability to raise profitably prices of the goods he sells above their competitive level (see Chapter 12). In this case, there is no reason to believe that this market power will not be exercised. To rescue the price-taking assumption, one needs to argue that under appropriate (competitive) conditions such market power does not exist. This we do in Sections 12.F and 18.C, where we formalize the idea that if market participants' desired trades are small relative to the size of the market, then they will have little incentive to depart from market prices. Thus, in a suitably defined equilibrium, they will act approximately like price takers.

---

Note from Definition 10.B.3 that if the allocation $(x_1^*, \ldots, x_I^*, y_1^*, \ldots, y_J^*)$ and price vector $p^* \gg 0$ constitute a competitive equilibrium, then so do the allocation

---

2. Strictly speaking, this second part of the argument requires the price to be positive; indeed, if the price is zero (i.e., if the good is free), then excess supply should be permissible at equilibrium. In the remainder of this chapter, however, consumer preferences will be such as to preclude this possibility (goods will be assumed to be desirable). Hence, we neglect this possibility here.

$(x_1^*, \ldots, x_I^*, y_1^*, \ldots, y_J^*)$ and price vector $\alpha p^* = (\alpha p_1^*, \ldots, \alpha p_L^*)$ for any scalar $\alpha > 0$ (see Exercise 10.B.2). As a result, we can normalize prices without loss of generality. In this chapter, we always normalize by setting one good's price equal to 1.

Lemma 10.B.1 will also prove useful in identifying competitive equilibria.

**Lemma 10.B.1:** If the allocation $(x_1, \ldots, x_I, y_1, \ldots, y_J)$ and price vector $p \gg 0$ satisfy the market clearing condition (10.B.3) for all goods $\ell \neq k$, and if every consumer's budget constraint is satisfied with equality, so that $p \cdot x_i = p \cdot \omega_i + \sum_j \theta_{ij} p \cdot y_j$ for all $i$, then the market for good $k$ also clears.

**Proof:** Adding up the consumers' budget constraints over the $I$ consumers and rearranging terms, we get

$$\sum_{\ell \neq k} p_\ell \left( \sum_{i=1}^{I} x_{\ell i} - \omega_\ell - \sum_{j=1}^{J} y_{\ell j} \right) = -p_k \left( \sum_{i=1}^{I} x_{ki} - \omega_k - \sum_{j=1}^{J} y_{kj} \right).$$

By market clearing in goods $\ell \neq k$, the left-hand side of this equation is equal to zero. Thus, the right-hand side must be equal to zero as well. Because $p_k > 0$, this implies that we have market clearing in good $k$. ∎

In the models studied in this chapter, Lemma 10.B.1 will allow us to identify competitive equilibria by checking for market clearing in only $L - 1$ markets. Lemma 10.B.1 is really just a matter of double-entry accountancy. If consumers' budget constraints hold with equality, the dollar value of each consumer's planned purchases equals the dollar value of what he plans to sell plus the dollar value of his share $(\theta_{ij})$ of the firms' (net) supply, and so the total value of planned purchases in the economy must equal the total value of planned sales. If those values are equal to each other in all markets but one, then equality must hold in the remaining market as well.

## 10.C  Partial Equilibrium Competitive Analysis

Marshallian partial equilibrium analysis envisions the market for one good (or several goods, as discussed in Section 10.G) that constitutes a small part of the overall economy. The small size of the market facilitates two important simplifications for the analysis of market equilibrium:[3] First, as Marshall (1920) emphasized, when the expenditure on the good under study is a small portion of a consumer's total expenditure, only a small fraction of any additional dollar of wealth will be spent on this good; consequently, we can expect wealth effects for it to be small. Second, with similarly dispersed substitution effects, the small size of the market under study should lead the prices of other goods to be approximately unaffected by changes in this market.[4] Because of this fixity of other prices, we are justified in treating the expenditure on these other goods as a single composite commodity, which we call the *numeraire* (see Exercise 3.G.5).

---

3. The following points have been formalized by Vives (1987). (See Exercise 10.C.1 for an illustration.)

4. This is not the only possible justification for taking other goods' prices as being unaffected by the market under study; see Section 10.G.

With this partial equilibrium interpretation as our motivation, we proceed to study a simple two-good quasilinear model. There are two commodities: good $\ell$ and the numeraire. We let $x_i$ and $m_i$ denote consumer $i$'s consumption of good $\ell$ and the numeraire, respectively. Each consumer $i = 1, \ldots, I$ has a utility function that takes the quasilinear form (see Sections 3.B and 3.C):

$$u_i(m_i, x_i) = m_i + \phi_i(x_i).$$

We let each consumer's consumption set be $\mathbb{R} \times \mathbb{R}_+$, and so we assume for convenience that consumption of the numeraire commodity $m$ can take negative values. This is to avoid dealing with boundary problems. We assume that $\phi_i(\cdot)$ is bounded above and twice differentiable, with $\phi_i'(x_i) > 0$ and $\phi_i''(x_i) < 0$ at all $x_i \geq 0$. We normalize $\phi_i(0) = 0$.

In terms of our partial equilibrium interpretation, we think of good $\ell$ as the good whose market is under study and of the numeraire as representing the composite of all other goods ($m$ stands for the total money expenditure on these other goods). Recall that with quasilinear utility functions, wealth effects for non-numeraire commodities are null.

In the discussion that follows, we normalize the price of the numeraire to equal 1, and we let $p$ denote the price of good $\ell$.

Each firm $j = 1, \ldots, J$ in this two-good economy is able to produce good $\ell$ from good $m$. The amount of the numeraire required by firm $j$ to produce $q_j \geq 0$ units of good $\ell$ is given by the cost function $c_j(q_j)$ (recall that the price of the numeraire is 1). Letting $z_j$ denote firm $j$'s use of good $m$ as an input, its production set is therefore

$$Y_j = \{(-z_j, q_j) \colon q_j \geq 0 \text{ and } z_j \geq c_j(q_j)\}.$$

In what follows, we assume that $c_j(\cdot)$ is twice differentiable, with $c_j'(q_j) > 0$ and $c_j''(q_j) \geq 0$ at all $q_j \geq 0$. [In terms of our partial equilibrium interpretation, we can think of $c_j(q_j)$ as actually arising from some multiple-input cost function $c_j(\bar{w}, q_j)$, given the fixed vector of factor prices $\bar{w}$.[5]]

For simplicity, we shall assume that there is no initial endowment of good $\ell$, so that all amounts consumed must be produced by the firms. Consumer $i$'s initial endowment of the numeraire is the scalar $\omega_{mi} > 0$, and we let $\omega_m = \sum_i \omega_{mi}$.

We now proceed to identify the competitive equilibria for this two-good quasilinear model. Applying Definition 10.B.3, we consider first the implications of profit and utility maximization.

Given the price $p^*$ for good $\ell$, firm $j$'s equilibrium output level $q_j^*$ must solve

$$\underset{q_j \geq 0}{\text{Max}} \quad p^* q_j - c_j(q_j),$$

which has the necessary and sufficient first-order condition

$$p^* \leq c_j'(q_j^*), \quad \text{with equality if } q_j^* > 0.$$

On the other hand, consumer $i$'s equilibrium consumption vector $(m_i^*, x_i^*)$ must

---

5. Some of the exercises at the end of the chapter investigate the effects of exogenous changes in these factor prices.

solve

$$\underset{m_i \in \mathbb{R}, \, x_i \in \mathbb{R}_+}{\text{Max}} \quad m_i + \phi_i(x_i)$$

$$\text{s.t.} \quad m_i + p^* x_i \leq \omega_{mi} + \sum_{j=1}^{J} \theta_{ij}(p^* q_j^* - c_j(q_j^*)).$$

In any solution to this problem, the budget constraint holds with equality. Substituting for $m_i$ from this constraint, we can rewrite consumer $i$'s problem solely in terms of choosing his optimal consumption of good $\ell$. Doing so, we see that $x_i^*$ must solve

$$\underset{x_i \geq 0}{\text{Max}} \quad \phi_i(x_i) - p^* x_i + \left[ \omega_{mi} + \sum_{j=1}^{J} \theta_{ij}(p^* q_j^* - c_j(q_j^*)) \right],$$

which has the necessary and sufficient first-order condition

$$\phi_i'(x_i^*) \leq p^*, \quad \text{with equality if } x_i^* > 0.$$

In what follows, it will be convenient to adopt the convention of identifying an equilibrium allocation by the levels of good $\ell$ consumed and produced, $(x_1^*, \ldots, x_I^*, q_1^*, \ldots, q_J^*)$, with the understanding that consumer $i$'s equilibrium consumption of the numeraire is then $m_i^* = [\omega_{mi} + \sum_j \theta_{ij}(p^* q_j^* - c_j(q_j^*))] - p^* x_i^*$ and that firm $j$'s equilibrium usage of the numeraire as an input is $z_j^* = c_j(q_j^*)$.

To complete the development of the equilibrium conditions for this model, recall that by Lemma 10.B.1, we need only check that the market for good $\ell$ clears.[6] Hence, we conclude that the allocation $(x_1^*, \ldots, x_I^*, q_1^*, \ldots, q_J^*)$ and the price $p^*$ constitute a competitive equilibrium if and only if

$$p^* \leq c_j'(q_j^*), \quad \text{with equality if } q_j^* > 0 \qquad j = 1, \ldots, J. \qquad (10.\text{C}.1)$$

$$\phi_i'(x_i^*) \leq p^*, \quad \text{with equality if } x_i^* > 0 \qquad i = 1, \ldots, I. \qquad (10.\text{C}.2)$$

$$\sum_{i=1}^{I} x_i^* = \sum_{j=1}^{J} q_j^*. \qquad (10.\text{C}.3)$$

At any interior solution, condition (10.C.1) says that firm $j$'s marginal benefit from selling an additional unit of good $\ell$, $p^*$, exactly equals its marginal cost $c_j'(q_j^*)$. Condition (10.C.2) says that consumer $i$'s marginal benefit from consuming an additional unit of good $\ell$, $\phi_i'(x_i^*)$, exactly equals its marginal cost $p^*$. Condition (10.C.3) is the market-clearing equation. Together, these $I + J + 1$ conditions characterize the $(I + J + 1)$ equilibrium values $(x_1^*, \ldots, x_I^*, q_1^*, \ldots, q_J^*)$ and $p^*$. Note that as long as $\text{Max}_i \, \phi_i'(0) > \text{Min}_j \, c_j'(0)$, the aggregate consumption and production of good $\ell$ must be strictly positive in a competitive equilibrium [this follows from conditions (10.C.1) and (10.C.2)]. For simplicity, we assume that this is the case in the discussion that follows.

Conditions (10.C.1) to (10.C.3) have a very important property: They do not involve, in any manner, the endowments or the ownership shares of the consumers. As a result, we see that *the equilibrium allocation and price are independent of the*

---

6. Note that we must have $p^* > 0$ in any competitive equilibrium; otherwise, consumers would demand an infinite amount of good $\ell$ [recall that $\phi_i'(\cdot) > 0$].

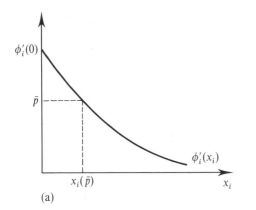

(a)

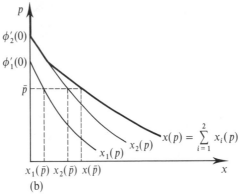

(b)

**Figure 10.C.1**

Construction of the aggregate demand function.
(a) Determination of consumer $i$'s demand.
(b) Construction of the aggregate demand function ($I = 2$).

*distribution of endowments and ownership shares.* This important simplification arises from the quasilinear form of consumer preferences.[7]

The competitive equilibrium of this model can be nicely represented using the traditional Marshallian graphical technique that identifies the equilibrium price as the point of intersection of aggregate demand and aggregate supply curves.

We can derive the aggregate demand function for good $\ell$ from condition (10.C.2). Because $\phi_i''(\cdot) < 0$ and $\phi_i(\cdot)$ is bounded, $\phi_i'(\cdot)$ is a strictly decreasing function of $x_i$ taking all values in the set $(0, \phi_i'(0)]$. Therefore, for each possible level of $p > 0$, we can solve for a unique level of $x_i$, denoted $x_i(p)$, that satisfies condition (10.C.2). Note that if $p \geq \phi_i'(0)$, then $x_i(p) = 0$. Figure 10.C.1(a) depicts this construction for a price $\bar{p} > 0$. The function $x_i(\cdot)$ is consumer $i$'s *Walrasian demand function* for good $\ell$ (see Section 3.D) which, because of quasilinearity, does not depend on the consumer's wealth. It is continuous and nonincreasing in $p$ at all $p > 0$, and is strictly decreasing at any $p < \phi_i'(0)$ [at any such $p$, we have $x_i'(p) = 1/\phi_i''(x_i(p)) < 0$].

The *aggregate demand function for good $\ell$* is then the function $x(p) = \sum_i x_i(p)$, which is continuous and nonincreasing at all $p > 0$, and is strictly decreasing at any $p < \text{Max}_i \, \phi_i'(0)$. Its construction is depicted in Figure 10.C.1(b) for the case in which $I = 2$; it is simply the horizontal summation of the individual demand functions and is drawn in the figure with a heavy trace. Note that $x(p) = 0$ whenever $p \geq \text{Max}_i \, \phi_i'(0)$.

The aggregate supply function can be similarly derived from condition (10.C.1).[8] Suppose, first, that every $c_j(\cdot)$ is strictly convex and that $c_j'(q_j) \to \infty$ as $q_j \to \infty$. Then, for any $p > 0$, we can let $q_j(p)$ denote the unique level of $q_j$ that satisfies condition (10.C.1). Note that for $p \leq c_j'(0)$, we have $q_j(p) = 0$. Figure 10.C.2(a) illustrates this construction for a price $\bar{p} > 0$. The function $q_j(\cdot)$ is firm $j$'s *supply function* for good $\ell$ (see Sections 5.C and 5.D). It is continuous and nondecreasing at all $p > 0$, and is strictly increasing at any $p > c_j'(0)$ [for any such $p$, $q_j'(p) = 1/c_j''(q_j(p)) > 0$].

The *aggregate* (or *industry*) *supply function* for good $\ell$ is then the function $q(p) = \sum_j q_j(p)$, which is continuous and nondecreasing at all $p > 0$, and is strictly increasing at any $p > \text{Min}_j \, c_j'(0)$. Its construction is depicted in Figure 10.C.2(b) for

---

7. See Section 10.G for a further discussion of this general feature of equilibrium in economies with quasilinear utility functions.

8. See Section 5.D for an extensive discussion of individual supply in the one-input, one-output case.

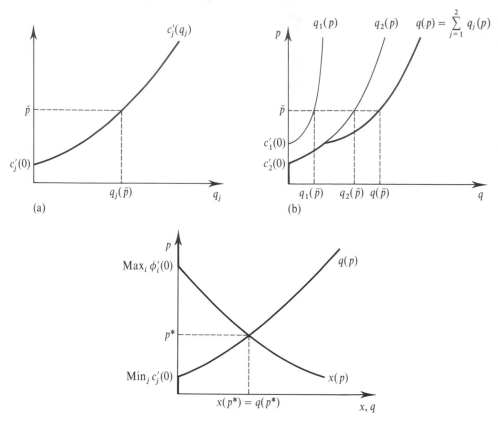

**Figure 10.C.2**

Construction of the aggregate supply function.
(a) Determination of firm $j$'s supply.
(b) Construction of the aggregate supply function ($J = 2$).

**Figure 10.C.3**

The equilibrium price equates demand and supply.

the case in which $J = 2$; it is equal to the horizontal sum of the individual firms' supply functions and is drawn in the figure with a heavy trace. Note that $q(p) = 0$ whenever $p \leq \text{Min}_j\, c_j'(0)$.

To find the equilibrium price of good $\ell$, we need only find the price $p^*$ at which aggregate demand equals aggregate supply, that is, at which $x(p^*) = q(p^*)$. When $\text{Max}_i\, \phi_i'(0) > \text{Min}_j\, c_j'(0)$ as we have assumed, at any $p \geq \text{Max}_i\, \phi_i'(0)$ we have $x(p) = 0$ and $q(p) > 0$. Likewise, at any $p \leq \text{Min}_j\, c_j'(0)$ we have $x(p) > 0$ and $q(p) = 0$. The existence of an equilibrium price $p^* \in (\text{Min}_j\, c_j'(0), \text{Max}_i\, \phi_i'(0))$ then follows from the continuity properties of $x(\cdot)$ and $q(\cdot)$. The solution is depicted in Figure 10.C.3. Note also that because $x(\cdot)$ is strictly decreasing at all $p < \text{Max}_i\, \phi_i'(0)$ and $q(\cdot)$ is strictly increasing at all $p > \text{Min}_j\, c_j'(0)$, this equilibrium price is uniquely defined.[9] The individual consumption and production levels of good $\ell$ in this equilibrium are then given by $x_i^* = x_i(p^*)$ for $i = 1, \ldots, I$ and $q_j^* = q_j(p^*)$ for $j = 1, \ldots, J$.

More generally, if some $c_j(\cdot)$ is merely convex [e.g., if $c_j(\cdot)$ is linear, as in the constant returns case], then $q_j(\cdot)$ is a convex-valued correspondence rather than a function and it may be well defined only on a subset of prices.[10] Nevertheless, the

---

9. Be warned, however, that the uniqueness of equilibrium is a property that need not hold in more general settings in which wealth effects are present. (See Chapter 17.)

10. For example, if firm $j$ has $c_j(q_j) = c_j q_j$ for some scalar $c_j > 0$, then when $p > c_j$, we have $q_j(p) = \infty$. As a result, if $p > c_j$, the aggregate supply is $q(p) = \sum_j q_j(p) = \infty$; consequently $q(\cdot)$ is not well defined for this $p$.

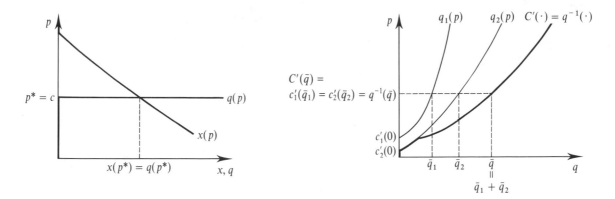

**Figure 10.C.4 (left)**

Equilibrium when $c_j(q_j) = cq_j$ for all $j = 1, \ldots, J$.

**Figure 10.C.5 (right)**

The industry marginal cost function.

basic features of the analysis do not change. Figure 10.C.4 depicts the determination of the equilibrium value of $p$ in the case where, for all $j$, $c_j(q_j) = cq_j$ for some scalar $c > 0$. The only difference from the strictly convex case is that, when $J > 1$, individual firms' equilibrium production levels are not uniquely determined.

The inverses of the aggregate demand and supply functions also have interpretations that are of interest. At any given level of aggregate output of good $\ell$, say $\bar{q}$, the inverse of the industry supply function, $q^{-1}(\bar{q})$, gives the price that brings forth aggregate supply $\bar{q}$. That is, when each firm chooses its optimal output level facing the price $p = q^{-1}(\bar{q})$, aggregate supply is exactly $\bar{q}$. Figure 10.C.5 illustrates this point. Note that in selecting these output levels, all active firms set their marginal cost equal to $q^{-1}(\bar{q})$. As a result, the marginal cost of producing an additional unit of good $\ell$ at $\bar{q}$ is precisely $q^{-1}(\bar{q})$, regardless of which active firm produces it. Thus $q^{-1}(\cdot)$, the inverse of the industry supply function, can be viewed as the *industry marginal cost function*, which we now denote by $C'(\cdot) = q^{-1}(\cdot)$.[11]

The derivation of $C'(\cdot)$ just given accords fully with our discussion in Section 5.E. We saw there that the aggregate supply of the $J$ firms, $q(p)$, maximizes aggregate profits given $p$; therefore, we can relate $q(\cdot)$ to the industry marginal cost function $C'(\cdot)$ in exactly the same manner as we did in Section 5.D for the case of a single firm's marginal cost function and supply behavior. With convex technologies, the aggregate supply locus for good $\ell$ therefore coincides with the graph of the industry marginal cost function $C'(\cdot)$, and so $q^{-1}(\cdot) = C'(\cdot)$.[12]

Likewise, at any given level of aggregate demand $\bar{x}$, the *inverse demand function* $P(\bar{x}) = x^{-1}(\bar{x})$ gives the price that results in aggregate demand of $\bar{x}$. That is, when each consumer optimally chooses his demand for good $\ell$ at this price, total demand exactly equals $\bar{x}$. Note that at these individual demand levels (assuming that they are positive), each consumer's marginal benefit in terms of the numeraire from an additional unit of good $\ell$, $\phi_i'(x_i)$, is exactly equal to $P(\bar{x})$. This is illustrated in Figure

---

11. Formally, the industry marginal cost function $C'(\cdot)$ is the derivative of the aggregate cost function $C(\cdot)$ that gives the total production cost that would be incurred by a central authority who operates all $J$ firms and seeks to produce any given aggregate level of good $\ell$ at minimum total cost. (See Exercise 10.C.3.)

12. More formally, by Proposition 5.E.1, aggregate supply behavior can be determined by maximizing profit given the aggregate cost function $C(\cdot)$. This yields first-order condition $p = C'(q(p))$. Hence, $q(\cdot) = C'^{-1}(\cdot)$, or equivalently $q^{-1}(\cdot) = C'(\cdot)$.

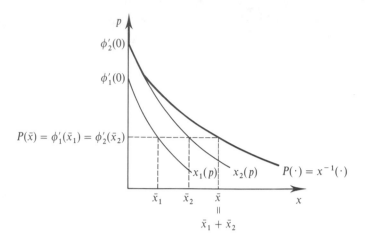

**Figure 10.C.6**

The inverse demand function.

10.C.6. The value of the inverse demand function at quantity $\bar{x}$, $P(\bar{x})$, can thus be viewed as giving the *marginal social benefit of good* $\ell$ given that the aggregate quantity $\bar{x}$ is efficiently distributed among the $I$ consumers (see Exercise 10.C.4 for a precise statement of this fact).

Given these interpretations, we can view the competitive equilibrium as involving an aggregate output level at which the marginal social benefit of good $\ell$ is exactly equal to its marginal cost. This suggests a social optimality property of the competitive allocation, a topic that we investigate further in Section 10.D.

### Comparative Statics

It is often of interest to determine how a change in underlying market conditions affects the equilibrium outcome of a competitive market. Such questions may arise, for example, because we may be interested in comparing market outcomes across several similar markets that differ in some measurable way (e.g., we might compare the price of ice cream in a number of cities whose average temperatures differ) or because we want to know how a change in market conditions will alter the outcome in a particular market. The analysis of these sorts of questions is known as *comparative statics analysis*.

As a general matter, we might imagine that each consumer's preferences are affected by a vector of exogenous parameters $\alpha \in \mathbb{R}^M$, so that the utility function $\phi_i(\cdot)$ can be written as $\phi_i(x_i, \alpha)$. Similarly, each firm's technology may be affected by a vector of exogenous parameters $\beta \in \mathbb{R}^S$, so that the cost function $c_j(\cdot)$ can be written as $c_j(q_j, \beta)$. In addition, in some circumstances, consumers and firms face taxes or subsidies that may make the effective (i.e., net of taxes and subsidies) price paid or received differ from the market price $p$. We let $\hat{p}_i(p, t)$ and $\hat{p}_j(p, t)$ denote, respectively, the effective price paid by consumer $i$ and the effective price received by firm $j$ given tax and subsidy parameters $t \in \mathbb{R}^K$. For example, if consumer $i$ must pay a tax of $t_i$ (in units of the numeraire) per unit of good $i$ purchased, then $\hat{p}_i(p, t) = p + t_i$. If consumer $i$ instead faces a tax that is a percentage $t_i$ of the sales price, then $\hat{p}_i(p, t) = p(1 + t_i)$.

For given values $(\alpha, \beta, t)$ of the parameters, the $I + J$ equilibrium quantities $(x_1^*, \ldots, x_I^*, q_1^*, \ldots, q_J^*)$ and the equilibrium price $p^*$ are determined as the solution to the following $I + J + 1$ equations (we assume, for simplicity, that $x_i^* > 0$ for all

$i$ and $q_j^* > 0$ for all $j$):

$$\phi_i'(x_i^*, \alpha) = \hat{p}_i(p^*, t) \qquad i = 1, \ldots, I. \tag{10.C.4}$$

$$c_j'(q_j^*, \beta) = \hat{p}_j(p^*, t) \qquad j = 1, \ldots, J. \tag{10.C.5}$$

$$\sum_{i=1}^{I} x_i^* = \sum_{j=1}^{J} q_j^*. \tag{10.C.6}$$

These $I + J + 1$ equations implicitly define the equilibrium allocation and price as functions of the exogenous parameters $(\alpha, \beta, t)$. If all the relevant functions are differentiable, we can use the implicit function theorem to derive the marginal change in the equilibrium allocation and price in response to a differential change in the values of these parameters (see Section M.E of the Mathematical Appendix). In Example 10.C.1, we consider one such comparative statics exercise; it is only one among a large number of possibilities that arise naturally in economic applications. (The exercises at the end of this chapter include additional examples.)

**Example 10.C.1:** *Comparative Statics Effects of a Sales Tax.* Suppose that a new sales tax is proposed under which consumers must pay an amount $t \geq 0$ (in units of the numeraire) for each unit of good $\ell$ consumed. We wish to determine the effect of this tax on the market price. Let $x(p)$ and $q(p)$ denote the aggregate demand and supply functions, respectively, for good $\ell$ in the absence of the tax (we maintain all our previous assumptions regarding these functions).

In terms of our previous notation, the $\phi_i(\cdot)$ and $c_j(\cdot)$ functions do not depend on any exogenous parameters, $\hat{p}_i(p, t) = p + t$ for all $i$, and $\hat{p}_j(p, t) = p$ for all $j$. In principle, by substituting these expressions into the system of equilbrium equations (10.C.4) to (10.C.6), we can derive the effect of a marginal increase in the tax on the price by direct use of the implicit function theorem (see Exercise 10.C.5). Here, however, we pursue a more instructive way to get the answer. In particular, note that aggregate demand with a tax of $t$ and price $p$ is exactly $x(p + t)$ because the tax is equivalent for consumers to the price being increased by $t$. Thus, the equilibrium market price when the tax is $t$, which we denote by $p^*(t)$, must satisfy

$$x(p^*(t) + t) = q(p^*(t)). \tag{10.C.7}$$

Suppose that we now want to determine the effect on prices paid and received of a marginal increase in the tax. Assuming that $x(\cdot)$ and $q(\cdot)$ are differentiable at $p = p^*(t)$, differentiating (10.C.7) yields

$$p^{*\prime}(t) = -\frac{x'(p^*(t) + t)}{x'(p^*(t) + t) - q'(p^*(t))}. \tag{10.C.8}$$

It is immediate from (10.C.8) and our assumptions on $x'(\cdot)$ and $q'(\cdot)$ that $-1 \leq p^{*\prime}(t) < 0$ at any $t$. Therefore, the price $p^*(t)$ received by producers falls as $t$ increases while the overall cost of the good to consumers $p^*(t) + t$ rises (weakly). The total quantities produced and consumed fall (again weakly). See Figure 10.C.7(a), where the equilibrium level of aggregate consumption at tax rate $t$ is denoted by $x^*(t)$. Notice from (10.C.8) that when $q'(p^*(t))$ is large we have $p^{*\prime}(t) \approx 0$, and so the price received by the firms is hardly affected by the tax; nearly all the impact of the tax is felt by consumers. In contrast, when $q'(p^*(t)) = 0$, we have $p^{*\prime}(t) = -1$, and so the impact of the tax is felt entirely by the firms. Figures 10.C.7(b) and (c) depict these two cases.

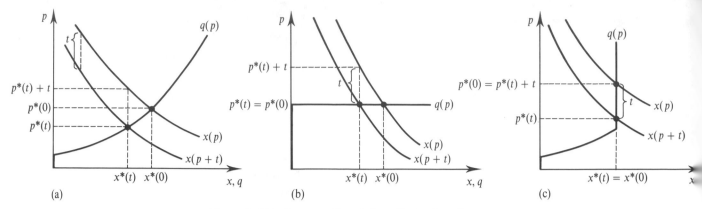

**Figure 10.C.7**    Comparative statics effects of a sales tax.

By substituting into (10.C.8) for $x'(\cdot)$ and $q'(\cdot)$, the marginal change in $p^*$ can be expressed in terms of derivatives of the underlying individual utility and cost functions. For example, if we let $p^* = p^*(0)$ be the pretax price, we see that

$$p^{*\prime}(0) = -\frac{\sum_{i=1}^{I} [\phi_i''(x_i(p^*))]^{-1}}{\sum_{i=1}^{I} [\phi_i''(x_i(p^*))]^{-1} - \sum_{j=1}^{J} [c_j''(q_j(p^*))]^{-1}}.$$

■

We have assumed throughout this section that consumers' preferences and firms' technologies are convex (and strictly so in the case of consumer preferences). What if this is not the case? Figure 10.C.8 illustrates one problem that can then arise; it shows the demand function and

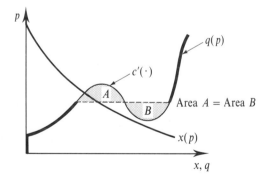

**Figure 10.C.8**

Nonexistence of competitive equilibrium with a nonconvex technology.

supply correspondence for an economy in which there is a single firm (so $J = 1$).[13] This firm's cost function $c(\cdot)$ is continuous and differentiable but not convex. In the figure, the light curve is the graph of the firm's marginal cost function $c'(\cdot)$. As the figure illustrates, $c'(\cdot)$ fails to be nondecreasing. The heavier curve is the firm's actual supply correspondence $q(\cdot)$ (you should verify that it is determined as indicated in the figure).[14] The graph of the supply correspondence no longer coincides with the marginal cost curve and, as is evident in the figure, no intersection exists between the graph of the supply correspondence and the demand curve. Thus, in this case, *no competitive equilibrium exists.*

---

13. We set $J = 1$ here solely for expositional purposes.

14. See Section 5.D for a more detailed discussion of the relation between a firm's supply correspondence and its marginal cost function when its technology is nonconvex.

This observation suggests that convexity assumptions are key to the existence of a competitive equilibrium. We shall confirm this in Chapter 17, where we provide a more general discussion of the conditions under which existence of a competitive equilibrium is assured.

## 10.D  The Fundamental Welfare Theorems in a Partial Equilibrium Context

In this section, we study the properties of Pareto optimal allocations in the framework of the two-good quasilinear economy introduced in Section 10.C, and we establish a fundamental link between the set of Pareto optimal allocations and the set of competitive equilibria.

The identification of Pareto optimal allocations is considerably facilitated by the quasilinear specification. In particular, *when consumer preferences are quasilinear, the boundary of the economy's utility possibility set is linear* (see Section 10.B for the definition of this set) *and all points in this boundary are associated with consumption allocations that differ only in the distribution of the numeraire among consumers.*

To see this important fact, suppose that we fix the consumption and production levels of good $\ell$ at $(\bar{x}_1, \ldots, \bar{x}_I, \bar{q}_1, \ldots, \bar{q}_J)$. With these production levels, the total amount of the numeraire available for distribution among consumers is $\omega_m - \sum_j c_j(\bar{q}_j)$. Because the quasilinear form of the utility functions allows for an unlimited unit-for-unit transfer of utility across consumers through transfers of the numeraire, the set of utilities that can be attained for the $I$ consumers by appropriately distributing the available amounts of the numeraire is given by

$$\left\{(u_1, \ldots, u_I): \sum_{i=1}^{I} u_i \leq \sum_{i=1}^{I} \phi_i(\bar{x}_i) + \omega_m - \sum_{j=1}^{J} c_j(\bar{q}_j)\right\}. \qquad (10.D.1)$$

The boundary of this set is a hyperplane with normal vector $(1, \ldots, 1)$. The set is depicted for the case $I = 2$ by the hatched set in Figure 10.D.1.

Note that by altering the consumption and production levels of good $\ell$, we necessarily shift the boundary of this set in a parallel manner. Thus, every Pareto optimal allocation must involve the quantities $(x_1^*, \ldots, x_I^*, q_1^*, \ldots, q_J^*)$ that extend this boundary as far out as possible, as illustrated by the heavily drawn boundary of the shaded utility possibility set in Figure 10.D.1. We call these quantities the *optimal consumption and production levels* for good $\ell$. As long as these optimal consumption and production levels for good $\ell$ are uniquely determined, Pareto optimal allocations can differ only in the distribution of the numeraire among consumers.[15]

---

15. The optimal individual production levels need not be unique if firms' cost functions are convex but not strictly so. Indeterminacy of optimal individual production levels arises, for example, when all firms have identical constant returns to scale technologies. However, under our assumptions that the $\phi_i(\cdot)$ functions are strictly concave and that the $c_j(\cdot)$ functions are convex, the optimal individual consumption levels of good $\ell$ are necessarily unique and, hence, so is the optimal aggregate production level $\sum_j q_j^*$ of good $\ell$. This implies that, under our assumptions, the consumption allocations in two different Pareto optimal allocations can differ only in the distribution of numeraire among consumers. If, moreover, the $c_j(\cdot)$ functions are strictly convex, then the optimal individual production levels are also uniquely determined. (See Exercise 10.D.1.)

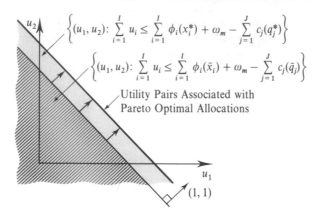

**Figure 10.D.1**

The utility possibility set in a quasilinear economy.

It follows from expression (10.D.1) that the optimal consumption and production levels of good $\ell$ can be obtained as the solution to

$$\underset{\substack{(x_1,\dots,x_I)\geq 0 \\ (q_1,\dots,q_J)\geq 0}}{\text{Max}} \quad \sum_{i=1}^{I} \phi_i(x_i) - \sum_{j=1}^{J} c_j(q_j) + \omega_m \tag{10.D.2}$$

$$\text{s.t.} \quad \sum_{i=1}^{I} x_i - \sum_{j=1}^{J} q_j = 0.$$

The value of the term $\sum_i \phi_i(x_i) - \sum_j c_j(q_j)$ in the objective function of problem (10.D.2) is known as the *Marshallian aggregate surplus* (or, simply, the *aggregate surplus*). It can be thought of as the total utility generated from consumption of good $\ell$ less its costs of production (in terms of the numeraire). The optimal consumption and production levels for good $\ell$ maximize this aggregate surplus measure.

Given our convexity assumptions, the first-order conditions of problem (10.D.2) yield necessary and sufficient conditions that characterize the optimal quantities. If we let $\mu$ be the multiplier on the constraint in problem (10.D.2), the $I + J$ optimal values $(x_1^*, \dots, x_I^*, q_1^*, \dots, q_J^*)$ and the multiplier $\mu$ satisfy the following $I + J + 1$ conditions:

$$\mu \leq c_j'(q_j^*), \quad \text{with equality if } q_j^* > 0 \qquad j = 1, \dots, J. \tag{10.D.3}$$

$$\phi_i'(x_i^*) \leq \mu, \quad \text{with equality if } x_i^* > 0 \qquad i = 1, \dots, I. \tag{10.D.4}$$

$$\sum_{i=1}^{I} x_i^* = \sum_{j=1}^{J} q_j^*. \tag{10.D.5}$$

These conditions should look familiar: They exactly parallel conditions (10.C.1) to (10.C.3) in Section 10.C, with $\mu$ replacing $p^*$. This observation has an important implication. We can immediately infer from it that any competitive equilibrium outcome in this model is Pareto optimal because any competitive equilibrium allocation has consumption and production levels of good $\ell$, $(x_1^*, \dots, x_I^*, q_1^*, \dots, q_J^*)$, that satisfy conditions (10.D.3) to (10.D.5) when we set $\mu = p^*$. Thus, we have established the *first fundamental theorem of welfare economics* (Proposition 10.D.1) in the context of this quasilinear two-good model.

**Proposition 10.D.1:** (*The First Fundamental Theorem of Welfare Economics*) If the price $p^*$ and allocation $(x_1^*, \dots, x_I^*, q_1^*, \dots, q_J^*)$ constitute a competitive equilibrium, then this allocation is Pareto optimal.

The first fundamental welfare theorem establishes conditions under which market equilibria are necessarily Pareto optimal. It is a formal expression of Adam Smith's "invisible hand" and is a result that holds with considerable generality (see Section 16.C for a much more extensive discussion). Equally important, however, are the conditions under which it fails to hold. In the models for which we establish the first fundamental welfare theorem here and in Section 16.C, markets are "complete" in the sense that there is a market for every relevant commodity and all market participants act as price takers. In Chapters 11 to 14, we study situations in which at least one of these conditions fails, and market outcomes fail to be Pareto optimal as a result.

We can also develop a converse to Proposition 10.D.1, known as the *second fundamental theorem of welfare economics*. In Section 10.C, we saw that good $\ell$'s equilibrium price $p^*$, its equilibrium consumption and production levels $(x_1^*, \ldots, x_I^*, q_1^*, \ldots, q_J^*)$, and firms' profits are unaffected by changes in consumers' wealth levels. As a result, a transfer of one unit of the numeraire from consumer $i$ to consumer $i'$ will cause each of these consumers' equilibrium consumption of the numeraire to change by exactly the amount of the transfer and will cause no other changes. Thus, by appropriately transferring endowments of the numeraire commodity, the resulting competitive equilibrium allocation can be made to yield any utility vector in the boundary of the utility possibility set. The second welfare theorem therefore tells us that, in this two-good quasilinear economy, a central authority interested in achieving a particular Pareto optimal allocation can always implement this outcome by transferring the numeraire among consumers and then "allowing the market to work." This is stated formally in Proposition 10.D.2.

**Proposition 10.D.2:** (*The Second Fundamental Theorem of Welfare Economics*) For any Pareto optimal levels of utility $(u_1^*, \ldots, u_I^*)$, there are transfers of the numeraire commodity $(T_1, \ldots, T_I)$ satisfying $\sum_i T_i = 0$, such that a competitive equilibrium reached from the endowments $(\omega_{m1} + T_1, \ldots, \omega_{mI} + T_I)$ yields precisely the utilities $(u_1^*, \ldots, u_I^*)$.

In Section 16.D, we study the conditions under which the second welfare theorem holds in more general competitive economies. A critical requirement, in addition to those needed for the first welfare theorem, turns out to be convexity of preferences and production sets, an assumption we have made in the model under consideration here. In contrast, we shall see in Chapter 16 that no such convexity assumptions are needed for the first welfare theorem.

The correspondence between $p$ and $\mu$ in the equilibrium conditions (10.C.1) to (10.C.3) and the Pareto optimality conditions (10.D.3) to (10.D.5) is worthy of emphasis: The competitive price is exactly equal to the shadow price on the resource constraint for good $\ell$ in the Pareto optimality problem (10.D.2). In this sense, then, we can say that a good's price in a competitive equilibrium reflects precisely its marginal social value. In a competitive equilibrium, each firm, by operating at a point where price equals marginal cost, equates its marginal production cost to the marginal social value of its output. Similarly, each consumer, by consuming up to the point where marginal utility from a good equals its price, is at a point where the marginal benefit from consumption of the good exactly equals its marginal cost. This correspondence between equilibrium market prices and optimal shadow prices holds quite generally in competitive economies (see Section 16.F for further discussion of this point).

---

An alternative way to characterize the set of Pareto optimal allocations is to solve

$$\underset{\{x_i, m_i\}_{i=1}^I, \{z_j, q_j\}_{j=1}^J}{\text{Max}} \quad m_1 + \phi_1(x_1) \tag{10.D.6}$$

$$\text{s.t.} \quad (1) \quad m_i + \phi_i(x_i) \geq \bar{u}_i \quad i = 2, \ldots, I$$

$$(2\ell) \quad \sum_{i=1}^I x_i - \sum_{j=1}^J q_j \leq 0$$

$$(2m) \quad \sum_{i=1}^I m_i + \sum_{j=1}^J z_j \leq \omega_m$$

$$(3) \quad z_j \geq c_j(q_j) \quad j = 1, \ldots, J.$$

Problem (10.D.6) expresses the Pareto optimality problem as one of trying to maximize the well-being of individual 1 subject to meeting certain required utility levels for the other individuals in the economy [constraints (1)], resource constraints [constraints $(2\ell)$ and $(2m)$], and technological constraints [constraints (3)]. By solving problem (10.D.6) for various required levels of utility for these other individuals, $(\bar{u}_2, \ldots, \bar{u}_I)$, we can identify all the Pareto optimal outcomes for this economy (see Exercise 10.D.3; more generally, we can do this whenever consumer preferences are strongly monotone). Exercise 10.D.4 asks you to derive conditions (10.D.3) to (10.D.5) in this alternative manner.

---

# 10.E   Welfare Analysis in the Partial Equilibrium Model

It is often of interest to measure the change in the level of social welfare that would be generated by a change in market conditions such as an improvement in technology, a new government tax policy, or the elimination of some existing market imperfection. In the partial equilibrium model, it is particularly simple to carry out this welfare analysis. This fact accounts to a large extent for the popularity of the model.

In the discussion that follows, we assume that the welfare judgments of society are embodied in a social welfare function $W(u_1, \ldots, u_I)$ assigning a social welfare value to every utility vector $(u_1, \ldots, u_I)$ (see Chapters 4, 16, and 22 for more on this concept). In addition, we suppose that (as in the theory of the normative representative consumer discussed in Section 4.D) there is some central authority who redistributes wealth by means of transfers of the numeraire commodity in order to maximize social welfare.[16] The critical simplification offered by the quasilinear specification of individual utility functions is that when there is a central authority who redistributes wealth in this manner, *changes in social welfare can be measured by changes in the Marshallian aggregate surplus* (introduced in Section 10.D) *for any social welfare function that society may have.*

To see this point (which we have in fact already examined in Example 4.D.2), consider some given consumption and production levels of good $\ell$, $(x_1, \ldots, x_I, q_1, \ldots, q_J)$,

---

16. As in Section 4.D, we assume that consumers treat these transfers as independent of their own actions; that is, in the standard terminology, they are *lump-sum* transfers. You should think of the central authority as making the transfers prior to the opening of markets.

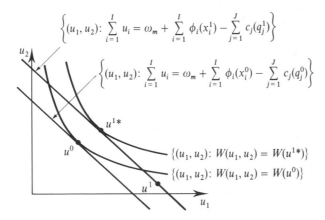

**Figure 10.E.1**

With lump-sum redistribution occurring to maximize social welfare, changes in welfare correspond to changes in aggregate surplus in a quasilinear model.

having $\sum_i x_i = \sum_j q_j$. From Section 10.D and Figure 10.D.1 we know that the utility vectors $(u_1, \ldots, u_I)$ that are achievable through reallocation of the numeraire given these consumption and production levels of good $\ell$ are

$$\left\{ (u_1, \ldots, u_I): \sum_{i=1}^{I} u_i \leq \omega_m + \sum_{i=1}^{I} \phi_i(x_i) - \sum_{j=1}^{J} c_j(q_j) \right\}.$$

Now, if a central authority is redistributing the numeraire to maximize $W(u_1, \ldots, u_I)$, the ultimate maximized value of welfare must be greater the larger this set is (i.e., the farther out the boundary of the set is). Hence, we see that a change in the consumption and production levels of good $\ell$ leads to an increase in welfare (given optimal redistribution of the numeraire) if and only if it increases the Marshallian aggregate surplus

$$S(x_1, \ldots, x_I, q_1, \ldots, q_J) = \sum_{i=1}^{I} \phi_i(x_i) - \sum_{j=1}^{J} c_j(q_j). \tag{10.E.1}$$

Figure 10.E.1 provides an illustration. It shows three utility vectors for the case $I = 2$: An initial utility vector $u^0 = (u_1^0, u_2^0)$ associated with an allocation in which the consumption and production levels of good $\ell$ are $(x_1^0, \ldots, x_I^0, q_1^0, \ldots, q_J^0)$ and in which the wealth distribution has been optimized, a utility vector $u^1 = (u_1^1, u_2^1)$ that results from a change in the consumption and production levels of good $\ell$ to $(x_1^1, \ldots, x_I^1, q_1^1, \ldots, q_J^1)$ in the absence of any transfers of the numeraire, and a utility vector $u^{1*} = (u_1^{1*}, u_2^{1*})$ that results from this change once redistribution of the numeraire occurs to optimize social welfare. As can be seen in the figure, the change increases aggregate surplus and also increases welfare once optimal transfers of the numeraire occur, even though welfare would decrease in the absence of the transfers. Thus, as long as redistribution of wealth is occurring to maximize a social welfare function, changes in welfare can be measured by changes in Marshallian aggregate surplus (to repeat: for *any* social welfare function).[17]

In many circumstances of interest, the Marshallian surplus has a convenient and

---

17. Notice that no transfers would be necessary in the special case in which the social welfare function is in fact the "utilitarian" social welfare function $\sum_i u_i$; in this case, it is sufficient that all available units of the numeraire go to consumers (i.e., none goes to waste or is otherwise withheld).

historically important formulation in terms of areas lying vertically between the aggregate demand and supply functions for good $\ell$.

To expand on this point, we begin by making two key assumptions. Denoting by $x = \sum_i x_i$ the aggregate consumption of good $\ell$, we assume, first, that for any $x$, the individual consumptions of good $\ell$ are distributed optimally across consumers. That is, recalling our discussion of the inverse demand function $P(\cdot)$ in Section 10.C (see Figure 10.C.6), that we have $\phi_i'(x_i) = P(x)$ for every $i$. This condition will be satisfied if, for example, consumers act as price-takers and all consumers face the same price. Similarly, denoting by $q = \sum_j q_j$ the aggregate output of good $\ell$, we assume that the production of any total amount $q$ is distributed optimally across firms. That is, recalling our discussion of the industry marginal cost curve $C'(\cdot)$ in Section 10.C (see Figure 10.C.5), that we have $c_j'(q_j) = C'(q)$ for every $j$. This will be satisfied if, for example, firms act as price takers and all firms face the same price. Observe that we do not require that the price faced by consumers and firms be the same.[18]

Consider now a differential change $(dx_1, \ldots, dx_I, dq_1, \ldots, dq_J)$ in the quantities of good $\ell$ consumed and produced satisfying $\sum_i dx_i = \sum_j dq_j$, and denote $dx = \sum_i dx_i$. The change in aggregate Marshallian surplus is then

$$dS = \sum_{i=1}^{I} \phi_i'(x_i)\, dx_i - \sum_{j=1}^{J} c_j'(q_j)\, dq_j. \tag{10.E.2}$$

Since $\phi_i'(x_i) = P(x)$ for all $i$, and $c_j'(q_j) = C'(q)$ for all $j$, we get

$$dS = P(x) \sum_{i=1}^{I} dx_i - C'(q) \sum_{j=1}^{J} dq_j. \tag{10.E.3}$$

Finally, since $x = q$ (by market feasibility) and $\sum_j dq_j = \sum_i dx_i = dx$, this becomes

$$dS = [P(x) - C'(x)]\, dx. \tag{10.E.4}$$

This differential change in Marshallian surplus is depicted in Figure 10.E.2(a). Expression (10.E.4) is quite intuitive; it tells us that starting at aggregate consumption level $x$ the marginal effect on social welfare of an increase in the aggregate quantity consumed, $dx$, is equal to consumers' marginal benefit from this consumption, $P(x)\, dx$, less the marginal cost of this extra production, $C'(x)\, dx$ (both in terms of the numeraire).

We can also integrate (10.E.4) to express the total value of the aggregate Marshallian surplus at the aggregate consumption level $x$, denoted $S(x)$, in terms of an integral of the difference between the inverse demand function and the industry marginal cost function,

$$S(x) = S_0 + \int_0^x [P(s) - C'(s)]\, ds, \tag{10.E.5}$$

---

18. For example, consumers may face a tax per unit purchased that makes the price they pay differ from the price received by the firms (see Example 10.C.1). The assumptions made here also hold in the monopoly model to be studied in Section 12.B. In that model, there is a single firm (and so there is no issue of optimal allocation of production), and all consumers act as price takers facing the same price. An example where the assumption of an optimal allocation of production is not valid is the Cournot duopoly model of Chapter 12 when firms have different efficiencies. There, firms with different costs have different levels of marginal cost in an equilibrium.

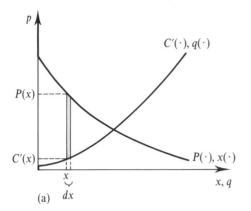

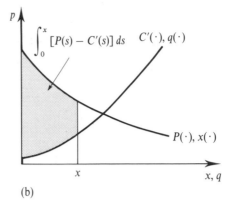

**Figure 10.E.2**

(a) A differential change in Marshallian surplus. (b) The Marshallian surplus at aggregate consumption level $x$.

where $S_0$ is a constant of integration equal to the value of the aggregate surplus when there is no consumption or production of good $\ell$ [it is equal to zero if $c_j(0) = 0$ for all $j$]. The integral in (10.E.5) is depicted in Figure 10.E.2(b); it is exactly equal to the area lying vertically between the aggregate demand and supply curves for good $\ell$ up to quantity $x$.

Note from (10.E.5) that the value of the aggregate Marshallian surplus is maximized at the aggregate consumption level $x^*$ such that $P(x^*) = C'(x^*)$, which is exactly the competitive equilibrium aggregate consumption level.[19] This accords with Proposition 10.D.1, the first fundamental welfare theorem, which states that the competitive allocation is Pareto optimal.

**Example 10.E.1:** *The Welfare Effects of a Distortionary Tax.* Consider again the commodity tax problem studied in Example 10.C.1. Suppose now that the welfare authority keeps a balanced budget and returns the tax revenue raised to consumers by means of lump-sum transfers. What impact does this tax-and-transfer scheme have on welfare?[20]

To answer this question, it is convenient to let $(x_1^*(t), \ldots, x_I^*(t), q_1^*(t), \ldots, q_J^*(t))$ and $p^*(t)$ denote the equilibrium consumption, production, and price levels of good $\ell$ when the tax rate is $t$. Note that $\phi_i'(x_i^*(t)) = p^*(t) + t$ for all $i$ and that $c_j'(q_j^*(t)) = p^*(t)$ for all $j$. Thus, letting $x^*(t) = \sum_i x_i^*(t)$ and $S^*(t) = S(x^*(t))$, we can use (10.E.5) to express the change in aggregate Marshallian surplus resulting from

---

19. To see this, check first that $S''(x) \leq 0$ at all $x$. Hence, $S(\cdot)$ is a concave function and therefore $x^* > 0$ maximizes aggregate surplus if and only if $S'(x^*) = 0$. Then verify that $S'(x) = P(x) - C'(x)$ at all $x > 0$.

20. This problem is closely related to that studied in Example 3.I.1 (we could equally well motivate the analysis here by asking, as we did there, about the welfare cost of the distortionary tax relative to the use of a lump-sum tax that raises the same revenue; the measure of deadweight loss that emerges would be the same as that developed here). The discussion that follows amounts to an extension, in the quasilinear context, of the analysis of Example 3.I.1 to situations with many consumers and the presence of firms. For an approach that uses the theory of a normative representative consumer presented in Section 4.D, see the small-type discussion at the end of this section.

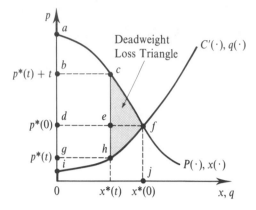

**Figure 10.E.3**

The deadweight welfare loss from distortionary taxation.

the introduction of the tax as

$$S^*(t) - S^*(0) = \int_{x^*(0)}^{x^*(t)} [P(s) - C'(s)] \, ds. \tag{10.E.6}$$

Expression (10.E.6) is negative because $x^*(t) < x^*(0)$ (recall the analysis of Example 10.C.1) and $P(x) \geq C'(x)$ for all $x \leq x^*(0)$, with strict inequality for $x < x^*(0)$. Hence, social welfare is optimized by setting $t = 0$. The loss in welfare from $t > 0$ is known as the *deadweight loss of distortionary taxation* and is equal to the area of the shaded region in Figure 10.E.3, called the *deadweight loss triangle*.

Notice that since $S^{*\prime}(t) = [P(x^*(t)) - C'(x^*(t))]x^{*\prime}(t)$, we have $S^{*\prime}(0) = 0$. That is, starting from a position without any tax, the first-order welfare effect of an infinitesimal tax is zero. Only as the tax rate increases above zero does the marginal effect become strictly negative. This is as it should be: if we start at an (interior) welfare maximum, then a small displacement from the optimum cannot have a first-order effect on welfare.

It is sometimes of interest to distinguish between the various components of aggregate Marshallian surplus that accrue directly to consumers, firms, and the tax authority.[21] The *aggregate consumer surplus* when consumers' effective price is $\hat{p}$ and therefore aggregate consumption is $x(\hat{p})$ is defined as the gross consumer benefits from consumption of good $\ell$ minus the consumers' total expenditure on this good (the latter is the cost to consumers in terms of forgone consumption of the numeraire):

$$CS(\hat{p}) = \sum_{i=1}^{I} \phi_i(x_i(\hat{p})) - \hat{p}x(\hat{p}).$$

Using again the fact that consumption is distributed optimally, we have

$$CS(\hat{p}) = \int_0^{x(\hat{p})} P(s) \, ds - \hat{p}x(\hat{p})$$

$$= \int_0^{x(\hat{p})} [P(s) - \hat{p}] \, ds \tag{10.E.7}$$

---

21. For example, if the set of active consumers of good $\ell$ is distinct from the set of owners of the firms producing the good, then this distinction tells us something about the distributional effects of the tax in the absence of transfers between owners and consumers.

Finally, the integral in (10.E.7) is equal to[22]

$$CS(\hat{p}) = \int_{\hat{p}}^{\infty} x(s) \, ds. \tag{10.E.8}$$

Thus, because consumers face an effective price of $p^*(t) + t$ when the tax is $t$, the change in consumer surplus from imposition of the tax is

$$CS(p^*(t) + t) - CS(p^*(0)) = -\int_{p^*(0)}^{p^*(t)+t} x(s) \, ds. \tag{10.E.9}$$

In Figure 10.E.3, the reduction in consumer surplus is depicted by area $(dbcf)$.

The aggregate profit, or *aggregate producer surplus*, when firms face effective price $\hat{p}$ is

$$\Pi(\hat{p}) = \hat{p}q(\hat{p}) - \sum_{j=1}^{J} c_j(q_j(\hat{p})).$$

Again, using the optimality of the allocation of production across firms, we have[23]

$$\Pi(\hat{p}) = \Pi_0 + \int_0^{q(\hat{p})} [\hat{p} - C'(s)] \, ds \tag{10.E.10}$$

$$= \Pi_0 + \int_0^{\hat{p}} q(s) \, ds, \tag{10.E.11}$$

where $\Pi_0$ is a constant of integration equal to profits when $q_j = 0$ for all $j$ [$\Pi_0 = 0$ if $c_j(0) = 0$ for all $j$]. Since producers pay no tax, they face price $p^*(t)$ when the tax rate is $t$. The change in producer surplus is therefore

$$\Pi(p^*(t)) - \Pi(p^*(0)) = -\int_{p^*(t)}^{p^*(0)} q(s) \, ds. \tag{10.E.12}$$

The reduction in producer surplus is depicted by area $(gdfh)$ in Figure 10.E.3.

Finally, the *tax revenue* is $tx^*(t)$; it is depicted in Figure 10.E.3 by area $(gbch)$.

The total deadweight welfare loss from the tax is then equal to the sum of the reductions in consumer and producer surplus less the tax revenue. ∎

The welfare measure developed here is closely related to our discussion of normative representative consumers in Section 4.D. We showed there that if a central authority is redistributing wealth to maximize a social welfare function given prices $p$, leading to a wealth distribution rule $(w_1(p, w), \dots, w_I(p, w))$, then there is a normative representative consumer with indirect utility function $v(p, w)$ whose demand $x(p, w)$ is exactly equal to aggregate demand [i.e., $x(p, w) = \sum_i x_i(p, w_i(p, w))$] and whose utility can be used as a measure of social welfare. Recalling our discussion in Section 3.I, this means that we can measure the change in welfare resulting from a price–wealth change by adding the representative consumer's

---

22. This can be seen geometrically. For example, when $\hat{p} = p^*(0)$, the integrals in both (10.E.7) and (10.E.8) are equal to area $(daf)$ in Figure 10.E.3. Formally, the equivalence follows from a change of variables and integration by parts (see Exercise 10.E.2).

23. When $\hat{p} = p^*(0)$, the integrals in both (10.E.10) and (10.E.11) are equal to area $(idf)$ in Figure 10.E.3. The equivalence of these two integrals again follows formally by a change of variables and integration by parts.

compensating or equivalent variation for the price change to the change in the representative consumer's wealth (see Exercise 3.I.12). But in the quasilinear case, the representative consumer's compensating and equivalent variations are the same and can be calculated by direct integration of the representative consumer's Walrasian demand function, that is, by integration of the aggregate demand function. Hence, in Example 10.E.1, the representative consumer's compensating variation for the price change is exactly equal to the change in aggregate consumer surplus, expression (10.E.9). The change in the representative consumer's wealth, on the other hand, is equal to the change in aggregate profits plus the tax revenue rebated to consumers. Thus, the total welfare change arising from the introduction of the tax-and-transfer scheme, as measured using the normative representative consumer, is exactly equal to the deadweight loss calculated in Example 10.E.1.[24]

Another way to justify the use of aggregate surplus as a welfare measure in the quasilinear model is as a measure of *potential Pareto improvement*. Consider the tax example. We could say that a change in the tax represents a *potential* Pareto improvement if there is a set of lump-sum transfers of the numeraire that would make all consumers better off than they were before the tax change. In the present quasilinear context, this is true if and only if aggregate surplus increases with the change in the tax. This approach is sometimes referred to as the *compensation principle* because it asks whether, in principle, it is possible given the change for the winners to compensate the losers so that all are better off than before. (See also the discussion in Example 4.D.2 and especially Section 22.C.)

We conclude this section with a warning: When the numeraire represents many goods, the welfare analysis we have performed is justified only if the prices of goods other than good $\ell$ are undistorted in the sense that they equal these goods' true marginal utilities and production costs. Hence, these other markets must be competitive, and all market participants must face the same price. If this condition does not hold, then the costs of production faced by producers of good $\ell$ do not reflect the true social costs incurred from their use of these goods as inputs. Exercise 10.G.3 provides an illustration of this problem.

# 10.F  Free-Entry and Long-Run Competitive Equilibria

Up to this point, we have taken the set of firms and their technological capabilities as fixed. In this section, we consider the case in which an infinite number of firms can potentially be formed, each with access to the most efficient production technology. Moreover, firms may enter or exit the market in response to profit opportunities. This scenario, known as a situation of *free entry*, is often a reasonable approximation when we think of long-run outcomes in a market. In the discussion that follows, we introduce and study a notion of *long-run competitive equilibrium* and then discuss how this concept can be used to analyze long-run and short-run comparative statics effects.

To begin, suppose that each of an infinite number of potential firms has access to a technology for producing good $\ell$ with cost function $c(q)$, where $q$ is the *individual* firm's output of good $\ell$. We assume that $c(0) = 0$; that is, a firm can earn zero profits by simply deciding to be inactive and setting $q = 0$. In the terminology of Section

---

24. This deadweight loss measure corresponds also to the measure developed for the one-consumer case in Example 3.I.1, where we implicitly limited ourselves to the case in which the taxed good has a constant unit cost.

5.B, there are no sunk costs in the long run. The aggregate demand function is $x(\cdot)$, with inverse demand function $P(\cdot)$.

In a long-run competitive equilibrium, we would like to determine not only the price and output levels for the firms but also the number of firms that are active in the industry. Given our assumption of identical firms, we focus on equilibria in which all active firms produce the same output level, so that a long-run competitive equilibrium can be described by a triple $(p, q, J)$ formed by a price $p$, an output per firm $q$, and an integer number of active firms $J$ (hence the total industry output is $Q = Jq$).[25] The central assumption determining the number of active firms is one of free entry and exit: A firm will enter the market if it can earn positive profits at the going market price and will exit if it can make only negative profits at any positive production level given this price. If all firms, active and potential, take prices as unaffected by their own actions, this implies that active firms must earn exactly zero profits in any long-run competitive equilibrium; otherwise, we would have either no firms willing to be active in the market (if profits were negative) or an infinite number of firms entering the market (if profits were positive). This leads us to the formulation given in Definition 10.F.1.

**Definition 10.F.1:** Given an aggregate demand function $x(p)$ and a cost function $c(q)$ for each potentially active firm having $c(0) = 0$, a triple $(p^*, q^*, J^*)$ is a *long-run competitive equilibrium* if

(i) $q^*$ solves $\underset{q \geq 0}{\mathrm{Max}}\ p^*q - c(q)$     (Profit maximization)

(ii) $x(p^*) = J^*q^*$     (Demand = supply)

(iii) $p^*q^* - c(q^*) = 0$     (Free Entry Condition).

The long-run equilibrium price can be thought of as equating demand with long-run supply, where the long-run supply takes into account firms' entry and exit decisions. In particular, if $q(\cdot)$ is the supply correspondence of an individual firm with cost function $c(\cdot)$ and $\pi(\cdot)$ is its profit function, we can define a *long-run aggregate supply correspondence* by[26]

$$Q(p) = \begin{cases} \infty & \text{if } \pi(p) > 0, \\ \{Q \geq 0: Q = Jq \text{ for some integer } J \geq 0 \text{ and } q \in q(p)\} & \text{if } \pi(p) = 0. \end{cases}$$

If $\pi(p) > 0$, then every firm wants to supply an amount strictly bounded away from zero. Hence, the aggregate supply is infinite. If $\pi(p) = 0$ and $Q = Jq$ for some $q \in q(p)$, then we can have $J$ firms each supply $q$ and have the rest remain inactive [since $c(0) = 0$, this is a profit-maximizing choice for the inactive firms as well]. With this

---

25. The assumption that all active firms produce the same output level is without loss of generality whenever $c(\cdot)$ is strictly convex on the set $(0, \infty]$. A firm's supply correspondence can then include at most one positive output level at any given price $p$.

26. In terms of the basic properties of production sets presented in Section 5.B, the long-run supply correspondence is the supply correspondence of the production set $Y^+$, where $Y$ is the production set associated with the individual firm [i.e., with $c(\cdot)$], and $Y^+$ is its "additive closure" (i.e., the smallest set that contains $Y$ and is additive: $Y^+ + Y^+ \subset Y^+$; see Exercise 5.B.4).

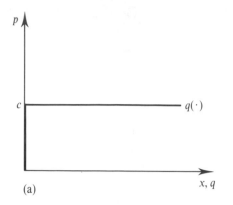

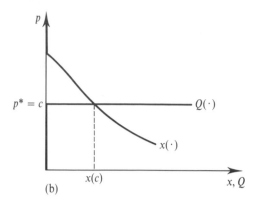

**Figure 10.F.1**

Long-run competitive equilibrium with constant returns to scale. (a) A firm's supply correspondence. (b) Long-run equilibrium.

notion of a long-run supply correspondence, $p^*$ is a long-run competitive equilibrium price if and only if $x(p^*) \in Q(p^*)$.[27]

We now investigate this long-run competitive equilibrium notion. Consider first the case in which the cost function $c(\cdot)$ exhibits constant returns to scale, so that $c(q) = cq$ for some $c > 0$, and assume that $x(c) > 0$. In this case, condition (i) of Definition 10.F.1 tells us that in any long-run competitive equilbrium we have $p^* \leq c$ (otherwise, there is no profit-maximizing production). However, at any such price, aggregate consumption is strictly positive since $x(c) > 0$, so condition (ii) requires that $q^* > 0$, By condition (iii), we must have $(p^* - c)q^* = 0$. Hence, we conclude that $p^* = c$ and aggregate consumption is $x(c)$. Note, however, that $J^*$ and $q^*$ are *indeterminate*: any $J^*$ and $q^*$ such that $J^*q^* = x(c)$ satisfies conditions (i) and (ii).

Figure 10.F.1 depicts this long-run equilibrium. The supply correspondence of an individual firm $q(\cdot)$ is illustrated in Figure 10.F.1(a); Figure 10.F.1(b) shows the long-run equilibrium price and aggregate output as the intersection of the graph of the aggregate demand function $x(\cdot)$ with the graph of the long-run aggregate supply correspondence

$$
Q(p) = \begin{cases} \infty & \text{if } p > c \\ [0, \infty) & \text{if } p = c \\ 0 & \text{if } p < c. \end{cases}
$$

We move next to the case in which $c(\cdot)$ is increasing and strictly convex (i.e., the production technology of an individual firm displays strictly decreasing returns to scale). We assume also that $x(c'(0)) > 0$. With this type of cost function, *no long-run competitive equilibrium can exist*. To see why this is so, note that if $p > c'(0)$, then $\pi(p) > 0$ and therefore the long-run supply is infinite. On the other hand, if $p \leq c'(0)$, then the long-run supply is zero while $x(p) > 0$. The problem is illustrated in Figure 10.F.2, where the graph of the demand function $x(\cdot)$ has no intersection with the

---

27. In particular, if $(p^*, q^*, J^*)$ is a long-run equilibrium, then condition (i) of Definition 10.F.1 implies that $q^* \in q(p^*)$ and condition (iii) implies that $\pi(p^*) = 0$. Hence, by condition (ii), $x(p^*) \in Q(p^*)$. In the other direction, if $x(p^*) \in Q(p^*)$, then $\pi(p^*) = 0$ and there exists $q^* \in q(p^*)$ and $J^*$ with $x(p^*) = J^*q^*$. Therefore, the three conditions of Definition 10.F.1 are satisfied.

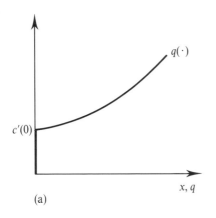

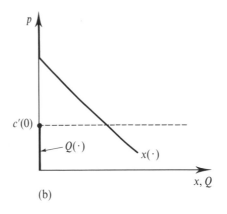

(a)

(b)

**Figure 10.F.2**

Nonexistence of long-run competitive equilibrium with strictly convex costs. (a) A firm's supply correspondence. (b) No intersection of long-run supply and demand.

graph of the long-run aggregate supply correspondence

$$Q(p) = \begin{cases} \infty & \text{if } p > c'(0) \\ 0 & \text{if } p \leq c'(0). \end{cases}$$

The difficulty can be understood in a related way. As discussed in Exercise 5.B.4, the long-run aggregate production set in the situation just described is convex but not closed. This can be seen in Figure 10.F.3, where the industry marginal cost function with $J$ firms,

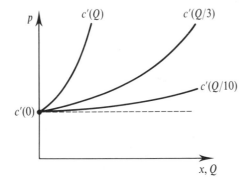

**Figure 10.F.3**

The limiting behavior of industry marginal cost as $J \to \infty$ with strictly convex costs.

$c'(Q/J)$, is shown for various values of $J$ (in particular, for $J = 1$, $J = 3$, and $J = 10$). Note that as $J$ increases, this marginal cost function approaches *but never reaches* the marginal cost function corresponding to a constant marginal cost of $c'(0)$.

Perhaps not surprisingly, to generate the existence of an equilibrium with a determinate number of firms, the long-run cost function must exhibit a strictly positive efficient scale; that is, *there must exist a strictly positive output level $\bar{q}$ at which a firm's average costs of production are minimized* (see Section 5.D for a further discussion of the efficient scale concept).

Suppose, in particular, that $c(\cdot)$ has a unique efficient scale $\bar{q} > 0$, and let the minimized level of average cost be $\bar{c} = c(\bar{q})/\bar{q}$. Assume, moreover, that $x(\bar{c}) > 0$. If at a long-run equilibrium $(p^*, q^*, J^*)$ we had $p^* > \bar{c}$, then $p^*\bar{q} > \bar{c}\bar{q}$, and so we would have $\pi(p^*) > 0$. Thus, at any long-run equilibrium we must have $p^* \leq \bar{c}$. In contrast, if $p^* < \bar{c}$, then $x(p^*) > 0$; but since $p^*q - c(q) = p^*q - (c(q)/q)q \leq (p^* - \bar{c})q < 0$

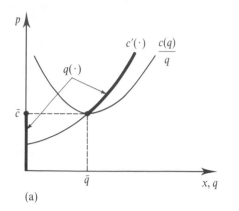

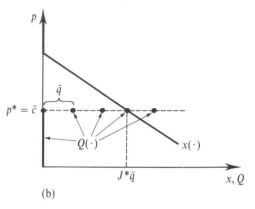

**Figure 10.F.4**

Long-run competitive equilibrium when average costs exhibit a strictly positive efficient scale. (a) A firm's supply correspondence. (b) Long-run equilibrium.

for all $q > 0$, a firm would earn strictly negative profits at any positive level of output. So $p^* < \bar{c}$ also cannot be a long-run equilibrium price. Thus, at any long-run equilibrium we must have $p^* = \bar{c}$. Moreover, if $p^* = \bar{c}$, then each active firm's supply must be $q^* = \bar{q}$ (this is the only strictly positive output level at which the firm earns nonnegative profits), and the equilibrium number of active firms is therefore $J^* = x(\bar{c})/\bar{q}$.[28] In conclusion, the number of active firms is a well-determined quantity at long-run equilibrium. Figure 10.F.4 depicts such an equilibrium. The long-run aggregate supply correspondence is

$$Q(p) = \begin{cases} \infty & \text{if } p > \bar{c} \\ \{Q \geq 0 : Q = J\bar{q} \text{ for some integer } J \geq 0\} & \text{if } p = \bar{c} \\ 0 & \text{if } p < \bar{c}. \end{cases}$$

Observe that the equilibrium price and aggregate output are exactly the same as if the firms had a constant returns to scale technology with unit cost $\bar{c}$.

Several points should be noted about the equilibrium depicted in Figure 10.F.4. First, if the efficient scale of operation is large relative to the size of market demand, it could well turn out that the equilibrium number of active firms is small. In these cases, we may reasonably question the appropriateness of the price-taking assumption (e.g., what if $J^* = 1$?). Indeed, we are then likely to be in the realm of the situations with market power studied in Chapter 12.

Second, we have conveniently shown the demand at price $\bar{c}$, $x(\bar{c})$, to be an integer multiple of $\bar{q}$. Were this not so, no long-run equilibrium would exist because the graphs of the demand function and the long-run supply correspondence would

---

28. Note that when $c(\cdot)$ is differentiable, condition (i) of Definition 10.F.1 implies that $c'(q^*) = p^*$, while condition (iii) implies $p^* = c(q^*)/q^*$. Thus, a *necessary* condition for an equilibrium is that $c'(q^*) = c(q^*)/q^*$. This is the condition for $q^*$ to be a critical point of average costs [differentiate $c(q)/q$ and see Exercise 5.D.1]. In the case where average cost $c(q)/q$ is U-shaped (i.e., with no critical point other than the global minimum, as shown in Figure 10.F.4), this implies that $q^* = \bar{q}$, and so $p^* = \bar{c}$ and $J^* = x(\bar{c})/\bar{q}$. Note, however, that the argument in the text does not require this assumption about the shape of average costs.

not intersect.[29] The nonexistence of competitive equilibrium can occur here for the same reason that we have already alluded to in small type in Section 10.C: The long-run production technologies we are considering exhibit nonconvexities.

It seems plausible, however, that when the efficient scale of a firm is small relative to the size of the market, this "integer problem" should not be too much of a concern. In fact, when we study oligopolistic markets in Chapter 12, we shall see that when firms' efficient scales are small in this sense, the oligopolistic equilibrium price is close to $\bar{c}$, the equilibrium price we would derive if we simply ignored the integer constraint on the number of firms $J^*$. Intuitively, when the efficient scale is small, we will have many firms in the industry and the equilibrium, although not strictly competitive, will involve a price close to $\bar{c}$. Thus, if the efficient scale is small relative to the size of the market [as measured by $x(\bar{c})$], then ignoring the integer problem and treating firms as price takers gives approximately the correct answer.

Third, when an equilibrium exists, as in Figure 10.F.4, the equilibrium outcome maximizes Marshallian aggregate surplus and therefore is Pareto optimal. To see this, note from Figure 10.F.4 that aggregate surplus at the considered equilibrium is equal to

$$\operatorname*{Max}_{x \geq 0} \int_0^x P(s)\, ds - \bar{c}x,$$

the maximized value of aggregate surplus when firms' cost functions are $\bar{c}q$. But because $c(q) \geq \bar{c}q$ for all $q$, this must be the largest attainable value of aggregate surplus given the actual cost function $c(\cdot)$; that is,

$$\operatorname*{Max}_{x \geq 0} \int_0^x P(s)\, ds - \bar{c}x \geq \int_0^{\hat{x}} P(s)\, ds - Jc(\hat{x}/J),$$

for all $\hat{x}$ and $J$. This fact provides an example of a point we raised at the end of Section 10.D (and will substantiate with considerable generality in Chapter 16): The first welfare theorem continues to be valid even in the absence of convexity of individual production sets.

### Short-Run and Long-Run Comparative Statics

Although firms may enter and exit the market in response to profit opportunities in the long run, these changes may take time. For example, factories may need to be shut down, the workforce reduced, and machinery sold when a firm exits an industry. It may even pay a firm to continue operating until a suitable buyer for its plant and equipment can be found. When examining the comparative statics effects of a shock to a market, it is therefore important to distinguish between long-run and short-run effects.

Suppose, for example, that we are at a long-run equilibrium with $J^*$ active firms

---

29. An intermediate case between constant returns (where any scale is efficient) and the case of a unique efficient scale occurs when there is a range $[\underline{q}, \bar{q}]$ of efficient scales (the average cost curve has a flat bottom). In this case, the integer problem is mitigated. For a long-run competitive equilibrium to exist, we now only need there to be some $q \in [\underline{q}, \bar{q}]$ such that $x(\bar{c})/q$ is an integer. Of course, as the interval $[\underline{q}, \bar{q}]$ grows larger, not only are the chances of a long-run equilibrium existing greater, but so are the chances of indeterminacy of the equilibrium number of firms (i.e., of multiple equilibria involving differing numbers of firms).

each producing $q*$ units of output and that there is some shock to demand (similar points can be made for supply shocks). In the short run, it may be impossible for any new firms to organize and enter the industry, and so we will continue to have $J*$ firms for at least some period of time. Moreover, these $J*$ firms may face a short-run cost function $c_s(\cdot)$ that differs from the long-run cost function $c(\cdot)$ because various input levels may be fixed in the short run. For example, firms may have the long-run cost function

$$c(q) = \begin{cases} K + \psi(q) & \text{if } q > 0 \\ 0 & \text{if } q = 0, \end{cases} \qquad (10.F.1)$$

where $\psi(0) = 0$, $\psi'(q) > 0$, and $\psi''(q) > 0$. But in the short run, it may be impossible for an active firm to recover its fixed costs if it exits and sets $q = 0$. Hence, in the short run the firm has the cost function

$$c_s(q) = K + \psi(q) \qquad \text{for all } q \geq 0. \qquad (10.F.2)$$

Another possibility is that $c(q)$ might be the cost function of some multiple-input production process, and in the short run an active firm may be unable to vary its level of some inputs. (See the discussion in Section 5.B on this point and also Exercises 10.F.5 and 10.F.6 for illustrations.)

   Whenever the distinction between short run and long run is significant, the *short-run comparative statics effects* of a demand shock may best be determined by solving for the competitive equilibrium given $J*$ firms, each with cost function $c_s(\cdot)$, and the new demand function. This is just the equilibrium notion studied in Section 10.C, where we take firms' cost functions to be $c_s(\cdot)$. The *long-run comparative statics effects* can then be determined by solving for the long-run (i.e., free entry) equilibrium given the new demand function and long-run cost function $c(\cdot)$.

**Example 10.F.1:** *Short-Run and Long-Run Comparative Statics with Lumpy Fixed Costs that Are Sunk in the Short Run.* Suppose that the long-run cost function $c(\cdot)$ is given by (10.F.1) but that in the short run the fixed cost $K$ is sunk so that $c_s(\cdot)$ is given by (10.F.2). The aggregate demand function is initially $x(\cdot, \alpha_0)$, and the industry is at a long-run equilibrium with $J_0$ firms, each producing $\bar{q}$ units of output [the efficient scale for cost function $c(\cdot)$], and a price of $p* = \bar{c} = c(\bar{q})/\bar{q}$. This equilibrium position is depicted in Figure 10.F.5.

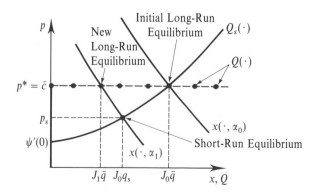

**Figure 10.F.5**

Short-run and long-run comparative statics in Example 10.F.1.

Now suppose that we have a shift to the demand function $x(\cdot, \alpha_1)$ shown in Figure 10.F.5. The short-run equilibrium is determined by the intersection of the graph of this demand function with the graph of the industry supply correspondence of the $J_0$ firms, each of which has short-run cost function $c_s(\cdot)$. The short-run aggregate supply correspondence is depicted as $Q_s(\cdot)$ in the figure. Thus, in the short run, the shock to demand causes price to fall to $p_s$ and output per firm to fall to $q_s$. Firms' profits also fall; since $p_s < \bar{c}$, active firms lose money in the short run.

In the long run, however, firms exit in response to the decrease in demand, with the number of firms falling to $J_1 < J_0$, each producing output $\bar{q}$. Price returns to $p^* = \bar{c}$, aggregate consumption is $x(\bar{c}, \alpha_1)$, and all active firms once again earn zero profits. This new long-run equilibrium is also shown in Figure 10.F.5. ∎

---

This division of dynamic adjustment into two periods, although useful as a first approximation, is admittedly crude. It may often be reasonable to think that there are several distinct short-run stages corresponding to different levels of adjustment costs associated with different decisions: in the very short run, production may be completely fixed; in the medium run, some inputs may be adjusted while others may not be; perhaps entry and exit take place only in the "very long run." Moreover, the methodology that we have discussed treats the two periods in isolation from each other. This approach ignores, for example, the possibility of intertemporal substitution by consumers when tomorow's price is expected to differ from today's (intertemporal substitution might be particularly important for very short-run periods when the fact that many production decisions are fixed can make prices very sensitive to demand shocks).

These weaknesses are not flaws in the competitive model per se, but rather only in the somewhat extreme methodological simplification adopted here. A fully satisfactory treatment of these issues requires an explicitly dynamic model that places expectations at center stage. In Chapter 20 we study dynamic models of competitive markets in greater depth. Nevertheless, this simple dichotomization into long-run and short-run periods of adjustment is often a useful starting point for analysis.

---

# 10.G  Concluding Remarks on Partial Equilibrium Analysis

In principle, the analysis of Pareto optimal outcomes and competitive equilibria requires the simultaneous consideration of the entire economy (a task we undertake in Part IV). Partial equilibrium analysis can be thought of as facilitating matters on two accounts. On the positive side, it allows us to determine the equilibrium outcome in the particular market under study in isolation from all other markets. On the normative side, it allows us to use Marshallian aggregate surplus as a welfare measure that, in many cases of interest, has a very convenient representation in terms of the area lying vertically between the aggregate demand and supply curves.

In the model considered in Sections 10.C to 10.F, the validity of both of these simplifications rested, implicitly, on two premises: first, that the prices of all commodities other than the one under consideration remain fixed; second, that there are no wealth effects in the market under study. We devote this section to a few additional interpretative comments regarding these assumptions. (See also Section 15.E for an example illustrating the limits of partial equilibrium analysis.)

The assumption that the prices of goods other than the good under consideration (say, good $\ell$) remain fixed is essential for limiting our positive and normative analysis to a single market. In Section 10.B, we justified this assumption in terms of the market for good $\ell$ being small and having a diffuse influence over the remaining markets. However, this is not its only possible justification. For example, the nonsubstitution theorem (see Appendix A of Chapter 5) implies that the prices of all other goods will remain fixed if the numeraire is the only primary (i.e., nonproduced) factor, all produced goods other than $\ell$ are produced under conditions of constant returns using the numeraire and produced commodities other than $\ell$ as inputs, and there is no joint production.[30]

Even when we cannot assume that all other prices are fixed, however, a generalization of our single-market partial equilibrium analysis is sometimes possible. Often we are interested not in a single market but in a group of commodities that are strongly interrelated either in consumers' tastes (tea and coffee are the classic examples) or in firms' technologies. In this case, studying one market at a time while keeping other prices fixed is no longer a useful approach because what matters is the *simultaneous* determination of *all* prices in the group. However, if the prices of goods outside the group may be regarded as unaffected by changes within the markets for this group of commodities, and if there are no wealth effects for commodities in the group, then we can extend much of the analysis presented in Sections 10.C to 10.F.

To this effect, suppose that the group is composed of $M$ goods, and let $x_i \in \mathbb{R}_+^M$ and $q_j \in \mathbb{R}^M$ be vectors of consumptions and productions for these $M$ goods. Each consumer has a utility function of the form

$$u_i(m_i, x_i) = m_i + \phi_i(x_i),$$

where $m_i$ is the consumption of the numeraire commodity (i.e., the total expenditure on commodities outside the group). Firms' cost functions are $c_j(q_j)$. With this specification, many of the basic results of the previous sections go through unmodified (often it is just a matter of reinterpreting $x_i$ and $q_j$ as vectors). In particular, the results discussed in Section 10.C on the uniqueness of equilibrium and its independence from initial endowments still hold (see Exercise 10.G.1), as do the welfare theorems of Section 10.D. However, our ability to conduct welfare analysis using the areas lying vertically between demand and supply curves becomes much more limited. The cross-effects among markets with changing and interrelated prices cannot be

---

30. A simple example of this result arises when all produced goods other than $\ell$ are produced directly from the numeraire with constant returns to scale. In this case, the equilibrium price of each of these goods is equal to the amount of the numeraire that must be used as an input in its production per unit of output produced. More generally, prices for produced goods other than $\ell$ will remain fixed under the conditions of the nonsubstitution theorem because all efficient production vectors can be generated using a single set of techniques. In any equilibrium, the price of each produced good other than $\ell$ must be equal to the amount of the numeraire embodied in a unit of the good in the efficient production technique, either directly through the use of the numeraire as an input or indirectly through the use as inputs of produced goods other than $\ell$ that are in turn produced using the numeraire (or using other produced goods that are themselves produced using the numeraire, and so on).

ignored.[31] (Exercises 10.G.3 to 10.G.5 ask you to consider some issues related to this point.)

The assumption of no wealth effects for good $\ell$, on the other hand, is critical for the validity of the style of welfare analysis that we have carried out in this chapter. Without it, as we shall see in Part IV, Pareto optimality cannot be determined independently from the particular distribution of welfare sought, and we already know from Section 3.I that area measures calculated from Walrasian demand functions are not generally correct measures of compensating or equivalent variations (for which the Hicksian demand functions should be used). However, the assumption of no wealth effects is much less critical for positive analysis (determination of equilibrium, comparative statics effects, and so on). Even with wealth effects, the demand-and-supply apparatus can still be quite helpful for the positive part of the theory. The behavior of firms, for example, is not changed in any way. Consumers, on the other hand, have a demand function that, with prices of the other goods kept fixed, now depends only on the price for good $\ell$ and wealth. If wealth is determined from initial endowments and shareholdings, then we can view wealth as itself a function of the price of good $\ell$ (recall that other prices are fixed), and so we can again express demand as a function of this good's price alone. Formally, the analysis reduces to that presented in Section 10.C: The equilibrium in market $\ell$ can be identified as an intersection point of demand and supply curves.[32]

---

31. A case in which the single-market analysis for good $\ell$ is still fully justified is when utility and cost functions have the form

$$u_i(m_i, x_i) = m_i + \phi_{\ell i}(x_{\ell i}) + \phi_{-\ell, i}(x_{-\ell, i}),$$

and

$$c_j(q_j) = c_{\ell j}(q_{\ell j}) + c_{-\ell, j}(q_{-\ell, j}),$$

where $x_{-\ell, i}$ and $q_{-\ell, j}$ are consumption and production vectors for goods in the group other than $\ell$. With this additive separability in good $\ell$, the markets for goods in the group other than $\ell$ do not influence the equilibrium price in market $\ell$. Good $\ell$ is effectively independent of the group, and we can treat it in isolation, as we have done in the previous sections. (In point of fact, we do not even need to assume that the remaining markets in the group keep their prices fixed. What happens in them is simply irrelevant for equilibrium and welfare analysis in the market for good $\ell$.) See Exercise 10.G.2.

32. The presence of wealth effects can lead, however, to some interesting new phenomena on the consumer's side. One is the *backward-bending* demand curve, where demand for a good is *increasing* in its price over some range. This can happen if consumers have endowments of good $\ell$, because then an increase in its price increases consumers' wealth and could lead to a net increase in their demands for good $\ell$, even if it is a normal good.

## REFERENCES

Marshall, A. (1920). *Principles of Economics*. New York: Macmillan.

Stigler, G. (1987). *The Theory of Price*, 4th ed. New York: Macmillan.

Vives, X. (1987). Small income effects: A Marshallian theory of consumer surplus and downward sloping demand. *Review of Economic Studies* **54**: 87–103.

## EXERCISES

**10.B.1$^B$** The concept defined in Definition 10.B.2 is sometimes known as *strong Pareto efficiency*. An outcome is *weakly Pareto efficient* if there is no alternative feasible allocation that makes *all* individuals *strictly* better off.

(a) Argue that if an outcome is strongly Pareto efficient, then it is weakly Pareto efficient as well.

(b) Show that if all consumers' preferences are continuous and strongly monotone, then these two notions of Pareto efficiency are equivalent for any *interior* outcome (i.e., an outcome in which each consumer's consumption lies in the interior of his consumption set). Assume for simplicity that $X_i = \mathbb{R}_+^L$ for all $i$.

(c) Construct an example where the two notions are not equivalent. Why is the strong monotonicity assumption important in (b)? What about interiority?

**10.B.2$^A$** Show that if allocation $(x_1^*, \ldots, x_I^*, y_1^*, \ldots, y_J^*)$ and price vector $p^* \gg 0$ constitute a competitive equilibrium, then allocation $(x_1^*, \ldots, x_I^*, y_1^*, \ldots, y_J^*)$ and price vector $\alpha p^*$ also constitute a competitive equilibrium for any scalar $\alpha > 0$.

**10.C.1$^B$** Suppose that consumer $i$'s preferences can be represented by the utility function $u_i(x_{1i}, \ldots, x_{Li}) = \sum_{\ell} \log(x_{\ell i})$ (these are Cobb–Douglas preferences).

(a) Derive his demand for good $\ell$. What is the wealth effect?

(b) Now consider a sequence of situations in which we proportionately increase both the number of goods and the consumer's wealth. What happens to the wealth effect in the limit?

**10.C.2$^B$** Consider the two-good quasilinear model presented in Section 10.C with one consumer and one firm (so that $I = 1$ and $J = 1$). The initial endowment of the numeraire is $\omega_m > 0$, and the initial endowment of good $\ell$ is 0. Let the consumer's quasilinear utility function be $\phi(x) + m$, where $\phi(x) = \alpha + \beta \ln x$ for some $(\alpha, \beta) \gg 0$. Also, let the firm's cost function be $c(q) = \sigma q$ for some scalar $\sigma > 0$. Assume that the consumer receives all the profits of the firm. Both the firm and the consumer act as price takers. Normalize the price of good $m$ to equal 1, and denote the price of good $\ell$ by $p$.

(a) Derive the consumer's and the firm's first-order conditions.

(b) Derive the competitive equilibrium price and output of good $\ell$. How do these vary with $\alpha$, $\beta$, and $\sigma$?

**10.C.3$^B$** Consider a central authority who operates $J$ firms with differentiable convex cost functions $c_j(q_j)$ for producing good $\ell$ from the numeraire. Define $C(q)$ to be the central authority's minimized cost level for producing aggregate quantity $q$; that is

$$C(q) = \underset{(q_1, \ldots, q_J) \geq 0}{\text{Min}} \sum_{j=1}^{J} c_j(q_j)$$

$$\text{s.t.} \sum_{j=1}^{J} q_j \geq q.$$

(a) Derive the first-order conditions for this cost-minimization problem.

(b) Show that at the cost-minimizing production allocation $(q_1^*, \ldots, q_J^*)$, $C'(q) = c_j'(q_j^*)$ for all $j$ with $q_j^* > 0$ (i.e., the central authority's marginal cost at aggregate output level $q$ equals each firm's marginal cost level at the optimal production allocation for producing $q$).

(c) Show that if firms all maximize profit facing output price $p = C'(q)$ (with the price of the numeraire equal to 1), then the consequent output choices result in an aggregate output of $q$. Conclude that $C'(\cdot)$ is the inverse of the industry supply function $q(\cdot)$.

**10.C.4$^B$** Consider a central authority who has $x$ units of good $\ell$ to allocate among $I$ consumers, each of whom has a quasilinear utility function of the form $\phi_i(x_i) + m_i$, with $\phi_i(\cdot)$ a differentiable, increasing, and strictly concave function. The central authority allocates good $\ell$ to maximize the sum of consumers' utilities $\sum_i u_i$.

**(a)** Set up the central authority's problem and derive its first-order condition.

**(b)** Let $\gamma(x)$ be the value function of the central authority's problem, and let $P(x) = \gamma'(x)$ be its derivative. Show that if $(x_1^*, \ldots, x_I^*)$ is the optimal allocation of good $\ell$ given available quantity $x$, then $P(x) = \phi_i'(x_i^*)$ for all $i$ with $x_i^* > 0$.

**(c)** Argue that if all consumers maximize utility facing a price for good $\ell$ of $P(x)$ (with the price of the numeraire equal to 1), then the aggregate demand for good $\ell$ is exactly $x$. Conclude that $P(\cdot)$ is, in fact, the inverse of the aggregate demand function $x(\cdot)$.

**10.C.5$^B$** Derive the differential change in the equilibrium price in response to a differential change in the tax in Example 10.C.1 by applying the implicit function theorem to the system of equations (10.C.4) to (10.C.6).

**10.C.6$^B$** A tax is to be levied on a commodity bought and sold in a competitive market. Two possible forms of tax may be used: In one case, a *specific* tax is levied, where an amount $t$ is paid per unit bought or sold (this is the case considered in the text); in the other case, an *ad valorem* tax is levied, where the government collects a tax equal to $\tau$ times the amount the seller receives from the buyer. Assume that a partial equilibrium approach is valid.

**(a)** Show that, with a specific tax, the ultimate cost of the good to consumers and the amounts purchased are independent of whether the consumers or the producers pay the tax.

**(b)** Show that this is not generally true with an ad valorem tax. In this case, which collection method leads to a higher cost to consumers? Are there special cases in which the collection method is irrelevant with an ad valorem tax?

**10.C.7$^B$** An ad valorem tax of $\tau$ (see Exercise 10.C.6 for a definition) is to be levied on consumers in a competitive market with aggregate demand curve $x(p) = Ap^\varepsilon$, where $A > 0$ and $\varepsilon < 0$, and aggregate supply curve $q(p) = \alpha p^\gamma$, where $\alpha > 0$ and $\gamma > 0$. Calculate the percentage change in consumer cost and producer receipts per unit sold for a small ("marginal") tax. Denote $\kappa = (1 + \tau)$. Assume that a partial equilibrium approach is valid.

Compute the elasticity of the equilibrium price with respect to $\kappa$. Argue that when $\gamma = 0$ producers bear the full effect of the tax while consumers' total costs of purchase are unaffected, and that when $\varepsilon = 0$ it is consumers who bear the full burden of the tax. What happens when each of these elasticities approaches $\infty$ in absolute value?

**10.C.8$^B$** Suppose that there are $J$ firms producing good $\ell$, each with a differentiable cost function $c(q, \alpha)$ that is strictly convex in $q$, where $\alpha$ is an exogenous parameter that affects costs (it could be a technological parameter or an input price). Assume that $\partial c(q, \alpha)/\partial \alpha > 0$. The differentiable aggregate demand function for good $\ell$ is $x(p)$, with $x'(\cdot) \leq 0$. Assume that partial equilibrium analysis is justified.

Let $q^*(\alpha)$ be the *per firm* output and $p^*(\alpha)$ be the equilibrium price in the competitive equilibrium given $\alpha$.

**(a)** Derive the marginal change in a firm's profits with respect to $\alpha$.

**(b)** Give the weakest possible sufficient condition, stated in terms of marginal and average costs and/or their derivatives, that guarantees that if $\alpha$ increases marginally, then firms' equilibrium profits decline for any demand function $x(\cdot)$ having $x'(\cdot) \leq 0$. Show that if this condition is not satisfied, then there are demand functions such that profits increase when $\alpha$ increases.

**(c)** In the case where $\alpha$ is the price of factor input $k$, interpret the condition in **(b)** in terms of the conditional factor demand for input $k$.

**10.C.9$^B$** Suppose that in a partial equilibrium context there are $J$ identical firms that produce good $\ell$ with cost function $c(w, q)$, where $w$ is a vector of factor input prices. Show that an increase in the price of factor $k$, $w_k$, lowers the equilibrium price of good $\ell$ if and only if factor $k$ is an *inferior* factor, that is, if at fixed input prices, the use of factor $k$ is decreasing in a firm's output level.

**10.C.10$^B$** Consider a market with demand curve $x(p) = \alpha p^\varepsilon$ and with $J$ firms, each of which has marginal cost function $c'(q) = \beta q^\eta$, where $(\alpha, \beta, \eta) \gg 0$ and $\varepsilon < 0$. Calculate the competitive equilibrium price and output levels. Examine the comparative statics change in these variables as a result of changes in $\alpha$ and $\beta$. How are these changes affected by $\varepsilon$ and $\eta$?

**10.C.11$^B$** Assume that partial equilibrium analysis is valid. Suppose that firms 1 and 2 are producing a positive level of output in a competitive equilibrium. The cost function for firm $j$ is given by $c(q, \alpha_j)$, where $\alpha_j$ is an exogenous technological parameter. If $\alpha_1$ differs from $\alpha_2$ marginally, what is the difference in the two firms' profits?

**10.D.1$^B$** Prove that under the assumptions that the $\phi_i(\cdot)$ functions are strictly concave and the cost functions $c_j(\cdot)$ are convex, the optimal individual consumption levels of good $\ell$ in problem (10.D.2) are uniquely defined. Conclude that the optimal aggregate production level of good $\ell$ is therefore also uniquely defined. Show that if the cost functions $c_j(\cdot)$ are *strictly* convex, then the optimal individual production levels of good $\ell$ in problem (10.D.2) are also uniquely defined.

**10.D.2$^B$** Determine the optimal consumption and production levels of good $\ell$ for the economy described in Exercise 10.C.2. Compare these with the equilibrium levels you identified in that exercise.

**10.D.3$^B$** In the context of the two-good quasilinear economy studied in Section 10.D, show that any allocation that is a solution to problem (10.D.6) is Pareto optimal and that any Pareto optimal allocation is a solution to problem (10.D.6) for *some* choice of utility levels $(\bar{u}_2, \ldots, \bar{u}_I)$.

**10.D.4$^B$** Derive the first-order conditions for problem (10.D.6) and compare them with conditions (10.D.3) to (10.D.5).

**10.E.1$^C$** Suppose that $J_d > 0$ of the firms that produce good $\ell$ are domestic firms, and $J_f > 0$ are foreign firms. All domestic firms have the same convex cost function for producing good $\ell$, $c_d(q_j)$. All foreign firms have the same convex cost function $c_f(q_j)$. Assume that partial equilibrium analysis is valid.

The government of the domestic country is considering imposing a per-unit tariff of $\tau$ on imports of good $\ell$. The government wants to maximize domestic welfare as measured by the *domestic* Marshallian surplus (i.e., the sum of domestic consumers' utilities less domestic firms' costs).

**(a)** Show that if $c_f(\cdot)$ is strictly convex, then imposition of a small tariff raises domestic welfare.

**(b)** Show that if $c_f(\cdot)$ exhibits constant returns to scale, then imposition of a small tariff lowers domestic welfare.

**10.E.2$^B$** Consumer surplus when consumers face effective price $\hat{p}$ can be written as

$$CS(\hat{p}) = \int_0^{x(\hat{p})} [P(s) - \hat{p}]\, ds.$$

Prove by means of a change of variables and integration by parts that this integral is equal to $\int_{\bar{p}}^{\infty} x(s)\, ds$.

**10.E.3$^C$** (*Ramsey tax problem*) Consider a fully separable quasilinear model with $L$ goods in which each consumer has preferences of the form $u_i(x_i) = x_{1i} + \sum_{\ell=2}^{L} \phi_{\ell i}(x_{\ell i})$ and each good $2, \ldots, L$ is produced with constant returns to scale from good 1, using $c_\ell$ units of good 1 per unit of good $\ell$ produced. Assume that consumers initially hold endowments only of the numeraire, good 1. Hence, consumers are net sellers of good 1 to the firms and net purchasers of goods $2, \ldots, L$.

In this setting, consumer $i$'s demand for each good $\ell \neq 1$ can be written in the form $x_{\ell i}(p_\ell)$, so that demand for good $\ell$ is independent of the consumer's wealth and all other prices, and welfare can be measured by the sum of the Marshallian aggregate surpluses in the $L-1$ markets for nonnumeraire commodities (see Section 10.G and Exercise 10.G.2 for more on this).

Suppose that the government must raise $R$ units of good 1 through (specific) commodity taxes. Note, in particular, that such taxes involve taxing a *transaction* of a good, *not* an individual's consumption level of that good.

Let $t_\ell$ denote the tax to be paid by a consumer in units of good 1 for each unit of good $\ell \neq 1$ purchased, and let $t_1$ be the tax in units of good 1 to be paid by consumers for each unit of good 1 sold to a firm. Normalize the price paid by firms for good 1 to equal 1. Under our assumptions, each choice of $t = (t_1, \ldots, t_L)$ results in a consumer paying a total of $c_\ell + t_\ell$ per unit of good $\ell \neq 1$ purchased and having to part with $(1 + t_1)$ units of good 1 for each unit of good 1 sold to a firm.

**(a)** Consider two possible tax vectors $t$ and $t'$. Show that if $t'$ is such that $(c_\ell + t'_\ell) = \alpha(c_\ell + t_\ell)$ and $(1 + t'_1) = (1/\alpha)(1 + t_1)$ for some scalar $\alpha > 0$, then the two sets of taxes raise the same revenue. Conclude from this fact that the government can restrict attention to tax vectors that leave one good untaxed.

**(b)** Let good 1 be the untaxed good (i.e., set $t_1 = 0$). Derive conditions describing the taxes that should be set on goods $2, \ldots, L$ if the government wishes to minimize the welfare loss arising from this taxation. Express this formula in terms of the elasticity of demand for each good.

**(c)** Under what circumstances should the tax rate on all goods be equal? In general, which goods should have higher tax rates? When would taxing only good 1 be optimal?

**10.F.1$^A$** Show that if $c(q)$ is strictly convex in $q$ and $c(0) = 0$, then $\pi(p) > 0$ if and only if $p > c'(0)$.

**10.F.2$^B$** Consider a market with demand function $x(p) = A - Bp$ in which every potential firm has cost function $c(q) = K + \alpha q + \beta q^2$, where $\alpha > 0$ and $\beta > 0$.

**(a)** Calculate the long-run competitive equilibrium price, output per firm, aggregate output, and number of firms. Ignore the integer constraint on the number of firms. How does each of these vary with $A$?

**(b)** Now examine the short-run competitive equilibrium response to a change in $A$ starting from the long-run equilibrium you identified in (a). How does the change in price depend on the level of $A$ in the initial equilibrium? What happens as $A \to \infty$? What accounts for this effect of market size?

**10.F.3$^B$** (D. Pearce) Consider a partial equilibrium setting in which each (potential) firm has a long-run cost function $c(\cdot)$, where $c(q) = K + \phi(q)$ for $q > 0$ and $c(0) = 0$. Assume that $\phi'(q) > 0$ and $\phi''(q) < 0$, and denote the firm's efficient scale by $\bar{q}$. Suppose that there is initially a long-run equilibrium with $J^*$ firms. The government considers imposing two different types of taxes: The first is an ad valorem tax of $\tau$ (see Exercise 10.C.6) on sales of the good. The second is a tax $T$ that must be paid by any operating firm (where a firm is considered to be "operating" if it sells a positive amount). If the two taxes would raise an equal amount of revenue with the initial level of sales and number of firms, which will raise more after the industry adjusts to a new long-run equilibrium? (You should ignore the integer constraint on the number of firms.)

**10.F.4$^B$** (J. Panzar) Assume that partial equilibrium analysis is valid. The single-output, many-input technology for producing good $\ell$ has a differentiable cost function $c(w, q)$, where $w = (w_1, \ldots, w_K)$ is a vector of factor input prices and $q$ is the firm's output of good $\ell$. Given factor prices $w$, let $\bar{q}(w)$ denote the firm's efficient scale. Assume that $\bar{q}(w) > 0$ for all $w$. Also let $p_\ell^*(w)$ denote the long-run equilibrium price of good $\ell$ when factor prices are $w$. Show that the function $p_\ell^*(w)$ is nondecreasing, homogeneous of degree one, and concave. (You should ignore the integer constraint on the number of firms.)

**10.F.5$^C$** Suppose that there are $J$ firms that can produce good $\ell$ from $K$ factor inputs with differentiable cost function $c(w, q)$. Assume that this function is strictly convex in $q$. The differentiable aggregate demand function for good $\ell$ is $x(p, \alpha)$, where $\partial x(p, \alpha)/\partial p < 0$ and $\partial x(p, \alpha)/\partial \alpha > 0$ ($\alpha$ is an exogenous parameter affecting demand). However, although $c(w, q)$ is the cost function when all factors can be freely adjusted, factor $k$ cannot be adjusted in the short run.

Suppose that we are initially at an equilibrium in which all inputs are optimally adjusted to the equilibrium level of output $q^*$ and factor prices $w$ so that, letting $z_k(w, q)$ denote a firm's conditional factor demand for input $k$ when all inputs can be adjusted, $z_k^* = z_k(w, q^*)$.

**(a)** Show that a firm's equilibrium response to an increase in the price of good $\ell$ is larger in the long run than in the short run.

**(b)** Show that this implies that the long-run equilibrium response of $p_\ell$ to a marginal increase in $\alpha$ is smaller than the short-run response. Show that the reverse is true for the response of the equilibrium aggregate consumption of good $\ell$ (hold the number of firms equal to $J$ in both the short run and long run).

**10.F.6$^B$** Suppose that the technology for producing a good uses capital ($z_1$) and labor ($z_2$) and takes the Cobb–Douglas form $f(z_1, z_2) = z_1^\alpha z_2^{1-\alpha}$, where $\alpha \in (0, 1)$. In the long run, both factors can be adjusted; but in the short run, the use of capital is fixed. The industry demand function takes the form $x(p) = a - bp$. The vector of input prices is $(w_1, w_2)$. Find the long-run equilibrium price and aggregate quantity. Holding the number of firms and the level of capital fixed at their long-run equilibrium levels, what is the short-run industry supply function?

**10.F.7$^B$** Consider a case where in the short run active firms can increase their use of a factor but cannot decrease it. Show that the short-run cost curve will exhibit a kink (i.e., be nondifferentiable) at the current (long-run) equilibrium. Analyze the implications of this fact for the relative variability of short-run prices and quantities.

**10.G.1$^B$** Consider the case of an interrelated group of $M$ commodities. Let consumer $i$'s utility function take the form $u_i(x_{1i}, \ldots, x_{Mi}) = m_i + \phi_i(x_{1i}, \ldots, x_{Mi})$. Assume that $\phi_i(\cdot)$ is differentiable and strictly concave. Let firm $j$'s cost function be the differentiable convex function $c_j(q_{1j}, \ldots, q_{Mj})$.

Normalize the price of the numeraire to be 1. Derive $(I + J + 1)M$ equations characterizing the $(I + J + 1)M$ equilibrium quantities $(x_{1i}^*, \ldots, x_{Mi}^*)$ for $i = 1, \ldots, I$, $(q_{1j}^*, \ldots, q_{Mj}^*)$ for $j = 1, \ldots, J$, and $(p_1^*, \ldots, p_M^*)$. [*Hint*: Derive consumers' and firms' first-order conditions and the $M - 1$ market-clearing conditions in parallel to our analysis of the single-market case.] Argue that the equilibrium prices and quantities of these $M$ goods are independent of consumers' wealths, that equilibrium individual consumptions and aggregate production levels are unique, and that if the $c_j(\cdot)$ functions are strictly convex, then equilibrium individual production levels are also unique.

**10.G.2$^B$** Consider the case in which the functions $\phi_i(\cdot)$ and $c_j(\cdot)$ in Exercise 10.G.1 are separable in good $\ell$ (one of the goods in the group): $\phi_i(\cdot) = \phi_{\ell i}(x_{\ell i}) + \phi_{-\ell, i}(x_{-\ell, i})$ and $c_j(\cdot) = c_{\ell j}(q_{\ell j}) + c_{-\ell, j}(q_{-\ell, j})$. Argue that in this case, the equilibrium price, consumption, and production of good $\ell$ can be determined independently of other goods in the group. Also argue that under the same assumptions as in the single-market case studied in Section 10.E, changes in welfare caused by changes in the market for this good can be captured by the Marshallian aggregate surplus for this good, $\sum_i \phi_{\ell i}(x_{\ell i}) - \sum_j c_{\ell j}(q_{\ell j})$, which can be represented in terms of the areas lying vertically between the demand and supply curves for good $\ell$. Note the implication of these results for the case in which we have separability of all goods: $\phi_i(\cdot) = \sum_\ell \phi_{\ell i}(x_{\ell i})$ and $c_j(\cdot) = \sum_\ell c_{\ell j}(q_{\ell j})$.

**10.G.3$^B$** Consider a three-good economy ($\ell = 1, 2, 3$) in which every consumer has preferences that can be described by the utility function $u(x) = x_1 + \phi(x_2, x_3)$ and there is a single production process that produces goods 2 and 3 from good 1 having $c(q_2, q_3) = c_2 q_2 + c_3 q_3$. Suppose that we are considering a tax change in only a single market, say market 2.

(a) Show that if the price in market 3 is undistorted (i.e., if $t_3 = 0$), then the change in aggregate surplus caused by the tax change can be captured solely through the change in the area lying vertically between market 2's demand and supply curves holding the price of good 3 at its initial level.

(b) Show that if market 3 is initially distorted because $t_3 > 0$, then by using only the single-market measure in (a), we would overstate the decrease in aggregate surplus if good 3 is a substitute for good 2 and would understate it if good 3 is a complement. Provide an intuitive explanation of this result. What is the correct measure of welfare change?

**10.G.4$^B$** Consider a three-good economy ($\ell = 1, 2, 3$) in which every consumer has preferences that can be described by the utility function $u(x) = x_1 + \phi(x_2, x_3)$ and there is a single production process that produces goods 2 and 3 from good 1 having $c(q_2, q_3) = c_2 q_2 + c_3 q_3$. Derive an expression for the welfare loss from an increase in the tax rates on both goods.

**10.G.5$^B$** Consider a three-good economy ($\ell = 1, 2, 3$) in which every consumer has preferences that can be described by the utility function $u(x) = x_1 + \phi(x_2, x_3)$ and there is a single production process that produces goods 2 and 3 from good 1 having $c(q_2, q_3) = c_2(q_2) + c_3(q_3)$, where $c_2(\cdot)$ and $c_3(\cdot)$ are strictly increasing and strictly convex.

(a) If goods 2 and 3 are substitutes, what effect does an increase in the tax on good 2 have on the price paid by consumers for good 3? What if they are complements?

(b) What is the bias from applying the formula for welfare loss you derived in part (b) of Exercise 10.G.3 using the price paid by consumers for good 3 prior to the tax change in both the case of substitutes and that of complements?

# Externalities and Public Goods ## 11

## 11.A Introduction

In Chapter 10, we saw a close connection between competitive, price-taking equilibria and Pareto optimality (or, Pareto efficiency).[1] The first welfare theorem tells us that competitive equilibria are necessarily Pareto optimal. From the second welfare theorem, we know that under suitable convexity hypotheses, any Pareto optimal allocation can be achieved as a competitive allocation after an appropriate lump-sum redistribution of wealth. Under the assumptions of these theorems, the possibilities for welfare-enhancing intervention in the marketplace are strictly limited to the carrying out of wealth transfers for the purposes of achieving distributional aims.

With this chapter, we begin our study of *market failures*: situations in which some of the assumptions of the welfare theorems do *not* hold and in which, as a consequence, market equilibria cannot be relied on to yield Pareto optimal outcomes. In this chapter, we study two types of market failure, known as *externalities* and *public goods*.

In Chapter 10, we assumed that the preferences of a consumer were defined solely over the set of goods that she might herself decide to consume. Similarly, the production of a firm depended only on its own input choices. In reality, however, a consumer or firm may in some circumstances be directly affected by the actions of other agents in the economy; that is, there may be *external effects* from the activities of other consumers or firms. For example, the consumption by consumer $i$'s neighbor of loud music at three in the morning may prevent her from sleeping. Likewise, a fishery's catch may be impaired by the discharges of an upstream chemical plant. Incorporating these concerns into our preference and technology formalism is, in principle, a simple matter: We need only define an agent's preferences or production set over both her own actions and those of the agent creating the external effect. But the effect on market equilibrium is significant: In general, when external effects are present, competitive equilibria are not Pareto optimal.

Public goods, as the name suggests, are commodities that have an inherently "public" character, in that consumption of a unit of the good by one agent does not preclude its consumption by another. Examples abound: Roadways, national defense,

---

1. See also Chapter 16.

flood-control projects, and knowledge all share this characteristic. The private provision of public goods generates a special type of externality: if one individual provides a unit of a public good, all individuals benefit. As a result, private provision of public goods is typically Pareto inefficient.

We begin our investigation of externalities and public goods in Section 11.B by considering the simplest possible externality: one that involves only two agents in the economy, where one of the agents engages in an activity that directly affects the other. In this setting, we illustrate the inefficiency of competitive equilibria when an externality is present. We then go on to consider three traditional solutions to this problem: quotas, taxes, and the fostering of decentralized bargaining over the extent of the externality. The last of these possibilities also suggests a connection between the presence of externalities and the nonexistence of certain commodity markets, a topic that we explore in some detail.

In Section 11.C, we study public goods. We first derive a condition that characterizes the optimal level of a public good and we then illustrate the inefficiency resulting from private provision. This Pareto inefficiency can be seen as arising from an externality among the consumers of the good, which in this context is known as the *free-rider problem*. We also discuss possible solutions to this free-rider problem. Both quantity-based intervention (here, direct governmental provision) and price-based intervention (taxes and subsidies) can, in principle, correct it. In contrast, decentralized bargaining and competitive market-based solutions are unlikely to be viable in the context of public goods.

In Section 11.D, we return to the analysis of externalities. We study cases in which many agents both produce and are affected by the externality. Multilateral externalities can be classified according to whether the externality is *depletable* (or *private* or *rivalrous*) or *nondepletable* (or *public* or *nonrivalrous*). We argue that market solutions are likely to work well in the former set of cases but poorly in the latter, where the externality possesses the characteristics of a public good (or bad). Indeed, this may well explain why most externalities that are regarded as serious social problems (e.g., water pollution, acid rain, congestion) take the form of nondepletable multilateral externalities.

In Section 11.E, we examine another problem that may arise in these settings: Individuals may have privately held information about the effects of externalities on their well-being. We see there that this type of informational asymmetry may confound both private and government efforts to achieve optimal outcomes.

In Appendix A, we study the connection between externalities and the presence of technological nonconvexities, and we examine the implications of these nonconvexities for our analysis.

The literature on externalities and public goods is voluminous. Useful introductions and further references to these subjects may be found in Baumol and Oates (1988) and Laffont (1988).

# 11.B A Simple Bilateral Externality

Surprisingly, perhaps, a fully satisfying definition of an externality has proved somewhat elusive. Nevertheless, informal Definition 11.B.1 provides a serviceable point of departure.

**Definition 11.B.1:** An *externality* is present whenever the well-being of a consumer or the production possibilities of a firm are directly affected by the actions of another agent in the economy.

Simple as Definition 11.B.1 sounds, it contains a subtle point that has been a source of some confusion. When we say "directly," we mean to exclude any effects that are mediated by prices. That is, an externality is present if, say, a fishery's productivity is affected by the emissions from a nearby oil refinery, but not simply because the fishery's profitability is affected by the price of oil (which, in turn, is to some degree affected by the oil refinery's output of oil). The latter type of effect [referred to as a *pecuniary externality* by Viner (1931)] is present in any competitive market but, as we saw in Chapter 10, creates no inefficiency. Indeed, with price-taking behavior, the market is precisely the mechanism that guarantees a Pareto optimal outcome. This suggests that the presence of an externality is not merely a technological phenomenon but also a function of the set of markets in existence. We return to this point later in the section.

In the remainder of this section, we explore the implications of external effects for competitive equilibria and public policy in the context of a very simple two-agent, partial equilibrium model. We consider two consumers, indexed by $i = 1, 2$, who constitute a small part of the overall economy. In line with this interpretation, we suppose that the actions of these consumers do not affect the prices $p \in \mathbb{R}^L$ of the $L$ traded goods in the economy. At these prices, consumer $i$'s wealth is $w_i$.

In contrast with the standard competitive model, however, we assume that each consumer has preferences not only over her consumption of the $L$ traded goods $(x_{1i}, \ldots, x_{Li})$ but also over some action $h \in \mathbb{R}_+$ taken by consumer 1. Thus, consumer $i$'s (differentiable) utility function takes the form $u_i(x_{1i}, \ldots, x_{Li}, h)$, and we assume that $\partial u_2(x_{12}, \ldots, x_{L2}, h)/\partial h \neq 0$. Because consumer 1's choice of $h$ affects consumer 2's well-being, it generates an externality. For example, the two consumers may live next door to each other, and $h$ may be a measure of how loudly consumer 1 plays music. Or the consumers may live on a river, with consumer 1 further upstream. In this case, $h$ could represent the amount of pollution put into the river by consumer 1; more pollution lowers consumer 2's enjoyment of the river. We should hasten to add that external effects need not be detrimental to those affected by them. Action $h$ could, for example, be consumer 1's beautification of her property, which her neighbor, consumer 2, also gets to enjoy.[2]

In what follows, it will be convenient to define for each consumer $i$ a derived utility function over the level of $h$, assuming optimal commodity purchases by consumer $i$ at prices $p \in \mathbb{R}^L$ and wealth $w_i$:

$$v_i(p, w_i, h) = \underset{x_i \geq 0}{\text{Max}} \quad u_i(x_i, h)$$

$$\text{s.t. } p \cdot x_i \leq w_i.$$

For expositional purposes, we shall also assume that the consumers' utility functions

---

2. An externality favorable to the recipient is usually called a *positive externality*, and conversely for a *negative externality*.

take a quasilinear form with respect to a numeraire commodity (we comment below, in small type, on the simplifications afforded by this assumption). In this case, we can write the derived utility function $v_i(\cdot)$ as $v_i(p, w_i, h) = \phi_i(p, h) + w_i$.[3] Since prices of the $L$ traded goods are assumed to be unaffected by any of the changes we are considering, we shall suppress the price vector $p$ and simply write $\phi_i(h)$. We assume that $\phi_i(\cdot)$ is twice differentiable with $\phi_i''(\cdot) < 0$. Be warned, however, that the concavity assumption is less innocent than it looks: see Appendix A for further discussion of this point.

Although we shall speak in terms of this consumer interpretation, everything we do here applies equally well to the case in which the two agents are firms (or, for that matter, one firm and one consumer). For example, we could consider a firm $j$ that has a derived profit function $\pi_j(p, h)$ over $h$ given prices $p$. Suppressing the price vector $p$, the firm's profit can be written as $\pi_j(h)$, which plays the same role as the function $\phi_i(h)$ in the analysis that follows.

### Nonoptimality of the Competitive Outcome

Suppose that we are at a competitive equilibrium in which commodity prices are $p$. That is, at the equilibrium position, each of the two consumers maximizes her utility limited only by her wealth and the prices $p$ of the traded goods. It must therefore be the case that consumer 1 chooses her level of $h \geq 0$ to maximize $\phi_1(h)$. Thus, the equilibrium level of $h$, $h^*$, satisfies the necessary and sufficient first-order condition

$$\phi_1'(h^*) \leq 0, \quad \text{with equality if } h^* > 0. \tag{11.B.1}$$

For an interior solution, we therefore have $\phi_1'(h^*) = 0$.

In contrast, in any Pareto optimal allocation, the optimal level of $h$, $h^\circ$, must maximize the *joint surplus* of the two consumers, and so must solve[4]

$$\underset{h \geq 0}{\text{Max}} \quad \phi_1(h) + \phi_2(h).$$

This problem gives us the necessary and sufficient first-order condition for $h^\circ$ of

$$\phi_1'(h^\circ) \leq -\phi_2'(h^\circ), \text{ with equality if } h^\circ > 0. \tag{11.B.2}$$

Hence, for an interior solution to the Pareto optimality problem, $\phi_1'(h^\circ) = -\phi_2'(h^\circ)$.

When external effects are present, so that $\phi_2'(h) \neq 0$ at all $h$, the equilibrium level of $h$ is not optimal unless $h^\circ = h^* = 0$. Consider, for example, the case in which we have interior solutions, that is, where $(h^*, h^\circ) \gg 0$. If $\phi_2'(\cdot) < 0$, so that $h$ generates

---

3. Indeed, suppose that $u_i(x_i, h) = g_i(x_{-1i}, h) + x_{1i}$, where $x_{-1i}$ is consumer $i$'s consumption of traded goods other than good 1. Then, the consumer's Walrasian demand function for these $L - 1$ traded goods, $x_{-1i}(\cdot)$, is independent of her wealth, and $v_i(p, w_i, h) = g_i(x_{-1i}(p, h), h) - p \cdot x_{-1i}(p, h) + w_i$. Thus, denoting $\phi_i(p, h) = g_i(x_{-1i}(p, h), h) - p \cdot x_{-1i}(p, h)$, we have obtained the desired form.

4. Recall the reasoning of Sections 10.D and 10.E, or note that at any Pareto optimal allocation in which $h^\circ$ is the level of $h$ and $w_i$ is consumer $i$'s wealth level for $i = 1, 2$, it must be impossible to change $h$ and reallocate wealth so as to make one consumer better off without making the other worse off. Thus, $(h^\circ, 0)$ must solve $\text{Max}_{h, T} \; \phi_1(h) + w_1 - T$ subject to $\phi_2(h) + w_2 + T \geq \bar{u}_2$, for some $\bar{u}_2$. Because the constraint holds with equality in any solution to this problem, substituting from the constraint for $T$ in the objective function shows that $h^\circ$ must maximize the joint surplus of the two consumers $\phi_1(h) + \phi_2(h)$.

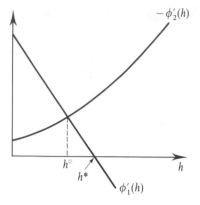

**Figure 11.B.1**

The equilibrium ($h^*$) and optimal ($h^\circ$) levels of a negative externality.

a negative externality, then we have $\phi_1'(h^\circ) = -\phi_2'(h^\circ) > 0$; because $\phi_1'(\cdot)$ is decreasing and $\phi_1'(h^*) = 0$, this implies that $h^* > h^\circ$. In contrast, when $\phi_2'(\cdot) > 0$, $h$ represents a positive externality, and $\phi_1'(h^\circ) = -\phi_2'(h^\circ) < 0$ implies that $h^* < h^\circ$.

Figure 11.B.1 depicts the solution for a case in which $h$ constitutes a negative external effect, so that $\phi_2'(h) < 0$ at all $h$. In the figure, we graph $\phi_1'(\cdot)$ and $-\phi_2'(\cdot)$. The competitive equilibrium level of the externality $h^*$ occurs at the point where the graph of $\phi_1'(\cdot)$ crosses the horizontal axis. In contrast, the optimal externality level $h^\circ$ corresponds to the point of intersection between the graphs of the two functions.

Note that optimality does not usually entail the complete elimination of a negative externality. Rather, the externality's level is adjusted to the point where the marginal benefit to consumer 1 of an additional unit of the externality-generating activity, $\phi_1'(h^\circ)$, equals its marginal cost to consumer 2, $-\phi_2'(h^\circ)$.

---

In the current example, quasilinear utilities lead the optimal level of the externality to be independent of the consumers' wealth levels. In the absence of quasilinearity, however, wealth effects for the consumption of the externality make its optimal level depend on the consumers' wealths. See Exercise 11.B.2 for an illustration. Note, however, that when the agents under consideration are firms, wealth effects are always absent.

---

## Traditional Solutions to the Externality Problem

Having identified the inefficiency of the competitive market outcome in the presence of an externality, we now consider three possible solutions to the problem. We first look at government-implemented quotas and taxes, and then analyze the possibility that an efficient outcome can be achieved in a much less intrusive manner by simply fostering bargaining between the consumers over the extent of the externality.

### Quotas and taxes

To fix ideas, suppose that $h$ generates a negative external effect, so that $h^\circ < h^*$. The most direct sort of government intervention to achieve efficiency is the direct control of the externality-generating activity itself. The government can simply mandate that $h$ be no larger than $h^\circ$, its optimal level. With this constraint, consumer 1 will indeed fix the level of the externality at $h^\circ$.

A second option is for the government to attempt to restore optimality by imposing a tax on the externality-generating activity. This solution is known as

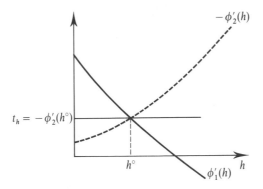

**Figure 11.B.2**

The optimality-restoring Pigouvian tax.

*Pigouvian taxation*, after Pigou (1932). To this effect, suppose that consumer 1 is made to pay a tax of $t_h$ per unit of $h$. It is then not difficult to see that a tax of

$$t_h = -\phi_2'(h^\circ) > 0$$

will implement the optimal level of the externality. Indeed, consumer 1 will then choose the level of $h$ that solves

$$\underset{h \geq 0}{\text{Max}} \quad \phi_1(h) - t_h h, \tag{11.B.3}$$

which has the necessary and sufficient first-order condition

$$\phi_1'(h) \leq t_h, \quad \text{with equality if } h > 0. \tag{11.B.4}$$

Given $t_h = -\phi_2'(h^\circ)$, $h = h^\circ$ satisfies condition (11.B.4) [recall that $h^\circ$ is defined by the condition: $\phi_1'(h^\circ) \leq -\phi_2'(h^\circ)$, with equality if $h^\circ > 0$]. Moreover, given $\phi_1''(\cdot) < 0$, $h^\circ$ must be the unique solution to problem (11.B.3). Figure 11.B.2 illustrates this solution for a case in which $h^\circ > 0$.

Note that the optimality-restoring tax is exactly equal to the *marginal externality* at the optimal solution.[5] That is, it is exactly equal to the amount that consumer 2 would be willing to pay to reduce $h$ slightly from its optimal level $h^\circ$. When faced with this tax, consumer 1 is effectively led to carry out an individual cost–benefit computation that *internalizes* the externality that she imposes on consumer 2.

The principles for the case of a positive externality are exactly the same, only now when we set $t_h = -\phi_2'(h^\circ) < 0$, $t_h$ takes the form of a per-unit *subsidy* (i.e., consumer 1 *receives* a payment for each unit of the externality she generates).

Several additional points are worth noting about this Pigouvian solution. First, we can actually achieve optimality either by taxing the externality or by subsidizing its reduction. Consider, for example, the case of a negative externality. Suppose the government pays a subsidy of $s_h = -\phi_2'(h^\circ) > 0$ for every unit that consumer 1's choice of $h$ is below $h^*$, its level in the competitive equilibrium. If so, then consumer 1 will maximize $\phi_1(h) + s_h(h^* - h) = \phi_1(h) - t_h h + t_h h^*$. But this is equivalent to a tax of $t_h$ per unit on $h$ combined with a lump-sum payment of $t_h h^*$. Hence, a subsidy for the reduction of the externality combined with a lump-sum transfer can exactly replicate the outcome of the tax.

Second, a point implicit in the derivation above is that, in general, it is essential

5. In the case where $h^\circ = 0$, any tax greater than $-\phi_2'(0)$ also implements the optimal outcome.

to tax the externality-producing activity directly. For instance, suppose that, in the example of consumer 1 playing loud music, we tax purchases of music equipment instead of taxing the playing of loud music itself. In general, this will not restore optimality. Consumer 1 will be led to lower her consumption of music equipment (perhaps she will purchase only a CD player, rather than a CD player and a tape player) but may nevertheless play whatever equipment she does purchase too loudly. A common example of this sort arises when a firm pollutes in the process of producing output. A tax on its output leads the firm to reduce its output level but may not have any effect (or, more generally, may have too little effect) on its pollution emissions. Taxing output achieves optimality only in the special case in which emissions bear a fixed monotonic relationship to the level of output. In this special case, emissions can be measured by the level of output, and a tax on output is essentially equivalent to a tax on emissions. (See Exercise 11.B.5 for an illustration.)

Third, note that the tax/subsidy and the quota approaches are equally effective in achieving an optimal outcome. However, the government must have a great deal of information about the benefits and costs of the externality for the two consumers to set the optimal levels of either the quota or the tax. In Section 11.E we will see that when the government does not possess this information the two approaches typically are not equivalent.

*Fostering bargaining over externalities: enforceable property rights*

Another approach to the externality problem aims at a less intrusive form of intervention, merely seeking to insure that conditions are met for the parties to themselves reach an optimal agreement on the level of the externality.

Suppose that we establish enforceable property rights with regard to the externality-generating activity. Say, for example, that we assign the right to an "externality-free" environment to consumer 2. In this case, consumer 1 is unable to engage in the externality-producing activity without consumer 2's permission. For simplicity, imagine that the bargaining between the parties takes a form in which consumer 2 makes consumer 1 a take-it-or-leave-it offer, demanding a payment of $T$ in return for permission to generate externality level $h$.[6] Consumer 1 will agree to this demand if and only if she will be at least as well off as she would be by rejecting it, that is, if and only if $\phi_1(h) - T \geq \phi_1(0)$. Hence, consumer 2 will choose her offer $(h, T)$ to solve

$$\underset{h \geq 0, T}{\text{Max}} \quad \phi_2(h) + T$$

$$\text{s.t. } \phi_1(h) - T \geq \phi_1(0).$$

Since the constraint is binding in any solution to this problem, $T = \phi_1(h) - \phi_1(0)$. Therefore, consumer 2's optimal offer involves the level of $h$ that solves

$$\underset{h \geq 0}{\text{Max}} \quad \phi_2(h) + \phi_1(h) - \phi_1(0). \tag{11.B.5}$$

But this is precisely $h°$, the socially optimal level.

Note, moreover, that the precise allocation of these rights between the two

---

6. Either of the bargaining processes discussed in Appendix A of Chapter 9 would yield the same conclusions.

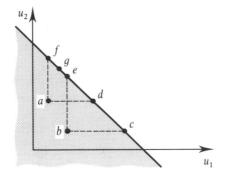

**Figure 11.B.3**

The final distribution of utilities under different property rights institutions and different bargaining procedures.

consumers is inessential to the achievement of optimality. Suppose, for example, that consumer 1 instead has the right to generate as much of the externality as she wants. In this case, in the absence of any agreement, consumer 1 will generate externality level $h^*$. Now consumer 2 will need to offer a $T < 0$ (i.e., to pay consumer 1) to have $h < h^*$. In particular, consumer 1 will agree to externality level $h$ if and only if $\phi_1(h) - T \geq \phi_1(h^*)$. As a consequence, consumer 2 will offer to set $h$ at the level that solves $\text{Max}_{h \geq 0} (\phi_2(h) + \phi_1(h) - \phi_1(h^*))$. Once again, the optimal externality level $h^\circ$ results. The allocation of rights affects only the final wealth of the two consumers by altering the payment made by consumer 1 to consumer 2. In the first case, consumer 1 pays $\phi_1(h^\circ) - \phi_1(0) > 0$ to be allowed to set $h^\circ > 0$; in the second, she "pays" $\phi_1(h^\circ) - \phi_1(h^*) < 0$ in return for setting $h^\circ < h^*$.

We have here an instance of what is known as the *Coase theorem* [for Coase (1960)]: If trade of the externality can occur, then bargaining will lead to an efficient outcome no matter how property rights are allocated.

All this is illustrated in Figure 11.B.3, in which we represent the utility possibility set for the two consumers. Every point in the boundary of this set corresponds to an allocation with externality level $h^\circ$. The points $a$ and $b$ correspond to the utility levels arising, respectively, from externality levels 0 and $h^*$ in the absence of any transfers. They constitute the initial situation after the assignment of property rights (to consumers 2 and 1, respectively) but before bargaining. In the particular bargaining procedure we have adopted (which gives the power to make a take-it-or-leave-it offer to consumer 2), the utility levels after bargaining are points $f$ and $e$, respectively. If the bargaining power (i.e., the power to make the take-it-or-leave-it offer) had been instead in the hands of consumer 1, the post-bargaining utility levels would have been points $d$ and $c$, respectively. Other bargaining procedures (such as the ones studied in Appendix A of Chapter 9) may yield other points in the segments $[f, d]$ and $[e, c]$, respectively.

Note that the existence of both well-defined and enforceable property rights is essential for this type of bargaining to occur. If property rights are not well defined, it will be unclear whether consumer 1 must gain consumer 2's permission to generate the externality. If property rights cannot be enforced (perhaps the level of $h$ is not easily measured), then consumer 1 has no need to purchase the right to engage in the externality-generating activity from consumer 2. For this reason, proponents of this type of approach focus on the absence of these legal institutions as a central impediment to optimality.

This solution to the externality problem has a significant advantage over the tax and quota schemes in terms of the level of knowledge required of the government. The consumers must know each other's preferences, but the government need not. We should emphasize, however, that for bargaining over the externality to lead to efficiency, it is important that the consumers know this information. In Section 11.E, we will see that when the agents are to some extent ignorant of each others' preferences, bargaining need *not* lead to an efficient outcome.

---

Two further points regarding these three types of solutions to the externality problem are worthy of note. First, in the case in which the two agents are firms, one form that an efficient bargain might take is the sale of one of the firms to the other. The resulting merged firm would then fully internalize the externality in the process of maximizing its profits.[7]

Second, note that all three approaches require that the externality-generating activity be measureable. This is not a trivial requirement; in many cases, such measurement may be either technologically infeasible or very costly (consider the cost of measuring air pollution or noise). A proper computation of costs and benefits should take these costs into account. If measurement is very costly, then it may be optimal to simply allow the externality to persist.

---

## Externalities and Missing Markets

The observation that bargaining can generate an optimal outcome suggests a connection between externalities and missing markets. After all, a market system can be viewed as a particular type of trading procedure.

Suppose that property rights are well defined and enforceable and that a competitive market for the right to engage in the externality-generating activity exists. For simplicity, we assume that consumer 2 has the right to an externality-free environment. Let $p_h$ denote the price of the right to engage in one unit of the activity. In choosing how many of these rights to purchase, say $h_1$, consumer 1 will solve

$$\underset{h_1 \geq 0}{\text{Max}} \; \phi_1(h_1) - p_h h_1,$$

which has the first-order condition

$$\phi_1'(h_1) \leq p_h, \quad \text{with equality if } h_1 > 0. \tag{11.B.6}$$

In deciding how many rights to sell, $h_2$, consumer 2 will solve

$$\underset{h_2 \geq 0}{\text{Max}} \; \phi_2(h_2) + p_h h_2,$$

which has the first-order condition

$$\phi_2'(h_2) \leq -p_h, \quad \text{with equality if } h_2 > 0. \tag{11.B.7}$$

---

7. Note, however, that this conclusion presumes that the owner of a firm has full control over all its functions. In more complicated (but realistic) settings in which this is not true, say because owners must hire managers whose actions cannot be perfectly controlled, the results of a merger and of an agreement over the level of the externality need not be the same. Chapters 14 and 23 provide an introduction to the topic of incentive design. See Holmstrom and Tirole (1989) for a discussion of these issues in the theory of the firm.

In a competitive equilibrium, the market for these rights must clear; that is, we must have $h_1 = h_2$. Hence, (11.B.6) and (11.B.7) imply that the level of rights traded in this competitive rights market, say $h^{**}$, satisfies

$$\phi_1'(h^{**}) \le -\phi_2'(h^{**}), \quad \text{with equality if } h^{**} > 0.$$

Comparing this expression with (11.B.2), we see that $h^{**}$ equals the optimal level $h^\circ$. The equilibrium price of the externality is $p_h^* = \phi_1'(h^\circ) = -\phi_2'(h^\circ)$.

Consumer 1 and 2's equilibrium utilities are then $\phi_1(h^\circ) - p_h^* h^\circ$ and $\phi_2(h^\circ) + p_h^* h^\circ$, respectively. The market therefore works as a particular bargaining procedure for splitting the gains from trade; for example, point $g$ in Figure 11.B.3 could represent the utilities in the competitive equilibrium.

We see that if a competitive market exists for the externality, then optimality results. Thus, externalities can be seen as being inherently tied to the absence of certain competitive markets, a point originally noted by Meade (1952) and substantially extended by Arrow (1969). Indeed, recall that our original definition of an externality, Definition 11.B.1, explicitly required that an action chosen by one agent must *directly* affect the well-being or production capabilities of another. Once a market exists for an externality, however, each consumer decides for herself how much of the externality to consume at the going prices.

Unfortunately, the idea of a competitive market for the externality in the present example is rather unrealistic; in a market with only one seller and one buyer, price taking would be unlikely.[8] However, most important externalities are produced and felt by *many* agents. Thus, we might hope that in these multilateral settings, price taking would be a more reasonable assumption and, as a result, that a competitive market for the externality would lead to an efficient outcome. In Section 11.D, where we study multilateral externalities, we see that the correctness of this conclusion depends on whether the externality is "private" or "public" in nature. Before coming to this, however, we first study the nature of public goods.

# 11.C Public Goods

In this section, we study commodities that, in contrast with those considered so far, have a feature of "publicness" to their consumption. These commodities are known as *public goods*.

**Definition 11.C.1:** A *public good* is a commodity for which use of a unit of the good by one agent does not preclude its use by other agents.

Put somewhat differently, public goods possess the feature that they are *nondepletable*: Consumption by one individual does not affect the supply available for other individuals. Knowledge provides a good illustration. The use of a piece of knowledge for one purpose does not preclude its use for others. In contrast, the commodities studied up to this point have been assumed to be of a *private*, or *depletable*, nature;

---

8. For that matter, the idea that the externality rights are all sold at the same price lacks justification here, because there is no natural unit of measurement for the externality.

that is, for each additional unit consumed by individual $i$, there is one unit less available for individuals $j \neq i$.[9]

A distinction can also be made according to whether *exclusion* of an individual from the benefits of a public good is possible. Every private good is automatically excludable, but public goods may or may not be. The patent system, for example, is a mechanism for excluding individuals (although imperfectly) from the use of knowledge developed by others. On the other hand, it might be technologically impossible, or at the least very costly, to exclude some consumers from the benefits of national defense or of a project to improve air quality. For simplicity, our discussion here will focus primarily on the case in which exclusion is not possible.

Note that a public "good" need not necessarily be desirable; that is, we may have public *bads* (e.g., foul air). In this case, we should read the phrase "does not preclude" in Definition 11.C.1 to mean "does not decrease."

### Conditions for Pareto Optimality

Consider a setting with $I$ consumers and one public good, in addition to $L$ traded goods of the usual, private, kind. We again adopt a partial equilibrium perspective by assuming that the quantity of the public good has no effect on the prices of the $L$ traded goods and that each consumer's utility function is quasilinear with respect to the same numeraire, traded commodity. As in Section 11.B, we can therefore define, for each consumer $i$, a derived utility function over the level of the public good. Letting $x$ denote the quantity of the public good, we denote consumer $i$'s utility from the public good by $\phi_i(x)$. We assume that this function is twice differentiable, with $\phi_i''(x) < 0$ at all $x \geq 0$. Note that precisely because we are dealing with a public good, the argument $x$ does not have an $i$ subscript.

The cost of supplying $q$ units of the public good is $c(q)$. We assume that $c(\cdot)$ is twice differentiable, with $c''(q) > 0$ at all $q \geq 0$.

To describe the case of a desirable public good whose production is costly, we take $\phi_i'(\cdot) > 0$ for all $i$ and $c'(\cdot) > 0$. Except where otherwise noted, however, the analysis applies equally well to the case of a public bad whose reduction is costly, where $\phi_i'(\cdot) < 0$ for all $i$ and $c'(\cdot) < 0$.

In this quasilinear model, any Pareto optimal allocation must maximize aggregate surplus (see Section 10.D) and therefore must involve a level of the public good that solves

$$\underset{q \geq 0}{\text{Max}} \ \sum_{i=1}^{I} \phi_i(q) - c(q).$$

The necessary and sufficient first-order condition for the optimal quantity $q^\circ$ is then

$$\sum_{i=1}^{I} \phi_i'(q^\circ) \leq c'(q^\circ), \quad \text{with equality if } q^\circ > 0. \qquad (11.C.1)$$

Condition (11.C.1) is the classic optimality condition for a public good first derived by Samuelson (1954; 1955). (Here it is specialized to the partial equilibrium setting;

---

9. Intermediate cases are also possible in which the consumption of the good by one individual affects to some degree its availability to others. A classic example is the presence of congestion effects. For this reason, goods for which there is no depletability whatsoever are sometimes referred to as *pure* public goods.

see Section 16.G for a more general treatment.) At an interior solution, we have $\sum_i \phi_i'(q^\circ) = c'(q^\circ)$, so that at the optimal level of the public good *the sum of consumers' marginal benefits from the public good is set equal to its marginal cost*. This condition should be contrasted with conditions (10.D.3) to (10.D.5) for a private good, where *each* consumer's marginal benefit from the good is equated to its marginal cost.

### Inefficiency of Private Provision of Public Goods

Consider the circumstance in which the public good is provided by means of private purchases by consumers. We imagine that a market exists for the public good and that each consumer $i$ chooses how much of the public good to buy, denoted by $x_i \geq 0$, taking as given its market price $p$. The total amount of the public good purchased by consumers is then $x = \sum_i x_i$. Formally, we treat the supply side as consisting of a single profit-maximizing firm with cost function $c(\cdot)$ that chooses its production level taking the market price as given. Note, however, that by the analysis of Section 5.E, we can actually think of the supply behavior of this firm as representing the industry supply of $J$ price-taking firms whose aggregate cost function is $c(\cdot)$.

At a competitive equilibrium involving price $p^*$, each consumer $i$'s purchase of the public good $x_i^*$ must maximize her utility and so must solve

$$\underset{x_i \geq 0}{\text{Max}} \quad \phi_i\left(x_i + \sum_{k \neq i} x_k^*\right) - p^* x_i. \tag{11.C.2}$$

In determining her optimal purchases, consumer $i$ takes as given the amount of the private good being purchased by each other consumer (as in the Nash equilibrium concept studied in Section 8.D). Consumer $i$'s purchases $x_i^*$ must therefore satisfy the necessary and sufficient first-order condition

$$\phi_i'\left(x_i^* + \sum_{k \neq i} x_k^*\right) \leq p^*, \quad \text{with equality if } x_i^* > 0.$$

Letting $x^* = \sum_i x_i^*$ denote the equilibrium level of the public good, for each consumer $i$ we must therefore have

$$\phi_i'(x^*) \leq p^*, \quad \text{with equality if } x_i^* > 0. \tag{11.C.3}$$

The firm's supply $q^*$, on the other hand, must solve $\text{Max}_{q \geq 0}\,(p^* q - c(q))$ and therefore must satisfy the standard necessary and sufficient first-order condition

$$p^* \leq c'(q^*), \quad \text{with equality if } q^* > 0. \tag{11.C.4}$$

At a competitive equilibrium, $q^* = x^*$. Thus, letting $\delta_i = 1$ if $x_i^* > 0$ and $\delta_i = 0$ if $x_i^* = 0$, (11.C.3) and (11.C.4) tell us that $\sum_i \delta_i[\phi_i'(q^*) - c'(q^*)] = 0$. Recalling that $\phi_i'(\cdot) > 0$ and $c'(\cdot) > 0$, this implies that whenever $I > 1$ and $q^* > 0$ (so that $\delta_i = 1$ for some $i$) we have

$$\sum_{i=1}^{I} \phi_i'(q^*) > c'(q^*). \tag{11.C.5}$$

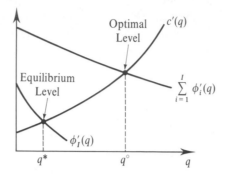

**Figure 11.C.1**

Private provision leads to an insufficient level of a desirable public good.

Comparing (11.C.5) with (11.C.1), we see that whenever $q° > 0$ and $I > 1$, the level of the public good provided is too low; that is, $q^* < q°$.[10]

The cause of this inefficiency can be understood in terms of our discussion of externalities in Section 11.B. Here each consumer's purchase of the public good provides a direct benefit not only to the consumer herself but also to every other consumer. Hence, private provision creates a situation in which externalities are present. The failure of each consumer to consider the benefits for others of her public good provision is often referred to as the *free-rider problem*: Each consumer has an incentive to enjoy the benefits of the public good provided by others while providing it insufficiently herself.

In fact, in the present model, the free-rider problem takes a very stark form. To see this most simply, suppose that we can order the consumers according to their marginal benefits, in the sense that $\phi_1'(x) < \cdots < \phi_I'(x)$ at all $x \geq 0$. Then condition (11.C.3) can hold with equality only for a *single* consumer and, moreover, this must be the consumer labeled $I$. Therefore, only the consumer who derives the largest (marginal) benefit from the public good will provide it; all others will set their purchases equal to zero in the equilibrium. The equilibrium level of the public good is then the level $q^*$ that satisfies $\phi_I'(q^*) = c'(q^*)$. Figure 11.C.1 depicts both this equilibrium and the Pareto optimal level. Note that the curve representing $\sum_i \phi_i'(q)$ geometrically corresponds to a *vertical* summation of the individual curves representing $\phi_i(q)$ for $i = 1, \ldots, I$ (whereas in the case of a private good, the market demand curve is identified by adding the individual demand curves *horizontally*).

The inefficiency of private provision is often remedied by governmental intervention in the provision of public goods. Just as with externalities, this can happen not only through quantity-based intervention (such as direct governmental provision) but also through "price-based" intervention in the form of taxes or subsidies. For example, suppose that there are two consumers with benefit functions $\phi_1(x_1 + x_2)$ and $\phi_2(x_1 + x_2)$, where $x_i$ is the amount of the public good purchased by consumer $i$, and that $q° > 0$. By analogy with the analysis in Section 11.B, a subsidy to each consumer $i$ per unit purchased of $s_i = \phi_{-i}'(q°)$ [or, equivalently, a tax of $-\phi_{-i}'(q°)$ per unit that consumer $i$'s purchases of the public good fall below some specified

---

10. The conclusion follows immediately if $q^* = 0$. So suppose instead that $q^* > 0$. Then since $\sum_i \phi_i'(q^*) - c'(q^*) > 0$ and $\sum_i \phi_i'(\cdot) - c'(\cdot)$ is decreasing, any solution to (11.C.1) must have a larger value than $q^*$. Note that, in contrast, if we are dealing with a public bad, so that $\phi_i'(\cdot) < 0$ and $c'(\cdot) < 0$, then the inequalities reverse and $q° < q^*$.

level] faces each consumer with the marginal external effect of her actions and so generates an optimal level of public good provision by consumer $i$. Formally, if $(\tilde{x}_1, \tilde{x}_2)$ are the competitive equilibrium levels of the public good purchased by the two consumers given these subsidies, and if $\tilde{p}$ is the equilbrium price, then consumer $i$'s purchases of the public good, $\tilde{x}_i$, must solve $\text{Max}_{x_i \geq 0}\ \phi_i(x_i + \tilde{x}_j) + s_i x_i - \tilde{p} x_i$, and so $\tilde{x}_i$ must satisfy the necessary and sufficient first-order condition

$$\phi_i'(\tilde{x}_1 + \tilde{x}_2) + s_i \leq \tilde{p}, \text{ with equality of } \tilde{x}_i > 0.$$

Substituting for $s_i$, and using both condition (11.C.4) and the market-clearing condition that $\tilde{x}_1 + \tilde{x}_2 = \tilde{q}$, we conclude that $\tilde{q}$ is the total amount of the public good in the competitive equilibrium given these subsidies if and only if

$$\phi_i'(\tilde{q}) + \phi_{-i}'(q^\circ) \leq c'(\tilde{q}),$$

with equality for some $i$ if $\tilde{q} > 0$. Recalling (11.C.1) we see that $\tilde{q} = q^\circ$. (Exercise 11.C.1 asks you to extend this argument to the case where $I > 2$; formally, we then have a multilateral externality of the sort studied in Section 11.D.)

Note that both optimal direct public provision and this subsidy scheme require that the government know the benefits derived by consumers from the public good (i.e., their willingness to pay in terms of private goods). In Section 11.E, we study the case in which this is not so.

### Lindahl Equilibria

Although private provision of the sort studied above results in an inefficient level of the public good, there is *in principle* a market institution that can achieve optimality. Suppose that, for each consumer $i$, we have a market for the public good "as experienced by consumer $i$." That is, we think of each consumer's consumption of the public good as a distinct commodity with its own market. We denote the price of this personalized good by $p_i$. Note that $p_i$ may differ across consumers. Suppose also that, given the equilibrium price $p_i^{**}$, each consumer $i$ sees herself as deciding on the *total amount of the public good she will consume*, $x_i$, so as to solve

$$\underset{x_i \geq 0}{\text{Max}} \quad \phi_i(x_i) - p_i^{**} x_i.$$

Her equilibrium consumption level $x_i^{**}$ must therefore satisfy the necessary and sufficient first-order condition

$$\phi_i'(x_i^{**}) \leq p_i^{**}, \quad \text{with equality if } x_i^{**} > 0. \tag{11.C.6}$$

The firm is now viewed as producing a bundle of $I$ goods with a fixed-proportions technology (i.e., the level of production of each personalized good is necessarily the same). Thus, the firm solves

$$\underset{q \geq 0}{\text{Max}} \quad \left( \sum_{i=1}^{I} p_i^{**} q \right) - c(q).$$

The firm's equilibrium level of output $q^{**}$ therefore satisfies the necessary and sufficient first-order condition

$$\sum_{i=1}^{I} p_i^{**} \leq c'(q^{**}), \quad \text{with equality if } q^{**} > 0. \tag{11.C.7}$$

Together, (11.C.6), (11.C.7), and the market-clearing condition that $x_i^{**} = q^{**}$ for all $i$ imply that

$$\sum_{i=1}^{I} \phi_i'(q^{**}) \leq c'(q^{**}), \quad \text{with equality if } q^{**} > 0. \tag{11.C.8}$$

Comparing (11.C.8) with (11.C.1), we see that the equilibrium level of the public good consumed by each consumer is exactly the efficient level: $q^{**} = q^\circ$.

This type of equilibrium in personalized markets for the public good is known as a *Lindahl equilibrium*, after Lindahl (1919). [See also Milleron (1972) for a further discussion.] To understand why we obtain efficiency, note that once we have defined personalized markets for the public good, each consumer, taking the price in her personalized market as given, fully determines her own level of consumption of the public good; externalities are eliminated.

Yet, despite the attractive properties of Lindahl equilibria, their realism is questionable. Note, first, that the ability to exclude a consumer from use of the public good is essential if this equilibrium concept is to make sense; otherwise a consumer would have no reason to believe that in the absence of making any purchases of the public good she would get to consume none of it.[11] Moreover, even if exclusion is possible, these are markets with only a single agent on the demand side. As a result, price-taking behavior of the sort presumed is unlikely to occur.

The idea that inefficiencies can in principle be corrected by introducing the right kind of markets, encountered here and in Section 11.B, is a very general one. In particular cases, however, this "solution" may or may not be a realistic possibility. We encounter this issue again in our study of multilateral externalities in Section 11.D. As we shall see, these types of externalities often share many of the features of public goods.

# 11.D Multilateral Externalities

In most cases, externalities are felt and generated by numerous parties. This is particularly true of those externalities, such as industrial pollution, smog caused by automobile use, or congestion, that are widely considered to be "important" policy problems. In this section, we extend our analysis of externalities to these multilateral settings.

An important distinction can be made in the case of multilateral externalities according to whether the externality is *depletable* (or *private*, or *rivalrous*) or *nondepletable* (or *public*, or *nonrivalrous*). Depletable externalities have the feature that experience of the externality by one agent reduces the amount that will be felt by other agents. For example, if the externality takes the form of the dumping of garbage on people's property, if an additional unit of garbage is dumped on one

---

11. Thus, the possibility of exclusion can be important for efficient supply of the public good, even though the use of an exclusion technology is itself inefficient (a Pareto optimal allocation cannot involve any exclusion).

piece of property, that much less is left to be dumped on others.[12] Depletable externalities therefore share the characteristics of our usual (private) sort of commodity. In contrast, air pollution is a nondepletable externality; the amount of air pollution experienced by one agent is not affected by the fact that others are also experiencing it. Nondepletable externalities therefore have the characteristics of public goods (or bads).

In this section we argue that a decentralized market solution can be expected to work well for multilateral depletable externalities as long as well-defined and enforceable property rights can be created. In contrast, market-based solutions are unlikely to work in the nondepletable case, in parallel to our conclusions regarding public goods in Section 11.C.

We shall assume throughout this section that the agents who generate externalities are distinct from those who experience them. This simplification is inessential but eases the exposition and facilitates comparison with the previous sections (Exercise 11.D.2 asks you to consider the general case). For ease of reference, we assume here that the generators of the externality are firms and that those experiencing the externality are consumers. We also focus on the special, but central, case in which the externality generated by the firms is homogeneous (i.e., consumers are indifferent to the source of the externality). (Exercise 11.D.4 asks you to consider the case in which the source matters.)

We again adopt a partial equilibrium approach and assume that agents take as given the price vector $p$ of $L$ traded goods. There are $J$ firms that generate the externality in the process of production. As discussed in Section 11.B, given price vector $p$, we can determine firm $j$'s derived profit function over the level of the externality it generates, $h_j \geq 0$, which we denote by $\pi_j(h_j)$. There are also $I$ consumers, who have quasilinear utility functions with respect to a numeraire, traded commodity. Given price vector $p$, we denote by $\phi_i(\tilde{h}_i)$ consumer $i$'s derived utility function over the amount of the externality $\tilde{h}_i$ she experiences. We assume that $\pi_j(\cdot)$ and $\phi_i(\cdot)$ are twice differentiable with $\pi_j''(\cdot) < 0$ and $\phi_i''(\cdot) < 0$. To fix ideas, we shall focus on the case where $\phi_i'(\cdot) < 0$ for all $i$, so that we are dealing with a negative externality.

## Depletable Externalities

We begin by examining the case of depletable externalities. As in Section 11.B, it is easy to see that the level of the (negative) externality is excessive at an unfettered competitive equilibrium. Indeed, at any competitive equilibrium, each firm $j$ will wish to set the externality-generating activity at the level $h_j^*$ satisfying the condition

$$\pi_j(h_j^*) \leq 0, \quad \text{with equality if } h_j^* > 0.^{13} \tag{11.D.1}$$

In contrast, any Pareto optimal allocation involves the levels $(\tilde{h}_1^\circ, \ldots, \tilde{h}_I^\circ, h_1^\circ, \ldots, h_J^\circ)$

---

12. A distinction can also be made as to whether a depletable externality is *allocable*. For example, acid rain is depletable in the sense that the total amount of chemicals put into the air will fall somewhere, but it is not readily allocable because where it falls is determined by weather patterns. Throughout this section, we take depletable externalities to be allocable. The analytical implications of nonallocable depletable externalities parallel those of nondepletable ones.

13. The firms are indifferent about which consumer is affected by their externality. Therefore, apart from the fact that $\sum_i \tilde{h}_i = \sum_j h_j^*$, the particular values of the individual $\tilde{h}_i$'s are indeterminate.

that solve[14]

$$\underset{\substack{(h_1,\dots,h_J)\geq 0 \\ (\tilde{h}_1,\dots,\tilde{h}_I)\geq 0}}{\text{Max}} \quad \sum_{i=1}^{I} \phi_i(\tilde{h}_i) + \sum_{j=1}^{J} \pi_j(h_j) \tag{11.D.2}$$

$$\text{s.t.} \sum_{j=1}^{J} h_j = \sum_{i=1}^{I} \tilde{h}_i.$$

The constraint in (11.D.2) reflects the depletability of the externality: If $\tilde{h}_i$ is increased by one unit, there is one unit less of the externality that needs to be experienced by others. Letting $\mu$ be the multiplier on this constraint, the necessary and sufficient first-order conditions to problem (11.D.2) are

$$\phi_i'(\tilde{h}_i^{\circ}) \leq \mu, \quad \text{with equality if } \tilde{h}_i^{\circ} > 0, \, i = 1, \dots, I, \tag{11.D.3}$$

and

$$\mu \leq -\pi_j'(h_j^{\circ}), \quad \text{with equality if } h_j^{\circ} > 0, \, j = 1, \dots, J. \tag{11.D.4}$$

Conditions (11.D.3) and (11.D.4), along with the constraint in problem (11.D.2), characterize the optimal levels of externality generation and consumption. Note that they exactly parallel the efficiency conditions for a private good derived in Chapter 10, conditions (10.D.3) to (10.D.5), where we interpret $-\pi_j'(\cdot)$ as firm $j$'s marginal cost of producing more of the externality. If well-defined and enforceable property rights can be specified over the externality, and if $I$ and $J$ are large numbers so that price taking is a reasonable hypothesis, then by analogy with the analysis of competitive markets for private goods in Chapter 10, a market for the externality can be expected to lead to the optimal levels of externality production and consumption in the depletable case.

### Nondepletable Externalities

We now move to the case in which the externality is nondepletable. To be specific, assume that the level of the externality experienced by *each* consumer is $\sum_j h_j$, the total amount of the externality produced by the firms.

In an unfettered competitive equilibrium, each firm $j$'s externality generation $h_j^*$ again satisfies condition (11.D.1). In contrast, any Pareto optimal allocation involves externality generation levels $(h_1^{\circ}, \dots, h_J^{\circ})$ that solve

$$\underset{(h_1,\dots,h_J)\geq 0}{\text{Max}} \quad \sum_{i=1}^{I} \phi_i(\textstyle\sum_j h_j) + \sum_{j=1}^{J} \pi_j(h_j). \tag{11.D.5}$$

This problem has necessary and sufficient first-order conditions for each firm $j$'s optimal level of externality generation, $h_j^{\circ}$, of

$$\sum_{i=1}^{I} \phi_i'(\textstyle\sum_j h_j^{\circ}) \leq -\pi_j'(h_j^{\circ}), \quad \text{with equality if } h_j^{\circ} > 0. \tag{11.D.6}$$

---

14. The objective function in (11.D.2) amounts to the usual difference between benefits and costs arising in the aggregate surplus measure. Note, to this effect, that $-\pi_j(\cdot)$ can be viewed as firm $j$'s cost function for producing the externality.

Condition (11.D.6) is exactly analogous to the optimality condition for a public good, condition (11.C.1), where $-\pi'_j(\cdot)$ is firm $j$'s marginal cost of externality production.[15]

By analogy with our discussion of private provision of public goods in Section 11.C, the introduction of a standard sort of market for the externality will *not* lead here, as it did in the bilateral case of Section 11.B, to an optimal outcome. The free-rider problem reappears, and the equilibrium level of the (negative) externality will exceed its optimal level. Instead, in the case of a multilateral nondepletable externality, a market-based solution would require personalized markets for the externality, as in the Lindahl equilibrium concept. However, all the problems with Lindahl equilibrium discussed in Section 11.C will similarly afflict these markets. As a result, purely market-based solutions, personalized or not, are unlikely to work in the case of a depletable externality.[16]

In contrast, given adequate information (a strong assumption!), the government *can* achieve optimality using quotas or taxes. With quotas, the government simply sets an upper bound on each firm $j$'s level of externality generation equal to its optimal level $h^\circ_j$. On the other hand, as in Section 11.B, optimality-restoring taxes face each firm with the marginal social cost of their externality. Here the optimal tax is identical for each firm and is equal to $t_h = -\sum_i \phi'_i(\sum_j h^\circ_j)$ per unit of the externality generated. Given this tax, each firm $j$ solves

$$\underset{h_j \geq 0}{\text{Max}} \quad \pi_j(h_j) - t_h h_j,$$

which has the necessary and sufficient first-order condition

$$\pi'_j(h_j) \leq t_h, \quad \text{with equality if } h_j > 0.$$

Given $t_h = -\sum_i \phi'_i(\sum_j h^\circ_j)$, firm $j$'s optimal choice is $h_j = h^\circ_j$.

---

A partial market-based approach that can achieve optimality with a nondepletable multilateral externality involves specification of a quota on the *total* level of the externality and distribution of that number of *tradeable externality permits* (each permit grants a firm the right to generate one unit of the externality). Suppose that $h^\circ = \sum_j h^\circ_j$ permits are given to the firms, with firm $j$ receiving $\bar{h}_j$ of them. Let $p^*_h$ denote the equilibrium price of these permits. Then each firm $j$'s demand for permits, $h_j$, solves $\text{Max}_{h_j \geq 0} (\pi_j(h_j) + p^*_h(\bar{h}_j - h_j))$ and so satisfies the necessary and sufficient first-order condition $\pi'_j(h_j) \leq p^*_h$, with equality if $h_j > 0$. In addition, market clearing in the permits market requires that $\sum_j h_j = h^\circ$. The competitive equilibrium in the market for permits then has price $p^*_h = -\sum_i \phi'_i(h^\circ)$ and each firm $j$ using $h^\circ_j$ permits and so yields an optimal allocation. The advantage of this scheme relative to a strict quota method arises when the government has limited information about the $\pi_j(\cdot)$ functions and cannot tell which particular firms can efficiently bear the burden of externality reduction, although it has enough information, perhaps of a statistical sort, to allow the computation of the optimal aggregate level of the externality, $h^\circ$.

---

15. Recall that the single firm's cost function $c(\cdot)$ in Section 11.C could be viewed as the aggregate cost function of $J$ separate profit-maximizing firms. Were we to explicitly model these $J$ firms in Section 11.C, the optimality conditions for public good production would take exactly the form in (11.D.6) with $c'_j(h^\circ_j)$ replacing $-\pi'_j(h^\circ_j)$.

16. The public nature of the externality leads to similar free-rider problems in any bargaining solution. (See Exercise 11.D.6 for an illustration.)

## 11.E  Private Information and Second-Best Solutions

In practice, the degree to which an agent is affected by an externality or benefits from a public good will often be known only to her. The presence of *privately held* (or *asymmetrically held*) information can confound both centralized (e.g., quotas and taxes) and decentralized (e.g., bargaining) attempts to achieve optimality. In this section, we provide an introduction to these issues, focusing for the sake of specificity on the case of a bilateral externality such as that studied in Section 11.B. Following the convention adopted in Section 11.D, we shall assume here that the externality-generating agent is a firm and the affected agent is a consumer. (For a more general treatment of some of the topics covered in this section, see Chapter 23.)

Suppose, then, that we can write the consumer's derived utility function from externality level $h$ (see Section 11.B for more on this construction) as $\phi(h, \eta)$, where $\eta \in \mathbb{R}$ is a parameter, to be called the consumer's *type*, that affects the consumer's costs from the externality. Similarly, we let $\pi(h, \theta)$ denote the firm's derived profit given its type $\theta \in \mathbb{R}$. The actual values of $\theta$ and $\eta$ are *privately observed*: Only the consumer knows her type $\eta$, and only the firm observes its type $\theta$. The ex ante likelihoods (probability distributions) of various values of $\theta$ and $\eta$ are, however, publicly known. For convenience, we assume that $\theta$ and $\eta$ are independently distributed. As previously, we assume that $\pi(h, \theta)$ and $\phi(h, \eta)$ are strictly concave in $h$ for any given values of $\theta$ and $\eta$.

### Decentralized Bargaining

Consider the decentralized approach to the externality problem first. In general, bargaining in the presence of bilateral asymmetric information will *not* lead to an efficient level of the externality. To see this, consider again the case in which the consumer has the right to an externality-free environment, and the simple bargaining process in which the consumer makes a take-it-or-leave-it offer to the firm. For simplicity, we assume that there are only two possible levels of the externality, 0 and $\bar{h} > 0$, and we focus on the case of a negative externality in which externality level $\bar{h}$, relative to the level 0, is detrimental for the consumer and beneficial for the firm (the analysis is readily applied to the case of a positive externality).

It is convenient to define $b(\theta) = \pi(\bar{h}, \theta) - \pi(0, \theta) > 0$ as the measure of the firm's benefit from the externality-generating activity when its type is $\theta$. Similarly, we let $c(\eta) = \phi(0, \eta) - \phi(\bar{h}, \eta) > 0$ give the consumer's cost from externality level $\bar{h}$. In this simplified setting, the only aspects of the consumer's and firm's types that matter are the values of $b$ and $c$ that these types generate. Hence, we can focus directly on the various possible values of $b$ and $c$ that the two agents might have. Denote by $G(b)$ and $F(c)$ the distribution functions of these two variables induced by the underlying probability distributions of $\theta$ and $\eta$ (note that, given the independence of $\theta$ and $\eta$, $b$ and $c$ are independent). For simplicity, we assume that these distributions have associated density functions $g(b)$ and $f(c)$, with $g(b) > 0$ and $f(c) > 0$ for all $b > 0$ and $c > 0$.

Since the consumer has the right to an externality-free environment, in the absence of any agreement with the firm she will always insist that the firm set $h = 0$ (recall that $c > 0$). However, in any arrangement that guarantees Pareto optimal outcomes for all values of $b$ and $c$, the firm should be allowed to set $h = \bar{h}$ whenever $b > c$.

Now consider the amount that the consumer will demand from the firm when her cost is $c$ in exchange for permission to engage in the externality-generating activity. Since the firm knows that the consumer will insist on $h = 0$ if there is no agreement, the firm will agree to pay the amount $T$ if and only if $b \geq T$. Hence, the consumer knows that if she demands a payment of $T$, the probability that the firm will accept her offer equals the probability that $b \geq T$; that is, it is equal to $1 - G(T)$. Given her cost $c > 0$ (and assuming risk neutrality), the consumer optimally chooses the value of $T$ she demands to solve

$$\underset{T}{\text{Max}} \quad (1 - G(T))(T - c). \qquad \text{(11.E.1)}$$

The objective function of problem (11.E.1) is the probability that the firm accepts the demand, multiplied by the net gain to the consumer when this happens ($T - c$). Under our assumptions, the objective function in (11.E.1) is strictly positive for all $T > c$ and equal to zero when $T = c$. Therefore, the solution, say $T_c^*$, is such that $T_c^* > c$. But this implies that this bargaining process must result in a strictly positive probability of an inefficient outcome, since whenever the firm's benefit $b$ satisfies $c < b < T_c^*$, the firm will reject the consumer's offer, resulting in an externality level of zero, even though optimality requires that $h = \bar{h}$.[17,18]

### Quotas and Taxes

Just as decentralized bargaining will involve inefficiencies in the presence of privately held information, so too will the use of quotas and taxes. Moreover, as originally noted by Weitzman (1974), the presence of asymmetrically held information causes these two policy instruments to no longer be perfect substitutes for one another, as they were in the model of Section 11.B.[19]

To begin, note that given $\theta$ and $\eta$, the aggregate surplus resulting from externality level $h$ (we return to a continuum of possible externality levels here) is $\phi(h, \eta) + \pi(h, \theta)$. Thus, the externality level that maximizes aggregate surplus depends in general on the realized values of $(\theta, \eta)$. We denote this optimal value by the function $h^\circ(\theta, \eta)$. Figure 11.E.1 depicts this optimum value for two different pairs of parameters, $(\theta', \eta')$ and $(\theta'', \eta'')$.

Suppose, first, that a quota level of $\hat{h}$ is fixed. The firm will then choose the level of the externality to solve

$$\underset{h \geq 0}{\text{Max}} \quad \pi(h, \theta)$$
$$\text{s.t.} \quad h \leq \hat{h}.$$

Denote its optimal choice by $h^q(\hat{h}, \theta)$. The typical effect of the quota will be to make

---

17. Note the similarity between problem (11.E.1) and the monopolist's problem studied in Section 12.B. Here the consumer's inability to discriminate among firms of different types leads her optimal offer to be one that yields an inefficient outcome.

18. We could, of course, also consider the outcomes from other, perhaps more elaborate, bargaining procedures. In Chapter 23, however, we shall study a result due to Myerson and Satterthwaite (1983) that implies that *no* bargaining procedure can lead to an efficient outcome for all values of $b$ and $c$ in this setting.

19. The discussion that follows also has implications for the relative advantages of quantity- versus price-based control mechanisms in organizations.

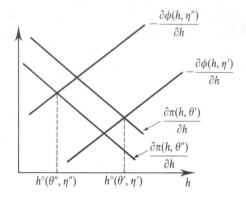

**Figure 11.E.1**

The surplus-maximizing aggregate externality level for two different pairs of parameters, $(\theta', \eta')$ and $(\theta'', \eta'')$.

the actual level of the externality much less sensitive to the values of $\theta$ and $\eta$ than is required by optimality. The firm's externality level will be completely insensitive to $\eta$. Moreover, if the level of the quota $\hat{h}$ is such that $\partial\pi(\hat{h}, \theta)/\partial h > 0$ for all $\theta$, we will have $h^q(\hat{h}, \theta) = \hat{h}$ for every $\theta$. The loss in aggregate surplus arising under the quota for types $(\theta, \eta)$ is given by

$$\phi(h^q(\hat{h}, \theta), \eta) + \pi(h^q(\hat{h}, \theta), \theta) - \phi(h^\circ(\theta, \eta), \eta) - \pi(h^\circ(\theta, \eta), \theta)$$
$$= \int_{h^\circ(\theta, \eta)}^{h^q(\hat{h}, \theta)} \left( \frac{\partial\pi(h, \theta)}{\partial h} + \frac{\partial\phi(h, \eta)}{\partial h} \right) dh.$$

This loss is represented by the shaded region in Figure 11.E.2 for a case in which the quota is set equal to $\hat{h} = h^\circ(\bar{\theta}, \bar{\eta})$, the externality level that maximizes social surplus when $\theta$ and $\eta$ each take their mean values, $\bar{\theta}$ and $\bar{\eta}$ [the dashed lines in the figure are the graphs of $\partial\pi(h, \bar{\theta})/\partial h$ and $-\partial\phi(h, \bar{\eta})/\partial h$ and the solid lines are the graphs of $\partial\pi(h, \theta)/\partial h$ and $-\partial\phi(h, \eta)/\partial h$; note that in the case depicted, the firm wishes to produce the externality up to the allowed quota $\hat{h}$].

Consider next the use of a tax on the firm of $t$ units of the numeraire per unit of the externality. For any given value of $\theta$, the firm will then choose the level of externality to solve

$$\underset{h \geq 0}{\text{Max}} \quad \pi(h, \theta) - th.$$

Denote its optimal choice by $h^t(t, \theta)$. The loss in aggregate surplus from the tax relative to the optimal outcome for types $(\theta, \eta)$ is therefore given by

$$\phi(h^t(t, \theta), \eta) + \pi(h^t(t, \theta), \theta) - \phi(h^\circ(\theta, \eta), \eta) - \pi(h^\circ(\theta, \eta), \theta)$$
$$= \int_{h^\circ(\theta, \eta)}^{h^t(t, \theta)} \left( \frac{\partial\pi(h, \theta)}{\partial h} + \frac{\partial\phi(h, \eta)}{\partial h} \right) dh.$$

Its value is depicted by the shaded region in Figure 11.E.3 for the same situation as in Figure 11.E.2, but now assuming that a tax is set at $t = -\partial\phi(h^\circ(\bar{\theta}, \bar{\eta}), \bar{\eta})/\partial h$, the value that results in the maximization of aggregate surplus when $(\theta, \eta) = (\bar{\theta}, \bar{\eta})$. Note that under a tax, as under a quota, the level of the externality is responsive to changes in the marginal benefits of the firm but not to changes in the marginal costs of the consumer.

Which of these instruments, quota or tax, performs better? The answer is that it depends. Imagine, for example, that $\eta$ is a constant, say equal to $\bar{\eta}$. Then, for $\theta$ such that the benefits of the externality's use to the firm are high, a quota will typically miss the optimal externality level by not allowing the externality to increase above the quota level. On the other hand, because a fixed tax rate $t$ does not reflect any

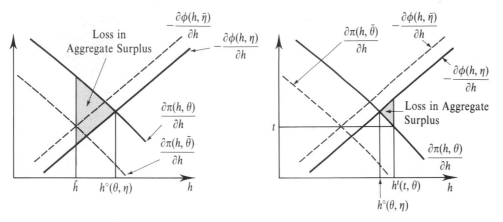

**Figure 11.E.2 (left)**

The loss in aggregate surplus under a quota for types $(\theta, \eta)$.

**Figure 11.E.3 (right)**

The loss in aggregate surplus under a tax for types $(\theta, \eta)$.

increasing marginal costs of the externality to the consumer at higher externality levels, for such values of $\theta$ the tax may result in excess production of the externality.

Intuitively, when the optimal externality level varies little with $\theta$, we expect a quota to be better. Figure 11.E.4(a), for example, depicts a case in which the marginal cost to the consumer of the externality is zero up to some point $h^*$ and infinite thereafter. In this case, by setting a quota of $\hat{h} = h^*$, we can maximize aggregate surplus for any value of $(\theta, \eta)$, but no tax can accomplish this. A tax would have to be very high to guarantee that with probability one the externality level fixed by the firm is not larger than $h^*$. But if so, the resulting externality level would be too low most of the time.

In contrast, in Figure 11.E.4(b) we depict a case in which the marginal cost to the consumer of the externality is independent of the level of $h$. In this case, a tax equal to this marginal cost ($t = t^*$) achieves the surplus-maximizing externality level for all $(\theta, \eta)$, but no quota can do so.

If we take the expected value of aggregate surplus as our welfare measure, we therefore see from these two examples that either policy instrument may be preferable, depending on the circumstances.[20] (Exercise 11.E.1 asks you to provide a full analysis for a linear-quadratic example.) Note also that the bargaining procedure we have discussed will not result in optimality in *either* case depicted in Figure 11.E.4.[21] Thus, we have here two cases in which either a quota or a tax performs better than a particular decentralized outcome.[22]

---

20. In Chapter 13, we discuss in greater detail some of the issues that arise in making welfare comparisons in settings with privately held information. There we shall justify the maximization of expected aggregate surplus in this partial equilibrium setting as a requirement of a notion of ex ante Pareto optimality for the two agents. See also the discussion in Section 23.F.

21. Strictly speaking, our previous discussion of bargaining assumed only two possible levels of the externality, while here we have a continuum of levels. This difference is not important. The inefficiency of the bargaining procedure previously studied would hold in this continuous environment as well.

22. We should emphasize that in these two examples other bargaining procedures will perform better than the procedure involving a take-it-or-leave-it offer by the consumer. For example, if a take-or-leave offer is made by the firm, then full optimality results in *both* of these cases because the type of the consumer is known with certainty. The conclusion of our discussion is therefore a qualitative one: With asymmetric information, it is difficult to make very general assertions about the relative performance of centralized versus decentralized approaches.

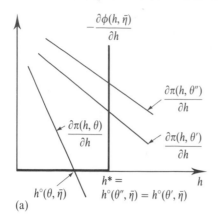

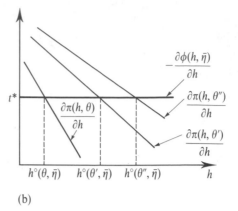

**Figure 11.E.4**

Two cases in which a quota or tax maximizes aggregate surplus for every realization of $\theta$.
(a) Quota $\hat{h} = h^*$ maximizes aggregate surplus for all $\theta$.
(b) Tax $t = t^*$ maximizes aggregate surplus for all $\theta$.

In Exercise 11.E.2, you are asked to extend the analysis just given to a case with two firms ($j = 1, 2$) generating an externality, where the two firms are identical except possibly for their realized levels of $\theta_j$. The exercise illustrates the importance of the degree of correlation between the $\theta_j$'s for the relative performance of quotas versus taxes. In comparing a uniform quota policy versus a uniform tax policy ("uniform" here means that the two firms face the same quota or tax rate), the less correlated the shocks across the firms, the better the tax looks. The reason is not difficult to discern. With imperfect correlation, a uniform tax has a benefit that is not achieved with a uniform quota: It allows for the individual levels of externalities generated to be responsive to the realized values of the $\theta_j$'s. Indeed, with a uniform tax, the production of the total amount of externality generated is always efficiently distributed across the two firms.

The presence of multiple generators of an externality also raises the possibility that a market for tradeable emissions permits could be created, as discussed at the end of Section 11.D. This simple addition to the quota policy can potentially eliminate the inefficient distribution of externality generation across different generators that is often a feature of a quota policy. In particular, suppose that instead of simply giving each firm a quota level, we now give them tradeable externality permits entitling them to generate the same number of units of the externality as in the quota. Suppose also that each firm would always fully use its quota if no trade was possible. Then trade must result in *at least* as large a value of aggregate surplus as the simple quota scheme for any realization of the firms' and consumer's types, because we still get the same total level of emissions and we can never get a trade between firms that lowers aggregate profits.[23] Of course, the same bargaining problems that we studied above can prevent a fully efficient distribution of externality generation from arising; but if the firms know each others' values of $\theta_j$ or are numerous enough to act competitively in the market for these rights, then we can expect a distribution of the total externality generation that is efficient across generators. In fact, in the case where the statistical distribution of costs among the firms is known but the particular realizations for individual firms are not known, this type of policy can achieve a fully optimal outcome.

---

23. Note, however, that the assumption that the externalities generated by the different firms are perfect substitutes to the consumer is crucial to this conclusion. If this is not true, then the reallocation of externality generation can reduce aggregate surplus by lowering the well-being of the agents affected by the externality.

## More General Policy Mechanisms

The tax and quota schemes considered above are, as we have seen, completely unresponsive to changes in the marginal costs of the externality to the affected agent (the consumer in this case). It is natural to wonder whether any other sorts of schemes can do better, perhaps by making the level of the externality responsive to the consumer's costs. The problem in doing so is that these benefits and costs are unobservable, and the parties involved may not have incentives to reveal them truthfully if asked. For example, suppose that the government simply asks the consumer and the firm to report their benefits and costs from the externality and then enforces whatever appears to be the optimal outcome based on these reports. In this case, the consumer will have an incentive to exaggerate her costs when asked in order to prevent the firm from being allowed to generate the externality. The question, then, is how to design mechanisms that control these incentives for misreporting and, as a consequence, enable the government to achieve an efficient outcome. This problem is studied in a very general form in Chapter 23; here we confine ourselves to a brief examination of one well-known scheme.

Return to the case in which there are only two possible levels of the externality, $0$ and $\bar{h}$. Can we design a scheme that achieves the optimal level of externality generation for every realization of $b$ (the firm's benefit from the externality) and $c$ (the consumer's cost)? We now verify that the answer is "yes."

Imagine the government setting up the following *revelation mechanism*: The firm and the consumer are each asked to report their values of $b$ and $c$, respectively. Let $\hat{b}$ and $\hat{c}$ denote these announcements. For each possible pair of announcements $(\hat{b}, \hat{c})$, the government sets an allowed level of the externality as well as a tax or subsidy payment for each of the two agents. Suppose, in particular, that the government declares that it will set the allowed externality level $h$ to maximize aggregate surplus given the announcements. That is, $h = \bar{h}$ if and only if $\hat{b} > \hat{c}$. In addition, if externality generation is allowed (i.e., if $h = \bar{h}$), the government will tax the firm an amount equal to $\hat{c}$ and will subsidize the consumer with a payment equal to $\hat{b}$. That is, if the firm wants to generate the externality (which it indicates by reporting a large value of $b$), it is asked to pay the externality's cost as declared by the consumer; and if the consumer allows the externality (by reporting a low value of $c$) she receives a payment equal to the externality's benefit as declared by the firm.

In fact, *under this scheme both the firm and the consumer will tell the truth*, so that an optimal level of externality generation will, indeed, result for every possible $(b, c)$ pair. To see this, consider the consumer's optimal announcement when her cost level is $c$. If the firm announces some $\hat{b} > c$, then the consumer prefers to have the externality-generating activity allowed (she does $\hat{b} - c$ better than if it is prevented). Hence, her optimal announcement satisfies $\hat{c} < \hat{b}$; moreover, because any such announcement will give her the same payoff, she might as well announce the truth, that is, $\hat{c} = c < \hat{b}$. On the other hand, if the firm announces $\hat{b} \leq c$, the consumer prefers to have the externality level set to zero. Hence, she would like announce $\hat{c} \geq \hat{b}$; and again, because any of these announcements will give her the same payoff, she may as well announce the truth, that is, $\hat{c} = c \geq \hat{b}$. Thus, whatever the firm's announcement, truth-telling is an optimal strategy for the consumer. (Formally, telling the truth is a *weakly dominant strategy* for the consumer in the sense studied in Section 8.B. In fact, it is the consumer's *only* weakly dominant strategy; see Exercise 11.E.3.) A parallel analysis yields the same conclusion for the firm.

**Exercise 11.E.4:** Show that in the tax-subsidy part of the mechanism above we could add, without affecting the mechanism's truth-telling or optimality properties, an additional payment to each agent that depends in an arbitrary way on the other agent's announcement.

The scheme we have described here is an example of the *Groves–Clarke mechanism* [due to Groves (1973) and Clarke (1971); see also Section 23.C] and was originally proposed as a mechanism for deciding whether to carry out public good projects. Some examples for the public goods context are contained in the exercises at the end of the chapter.

---

The Groves–Clarke mechanism has two very attractive features: it implements the optimal level of the externality for every $(b, c)$ pair, and it induces truth-telling in a very strong (i.e., dominant strategy) sense. But the mechanism has some unattractive features as well. In particular, it does not result in a balanced budget for the government: The government has a deficit equal to $(b - c)$ whenever $b > c$. We could use the flexibility offered by Exercise 11.E.4 to eliminate this deficit for all possible $(b, c)$, but then we would necessarily create a budget surplus and therefore a Pareto inefficient outcome for some values of $(b, c)$ (not all units of the numeraire will be left in the hands of the firm or the consumer).

In fact, this problem is unavoidable with this type of mechanism: If we want to preserve the properties that, for every $(b, c)$, truth-telling is a dominant strategy and the optimal level of externality is implemented, then we generally cannot achieve budget balance for every $(b, c)$. In Chapter 23 we discuss this issue in greater detail and also consider other mechanisms that can, under certain circumstances, get around the problem. (See also Exercise 11.E.5 for an analysis in which budget balance is required only on average.)

---

## APPENDIX A: NONCONVEXITIES AND THE THEORY OF EXTERNALITIES

Throughout this chapter, we have maintained the assumption that preferences and production sets are convex, leading the derived utility and profit functions we have considered to be concave. With these assumptions, all the decision problems we have studied have been well behaved; they had unique solutions (or, more generally, convex-valued solutions) that varied continuously with the underlying parameters of the problems (e.g., the prices of the $L$ traded commodities or the price of the externality if a market existed for it). Yet, this is not a completely innocent assumption. In this appendix, we present some simple examples designed to illustrate that externalities may themselves generate nonconvexities, and we comment on some of the implications of this fact.

We consider here a bilateral externality situation involving two firms. We suppose that firm 1 may engage in an externality-generating activity that affects firm 2's production. The level of externality generated by firm 1 is denoted by $h$, and firm $j$'s profits conditional on the production of externality level $h$ are $\pi_j(h)$ for $j = 1, 2$. It is perfectly natural to assume that $\pi_1(\cdot)$ is concave: The level $h$ could, for example,

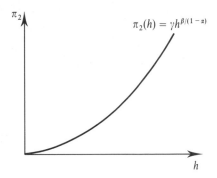

$\pi_2(h) = \gamma h^{\beta/(1-\alpha)}$

**Figure 11.AA.1**

The derived profit function of firm 2 (the externality recipient) in Example 11.AA.1 when $\alpha + \beta > 1$.

be equal to firm 1's output.[24] As Examples 11.AA.1 and 11.AA.2 illustrate, however, this may not be true of firm 2's profit function.

**Example 11.AA.1:** *Positive Externalities as a Source of Increasing Returns.*  Suppose that firm 2 produces an output whose price is 1, using an input whose price, for simplicity, we also take to equal 1. Firm 2's production function is $q = h^\beta z^\alpha$, where $\alpha, \beta \in [0, 1]$. Thus, the externality is a positive one.[25] Note that, for fixed $h$, the problem of firm 2 is concave and perfectly well behaved. Given a level of $h$, the maximized profits of firm 2 can be calculated to be $\pi_2(h) = \gamma h^{\beta/(1-\alpha)}$, where $\gamma > 0$ is a constant. In Figure 11.AA.1, we represent $\pi_2(h)$ for $\beta > 1 - \alpha$. We see there that firm 2's derived profit function is *not* concave in $h$; in fact, it is convex. This reflects the fact that if we think of the externality $h$ as an input to firm 2's production process, then firm 2's overall production function exhibits increasing returns to scale because $\alpha + \beta > 1$. ∎

**Example 11.AA.2:** *Negative Externalities as a Source of Nonconvexities.*  In Example 11.AA.1, the nonconvexity in firm 2's production set, and the resulting failure of concavity in its derived profit function, were caused by a positive externality. In this example the failure of concavity of firm 2's derived profit function is the result of a negative externality.

Suppose, in particular, that $\pi_2'(h) \le 0$ for all $h$, with strict inequality for some $h$, and that firm 2 has the option of shutting down when experiencing externality level $h$ and receiving profits of zero.[26] In this case, the function $\pi_2(\cdot)$ can *never* be concave

---

24. Note also that we may well have $\pi_1(h) < 0$ for some levels $h \ge 0$ because $\pi_1(h)$ is firm 1's maximized profit *conditional* on producing externality level $h$ (and so shutting down is not possible if $h > 0$).

25. More generally, we could think that there is an industry composed of many firms and that the externality is produced and felt by all firms in the industry (e.g., $h$ could be an index, correlated with output, of accumulated know-how in the industry). Externalities were first studied by Marshall (1920) in this context. See also Chipman (1970) and Romer (1986).

26. In the more typical case of a multilateral externality, the ability of affected parties to shut down in this manner often depends on whether the externality is depletable. In the case of a nondepletable externality, such as air pollution, affected firms can always shut down and receive zero profits. In contrast, in the case of a depletable externality (such as garbage), where $\pi_j(h)$ reflects firm $j$'s profits when it individually absorbs $h$ units of the externality, the absorption of the externality may itself require the use of some inputs (e.g., land to absorb garbage). Indeed, were this not the case for a depletable externality, the externality could always be absorbed in a manner that creates no social costs by allocating all of the externality to a firm that shuts down.

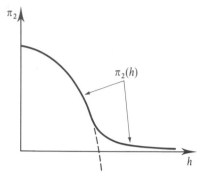

**Figure 11.AA.2**

If the recipient of a negative externality can shut down and earn zero profits for any level of the externality, then its derived profit function $\pi_2(h)$ cannot be concave over $h \in [0, \infty]$.

over all $h \in [0, \infty)$, a point originally noted by Starrett (1972). The reason can be seen in Figure 11.AA.2: If $\pi_2(\cdot)$ were a strictly decreasing concave function, then it would have to become negative at some level of $h$ (see the dashed curve), but $\pi_2(\cdot)$ must be nonnegative if firm 2 can always choose to shut down. ∎

The failure of $\pi_2(\cdot)$ to be concave can create problems for both centralized and decentralized solutions to the externality problem. For example, if property rights over the externality are defined and a market for the externality is introduced in either Example 11.AA.1 or Example 11.AA.2, a competitive equilibrium may fail to exist (even assuming that the two agents act as price takers). Firm 2's objective function will not be concave, and so its optimal demand may fail to be well defined and continuous (recall our discussion in Section 10.C of the equilibrium existence problems caused by nonconvexities in firms' cost functions).

In contrast, taxes and quotas can, in principle, still implement the optimal outcome despite the failure of firm 2's profit function to be concave because their use depends only on the profit function of the externality generator (here, firm 1) being well behaved. In practice, however, nonconvexities in firm 2's profit function may create problems for these centralized solutions as well. Example 11.AA.3 illustrates this point.

**Example 11.AA.3:** *Externalities as a Source of Multiple Local Social Optima.* It is, in principle, true that if the decision problem of the generator of an externality is concave, then the optimum can be sustained by means of quotas or taxes. But if $\pi_2(\cdot)$ is not concave, then the aggregate surplus function $\pi_1(h) + \pi_2(h)$ may not be concave and, as a result, the first-order conditions for aggregate surplus maximization may suffice only for determining local optima. In fact, as emphasized by Baumol and Oates (1988), the nonconvexities created by externalities may easily generate situations with multiple local social optima, so that identifying a global optimum may be a formidable task.

Suppose, for example, that the profit functions of the two firms are

$$\pi_1(h) = \begin{cases} h & \text{for } h \leq 1 \\ 1 & \text{for } h > 1 \end{cases}$$

and

$$\pi_2(h) = \begin{cases} 2(1 - h)^2 & \text{for } h \leq 1 \\ 0 & \text{for } h > 1. \end{cases}$$

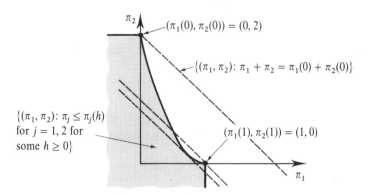

**Figure 11.AA.3**

The set of possible profit pairs $(\pi_1, \pi_2)$ in Example 11.AA.3 exhibits multiple local maxima of aggregate surplus $\pi_1(h) + \pi_2(h)$.

The function $\pi_2(\cdot)$ is not concave, something that the two previous examples have shown us can easily happen with externalities. The profit levels for the two firms that are attainable for different levels of $h$ are depicted in Figure 11.AA.3 by the shaded set $\{(\pi_1, \pi_2): \pi_j \leq \pi_j(h)$ for $j = 1, 2$ for some $h > 0\}$ (note that this definition allows for free disposal of profits). The social optimum has $h = 0$ (joint profits are then equal to 2), in which case firm 2 is able to operate in an environment free from the externality. This can be implemented by setting a tax rate on firm 1 of $t > 1$ per unit of the externality. But note that the outcome $h = 1$ (implemented by setting a tax rate on firm 1 of $t = 0$) is a local social optimum: As we decrease $h$, it is not until $h < \frac{1}{2}$ that we get an aggregate surplus level higher than that at $h = 1$. Hence, this latter outcome satisfies both the first-order and second-order conditions for the maximization of aggregate surplus (e.g., at this point, the marginal benefits of the externality exactly equal its marginal costs), and it will be easy for a social planner to be misled into thinking that she is at a welfare maximum. ∎

## REFERENCES

Arrow, K. J. (1969). The organization of economic activity: Issues pertinent to the choice of market versus non-market allocation. In *Collected Papers of K. J. Arrow*, Vol. 2. Cambridge, Mass.: Harvard University Press, 1983.

Baumol, W. J. (1964). External economies and second-order optimality conditions. *American Economic Review* **54**: 368–72.

Baumol, W. J., and W. E. Oates. (1988). *The Theory of Environmental Policy*, 2nd. ed. New York: Cambridge University Press.

Chipman, J. S. (1970). External economies of scale and competitive equilibrium. *Quarterly Journal of Economics* **84**: 347–85.

Clarke, E. H. (1971). Multipart pricing of public goods. *Public Choice* **11**: 17–33.

Coase, R. (1960). The problem of social cost. *Journal of Law and Economics* **1**: 1–44.

Groves, T. (1973). Incentives in teams. *Econometrica* **41**: 617–31.

Holmstrom, B., and J. Tirole. (1989). The theory of the firm. In *Handbook of Industrial Organization*, edited by R. Schmalensee and R. D. Willig. Amsterdam: North-Holland.

Laffont, J.-J. (1988). *Fundamentals of Public Economics*. Cambridge, Mass.: MIT Press.

Lindahl, E. (1919). *Die Gerechtigkeit der Besteurung*. Lund: Gleerup. [English translation: Just taxation—a positive solution. In *Classics in the Theory of Public Finance*, edited by R. A. Musgrave and A. T. Peacock. London: Macmillan, 1958.]

Marshall, A. (1920). *Principles of Economics*. London: Macmillan.

Meade, J. (1952). External economies and diseconomies in a competitive situation. *Economic Journal* **62**: 54–67.

Milleron, J.-C. (1972). Theory of value with public goods: A survey article. *Journal of Economic Theory* **5**: 419–77.

Myerson, R., and M. Satterthwaite. (1983). Efficient mechanisms for bilateral trading. *Journal of Economic Theory* **29**: 265–81.

Pigou, A. C. (1932). *The Economics of Welfare*. London: Macmillan.

Romer, P. (1986). Increasing returns and long-run growth. *Journal of Political Economy* **94**: 1002–36.

Samuelson, P. A. (1954). The pure theory of public expenditure. *Review of Economics and Statistics* **36**: 387–89.

Samuelson, P. A. (1955). Diagrammatic exposition of a pure theory of public expenditure. *Review of Economics and Statistics* **37**: 350–56.

Starrett, D. A. (1972). Fundamental non-convexities in the theory of externalities. *Journal of Economic Theory* **4**: 180–99.

Viner, J. (1931). Cost curves and supply curves. *Zeitschrift für Nationalökonomie* **111**: 23–46.

Weitzman, M. (1974). Prices vs. quantities. *Review of Economic Studies* **41**: 477–91.

## EXERCISES

**11.B.1[B]** (M. Weitzman)  On Farmer Jones' farm, only honey is produced. There are two ways to make honey: with and without bees. A bucket full of artificial honey, absolutely indistinguishable from the real thing, is made out of 1 gallon of maple syrup with one unit of labor. If the same honey is made the old-fashioned way (with bees), $k$ total units of labor are required (including bee-keeping) and $b$ bees are required per bucket. Either way, Farmer Jones has the capacity to produce up to $H$ buckets of honey on his farm.

The neighboring farm, belonging to Smith, produces apples. If bees are present, less labor is needed because bees pollinate the blossoms instead of workers doing it. For this reason, $c$ bees replace one worker in the task of pollinating. Up to $A$ bushels of apples can be grown on Smith's farm.

Suppose that the market wage rate is $w$, bees cost $p_b$ per bee, and maple syrup costs $p_m$ per gallon. If each farmer produces her maximal output at the cheapest cost to her (assume the output prices they face make maximal production efficient), is the resulting outcome efficient? How does the answer depend on $k$, $b$, $c$, $w$, $p_b$, and $p_m$? Give an intuitive explanation of your result. Up to how much would Smith be willing to bribe Jones to produce honey with bees? What would happen to efficiency if both farms belonged to the same owner? How could the government achieve efficient production through taxes?

**11.B.2[C]**  Consider the two-consumer externality problem studied in Section 11.B, but now assume that consumer 2's derived utility function over the externality level $h$ and her wealth available for commodity purchases $w_2$ takes the form $\phi_2(h, w_2)$. Assume that $\phi_2(h, w_2)$ is a twice-differentiable, strictly quasiconcave function with $\partial \phi_2(h, w_2)/\partial w_2 > 0$ and, for simplicity, that we have a positive externality so that $\partial \phi_2(h, w_2)/\partial h > 0$.

**(a)**  Set up the Pareto optimality problem as one of choosing $h$ and a wealth transfer $T$ to maximize consumer 1's welfare subject to giving consumer 2 a utility level of at least $\bar{u}_2$. Derive the (necessary and sufficient) first-order condition characterizing the optimal levels of $h$ and $T$, say $h^\circ$ and $T^\circ$.

**(b)**  Imagine that consumer 1 could purchase $h$ on an externality market. Let $p_h$ be the price per unit, and let $h(p_h, w_2)$ be consumer 2's demand function for $h$. Express the wealth effect $\partial h(p_h, w_2)/\partial w_2$ in terms of first-order and second-order partial derivatives of consumer 2's utility function.

**(c)** Derive the comparative statics change in the Pareto optimal level of the externality $h^\circ$ (for a given $\bar{u}_2$) with respect to a differential increase $dw_2 > 0$ in consumer 2's wealth. Show that if consumer 2's demand for the externality, derived in **(b)**, is normal at price $\bar{p}_h = [\partial \phi_2(h^\circ, w_2 - T^\circ)/\partial h]/ [\partial \phi_2(h^\circ, w_2 - T^\circ)/\partial w_2]$ and wealth level $\bar{w}_2 = w_2 - T^\circ$ [i.e., if $\partial h(\bar{p}_h, \bar{w}_2)/\partial w_2 > 0$], then a marginal increase in consumer 2's wealth $w_2$ causes the Pareto optimal level of the externality $h^\circ$ to increase. (Similarly, in the case of a negative externality, if consumer 2's demand for reductions in the externality is a normal good, then when consumer 2 becomes wealthier, the Pareto optimal level of the externality declines.)

**11.B.3**[B] Consider the optimal Pigouvian tax identified in Section 11.B for the two-consumer externality problem studied there. What happens if, given this tax, the two consumers are able to bargain with each other? Will the efficient level of the externality still result? What about with the optimal quota?

**11.B.4**[B] Consider again the two-consumer externality problem studied in Section 11.B. Suppose that consumer 2 can take some action, say $e \in \mathbb{R}$, that affects the degree to which she is affected by the externality, so that we now write her derived utility function as $\phi_2(h, e) + w_2$. To fix ideas, let $h$ be a negative externality, and suppose that $\partial^2 \phi_2(h, e)/\partial h \partial e > 0$, so that increases in $e$ reduce the negative effect of the externality on the margin. Suppose that both $h$ and $e$ can in principle be taxed or subsidized. Should $e$ be taxed or subsidized in the optimal tax scheme? Why or why not?

**11.B.5**[B] Suppose that at fixed input prices of $\bar{w}$ a firm produces output with the differentiable and strictly convex cost function $c(q, h)$, where $q \geq 0$ is its output level (whose price is $p > 0$) and $h$ is the level of a negative externality generated by the firm. The externality affects a single consumer, whose derived utility function takes the form $\phi(h) + w$. The actions of the firm and consumer do not affect any market prices.

**(a)** Derive the first-order condition for the firm's choice of $q$ and $h$.

**(b)** Derive the first-order conditions characterizing the Pareto optimal levels of $q$ and $h$.

**(c)** Suppose that the government taxes the firm's output level. Show that this cannot restore efficiency. Show that a direct tax on the externality *can* restore efficiency.

**(d)** Show, however, that in the limiting case where $h$ is necessarily produced in fixed proportions with $q$, so that $h(q) = \alpha q$ for some $\alpha > 0$, a tax on the firm's output *can* restore efficiency. What is the efficiency-restoring tax?

**11.C.1**[A] Consider the model discussed in Section 11.C, in which $I$ consumers privately purchase a public good. Identify per-unit subsidies $s_1, \ldots, s_I$, such that when each consumer $i$ faces subsidy rate $s_i$, the total level of the public good provided is optimal.

**11.C.2**[A] Consider the model discussed in Section 11.C, in which $I$ consumers privately purchase a public good. Show that a per-unit subsidy on the firm's output (paid to the firm) can also restore efficiency.

**11.C.3**[C] Reconsider the Ramsey tax problem from Exercise 10.E.3, but now suppose that the government can also provide a public good $x_0$ that can be produced from good 1 at cost $c(x_0)$. However, the government must still balance its budget (including any expenditures on the public good). Consumer $i$'s utility function now takes the form $x_{1i} + \sum_{\ell=2}^{L} \phi_{\ell i}(x_{\ell i}, x_0)$. Derive and interpret the conditions characterizing the optimal commodity taxes and the optimal level of the public good. How do the two problems of Ramsey taxation and provision of the public good interact?

**11.D.1**[B] (M. Weitzman) First-year graduate students are a hard-working group. Consider a typical class of $I$ students. Suppose that each student $i$ puts in $h_i$ hours of work on her classes. This effort involves a disutility of $h_i^2/2$. Her benefits depend on how she performs relative to her peers and take the form $\phi(h_i/\bar{h})$ for all $i$, where $\bar{h} = (1/I)\sum_i h_i$ is the average number of hours put in by all students in the class and $\phi(\cdot)$ is a differentiable concave function, with

$\phi'(\cdot) > 0$ and $\lim_{h \to 0} \phi'(h) = \infty$. Characterize the symmetric (Nash) equilibrium. Compare it with the Pareto optimal symmetric outcome. Interpret.

**11.D.2**[B] Consider a setting with $I$ consumers. Each consumer $i$ chooses an action $h_i \in \mathbb{R}_+$. Consumer $i$'s derived utility function over her choice of $h$ and the choices of other consumers takes the form $\phi_i(h_i, \sum_i h_i) + w_i$, where $\phi_i(\cdot)$ is strictly concave. Characterize the optimal levels of $h_1, \ldots, h_I$. Compare these with the equilibrium levels. What tax/subsidy scheme induces the optimal outcome?

**11.D.3**[B] Consider an industry composed of $J > 1$ identical firms that act as price takers. The price of their output is $p$, and the prices of their inputs are unaffected by their actions. Suppose that partial equilibrium analysis is valid and that the aggregate demand for their product is given by the function $x(p)$. The industry is characterized by "learning by doing," in that each firm's total cost of producing a given level of output is declining in the level of total industry output; that is, each firm $j$ has a twice-differentiable cost function of the form $c(q_j, Q)$ for $Q = \sum_j q_j$, where $c(\cdot)$ is strictly increasing in its first argument and strictly decreasing in its second. Letting subscripts denote partial derivatives, assume that $c_q + Jc_Q > 0$ and $(1/n)c_{qq} + 2c_{qQ} + nc_{QQ} > 0$ for $n = 1$ and $J$. Compare the equilibrium and optimal industry output levels. Interpret. What tax or subsidy restores efficiency?

**11.D.4**[B] Reconsider the nondepletable externality example discussed in Section 11.D, but now assume that the externalities produced by the $J$ firms are not homogeneous. In particular, suppose that if $h_1, \ldots, h_J$ are the firms' externality levels, then consumer $i$'s derived utility is given by $\phi_i(h_1, \ldots, h_J) + w_i$ for each $i = 1, \ldots, I$. Compare the equilibrium and efficient levels of $h_1, \ldots, h_J$. What tax/subsidy scheme can restore efficiency? Under what condition should each firm face the same tax/subsidy rate?

**11.D.5**[B] (*The problem of the commons*) Lake Ec can be freely accessed by fishermen. The cost of sending a boat out on the lake is $r > 0$. When $b$ boats are sent out onto the lake, $f(b)$ fish are caught in total [so each boat catches $f(b)/b$ fish], where $f'(b) > 0$ and $f''(b) < 0$ at all $b \geq 0$. The price of fish is $p > 0$, which is unaffected by the level of the catch from Lake Ec.

(a) Characterize the equilibrium number of boats that are sent out on the lake.

(b) Characterize the optimal number of boats that should be sent out on the lake. Compare this with your answer to (a).

(c) What per-boat fishing tax would restore efficiency?

(d) Suppose that the lake is instead owned by a single individual who can choose how many boats to send out. What level would this owner choose?

**11.D.6**[B] Suppose that there is a piece of land that is affected adversely by an externality produced by a single firm. The firm's derived profit function for the externality is $\pi(h) = \alpha + \beta h - \mu h^2$, where $h$ is the level of the externality and $(\alpha, \beta, \mu) \gg 0$. There are $I$ consumers who farm the land, each owning a fraction $1/I$ of it. The total yield of the land is $\phi(h) = \gamma - \eta h$, where $(\gamma, \eta) \gg 0$. Each of the $I$ consumers then has a derived utility function of $\phi(h)/I + w$.

Bargaining among the consumers and the firm works as follows: Each consumer simultaneously decides whether to be in or out of a bargaining coalition. After this, the bargaining coalition makes the firm a take-it-or-leave-it offer specifying a level of $h$ and a transfer. The firm then accepts or rejects this offer. In the absence of any agreement, the firm can generate any level of the externality it wishes.

(a) Let $\theta$ denote the fraction of the $I$ consumers who join the bargaining coalition. Characterize the subgame perfect Nash equilibrium level of $\theta$ (for simplicity, treat $\theta$ as a continuous variable). Show that when $I = 1$ the optimal level of the externality results, but that when $I > 1$ we have $\theta < 1$ in equilibrium and too much of the externality is generated.

**(b)** Show that as $I$ increases, the equilibrium level of $\theta$ declines. Also show that $\lim_{I \to \infty} \theta = 0$.

**11.D.7$^C$** Individuals can build their houses in one of two neighborhoods, A or B. It costs $c_A$ to build a house in neighborhood A and $c_B < c_A$ to build in neighborhood B. Individuals care about the prestige of the people living in their neighborhood. Individuals have varying levels of prestige, denoted by the parameter $\theta$. Prestige varies between 0 and 1 and is uniformly distributed across the population. The prestige of neighborhood $k$ ($k = A, B$) is a function of the average value of $\theta$ in that neighborhood, denoted by $\bar{\theta}_k$. If individual $i$ has prestige parameter $\theta$ and builds her house in neighborhood $k$, her derived utility net of building costs is $(1 + \theta)(1 + \bar{\theta}_k) - c_k$. Thus, individuals with more prestige value a prestigous neighborhood more. Assume that $c_A$ and $c_B$ are less than 1 and that $c_A - c_B \in (\frac{1}{2}, 1)$.

**(a)** Show that in any building-choice equilibrium (technically, the Nash equilibrium of the simultaneous-move game in which individuals simultaneously choose where to build their house) both neighborhoods must be occupied.

**(b)** Show that in any equilibrium in which the prestige levels of the two neighborhoods differ, every resident of neighborhood A must have at least as high a prestige level as every resident of neighborhood B; that is, there is a cutoff level of $\theta$, say $\hat{\theta}$, such that all types $\theta \geq \hat{\theta}$ build in neighborhood A and all $\theta < \hat{\theta}$ build in neighborhood B. Characterize this cutoff level.

**(c)** Show that in any equilibrium of the type identified in (b), a Pareto improvement can be achieved by altering the cutoff value of $\theta$ slightly.

**11.E.1$^B$** Consider the setting studied in Section 11.E, and suppose that $\partial \pi(h, \theta)/\partial h = \beta - bh + \theta$ and $\partial \phi(h, \eta)/\partial h = \gamma - ch + \eta$, where $\theta$ and $\eta$ are random variables with $E[\theta] = E[\eta] = E[\theta\eta] = 0$, $(\beta, b, c) \gg 0$, and $\gamma < 0$. Denote $E[\theta^2] = \sigma_\theta^2$ and $E[\eta^2] = \sigma_\eta^2$.

**(a)** Identify the best quota $\hat{h}*$ for a planner who wants to maximize the expected value of aggregate surplus. (Assume the firm must produce an amount exactly equal to the quota.)

**(b)** Identify the best tax $t*$ for this same planner.

**(c)** Compare the two instruments: Which is better and when?

**11.E.2$^C$** Extend the model in Exercise 11.E.1 to the case of two producers. Now let $\partial \pi_i(h_i, \theta_i)/\partial h = \beta - bh_i + \theta_i$ for $i = 1, 2$. Let $\sigma_{12} = E[\theta_1 \theta_2]$. Calculate and compare the optimal quotas and taxes. How does the choice depend on $\sigma_{12}$?

**11.E.3$^B$** Show that truth-telling is the consumer's only weakly dominant strategy in the (Groves–Clarke) revelation mechanism studied in Section 11.E.

**11.E.4$^A$** In text.

**11.E.5$^B$** Suppose that the government is considering building a public project. The cost is $K$. There are $I$ individuals indexed by $i$. Individual $i$'s privately known benefit from the project is $b_i$. The government's objective is to maximize the expected value of aggregate surplus. Derive the extension of the Groves–Clarke mechanism discussed in Section 11.E for this case. Can you construct your scheme so that the government balances its budget on average (over all realizations of the $b_i$'s)?

**11.E.6$^B$** Extend Exercise 11.E.5 to the case in which there are $N$ possible projects, $n = 1, \ldots, N$, with individual $i$ deriving a (privately known) benefit of $b_i(n)$ from project $n$.

**11.E.7$^B$** Suppose that in the model of Section 11.E the consumer's type $\eta$ takes only one possible value, $\bar{\eta}$. We have seen in the text that in this case neither a quota nor a tax will maximize aggregate surplus for all realizations of $\theta$ when the derived utility function $\phi(h, \bar{\eta})$ for the consumer has $\partial\phi(h, \bar{\eta})/\partial h \in (0, -\infty)$. Show, however, that a variable tax per unit in which the total tax collected from the firm is $\phi(h, \bar{\eta})$ when the level of the externality is $h$ will maximize aggregate surplus for all values of $\theta$ for *any* derived utility function $\phi(h, \bar{\eta})$.

# 12

# Market Power

## 12.A Introduction

In the competitive model, all consumers and producers are assumed to act as price takers, in effect behaving as if the demand or supply functions that they face are infinitely elastic at going market prices. However, this assumption may not be a good one when there are only a few agents on one side of a market, for these agents will often possess *market power*—the ability to alter profitably prices away from competitive levels.

The simplest example of market power arises when there is only a single seller, a *monopolist*, of some good. If this good's market demand is a continuous decreasing function of price, then the monopolist, recognizing that a small increase in its price above the competitive level leads to only a small reduction in its sales, will find it worthwhile to raise its price above the competitive level.

Similar effects can occur when there is more than one agent, but still not many, on one side of a market. Most often, these agents with market power are firms, whose fewness arises from nonconvexities in production technologies (recall the discussion of entry in Section 10.F).

In this chapter, we study the functioning of markets in which market power is present. We begin, in Section 12.B, by considering the case in which there is a monopolist seller of some good. We review the theory of monopoly pricing and identify the welfare loss that it creates.

The remaining sections focus on situations of *oligopoly*, in which a number of firms compete in a market. In Sections 12.C and 12.D, we discuss several models of oligopolistic pricing. Each incorporates different assumptions about the underlying structure of the market and behavior of firms. The discussion highlights the implicatons of these differing assumptions for market outcomes. In Section 12.C, we focus on static models of oligopolistic pricing, where competition is viewed as a one-shot, simultaneous event. In contrast, in Section 12.D, we study how repeated interaction among firms may affect pricing in oligopolistic markets. This discussion constitutes an application of the theory of repeated games, a subject that we discuss in greater generality in Appendix A.

The analysis in Sections 12.B to 12.D treats the number of firms in the market as exogeneously given. In reality, however, the number of active firms in a market is likely to be affected by factors such as the size of market demand and the nature of competition within the market. Sections 12.E and 12.F consider issues that arise when the number of active firms in a market is determined endogenously.

Section 12.E specifies a simple model of entry into an oligopolistic market and studies the determinants of the number of active firms. It offers an analysis that parallels that considered in Section 10.F for competitive markets.

Section 12.F returns to a theme raised in Chapter 10. We illustrate how the competitive (price-taking) model can be viewed as a limiting case of oligopoly in which the size of the market, and hence the number of firms that can profitably operate in it, grows large. In the model we study, an active firm's market power diminishes as the market size expands; in the limit, the equilibrium market price comes to approximate the competitive level.

In Section 12.G, we briefly consider how firms in oligopolistic markets can make strategic precommitments to affect the conditions of future competition in a manner favorable to themselves. This issue nicely illustrates the importance of credible commitments in strategic settings, an issue we studied extensively in Chapter 9. In Appendix B, we consider in greater detail a particularly striking example of strategic precommitment to affect future market conditions, the case of entry deterrence through capacity choice.

If you have not done so already, you should review the game theory chapters in Part II before studying Sections 12.C to 12.G (in particular, review all of Chapter 7, Sections 8.A to 8.D, and Sections 9.A and 9.B).

An excellent source for further study of the topics covered in this chapter is Tirole (1988).[1]

# 12.B   Monopoly Pricing

In this section, we study the pricing behavior of a profit-maximizing *monopolist*, a firm that is the only producer of a good. The demand for this good at price $p$ is given by the function $x(p)$, which we take to be continuous and strictly decreasing at all $p$ such that $x(p) > 0$.[2] For convenience, we also assume that there exists a price $\bar{p} < \infty$ such that $x(p) = 0$ for all $p \geq \bar{p}$.[3] Throughout, we suppose that the monopolist knows the demand function for its product and can produce output level $q$ at a cost of $c(q)$.

The monopolist's decision problem consists of choosing its price $p$ so as to maximize its profits (in terms of the numeraire), or formally, of solving

$$\underset{p}{\text{Max}} \quad px(p) - c(x(p)). \tag{12.B.1}$$

---

1. See also the survey by Shapiro (1989) for the topics covered in Sections 12.C, 12.D, and 12.G.

2. Throughout this chapter we take a partial equilibrium approach; see Chapter 10 for a discussion of this approach.

3. This assumption helps to insure that an optimal solution to the monopolist's problem exists. (See Exercise 12.B.2 for an example in which the failure of this condition leads to nonexistence.)

An equivalent formulation in terms of quantity choices can be derived by thinking instead of the monopolist as deciding on the level of output that it desires to sell, $q \geq 0$, letting the price at which it can sell this output be given by the *inverse demand function* $p(\cdot) = x^{-1}(\cdot)$.[4] Using this inverse demand function, the monopolist's problem can then be stated as

$$\underset{q \geq 0}{\text{Max}} \quad p(q)q - c(q). \tag{12.B.2}$$

We shall focus our analysis on this quantity formulation of the monopolist's problem [identical conclusions could equally well be developed from problem (12.B.1)]. We assume throughout that $p(\cdot)$ and $c(\cdot)$ are continuous and twice differentiable at all $q \geq 0$, that $p(0) > c'(0)$, and that there exists a unique output level $q° \in (0, \infty)$ such that $p(q°) = c'(q°)$. Thus, $q°$ is the unique socially optimal (competitive) output level in this market (see Chapter 10).

Under these assumptions, a solution to problem (12.B.2) can be shown to exist.[5] Given the differentiability assumed, the monopolist's optimal quantity, which we denote by $q^m$, must satisfy the first-order condition[6]

$$p'(q^m) q^m + p(q^m) \leq c'(q^m), \quad \text{with equality if } q^m > 0. \tag{12.B.3}$$

The left-hand side of (12.B.3) is the *marginal revenue* from a differential increase in $q$ at $q^m$, which is equal to the derivative of revenue $d[p(q)q]/dq$, while the right-hand side is the corresponding marginal cost at $q^m$. Since $p(0) > c'(0)$, condition (12.B.3) can be satisfied only at $q^m > 0$. Hence, under our assumptions, *marginal revenue must equal marginal cost* at the monopolist's optimal output level:

$$p'(q^m)q^m + p(q^m) = c'(q^m). \tag{12.B.4}$$

For the typical case in which $p'(q) < 0$ at all $q \geq 0$, condition (12.B.4) implies that we must have $p(q^m) > c'(q^m)$, and so *the price under monopoly exceeds marginal cost*. Correspondingly, the monopolist's optimal output $q^m$ must be below the socially optimal (competitive) output level $q°$. The cause of this quantity distortion is the monopolist's recognition that a reduction in the quantity it sells allows it to increase the price charged on its remaining sales, an increase whose effect on profits is captured by the term $p'(q^m)q^m$ in condition (12.B.4).

The welfare loss from this quantity distortion, known as the *deadweight loss of monopoly*, can be measured using the change in Marshallian aggregate surplus

---

4. More precisely, to take account of the fact that $x(p) = 0$ for more than one value of $p$, we take $p(q) = \text{Min} \{p: x(p) = q\}$ at all $q \geq 0$. Thus, $p(0) = \bar{p}$, the lowest price at which $x(p) = 0$.

5. In particular, it follows from condition (12.B.3) and from the facts that $p'(q) \leq 0$ for all $q \geq 0$ and $p(q) < c'(q)$ for all $q > q°$, that the monopolist's optimal choice must lie in the compact set $[0, q°]$. Because the objective function in problem (12.B.2) is continuous, a solution must therefore exist (see Section M.F of the Mathematical Appendix).

6. Satisfaction of first-order condition (12.B.3) is sufficient for $q^m$ to be an optimal choice if the objective function of problem (12.B.2) is concave on $[0, q°]$. Note, however, that concavity of this objective function depends not only on the technology of the firm, as in the competitive model, but also on the shape of the inverse demand function. In particular, even with a convex cost function, the monopolist's profit function can violate this concavity condition if demand is a convex function of price.

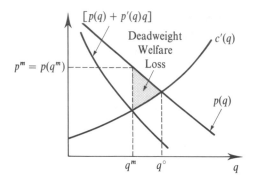

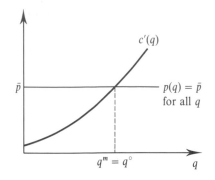

**Figure 12.B.1 (left)**

The monopoly solution and welfare loss when $p'(\cdot) < 0$.

**Figure 12.B.2 (right)**

The monopoly solution when $p'(q) = 0$ for all $q$.

(see Section 10.E),

$$\int_{q^m}^{q^\circ} [p(s) - c'(s)] \, ds > 0,$$

where $q^\circ$ is the socially optimal (competitive) output level.

Figure 12.B.1 illustrates the monopoly outcome in this case. The monopolist's quantity $q^m$ is determined by the intersection of the graphs of marginal revenue $p'(q)q + p(q)$ and marginal cost $c'(q)$. The monopoly price $p(q^m)$ can then be determined from the inverse demand curve. The deadweight welfare loss is equal to the area of the shaded region.

Note from condition (12.B.4) that the monopoly quantity distortion is absent in the special case in which $p'(q) = 0$ for all $q$. In this case, where $p(q)$ equals some constant $\bar{p}$ at all $q > 0$, the monopolist sells the same quantity as a price-taking competitive firm because it perceives that any increase in its price above the competitive price $\bar{p}$ causes it to lose all its sales.[7] Figure 12.B.2 depicts this special case.

**Example 12.B.1:** *Monopoly Pricing with a Linear Inverse Demand Function and Constant Returns to Scale.* Suppose that the inverse demand function in a monopolized market is $p(q) = a - bq$ and that the monopolist's cost function is $c(q) = cq$, where $a > c \geq 0$ [so that $p(0) > c'(0)$] and $b > 0$. In this case, the objective function of the monopolist's problem (12.B.2) is concave, and so condition (12.B.4) is both necessary and sufficient for a solution to the monopolist's problem. From condition (12.B.4), we can calculate the monopolist's optimal quantity and price to be $q^m = (a - c)/2b$ and $p^m = (a + c)/2$. In contrast, the socially optimal (competitive) output level and price are $q^\circ = (a - c)/b$ and $p^\circ = p(q^\circ) = c$. ∎

Although we do not discuss these issues here, we point out that the behavioral distortions arising under monopoly are not limited to pricing decisions. (Exercises 12.B.9 and 12.B.10 ask you to investigate two examples.)

---

The monopoly quantity distortion is fundamentally linked to the fact that if the monopolist wants to increase the quantity it sells, it must lower its price on *all* its existing sales. In fact,

---

7. This inverse demand function arises, for example, when each consumer $i$ has quasilinear preferences of the form $u_i(q_i) + m_i$ with $u_i(q_i) = \bar{p}q_i$, where $q_i$ is consumer $i$'s consumption of the good under study and $m_i$ is his consumption of the numeraire commodity. [Strictly speaking, with these preferences we now have a multivalued demand correspondence rather than a demand function, but $p(\cdot)$ is nevertheless a function as before.]

if the monopolist were able to *perfectly discriminate* among its customers in the sense that it could make a distinct offer to each consumer, knowing the consumer's preferences for its product, then the monopoly quantity distortion would disappear.

To see this formally, let each consumer $i$ have a quasilinear utility function of the form $u_i(q_i) + m_i$ over the amount $q_i$ of the monopolist's good that he consumes and the amount $m_i$ that he consumes of the numeraire good, and normalize $u_i(0) = 0$. Suppose that the monopolist makes a take-it-or-leave-it offer to each consumer $i$ of the form $(q_i, T_i)$, where $q_i$ is the quantity offered to consumer $i$ and $T_i$ is the total payment that the consumer must make in return. Given offer $(q_i, T_i)$, consumer $i$ will accept the monopolist's offer if and only if $u_i(q_i) - T_i \geq 0$. As a result, the monopolist can extract a payment of exactly $u_i(q_i)$ from consumer $i$ in return for $q_i$ units of its product, leaving the consumer with a surplus of exactly zero from consumption of the good. Given this fact, the monopolist will choose the quantities it sells to the $I$ consumers $(q_1, \ldots, q_I)$ to solve

$$\underset{(q_1,\ldots,q_I) \geq 0}{\text{Max}} \sum_{i=1}^{I} u_i(q_i) - c(\textstyle\sum_i q_i). \tag{12.B.5}$$

Note, however, that any solution to problem (12.B.5) maximizes the aggregate surplus in the market, and so the monopolist will sell each consumer exactly the socially optimal (competitive) quantity. Of course, the distributional properties of this outcome would not be terribly attractive in the absence of wealth redistribution: The monopolist would get all the aggregate surplus generated by its product, and each consumer $i$ would receive a surplus of zero (i.e., each consumer $i$'s welfare would be exactly equal to the level he would achieve if he consumed none of the monopolist's product). But in principle, these distributional problems can be corrected through lump-sum redistribution of the numeraire.

Thus, the welfare loss from monopoly pricing can be seen as arising from constraints that prevent the monopolist from charging fully discriminatory prices. In practice, however, these constraints can be significant. They may include the costs of assessing separate charges for different consumers, the monopolist's lack of information about consumer preferences, and the possibility of consumer resale. Exercise 12.B.5 explores some of these factors. It provides conditions under which the best the monopolist can do is to name a single per-unit price, as we assumed at the beginning of this section.

# 12.C   Static Models of Oligopoly

We now turn to cases in which more than one, but still not many, firms compete in a market. These are known as situations of *oligopoly*. Competition among firms in an oligopolistic market is inherently a setting of strategic interaction. For this reason, the appropriate tool for its analysis is game theory. Because this discussion constitutes our first application of the theory of games, we focus on relatively simple *static* models of oligopoly, in which there is only one period of competitive interaction and firms take their actions simultaneously.

We begin by studying a model of simultaneous price choices by firms with constant returns to scale technologies, known as the *Bertrand model*. This model displays a striking feature: With just two firms in a market, we obtain a perfectly competitive outcome. Motivated by this finding, we then consider three alterations of this model that weaken its strong and often implausible conclusion: a change in the firm's strategy from choosing its price to choosing its quantity of output (the *Cournot model*); the introduction of capacity constraints (or, more generally, decreasing returns to scale); and the presence of product differentiation.[8]

One lesson of this analysis is that a critical part of game-theoretic modeling goes into choosing the strategies and payoff functions of the players. In the context of oligopolistic markets, this choice requires that considerable thought be given both to the demand and technological features of the market and to the underlying processes of competition.

Unless otherwise noted, we restrict our attention to pure strategy equilibria of the models we study.

### The Bertrand Model of Price Competition

We begin by considering the model of oligopolistic competition proposed by Bertrand (1883). There are two profit-maximizing firms, firms 1 and 2 (a *duopoly*), in a market whose demand function is given by $x(p)$. As in Section 10.B, we assume that $x(\cdot)$ is continuous and strictly decreasing at all $p$ such that $x(p) > 0$ and that there exists a $\bar{p} < \infty$ such that $x(p) = 0$ for all $p \geq \bar{p}$. The two firms have constant returns to scale technologies with the same cost, $c > 0$, per unit produced. We assume that $x(c) \in (0, \infty)$, which implies that the socially optimal (competitive) output level in this market is strictly positive and finite (see Chapter 10).

Competition takes place as follows: The two firms simultaneously name their prices $p_1$ and $p_2$. Sales for firm $j$ are then given by

$$x_j(p_j, p_k) = \begin{cases} x(p_j) & \text{if } p_j < p_k \\ \frac{1}{2}x(p_j) & \text{if } p_j = p_k \\ 0 & \text{if } p_j > p_k. \end{cases}$$

The firms produce to order and so they incur production costs only for an output level equal to their actual sales. Given prices $p_j$ and $p_k$, firm $j$'s profits are therefore equal to $(p_j - c)x_j(p_j, p_k)$.

The Bertrand model constitutes a well-defined simultaneous-move game to which we can apply the concepts developed in Chapter 8. In fact, the Nash equilibrium outcome of this model, presented in Proposition 12.C.1, is relatively simple to discern.

**Proposition 12.C.1:** There is a unique Nash equilibrium $(p_1^*, p_2^*)$ in the Bertrand duopoly model. In this equilibrium, both firms set their prices equal to cost: $p_1^* = p_2^* = c$.

**Proof:** To begin, note that both firms setting their prices equal to $c$ is indeed a Nash equilibrium. At these prices, both firms earn zero profits. Neither firm can gain by raising its price because it will then make no sales (thereby still earning zero); and by lowering its price below $c$ a firm increases its sales but incurs losses. What remains is to show that there can be no other Nash equilibrium.[9] Suppose, first, that the lower of the two prices named is less than $c$. In this case, the firm naming this price

---

8. Section 12.D studies a fourth variation that involves repeated interaction among firms.

9. Recall that we restrict attention to pure strategy equilibria here. See Exercise 12.C.2 for a consideration of mixed strategy equilibria. There you are asked to show that under the conditions assumed here, Proposition 12.C.1 continues to hold: $p_1^* = p_2^* = c$ is the unique Nash equilibrium, pure or mixed, of the Bertrand model.

incurs losses. But by raising its price above $c$, the worst it can do is earn zero. Thus, these price choices could not constitute a Nash equilibrium.

Now suppose that one firm's price is equal to $c$ and that the other's price is strictly greater than $c$: $p_j = c$, $p_k > c$. In this case, firm $j$ is selling to the entire market but making zero profits. By raising its price a little, say to $\hat{p}_j = c + (p_k - c)/2$, firm $j$ would still make all the sales in the market, but at a strictly positive profit. Thus, these price choices also could not constitute an equilibrium.

Finally, suppose that both price choices are strictly greater than $c$: $p_j > c$, $p_k > c$. Without loss of generality, assume that $p_j \leq p_k$. In this case, firm $k$ can be earning at most $\frac{1}{2}(p_j - c)x(p_j)$. But by setting its price equal to $p_j - \varepsilon$ for $\varepsilon > 0$, that is, by undercutting firm $j$'s price, firm $k$ will get the entire market and earn $(p_j - \varepsilon - c)x(p_j - \varepsilon)$. Since $(p_j - \varepsilon - c)x(p_j - \varepsilon) > \frac{1}{2}(p_j - c)x(p_j)$ for small-enough $\varepsilon > 0$, firm $k$ can strictly increase its profits by doing so. Thus, these price choices are also not an equilibrium.

The three types of price configurations that we have just ruled out constitute all the possible price configurations other than $p_1 = p_2 = c$, and so we are done. ■

The striking implication of Proposition 12.C.1 is that with only two firms we get the perfectly competitive outcome. In effect, competition between the two firms makes each firm face an infinitely elastic demand curve at the price charged by its rival.

The basic idea of Proposition 12.C.1 can also be readily extended to any number of firms greater than two. [In this case, if firm $j$ names the lowest price in the market, say $\tilde{p}$, along with $\tilde{J} - 1$ other firms, it earns $(1/\tilde{J})x(\tilde{p})$.] You are asked to show this in Exercise 12.C.1.

**Exercise 12.C.1:** Show that in any Nash equilibrium of the Bertrand model with $J > 2$ firms, all sales take place at a price equal to cost.

Thus, the Bertrand model predicts that the distortions arising from the exercise of market power are limited to the special case of monopoly. Notable as this result is, it also seems an unrealistic conclusion in many (although not all) settings. In the remainder of this section, we examine three changes in the Bertrand model that considerably weaken this strong conclusion: First, we make *quantity* the firms' strategic variable. Second, we introduce *capacity constraints* (or, more generally, decreasing returns to scale). Third, we allow for *product differentiation*.

### Quantity Competition (*The Cournot Model*)

Suppose now that competition between the two firms takes a somewhat different form: The two firms simultaneously decide how much to produce, $q_1$ and $q_2$. Given these quantity choices, price adjusts to the level that clears the market, $p(q_1 + q_2)$, where $p(\cdot) = x^{-1}(\cdot)$ is the inverse demand function. This model is known as the *Cournot model*, after Cournot (1838). You can imagine farmers deciding how much of a perishable crop to pick each morning and send to a market. Once they have done so, the price at the market ends up being the level at which all the crops that have been sent are sold.[10] In this discussion, we assume that $p(\cdot)$ is differentiable

---

10. One scenario that will lead to this outcome arises when buyers bid for the crops sent that day (very much like sellers in the Bertrand model; see Exercise 12.C.5).

with $p'(q) < 0$ at all $q \geq 0$. As before, both firms produce output at a cost of $c > 0$ per unit. We also assume that $p(0) > c$ and that there exists a unique output level $q° \in (0, \infty)$ such that $p(q°) = c$ [in terms of the demand function $x(\cdot)$, $q° = x(c)$]. Quantity $q°$ is therefore the socially optimal (competitive) output level in this market.

To find a (pure strategy) Nash equilibrium of this model, consider firm $j$'s maximization problem given an output level $\bar{q}_k$ of the other firm, $k \neq j$:

$$\underset{q_j \geq 0}{\text{Max}} \quad p(q_j + \bar{q}_k)q_j - cq_j. \tag{12.C.1}$$

In solving problem (12.C.1), firm $j$ acts exactly like a monopolist who faces inverse demand function $\tilde{p}(q_j) = p(q_j + \bar{q}_k)$. An optimal quantity choice for firm $j$ given its rival's output $\bar{q}_k$ must therefore satisfy the first-order condition

$$p'(q_j + \bar{q}_k)\, q_j + p(q_j + \bar{q}_k) \leq c, \quad \text{with equality if } q_j > 0. \tag{12.C.2}$$

For each $\bar{q}_k$, we let $b_j(\bar{q}_k)$ denote firm $j$'s set of optimal quantity choices; $b_j(\cdot)$ is firm $j$'s *best-response correspondence* (or *function* if it is single-valued).

A pair of quantity choices $(q_1^*, q_2^*)$ is a Nash equilibrium if and only if $q_j^* \in b_j(q_k^*)$ for $k \neq j$ and $j = 1, 2$. Hence, if $(q_1^*, q_2^*)$ is a Nash equilibrium, these quantities must satisfy[11]

$$p'(q_1^* + q_2^*)q_1^* + p(q_1^* + q_2^*) \leq c, \quad \text{with equality if } q_1^* > 0 \tag{12.C.3}$$

and

$$p'(q_1^* + q_2^*)q_2^* + p(q_1^* + q_2^*) \leq c, \quad \text{with equality if } q_2^* > 0. \tag{12.C.4}$$

It can be shown that under our assumptions we must have $(q_1^*, q_2^*) \gg 0$, and so conditions (12.C.3) and (12.C.4) must both hold with equality in any Nash equilibrium.[12] Adding these two equalities tells us that in any Nash equilibrium we must have

$$p'(q_1^* + q_2^*)\left(\frac{q_1^* + q_2^*}{2}\right) + p(q_1^* + q_2^*) = c. \tag{12.C.5}$$

Condition (12.C.5) allows us to reach the conclusion presented in Proposition 12.C.2.

**Proposition 12.C.2:** In any Nash equilibrium of the Cournot duopoly model with cost $c > 0$ per unit for the two firms and an inverse demand function $p(\cdot)$ satisfying $p'(q) < 0$ for all $q \geq 0$ and $p(0) > c$, the market price is greater than $c$ (the competitive price) and smaller than the monopoly price.

---

11. Note that this method of analysis, which relies on the use of first-order conditions to calculate best responses, differs from the method used in the analysis of the Bertrand model. The reason is that in the Bertrand model each firm's objective function is discontinuous in its decision variable, so that differential optimization techniques cannot be used. Fortunately, the determination of the Nash equilibrium in the Bertrand model turned out, nevertheless, to be quite simple.

12. To see this, suppose that $q_1^* = 0$. Condition (12.C.3) then implies that $p(q_2^*) \leq c$. By condition (12.C.4) and the fact that $p'(\cdot) < 0$, this implies that were $q_2^* > 0$ we would have $p'(q_2^*)q_2^* + p(q_2^*) < c$, and so $q_2^* = 0$. But this means that $p(0) \leq c$, contradicting the assumption that $p(0) > c$. Hence, we must have $q_1^* > 0$. A similar argument shows that $q_2^* > 0$. Note, however, that this conclusion depends on our assumption of equal costs for the two firms. For example, a firm might set its output equal to zero if it is much less efficient than its rival. Exercise 12.C.9 considers some of the issues that arise when firms have differing costs.

**Proof:** That the equilibrium price is above $c$ (the competitive price) follows immediately from condition (12.C.5) and the facts that $q_1^* + q_2^* > 0$ and $p'(q) < 0$ at all $q \geq 0$. We next argue that $(q_1^* + q_2^*) > q^m$, that is, that the equilibrium duopoly price $p(q_1^* + q_2^*)$ is strictly less than the monopoly price $p(q^m)$. The argument is in two parts.

First, we argue that $(q_1^* + q_2^*) \geq q^m$. To see this, suppose that $q^m > (q_1^* + q_2^*)$. By increasing its quantity to $\hat{q}_j = q^m - q_k^*$, firm $j$ would (weakly) increase the joint profit of the two firms (the firms' joint profit then equals the monopoly profit level, its largest possible level). In addition, because aggregate quantity increases, price must fall, and so firm $k$ is strictly worse off. This implies that firm $j$ is strictly better off, and so firm $j$ would have a profitable deviation if $q^m > (q_1^* + q_2^*)$. We conclude that we must have $(q_1^* + q_2^*) \geq q^m$.

Second, condition (12.C.5) implies that we cannot have $(q_1^* + q_2^*) = q^m$ because then

$$p'(q^m) \frac{q^m}{2} + p(q^m) = c,$$

in violation of the monopoly first-order condition (12.B.4). Thus, we must in fact have $(q_1^* + q_2^*) > q^m$. ∎

Proposition 12.C.2 tells us that the presence of two firms is *not* sufficient to obtain a competitive outcome in the Cournot model, in contrast with the prediction of the Bertrand model. The reason is straightforward. In this model, a firm no longer sees itself as facing an infinitely elastic demand. Rather, if the firm reduces its quantity by a (differential) unit, it increases the market price by $-p'(q_1 + q_2)$. If the firms found themselves jointly producing the competitive quantity and consequently earning zero profits, either one could do strictly better by reducing its output slightly.

At the same time, competition does lower the price below the monopoly level, the price that would maximize the firms' joint profit. This occurs because when each firm determines the profitability of selling an additional unit it fails to consider the reduction in its rival's profit that is caused by the ensuing decrease in the market price [note that in firm $j$'s first-order condition (12.C.2), only $q_j$ multiplies the term $p'(\cdot)$, whereas in the first-order condition for joint profit maximization $(q_1 + q_2)$ does].

**Example 12.C.1:** *Cournot Duopoly with a Linear Inverse Demand Function and Constant Returns to Scale.* Consider a Cournot duopoly in which the firms have a cost per unit produced of $c$ and the inverse demand function is $p(q) = a - bq$, with $a > c \geq 0$ and $b > 0$. Recall that the monopoly quantity and price are $q^m = (a - c)/2b$ and $p^m = (a + c)/2$ and that the socially optimal (competitive) output and price are $q^\circ = (a - c)/b$ and $p^\circ = p(q^\circ) = c$. Using the first-order condition (12.C.2), we find that firm $j$'s best-response function in this Cournot model is given by $b_j(q_k) = \text{Max }\{0, (a - c - bq_k)/2b\}$.

Firm 1's best-response function $b_1(q_2)$ is depicted graphically in Figure 12.C.1. Since $b_1(0) = (a - c)/2b$, its graph hits the $q_1$ axis at the monopoly output level $(a - c)/2b$. This makes sense: Firm 1's best response to firm 2 producing no output is to produce exactly its monopoly output level. Similarly, since $b_1(q_2) = 0$ for all

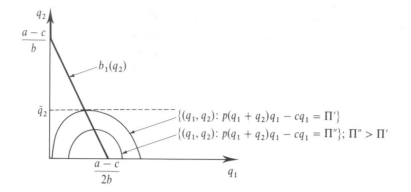

**Figure 12.C.1**

Firm 1's best-response function in the Cournot duopoly model of Example 12.C.1.

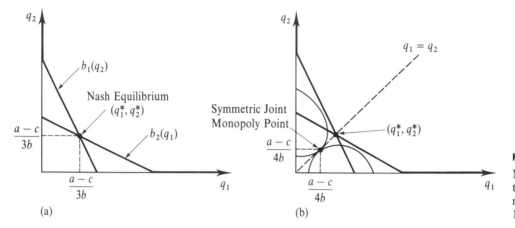

**Figure 12.C.2**

Nash equilibrium in the Cournot duopoly model of Example 12.C.1.

$q_2 \geq (a - c)/b$, the graph of firm 1's best-response function hits the $q_2$ axis at the socially optimal (competitive) output level $(a - c)/b$. Again, this makes sense: If firm 2 chooses an output level of at least $(a - c)/b$, any attempt by firm 1 to make sales results in a price below $c$. Two isoprofit loci of firm 1 are also drawn in the figure; these are sets of the form $\{(q_1, q_2): p(q_1 + q_2)q_1 - cq_1 = \Pi\}$ for some profit level $\Pi$. The profit levels associated with these loci increase as we move toward firm 1's monopoly point $(q_1, q_2) = ((a - c)/2b, 0)$. Observe that firm 1's isoprofit loci have a zero slope where they cross the graph of firm 1's best-response function. This is because the best response $b_1(\bar{q}_2)$ identifies firm 1's maximal profit point on the line $q_2 = \bar{q}_2$ and must therefore correspond to a point of tangency between this line and an isoprofit locus. Firm 2's best-response function can be depicted similarly; given the symmetry of the firms, it is located symmetrically with respect to firm 1's best-response function in $(q_1, q_2)$-space [i.e., it hits the $q_2$ axis at $(a - c)/2b$ and hits the $q_1$ axis at $(a - c)/b$].

The Nash equilibrium, which in this example is unique, can be computed by finding the output pair $(q_1^*, q_2^*)$ at which the graphs of the two best-response functions intersect, that is, at which $q_1^* = b_1(q_2^*)$ and $q_2^* = b_2(q_1^*)$. It is depicted in Figure 12.C.2(a) and corresponds to individual outputs of $q_1^* = q_2^* = \frac{1}{3}[(a - c)/b]$, total output of $\frac{2}{3}[(a - c)/b]$, and a market price of $p(q_1^* + q_2^*) = \frac{1}{3}(a + 2c) \in (c, p^m)$.

Also shown in Figure 12.C.2(b) is the symmetric joint monopoly point $(q^m/2, q^m/2) = ((a - c)/4b, (a - c)/4b)$. It can be seen that this point, at which each

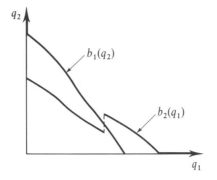

**Figure 12.C.3**

Nonexistence of (pure strategy) Nash equilibrium in the Cournot model.

firm produces half of the monopoly output of $(a - c)/2b$, is each firm's most profitable point on the $q_1 = q_2$ ray. ∎

**Exercise 12.C.6:** Verify the computations and other claims in Example 12.C.1.

Up to this point we have not made any assumptions about the quasiconcavity in $q_j$ of each firm $j$'s objective function in problem (12.C.1). Without quasiconcavity of these functions, however, a pure strategy Nash equilibrium of this quantity game may not exist. For example, as happens in Figure 12.C.3, the best-response function of a firm lacking a quasiconcave objective function may "jump," leading to the possibility of nonexistence. (Strictly speaking, for a situation like the one depicted in Figure 12.C.3 to arise, the two firms must have different cost functions; see Exercise 12.C.8.) With quasiconcavity, we can use Proposition 8.D.3 to show that a pure strategy Nash equilibrium necessarily exists.

Suppose now that we have $J > 2$ identical firms facing the same cost and demand functions as above. Letting $Q_J^*$ be aggregate output at equilibrium, an argument parallel to that above leads to the following generalization of condition (12.C.5):

$$p'(Q_J^*) \frac{Q_J^*}{J} + p(Q_J^*) = c. \tag{12.C.6}$$

At one extreme, when $J = 1$, condition (12.C.6) coincides with the monopoly first-order condition that we have seen in Section 12.B. At the other extreme, we must have $p(Q_J^*) \to c$ as $J \to \infty$. To see this, note that since $Q_J^*$ is always less than the socially optimal (competitive) quantity $q^\circ$, it must be the case that $p'(Q_J^*)(Q_J^*/J) \to 0$ as $J \to \infty$. Hence, condition (12.C.6) implies that price must approach marginal cost as the number of firms grows infinitely large. This provides us with our first taste of a "competitive limit" result, a topic we shall return to in Section 12.F. Exercise 12.C.7 asks you to verify these claims for the model of Example 12.C.1.

**Exercise 12.C.7:** Derive the Nash equilibrium price and quantity levels in the Cournot model with $J$ firms where each firm has a constant unit production cost of $c$ and the inverse demand function in the market is $p(q) = a - bq$, with $a > c \geq 0$ and $b > 0$. Verify that when $J = 1$, we get the monopoly outcome; that output rises and price falls as $J$ increases; and that as $J \to \infty$ the price and aggregate output in the market approach their competitive levels.

In contrast with the Bertrand model, the Cournot model displays a gradual reduction in market power as the number of firms increases. Yet, the "farmer sending crops to market" scenario may not seem relevant to a wide class of situations. After all, most firms seem to choose their prices, not their quantities. For this reason, many economists have thought that the Cournot model gives the right answer for the wrong reason. Fortunately, the departure from the Bertrand model that we study next offers an alternative interpretation of the Cournot model. The basic idea is that we can think of the quantity choices in the Cournot model as long-run choices of *capacity*, with the determination of price from the inverse demand function being a proxy for the outcome of short-run price competition given these capacity choices.

### *Capacity Constraints and Decreasing Returns to Scale*

In many settings, it is natural to suppose that firms operate under conditions of eventual decreasing returns to scale, at least in the short run when capital is fixed. One special case of decreasing returns occurs when a firm has a capacity constraint that prevents it from producing more than some maximal amount, say $\bar{q}$. Here we consider, somewhat informally, how the introduction of capacity constraints affects the prediction of the Bertrand model.

With capacity constraints (or, for that matter, costs that exhibit decreasing returns to scale in a smoother way), it is no longer sensible to assume that a price announcement represents a commitment to provide *any* demanded quantity, since the costs of an order larger than capacity are infinite. We therefore make a minimal adjustment to the rules of the Bertrand model by taking price announcements to be a commitment to supply demand only up to capacity. We also assume that capacities are commonly known among the firms.

To see how capacity constraints can affect the outcome of the duopoly pricing game, suppose that each of the two firms has a constant marginal cost of $c > 0$ and a capacity constraint of $\bar{q} = \frac{3}{4}x(c)$. As before, the market demand function $x(\cdot)$ is continuous, is strictly decreasing at all $p$ such that $x(p) > 0$, and has $x(c) > 0$.

In this case, the Bertrand outcome $p_1^* = p_2^* = c$ is no longer an equilibrium. To see this, note that because firm 2 cannot supply all demand at price $p_2^* = c$, firm 1 can anticipate making a strictly positive level of sales if it raises $p_1$ slightly above $c$. As a result, it has an incentive to deviate from $p_1^* = c$.

In fact, whenever the capacity level $\bar{q}$ satisfies $\bar{q} < x(c)$, each firm can *assure* itself of a strictly positive level of sales at a strictly positive profit margin by setting its price below $p(\bar{q})$ but above $c$. This is illustrated in Figure 12.C.4. In the figure, we assume that the lower-priced firm 2 fills the highest-valuation demands. By charging

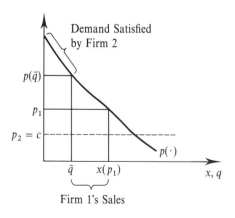

**Figure 12.C.4**

Calculation of demand in the presence of capacity constraints when the low-priced firm satisfies high-valuation demands first.

a price $p_1 \in (c, p(\bar{q}))$, firm 1 sells to the remaining demand at price $p_1$, making sales of $x(p_1) - \bar{q} > 0$. Hence, with capacity constraints, competition will not generally drive price down to cost, a point originally noted by Edgeworth (1897).

Determining the equilibrium outcome in situations in which capacity constraints are present can be tricky because knowledge of prices is no longer enough to determine each firm's sales. When the prices quoted are such that the low-priced firm cannot supply all demand at its quoted price, the demand for the higher-priced firm will generally depend on precisely *who* manages to buy from the low-priced firm. The high-priced firm will typically have greater sales if consumers with low valuations buy from the low-priced firm (in contrast with the assumption made in Figure 12.C.4) than if high-valuation consumers do. Thus, to determine demand functions for the firms, we now need to state a *rationing rule* specifying which consumers manage to buy from the low-priced firm when demand exceeds its capacity. In fact, the choice of a rationing rule can have important effects on equilibrium behavior. Exercise 12.C.11 asks you to explore some of the features of the equilibrium outcome when the highest valuation demands are served first, as in Figure 12.C.4. This is the rationing rule that tends to give the nicest results. Yet, it is neither more nor less plausible than other rules, such as a queue system or a random allocation of available units among possible buyers.

Up to this point in our discussion, we have taken a firm's capacity level as exogenous. Typically, however, we think of firms as *choosing* their capacity levels. This raises a natural question: What is the outcome in a model in which firms first choose their capacity levels and then compete in prices? Kreps and Scheinkman (1983) address this question and show that under certain conditions (among these is the assumption that high-valuation demands get served first when demand for a low-priced firm outstrips its capacity), the unique subgame perfect Nash equilibrium in this two-stage model is the *Cournot outcome*. This result is natural: the computation of price from the inverse demand curve in the Cournot model can be thought of as a proxy for this second-stage price competition. Indeed, for a wide range of capacity choices $(\bar{q}_1, \bar{q}_2)$, the unique equilibrium of the pricing subgame involves both firms setting their prices equal to $p(\bar{q}_1 + \bar{q}_2)$ (see Exercise 12.C.11). Thus, this two-stage model of capacity choice/price competition gives us the promised reinterpretation of the Cournot model: We can think of Cournot quantity competition as capturing long-run competition through capacity choice, with price competition occurring in the short run given the chosen levels of capacity.

*Product Differentiation*

In the Bertrand model, firms faced an infinitely elastic demand curve in equilibrium: With an arbitrarily small price differential, every consumer would prefer to buy from the lowest-priced firm. Often, however, consumers perceive differences among the products of different firms. When product differentiation exists, each firm will possess some market power as a result of the uniqueness of its product. Suppose, for example, that there are $J > 1$ firms. Each firm produces at a constant marginal cost of $c > 0$. The demand for firm $j$'s product is given by the continuous function $x_j(p_j, p_{-j})$, where $p_{-j}$ is a vector of prices of firm $j$'s rivals.[13] In a setting of simultaneous price

---

13. Note the departure from the Bertrand model: In the Bertrand model, $x_j(p_j, p_{-j})$ is discontinuous at $p_j = \mathrm{Min}_{k \neq j}\, p_k$.

**Figure 12.C.5**

The linear city.

choices, each firm $j$ takes its rivals' price choices $\bar{p}_{-j}$ as given and chooses $p_j$ to solve

$$\underset{p_j}{\text{Max}} \quad (p_j - c)x_j(p_j, \bar{p}_{-j}).$$

Note that as long as $x_j(c, \bar{p}_{-j}) > 0$, firm $j$'s best response necessarily involves a price in excess of its costs ($p_j > c$) because it can assure itself of strictly positive profits by setting its price slightly above $c$. Thus, in the presence of product differentiation, equilibrium prices will be above the competitive level. As with quantity competition and capacity constraints, the presence of product differentiation softens the strongly competitive result of the Bertrand model.

A number of models of product differentiation are popular in the applied literature. Example 12.C.2 describes one in some detail.

**Example 12.C.2:** *The Linear City Model of Product Differentiation.* Consider a city that can be represented as lying on a line segment of length 1, as shown in Figure 12.C.5. There is a continuum of consumers whose total number (or, more precisely, measure) is $M$ and who are assumed to be located uniformly along this line segment. A consumer's location is indexed by $z \in [0, 1]$, the distance from the left end of the city. At each end of the city is located one supplier of widgets: Firm 1 is at the left end; firm 2, at the right. Widgets are produced at a constant unit cost of $c > 0$. Every consumer wants at most 1 widget and derives a gross benefit of $v$ from its consumption. The total cost of buying from firm $j$ for a consumer located a distance $d$ from firm $j$ is $p_j + td$, where $t/2 > 0$ can be thought of as the cost or disutility per unit of distance traveled by the consumer in going to and from firm $j$'s location. The presence of travel costs introduces differentiation between the two firms' products because various consumers may now strictly prefer purchasing from one of the two firms even when the goods sell at the same price.

Figure 12.C.6(a) illustrates the purchase decisions of consumers located at various points in the city for a given pair of prices $p_1$ and $p_2$. Consumers at locations $[0, z_1)$

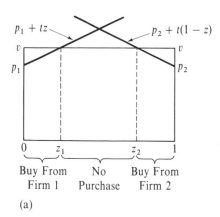

(a)

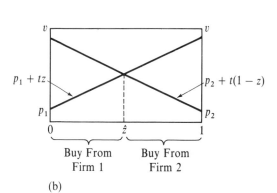

(b)

**Figure 12.C.6**

Consumer purchase decisions given $p_1$ and $p_2$. (a) Some consumers do not buy. (b) All consumers buy.

buy from firm 1. At these locations, $p_1 + tz < p_2 + t(1 - z)$ (purchasing from firm 1 is better than purchasing from firm 2), and $v - p_1 - tz > 0$ (purchasing from firm 1 is better than not purchasing at all). At location $z_1$, a consumer is indifferent between purchasing from firm 1 and not purchasing at all; that is, $z_1$ satisfies $v - p_1 - tz_1 = 0$. In Figure 12.C.6(a), consumers in the interval $(z_1, z_2)$ do not purchase from either firm, while those in the interval $(z_2, 1]$ buy from firm 2.

Figure 12.C.6(b), by contrast, depicts a case in which, given prices $p_1$ and $p_2$, all consumers can obtain a strictly positive surplus by purchasing the good from one of the firms. The location of the consumer who is indifferent between the two firms is the point $\hat{z}$ such that

$$p_1 + t\hat{z} = p_2 + t(1 - \hat{z})$$

or

$$\hat{z} = \frac{t + p_2 - p_1}{2t}. \qquad (12.C.7)$$

In general, the analysis of this model is complicated by the fact that depending on the parameters $(v, c, t)$, the equilibria may involve market areas for the firms that do not touch [as in Figure 12.C.6(a)], or may have the firms battling for consumers in the middle of the market [as in Figure 12.C.6(b)]. To keep things as simple as possible here, we shall assume that consumers' value from a widget is large relative to production and travel costs, or more precisely, that $v > c + 3t$. In this case, it can be shown that a firm never wants to set its price at a level that causes some consumers not to purchase from either firm (see Exercise 12.C.13). In what follows, we shall therefore ignore the possibility of nonpurchase.

Given $p_1$ and $p_2$, let $\hat{z}$ be defined as in (12.C.7). Then firm 1's demand, given a pair of prices $(p_1, p_2)$, equals $M\hat{z}$ when $\hat{z} \in [0, 1]$, $M$ when $\hat{z} > 1$, and 0 when $\hat{z} < 0$.[14] Substituting for $\hat{z}$ from (12.C.7), we have

$$x_1(p_1, p_2) = \begin{cases} 0 & \text{if } p_1 > p_2 + t \\ (t + p_2 - p_1)M/2t & \text{if } p_1 \in [p_2 - t, p_2 + t] \\ M & \text{if } p_1 < p_2 - t. \end{cases} \qquad (12.C.8)$$

By the symmetry of the two firms, the demand function of firm 2, $x_2(p_1, p_2)$, is

$$x_2(p_1, p_2) = \begin{cases} 0 & \text{if } p_2 > p_1 + t \\ (t + p_1 - p_2)M/2t & \text{if } p_2 \in [p_1 - t, p_1 + t] \\ M & \text{if } p_2 < p_1 - t. \end{cases} \qquad (12.C.9)$$

Note from (12.C.8) and (12.C.9) that each firm $j$, in searching for its best response to any price choice $\bar{p}_{-j}$ by its rival, can restrict itself to prices in the interval $[\bar{p}_{-j} - t, \bar{p}_{-j} + t]$. Any price $p_j > \bar{p}_{-j} + t$ yields the same profits as setting $p_j = \bar{p}_{-j} + t$ (namely, zero), and any price $p_j < \bar{p}_{-j} - t$ yields lower profits than setting $p_j = \bar{p}_{-j} - t$ (all such prices result in sales of $M$ units). Thus, firm $j$'s best

---

14. Recall that the $M$ consumers are uniformly distributed on the line segment, so $\hat{z}$ is the fraction who buy from firm 1.

response to $\bar{p}_{-j}$ solves

$$\underset{p_j}{\text{Max}} \quad (p_j - c)(t + \bar{p}_{-j} - p_j)\frac{M}{2t} \tag{12.C.10}$$

$$\text{s.t. } p_j \in [\bar{p}_{-j} - t, \bar{p}_{-j} + t].$$

The necessary and sufficient (Kuhn–Tucker) first-order condition for this problem is

$$t + \bar{p}_{-j} + c - 2p_j \begin{cases} \leq 0 & \text{if } p_j = \bar{p}_{-j} - t \\ = 0 & \text{if } p_j \in (\bar{p}_{-j} - t, \bar{p}_{-j} + t) \\ \geq 0 & \text{if } p_j = \bar{p}_{-j} + t. \end{cases} \tag{12.C.11}$$

Solving (12.C.11), we find that each firm $j$'s best-response function is

$$b(\bar{p}_{-j}) = \begin{cases} \bar{p}_{-j} + t & \text{if } \bar{p}_{-j} \leq c - t \\ (t + \bar{p}_{-j} + c)/2 & \text{if } \bar{p}_{-j} \in (c - t, c + 3t) \\ \bar{p}_{-j} - t & \text{if } \bar{p}_{-j} \geq c + 3t. \end{cases} \tag{12.C.12}$$

When $\bar{p}_{-j} < c - t$, firm $j$ prices in a manner that leads its sales to equal zero (it cannot make profits because it cannot make sales at any price above $c$). When $\bar{p}_{-j} > c + 3t$, firm $j$ prices in a manner that captures the entire market. In the intermediate case, firm $j$'s best response to $\bar{p}_{-j}$ leaves both firms with strictly positive sales levels.

Given the symmetry of the model, we look for a symmetric equilibrium, that is, an equilibrium in which $p_1^* = p_2^* = p^*$. In any symmetric equilibrium, $p^* = b(p^*)$. Examining (12.C.12), we see that this condition can be satisfied only in the middle case (note also that this is the only case in which both firms can have strictly positive sales, as they must in any symmetric equilibrium). Thus, $p^*$ must satisfy

$$p^* = \tfrac{1}{2}(t + p^* + c),$$

and so

$$p^* = c + t.$$

In this Nash equilibrium, each firm has sales of $M/2$ and a profit of $tM/2$. Note that as $t$ approaches zero, the firms' products become completely undifferentiated and the equilibrium prices approach $c$, as in the Bertrand model. In the other direction, as the travel cost $t$ becomes greater, thereby increasing the differentiation between the firms' products, equilibrium prices and profits increase.

Figure 12.C.7 depicts the best-response functions for the two firms (for prices greater than or equal to $c$) and the Nash equilibrium. As usual, the Nash equilibrium lies at the intersection of the graphs of these best-response functions. Note that there are no asymmetric equilibria here. ∎

---

Matters become more complicated when $v < c + 3t$ because firms may wish to set prices at which some consumers do not want to purchase from either firm. One can show, however, that the equilibrium just derived remains valid as long as $v \geq c + \frac{3}{2}t$. In contrast, when $v < c + t$, in equilibrium the firms' market areas do not touch (the firms are like "local monopolists"). In the intermediate case where $v \in [c + t, c + \frac{3}{2}t]$, firms are at a "kink" in their demand functions and the consumer at the indifferent location $\hat{z}$ receives no surplus from his purchase in the equilibrium. Exercise 12.C.14 asks you to investigate these cases.

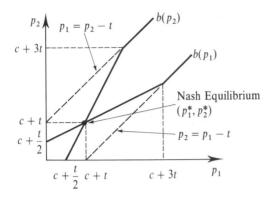

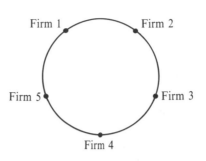

**Figure 12.C.7 (left)**

Best-response functions and Nash equilibrium in the linear city model when $v > c + 3t$.

**Figure 12.C.8 (right)**

The circular city model when $J = 5$.

The essential features of the linear city model can be extended to the case in which $J > 2$. In doing so, it is often most convenient for analytical purposes to consider instead a model of a *circular city*, so that firms can be kept in symmetric positions.[15] In this model, which is due to Salop (1979), consumers are uniformly distributed along a circle of circumference 1, and the firms are positioned at equal intervals from one another. Figure 12.C.8 depicts a case where $J = 5$.

Models like the linear and circular city models are known as *spatial* models of product differentiation because each firm is identified with an "address" in product space. More generally, we can imagine firms' products located in some $N$-dimensional characteristics space, with consumers' "addresses" (their ideal points of consumption) distributed over this space.

Spatial models share the characteristic that each firm competes for customers only locally, that is, solely with the firms offering similar products. A commonly used alternative to spatial formulations, in which each product competes instead for sales with *all* other products, is the *representative consumer model* introduced by Spence (1976) and Dixit and Stiglitz (1977). In this model, a representative consumer is postulated whose preferences over consumption of the $J$ products $(x_1, \ldots, x_J)$ and a numeraire good $m$ take the quasilinear form

$$u(m, x_1, \ldots, x_J) = G\left(\sum_{j=1}^{J} f(x_j)\right) + m,$$

where both $G(\cdot)$ and $f(\cdot)$ are concave.[16] Normalizing the price of the numeraire to be 1, the first-order conditions for the representative consumer's maximization problem are

$$G'\left(\sum_{j=1}^{J} f(x_j)\right)f'(x_j) = p_j \qquad \text{for } j = 1, \ldots, J. \tag{12.C.13}$$

These first-order conditions can be inverted to yield demand functions $x_j(p_1, \ldots, p_J)$ for $j = 1, \ldots, J$, which can then be used to specify a game of simultaneous price choices.[17]

An important variant of this representative consumer model arises in the limiting case where we have many products, each of which constitutes a small fraction of the sales in the overall market. In the limit, we can write the representative consumer's utility function as $G(\int f(x_j)\, dj) + m$, where $x_j$ is now viewed as a function of the continuous index variable $j$.

---

15. In the segment $[0, 1]$, only with two firms can we have symmetric positioning. With more than two firms, the two firms closest to the endpoints of the segment would have only one nearest neighbor but the firms in the interior would have two.

16. Dixit and Stiglitz (1977) actually consider more general utility functions of the form $u(G(\sum_j f(x_j)), m)$.

17. It is also common in the literature to study games of simultaneous quantity choices, using the expression in (12.C.13) directly as the inverse demand functions for the firms.

This leads to a considerable simplification because each firm $j$, in deciding on its price choice, can take the value of $\bar{x} = \int f(x_j)\,dj$, called the *index of aggregate output*, as given; its own production has no effect on the value of this index. Given the value of $\bar{x}$, firm $j$ faces the demand function

$$x_j(p_j, \bar{x}) = \psi\left(\frac{p_j}{G'(\bar{x})}\right),$$

where $\psi(\cdot) = f'^{-1}(\cdot)$. Its optimal choice can then be viewed as a function $p_j^*(\bar{x})$ of the index $\bar{x}$. Thus, the equilibrium value of the aggregate output index, say $\bar{x}^*$, satisfies $\bar{x}^* = \int f(x_j(p_j^*(\bar{x}^*), \bar{x}^*))\,dj$.

This limiting case is known as the *monopolistic competition model*. It originates in Chamberlin (1933); see Hart (1985) for a modern treatment. In markets characterized by monopolistic competition, market power is accompanied by a low level of strategic interaction, in that the strategies of any particular firm do not affect the payoff of any other firm.[18]

# 12.D   Repeated Interaction

One unrealistic assumption in the models presented in Section 12.C was their static, one-shot nature. In these models, a firm never had to consider the reaction of its competitors to its price or quantity choice. In the Bertrand model, for instance, a firm could undercut its rival's price by a penny and steal all the rival's customers. In practice, however, a firm in this circumstance may well worry that if it does undercut its rival in this manner, the rival will respond by cutting its own price, ultimately leading to only a short-run gain in sales but a long-run reduction in the price level in the market.

In this section, we consider the simplest type of dynamic model in which these concerns arise. Two identical firms complete for sales repeatedly, with competition in each period $t$ described by the Bertrand model. When they do so, the two firms know all the prices that have been chosen (by *both* firms) previously. There is a discount factor $\delta < 1$, and each firm $j$ attempts to maximize the discounted value of profits, $\sum_{t=1}^{\infty} \delta^{t-1}\pi_{jt}$, where $\pi_{jt}$ is firm $j$'s profit in period $t$. The game that this situation gives rise to is a dynamic game (see Chapter 9) of a special kind: it is obtained by repeated play of the same static simultaneous-move game and is known as a *repeated game*.

In this repeated Bertrand game, firm $j$'s strategy specifies what price $p_{jt}$ it will charge in each period $t$ as a function of the history of all past price choices by the two firms, $H_{t-1} = \{p_{1\tau}, p_{2\tau}\}_{\tau=1}^{t-1}$. Strategies of this form allow for a range of interesting behaviors. For example, a firm's strategy could call for retaliation if the firm's rival ever lowers its price below some "threshold price." This retaliation could be brief, calling for the firm to lower its price for only a few periods after the rival "crosses the line," or it could be unrelenting. The retaliation could be tailored to the amount by which the firm's rival undercut it, or it could be severe no matter how minor the rival's transgression. The firm could also respond with increasingly cooperative

---

18. In contrast, in spatial models, even in the limit of a continuum of firms, strategic interaction remains. In that case, firms interact locally, and neighbors count, no matter how large the economy is.

behavior in return for its rival acting cooperatively in the past. And, of course, the firm's strategy could also make the firm's behavior in any period $t$ independent of past history (a strategy involving no retaliation or rewards).

Of particular interest to us is the possibility that these types of behavioral responses could allow firms, in settings of repeated interaction, to sustain behavior more cooperative than the outcome predicted by the simple one-shot Bertrand model. We explore this possibility in the remainder of this section.

We begin by considering the case in which the firms compete only a finite number of times $T$ (this is known as a *finitely repeated game*). Can the rich set of possible behaviors just described actually arise in a subgame perfect Nash equilibrium of this model? Recalling Proposition 9.B.4, we see the answer is "no." The unique subgame perfect Nash equilibrium of the finitely repeated Bertrand game simply involves $T$ repetitions of the static Bertrand equilibrium in which prices equal cost. This is a simple consequence of backward induction: In the last period, $T$, we must be at the Bertrand solution, and therefore profits are zero in that period *regardless of what has happened earlier*. But, then, in period $T - 1$ we are, strategically speaking, at the last period, and the Bertrand solution must arise again. And so on, until we get to the first period. In summary, backward induction rules out the possibility of more cooperative behavior in the finitely repeated Bertrand game.

Things can change dramatically, however, when the horizon is extended to an infinite number of periods (this is known as an *infinitely repeated game*). To see this, consider the following strategies for firms $j = 1, 2$:

$$p_{jt}(H_{t-1}) = \begin{cases} p^m & \text{if all elements of } H_{t-1} \text{ equal } (p^m, p^m) \text{ or } t = 1 \\ c & \text{otherwise.} \end{cases} \quad (12.D.1)$$

In words, firm $j$'s strategy calls for it to initially play the monopoly price $p^m$ in period 1. Then, in each period $t > 1$, firm $j$ plays $p^m$ if in every previous period both firms have charged price $p^m$ and otherwise charges a price equal to cost. This type of strategy is called a *Nash reversion strategy*: Firms cooperate until someone deviates, and any deviation triggers a permanent retaliation in which both firms thereafter set their prices equal to cost, the one-period Nash strategy. Note that if both firms follow the strategies in (12.D.1), then both firms will end up charging the monopoly price in every period. They start by charging $p^m$, and therefore no deviation from $p^m$ will ever be triggered.

For the strategies in (12.D.1), we have the result presented in Proposition 12.D.1.

**Proposition 12.D.1:** The strategies described in (12.D.1) constitute a subgame perfect Nash equilibrium (SPNE) of the infinitely repeated Bertrand duopoly game if and only if $\delta \geq \frac{1}{2}$.

**Proof:** Recall that a set of strategies is an SPNE of an infinite horizon game if and only if it specifies Nash equilibrium play in every subgame (see Section 9.B). To start, note that although each subgame of this repeated game has a distinct history of play leading to it, all of these subgames have an identical structure: Each is an infinitely repeated Bertrand duopoly game exactly like the game as a whole. Thus, to establish that the strategies in (12.D.1) constitute an SPNE, we need to show that after any previous history of play, the strategies specified for the remainder of the game constitute a Nash equilibrium of an infinitely repeated Bertrand game.

In fact, given the form of the strategies in (12.D.1), we need to be concerned with only two types of previous histories: those in which there has been a previous deviation (a price not equal to $p^m$) and those in which there has been no deviation.

Consider, first, a subgame arising after a deviation has occurred. The strategies call for each firm to set its price equal to $c$ in every future period regardless of its rival's behavior. This pair of strategies is a Nash equilibrium of an infinitely repeated Bertrand game because each firm $j$ can earn at most zero when its opponent always sets its price equal to $c$, and it earns exactly this amount by itself setting its price equal to $c$ in every remaining period.

Now consider a subgame starting in, say, period $t$ after no previous deviation has occurred. Each firm $j$ knows that its rival's strategy calls for it to charge $p^m$ until it encounters a deviation from $p^m$ and to charge $c$ thereafter. Is it in firm $j$'s interest to use this strategy itself given that its rival does? That is, do these strategies constitute a Nash equilibrium in this subgame?

Suppose that firm $j$ contemplates deviating from price $p^m$ in period $\tau \geq t$ of the subgame if no deviation has occurred prior to period $\tau$.[19] From period $t$ through period $\tau - 1$, firm $j$ will earn $\frac{1}{2}(p^m - c)x(p^m)$ in each period, exactly as it does if it never deviates. Starting in period $\tau$, however, its payoffs will differ from those that would arise if it does not deviate. In periods after it deviates (periods $\tau + 1, \tau + 2, \ldots$), firm $j$'s rival charges a price of $c$ regardless of the form of firm $j$'s deviation in period $\tau$, and so firm $j$ can earn at most zero in each of these periods. In period $\tau$, firm $j$ optimally deviates in a manner that maximizes its payoff in that period (note that the payoffs firm $j$ receives in later periods are the same for any deviation from $p^m$ that it makes). It will therefore charge $p^m - \varepsilon$ for some arbitrarily small $\varepsilon > 0$, make all sales in the market, and earn a one-period payoff of $(p^m - c - \varepsilon)x(p^m)$. Thus, its overall discounted payoff from period $\tau$ onward as a result of following this deviation strategy, discounted to period $\tau$, can be made arbitrarily close to $(p^m - c)x(p^m)$.

On the other hand, if firm $j$ never deviates, it earns a discounted payoff from period $\tau$ onward, discounted to period $\tau$, of $[\frac{1}{2}(p^m - c)x(p^m)]/(1 - \delta)$. Hence, for any $t$ and $\tau \geq t$, firm $j$ will prefer no deviation to deviation in period $\tau$ if and only if

$$\frac{1}{1 - \delta}\left[\tfrac{1}{2}(p^m - c)x(p^m)\right] \geq (p^m - c)x(p^m),$$

or

$$\delta \geq \tfrac{1}{2}. \tag{12.D.2}$$

Thus, the strategies in (12.D.1) constitute an SPNE if and only if $\delta \geq \frac{1}{2}$. ■

The implication of Proposition 12.D.1 is that the perfectly competitive outcome of the static Bertrand game may be avoided if the firms foresee infinitely repeated interaction. The reason is that, in contemplating a deviation, each firm takes into account not only the one-period gain it earns from undercutting its rival but also the profits forgone by triggering retaliation. The size of the discount factor $\delta$ is

---

19. From our previous argument, we know that once a deviation has occurred within this subgame, firm $j$ can do no better than to play $c$ in every period given that its rival will do so. Hence, to check whether these strategies form a Nash equilibrium in this subgame, we need only check whether firm $j$ will wish to deviate from $p^m$ if no such deviation has yet occurred.

important here because it affects the relative weights put on the future losses versus the present gain from a deviation. The monopoly price is sustainable if and only if the present value of these future losses is large enough relative to the possible current gain from deviation to keep the firms from going for short-run profits.

The discount factor need not be interpreted literally. For example, in a model in which market demand is growing at rate $\gamma$ [i.e., $x_t(p) = \gamma^t x(p)$], larger values of $\gamma$ make the model behave as if there is a larger discount factor because demand growth increases the size of any future losses caused by a current deviation. Alternatively, we can imagine that in each period there is a probability $\gamma$ that the firms' interaction might end. The larger $\gamma$ is, the more firms will effectively discount the future. (This interpretation makes clear that the infinitely repeated game framework can be relevant even when the firms may cease their interaction within some finite amount of time; what is needed to fit the analysis into the framework above is a strictly positive probability of continuing upon having reached any period.) Finally, the value of $\delta$ can reflect how long it takes to detect a deviation. These interpretations are developed in Exercise 12.D.1.

Although the strategies in (12.D.1) constitute an SPNE when $\delta \geq \frac{1}{2}$, they are *not* the only SPNE of the repeated Bertrand model. In particular, we can obtain the result presented in Proposition 12.D.2.

**Proposition 12.D.2:** In the infinitely repeated Bertand duopoly game, when $\delta \geq \frac{1}{2}$ repeated choice of any price $p \subset [c, p^m]$ can be supported as a subgame perfect Nash equilibrium outcome path using Nash reversion strategies. By contrast, when $\delta < \frac{1}{2}$, any subgame perfect Nash equilibrium outcome path must have all sales occurring at a price equal to $c$ in every period.

**Proof:** For the first part of the result, we have already shown in Proposition 12.D.1 that repeated choice of price $p^m$ can be sustained as an SPNE outcome when $\delta \geq \frac{1}{2}$. The proof for any price $p \in [c, p^m)$ follows exactly the same lines; simply change price $p^m$ in the strategies of (12.D.1) to $p \in [c, p^m)$.

The proof of the second part of the result is presented in small type.

We now show that all sales must occur at a price equal to $c$ when $\delta < \frac{1}{2}$. To begin, let $v_{jt} = \sum_{\tau \geq t} \delta^{\tau - t} \pi_{jt}$ denote firm $j$'s profits, discounted to period $t$, when the equilibrium strategies are played from period $t$ onward. Also define $\pi_t = \pi_{1t} + \pi_{2t}$.

Observe that, because every firm $j$ finds it optimal to conform to the equilibrium strategies in every period $t$, it must be that

$$\pi_t \leq v_{jt} \quad \text{for } j = 1, 2 \text{ and every } t, \tag{12.D.3}$$

since each firm $j$ can obtain a payoff arbitrarily close to $\pi_t$ in period $t$ by deviating and undercutting the lowest price in the market by an arbitrarily small amount and can assure itself a nonnegative payoff in any period thereafter.

Suppose that there exists at least one period $t$ in which $\pi_t > 0$. We will derive a contradiction. There are two cases to consider:

(i) Suppose, first, that there is a period $\tau$ with $\pi_\tau > 0$ such that $\pi_\tau \geq \pi_t$ for all $t$. If so, then adding (12.D.3) for $t = \tau$ over $j = 1, 2$, we have

$$2\pi_\tau \leq (v_{1\tau} + v_{2\tau}).$$

But $(v_{1\tau} + v_{2\tau}) \leq [1/(1 - \delta)]\pi_\tau$, and so this is impossible if $\delta < \frac{1}{2}$.

(ii) Suppose, instead, that no such period exists; that is, for any period $t$, there is a period $\tau > t$ such that $\pi_\tau > \pi_t$. Define $\tau(t)$ for $t \geq 1$ recursively as follows: Let $\tau(1) = 1$ and for $t \geq 2$ define $\tau(t) = \text{Min} \{\tau > \tau(t-1): \pi_\tau > \pi_{\tau(t-1)}\}$. Note that, for all $t$, $\pi_t$ is bounded above by the monopoly profit level $\pi^m = (p^m - c)x(p^m)$ and that the sequence $\{\pi_{\tau(t)}\}_{t=1}^\infty$ is monotonically increasing. Hence, as $t \to \infty$, $\pi_{\tau(t)}$ must converge to some $\bar{\pi} \in (0, \pi^m]$ such that $\pi_t < \bar{\pi}$ for all $t$. Now, adding (12.D.3) over $j = 1, 2$, we see that we must have

$$2\pi_{\tau(t)} \leq v_{1\tau(t)} + v_{2\tau(t)} \tag{12.D.4}$$

for all $t$. Moreover, $v_{1\tau(t)} + v_{2\tau(t)} \leq [1/(1-\delta)]\bar{\pi}$ for all $t$, and so we must have

$$2\pi_{\tau(t)} \leq \frac{1}{1-\delta}\bar{\pi} \tag{12.D.5}$$

for all $t$. But when $\delta < \frac{1}{2}$, condition (12.D.5) must be violated for $t$ sufficiently large.

---

This completes the proof of the proposition. ∎

The presence of multiple equilibria identified in Proposition 12.D.2 for $\delta \geq \frac{1}{2}$ is common in infinitely repeated games. Typically, a range of cooperative equilibria is possible for a given level of $\delta$, as is a complete lack of cooperation in the form of the static Nash equilibrium outcome repeated forever.

Proposition 12.D.2 also tells us that the set of SPNE of the repeated Bertrand game grows as $\delta$ gets larger.[20] The discontinuous behavior as a function of $\delta$ of the set of SPNE displayed in Proposition 12.D.2 is, however, a special feature of the repeated Bertrand model. The repeated Cournot model and models of repeated price competition with differentiated products generally display a smoother increase in the maximal level of joint profits that can be sustained as $\delta$ increases (see Exercise 12.D.3).

In fact, a general result in the theory of repeated games, known as the *folk theorem*, tells us the following: In an infinitely repeated game, *any feasible discounted payoffs that give each player, on a per-period basis, more than the lowest payoff that he could guarantee himself in a single play of the simultaneous-move component game can be sustained as the payoffs of an SPNE if players discount the future to a sufficiently small degree.* In Appendix A, we provide a more precise statement and extended discussion of the folk theorem for general repeated games. Its message is clear: Although infinitely repeated games allow for cooperative behavior, they also allow for an *extremely wide range* of possible behavior.

The wide range of equilibria in repeated game models of oligopoly is somewhat disconcerting. From a practical point of view, how do we know which equilibrium behavior will arise? Can "anything happen" in oligopolistic markets? To get around this problem, researchers often assume that symmetrically placed firms will find the symmetric profit-maximizing equilibrium focal (see Section 8.D). However, even restricting attention to the case of symmetric firms, the validity of this assumption is likely to depend on the setting. For example, the history of an industry could make other equilibria focal: An industry that has historically been very noncooperative (maybe because $\delta$ has always been low) may find noncooperative outcomes more focal. The assumption that the symmetric profit-maximizing equilibrium arises is

---

20. Strictly speaking, Proposition 12.D.2 shows this only for the class of stationary, symmetric equilibria (i.e., equilibria in which the firms adopt identical strategies and in which, on the equilibrium path, the actions taken are the same in every period).

more natural when the self-enforcing agreement interpretation of these equilibria is relevant, as when oligopolists secretly meet to discuss their pricing plans. Because antitrust laws preclude oligopolists from writing a formal contract specifying their behavior, any secret collusive agreement among them must be self-enforcing and so must constitute an SPNE. It seems reasonable to think that, in such circumstances, identical firms will therefore agree to the most profitable symmetric SPNE. (If the firms are not identical, similar logic suggests that the firms would agree to an SPNE corresponding to a point on the frontier of their set of SPNE payoffs.)

Finally, just as with the static models discussed in Section 12.C, it is of interest to investigate how the number of firms in a market affects its competitiveness. You are asked to do so in Exercise 12.D.2.

**Exercise 12.D.2:** Show that with $J$ firms, repeated choice of any price $p \in (c, p^m]$ can be sustained as a stationary SPNE outcome path of the infinitely repeated Bertrand game using Nash reversion strategies if and only if $\delta \geq (J - 1)/J$. What does this say about the effect of having more firms in a market on the difficulty of sustaining collusion?

---

In practice, an important feature of many settings of oligopolistic collusion (as well as other settings of cooperation) is that firms are likely to be able to observe their rivals' behavior only imperfectly. For example, as emphasized by Stigler (1960), an oligopolist's rivals may make secret price cuts to consumers. If the market demand is stochastic, a firm will be unable to tell with certainty whether there have been any deviations from collusive pricing simply from observation of its own demand. This possibility leads formally to study of *repeated games with imperfect observability*; see, for example, Green and Porter (1984) and Abreu, Pearce, and Stachetti (1990). A feature of this class of models is that they are able to explain observed breakdowns of cooperation as being an inevitable result of attempts to cooperate in environments characterized by imperfect observability. This is so because equilibrium strategies must be such that some negative realizations of demand result in a breakdown of cooperation if firms are to be prevented from secretly deviating from a collusive scheme.

---

# 12.E  Entry

In Sections 12.B to 12.D, we analyzed monopolistic and oligopolistic market outcomes, keeping the number of active firms exogenously fixed. In most cases, however, we wish to view the number of firms that will be operating in an industry as an endogenous variable. Doing so also raises a new question regarding the welfare properties of situations in which market power is present: Is the equilibrium number of firms that enter the market socially efficient? In Section 10.F, we saw that the answer to this question is "yes" in the case of competitive markets as long as an equilibrium exists. In this section, however, we shall see that this is no longer true when market power is present.

We now take the view that there is an infinite (or finite but very large) number of potential firms, each of which could enter and produce the good under consideration if it were profitable to do so. As in Section 10.F, we focus on the case in which all potential firms are identical. (See Exercise 12.E.1 for a case in which they are not.)

A natural way to conceptualize entry in oligopolistic settings is as a two-stage process in which a firm first incurs some setup cost $K > 0$ in entering the industry and then, once this cost is sunk, competes for business. The simplest sort of model that captures this idea has the following structure:

*Stage* 1:  All potential firms simultaneously decide "in" or "out." If a firm decides "in," it pays a setup cost $K > 0$.

*Stage* 2:  All firms that have entered play some oligopolistic game.

The oligopoly game in stage 2 could be any of those considered in Sections 12.C and 12.D.

Formally, this two-stage entry model defines a dynamic game (see Chapter 9). Note that its stage 2 subgames are exactly like the games we have analyzed in the previous sections because, at that stage, the number of firms is fixed. Throughout our discussion we shall assume that for each possible number of active firms, there is a unique, symmetric (across firms) equilibrium in stage 2, and we let $\pi_J$ denote the profits of a firm in this stage 2 equilibrium when $J$ firms have entered ($\pi_J$ does not include the entry cost $K$).

This two-stage entry model provides a very simple representation of the entry process. There is very little dynamic structure, and no firm has any "first-mover" advantage that enables it to deter entry or lessen competition from other firms (see Section 12.G and Appendix B for a discussion of these possibilities).

Consider now the (pure strategy) subgame perfect Nash equilibria (SPNEs) of this model. In any SPNE of this game, no firm must want to change its entry decision given the entry decisions of the other firms. For expositional purposes, we shall also adopt the convention that a firm chooses to enter the market when it is indifferent. With this assumption, there is an equilibrium with $J^*$ firms choosing to enter the market if and only if

$$\pi_{J*} \geq K \tag{12.E.1}$$

and

$$\pi_{J*+1} < K. \tag{12.E.2}$$

Condition (12.E.1) says that a firm that has chosen to enter does at least as well by doing so as it would do if it were to change its decision to "out," given the anticipated result of competition with $J^*$ firms. Condition (12.E.2) says that a firm that has decided to remain out of the market does strictly worse by changing its decision to "in," given the anticipated result of competition with $J^* + 1$ firms.

Typically, we expect that $\pi_J$ is decreasing in $J$ and that $\pi_J \to 0$ and $J \to \infty$. In this case, there is a unique integer $\hat{J}$ such that $\pi_J \geq K$ for all $J \leq \hat{J}$ and $\pi_J < K$ for all $J > \hat{J}$, and so $J^* = \hat{J}$ is the unique equilibrium number of firms.[21,22]

21. Note, however, that although there is a unique number of entrants, there are many equilibria, in each of which the particular firms choosing to enter differ.

22. Without the assumption that firms enter when indifferent, condition (12.E.2) would be a weak inequality. This change in (12.E.2) matters for the identification of the equilibrium number of firms only in the case in which there is an integer number of firms $\tilde{J}$ such that $\pi_{\tilde{J}} = K$ (so that with $\tilde{J}$ firms in the market each firm earns exactly zero net of its entry cost $K$). When this is so, this change allows both $\tilde{J}$ and $\tilde{J} - 1$ to be equilibria. With minor adaptations but some loss of expositional simplicity, all the points made in this section can be extended to cover this case.

We illustrate the determination of the equilibrium number of firms with two examples in which the stage 2 oligopoly games correspond, respectively, to the Cournot and Bertrand models discussed in Section 12.C.

**Example 12.E.1:** *Equilibrium Entry with Cournot Competition.* Suppose that competition in stage 2 of the two-stage entry game corresponds to the Cournot model studied in Section 12.C, with $c(q) = cq$, $p(q) = a - bq$, $a > c \geq 0$, and $b > 0$. The stage 2 output per firm, $q_J$, and profit per firm, $\pi_J$, are given (see Exercise 12.C.7) by

$$q_J = \left(\frac{a-c}{b}\right)\left(\frac{1}{J+1}\right), \tag{12.E.3}$$

$$\pi_J = \left(\frac{a-c}{J+1}\right)^2\left(\frac{1}{b}\right). \tag{12.E.4}$$

Note that $\pi_J$ is strictly decreasing in $J$ and that $\pi_J \to 0$ as $J \to \infty$. Also, $Jq_J \to (a-c)/b$ as $J \to \infty$, so that aggregate quantity approaches the competitive level. Solving for the real number $\tilde{J} \in \mathbb{R}$ at which $\pi_{\tilde{J}} = K$ gives

$$(\tilde{J} + 1)^2 = \frac{(a-c)^2}{bK}$$

or

$$\tilde{J} = \frac{(a-c)}{\sqrt{bK}} - 1.$$

The equilibrium number of entrants $J^*$ is the largest integer that is less than or equal to $\tilde{J}$. Note that as $K$ decreases, the number of firms active in the market (weakly) increases, and that as more firms become active, aggregate output increases and price decreases. Indeed, $J^* \to \infty$ as $K \to 0$, and output and price approach their competitive levels. Note also that a proportional increase in demand at every price, captured by a reduction in $b$, changes the equilibrium number of firms and price in a manner that is identical to a decrease in $K$. ∎

**Example 12.E.2:** *Equilibrium Entry with Bertrand Competition.* Suppose now that competition in stage 2 of the two-stage entry game takes the form of the Bertrand model studied in Section 10.C. Once again, $c(q) = cq$, $p(q) = a - bq$, $a > c \geq 0$, and $b > 0$. Now $\pi_1 = \pi^m$, the monopoly profit level, and $\pi_J = 0$ for all $J \geq 2$. Thus, assuming that $\pi^m > K$, the SPNE must have $J^* = 1$ and result in the monopoly price and quantity levels. Comparing this result with the result in Example 12.E.1 for the Cournot model, we see that the presence of more intense stage 2 competition here actually *lowers* the ultimate level of competition in the market! ∎

### Entry and Welfare

Consider now how the number of firms entering an oligopolistic market compares with the number that would maximize social welfare given the presence of oligopolistic competition in the market. We begin by considering this issue for the case of a homogeneous-good industry.

Let $q_J$ be the symmetric equilibrium output per firm when there are $J$ firms in the market. As usual, the inverse demand function is denoted by $p(\cdot)$. Thus, $p(Jq_J)$ is the price when there are $J$ active firms; and so $\pi_J = p(Jq_J)q_J - c(q_J)$, where $c(\cdot)$ is the cost function of a firm after entry. We assume that $c(0) = 0$.

We measure welfare here by means of Marshallian aggregate surplus (see Section 10.E). In this case, social welfare when there are $J$ active firms is given by

$$W(J) = \int_0^{Jq_J} p(s)\,ds - Jc(q_J) - JK. \tag{12.E.5}$$

The socially optimal number of active firms in this oligopolistic industry, which we denote by $J^\circ$, is any integer number that solves $\mathrm{Max}_J\, W(J)$. Example 12.E.3 illustrates that in contrast with the conclusion arising in the case of a competitive market, the equilibrium number of firms here need not be socially optimal.

**Example 12.E.3:** Consider the Cournot model of Example 12.E.1. For the moment, ignore the requirement that the number of firms is an integer, and solve for the number of firms $\bar{J}$ at which $W'(\bar{J}) = 0$. This gives

$$(\bar{J} + 1)^3 = \frac{(a - c)^2}{bK}. \tag{12.E.6}$$

If $\bar{J}$ turns out to be an integer, then the socially optimal number of firms is $J^\circ = \bar{J}$. Otherwise, $J^\circ$ is one of the two integers on either side of $\bar{J}$ [recall that $W(\cdot)$ is concave]. Now, recall from (12.E.4) that $\pi_J = (1/b)[(a - c)/(J + 1)]^2$. As noted in Example 12.E.1, if we let $\tilde{J}$ be the real number such that

$$(\tilde{J} + 1)^2 = \frac{(a - c)^2}{bK}, \tag{12.E.7}$$

the equilibrium number of firms is the largest integer less than or equal to $\tilde{J}$. From (12.E.6) and (12.E.7), we see that

$$(\tilde{J} + 1) = (\bar{J} + 1)^{3/2}.$$

Thus, when the demand and cost parameters are such that the optimal number of firms is exactly two ($J^\circ = \bar{J} = 2$), four firms actually enter this market ($J^* = 4$, since $\tilde{J} \cong 4.2$); when the social optimum is for exactly three firms to enter ($J^\circ = \bar{J} = 3$), seven firms actually do ($J^* = 7$, since $\tilde{J} = 7$); when the social optimum is for exactly eight firms to enter ($J^\circ = \bar{J} = 8$), 26 actually enter ($J^* = 26$, since $\tilde{J} = 26$). ∎

Can we say anything general about the nature of the entry bias? It turns out that we can as long as stage 2 competition satisfies three weak conditions [we follow Mankiw and Whinston (1986) here]:

(A1) $Jq_J \geq J'q_{J'}$ whenever $J > J'$;
(A2) $q_J \leq q_{J'}$ whenever $J > J'$;
(A3) $p(Jq_J) - c'(q_J) \geq 0$ for all $J$.

Conditions (A1) and (A3) are straightforward: (A1) requires that aggregate output increases (price falls) when more firms enter the industry, and (A3) says that price is not below marginal cost regardless of the number of firms entering the industry. Condition (A2) is more interesting. It is the assumption of *business stealing*. It says that when an additional firm enters the market, the sales of existing firms fall (weakly). Hence, part of the new firm's sales come at the expense of existing firms. These conditions are satisfied by most, although not all, oligopoly models. [In the Bertrand model, for example, condition (A3) does not hold.]

For markets satisfying these three conditions we have the result shown in Proposition 12.E.1.

**Proposition 12.E.1:** Suppose that conditions (A1) to (A3) are satisfied by the post-entry oligopoly game, that $p'(\cdot) < 0$, and that $c''(\cdot) \geq 0$. Then the equilibrium number of entrants, $J^*$, is at least $J^\circ - 1$, where $J^\circ$ is the socially optimal number of entrants.[23]

**Proof:** The result is trivial for $J^\circ = 1$, so suppose that $J^\circ > 1$. Under the assumptions of the proposition, $\pi_J$ is decreasing in $J$ (Exercise 12.E.2 asks you to show this). To establish the result, we therefore need only show that $\pi_{J^\circ - 1} \geq K$.

To prove this, note first that by the definition of $J^\circ$ we must have $W(J^\circ) - W(J^\circ - 1) \geq 0$, or

$$\int_{Q_{J^\circ - 1}}^{Q_{J^\circ}} p(s)\, ds - J^\circ c(q_{J^\circ}) + (J^\circ - 1)c(q_{J^\circ - 1}) \geq K,$$

where we let $Q_J = Jq_J$. We can rearrange this expression to yield

$$\pi_{J^\circ - 1} - K \geq p(Q_{J^\circ - 1})q_{J^\circ - 1} - \int_{Q_{J^\circ - 1}}^{Q_{J^\circ}} p(s)\, ds + J^\circ[c(q_{J^\circ}) - c(q_{J^\circ - 1})].$$

Given $p'(\cdot) < 0$ and condition (A1), this implies that

$$\pi_{J^\circ - 1} - K \geq p(Q_{J^\circ - 1})[q_{J^\circ - 1} + Q_{J^\circ - 1} - Q_{J^\circ}] + J^\circ[c(q_{J^\circ}) - c(q_{J^\circ - 1})]. \quad (12.E.8)$$

But since $c''(\cdot) \geq 0$, we know that $c'(q_{J^\circ - 1})[q_{J^\circ} - q_{J^\circ - 1}] \leq c(q_{J^\circ}) - c(q_{J^\circ - 1})$. Using this inequality with (12.E.8) and the fact that $q_{J^\circ - 1} + Q_{J^\circ - 1} - Q_{J^\circ} = J^\circ(q_{J^\circ - 1} - q_{J^\circ})$ yields

$$\pi_{J^\circ - 1} - K \geq [p(Q_{J^\circ - 1}) - c'(q_{J^\circ - 1})]J^\circ(q_{J^\circ - 1} - q_{J^\circ}).$$

Conditions (A2) and (A3) then imply that $\pi_{J^\circ - 1} \geq K$.[24] ∎

The idea behind the proof of Proposition 12.E.1 is illustrated in Figure 12.E.1 for the case where $c(q) = 0$ for all $q$. In the figure, the incremental welfare benefit of the $J^\circ$th firm, before taking its entry cost into account, is represented by the shaded area $(abcd)$. Since entry of this firm is socially efficient, this area must be at least $K$. But area $(abcd)$ is less than area $(abce)$, which equals $p(Q_{J^\circ - 1})(Q_{J^\circ} - Q_{J^\circ - 1})$. Moreover, business stealing implies that $(Q_{J^\circ} - Q_{J^\circ - 1}) = J^\circ q_{J^\circ} - (J^\circ - 1)q_{J^\circ - 1} \leq q_{J^\circ - 1}$, and so we see that area $(abce) \leq p(Q_{J^\circ - 1})q_{J^\circ - 1} = \pi_{J^\circ - 1}$ [the value of $\pi_{J^\circ - 1}$ is represented in Figure 12.E.1 by area $(abfg)$]. Hence $\pi_{J^\circ - 1} \geq K$.

The tendency for excess entry in the presence of market power is fundamentally driven by the business-stealing effect. When business stealing accompanies new entry and price exceeds marginal cost, part of a new entrant's profit comes at the expense of existing firms, creating an excess incentive for the new firm to enter.

Of course, as Proposition 12.E.1 indicates, we may also see too few firms in an industry. The classic example concerns a situation in which the socially optimal number of firms is one. A single firm deciding whether to enter a market as a

---

23. If there is more than one maximizer of $W(J)$, say $\{J_1^\circ, \ldots, J_N^\circ\}$, then $J^* \geq \mathrm{Max}\,\{J_1^\circ, \ldots, J_N^\circ\} - 1$.

24. Note that if (A1) holds with strict inequality, then this conclusion can be strengthened to $\pi_{J^\circ - 1} > K$ [a strict inequality appears in (12.E.8)]. In this case, $J^* \geq J^\circ - 1$ even if firms do not enter when indifferent.

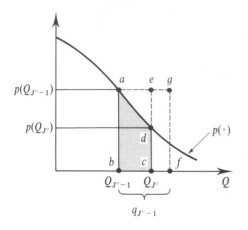

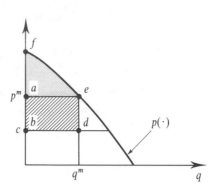

**Figure 12.E.1 (left)**

Diagrammatic explanation of Proposition 12.E.1.

**Figure 12.E.2 (right)**

An insufficient entry incentive.

monopolist compares its monopoly profit—the hatched area (*abde*) in Figure 12.E.2—with the entry cost $K$. However, the firm fails to capture, and therefore ignores, the increase in consumer surplus that its entry generates—the shaded area (*fae*). As a result, the firm may find entry unprofitable even though it is socially desirable. Proposition 12.E.1 tells us, however, that if we have too little entry in a homogeneous-good market, this can be at most by a single firm.

What happens when product differentiation is present? It turns out that we can then say very little of a general nature. The reason is that the sort of problem illustrated in Figure 12.E.2 can now happen for many products, leading to many "too few by one" conclusions. An additional issue is that, with product differentiation, the number of firms is not all that matters. We may also fail to have the right selection of products.[25]

---

An alternative approach to the two-stage entry game models the actions of entry and quantity/price choice as simultaneous. In this *one-stage entry game*, a firm incurs its setup cost only if it sells a positive amount. For example, the one-stage versions of Examples 12.E.1 and 12.E.2 are Cournot and Bertrand games, respectively, with cost functions

$$C(q) = \begin{cases} K + c(q) & \text{if } q > 0 \\ 0 & \text{if } q = 0 \end{cases}$$

and an infinite (or very large) number of firms. For models of price competition, this change can have dramatic consequences. Consider the effect on the result of Example 12.E.2 that is illustrated in Example 12.E.4.

**Example 12.E.4:** *The One-Stage Entry Model with Bertrand Competition.* Suppose that $p > [K + cx(p)]/x(p)$ for some $p$ (the parameter $c > 0$ is the cost per unit); that is, suppose there is some price level at which a monopolist can earn strictly positive profits after paying its set up cost $K$. Assume that many firms simultaneously name prices and that a firm incurs the setup cost $K$ only if it actually makes sales. Any equilibrium of this game has all sales occurring at price $p^* = \text{Min}\{p: p \geq [K + cx(p)]/x(p)\}$ (if price is above $p^*$, some firm could gain by setting a price $p^* - \varepsilon$; if price is below $p^*$, some firm must be making strictly negative profits), and one firm satisfying all demand at this price (if the demand were split among

---

25. See Spence (1976), Dixit and Stiglitz (1977), Salop (1979), and Mankiw and Whinston (1986) for more on the case of product differentiation.

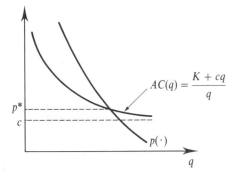

**Figure 12.E.3**

Equilibrium in the one-stage entry game discussed in Example 12.E.4.

several firms at price $p^*$, none of them could cover their cost).[26] In this equilibrium, all firms make zero profits. The equilibrium outcome is depicted in Figure 12.E.3. Observe that it is strictly superior in welfare terms to the outcome that arises in the two-stage entry process considered in Example 12.E.2, where there is also a single firm active but it quotes a monopoly price.[27] ■

What is the critical difference between the one-stage and two-stage entry processes? In the two-stage model an entrant must sink its fixed costs prior to competing, whereas in the one-stage model it can compete for sales while retaining the option not to sink these costs if it does not make any sales. We can think of the two-stage case as a model of a firm incurring a once-and-for-all sunk entry cost that allows for many later periods of competitive interaction, whereas the one-stage case captures a setting in which "hit-and-run" entry is possible (i.e., entry for just one period while paying only the one-period rental price of capital). When a firm must incur a sunk cost in entering it must consider the reaction of other firms to its entry. In the Bertrand model with constant costs this reaction is severe: price falls to cost and the firm loses money by entering. In contrast, in the one-stage game the firm can enter and undercut active firms' prices without fearing their reactions. This makes entry more aggressive and leads to a lower equilibrium price. This one-stage entry model with price competition provides one formalization of what Baumol, Panzar, and Willig (1982) call a *contestable market*.

## 12.F  The Competitive Limit

In Chapter 10, we introduced the idea that a competitive market might usefully be thought of as a limiting case of an oligopolistic market in which firms' market power grows increasingly small (see Section 10.B). We also noted that this view could provide a framework for reconciling cases in which competitive equilibria fail to exist in the presence of free entry and average costs that exhibit a strictly positive efficient

---

26. Note that we now allow consumer demand to be given entirely to one firm when several firms name the same price (before, we had taken the division of demand in this case to be exogenously given). This is the only division of demand that is compatible with equilibrium in this example. It can be formally justified as the limit of the equilibria that arise when prices must be quoted in discrete units as the size of these units grows small.

27. In fact, this equilibrium outcome is the solution to the problem faced by a welfare-maximizing planner who can control the outputs $q_j$ of the firms but must guarantee a nonnegative profit to all active firms, that is, who faces the constraint that $p(\sum_k q_k)q_j \geq cq_j + K$ for every $j$ with $q_j > 0$.

scale (see Section 10.F). In this situation, we argued, as long as many firms could fit into the market, the market outcome ought to be close to the competitive outcome that would arise if industry average costs were actually constant at the level of minimum average cost. In this section, we elaborate on these points and develop, in a setting of free entry, the theme that if the size of individual firms is small relative to the size of the market, then the equilibrium will be nearly competitive.

We have already seen one example of this phenomenon in Example 12.E.1. Here we establish the point in a more general way. We now let market demand be $x_\alpha(p) = \alpha x(p)$, where $x(p)$ is differentiable and $x'(\cdot) < 0$. Increases in $\alpha$ correspond to proportional increases in demand at all prices. Letting $p(q)$ be the inverse demand function associated with $x(p)$, the inverse demand function associated with $x_\alpha(p)$ is then $p_\alpha(q) = p(q/\alpha)$. All potential firms have a strictly convex cost function $c(q)$ and entry cost $K > 0$. We denote the level of minimum average cost for a firm by $\bar{c} = \mathrm{Min}_{q>0}\,[K + c(q)]/q$, and we let $\bar{q} > 0$ denote a firm's (unique) efficient scale.

As in Example 12.E.1, we focus on the case of a two-stage entry model with Cournot competition in the second stage, in which the cost $K$ is incurred only if the firm decides to enter in stage 1. We let $b(Q_{-j})$ denote active firm $j$'s optimal output level for any given level of aggregate output by its rivals, $Q_{-j}$, and we assume that this best response is unique for all $Q_{-j}$.

Finally, we let $p_\alpha$ and $Q_\alpha$ denote the price and aggregate output in a subgame perfect Nash equilibrium (SPNE) of the two-stage Cournot entry model when the market size is $\alpha$. We denote by $P_\alpha$ the set of all SPNE prices for market size $\alpha$.

**Proposition 12.F.1:** As the market size grows, the price in any subgame perfect Nash equilibrium of the two-stage Cournot entry model converges to the level of minimum average cost (the ''competitive'' price). Formally,

$$\mathrm{Max}_{p_\alpha \in P_\alpha} |p_\alpha - \bar{c}| \to 0 \quad \text{as} \quad \alpha \to \infty.$$

**Proof:** The argument consists of three steps:

(i) First, you are asked in Exercise 12.F.1 to show that for large enough $\alpha$, an active firm's best-response function $b(Q_{-j})$ is (weakly) decreasing in $Q_{-j}$.

(ii) Second, we argue that if $b(Q_{-j})$ is decreasing, then we must have $Q_\alpha \geq \alpha x(\bar{c}) - \bar{q}$ in any SPNE of the two-stage entry game with market size $\alpha$. To see why this is so, suppose that with market size $\alpha$ we had an SPNE with $J_\alpha$ firms entering and an aggregate output level $Q_\alpha < \alpha x(\bar{c}) - \bar{q}$. Consider any firm $j$ whose equilibrium entry choice is "out" in this equilibrium, and suppose that firm $j$ instead decided to enter and produce quantity $\bar{q}$. Because $b(\cdot)$ is decreasing, it is intuitively plausible that the aggregate output level of the original $J_\alpha$ active firms cannot increase when firm $j$ enters in this way (see the small-type paragraph that follows for the formal argument behind this claim). As a result, aggregate output in the market following firm $j$'s entry is no more than $(Q_\alpha + \bar{q})$; and since $(Q_\alpha + \bar{q}) < \alpha x(\bar{c})$, the resulting (post-entry) price is above $\bar{c}$. Hence, firm $j$ would earn strictly positive profits by entering in this fashion, contradicting the hypothesis that we were at an SPNE to start with.

---

The argument that the output of the existing $J_\alpha$ firms cannot increase following entry of firm $j$ is as follows: Let $Q_{-j}$ be the initial equilibrium level of these firms' aggregate output, and let $\tilde{Q}_{-j}$ be their post-entry aggregate output. Suppose that $\tilde{Q}_{-j} > Q_{-j}$. Then at least one of these firms, say firm $k$, must have increased its output level in response to firm $j$'s entry, say from $q_k$ to $\tilde{q}_k > q_k$. Because $b(\cdot)$ is decreasing, it must be that $\tilde{Q}_{-k} < Q_{-k}$; that is, the post-entry output $\tilde{Q}_{-k}$ of active firms other than $k$ (which includes firm $j$) must be less than their pre-entry output, $Q_{-k}$. By part (c) of Exercise 12.C.8, this implies that $q_k + Q_{-k} \geq \tilde{q}_k + \tilde{Q}_{-k}$. But $Q_{-j} = q_k + Q_{-k}$ (since firm $j$ initially produces nothing), and $\tilde{q}_k + \tilde{Q}_{-k} \geq \tilde{Q}_{-j}$ (because firm $j$'s post-entry output is nonnegative). Hence, $Q_{-j} \geq \tilde{Q}_{-j}$, which is a contradiction.

---

(iii) Finally, we argue that the conclusion of (ii) implies the result. To see this, consider how much above $\bar{c}$ the price can be if aggregate output is no more than $\bar{q}$ below $\alpha x(\bar{c})$. This is given by

$$\Delta p_\alpha = p_\alpha(\alpha x(\bar{c}) - \bar{q}) - p_\alpha(\alpha x(\bar{c}))$$
$$= p\left(\frac{\alpha x(\bar{c}) - \bar{q}}{\alpha}\right) - p(x(\bar{c})).$$

But as $\alpha \to \infty$, $[\alpha x(\bar{c}) - \bar{q}]/\alpha \to x(\bar{c})$, so that $\Delta p_\alpha \to 0$.  ■

There are two forces driving Proposition 12.F.1. First, the entry process ensures that firms will enter if there is too much "room" left in the market. Second, in a market that is very large relative to the minimum efficient scale, a reduction of output equal to the level of minimum efficient scale has very little effect on price. The consequence of these two facts is that as the market size grows large, firms' market power is dissipated and price approaches the level of minimum average cost (the competitive level). In this limiting outcome, welfare approaches its optimal level.[28]

In Example 12.E.2, we saw that in a two-stage Bertrand market, no such limiting result holds.[29] Because price drops to marginal cost if even two firms enter, the market is always monopolized, no matter what its size. However, the two-stage Bertrand model's limiting properties are quite special. As long as, for any market size, price is above marginal cost for any finite number of firms that enter the market, and approaches marginal cost as the number of firms grows large, a limiting result like that in Proposition 12.F.1 holds.

Finally, Proposition 12.F.1 applies only for the case of homogeneous-good markets. With product differentiation, we must be careful. Firms may be small relative to the size of the entire set of interrelated markets, but they may still be large relative to their own particular niche. In this case, each firm may maintain substantial market power even in the limit, and the limiting equilibrium can be far from efficient (see Exercise 12.F.4).

---

28. The sense of approximation is relative to the size parameter of the market $\alpha$. Assuming that $\alpha$ is a proxy for the number of consumers, this means that the welfare loss per consumer relative to the social optimum goes to zero.

29. Strictly speaking, firms' cost functions in Example 12.E.2 differ from the cost functions assumed in Proposition 12.F.1 (average costs including $K$ are declining everywhere in Example 12.E.2). Nevertheless, for the two-stage Cournot model, Proposition 12.F.1 can be shown to be valid for the cost function of Example 12.E.2 (letting $\bar{c}$ in the statement of the proposition now be the limiting value of average cost as a firm's output grows large).

# 12.G Strategic Precommitments to Affect Future Competition

An important feature of many oligopolistic settings is that firms attempt to make strategic precommitments in order to alter the conditions of future competition in a manner that is favorable to them. Examples of strategic precommitments abound. For example, investments in cost reduction, capacity, and new-product development all lead to long-lasting changes that can affect the nature of future competition. In practice, these types of decisions can be among the most important competitive decisions that firms make.

Some general features of these types of strategic precommitments can be usefully illuminated through examination of the following simple two-stage duopoly model:

*Stage* 1: Firm 1 has the option to make a strategic investment, whose level we denote by $k \in \mathbb{R}$. This choice is observable.

*Stage* 2: Firms 1 and 2 play some oligopoly game, choosing strategies $s_1 \in S_1 \subset \mathbb{R}$ and $s_2 \in S_2 \subset \mathbb{R}$, respectively. Given investment level $k$ and strategy choices $(s_1, s_2)$, profits for firms 1 and 2 are given by $\pi_1(s_1, s_2, k)$ and $\pi_2(s_1, s_2)$, respectively.

For example, $k$ might be an investment that reduces firm 1's marginal cost of production with the stage 2 game being Cournot competition (so $s_j = q_j$, firm $j$'s quantity choice). Alternatively, stage 2 competition could be differentiated products price competition.

We suppose that there is a unique Nash equilibrium in stage 2 given any choice of $k$, $(s_1^*(k), s_2^*(k))$, and we assume for convenience that it is differentiable in $k$. We also assume for purposes of our discussion that $\partial \pi_1(s_1, s_2, k)/\partial s_2 < 0$ and $\partial \pi_2(s_1, s_2)/\partial s_1 < 0$, that is, that stage 2 actions are "aggressive" in the sense that a higher level of $s_{-j}$ by firm $j$'s rival lowers firm $j$'s profit. Hence, firm 1 would be better off, all else being equal, if it could induce firm 2 to lower its choice of $s_2$.

When can investment by firm 1 cause firm 2 to lower $s_2$? Letting $b_1(s_2, k)$ and $b_2(s_1)$ denote firm 1's and firm 2's stage 2 best-response functions (note that firm 1's best response depends on $k$), we can differentiate the equilibrium condition $s_2^* = b_2(b_1(s_2^*, k))$ to get

$$\frac{ds_2^*(k)}{dk} = \frac{db_2(s_1^*(k))}{ds_1} \left( \frac{\partial b_1(s_2^*(k), k)/\partial k}{1 - [\partial b_1(s_2^*(k), k)/\partial s_2][db_2(s_1^*(k))/ds_1]} \right). \quad (12.G.1)$$

The denominator of the second term on the right-hand side of (12.G.1) being nonegative is often called the *stability condition*. It implies that the simple dynamic adjustment process in which the firms take turns myopically playing a best response to each others' current strategies converges to the Nash equilibrium from any strategy pair in a neighborhood of the equilibrium. We shall maintain this assumption for the remainder of our discussion. Thus, the effect of $k$ on $s_2$ can be seen to depend on two factors: (i) Does $k$ make firm 1 more or less "aggressive" in stage 2 competition [i.e., what is the sign of $\partial b_1(s_2^*(k), k)/\partial k$?] and (ii) Does firm 2 respond to the anticipation of more aggressive play by firm 1 with more aggression itself or with less [i.e., what is the sign of $db_2(s_1^*(k))/ds_1$?]

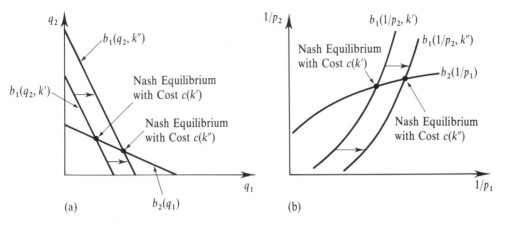

**Figure 12.G.1**

Determinants of the sign of $ds_2^*(k)/dk$.

**Figure 12.G.2**

Strategic effects of a reduction in marginal cost from $c(k')$ to $c(k'') < c(k')$.
(a) Quantity model.
(b) Price model.

When firm 2 responds in kind to more aggressive choices of $s_1$ by firm 1 [i.e., when $db_2(s_1^*(k))/ds_1 > 0$], we say that $s_2$ is a *strategic complement* of $s_1$; and if firm 2 becomes less aggressive in the face of more aggressive play by firm 1 [i.e., if $db_2(s_1^*(k))/ds_1 < 0$], $s_2$ is a *strategic substitute* of $s_1$. [This terminology is derived from Bulow, Geanakoplos, and Klemperer (1985); see also Fudenberg and Tirole (1984) for a related taxonomy.]

Figure 12.G.1 summarizes these two determinants of firm 2's response, $ds_2^*(k)/dk$.

**Example 12.G.1:** *The Strategic Effects from Investment in Marginal Cost Reduction.* The importance for strategic behavior of the distinction between cases of strategic complements and strategic substitutes is nicely illustrated by examining the strategic effects of investments in marginal cost reduction for models of quantity versus price competition.

Suppose that if firm 1 invests $k$ then its (constant) per-unit production costs are $c(k)$, where $c'(k) < 0$. Consider, first, the case in which stage 2 competition takes the form of the Cournot model of Example 12.C.1, so that the stage 2 strategic variable is $s_j = q_j$, firm $j$'s quantity choice. In this model, we have a situation of strategic substitutes because firm 2's best-response function in stage 2 is downward sloping [$db_2(q_1)/dq_1 < 0$ at all $q_1$ such that $b_2(q_1) > 0$]. As shown in Figure 12.G.2(a), the lowering of firm 1's marginal cost because of an increase in $k$ from, say, $k'$ to $k'' > k'$, shifts firm 1's best-response function outward from $b_1(q_2, k')$ to $b_1(q_2, k'')$; with lower marginal costs, firm 1 will wish to produce more for any quantity choice of its rival [and so, in terms of our earlier analysis, $\partial b_1(q_2^*(k), k)/\partial k > 0$]. Thus, in this model, investment in cost reduction leads to a reduction in firm 2's output level, an effect that is beneficial for firm 1 [see Figure 12.G.2(a)].

In contrast, suppose that stage 2 competition takes the form of the differentiated price competition model of Example 12.C.2. Here we take $s_j = (1/p_j)$ to conform with the interpretation of $s_j$ as an "aggressive" variable [i.e., $\partial \pi_1(s_1, s_2, k)/\partial s_2 < 0$]. In this model, we have a situation of strategic complements: an anticipated reduction in firm 1's price causes firm 2 to reduce its price also [i.e., $db_2(1/p_1)/d(1/p_1) > 0$]. As depicted in Figure 12.G.2(b), a reduction in firm 1's marginal cost because of an increase in $k$ from $k'$ to $k'' > k'$ once again makes firm 1 more aggressive, leading it to choose a lower price given any price choice of its rival; its best-response function shifts to the right from $b_1(1/p_2, k')$ to $b_1(1/p_2, k'')$ [hence, in terms of our earlier analysis, $\partial b_1(1/p_2^*(k), k)/\partial k > 0$]. With strategic complements, the result of the reduction in firm 1's marginal cost is therefore to lower firm 2's equilibrium price, an effect that is undesirable for firm 1.

Thus, the strategic effects of a reduction in firm 1's marginal cost differ between the two models, being beneficial to firm 1 in the quantity model and detrimental in the price model.[30] Which model more accurately captures the nature of competitive interaction depends on the particulars of an industry's situation. For example, if firms in a mature industry have excess capacity, the price model is likely to be more descriptive, and the strategic effect will be detrimental. On the other hand, in a new market where firms are investing in capacity, the strategic effect is likely to be better captured by the quantity model (recall our interpretation of the Cournot model in terms of capacity choices in Section 12.C). ∎

In deciding on its level of investment, firm 1 must therefore consider not only the direct effects of its investment (say, the direct benefit of lower costs), but also the strategic effects that arise through induced changes in its its rival's behavior. Formally, the derivative of firm 1's profits with respect to a change in $k$ can be written as

$$\frac{d\pi_1(s_1^*(k), s_2^*(k), k)}{dk} = \frac{\partial \pi_1(s_1^*(k), s_2^*(k), k)}{\partial k} + \frac{\partial \pi_1(s_1^*(k), s_2^*(k), k)}{\partial s_1} \frac{ds_1^*(k)}{dk}$$

$$+ \frac{\partial \pi_1(s_1^*(k), s_2^*(k), k)}{\partial s_2} \frac{ds_2^*(k)}{dk}.$$

Since at a Nash equilibrium in stage 2 given investment level $k$ we have $\partial \pi_1(s_1^*(k), s_2^*(k), k)/\partial s_1 = 0$, this simplifies to

$$\frac{d\pi_1(s_1^*(k), s_2^*(k), k)}{dk} = \frac{\partial \pi_1(s_1^*(k), s_2^*(k), k)}{\partial k} + \frac{\partial \pi_1(s_1^*(k), s_2^*(k), k)}{\partial s_2} \frac{ds_2^*(k)}{dk}. \quad (12.G.2)$$

The first term on the right-hand side of (12.G.2) is the *direct effect* on firm 1's profits from changing $k$; the second term is the *strategic effect* that arises because of firm 2's equilibrium response to the change in $k$. Since $\partial \pi_1(s_1^*(k), s_2^*(k), k)/\partial s_2 < 0$, the strategic effect on firm 1's profits is positive if $ds_2^*(k)/dk < 0$, that is, if firm 2's response to increases in firm 1's investment is to lower its choice of $s_2$.

---

30. Best-response functions need not always slope this way in the price and quantity models, but the particular examples considered here represent the "normal" cases; see Exercise 12.C.12.

In the above discussion, we have considered situations in which a firm makes a strategic precommitment to affect future competition with another firm who is (or will be) in the market. A particularly striking example of strategic precommitment to affect future market conditions, however, arises when one firm is the first into an industry and seeks to use its first-mover advantage to deter further entry into its market. We can analyze this case formally by introducing a stage between stages 1 and 2, say stage 1.5, at which firm 2 decides whether to be in the market and by supposing that if firm 2 chooses "in" then it must pay a set-up cost $F > 0$. Firm 2 will therefore choose "out" given firm 1's stage 1 choice of $k$ if its anticipated profit in stage 3, $\pi_2(s_1^*(k), s_2^*(k))$, is less than $F$. Given this fact, the incumbent would, of course, like simply to announce that in response to any entry it will engage in predatory pricing (i.e., it will choose a very high level of $s_1$ in stage 3). The problem, however, is that this threat must be *credible* (recall the discussion in Chapter 9). Thus, what the incumbent needs to do to deter entry is choose a level of $k$ that precommits it to sufficiently aggressive behavior that firm 2 chooses not to enter. In any particular problem, this may or may not be possible, and it may or may not be profitable. As a general matter, there are many potential mechanisms (i.e., many types of variables $k$) by which such precommitments can be made. In Appendix B, we examine in some detail the classic mechanism of entry deterrence through capacity expansion first studied by Spence (1977) and Dixit (1980).

## APPENDIX A: INFINITELY REPEATED GAMES AND THE FOLK THEOREM

In this appendix, we extend the discussion in Section 12.D of infinitely repeated games to a more general setting. Our primary aim is to develop a formal statement of a version of the *folk theorem* of infinitely repeated games. Infinitely repeated games have a very rich theoretical structure and we shall only touch on a limited number of their properties. Fudenberg and Tirole (1992) and Osborne and Rubinstein (1994) provide more extended discussions.

### *The Model*

An infinitely repeated game consists of an infinite sequence of repetitions of a one-period simultaneous-move game, known as the *stage game*. For expositional simplicity, we focus here on the case in which there are two players.

In the one-period stage game, each player $i$ has a compact strategy set $S_i$; $q_i \in S_i$ is a particular feasible action for player $i$. Denote $q = (q_1, q_2)$ and $S = S_1 \times S_2$. Player $i$'s payoff function is $\pi_i(q_i, q_j)$. We restrict our attention throughout to pure strategies. It will be convenient to define player $i$'s one-period best-response payoff given that his rival plays $q_j$ by $\hat{\pi}_i(q_j) = \text{Max}_{q \in S_i} \pi_i(q, q_j)$.[31] We assume that the stage game has a unique pure strategy Nash equilibrium $q^* = (q_1^*, q_2^*)$ (the assumption of uniqueness is for expositional simplicity only).

In the infinitely repeated game, actions are taken and payoffs are earned at the beginning of each period. The players discount payoffs with discount factor $\delta < 1$.

---

31. We assume that conditions on the sets $S_i$ and functions $\pi_i(q_i, q_j)$ hold such that this function exists (i.e., such that each player's best response is always well defined).

Players observe each other's action choices in each period and have perfect recall. A pure strategy in this game for player $i$, $s_i$, is a sequence of functions $\{s_{it}(\cdot)\}_{t=1}^{\infty}$ mapping from the history of previous action choices (denoted $H_{t-1}$) to his action choice in period $t$, $s_{it}(H_{t-1}) \in S_i$. The set of all such pure strategies for player $i$ is denoted by $\Sigma_i$, and $s = (s_1, s_2) \in \Sigma_1 \times \Sigma_2$ is a profile of pure strategies for the two players.

Any pure strategy profile $s = (s_1, s_2)$ induces an *outcome path* $Q(s)$, an infinite sequence of actions $\{q_t = (q_{1t}, q_{2t})\}_{t=1}^{\infty}$ that will actually be played when the players follow strategies $s_1$ and $s_2$. Player $i$'s discounted payoff from outcome path $Q$ is given by $v_i(Q) = \sum_{\tau=0}^{\infty} \delta^{\tau} \pi_i(q_{1+\tau})$. We also define player $i$'s *average payoff* from outcome path $Q$ to be $(1 - \delta)v_i(Q)$; this is the per-period payoff that, if infinitely repeated, would give player $i$ a discounted payoff of $v_i(Q)$. Finally, it is also useful to define the discounted continuation payoff from outcome path $Q$ from some period $t$ onward (discounted to period $t$) by $v_i(Q, t) = \sum_{\tau=0}^{\infty} \delta^{\tau} \pi_i(q_{t+\tau})$.

We can note immediately the following fact: The strategies that call for each player $i$ to play his stage game Nash equilibrium action $q_i^*$ in every period, regardless of the prior history of play, constitute an SPNE for *any* value of $\delta < 1$. In the discussion that follows, we are interested in determining to what extent repetition allows other outcomes to emerge as SPNEs.

### Nash Reversion and the Nash Reversion Folk Theorem

We begin by considering strategies with the Nash reversion form that we considered for the Bertrand pricing game in Section 12.D.

**Definition 12.AA.1:** A strategy profile $s = (s_1, s_2)$ in an infinitely repeated game is one of *Nash reversion* if each player's strategy calls for playing some outcome path $Q$ until someone defects and playing the stage game Nash equilibrium $q^* = (q_1^*, q_2^*)$ thereafter.

What outcome paths $Q$ can be supported as outcome paths of an SPNE using Nash reversion strategies? Following logic similar to that discussed in Section 12.D, we can derive the test in Lemma 12.AA.1.

**Lemma 12.AA.1:** A Nash reversion strategy profile that calls for playing outcome path $Q = \{q_{1t}, q_{2t}\}_{t=1}^{\infty}$ prior to any deviation is an SPNE if and only if

$$\hat{\pi}_i(q_{jt}) + \frac{\delta}{1-\delta}\pi_i(q_1^*, q_2^*) \le v_i(Q, t) \qquad (12.AA.1)$$

(where $j \neq i$) for all $t$ and $i = 1, 2$.

**Proof:** As discussed in Section 12.D, the prescribed play after any deviation is a Nash equilibrium in the continuation subgame; so we need only check whether these strategies induce a Nash equilibrium in the subgame starting in any period $t$ when there has been no previous deviation. Note first that if for some $i$ and $t$ condition (12.AA.1) did not hold, then we could not have an SPNE. That is, if no deviation had occurred prior to period $t$, then in the continuation subgame, player $i$ would not find following path $Q$ to be his best response to player $j$'s doing so (in particular, a deviation by player $i$ in period $t$ that maximizes his payoff in that period, followed by his playing $q_i^*$ thereafter, would be superior for him).

In the other direction, suppose that condition (12.AA.1) is satisfied for all $i$ and $t$ but that we do not have an SPNE. Then there must be some period $t$ in which some player $i$ finds it worthwhile to deviate from outcome path $Q$ if no previous deviation has occurred. Now, when his opponent follows a Nash revision strategy, player $i$'s optimal deviation will involve deviating in a manner that maximizes his payoff in period $t$ and then playing $q_i^*$ thereafter. But his payoff from this deviation is exactly that on the left side of condition (12.AA.1), and so this deviation cannot raise his payoff. ■

Condition (12.AA.1) can be written to emphasize the trade-off between one-period gains and future losses as follows:

$$\hat{\pi}_i(q_{jt}) - \pi_i(q_{1t}, q_{2t}) \leq \delta\left(v_i(Q, t+1) - \frac{\pi_i(q_1^*, q_2^*)}{1-\delta}\right) \qquad (12.AA.2)$$

for all $t$ and $i = 1, 2$. The left-hand side of condition (12.AA.2) gives player $i$'s one-period gain from deviating in period $t$, and the right-hand side gives player $i$'s discounted future losses from reversion to the Nash equilibrium starting in period $t + 1$.

For stationary outcome paths of the sort considered in Section 12.D [where each player $i$ takes the same action $q_i$ in every period, so that $Q = (q_1, q_2), (q_1, q_2), \ldots$], the infinite set of inequalities that must be checked in condition (12.AA.2) reduce to just two: infinite repetition of $(q_1, q_2)$ is an outcome path of an SPNE that uses Nash reversion if and only if, for $i = 1$ and 2,

$$\hat{\pi}_i(q_j) - \pi_i(q_1, q_2) \leq \frac{\delta}{1-\delta}[\pi_i(q_1, q_2) - \pi_i(q_1^*, q_2^*)]. \qquad (12.AA.3)$$

How much better than the static Nash equilibrium outcome $q^* = (q_1^*, q_2^*)$ can the players do using Nash reversion? First, under relatively mild conditions (which the Bertrand game considered in Section 12.D does not satisfy), the players can sustain a stationary outcome path that has strictly higher discounted payoffs than does infinite repetition of $q^* = (q_1^*, q_2^*)$ as long as $\delta > 0$. This fact is developed formally in Proposition 12.AA.1.

**Proposition 12.AA.1:** Consider an infinitely repeated game with $\delta > 0$ and $S_i \subset \mathbb{R}$ for $i = 1, 2$. Suppose also that $\pi_i(q)$ is differentiable at $q^* = (q_1^*, q_2^*)$, with $\partial\pi_i(q_i^*, q_j^*)/\partial q_j \neq 0$ for $j \neq i$ and $i = 1, 2$. Then there is some $q' = (q_1', q_2')$, with $[\pi_1(q'), \pi_2(q')] \gg [\pi_1(q^*), \pi_2(q^*)]$ whose infinite repetition is the outcome path of an SPNE that uses Nash reversion.

---

**Proof:** At $q = (q_1^*, q_2^*)$, condition (12.AA.3) holds with equality. Consider a differential change in $q$, $(dq_1, dq_2)$, such that $[\partial\pi_i(q_i^*, q_j^*)/\partial q_j]\, dq_j > 0$ for $i = 1, 2$. The differential change in firm $i$'s profits from this change is

$$d\pi_i(q_i^*, q_j^*) = \frac{\partial\pi_i(q_i^*, q_j^*)}{\partial q_i}\, dq_i + \frac{\partial\pi_i(q_i^*, q_j^*)}{\partial q_j}\, dq_j$$

$$= \frac{\partial\pi_i(q_i^*, q_j^*)}{\partial q_j}\, dq_j, \qquad (12.AA.4)$$

since $q_i^*$ is a best response to $q_j^*$. Thus,

$$d\pi_i(q_i^*, q_j^*) > 0. \qquad (12.AA.5)$$

On the other hand, the envelope theorem (see Section M.L of the Mathematical Appendix) tells us that at any $q_j$

$$d\hat{\pi}_i(q_j) = \frac{\partial \pi_i(b_i(q_j), q_j)}{\partial q_j} dq_j,$$

where $b_i(\cdot)$ is player $i$'s best response to $q_j$ in the stage game. Hence,

$$d\hat{\pi}_i(q_j^*) = \frac{\partial \pi_i(q_i^*, q_j^*)}{\partial q_j} dq_j. \tag{12.AA.6}$$

Together, (12.AA.4) and (12.AA.6) imply that, to first order, the value of the left-hand side of condition (12.AA.3) is unaffected by this change. However, (12.AA.5) implies that the right-hand side of (12.AA.3), to first order, increases. Hence, for a small enough change $(\Delta q_1, \Delta q_2)$ in direction $(dq_1, dq_2)$, infinite repetition of $(q_1 + \Delta q_1, q_2 + \Delta q_2)$ is sustainable as the outcome path of an SPNE using Nash reversion strategies and, by (12.AA.5), yields strictly higher discounted payoffs to the two players than does infinite repetition of $q^* = (q_1^*, q_2^*)$. ∎

Proposition 12.AA.1 tells us that with continuous strategy sets and differentiable payoff functions, as long as there is some possibility for a joint improvement in payoffs around the stage game Nash equilibrium, some cooperation can be sustained.

Going further, examination of condition (12.AA.2) tells us that cooperation becomes easier as $\delta$ grows.

**Proposition 12.AA.2:** Suppose that outcome path $Q$ can be sustained as an SPNE outcome path using Nash reversion when the discount rate is $\delta$. Then it can be so sustained for any $\delta' \geq \delta$.

In fact, as $\delta$ gets very large, a great number of outcomes become sustainable. The result presented in Proposition 12.AA.3, a version of the *Nash reversion folk theorem* [originally due to Friedman (1971)], shows that *any* stationary outcome path that gives each player a discounted payoff that exceeds that arising from infinite repetition of the stage game Nash equilibrium $q^* = (q_1^*, q_2^*)$ can be sustained as an SPNE if $\delta$ is sufficiently close to 1.

**Proposition 12.AA.3:** For any pair of actions $q = (q_1, q_2)$ such that $\pi_i(q_1, q_2) > \pi_i(q_1^*, q_2^*)$ for $i = 1, 2$, there exists a $\underline{\delta} < 1$ such that, for all $\delta > \underline{\delta}$, infinite repetition of $q = (q_1, q_2)$ is the outcome path of an SPNE using Nash reversion strategies.

The proof of Proposition 12.AA.3 follows immediately from condition (12.AA.3) letting $\delta \rightarrow 1$. In fact, with a more sophisticated argument, the logic of Proposition 12.AA.3 can be extended to nonstationary outcome paths. By doing so, it is possible to convexify the set of possible payoffs identified in Proposition 12.AA.3 by alternating between various action pairs $(q_1, q_2)$. In this way, we can support any payoffs in the shaded region of Figure 12.AA.1 as the average payoffs of an SPNE.[32]

**Exercise 12.AA.1:** Argue that no pair of actions $q$ such that $\pi_i(q_1, q_2) < \pi_i(q_1^*, q_2^*)$ for some $i$ can be sustained as a stationary SPNE outcome path using Nash reversion.

*More Severe Punishments and the Folk Theorem*

It is intuitively clear that, for a given level of $\delta < 1$, the more severe the punishments that can be credibly threatened in response to a deviation, the easier it is to prevent

---

32. See Fudenberg and Maskin (1991) for details.

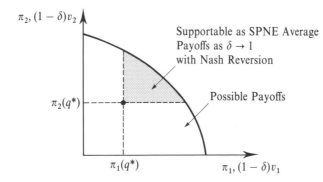

**Figure 12.AA.1**
The Nash reversion folk theorem.

players from deviating from any given outcome path. In general, Nash reversion is not the most severe credible punishment that is possible. Just as players can be induced to cooperate through the use of threatened punishments, they can also be induced to punish each other.

To consider this issue, it is useful to let $\underline{\pi}_i = \text{Min}_{q_j}[\text{Max}_{q_i} \pi_i(q_i, q_j)]$ denote player $i$'s *minimax payoff*.[33] Payoff $\underline{\pi}_i$ is the lowest payoff that player $i$'s rival can hold him to in the stage game if player $i$ anticipates the action that his rival will play. Note, first, that player $i$'s payoff in the stage game Nash equilibrium $q^* = (q_1^*, q_2^*)$ cannot be below $\underline{\pi}_i$. More importantly, regardless of the strategies played by his rival, player $i$'s average payoff in the infinitely repeated game or in any subgame within it cannot be below $\underline{\pi}_i$. Thus, no punishment following a deviation can give player $i$ an average payoff below $\underline{\pi}_i$. Payoffs that strictly exceed $\underline{\pi}_i$ for each player $i$ are known as *individually rational payoffs*.

Note that for a punishment to be credible we must be sure that after an initial deviation occurs and the punishment is called for, no player wants to deviate from the prescribed punishment path. This means that a punishment is credible if and only if it itself constitutes an SPNE outcome path. Proposition 12.AA.4 tells us that as long as $\delta > 0$ and conditions similar to those in Proposition 12.AA.1 hold, SPNEs that yield more severe punishments than Nash reversion can be constructed whenever each player $i$'s stage game Nash equilibrium payoff strictly exceeds $\underline{\pi}_i$. (You are asked to prove this result in Exercise 12.AA.2.)

**Proposition 12.AA.4:** Consider an infinitely repeated game with $\delta > 0$ and $S_i \subset \mathbb{R}$ for $i = 1, 2$. Suppose also that $\pi_i(q)$ is differentiable at $q^* = (q_1^*, q_2^*)$, with $\partial\pi_i(q_i^*, q_j^*)/\partial q_j \neq 0$ for $j \neq i$ and $i = 1, 2$, and that $\pi_i(q_1^*, q_2^*) > \underline{\pi}_i$ for $i = 1, 2$. Then there is some SPNE with discounted payoffs to the two players of $(v_1', v_2')$ such that $(1 - \delta)v_i' < \pi_i(q_1^*, q_2^*)$ for $i = 1, 2$.

Under the conditions of Proposition 12.AA.4, for any $\delta \in (0, 1)$, more severe punishments than Nash reversion can credibly be threatened. We should therefore expect that more cooperative outcomes can be sustained than those sustainable through the threat of Nash reversion whenever a fully cooperative outcome is not already achievable using Nash reversion strategies.

---

33. In general, a player's minimax payoff will be lower if mixed strategies are allowed. In this case, the statement of the folk theorem given in Proposition 12.AA.5 remains unchanged, but with these (potentially) lower levels of $\underline{\pi}_i$.

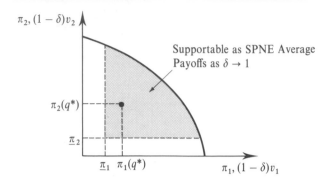

**Figure 12.AA.2**
The folk theorem.

For arbitrary $\delta < 1$, constructing the full set of SPNEs is a delicate process. Each SPNE, whether collusive or punishing, uses other SPNEs as threatened punishments. For details on how this is done, see the original contributions by Abreu (1986) and (1988) and the presentation in Fudenberg and Tirole (1992). As with SPNEs using Nash reversion strategies, the full set of SPNEs grows as $\delta$ increases, making possible both more cooperation and more severe punishments. In fact, the result presented in Proposition 12.AA.5, known as the *folk theorem*, tells us that *any* feasible individually rational payoffs can be supported as the average payoffs in an SPNE as long as players discount the future to a sufficiently small degree.[34] (Feasibility simply means that there is some outcome path $Q$ that generates these average payoffs.)

**Proposition 12.AA.5:** (*The Folk Theorem*)  For any feasible pair of individually rational payoffs $(\pi_1, \pi_2) \gg (\underline{\pi}_1, \underline{\pi}_2)$, there exists a $\underline{\delta} < 1$ such that, for all $\delta > \underline{\delta}$, $(\pi_1, \pi_2)$ are the average payoffs arising in an SPNE.

In comparison with Proposition 12.AA.3, Proposition 12.AA.5 tells us that as $\delta \to 1$ we can support any average payoffs that exceed each player's minimax payoff.[35] This limiting set of SPNE average payoffs is shown in Figure 12.AA.2.

Example 12.AA.1 gives some idea of how this can be done.

**Example 12.AA.1:** *Sustaining an Average Payoff of Zero in the Infinitely Repeated Cournot Game.*  In this example, we construct an SPNE in which both firms earn an average payoff of zero in an infinitely repeated Cournot game. In particular, let the stage game be a symmetric Cournot duopoly game with cost function $c(q) = cq$, where $c > 0$, and a continuous inverse demand function $p(\cdot)$ such that $p(x) \to 0$ as $x \to \infty$. It will be convenient to write a firm's profit when both firms choose quantity $q$ as $\pi(q) = [p(2q) - c]q$ and, as before, a firm's best-response profits when its rival

34. The theorem's name refers to the fact that some version of the result was known in game theory "folk wisdom" well before its formal appearance in the literature. See Fudenberg and Maskin (1986) and (1991) for a proof of the result. When there are more than two players, the result requires that the set of feasible payoffs satisfy an additional "dimensionality" condition. The original appearances of the result in the literature actually analyzed infinitely repeated games *without* discounting [see, for example, Rubinstein (1979)].

35. We may also be able in some cases to give each player exactly his minimax payoff. This is the case, for example, in the repeated Bertrand game, where the stage game's Nash equilibrium yields the minimax payoffs. In Example 12.AA.1, we show that we can also do this for large enough $\delta$ in the repeated Cournot duopoly game.

chooses quantity $q$ as $\hat{\pi}(q)$.[36] Note that $\underline{\pi}_j = 0$ for $j = 1, 2$ here; if firm $j$'s rival chooses a quantity at least as large as the competitive quantity $q_c$ satisfying $p(q_c) = c$, then the best firm $j$ can do is to produce nothing and earn zero, and firm $j$ can never be forced to a payoff worse than zero.

Consider strategies for the players that take the following form:

(i) Both firms play quantity $\tilde{q}$ in period 1 followed by the monopoly quantity $q^m$ in every period $t > 1$ as long as no one deviates, where quantity $\tilde{q}$ satisfies

$$\pi(\tilde{q}) + \frac{\delta}{1 - \delta} \pi(q^m) = 0. \tag{12.AA.7}$$

(ii) If anyone deviates when $\tilde{q}$ is meant to be played, the outcome path described in (i) is restarted.

(iii) If anyone deviates when $q^m$ is meant to be played, Nash reversion occurs.

Note that the outcome path described in (i), if followed by both players, gives both players an average payoff of zero by construction [recall (12.AA.7)].

By Proposition 12.AA.3, we know that for some $\underline{\delta} < 1$ we can sustain infinite repetition of $q^m$ through Nash reversion for all $\delta > \underline{\delta}$. Thus, for $\delta > \underline{\delta}$, neither firm will deviate from the above strategies when $q^m$ is supposed to be played. Will they deviate when $\tilde{q}$ is supposed to be played? Consider firm $j$'s payoff from deviating from $\tilde{q}$ in a single period and conforming with the prescribed strategy thereafter. Firm $j$ earns $\hat{\pi}(\tilde{q}) + (\delta)(0)$ because it plays a best response when deviating, and then the original path is restarted. Thus, this deviation does not improve firm $j$'s payoff if $\hat{\pi}(\tilde{q}) = 0$ (it cannot be less than zero because $\underline{\pi}_i = 0$). This is so if $\tilde{q} \geq q_c$. But examining condition (12.AA.7), we see that as $\delta$ approaches 1, $\pi(\tilde{q})$ must get increasingly negative for (12.AA.7) to hold and, in particular, that there exists a $\delta_c < 1$ such that $\tilde{q}$ will exceed $q_c$ for all $\delta > \delta_c$. Thus, for $\delta > \text{Max}\{\delta_c, \underline{\delta}\}$, these strategies constitute an SPNE that gives both firms an average payoff of 0.[37] ∎

## APPENDIX B: STRATEGIC ENTRY DETERRENCE AND ACCOMMODATION

In this appendix, we discuss an important example of credible precommitments to affect future market conditions in which an incumbent firm engages in pre-entry capacity expansion to gain a strategic advantage over a potential entrant and possibly to deter this firm's entry altogether [the original analyses of this issue are due to Spence (1977) and Dixit (1980)]. In what follows, we study the following three-stage game that is adapted from Dixit (1980).

---

36. We can make the strategy sets compact by noting that in no period will any firm ever choose a quantity larger than the level $\bar{q}$ such that $\pi(\bar{q}) + [\delta/(1 - \delta)](\text{Max}_q \pi(q)) = 0$, because it would do better setting its quantity equal to zero forever. Then, without loss, we can let each firm choose its output from the compact set $[0, \bar{q}]$.

37. We have not considered any multiperiod deviations, but it can be shown that if no single-period deviation followed by conformity with the strategies is worthwhile, then neither is any multiperiod deviation (this is a general principle of dynamic programming).

*Stage* 1: An incumbent, firm I, chooses the capacity level of its plant, denoted by $k_I$. Capacity costs $r$ per unit.

*Stage* 2: A potential entrant, firm E, decides whether to enter the market. If it does, it pays an entry cost of $F$.

*Stage* 3: If firm E enters, the two firms choose their output levels, $q_I$ and $q_E$, simultaneously. The resulting price is $p(q_I + q_E)$. For firm E, output costs $(w + r)$ per unit: for each unit of output produced, firm E incurs both a capacity cost of $r$ and a labor cost of $w$. For firm I, production must not exceed its previously chosen capacity level. Its production cost, however, is only $w$ per unit because it has already built its capacity. If, on the other hand, firm E does not enter, then firm $I$ acts as a monopolist who can produce up to $k_I$ units of output at cost $w$ per unit.

To determine the subgame perfect Nash equilibrium (SPNE) of this game, we begin by analyzing behavior in the stage 3 subgames and then work backward.

### Stage 3: Quantity Competition

The subgames in stage 3 are distinguished by two previous events: whether firm E has entered and the previous capacity choice of firm I. We first consider the outcome of stage 3 competition following entry and then discuss firm I's behavior in stage 3 if entry does not occur. For simplicity, we assume throughout that firms' profit functions are strictly concave in own quantity; a sufficient condition for this is for $p(\cdot)$ to be concave. The concavity of $p(\cdot)$ also implies that firms' best-response functions are downward sloping.

*Stage 3 competition after entry.* Figure 12.BB.1 depicts firm E's best-response function in stage 3, which we denote by $b(q|w + r)$ to emphasize that it is the best-response function for a firm with marginal cost $w + r$. Firm E's stage 3 profits decline as we move along this curve to the right (involving higher levels of $q_I$) and, at some point, denoted $Z$ in the figure, they fall below the entry cost $F$.

Now consider firm I's optimal behavior. The key difference between firm I and firm E is that firm I has already built its capacity. Hence, firm I's expenditure on this capacity is sunk (it cannot recover it by reducing its capacity), its capacity level is fixed, and its marginal cost is only $w$. Suppose we let $b(q|w)$ denote the best-response function of a firm with marginal cost $w$. Then firm $I$'s best-response function in stage 3 is

$$b_I(q_E|k_I) = \mathrm{Min}\{b(q_E|w), k_I\}.$$

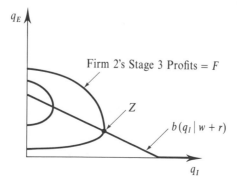

**Figure 12.BB.1**

Firm E's stage 3 best-response function after entry.

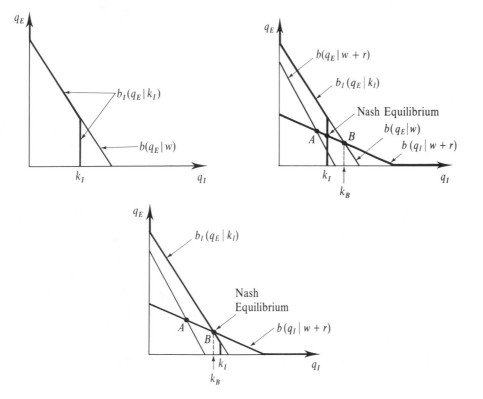

**Figure 12.BB.2 (left)**

Firm I's stage 3 best-response function after entry.

**Figure 12.BB.3 (right)**

Stage 3 Nash equilibrium after entry.

**Figure 12.BB.4**

A stage 3 equilibrium in which firm I does not use all of its capacity.

That is, firm $I$'s best response to an output choice of $q_E$ by firm E is the same as that for a firm with marginal cost level $w$ as long as this output level does not exceed its previously chosen capacity. Figure 12.BB.2 illustrates firm I's best-response function.

We can now put together the best-response functions for the two firms to determine the equilibrium in stage 3 following firm E's decision to enter, for any given level of $k_I$. This equilibrium is shown in Figure 12.BB.3.

In Figure 12.BB.3, point $A$ is the outcome that would arise if there were no first-mover advantage for firm I, that is, if the two firms chose both their capacity and output levels simultaneously. However, when firm I is able to choose its capacity level first, by choosing an appropriate level of $k_I$, it can get the post-entry equilibrium to lie anywhere on firm E's best-response function up to point $B$. Firm I is able to induce points to the right of point $A$ because its ability to incur its capacity costs prior to stage 3 competition allows it to have a marginal cost in stage 3 of only $w$, rather than $w + r$. Note, however, that firm I cannot induce a point on firm 2's best-response function beyond point $B$, even though it might want to; if it built a capacity greater than level $k_B$, it would not have an incentive to actually use all of it. Figure 12.BB.4 depicts this situation. A threat to produce up to capacity following entry would in this case not be credible.

*Stage 3 outcomes if firm E does not enter.* If firm E decides not to enter, then firm I will be a monopolist in stage 3. Its optimal monopoly output is then the point where its best-response function hits the $q_E = 0$ axis, $b_I(0|k_I)$.

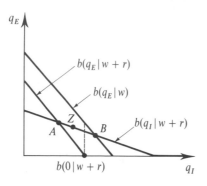

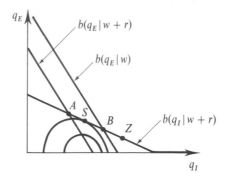

**Figure 12.BB.5 (left)**
Blockaded entry.

**Figure 12.BB.6 (right)**
Strategic entry accommodation when entry is inevitable.

*Stage 2: Firm E's Entry Decision*

Firm E's entry decision is straightforward: Given the level of capacity $k_I$ chosen by firm I in stage 1, firm E will enter if it expects nonnegative profits net of its entry cost F. This means that firm E will enter when it expects that the post-entry equilibrium will lie to the left of point Z on its best-response function in Figure 12.BB.1.

*Stage 1: Firm I's Stage 1 Capacity Investment*

Now consider firm I's optimal capacity choice in stage 1. There are three situations in which firm I could find itself: Entry could be blockaded, entry could be inevitable, or entry deterrence could be possible but not inevitable. Let us consider each in turn.

*Entry is blockaded.* One possibility is that the entry cost F is large enough that firm E does not find it worthwhile to enter even if firm I ignores the possibility of entry and simply builds the same capacity that it would if it were an uncontested monopolist, $b(0 | w + r)$. This situation, in which we say that *entry is blockaded*, is shown in Figure 12.BB.5. In this case, firm I achieves its best possible outcome: it builds a capacity of $b(0 | w + r)$, no entry occurs, and then it sells $b(0 | w + r)$ units of output.

*Entry deterrence is impossible: strategic entry accommodation.* Suppose that point Z is to the right of point B. In this case, entry deterrence is impossible; firm E will find it profitable to enter regardless of $k_I$. What is firm I's optimal choice of $k_I$ in this case? In Figure 12.BB.6, we have drawn isoprofit curves for firm I; note that because these include the cost of capacity, they are the isoprofit curves corresponding to those of a firm with marginal cost $(w + r)$. Now recall that firm I can induce any point on firm E's best-response function up to point B through an appropriate choice of capacity. It will choose the point that maximizes its profit. In Figure 12.BB.6, this point, which involves a tangency between firm E's best-response function and firm I's isoprofit curves, is denoted as point S. This outcome corresponds to exactly the outcome that would emerge in a model of sequential quantity choice, known as a *Stackleberg leadership model* (see Exercise 12.C.18). Note that firm I's first-mover advantage allows it to earn higher profits than the otherwise identical firm E.

The point of tangency, S, could also lie to the right of point B. In this case, the optimal capacity choice will be $k_I = k_B$, and the outcome will not be as desirable for firm I as the Stackleberg point. Here firm I is unable to credibly

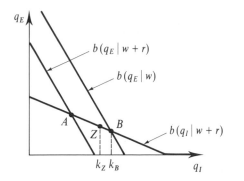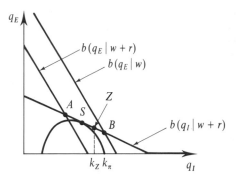

**Figure 12.BB.7 (left)**
Entry deterrence is possible but not inevitable.

**Figure 12.BB.8 (right)**
Entry deterrence versus entry accommodation.

commit to produce the output associated with point $S$, even if it builds sufficient capacity in stage 1.

*Entry deterrence is possible but not inevitable.* Suppose now that point $Z$ lies to the left of point $B$ but not so far that entry is blockaded, as shown in Figure 12.BB.7. Firm I can deter firm E's entry by picking a capacity level at least as large as point $k_Z$ in the figure. The only question is whether this will be optimal for firm I, or whether firm I is better off accommodating firm E's entry. To judge this, firm I will compare its profits at point $(k_Z, 0)$ to those at point $S$ (or at point $B$ if point $S$ lies to the right of $B$). This can be done by comparing the capacity level $k_\pi$ in Figure 12.BB.8, the output level under monopoly that gives the same profit as the optimal accommodation point $S$, with $k_Z$. If $k_\pi > k_Z$, then firm I prefers to deter entry because its profits are higher in this case; but if $k_\pi < k_Z$, then it will prefer accommodation. Note that if deterrence is optimal, then even though entry does not occur its *threat* nevertheless has an effect on the market outcome, raising the level of output and welfare relative to a situation in which no entry is possible.

**Exercise 12.BB.1:** Show that when entry deterrence is possible but not inevitable, if point $S$ lies to the right of point $Z$, then entry deterrence is better than entry accommodation.

## REFERENCES

Abreu, D. (1986). Extremal equilibria of oligopolistic supergames. *Journal of Economic Theory* **39**: 191–225.

Abreu, D. (1988). On the theory of infinitely repeated games with discounting. *Econometrica* **56**: 383–96.

Abreu, D., D. Pearce, and E. Stachetti. (1990). Toward a theory of discounted repeated games with imperfect monitoring. *Econometrica* **58**: 1041–64.

Baumol, W., J. Panzar, and R. Willig. (1982). *Contestable Markets and the Theory of Industry Structure*. San Diego: Harcourt, Brace, Jovanovich.

Bertrand, J. (1883). Théorie mathématique de la richesse sociale. *Journal des Savants* **67**: 499–508.

Bulow, J., J. Geanakoplos, and P. Klemperer. (1985). Multimarket oligopoly: strategic substitutes and complements. *Journal of Political Economy* **93**: 488–511.

Chamberlin, E. (1933). *The Theory of Monopolistic Competition*. Cambridge, Mass.: Harvard University Press.

Cournot, A. (1838). *Recherches sur les Principes Mathématiques de la Théorie des Richesses.* [English edition: *Researches into the Mathematical Principles of the Theory of Wealth*, edited by N. Bacon. London: Macmillan, 1897.]

Dixit, A. (1980). The role of investment in entry deterrence. *Economic Journal* **90**: 95–106.

Dixit, A., and J. E. Stiglitz. (1977). Monopolistic competition and optimal product diversity. *American Economic Review* **67**: 297–308.

Edgeworth, F. (1897). Me teoria pura del monopolio. *Giornale degli Economisti* **40**: 13–31. [English translation: The pure theory of monopoly. In *Papers Relating to Political Economy*, Vol. I, edited by F. Edgeworth. London: Macmillan, 1925.]

Friedman, J. (1971). A non-cooperative equilibrium for supergames. *Review of Economic Studies* **28**: 1–12.

Fudenberg, D., and E. Maskin. (1986). The folk theorem in repeated games with discounting or with incomplete information. *Econometrica* **52**: 533–54.

Fudenberg, D., and E. Maskin. (1991). On the dispensibility of public randomizaton in discounted repeated games. *Journal of Economic Theory* **53**: 428–38.

Fudenberg, D., and J. Tirole. (1984). The fat cat effect, the puppy dog ploy, and the lean and hungry look. *American Economic Review, Papers and Proceedings* **74**: 361–68.

Fudenberg, D., and J. Tirole. (1992). *Game Theory.* Cambridge, Mass.: MIT Press.

Green, E., and R. Porter. (1984). Noncooperative collusion under imperfect price information. *Econometrica* **52**: 87–100.

Hart, O. D. (1985). Monopolistic competition in the spirit of Chamberlin: A general model. *Review of Economic Studies* **52**: 529–46.

Kreps, D. M., and J. Scheinkman. (1983). Quantity precommitment and Bertrand competition yield Cournot outcomes. *Rand Journal of Economics* **14**: 326–37.

Mankiw, N. G., and M. D. Whinston. (1986). Free entry and social inefficiency. *Rand Journal of Economics* **17**: 48–58.

Osborne, M. J., and A. Rubinstein. (1994). *A Course in Game Theory.* Cambridge, Mass.: MIT Press.

Rotemberg, J., and G. Saloner. (1986). A supergame-theoretic model of business cycles and price wars during booms. *American Economic Review* **76**: 390–407.

Rubinstein, A. (1979). Equilibrium in supergames with the overtaking criterion. *Journal of Economic Theory* **21**: 1–9.

Salop, S. (1979). Monopolistic competition with outside goods. *Bell Journal of Economics* **10**: 141–56.

Shapiro, C. (1989). Theories of oligopoly behavior. In *Handbook of Industrial Organization*, edited by R. Schmalensee and R. D. Willig. Amsterdam: North-Holland.

Spence, A. M. (1976). Product selection, fixed costs, and monopolistic competition. *Review of Economic Studies* **43**: 217–35.

Spence, A. M. (1977). Entry, capacity investment, and oligopolistic pricing. *Bell Journal of Economics* **8**: 534–44.

Stigler, G. (1960). A theory of oligopoly. *Journal of Political Economy* **72**: 44–61.

Tirole, J. (1988). *The Theory of Industrial Organization.* Cambridge, Mass.: MIT Press.

## EXERCISES

**12.B.1**[A] The expression $[p^m - c'(q^m)]/p^m$, where $p^m$ and $q^m$ are the monopolist's price and output level, respectively, is known as the monopolist's *price–cost margin* (or as the *Lerner index of monopoly power*). It measures the distortion of the monopolist's price above its marginal cost as a proportion of its price.

**(a)** Show the monopolist's price–cost margin is always equal to the inverse of the price elasticity of demand at price $p^m$.

**(b)** Also argue that if the monopolist's marginal cost is positive at every output level, then demand must be *elastic* (i.e., the price elasticity of demand is greater than 1) at the monopolist's optimal price.

**12.B.2$^B$** Consider a monopolist with cost function $c(q) = cq$, with $c > 0$, facing demand function $x(p) = \alpha p^{-\varepsilon}$, where $\varepsilon > 0$.

**(a)** Show that if $\varepsilon \le 1$, then the monopolist's optimal price is not well defined.

**(b)** Assume that $\varepsilon > 1$. Derive the monopolist's optimal price, quantity, and price–cost margin $(p^m - c)/p^m$. Calculate the resulting deadweight welfare loss.

**(c)** (Harder) Consider a sequence of demand functions that differ in their levels of $\varepsilon$ and $\alpha$ but that all involve the same competitive quantity $x(c)$ [i.e., for each level of $\varepsilon$, $\alpha$ is adjusted to keep $x(c)$ the same]. How does the deadweight loss vary with $\varepsilon$? (If you cannot derive an analytic answer, try calculating some values on a computer.)

**12.B.3$^B$** Suppose that we consider a monopolist facing demand function $x(p, \theta)$ with cost function $c(q, \phi)$, where $\theta$ and $\phi$ are parameters. Use the implicit function theorem to compute the changes in the monopolist's price and quantity as a function of a differential change in either $\theta$ or $\phi$. When will each lead to a price increase?

**12.B.4$^B$** Consider a monopolist with a cost of $c$ per unit. Use a "revealed preference" proof to show that the monopoly price is nondecreasing in $c$. Then extend your argument to the case in which the monopolist's cost function is $c(q, \phi)$, with $[c(q'', \phi) - c(q', \phi)]$ increasing in $\phi$ for all $q'' > q'$, by showing that the monopoly price is nondecreasing in $\phi$. (If you did Exercise 12.B.3, also relate this condition to the one you derived there.)

**12.B.5$^B$** Suppose that a monopolist faces many consumers. Argue that in each of the following two cases, the monopolist can do no better than it does by restricting itself to simply charging a price per unit, say $p$.

**(a)** Suppose that each consumer $i$ wants either one or no units of the monopolist's good and that the monopolist is unable to discern any particular consumer's preferences.

**(b)** Suppose that consumers may desire to consume multiple units of the good. The monopolist cannot discern any particular consumer's preferences. In addition, resale of the good is costless and after the monopolist has made its sales to consumers a competitive market develops among consumers for the good.

**12.B.6$^A$** Suppose that the government can tax or subsidize a monopolist who faces inverse demand function $p(q)$ and has cost function $c(q)$ [assume both are differentiable and that $p(q)q - c(q)$ is concave in $q$]. What tax or subsidy per unit of output would lead the monopolist to act efficiently?

**12.B.7$^B$** Consider the widget market. The total demand by men for widgets is given by $x_m(p) = a - \theta_m p$, and the total demand by women is given by $x_w(p) = a - \theta_w p$, where $\theta_w < \theta_m$. The cost of production is $c$ per widget.

**(a)** Suppose the widget market is competitive. Find the equilibrium price and quantity sold.

**(b)** Suppose, instead, that firm A is a monopolist of widgets [also make this assumption in **(c)** and **(d)**]. If firm A is prohibited from "discriminating" (i.e., charging different prices to men and women), what is its profit-maximizing price? Under what conditions do both men and women consume a positive level of widgets in this solution?

**(c)** If firm A has produced some total level of output $X$, what is the welfare-maximizing way to distribute it between the men and the women? (Assume here and below that Marshallian aggregrate surplus is a valid measure of welfare.)

**(d)** Suppose that firm A is allowed to discriminate. What prices does it charge? In the case where the nondiscriminatory solution in **(b)** has positive consumption of widgets by both men and women, does aggregate welfare as measured by the Marshallian aggregate surplus rise or fall relative to when discrimination is allowed? Relate your conclusion to your answer in (c). What if the nondiscriminatory solution in (b) has only one type of consumers being served?

**12.B.8**[B] Consider the following two-period model: A firm is a monopolist in a market with an inverse demand function (in each period) of $p(q) = a - bq$. The cost per unit in period 1 is $c_1$. In period 2, however, the monopolist has "learned by doing," and so its constant cost per unit of output is $c_2 = c_1 - mq_1$, where $q_1$ is the monopolist's period 1 output level. Assume $a > c$ and $b > m$. Also assume that the monopolist does not discount future earnings.

(a) What is the monopolist's level of output in each of the periods?

(b) What outcome would be implemented by a benevolent social planner who fully controlled the monopolist? Is there any sense in which the planner's period 1 output is selected so that "price equals marginal cost"?

(c) Given that the monopolist will be selecting the period 2 output level, would the planner like the monopolist to slightly increase the level of period 1 output above that identified in (a)? Can you give any intuition for this?

**12.B.9**[C] Consider a situation in which there is a monopolist in a market with inverse demand function $p(q)$. The monopolist makes two choices: How much to invest in cost reduction, $I$, and how much to sell, $q$. If the monopolist invests $I$ in cost reduction, his (constant) per-unit cost of production is $c(I)$. Assume that $c'(I) < 0$ and that $c''(I) > 0$. Assume throughout that the monopolist's objective function is concave in $q$ and $I$.

(a) Derive the first-order conditions for the monopolist's choices.

(b) Compare the monopolist's choices with those of a benevolent social planner who can control both $q$ and $I$ (a "first-best" comparison).

(c) Compare the monopolist's choices with those of a benevolent social planner who can control $I$ but not $q$ (a "second-best" comparison). Suppose that the planner chooses $I$ and then the monopolist chooses $q$.

**12.B.10**[B] Consider a monopolist that can choose both its product's price $p$ and its quality $q$. The demand for its product is given by $x(p, q)$, which is increasing in $q$ and decreasing in $p$. Given the price chosen by the monopolist, does the monopolist choose the socially efficient quality level?

**12.C.1**[A] In text.

**12.C.2**[C] Extend the argument of Proposition 12.C.1 to show that under the assumptions made in the text [in particular, the assumption that there is a price $\bar{p} < \infty$ such that $x(p) = 0$ for all $p \geq \bar{p}$], both firms setting their price equal to $c$ with certainty is the unique Nash equilibrium of the Bertrand duopoly model even when we allow for mixed strategies.

**12.C.3**[B] Note that the unique Nash equilibrium of the Bertrand duopoly model has each firm playing a weakly dominated strategy. Consider an alteration of the model in which prices must be named in some discrete unit of account (e.g., pennies) of size $\Delta$.

(a) Show that both firms naming prices equal to the smallest multiple of $\Delta$ that is strictly greater than $c$ is a pure strategy equilibrium of this game. Argue that it does not involve either firm playing a weakly dominated strategy.

(b) Argue that as $\Delta \to 0$, this equilibrium converges to both firms charging prices equal to $c$.

**12.C.4**[B] Consider altering the Bertrand duopoly model to a case in which each firm $j$'s cost per unit is $c_j$ and $c_1 < c_2$.

(a) What are the pure strategy Nash equilibria of this game?

**(b)** Examine a model in which prices must be named in discrete units, as in Exercise 12.C.3. What are the pure strategy Nash equilibria of such a game? Which do not involve the play of weakly dominated strategies? As the grid becomes finer, what is the limit of these equilibria in undominated strategies?

**12.C.5$^B$** Suppose that we have a market with $I$ buyers, each of whom wants at most one unit of the good. Buyer $i$ is willing to pay up to $v_i$ for his unit, and $v_1 > v_2 > \cdots > v_I$. There are a total of $q < I$ units available. Suppose that buyers simultaneously submit bids for a unit of the output and that the output goes to the $q$ highest bidders, who pay the amounts of their bids. Show that every buyer making a bid of $v_{q+1}$ and the good being assigned to buyers $1, \ldots, q$ is a Nash equilibrium of this game. Argue that this is a competitive equilibrium price. Also show that in *any* pure strategy Nash equilibrium of this game, buyers 1 through $q$ receive a unit and buyers $q + 1$ through $I$ do not.

**12.C.6$^A$** In text.

**12.C.7$^B$** In text.

**12.C.8$^C$** Consider a homogeneous-good $J$-firm Cournot model in which the demand function $x(p)$ is downward sloping but otherwise arbitrary. The firms all have an identical cost function $c(q)$ that is increasing in $q$ and convex. Denote by $Q$ the aggregate output of the $J$ firms, and let $Q_{-j} = \sum_{k \ne j} q_k$.

**(a)** Show that firm j's best response can be written as $b(Q_{-j})$.

**(b)** Show that $b(Q_{-j})$ need not be unique (i.e., that it is in general a correspondence, not a function).

**(c)** Show that if $\hat{Q}_{-j} > Q_{-j}, q_j \in b(Q_{-j})$, and $\hat{q}_j \in b(\hat{Q}_{-j})$, then $(\hat{q}_j + \hat{Q}_{-j}) \ge (q_j + Q_{-j})$. Deduce from this that $b(\cdot)$ can jump only upward and that $b'(Q_{-j}) \ge -1$ whenever this derivative is defined.

**(d)** Use you result in **(c)** to prove that a symmetric pure strategy Nash equilibrium exists in this model.

**(e)** Show that multiple equilibria are possible.

**(f)** Give sufficient conditions (they are very weak) for the symmetric equilibrium to be the only equilibrium in pure strategies.

**12.C.9$^B$** Consider a two-firm Cournot model with constant returns to scale but in which firms' costs may differ. Let $c_j$ denote firm $j$'s cost per unit of output produced, and assume that $c_1 > c_2$. Assume also that the inverse demand function is $p(q) = a - bq$, with $a > c_1$.

**(a)** Derive the Nash equilibrium of this model. Under what conditions does it involve only one firm producing? Which will this be?

**(b)** When the equilibrium involves both firms producing, how do equilibrium outputs and profits vary when firm 1's cost changes?

**(c)** Now consider the general case of $J$ firms. Show that the ratio of industry profits divided by industry revenue in any (pure strategy) Nash equilibrium is exactly $H/\varepsilon$, where $\varepsilon$ is the elasticity of the market demand curve at the equilibrium price and $H$, the *Herfindahl index of concentration*, is equal to the sum of the firms' squared market shares $\sum_j (q_j^*/Q^*)^2$. (*Note:* This result depends on the assumption of constant returns to scale.)

**12.C.10$^B$** Consider a $J$-firm Cournot model in which firms' costs differ. Let $c_j(q_j) = \alpha_j \tilde{c}(q_j)$ denote firm $j$'s cost function, and assume that $\tilde{c}(\cdot)$ is strictly increasing and convex. Assume that $\alpha_1 > \cdots > \alpha_J$.

**(a)** Show that if more than one firm is making positive sales in a Nash equilibrium of this model, then we cannot have productive efficiency; that is, the equilibrium aggregate output $Q^*$ is produced inefficiently.

**(b)** If so, what is the correct measure of welfare loss relative to a fully efficient (competitive) outcome? [*Hint:* Reconsider the discussion in Section 10.E.]

**(c)** Provide an example in which welfare decreases when a firm becomes more productive (i.e., when $\alpha_j$ falls for some $j$). [*Hint:* Consider an improvement in cost for firm 1 in the model of Exercise 12.C.9.] Why can this happen?

**12.C.11$^C$** Consider a capacity-constrained duopoly pricing game. Firm $j$'s capacity is $q_j$ for $j = 1, 2$, and it has a constant cost per unit of output of $c \geq 0$ up to this capacity limit. Assume that the market demand function $x(p)$ is continuous and strictly decreasing at all $p$ such that $x(p) > 0$ and that there exists a price $\tilde{p}$ such that $x(\tilde{p}) = q_1 + q_2$. Suppose also that $x(p)$ is concave. Let $p(\cdot) = x^{-1}(\cdot)$ denote the inverse demand function.

Given a pair of prices charged, sales are determined as follows: consumers try to buy at the low-priced firm first. If demand exceeds this firm's capacity, consumers are served in order of their valuations, starting with high-valuation consumers. If prices are the same, demand is split evenly unless one firm's demand exceeds its capacity, in which case the extra demand spills over to the other firm. Formally, the firms' sales are given by the functions $x_1(p_1, p_2)$ and $x_2(p_1, p_2)$ satisfying [$x_i(\cdot)$ gives the amount firm $i$ sells taking account of its capacity limitation in fulfilling demand]

$$\text{If } p_j > p_i: \quad x_i(p_1, p_2) = \text{Min}\{q_i, x(p_i)\}$$
$$x_j(p_1, p_2) = \text{Min}\{q_j, \text{Max}\{x(p_j) - q_i, 0\}\}$$
$$\text{If } p_2 = p_1 = p: \; x_i(p_1, p_2) = \text{Min}\{q_i, \text{Max}\{x(p)/2, x(p) - q_j\}\} \quad \text{for } i = 1, 2.$$

**(a)** Suppose that $q_1 < b_c(q_2)$ and $q_2 < b_c(q_1)$, where $b_c(\cdot)$ is the best-response function for a firm with constant marginal costs of $c$. Show that $p_1^* = p_2^* = p(q_1 + q_2)$ is a Nash equilibrium of this game.

**(b)** Argue that if either $q_1 > b_c(q_2)$ or $q_2 > b_c(q_1)$, then no pure strategy Nash equilibrium exists.

**12.C.12$^B$** Consider two strictly concave and differentiable profit functions $\pi_j(q_j, q_k), j = 1, 2$, defined on $q_j \in [0, q]$.

**(a)** Give sufficient conditions for the best-response functions $b_j(q_j)$ to be increasing or decreasing.

**(b)** Specialize to the Cournot model. Argue that a decreasing (downward-sloping) best-response function is the "normal" case.

**12.C.13$^B$** Show that when $v > c + 3t$ in the linear city model discussed in Example 12.C.2, a firm $j$'s best response to any price of its rival $p_{-j}$ always results in all consumers purchasing from one of the two firms.

**12.C.14$^C$** Consider the linear city model discussed in Example 12.C.2.

**(a)** Derive the best-response functions when $v \in (c + 2t, c + 3t)$. Show that the unique Nash equilibrium in this case is $p_1^* = p_2^* = c + t$.

**(b)** Repeat **(a)** for the case in which $v \in (c + \frac{3}{2}t, c + 2t)$.

**(c)** Show that when $v < c + t$, the unique Nash equilibrium involves prices of $p_1^* = p_2^* = (v + c)/2$ and some consumers not purchasing from either firm.

**(d)** Show that when $v \in (c + t, c + \frac{3}{2}t)$, the unique symmetric equilibrium is $p_1^* = p_2^* = v - t/2$. Are there asymmetric equilibria in this case?

(e) Compare the change in equilibrium prices and profits from a reduction in $t$ in the case studied in (d) with that in the equilibria of (a) and (b).

**12.C.15$^B$** Derive the Nash equilibrium prices of the linear city model where a consumer's travel cost is quadratic in distance, that is, where the total cost of purchasing from firm $j$ is $p_j + td^2$, where $d$ is the consumer's distance from firm $j$. Restrict attention to the case in which $v$ is large enough that the possibility of nonpurchase can be ignored.

**12.C.16$^B$** Derive the Nash equilibrium prices and profits in the circular city model with $J$ firms when travel costs are quadratic, as in Exercise 12.C.15. Restrict attention to the case in which $v$ is large enough that the possibility of nonpurchase can be ignored. What happens as $J$ grows large? As $t$ falls?

**12.C.17$^B$** Consider the linear city model in which the two firms may have different constant unit production costs $c_1 > 0$ and $c_2 > 0$. Without loss of generality, take $c_1 \leq c_2$ and suppose that $v$ is large enough that nonpurchase can be ignored. Determine the Nash equilibrium prices and sales levels for equilibria in which both firms make strictly positive sales. How do local changes in $c_1$ affect the equilibrium prices and profits of firms 1 and 2? For what values of $c_1$ and $c_2$ does the equilibrium involve one firm making no sales?

**12.C.18$^B$** (*The Stackleberg leadership model*) There are two firms in a market. Firm 1 is the "leader" and picks its quantity first. Firm 2, the "follower," observes firm 1's choice and then chooses its quantity. Profits for each firm $i$ given quantity choices $q_1$ and $q_2$ are $p(q_1 + q_2)q_i - cq_i$, where $p'(q) < 0$ and $p'(q) + p''(q)q < 0$ at all $q \geq 0$.

(a) Prove formally that firm 1's quantity choice is larger than its quantity choice would be if the firms chose quantities simultaneously and that its profits are larger as well. Also show that aggregate output is larger and that firm 2's profits are smaller.

(b) Draw a picture of this outcome using best-response functions and isoprofit contours.

**12.C.19$^C$** Do Exercise 8.B.5.

**12.C.20$^B$** Prove Proposition 12.C.2 for the case of a general convex cost function $c(q)$.

**12.D.1$^B$** Consider an infinitely repeated Bertrand duopoly with discount factor $\delta < 1$. Determine the conditions under which strategies of the form in (12.D.1) sustain the monopoly price in each of the following cases:

(a) Market demand in period $t$ is $x_t(p) = \gamma^t x(p)$ where $\gamma > 0$.

(b) At the end of each period, the market ceases to exist with probability $\gamma$.

(c) It takes $K$ periods to respond to a deviation.

**12.D.2$^B$** In text.

**12.D.3$^B$** Consider an infinitely repeated Cournot duopoly with discount factor $\delta < 1$, unit costs of $c > 0$, and inverse demand function $p(q) = a - bq$, with $a > c$ and $b > 0$.

(a) Under what conditions can the symmetric joint monopoly outputs $(q_1, q_2) = (q^m/2, q^m/2)$ be sustained with strategies that call for $(q^m/2, q^m/2)$ to be played if no one has yet deviated and for the single-period Cournot (Nash) equilibrium to be played otherwise?

(b) Derive the minimal level of $\delta$ such that output levels $(q_1, q_2) = (q, q)$ with $q \in [((a - c)/2b), ((a - c)/b)]$ are sustainable through Nash reversion strategies. Show that this level of $\delta$, $\delta(q)$, is an increasing, differentiable function of $q$.

**12.D.4$^B$** Consider an infinitely repeated Bertrand oligopoly with discount factor $\delta \in [\frac{1}{2}, 1)$.

  **(a)** If the cost of production changes, what happens to the most profitable price that can be sustained?

  **(b)** Suppose, instead, that the cost of production will increase permanently in period 2 (i.e., from period 2 on, it will be higher than in period 1). What effect does this have on the maximal price that can be sustained in period 1?

**12.D.5$^C$** [Based on Rotemberg and Saloner (1986)] Consider a model of infinitely repeated Bertrand interaction where in each period there is a probability $\lambda \in (0, 1)$ of a "high-demand" state in which demand is $x(p)$ and a probability $(1 - \lambda)$ of a "low-demand" state in which demand is $\alpha x(p)$, where $\alpha \in (0, 1)$. The cost of production is $c > 0$ per unit. Consider Nash reversion strategies of the following form: charge price $p_H$ in a high-demand state if no previous deviation has occurred, charge $p_L$ in a low-demand state if no previous deviation has occurred, and set price equal to $c$ if a deviation has previously occurred.

  **(a)** Show that if $\delta$ is sufficiently high, then there is an SPNE in which the firms set $p_H = p_L = p^m$, the monopoly price.

  **(b)** Show that for some $\underline{\delta}$ above $\frac{1}{2}$, a firm will want to deviate from price $p^m$ in the high-demand state whenever $\delta < \underline{\delta}$. Identify the highest price $p_H$ that the firms can sustain when $\delta \in [\frac{1}{2}, \underline{\delta})$ (verify that they can still sustain price $p_L = p^m$ in the low-demand state). Notice that this equilibrium may involve "countercyclical" pricing; that is, $p_L > p_H$. Intuitively, what drives this result?

  **(c)** Show that when $\delta < \frac{1}{2}$ we must have $p_H = p_L = c$.

**12.E.1$^B$** Suppose that we have a two-stage model of entry into a homogeneous-good market characterized by price competition. If potential firms differ in efficiency, need the equilibrium have the most efficient firm being active?

**12.E.2$^B$** Prove that $\pi_J$ is decreasing in $J$ under assumptions (A1) to (A3) of Proposition 12.E.1.

**12.E.3$^B$** Calculate the welfare loss from the free-entry equilibrium number of firms relative to the socially optimal number of firms in the models discussed in Examples 12.E.1 and 12.E.2. What happens to this loss as $K \to 0$?

**12.E.4$^B$** Consider a two-stage model of entry in which all potential entrants have a cost per unit of $c$ (in additional to an entry cost of $K$) and in which, whatever number of firms enter, a perfect cartel is formed. What is the socially optimal number of firms for a planner who cannot control this cartel behavior? What are the welfare consequences if the planner cannot control entry?

**12.E.5$^C$** Consider a two-stage entry model with a market that looks like the market in Exercise 12.C.16. The entry cost is $K$. Compare the equilibrium number of firms to the number that a planner would pick who can control (a) entry and pricing and (b) only entry.

**12.E.6$^B$** Compare a one-stage and a two-stage model of entry with Cournot competition [all potential entrants are identical and production costs are $c(q) = cq$]. Argue that any (SPNE) equilibrium outcome of the two-stage game is also an outcome of the one-stage game. Show by example that the reverse is not true. Argue that we cannot, however, have more firms active in the one-stage game than in the two-stage game.

**12.E.7$^B$** Consider a one-stage entry model in which firms announce prices and all potential firms have average costs of $AC(q)$ (including their fixed setup costs) with a minimum average cost of $\bar{c}$ reached at $\bar{q}$. Show that if there exists a $J^*$ such that $J^*\bar{q} = x(\bar{c})$, then any equilibrium of this model produces the perfectly competitive outcome and, hence, the outcome is (first-best) efficient.

**12.F.1$^B$** Show that in the Cournot model discussed in Section 12.F with demand function $\alpha x(p)$, a firm's best-response function $b(Q_{-j})$ is (weakly) decreasing in $Q_{-j}$ provided $\alpha$ is large enough.

**12.F.2$^B$** Suppose each of the $I$ consumers in the economy has quasilinear preferences and a demand function for good $\ell$ of $x_{\ell i}(p) = a - bp$.

(a) Derive the market inverse demand function.

(b) Now consider a Cournot entry model with this market inverse demand function, technology $c(q) = cq$, and entry cost $K$. Analyze what happens to the equilibrium prices and output levels, as well as what happens to consumer welfare (measured by consumer surplus), as $I \to \infty$ for both a one-stage and a two-stage entry model.

**12.F.3$^B$** Analyze the two-stage Cournot entry model discussed in Section 12.F when $\alpha$ remains fixed but $K \to 0$. Show, in particular, that the welfare loss goes to zero.

**12.F.4$^B$** Consider the following two-stage entry model with differentiated products and price competition following entry: All potential firms have zero marginal costs and an entry cost of $K > 0$. In stage 2, the demand function for firm $j$ as a function of the price vector $p = (p_1, \ldots, p_J)$ of the $J$ active firms is $x_j(p) = \alpha[\gamma - \beta(Jp_j/\sum_k p_k)]$. Analyze the welfare properties as the size ($\alpha$) and the substitution ($\beta$) parameters change.

**12.G.1$^B$** Consider the linear inverse demand Cournot duopoly model and the linear city differentiated-price duopoly model with differing unit costs that you examined in Exercises 12.C.9 and 12.C.17. Find the derivative, with respect to a change in firm 1's unit cost, of firm 2's equilibrium quantity in the Cournot model and equilibrium price in the linear city model. In which model is this change in firm 2's behavior beneficial to firm 1?

**12.AA.1$^A$** In text.

**12.AA.2$^C$** Prove Proposition 12.AA.4. [*Hint:* Consider a strategy profile of the following form: the players are to play an outcome path involving some pair $(q_1, q_2)$ in period 1 and $(q_1^*, q_2^*)$ in every period thereafter. If either player deviates, this outcome path is restarted.]

**12.BB.1$^A$** In text.

**12.BB.2$^B$** Show that if the incumbent in the entry deterrence model discussed in Appendix B is indifferent between deterring entry and accommodating it, social welfare is strictly greater if he chooses deterrence. Discuss generally why we might not be too surprised if entry deterrence could in some cases raise social welfare.

**12.BB.3$^C$** Consider the linear city model of Exercise 12.C.2 with $v > c + 3t$. Suppose that firm 1 enters the market first and can choose to set up either one plant at one end of the city or two plants, one at each end. Each plant costs $F$. Then firm E decides whether to enter (for simplicity, restrict it to building one plant) and at which end it wants to locate its plant. Determine the equilibrium of this model. How is it affected by the underlying parameter values? Compare the welfare of this outcome with the welfare if there were no entrant. Compare with the case where there is an entrant but firm 1 is allowed to build only one plant.

# Adverse Selection, Signaling, and Screening

## 13.A Introduction

One of the implicit assumptions of the fundamental welfare theorems is that the characteristics of all commodities are observable to all market participants. Without this condition, distinct markets cannot exist for goods having differing characteristics, and so the complete markets assumption cannot hold. In reality, however, this kind of information is often asymmetrically held by market participants. Consider the following three examples:

(i) When a firm hires a worker, the firm may know less than the worker does about the worker's innate ability.

(ii) When an automobile insurance company insures an individual, the individual may know more than the company about her inherent driving skill and hence about her probability of having an accident.

(iii) In the used-car market, the seller of a car may have much better information about her car's quality than a prospective buyer does.

A number of questions immediately arise about these settings of *asymmetric information*: How do we characterize market equilibria in the presence of asymmetric information? What are the properties of these equilibria? Are there possibilities for welfare-improving market intervention? In this chapter, we study these questions, which have been among the most active areas of research in microeconomic theory during the last twenty years.

We begin, in Section 13.B, by introducing asymmetric information into a simple competitive market model. We see that in the presence of asymmetric information, market equilibria often fail to be Pareto optimal. The tendency for inefficiency in these settings can be strikingly exacerbated by the phenomenon known as *adverse selection*. Adverse selection arises when an informed individual's trading decisions depend on her privately held information in a manner that adversely affects uninformed market participants. In the used-car market, for example, an individual is more likely to decide to sell her car when she knows that it is not very good. When adverse selection is present, uninformed traders will be wary of any informed trader who wishes to trade with them, and their willingness to pay for the product offered will be low. Moreover, this fact may even further exacerbate the adverse selection problem: If the price that can be received by selling a used car is very low, only sellers with *really* bad cars will offer them for sale. As a result, we may see little trade in markets in which adverse selection is present, even if a great deal of trade would occur were information symmetrically held by all market participants.

We also introduce and study in Section 13.B an important concept for the analysis of market intervention in settings of asymmetric information: the notion of a *constrained Pareto optimal allocation*. These are allocations that cannot be Pareto improved upon by a central authority who, like market participants, cannot observe individuals' privately held information. A Pareto-improving market intervention can be achieved by such an authority only when the equilibrium allocation fails to be a constrained Pareto optimum. In general, the central authority's inability to observe individuals' privately held information leads to a more stringent test for Pareto-improving market intervention.

In Sections 13.C and 13.D, we study how market behavior may adapt in response to these informational asymmetries. In Section 13.C, we consider the possibility that informed individuals may find ways to *signal* information about their unobservable knowledge through observable actions. For example, a seller of a used car could offer to allow a prospective buyer to take the car to a mechanic. Because sellers who have good cars are more likely to be willing to take such an action, this offer can serve as a signal of quality. In Section 13.D, we consider the possibility that uninformed parties may develop mechanisms to distinguish, or *screen*, informed individuals who have differing information. For example, an insurance company may offer two policies: one with no deductible at a high premium and another with a significant deductible at a much lower premium. Potential insureds then *self-select*, with high-ability drivers choosing the policy with a deductible and low-ability drivers choosing the no-deductible policy. In both sections, we consider the welfare characteristics of the resulting market equilibria and the potential for Pareto-improving market intervention.

For expositional purposes, we present all the analysis that follows in terms of the labor market example (i). We should nevertheless emphasize the wide range of settings and fields within economics in which these issues arise. Some of these examples are developed in the exercises at the end of the chapter.

# 13.B  Informational Asymmetries and Adverse Selection

Consider the following simple labor market model adapted from Akerlof's (1970) pioneering work:[1] there are many identical potential firms that can hire workers. Each produces the same output using an identical constant returns to scale technology in which labor is the only input. The firms are risk neutral, seek to maximize their expected profits, and act as price takers. For simplicity, we take the price of the firms' output to equal 1 (in units of a numeraire good).

Workers differ in the number of units of output they produce if hired by a firm,

---

1. Akerlof (1970) used the example of a used-car market in which only the seller of a used car knows if the car is a "lemon." For this reason, this type of model is sometimes referred to as a *lemons* model.

which we denote by $\theta$.[2] We let $[\underline{\theta}, \bar{\theta}] \subset \mathbb{R}$ denote the set of possible worker productivity levels, where $0 \le \underline{\theta} < \bar{\theta} < \infty$. The proportion of workers with productivity of $\theta$ or less is given by the distribution function $F(\theta)$, and we assume that $F(\cdot)$ is nondegenerate, so that there are at least two types of workers. The total number (or, more precisely, measure) of workers is $N$.

Workers seek to maximize the amount that they earn from their labor (in units of the numeraire good). A worker can choose to work either at a firm or at home, and we suppose that a worker of type $\theta$ can earn $r(\theta)$ on her own through home production. Thus, $r(\theta)$ is the opportunity cost to a worker of type $\theta$ of accepting employment; she will accept employment at a firm if and only if she receives a wage of at least $r(\theta)$ (for convenience, we assume that she accepts if she is indifferent).[3]

As a point of comparison, consider first the competitive equilibrium arising in this model when workers' productivity levels are *publicly observable*. Because the labor of each different type of worker is a distinct good, there is a distinct equilibrium wage $w^*(\theta)$ for each type $\theta$. Given the competitive, constant returns nature of the firms, in a competitive equilibrium we have $w^*(\theta) = \theta$ for all $\theta$ (recall that the price of their output is 1), and the set of workers accepting employment in a firm is $\{\theta : r(\theta) \le \theta\}$.[4]

As would be expected from the first fundamental welfare theorem, this competitive outcome is Pareto optimal. To verify this, recall that any Pareto optimal allocation of labor must maximize aggregate surplus (see Section 10.E). Letting $I(\theta)$ be a binary variable that equals 1 if a worker of type $\theta$ works for a firm and 0 otherwise, the sum of the aggregate surplus in these labor markets is equal to

$$\int_{\underline{\theta}}^{\bar{\theta}} N[I(\theta)\theta + (1 - I(\theta))r(\theta)] \, dF(\theta). \tag{13.B.1}$$

(This is simply the total revenue generated by the workers' labor.)[5] Aggregate surplus is therefore maximized by setting $I(\theta) = 1$ for those $\theta$ with $r(\theta) \le \theta$ and $I(\theta) = 0$ otherwise (we again resolve indifference in favor of working at a firm). Put simply,

---

2. A worker's productivity could be random without requiring any change in the analysis that follows; in this case, $\theta$ is her *expected* (in a statistical sense) level of productivity.

3. An equivalent model arises from instead specifying $r(\theta)$ as the disutility of labor. In this alternative model, a worker of type $\theta$ has quasilinear preferences of the form $u(m, I) = m - r(\theta)I$, where $m$ is the worker's consumption of the numeraire good and $I \in \{0, 1\}$ is a binary variable with $I = 1$ if the worker works and $I = 0$ if not. With these preferences, a worker again accepts employment if and only if she receives a wage of at least $r(\theta)$, and the rest of our analysis remains unaltered.

4. More precisely, there are also competitive equilibria in which $w^*(\theta) = \theta$ for all types of workers who are employed in the equilibrium [those with $r(\theta) \le \theta$] and $w^*(\theta) \ge \theta$ for those types who are not [those with $r(\theta) > \theta$]. However, for the sake of expositional simplicity, when discussing competitive equilibria that involve no trade in this section we shall restrict attention to equilibrium wages that are equal to workers' (expected) productivity.

5. In Section 10.E, the aggregate surplus from an allocation in a product market (where firms produce output) was written as consumers' direct benefits from consumption of the good less firms' total costs of production. Here, in a labor market setting, a firm's "cost" of employing a worker is the positive revenue it earns, and a worker receives a direct utility (exclusive of any wage payments) of 0 if she works for a firm and $r(\theta)$ if she does not. Hence, aggregate surplus in these markets is equal to firms' total revenues, $\int NI(\theta)\theta \, dF(\theta)$, plus consumers' total revenue from home production, $\int N(1 - I(\theta))r(\theta) \, dF(\theta)$.

since a type $\theta$ worker produces at least as much at a firm as at home if and only if $r(\theta) \leq \theta$, in any Pareto optimal allocation the set of workers who are employed by the firms must be $\{\theta : r(\theta) \leq \theta\}$.

We now investigate the nature of competitive equilibrium when workers' productivity levels are *unobservable* by the firms. We begin by developing a notion of competitive equilibrium for this environment with asymmetric information.

To do so, note first that when workers' types are not observable, the wage rate must be independent of a worker's type, and so we will have a single wage rate $w$ for all workers. Consider, then, the supply of labor as a function of the wage rate $w$. A worker of type $\theta$ is willing to work for a firm if and only if $r(\theta) \leq w$. Hence, the set of worker types who are willing to accept employment at wage rate $w$ is

$$\Theta(w) = \{\theta : r(\theta) \leq w\}. \tag{13.B.2}$$

Consider, next, the demand for labor as a function of $w$. If a firm believes that the average productivity of workers who accept employment is $\mu$, its demand for labor is given by

$$z(w) = \begin{cases} 0 & \text{if } \mu < w \\ [0, \infty] & \text{if } \mu = w \\ \infty & \text{if } \mu > w. \end{cases} \tag{13.B.3}$$

Now, if worker types in set $\Theta^*$ are accepting employment offers in a competitive equilibrium, and if firms' beliefs about the productivity of potential employees correctly reflect the actual average productivity of the workers hired in this equilibrium, then we must have $\mu = E[\theta \mid \theta \in \Theta^*]$. Hence, (13.B.3) implies that the demand for labor can equal its supply in an equilibrium with a positive level of employment if and only if $w = E[\theta \mid \theta \in \Theta^*]$. This leads to the notion of a competitive equilibrium presented in Definition 13.B.1.

**Definition 13.B.1:** In the competitive labor market model with unobservable worker productivity levels, a *competitive equilibrium* is a wage rate $w^*$ and a set $\Theta^*$ of worker types who accept employment such that

$$\Theta^* = \{\theta : r(\theta) \leq w^*\} \tag{13.B.4}$$

and

$$w^* = E[\theta \mid \theta \in \Theta^*]. \tag{13.B.5}$$

Condition (13.B.5) involves *rational expectations* on the part of the firms. That is, firms correctly anticipate the average productivity of those workers who accept employment in the equilibrium.

Note, however, that the expectation in (13.B.5) is not well defined when *no* workers are accepting employment in an equilibrium (i.e., when $\Theta^* = \varnothing$). In the discussion that follows, we assume for simplicity that in this circumstance each firm's expectation of potential employees' average productivity is simply the unconditional expectation $E[\theta]$, and we take $w^* = E[\theta]$ in any such equilibrium. (As discussed in footnote 4, we restrict attention to wages that equal workers' expected productivity in any no-trade equilibrium. See Exercise 13.B.5 for the consequences of altering the assumption that expected productivity is $E[\theta]$ when $\Theta^* = \varnothing$.)

*Asymmetric Information and Pareto Inefficiency*

Typically, a competitive equilibrium as defined in Definition 13.B.1 will fail to be Pareto optimal. To see this point in the simplest-possible setting, consider the case where $r(\theta) = r$ for all $\theta$ (every worker is equally productive at home) and suppose that $F(r) \in (0, 1)$, so that there are some workers with $\theta > r$ and some with $\theta < r$. In this setting, the Pareto optimal allocation of labor has workers with $\theta \geq r$ accepting employment at a firm and those with $\theta < r$ not doing so.

Now consider the competitive equilibrium. When $r(\theta) = r$ for all $\theta$, the set of workers who are willing to accept employment at a given wage, $\Theta(w)$, is either $[\underline{\theta}, \bar{\theta}]$ (if $w \geq r$) or $\varnothing$ (if $w < r$). Thus, $E[\theta \,|\, \theta \in \Theta(w)] = E[\theta]$ for all $w$ and so by (13.B.5) the equilibrium wage rate must be $w^* = E[\theta]$. If $E[\theta] \geq r$, then *all* workers accept employment at a firm; if $E[\theta] < r$, then none do. Which type of equilibrium arises depends on the relative fractions of good and bad workers. For example, if there is a high fraction of low-productivity workers then, because firms cannot distinguish good workers from bad, they will be unwilling to hire any workers at a wage rate that is sufficient to have them accept employment (i.e., a wage of at least $r$). On the other hand, if there are very few low-productivity workers, then the average productivity of the workforce will be above $r$, and so the firms will be willing to hire workers at a wage that they are willing to accept. In one case, too many workers are employed relative to the Pareto optimal allocation, and in the other too few.

The cause of this failure of the competitive allocation to be Pareto optimal is simple to see: because firms are unable to distinguish among workers of differing productivities, the market is unable to allocate workers efficiently between firms and home production.[6]

*Adverse Selection and Market Unraveling*

A particularly striking breakdown in efficiency can arise when $r(\theta)$ varies with $\theta$. In this case, the average productivity of those workers who are willing to accept employment in a firm depends on the wage, and a phenomenon known as *adverse selection* may arise. Adverse selection is said to occur when an informed individual's trading decision depends on her unobservable characteristics in a manner that adversely affects the uninformed agents in the market. In the present context, adverse selection arises when only relatively less capable workers are willing to accept a firm's employment offer at any given wage.

Adverse selection can have a striking effect on market equilibrium. For example, it may seem from our discussion of the case in which $r(\theta) = r$ for all $\theta$ that problems arise for the Pareto optimality of competitive equilibrium in the presence of asymmetric information only if there are some workers who should work for a firm and some who should not (since when either $\bar{\theta} < r$ or $\underline{\theta} > r$ the competitive equilibrium outcome is Pareto optimal). In fact, because of adverse selection, this is

---

6. Another way to understand the difficulty here is that asymmetric information leads to a situation with missing markets and thereby creates externalities (recall Chapter 11). When a worker of type $\theta > E[\theta] = w$ marginally reduces her supply of labor to a firm here, the firm is made worse off, in contrast with the situation in a competitive market with perfect information, where the wage exactly equals a worker's marginal productivity.

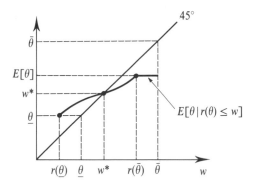

**Figure 13.B.1**

A competitive equilibrium with adverse selection.

not so; indeed, the market may fail completely despite the fact that *every* worker type should work at a firm.

To see the power of adverse selection, suppose that $r(\theta) \leq \theta$ for all $\theta \in [\underline{\theta}, \bar{\theta}]$ and that $r(\cdot)$ is a strictly increasing function. The first of these assumptions implies that the Pareto optimal labor allocation has every worker type employed by a firm. The second assumption says that workers who are more productive at a firm are also more productive at home. It is this assumption that generates adverse selection: Because the payoff of home production is greater for more capable workers, only less capable workers accept employment at any given wage $w$ [i.e., those with $r(\theta) \leq w$].

The expected value of worker productivity in condition (13.B.5) now depends on the wage rate. As the wage rate increases, more productive workers become willing to accept employment at a firm, and the average productivity of those workers accepting employment rises. For simplicity, from this point on, we assume that $F(\cdot)$ has an associated density function $f(\cdot)$, with $f(\theta) > 0$ for all $\theta \in [\underline{\theta}, \bar{\theta}]$. This insures that the average productivity of those workers willing to accept employment, $E[\theta \mid r(\theta) \leq w]$, varies continuously with the wage rate on the set $w \in [r(\underline{\theta}), \infty]$.

To determine the equilibrium wage, we use conditions (13.B.4) and (13.B.5). Together they imply that the competitive equilibrium wage $w^*$ must satisfy

$$w^* = E[\theta \mid r(\theta) \leq w^*]. \tag{13.B.6}$$

We can use Figure 13.B.1 to study the determination of the equilibrium wage $w^*$. There we graph the values of $E[\theta \mid r(\theta) \leq w]$ as a function of $w$. This function gives the expected value of $\theta$ for workers who would choose to work for a firm when the prevailing wage is $w$. It is increasing in the level $w$ for wages between $r(\underline{\theta})$ and $r(\bar{\theta})$, has a minimum value of $\underline{\theta}$ when $w = r(\underline{\theta})$, and attains a maximum value of $E[\theta]$ for $w \geq r(\bar{\theta})$.[7] The competitive equilibrium wage $w^*$ is found by locating the wage rate at which this function crosses the 45-degree line; at this point, condition (13.B.6) is satisfied. The set of workers accepting employment at a firm is then $\Theta^* = \{\theta: r(\theta) \leq w^*\}$. Their average productivity is exactly $w^*$.[8]

---

7. The figure does not depict this function for wages below $r(\underline{\theta})$. Because $E[\theta] > r(\underline{\theta})$ in this model, no wage below $r(\underline{\theta})$ can be an equilibrium wage under our assumption that $E[\theta \mid \Theta(w) = \varnothing] = E[\theta]$.

8. For another diagrammatic determination of equilibrium, see Exercise 13.B.1.

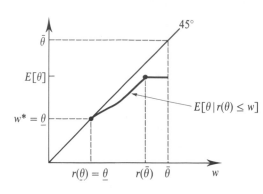

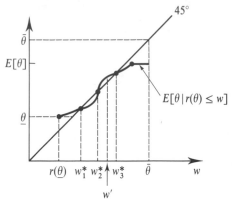

**Figure 13.B.2 (left)**
Complete market failure.

**Figure 13.B.3 (right)**
Multiple competitive equilibria.

We can see immediately from Figure 13.B.1 that the market equilibrium need not be efficient. The problem is that to get the best workers to accept employment at a firm, we need the wage to be at least $r(\bar{\theta})$. But in the case depicted, firms cannot break even at this wage because their inability to distinguish among different types of workers leaves them receiving only an expected output of $E[\theta] < r(\bar{\theta})$ from each worker that they hire. The presence of enough low-productivity workers therefore forces the wage down below $r(\bar{\theta})$, which in turn drives the best workers out of the market. But once the best workers are driven out of the market, the average productivity of the workforce falls, thereby further lowering the wage that firms are willing to pay. As a result, once the best workers are driven out of the market, the next-best may follow; the good may then be driven out by the mediocre.

How far can this process go? Potentially *very* far. To see this, consider the case depicted in Figure 13.B.2, where we have $r(\underline{\theta}) = \underline{\theta}$ and $r(\theta) < \theta$ for all other $\theta$. There the equilibrium wage rate is $w^* = \underline{\theta}$, and only type $\underline{\theta}$ workers accept employment in the equilibrium. Because of adverse selection, essentially *no* workers are hired by firms (more precisely, a set of measure zero) even though the social optimum calls for *all* to be hired![9]

**Example 13.B.1:** To see an explicit example in which the market completely unravels let $r(\theta) = \alpha\theta$, where $\alpha < 1$, and let $\theta$ be distributed uniformly on $[0, 2]$. Thus, $r(\underline{\theta}) = \underline{\theta}$ (since $\underline{\theta} = 0$), and $r(\theta) < \theta$ for $\theta > 0$. In this case, $E[\theta \mid r(\theta) \le w] = (w/2\alpha)$. For $\alpha > \frac{1}{2}$, $E[\theta \mid r(\theta) \le 0] = 0$ and $E[\theta \mid r(\theta) \le w] < w$ for all $w > 0$, as in Figure 13.B.2.[10]

The competitive equilibrium defined in Definition 13.B.1 need not be unique. Figure 13.B.3, for example, depicts a case in which there are three equilibria with strictly positive employment levels. Multiple competitive equilibria can arise because there is virtually no restriction on the slope of the function $E[\theta \mid r(\theta) \le w]$. At any wage $w$, this slope depends on the density of workers who are just indifferent about accepting employment and so it can vary greatly if this density varies.

---

9. In this equilibrium, every agent receives the same payoff as if the market were abolished: every firm earns zero and a worker of type $\theta$ earns $r(\theta)$ for all $\theta$ (including $\theta = \underline{\theta}$).

10. This example is essentially the one developed in Akerlof (1970). His example corresponds to the case $\alpha = \frac{2}{3}$.

Note that the equilibria in Figure 13.B.3 can be *Pareto ranked*. Firms earn zero profits in any equilibrium, and workers are better off if the wage rate is higher (those workers who do not accept employment are indifferent; all other workers are strictly better off). Thus, the equilibrium with the highest wage Pareto dominates all the others. The low-wage, Pareto-dominated equilibria arise because of a *coordination failure*: the wage is too low because firms expect that the productivity of workers accepting employment is poor and, at the same time, only bad workers accept employment precisely because the wage is low.

### A Game-Theoretic Approach

The notion of competitive equilibrium that we have employed above is that used by Akerlof (1970). We might ask whether these competitive equilibria can be viewed as the outcome of a richer model in which firms *could* change their offered wages but choose not to in equilibrium.

The situation depicted in Figure 13.B.3 might give you some concern in this regard. For example, consider the equilibrium with wage rate $w_2^*$. In this equilibrium, a firm that experimented with small changes in its wage offer would find that a small increase in its wage, say to the level $w' > w_2^*$ depicted in the figure, would raise its profits because it would then attract workers with an average productivity of $E[\theta \mid r(\theta) \leq w'] > w'$. Hence, it seems unlikely that a model in which firms could change their offered wages would ever lead to this equilibrium outcome. Similarly, at the equilibrium involving wage $w_1^*$, a firm that understood the structure of the market would realize that it could earn a strictly positive profit by raising its offered wage to $w'$.

To be more formal about this idea, consider the following game-theoretic model: The underlying structure of the market [e.g., the distribution of worker productivities $F(\cdot)$ and the reservation wage function $r(\cdot)$] is assumed to be common knowledge. Market behavior is captured in the following two-stage game: In stage 1, two firms simultaneously announce their wage offers (the restriction to two firms is without loss of generality). Then, in stage 2, workers decide whether to work for a firm and, if so, which one. (We suppose that if they are indifferent among some set of firms, then they randomize among them with equal probabilities.)[11]

Proposition 13.B.1 characterizes the subgame perfect Nash equilibria (SPNEs) of this game for the adverse selection model in which $r(\cdot)$ is strictly increasing with $r(\theta) \leq \theta$ for all $\theta \in [\underline{\theta}, \bar{\theta}]$ and $F(\cdot)$ has an associated density $f(\cdot)$ with $f(\theta) > 0$ for all $\theta \in [\underline{\theta}, \bar{\theta}]$.

**Proposition 13.B.1:** Let $W^*$ denote the set of competitive equilibrium wages for the adverse selection labor market model, and let $w^* = \text{Max}\{w : w \in W^*\}$.

(i) If $w^* > r(\underline{\theta})$ and there is an $\varepsilon > 0$ such that $E[\theta \mid r(\theta) \leq w'] > w'$ for all $w' \in (w^* - \varepsilon, w^*)$, then there is a unique pure strategy SPNE of the two-stage game-theoretic model. In this SPNE, employed workers receive

---

11. Note that if there is a single type of worker with productivity $\theta$, this model is simply the labor market version of the Bertrand model of Section 12.C and has an equilibrium wage equal to $\theta$, the competitive wage.

a wage of $w^*$, and workers with types in the set $\Theta(w^*) = \{\theta : r(\theta) \leq w^*\}$ accept employment in firms.

(ii) If $w^* = r(\underline{\theta})$, then there are multiple pure strategy SPNEs. However, in every pure strategy SPNE each agent's payoff exactly equals her payoff in the highest-wage competitive equilibrium.

**Proof:** To begin, note that in any SPNE a worker of type $\theta$ must follow the strategy of accepting employment only at one of the highest-wage firms, and of doing so if and only if its wage is at least $r(\theta)$.[12] Using this fact, we can determine the equilibrium behavior of the firms. We do so for each of the two cases in turn.

(i) $w^* > r(\underline{\theta})$: Note, first, that in any SPNE both firms must earn exactly zero. To see this, suppose that there is an SPNE in which a total of $M$ workers are hired at a wage $\bar{w}$ and in which the aggregate profits of the two firms are

$$\Pi = M\big(E[\theta \mid r(\theta) \leq \bar{w}] - \bar{w}\big) > 0.$$

Note that $\Pi > 0$ implies that $M > 0$, which in turn implies that $\bar{w} \geq r(\underline{\theta})$. In this case, the (weakly) less-profitable firm, say firm $j$, must be earning no more than $\Pi/2$. But firm $j$ can earn profits of at least $M(E[\theta \mid r(\theta) \leq \bar{w} + \alpha] - \bar{w} - \alpha)$ by instead offering wage $\bar{w} + \alpha$ for $\alpha > 0$. Since $E[\theta \mid r(\theta) \leq w]$ is continuous in $w$, these profits can be made arbitrarily close to $\Pi$ by choosing $\alpha$ small enough. Thus, firm $j$ would be better off deviating, which yields a contradiction: we must therefore have $\Pi \leq 0$. Because neither firm can have strictly negative profits in an SPNE (a firm can always offer a wage of zero), we conclude that both firms must be earning exactly zero in any SPNE.

From this fact, we know that if $\bar{w}$ is the highest wage rate offered by either of the two firms in an SPNE, then either $\bar{w} \in W^*$ (i.e., it must be a competitive equilibrium wage rate) or $\bar{w} < r(\underline{\theta})$ (it must be so low that no workers accept employment). But suppose that $\bar{w} < w^* = \text{Max}\,\{w : w \in W^*\}$. Then either firm can earn strictly positive expected profits by deviating and offering any wage rate $w' \in (w^* - \varepsilon, w^*)$. We conclude that the highest wage rate offered must equal $w^*$ in any SPNE.

Finally, we argue that both firms naming $w^*$ as their wage, plus the strategies for workers described above, constitute an SPNE. With these strategies, both firms earn zero. Neither firm can earn a positive profit by unilaterally lowering its wage because it gets no workers if it does so. To complete the argument, we show that $E[\theta \mid r(\theta) \leq w] < w$ at every $w > w^*$, so that no unilateral deviation to a higher wage can yield a firm positive profits either. By hypothesis, $w^*$ is the highest competitive wage. Hence, there is no $w > w^*$ at which $E[\theta \mid r(\theta) \leq w] = w$. Therefore, because $E[\theta \mid r(\theta) \leq w]$ is continuous in $w$, $E[\theta \mid r(\theta) \leq w] - w$ must have the same sign for all $w > w^*$. But we cannot have $E[\theta \mid r(\theta) \leq w] > w$ for all $w > w^*$ because, as $w \to \infty$, $E[\theta \mid r(\theta) \leq w] \to E[\theta]$, which, under our assumptions, is finite. We must therefore have $E[\theta \mid r(\theta) \leq w] < w$ at all $w > w^*$. This completes the argument for case (i).

The assumption that there exists an $\varepsilon > 0$ such that $E[\theta \mid r(\theta) \leq w'] > w'$ for all $w' \in (w^* - \varepsilon, w^*)$ rules out pathological cases such as that depicted in Figure 13.B.4.

(ii) $w^* = r(\underline{\theta})$: In this case, $E[\theta \mid r(\theta) \leq w] < w$ for all $w > w^*$, so that any firm attracting workers at a wage in excess of $w^*$ incurs losses. Moreover, a firm must

---

12. Recall that we assume that a worker accepts employment whenever she is indifferent.

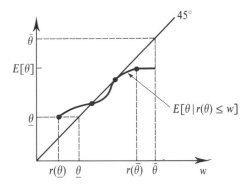

**Figure 13.B.4**

A pathological example.

earn exactly zero by announcing any $w \leq w^*$. Hence, the set of wage offers $(w_1, w_2)$ that can arise in an SPNE is $\{(w_1, w_2): w_j \leq w^*$ for $j = 1, 2\}$. In every one of these SPNEs, all agents earn exactly what they earn at the competitive equilibrium involving wage rate $w^*$: both firms earn zero, and a worker of type $\theta$ earns $r(\theta)$ for all $\theta \in [\underline{\theta}, \bar{\theta}]$. ∎

One difference between this game-theoretical model and the notion of competitive equilibrium specified in Definition 13.B.1 involves the level of firms' sophistication. In the competitive equilibria of Definition 13.B.1, firms can be fairly unsophisticated. They need know only the average productivity level of the workers who accept employment at the going equilibrium wage; they need not have any idea of the underlying market mechanism. In contrast, in the game-theoretic model, firms understand the entire structure of the market, including the full relationship that exists between the wage rate and the quality of employed workers. The game-theoretic model tells us that if sophisticated firms have the ability to make wage offers, then we break the coordination problem described above. If the wage is too low, some firm will find it in its interest to offer a higher wage and attract better workers; the highest-wage competitive outcome must then arise.[13]

### Constrained Pareto Optima and Market Intervention

We have seen that the presence of asymmetric information often results in market equilibria that fail to be Pareto optimal. As a consequence, a central authority who knows all agents' private information (e.g., worker types in the models above), and can engage in lump-sum transfers among agents in the economy, can achieve a Pareto improvement over these outcomes.

In practice, however, a central authority may be no more able to observe agents' private information than are market participants. Without this information, the authority will face additional constraints in trying to achieve a Pareto improvement. For example, arranging lump-sum transfers among workers of different types will be impossible because the authority cannot observe workers' types directly. For Pareto-improving market intervention to be possible in this case, a more stringent test must therefore be passed. An allocation that cannot be Pareto improved by an

---

13. See Exercise 13.B.6, however, for an example of a model of adverse selection in which, for some parameter values, the highest-wage competitive equilibrium is *not* an SPNE of our game-theoretic model.

authority who is unable to observe agents' private information is known as a *constrained* (or *second-best*) *Pareto optimum*. Because it is more difficult to generate a Pareto improvement in the absence of an ability to observe agents' types, a constrained Pareto optimal allocation need not be (fully) Pareto optimal [however, a (full) Pareto optimum is necessarily a constrained Pareto optimum].

Here, as an example, we shall study whether Pareto-improving market intervention is possible in the context of our adverse selection model (where $r(\cdot)$ is strictly increasing with $r(\theta) \leq \theta$ for all $\theta \in [\underline{\theta}, \bar{\theta}]$ and $F(\cdot)$ has an associated density $f(\cdot)$ with $f(\theta) > 0$ for all $\theta \in [\underline{\theta}, \bar{\theta}]$) when the central authority cannot observe worker types. That is, we study whether the competitive equilibria of this adverse selection model are constrained Pareto optima.

In general, the formal analysis of this problem uses tools that we develop in Section 14.C in our study of principal-agent models with hidden information (see, in particular, the discussion of monopolistic screening). As these techniques have yet to be introduced, we shall not analyze this problem fully here. (Once you have studied Section 14.C, however, refer back to the discussion in small type at the end of this section.) Nevertheless, we can convey much of the analysis here.

By way of motivation, note first that in examining whether a Pareto improvement relative to a market equilibrium is possible, we might as well simply think of intervention schemes in which the authority runs the firms herself and tries to achieve a Pareto improvement for the workers (the firms' owners will then earn exactly what they were earning in the equilibrium, namely zero profits). Second, because the authority cannot distinguish directly among different types of workers, any differences in lump-sum transfers to or from a worker can depend only on whether the worker is employed (the workers otherwise appear identical). Thus, intuitively, there should be no loss of generality in restricting attention to interventions in which the authority runs the firms herself, offers a wage of $w_e$ to those accepting employment, an unemployment benefit of $w_u$ to those who do not [these workers also receive $r(\theta)$], leaves the workers free to choose whether to accept employment in a firm, and balances her budget. (In the small-type discussion at the end of this section, we show formally that this is the case.)

Given this background, can the competitive equilibria of our adverse selection model be Pareto-improved upon in this way? Consider, first, dominated competitive equilibria, that is, competitive equilibria that are Pareto dominated by some other competitive equilibrium (e.g., the equilibrium with wage rate $w_1^*$ shown in Figure 13.B.3). A central authority who is unable to observe worker types can always implement the best (highest-wage) competitive equilibrium outcome. She need only set $w_e = w^*$, the highest competitive equilibrium wage, and $w_u = 0$. All workers in set $\Theta(w^*)$ then accept employment in a firm and, since $w^* = E[\theta \,|\, r(\theta) \leq w^*]$, the authority exactly balances her budget.[14] Thus, the outcome in such an equilibrium is *not* a constrained Pareto optimum. In this case, the planner is essentially able to step in and solve the coordination failure that is keeping the market at the low-wage equilibrium.

---

14. An equivalent but less heavy-handed intervention would have the authority simply require any operating firm to pay a wage rate equal to $w^*$. Firms will be willing to remain operational because they break even at this wage rate, and a Pareto improvement results.

What about the highest-wage competitive equilibrium (i.e., the SPNE outcome in the game-theoretic model of Proposition 13.B.1)? As Proposition 13.B.2 shows, any such equilibrium *is* a constrained Pareto optimum in this model.

**Proposition 13.B.2:** In the adverse selection labor market model (where $r(\cdot)$ is strictly increasing with $r(\theta) \leq \theta$ for all $\theta \in [\underline{\theta}, \bar{\theta}]$ and $F(\cdot)$ has an associated density $f(\cdot)$ with $f(\theta) > 0$ for all $\theta \in [\underline{\theta}, \bar{\theta}]$), the highest-wage competitive equilibrium is a constrained Pareto optimum.

**Proof:** If all workers are employed in the highest wage competitive equilibrium then the outcome is fully (and, hence, constrained) Pareto optimal. So suppose some are not employed. Note, first, that for any wage $w_e$ and unemployment benefit $w_u$ offered by the central authority the set of worker types accepting employment has the form $[\underline{\theta}, \hat{\theta}]$ for some $\hat{\theta}$ [it is $\{\theta: w_u + r(\theta) \leq w_e\}$]. Suppose, then, that the authority attempts to implement an outcome in which worker types $\theta \leq \hat{\theta}$ for $\hat{\theta} \in [\underline{\theta}, \bar{\theta}]$ accept employment. To do so, she must choose $w_e$ and $w_u$ so that

$$w_u + r(\hat{\theta}) = w_e. \tag{13.B.7}$$

In addition, to balance her budget, $w_u$ and $w_e$ must also satisfy[15]

$$w_e F(\hat{\theta}) + w_u(1 - F(\hat{\theta})) = \int_{\underline{\theta}}^{\hat{\theta}} \theta f(\theta)\, d\theta. \tag{13.B.8}$$

Substituting into (13.B.7) from (13.B.8), we find that, given the choice of $\hat{\theta}$, the values of $w_u$ and $w_e$ must be

$$w_u(\hat{\theta}) = \int_{\underline{\theta}}^{\hat{\theta}} \theta f(\theta)\, d\theta - r(\hat{\theta})F(\hat{\theta}) \tag{13.B.9}$$

and

$$w_e(\hat{\theta}) = \int_{\underline{\theta}}^{\hat{\theta}} \theta f(\theta)\, d\theta + r(\hat{\theta})(1 - F(\hat{\theta})), \tag{13.B.10}$$

or, equivalently,

$$w_u(\hat{\theta}) = F(\hat{\theta})\big(E[\theta \mid \theta \leq \hat{\theta}] - r(\hat{\theta})\big) \tag{13.B.11}$$

$$w_e(\hat{\theta}) = F(\hat{\theta})\big(E[\theta \mid \theta \leq \hat{\theta}] - r(\hat{\theta})\big) + r(\hat{\theta}). \tag{13.B.12}$$

Now, let $\theta^*$ denote the highest worker type who accepts employment in the highest-wage competitive equilibrium. We know that $r(\theta^*) = E[\theta \mid \theta \leq \theta^*]$. Hence, from conditions (13.B.11) and (13.B.12), we see that $w_u(\theta^*) = 0$ and $w_e(\theta^*) = r(\theta^*)$. Thus, the outcome when the authority sets $\hat{\theta} = \theta^*$ is exactly the same as in the highest-wage competitive equilibrium.

We now examine whether a Pareto improvement can be achieved by setting $\hat{\theta} \neq \theta^*$. Note that for any $\hat{\theta} \in [\underline{\theta}, \bar{\theta}]$ with $\hat{\theta} \neq \theta^*$, type $\underline{\theta}$ workers are worse off than in the equilibrium if $w_e(\hat{\theta}) < r(\theta^*)$ [$r(\theta^*)$ is their wage in the equilibrium] and type $\bar{\theta}$ workers are worse off if $w_u(\hat{\theta}) < 0$.

Consider $\hat{\theta} < \theta^*$ first. Since $r(\theta^*) > r(\hat{\theta})$, condition (13.B.10) implies that

$$w_e(\hat{\theta}) \leq \int_{\underline{\theta}}^{\hat{\theta}} \theta f(\theta)\, d\theta + r(\theta^*)(1 - F(\hat{\theta})),$$

---

15. The authority will never wish to run a budget surplus. If $w_u$ and $w_e$ lead to a budget surplus, then setting $\hat{w}_u = w_u + \varepsilon$ and $\hat{w}_e = w_e + \varepsilon$ for some $\varepsilon > 0$ is budget feasible and is Pareto superior. (Note that the set of workers accepting employment would be unchanged.)

and so

$$w_e(\hat{\theta}) - r(\theta^*) \leq F(\hat{\theta})(E[\theta \,|\, \theta \leq \hat{\theta}] - r(\theta^*))$$

$$= F(\hat{\theta})(E[\theta \,|\, \theta \leq \hat{\theta}] - E[\theta \,|\, \theta \leq \theta^*])$$

$$< 0.$$

Thus, type $\underline{\theta}$ workers must be made worse off by any such intervention.

Now consider $\hat{\theta} > \theta^*$. We know that $E[\theta \,|\, r(\theta) \leq w] < w$ for all $w > w^*$ (see the proof of Proposition 13.B.1). Thus, since $r(\theta^*) = w^*$ and $r(\cdot)$ is strictly increasing, we have $E[\theta \,|\, r(\theta) \leq r(\hat{\theta})] < r(\hat{\theta})$ for all $\hat{\theta} > \theta^*$. Moreover,

$$E[\theta \,|\, r(\theta) \leq r(\hat{\theta})] = E[\theta \,|\, \theta \leq \hat{\theta}],$$

and so $E[\theta \,|\, \theta \leq \hat{\theta}] - r(\hat{\theta}) < 0$ for all $\hat{\theta} > \theta^*$. But condition (13.B.11) then implies that $w_u(\hat{\theta}) < 0$ for all $\hat{\theta} > \theta^*$, and so type $\bar{\theta}$ workers are made worse off by any such intervention. ∎

Hence, when a central authority cannot observe worker types, her options may be severely limited. Indeed, in the adverse selection model just considered, the authority is unable to create a Pareto improvement as long as the highest-wage competitive equilibrium (the SPNE outcome of the game-theoretic model of Proposition 13.B.1) is the market outcome.[16] More generally, whether Pareto-improving market intervention is possible in situations of asymmetric information depends on the specifics of the market under study (and as we have already seen, possibly on which equilibria result). Exercises 13.B.8 and 13.B.9 provide two examples of models in which the highest-wage competitive equilibrium may fail to be a constrained Pareto optimum.

---

Although it is impossible to Pareto improve a constrained Pareto optimal allocation, market intervention could still be justified in the pursuit of distributional aims. For example, if social welfare is given by the sum of weighted worker utilities

$$\int_{\underline{\theta}}^{\bar{\theta}} [I(\theta)\theta + (1 - I(\theta))r(\theta)]\lambda(\theta)\, dF(\theta), \tag{13.B.13}$$

where $\lambda(\theta) > 0$ for all $\theta$, then social welfare may be increased even though some worker types end up worse off. In the applied literature, for example, it is common to see aggregate surplus used as the social welfare function, which is equivalent to the choice of $\lambda(\theta) = N$ for all $\theta$.[17] When society has this social welfare function, social welfare can be raised relative to the competitive equilibrium in Figure 13.B.1 (which, by Proposition 13.B.2, is a constrained Pareto optimum) simply by mandating that all workers must work for a firm and that all firms must

---

16. Proposition 13.B.2 can also be readily generalized to allow $r(\theta) > \theta$ for some $\theta$. (See Exercise 13.B.10.)

17. Note that when types cannot be observed, aggregate surplus is no longer a valid welfare measure for *any* social welfare function because, unlike the case of perfect information, lump-sum transfers across worker types are infeasible. (See Section 10.E for a discussion of the need for lump-sum transfers to justify aggregate surplus as a welfare measure for any social welfare function.)

pay workers a wage of $E(\theta)$. Although workers of type $\bar{\theta}$ are made worse off by this intervention, welfare as measured by aggregate surplus increases.[18]

An interesting interpretation of the choice of aggregate surplus as a social welfare function is in terms of an unborn worker's ex ante expected utility. In particular, imagine that each worker originally has a probability $f(\theta)$ of ending up a type $\theta$ worker. If this unborn worker is risk neutral, then her ex ante expected utility is exactly equal to expression (13.B.13) with $\lambda(\theta) = 1$ for all $\theta$. Thus, maximization of aggregate surplus is equivalent to maximization of this unborn worker's expected utility. We might then say that an allocation is an *ex ante constrained Pareto optimum* in this model if, in the absence of an ability to observe worker types, it is impossible to devise a market intervention that raises aggregate surplus. We see, therefore, that whether an allocation is a constrained optimum (and, thus, whether a planned intervention leads to a Pareto improvement) can depend on the point at which the welfare evaluation is conducted (i.e., before the workers know their types, or after).[19]

Let us now use the techniques of Section 14.C to show formally that we can restrict attention in searching for a Pareto improvement to interventions of the type considered above. We shall look for a Pareto improvement for the workers keeping the profits of the firms' owners nonnegative. For notational simplicity, we shall treat the firms as a single aggregate firm.

By the revelation principle (see Section 14.C), we know that we can restrict attention to direct revelation mechanisms in which every worker type tells the truth. Here a direct revelation mechanism assigns, for each worker type $\theta \in [\underline{\theta}, \bar{\theta}]$, a payment from the authority to the worker of $w(\theta) \in \mathbb{R}$, a tax $t(\theta)$ paid by the firm to the authority, and an employment decision $I(\theta) \in \{0, 1\}$. The set of feasible mechanisms here are those that satisfy the *individual rationality constraint* for the firm,

$$\int_{\underline{\theta}}^{\bar{\theta}} [I(\theta)\theta - t(\theta)] \, dF(\theta) \geq 0, \tag{13.B.14}$$

the *budget balance condition* for the central authority,

$$\int_{\underline{\theta}}^{\bar{\theta}} [t(\theta) - w(\theta)] \, dF(\theta) \geq 0, \tag{13.B.15}$$

and the *truth-telling* (or *incentive compatibility*, or *self-selection*) *constraints* that say that for all $\theta$ and $\hat{\theta}$

$$w(\theta) + (1 - I(\theta))r(\theta) \geq w(\hat{\theta}) + (1 - I(\hat{\theta}))r(\theta). \tag{13.B.16}$$

Note, first, that mechanism $[w(\cdot), t(\cdot), I(\cdot)]$ is feasible only if $[w(\cdot), I(\cdot)]$ satisfies both condition (13.B.16) and

$$\int_{\underline{\theta}}^{\bar{\theta}} [I(\theta)\theta - w(\theta)] \, dF(\theta) \geq 0. \tag{13.B.17}$$

---

18. Moreover, because lump-sum transfers among different types of workers are not possible in the absence of an ability to observe worker types, the achievement of these distributional aims actually *requires* direct intervention in the labor market, in contrast with the case of perfect information.

19. Holmstrom and Myerson (1983) call this ex ante notion of constrained Pareto optimality *ex ante incentive efficiency*. Their terminology refers to the fact that we are taking an ex ante perspective in evaluating welfare (before the realization of worker types) and that a central authority who cannot observe worker types faces *incentive constraints* if she wants to induce workers to reveal their types. Holmstrom and Myerson call our previous notion of constrained Pareto efficiency *interim incentive efficiency* because the perspective used to assess Pareto optimality is that of workers who already know their types. See Section 23.F for a more general discussion of these concepts.

Moreover, if $[w(\cdot), I(\cdot)]$ satisfies (13.B.16) and (13.B.17), then there exists a $t(\cdot)$ such that $[w(\cdot), t(\cdot), I(\cdot)]$ satisfies (13.B.14)–(13.B.16). Condition (13.B.17), however, is exactly the budget constraint faced by a central authority who runs the firms herself. Hence, we can restrict attention to schemes in which the authority runs the firms herself and uses a direct revelation mechanism $[w(\cdot), I(\cdot)]$ satisfying (13.B.16) and (13.B.17).

Now consider any two types $\theta'$ and $\theta''$ for which $I(\theta') = I(\theta'')$. Setting $\theta = \theta'$ and $\hat{\theta} = \theta''$ in condition (13.B.16), we see that we must have $w(\theta') \geq w(\theta'')$. Likewise, letting $\theta = \theta''$ and $\hat{\theta} = \theta'$, we must have $w(\theta'') \geq w(\theta')$. Together, this implies that $w(\theta') = w(\theta'')$. Since $I(\theta) \in \{0, 1\}$, we see that any feasible mechanism $[w(\cdot), I(\cdot)]$ can be viewed as a scheme that gives each worker a choice between two outcomes, $(w_e, I = 1)$ and $(w_u, I = 0)$ and satisfies the budget balance condition (13.B.17). This is exactly the class of mechanisms studied above.

# 13.C  Signaling

Given the problems observed in Section 13.B, one might expect mechanisms to develop in the marketplace to help firms distinguish among workers. This seems plausible because both the firms and the high-ability workers have incentives to try to accomplish this objective. The mechanism that we examine in this section is that of *signaling*, which was first investigated by Spence (1973, 1974). The basic idea is that high-ability workers may have actions they can take to distinguish themselves from their low-ability counterparts.

The simplest example of such a signal occurs when workers can submit to some costless test that reliably reveals their type. It is relatively straightforward to show that in any subgame perfect Nash equilibrium all workers with ability greater than $\underline{\theta}$ will submit to the test and the market will achieve the full information outcome (see Exercise 13.C.1). Any worker who chooses not to take the test will be correctly treated as being no better than the worst type of worker.

However, in many instances, no procedure exists that directly reveals a worker's type. Nevertheless, as the analysis in this section reveals, the potential for signaling may still exist.

Consider the following adaptation of the model discussed in Section 13.B. For simplicity, we restrict attention to the case of two types of workers with productivities $\theta_H$ and $\theta_L$, where $\theta_H > \theta_L > 0$ and $\lambda = \text{Prob}\,(\theta = \theta_H) \in (0, 1)$. The important extension of our previous model is that before entering the job market a worker can get some education, and the amount of education that a worker receives is observable. To make matters particularly stark, we assume that education does *nothing* for a worker's productivity (see Exercise 13.C.2 for the case of productive signaling). The cost of obtaining education level $e$ for a type $\theta$ worker (the cost may be of either monetary or psychic origin) is given by the twice continuously differentiable function $c(e, \theta)$, with $c(0, \theta) = 0$, $c_e(e, \theta) > 0$, $c_{ee}(e, \theta) > 0$, $c_\theta(e, \theta) < 0$ for all $e > 0$, and $c_{e\theta}(e, \theta) < 0$ (subscripts denote partial derivatives). Thus, both the cost and the marginal cost of education are assumed to be lower for high-ability workers; for example, the work required to obtain a degree might be easier for a high-ability individual. Letting $u(w, e \,|\, \theta)$ denote the utility of a type $\theta$ worker who chooses education level $e$ and receives wage $w$, we take $u(w, e \,|\, \theta)$ to equal her wage less any educational costs incurred: $u(w, e \,|\, \theta) = w - c(e, \theta)$. As in Section 13.B, a worker of type $\theta$ can earn $r(\theta)$ by working at home.

In the analysis that follows, we shall see that this otherwise useless education may serve as a signal of unobservable worker productivity. In particular, equilibria emerge in which high-productivity workers choose to get more education than low-productivity workers and firms correctly take differences in education levels as a signal of ability. The welfare effects of signaling activities are generally ambiguous. By revealing information about worker types, signaling can lead to a more efficient allocation of workers' labor, and in some instances to a Pareto improvement. At the same time, because signaling activity is costly, workers' welfare may be reduced if they are compelled to engage in a high level of signaling activity to distinguish themselves.

To keep things simple, throughout most of this section we concentrate on the special case in which $r(\theta_H) = r(\theta_L) = 0$. Note that under this assumption the unique equilibrium that arises in the absence of the ability to signal (analyzed in Section 13.B) has all workers employed by firms at a wage of $w^* = E[\theta]$ and is Pareto efficient. Hence, our study of this case emphasizes the potential inefficiencies created by signaling. After studying this case in detail, we briefly illustrate (in small type) how, with alternative assumptions about the function $r(\cdot)$, signaling may instead generate a Pareto improvement.

A portion of the game tree for this model is shown in Figure 13.C.1. Initially, a random move of nature determines whether a worker is of high or low ability. Then, conditional on her type, the worker chooses how much education to obtain. After obtaining her chosen education level, the worker enters the job market. Conditional on the observed education level of the worker, two firms simultaneously make wage offers to her. Finally, the worker decides whether to work for a firm and, if so, which one.

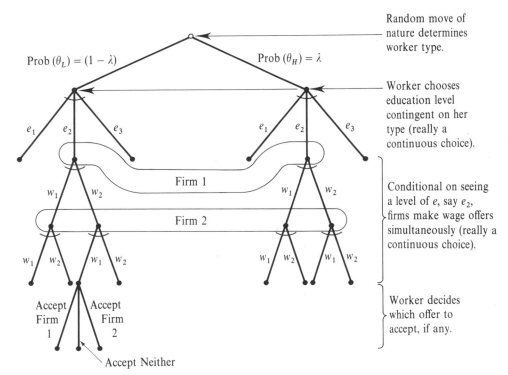

Random move of nature determines worker type.

Worker chooses education level contingent on her type (really a continuous choice).

Conditional on seeing a level of $e$, say $e_2$, firms make wage offers simultaneously (really a continuous choice).

Worker decides which offer to accept, if any.

**Figure 13.C.1**

The extensive form of the education signaling game.

Note that, in contrast with the model of Section 13.B, here we explicitly model only a single worker of unknown type; the model with many workers can be thought of as simply having many of these single-worker games going on simultaneously, with the fraction of high-ability workers in the market being $\lambda$. In discussing the equilibria of this game, we often speak of the "high-ability workers" and "low-ability workers," having the many-workers case in mind.

The equilibrium concept we employ is that of a weak perfect Bayesian equilibrium (see Definition 9.C.3), but with an added condition. Put formally, we require that, in the game tree depicted in Figure 13.C.1, the firms' beliefs have the property that, for each possible choice of $e$, there exists a number $\mu(e) \in [0, 1]$ such that: (i) firm 1's belief that the worker is of type $\theta_H$ after seeing her choose $e$ is $\mu(e)$ and (ii) after the worker has chosen $e$, firm 2's belief that the worker is of type $\theta_H$ and that firm 1 has chosen wage offer $w$ is precisely $\mu(e)\sigma_1^*(w \mid e)$, where $\sigma_1^*(w \mid e)$ is firm 1's equilibrium probability of choosing wage offer $w$ after observing education level $e$. This extra condition adds an element of commonality to the firms' beliefs about the type of worker who has chosen $e$, and requires that the firms' beliefs about each others' wage offers following $e$ are consistent with the equilibrium strategies both on and off the equilibrium path.

We refer to a weak perfect Bayesian equilibrium satisfying this extra condition on beliefs as a *perfect Bayesian equilibrium* (PBE). Fortunately, this PBE notion can more easily, and equivalently, be stated as follows: A set of strategies and a belief function $\mu(e) \in [0, 1]$ giving the firms' common probability assessment that the worker is of high ability after observing education level $e$ is a PBE if

(i)   The worker's strategy is optimal given the firm's strategies.
(ii)  The belief function $\mu(e)$ is derived from the worker's strategy using Bayes' rule where possible.
(iii) The firms' wage offers following each choice $e$ constitute a Nash equilibrium of the simultaneous-move wage offer game in which the probability that the worker is of high ability is $\mu(e)$.[20]

In the context of the model studied here, this notion of a PBE is equivalent to the sequential equilibrium concept discussed in Section 9.C. We also restrict our attention throughout to pure strategy equilibria.

We begin our analysis at the end of the game. Suppose that after seeing some education level $e$, the firms attach a probability of $\mu(e)$ that the worker is type $\theta_H$. If so, the expected productivity of the worker is $\mu(e)\theta_H + (1 - \mu(e))\theta_L$. In a simultaneous-move wage offer game, the firms' (pure strategy) Nash equilibrium wage offers equal the worker's expected productivity (this game is very much like the Bertrand pricing game discussed in Section 12.C). Thus, in any (pure strategy) PBE, we must have both firms offering a wage exactly equal to the worker's expected productivity, $\mu(e)\theta_H + (1 - \mu(e))\theta_L$.

---

20. Thus, the extra condition we add imposes equilibrium-like play in parts of the tree off the equilibrium path. See Section 9.C for a discussion of the need to augment the weak perfect Bayesian equilibrium concept to achieve this end.

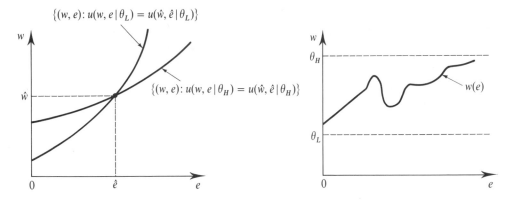

**Figure 13.C.2 (left)**
Indifference curves for high- and low-ability workers: the single-crossing property.

**Figure 13.C.3 (right)**
A wage schedule.

Knowing this fact, we turn to the issue of the worker's equilibrium strategy, her choice of an education level contingent on her type. As a first step in this analysis, it is useful to examine the worker's preferences over (wage rate, education level) pairs. Figure 13.C.2 depicts an indifference curve for each of the two types of workers (with wages measured on the vertical axis and education levels measured on the horizontal axis). Note that these indifference curves cross only once and that, where they do, the indifference curve of the high-ability worker has a smaller slope. This property of preferences, known as the *single-crossing property*, plays an important role in the analysis of signaling models and in models of asymmetric information more generally. It arises here because the worker's marginal rate of substitution between wages and education at any given $(w, e)$ pair is $(dw/de)_{\bar{u}} = c_e(e, \theta)$, which is decreasing in $\theta$ because $c_{e\theta}(e, \theta) < 0$.

We can also graph a function giving the equilibrium wage offer that results for each education level, which we denote by $w(e)$. Note that since in any PBE $w(e) = \mu(e)\theta_H + (1 - \mu(e))\theta_L$ for the equilibrium belief function $\mu(e)$, the equilibrium wage offer resulting from any choice of $e$ must lie in the interval $[\theta_L, \theta_H]$. A possible wage offer function $w(e)$ is shown in Figure 13.C.3.

We are now ready to determine the equilibrium education choices for the two types of workers. It is useful to consider separately two different types of equilibria that might arise: *separating equilibria*, in which the two types of workers choose different education levels, and *pooling equilibria*, in which the two types choose the same education level.

### Separating Equilibria

To analyze separating equilibria, let $e^*(\theta)$ be the worker's equilibrium education choice as a function of her type, and let $w^*(e)$ be the firms' equilibrium wage offer as a function of the worker's education level. We first establish two useful lemmas.

**Lemma 13.C.1:** In any separating perfect Bayesian equilibrium, $w^*(e^*(\theta_H)) = \theta_H$ and $w^*(e^*(\theta_L)) = \theta_L$; that is, each worker type receives a wage equal to her productivity level.

**Proof:** In any PBE, beliefs on the equilibrium path must be correctly derived from the equilibrium strategies using Bayes' rule. Here this implies that upon seeing education level $e^*(\theta_L)$, firms must assign probability one to the worker being type $\theta_L$. Likewise, upon seeing education level $e^*(\theta_H)$, firms must assign probability one

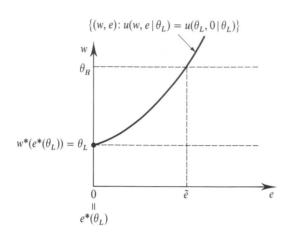

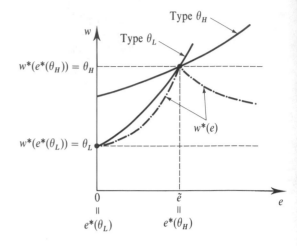

to the worker being type $\theta_H$. The resulting wages are then exactly $\theta_L$ and $\theta_H$, respectively. ■

**Figure 13.C.4 (left)**
Low-ability worker's outcome in a separating equilibrium.

**Lemma 13.C.2:** In any separating perfect Bayesian equilibrium, $e^*(\theta_L) = 0$; that is, a low-ability worker chooses to get no education.

**Figure 13.C.5 (right)**
A separating equilibrium: Type is inferred from education level.

**Proof:** Suppose not, that is, that when the worker is type $\theta_L$, she chooses some strictly positive education level $\hat{e} > 0$. According to Lemma 13.C.1, by doing so, the worker receives a wage equal to $\theta_L$. However, she would receive a wage of at least $\theta_L$ if she instead chose $e = 0$. Since choosing $e = 0$ would have save her the cost of education, she would be strictly better off by doing so, which is a contradiction to the assumption that $\hat{e} > 0$ is her equilibrium education level. ■

Lemma 13.C.2 implies that, in any separating equilibrium, type $\theta_L$'s indifference curve through her equilibrium level of education and wage must look as depicted in Figure 13.C.4.

Using Figure 13.C.4, we can construct a separating equilibrium as follows: Let $e^*(\theta_H) = \tilde{e}$, let $e^*(\theta_L) = 0$, and let the schedule $w^*(e)$ be as drawn in Figure 13.C.5. The firms' equilibrium beliefs following education choice $e$ are $\mu^*(e) = (w^*(e) - \theta_L)/(\theta_H - \theta_L)$. Note that they satisfy $\mu^*(e) \in [0, 1]$ for all $e \geq 0$, since $w^*(e) \in [\theta_L, \theta_H]$.

To verify that this is indeed a PBE, note that we are completely free to let firms have any beliefs when $e$ is neither 0 nor $\tilde{e}$. On the other hand, we must have $\mu(0) = 0$ and $\mu(\tilde{e}) = 1$. The wage offers drawn, which have $w^*(0) = \theta_L$ and $w^*(\tilde{e}) = \theta_H$, reflect exactly these beliefs.

What about the worker's strategy? It is not hard to see that, given the wage function $w^*(e)$, the worker is maximizing her utility by choosing $e = 0$ when she is type $\theta_L$ and by choosing $e = \tilde{e}$ when she is type $\theta_H$. This can be seen in Figure 13.C.5 by noting that, for each type that she may be, the worker's indifference curve is at its highest-possible level along the schedule $w^*(e)$. Thus, strategies $[e^*(\theta), w^*(e)]$ and the associated beliefs $\mu(e)$ of the firms do in fact constitute a PBE.

Note that this is not the only PBE involving these education choices by the two types of workers. Because we have so much freedom to choose the firms' beliefs off the equilibrium path, many wage schedules can arise that support these education

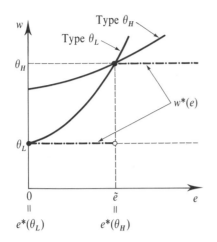 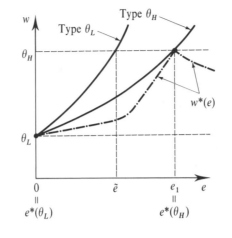

**Figure 13.C.6 (left)**

A separating
equilibrium with the
same education
choices as in Figure
13.C.5 but different
off-equilibrium-
path beliefs.

**Figure 13.C.7 (right)**

A separating
equilibrium with an
education choice
$e^*(\theta_H) > \tilde{e}$ by
high-ability workers.

choices. Figure 13.C.6 depicts another one; in this PBE, firms believe that the worker
is certain to be of high quality if $e \geq \tilde{e}$ and is certain to be of low quality if $e < \tilde{e}$.
The resulting wage schedule has $w^*(e) = \theta_H$ if $e \geq \tilde{e}$ and $w^*(e) = \theta_L$ if $e < \tilde{e}$.

In these separating equilibria, high-ability workers are willing to get otherwise
useless education simply because it allows them to distinguish themselves from
low-ability workers and receive higher wages. The fundamental reason that education
can serve as a signal here is that the marginal cost of education depends on a worker's
type. Because the marginal cost of education is higher for a low-ability worker [since
$c_{e\theta}(e, \theta) < 0$], a type $\theta_H$ worker may find it worthwhile to get some positive level of
education $e' > 0$ to raise her wage by some amount $\Delta w > 0$, whereas a type $\theta_L$ worker
may be unwilling to get this same level of education in return for the same wage
increase. As a result, firms can reasonably come to regard education level as a signal
of worker quality.

The education level for the high-ability type observed above is not the only one
that can arise in a separating equilibrium in this model. Indeed, many education
levels for the high-ability type are possible. In particular, any education level between
$\tilde{e}$ and $e_1$ in Figure 13.C.7 can be the equilibrium education level of the high-ability
workers. A wage schedule that supports education level $e^*(\theta_H) = e_1$ is depicted in
the figure. Note that the education level of the high-ability worker cannot be below
$\tilde{e}$ in a separating equilibrium because, if it were, the low-ability worker would deviate
and pretend to be of high ability by choosing the high-ability education level. On the
other hand, the education level of the high-ability worker cannot be above $e_1$ because,
if it were, the high-ability worker would prefer to get no education, even if this resulted
in her being thought to be of low ability.

Note that these various separating equilibria can be Pareto ranked. In all of them,
firms earn zero profits, and a low-ability worker's utility is $\theta_L$. However, a high-ability
worker does strictly better in equilibria in which she gets a lower level of education.
Thus, separating equilibria in which the high-ability worker gets education level $\tilde{e}$
(e.g., the equilibria depicted in Figures 13.C.5 and 13.C.6) Pareto dominate all the
others. The Pareto-dominated equilibria are sustained because of the high-ability
worker's fear that if she chooses a lower level of education than that prescribed in
the equilibrium firms will believe that she is not a high-ability worker. These beliefs
can be maintained because in equilibrium they are never disconfirmed.

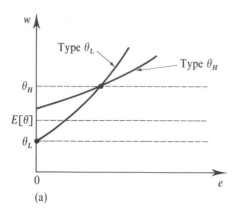

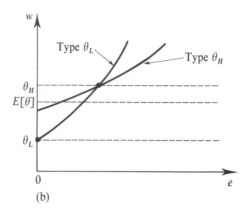

**Figure 13.C.8**

Separating equilibria may be Pareto dominated by the no-signaling outcome. (a) A separating equilibrium that is not Pareto dominated by the no-signaling outcome. (b) A separating equilibrium that is Pareto dominated by the no-signaling outcome.

It is of interest to compare welfare in these equilibria with that arising when worker types are unobservable but no opportunity for signaling is available. When education is not available as a signal (so workers also incur no education costs), we are back in the situation studied in Section 13.B. In both cases, firms earn expected profits of zero. However, low-ability workers are strictly worse off when signaling is possible. In both cases they incur no education costs, but when signaling is possible they receive a wage of $\theta_L$ rather than $E(\theta)$.

What about high-ability workers? The somewhat surprising answer is that high-ability workers may be either better or worse off when signaling is possible. In Figure 13.C.8(a), the high-ability workers are better off because of the increase in their wages arising through signaling. However, in Figure 13.C.8(b), even though high-ability workers seek to take advantage of the signaling mechanism to distinguish themselves, they are *worse* off than when signaling is impossible! Although this may seem paradoxical (if high-ability workers choose to signal, how can they be worse off?), its cause lies in the fact that in a separating signaling equilibrium firms' expectations are such that the wage–education outcome from the no-signaling situation, $(w, e) = (E[\theta], 0)$, is no longer available to the high-ability workers; if they get no education in the separating signaling equilibrium, they are thought to be of low ability and offered a wage of $\theta_L$. Thus, they can be worse off when signaling is possible, even though they are choosing to signal.

Note that because the set of separating equilibria is completely unaffected by the fraction $\lambda$ of high-ability workers, as this fraction grows it becomes more likely that the high-ability workers are made worse off by the possibility of signaling [compare Figures 13.C.8(a) and 13.C.8(b)]. In fact, as this fraction gets close to 1, nearly every worker is getting costly education just to avoid being thought to be one of the handful of bad workers!

*Pooling Equilibria*

Consider now pooling equilibria, in which the two types of workers choose the same level of education, $e^*(\theta_L) = e^*(\theta_H) = e^*$. Since the firms' beliefs must be correctly derived from the equilibrium strategies and Bayes' rule when possible, their beliefs when they see education level $e^*$ must assign probability $\lambda$ to the worker being type $\theta_H$. Thus, in any pooling equilibrium, we must have $w^*(e^*) = \lambda\theta_H + (1 - \lambda)\theta_L = E[\theta]$.

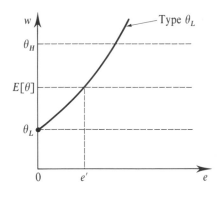

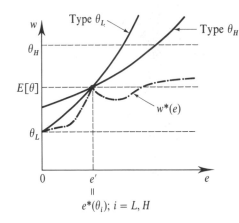

**Figure 13.C.9 (left)**
The highest-possible education level in a pooling equilibrium.

**Figure 13.C.10 (right)**
A pooling equilibrium.

The only remaining issue therefore concerns what levels of education can arise in a pooling equilibrium. It turns out that any education level between 0 and the level $e'$ depicted in Figure 13.C.9 can be sustained.

Figure 13.C.10 shows an equilibrium supporting education level $e'$. Given the wage schedule depicted, each type of worker maximizes her payoff by choosing education level $e'$. This wage schedule is consistent with Bayesian updating on the equilibrium path because it gives a wage offer of $E[\theta]$ when education level $e'$ is observed.

Education levels between 0 and $e'$ can be supported in a similar manner. Education levels greater than $e'$ cannot be sustained because a low-ability worker would rather set $e = 0$ than $e > e'$ even if this results in a wage payment of $\theta_L$. Note that a pooling equilibrium in which both types of worker get no education Pareto dominates any pooling equilibrium with a positive education level. Once again, the Pareto-dominated pooling equilibria are sustained by the worker's fear that a deviation will lead firms to have an unfavorable impression of her ability. Note also that a pooling equilibrium in which both types of worker obtain no education results in exactly the same outcome as that which arises in the absence of an ability to signal. Thus, pooling equilibria are (weakly) Pareto dominated by the no-signaling outcome.

### Multiple Equilibria and Equilibrium Refinement

The multiplicity of equilibria observed here is somewhat disconcerting. As we have seen, we can have separating equilibria in which firms learn the worker's type, but we can also have pooling equilibria where they do not; and within each type of equilibrium, many different equilibrium levels of education can arise. In large part, this multiplicity stems from the great freedom that we have to choose beliefs off the equilibrium path. Recently, a great deal of research has investigated the implications of putting "reasonable" restrictions on such beliefs along the lines we discussed in Section 9.D.

To see a simple example of this kind of reasoning, consider the separating equilibrium depicted in Figure 13.C.7. To sustain $e_1$ as the equilibrium education level of high-ability workers, firms must believe that any worker with an education level below $e_1$ has a positive probability of being of type $\theta_L$. But consider any education level $\hat{e} \in (\tilde{e}, e_1)$. A type $\theta_L$ worker could never be made better off choosing such an education level than she is getting education level $e = 0$ *regardless of what firms believe about her as a result*. Hence, any belief by firms upon seeing education level $\hat{e} > \tilde{e}$ other than $\mu(\hat{e}) = 1$ seems unreasonable. But if this is so, then we must have $w(\hat{e}) = \theta_H$, and so the high-ability worker would deviate to $\hat{e}$. In fact, by this logic, the only education level that can be chosen by type $\theta_H$ workers in a separating equilibrium involving reasonable beliefs is $\tilde{e}$.

In Appendix A we discuss in greater detail the use of these types of reasonable-beliefs refinements. One refinement proposed by Cho and Kreps (1987), known as the *intuitive criterion*, extends the idea discussed in the previous paragraph to rule out not only the dominated separating equilibria but also all pooling equilibria. Thus, if we accept the Cho and Kreps (1987) argument, we predict a *unique* outcome to this two-type signaling game: the best separating equilibrium outcome, which is shown in Figures 13.C.5 and 13.C.6.

## Second-Best Market Intervention

In contrast with the market outcome predicted by the game-theoretic model studied in Section 13.B (the highest-wage competitive equilibrium), in the presence of signaling a central authority who cannot observe worker types may be able to achieve a Pareto improvement relative to the market outcome. To see this in the simplest manner, suppose that the Cho and Kreps (1987) argument predicting the best separating equilibrium outcome is correct. We have already seen that the best separating equilibrium can be Pareto dominated by the outcome that arises when signaling is impossible. When it is, a Pareto improvement can be achieved simply by banning the signaling activity.

In fact, it may be possible to achieve a Pareto improvement even when the no-signaling outcome does not Pareto dominate the best separating equilibrium. To see how, consider Figure 13.C.11. In the figure, the best separating equilibrium has low-ability workers at point $(\theta_L, 0)$ and high-ability workers at point $(\theta_H, \tilde{e})$. Note that the high-ability workers would be worse off if signaling were banned, since the point $(E[\theta], 0)$ gives them less than their equilibrium level of utility. Nevertheless, note that if we gave the low- and high-ability workers outcomes of $(\hat{w}_L, 0)$ and $(\hat{w}_H, \hat{e}_H)$, respectively, both types would be better off. The central authority can achieve this outcome by mandating that workers with education levels below $\hat{e}_H$ receive a wage of $\hat{w}_L$ and that workers with education levels of at least $\hat{e}_H$ receive a

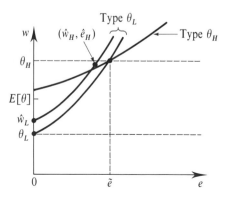

**Figure 13.C.11**

Achieving a Pareto improvement through cross-subsidization.

wage of $\hat{w}_H$. If so, low-ability workers would choose $e = 0$ and high-ability workers would choose $e = \hat{e}_H$. This alternative outcome involves firms incurring losses on low-ability workers and making profits on high-ability workers. However, as long as the firms break even on *average*, they are no worse off than before and a Pareto improvement has been achieved. The key to this Pareto improvement is that the central authority introduces *cross-subsidization*, where high-ability workers are paid less than their productivity level while low-ability workers are paid more than theirs, an outcome that cannot occur in a separating signaling equilibrium. (Note that the outcome when signaling is banned is an extreme case of cross-subsidization.)

**Exercise 13.C.3:** In the signaling model discussed in Section 13.C with $r(\theta_H) = r(\theta_L) = 0$, construct an example in which a central authority who does not observe worker types can achieve a Pareto improvement over the best separating equilibrium through a policy that involves cross-subsidization, but cannot achieve a Pareto improvement by simply banning the signaling activity. [*Hint*: Consider first a case with linear indifference curves.]

The case with $r(\theta_H) = r(\theta_L) = 0$ studied above, in which the market outcome in the absence of signaling is Pareto optimal, illustrates how the use of costly signaling can reduce welfare. Yet, when the market outcome in the absence of signaling is not efficient, signaling's ability to reveal information about worker types may instead create a Pareto improvement by leading to a more efficient allocation of labor. To see this point, suppose that we have $r = r(\theta_L) = r(\theta_H)$, with $\theta_L < r < \theta_H$ and $E[\theta] < r$. In this case, the equilibrium outcome without signaling has no workers employed. In contrast, any Pareto efficient outcome must have the high-ability workers employed by firms.

We now study the equilibrium outcome when signaling is possible. Consider, first, the wage and employment outcome that results after educational choice $e$ by the worker. Following the worker's choice of educational level $e$, equilibrium behavior involves a wage of $w^*(e) = \mu(e)\theta_H + (1 - \mu(e))\theta_L$. If $w^*(e) \geq r$, then both types of workers would accept employment; if $w^*(e) < r$, then neither type would do so.

We now determine the equilibrium education choices of the two types of workers. Note first that any pooling equilibrium must have both types choosing $e = 0$ and neither type accepting employment. To see this, suppose that both types are choosing education level $\hat{e}$. Then $\mu(\hat{e}) = \lambda$ and $w^*(e) = E[\theta] < r$, and so neither type accepts employment. Hence, if $\hat{e} > 0$, both types would be better off choosing $e = 0$ instead. Thus, only an education level of zero is possible in a pooling equilibrium. In this zero education pooling equilibrium, the outcome is identical to the equilibrium outcome arising in the absence of the opportunity to signal.

The set of separating equilibria, on the other hand, is illustrated in Figure 13.C.12. In any separating equilibrium, a low-ability worker sets $e = 0$, is offered a wage of $\theta_L$, and chooses to work at home, thereby achieving a utility of $r$. High-ability workers, on the other hand, select an education level in the interval $[\hat{e}, e_2]$ depicted in the figure, are offered a wage of $\theta_H$, and accept employment. Note that no separating equilibrium can have $e^*(\theta_H) < \hat{e}$, since then low-ability workers would deviate and set $e = e^*(\theta_H)$; also, no separating equilibrium can have $e^*(\theta_H) > e_2$, since high-ability workers would then be better off setting $e = 0$ and working at home.

Note that in all these equilibria, both pooling and separating, the high-ability workers are weakly better off compared with the equilibrium arising without signaling opportunities and are strictly better off in separating equilibria with $e^*(\theta_H) < e_2$. Moreover, both the low-ability workers and the firms are equally well off. Thus, in the case with $\theta_L < r < \theta_H$ and $E[\theta] < r$, any pooling or separating signaling equilibrium weakly *Pareto dominates* the outcome arising

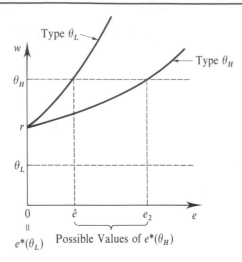

**Figure 13.C.12**

Separating equilibria when $r(\theta_L) = r(\theta_H) = r \in (\theta_L, \theta_H)$.

in the absence of signaling, and this Pareto dominance is *strict* for (essentially) all separating equilibria.

## 13.D Screening

In Section 13.C, we considered how signaling may develop in the marketplace as a response to the problem of asymmetric information about a good to be traded. There, individuals on the *more informed* side of the market (workers) chose their level of education in an attempt to signal information about their abilities to uninformed parties (the firms). In this section, we consider an alternative market response to the problem of unobservable worker productivity in which the *uninformed* parties take steps to try to distinguish, or *screen*, the various types of individuals on the other side of the market.[21] This possibility was first studied by Rothschild and Stiglitz (1976) and Wilson (1977) in the context of insurance markets (see Exercise 13.D.2).

As in Section 13.C, we focus on the case in which there are two types of workers, $\theta_L$ and $\theta_H$, with $\theta_H > \theta_L > 0$ and where the fraction of workers who are of type $\theta_H$ is $\lambda \in (0, 1)$. In addition, workers earn nothing if they do not accept employment in a firm [in the notation used in Section 13.B, $r(\theta_L) = r(\theta_H) = 0$]. However, we now suppose that jobs may differ in the "task level" required of the worker. For example, jobs could differ in the number of hours per week that the worker is required to work. Or the task level might represent the speed at which a production line is run in a factory.

To make matters particularly simple, and to make the model parallel that in Section 13.C, we suppose that higher task levels add *nothing* to the output of the worker; rather, their *only* effect is to lower the utility of the worker.[22] The output of a type $\theta$ worker is therefore $\theta$ regardless of the worker's task level.

21. The setting analyzed here is one of *competitive screening* of workers, since we assume that there are several competing firms. See Section 14.C for a discussion of the *monopolistic screening* case, where a single firm screens workers.

22. As was true in the case of educational signaling, the assumption that higher task levels do not raise productivity is made purely for expositional purposes. Exercise 13.D.1 considers the case in which the firms' profits are increasing in the task level.

We assume that the utility of a type $\theta$ worker who receives wage $w$ and faces task level $t \geq 0$ is

$$u(w, t \mid \theta) = w - c(t, \theta),$$

where $c(t, \theta)$ has all the properties assumed of the function $c(e, \theta)$ in Section 13.C. In particular, $c(0, \theta) = 0$, $c_t(t, \theta) > 0$, $c_{tt}(t, \theta) > 0$, $c_\theta(t, \theta) < 0$ for all $t > 0$, and $c_{t\theta}(t, \theta) < 0$. As will be clear shortly, the task level $t$ serves to distinguish among types here in a manner that parallels the role of education in the signaling model discussed in Section 13.C.

Here we study the pure strategy subgame perfect Nash equilibria (SPNEs) of the following two-stage game:[23]

*Stage 1:*  Two firms simultaneously announce sets of offered contracts. A contract is a pair $(w, t)$. Each firm may announce any finite number of contracts.

*Stage 2:*  Given the offers made by the firms, workers of each type choose whether to accept a contract and, if so, which one. For simplicity, we assume that if a worker is indifferent between two contracts, she always chooses the one with the lower task level and that she accepts employment if she is indifferent about doing so. If a worker's most preferred contract is offered by both firms, she accepts each firm's offer with probability $\frac{1}{2}$.

Thus, a firm can offer a variety of contracts; for example, it might have several production lines, each running at a different speed. Different types of workers may then end up choosing different contracts.[24]

It is helpful to start by considering what the outcome of this game would be if worker types were *observable*. To address this case, we allow firms to condition their offer on a worker's type (so that a firm can offer a contract $(w_L, t_L)$ solely to type $\theta_L$ workers and another contract $(w_H, t_H)$ solely to type $\theta_H$ workers).

**Proposition 13.D.1:** In any SPNE of the screening game with observable worker types, a type $\theta_i$ worker accepts contract $(w_i^*, t_i^*) = (\theta_i, 0)$, and firms earn zero profits.

**Proof:** We first argue that any contract $(w_i^*, t_i^*)$ that workers of type $\theta_i$ accept in equilibrium must produce exactly zero profits; that is, it must involve a wage $w_i^* = \theta_i$. To see this, note that if $w_i^* > \theta_i$, then some firm is making a loss offering this contract and it would do better by not offering any contract to type $\theta_i$ workers. Suppose, on the other hand, that $w_i^* < \theta_i$, and let $\Pi > 0$ be the aggregate profits earned by the two firms on type $\theta_i$ workers. One of the two firms must be earning no more than $\Pi/2$ from these workers. If it deviates by offering a contract $(w_i^* + \varepsilon, t_i^*)$ for any

23. For this game, the set of subgame perfect Nash equilibria is identical to the sets of strategy profiles in weak perfect Bayesian equilibria or sequential equilibria.

24. The models in the original Rothschild and Stiglitz (1976) and Wilson (1977) analyses differ from our model in two respects. First, firms in those papers were restricted to offering only a single contract. This could make sense in the production line interpretation, for example, if each firm had only a single production line. Second, those authors allowed for "free entry," so that an additional firm could always enter if a profitable contracting opportunity existed. In fact, making these two changes has little effect on our conclusions. The only difference is in the precise conditions under which an equilibrium exists. (For more on this, see Exercise 13.D.4.)

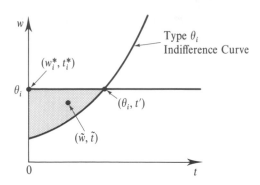

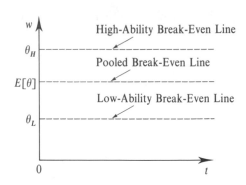

**Figure 13.D.1 (left)**

The equilibrium contract $(w_i^*, t_i^*)$ for type $\theta_i$ with perfect observability.

**Figure 13.D.2 (right)**

Break-even lines.

$\varepsilon > 0$, it will attract all type $\theta_i$ workers. Since $\varepsilon$ can be made arbitrarily small, its profits from type $\theta_i$ workers can be made arbitrarily close to $\Pi$, and so this deviation will increase its profits. Thus, we must have $w_i^* = \theta_i$.

Now suppose that $(w_i^*, t_i^*) = (\theta_i, t')$ for some $t' > 0$. Then, as shown in Figure 13.D.1 (where the wage is measured on the vertical axis and the task level is measured on the horizontal axis), either firm could deviate and earn strictly positive profits by offering a contract in the shaded area of the figure, such as $(\tilde{w}, \tilde{t})$. The only contract at which there are no profitable deviations is $(w_i^*, t_i^*) = (\theta_i, 0)$, the contract that maximizes a type $\theta_i$ worker's utility subject to the constraint that the firms offering the contract break even. ∎

We now turn to the situation in which worker types are *not observable*. In this case, each contract offered by a firm may in principle be accepted by either type of worker. We can note immediately that the complete information outcome identified in Proposition 13.D.1 cannot arise when worker types are unobservable: Because every low-ability worker prefers the high-ability contract $(\theta_H, 0)$ to contract $(\theta_L, 0)$, if these were the two contracts being offered by the firms then *all* workers would accept contract $(\theta_H, 0)$ and the firms would end up losing money.

To determine the equilibrium outcome with unobservable worker types, it is useful to begin by drawing three break-even lines: the zero-profit lines for productivity levels $\theta_L$, $E[\theta]$, and $\theta_H$, respectively. These three break-even lines are depicted by the dashed lines in Figure 13.D.2. The middle line represents the break-even line for a contract that attracts both types of workers, and we therefore refer to it as the *pooled* break-even line.

As in Section 13.C, we can in principle have two types of (pure strategy) equilibria: *separating* equilibria, in which the two types of workers accept different contracts, and *pooling* equilibria, in which both types of workers sign the same contract. (It can be shown that in any equilibrium both types of workers will accept some contract; we assume that this is so in the discussion that follows.) We proceed with a series of lemmas. Lemma 13.D.1 applies to both pooling and separating equilibria.

**Lemma 13.D.1:** In any equilibrium, whether pooling or separating, both firms must earn zero profits.

**Proof:** Let $(w_L, t_L)$ and $(w_H, t_H)$ be the contracts chosen by the low- and high-ability workers, respectively (these could be the same contract), and suppose that the two firms' aggregate profits are $\Pi > 0$. Then one firm must be making no more than $\Pi/2$. Consider a deviation by this firm in which it offers contracts $(w_L + \varepsilon, t_L)$ and

$(w_H + \varepsilon, t_H)$ for $\varepsilon > 0$. Contract $(w_L + \varepsilon, t_L)$ will attract all type $\theta_L$ workers, and contract $(w_H + \varepsilon, t_H)$ will attract all type $\theta_H$ workers. [Note that since type $\theta_i$ initially prefers contract $(w_i, t_i)$ to $(w_j, t_j)$, we have $w_i - c(t_i, \theta_i) \geq w_j - c(t_j, \theta_i)$, and so $(w_i + \varepsilon) - c(t_i, \theta_i) \geq (w_j + \varepsilon) - c(t_j, \theta_i)$.] Since $\varepsilon$ can be chosen to be arbitrarily small, this deviation yields this firm profits arbitrarily close to $\Pi$, and so the firm has a profitable deviation. Thus, we must have $\Pi \leq 0$. Because no firm can incur a loss in any equilibrium (it could always earn zero by offering no contracts), both firms must in fact earn a profit of zero. ∎

An important implication of Lemma 13.D.1 is that, in any equilibrium, no firm can have a deviation that allows it to earn strictly positive profits. We shall use this fact repeatedly in the discussion that follows. Using it, we immediately get the result given in Lemma 13.D.2 regarding pooling equilibria.

**Lemma 13.D.2:** No pooling equilibria exist.

**Proof:** Suppose that there is a pooling equilibrium contract $(w^p, t^p)$. By Lemma 13.D.1, it lies on the pooled break-even line, as shown in Figure 13.D.3. Suppose that firm $j$ is offering contract $(w^p, t^p)$. Then firm $k \neq j$ has a deviation that yields it a strictly positive profit: It offers a single contract $(\tilde{w}, \tilde{t})$ that lies somewhere in the shaded region in Figure 13.D.3 and has $\tilde{w} < \theta_H$. This contract attracts all the type $\theta_H$ workers and none of the type $\theta_L$ workers, who prefer $(w^p, t^p)$ over $(\tilde{w}, \tilde{t})$. Moreover, since $\tilde{w} < \theta_H$, firm $k$ makes strictly positive profits from this contract when the high-ability workers accept it. ∎

We now consider the possibilities for separating equilibria. Lemma 13.D.3 shows that all contracts accepted in a separating equilibrium must yield zero profits.

**Lemma 13.D.3:** If $(w_L, t_L)$ and $(w_H, t_H)$ are the contracts signed by the low- and high-ability workers in a separating equilibrium, then both contracts yield zero profits; that is, $w_L = \theta_L$ and $w_H = \theta_H$.

**Proof:** Suppose first that $w_L < \theta_L$. Then either firm could earn strictly positive profits by instead offering only contract $(\tilde{w}_L, t_L)$, where $\theta_L > \tilde{w}_L > w_L$. All low-ability workers would accept this contract; moreover, the deviating firm earns strictly positive profits from any worker (of low or high ability) who accepts it. Since Lemma 13.D.1 implies that no such deviation can exist in an equilibrium, we must have $w_L \geq \theta_L$ in any separating equilibrium.

Suppose, instead, that $w_H < \theta_H$, as in Figure 13.D.4. If we have a separating

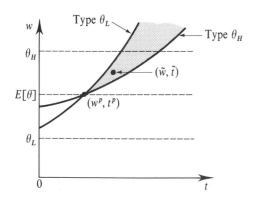

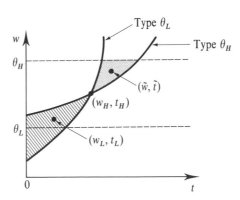

**Figure 13.D.3 (left)**

No pooling equilibria exist.

**Figure 13.D.4 (right)**

The high-ability contract in a separating equilibrium cannot have $w_H < \theta_H$.

equilibrium, then the type $\theta_L$ contract $(w_L, t_L)$ must lie in the hatched region of the figure (by Lemma 13.D.1, it must also have $w_L > \theta_L$). To see this, note that since type $\theta_H$ workers choose contract $(w_H, t_H)$, contract $(w_L, t_L)$ must lie on or below the type $\theta_H$ indifference curve through $(w_H, t_H)$, and since type $\theta_L$ workers choose $(w_L, t_L)$ over $(w_H, t_H)$, contract $(w_L, t_L)$ must lie on or above the type $\theta_L$ indifference curve through $(w_H, t_H)$. Suppose that firm $j$ is offering the low-ability contract $(w_L, t_L)$. Then firm $k \neq j$ could earn strictly positive profits by deviating and offering only a contract lying in the shaded region of the figure with a wage strictly less than $\theta_H$, such as $(\tilde{w}, \tilde{t})$. This contract, which has $w_H < \theta_H$, will be accepted by all the type $\theta_H$ workers and by none of the type $\theta_L$ workers [since firm $j$ will still be offering contract $(w_L, t_L)$]. So we must have $w_H \geq \theta_H$ in any separating equilibrium.

Since, by Lemma 13.D.1, firms break even in any equilibrium, we must in fact have $w_L = \theta_L$ and $w_H = \theta_H$.  ∎

Lemma 13.D.4 identifies the contract that must be accepted by low-ability workers in any separating equilibrium.

**Lemma 13.D.4:** In any separating equilibrium, the low-ability workers accept contract $(\theta_L, 0)$; that is, they receive the same contract as when no informational imperfections are present in the market.

**Proof:** By Lemma 13.D.3, $w_L = \theta_L$ in any separating equilibrium. Suppose that the low-ability workers' contract is instead some point $(\theta_L, t'_L)$ with $t'_L > 0$, as in Figure 13.D.5. (Although it is not important for the proof, the high-ability contract must then lie on the segment of the high-ability break-even line lying in the hatched region of the figure, as shown.) If so, then a firm can make strictly positive profits by offering only a contract lying in the shaded region of the figure, such as $(\tilde{w}, \tilde{t})$. All low-ability workers accept this contract, and the contract yields the firm strictly positive profits from any worker (of low or high ability) who accepts it.  ∎

We can now derive the high-ability workers' contract.

**Lemma 13.D.5:** In any separating equilibrium, the high-ability workers accept contract $(\theta_H, \hat{t}_H)$, where $\hat{t}_H$ satisfies $\theta_H - c(\hat{t}_H, \theta_L) = \theta_L - c(0, \theta_L)$.

**Proof:** Consider Figure 13.D.6. By Lemmas 13.D.3 and 13.D.4, we know that $(w_L, t_L) = (\theta_L, 0)$ and that $w_H = \theta_H$. In addition, if the type $\theta_L$ workers are willing to accept contract $(\theta_L, 0)$, $t_H$ must be at least as large as the level $\hat{t}_H$ depicted in the

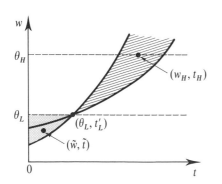

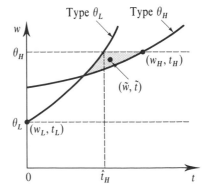

**Figure 13.D.5 (left)**

The low-ability workers must receive contract $(\theta_L, 0)$ in any separating equilibrium.

**Figure 13.D.6 (right)**

The high-ability workers must receive contract $(\theta_H, \hat{t}_H)$ in any separating equilibrium.

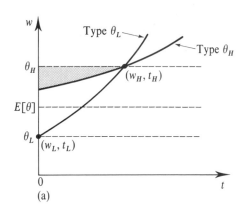 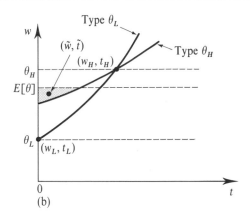

**Figure 13.D.7**

An equilibrium may not exist. (a) No pooling contract breaks the separating equilibrium. (b) The pooling contract $(\tilde{w}, \tilde{t})$ breaks the separating equilibrium.

figure. Note that low-ability workers are indifferent between contracts $(\theta_L, 0)$ and $(\theta_H, \hat{t}_H)$, and so $\theta_H - c(\hat{t}_H, \theta_L) = \theta_L - c(0, \theta_L)$. Suppose, then, that the high-ability contract $(\theta_H, t_H)$ has $t_H > \hat{t}_H$, as in the figure. Then either firm can earn a strictly positive profit by also offering, in addition to its current contracts, a contract lying in the shaded region of the figure with $w_H < \theta_H$, such as $(\tilde{w}, \tilde{t})$. This contract attracts all the high-ability workers and does not change the choice of the low-ability workers. Thus, in any separating equilibrium, the high-ability contract must be $(\theta_H, \hat{t}_H)$. ∎

Proposition 13.D.2 summarizes the discussion so far.

**Proposition 13.D.2:** In any subgame perfect Nash equilibrium of the screening game, low-ability workers accept contract $(\theta_L, 0)$, and high-ability workers accept contract $(\theta_H, \hat{t}_H)$, where $\hat{t}_H$ satisfies $\theta_H - c(\hat{t}_H, \theta_L) = \theta_L - c(0, \theta_L)$.

Proposition 13.D.2 does not complete our analysis, however. Although we have established what any equilibrium must look like, we have not established that one exists. In fact, we now show that *one may not exist.*

Suppose that both firms are offering the two contracts identified in Proposition 13.D.2 and illustrated in Figure 13.D.7(a). Does either firm have an incentive to deviate? No firm can earn strictly positive profits by deviating in a manner that attracts either only high-ability or only low-ability workers (just try to find such a deviation). But what about a deviation that attracts *all* workers? Consider a deviation in which the deviating firm attracts all workers to a single pooling contract. In Figure 13.D.7(a), a contract can attract both types of workers if and only if it lies in the shaded region. There is no profitable deviation of this type if, as depicted in the figure, this shaded area lies completely above the pooled break-even line. However, when some of the shaded area lies strictly below the pooled break-even line, as in Figure 13.D.7(b), a profitable deviation to a pooling contract such as $(\tilde{w}, \tilde{t})$ exists. In this case, *no equilibrium exists.*

Even when no single pooling contract breaks the separating equilibrium, it is possible that a profitable deviation involving a pair of contracts may do so. For example, a firm can attract both types of workers by offering the contracts $(\tilde{w}_L, \tilde{t}_L)$ and $(\tilde{w}_H, \tilde{t}_H)$ depicted in Figure 13.D.8. When it does so, type $\theta_L$ workers accept contract $(\tilde{w}_L, \tilde{t}_L)$ and type $\theta_H$ workers accept $(\tilde{w}_H, \tilde{t}_H)$. If this pair of contracts yields the firm a positive profit, then this deviation breaks the separating contracts identified

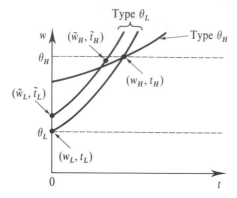

**Figure 13.D.8**

A profitable deviation using a pair of contracts may exist that breaks the separating equilibrium.

in Proposition 13.D.2 and no equilibrium exists. More generally, an equilibrium exists only if there is no such profitable deviation.

### Welfare Properties of Screening Equilibria

Restricting attention to cases in which an equilibrium does exist, the screening equilibrium has welfare properties parallel to those of the signaling model's best separating equilibrium [with $r(\theta_L) = r(\theta_H) = 0$]. First, as in the earlier model, asymmetric information leads to Pareto inefficient outcomes. Here high-ability workers end up signing contracts that make them engage in completely unproductive and disutility-producing tasks merely to distinguish themselves from their less able counterparts. As in the signaling model, the low-ability workers are always worse off here when screening is possible than when it is not. One difference from the signaling model, however, is that in cases where an equilibrium exists, screening must make the high-ability workers better off; it is precisely in those cases where it would not that a move to a pooling contract breaks the separating equilibrium [see Figure 13.D.7(b)]. Indeed, when an equilibrium does exist, it is a constrained Pareto optimal outcome; if no firm has a deviation that can attract both types of workers and yield it a positive profit, then a central authority who is unable to observe worker types cannot achieve a Pareto improvement either.[25]

---

What can be said about the potential nonexistence of equilibrium in this model? Two paths have been followed in the literature. One approach is to establish existence of equilibria in the larger strategy space that allows for mixed strategies; on this, see Dasgupta and Maskin (1986). The other is to take the position that the lack of equilibria indicates that, in some important way, the model is incompletely specified. The aspect the literature has emphasized in this regard is the lack of any dynamic reactions to new contract offers [see Wilson (1977), Riley (1979), and Hellwig (1986)]. Wilson (1977), for example, uses a definition of equilibrium that captures the idea that firms are able to withdraw unprofitable contracts from the market. A set of contracts is a *Wilson equilibrium* if no firm has a profitable deviation that remains profitable once existing contracts that lose money after the deviation are withdrawn. This extra requirement may make deviations less attractive. In the deviation considered in Figure 13.D.3, for example, once contract $(\tilde{w}, \tilde{t})$ is introduced, the original contract $(w^p, t^p)$ loses

---

25. Actually, there is a small gap: An equilibrium may exist when there is another pair of contracts that would give higher utility to both types of workers and that would yield the firm deviating to it exactly zero profits. In this case, the equilibrium is not a constrained Pareto optimum.

money. But if $(w^p, t^p)$ is withdrawn as a result, then low-ability workers will accept $(\tilde{w}, \tilde{t})$ and this deviation ends up being unprofitable. Hellwig (1986) examines sequential equilibria and their refinements in a game that explicitly allows for such withdrawals.

By introducing such reactions, these papers establish the existence of pure strategy equilibria. Introducing reactions of this sort does not simply eliminate the nonexistence problem, however, but also yields somewhat different predictions regarding the characteristics of market equilibria and their welfare properties. For example, when firms can make multiple offers as we have allowed here, cross-subsidization can arise in Wilson equilibria. Indeed, Miyazaki (1977) shows that in the case in which multiple offers are possible, a Wilson equilibrium always exists and is necessarily a constrained Pareto optimum.

In the screening model examined above, we took the view that the uninformed firms made employment offers to the informed workers. Yet we could equally well imagine a model in which informed workers instead make contract offers to the firms. For example, each worker might propose a task level at which she is willing to work, and firms might then offer a wage for that task level. Note, however, that this alternative model exactly parallels the signaling model in Section 13.C and, as we have seen, yields quite different predictions. For example, the signaling model has numerous equilibria, but here we have at most a single equilibrium. This is somewhat disturbing. Given that our models are inevitably simplifications of actual market processes, if market outcomes are really very sensitive to issues such as this our models may provide us with little predictive ability.

One approach to this problem is offered by Maskin and Tirole (1992). They note that contracts like those we have allowed firms to offer in the screening model discussed in this section are still somewhat restricted. In particular, we could imagine a firm offering a worker a contract that involved an ex post (after signing) choice among a set of wage–task pairs (you will see more about contracts of this type in Section 14.C). Similarly, in considering the counterpart model in which workers make offers, we could allow a worker to propose such a contract. Maskin and Tirole (1992) show that with this enrichment of the allowed contracts (and a weak additional assumption) the sets of sequential equilibria of the two models coincide (there may be multiple equilibria in both cases).

---

## APPENDIX A: REASONABLE-BELIEFS REFINEMENTS IN SIGNALING GAMES

In this appendix, we describe several commonly used reasonable-beliefs refinements of the perfect Bayesian and sequential equilibrium concepts for signaling games, and we apply them to the education signaling model discussed in Section 13.C. Excellent sources for further details and discussion are Cho and Kreps (1987) and Fudenberg and Tirole (1992).

Consider the following class of signaling games: There are $I$ players plus nature. The first move of the game is nature's, who picks a "type" for player 1, $\theta \in \Theta = \{\theta_1, \ldots, \theta_N\}$. The probability of type $\theta$ is $f(\theta)$, and this is common knowledge among the players. However, only player 1 observes $\theta$. The second move is player 1's, who picks an action $a$ from set $A$ after observing $\theta$. Then, after seeing player 1's action choice (but not her type), each player $i = 2, \ldots, I$ simultaneously chooses an action $s_i$ from set $S_i$. We define $S = S_2 \times \cdots \times S_I$. If player 1 is of type $\theta$, her utility from choosing action $a$ and having players $2, \ldots, I$ choose $s = (s_2, \ldots, s_I)$ is $u_1(a, s, \theta)$. Player $i \neq 1$ receives payoff $u_i(a, s, \theta)$ in this event. A perfect Bayesian equilibrium (PBE) in the sense used in Section 13.C is a profile of strategies $(a(\theta), s_2(a), \ldots, s_I(a))$, combined with a common belief function $\mu(\theta \,|\, a)$ for players $2, \ldots, I$ that assigns a probability $\mu(\theta \,|\, a)$ to type $\theta$ of player 1 conditional on observing action $a \in A$, such that

   (i) Player 1's strategy is optimal given the strategies of players $2, \ldots, I$.

   (ii) The belief function $\mu(\theta \,|\, a)$ is derived from player 1's strategy using Bayes' rule where possible.

  (iii) The strategies of players $2, \ldots, I$ specify actions following each choice $a \in A$ that constitute a Nash equilibrium of the simultaneous-move game in which the probability that player 1 is of type $\theta$ is $\mu(\theta \,|\, a)$ for all $\theta \in \Theta$.

In the context of the model under study here, this notion of a PBE is equivalent to the sequential equilibrium notion.

The education signaling model in Section 13.C falls into this category of signaling games if we do not explicitly model the worker's choice between the firms' offers and instead simply incorporate into the payoff functions the implications of her optimal choice (she chooses from among the firms offering the highest wage if this wage is positive and refuses both firms' offers otherwise). In that model, $I = 3$, $\Theta = \{\theta_L, \theta_H\}$, the set $A = \{e : e \geq 0\}$ contains the possible education choices of the worker, and the set $S_i = \{w : w \in \mathbb{R}\}$ contains the possible wage offers by firm $i$.

*Domination-Based Refinements of Beliefs*

The simplest reasonable-belief refinement of the PBE notion arises from the idea (discussed in Section 9.D) that reasonable beliefs should not assign positive probability to a player taking an action that is strictly dominated for her. In a signaling game, this problem can arise when players $2, \ldots, I$ (the firms in the education signaling model) assign a probability $\mu(\theta \,|\, a) > 0$ to player 1 (the worker) being of type $\theta$ after observing action $a$, even though action $a$ is a strictly dominated choice for player 1 when she is of type $\theta$.

Formally, we say that action $a \in A$ is a strictly dominated choice for type $\theta$ if there is an action $a' \in A$ such that

$$\underset{s' \in S}{\text{Min}}\; u_1(a', s', \theta) > \underset{s \in S}{\text{Max}}\; u_1(a, s, \theta).^{26} \qquad (13.\text{AA}.1)$$

For each action $a \in A$, it is useful to define the set

$$\Theta(a) = \{\theta : \text{there is no } a' \in A \text{ satisfying } (13.\text{AA}.1)\}.$$

This is the set of types of player 1 for whom action $a$ is not a strictly dominated choice. We can then say that a PBE has reasonable beliefs if, for all $a \in A$ with $\Theta(a) \neq \varnothing$,

$$\mu(\theta \,|\, a) > 0 \quad \text{only if} \quad \theta \in \Theta(a)$$

and we consider a PBE to be a sensible prediction only if it has reasonable beliefs.[27]

---

26. Note that a strategy $a(\theta)$ is strictly dominated for player 1 if and only if it involves play of a strictly dominated action for some type $\theta$.

27. Doing this is equivalent to first eliminating each type $\theta$'s dominated actions from the game and then identifying the PBEs of this simplified game.

Unfortunately, in the education signaling model discussed in Section 13.C, this refinement does not narrow down our predictions at all. The set $\Theta(e)$ equals $\{\theta_L, \theta_H\}$ for all education levels $e$ because either worker type will find $e$ to be her optimal choice if the wage offered in response to $e$ is sufficiently in excess of the wage offered at other education levels. Thus, no beliefs are ruled out, and all PBEs of the signaling game pass this test. If we want to narrow down our predictions for this model, we need to go beyond the use of refinements based only on notions of strict dominance.[28]

Recall the argument we made in Section 13.C for eliminating all separating equilibria but the best one. We argued that since, in Figure 13.C.7, a worker of type $\theta_L$ would be better off choosing $e = 0$ than she would choosing an education level above $\tilde{e}$ *for any beliefs and resulting equilibrium wage that might follow these two education levels*, no reasonable belief should assign a positive probability to a worker of type $\theta_L$ choosing any $e > \tilde{e}$. This is close to an argument that education levels $e > \tilde{e}$ are dominated choices for a type $\theta_L$ worker, but with the critical difference reflected in the italicized phrase: Only *equilibrium* responses of the firms are considered, rather than all conceivable responses. That is, we take a backward-induction-like view that the worker should only concern herself with possible equilibrium reactions to her education choices.

To be more formal about this idea, for any nonempty set $\hat{\Theta} \subset \Theta$, let $S^*(\hat{\Theta}, a) \subset S_2 \times \cdots \times S_I$ denote the set of possible equilibrium responses that can arise after action $a$ is observed for *some* beliefs satisfying the property that $\mu(\theta \,|\, a) > 0$ only if $\theta \in \hat{\Theta}$. The set $S^*(\hat{\Theta}, a)$ contains the set of equilibrium responses by players $2, \ldots, I$ that can follow action choice $a$ for some beliefs that assign positive probability only to types in $\hat{\Theta}$. When $\hat{\Theta} = \Theta$, the set of all conceivable types of player 1, this construction allows for all possible beliefs.[29] We can now say that action $a \in A$ is strictly dominated for type $\theta$ in this stronger sense if there exists an action $a'$ with

$$\underset{s' \in S^*(\Theta, a')}{\text{Min}} \ u_1(a', s', \theta) > \underset{s \in S^*(\Theta, a)}{\text{Max}} \ u_1(a, s, \theta). \qquad (13.\text{AA}.2)$$

Using this stronger notion of dominance, we can define the set

$$\Theta^*(a) = \{\theta\colon \text{there is no } a' \in A \text{ satisfying } (13.\text{AA}.2)\},$$

containing those types of player 1 for whom action $a$ is not strictly dominated in the sense of (13.AA.2). We can now say that a PBE has reasonable beliefs if for all $a \in A$ with $\Theta^*(a) \neq \varnothing$, $\mu(a, \theta) > 0$ only if $\theta \in \Theta^*(a)$.

Using this reasonable-beliefs refinement significantly reduces the set of possible outcomes in the educational signaling model, sometimes even to a unique prediction. In that model, $S^*(\Theta, e) = [\theta_L, \theta_H]$ for all education choices $e$ because, for any belief $\mu \in [0, 1]$, the resulting Nash equilibrium wage must lie between $\theta_L$ and $\theta_H$. As a

---

28. We could, in principle, go further with this identification of strictly dominated strategies for player 1 by also eliminating any strictly dominated strategies for players $2, \ldots, I$, then looking to see whether we have any more strictly dominated actions for any of player 1's types, and so on. However, in the educational signaling model, this does not help us because the firms have no strictly dominated strategies.

29. Note that when there is only one player responding (so $I = 2$), the set $S^*(\Theta, a)$ is exactly the set of responses that are not strictly dominated for player 2 conditional on following action $a$. Note also that in this case a strategy $s_2(a)$ is weakly dominated for player 2 if, for any $a \in A$, it involves play of some $s \notin S^*(\Theta, a)$.

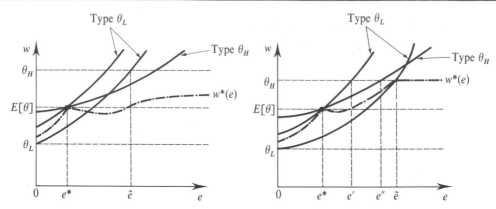

**Figure 13.AA.1 (left)**

A pooling equilibrium that is eliminated using the dominance test in (13.AA.2).

**Figure 13.AA.2 (right)**

A pooling equilibrium that is eliminated using the dominance test in (13.AA.3).

consequence, an education choice in excess of $\tilde{e}$ in Figure 13.C.7 is dominated for a type $\theta_L$ worker according to the test in (13.AA.2) by the education choice $e = 0$. Hence, in any PBE with reasonable beliefs, $\mu(\theta_H \mid e) = 1$ for all $e > \tilde{e}$. But if this is so, then no separating equilibrium with $e^*(\theta_H) > \tilde{e}$ can survive because, as we argued in Section 13.C, the high-ability worker will do better by deviating to an education level slightly in excess of $\tilde{e}$. Furthermore, we can also eliminate any pooling equilibrium in which the equilibrium outcome is worse for a high-ability worker than outcome $(\theta_H, \tilde{e})$, such as in the equilibrium depicted in Figure 13.AA.1, since any such equilibrium must involve unreasonable beliefs: If $\mu(\theta_H \mid e) = 1$ for all $e > \tilde{e}$, then a type $\theta_H$ worker could do better deviating to an education level just above $\tilde{e}$ where she would receive a wage of $\theta_H$. In fact, when the high-ability worker prefers outcome $(\theta_H, \tilde{e})$ to $(E[\theta], 0)$, this argument rules out all pooling equilibria, and so we get the unique prediction of the best separating equilibrium.

### Equilibrium Domination and the Intuitive Criterion

We now consider a further strengthening of the notion of dominance, known as *equilibrium dominance*. This leads to a refinement known as the *intuitive criterion* [Cho and Kreps (1987)] that always gives us the unique prediction of the best separating equilibrium in the two-type education signaling model studied in Section 13.C.

The idea behind this refinement can be seen by considering the pooling equilibrium of the education signaling model that is shown in Figure 13.AA.2, an equilibrium that is not eliminated by our previous refinements. Note that, as illustrated in the figure, to support education choice $e^*$ as a pooling equilibrium outcome we must have beliefs for the firms satisfying $\mu(\theta_H \mid e) < 1$ for all $e \in (e', e'')$. Indeed, if $\mu(\theta_H \mid e) = 1$ at any such education level, then the wage offered would be $\theta_H$ and the type $\theta_H$ worker would find it optimal to deviate.

Suppose, however, that a firm is confronted with a deviation to some education level $\hat{e} \in (e', e'')$ when it was expecting the equilibrium level of education $e^*$ to be chosen. It might reason as follows: "Either type of worker could be sure of getting outcome $(w, e) = (E[\theta], e^*)$ by choosing the equilibrium education level $e^*$. But a low-ability worker would be worse off deviating to education level $e'$ *regardless* of what beliefs firms have after this choice, while a high-ability worker might be made better off by doing this. Thus, this must not be a low-ability worker." In this case, the choice of $e'$ by the low-ability worker is dominated by her *equilibrium* payoff.

To formalize this idea in terms of our general specification, denote the equilibrium payoff to type $\theta$ in PBE $(a^*(\theta), s^*(a), \mu)$ by $u_1^*(\theta) = u_1(a^*(\theta), s^*(a^*(\theta)), \theta)$. We then say that action $a$ is *equilibrium dominated* for type $\theta$ in PBE $(a^*(\theta), s^*(a), \mu)$ if

$$u_1^*(\theta) > \underset{s \in S^*(\Theta, a)}{\text{Max}} \ u_1(a, s, \theta). \qquad (13.\text{AA}.3)$$

Using this notion of dominance, define for each $a \in A$ the set $\Theta^{**}(a) = \{\theta:$ condition $(13.\text{AA}.3)$ does not hold$\}$. We can now say that a PBE has reasonable beliefs if for all actions $a$ with $\Theta^{**}(a) \neq \varnothing$, $\mu(\theta \,|\, a) > 0$ only if $\theta \in \Theta^{**}(a)$, and we can restrict attention to those PBEs that have reasonable beliefs.

Note that any action $a$ that is dominated in the sense of $(13.\text{AA}.2)$ for type $\theta$ must also be equilibrium dominated for this type because $u_1^*(\theta) = u_1^*(a^*(\theta), s^*(a^*(\theta)), \theta) > \text{Min}_{s' \in S^*(\Theta, a')} \, u_1(a', s', \theta)$ by the definition of a PBE. Thus, this equilibrium dominance-based procedure must rule out all the PBEs that were ruled out by our earlier procedure and may rule out more.

Consider the use of this refinement in the education signaling model of Section 13.C. Since it is stronger than the refinement based on $(13.\text{AA}.2)$, this refinement also eliminates all but the best separating equilibrium. However, unlike our earlier dominance-based refinements, the equilibrium dominance-based refinement also eliminates *all* pooling equilibria. For example, in the pooling equilibrium depicted in Figure 13.AA.2, any education choice $\hat{e} \in (e', e'')$ is equilibrium dominated for the low-ability worker. Moreover, once the firms' beliefs following this education choice are restricted to assigning probability 1 to the worker being type $\theta_H$, the high-ability worker wishes to deviate to this education level. Thus, we get a unique prediction for the outcome in this game: the best separating equilibrium.

In signaling games with two types, this equilibrium dominance-based refinement is equivalent to the *intuitive criterion* proposed in Cho and Kreps (1987). Formally, a PBE is said to violate the intuitive criterion if there exists a type $\theta$ and an action $a \in A$ such that

$$\underset{s \in S^*(\Theta^{**}(a), a)}{\text{Min}} \ u_1(a, s, \theta) > u_1^*(\theta). \qquad (13.\text{AA}.4)$$

Thus, we eliminate a PBE using the intuitive criterion if there is some type $\theta$ who has a deviation that is *assured* of yielding her a payoff above her equilibrium payoff as long as players $2, \ldots, I$ do not assign a positive probability to the deviation having been made by any type $\theta$ for whom this action is equilibrium dominated. We can think of the intuitive criterion as saying that to eliminate a PBE we must find a type of player 1 who wants to deviate even if she is not sure what exact belief of players $2, \ldots, I$ will result, she is only sure that they will not think she is a type who would find the deviation to be an equilibrium-dominated action. In general, the intuitive criterion is a more conservative elimination procedure than just insisting on PBEs involving reasonable beliefs using set $\Theta^{**}(a)$ because any PBE with reasonable beliefs using set $\Theta^{**}(a)$ passes the intuitive criterion's test, but as Example 13.AA.1 illustrates, a PBE could satisfy the intuitive criterion's test but fail to have reasonable beliefs. However, when there are only two types of player 1, the two notions are equivalent.

**Example 13.AA.1:** Suppose that there are three types of player 1, $\{\theta_1, \theta_2, \theta_3\}$, and that in some PBE the out-of-equilibrium action $\hat{a}$ is equilibrium dominated for type $\theta_1$ only, so that $\Theta^{**}(\hat{a}) = \{\theta_2, \theta_3\}$. Suppose also that type $\theta_2$ strictly prefers to deviate to action $\hat{a}$ if and only if beliefs over types $\theta_2$ and $\theta_3$ have $\mu(\theta_2 \mid \hat{a}) \geq \frac{1}{4}$ while type $\theta_3$ strictly prefers to deviate to action $\hat{a}$ if and only if $\mu(\theta_2 \mid \hat{a}) \leq \frac{3}{4}$. This situation will not violate the intuitive criterion because condition (13.AA.4) does not hold for either type $\theta_2$ or type $\theta_3$. But in any PBE with reasonable beliefs using set $\Theta^{**}(a)$, one of the two types will deviate to action $\hat{a}$; therefore, this PBE must not have reasonable beliefs in this sense. When there are only two possible types for player 1, say $\theta_1$ and $\theta_2$, this difference disappears because whenever equilibrium domination eliminates a type from consideration, so that $\Theta^*(a) = \{\theta_i\}$ for $i = 1$ or 2, there is only one possible belief for players $2, \ldots, I$ to hold. ∎

Although the use of either equilibrium domination or the intuitive criterion yields a unique prediction in the education signaling model when there are two types of workers, they do not accomplish this when there are three or more possible worker types (see Exercise 13.AA.1). Stronger refinements such as Banks and Sobel's (1987) notions of *divinity* and *universal divinity*, Cho and Kreps' (1987) related notion called *D1*, and Kohlberg and Mertens' (1986) *stability* do yield the unique prediction of the best separating equilibrium in these games with many worker types. See Cho and Kreps (1987) and Fudenberg and Tirole (1992) for further details.

## REFERENCES

Akerlof, G. (1970). The market for lemons: Quality uncertainty and the market mechanism. *Quarterly Journal of Economics* **89**: 488–500.

Banks, J., and J. Sobel. (1987). Equilibrium selection in signaling games. *Econometrica* **55**: 647–62.

Cho, I-K., and D. M. Kreps. (1987). Signaling games and stable equilibria. *Quarterly Journal of Economics* **102**: 179–221.

Dasgupta, P., and E. Maskin. (1986). The existence of equilibrium in discontinuous economic games. *Review of Economic Studies* **46**: 1–41.

Fudenberg, D., and J. Tirole. (1992). *Game Theory*. Cambridge, Mass.: MIT Press.

Hellwig, M. (1986). Some recent developments in the theory of competition in markets with adverse selection. (University of Bonn, mimeographed).

Holmstrom, B., and R. B. Myerson. (1983). Efficient and durable decision rules with incomplete information. *Econometrica* **51**: 1799–819.

Kohlberg, E., and J.-F. Mertens. (1986). On the strategic stability of equilibria. *Econometrica* **54**: 1003–38.

Maskin, E., and J. Tirole. (1992). The principal-agent relationship with an informed principal, II: Common values. *Econometrica* **60**: 1–42.

Miyazaki, H. (1977). The rat race and internal labor markets. *Bell Journal of Economics* **8**: 394–418.

Riley, J. (1979). Informational equilibrium. *Econometrica* **47**: 331–59.

Rothschild, M., and J. E. Stiglitz. (1976). Equilibrium in competitive insurance markets: An essay in the economics of imperfect information. *Quarterly Journal of Economics* **80**: 629–49.

Spence, A. M. (1973). Job market signaling. *Quarterly Journal of Economics* **87**: 355–74.

Spence, A. M. (1974). *Market Signaling*. Cambridge, Mass.: Harvard University Press.

Wilson, C. (1977). A model of insurance markets with incomplete information. *Journal of Economic Theory* **16**: 167–207.

Wilson, C. (1980). The nature of equilibrium in markets with adverse selection. *Bell Journal of Economics* **11**: 108–30.

## EXERCISES

**13.B.1**[A] Consider three functions of $\hat{\theta}$: $r(\hat{\theta})$, $E[\theta \mid \theta \le \hat{\theta}]$, and $\hat{\theta}$. Graph these three functions over the domain $[\underline{\theta}, \bar{\theta}]$, assuming that the first two functions are continuous in $\hat{\theta}$ but allowing them to be otherwise quite arbitrary. Identify the competitive equilibria of the adverse selection model of Section 13.B using this diagram. What about the Pareto optimal labor allocation? Now produce a diagram to depict each of the situations in Figures 13.B.1 to 13.B.3.

**13.B.2**[B] Suppose that $r(\cdot)$ is a continuous and strictly increasing function and that there exists $\hat{\theta} \in (\underline{\theta}, \bar{\theta})$ such that $r(\theta) > \theta$ for $\theta > \hat{\theta}$ and $r(\theta) < \theta$ for $\theta < \hat{\theta}$. Let the density of workers of type $\theta$ be $f(\theta)$, with $f(\theta) > 0$ for all $\theta \in [\underline{\theta}, \bar{\theta}]$. Show that a competitive equilibrium with unobservable worker types necessarily involves a Pareto inefficient outcome.

**13.B.3**[B] Consider a *positive selection* version of the model discussed in Section 13.B in which $r(\cdot)$ is a continuous, strictly *decreasing* function of $\theta$. Let the density of workers of type $\theta$ be $f(\theta)$, with $f(\theta) > 0$ for all $\theta \in [\underline{\theta}, \bar{\theta}]$.

(a) Show that the *more capable* workers are the ones choosing to work at any given wage.

(b) Show that if $r(\theta) > \theta$ for all $\theta$, then the resulting competitive equilibrium is Pareto efficient.

(c) Suppose that there exists a $\hat{\theta}$ such that $r(\theta) < \theta$ for $\theta > \hat{\theta}$ and $r(\theta) > \theta$ for $\theta < \hat{\theta}$. Show that any competitive equilibrium with strictly positive employment necessarily involves *too much* employment relative to the Pareto optimal allocation of workers.

**13.B.4**[B] Suppose two individuals, 1 and 2, are considering a trade at price $p$ of an asset that they both use only as a store of wealth. Ms. 1 is currently the owner. Each individual $i$ has a privately observed signal of the asset's worth $y_i$. In addition, each cares only about the expected value of the asset one year from now. Assume that a trade at price $p$ takes place only if both parties think they are being made strictly better off. Prove that the probability of trade occurring is zero. [*Hint*: Study the following trading game: The two individuals simultaneously say either "trade" or "no trade," and a trade at price $p$ takes place only if they both say "trade."]

**13.B.5**[B] Reconsider the case where $r(\theta) = r$ for all $\theta$, but now assume that when the wage is such that no workers are accepting employment firms believe that any worker who might accept would be of the lowest quality, that is, $E[\theta \mid \Theta = \varnothing] = \underline{\theta}$. Maintain the assumption that all workers accept employment when indifferent.

(a) Argue that when $E[\theta] \ge r > \underline{\theta}$, there are now two competitive equilibria: one with $w^* = E[\theta]$ and $\Theta^* = [\underline{\theta}, \bar{\theta}]$ and one with $w^* = \underline{\theta}$ and $\Theta^* = \varnothing$. Also show that when $\underline{\theta} \ge r$ the unique competitive equilibrium is $w^* = E[\theta]$ and $\Theta^* = [\underline{\theta}, \bar{\theta}]$, and when $r > E[\theta]$ the unique competitive equilibrium is $w^* = \underline{\theta}$ and $\Theta^* = \varnothing$.

(b) Show that when $E[\theta] > r$ and there are two equilibria, the full-employment equilibrium Pareto dominates the no-employment one.

(c) Argue that when $E[\theta] \ge r$ the unique SPNE of the game-theoretic model in which two firms simultaneously make wage offers is the competitive equilibrium when this equilibrium is unique, and is the full-employment (highest-wage) competitive equilibrium when the competitive equilibrium is not unique and $E[\theta] > r$. What happens when $E[\theta] = r$? What about the case where $E[\theta] < r$?

(d) Argue that the highest-wage competitive equilibrium is a constrained Pareto optimum.

**13.B.6**[C] [Based on Wilson (1980)] Consider the following change in the adverse selection model of Section 13.B. Now there are $N$ firms, each of which wants to hire at most 1 worker. The $N$ firms differ in their productivity: In a firm of type $\gamma$ a worker of type $\theta$ produces $\gamma\theta$ units of output. The parameter $\gamma$ is distributed with density function $g(\cdot)$ on $[0, \infty]$, and $g(\gamma) > 0$ for all $\gamma \in [0, \infty]$.

**(a)** Let $z(w, \mu)$ denote the aggregate demand for labor when the wage is $w$ and the average productivity of workers accepting employment at that wage is $\mu$. Derive an expression for this function in terms of the density function $g(\cdot)$.

**(b)** Let $\mu(w) = E[\theta \mid r(\theta) \le w]$, and define the *aggregate demand function for labor* by $z^*(w) = z(w, \mu(w))$. Show that $z^*(w)$ is strictly increasing in $w$ at wage $\bar{w}$ if and only if the elasticity of $\mu$ with respect to $w$ exceeds 1 at wage $\bar{w}$ (assume that all relevant functions are differentiable).

**(c)** Let $s(w) = \int_{\underline\theta}^{r^{-1}(w)} f(\theta)\, d\theta$ denote the *aggregate supply function of labor*, and define a competitive equilibrium wage $w^*$ as one where $z^*(w^*) = s(w^*)$. Show that if there are multiple competitive equilibria, then the one with the highest wage Pareto dominates all the others.

**(d)** Consider a game-theoretic model in which the firms make simultaneous wage offers, and denote the highest competitive equilibrium wage by $w^*$. Show that (i) only the highest-wage competitive equilibrium can arise as an SPNE, and (ii) the highest-wage competitive equilibrium is an SPNE if and only if $z^*(w) \le z^*(w^*)$ for all $w > w^*$.

**13.B.7**[B] Suppose that it is impossible to observe worker types and consider a competitive equilibrium with wage rate $w^*$. Show that there is a Pareto-improving market intervention $(\tilde{w}_e, \tilde{w}_u)$ that reduces employment if and only if there is one of the form $(w_e, w_u) = (w^*, \hat{w}_u)$ with $\hat{w}_u > 0$. Similarly, argue that there is a Pareto-improving market intervention $(\tilde{w}_e, \tilde{w}_u)$ that increases employment if and only if there is one of the form $(w_e, w_u) = (\hat{w}_e, 0)$ with $\hat{w}_e > w^*$. Can you use these facts to give a simple proof of Proposition 13.B.2?

**13.B.8**[B] Consider the following alteration to the adverse selection model in Section 13.B. Imagine that when workers engage in home production, they use product $x$. Suppose that the amount consumed is related to a worker's type, with the relation given by the increasing function $x(\theta)$. Show that if a central authority can observe purchases of good $x$ but not worker types, then there is a market intervention that results in a Pareto improvement even if the market is at the highest-wage competitive equilibrium.

**13.B.9**[B] Consider a model of *positive selection* in which $r(\cdot)$ is strictly decreasing and there are two types of workers, $\theta_H$ and $\theta_L$, with $\infty > \theta_H > \theta_L > 0$. Let $\lambda = \text{Prob}\,(\theta = \theta_H) \in (0, 1)$. Assume that $r(\theta_H) < \theta_H$ and that $r(\theta_L) > \theta_L$. Show that the highest-wage competitive equilibrium need not be a constrained Pareto optimum. [*Hint*: Consider introducing a small unemployment benefit for a case in which $E[\theta] = r(\theta_L)$. Can you use the result in Exercise 13.B.7 to give an exact condition for when a competitive equilibrium involving full employment is a constrained Pareto optimum?]

**13.B.10**[B] Show that Proposition 13.B.2 continues to hold when $r(\theta) > \theta$ for some $\theta$.

**13.C.1**[B] Consider a game in which, first, nature draws a worker's type from some continuous distribution on $[\underline\theta, \bar\theta]$. Once the worker observes her type, she can choose whether to submit to a costless test that reveals her ability perfectly. Finally, after observing whether the worker has taken the test and its outcome if she has, two firms bid for the worker's services. Prove that in any subgame perfect Nash equilibrium of this model all worker types submit to the test, and firms offer a wage no greater than $\underline\theta$ to any worker not doing so.

**13.C.2$^C$** Reconsider the two-type signaling model with $r(\theta_L) = r(\theta_H) = 0$, assuming a worker's productivity is $\theta(1 + \mu e)$ with $\mu > 0$. Identify the separating and pooling perfect Bayesian equilibria, and relate them to the perfect information competitive outcome.

**13.C.3$^B$** In text.

**13.C.4$^B$** Reconsider the signaling model discussed in Section 13.C, now assuming that worker types are drawn from the interval $[\underline{\theta}, \bar{\theta}]$ with a density function $f(\theta)$ that is strictly positive everywhere on this interval. Let the cost function be $c(e, \theta) = (e^2/\theta)$. Derive the (unique) perfect Bayesian equilibrium.

**13.C.5$^B$** Assume a single firm and a single consumer. The firm's product may be either high or low quality and is of high quality with probability $\lambda$. The consumer cannot observe quality before purchase and is risk neutral. The consumer's valuation of a high-quality product is $v_H$; her valuation of a low-quality product is $v_L$. The costs of production for high ($H$) and low ($L$) quality are $c_H$ and $c_L$, respectively. The consumer desires at most one unit of the product. Finally, the firm's price is regulated and is set at $p$. Assume that $v_H > p > v_L > c_H > c_L$.

**(a)** Given the level of $p$, under what conditions will the consumer buy the product?

**(b)** Suppose that before the consumer decides whether to buy, the firm (which knows its type) can advertise. Advertising conveys no information directly, but consumers can observe the total amount of money that the firm is spending on advertising, denoted by $A$. Can there be a separating perfect Bayesian equilibrium, that is, an equilibrium in which the consumer rationally expects firms with different quality levels to pick different levels of advertising?

**13.C.6$^C$** Consider a market for loans to finance investment projects. All investment projects require an outlay of 1 dollar. There are two types of projects: good and bad. A good project has a probability of $p_G$ of yielding profits of $\Pi > 0$ and a probability $(1 - p_G)$ of yielding profits of zero. For a bad project, the relative probabilities are $p_B$ and $(1 - p_B)$, respectively, where $p_G > p_B$. The fraction of projects that are good is $\lambda \in (0, 1)$.

Entrepreneurs go to banks to borrow the cash to make the initial outlay (assume for now that they borrow the entire amount). A loan contract specifies an amount $R$ that is supposed to be repaid to the bank. Entrepreneurs know the type of project they have, but the banks do not. In the event that a project yields profits of zero, the entrepreneur defaults on her loan contract, and the bank receives nothing. Banks are competitive and risk neutral. The risk-free rate of interest (the rate the banks pay to borrow funds) is $r$. Assume that

$$p_G\Pi - (1 + r) > 0 > p_B\Pi - (1 + r).$$

**(a)** Find the equilibrium level of $R$ and the set of projects financed. How does this depend on $p_G$, $p_B$, $\lambda$, $\Pi$, and $r$?

**(b)** Now suppose that the entrepreneur can offer to contribute some fraction $x$ of the 1 dollar initial outlay from her own funds ($x \in [0, 1]$). The entrepreneur is liquidity constrained, however, so that the effective cost of doing so is $(1 + \rho)x$, where $\rho > r$.
  (i) What is an entrepreneur's payoff as a function of her project type, her loan-repayment amount $R$, and her contribution $x$?
  (ii) Describe the best (from a welfare perspective) separating perfect Bayesian equilibrium of a game in which the entrepreneur first makes an offer that specifies the level of $x$ she is willing to put into a project, banks then respond by making offers specifying the level of $R$ they would require, and finally the entrepreneur accepts a bank's offer or decides not to go ahead with the project. How does the amount contributed by entrepreneurs with good projects change with small changes in $p_B$, $p_G$, $\lambda$, $\Pi$, and $r$?

(iii) How do the two types of entrepreneurs do in the separating equilibrium of (b)(ii) compared with the equilibrium in (a)?

**13.D.1**[B] Extend the screening model to a case in which tasks are productive. Assume that a type $\theta$ worker produces $\theta(1 + \mu t)$ units of output when her task level is $t$ where $\mu > 0$. Identify the subgame perfect Nash equilibria of this model.

**13.D.2**[B] Consider the following model of the insurance market. There are two types of individuals: high risk and low risk. Each starts with initial wealth $W$ but has a chance that an accident (e.g., a fire) will reduce her wealth by $L$. The probability of this happening is $p_L$ for low-risk types and $p_H$ for high-risk types, where $p_H > p_L$. Both types are expected utility maximizers with a Bernoulli utility function over wealth of $u(w)$, with $u'(w) > 0$ and $u''(w) < 0$ at all $w$. There are two risk-neutral insurance companies. An insurance policy consists of a premium payment $M$ made by the insured individual to her insurance firm and a payment $R$ from the insurance company to the insured individual in the event of a loss.

(a) Suppose that individuals are prohibited from buying more than one insurance policy. Argue that a policy can be thought of as specifying the wealth levels of the insured individual in the two states "no loss" and "loss."

(b) Assume that the insurance companies simultaneously offer policies; as in Section 13.D, they can each offer any finite number of policies. What are the subgame perfect Nash equilibrium outcomes of the model? Does an equilibrium necessarily exist?

**13.D.3**[C] Consider the following extension of the model you developed in Exercise 13.D.1. Suppose that there is a fixed task level $T$ that all workers face. The monetary equivalent cost of accepting employment at this task level is $c > 0$, which is independent of worker type. However, now a worker's actual output is observable and verifiable, and so contracts can base compensation on the worker's ex post observed output level.

(a) What is the subgame perfect Nash equilibrium outcome of this model?

(b) Now suppose that the output realization is random. It can be either good ($q_G$) or bad ($q_B$). The probability that it is good is $p_H$ for a high-ability worker and $p_L$ for a low-ability worker ($p_H > p_L$). If workers are risk-neutral expected utility maximizers with a Bernoulli utility function over wealth of $u(w) = w$, what is the subgame perfect Nash equilibrium outcome?

(c) What if workers are strictly risk averse with $u''(w) < 0$ at all $w$?

**13.D.4**[B] Reconsider the screening model in Section 13.D, but assume that (i) there is an infinite number of firms that could potentially enter the industry and (ii) firms can each offer at most one contract. [The implication of (i) is that, in any SPNE, no firm can have a profitable entry opportunity.] Characterize the equilibria for this case.

**13.AA.1**[C] Consider the extension of the signaling model discussed in Section 13.C to the case of three types. Assume all three types have $r(\theta) = 0$. Provide an example in which more than one perfect Bayesian equilibrium satisfies the intuitive criterion.

# The Principal-Agent Problem

## 14.A Introduction

In Chapter 13, we considered situations in which asymmetries of information exist between individuals at the time of contracting. In this chapter, we shift our attention to asymmetries of information that develop *subsequent* to the signing of a contract.

Even when informational asymmetries do not exist at the time of contracting, the parties to a contract often anticipate that asymmetries will develop sometime after the contract is signed. For example, after an owner of a firm hires a manager, the owner may be unable to observe how much effort the manager puts into the job. Similarly, the manager will often end up having better information than the owner about the opportunities available to the firm.

Anticipating the development of such informational asymmetries, the contracting parties seek to design a contract that mitigates the difficulties they cause. These problems are endemic to situations in which one individual hires another to take some action for him as his "agent." For this reason, this contract design problem has come to be known as the *principal-agent problem*.

The literature has traditionally distinguished between two types of informational problems that can arise in these settings: those resulting from *hidden actions* and those resulting from *hidden information*. The hidden action case, also known as *moral hazard*, is illustrated by the owner's inability to observe how hard his manager is working; the manager's coming to possess superior information about the firm's opportunities, on the other hand, is an example of hidden information.[1]

Although many economic situations (and some of the literature) contain elements of both types of problems, it is useful to begin by studying each in isolation. In Section 14.B, we introduce and study a model of hidden actions. Section 14.C analyzes

---

1. The literature's use of the term *moral hazard* is not entirely uniform. The term originates in the insurance literature, which first focused attention on two types of informational imperfections: the "moral hazard" that arises when an insurance company cannot observe whether the insured exerts effort to prevent a loss and the "adverse selection" (see Section 13.B) that occurs when the insured knows more than the company at the time he purchases a policy about his likelihood of an accident. Some authors use moral hazard to refer to either of the hidden action or hidden information variants of the principal-agent problem [see, for example, Hart and Holmstrom (1987)]. Here, however, we use the term in the original sense.

a hidden information model. Then, in Section 14.D, we provide a brief discussion of hybrid models that contain both of these features. We shall see that the presence of postcontractual asymmetric information often leads to welfare losses for the contracting parties relative to what would be achievable in the absence of these informational imperfections.

It is important to emphasize the broad range of economic relationships that fit into the general framework of the principal-agent problem. The owner–manager relationship is only one example; others include insurance companies and insured individuals (the insurance company cannot observe how much care is exercised by the insured), manufacturers and their distributors (the manufacturer may not be able to observe the market conditions faced by the distributor), a firm and its workforce (the firm may have more information than its workers about the true state of demand for its products and therefore about the value of the workers' product), and banks and borrowers (the bank may have difficulty observing whether the borrower uses the loaned funds for the purpose for which the loan was granted). As would be expected given this diversity of examples, the principal-agent framework has found application in a broad range of applied fields in economics. Our discussion will focus on the owner–manager problem.

The analysis in this chapter, particularly that in Section 14.C, is closely related to that in two other chapters. First, the techniques developed in Section 14.C can be applied to the analysis of screening problems in which, in contrast with the case studied in Section 13.D, only one uninformed party screens informed individuals. We discuss the analysis of this *monopolistic screening problem* in small type at the end of Section 14.C. Second, the principal-agent problem is actually a special case of "mechanism design," the topic of Chapter 23. Thus, the material here constitutes a first pass at this more general issue. Mastery of the fundamentals of the principal-agent problem, particularly the material in Section 14.C, will be helpful when you study Chapter 23.

A good source for further reading on topics of this chapter is Hart and Holmstrom (1987).

# 14.B  Hidden Actions (Moral Hazard)

Imagine that the owner of a firm (the *principal*) wishes to hire a manager (the *agent*) for a one-time project. The project's profits are affected, at least in part, by the manager's actions. If these actions were observable, the contracting problem between the owner and the manager would be relatively straightforward; the contract would simply specify the exact actions to be taken by the manager and the compensation (wage payment) that the owner is to provide in return.[2] When the manager's actions are not observable, however, the contract can no longer specify them in an effective manner, because there is simply no way to verify whether the manager has fulfilled his obligations. In this circumstance, the owner must design the manager's compensation scheme in a way that *indirectly* gives him the incentive to take the correct

---

2. Note that this requires not only that the manager's actions be observable to the owner but also that they be observable to any court that might be called upon to enforce the contract.

actions (those that would be contracted for if his actions were observable). In this section, we study this contract design problem.

To be more specific, let $\pi$ denote the project's (observable) profits, and let $e$ denote the manager's action choice. The set of possible actions is denoted by $E$. We interpret $e$ as measuring managerial effort. In the simplest case that is widely studied in the literature, $e$ is a one-dimensional measure of how "hard" the manager works, and so $E \subset \mathbb{R}$. More generally, however, managerial effort can have many dimensions— how hard the manager works to reduce costs, how much time he spends soliciting customers, and so on—and so $e$ could be a vector with each of its elements measuring managerial effort in a distinct activity. In this case, $E \subset \mathbb{R}^M$ for some $M$.[3] In our discussion, we shall refer to $e$ as the manager's *effort choice* or *effort level*.

For the nonobservability of managerial effort to have any consequence, the manager's effort must not be perfectly deducible from observation of $\pi$. Hence, to make things interesting (and realistic), we assume that although the project's profits are affected by $e$, they are not fully determined by it. In particular, we assume that the firm's profit can take values in $[\underline{\pi}, \bar{\pi}]$ and that it is stochastically related to $e$ in a manner described by the conditional density function $f(\pi \mid e)$, with $f(\pi \mid e) > 0$ for all $e \in E$ and all $\pi \in [\underline{\pi}, \bar{\pi}]$. Thus, any potential realization of $\pi$ can arise following any given effort choice by the manager.

In the discussion that follows, we restrict our attention to the case in which the manager has only two possible effort choices, $e_H$ and $e_L$ (see Appendix A for a discussion of the case in which the manager has many possible actions), and we make assumptions implying that $e_H$ is a "high-effort" choice that leads to a higher profit level for the firm than $e_L$ but entails greater difficulty for the manager. This fact will mean that there is a conflict between the interests of the owner and those of the manager.

More specifically, we assume that the distribution of $\pi$ conditional on $e_H$ first-order stochastically dominates the distribution conditional on $e_L$; that is, the distribution functions $F(\pi \mid e_L)$ and $F(\pi \mid e_H)$ satisfy $F(\pi \mid e_H) \leq F(\pi \mid e_L)$ at all $\pi \in [\underline{\pi}, \bar{\pi}]$, with strict inequality on some open set $\Pi \subset [\underline{\pi}, \bar{\pi}]$ (see Section 6.D). This implies that the level of expected profits when the manager chooses $e_H$ is larger than that from $e_L$: $\int \pi f(\pi \mid e_H) \, d\pi > \int \pi f(\pi \mid e_L) \, d\pi$.

The manager is an expected utility maximizer with a Bernoulli utility function $u(w, e)$ over his wage $w$ and effort level $e$. This function satisfies $u_w(w, e) > 0$ and $u_{ww}(w, e) \leq 0$ at all $(w, e)$ (subscripts here denote partial derivatives) and $u(w, e_H) < u(w, e_L)$ at all $w$; that is, the manager prefers more income to less, is weakly risk averse over income lotteries, and dislikes a high level of effort.[4] In what follows, we focus on a special case of this utility function that has attracted much of the

---

3. In fact, more general interpretations are possible. For example, $e$ could include non-effort-related managerial decisions such as what kind of inputs are purchased or the strategies that are adopted for appealing to buyers. We stick to the effort interpretation largely because it helps with intuition.

4. Note that in the multidimensional-effort case, it need not be that $e_H$ has higher effort in every dimension; the only important thing for our analysis is that it leads to higher profits and entails a larger managerial disutility than does $e_L$.

attention in the literature: $u(w, e) = v(w) - g(e)$.[5] For this case, our assumptions on $u(w, e)$ imply that $v'(w) > 0$, $v''(w) \leq 0$, and $g(e_H) > g(e_L)$.

The owner receives the project's profits less any wage payments made to the manager. We assume that the owner is risk neutral and therefore that his objective is to maximize his expected return. The idea behind this simplifying assumption is that the owner may hold a well-diversified portfolio that allows him to diversify away the risk from this project. (Exercise 14.B.2 asks you to consider the case of a risk-averse owner.)

### The Optimal Contract when Effort is Observable

It is useful to begin our analysis by looking at the optimal contracting problem when effort is observable.

Suppose that the owner chooses a contract to offer the manager that the manager can then either accept or reject. A contract here specifies the manager's effort $e \in \{e_L, e_H\}$ and his wage payment as a function of observed profits $w(\pi)$. We assume that a competitive market for managers dictates that the owner must provide the manager with an expected utility level of at least $\bar{u}$ if he is to accept the owner's contract offer ($\bar{u}$ is the manager's *reservation utility level*). If the manager rejects the owner's contract offer, the owner receives a payoff of zero.

We assume throughout that the owner finds it worthwhile to make the manager an offer that he will accept. The optimal contract for the owner then solves the following problem (for notational simplicity, we suppress the lower and upper limits of integration $\underline{\pi}$ and $\bar{\pi}$):

$$\underset{e \in \{e_L, e_H\}, \, w(\pi)}{\text{Max}} \int (\pi - w(\pi)) f(\pi \,|\, e) \, d\pi \tag{14.B.1}$$

$$\text{s.t.} \int v(w(\pi)) f(\pi \,|\, e) \, d\pi - g(e) \geq \bar{u}.$$

It is convenient to think of this problem in two stages. First, for each choice of $e$ that might be specified in the contract, what is the best compensation scheme $w(\pi)$ to offer the manager? Second, what is the best choice of $e$?

Given that the contract specifies effort level $e$, choosing $w(\pi)$ to maximize $\int (\pi - w(\pi)) f(\pi \,|\, e) \, d\pi = (\int \pi f(\pi \,|\, e) \, d\pi) - (\int w(\pi) f(\pi \,|\, e) \, d\pi)$ is equivalent to minimizing the expected value of the owner's compensation costs, $\int w(\pi) f(\pi \,|\, e) \, d\pi$, so (14.B.1) tells us that the optimal compensation scheme in this case solves

$$\underset{w(\pi)}{\text{Min}} \int w(\pi) f(\pi \,|\, e) \, d\pi \tag{14.B.2}$$

$$\text{s.t.} \int v(w(\pi)) f(\pi \,|\, e) \, d\pi - g(e) \geq \bar{u}.$$

The constraint in (14.B.2) always binds at a solution to this problem; otherwise, the owner could lower the manager's wages while still getting him to accept the contract. Letting $\gamma$ denote the multiplier on this constraint, at a solution to problem (14.B.2) the manager's wage $w(\pi)$ at each level of $\pi \in [\underline{\pi}, \bar{\pi}]$ must satisfy the first-order

---

5. Exercise 14.B.1 considers one implication of relaxing this assumption.

condition[6]

$$-f(\pi \,|\, e) + \gamma v'(w(\pi)) f(\pi \,|\, e) = 0,$$

or

$$\frac{1}{v'(w(\pi))} = \gamma. \qquad (14.\text{B}.3)$$

If the manager is strictly risk averse [so that $v'(w)$ is strictly decreasing in $w$], the implication of condition (14.B.3) is that the optimal compensation scheme $w(\pi)$ is a constant; that is, the owner should provide the manager with a fixed wage payment. This finding is just a risk-sharing result: Given that the contract explicitly dictates the manager's effort choice and that there is no problem with providing incentives, the risk-neutral owner should fully insure the risk-averse manager against any risk in his income stream (in a manner similar to that in Example 6.C.1). Hence, given the contract's specification of $e$, the owner offers a fixed wage payment $w_e^*$ such that the manager receives exactly his reservation utility level:

$$v(w_e^*) - g(e) = \bar{u}. \qquad (14.\text{B}.4)$$

Note that since $g(e_H) > g(e_L)$, the manager's wage will be higher if the contract calls for effort $e_H$ than if it calls for $e_L$.

On the other hand, when the manager is risk neutral, say with $v(w) = w$, condition (14.B.3) is necessarily satisfied for *any* compensation function. In this case, because there is no need for insurance, a fixed wage scheme is merely one of many possible optimal compensation schemes. Any compensation function $w(\pi)$ that gives the manager an expected wage payment equal to $\bar{u} + g(e)$ [the level derived from condition (14.B.4) when $v(w) = w$] is also optimal.

Now consider the optimal choice of $e$. The owner optimally specifies the effort level $e \in \{e_L, e_H\}$ that maximizes his expected profits less wage payments,

$$\int \pi f(\pi \,|\, e) \, d\pi - v^{-1}(\bar{u} + g(e)). \qquad (14.\text{B}.5)$$

The first term in (14.B.5) represents the gross profit when the manager puts forth effort $e$; the second term represents the wages that must be paid to compensate the manager for this effort [derived from condition (14.B.4)]. Whether $e_H$ or $e_L$ is optimal depends on the incremental increase in expected profits from $e_H$ over $e_L$ compared with the monetary cost of the incremental disutility it causes the manager.

This is summarized in Proposition 14.B.1.

**Proposition 14.B.1:** In the principal-agent model with observable managerial effort, an optimal contract specifies that the manager choose the effort $e^*$ that maximizes $[\int \pi f(\pi \,|\, e) \, d\pi - v^{-1}(\bar{u} + g(e))]$ and pays the manager a fixed wage $w^* = v^{-1}(\bar{u} + g(e^*))$. This is the uniquely optimal contract if $v''(w) < 0$ at all $w$.

---

6. The first-order condition for $w(\pi)$ is derived by taking the derivative with respect to the manager's wage at each level of $\pi$ separately. To see this point, consider a discrete version of the model in which there is a finite number of possible profit levels $(\pi_1, \ldots, \pi_N)$ and associated wage levels $(w_1, \ldots, w_N)$. The first-order condition (14.B.3) is analogous to the condition one gets in the discrete model by examining the first-order conditions for each $w_n$, $n = 1, \ldots, N$ (note that we allow the wage payment to be negative). To be rigorous, we should add that when we have a continuum of possible levels of $\pi$, an optimal compensation scheme need only satisfy condition (14.B.3) at a set of profit levels that is of full measure.

### The Optimal Contract when Effort is Not Observable

The optimal contract described in Proposition 14.B.1 accomplishes two goals: it specifies an efficient effort choice by the manager, and it fully insures him against income risk. When effort is not observable, however, these two goals often come into conflict because the only way to get the manager to work hard is to relate his pay to the realization of profits, which is random. When these goals come into conflict, the nonobservability of effort leads to inefficiencies.

To highlight this point, we first study the case in which the manager is risk neutral. We show that in this case, where the risk-bearing concern is absent, the owner can still achieve the same outcome as when effort is observable. We then study the optimal contract when the manager is risk averse. In this case, whenever the first-best (full observability) contract would involve the high-effort level, efficient risk bearing and efficient incentive provision come into conflict, and the presence of nonobservable actions leads to a welfare loss.

### A risk-neutral manager

Suppose that $v(w) = w$. Applying Proposition 14.B.1, the optimal effort level $e^*$ when effort is observable solves

$$\max_{e \in \{e_L, e_H\}} \int \pi f(\pi \mid e) \, d\pi - g(e) - \bar{u}. \tag{14.B.6}$$

The owner's profit in this case is the value of expression (14.B.6), and the manager receives an expected utility of exactly $\bar{u}$.

Now consider the owner's payoff when the manager's effort is not observable. In Proposition 14.B.2, we establish that the owner can still achieve his full-information payoff.

**Proposition 14.B.2:** In the principal-agent model with unobservable managerial effort and a risk-neutral manager, an optimal contract generates the same effort choice and expected utilities for the manager and the owner as when effort is observable.

**Proof:** We show explicitly that there is a contract the owner can offer that gives him the same payoff that he receives under full information. This contract must therefore be an optimal contract for the owner because the owner can never do better when effort is not observable than when it is (when effort is observable, the owner is always free to offer the optimal nonobservability contract and simply leave the choice of an effort level up to the manager).

Suppose that the owner offers a compensation schedule of the form $w(\pi) = \pi - \alpha$, where $\alpha$ is some constant. This compensation schedule can be interpreted as "selling the project to the manager" because it gives the manager the full return $\pi$ except for the fixed payment $\alpha$ (the "sales price"). If the manager accepts this contract, he chooses $e$ to maximize his expected utility,

$$\int w(\pi) f(\pi \mid e) \, d\pi - g(e) = \int \pi f(\pi \mid e) \, d\pi - \alpha - g(e). \tag{14.B.7}$$

Comparing (14.B.7) with (14.B.6), we see that $e^*$ maximizes (14.B.7). Thus, this contract induces the first-best (full observability) effort level $e^*$.

The manager is willing to accept this contract as long as it gives him an expected utility of at least $\bar{u}$, that is, as long as

$$\int \pi f(\pi \,|\, e^*) \, d\pi - \alpha - g(e^*) \geq \bar{u}. \tag{14.B.8}$$

Let $\alpha^*$ be the level of $\alpha$ at which (14.B.8) holds with equality. Note that the owner's payoff if the compensation scheme is $w(\pi) = \pi - \alpha^*$ is exactly $\alpha^*$ (the manager gets all of $\pi$ except for the fixed payment $\alpha^*$). Rearranging (14.B.8), we see that $\alpha^* = \int \pi f(\pi \,|\, e^*) \, d\pi - g(e^*) - \bar{u}$. Hence, with compensation scheme $w(\pi) = \pi - \alpha^*$, both the owner and the manager get exactly the same payoff as when effort is observable. ∎

The basic idea behind Proposition 14.B.2 is straightforward. If the manager is risk neutral, the problem of risk sharing disappears. Efficient incentives can be provided without incurring any risk-bearing losses by having the manager receive the full marginal returns from his effort.

### A risk-averse manager

When the manager is strictly risk averse over income lotteries, matters become more complicated. Now incentives for high effort can be provided only at the cost of having the manager face risk. To characterize the optimal contract in these circumstances, we again consider the contract design problem in two steps: first, we characterize the optimal incentive scheme for each effort level that the owner might want the manager to select; second, we consider which effort level the owner should induce.

The optimal incentive scheme for implementing a specific effort level $e$ minimizes the owner's expected wage payment subject to two constraints. As before, the manager must receive an expected utility of at least $\bar{u}$ if he is to accept the contract. When the manager's effort is unobservable, however, the owner also faces a second constraint: The manager must actually *desire* to choose effort $e$ when facing the incentive scheme. Formally, the optimal incentive scheme for implementing $e$ must therefore solve

$$\underset{w(\pi)}{\text{Min}} \ \int w(\pi) \, f(\pi \,|\, e) \, d\pi \tag{14.B.9}$$

$$\text{s.t.} \quad \text{(i)} \ \int v(w(\pi)) \, f(\pi \,|\, e) \, d\pi - g(e) \geq \bar{u}$$

$$\text{(ii)} \ \ e \text{ solves } \underset{\tilde{e}}{\text{Max}} \int v(w(\pi)) \, f(\pi \,|\, \tilde{e}) \, d\pi - g(\tilde{e}).$$

Constraint (ii) is known as the *incentive constraint*: it insures that under compensation scheme $w(\pi)$ the manager's optimal effort choice is $e$.

How does the owner optimally implement each of the two possible levels of $e$? We consider each in turn.

*Implementing $e_L$:* Suppose, first, that the owner wishes to implement effort level $e_L$. In this case, the owner optimally offers the manager the fixed wage payment $w_e^* = v^{-1}(\bar{u} + g(e_L))$, the same payment he would offer if contractually specifying effort $e_L$ when effort is observable. To see this, note that with this compensation scheme the manager selects $e_L$: His wage payment is unaffected by his effort, and so he will choose the effort level that involves the lowest disutility, namely $e_L$. Doing so, he earns exactly $\bar{u}$. Hence, this contract implements $e_L$ at exactly the same cost as when effort is observable. But, as we noted in the proof of Proposition 14.B.2, the owner can never do better when effort is unobservable than when effort is observable [formally, in problem (14.B.9), the owner faces the additional constraint (ii) relative to problem (14.B.2)]; therefore, this must be a solution to problem (14.B.9).

*Implementing $e_H$*: The more interesting case arises when the owner decides to induce effort level $e_H$. In this case, constraint (ii) of (14.B.9) can be written as

$$(\text{ii}_H) \quad \int v(w(\pi))\, f(\pi\,|\,e_H)\, d\pi - g(e_H) \geq \int v(w(\pi))\, f(\pi\,|\,e_L)\, d\pi - g(e_L).$$

Letting $\gamma \geq 0$ and $\mu \geq 0$ denote the multipliers on constraints (i) and (ii$_H$), respectively, $w(\pi)$ must satisfy the following Kuhn–Tucker first-order condition at every $\pi \in [\underline{\pi}, \bar{\pi}]$:[7]

$$-f(\pi\,|\,e_H) + \gamma v'(w(\pi))\, f(\pi\,|\,e_H) + \mu[f(\pi\,|\,e_H) - f(\pi\,|\,e_L)]v'(w(\pi)) = 0$$

or

$$\frac{1}{v'(w(\pi))} = \gamma + \mu\left[1 - \frac{f(\pi\,|\,e_L)}{f(\pi\,|\,e_H)}\right]. \tag{14.B.10}$$

We first establish that in any solution to problem (14.B.9), where $e = e_H$, both $\gamma$ and $\mu$ are strictly positive.

**Lemma 14.B.1:** In any solution to problem (14.B.9) with $e = e_H$, both $\gamma > 0$ and $\mu > 0$.

**Proof:** Suppose that $\gamma = 0$. Because $F(\pi\,|\,e_H)$ first-order stochastically dominates $F(\pi\,|\,e_L)$, there must exist an open set of profit levels $\tilde{\Pi} \subset [\underline{\pi}, \bar{\pi}]$ such that $[f(\pi\,|\,e_L)/f(\pi\,|\,e_H)] > 1$ at all $\pi \in \tilde{\Pi}$. But if $\gamma = 0$, condition (14.B.10) then implies that $v'(w(\pi)) \leq 0$ at any such $\pi$ (recall that $\mu \geq 0$), which is impossible. Hence, $\gamma > 0$.

On the other hand, if $\mu = 0$ in the solution to problem (14.B.9) then, by condition (14.B.10), the optimal compensation schedule gives a fixed wage payment for every profit realization. But we know that this would lead the manager to choose $e_L$ rather than $e_H$, violating constraint (ii$_H$) of problem (14.B.9). Hence, $\mu > 0$. ∎

---

7. Although problem (14.B.9) may not appear to be a convex programming problem, a simple transformation of the problem shows that (14.B.10) is both a necessary and a sufficient condition for a solution. To see this, reformulate (14.B.9) as a problem of choosing the manager's level of utility for each profit outcome $\pi$, say $\bar{v}(\pi)$. Letting $\phi(\cdot) = v^{-1}(\cdot)$, the objective function becomes $\int \phi(\bar{v}(\pi))\, f(\pi\,|\,e_H)\, d\pi$, which is convex in $\bar{v}(\pi)$, and the constraints are then all linear in $\bar{v}(\pi)$. Thus, (Kuhn–Tucker) first-order conditions are both necessary and sufficient for a maximum of this reformulated problem (see Section M.K of the Mathematical Appendix). The first-order condition for this problem is

$$-\phi'(\bar{v}(\pi))f(\pi\,|\,e_H) + \gamma f(\pi\,|\,e_H) + \mu[f(\pi\,|\,e_H) - f(\pi\,|\,e_L)] = 0 \quad \text{for all } \pi \in [\underline{\pi}, \bar{\pi}].$$

Defining $w(\pi)$ by $v(w(\pi)) = \bar{v}(\pi)$, and noting that $\phi'(v(w(\pi))) = 1/v'(w(\pi))$, this gives (14.B.10).

Lemma 14.B.1 tells us that both constraints in problem (14.B.9) bind when $e = e_H$.[8] Moreover, given Lemma 14.B.1, condition (14.B.10) can be used to derive some useful insights into the shape of the optimal compensation schedule. Consider, for example, the fixed wage payment $\hat{w}$ such that $(1/v'(\hat{w})) = \gamma$. According to condition (14.B.10),

$$w(\pi) > \hat{w} \quad \text{if} \quad \frac{f(\pi \mid e_L)}{f(\pi \mid e_H)} < 1$$

and

$$w(\pi) < \hat{w} \quad \text{if} \quad \frac{f(\pi \mid e_L)}{f(\pi \mid e_H)} > 1.$$

This relationship is fairly intuitive. The optimal compensation scheme pays more than $\hat{w}$ for outcomes that are statistically relatively more likely to occur under $e_H$ than under $e_L$ in the sense of having a likelihood ratio $[f(\pi \mid e_L)/f(\pi \mid e_H)]$ less than 1. Similarly, it offers less compensation for outcomes that are relatively more likely when $e_L$ is chosen. We should stress, however, that while this condition evokes a statistical interpretation, there is no actual statistical inference going on here; the owner *knows* what level of effort will be chosen given the compensation schedule he offers. Rather, the compensation package has this form because of its *incentive effects*. That is, by structuring compensation in this way, it provides the manager with an incentive for choosing $e_H$ instead of $e_L$.

This point leads to what may at first seem a somewhat surprising implication: in an optimal incentive scheme, compensation is not necessarily monotonically increasing in profits. As is clear from examination of condition (14.B.10), for the optimal compensation scheme to be monotonically increasing, it must be that the likelihood ratio $[f(\pi \mid e_L)/f(\pi \mid e_H)]$ is decreasing in $\pi$; that is, as $\pi$ increases, the likelihood of getting profit level $\pi$ if effort is $e_H$ relative to the likelihood if effort is $e_L$ must increase. This property, known as the *monotone likelihood ratio property* [see Milgrom (1981)], is *not* implied by first-order stochastic dominance. Figures 14.B.1(a) and (b), for example, depict a case in which the distribution of $\pi$ conditional on $e_H$ stochastically dominates the distribution of $\pi$ conditional on $e_L$ but the monotone likelihood ratio property does not hold. In this example, increases in effort serve to convert low profit realizations into intermediate ones but have no effect on the likelihood of very high profit realizations. Condition (14.B.10) tells us that in this case, we should have higher wages at intermediate levels of profit than at very high ones because it is the likelihood of intermediate profit levels that is sensitive to increases in effort. The optimal compensation function for this example is shown in Figure 14.B.1(c).

---

8. A more direct argument for constraint (i) being binding goes as follows: Suppose that $w(\pi)$ is a solution to (14.B.9) in which constraint (i) is not binding. Consider a change in the compensation function that lowers the wage paid at each level of $\pi$ in such a way that the resulting decrease in utility is equal at all $\pi$, that is, to a new function $\hat{w}(\pi)$ with $[v(w(\pi)) - v(\hat{w}(\pi))] = \Delta v > 0$ at all $\pi \in [\underline{\pi}, \bar{\pi}]$. This change does not affect the satisfaction of the incentive constraint $(ii_H)$ since if the manager was willing to pick $e_H$ when faced with $w(\pi)$, he will do so when faced with $\hat{w}(\pi)$. Furthermore, because constraint (i) is not binding, the manager will still accept this new contract if $\Delta v$ is small enough. Lastly, the owner's expected wage payments will be lower than under $w(\pi)$. This yields a contradiction.

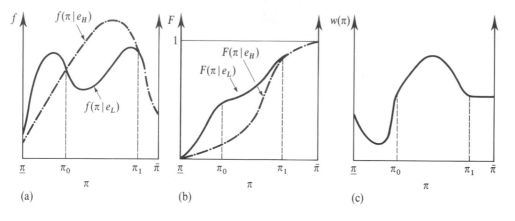

**Figure 14.B.1**

A violation of the monotone likelihood ratio property. (a) Densities. (b) Distribution functions. (c) Optimal wage scheme.

Condition (14.B.10) also implies that the optimal contract is not likely to take a simple (e.g., linear) form. The optimal shape of $w(\pi)$ is a function of the informational content of various profit levels (through the likelihood ratio), and this is unlikely to vary with $\pi$ in a simple manner in most problems.

Finally, note that given the variability that is optimally introduced into the manager's compensation, the expected value of the manager's wage payment must be strictly greater than his (fixed) wage payment in the observable case, $w_{e_H}^* = v^{-1}(\bar{u} + g(e_H))$. Intuitively, because the manager must be assured an expected utility level of $\bar{u}$, the owner must compensate him through a higher average wage payment for any risk he bears. To see this point formally, note that since $E[v(w(\pi))|e_H] = \bar{u} + g(e_H)$ and $v''(\cdot) < 0$, Jensen's inequality (see Section M.C of the Mathematical Appendix) tells us that $v(E[w(\pi)|e_H]) > \bar{u} + g(e_H)$. But we know that $v(w_{e_H}^*) = \bar{u} + g(e_H)$, and so $E[w(\pi)|e_H] > w_{e_H}^*$. As a result, nonobservability increases the owner's expected compensation costs of implementing effort level $e_H$.

Given the preceding analysis, which effort level should the owner induce? As before, the owner compares the incremental change in expected profits from the two effort levels $[\int \pi f(\pi|e_H) \, d\pi - \int \pi f(\pi|e_L) \, d\pi]$ with the difference in expected wage payments in the contracts that optimally implement each of them, that is, with the difference in the value of problem (14.B.9) for $e = e_H$ compared with $e = e_L$.

From the preceding analysis, we know that the wage payment when implementing $e_L$ is exactly the same as when effort is observable, whereas the expected wage payment when the owner implements $e_H$ under nonobservability is strictly larger than his payment in the observable case. Thus, in this model, nonobservability raises the cost of implementing $e_H$ and does not change the cost of implementing $e_L$. The implication of this fact is that nonobservability of effort can lead to an inefficiently low level of effort being implemented. When $e_L$ would be the optimal effort level if effort were observable, then it still is when effort is nonobservable. In this case, nonobservability causes no losses. In contrast, when $e_H$ would be optimal if effort were observable, then one of two things may happen: it may be optimal to implement $e_H$ using an incentive scheme that faces the manager with risk; alternatively, the risk-bearing costs may be high enough that the owner decides that it is better to simply implement $e_L$. In either case, nonobservability causes a welfare loss to the owner (the manager's expected utility is $\bar{u}$ in either case).[9]

These observations are summarized in Proposition 14.B.3.

**Proposition 14.B.3:** In the principal-agent model with unobservable manager effort, a risk-averse manager, and two possible effort choices, the optimal compensation scheme for implementing $e_H$ satisfies condition (14.B.10), gives the manager expected utility $\bar{u}$, and involves a larger expected wage payment than is required when effort is observable. The optimal compensation scheme for implementing $e_L$ involves the same fixed wage payment as if effort were observable. Whenever the optimal effort level with observable effort would be $e_H$, nonobservability causes a welfare loss.

The fact that nonobservability leads in this model only to *downward* distortions in the manager's effort level is a special feature of the two-effort-level specification. With many possible effort choices, nonobservability may still alter the level of managerial effort induced in an optimal contract from its level under full observability, but the direction of the bias can be upward as well as downward. (See Exercise 14.B.4 for an illustration.)

---

Imagine that another statistical signal of effort, say $y$, is available to the owner in addition to the realization of profits, and that the joint density of $\pi$ and $y$ given $e$ is given by $f(\pi, y \mid e)$. In this case, the manager's compensation can, in principle, be made to depend on both $\pi$ and $y$. When should compensation be made a function of this variable as well? That is, when does the optimal compensation function $w(\pi, y)$ actually depend on $y$?

To answer this question, suppose that the owner wishes to implement $e_H$. Following along the same lines as above, we can derive a condition analogous to condition (14.B.10):

$$\frac{1}{v'(w(\pi, y))} = \gamma + \mu\left[1 - \frac{f(\pi, y \mid e_L)}{f(\pi, y \mid e_H)}\right]. \tag{14.B.11}$$

Consider, first, the case in which $y$ is simply a noisy random variable that is unrelated to $e$. Then we can write the density $f(\pi, y \mid e)$ as the product of two densities, $f_1(\pi \mid e)$ and $f_2(y)$: $f(\pi, y \mid e) = f_1(\pi \mid e)f_2(y)$. Substituting into (14.B.11), the $f_2(\cdot)$ terms cancel out, and so the optimal compensation package is independent of $y$.

The intuition behind this result is straightforward. Suppose that the owner is initially offering a contract that has wage payments dependent on $y$. Intuitively, this contract induces a randomness in the manager's wage that is unrelated to $e$ and therefore makes the manager face risk without achieving any beneficial incentive effect. If the owner instead offers, for each realization of $\pi$, the certain payment $\bar{w}(\pi)$ such that

$$v(\bar{w}(\pi)) = E[v(w(\pi, y)) \mid \pi] = \int v(w(\pi, y))f_2(y)\, dy,$$

---

9. Note, however, that although nonobservability leads to a welfare loss, the outcome here is a constrained Pareto optimum in the sense introduced in Section 13.B. To see this, note that the owner maximizes his profit subject to giving the manager an expected utility level no less than $\bar{u}$ and subject to constraints deriving from his inability to observe the manager's effort choice. As a result, no allocation that Pareto dominates this outcome can be achieved by a central authority who cannot observe the manager's effort choice. For market intervention by such an authority to generate a Pareto improvement, there must be externalities among the contracts signed by different pairs of individuals.

then the manager gets exactly the same expected utility under $\bar{w}(\pi)$ as under $w(\pi, y)$ for any level of effort he chooses. Thus, the manager's effort choice will be unchanged, and he will still accept the contract. However, because the manager faces less risk, the expected wage payments are lower and the owner is better off (this again follows from Jensen's inequality: for all $\pi$, $v(E[w(\pi, y)|\pi]) > E[v(w(\pi, y))|\pi]$, and so $\bar{w}(\pi) < E[w(\pi, y)|\pi]$).

This point can be pushed further. Note that we can always write

$$f(\pi, y \,|\, e) = f_1(\pi \,|\, e) f_2(y \,|\, \pi, e).$$

If $f_2(y \,|\, \pi, e)$ does not depend on $e$, then the $f_2(\cdot)$ terms in condition (14.B.11) again cancel out and the optimal compensation package does not depend on $y$. This condition on $f_2(y \,|\, \pi, e)$ is equivalent to the statistical concept that $\pi$ is a *sufficient statistic* for $y$ with respect to $e$. The converse is also true: As long as $\pi$ is *not* a sufficient statistic for $y$, then wages *should* be made to depend on $y$, at least to some degree. See Holmstrom (1979) for further details.

---

A number of extensions of this basic analysis have been studied in the literature. For example, Holmstrom (1982), Nalebuff and Stiglitz (1983), and Green and Stokey (1983) examine cases in which many managers are being hired and consider the use of relative performance evaluation in such settings; Bernheim and Whinston (1986), on the other hand, extend the model in the other direction, examining settings in which a single agent is hired simultaneously by several principals; Dye (1986) considers cases in which effort may be observed through costly monitoring; Rogerson (1985a), Allen (1985), and Fudenberg, Holmstrom, and Milgrom (1990) examine situations in which the agency relationship is repeated over many periods, with a particular focus on the extent to which long-term contracts are more effective at resolving agency problems than is a sequence of short-term contracts of the type we analyzed in this section. (This list of extensions is hardly exhaustive.) Many of these analyses focus on the case in which effort is single-dimensional; Holmstrom and Milgrom (1991) discuss some interesting aspects of the more realistic case of multidimensional effort.

Holmstrom and Milgrom (1987) have pursued another interesting extension. Bothered by the simplicity of real-world compensation schemes relative to the optimal contracts derived in models like the one we have studied here, they investigate a model in which profits accrue incrementally over time and the manager is able to adjust his effort during the course of the project in response to early profit realizations. They identify conditions under which the owner can restrict himself without loss to the use of compensation schemes that are *linear* functions of the project's total profit. The optimality of linear compensation schemes arises because of the need to offer incentives that are "robust" in the sense that they continue to provide incentives regardless of how early profit realizations turn out. Their analysis illustrates a more general idea, namely, that complicating the nature of the incentive problem can actually lead to simpler forms for optimal contracts. For illustrations of this point, see Exercises 14.B.5 and 14.B.6.

The exercises at the end of the chapter explore some of these extensions.

# 14.C  Hidden Information (and Monopolistic Screening)

In this section, we shift our focus to a setting in which the postcontractual informational asymmetry takes the form of hidden information.

Once again, an owner wishes to hire a manager to run a one-time project. Now, however, the manager's effort level, denoted by $e$, is fully observable. What is not observable after the contract is signed is the random realization of the manager's disutility from effort. For example, the manager may come to find himself well suited to the tasks required at the firm, in which case high effort has a relatively low disutility associated with it, or the opposite may be true. However, only the manager comes to know which case obtains.[10]

Before proceeding, we note that the techniques we develop here can also be applied to models of *monopolistic screening* where, in a setting characterized by *precontractual* informational asymmetries, a single uninformed individual offers a menu of contracts in order to distinguish, or *screen*, informed agents who have differing information at the time of contracting (see Section 13.D for an analysis of a competitive screening model). We discuss this connection further in small type at the end of this section.

To formulate our hidden information principal-agent model, we suppose that effort can be measured by a one-dimensional variable $e \in [0, \infty)$. Gross profits (excluding any wage payments to the manager) are a simple deterministic function of effort, $\pi(e)$, with $\pi(0) = 0$, $\pi'(e) > 0$, and $\pi''(e) < 0$ for all $e$.

The manager is an expected utility maximizer whose Bernoulli utility function over wages and effort, $u(w, e, \theta)$, depends on a state of nature $\theta$ that is realized after the contract is signed and that only the manager observes. We assume that $\theta \in \mathbb{R}$, and we focus on a special form of $u(w, e, \theta)$ that is widely used in the literature:[11]

$$u(w, e, \theta) = v(w - g(e, \theta)).$$

The function $g(e, \theta)$ measures the disutility of effort in monetary units. We assume that $g(0, \theta) = 0$ for all $\theta$ and, letting subscripts denote partial derivatives, that

$$g_e(e, \theta) \begin{cases} > 0 & \text{for } e > 0 \\ = 0 & \text{for } e = 0 \end{cases}$$

$$g_{ee}(e, \theta) \quad > 0 \qquad \text{for all } e$$

$$g_\theta(e, \theta) \quad < 0 \qquad \text{for all } e$$

$$g_{e\theta}(e, \theta) \begin{cases} < 0 & \text{for } e > 0 \\ = 0 & \text{for } e = 0. \end{cases}$$

Thus, the manager is averse to increases in effort, and this aversion is larger the greater the current level of effort. In addition, higher values of $\theta$ are more productive states in the sense that both the manager's total disutility from effort, $g(e, \theta)$, and his marginal disutility from effort at any current effort level, $g_e(e, \theta)$, are lower when $\theta$

---

10. A seemingly more important source of hidden information between managers and owners is that the manager of a firm often comes to know more about the potential profitability of various actions than does the owner. In Section 14.D, we discuss one hybrid hidden action–hidden information model that captures this alternative sort of informational asymmetry; its formal analysis reduces to that of the model studied here.

11. Exercise 14.C.3 asks you to consider an alternative form for the manager's utility function.

is greater. We also assume that the manager is strictly risk averse, with $v''(\cdot) < 0$.[12] As in Section 14.B, the manager's reservation utility level, the level of expected utility he must receive if he is to accept the owner's contract offer, is denoted by $\bar{u}$. Note that our assumptions about $g(e, \theta)$ imply that the manager's indifference curves have the single-crossing property discussed in Section 13.C.

Finally, for expositional purposes, we focus on the simple case in which $\theta$ can take only one of two values, $\theta_H$ and $\theta_L$, with $\theta_H > \theta_L$ and Prob $(\theta_H) = \lambda \in (0, 1)$. (Exercise 14.C.1 asks you to consider the case of an arbitrary finite number of states.)

A contract must try to accomplish two objectives here: first, as in Section 14.B, the risk-neutral owner should insure the manager against fluctuations in his income; second, although there is no problem here in insuring that the manager puts in effort (because the contract can explicitly state the effort level required), a contract that maximizes the surplus available in the relationship (and hence, the owner's payoff) must make the level of managerial effort responsive to the disutility incurred by the manager, that is, to the state $\theta$. To fix ideas, we first illustrate how these goals are accomplished when $\theta$ is observable; we then turn to an analysis of the problems that arise when $\theta$ is observed only by the manager.

### The State $\theta$ is Observable

If $\theta$ is observable, a contract can directly specify the effort level and remuneration of the manager contingent on each realization of $\theta$ (note that these variables fully determine the economic outcomes for the two parties). Thus, a complete information contract consists of two wage–effort pairs: $(w_H, e_H) \in \mathbb{R} \times \mathbb{R}_+$ for state $\theta_H$ and $(w_L, e_L) \in \mathbb{R} \times \mathbb{R}_+$ for state $\theta_L$. The owner optimally chooses these pairs to solve the following problem:

$$\underset{\substack{w_L, e_L \geq 0 \\ w_H, e_H \geq 0}}{\text{Max}} \quad \lambda[\pi(e_H) - w_H] + (1 - \lambda)[\pi(e_L) - w_L] \qquad (14.C.1)$$

$$\text{s.t.} \quad \lambda\, v(w_H - g(e_H, \theta_H)) + (1 - \lambda)v(w_L - g(e_L, \theta_L)) \geq \bar{u}.$$

In any solution $[(w_L^*, e_L^*), (w_H^*, e_H^*)]$ to problem (14.C.1) the reservation utility constraint must bind; otherwise, the owner could lower the level of wages offered and still have the manager accept the contract. In addition, letting $\gamma \geq 0$ denote the multiplier on this constraint, the solution must satisfy the following first-order conditions:

$$-\lambda + \gamma\lambda v'(w_H^* - g(e_H^*, \theta_H)) = 0. \qquad (14.C.2)$$

$$-(1 - \lambda) + \gamma(1 - \lambda) v'(w_L^* - g(e_L^*, \theta_L)) = 0. \qquad (14.C.3)$$

$$\lambda\pi'(e_H^*) - \gamma\lambda v'(w_H^* - g(e_H^*, \theta_H))\, g_e(e_H^*, \theta_H) \begin{cases} \leq 0, \\ = 0 & \text{if } e_H^* > 0. \end{cases} \qquad (14.C.4)$$

$$(1 - \lambda)\pi'(e_L^*) - \gamma(1 - \lambda) v'(w_L^* - g(e_L^*, \theta_L))\, g_e(e_L^*, \theta_L) \begin{cases} \leq 0, \\ = 0 & \text{if } e_L^* > 0. \end{cases} \qquad (14.C.5)$$

---

12. As with the case of hidden actions studied in Section 14.B, nonobservability causes no welfare loss in the case of managerial risk neutrality. As there, a "sellout" contract that faces the manager with the full marginal returns from his actions can generate the first-best outcome. (See Exercise 14.C.2.)

These conditions indicate how the two objectives of insuring the manager and making effort sensitive to the state are handled. First, rearranging and combining conditions (14.C.2) and (14.C.3), we see that

$$v'(w_H^* - g(e_H^*, \theta_H)) = v'(w_L^* - g(e_L^*, \theta_L)),  \tag{14.C.6}$$

so the manager's marginal utility of income is equalized across states. This is the usual condition for a risk-neutral party optimally insuring a risk-averse individual. Condition (14.C.6) implies that $w_H^* - g(e_H^*, \theta_H) = w_L^* - g(e_L^*, \theta_L)$, which in turn implies that $v(w_H^* - g(e_H^*, \theta_H)) = v(w_L^* - g(e_L^*, \theta_L))$; that is, the manager's utility is equalized across states. Given the reservation utility constraint in (14.C.1), the manager therefore has utility level $\bar{u}$ in each state.

Now consider the optimal effort levels in the two states. Since $g_e(0, \theta) = 0$ and $\pi'(0) > 0$, conditions (14.C.4) and (14.C.5) must hold with equality and $e_i^* > 0$ for $i = 1, 2$. Combining condition (14.C.2) with (14.C.4), and condition (14.C.3) with (14.C.5), we see that the optimal level of effort in state $\theta_i$, $e_i^*$, satisfies

$$\pi'(e_i^*) = g_e(e_i^*, \theta_i)  \qquad \text{for } i = L, H.  \tag{14.C.7}$$

This condition says that the optimal level of effort in state $\theta_i$ equates the marginal benefit of effort in terms of increased profit with its marginal disutility cost.

The pair $(w_i^*, e_i^*)$ is illustrated in Figure 14.C.1 (note that the wage is depicted on the vertical axis and the effort level on the horizontal axis). As shown, the manager is better off as we move to the northwest (higher wages and less effort), and the owner is better off as we move toward the southeast. Because the manager receives utility level $\bar{u}$ in state $\theta_i$, the owner seeks to find the most profitable point on the manager's state $\theta_i$ indifference curve with utility level $\bar{u}$. This is a point of tangency between the manager's indifference curve and one of the owner's isoprofit curves. At this point, the marginal benefit to additional effort in terms of increased profit is exactly equal to the marginal cost borne by the manager.

The owner's profit level in state $\theta_i$ is $\Pi_i^* = \pi(e_i^*) - v^{-1}(\bar{u}) - g(e_i^*, \theta_i)$. As shown in Figure 14.C.1, this profit is exactly equal to the distance from the origin to the point at which the owner's isoprofit curve through point $(w_i^*, e_i^*)$ hits the vertical

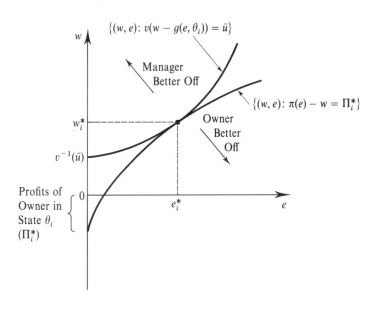

**Figure 14.C.1**

The optimal wage–effort pair for state $\theta_i$ when states are observable.

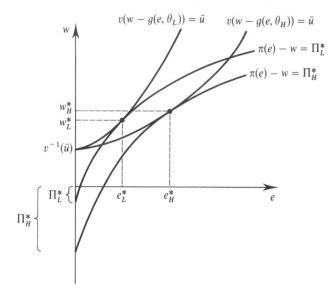

**Figure 14.C.2**

The optimal contract with full observability of $\theta$.

axis [since $\pi(0) = 0$, if the wage payment at this point on the vertical axis is $\hat{w} < 0$, the owner's profit at $(w_i^*, e_i^*)$ is exactly $-\hat{w}$].

From condition (14.C.7), we see that $g_{e\theta}(e, \theta) < 0$, $\pi''(e) < 0$, and $g_{ee}(e, \theta) > 0$ imply that $e_H^* > e_L^*$. Figure 14.C.2 depicts the optimal contract, $[(w_H^*, e_H^*), (w_L^*, e_L^*)]$. These observations are summarized in Proposition 14.C.1.

**Proposition 14.C.1:** In the principal-agent model with an observable state variable $\theta$, the optimal contract involves an effort level $e_i^*$ in state $\theta_i$ such that $\pi'(e_i^*) = g_e(e_i^*, \theta_i)$ and fully insures the manager, setting his wage in each state $\theta_i$ at the level $w_i^*$ such that $v(w_i^* - g(e_i^*, \theta_i)) = \bar{u}$.

Thus, with a strictly risk-averse manager, the first-best contract is characterized by two basic features: first, the owner fully insures the manager against risk; second, he requires the manager to work to the point at which the marginal benefit of effort exactly equals its marginal cost. Because the marginal cost of effort is lower in state $\theta_H$ than in state $\theta_L$, the contract calls for more effort in state $\theta_H$.

### The State $\theta$ is Observed Only by the Manager

As in Section 14.B, the desire both to insure the risk-averse manager and to elicit the proper levels of effort come into conflict when informational asymmetries are present. Suppose, for example, that the owner offers a risk-averse manager the contract depicted in Figure 14.C.2 and relies on the manager to reveal the state voluntarily. If so, the owner will run into problems. As is evident in the figure, in state $\theta_H$, the manager prefers point $(w_L^*, e_L^*)$ to point $(w_H^*, e_H^*)$. Consequently, in state $\theta_H$ he will *lie* to the owner, claiming that it is actually state $\theta_L$. As is also evident in the figure, this misrepresentation lowers the owner's profit.

Given this problem, what is the optimal contract for the owner to offer? To answer this question, it is necessary to start by identifying the set of possible contracts that the owner can offer. One can imagine many different forms that a contract could conceivably take. For example, the owner might offer a compensation function $w(\pi)$ that pays the manager as a function of realized profit and that leaves the effort choice in each state to the manager's discretion. Alternatively, the owner could offer a compensation schedule $w(\pi)$ but restrict the possible effort choices by the manager to some degree. Another possibility is that the owner could offer compensation as a function of the observable effort level chosen by the manager, possibly again with some restriction on the allowable choices. Finally, more complicated arrangements might be imagined. For example, the manager might be required to make an announcement about what the state is and then be free to choose his effort level while facing a compensation function $w(\pi \mid \hat{\theta})$ that depends on his announcement $\hat{\theta}$.

Although finding an optimal contract from among all these possibilities may seem a daunting task, an important result known as the *revelation principle* greatly simplifies the analysis of these types of contracting problems:[13]

**Proposition 14.C.2:** (*The Revelation Principle*) Denote the set of possible states by $\Theta$. In searching for an optimal contract, the owner can without loss restrict himself to contracts of the following form:

   (i) After the state $\theta$ is realized, the manager is required to announce which state has occurred.
   (ii) The contract specifies an outcome $[w(\hat{\theta}), e(\hat{\theta})]$ for each possible announcement $\hat{\theta} \in \Theta$.
   (iii) In every state $\theta \in \Theta$, the manager finds it optimal to report the state *truthfully*.

A contract that asks the manager to announce the state $\theta$ and associates outcomes with the various possible announcements is known as a *revelation mechanism*. The revelation principle tells us that the owner can restrict himself to using a revelation mechanism for which the manager always responds truthfully; revelation mechanisms with this truthfulness property are known as *incentive compatible* (or *truthful*) revelation mechanisms. The revelation principle holds in an extremely wide array of incentive problems. Although we defer its formal (and very general) proof to Chapter 23 (see Sections 23.C and 23.D), its basic idea is relatively straightforward.

For example, imagine that the owner is offering a contract with a compensation schedule $w(\pi)$ that leaves the choice of effort up to the manager. Let the resulting levels of effort in states $\theta_L$ and $\theta_H$ be $e_L$ and $e_H$, respectively. We can now show that there is a truthful revelation mechanism that generates exactly the same outcome as this contract. In particular, suppose that the owner uses a revelation mechanism that assigns outcome $[w(\pi(e_L)), e_L]$ if the manager announces that the state is $\theta_L$ and outcome $[w(\pi(e_H)), e_H]$ if the manager announces that the state is $\theta_H$. Consider the manager's incentives for truth telling when facing this revelation mechanism. Suppose, first, that the state is $\theta_L$. Under the initial contract with compensation schedule $w(\pi)$, the manager could have achieved outcome $[w(\pi(e_H)), e_H]$ in state $\theta_L$ by choosing effort level $e_H$. Since he instead chose $e_L$, it must be that in state $\theta_L$ outcome $[w(\pi(e_L)), e_L]$ is at least as good for the manager as outcome $[w(\pi(e_H)), e_H]$. Thus, under the proposed revelation mechanism, the manager will find telling the truth to be an optimal response when the state is $\theta_L$. A similar argument applies for state $\theta_H$. We see therefore that this revelation mechanism results in truthful announcements

---

13. Two early discussions of the revelation principle are Myerson (1979) and Dasgupta, Hammond, and Maskin (1979).

by the manager and yields exactly the same outcome as the initial contract. In fact, a similar argument can be constructed for *any* initial contract (see Chapter 23), and so the owner can restrict his attention without loss to truthful revelation mechanisms.[14]

To simplify the characterization of the optimal contract, we restrict attention from this point on to a specific and extreme case of managerial risk aversion: *infinite risk aversion*. In particular, we take the expected utility of the manager to equal the manager's lowest utility level across the two states. Thus, for the manager to accept the owner's contract, it must be that the manager receives a utility of at least $\bar{u}$ in each state.[15] As above, efficient risk sharing requires that an infinitely risk-averse manager have a utility level equal to $\bar{u}$ in each state. If, for example, his utility is $\bar{u}$ in one state and $u' > \bar{u}$ in the other, then the owner's expected wage payment is larger than necessary for giving the manager an expected utility of $\bar{u}$.

Given this assumption about managerial risk preferences, the revelation principle allows us to write the owner's problem as follows:

$$\max_{w_H, e_H \geq 0, w_L, e_L \geq 0} \lambda[\pi(e_H) - w_H] + (1 - \lambda)[\pi(e_L) - w_L] \qquad (14.C.8)$$

$$\text{s.t.} \quad \begin{array}{l} \text{(i)} \;\; w_L - g(e_L, \theta_L) \geq v^{-1}(\bar{u}) \\ \text{(ii)} \; w_H - g(e_H, \theta_H) \geq v^{-1}(\bar{u}) \end{array} \left.\begin{array}{l} \\ \\ \end{array}\right\} \begin{array}{l} \textit{reservation utility} \\ (\text{or } \textit{individual rationality}) \\ \textit{constraint} \end{array}$$

$$\begin{array}{l} \text{(iii)} \; w_H - g(e_H, \theta_H) \geq w_L - g(e_L, \theta_H) \\ \text{(iv)} \;\; w_L - g(e_L, \theta_L) \; \geq w_H - g(e_H, \theta_L) \end{array} \left.\begin{array}{l} \\ \\ \end{array}\right\} \begin{array}{l} \textit{incentive compatibility} \\ (\text{or } \textit{truth-telling} \\ \text{or } \textit{self-selection}) \\ \textit{constraints.} \end{array}$$

The pairs $(w_H, e_H)$ and $(w_L, e_L)$ that the contract specifies are now the wage and effort levels that result from different *announcements* of the state by the manager; that is, the outcome if the manager announces that the state is $\theta_i$ is $(w_i, e_i)$. Constraints (i) and (ii) make up the *reservation utility* (or *individual rationality*) *constraint* for the infinitely risk-averse manager; if he is to accept the contract, he must be guaranteed a utility of at least $\bar{u}$ in each state. Hence, we must have $v(w_i - g(e_i, \theta_i)) \geq \bar{u}$ for $i = L, H$ or, equivalently, $w_i - g(e_i, \theta_i) \geq v^{-1}(\bar{u})$ for $i = L, H$. Constraints (iii) and (iv) are the *incentive compatibility* (or *truth-telling* or *self-selection*) *constraints* for the manager in states $\theta_H$ and $\theta_L$, respectively. Consider, for example, constraint (iii). The

---

14. One restriction that we have imposed here for expositional purposes is to limit the outcomes specified following the manager's announcement to being nonstochastic (in fact, much of the literature does so as well). Randomization can sometimes be desirable in these settings because it can aid in satisfying the incentive compatibility constraints that we introduce in problem (14.C.8). See Maskin and Riley (1984a) for an example.

15. This can be thought of as the limiting case in which, starting from the concave utility function $v(x)$, we take the concave transformation $v_\rho(v) = -v(x)^\rho$ for $\rho < 0$ as the manager's Bernoulli utility function and let $\rho \to -\infty$. To see this, note that the manager's expected utility over the random outcome giving $(w_H - g(e_H, \theta_H))$ with probability $\lambda$ and $(w_L - g(e_L, \theta_L))$ with probability $(1 - \lambda)$ is then $EU = -[\lambda v_H^\rho + (1 - \lambda)v_L^\rho]$, where $v_i = v(w_i - g(e_i, \theta_i))$ for $i = L, H$. This expected utility is correctly ordered by $(-EU)^{1/\rho} = [\lambda v_H^\rho + (1 - \lambda)v_L^\rho]^{1/\rho}$. Now as $\rho \to -\infty$, $[\lambda v_H^\rho + (1 - \lambda)v_L^\rho]^{1/\rho} \to \text{Min}\{v_H, v_L\}$ (see Exercise 3.C.6). Hence, a contract gives the manager an expected utility greater than his (certain) reservation utility if and only if $\text{Min}\{v(w_H - g(e_H, \theta_H)), v(w_L - g(e_L, \theta_L))\} \geq \bar{u}$.

manager's utility in state $\theta_H$ is $v(w_H - g(e_H, \theta_H))$ if he tells the truth, but it is $v(w_L - g(e_L, \theta_H))$ if he instead claims that it is state $\theta_L$. Thus, he will tell the truth if $w_H - g(e_H, \theta_H) \geq w_L - g(e_L, \theta_H)$. Constraint (iv) follows similarly.

Note that the first-best (full observability) contract depicted in Figure 14.C.2 does not satisfy the constraints of problem (14.C.8) because it violates constraint (iii).

We analyze problem (14.C.8) through a sequence of lemmas. Our arguments for these results make extensive use of graphical analysis to build intuition. An analysis of this problem using Kuhn–Tucker conditions is presented in Appendix B.

**Lemma 14.C.1:** We can ignore constraint (ii). That is, a contract is a solution to problem (14.C.8) if and only if it is the solution to the problem derived from (14.C.8) by dropping constraint (ii).

**Proof:** Whenever both constraints (i) and (iii) are satisfied, it must be that $w_H - g(e_H, \theta_H) \geq w_L - g(e_L, \theta_H) \geq w_L - g(e_L, \theta_L) \geq v^{-1}(\bar{u})$, and so constraint (ii) is also satisfied. This implies that the set of feasible contracts in the problem derived from (14.C.8) by dropping constraint (ii) is exactly the same as the set of feasible contracts in problem (14.C.8). ■

Lemma 14.C.1 is illustrated in Figure 14.C.3. By constraint (i), $(w_L, e_L)$ must lie in the shaded region of the figure. But by constraint (iii), $(w_H, e_H)$ must lie on or above the state $\theta_H$ indifference curve through point $(w_L, e_L)$. As can be seen, this implies that the manager's state $\theta_H$ utility is at least $\bar{u}$, the utility he gets at point $(w, e) = (v^{-1}(\bar{u}), 0)$.

Therefore, from this point on we can ignore constraint (ii).

**Lemma 14.C.2:** An optimal contract in problem (14.C.8) must have $w_L - g(e_L, \theta_L) = v^{-1}(\bar{u})$.

**Proof:** Suppose not, that is, that there is an optimal solution $[(w_L, e_L), (w_H, e_H)]$ in which $w_L - g(e_L, \theta_L) > v^{-1}(\bar{u})$. Now, consider an alteration to the owner's contract

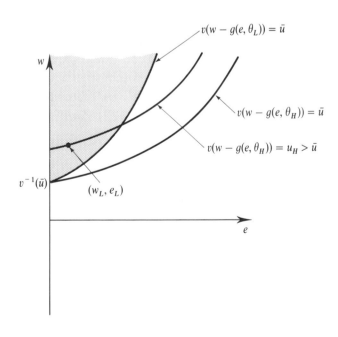

**Figure 14.C.3**

Constraint (ii) in problem (14.C.8) is satisfied by any contract satisfying constraints (i) and (iii).

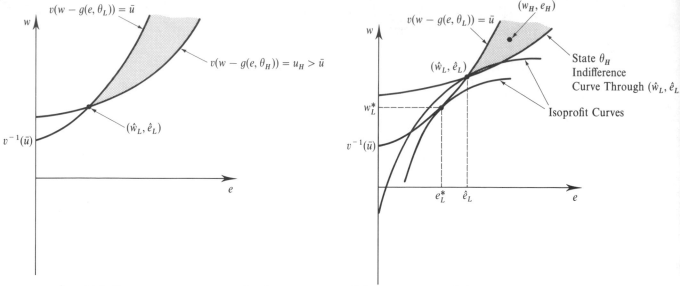

in which the owner pays wages in the two states of $\hat{w}_L = w_L - \varepsilon$ and $\hat{w}_H = w_H - \varepsilon$, where $\varepsilon > 0$ (i.e., the owner lowers the wage payments in both states by $\varepsilon$). This new contract still satisfies constraint (i) as long as $\varepsilon$ is chosen small enough. In addition, the incentive compatibility constraints are still satisfied because this change just subtracts a constant, $\varepsilon$, from each side of these constraints. But if this new contract satisfies all the constraints, the original contract could not have been optimal because the owner now has higher profits, which is a contradiction. ∎

**Figure 14.C.4 (left)**

In a feasible contract offering $(\hat{w}_L, \hat{e}_L)$ for state $\theta_L$, the pair $(w_H, e_H)$ must lie in the shaded region.

**Lemma 14.C.3:** In any optimal contract:
  (i) $e_L \leq e_L^*$; that is, the manager's effort level in state $\theta_L$ is no more than the level that would arise if $\theta$ were observable.
  (ii) $e_H = e_H^*$; that is, the manager's effort level in state $\theta_H$ is exactly equal to the level that would arise if $\theta$ were observable.

**Figure 14.C.5 (right)**

An optimal contract has $e_L \leq e_L^*$.

**Proof:** Lemma 14.C.3 can best be seen graphically. By Lemma 14.C.2, $(w_L, e_L)$ lies on the locus $\{(w, e): v(w - g(e, \theta_L)) = \bar{u}\}$ in any optimal contract. Figure 14.C.4 depicts one possible pair $(\hat{w}_L, \hat{e}_L)$. In addition, the truth-telling constraints imply that the outcome for state $\theta_H$, $(w_H, e_H)$, must lie in the shaded region of Figure 14.C.4. To see this, note that by constraint (iv), $(w_H, e_H)$ must lie on or below the state $\theta_L$ indifference curve through $(\hat{w}_L, \hat{e}_L)$. In addition, by constraint (iii), $(w_H, e_H)$ must lie on or above the state $\theta_H$ indifference curve through $(\hat{w}_L, \hat{e}_L)$.

To see part (i), suppose that we have a contract with $\hat{e}_L > e_L^*$. Figure 14.C.5 depicts such a contract offer: $(\hat{w}_L, \hat{e}_L)$ lies on the manager's state $\theta_L$ indifference curve with utility level $\bar{u}$, and $(w_H, e_H)$ lies in the shaded region defined by the truth-telling constraints. The state $\theta_L$ indifference curve for the manager and the isoprofit curve for the owner which go through point $(\hat{w}_L, \hat{e}_L)$ have the relation depicted at point $(\hat{\omega}_L, \hat{e}_L)$ because $\hat{e}_L > e_L^*$.

As can be seen in the figure, the owner can raise his profit level in state $\theta_L$ by moving the state $\theta_L$ wage–effort pair down the manager's indifference curve from $(\hat{w}_L, \hat{e}_L)$ to its first-best point $(w_L^*, e_L^*)$. This change continues to satisfy all the constraints in problem (14.C.8): The manager's utility in each state is unchanged,

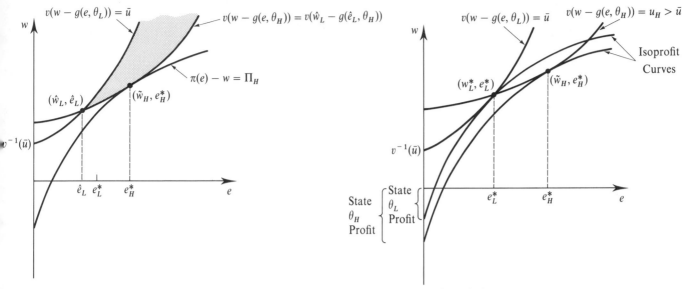

and, as is evident in Figure 14.C.5, the truth-telling constraints are still satisfied. Thus, a contract with $\hat{e}_L > e_L^*$ cannot be optimal.

Now consider part (ii). Given any wage–effort pair $(\hat{w}_L, \hat{e}_L)$ with $\hat{e}_L \leq e_L^*$, such as that shown in Figure 14.C.6, the owner's problem is to find the location for $(w_H, e_H)$ in the shaded region that maximizes his profit in state $\theta_H$. The solution occurs at a point of tangency between the manager's state $\theta_H$ indifference curve through point $(\hat{w}_L, \hat{e}_H)$ and an isoprofit curve for the owner. This tangency occurs at point $(\tilde{w}_H, e_H^*)$ in the figure, and necessarily involves effort level $e_H^*$ because all points of tangency between the manager's state $\theta_H$ indifference curves and the owner's isoprofit curves occur at effort level $e_H^*$ [they are characterized by condition (14.C.7) for $i = H$]. Note that this point of tangency occurs strictly to the right of effort level $\hat{e}_L$ because $\hat{e}_L \leq e_L^* < e_H^*$. ■

A secondary point emerging from the proof of Lemma 14.C.3 is that only the truth-telling constraint for state $\theta_H$ is binding in the optimal contract. This property is common to many of the other applications in the literature.[16]

**Lemma 14.C.4:** In any optimal contract, $e_L < e_L^*$; that is, the effort level in state $\theta_L$ is necessarily *strictly* below the level that would arise in state $\theta_L$ if $\theta$ were observable.

**Proof:** Again, this point can be seen graphically. Suppose we start with $(w_L, e_L) = (w_L^*, e_L^*)$, as in Figure 14.C.7. By Lemma 14.C.3, this determines the state $\theta_H$ outcome, denoted by $(\tilde{w}_H, e_H^*)$ in the figure. Note that by the definition of $(w_L^*, e_L^*)$, the isoprofit curve through this point is tangent to the manager's state $\theta_L$ indifference curve.

Recall that the absolute distance between the origin and the point where each state's isoprofit curve hits the vertical axis represents the profit the owner earns in that state. The owner's overall expected profit with this contract offer is therefore

**Figure 14.C.6 (left)**
An optimal contract has $e_H = e_H^*$.

**Figure 14.C.7 (right)**
The best contract with $e_L = e_L^*$.

---

16. In models with more than two types, this property takes the form that only the incentive constraints between adjacent types bind, and they do so only in one direction. (See Exercise 14.C.1.)

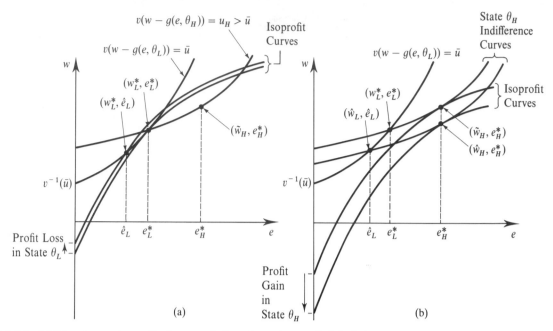

**Figure 14.C.8**   (a) The change in profits in state $\theta_L$ from lowering $e_L$ slightly below $e_L^*$. (b) The change in profits in state $\theta_H$ from lowering $e_L$ slightly below $e_L^*$ and optimally adjusting $w_H$.

equal to the average of these two profit levels (with weights equal to the relative probabilities of the two states).

We now argue that a change in the state $\theta_L$ outcome that lowers this state's effort level to one slightly below $e_L^*$ necessarily raises the owner's expected profit. To see this, start by moving the state $\theta_L$ outcome to a slightly lower point, $(\hat{w}_L, \hat{e}_L)$, on the manager's state $\theta_L$ indifference curve. This change is illustrated in Figure 14.C.8, along with the owner's isoprofit curve through this new point. As is evident in Figure 14.C.8(a), this change lowers the profit that the owner earns in state $\theta_L$. However, it also relaxes the incentive constraint on the state $\theta_H$ outcome and, by doing so, it allows the owner to offer a lower wage in that state. Figure 14.C.8(b) shows the new state $\theta_H$ outcome, say $(\hat{w}_H, e_H^*)$, and the new (higher-profit) isoprofit curve through this point.

Overall, this change results in a lower profit for the owner in state $\theta_L$ and a higher profit for the owner in state $\theta_H$. Note, however, that because we started at a point of tangency at $(w_L^*, e_L^*)$, the profit loss in state $\theta_L$ is small relative to the gain in state $\theta_H$. Indeed, if we were to look at the derivative of the owner's profit in state $\theta_L$ with respect to an *infinitesimal* change in that state's outcome, we would find that it is *zero*. In contrast, the derivative of profit in state $\theta_H$ with respect to this infinitesimal change would be strictly positive. The zero derivative in state $\theta_L$ is an envelope theorem result: because we started out at the first-best level of effort in state $\theta_L$, a small change in $(w_L, e_L)$ that keeps the manager's state $\theta_L$ utility at $\bar{u}$ has no first-order effect on the owner's profit in that state; but because it relaxes the state $\theta_H$ incentive constraint, for a small-enough change the owner's expected profit is increased. ∎

How far should the owner go in lowering $e$? In answering this question, the owner must weigh the marginal loss in profit in state $\theta_L$ against the marginal gain in state $\theta_H$

$\theta_H$ [note that once we move away from $(w_L^*, e_L^*)$, the envelope result no longer holds and the marginal reduction in state $\theta_L$'s profit is strictly positive]. It should not be surprising that the extent to which the owner wants to make this trade-off depends on the relative probabilities of the two states. In particular, the greater the likelihood of state $\theta_H$, the more the owner is willing to distort the state $\theta_L$ outcome to increase profit in state $\theta_H$. In the extreme case in which the probability of state $\theta_L$ gets close to zero, the owner may set $e_L = 0$ and hire the manager to work only in state $\theta_H$.[17]

The analysis in Appendix B confirms this intuition. There we show that the optimal level of $e_L$ satisfies the following first-order condition:

$$[\pi'(e_L) - g_e(e_L, \theta_L)] + \frac{\lambda}{1 - \lambda}[g_e(e_L, \theta_H) - g_e(e_L, \theta_L)] = 0. \qquad (14.C.9)$$

The first term of this expression is zero at $e_L = e_L^*$ and is strictly positive at $e_L < e_L^*$; the second term is always strictly negative. Thus, we must have $e_L < e_L^*$ to satisfy this condition, confirming our finding in Lemma 14.C.4. Differentiating this expression reveals that the optimal level of $e_L$ falls as $\lambda/(1 - \lambda)$ rises.

These findings are summarized in Proposition 14.C.3.

**Proposition 14.C.3:** In the hidden information principal-agent model with an infinitely risk-averse manager the optimal contract sets the level of effort in state $\theta_H$ at its first-best (full observability) level $e_H^*$. The effort level in state $\theta_L$ is distorted downward from its first-best level $e_L^*$. In addition, the manager is inefficiently insured, receiving a utility greater than $\bar{u}$ in state $\theta_H$ and a utility equal to $\bar{u}$ in state $\theta_L$. The owner's expected payoff is strictly lower than the expected payoff he receives when $\theta$ is observable, while the infinitely risk-averse manager's expected utility is the same as when $\theta$ is observable (it equals $\bar{u}$).[18,19]

A basic, and very general, point that emerges from this analysis is that the optimal contract for the owner in this setting of hidden information necessarily *distorts* the effort choice of the manager in order to ameliorate the costs of asymmetric information, which here take the form of the higher expected wage payment that the owner makes because the manager has a utility in state $\theta_H$ in excess of $\bar{u}$.

Note that nothing would change if the profit level $\pi$ were not publicly observable (and so could not be contracted on), since our analysis relied only on the fact that the effort level $e$ was observable. Moreover, in the case in which $\pi$ is not publicly observable, we can extend the model to allow the relationship between profits and effort to depend on the state; that is, the owner's profits in states $\theta_L$ and $\theta_H$ given effort level $e$ might be given by the functions $\pi_L(e)$ and $\pi_H(e)$.[20] As long as

---

17. In fact, this can happen only if $g_e(0, \theta_L) > 0$.

18. Recall that an infinitely risk-averse manager's expected utility is equal to his lowest utility level across the two states.

19. Note, however, that while the outcome here is Pareto inefficient, it is a constrained Pareto optimum in the sense introduced in Section 13.B; the reasons parallel those given in footnote 9 of Section 14.B for the hidden action model (although here it is $\theta$ that the authority cannot observe rather than $e$).

20. The nonobservability of profits is important for this extension because if $\pi$ could be contracted upon, the manager could be punished for misrepresenting the state by simply comparing the realized profit level with the profit level that should have been realized in the announced state for the specified level of effort.

$\pi'_H(e) \geq \pi'_L(e) > 0$ for all $e \geq 0$, the analysis of this model follows exactly along the lines of the analysis we have just conducted (see Exercise 14.C.5).

As in the case of hidden action models, a number of extensions of this basic hidden information model have been explored in the literature. Some of the most general treatments appear in the context of the "mechanism design" literature associated with social choice theory. A discussion of these models can be found in Chapter 23.

---

## The Monopolistic Screening Model

In Section 13.D, we studied a model of *competitive screening* in which firms try to design their employment contracts in a manner that distinguishes among workers who, at the time of contracting, have different unobservable productivity levels (i.e., there is *precontractual* asymmetric information). The techniques that we have developed in our study of the principal-agent model with hidden information enable us to formulate and solve a model of *monopolistic screening* in which, in contrast with the analysis in Section 13.D, only a single firm offers employment contracts (actually, this might more properly be called a *monopsonistic* screening model because the single firm is on the demand side of the market).

To see this, suppose that, as in the model in Section 13.D, there are two possible types of workers who differ in their productivity. A worker of type $\theta$ has utility $u(w, t \mid \theta) = w - g(t, \theta)$ when he receives a wage of $w$ and faces task level $t$. His reservation utility level is $\bar{u}$. The productivities of the two types of workers are $\theta_H$ and $\theta_L$, with $\theta_H > \theta_L > 0$. The fraction of workers of type $\theta_H$ is $\lambda \in (0, 1)$. We assume that the firm's profits, which are not publicly observable, are given by the function $\pi_H(t)$ for a type $\theta_H$ worker and by $\pi_L(t)$ for a type $\theta_L$ worker, and that $\pi'_H(t) \geq \pi'_L(t) > 0$ for all $t \geq 0$ [e.g., as in Exercise 13.D.1, we could have $\pi_i(t) = \theta_i(1 - \mu t)$ for $\mu > 0$].[21]

The firm's problem is to offer a set of contracts that maximizes its profits given worker self-selection among, and behavior within, its offered contracts. Once again, the revelation principle can be invoked to greatly simplify the firm's problem. Here the firm can restrict its attention to offering a menu of wage–task pairs $[(w_H, t_H), (w_L, t_L)]$ to solve

$$\operatorname*{Max}_{w_H, t_H \geq 0, \, w_L, t_L \geq 0} \quad \lambda[\pi_H(t_H) - w_H] + (1 - \lambda)[\pi_L(t_L) - w_L] \qquad (14.C.10)$$

$$\text{s.t.} \quad \text{(i)} \quad w_L - g(t_L, \theta_L) \geq \bar{u}$$

$$\text{(ii)} \quad w_H - g(t_H, \theta_H) \geq \bar{u}$$

$$\text{(iii)} \quad w_H - g(t_H, \theta_H) \geq w_L - g(t_L, \theta_H)$$

$$\text{(iv)} \quad w_L - g(t_L, \theta_L) \geq w_H - g(t_H, \theta_L).$$

This problem has exactly the same structure as (14.C.8) but with the principal's (here the firm's) profit being a function of the state. As noted above, the analysis of this problem follows exactly the same lines as our analysis of problem (14.C.8).

This class of models has seen wide application in the literature (although often with a continuum of types assumed). Maskin and Riley (1984b), for example, apply this model to the study of monopolistic price discrimination. In their model, a consumer of type $\theta$ has utility $v(x, \theta) - T$ when he consumes $x$ units of a monopolist's good and makes a total payment of $T$ to the monopolist, and can earn a reservation utility level of $v(0, \theta) = 0$ by not purchasing from the monopolist. The monopolist has a constant unit cost of production equal to $c > 0$

---

21. The model studied in Section 13.D with $\pi_i(t) = \theta_i$ corresponds to the limiting case where $\mu \to 0$.

and seeks to offer a menu of $(x_i, T_i)$ pairs to maximize its profit. The monopolist's problem then takes the form in (14.C.10) where we take $t_i = x_i$, $w_i = -T_i$, $\bar{u} = 0$, $g(t_i, \theta_i) = -v(x_i, \theta_i)$, and $\pi_i(t_i) = -cx_i$.

Baron and Myerson's (1982) analysis of optimal regulation of a monopolist with unknown costs provides another example. There, a regulated firm faces market demand function $x(p)$ and has unobservable unit costs of $\theta$. The regulator, who seeks to design a regulatory policy that maximizes consumer surplus, faces the monopolist with a choice among a set of pairs $(p_i, T_i)$, where $p_i$ is the allowed retail price and $T_i$ is a transfer payment from the regulator to the firm. The regulated firm is able to shut down if it cannot earn profits of at least zero from any of the regulator's offerings. The regulator's problem then corresponds to (14.C.10) with $t_i = p_i$, $w_i = T_i$, $\bar{u} = 0$, $g(t_i, \theta_i) = -(p_i - \theta_i)x(p_i)$, and $\pi_i(t_i) = \int_{p_i}^{\infty} x(s)\, ds$.[22]

Exercises 14.C.7 to 14.C.9 ask you to study some examples of monopolistic screening models.

# 14.D Hidden Actions and Hidden Information: Hybrid Models

Although the hidden action–hidden information dichotomization serves as a useful starting point for understanding principal-agent models, many real-world situations (and some of the literature as well) involve elements of both problems.

To consider an example of such a model, suppose that we augment the simple hidden information model considered in Section 14.C in the following manner: let the level of effort $e$ now be unobservable, and let profits be a stochastic function of effort, described by conditional density function $f(\pi \mid e)$. In essence, what we now have is a hidden action model, but one in which the owner also does not know something about the disutility of the manager (which is captured in the state variable $\theta$).

Formal analysis of this model is beyond the scope of this chapter, but the basic thrust of the revelation principle extends to the analysis of these types of hybrid problems. In particular, as Myerson (1982) shows, the owner can now restrict attention to contracts of the following form:

(i) After the state $\theta$ is realized, the manager announces which state has occurred.

(ii) The contract specifies, for each possible announcement $\hat{\theta} \in \Theta$, the effort level $e(\hat{\theta})$ that the manager should take and a compensation scheme $w(\pi \mid \hat{\theta})$.

(iii) In every state $\theta$, the manager is willing to be both *truthful* in stage (i) and *obedient* following stage (ii) [i.e., he finds it optimal to choose effort level $e(\theta)$ in state $\theta$].

This contract can be thought of as a revelation game, but one in which the outcome of the manager's announcement about the state is a hidden action-style contract, that is, a compensation scheme and a "recommended action." The requirement of "obedience" amounts to an incentive constraint that is like that in the hidden action

---

22. The regulator's objective function can be generalized to allow a weighted average of consumer and producer surplus, with greater weight on consumers. In this case, the function $\pi_i(\cdot)$ will depend on $\theta_i$.

model considered in Section 14.B; the "truthfulness" constraints are generalizations of those considered in our hidden information model. See Myerson (1982) for details.

One special case of this hybrid model deserves particular mention because its analysis reduces to that of the pure hidden information model considered in Section 14.C. In particular, suppose that effort is unobservable but that the relationship between effort and profits is *deterministic*, given by the function $\pi(e)$. In that case, for any particular announcement $\hat{\theta}$, it is possible to induce any wage–effort pair that is desired, say $(\hat{w}, \hat{e})$, by use of a simple "forcing" compensation scheme: Just reward the manager with a wage payment of $\hat{w}$ if profits are $\pi(\hat{e})$, and give him a wage payment of $-\infty$ otherwise. Thus, the combination of the observability of $\pi$ and the one-to-one relationship between $\pi$ and $e$ effectively allows the contract to specify $e$. The analysis of this model is therefore identical to that of the hidden information model considered in Section 14.C, where wage–effort pairs could be specified directly as functions of the manager's announcement.

To see this point in a slightly different way, note first that because of the ability to write forcing contracts, in this model an optimal contract can be thought of as specifying, for each announcement $\hat{\theta}$, a wage–profit pair $(w(\hat{\theta}), \pi(\hat{\theta}))$. Now, for any required profit level $\pi$, the effort level necessary to achieve a profit of $\pi$ is $\tilde{e}$ such that $\pi(\tilde{e}) = \pi$. Let the function $\tilde{e}(\pi)$ describe this effort level. We can now think of the manager as having a disutility function defined directly over the profit level which is given by $\tilde{g}(\pi, \theta) = g(\tilde{e}(\pi), \theta)$. But this model looks just like a model with *observable* effort where the effort variable is $\pi$, the disutility function over this effort is $\tilde{g}(\pi, \theta)$, and the profit function is $\tilde{\pi}(\pi) = \pi$. Thus, the analysis of this model is identical to that in a pure hidden information model.

A similar point applies to a closely related hybrid model in which, instead of the manager's disutility of effort, it is the relation between profit and effort that depends on the state. In particular, suppose that the disutility of effort is given by the function $g(e)$ and profits are given by the function $\pi(e, \theta)$, where $\pi_e(\cdot) > 0$, $\pi_{ee}(\cdot) < 0$, $\pi_\theta(\cdot) > 0$, and $\pi_{e\theta}(\cdot) > 0$. Effort is not observable, but profits are. The idea is that the manager knows more than the owner does about the true profit opportunities facing the firm (e.g., the marginal productivity of effort). Again, we can think of a contract as specifying, for each announcement by the manager, a wage–profit pair (implicitly using forcing contracts). In this context, the effort needed to achieve any given level of profit $\pi$ in state $\theta$ is given by some function $\hat{e}(\pi, \theta)$, and the disutility associated with this effort is then $\hat{g}(\pi, \theta) = g(\hat{e}(\pi, \theta))$. But this model is also equivalent to our basic hidden information model with observable effort: just let the effort variable be $\pi$, the disutility of this effort be $\hat{g}(\pi, \theta)$, and the profit function be $\hat{\pi}(\pi) = \pi$. Again, our results from Section 14.C apply.

## APPENDIX A: MULTIPLE EFFORT LEVELS IN THE HIDDEN ACTION MODEL

In this appendix, we discuss additional issues that arise when the effort choice in the hidden action (moral hazard) model discussed in Section 14.B is more complex than the simple two-effort-choice specification $e \in \{e_L, e_H\}$ analyzed there. Here, we return

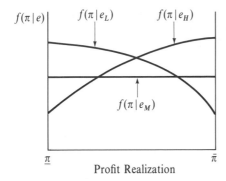

**Figure 14.AA.1**
Density functions for $E = \{e_L, e_M, e_H\}$: effort choice $e_M$ may not be implementable.

to the more general specification initially introduced in Section 14.B in which $E$ is the feasible set of effort choices.

As in Section 14.B, we can break up the principal's (the owner's) problem into several parts:

(a) What are the effort levels $e$ that it is possible to induce?
(b) What is the optimal contract for inducing each specific effort level $e \in E$?
(c) Which effort level $e \in E$ is optimal?

In a multiple-action setting, each of these three parts becomes somewhat more complicated. For example, with just two actions, part (a) was trivial: $e_L$ could be induced with a fixed wage contract, and $e_H$ could always be induced by giving incentives that were sufficiently high at outcomes that were more likely to arise when $e_H$ is chosen. With more than two actions, however, this may not be so. For example, consider the three-action case in which $E = \{e_L, e_M, e_H\}$ and the conditional density functions are those depicted in Figure 14.AA.1. As is suggested by the figure, it may be impossible to design incentives such that $e_M$ is chosen because for any $w(\pi)$ the agent may prefer either $e_L$ or $e_H$ to $e_M$. (Exercise 14.B.4 provides an example along these lines.)

Part (b) also becomes more involved. The optimal contract for implementing effort choice $e$ solves

$$\underset{w(\pi)}{\text{Min}} \int w(\pi) f(\pi \mid e) \, d\pi \qquad\qquad (14.AA.1)$$

$$\text{s.t. (i)} \int v(w(\pi)) f(\pi \mid e) \, d\pi - g(e) \geq \bar{u}$$

(ii) $e$ solves $\underset{\tilde{e} \in E}{\text{Max}} \int v(w(\pi)) f(\pi \mid \tilde{e}) \, d\pi - g(\tilde{e})$.

If we have $K$ possible actions in set $E$, the incentive constraints in problem (14.AA.1) [constraints (ii)] consist of $(K-1)$ constraints that must be satisfied. In this case, with a change of variables in which we maximize over the level of utility that the manager gets conditional on $\pi$, say $\bar{v}(\pi)$, we have a problem with $K$ linear constraints and a convex objective function [see Grossman and Hart (1983) and footnote 7 for more on this].

However, if $E$ is a continuous set of possible actions, say $E = [0, \bar{e}] \subset \mathbb{R}$, then we have an *infinity* of incentive constraints. One trick sometimes used in this case to simplify problem (14.AA.1) is to replace constraint (ii) with a *first-order condition* (this is sometimes called the *first-order approach*). For example, if $e$ is a one-dimensional measure of effort, then the manager's first-order condition is

$$\int v(w(\pi)) f_e(\pi \,|\, e) \, d\pi - g'(e) = 0, \tag{14.AA.2}$$

where $f_e(\pi \,|\, e) = \partial f(\pi \,|\, e)/\partial e$. If we replace constraint (ii) with (14.AA.2) and solve the resulting problem, we can derive a condition for $w(\pi)$ that parallels condition (14.B.10):

$$\frac{1}{v'(w(\pi))} = \lambda + \mu \left[ \frac{f_e(\pi \,|\, e)}{f(\pi \,|\, e)} \right]. \tag{14.AA.3}$$

The condition that ratio $[f_e(\pi \,|\, e)/f(\pi \,|\, e)]$ be increasing in $\pi$ is the differential version of the monotone likelihood ratio property (see Exercise 14.AA.1).

In general, however, a solution to the problem resulting from this substitution is not necessarily a solution to the actual problem (14.AA.1). The reason is that the agent may satisfy first-order condition (14.AA.2) even when effort level $e$ is not his optimal effort choice. First, effort level $e$ could be a *minimum* rather than a maximum; therefore, we at least want the agent to also be satisfying a local second-order condition. But even this will not be sufficient. In general, we need to be sure that the agent's objective function is concave in $e$. Note that this is not a simple matter because the concavity of his objective function in $e$ will depend both on the shape of $f(\pi \,|\, e)$ *and* on the shape of the incentive contract $w(\pi)$ that is offered. The known conditions which insure that this condition is met are very restrictive. See Grossman and Hart (1983) and Rogerson (1985b) for details. Exercise 14.AA.2 provides a very simple example.

Finally, to answer part (c), we need to compute the optimal contract from part (b) for each action that part (a) reveals is implementable and then compare their relative profits for the principal. With more than two effort choices, two features of the two-effort-choice case fail to generalize. First, nonobservability can lead to an upward distortion in effort. (Exercise 14.B.4 provides an example.) Second, at the optimal contract under nonobservability we can get *both* an inefficient effort choice and inefficiencies resulting from managerial risk bearing.

## APPENDIX B: A FORMAL SOLUTION OF THE PRINCIPAL-AGENT PROBLEM WITH HIDDEN INFORMATION

Recall problem (14.C.8):

$$\underset{w_H, e_H \geq 0, \, w_L, e_L \geq 0}{\text{Max}} \quad \lambda[\pi(e_H) - w_H] + (1 - \lambda)[\pi(e_L) - w_L]$$

$$\text{s.t.} \quad \text{(i)} \quad w_L - g(e_L, \theta_L) \geq v^{-1}(\bar{u})$$

$$\text{(ii)} \quad w_H - g(e_H, \theta_H) \geq v^{-1}(\bar{u})$$

$$\text{(iii)} \quad w_H - g(e_H, \theta_H) \geq w_L - g(e_L, \theta_H)$$

$$\text{(iv)} \quad w_L - g(e_L, \theta_L) \geq w_H - g(e_H, \theta_L).$$

Using Lemma 14.C.1 we can restate problem (14.C.8) as

$$\underset{w_H, e_H \geq 0, \, w_L, e_L \geq 0}{\text{Max}} \quad \lambda[\pi(e_H) - w_H] + (1 - \lambda)[\pi(e_L) - w_L] \qquad (14.\text{BB}.1)$$

$$\text{s.t.} \quad \text{(i)} \ w_L - g(e_L, \theta_L) \geq v^{-1}(\bar{u})$$

$$\text{(iii)} \ w_H - g(e_H, \theta_H) \geq w_L - g(e_L, \theta_H)$$

$$\text{(iv)} \ w_L - g(e_L, \theta_L) \geq w_H - g(e_H, \theta_L).$$

Letting $(\gamma, \phi_H, \phi_L) \geq 0$ be the multipliers on constraints (i), (iii), and (iv), respectively, the Kuhn–Tucker conditions for this problem can be written (see Section M.K of the Mathematical Appendix)

$$-\lambda + \phi_H - \phi_L = 0. \qquad (14.\text{BB}.2)$$

$$-(1 - \lambda) + \gamma - \phi_H + \phi_L = 0. \qquad (14.\text{BB}.3)$$

$$\lambda\pi'(e_H) - \phi_H g_e(e_H, \theta_H) + \phi_L g_e(e_H, \theta_L) \begin{cases} \leq 0 \\ = 0 \end{cases} \quad \text{if } e_H > 0 \qquad (14.\text{BB}.4)$$

$$(1 - \lambda)\pi'(e_L) - (\gamma + \phi_L)g_e(e_L, \theta_L) + \phi_H g_e(e_L, \theta_H) \begin{cases} \leq 0 \\ = 0 \end{cases} \quad \text{if } e_L > 0 \qquad (14.\text{BB}.5)$$

along with the complementary slackness conditions for constraints (i), (iii), and (iv) [conditions (M.K.7)].

Let us break up the analysis of these conditions into several steps.

*Step 1:* Condition (14.BB.2) implies that $\phi_H > 0$. Thus, constraint (iii) must bind (hold with equality) at an optimal solution.

*Step 2:* Adding conditions (14.BB.2) and (14.BB.3) implies that $\gamma = 1$. Hence, constraint (i) must bind at an optimal solution.

*Step 3:* Both $e_L$ and $e_H$ are strictly positive. To see this, note that condition (14.BB.4) cannot hold at $e_H = 0$ because $\pi'(0) > 0$ and $g_e(0, \theta_i) = 0$ for $i = L, H$. Similarly for condition (14.BB.5) and $e_L$.

*Step 4:* Steps 1 to 3 imply that $\phi_L = 0$. Suppose not: i.e., that $\phi_L > 0$. Then constraint (iv) must be binding. We shall now derive a contradiction. First, substitute for $\phi_H$ in conditions (14.BB.4) and (14.BB.5) using the fact that $\phi_H = \phi_L + \lambda$ from condition (14.BB.2). Then, using the fact that $(e_L, e_H) \gg 0$, we can write conditions (14.BB.4) and (14.BB.5) as

$$\lambda[\pi'(e_H) - g_e(e_H, \theta_H)] + \phi_L[g_e(e_H, \theta_L) - g_e(e_H, \theta_H)] = 0$$

and

$$(1 - \lambda)[\pi'(e_L) - g_e(e_L, \theta_H)] + (1 + \phi_L)[g_e(e_L, \theta_H) - g_e(e_L, \theta_L)] = 0.$$

But $\phi_L > 0$ then implies that

$$\pi'(e_L) - g_e(e_L, \theta_H) > 0 > \pi'(e_H) - g_e(e_H, \theta_H),$$

which implies $e_H > e_L$ since $\pi(e) - g(e, \theta_H)$ is concave in $e$. But if $e_H > e_L$ and constraint (iii) binds (which it does from Step 1), then constraint (iv) must be slack because we then have

$$(w_H - w_L) = g(e_H, \theta_H) - g(e_L, \theta_H)$$
$$= \int_{e_L}^{e_H} g_e(e, \theta_H) \, de$$
$$< \int_{e_L}^{e_H} g_e(e, \theta_L) \, de$$
$$= g(e_H, \theta_L) - g(e_L, \theta_L).$$

This is our desired contradiction.

*Step 5:* Since $\phi_L = 0$, we know from (14.BB.2) that $\phi_H = \lambda$. Substituting these two values into conditions (14.BB.4) and (14.BB.5) we have

$$\pi'(e_H) - g_e(e_H, \theta_H) = 0 \qquad (14.BB.6)$$

and

$$[\pi'(e_L) - g_e(e_L, \theta_L)] + \frac{\lambda}{1 - \lambda}[g_e(e_L, \theta_H) - g_e(e_L, \theta_L)] = 0. \qquad (14.BB.7)$$

Conditions (14.BB.6) and (14.BB.7) characterize the optimal values of $e_H$ and $e_L$, respectively. The optimal values for $w_L$ and $w_H$ are then determined from constraints (i) and (iii), which we have seen hold with equality at the solution.

An alternative approach to solving problem (14.BB.1) that avoids this somewhat cumbersome argument involves the following "trick": Solve problem (14.BB.1) ignoring constraint (iv). Then show that the solution derived in this way also satisfies constraint (iv). If so, this must be a solution to the (more constrained) problem (14.BB.1). (Exercise 14.BB.1 asks you to try this approach.)

## REFERENCES

Allen, F. (1985). Repeated principal-agent relationships with lending and borrowing. *Economic Letters* **17**: 27–31.

Baron, D., and R. Myerson. (1982). Regulating a monopolist with unknown costs. *Econometrica* **50**: 911–30.

Bernheim, B. D., and M. D. Whinston. (1986). Common agency. *Econometrica* **54**: 923–42.

Dasgupta, P., P. Hammond, and E. Maskin. (1979). The implementation of social choice rules: Some results on incentive compatibility. *Review of Economic Studies* **46**: 185–216.

Dye, R. (1986). Optimal monitoring policies in agencies. *Rand Journal of Economics* **17**: 339–50.

Fudenberg, D., B. Holmstrom, and P. Milgrom. (1990). Short-term contracts and long-term agency relationships. *Journal of Economic Theory* **52**: 194–206.

Green, J., and N. Stokey. (1983). A comparison of tournaments and contests. *Journal of Political Economy* **91**: 349–64.

Grossman, S. J., and O. D. Hart. (1983). An analysis of the principal-agent problem. *Econometrica* **51**: 7–45.

Hart, O. D., and B. Holmstrom. (1987). The theory of contracts. In *Advances in Economic Theory, Fifth World Congress*, edited by T. Bewley. New York: Cambridge University Press.

Holmstrom, B. (1979). Moral hazard and observability. *Bell Journal of Economics* **10**: 74–91.

Holmstrom, B. (1982). Moral hazard in teams. *Bell Journal of Economics* **13**: 324–40.

Holmstrom, B., and P. Milgrom. (1987). Aggregation and linearity in the provision of intertemporal incentives. *Econometrica* **55**: 303–28.

Holmstrom, B., and P. Milgrom. (1991). Multitask principal-agent analyses: Incentive contracts, asset ownership, and job design. *Journal of Law, Economics, and Organizations* **7**: 24–52.

Maskin, E., and J. Riley. (1984a). Optimal auctions with risk averse buyers. *Econometrica* **52**: 1473–1518.

Maskin, E., and J. Riley. (1984b). Monopoly with incomplete information. *Rand Journal of Economics* **15**: 171–96.

Milgrom, P. (1981). Good news and bad news: Representation theorems and applications. *Bell Journal of Economics* **12**: 380–91.

Myerson, R. (1979). Incentive compatibility and the bargaining problem. *Econometrica* **47**: 61–74.

Myerson, R. (1982). Optimal coordination mechanisms in generalized principal-agent problems. *Journal of Mathematical Economics* **10**: 67–81.

Nalebuff, B., and J. E. Stiglitz. (1983). Prizes and incentives: Towards a general theory of compensation and competition. *Bell Journal of Economics* **13**: 21–43.

Rogerson, W. (1985a). Repeated moral hazard. *Econometrica* **53**: 69–76.

Rogerson, W. (1985b). The first-order approach to principal-agent problems. *Econometrica* **53**: 1357–68.

## EXERCISES

**14.B.1$^B$** Consider the two-effort-level hidden action model discussed in Section 14.B with the general utility function $u(w, e)$ for the agent. Must the reservation utility constraint be binding in an optimal contract?

**14.B.2$^B$** Derive the first-order condition characterizing the optimal compensation scheme for the two-effort-level hidden action model studied in Section 14.B when the principal is strictly risk averse.

**14.B.3$^B$** Consider a hidden action model in which the owner is risk neutral while the manager has preferences defined over the mean and the variance of his income $w$ and his effort level $e$ as follows: Expected utility $= E[w] - \phi \text{Var}(w) - g(e)$, where $g'(0) = 0$, $(g'(e), g''(e), g'''(e)) \gg 0$ for $e > 0$, and $\text{Lim}_{e \to \infty} g'(e) = \infty$. Possible effort choices are $e \in \mathbb{R}_+$. Conditional on effort level $e$, the realization of profit is normally distributed with mean $e$ and variance $\sigma^2$.

   **(a)** Restrict attention to linear compensation schemes $w(\pi) = \alpha + \beta\pi$. Show that the manager's expected utility given $w(\pi)$, $e$, and $\sigma^2$ is given by $\alpha + \beta e - \phi\beta^2\sigma^2 - g(e)$.

   **(b)** Derive the optimal contract when $e$ is observable.

   **(c)** Derive the optimal linear compensation scheme when $e$ is not observable. What effects do changes in $\beta$ and $\sigma^2$ have?

**14.B.4$^B$** Consider the following hidden action model with three possible actions $E = \{e_1, e_2, e_3\}$. There are two possible profit outcomes: $\pi_H = 10$ and $\pi_L = 0$. The probabilities of $\pi_H$ conditional on the three effort levels are $f(\pi_H | e_1) = \frac{2}{3}$, $f(\pi_H | e_2) = \frac{1}{2}$, and $f(\pi_H | e_3) = \frac{1}{3}$. The agent's effort cost function has $g(e_1) = \frac{5}{3}$, $g(e_2) = \frac{8}{5}$, $g(e_3) = \frac{4}{3}$. Finally, $v(w) = \sqrt{w}$, and the manager's reservation utility is $\bar{u} = 0$.

   **(a)** What is the optimal contract when effort is observable?

   **(b)** Show that if effort is not observable, then $e_2$ is not implementable. For what levels of $g(e_2)$ would $e_2$ be implementable? [*Hint:* Focus on the utility levels the manager will get for the two outcomes, $v_1$ and $v_2$, rather than on the wage payments themselves.]

   **(c)** What is the optimal contract when effort is not observable?

   **(d)** Suppose, instead, that $g(e_1) = \sqrt{8}$, and let $f(\pi_H | e_1) = x \in (0, 1)$. What is the optimal contract if effort is observable as $x$ approaches 1? What is the optimal contract as $x$ approaches 1 if it is not observable? As $x$ approaches 1, is the level of effort implemented higher or lower when effort is not observable than when it is observable?

**14.B.5$^B$** Suppose that in the hidden action model explored in Section 14.B the manager can not only choose how much effort to exert but can also, after observing the realization of the firm's profits $\pi$, unobservably reduce them in a way that is of no direct benefit to him (e.g., he can voluntarily offer to pay more for his inputs). Show that in this case there is always an optimal incentive scheme that is nondecreasing in observed profits.

**14.B.6$^B$** Amend the two-effort-level model studied in Section 14.B as follows: Suppose now that effort has distinct effects on revenues $R$ and costs $C$, where $\pi = R - C$. Let $f_R(R\,|\,e)$ and $f_C(C\,|\,e)$ denote the density functions of $R$ and $C$ conditional on $e$, and assume that, conditional on $e$, $R$ and $C$ are independently distributed. Assume $R \in [\underline{R}, \bar{R}]$, $C \in [\underline{C}, \bar{C}]$, and that for all $e$, $f_R(R\,|\,e) > 0$ for all $R \in [\underline{R}, \bar{R}]$ and $f_C(C\,|\,e) > 0$ for all $C \in [\underline{C}, \bar{C}]$.

The two effort choices are now $\{e_R, e_C\}$, where $e_R$ is an effort choice that devotes more time to revenue enhancement and less to cost reduction, and the opposite is true for $e_C$. In particular, assume that $F_R(R\,|\,e_R) < F_R(R\,|\,e_C)$ for all $R \in (\underline{R}, \bar{R})$ and that $F_C(C\,|\,e_C) > F_C(C\,|\,e_R)$ for all $C \in (\underline{C}, \bar{C})$. Moreover, assume that the monotone likelihood ratio property holds for each of these variables in the following form: $[f_R(R\,|\,e_R)/f_R(R\,|\,e_C)]$ is increasing in $R$, and $[f_C(C\,|\,e_R)/f_C(C\,|\,e_C)]$ is increasing in $C$. Finally, the manager prefers revenue enhancement over cost reduction: that is, $g(e_C) > g(e_R)$.

**(a)** Suppose that the owner wants to implement effort choice $e_C$ and that both $R$ and $C$ are observable. Derive the first-order condition for the optimal compensation scheme $w(R, C)$. How does it depend on $R$ and $C$?

**(b)** How would your answer to **(a)** change if the manager could always unobservably reduce the revenues of the firm (in a way that is of no direct benefit to him)?

**(c)** What if, in addition, costs are now unobservable by a court (so that compensation can be made contingent only on revenues)?

**14.B.7$^C$** Consider a two-period model that involves two repetitions of the two-effort-level hidden action model studied in Section 14.B. There is no discounting by either the firm or the manager. The manager's expected utility over the two periods is the sum of his two single-period expected utilities $E[v(w) - g(e)]$, where $v'(\cdot) > 0$ and $v''(\cdot) < 0$.

Suppose that a contract can be signed ex ante that gives payoffs in each period as a function of performance up until then. Will period 2 wages depend on period 1 profits in the optimal contract?

**14.B.8$^C$** Amend the two-effort-choice hidden action model discussed in Section 14.B as follows: Suppose the principal can, for a cost of $c$, observe an extra signal $\tilde{y}$ of the agent's effort. Profits $\pi$ and the signal $y$ have a joint distribution $f(\pi, y\,|\,e)$ conditional on $e$. The decision to investigate the value of $y$ can be made after observing $\pi$.

A contract now specifies a wage schedule $w(\pi)$ in the event of no investigation, a wage schedule $w(\pi, y)$ if an investigation occurs, and a probability $p(\pi)$ of investigation conditional on $\pi$. Characterize the optimal contract for implementing effort level $e_H$.

**14.C.1$^C$** Analyze the extension of the hidden information model discussed in Section 14.C where there are an arbitrary finite number of states $(\theta_1, \ldots, \theta_N)$ where $\theta_{i+1} > \theta_i$ for all $i$.

**14.C.2$^B$** Consider the hidden information model in Section 14.C, but now let the manager be risk neutral with utility function $v(w) = w$. Show that the owner can do as well when $\theta$ is unobservable as when it is observable. In particular, show that he can accomplish this with a contract that offers the manager a compensation scheme of the form $w(\pi) = \pi - \alpha$ and allows him to choose any effort level he wants. Graph this function and the manager's choices in $(w, e)$-space. What revelation mechanism would give this same outcome?

**14.C.3$^B$** Suppose that in the two-state hidden information model examined in Section 14.C, $u(w, e, \theta) = v(w) - g(e, \theta)$.

   **(a)** Characterize the optimal contract under full observability.

   **(b)** Is this contract feasible when the state $\theta$ is not observable?

**14.C.4$^C$** Characterize the solution to the two-state principal-agent model with hidden information when the manager is risk averse, but not infinitely so.

**14.C.5$^B$** Confirm that the analysis in Section 14.C could not change if the owner's profits depended on the state and were not publicly observable and if, letting $\pi_i(e)$ denote the profits in state $\theta_i$ for $i = L, H$, $\pi'_H(e) \geq \pi'_L(e) > 0$ for all $e \geq 0$. What happens if this condition is not satisfied?

**14.C.6$^C$** Reconsider the labor market screening model in Exercise 13.D.1, but now suppose that there is a single employer. Characterize the solution to this firm's screening problem (assume that both types of workers have a reservation utility level of 0). Compare the task levels in this solution with those in the equilibrium of the competitive screening model (assuming an equilibrium exists) that you derived in Exercise 13.D.1.

**14.C.7$^B$** (J. Tirole) Assume that there are two types of consumers for a firm's product, $\theta_H$ and $\theta_L$. The proportion of type $\theta_L$ consumers is $\lambda$. A type $\theta$'s utility when consuming amount $x$ of the good and paying a total of $T$ for it is $u(x, T) = \theta v(x) - T$, where

$$v(x) = \frac{1 - (1 - x)^2}{2}.$$

The firm is the sole producer of this good, and its cost of production per unit is $c > 0$.

   **(a)** Consider a nondiscriminating monopolist. Derive his optimal pricing policy. Show that he serves both classes of consumers if either $\theta_L$ or $\lambda$ is "large enough."

   **(b)** Consider a monopolist who can distinguish the two types (by some characteristic) but can only charge a simple price $p_i$ to each type $\theta_i$. Characterize his optimal prices.

   **(c)** Suppose the monopolist cannot distinguish the types. Derive the optimal two-part tariff (a pricing policy consisting of a lump-sum charge $F$ plus a linear price per unit purchased of $p$) under the assumption that the monopolist serves both types. Interpret. When will the monopolist serve both types?

   **(d)** Compute the fully optimal nonlinear tariff. How do the quantities purchased by the two types compare with the levels in **(a)** to **(c)**?

**14.C.8$^B$** Air Shangri-la is the only airline allowed to fly between the islands of Shangri-la and Nirvana. There are two types of passengers, tourist and business. Business travelers are willing to pay more than tourists. The airline, however, cannot tell directly whether a ticket purchaser is a tourist or a business traveler. The two types do differ, though, in how much they are willing to pay to avoid having to purchase their tickets in advance. (Passengers do not like to commit themselves in advance to traveling at a particular time.)

   More specifically, the utility levels of each of the two types net of the price of the ticket, $P$, for any given amount of time $W$ prior to the flight that the ticket is purchased are given by

$$\begin{aligned} \textit{Business:} \quad & v - \theta_B P - W, \\ \textit{Tourist:} \quad & v - \theta_T P - W, \end{aligned}$$

where $0 < \theta_B < \theta_T$. (Note that for any given level of $W$, the business traveler is willing to pay more for his ticket. Also, the business traveler is willing to pay more for any given reduction in $W$.)

The proportion of travelers who are tourists is $\lambda$. Assume that the cost of transporting a passenger is $c$.

Assume in (a) to (d) that Air Shangri-la wants to carry both types of passengers.

(a) Draw the indifference curves of the two types in $(P, W)$-space. Draw the airline's isoprofit curves. Now formulate the optimal (profit-maximizing) price discrimination problem mathematically that Air Shangri-la would want to solve. [*Hint*: Impose nonnegativity of prices as a constraint since, if it charged a negative price, it would sell an infinite number of tickets at this price.]

(b) Show that in the optimal solution, tourists are indifferent between buying a ticket and not going at all.

(c) Show that in the optimal solution, business travelers never buy their ticket prior to the flight and are just indifferent between doing this and buying when tourists buy.

(d) Describe fully the optimal price discrimination scheme under the assumption that they sell to both types. How does it depend on the underlying parameters $\lambda$, $\theta_B$, $\theta_T$, and $c$?

(e) Under what circumstances will Air Shangri-la choose to serve only business travelers?

**14.C.9$^C$** Consider a risk-averse individual who is an expected utility maximizer with a Bernoulli utility function over wealth $u(\cdot)$. The individual has initial wealth $W$ and faces a probability $\theta$ of suffering a loss of size $L$, where $W > L > 0$.

An insurance contract may be described by a pair $(c_1, c_2)$, where $c_1$ is the amount of wealth the individual has in the event of no loss and $c_2$ is the amount the individual has if a loss is suffered. That is, in the event no loss occurs the individual pays the insurance company an amount $(W - c_1)$, whereas if a loss occurs the individual receives a payment $[c_2 - (W - L)]$ from the company.

(a) Suppose that the individual's only source of insurance is a risk-neutral monopolist (i.e., the monopolist seeks to maximize its expected profits). Characterize the contract the monopolist will offer the individual in the case in which the individual's probability of loss, $\theta$, is observable.

(b) Suppose, instead, that $\theta$ is not observable by the insurance company (the individual knows $\theta$). The parameter $\theta$ can take one of two values $\{\theta_L, \theta_H\}$, where $\theta_H > \theta_L > 0$ and $\text{Prob}\,(\theta_L) = \lambda$. Characterize the optimal contract offers of the monopolist. Can one speak of one type of insured individual being "rationed" in his purchases of insurance (i.e., he would want to purchase more insurance if allowed to at fair odds)? Intuitively, why does this rationing occur? [*Hint*: It might be helpful to draw a picture in $(c_1, c_2)$-space. To do so, start by locating the individual's endowment point, that is, what he gets if he does not purchase any insurance.]

(c) Compare your solution in (b) with your answer to Exercise 13.D.2.

**14.AA.1$^B$** Show that $[f_e(\pi\,|\,e)/f(\pi\,|\,e)]$ is increasing in $\pi$ for all $e \in [a, b] \subset \mathbb{R}$ if and only if for any $e', e'' \in [a, b]$, with $e'' > e'$, $[f(\pi\,|\,e'')/f(\pi\,|\,e')]$ is increasing in $\pi$.

**14.AA.2$^B$** Consider a hidden action model with $e \in [0, \bar{e}]$ and two outcomes $\pi_H$ and $\pi_L$, with $\pi_H > \pi_L$. The probability of $\pi_H$ given effort level $e$ is $f(\pi_H\,|\,e)$. Give sufficient conditions for the first-order approach to be valid. Characterize the optimal contract when these conditions are satisfied.

**14.BB.1$^B$** Try solving problem (14.BB.1) by first solving it while ignoring constraint (iv) and then arguing that the solution you derive to this "relaxed" problem is actually the solution to problem (14.BB.1).

# General Equilibrium

Part IV is devoted to an examination of competitive market economies from a *general equilibrium* perspective. Our use of the term "general equilibrium" refers both to a methodological point of view and to a substantive theory.

Methodologically, the general equilibrium approach has two central features. First, it views the economy as a *closed* and *interrelated* system in which we must simultaneously determine the equilibrium values of all variables of interest. Thus, when we evaluate the effects of a perturbation in the economic environment, the equilibrium levels of the entire set of endogenous variables in the economy needs to be recomputed. This stands in contrast to the *partial equilibrium* approach, where the impact on endogenous variables not directly related to the problem at hand is explicitly or implicitly disregarded.

A second central feature of the general equilibrium approach is that it aims at reducing the set of variables taken as exogenous to a small number of physical realities (e.g., the set of economic agents, the available technologies, the preferences and physical endowments of goods of various agents).

From a substantive viewpoint, general equilibrium theory has a more specific meaning: It is a theory of the determination of equilibrium prices and quantities in a system of perfectly competitive markets. This theory is often referred to as the *Walrasian theory* of markets [from L. Walras (1874)], and it is the object of our study in Part IV. The Walrasian theory of markets is very ambitious. It attempts no less than to predict the complete vector of final consumptions and productions using only the fundamentals of the economy (the list of commodities, the state of technology, preferences and endowments), the institutional assumption that a price is quoted for every commodity (including those that will not be traded at equilibrium), and the behavioral assumption of price taking by consumers and firms.

Strictly speaking, we introduced a particular case of the general equilibrium model in Chapter 10. There, we carried out an equilibrium and welfare analysis of perfectly competitive markets under the assumption that consumers had quasilinear preferences. In that setting, consumer demand functions do not display wealth effects (except for a single commodity, called the *numeraire*); as a consequence, the analysis of a single market (or small group of markets) could be pursued in a manner understandable as traditional partial equilibrium analysis. A good deal of what we do in Part IV can be viewed as an attempt to extend the ideas of Chapter 10 to a world in which wealth effects are significant. The primary motivation for this is the increase in realism it brings. To make practical use of equilibrium analysis for studying the performance of an entire economy, or for evaluating policy interventions that affect large numbers of markets simultaneously, wealth effects, a primary source of linkages across markets, cannot be neglected, and therefore the general equilibrium approach is essential.

Although knowledge of the material discussed in Chapter 10 is not a strict prerequisite for Part IV, we nonetheless strongly recommend that you study it, especially Sections 10.B to 10.D. It constitutes an introduction to the main issues and provides a simple and analytically very useful example. We will see in the different chapters of Part IV that quite a number of the important results established in Chapter 10 for the quasilinear situation carry over to the case of general preferences. But many others do not. To understand why this may be so, recall from Chapters 4 and 10 that a group of consumers with quasilinear preferences (with respect to the same numeraire) admits the existence of a (normative) representative consumer. This is a powerful restriction on the behavior of aggregate demand that will not be available to us in the more general settings that we study here.

It is important to note that, relative to the analysis carried out in Part III, we incur a cost for accomplishing the task that general equilibrium sets itself to do: the assumptions of price-taking behavior and universal price quoting—that is, the existence of markets for every relevant commodity (with the implication of symmetric information)—are present in nearly all the theory studied in Part IV. Thus, in many respects, we are not going as deep as we did in Part III in the microanalysis of markets, of market failure, and of the strategic interdependence of market actors. The trade-off in conceptual structure between Parts III and IV reflects, in a sense, the current state of the frontier of microeconomic research.

The content of Part IV is organized into six chapters.

Chapter 15 presents a preliminary discussion. Its main purpose is to illustrate the issues that concern general equilibrium theory by means of three simple examples: the *two-consumer Edgeworth box economy*; the *one-consumer, one-firm economy*, and the *small open economy* model.

Chapters 16 and 17 constitute the heart of the formal analysis in Part IV. Chapter 16 presents the formal structure of the general equilibrium model and introduces two central concepts of the theory: the notions of *Pareto optimality* and *price-taking equilibrium* (and, in particular, *Walrasian equilibrium*). The chapter is devoted to the examination of the relationship between these two concepts. The emphasis is therefore *normative*, focusing on the welfare properties of price-taking equilibria. The core of the chapter is concerned with the formulation and proof of the two *fundamental theorems of welfare economics*.

In Chapter 17, the emphasis is, instead, on *positive* (or *descriptive*) properties of Walrasian equilibria. We study a number of questions pertaining to the predictive power of the Walrasian theory, including the existence, local and global uniqueness, and comparative statics behavior of Walrasian equilibria.

Chapters 18 to 20 explore extensions of the basic analysis presented in Chapters 16 and 17. Chapter 18 covers a number of topics whose origins lie in normative theory or the cooperative theory of games; these topics share the feature that they provide a deeper look at the foundations of price-taking equilibria by exploiting properties derived from the mass nature of markets. We study the important *core equivalence theorem*, examine further the idea of Walrasian equilibria as the limit of noncooperative equilibria as markets grow large (a subject already broached in Section 12.F), and present two normative characterizations of Walrasian equilibria: one in terms of *envy-freeness* (or *anonymity*) and the other in terms of a *marginal productivity principle*. Appendix A of Chapter 18 offers a brief introduction to the cooperative theory of games.

Chapter 19 covers the modeling of uncertainty in a general equilibrium context. The ability to do this in a theoretically satisfying way has been one of the success stories of general equilibrium theory. The concepts of *contingent commodities*, *Arrow–Debreu equilibrium*, *sequential trade* (in a two-period setting), *Radner equilibrium*, *arbitrage*, *rational expectations equilibrium*, and *incomplete markets* are all introduced and studied here. The chapter provides a natural link to the modern theory of finance.

Chapter 20 considers the application of the general theory to dynamic competitive economies (but with no uncertainty) and also studies a number of issues specific to this environment. Notions such as *impatience*, *dynamic efficiency*, and *myopic* versus *overall utility maximization* are introduced. The chapter first analyzes dynamic representative consumer economies (including the *Ramsey–Solow model*), then generalizes to the case of a finite number of consumers, and concludes with a brief presentation of the *overlapping generations model*. In the process, we explore a wide range of dynamic behaviors. The chapter provides a natural link to macroeconomic theory.

The modern classics of general equilibrium theory are Debreu (1959) and Arrow and Hahn (1971). These texts provide further discussion of topics treated here. For extensions, we recommend the encyclopedic coverage of Arrow and Intriligator (1981, 1982, 1986) and Hildenbrand and Sonnenschein (1991). See also the more recent textbook account of Ellickson (1993). General equilibrium analysis has a very important applied dimension that we do not touch on in this book but that accounts in good part for the importance of the theory. For a review, we recommend Shoven and Whalley (1992).

## REFERENCES

Arrow, K., and F. Hahn. (1971). *General Competitive Analysis.* San Francisco: Holden-Day.

Arrow, K., and M. Intriligator, eds. (1981). *Handbook of Mathematical Economics*, Vol. 1. Amsterdam: North-Holland.

Arrow, K., and M. Intriligator, eds. (1982). *Handbook of Mathematical Economics*, Vol. 2. Amsterdam: North-Holland.

Arrow, K., and M. Intriligator, eds. (1986). *Handbook of Mathematical Economics*, Vol. 3. Amsterdam: North-Holland.

Debreu, G. (1959). *Theory of Value.* New York: Wiley.

Ellickson, B. (1993). *Competitive Equilibrium: Theory and Applications*, Cambridge, UK: Cambridge University Press.

Hildenbrand, W., and H. Sonnenschein, eds. (1991). *Handbook of Mathematical Economics*, Vol. 4. Amsterdam: North-Holland.

Shoven, J., and J. Whalley. (1992). *Applying General Equilibrium Analysis.* Cambridge, UK: Cambridge University Press.

Walras, L. (1874). *Eléments d'économie politique pure.* Lausanne: Corbaz.

# General Equilibrium Theory: Some Examples

## 15.A Introduction

The purpose of this chapter is to present a preliminary discussion. In it, we describe and analyze three simple examples of general equilibrium models. These examples introduce some of the questions, concepts, and common techniques that will occupy us for the rest of Part IV.

In most economies, three basic economic activities occur: production, exchange, and consumption. In Section 15.B, we restrict our focus to exchange and consumption. We analyze the case of a *pure exchange economy*, in which no production is possible and the commodities that are ultimately consumed are those that individuals possess as *endowments*. Individuals trade these endowments among themselves in the marketplace for mutual advantage. The model we present is the simplest-possible exchange problem: two consumers trading two goods between each other. In this connection, we introduce an extremely handy graphical device, the *Edgeworth box*.

In Section 15.C, we introduce production by studying an economy formed by one firm and one consumer. Using this simple model, we explore how the production and consumption sides of the economy fit together.

In Section 15.D, we examine the production side of the economy in greater detail by discussing the allocation of resources among several firms. To analyze this issue in isolation, we study the case of a small open economy that takes the world prices of its outputs as fixed, a central model in international trade literature.

Section 15.E illustrates, by means of an example, some of the potential dangers of adopting a partial equilibrium perspective when a general equilibrium approach is called for.

As we noted in the introduction of Part IV, Chapter 10 contains another simple example of a general equilibrium model: that of an economy in which consumers have preferences admitting a quasilinear representation.

## 15.B Pure Exchange: The Edgeworth Box

A *pure exchange economy* (or, simply, an *exchange economy*) is an economy in which there are no production opportunities. The economic agents of such an economy are consumers who possess initial stocks, or *endowments*, of commodities. Economic activity consists of trading and consumption.

The simplest economy with the possibility of profitable exchange is one with two commodities and two consumers. As it turns out, this case is amenable to analysis by a graphical device known as the *Edgeworth box*, which we use extensively in this section. Throughout, we assume that the two consumers act as price takers. Although this may not seem reasonable with only two traders, our aim here is to illustrate some of the features of general equilibrium models in the simplest-possible way.[1]

To begin, assume that there are two consumers, denoted by $i = 1, 2$, and two commodities, denoted by $\ell = 1, 2$. Consumer $i$'s consumption vector is $x_i = (x_{1i}, x_{2i})$; that is, consumer $i$'s consumption of commodity $\ell$ is $x_{\ell i}$. We assume that consumer $i$'s consumption set is $\mathbb{R}^2_+$ and that he has a preference relation $\succsim_i$ over consumption vectors in this set. Each consumer $i$ is initially endowed with an amount $\omega_{\ell i} \geq 0$ of good $\ell$. Thus, consumer $i$'s *endowment vector* is $\omega_i = (\omega_{1i}, \omega_{2i})$. The *total endowment* of good $\ell$ in the economy is denoted by $\bar{\omega}_\ell = \omega_{\ell 1} + \omega_{\ell 2}$; we assume that this quantity is strictly positive for both goods.

An *allocation* $x \in \mathbb{R}^4_+$ in this economy is an assignment of a nonnegative consumption vector to each consumer: $x = (x_1, x_2) = ((x_{11}, x_{21}), (x_{12}, x_{22}))$. We say that an allocation is *feasible* for the economy if

$$x_{\ell 1} + x_{\ell 2} \leq \bar{\omega}_\ell \qquad \text{for } \ell = 1, 2, \tag{15.B.1}$$

that is, if the total consumption of each commodity is no more than the economy's aggregate endowment of it (note that in this notion of feasibility, we are implicitly assuming that there is free disposal of commodities).

The feasible allocations for which equality holds in (15.B.1) could be called *nonwasteful*. Nonwasteful feasible allocations can be depicted by means of an *Edgeworth box*, shown in Figure 15.B.1. In the Edgeworth box, consumer 1's quantities are measured in the usual way, with the southwest corner as the origin. In contrast, consumer 2's quantities are measured using the northeast corner as the origin. For both consumers, the vertical dimension measures quantities of good 2, and the horizontal dimension measures quantities of good 1. The length of the box is $\bar{\omega}_1$, the economy's total endowment of good 1; its height is $\bar{\omega}_2$, the economy's total endowment of good 2. Any point in the box represents a (nonwasteful) division of the economy's total endowment between consumers 1 and 2. For example, Figure 15.B.1 depicts the endowment vector $\omega = ((\omega_{11}, \omega_{21}), (\omega_{12}, \omega_{22}))$ of the two consumers. Also depicted is another possible nonwasteful allocation, $x = ((x_{11}, x_{21}), (x_{12}, x_{22}))$; the fact that it is nonwasteful means that $(x_{12}, x_{22}) = (\bar{\omega}_1 - x_{11}, \bar{\omega}_2 - x_{21})$.

As is characteristic of general equilibrium theory, the wealth of a consumer is not given exogenously. Rather, for any prices $p = (p_1, p_2)$, consumer $i$'s wealth equals the market value of his endowments of commodities, $p \cdot \omega_i = p_1 \omega_{1i} + p_2 \omega_{2i}$. Wealth levels are therefore determined by the values of prices. Hence, given the consumer's endowment vector $\omega_i$, his budget set can be viewed solely as a

---

1. Alternatively, we could assume that each consumer (perhaps better called a *consumer type*) stands, not for an individual, but for a large number of identical consumers. This would make the price-taking assumption more plausible; and with equal numbers of the two types of consumers, the analysis in this section would be otherwise unaffected.

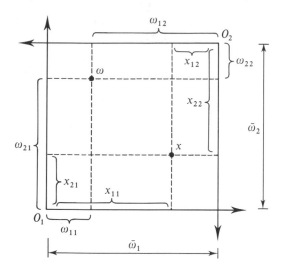

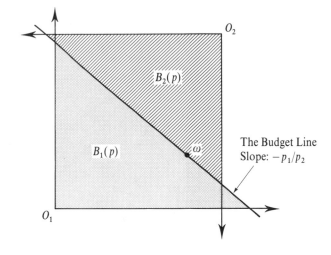

function of prices:

$$B_i(p) = \{x_i \in \mathbb{R}^2_+ : p \cdot x_i \leq p \cdot \omega_i\}.$$

**Figure 15.B.1 (left)**
An Edgeworth box.

**Figure 15.B.2 (right)**
Budget sets.

The budget sets of the two consumers can be represented in the Edgeworth box in a simple manner. To do so, we draw a line, known as the *budget line*, through the endowment point $\omega$ with slope $-(p_1/p_2)$, as shown in Figure 15.B.2. Consumer 1's budget set consists of all the nonnegative vectors below and to the left of this line (the shaded set). Consumer 2's budget set, on the other hand, consists of all the vectors above and to the right of this same line which give consumer 2 nonnegative consumption levels (the hatched set).[2] Observe that only allocations on the budget line are affordable to both consumers simultaneously at prices $(p_1, p_2)$.[3]

We can also depict the preferences $\succsim_i$ of each consumer $i$ in the Edgeworth box, as in Figure 15.B.3. Except where otherwise noted, we assume that $\succsim_i$ is strictly convex, continuous, and strongly monotone (see Sections 3.B and 3.C for discussion of these conditions).

Figure 15.B.4 illustrates how the consumption vector demanded by consumer 1 can be determined for any price vector $p$. Given $p$, the consumer demands his most preferred point in $B_1(p)$, which can be expressed using his demand function as $x_1(p, p \cdot \omega_1)$ (this is the same demand function studied in Chapters 2 to 4; here wealth is $w_1 = p \cdot \omega_1$). In Figure 15.B.5, we see that as the price vector $p$ varies, the budget line pivots around the endowment point $\omega$, and the demanded consumptions trace out a curve, denoted by $OC_1$, that is called the *offer curve* of consumer 1. Note that this curve passes through the endowment point. Because at every $p$ the endowment vector $\omega_1 = (\omega_{11}, \omega_{21})$ is affordable to consumer 1, it follows that this consumer must find every point on his offer curve at least as good as his endowment point.

---

2. Note, in particular, that the budget sets of the consumers may well extend outside the box.

3. There are other feasible allocations that are simultaneously affordable; but in these allocations some resources are not consumed by either consumer, and thus they cannot be depicted in an Edgeworth box. Because of the nonsatiation assumption to be made on preferences, we will not have to worry about such allocations.

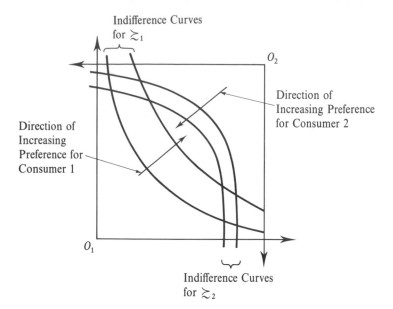

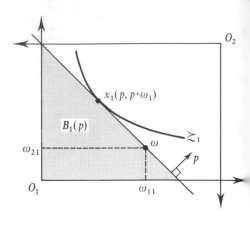

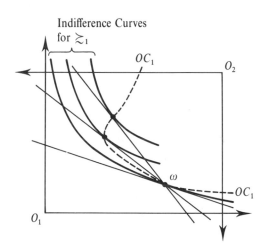

**Figure 15.B.3 (top left)**
Preferences in the Edgeworth box.

**Figure 15.B.4 (top right)**
Optimal consumption for consumer 1 at prices $p$.

**Figure 15.B.5 (bottom)**
Consumer 1's offer curve.

This implies that the consumer's offer curve lies within the upper contour set of $\omega_1$ and that, if indifference curves are smooth, the offer curve must be tangent to the consumer's indifference curve at the endowment point.

Figure 15.B.6 represents the demanded bundles of the two consumers at some arbitrary price vector $p$. Note that the demands expressed by the two consumers are not compatible. The total demand for good 2 exceeds its total supply in the economy $\bar{\omega}_2$, whereas the total demand for good 1 is strictly less than its endowment $\bar{\omega}_1$. Put somewhat differently, consumer 1 is a *net demander* of good 2 in the sense that he wants to consume more than his endowment of that commodity. Although consumer 2 is willing to be a *net supplier* of that good (he wants to consume less than his endowment), he is not willing to supply enough to satisfy consumer 1's needs. Good 2 is therefore in *excess demand* in the situation depicted in the figure. In contrast, good 1 is in *excess supply*.

At a market equilibrium where consumers take prices as given, markets should clear. That is, the consumers should be able to fulfill their desired purchases and

**Figure 15.B.6**

A price vector with excess demand for good 2 and excess supply for good 1.

sales of commodities at the going market prices. Thus, if one consumer wishes to be *a net demander* of some good, the other must be a *net supplier* of this good in exactly the same amount; that is, demand should equal supply. This gives us the notion of equilibrium presented in Definition 15.B.1.

**Definition 15.B.1:** A *Walrasian* (or *competitive*) *equilibrium* for an Edgeworth box economy is a price vector $p^*$ and an allocation $x^* = (x_1^*, x_2^*)$ in the Edgeworth box such that for $i = 1, 2$,

$$x_i^* \succsim_i x_i' \quad \text{for all} \quad x_i' \in B_i(p^*).$$

A Walrasian equilibrium is depicted in Figure 15.B.7. In Figure 15.B.7(a), we represent the equilibrium price vector $p^*$ and the equilibrium allocation $x^* = (x_1^*, x_2^*)$. Each consumer $i$'s demanded bundle at price vector $p^*$ is $x_i^*$, and one consumer's net demand for a good is exactly matched by the other's net supply. Figure 15.B.7(b) adds to the depiction the consumers' offer curves and their indifference curves through $\omega$. Note that at any equilibrium, the offer curves of the two consumers intersect. In fact, *any* intersection of the consumers' offer curves at an allocation different from the endowment point $\omega$ corresponds to an equilibrium because if $x^* = (x_1^*, x_2^*)$ is any such point of intersection, then $x_i^*$ is the optimal consumption bundle for each consumer $i$ for the budget line that goes through the two points $\omega$ and $x^*$.

In Figure 15.B.8, we show a Walrasian equilibrium where the equilibrium allocation lies on the boundary of the Edgeworth box. Once again, at price vector $p^*$, the two consumers' demands are compatible.

Note that each consumer's demand is homogeneous of degree zero in the price vector $p = (p_1, p_2)$; that is, if prices double, then the consumer's wealth also doubles and his budget set remains unchanged. Thus, from Definition 15.B.1, we see that if $p^* = (p_1^*, p_2^*)$ is a Walrasian equilibrium price vector, then so is $\alpha p^* = (\alpha p_1^*, \alpha p_2^*)$ for any $\alpha > 0$. In short, only the *relative* prices $p_1^*/p_2^*$ are determined in an equilibrium.

**Example 15.B.1:** Suppose that each consumer $i$ has the Cobb–Douglas utility function $u_i(x_{1i}, x_{2i}) = x_{1i}^\alpha x_{2i}^{1-\alpha}$. In addition, endowments are $\omega_1 = (1, 2)$ and $\omega_2 = (2, 1)$. At prices $p = (p_1, p_2)$, consumer 1's wealth is $(p_1 + 2p_2)$ and therefore his demands lie on the offer curve (recall the derivation in Example 3.D.1):

$$OC_1(p) = \left( \frac{\alpha(p_1 + 2p_2)}{p_1}, \frac{(1-\alpha)(p_1 + 2p_2)}{p_2} \right).$$

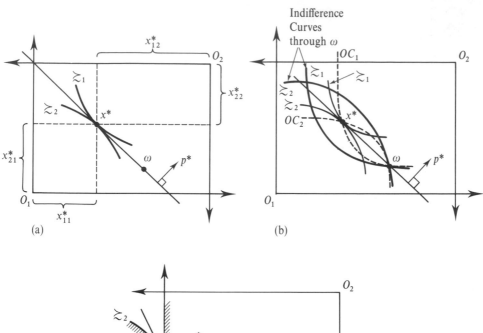

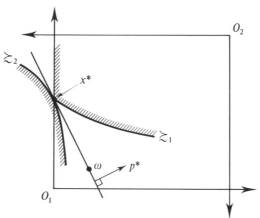

**Figure 15.B.7 (top)**

(a) A Walrasian equilibrium.
(b) The consumer's offer curves intersect at the Walrasian equilibrium allocation.

**Figure 15.B.8 (bottom)**

A Walrasian equilibrium allocation on the boundary of the Edgeworth box.

Observe that the demands for the first and the second good are, respectively, decreasing and increasing with $p_1$. This is how we have drawn $OC_1$ in Figure 15.B.7(b). Similarly, $OC_2(p) = (\alpha(2p_1 + p_2)/p_1, (1 - \alpha)(2p_1 + p_2)/p_2)$. To determine the Walrasian equilibrium prices, note that at these prices the total amount of good 1 consumed by the two consumers must equal 3 $(=\omega_{11} + \omega_{12})$. Thus,

$$\frac{\alpha(p_1^* + 2p_2^*)}{p_1^*} + \frac{\alpha(2p_1^* + p_2^*)}{p_1^*} = 3.$$

Solving this equation yields

$$\frac{p_1^*}{p_2^*} = \frac{\alpha}{1 - \alpha}. \tag{15.B.2}$$

Observe that at any prices $(p_1^*, p_2^*)$ satisfying condition (15.B.2), the market for good 2 clears as well (you should verify this). This is a general feature of an Edgeworth box economy: To determine equilibrium prices we need only determine prices at which one of the markets clears; the other market will necessarily clear at these prices. This point can be seen graphically in the Edgeworth box: Because both consumers' demanded bundles lie on the same budget line, if the amounts of commodity 1 demanded are compatible, then so must be those for commodity 2. (See also Exercise 15.B.1.) ∎

**Figure 15.B.9**

Multiple Walrasian equilibria.

The Edgeworth box, simple as it is, is remarkably powerful. There are virtually no phenomena or properties of general equilibrium exchange economies that cannot be depicted in it. Consider, for example, the issue of the uniqueness of Walrasian equilibrium. In Chapter 10, we saw that if there is a numeraire commodity relative to which preferences admit a quasilinear representation, then (with strict convexity of preferences) the equilibrium consumption allocation and relative prices are unique. In Figure 15.B.7, we also have uniqueness (see Exercise 15.B.2 for a more explicit discussion). Yet, as the Edgeworth box in Figure 15.B.9 shows, this property does not generalize. In that figure, preferences (which are entirely nonpathological) are such that the offer curves change curvature and interlace several times. In particular, they intersect for prices such that $p_1/p_2$ is equal to $\frac{1}{2}$, 1, and 2. For the sake of completeness, we present an analytical example with the features of the figure.

**Example 15.B.2:** Let the two consumers have utility functions

$$u_1(x_{11}, x_{21}) = x_{11} - \tfrac{1}{8}x_{21}^{-8} \text{ and } u_2(x_{12}, x_{22}) = -\tfrac{1}{8}x_{12}^{-8} + x_{22}.$$

Note that the utility functions are quasilinear (which, in particular, facilitates the computation of demand), but with respect to *different* numeraires. The endowments are $\omega_1 = (2, r)$ and $\omega_2 = (r, 2)$, where $r$ is chosen to guarantee that the equilibrium prices turn out to be round numbers. Precisely, $r = 2^{8/9} - 2^{1/9} > 0$. In Exercise 15.B.5, you are asked to compute the offer curves of the two consumers. They are:

$$OC_1(p_1, p_2) = \left(2 + r\left(\frac{p_2}{p_1}\right) - \left(\frac{p_2}{p_1}\right)^{8/9}, \left(\frac{p_2}{p_1}\right)^{-1/9}\right) \gg 0$$

and

$$OC_2(p_1, p_2) = \left(\left(\frac{p_1}{p_2}\right)^{-1/9}, 2 + r\left(\frac{p_1}{p_2}\right) - \left(\frac{p_1}{p_2}\right)^{8/9}\right) \gg 0.$$

Note that, as illustrated in Figure 15.B.9, and in contrast with Example 15.B.1, consumer 1's demand for good 1 (and symmetrically for consumer 2) may be increasing in $p_1$.

To compute the equilibria it is sufficient to solve the equation that equates the total demand of the second good to its total supply, or

$$\left(\frac{p_2}{p_1}\right)^{-1/9} + 2 + r\left(\frac{p_1}{p_2}\right) - \left(\frac{p_1}{p_2}\right)^{8/9} = 2 + r.$$

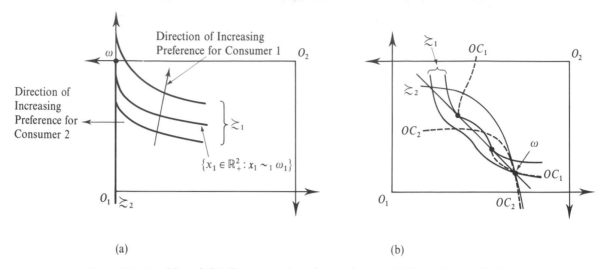

**Figure 15.B.10**  (a) and (b): Two examples of nonexistence of Walrasian equilibrium.

Recalling the value of $r$, this equation has three solutions for $p_1/p_2$: 2, 1, and $\frac{1}{2}$ (you should check this). ∎

It may also happen that a pure exchange economy does not have *any* Walrasian equilibria. For example, Figure 15.B.10(a) depicts a situation in which the endowment lies on the boundary of the Edgeworth box (in the northwest corner). Consumer 2 has all the endowment of good 1 and desires only good 1. Consumer 1 has all the endowment of good 2 and his indifference set containing $\omega_1$, $\{x_1 \in \mathbb{R}^2_+ : x_1 \sim_1 \omega_1\}$, has an infinite slope at $\omega_1$ (note, however, that at $\omega_1$, consumer 1 would strictly prefer receiving more of good 1). In this situation, there is no price vector $p^*$ at which the consumers' demands are compatible. If $p_2/p_1 > 0$ then consumer 2 optimal demand is to keep his initial bundle $\omega_2$, whereas the initial bundle $\omega_1$ is never consumer 1's optimal demand (no matter how large the relative price of the first good, consumer 1 always wishes to buy a strictly positive amount of it). On the other hand, consumer 1's demand for good 2 is infinite when $p_2/p_1 = 0$. Note for future reference that consumer 2's preferences in this example are not strongly monotone.

Figure 15.B.10(b) depicts a second example of nonexistence. There, consumer 1's preferences are nonconvex. As a result, consumer 1's offer curve is disconnected, and there is no crossing point of the two consumers' offer curves (other than the endowment point, which is not an equilibrium allocation here).

In Chapter 17, we will study the conditions under which the existence of a Walrasian equilibrium is assured.

*Welfare Properties of Walrasian Equilibria*

A central question in economic theory concerns the welfare properties of equilibria. Here we shall focus on the notion of Pareto optimality, which we have already encountered in Chapter 10 (see, in particular, Section 10.B). An economic outcome is *Pareto optimal* (or *Pareto efficient*) if there is no alternative feasible outcome at which every individual in the economy is at least as well off and some individual is

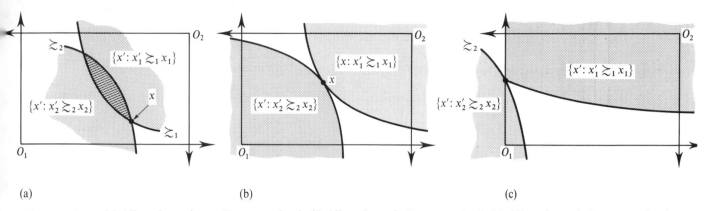

(a)                                  (b)                                  (c)

**Figure 15.B.11**   (a) Allocation $x$ is not Pareto optimal. (b) Allocation $x$ is Pareto optimal. (c) Allocation $x$ is Pareto optimal.

strictly better off. Definition 15.B.2 expresses this idea in the setting of our two-consumer, pure exchange economy.

**Definition 15.B.2:** An allocation $x$ in the Edgeworth box is *Pareto optimal* (or *Pareto efficient*) if there is no other allocaton $x'$ in the Edgeworth box with $x'_i \succsim_i x_i$ for $i = 1, 2$ and $x'_i \succ_i x_i$ for some $i$.

Figure 15.B.11(a) depicts an allocation $x$ that is not Pareto optimal. Any allocation in the interior of the crosshatched region of the figure, the intersection of the sets $\{x'_1 \in \mathbb{R}^2_+ : x'_1 \succsim_1 x_1\}$ and $\{x'_2 \in \mathbb{R}^2_+ : x'_2 \succsim_2 x_2\}$ within the Edgeworth box, is a feasible allocation that makes both consumers strictly better off than at $x$. The allocation $x$ depicted in Figure 15.B.11(b), on the other hand, is Pareto optimal because the intersection of the sets $\{x'_i \in \mathbb{R}^2_+ : x'_i \succsim_i x_i\}$ for $i = 1, 2$ consists only of the point $x$. Note that if a Pareto optimal allocation $x$ is an interior point of the Edgeworth box, then the consumers' indifference curves through $x$ must be tangent (assuming that they are smooth). Figure 15.B.11(c) depicts a Pareto optimal allocation $x$ that is not interior; at such a point, tangency need not hold.

The set of all Pareto optimal allocations is known as the *Pareto set*. An example is illustrated in Figure 15.B.12. The figure also displays the *contract curve*, the part of the

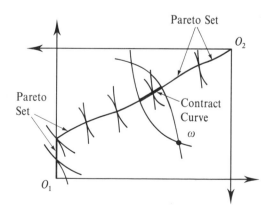

**Figure 15.B.12**

The Pareto set and the contract curve.

Pareto set where both consumers do at least as well as at their initial endowments. The reason for this term is that we might expect any bargaining between the two consumers to result in an agreement to trade to some point on the contract curve; these are the only points at which both of them do as well as at their initial endowments and for which there is no alternative trade that can make both consumers better off.

We can now verify a simple but important fact: *Any Walrasian equilibrium allocation x\* necessarily belongs to the Pareto set.* To see this, note that by the definition of a Walrasian equilibrium the budget line separates the two at-least-as-good-as sets associated with the equilibrium allocation, as seen in Figures 15.B.7(a) and 15.B.8. The only point in common between these two sets is $x^*$ itself. Thus, at any competitive allocation $x^*$, there is no alternative feasible allocation that can benefit one consumer without hurting the other. The conclusion that Walrasian allocations yield Pareto optimal allocations is an expression of the *first fundamental theorem of welfare economics,* a result that, as we shall see in Chapter 16, holds with great generality. Note, moreover, that since each consumer must be at least as well off in a Walrasian equilibrium as by simply consuming his endowment, any Walrasian equilibrium lies in the contract curve portion of the Pareto set.

The first fundamental welfare theorem provides, for competitive market economies, a formal expression of Adam Smith's "invisible hand." Under perfectly competitive conditions, any equilibrium allocation is a Pareto optimum, and the only possible welfare justification for intervention in the economy is the fulfillment of distributional objectives.

The *second fundamental theorem of welfare economics,* which we also discuss extensively in Chapter 16, offers a (partial) converse result. Roughly put, it says that *under convexity assumptions* (*not required for the first welfare theorem*), *a planner can achieve any desired Pareto optimal allocation by appropriately redistributing wealth in a lump-sum fashion and then "letting the market work."* Thus, the second welfare theorem provides a theoretical affirmation for the use of competitive markets in pursuing distributional objectives.

Definition 15.B.3 is a more formal statement of the concept of an equilibrium with lump-sum wealth redistribution.

**Definition 15.B.3:** An allocation $x^*$ in the Edgeworth box is supportable as an *equilibrium with transfers* if there is a price system $p^*$ and wealth transfers $T_1$ and $T_2$ satisfying $T_1 + T_2 = 0$, such that for each consumer $i$ we have

$$x_i^* \succsim_i x_i' \quad \text{for all } x_i' \in \mathbb{R}_+^2 \quad \text{such that} \quad p^* \cdot x_i' \leq p^* \cdot \omega_i + T_i.$$

Note that the transfers sum to zero in Definition 15.B.3; the planner runs a balanced budget, merely redistributing wealth between the consumers.

Equipped with Definition 15.B.3, we can state more formally a version of the second welfare theorem as follows: if the preferences of the two consumers in the Edgeworth box are continuous, convex, and strongly monotone, then *any Pareto optimal allocation is supportable as an equilibrium with transfers.* This result is illustrated in Figure 15.B.13(a), where the consumer's endowments are at point $\omega$. Suppose that for distributional reasons, the socially desired allocation is the Pareto optimal allocation $x^*$. Then if a tax authority constructs a transfer of wealth between the two consumers that shifts the budget line to the location

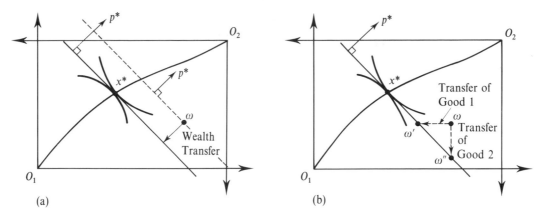

**Figure 15.B.13**  The second fundamental welfare theorem. (a) Using wealth transfers. (b) Using transfers of endowments.

indicated in the figure, the price vector $p^*$ clears the markets for the two goods, and allocation $x^*$ results.

Note that this wealth transfer may also be accomplished by directly transferring endowments. As Figure 15.B.13(b) illustrates, a transfer of good 1 that moves the endowment vector to $\omega'$ will have the price vector $p^*$ and allocation $x^*$ as a Walrasian equilibrium. A transfer of good 2 that changes endowments to $\omega''$ does so as well. In fact, if all commodities can be easily transferred, then we could equally well move the endowment vector directly to allocation $x^*$. From this new endowment point, the Walrasian equilibrium involves no trade.[4]

Figure 15.B.14 shows that the second welfare theorem may fail to hold when preferences are not convex. In the figure, $x^* = (x_1^*, x_2^*)$ is a Pareto optimal allocation that is not supportable as an equilibrium with transfers. At the budget line with the property that consumer 2 would demand $x_2^*$, consumer 1 would prefer a point other than $x_1^*$ (such as $x_1'$). Convexity, as it turns out, is a critical assumption for the second welfare theorem.

A failure of the second welfare theorem of a different kind is illustrated in Figure 15.B.10(a). There, the initial endowment allocation $\omega$ is a Pareto optimal allocation, but it cannot be supported as an equilibrium with transfers (you should check this). In this case, it is the assumption that consumers' preferences are strongly monotone that is violated.

For further illustrations of Edgeworth box economies see, for example, Newman (1965).

# 15.C  The One-Consumer, One-Producer Economy

We now introduce the possibility of production. To do so in the simplest-possible setting, we suppose that there are two price-taking economic agents, a single

---

4. In practice, endowments may be difficult to transfer (e.g., human capital), and so the ability to use wealth transfers (or transfers of only a limited number of commodities) may be important. It is worth observing that there is one attractive feature of transferring endowments directly to the desired Pareto optimal allocation: we can be assured that $x^*$ is the *unique* Walrasian equilibrium allocation after the transfers (strictly speaking this requires a strict convexity assumption on preferences).

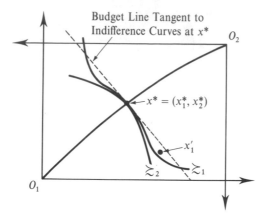

**Figure 15.B.14**

Failure of the second welfare theorem with nonconvex preferences.

consumer and a single firm, and two goods, the labor (or leisure) of the consumer and a consumption good produced by the firm.[5]

The consumer has continuous, convex, and strongly monotone preferences $\succsim$ defined over his consumption of leisure $x_1$ and the consumption good $x_2$. He has an endowment of $\bar{L}$ units of leisure (e.g., 24 hours in a day) and no endowment of the consumption good.

The firm uses labor to produce the consumption good according to the increasing and strictly concave production function $f(z)$, where $z$ is the firm's labor input. Thus, to produce output, the firm must hire the consumer, effectively purchasing some of the consumer's leisure from him. We assume that the firm seeks to maximize its profits taking market prices as given. Letting $p$ be the price of its output and $w$ be the price of labor, the firm solves

$$\underset{z \geq 0}{\text{Max}} \quad pf(z) - wz. \tag{15.C.1}$$

Given prices $(p, w)$, the firm's optimal labor demand is $z(p, w)$, its output is $q(p, w)$, and its profits are $\pi(p, w)$.

As we noted in Chapter 5, firms are owned by consumers. Thus, we assume that the consumer is the sole owner of the firm and receives the profits earned by the firm $\pi(p, w)$. As with the price-taking assumption, the idea of the consumer being hired by his own firm through an anonymous labor market may appear strange in this model with only two agents. Nevertheless, bear with us; our aim is to illustrate the workings of more complicated many-consumer general equilibrium models in the simplest-possible way.[6]

Letting $u(x_1, x_2)$ be a utility function representing $\succsim$, the consumer's problem given prices $(p, w)$ is

$$\underset{(x_1, x_2) \in \mathbb{R}_+^2}{\text{Max}} \quad u(x_1, x_2) \tag{15.C.2}$$
$$\text{s.t.} \quad px_2 \leq w(\bar{L} - x_1) + \pi(p, w).$$

---

5. One-consumer economies are sometimes referred to as *Robinson Crusoe economies*.

6. The point made in footnote 1 can be repeated here: we could imagine that the firm and the consumer stand for a large number of identical firms and consumers. We comment a bit more on this interpretation at the end of this Section.

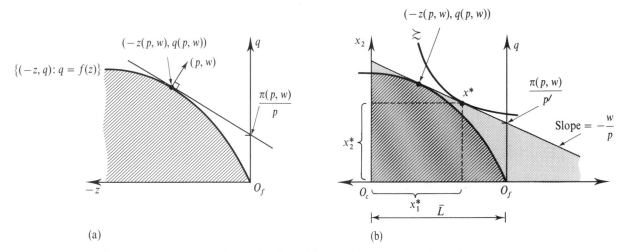

**Figure 15.C.1**  (a) The firm's problem. (b) The consumer's problem.

The budget constraint in (15.C.2) reflects the two sources of the consumer's purchasing power: If the consumer supplies an amount $(\bar{L} - x_1)$ of labor when prices are $(p, w)$, then the total amount he can spend on the consumption good is his labor earnings $w(\bar{L} - x_1)$ plus the profit distribution from the firm $\pi(p, w)$. The consumer's optimal demands in problem (15.C.2) for prices $(p, w)$ are denoted by $(x_1(p, w), x_2(p, w))$.

A Walrasian equilibrium in this economy involves a price vector $(p^*, w^*)$ at which the consumption and labor markets clear; that is, at which

$$x_2(p^*, w^*) = q(p^*, w^*) \tag{15.C.3}$$

and

$$z(p^*, w^*) = \bar{L} - x_1(p^*, w^*) \tag{15.C.4}$$

Figure 15.C.1 illustrates the working of this one-consumer, one-firm economy. Figure 15.C.1(a) depicts the firm's problem. As in Chapter 5, we measure the firm's use of labor input on the horizontal axis as a negative quantity. Its output is depicted on the vertical axis. The production set associated with the production function $f(z)$ is also shown, as are the profit-maximizing input and output levels at prices $(p, w)$, $z(p, w)$ and $q(p, w)$, respectively.

Figure 15.C.1(b) adapts this diagram to represent the consumer's problem. Leisure and consumption levels are measured from the origin denoted $O_c$ at the lower-left-hand corner of the diagram, which is determined by letting the length of the segment $[O_c, O_f]$ be equal to $\bar{L}$, the total labor endowment. The figure depicts the consumer's (shaded) budget set given prices $(p, w)$ and profits $\pi(p, w)$. Note that if the consumer consumes $\bar{L}$ units of leisure then since he sells no labor, he can purchase $\pi(p, w)/p$ units of the consumption good. Thus, the budget line must cut the vertical $q$-axis at height $\pi(p, w)/p$. In addition, for each unit of labor he sells, the consumer earns $w$ and can therefore afford to purchase $w/p$ units of $x_2$. Hence, the budget line has slope $-(w/p)$. Observe that the consumer's budget line is exactly the isoprofit line associated with the solution to the firm's profit-maximization problem in Figure 15.C.1(a), that is, the set of points $\{(-z, q): pq - wz = \pi(p, w)\}$ that yield profits of $\pi(p, w)$.

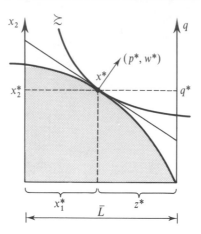

**Figure 15.C.2**

A Walrasian equilibrium.

The prices depicted in Figure 15.C.1(b) are not equilibrium prices; at these prices, there is an excess demand for labor (the firm wants more labor than the consumer is willing to supply) and an excess supply of the produced good. An equilibrium price vector $(p^*, w^*)$ that clears the markets for the two goods is depicted in Figure 15.C.2.

There is a very important fact to notice from Figure 15.C.2: *A particular consumption–leisure combination can arise in a competitive equilibrium if and only if it maximizes the consumer's utility subject to the economy's technological and endowment constraints.* That is, the Walrasian equilibrium allocation is the same allocation that would be obtained if a planner ran the economy in a manner that maximized the consumer's well-being. Thus, we see here an expression of the fundamental theorems of welfare economics: Any Walrasian equilibrium is Pareto optimal, and the Pareto optimal allocation is supportable as a Walrasian equilibrium.[7]

The indispensability of convexity for the second welfare theorem can again be observed in Figure 15.C.3(a). There, the allocation $x^*$ maximizes the welfare of the consumer, but for the only value of relative prices that could support $x^*$ as a utility-maximizing bundle, the firm does not maximize profits even locally (i.e., at the relative prices $w/p$, there are productions arbitrarily close to $x^*$ yielding higher profits). In contrast, the first welfare theorem remains applicable even in the presence of nonconvexities. As Figure 15.C.3(b) suggests, any Walrasian equilibrium maximizes the well-being of the consumer in the feasible production set.

---

Under certain circumstances, the model studied in this section can be rigorously justified as representing the outcome of a more general economy by interpreting the "firm" as a representative producer (see Section 5.E) and the "consumer" as a representative consumer (see Section 4.D). The former is always possible, but the latter—that is, the existence of a (normative) representative consumer—requires strong conditions. If, however, the economy

---

7. In a single-consumer economy, the test for Pareto optimality reduces to the question of whether the well-being of the single consumer is being maximized (subject to feasibility constraints). Note that given the convexity of preferences and the strict convexity of the aggregate production set assumed here, there is a unique Pareto optimal consumption vector (and therefore a unique equilibrium).

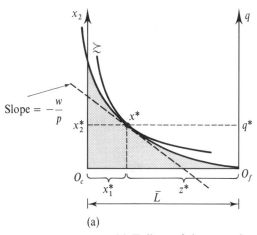 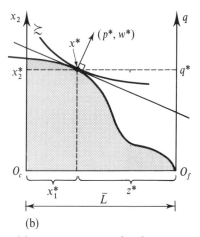

(a)                              (b)

**Figure 15.C.3**  (a) Failure of the second welfare theorem with a nonconvex technology.
(b) The first welfare theorem applies even with a nonconvex technology.

is composed of many consumers with identical concave utility functions and identical initial endowments, and if society has a strictly concave social welfare function in which these consumers are treated symmetrically, then a (normative) representative consumer exists who has the same utility function as the consumers over levels of per capita consumption.[8] (We can also think of the representative firm's input and output choices as being on a per capita basis). For more general conditions under which a representative consumer exists, see Section 4.D.

# 15.D The 2 × 2 Production Model

In this section, we discuss an example that concentrates on general equilibrium effects in production.

To begin, consider an economy in which the production sector consists of $J$ firms. Each firm $j$ produces a consumer good $q_j$ directly from a vector of $L$ primary (i.e., nonproduced) inputs, or *factors*, $z_j = (z_{1j}, \ldots, z_{Lj}) \geq 0$.[9] Firm $j$'s production takes place by means of a concave, strictly increasing, and differentiable production function $f_j(z_j)$. Note that there are no intermediate goods (i.e., produced goods that are used as inputs). The economy has total endowments of the $L$ factor inputs, $(\bar{z}_1, \ldots, \bar{z}_L) \gg 0$. These endowments are initially owned by consumers and have a use only as production inputs (i.e., consumers do not wish to consume them).

To concentrate on the factor markets of the economy, we suppose that the prices of the $J$ produced consumption goods are fixed at $p = (p_1, \ldots, p_J)$, The leading example for this assumption is that of a small open economy whose trading decisions in the world markets for consumption goods have little effect on the world prices of

---

8. To see this, note that an equal distribution of wealth (which is what occurs here in the absence of any wealth transfers given the identical endowments of the consumers) maximizes social welfare for any price vector and aggregate wealth level.

9. Some of these outputs may be the same good; that is, firms $j$ and $j'$ may produce the same commodity.

these goods.[10] Output is sold in world markets. Factors, on the other hand, are immobile and must be used for production within the country.

The central question for our analysis concerns the equilibrium in the factor markets; that is, we wish to determine the equilibrium factor prices $w = (w_1, \ldots, w_L)$ and the allocation of the economy's factor endowments among the $J$ firms.[11]

Given output prices $p = (p_1, \ldots, p_J)$ and input prices $w = (w_1, \ldots, w_L)$, a profit-maximizing production plan for firm $j$ solves

$$\underset{z_j \geq 0}{\text{Max}} \quad p_j f_j(z_j) - w \cdot z_j.$$

We denote firm $j$'s set of optimal input demands given prices $(p, w)$ by $z(p, w) \subset \mathbb{R}_+^L$. Because consumers have no direct use for their factor endowments, the total factor supply will be $(\bar{z}_1, \ldots, \bar{z}_L)$ as long as the input prices $w_\ell$ are strictly positive (the only case that will concern us here). An equilibrium for the factor markets of this economy given the fixed output prices $p$ therefore consists of an input price vector $w^* = (w_1^*, \ldots, w_L^*) \gg 0$ and a factor allocation

$$(z_1^*, \ldots, z_J^*) = ((z_{11}^*, \ldots, z_{L1}^*), \ldots, (z_{1J}^*, \ldots, z_{LJ}^*)),$$

such that firms receive their desired factor demands under prices $(p, w^*)$ and all the factor markets clear, that is, such that

$$z_j^* \in z_j(p, w) \qquad \text{for all } j = 1, \ldots, J$$

and

$$\sum_j z_{\ell j}^* = \bar{z}_\ell \qquad \text{for all } \ell = 1, \ldots, L.$$

Because of the concavity of firms' production functions, first-order conditions are both necessary and sufficient for the characterization of optimal factor demands. Therefore, the $L(J + 1)$ variables formed by the factor allocation $(z_1^*, \ldots, z_J^*) \in \mathbb{R}_+^{LJ}$ and the factor prices $w^* = (w_1^*, \ldots, w_L^*)$ constitute an equilibrium if and only if they satisfy the following $L(J + 1)$ equations (we assume an interior solution here):

$$p_j \frac{\partial f_j(z_j^*)}{\partial z_{\ell j}} = w_\ell^* \qquad \text{for } j = 1, \ldots, J \text{ and } \ell = 1, \ldots, L \qquad (15.\text{D}.1)$$

and

$$\sum_j z_{\ell j}^* = \bar{z}_\ell \qquad \text{for } \ell = 1, \ldots, L. \qquad (15.\text{D}.2)$$

The equilibrium output levels are then $q_j^* = f_j(z_j^*)$ for every $j$.

Equilibrium conditions for *outputs* and factor prices can alternatively be stated using the firms' cost functions $c_j(w, q_j)$ for $j = 1, \ldots, J$. Output levels $(q_1^*, \ldots, q_J^*) \gg 0$ and factor prices $w^* \gg 0$ constitute an equilibrium if and only if the following

---

10. See Exercise 15.D.4 for an endogenous determination (up to a scalar multiple) of the prices $p = (p_1, \ldots, p_J)$.

11. Note that once the factor prices and allocations are determined, each consumer's demands can be readily determined from his demand function given the exogenous prices $(p_1, \ldots, p_J)$ and the wealth derived from factor input sales and profit distributions. Recall that the current model is completed by assuming that this demand is met in the world markets.

conditions hold:

$$p_j = \frac{\partial c_j(w^*, q_j^*)}{\partial q_j} \qquad \text{for } j = 1, \ldots, J, \tag{15.D.3}$$

$$\sum_j \frac{\partial c_j(w^*, q_j^*)}{\partial w_\ell} = \bar{z}_\ell \qquad \text{for } \ell = 1, \ldots, L. \tag{15.D.4}$$

Conditions (15.D.3) and (15.D.4) constitute a system of $L + J$ equations in the $L + J$ endogenous variables $(w_1, \ldots, w_L)$ and $(q_1, \ldots, q_J)$. Condition (15.D.3) states that each firm must be at a profit-maximizing output level given prices $p$ and $w^*$. If so, firm $j$'s optimal demand for the $\ell$th input is $z_{\ell j}^* = \partial c_j(w, q_j^*)/\partial w_\ell$ (this is Shepard's lemma; see Proposition 5.C.2). Condition (15.D.4) is therefore the factor market-clearing condition.

Before examining the determinants of the equilibrium factor allocation in greater detail, we note that the equilibrium factor allocation $(z_1^*, \ldots, z_J^*)$ in this model is exactly the factor allocation that would be chosen by a revenue-maximizing planner, thus providing us with yet another expression of the welfare-maximizing property of competitive allocations (the first welfare theorem).[12] To see this, consider the problem faced by a planning authority who is charged with coordinating factor allocations for the economy in order to maximize the gross revenues from the economy's production activities:

$$\underset{(z_1, \ldots, z_J) \geq 0}{\text{Max}} \quad \sum_j p_j f_j(z_j) \tag{15.D.5}$$

$$\text{s.t.} \quad \sum_j z_j = \bar{z}.$$

How does the equilibrium factor allocation $(z_1^*, \ldots, z_J^*)$ compare with what this planner does? Recall from Section 5.E that whenever we have a collection of $J$ price-taking firms, their profit-maximizing behavior is compatible with the behavior we would observe if the firms were to maximize their profits jointly taking the prices of outputs and factors as given. That is, the factor demands $(z_1^*, \ldots, z_J^*)$ solve

$$\underset{(z_1, \ldots, z_J) \geq 0}{\text{Max}} \quad \sum_j (p_j f_j(z_j) - w^* \cdot z_j). \tag{15.D.6}$$

Since $\sum_j z_j^* = \bar{z}$ (by the equilibrium property of market clearing), the factor demands $(z_1^*, \ldots, z_J^*)$ must also solve problem (15.D.6) subject to the further constraint that $\sum_j z_j = \bar{z}$. But this implies that the factor demands $(z_1^*, \ldots, z_J^*)$ in fact solve problem (15.D.5): if we must have $\sum_j z_j = \bar{z}$, then the total cost $w^* \cdot (\sum_j z_j)$ is given, and so the joint profit-maximizing problem (15.D.6) reduces to the revenue-maximizing problem (15.D.5).

One benefit of the property just established is that it can be used to obtain the equilibrium factor allocation without a previous explicit computation of the equilibrium factor prices; we simply need to solve problem (15.D.5) directly. It also provides a useful way of viewing the equilibrium factor prices. To see this, consider again the joint profit-maximization problem (15.D.6). We can approach this problem in an equivalent manner by first deriving an aggregate

---

12. Note that maximization of economy-wide revenue from production would be the goal of any planner who wanted to maximize consumer welfare: it allows for the maximal purchases of consumption goods, at the fixed world prices.

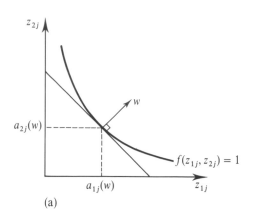

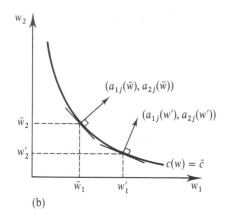

**Figure 15.D.1**

(a) A unit isoquant.
(b) The unit cost function.

production function for dollars:

$$f(z) = \underset{(z_1,\dots,z_J) \geq 0}{\text{Max}} \quad p_1 f_1(z_1) + \cdots + p_J f_J(z_J)$$

$$\text{s.t. } \sum_j z_j = z.$$

The aggregate factor demands must then solve $\text{Max}_{z \geq 0}(f(z) - w \cdot z)$. For every $\ell$, the first-order condition for this problem is $w_\ell = \partial f(z)/\partial z_\ell$. Moreover, at an equilibrium, the aggregate usage of factor $\ell$ must be exactly $\bar{z}_\ell$. Hence, the equilibrium factor price of factor $\ell$ must be $w_\ell = \partial f(\bar{z})/\partial z_\ell$; that is, *the price of factor $\ell$ must be exactly equal to its aggregate marginal productivity (in terms of revenue)*. Since $f(\cdot)$ is concave, this observation by itself generates some interesting comparative statics. For example, a change in the endowment of a single input must change the equilibrium price of the input in the opposite direction.

---

Let us now be more specific and take $J = L = 2$, so that the economy under study produces two outputs from two primary factors. We also assume that the production functions $f_1(z_{11}, z_{21})$, $f_2(z_{12}, z_{22})$ are homogeneous of degree one (so the technologies exhibit constant returns to scale; see Section 5.B). This model is known as the *2 × 2 production model*. In applications, factor 1 is often thought of as labor and factor 2 as capital.

For every vector of factor prices $w = (w_1, w_2)$, we denote by $c_j(w)$ the minimum cost of producing one unit of good $j$ and by $a_j(w) = (a_{1j}(w), a_{2j}(w))$ the input combination (assumed unique) at which this minimum cost is reached. Recall again from Proposition 5.C.2 that $\nabla c_j(w) = (a_{1j}(w), a_{2j}(w))$.

Figure 15.D.1(a) depicts the unit isoquant of firm $j$,

$$\{(z_{1j}, z_{2j}) \in \mathbb{R}_+^2 : f_j(z_{1j}, z_{2j}) = 1\},$$

along with the cost-minimizing input combination $(a_{1j}(w), a_{2j}(w))$. In Figure 15.D.1(b), we draw a level curve of the unit cost function, $\{(w_1, w_2): c_j(w_1, w_2) = \bar{c}\}$. This curve is downward sloping because as $w_1$ increases, $w_2$ must fall in order to keep the minimized costs of producing one unit of good $j$ unchanged. Moreover, the set $\{(w_1, w_2): c_j(w_1, w_2) \geq \bar{c}\}$ is convex because of the concavity of the cost function $c_j(w)$ in $w$. Note that the vector $\nabla c_j(\bar{w})$, which is normal to the level curve at $\bar{w} = (\bar{w}_1, \bar{w}_2)$, is exactly $(a_{1j}(\bar{w}), a_{2j}(\bar{w}))$. As we move along the curve toward higher $w_1$ and lower $w_2$, the ratio $a_{1j}(w)/a_{2j}(w)$ falls.

Consider, first, the efficient factor allocations for this model. In Figure 15.D.2, we

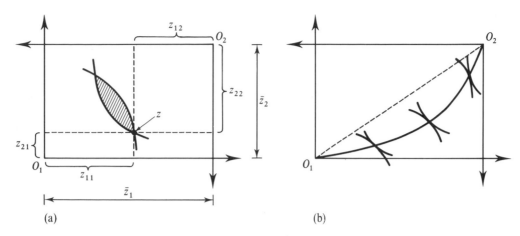

**Figure 15.D.2**    (a) An inefficient factor allocation. (b) The Pareto set of factor allocations.

represent the possible allocations of the factor endowments between the two firms in an Edgeworth box of size $\bar{z}_1$ by $\bar{z}_2$. The factors used by firm 1 are measured from the southwest corner; those used by firm 2 are measured from the northeast corner. We also represent the isoquants of the two firms in this Edgeworth box. Figure 15.D.2(a) depicts an inefficient allocation $z$ of the inputs between the two firms: Any allocation in the interior of the hatched region generates more output of *both* goods than does $z$. Figure 15.D.2(b), on the other hand, depicts the Pareto set of factor allocations, that is, the set of factor allocations at which it is not possible, with the given total factor endowments, to produce more of one good without producing less of the other.

The Pareto set (endpoints excluded) must lie all above or all below or be coincident with the diagonal of the Edgeworth box. If it ever cuts the diagonal then because of constant returns, the isoquants of the two firms must in fact be tangent all along the diagonal, and so the diagonal must be the Pareto set (see also Exercise 15.B.7). Moreover, you should convince yourself of the correctness of the following claims.

**Exercise 15.D.1:** Suppose that the Pareto set of the $2 \times 2$ production model does not coincide with the diagonal of the Edgeworth box.

(a) Show that in this case, the factor intensity (the ratio of a firm's use of factor 1 relative to factor 2) of one of the firms exceeds that of the other at every point along the Pareto set.

(b) Show that in this case, any ray from the origin of either of the firms can intersect the Pareto set at most once. Conclude that the factor intensities of the two firms and the supporting relative factor prices change monotonically as we move along the Pareto set from one origin to the other.

In Figure 15.D.3, we depict the set of nonnegative output pairs $(q_1, q_2)$ that can be produced using the economy's available factor inputs. This set is known as the *production possibility set*. Output pairs on the frontier of this set arise from factor allocations lying in the Pareto set of Figure 15.D.2(b). (Exercise 15.D.2 asks you to prove that the production possibility set is convex, as shown in Figure 15.D.3.)

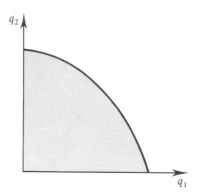

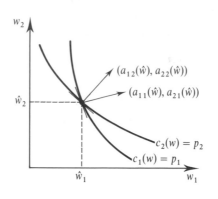

**Figure 15.D.3 (left)**

The production possibility set.

**Figure 15.D.4 (right)**

The equilibrium factor prices and factor intensities in an interior equilibrium.

With the purpose of examining more closely the determinants of the equilibrium factor allocation $(z_1^*, z_2^*)$ and the corresponding equilibrium factor prices $w^* = (w_1^*, w_2^*)$, we now assume that the *factor intensities* of the two firms bear a systematic relation to one another. In particular, we assume that in the production of good 1, there is, relative to good 2, a greater need for the first factor. In Definition 15.D.1 we make precise the meaning of "greater need".

**Definition 15.D.1:** The production of good 1 is *relatively more intensive in factor 1* than is the production of good 2 if

$$\frac{a_{11}(w)}{a_{21}(w)} > \frac{a_{12}(w)}{a_{22}(w)}$$

at *all* factor prices $w = (w_1, w_2)$.

To determine the equilibrium factor prices, suppose that we have an *interior* equilibrium in which the production levels of the two goods are strictly positive (otherwise, we say that the equilibrium is *specialized*). Given our constant returns assumption, a necessary condition for $(w_1^*, w_2^*)$ to be the factor prices in an interior equilibrium is that it satisfies the system of equations

$$c_1(w_1, w_2) = p_1 \qquad \text{and} \qquad c_2(w_1, w_2) = p_2. \tag{15.D.7}$$

That is, at an interior equilibrium, prices must be equal to unit cost. This gives us two equations for the two unknown factor prices $w_1$ and $w_2$.[13]

Figure 15.D.4 depicts the two unit cost functions in (15.D.7). By expression (15.D.7), a necessary condition for $(\hat{w}_1, \hat{w}_2)$ to be the factor prices of an interior equilibrium is that these curves cross at $(\hat{w}_1, \hat{w}_2)$. Moreover, the factor intensity assumption implies that whenever the two curves cross, the curve for firm 2 must be flatter (less negatively sloped) than that for firm 1 [recall that $\nabla c_j(w) = (a_{1j}(w), a_{2j}(w))$]. From this, it follows that the two curves can cross at most once.[14] Hence, under the

13. Expression (15.D.7) is the constant returns version of (15.D.3). Note that the effect of the constant returns to scale assumption is to make (15.D.3) independent of the output levels $(q_1, \ldots, q_J)$ (for interior equilibria).

14. If they crossed several times, then the curve for firm 2 must cross the curve for firm 1 at least once from above. At this crossing point, the curve for firm 2 would be steeper than the curve for firm 1, contradicting the factor intensity condition.

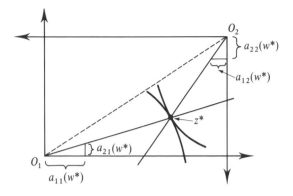

**Figure 15.D.5**

The equilibrium factor allocation.

factor intensity condition, there is at most a single pair of factor prices that can arise as the equilibrium factor prices of an interior equilibrium.[15]

Once the equilibrium factor prices $w^*$ are known, the equilibrium output levels can be found graphically by determining the unique point $(z_1^*, z_2^*)$ in the Edgeworth box of factor allocations at which both firms have the factor intensities associated with factor prices $w^*$, that is,

$$\frac{z_{11}^*}{z_{21}^*} = \frac{a_{11}(w^*)}{a_{21}(w^*)} \quad \text{and} \quad \frac{z_{12}^*}{z_{22}^*} = \frac{a_{12}(w^*)}{a_{22}(w^*)}.$$

The construction is depicted in Figure 15.D.5.

An important consequence of this discussion is that in the $2 \times 2$ production model, if the factor intensity condition holds, then as long as the economy does not specialize in the production of a single good [and therefore (15.D.7) holds], the equilibrium factor prices depend *only on the technologies of the two firms and on the output prices p*. Thus, the levels of the endowments matter only to the extent that they determine whether the economy specializes. This result is known in the international trade literature as the *factor price equalization theorem*. The theorem provides conditions (which include the presence of tradable consumption goods, identical production technologies in each country, and price-taking behavior) under which the prices of nontradable factors are equalized across nonspecialized countries.

We now present two comparative statics exercises. We first ask: How does a change in the price of one of the outputs, say $p_1$, affect the equilibrium factor prices and factor allocations? Figure 15.D.6(a), which depicts the induced change in Figure 15.D.4, identifies the change in factor prices. The increase in $p_1$ shifts firm 1's curve

---

15. Note, however, that although $(\hat{w}_1, \hat{w}_2)$ may solve (15.D.7), this is not sufficient to ensure that $(\hat{w}_1, \hat{w}_2)$ are equilibrium factor prices. In particular, even though $(\hat{w}_1, \hat{w}_2)$ solve (15.D.7), no interior equilibrium may exist. In Exercise 15.D.6, you are asked to show that under the factor intensity condition, the equilibrium will involve positive production of the two goods if and only if

$$\frac{a_{11}(\hat{w})}{a_{21}(\hat{w})} > \frac{\bar{z}_1}{\bar{z}_2} > \frac{a_{12}(\hat{w})}{a_{22}(\hat{w})},$$

where $\hat{w} = (\hat{w}_1, \hat{w}_2)$ is the unique solution to (15.D.7). In words, the factor intensity of the overall economy must be intermediate between the factor intensities of the two firms computed at the sole vector of factor prices at which diversification can conceivably occur.

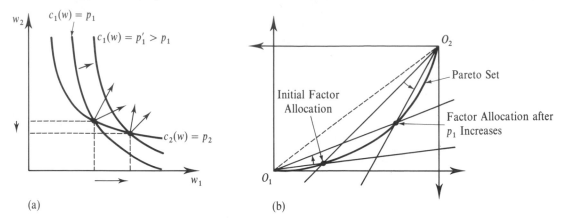

**Figure 15.D.6** The Stolper–Samuelson theorem. (a) The change in equilibrium factor prices. (b) The change in the equilibrium factor allocation.

[the set $\{(w_1, w_2): c_1(w_1, w_2) = p_1\}$] outward toward higher factor price levels; the point of intersection of the two curves moves out along firm 2's curve to a higher level of $w_1$ and a lower level of $w_2$.

Formally, this gives us the result presented in Proposition 15.D.1.

**Proposition 15.D.1:** (*Stolper–Samuelson Theorem*)   In the $2 \times 2$ production model with the factor intensity assumption, if $p_j$ increases, then the equilibrium price of the factor more intensively used in the production of good *j* increases, while the price of the other factor decreases (assuming interior equilibria both before and after the price change).[16]

---

**Proof:** For illustrative purposes, we provide a formal proof to go along with the graphical analysis of Figure 15.D.6 presented above. Note that it suffices to prove the result for an infinitesimal change $dp = (1, 0)$.

Differentiating conditions (15.D.7), we have

$$dp_1 = \nabla c_1(w^*) \cdot dw = a_{11}(w^*)\, dw_1 + a_{21}(w^*)\, dw_2,$$
$$dp_2 = \nabla c_2(w^*) \cdot dw = a_{12}(w^*)\, dw_1 + a_{22}(w^*)\, dw_2,$$

or in matrix notation,

$$dp = \begin{bmatrix} a_{11}(w^*) & a_{21}(w^*) \\ a_{12}(w^*) & a_{22}(w^*) \end{bmatrix} dw.$$

---

16. See Exercise 15.D.3 for a strengthening of this conclusion. We also note that, strictly speaking, the factor inensity condition is not required for this result. The reason is that, as we saw in Exercise 15.D.1, the firm that uses one factor, say factor 1, more intensively is the same for any point in the Pareto set of factor allocations. Suppose, for example, that we are as in Figure 15.D.2(b), where firm 1 uses factor 1 more intensively. Then, when $p_1$ rises, we can see from Figure 15.D.3, and the overall revenue-maximizing property of equilibrium discussed earlier in this section, that the output of good 1 increases and that of good 2 decreases. This implies that we move along the Pareto set in Figure 15.D.2(b) toward firm 2's origin. Therefore, recalling Exercise 15.D.1, both firms' intensity of use of factor 1 decreases. Hence, the equilibrium factor price ratio $w_1^*/w_2^*$ must increase. Finally, since firm 2 is still breaking even and its output price has not changed, this implies that $w_1^*$ increases and $w_2^*$ decreases.

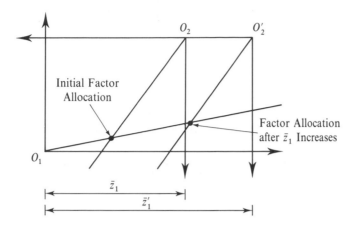

**Figure 15.D.7**

The Rybcszynski
theorem.

Denote this $2 \times 2$ matrix by $A$. The factor intensity assumption implies that $|A| = a_{11}(w^*)a_{22}(w^*) - a_{12}(w^*)a_{21}(w^*) > 0$. Therefore $A^{-1}$ exists and we can compute it to be

$$A^{-1} = \frac{1}{|A|} \begin{bmatrix} a_{22}(w^*) & -a_{21}(w^*) \\ -a_{12}(w^*) & a_{11}(w^*) \end{bmatrix}.$$

Hence, the entries of $A^{-1}$ are positive at the diagonal and negative off the diagonal. Since $dw = A^{-1}\,dp$, this implies that for $dp = (1, 0)$ we have $dw_1 > 0$ and $dw_2 < 0$, as we wanted. ■

We have just seen that if $p_1$ increases, then $w_1^*/w_2^*$ increases. Therefore, both firms must move to a less intensive use of factor 1. Figure 15.D.6(b) depicts the resulting change in the equilibrium allocation of factors. As can be seen, the factor allocation moves to a new point in the Pareto set at which the output of good 1 has risen and that of good 2 has fallen.

For the second comparative statics exercise, suppose that the total availability of factor 1 increases from $\bar{z}_1$ to $\bar{z}_1'$. What is the effect of this on equilibrium factor prices and output levels? Because neither the output prices nor the technologies have changed, the factor input prices remain unaltered (as long as the economy does not specialize). As a result, factor intensities also do not change. The new input allocation is then easily determined in the superimposed Edgeworth boxes of Figure 15.D.7; we merely find the new intersection of the two rays associated with the unaltered factor intensity levels.

Thus, examination of Figure 15.D.7 gives us the result presented in Proposition 15.D.2.

**Proposition 15.D.2:** (*Rybcszynski Theorem*) In the $2 \times 2$ production model with the factor intensity assumption, if the endowment of a factor increases, then the production of the good that uses this factor relatively more intensively increases and the production of the other good decreases (assuming interior equilibria both before and after the change of endowment).

For further discussion of the $2 \times 2$ production model see, for example, Johnson (1971).

Consider the general case of an arbitrary number of factors $L$ and outputs $J$. For given output prices, the zero-profit conditions [i.e., the general analog of expression (15.D.7)] constitute a (nonlinear) system of $J$ equations in $L$ unknowns. If $L > J$, then there are too many unknowns and we cannot hope that the zero-profit conditions alone will determine the factor prices. The total factor endowments will play a role. If $J > L$, then there are too many equations and, for typical world prices, they cannot all be satisfied simultaneously. What this means is that the economy will specialize in the production of a number of goods equal to the number of factors $L$. The set of goods chosen may well depend on the endowments of factors. Beyond the $2 \times 2$ situation (the analysis of which, as we have seen, is quite instructive), the case $L = J$ seems too coincidental to be of interest. Nevertheless, we point out that in this case the zero-profit conditions are nonlinear and that in order to guarantee a unique solution (and versions of the Stolper–Samuelson and the Rybcszynski theorems), we need a generalization of the factor intensity condition. These generalizations exist, but they cannot be interpreted economically in as simple a manner as can the factor intensity condition of the $2 \times 2$ model.

# 15.E   General Versus Partial Equilibrium Theory

There are some problems that are inherently general equilibrium problems. It would be hard to envision convincing analyses of economic growth, demographic change, international economic relations, or monetary policy that were restricted to only a subset of commodities and did not consider economy-wide feedback effects.

Partial equilibrium models of markets, or of systems of related markets, determine prices, profits, productions, and the other variables of interest adhering to the assumption that there are no feedback effects from these endogenous magnitudes to the underlying demand or cost curves that are specified in advance. Individuals' wealth is another variable that general equilibrium theory regards as endogenously determined but that is often treated as exogenous in partial equilibrium theory.

If general equilibrium analysis did not change any of the predictions or conclusions of partial equilibrium analysis, it would be of limited significance when applied to problems amenable to partial equilibrium treatment. It might be of comfort because we would then know that our partial equilibrium conclusions are valid, but it would not change our view of how markets work. However, things are not that simple. The choice of methodology may be far from innocuous. We now present an example [due to Bradford (1978)] in which a naive application of partial equilibrium analysis leads us seriously astray. See Sections 3.I and 10.G for some discussion of when partial equilibrium theory is (approximately) justified.

### A Tax Incidence Example

Consider an economy with a large number of towns, $N$. Each town has a single price-taking firm that produces a consumption good by means of the strictly concave production function $f(z)$ (once again, we could reinterpret the model as having many identical firms in each town to make the price-taking hypothesis more palatable). This consumption good, which is identical across towns, is traded in a national market. The overall economy has $M$ units of labor, inelastically supplied by workers who derive utility only from the output of the firms. Workers are free to move from town to town and do so to seek the highest wage. We normalize the price of the consumption good to be 1, and we denote the wage rate in town $n$'s labor market by $w_n$.

Given that workers can move freely in search of the highest wage, at an equilibrium the wage rates across towns must be equal; that is, we must have $w_1 = \cdots = w_N = \bar{w}$. From the symmetry of the problem, it must be that each firm hires exactly $M/N$ units of labor in an equilibrium. As a result, the equilibrium wage rate must be $\bar{w} = f'(M/N)$. The equilibrium profits of an individual firm are therefore $f(M/N) - f'(M/N)(M/N)$.

Now suppose that town 1 levies a tax on the labor used by the firm located there. We investigate the "incidence" of the tax on workers and firms (or, more properly, on the firms' owners); that is, we examine the extent to which each group bears the burden of the tax. If the tax rate is $t$ and the wage in town 1 is $w_1$, the labor demand of the firm in town 1 will be the amount $z_1$ such that $f'(z_1) = t + w_1$. At this point, we may be tempted to argue that, since $N$ is large, we can approximate and take the wage rates elsewhere, $\bar{w}$, to be unaffected by this change in town 1. Moreover, since labor moves freely, the supply correspondence of workers in town 1 should then be 0 at $w_1 < \bar{w}$, $\infty$ at $w_1 > \bar{w}$, and $[0, \infty]$ at $w_1 = \bar{w}$. Thus, taking a partial equilibrium view, the equilibrium wage rate in the town 1 labor market remains equal to $\bar{w}$, and the labor employed in town 1 falls to the level $z_1$ such that $f'(z_1) = t + \bar{w}$ (hence, some labor will shift to the other towns). By adopting this sort of partial equilibrium view of the labor market of town 1, we are therefore led to conclude that the income of workers remains the same, as does the profit of every firm not located in town 1. Only the profit of the firm in town 1 decreases. The qualitative conclusion is that firms (actually, firms' owners) "bear" all of the tax burden. Labor, because it is free to move and because the number of untaxed firms is large, "escapes."

Alas, this conclusion constitutes an egregious mistake, and it will be overturned by a general equilibrium view of the same model.

We now look at the general equilibrium across the labor markets of all the towns. We know that the equilibrium wage rate must be such that $w_1 = \cdots = w_N$ and that all $M$ units of labor are employed. Let $w(t)$ be this common equilibrium wage when the tax rate in town 1 is $t$. By symmetry, the firms in towns $2, \ldots, N$ will each employ the same amount of labor, $z(t)$. Let $z_1(t)$ be the equilibrium labor demand of the firm in town 1 when town 1's tax rate is $t$. Then the equilibrium conditions are

$$(N - 1)z(t) + z_1(t) = M. \tag{15.E.1}$$

$$f'(z(t)) = w(t). \tag{15.E.2}$$

$$f'(z_1(t)) = w(t) + t. \tag{15.E.3}$$

Consider the impact on wages of the introduction of a small tax $dt$. Substituting from (15.E.1) for $z_1(t)$ in (15.E.3), differentiating with respect to $t$, and evaluating at $t = 0$ [at which point $z_1(0) = z(0) = (M/N)$], we get

$$-f''(M/N)(N - 1)z'(0) = w'(0) + 1. \tag{15.E.4}$$

But from (15.E.2), we get

$$f''(M/N)z'(0) = w'(0). \tag{15.E.5}$$

Substituting from (15.E.5) into (15.E.4) yields

$$w'(0) = -\frac{1}{N}.$$

Therefore, once the general equilibrium effects are taken into account, we see that the wage rate in all towns falls with the imposition of the tax in town 1. However, we see that this fall in the wage rate approaches zero as $N$ grows large. Thus, at this point, it may still seem that our partial equilibrium approximation will have given us the correct answers for large $N$. But this is not so. Consider the effect of the tax on total profits. The partial equilibrium approach told us that workers escaped the tax; all the tax fell as a burden on firms. But letting $\pi(w)$ be the profit function of a representative firm, the change in aggregate profits from the imposition of this tax is[17]

$$(N - 1)\pi'(\bar{w})w'(0) + \pi'(\bar{w})(w'(0) + 1) = \pi'(\bar{w})\left(-\frac{N - 1}{N} + \frac{N - 1}{N}\right) = 0.$$

Aggregate profits stay constant! Thus, all of the burden of a small tax falls on laborers, not on the owners of firms. Although the partial equilibrium approximation is correct as far as getting prices and wages about right, it errs by just enough, and in just such a direction, that the conclusions of the tax incidence analysis based on it are completely reversed.[18]

---

17. Recall that the profits of the firm in town 1 are $\pi(w(t) + t)$.

18. We note that the justifications of partial equilibrium analysis in terms of small individual budget shares that we informally described in Sections 3.I and 10.G do not apply here because the "consumption" goods in this example (jobs in different towns) are perfect substitutes and therefore individual budget shares are not guaranteed to be small at all prices.

## REFERENCES

Bradford, D. (1978). Factor prices may be constant but factor returns are not. *Economic Letters*, 199–203.
Johnson, H. G. (1971). *The Two-Sector Model of General Equilibrium*. Chicago: Aldine-Atherton.
Newman, P. (1965). *The Theory of Exchange*. Englewood Cliffs, N.J.: Prentice-Hall.

## EXERCISES

**15.B.1[A]** Consider an Edgeworth box economy in which the two consumers have locally nonsatiated preferences. Let $x_{\ell i}(p)$ be consumer $i$'s demand for good $\ell$ at prices $p = (p_1, p_2)$.

(a) Show that $p_1(\sum_i x_{1i}(p) - \bar{\omega}_1) + p_2(\sum_i x_{2i}(p) - \bar{\omega}_2) = 0$ for all prices $p$.

(b) Argue that if the market for good 1 clears at prices $p^* \gg 0$, then so does the market for good 2; hence, $p^*$ is a Walrasian equilibrium price vector.

**15.B.2[A]** Consider an Edgeworth box economy in which the consumers have the Cobb–Douglas utility functions $u_1(x_{11}, x_{21}) = x_{11}^\alpha x_{21}^{1-\alpha}$ and $u_2(x_{12}, x_{22}) = x_{12}^\beta x_{22}^{1-\beta}$. Consumer $i$'s endowments are $(\omega_{1i}, \omega_{2i}) \gg 0$, for $i = 1, 2$. Solve for the equilibrium price ratio and allocation. How do these change with a differential change in $\omega_{11}$?

**15.B.3[B]** Argue (graphically) that in an Edgeworth box economy with locally nonsatiated preferences, a Walrasian equilibrium is Pareto optimal.

**15.B.4^C** Consider an Edgeworth box economy. An offer curve has the *gross substitute* property if an increase in the price of one commodity decreases the demand for that commodity and increases the demand for the other one.

**(a)** Represent in an Edgeworth box the shape of an offer curve with the gross substitute property.

**(b)** Assume that the offer curves of the two consumers have the gross substitute property. Show then that the offer curves can intersect only once (not counting the intersection at the initial endowments).

Let us denote an offer curve as *normal* if an increase in the price of one commodity leads to an increase in the demand for that commodity only if the demands of the two commodities both increase.

**(c)** Represent in the Edgeworth box the shape of a normal offer curve that does not satisfy the gross substitute property.

**(d)** Show that there are preferences giving rise to offer curves that are not normal. Show that the demand function for such preferences is not normal (i.e., at some prices some good is inferior).

**(e)** Show in the Edgeworth box that if the offer curve of one consumer is normal and that of the other satisfies the gross substitute property, then the offer curves can intersect at most once (not counting the intersection at the initial endowments).

**(f)** Show that two normal offer curves can intersect several times.

**15.B.5^A** Verify that the offer curves of Example 15.B.2 are as claimed. Solve also for the claimed values of relative prices.

**15.B.6^B** (D. Blair) Compute the equilibria of the following Edgeworth box economy (there is more than one):

$$u_1(x_{11}, x_{21}) = (x_{11}^{-2} + (12/37)^3 x_{21}^{-2})^{-1/2}, \qquad \omega_1 = (1, 0),$$
$$u_2(x_{12}, x_{22}) = ((12/37)^3 x_{12}^{-2} + x_{22}^{-2})^{-1/2}, \qquad \omega_2 = (0, 1).$$

**15.B.7^C** Show that if both consumers in an Edgeworth box economy have continuous, strongly monotone, and strictly convex preferences, then the Pareto set has no "holes": precisely, it is a connected set. Show that if, in addition, the preferences of both consumers are homothetic, then the Pareto set lies entirely on one side of the diagonal of the box.

**15.B.8^B** Suppose that both consumers in an Edgeworth box have continuous and strictly convex preferences that admit a quasilinear utility representation with the first good as numeraire. Show that any two Pareto optimal allocations in the interior of the Edgeworth box then involve the same consumptions of the second good. Connect this with the discussion of Chapter 10.

**15.B.9^B** Suppose that in a pure exchange economy (i.e., an economy without production), we have two consumers, Alphanse and Betatrix, and two goods, Perrier and Brie. Alphanse and Betatrix have the utility functions:

$$u_\alpha = \text{Min}\{x_{p\alpha}, x_{b\alpha}\} \qquad \text{and} \qquad u_\beta = \text{Min}\{x_{p\beta}, (x_{b\beta})^{1/2}\}$$

(where $x_{p\alpha}$ is Alphanse's consumption of Perrier, and so on). Alphanse starts with an endowment of 30 units of Perrier (and none of Brie); Betatrix starts with 20 units of Brie (and none of Perrier). Neither can consume negative amounts of a good. If the two consumers behave as price takers, what is the equilibrium?

Suppose instead that Alphanse begins with only 5 units of Perrier while Betatrix's initial endowment remains 20 units of Brie, 0 units of Perrier. What happens now?

**15.B.10$^C$** (*The Transfer Paradox*) In a two-consumer, two-commodity pure exchange economy with continuous, strictly convex and strongly monotone preferences, consider the comparative statics of the welfare of consumer 1 with changes in the initial endowments $\omega_1 = (\omega_{11}, \omega_{21})$ and $\omega_2 = (\omega_{12}, \omega_{22})$.

**(a)** Suppose first that the preferences of the two consumers are quasilinear with respect to the same numeraire. Show that if the endowments of consumer 1 are increased to $\omega_1' \gg \omega_1$ while $\omega_2$ remains the same, then at equilibrium the utility of consumer 1 *may* decrease. Interpret this observation and relate it to the theory of a quantity-setting monopoly.

**(b)** Suppose now that the increase in resources of consumer 1 constitute a transfer from consumer 2, that is, $\omega_1' = \omega_1 + z$ and $\omega_2' = \omega_2 - z$ with $z \geq 0$. Under the same assumption as in **(a)**, show that the utility of consumer 1 cannot decrease.

**(c)** Consider again a transfer as in **(b)**, but this time preferences may not be quasilinear. Suppose that the transfer $z$ is small and that similarly the change in the equilibrium (relative) price is restricted to be small. Show that it is possible for the utility of consumer 1 to decrease (this is called the *transfer paradox*). A graphical illustration in the Edgeworth box suffices to make the point. Interpret in terms of the interplay between substitution and wealth effects.

**(d)** Show that in this Edgeworth box example (but, be warned, not more generally) the transfer paradox can happen only if there is a multiplicity of equilibria. [*Hint:* Argue graphically in the Edgeworth box. Show that if a transfer to consumer 1 leads to a decrease of the utility of consumer 1, then there must be an equilibrium at the no-transfer situation where consumer 1 gets an even lower level of utility.]

**15.C.1$^B$** This exercise refers to the one-consumer, one-firm economy discussed in Section 15.C.

**(a)** Prove that in an economy with one firm, one consumer, and strictly convex preferences and technology, the equilibrium level of production is unique.

**(b)** Fix the price of output to be 1. Define the excess demand function for labor as

$$z_1(w) = x_1(w, w\bar{L} + \pi(w)) + y_1(w) - \bar{L},$$

where $w$ is the wage rate, $\pi(\cdot)$ is the profit function, and $x_1(\cdot, \cdot)$, $y_1(\cdot)$ are, respectively, the consumer's demand function for leisure and the firm's demand function for labor. Show that the slope of the excess demand function is not necessarily of one sign throughout the range of prices but that it is necessarily negative in a neighborhood of the equilibrium.

**(c)** Give an example to show that there can be multiple equilibria in a strictly convex economy with one firm and two individuals, each of whom is endowed with labor alone. (Assume that profits are split equally between the two consumers.) Can this happen if the firm operates under constant rather than strictly decreasing returns to scale?

**15.C.2$^A$** Consider the one-consumer, one-producer economy discussed in Section 15.C. Compute the equilibrium prices, profits, and consumptions when the production function is $f(z) = z^{1/2}$, the utility function is $u(x_1, x_2) = \ln x_1 + \ln x_2$, and the total endowment of labor is $\bar{L} = 1$.

**15.D.1$^B$** In text.

**15.D.2$^A$** Show that in the $2 \times 2$ production model the production possibility set is convex (assume free disposal).

**15.D.3[B]** Show that the Stolper–Samuelson theorem (Proposition 15.D.1) can be strengthened to assert that the increase in the price of the intensive factor is proportionally larger than the increase in the price of the good (and therefore the well-being of a consumer who owns only the intensive factor must increase).

**15.D.4[C]** Consider a general equilibrium problem with two consumer–workers ($i = 1, 2$), two constant returns firms ($j = 1, 2$) with concave technologies, two factors of production ($\ell = 1, 2$), and two consumption goods ($j = 1, 2$) produced, respectively, by the two firms. Assume that the production of consumption good 1 is relatively more intensive in factor 1. Neither consumer consumes either of the factors. Consumer 1 owns one unit of factor 1 while consumer 2 owns one unit of factor 2.

   **(a)** Set up the equilibrium problem as one of clearing the factor and goods markets (in a closed economy context) under the assumption that prices are taken as given and productions are profit maximizing.

   **(b)** Suppose that consumer 1 has a taste only for the second consumption good and that consumer 2 cares only for the first good. Argue that there is at most one equilibrium.

   **(c)** Suppose now that consumer 1 has a taste only for the first good and that consumer 2 cares only for the second good. Argue that a multiplicity of equilibria is possible.

[*Hint:* Parts **(b)** and **(c)** can be answered by graphical analysis in the Edgeworth box of factors of production.]

**15.D.5[B]** Show that the Rybczynski theorem (Proposition 15.D.2) can be strengthened to assert that the proportional increase in the production of the good that uses the increased factor relatively more intensively is greater than the proportional increase in the endowment of the factor.

**15.D.6[C]** Suppose you are in the $2 \times 2$ production model with output prices ($p_1, p_2$) given (the economy could be a small open economy). The factor intensity condition is satisfied (production of consumption good 1 uses factor 1 more intensely). The total endowment vector is $\bar{z} \in \mathbb{R}^2$.

   **(a)** Set up the equilibrium conditions for factor prices ($w_1^*, w_2^*$) and outputs ($q_1^*, q_2^*$) allowing for the possibility of specialization.

   **(b)** Suppose that $\hat{w} = (\hat{w}_1, \hat{w}_2)$ are factor prices with the property that for each of the two goods the unit cost equals the price. Show that the necessary and sufficient condition for the equilibrium determined in **(a)** to have ($q_1^*, q_2^*$) $\gg 0$ is that $\bar{z}$ belongs to the set

$$\{(z_1, z_2) \in \mathbb{R}_+^2 : a_{11}(\hat{w})/a_{21}(\hat{w}) > z_1/z_2 > a_{12}(\hat{w})/a_{22}(\hat{w})\},$$

where $a_{\ell j}(\hat{w})$ is the optimal usage (at factor prices $\hat{w}$) of the input $\ell$ in the production of one unit of good $j$. This set is called the *diversification cone.*

   **(c)** The unit-dollar isoquant of good $j$ is the set of factor combinations that produce an amount of good $j$ of 1 dollar value. Show that under the factor intensity condition the unit-dollar isoquants of the two goods can intersect at most once. Use the unit-dollar isoquants to construct graphically the diversification cone. [*Hint:* If they intersect twice then there are two points (one in each isoquant) proportional to each other and such that the slopes of the isoquants at these points are identical.]

   **(d)** When the total factor endowment is not in the diversification cone, the equilibrium is specialized. Can you determine, as a function of total factor endowments, in which good the economy will specialize and what the factor prices will be? Be sure to verify the inequality conditions in **(a)**. To answer this question you can make use of the graphical apparatus developed in **(c)**.

**15.D.7$^B$** Suppose there are two output goods and two factors. The production functions for the two outputs are

$$f_1(z_{11}, z_{21}) = 2(z_{11})^{1/2} + (z_{21})^{1/2} \qquad \text{and} \qquad f_2(z_{12}, z_{22}) = (z_{12})^{1/2} + 2(z_{22})^{1/2}.$$

The international prices for these goods are $p = (1, 1)$. Firms are price takers and maximize profits. The total factor endowments are $\bar{z} = (\bar{z}_1, \bar{z}_2)$. Consumers have no taste for the consumption of factors of production. Derive the equilibrium factor allocation $((z_{11}^*, z_{21}^*), (z_{12}^*, z_{22}^*))$ and the equilibrium factor prices $(w_1^*, w_2^*)$ as a function of $(\bar{z}_1, \bar{z}_2)$. Verify that you get the same result whether you proceed through equations (15.D.1) and (15.D.2) or by solving (15.D.5).

**15.D.8$^B$** The setting is as in the $2 \times 2$ production model. The production functions for the two outputs are of the Cobb–Douglas type:

$$f_1(z_{11}, z_{21}) = (z_{11})^{2/3}(z_{21})^{1/3} \qquad \text{and} \qquad f_2(z_{12}, z_{22}) = (z_{12})^{1/3}(z_{22})^{2/3}.$$

The international output price vector is $p = (1, 1)$ and the total factor endowments vector is $\bar{z} = (\bar{z}_1, \bar{z}_2) \gg 0$. Compute the equilibrium factor allocations and factor prices for all possible values of $\bar{z}$. Be careful in specifying the region of total endowment vectors where the economy will specialize in the production of a single good.

**15.D.9$^C$** (*The Heckscher–Ohlin Theorem*) Suppose there are two consumption goods, two factors, and two countries A and B. Each country has technologies as in the $2 \times 2$ production model. The technologies for the production of each consumption good are the same in the two countries. The technology for the production of the first consumption good is relatively more intensive in factor 1. The endowments of the two factors are $\bar{z}_A \in \mathbb{R}_+^2$ and $\bar{z}_B \in \mathbb{R}_+^2$ for countries A and B, respectively. We assume that country A is relatively better endowed with factor 1, that is, $\bar{z}_{1A}/\bar{z}_{2A} > \bar{z}_{1B}/\bar{z}_{2B}$. Consumers are identical within and between countries. Their preferences are representable by increasing, concave, and homogeneous utility functions that depend only on the amount consumed of the two consumption goods.

Suppose that factors are not mobile and that each country is a price taker with respect to the international prices for consumption goods. Suppose then that at the international prices $p = (p_1, p_2)$ we have that, first, neither of the two countries specializes and, second, the international markets for consumption goods clear. Prove that country A must be exporting good 1, the good whose production is relatively more intensive in the factor that is relatively more abundant in country A.

# Equilibrium and Its Basic Welfare Properties

## 16.A Introduction

With this chapter, we begin our systematic study of equilibrium in economies where agents act as price takers. We consider a world with $L$ commodities in which consumers and firms interact through a market system. In this market system, a price is quoted for every commodity, and economic agents take these prices as independent of their individual actions.

We concentrate in this chapter on a presentation of the basic welfare properties of equilibria. Some more advanced topics in welfare economics are discussed in Chapter 18 and in Part V.

We begin, in Section 16.B, by specifying the formal model of an economy to be studied here and for the rest of Part IV. Its essential ingredients—commodities, consumers, and firms—we have already encountered in Part I. The remainder of Section 16.B introduces the main concepts that will concern us throughout the chapter. We define first the normative notion of a *Pareto optimal allocation*, an allocation with the property that it is impossible to make any consumer better off without making some other consumer worse off. Then, we present two notions of price-taking equilibrium: *Walrasian* (or *competitive*) *equilibrium*, and its generalization, a *price equilibrium with transfers*. The Walrasian equilibrium concept applies to the case of a *private ownership economy*, in which a consumer's wealth is derived from her ownership of endowments and from claims to profit shares of firms. The more general notion of a price equilibrium with transfers allows instead for an arbitrary distribution of wealth among consumers.

The remaining sections of the chapter are devoted to exploring the relationships between these equilibrium concepts and Pareto optimality.

Section 16.C focuses on the statement of the (very weak) conditions implying that every price equilibrium with transfers (and, hence, every Walrasian equilibrium) results in a Pareto optimal allocation. This is the *first fundamental theorem of welfare economics*, a formal expression for competitive market economies of Adam Smith's claimed "invisible hand" property of markets.

In Section 16.D, we study the converse issue. We state conditions (convexity assumptions are the crucial ones) under which every Pareto optimal allocation can be supported as a price equilibrium with transfers. This result is known as the *second fundamental theorem of welfare economics*. It tells us that if its assumptions are satisfied, then through the use of appropriate lump-sum wealth transfers, a welfare authority can, in principle, implement any desired Pareto optimal allocation as a price-taking equilibrium. We also discuss the practical limitations of this result.

In Section 16.E, we introduce the problem of maximizing a *social welfare function* and relate it to the Pareto optimality concept. We uncover a close formal relationship between these two notions of welfare optimality.

Section 16.F reexamines the Pareto optimality concept and associated results by making differentiability assumptions and analyzing first-order conditions. There we see how equilibrium prices can be interpreted as the Lagrange multipliers, or shadow prices, that arise in the associated Pareto optimality problem.

Section 16.G discusses several applications of the concepts and results previously developed. We first present some examples that rely on particular interpretations of the $L$ abstract commodities; one of them concerns the case of *public goods*. We then consider an application of our results to a world with nonconvex production sets, which leads to a brief exposition of the theory of *marginal cost pricing*.

Appendix A deals with some technical issues concerning the boundedness of the set of feasible allocations and the existence of Pareto optima.

Classical accounts of the material at the heart of this chapter are given by Koopmans (1957), Debreu (1959), and Arrow and Hahn (1971).

# 16.B  The Basic Model and Definitions

In this chapter, we study an economy composed of $I > 0$ consumers and $J > 0$ firms in which there are $L$ commodities. These $L$ commodities can be given many possible interpretations; we discuss some examples in Section 16.G.

Each consumer $i = 1, \ldots, I$ is characterized by a consumption set $X_i \subset \mathbb{R}^L$ and a preference relation $\succsim_i$ defined on $X_i$. We assume that these preferences are rational (i.e., complete and transitive). Chapters 1 to 3 provide an extensive discussion of these concepts.

Each firm $j = 1, \ldots, J$ is characterized by a technology, or production set, $Y_j \subset \mathbb{R}^L$. We assume that every $Y_j$ is nonempty and closed. See Chapter 5 for a discussion of production sets and their properties.

The initial resources of commodities in the economy—that is, the economy's *endowments*—are given to us by a vector $\bar{\omega} = (\bar{\omega}_1, \ldots, \bar{\omega}_L) \in \mathbb{R}^L$.

Thus, the basic data on preferences, technologies, and resources for this economy are summarized by $(\{(X_i, \succsim_i)\}_{i=1}^I, \{Y_j\}_{j=1}^J, \bar{\omega})$.

The Edgeworth box pure exchange economy discussed in Section 15.B, for example, corresponds to the case in which $L = 2$, $I = 2$, $X_1 = X_2 = \mathbb{R}_+^L$, $J = 1$, and $Y_1 = -\mathbb{R}_+^2$ (the disposal technology). More generally, we say that an economy is a *pure exchange economy* if its only technological possibility is that of free disposal, that is, if $Y_j = -\mathbb{R}_+^L$ for all $j = 1, \ldots, J$.

**Definition 16.B.1:** An *allocation* $(x, y) = (x_1, \ldots, x_I, y_1, \ldots, y_J)$ is a specification of a consumption vector $x_i \in X_i$ for each consumer $i = 1, \ldots, I$ and a production vector $y_j \in Y_j$ for each firm $j = 1, \ldots, J$. An allocation $(x, y)$ is *feasible* if

$\sum_i x_{\ell i} = \bar{\omega}_\ell + \sum_j y_{\ell j}$ for every commodity $\ell$. That is, if

$$\sum_i x_i = \bar{\omega} + \sum_j y_j. \tag{16.B.1}$$

We denote the set of feasible allocations by

$$A = \{(x, y) \in X_1 \times \cdots \times X_I \times Y_1 \times \cdots \times Y_J : \sum_i x_i = \bar{\omega} + \sum_j y_j\} \subset \mathbb{R}^{L(I+J)}.$$

The notion of a socially desirable outcome that we focus on is that of a *Pareto optimal* allocation.

**Definition 16.B.2:** A feasible allocation $(x, y)$ is *Pareto optimal* (or *Pareto efficient*) if there is no other allocation $(x', y') \in A$ that *Pareto dominates* it, that is, if there is no feasible allocation $(x', y')$ such that $x_i' \succsim_i x_i$ for all $i$ and $x_i' \succ_i x_i$ for some $i$.

An allocation is Pareto optimal if there is no waste: It is impossible to make any consumer strictly better off without making some other consumer worse off. Note that the Pareto optimality concept does not concern itself with distributional issues. For example, in a pure exchange economy, an allocation that gives all of society's endowments to one consumer who has strongly monotone preferences is necessarily Pareto optimal.

In Appendix A, we provide conditions on the primitives of the economy implying that the set of feasible allocations $A$ is nonempty, closed, and bounded and that Pareto optimal allocations exist.

### Private Ownership Economies

Throughout Part IV, we study the properties of competitive *private ownership economies*. In such economies, every good is traded in a market at publicly known prices that consumers and firms take as unaffected by their own actions. Consumers trade in the marketplace to maximize their well-being, and firms produce and trade to maximize profits. The wealth of consumers is derived from individual endowments of commodities and from ownership claims (*shares*) to the profits of the firms, which are therefore thought of as being owned by consumers.[1]

Formally, consumer $i$ has an initial endowment vector of commodities $\omega_i \in \mathbb{R}^L$ and a claim to a share $\theta_{ij} \in [0, 1]$ of the profits of firm $j$ (where $\bar{\omega} = \sum_i \omega_i$ and $\sum_i \theta_{ij} = 1$ for every firm $j$). Thus, the basic preference, technological, resource, and ownership data of a private ownership economy are summarized by $(\{(X_i, \succsim_i)\}_{i=1}^I, \{Y_j\}_{j=1}^J, \{(\omega_i, \theta_{i1}, \ldots, \theta_{iJ})\}_{i=1}^I)$.

The notion of a price-taking equilibrium for a competitive private ownership economy is that of a *Walrasian equilibrium*.

**Definition 16.B.3:** Given a private ownership economy specified by $(\{(X_i, \succsim_i)\}_{i=1}^I, \{Y_j\}_{j=1}^J, \{(\omega_i, \theta_{i1}, \ldots, \theta_{iJ})\}_{i=1}^I)$, an allocation $(x^*, y^*)$ and a price vector $p = (p_1, \ldots, p_L)$ constitute a *Walrasian* (or *competitive*) *equilibrium* if:

    (i) For every $j$, $y_j^*$ maximizes profits in $Y_j$; that is,

$$p \cdot y_j \leq p \cdot y_j^* \qquad \text{for all } y_j \in Y_j.$$

---

1. Recall from Section 5.G that, under our present assumptions, the consumer–owners of a firm are unanimously in favor of the objective of profit maximization.

(ii) For every $i$, $x_i^*$ is maximal for $\succsim_i$ in the budget set

$$\{x_i \in X_i : p \cdot x_i \leq p \cdot \omega_i + \sum_j \theta_{ij} p \cdot y_j^*\}.^2$$

(iii) $\sum_i x_i^* = \bar{\omega} + \sum_j y_j^*$.

Condition (i) of Definition 16.B.3 says that at a Walrasian equilibrium, firms are maximizing their profits given the equilibrium prices $p$. The logic of profit maximization is examined extensively in Chapter 5. Condition (ii) says that consumers are maximizing their well-being given, first, the equilibrium prices and, second, the wealth derived from their holdings of commodities and from their shares of profits. See Chapter 3 for extensive discussion of preference maximization. Finally, condition (iii) says that markets must clear at an equilibrium; that is, all consumers and firms must be able to achieve their desired trades at the going market prices.

### Price Equilibria with Transfers

The aim of this chapter is to relate the idea of Pareto optimality to supportability by means of price-taking behavior. To this end, it is useful to introduce a notion of equilibrium that allows for a more general determination of consumers' wealth levels than that in a private ownership economy. By way of motivation, we can imagine a situation where a social planner is able to carry out (lump-sum) redistributions of wealth, and where society's aggregate wealth can therefore be redistributed among consumers in any desired manner.

**Definition 16.B.4:** Given an economy specified by $(\{(X_i, \succsim_i)\}_{i=1}^I, \{Y_j\}_{j=1}^J, \bar{\omega})$ an allocation $(x^*, y^*)$ and a price vector $p = (p_1, \ldots, p_L)$ constitute a *price equilibrium with transfers* if there is an assignment of wealth levels $(w_1, \ldots, w_I)$ with $\sum_i w_i = p \cdot \bar{\omega} + \sum_j p \cdot y_j^*$ such that

(i) For every $j$, $y_j^*$ maximizes profits in $Y_j$; that is,

$$p \cdot y_j \leq p \cdot y_j^* \qquad \text{for all } y_j \in Y_j.$$

(ii) For every $i$, $x_i^*$ is maximal for $\succsim_i$ in the budget set

$$\{x_i \in X_i : p \cdot x_i \leq w_i\}.$$

(iii) $\sum_i x_i^* = \bar{\omega} + \sum_j y_j^*$.

The concept of a price equilibrium with transfers requires only that there be *some* wealth distribution such that allocation $(x^*, y^*)$ and price vector $p \in \mathbb{R}^L$ constitute an equilibrium. It captures the idea of price-taking market behavior without any supposition about the determination of consumers' wealth levels. Note that a Walrasian equilibrium is a special case of an equilibrium with transfers. It amounts to the case in which, for every $i$, consumer $i$'s wealth level is determined by the initial endowment vector $\omega_i$ and by the profit shares $(\theta_{i1}, \ldots, \theta_{iJ})$ without any further wealth transfers, that is, where $w_i = p \cdot \omega_i + \sum_j \theta_{ij} p \cdot y_j^*$ for all $i = 1, \ldots, I$.

---

2. The terminology "$x_i$ is maximal for $\succsim_i$ in set $B$" means that $x_i$ is a preference-maximizing choice for consumer $i$ in the set $B$; that is, $x_i \in B$ and $x_i \succsim_i x_i'$ for all $x_i' \in B$.

# 16.C  The First Fundamental Theorem of Welfare Economics

The first fundamental theorem of welfare economics states conditions under which any price equilibrium with transfers, and in particular any Walrasian equilibrium, is a Pareto optimum. For competitive market economies, it provides a formal and very general confirmation of Adam Smith's asserted "invisible hand" property of the market. A single, very weak assumption, the *local nonsatiation of preferences* (see Section 3.B), is all that is required for the result. Notably, we need not appeal to any convexity assumption whatsoever.

Recall the definition of locally nonsatiated preferences from Section 3.B (Definition 3.B.3).

**Definition 16.C.1:** The preference relation $\succsim_i$ on the consumption set $X_i$ is *locally nonsatiated* if for every $x_i \in X_i$ and every $\varepsilon > 0$, there is an $x_i' \in X_i$ such that $\|x_i' - x_i\| \le \varepsilon$ and $x_i' \succ_i x_i$.

Intuitively, the local nonsatiation condition will be satisfied if there are some desirable commodities. Note also a significant implication of the condition: if $\succsim_i$ is continuous and locally nonsatiated, then any closed consumption set $X_i$ must be unbounded. Otherwise, there would by necessity exist a global (hence, local) satiation point (see Exercise 16.C.1).

**Proposition 16.C.1:** (*First Fundamental Theorem of Welfare Economics*) If preferences are locally nonsatiated, and if $(x^*, y^*, p)$ is a price equilibrium with transfers, then the allocation $(x^*, y^*)$ is Pareto optimal. In particular, any Walrasian equilibrium allocation is Pareto optimal.

**Proof:** Suppose that $(x^*, y^*, p)$ is a price equilibrium with transfers and that the associated wealth levels are $(w_1, \ldots, w_I)$. Recall that $\sum_i w_i = p \cdot \bar{\omega} + \sum_j p \cdot y_j^*$.

The preference maximization part of the definition of a price equilibrium with transfers [i.e., part (ii) of Definition 16.B.4] implies that

$$\text{If } x_i \succ_i x_i^* \qquad \text{then } p \cdot x_i > w_i. \qquad (16.C.1)$$

That is, anything that is strictly preferred by consumer $i$ to $x_i^*$ must be unaffordable to her. The significance of the local nonsatiation condition for the purpose at hand is that with it (16.C.1) implies an additional property:

$$\text{If } x_i \succsim_i x_i^* \qquad \text{then } p \cdot x_i \ge w_i. \qquad (16.C.2)$$

That is, anything that is at least as good as $x_i^*$ is at best just affordable. This property is easily verified (you are asked to do so in Exercise 16.C.2).

Now consider an allocation $(x, y)$ that Pareto dominates $(x^*, y^*)$. That is, $x_i \succsim_i x_i^*$ for all $i$ and $x_i \succ_i x_i^*$ for some $i$. By (16.C.2), we must have $p \cdot x_i \ge w_i$ for all $i$, and by (16.C.1) $p \cdot x_i > w_i$ for some $i$. Hence,

$$\sum_i p \cdot x_i > \sum_i w_i = p \cdot \bar{\omega} + \sum_j p \cdot y_j^*.$$

Moreover, because $y_j^*$ is profit maximizing for firm $j$ at price vector $p$,

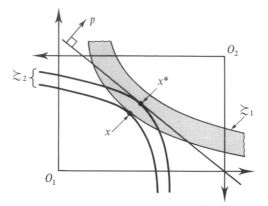

**Figure 16.C.1**

A price equilibrium
with transfers that is
not a Pareto optimum.

we have $p \cdot \bar{\omega} + \sum_j p \cdot y_j^* \geq p \cdot \bar{\omega} + \sum_j p \cdot y_j$. Thus,

$$\sum_i p \cdot x_i > p \cdot \bar{\omega} + \sum_j p \cdot y_j. \tag{16.C.3}$$

But then $(x, y)$ cannot be feasible. Indeed, $\sum_i x_i = \bar{\omega} + \sum_j y_j$ implies $\sum_i p \cdot x_i = p \cdot \bar{\omega} + \sum_j p \cdot y_j$, which contradicts (16.C.3). We conclude that the equilibrium allocation $(x^*, y^*)$ must be Pareto optimal. ∎

The central idea in the proof of Proposition 16.C.1 can be put as follows: At any feasible allocation $(x, y)$, the total cost of the consumption bundles $(x_1, \ldots, x_I)$, evaluated at prices $p$, must be equal to the social wealth at those prices, $p \cdot \bar{\omega} + \sum_j p \cdot y_j$. Moreover, because preferences are locally nonsatiated, if $(x, y)$ Pareto dominates $(x^*, y^*)$ then the total cost of consumption bundles $(x_1, \ldots, x_I)$ at prices $p$, and therefore the social wealth at those prices, must exceed the total cost of the equilibrium consumption allocation $p \cdot (\sum_i x_i^*) = p \cdot \bar{\omega} + \sum_j p \cdot y_j^*$. But by the profit-maximization of Definition 16.B.4, there are no technologically feasible production levels that attain a value of social wealth at prices $p$ in excess of $p \cdot \bar{\omega} + \sum_j p \cdot y_j^*$.

The importance of the nonsatiation assumption for the result can be seen in Figure 16.C.1, which depicts an Edgeworth box where local nonsatiation fails for consumer 1 (note that consumer 1's indifference "curve" is thick) and where the allocation $x^*$, a price equilibrium for the price vector $p = (p_1, p_2)$ (you should verify this), is not Pareto optimal. Consumer 1 is indifferent about a move to allocation $x$, and consumer 2, having strongly monotone preferences, is strictly better off. (See Exercise 16.C.3 for a first welfare theorem compatible with satiation.)

Two points about Proposition 16.C.1 should be noted. First, although the result may appear to follow from very weak hypotheses, our theoretical structure already incorporates two strong assumptions: *universal price quoting of commodities* (market completeness) and *price taking* by economic agents. In Part III, we studied a number of circumstances (externalities, market power, and asymmetric information) in which these conditions are not satisfied and market equilibria fail to be Pareto optimal. Second, the first welfare theorem is entirely silent about the desirability of the equilibrium allocation from a distributional standpoint. In Section 16.D, we study the second fundamental theorem of welfare economics. That result, a partial converse to the first welfare theorem, gives us conditions under which any desired distributional aims can be achieved through the use of competitive (price-taking) markets.

# 16.D  The Second Fundamental Theorem of Welfare Economics

The second fundamental welfare theorem gives conditions under which a Pareto optimum allocation can be supported as a price equilibrium with transfers. It is a converse of the first welfare theorem in the sense that it tells us that, under its assumptions, we can achieve any desired Pareto optimal allocation as a market-based equilibrium using an appropriate lump-sum wealth distribution scheme.

The second welfare theorem is more delicate than the first, and its validity requires additional assumptions. To see this, reconsider some of the examples discussed in Chapter 15. In Figure 15.C.3 (a) we saw that in a one-consumer, one-firm economy a Pareto optimal allocation may not be supportable as an equilibrium if the firm's technology is not convex. Figure 15.B.14 depicted a similar failure in a two-consumer Edgeworth box economy where the preferences of one consumer were not convex. Both figures suggest that the assumption of convexity will have to play a central role in establishing the second welfare theorem. Notice that convexity was not appealed to in any way for the first welfare theorem in Section 16.C.

The Edgeworth box of Figure 15.B.10(a) illustrates a different type of failure of supportability by means of prices. In that figure, both consumers have convex preferences, but the Pareto optimal allocation $(\omega_1, \omega_2)$ cannot be supported as a price equilibrium with transfers; $\omega_2$ is an optimal demand for consumer 2 for any price vector $p = (p_1, p_2) \geq 0$ when her wealth is $w_2 = p \cdot \omega_2$, but $\omega_1$ is an optimal demand for consumer 1 for *no* price vector $p \geq 0$ and wealth level $w_1$.

It is convenient to tackle the problems raised by these two types of examples in two steps. The first step consists of establishing a version of the second fundamental theorem in which the sort of failure arising in Figure 15.B.10(a) is allowed. This is accomplished by defining the concept of a *price quasiequilibrium with transfers*, a weakening of the notion of a price equilibrium with transfers. We prove that if all preferences and technologies are convex, any Pareto optimal allocation can be achieved as a price quasiequilibrium with transfers. The second step consists of giving sufficient conditions for a price quasiequilibrium to be a full-fledged equilibrium. This division of labor is convenient because the first step is very general and isolates the central role of convexity, whereas the assumptions for the second step tend to be more special, often being tailored to the particulars of the model under consideration.

The definition of a quasiequilibrium with transfers, Definition 16.D.1, is identical to Definition 16.B.4 except that the preference maximization condition that anything preferred to $x_i^*$ must cost more than $w_i$ (i.e., "if $x_i \succ_i x_i^*$, then $p \cdot x_i > w_i$") is replaced by the weaker requirement that anything preferred to $x_i^*$ cannot cost less than $w_i$ (i.e., "if $x_i \succ_i x_i^*$, then $p \cdot x_i \geq w_i$").

**Definition 16.D.1:** Given an economy specified by $(\{(X_i, \succsim_i)\}_{i=1}^{I}, \{Y_j\}_{j=1}^{J}, \bar{\omega})$ an allocation $(x^*, y^*)$ and a price vector $p = (p_1, \ldots, p_L) \neq 0$ constitute a *price quasiequilibrium with transfers* if there is an assignment of wealth levels $(w_1, \ldots, w_I)$ with $\sum_i w_i = p \cdot \bar{\omega} + \sum_j p \cdot y_j^*$ such that

(i) For every $j$, $y_j^*$ maximizes profits in $Y_j$; that is,

$$p \cdot y_j \leq p \cdot y_j^* \qquad \text{for all } y_j \in Y_j.$$

(ii) For every $i$, if $x_i \succ_i x_i^*$ then $p \cdot x_i \geq w_i$.

(iii) $\sum_i x_i^* = \bar{\omega} + \sum_j y_j^*.$

Part (ii) of Definition 16.D.1 is implied by the preference maximization condition of the definition of a price equilibrium with transfers [part (ii) of Definition 16.B.4]: If $x_i^*$ is preference maximizing in the set $\{x_i \in X_i : p \cdot x_i \leq w_i\}$, then no $x_i \succ_i x_i^*$ with $p \cdot x_i < w_i$ can exist. Hence, any price equilibrium with transfers is a price quasi-equilibrium with transfers. However, as we discuss later in this section, the converse is not true.

---

Note also that when consumers' preferences are locally nonsatiated, part (ii) of Definition 16.D.1 implies $p \cdot x_i^* \geq w_i$ for every $i$.[3] In addition, from part (iii), we get $\sum_i p \cdot x_i^* = p \cdot \bar{\omega} + \sum_j p \cdot y_j^* = \sum_i w_i$. Therefore, *under the assumption of locally nonsatiated preferences*, which we always make, *we must have $p \cdot x_i^* = w_i$ for every $i$*. This means that we could just as well not mention the $w_i$'s explicitly and replace part (ii) of Definition 16.D.1 by

(ii′) If $x_i \succ_i x_i^*$ then $p \cdot x_i \geq p \cdot x_i^*$.

That is, allocation $(x^*, y^*)$ and price vector $p$ constitute a price quasiequilibrium with transfers if and only if conditions (i), (ii′), and (iii) hold.[4] Moreover, with locally nonsatiated preferences, condition (ii′) is equivalent to saying that $x_i^*$ is expenditure minimizing on the set $\{x_i \in X : x_i \succsim_i x_i^*\}$ (see Exercise 16.D.1). Thus, our discussion later in this section of the conditions under which a price quasiequilibrium with transfers is a price equilibrium with transfers can be interpreted in the locally nonsatiated case as providing conditions under which expenditure minimization on the set $\{x_i \in X_i : x_i \succsim_i x_i^*\}$ implies preference maximization on the set $\{x_i \in X_i : p \cdot x_i \leq p \cdot x_i^*\} = \{x_i \in X_i : p \cdot x_i \leq w_i\}$. ∎

---

Proposition 16.D.1 states a version of the second fundamental welfare theorem.

**Proposition 16.D.1:** (*Second Fundamental Theorem of Welfare Economics*) Consider an economy specified by $(\{(X_i, \succsim_i)\}_{i=1}^I, \{Y_j\}_{j=1}^J, \bar{\omega})$, and suppose that every $Y_j$ is convex and every preference relation $\succsim_i$ is convex [i.e., the set $\{x_i' \in X_i : x_i' \succsim_i x_i\}$ is convex for every $x_i \in X_i$] and locally nonsatiated. Then, for every Pareto optimal allocation $(x^*, y^*)$, there is a price vector $p = (p_1, \ldots, p_L) \neq 0$ such that $(x^*, y^*, p)$ is a price quasiequilibrium with transfers.

**Proof:** In its essence, the proof is just an application of the separating hyperplane theorem for convex sets (see Section M.G. of the Mathematical Appendix). To facilitate comprehension, we organize the proof into a number of small steps.

---

3. To see this, observe that if preferences are locally nonsatiated and $p \cdot x_i^* < w_i$, then close to $x_i^*$ there is an $x_i$ with $x_i \succ_i x_i^*$ and $p \cdot x_i < w_i$, contradicting condition (ii) of Definition 16.D.1.

4. A similar observation applies, incidentally, to the definition of price equilibrium with transfers (Definition 16.B.4). If preferences are locally nonsatiated, we get an equivalent definition by not referring explicitly to the $w_i$'s and replacing part (ii) of the definition by (ii″): If $x_i \succ_i x_i^*$ then $p \cdot x_i > p \cdot x_i^*$. Thus, in this locally nonsatiated case, condition (ii″) says that $x_i^*$ is preference maximizing on $\{x_i \in X_i : p \cdot x_i \leq p \cdot x_i^*\}$.

We begin by defining, for every $i$, the set $V_i$ of consumptions preferred to $x_i^*$, that is, $V_i = \{x_i \in X_i \colon x_i \succ_i x_i^*\} \subset \mathbb{R}^L$. Then define

$$V = \sum_i V_i = \left\{ \sum_i x_i \in \mathbb{R}^L \colon x_1 \in V_1, \ldots, x_I \in V_I \right\}$$

and

$$Y = \sum_j Y_j = \left\{ \sum_j y_j \in \mathbb{R}^L \colon y_1 \in Y_1, \ldots, y_J \in Y_J \right\}.$$

Thus, $V$ is the set of aggregate consumption bundles that could be split into $I$ individual consumptions, each preferred by its corresponding consumer to $x_i^*$. The set $Y$ is simply the aggregate production set. Note that the set $Y + \{\bar{\omega}\}$, which geometrically is the aggregate production set with its origin shifted to $\bar{\omega}$, is the set of aggregate bundles producible with the given technology and endowments and usable, in principle, for consumption.

*Step 1: Every set $V_i$ is convex.* Suppose that $x_i \succ_i x_i^*$ and $x_i' \succ_i x_i^*$. Take $0 \leq \alpha \leq 1$. We want to prove that $\alpha x_i + (1 - \alpha)x_i' \succsim_i x_i^*$. Because preferences are complete, we can assume without loss of generality that $x_i \succsim_i x_i'$. Therefore, by convexity of preferences, we have $\alpha x_i + (1 - \alpha)x_i' \succsim_i x_i'$, which by transitivity yields the desired conclusion: $\alpha x_i + (1 - \alpha)x_i' \succ_i x_i^*$ [recall part (iii) of Proposition 1.B.1].

*Step 2: The sets $V$ and $Y + \{\bar{\omega}\}$ are convex.* This is just a general, and easy-to-prove, mathematical fact: The sum of any two (and therefore any number of) convex sets is convex.

*Step 3: $V \cap (Y + \{\bar{\omega}\}) = \varnothing$.* This is a consequence of the Pareto optimality of $(x^*, y^*)$. If there were a vector both in $V$ and in $Y + \{\bar{\omega}\}$, then this would mean that with the given endowments and technologies it would be possible to produce an aggregate vector that could be used to give every consumer $i$ a consumption bundle that is preferred to $x_i^*$.

*Step 4: There is $p = (p_1, \ldots, p_L) \neq 0$ and a number $r$ such that $p \cdot z \geq r$ for every $z \in V$ and $p \cdot z \leq r$ for every $z \in Y + \{\bar{\omega}\}$.* This follows directly from the separating hyperplane theorem (see Section M. G. the Mathematical Appendix). It is illustrated in Figure 16.D.1.

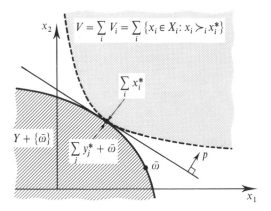

**Figure 16.D.1**

The separation argument in the proof of the second welfare theorem.

*Step 5: If $x_i \succsim_i x_i^*$ for every i then $p \cdot (\sum_i x_i) \geq r$.* Suppose that $x_i \succsim_i x_i^*$ for every i. By local nonsatiation, for each consumer i there is a consumption bundle $\hat{x}_i$ arbitrarily close to $x_i$ such that $\hat{x}_i \succ_i x_i$, and therefore $\hat{x}_i \in V_i$. Hence, $\sum_i \hat{x}_i \in V$, and so $p \cdot (\sum_i \hat{x}_i) \geq r$, which, taking the limit as $\hat{x}_i \to x_i$, gives $p \cdot (\sum_i x_i) \geq r$.[5]

*Step 6: $p \cdot (\sum_i x_i^*) = p \cdot (\bar{\omega} + \sum_j y_j^*) = r$.* Because of step 5, we have $p \cdot (\sum_i x_i^*) \geq r$. On the other hand, $\sum_i x_i^* = \sum_j y_j^* + \bar{\omega} \in Y + \{\bar{\omega}\}$, and therefore $p \cdot (\sum_i x_i^*) \leq r$. Thus, $p \cdot (\sum_i x_i^*) = r$. Since $\sum_i x_i^* = \bar{\omega} + \sum_j y_j^*$, we also have $p \cdot (\bar{\omega} + \sum_j y_j^*) = r$.

*Step 7: For every j, we have $p \cdot y_j \leq p \cdot y_j^*$ for all $y_j \in Y_j$.* For any firm j and $y_j \in Y_j$, we have $y_j + \sum_{h \neq j} y_h^* \in Y$. Therefore,

$$p \cdot \left( \bar{\omega} + y_j + \sum_{h \neq j} y_h^* \right) \leq r = p \cdot \left( \bar{\omega} + y_j^* + \sum_{h \neq j} y_h^* \right).$$

Hence, $p \cdot y_j \leq p \cdot y_j^*$.

*Step 8: For every i, if $x_i \succ_i x_i^*$, then $p \cdot x_i \geq p \cdot x_i^*$.* Consider any $x_i \succ_i x_i^*$. Because of steps 5 and 6, we have

$$p \cdot \left( x_i + \sum_{k \neq i} x_k^* \right) \geq r = p \cdot \left( x_i^* + \sum_{k \neq i} x_k^* \right).$$

Hence, $p \cdot x_i \geq p \cdot x_i^*$.

*Step 9: The wealth levels $w_i = p \cdot x_i^*$ for $i = 1, \ldots, I$ support $(x^*, y^*, p)$ as a price quasiequilibrium with transfers.* Conditions (i) and (ii) of Definition 16.D.1 follow from steps 7 and 8; condition (iii) follows from the feasibility of the Pareto optimal allocation $(x^*, y^*)$. ∎

In Exercise 16.D.2, you are asked to show that the local nonsatiation condition is required in Proposition 16.D.1.

When will a price quasiequilibrium with transfers be a price equilibrium with transfers? The example in Figure 15.B.10(a), reproduced in Figure 16.D.2, indicates that there is indeed a problem. Figure 16.D.2 depicts the quasiequilibrium associated with the Pareto optimal allocation labeled $x^*$. The unique price vector (normalizing $p_1 = 1$) that supports $x^*$ as a quasiequilibrium allocation is $p = (1, 0)$; the associated wealth levels are $w_1 = p \cdot x_1^* = (1, 0) \cdot (0, x_{21}^*) = 0$ and $w_2 = p \cdot x_2^*$. However, although the consumption bundle $x_1^*$ satisfies part (ii) of Definition 16.D.1 (indeed, $p \cdot x_1 \geq 0 = w_1$ for *any* $x_1 \geq 0$), it is *not* consumer 1's preference-maximizing bundle in her budget set $\{(x_{11}, x_{21}) \in \mathbb{R}_+^2 : (1, 0) \cdot (x_{11}, x_{21}) \leq 0\} = \{(x_{11}, x_{21}) \in \mathbb{R}_+^2 : x_{11} = 0\}$.

An important feature of the example just discussed, however, is that consumer 1's wealth level at the quasiequilibrium is zero. As we shall see, this is key to the failure of the quasiequilibrium to be an equilibrium. Our next result provides a sufficient condition under which the condition "$x_i \succ_i x_i^*$ implies $p \cdot x_i \geq w_i$" is equivalent to the preference maximization condition "$x_i \succ_i x_i^*$ implies $p \cdot x_i > w_i$."

---

5. Geometrically, what we have done here is show that the set $\sum_i \{x_i \in X_i : x_i \succsim_i x_i^*\}$ is contained in the closure of $V$ (see Section M.F of the Mathematical Appendix for this concept), which, in turn, is contained in the half-space $\{v \in \mathbb{R}^L : p \cdot v \geq r\}$.

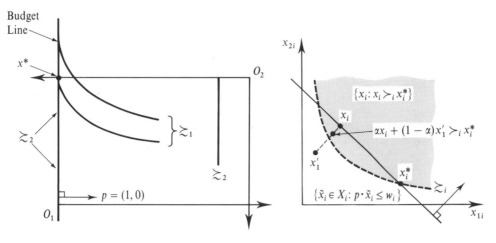

**Figure 16.D.2 (left)**

A price quasi-equilibrium that is not a price equilibrium.

**Figure 16.D.3 (right)**

Suppose there exists a "cheaper consumption" (an $x'_i \in X_i$ such that $p \cdot x'_i < w_i$). Then if the preferred set does intersect the budget set ($p \cdot x_i \leq w_i$ for some $x_i \succ_i x^*_i$), it follows that the preferred set does intersect the interior of the budget set ($p \cdot x_i < w_i$ for some $x_i \succ_i x^*_i$).

**Proposition 16.D.2:** Assume that $X_i$ is convex and $\succsim_i$ is continuous. Suppose also that the consumption vector $x^*_i \in X_i$, the price vector $p$, and the wealth level $w_i$ are such that $x_i \succ_i x^*_i$ implies $p \cdot x_i \geq w_i$. Then, if there is a consumption vector $x'_i \in X_i$ such that $p \cdot x'_i < w_i$ [a *cheaper consumption* for $(p, w_i)$], it follows that $x_i \succ_i x^*_i$ implies $p \cdot x_i > w_i$.[6]

**Proof:** The idea of the proof is indicated in Figure 16.D.3 (where we take $p \cdot x^*_i = w_i$ only because this is the leading case; the fact plays no role in the proof). Suppose that, contrary to the assertion of the proposition, there is an $x_i \succ_i x^*_i$ with $p \cdot x_i = w_i$. By the cheaper consumption assumption, there exists an $x'_i \in X_i$ such that $p \cdot x'_i < w_i$. Then for all $\alpha \in [0, 1)$, we have $\alpha x_i + (1 - \alpha) x'_i \in X_i$ and $p \cdot (\alpha x_i + (1 - \alpha) x'_i) < w_i$.[7] But if $\alpha$ is close enough to 1, the continuity of $\succsim_i$ implies that $\alpha x_i + (1 - \alpha) x'_i \succ_i x^*_i$, which constitutes a contradiction because we have then found a consumption bundle that is preferred to $x^*_i$ and costs less than $w_i$. ∎

Note that in the example of Figure 16.D.2, we have $w_1 = 0$ in the price quasiequilibrium supporting allocation $x^*$, and so there is no cheaper consumption for $(p, w_1)$.[8]

As a consequence of Proposition 16.D.2, we have Proposition 16.D.3.

**Proposition 16.D.3:** Suppose that for every $i$, $X_i$ is convex, $0 \in X_i$, and $\succsim_i$ is continuous. Then any price quasiequilibrium with transfers that has $(w_1, \ldots, w_I) \gg 0$ is a price equilibrium with transfers.

---

6. If, as in all our applications, $\succsim_i$ is locally nonsatiated and $w_i = p \cdot x^*$, then Proposition 16.D.2 offers sufficient conditions for the equivalence of the statements "$x^*_i$ minimizes expenditure relative to $p$ in the set $\{x_i \in X_i : x_i \succsim_i x^*_i\}$" and "$x^*_i$ is maximal for $\succsim_i$ in the budget set $\{x_i \in X_i : p \cdot x_i \leq p \cdot x^*_i\}$."

7. A similar argument can be used to show that if $X_i$ is convex and the Walrasian demand function $x_i(p, w_i)$ is well defined, then there is a cheaper consumption for $(p, w_i)$ if and only if there is an $x'_i$ arbitrarily close to $x_i(p, w_i)$ with $p \cdot x'_i < w_i$. In the Appendix A, of Chapter 3 the latter concept was called the *locally cheaper consumption condition*.

8. Note also that Proposition 16.D.2 generalizes the result in Proposition 3.E.1(ii), which assumed local nonsatiation, $w_i = p \cdot x^*_i > 0$, and $X_i = \mathbb{R}^L_+$.

Consider the implications of Proposition 16.D.3 for a pure exchange economy in which $\bar{\omega} \gg 0$ and every consumer has $X_i = \mathbb{R}_+^L$ and continuous, locally nonsatiated preferences. In such an economy, by free disposal and profit maximization, we must have $p \geq 0$ and $p \neq 0$ at any price quasiequilibrium.[9] Thus, under these assumptions, any price quasiequilibrium with transfers in which $x_i^* \gg 0$ for all $i$ is a price equilibrium with transfers (since then $w_i = p \cdot x_i^* > 0$ for all $i$). But there is more. Suppose that, in addition, preferences are strongly monotone. Then we must have $p \gg 0$ in any price quasiequilibrium with transfers. To see this, note that $p \geq 0$, $p \neq 0$, and $\bar{\omega} \gg 0$ imply that $\sum_i w_i = p \cdot \bar{\omega} > 0$ and therefore that $w_i > 0$ for *some i*. But by Proposition 16.D.2, this consumer must then be maximizing her preferences in her budget set $\{x_i \in \mathbb{R}_+^L : p \cdot x_i \leq w_i\}$, which, by strong monotonicity of preferences, cannot occur if prices are not strictly positive. Once we know that we must have $p \gg 0$, we can conclude that *any* price quasiequilibrium with transfers in this economy is a price equilibrium with transfers: if consumer $i$'s allocation satisfies $x_i^* \neq 0$, then $p \cdot x_i^* = w_i > 0$ and Proposition 16.D.2 applies. On the other hand, if $x_i^* = 0$, then $w_i = 0$ and the result follows from the fact that $x_i^* = 0$ is the only vector in the set $\{x_i \in \mathbb{R}_+^L : p \cdot x_i \leq 0\}$. (Exercise 16.D.3 asks you to extend the arguments presented in this paragraph to the case of an economy with production.)

The second welfare theorem (combined with Propositions 16.D.2 and 16.D.3) identifies conditions under which any Pareto optimal allocation can be implemented through competitive markets and offers a strong conceptual affirmation of the use of competitive markets, even for dealing with distributional concerns. Yet, it is important to discuss some of the practical limitations on the use of this theoretical result.

The first observation to make is that a planning authority wishing to implement a particular Pareto optimal allocation must be able to insure that the supporting prices $(p_1, \ldots, p_L)$ will be taken as given by consumers and firms. If the market structure is such that price-taking behavior would not automatically hold (say, because economic agents are not all of negligible size), then the planning authority must somehow enforce these prices, either by monitoring all transactions or, perhaps, by credibly offering to buy or sell any amount of any good $\ell$ at price $p_\ell$.

A second observation is that the information of a planning authority that wants to use the second welfare theorem must be very good indeed. To begin with, it must have sufficiently good information to identify the Pareto optimal allocation to be implemented and to compute the right supporting price vector. For this purpose, the authority must know, at least, the statistical joint distribution of preferences, endowments, and other relevant characteristics of the agents that actually exist in the economy. However, to implement the correct transfer levels for each consumer, the planning authority must know *more*: it must have the ability to tell who is who by observing each individual's private characteristics (e.g., preferences and endowments) perfectly. Such information is extremely unlikely to be available in practice; as a result, most common transfer schemes fail to be lump-sum schemes. For example, if the planning authority wants to transfer wealth from those who have a great deal of a highly valuable labor skill to those who do not, the only way it may have to tell which consumers are which may be by observing their *actual*

---

9. Indeed, if we had $p_\ell < 0$, then unboundedly large profits could be generated through disposal of the $\ell$th good.

earnings. But if transfers are based on observed earnings, they will cease to be lump-sum in nature. Individuals will recognize that by altering their earnings, they will change their tax burden.

Finally, even if the planning authority observes all the required information, it must actually have the power to enforce the necessary wealth transfers through some tax-and-transfer mechanism that individuals cannot evade.

Because of these informational and enforceability limitations, it is in practice unlikely that extensive lump-sum taxation will be possible.[10] We shall see in Section 18.D that if these types of transfers are not possible, then the second welfare theorem collapses in the sense that, for a typical economy, only a limited range of Pareto optima are supportable by means of prices supplemented by the usual sort of taxation systems. For the typical economy, redistribution schemes are *distortionary*; that is, they trade off distributional aims against Pareto optimality. The analysis of this trade-off is the subject of *second-best* welfare economics, some elements of which are presented in Chapter 22. (Chapter 23 discusses in much more depth what is and what is not implementable by a planning authority who faces informational and enforceability constraints.)

In summary, the second welfare theorem is a very useful *theoretical* reference point. But it is far from a direct prescription for policy practice. On the contrary, by pointing out what is necessary to achieve any desired Pareto optimal allocation, it serves a cautionary purpose.

---

It is clear from our discussion that convexity plays a central role in the second welfare theorem. But it is a role that deserves a very important qualification. The interpretation of the second welfare theorem is at its strongest when the number of economic agents is large. This is so because the price-taking assumption is then enforced by the market itself (otherwise, it is almost inescapable that there must be some sort of centralized mechanism guaranteeing the fixity of prices). It turns out, however, that if consumers are numerous (in the limit, a continuum), and if the nonconvexities of production sets are bounded in a certain sense, then the assumptions of convex preferences and production sets are *not* required for the second welfare theorem.

To see the idea behind this, it is useful to consider the one-consumer economy depicted in Figure 16.D.4 where, because of nonconvexities, the (trivially Pareto optimal) allocation $x_1 = \bar{\omega}$ cannot be price supported. Suppose, however, that we replicate the economy so that we have *two* consumers and the total endowments are *doubled* to $2\bar{\omega}$. Again, the allocation $x_1 = x_2 = \bar{\omega}$ cannot be price supported, but now *this symmetric allocation is no longer a Pareto optimum*. In Figure 16.D.5, we can see that the asymmetric allocation

$$x_1' = \bar{\omega} + (1, -1) \qquad \text{and} \qquad x_2' = \bar{\omega} + (-1, 1)$$

Pareto dominates $x_1 = x_2 = \bar{\omega}$. It certainly does not follow from this that with just two replicas any allocation that cannot be price supported is not a Pareto optimum. (In Figure 16.D.6, we represent the Edgeworth box associated with Figure 16.D.5. We have drawn it so that the allocation $x'$ is actually Pareto optimal and yet cannot be price supported). However, what

---

10. Note that the extent of the required lump-sum taxation depends not only on the final wealth levels $(w_1, \ldots, w_I)$ but also on the initial situation. For example, if we are in private ownership economy, then the net transfer to consumer $i$ is $w_i - p \cdot \omega_i - \sum_j \theta_{ij} p \cdot y_j^*$ and so depends on the consumer's initial endowments. The Walrasian equilibria correspond to the no-taxation situations; and the farther from the Walrasian wealth levels that we try to go, the larger the required transfer.

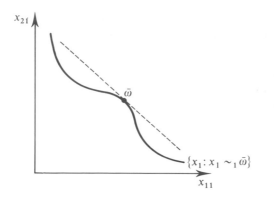

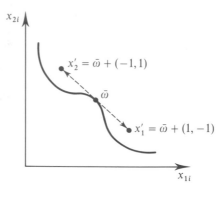

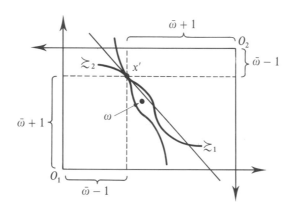

**Figure 16.D.4 (top left)**

A one-consumer economy (without production) where the initial endowment is not supportable by prices.

**Figure 16.D.5 (top right)**

Allocation $(x_1', x_2')$ Pareto dominates allocation $(\bar{\omega}, \bar{\omega})$ in a two-consumer replica of the economy in Figure 16.D.4.

**Figure 16.D.6 (bottom)**

Allocation $x' = (x_1', x_2')$ is Pareto optimal but not price supportable.

can be shown is that if the number of replicas is large enough, then any feasible allocation that fails (significantly) to be price supportable can be Pareto dominated, and therefore any Pareto optimum must be (almost) price supportable. (See Exercise 16.D.4 for more on this.)[11]

# 16.E  Pareto Optimality and Social Welfare Optima

In this section, we discuss the relationship between the Pareto optimality concept and the maximization of a social welfare function (see Section 4.D and Chapter 22 for more on this concept).

Given a family $u_i(\cdot)$ of (continuous) utility functions representing the preferences $\succsim_i$ of the $I$ consumers, we can capture the attainable vectors of utility levels for an economy specified by $(\{(X_i, \succsim_i)\}_{i=1}^I, \{Y_j\}_{j=1}^J, \bar{\omega})$ by means of the *utility possibility set*:

$$U = \{(u_1, \ldots, u_I) \in \mathbb{R}^I : \text{there is a feasible allocation } (x, y) \text{ such that}$$
$$u_i \le u_i(x_i) \text{ for } i = 1, \ldots, I\}.$$

11. Two facts established in Chapter 17 lend plausibility to this claim. First, in Section 17.I, we show that convexity is not required for the (approximate) existence of a Walrasian equilibrium in a large economy. Second, in Section 17.C, we argue that the second welfare theorem can be rephrased as an assertion of the existence of a Walrasian equilibrium for economies in which endowments are distributed in a particular manner, and it can therefore be seen as implied by the conditions guaranteeing the general existence of Walrasian equilibria.

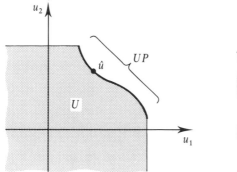

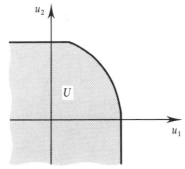

**Figure 16.E.1 (left)**

The utility possibility set.

**Figure 16.E.2 (right)**

A convex utility possibility set.

Figure 16.E.1 depicts this set for a two-consumer economy. (Note that we show $U \subset \mathbb{R}^I$ as a closed set; Appendix A discusses sufficient conditions to guarantee that the set is indeed closed.)

By the definition of Pareto optimality, the utility values of a Pareto optimal allocation must belong to the boundary of the utility possibility set.[12] More precisely, we define the *Pareto frontier UP*, also shown in Figure 16.E.1, by

$$UP = \{(u_1, \dots, u_I) \in U: \text{there is no } (u'_1, \dots, u'_I) \in U \text{ such that } u'_i \geq u_i$$
$$\text{for all } i \text{ and } u'_i > u_i \text{ for some } i\}.$$

Proposition 16.E.1 is then intuitive.

**Proposition 16.E.1:** A feasible allocation $(x, y) = (x_1, \dots, x_I, y_1, \dots, y_J)$ is a Pareto optimum if and only if $(u_1(x_1), \dots, u_I(x_I)) \in UP$.

**Proof:** If $(u_1(x_1), \dots, u_I(x_I)) \notin UP$, then there is $(u'_1, \dots, u'_I) \in U$ such that $u'_i \geq u_i(x_i)$ for all $i$ and $u'_i > u_i(x_i)$ for some $i$. But $(u'_1, \dots, u'_I) \in U$ only if there is a feasible allocation $(x', y')$ such that $u_i(x'_i) \geq u'_i$ for all $i$. It follows then that $(x', y')$ Pareto dominates $(x, y)$. Conversely, if $(x, y)$ is not a Pareto optimum, then it is Pareto dominated by some feasible $(x', y')$, which means that $u_i(x'_i) \geq u_i(x_i)$ for all $i$ and $u_i(x'_i) > u_i(x_i)$ for some $i$. Hence, $(u_1(x_1), \dots, u_I(x_I)) \notin UP$. ∎

We also note that if every $X_i$ and every $Y_j$ is convex, and if the utility functions $u_i(\cdot)$ are concave, then the utility possibility set $U$ is convex (see Exercise 16.E.2).[13] One such utility possibility set is represented in Figure 16.E.2.

Suppose now that society's distributional principles can be summarized in a *social welfare function* $W(u_1, \dots, u_I)$ assigning social utility values to the various possible vectors of utilities for the $I$ consumers. We concentrate here on a particularly simple class of social welfare functions: those that take the *linear* form

$$W(u_1, \dots, u_I) = \sum_i \lambda_i u_i$$

---

12. However, not every point in the boundary must be Pareto optimal. Go back, for example, to Figure 16.C.1: The utility values associated with $x^*$ belong to the boundary of the utility possibility set because it is impossible to make *both* consumers better off. Yet, $x^*$ is not a Pareto optimum.

13. It can be shown that under a mild technical strengthening of the strict convexity assumption on preferences (essentially the same condition used to guarantee differentiability of the Walrasian demand function in Appendix A of Chapter 3), there are in the family of utility functions $u_i(\cdot)$ that represent $\succsim_i$ some utility functions that are not only quasiconcave but also concave.

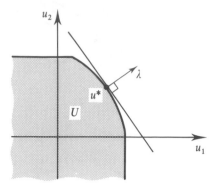

**Figure 16.E.3**

Maximizing a linear
social welfare function.

for some constants $\lambda = (\lambda_1, \ldots, \lambda_I)$.[14] Letting $u = (u_1, \ldots, u_I)$, we can also write
$W(u) = \lambda \cdot u$. Because social welfare should be nondecreasing in the consumer's utility
levels, we assume that $\lambda \geq 0$.

Armed with a linear social welfare function, we can select points in the utility
possibility set $U$ that maximize our measure of social welfare by solving

$$\underset{u \in U}{\text{Max}} \quad \lambda \cdot u. \tag{16.E.1}$$

Figure 16.E.3 depicts the solution to problem (16.E.1). As the figure suggests, we have
the result presented in Proposition 16.E.2.

**Proposition 16.E.2:** If $u^* = (u_1^*, \ldots, u_I^*)$ is a solution to the social welfare maximization problem (16.E.1) with $\lambda \gg 0$, then $u^* \in UP$; that is, $u^*$ is the utility
vector of a Pareto optimal allocation. Moreover, if the utility possibility set $U$ is
convex, then for any $\tilde{u} = (\tilde{u}_1, \ldots, \tilde{u}_I) \in UP$, there is a vector of welfare weights
$\lambda = (\lambda_1, \ldots, \lambda_I) \geq 0$, $\lambda \neq 0$, such that $\lambda \cdot \tilde{u} \geq \lambda \cdot u$ for all $u \in U$, that is, such that $\tilde{u}$
is a solution to the social welfare maximization problem (16.E.1).

**Proof:** The first part is immediate: if $u^*$ were not Pareto optimal, then there would
exist a $u \in U$ with $u \geq u^*$ and $u \neq u^*$; and so because $\lambda \gg 0$, we would have
$\lambda \cdot u > \lambda \cdot u^*$.

For the second part, note that if $\tilde{u} \in UP$, then $\tilde{u}$ is in the boundary of $U$. By the
supporting hyperplane theorem (see Section M.G of the Mathematical Appendix),
there exists a $\lambda \neq 0$ such that $\lambda \cdot \tilde{u} \geq \lambda \cdot u$ for all $u \in U$. Moreover, since the set $U$ has
been constructed so that $U - \mathbb{R}_+^I \subset U$, we must have $\lambda \geq 0$ (indeed, if $\lambda_i < 0$, then
by choosing a $u \in U$ with $u_i < 0$ large enough in absolute value, we would have
$\lambda \cdot u > \lambda \cdot \tilde{u}$). ∎

Proposition 16.E.2 tells us that for economies with convex utility possibility sets,
there is a close relation between Pareto optima and linear social welfare optima:
Every linear social welfare optimum with weights $\lambda \gg 0$ is Pareto optimal, and every
Pareto optimal allocation (and hence, every Walrasian equilibrium) is a social
welfare optimum for *some* welfare weights $(\lambda_1, \ldots, \lambda_I) \geq 0$.[15]

---

14. See Chapter 22 for a discussion of more general types of social welfare functions.

15. The necessity of allowing for some $\lambda_i$ to equal zero in the second part of this statement
parallels the similar feature encountered in the characterization of efficient production vectors in
Proposition 5.F.2.

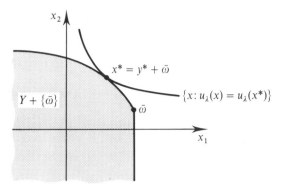

**Figure 16.E.4**

Maximizing the utility of a representative consumer.

As usual, in the absence of convexity of the set $U$, we cannot be assured that a Pareto optimum can be supported as a maximum of a linear social welfare function. The point $\hat{u}$ in Figure 16.E.1 provides an example where it cannot.

---

By using the social welfare weights associated with a particular Pareto optimal allocation (perhaps a Walrasian equilibrium), we can view the latter as the welfare optimum in a certain single-consumer, single-firm economy. To see this, let $(x^*, y^*)$ be a Pareto optimal allocation and suppose that $\lambda = (\lambda_1, \ldots, \lambda_I) \gg 0$ is a vector of welfare weights supporting $U$ at $(u_1(x_1^*), \ldots, u_I(x_I^*))$. Define then a utility function $u_\lambda(\bar{x})$ on aggregate consumption vectors in $X = \sum_i X_i \subset \mathbb{R}^L$ by

$$u_\lambda(\bar{x}) = \underset{(x_1, \ldots, x_I)}{\text{Max}} \sum_i \lambda_i u_i(x_i) \tag{16.E.2}$$

$$\text{s.t. } x_i \in X_i \text{ for all } i \text{ and } \sum_i x_i = \bar{x}.$$

The utility function $u_\lambda(\cdot)$ is the (direct) utility function of a normative representative consumer in the sense discussed in Section 4.D (see, in particular, Exercise 4.D.4). Letting $Y = \sum_j Y_j$ be the aggregate production set, the pair $(\sum_i x_i^*, \sum_j y_j^*)$ is then a solution to the problem

$$\text{Max } u_\lambda(\bar{x})$$

$$\text{s.t. } \bar{x} = \bar{\omega} + \bar{y}, \ \bar{x} \in X, \ \bar{y} \in Y.$$

This solution is depicted in Figure 16.E.4.

It is important to emphasize, however, that the particular utility function chosen for the representative consumer depends on the weights $(\lambda_1, \ldots, \lambda_I)$ and therefore on the Pareto optimal allocation under consideration.

---

# 16.F First-Order Conditions for Pareto Optimality

This section intends to be pedagogical. The emphasis is not on minimal assumptions, and its pace is deliberately slow. Making differentiability assumptions, we show how prices and the optimality properties of price-taking behavior emerge naturally from an examination of the first-order conditions associated with Pareto optimality problems. Along the way we redo, and in some aspects also generalize, the analysis in Sections 16.C and 16.D on the two fundamental welfare theorems.[16]

---

16. Early contributions along the line of the discussion in this section are Allais (1953), Lange (1942), and Samuelson (1947).

To begin with, we assume that the consumption set of every consumer is $\mathbb{R}^L_+$ and that preferences are represented by utility functions $u_i(x_i)$ that are twice continuously differentiable and satisfy $\nabla u_i(x_i) \gg 0$ at all $x_i$ (hence, preferences are strongly monotone). We also normalize so that $u_i(0) = 0$.

The production set of firm $j$ takes the form $Y_j = \{y \in \mathbb{R}^L : F_j(y) \le 0\}$, where $F_j(y) = 0$ defines firm $j$'s transformation frontier. We assume that $F_j : \mathbb{R}^L \to \mathbb{R}$ is twice continuously differentiable, that $F_j(0) \le 0$, and that $\nabla F_j(y_j) = (\partial F_j(y_j)/\partial y_{1j}, \ldots, \partial F_j(y_j)/\partial y_{Lj}) \gg 0$ for all $y_j \in \mathbb{R}^L$. The meaning of the last condition is that if $F_j(y_j) = 0$, so that $y_j$ is in the transformation frontier of $Y_j$, then any attempt to produce more of some output or use less of some input makes the value of $F_j(\cdot)$ positive and pushes us out of $Y_j$ (in other words, $y_j$ is production efficient, in the sense discussed in Section 5.F, in the production set $Y_j$).[17]

Note that, for the moment, no convexity assumptions have been made on preferences or production sets.

The problem of identifying the Pareto optimal allocations for this economy can be reduced to the selection of allocations

$$(x, y) = (x_1, \ldots, x_I, y_1, \ldots, y_J) \in \mathbb{R}^{LI}_+ \times \mathbb{R}^{LJ}$$

that solve the following problem:

$$\text{Max} \quad u_1(x_{11}, \ldots, x_{L1}) \tag{16.F.1}$$
$$\text{s.t. (1)} \quad u_i(x_{1i}, \ldots, x_{Li}) \ge \bar{u}_i \qquad i = 2, \ldots, I$$
$$(2) \quad \sum_i x_{\ell i} \le \bar{\omega}_\ell + \sum_j y_{\ell j} \qquad \ell = 1, \ldots, L$$
$$(3) \quad F_j(y_{1j}, \ldots, y_{Lj}) \le 0 \qquad j = 1, \ldots, J.$$

Problem (16.F.1) states the Pareto optimality problem as one of trying to maximize the well-being of consumer 1 subject to meeting certain required utility levels for the other consumers in the economy [constraints (1)] and the resource and technological limitations on what is feasible [constraints (2) and (3), respectively]. By solving problem (16.F.1) for varying required levels of utility for these other consumers $(\bar{u}_2, \ldots, \bar{u}_I)$, we can identify all the Pareto optimal allocations for this economy. Indeed, you should pause to convince yourself of this by solving Exercise 16.F.1.

**Exercise 16.F.1:** Show that any allocation that is a solution to problem (16.F.1) is Pareto optimal and that any Pareto optimal allocation for this economy must be a solution to problem (16.F.1) for *some* choice of utility levels $(\bar{u}_2, \ldots, \bar{u}_I)$. [*Hint:* Use the fact that preferences are strongly monotone.]

Because utility functions are normalized to take nonnegative values, from now on we consider only required utility levels that satisfy $\bar{u}_i \ge 0$ for all $i$.

The point of Exercise 16.F.1 can be seen by examining the utility possibility set $U$ in Figure 16.F.1. If we fix a required nonnegative utility level for consumer 2, we can locate a point on the frontier of the utility possibility set $U$ by maximizing

17. For expositional convenience, we have taken every $F_j(\cdot)$ to be defined on the entire $\mathbb{R}^L$. A consequence of this (and the assumption that $\nabla F_j(y_j) \gg 0$ for all $y_j$) is that every commodity is both an input and an output of the production process. Because this is unrealistic, we emphasize that no more than expositional ease is involved here.

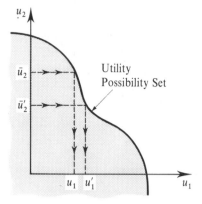

**Figure 16.F.1**

Parameterizing the frontier of the utility possibility set when $I = 2$ by the required utility level of consumer 2.

consumer 1's utility subject to the required utility constraint for consumer 2. By varying 2's required utility level, we trace out the set of Pareto optimal points.

Under our assumptions (recall that $\bar{u}_i \geq 0$ for $i \geq 2$), all the constraints of problem (16.F.1) will be binding at a solution. Denote by $(\delta_2, \ldots, \delta_I) \geq 0$, $(\mu_1, \ldots, \mu_L) \geq 0$, and $(\gamma_1, \ldots, \gamma_J) \geq 0$ the multipliers associated with the constraints (1), (2), and (3) of problem (16.F.1), respectively, and define $\delta_1 = 1$. In Exercise 16.F.2, you are asked to verify that the first-order (Kuhn–Tucker) necessary conditions for problem (16.F.1) can be written as follows (all the derivatives, here and elsewhere in this section, are evaluated at the solution):[18]

$$x_{\ell i}: \quad \delta_i \frac{\partial u_i}{\partial x_{\ell i}} - \mu_\ell \begin{cases} \leq 0 \\ = 0 \text{ if } x_{\ell i} > 0 \end{cases} \qquad \text{for all } i, \ell, \qquad (16.F.2)$$

$$y_{\ell j}: \quad \mu_\ell - \gamma_j \frac{\partial F_j}{\partial y_{\ell j}} = 0 \qquad \text{for all } j, \ell. \qquad (16.F.3)$$

As is well known from Kuhn–Tucker theory (see Section M.K of the Mathematical Appendix), the value of the multiplier $\mu_\ell$ at an optimal solution is exactly equal to the increase in consumer 1's utility derived from a relaxation of the corresponding constraint, that is, from a marginal increase in the available social endowment $\bar{\omega}_\ell$ of good $\ell$. Thus, the multiplier $\mu_\ell$ can be interpreted as the marginal value or "shadow price" (in terms of consumer 1's utility) of good $\ell$. The multiplier $\delta_i$, on the other hand, equals the marginal change in consumer 1's utility if we decrease the utility requirement $\bar{u}_i$ that must be met for consumer $i \neq 1$. Condition (16.F.2) therefore says that, at an optimal interior allocation, the increase in the utility of any consumer $i$ from receiving an additional unit of good $\ell$, weighted (if $i \neq 1$) by the amount that relaxing consumer $i$'s utility constraint is worth in terms of raising consumer 1's utility, should be equal to the marginal value $\mu_\ell$ of good $\ell$.

Similarly, the multiplier $\gamma_j$ can be interpreted as the marginal benefit from relaxing the $j$th production constraint or, equivalently, the marginal cost from tightening it.

---

18. Recall that for expositional ease we are not imposing any boundary constraints on the vectors $y_j$. We note also that the assumption of strictly positive gradients of the functions $u_i(\cdot)$ and $F_j(\cdot)$ implies that the constraint qualification for the necessity of the Kuhn–Tucker conditions is satisfied. (See Section M.K of the Mathematical Appendix for the specifics of first-order conditions for optimization problems under constraints.)

Hence, $\gamma_j(\partial F_j/\partial y_{\ell j})$ is the marginal cost of increasing $y_{\ell j}$ and thereby effectively tightening the constraint on the net outputs of the other goods. Condition (16.F.3) says, then, that at an optimum this marginal cost is equated, for every $j$, to the marginal benefit $\mu_\ell$ of good $\ell$.

If we suppose that we have an interior solution (i.e., $x_i \gg 0$ for all $i$), then conditions (16.F.2) and (16.F.3) imply that three types of ratio conditions must hold (see Exercise 16.F.3):

$$\frac{\partial u_i/\partial x_{\ell i}}{\partial u_i/\partial x_{\ell' i}} = \frac{\partial u_{i'}/\partial x_{\ell i'}}{\partial u_{i'}/\partial x_{\ell' i'}} \qquad \text{for all } i, i', \ell, \ell'. \qquad (16.F.4)$$

$$\frac{\partial F_j/\partial y_{\ell j}}{\partial F_j/\partial y_{\ell' j}} = \frac{\partial F_{j'}/\partial y_{\ell j'}}{\partial F_{j'}/\partial y_{\ell' j'}} \qquad \text{for all } j, j', \ell, \ell'. \qquad (16.F.5)$$

$$\frac{\partial u_i/\partial x_{\ell i}}{\partial u_i/\partial x_{\ell' i}} = \frac{\partial F_j/\partial y_{\ell j}}{\partial F_j/\partial y_{\ell' j}} \qquad \text{for all } i, j, \ell, \ell'. \qquad (16.F.6)$$

Condition (16.F.4) says that in any Pareto optimal allocation, all consumers' marginal rates of substitution between every pair of goods must be equalized [see Figures 15.B.11(b) and 15.B.12 for an illustration in the two-good, two-consumer case]; condition (16.F.5) says that all firms' marginal rates of transformation between every pair of goods must be equalized [see Figure 15.D.2(b) for an illustration in the two-good, two-firm case]; and condition (16.D.6) says that every consumer's marginal rate of substitution must equal every firm's marginal rate of transformation for all pairs of goods [see Figure 15.C.2 for an illustration in the case of the one-consumer, one-firm model with two goods].

---

Conditions (16.F.4) to (16.F.6) correspond to three types of efficiency embodied in a Pareto optimal allocation (see Exercise 16.F.4).

(i) *Optimal allocation of available goods across consumers.* Given some aggregate amounts $(\bar{x}_1, \ldots, \bar{x}_L)$ of goods available for consumption purposes, we want to distribute them to maximize consumer 1's well-being while meeting the utility requirements $(\bar{u}_2, \ldots, \bar{u}_I)$ for consumers $2, \ldots, I$. That is, we want to solve

$$\begin{aligned} \underset{(x_1, \ldots, x_I)}{\text{Max}} \quad & u_1(x_{11}, \ldots, x_{L1}) & (16.F.7) \\ \text{s.t. (1) } & u_i(x_{1i}, \ldots, x_{Li}) \geq \bar{u}_i & i = 2, \ldots, I \\ (2) \ & \textstyle\sum_i x_{\ell i} \leq \bar{x}_\ell & \ell = 1, \ldots, L. \end{aligned}$$

The first-order conditions for this problem lead to condition (16.F.4).

(ii) *Efficient production across technologies.* The aggregate production vector should be *efficient* in the sense discussed in Section 5.F. That is, it should be impossible to reassign production plans across individual production sets so as to produce, in the aggregate, more of a particular output (or use less of it as an input) without producing less of another. Focusing, in particular, on the first good, this means that given required total productions $(\bar{y}_2, \ldots, \bar{y}_L)$ of the other goods, we want to solve

$$\begin{aligned} \underset{(y_1, \ldots, y_J)}{\text{Max}} \quad & \textstyle\sum_j y_{1j} & (16.F.8) \\ \text{s.t. (1) } & \textstyle\sum_j y_{\ell j} \geq \bar{y}_\ell & \ell = 2, \ldots, L \\ (2) \ & F_j(y_j) \leq 0 & j = 1, \ldots, J. \end{aligned}$$

The first-order conditions for this problem lead to condition (16.F.5).

(iii) *Optimal aggregate production levels.* We also must have picked aggregate production levels that generate a desirable assortment of commodities available for consumption. Keeping the utility requirements $(\bar{u}_2, \dots, \bar{u}_I)$ fixed, let $u(\bar{x}_1, \dots, \bar{x}_L)$ and $f(\bar{y}_2, \dots, \bar{y}_L)$ denote, respectively, the value functions for problems (16.F.7) and (16.F.8). Then we want to solve

$$\underset{(\bar{y}_1, \dots, \bar{y}_L)}{\text{Max}} \quad u(\bar{\omega}_1 + \bar{y}_1, \dots, \bar{\omega}_L + \bar{y}_L) \tag{16.F.9}$$
$$\text{s.t. } \bar{y}_1 \leq f(\bar{y}_2, \dots, \bar{y}_L).$$

The first-order conditions of this problem lead to condition (16.F.6).

---

To explore the relationship of the first-order conditions (16.F.2) and (16.F.3) to the first and second welfare theorems, we make the further, and substantive, assumption that every $u_i(\cdot)$ is a quasiconcave function (hence, preferences are convex) and that every $F_j(\cdot)$ is a convex function (hence, production sets are convex). The virtue of this assumption is that with it we do not have to worry about second-order conditions; in all the maximization problems to be considered, the first-order necessary conditions are automatically sufficient.

In this differentiable, convex framework, conditions (16.F.2) and (16.F.3) can be used to establish a version of the two welfare theorems. To see this, note first that $(x^*, y^*, p)$ is a price equilibrium with transfers (with associated wealth levels $w_i = p \cdot x_i^*$ for $i = 1, \dots, I$) if and only if the first-order conditions for the budget-constrained utility maximization problems

$$\underset{x_i \geq 0}{\text{Max}} \quad u_i(x_i)$$
$$\text{s.t. } p \cdot x_i \leq w_i$$

and the profit maximization problems

$$\underset{y_j}{\text{Max}} \quad p \cdot y_j$$
$$\text{s.t. } F_j(y_j) \leq 0$$

are satisfied. Denoting by $\alpha_i$ and $\beta_j$ the respective multipliers for the constraints of these problems, the first-order conditions [evaluated at $(x^*, y^*)$] can be written as follows:

$$x_{\ell i}: \quad \frac{\partial u_i}{\partial x_{\ell i}} - \alpha_i p_\ell \begin{cases} \leq 0 \\ = 0 \text{ if } x_{\ell i} > 0 \end{cases} \qquad \text{for all } i, \ell, \tag{16.F.10}$$

$$y_{\ell j}: \quad p_\ell - \beta_j \frac{\partial F_j}{\partial y_{\ell j}} = 0 \qquad \text{for all } i, \ell. \tag{16.F.11}$$

Letting $\mu_\ell = p_\ell$, $\delta_i = 1/\alpha_i$, and $\gamma_j = \beta_j$, we see that there is an exact correspondence between conditions (16.F.2)–(16.F.3) and (16.F.10)–(16.F.11). Since both sets of conditions are necessary and sufficient for their respective problems, this implies that the allocation $(x^*, y^*)$ is Pareto optimal if and only if it is a price equilibrium with transfers with respect to some price vector $p = (p_1, \dots, p_L)$. Note, moreover, that the equilibrium price $p_\ell$ exactly equals $\mu_\ell$, the marginal value of good $\ell$ in the Pareto optimality problem.

Suppose that, in addition, every $u_i(\cdot)$ is concave. Then it is also instructive to examine the marginal conditions for the maximization of a linear social welfare function (see Section 16.E). Consider the problem

$$\underset{x,y}{\text{Max}} \quad \sum_i \lambda_i u_i(x_{1i}, \ldots, x_{Li}) \tag{16.F.12}$$

$$\text{s.t. (1)} \quad \sum_i x_{\ell i} \leq \bar{\omega}_\ell + \sum_j y_{\ell j} \qquad \ell = 1, \ldots, L$$

$$\text{(2)} \quad F_j(y_{1j}, \ldots, y_{Lj}) \leq 0 \qquad j = 1, \ldots, J.$$

where $\lambda_i > 0$ for all $i$. Letting $(\psi_1, \ldots, \psi_L)$ and $(\eta_1, \ldots, \eta_J)$ denote the multipliers on constraints (1) and (2), respectively, the necessary and sufficient first-order conditions for this problem can be written as follows:

$$x_{\ell i}: \quad \lambda_i \frac{\partial u_i}{\partial x_{\ell i}} - \psi_\ell \begin{cases} \leq 0 \\ = 0 \text{ if } x_{\ell i} > 0 \end{cases} \qquad \text{for all } i, \ell, \tag{16.F.13}$$

$$y_{\ell j}: \quad \psi_\ell - \eta_j \frac{\partial F_j}{\partial y_{\ell j}} = 0 \qquad \text{for all } j, \ell. \tag{16.F.14}$$

Note that by letting $\delta_1 = \lambda_i//\lambda_1, \mu_\ell = \psi_\ell/\lambda_1$, and $\gamma_j = \eta_j/\lambda_1$, we have an exact correspondence between (16.F.2)–(16.F.3) and (16.F.13)–(16.F.14). Therefore, any solution to (16.F.13) and (16.F.14) is a solution to (16.F.2) and (16.F.3) and, hence, a Pareto optimum.[19] Conversely, any Pareto optimum that for some multipliers satisfies (16.F.2) and (16.F.3) is also a solution of (16.F.13) and (16.F.14), and consequently of problem (16.F.12), for an appropriate choice of $\lambda = (\lambda_1, \ldots, \lambda_I)$.

It is also enlightening to compare (16.F.13) and (16.F.14) with the first-order conditions (16.F.10) and (16.F.11) for the optimization problems associated with a price equilibrium with transfers. We get an exact correspondence between them by letting $p_\ell = \psi_\ell$, $\alpha_i = 1/\lambda_i$, and $\beta_j = \eta_j$. Once again, the price $p_\ell$ represents the marginal social value of good $\ell$. In addition, note that $\alpha_i$, which is the marginal utility of wealth for consumer $i$ at prices $p$ and wealth level $w_i = p \cdot x_i^*$, equals the reciprocal of $\lambda_i$. Hence, we can draw the conclusion presented in Proposition 16.F.1.

**Proposition 16.F.1:** Under the assumptions made about the economy [in particular, the concavity of every $u_i(\cdot)$ and the convexity of every $F_j(\cdot)$], every Pareto optimal allocation (and, hence, every price equilibrium with transfers) maximizes a weighted sum of utilities subject to the resource and technological constraints. Moreover, the weight $\lambda_i$ of the utility of the $i$th consumer equals the reciprocal of consumer $i$'s marginal utility of wealth evaluated at the supporting prices and imputed wealth.

# 16.G  Some Applications

In this section, we present some applications of the ideas covered in the previous sections of the chapter. We first discuss three examples that introduce particular interpretations of the commodity space. We then present an extension of the second welfare theorem that relies on a concept of *marginal cost pricing*.

---

19. Recall that by the concavity–convexity assumptions, (16.F.2)–(16.F.3) and (16.F.13)–(16.F.14) are necessary and sufficient conditions for their respective problems.

*Interpretations of the Commodity Space*

Up to now we have treated our commodities as abstractly defined objects. This has not been for formalism's sake, but to facilitate a wide applicability of the theory.

It is easy to think of the case in which commodities are distinct, physically tradeable real objects. But there are many other interesting possibilities. The theory presented in the previous sections has proven to be remarkably flexible and subtle in the interpretations that can be given to the commodities, consumption sets, preferences, and production sets.

Two important examples, *commodities contingent on the state of the world* and *dated commodities*, are discussed extensively in Chapters 19 and 20, respectively. For the sake of completeness, we devote a few words to contingent commodities in this section. We then briefly discuss two other examples: *occupational choice* and *public goods*.

**Example 16.G.1:** *Contingent Commodities.* An interesting use of artificial commodities appears in the area of general equilibrium under uncertainty. A full formal description is presented in Chapter 19, but the basic idea can be conveyed here. The usefulness of a commodity may depend on uncertain, external circumstances. For example, medical care is much more important if one is ill than if one is healthy. To ensure an efficient allocation of resources, we have to make sure not only that the right commodities are delivered to the right people but also that they are allocated under the right circumstances, that is, according to the realization of the uncertain external states. To model this type of resource allocation problem, we can use the concept of a *contingent commodity*. A commodity such as medical care can be subdivided into many different "artificial commodities," each of which has the interpretation "medical care is provided under circumstance $s$." For example, suppose that there are $I$ consumers in the economy, each of whom may turn out ex post to be either "sick" or "healthy." A consumer's need for medical care depends, of course, on her state of health. From an economy-wide perspective, there are then $2^I$ different states of nature, each corresponding to a different configuration of ill health across the population. We can therefore imagine $2^I$ different commodities called "medical care," one for each of these configurations. A consumer buying "medical care in state $s$" receives care when state $s$ occurs.[20]

One of the strengths of general equilibrium theory is its ability to deal easily with an arbitrary number of commodities. There are very few results that depend on the number of commodities, and none of them is of general interest. Therefore, even though it seems difficult to conceive of a very large number of markets for a very large number of contingent commodities, all the welfare propositions that we have developed turn out to be easily applicable to this uncertainty setting (to be sure, we are taking a theoretical, rather than a practical perspective here). In Chapter 19, we discuss these points in more detail. ∎

---

20. Thus, to purchase medical care when she is sick, the consumer actually buys a large number of different "contingent medical care commodities" (in fact, $2^{I-1}$ of them).

**Example 16.G.2:** *Occupational Choice* Suppose that every individual could, in principle, work either as a classics scholar or as an economics professor. But not all individuals are equally good at both things. A way to capture the different comparative advantage is to assume that for every individual $i$, there is an $\alpha_i \geq 0$ measuring how many "effective hours of economics professorial services" it takes to produce "an effective hour of classical scholarship." A relatively low $\alpha_i$ indicates comparative advantage in classical scholarship. Suppose also that every individual $i$ has an amount $\bar{T}_i$ of professorial hours that she can supply; we assume that 1 professorial hour can produce 1 effective hour of economics professorial services or $1/\alpha_i$ effective hours of classical scholarship by individual $i$. There is a single consumption good on which the individual $i$ can spend her earnings.

It is important to be able to imbed this problem in our formal structure because we certainly want to be able to analyze how, for example, competitive labor markets will perform when individuals have *occupational choices* as well as choices about *how much* labor to supply.

This is how it can be done (it is not the only possible way): suppose we list consumption and effective hours supplied as a three-dimensional vector $(c_i, t_{ci}, t_{ei})$, where $c_i$ is individual $i$'s consumption and $t_{ci} \leq 0$ and $t_{ei} \leq 0$ are the effective hours spent working as a classics scholar and as an economics professor, respectively. Because the latter two quantities are supplies—that is, services offered by the individual to the market—we follow the convention of measuring them as negative numbers. We can then define the consumption set of individual $i$ as

$$X_i = \{(c_i, t_{ci}, t_{ei}): c_i \geq 0, t_{ci} \leq 0, t_{ei} \leq 0, \bar{T}_i + t_{ei} + \alpha_i t_{ci} \geq 0\}.$$

One should interpret the nonpositivity constraints as the inability to consume labor services. The amount $\bar{T}_i + t_{ei} + \alpha_i t_{ci}$ is the time available for leisure activities. Preferences are defined on $X_i$. Because the consumption good is desirable, the local nonsatiation condition is satisfied. The assumption that preferences are continuous and convex is also natural. We can complete the model by having a concave production function $f(z_c, z_e)$ that transforms input combinations $(z_c, z_e)$ of effective hours of classics and economics scholarship, respectively, into the consumption good.

We now have a complete general equilibrium system to which we can pose a number of interesting questions: If the occupational choice is directed by a competitive (i.e., price-taking) market system, will the outcome result in an efficient exploitation of comparative advantage? Conversely, can every efficient arrangement of occupations be sustained by a market system (supplemented perhaps by lump-sum transfers)? The results of Sections 16.C and 16.D tell us that the answer to both questions is in the affirmative. ∎

**Example 16.G.3:** *Public Goods.* The notion of a "public good" and the more general concept of an "externality" were discussed in Chapter 11, where we also introduced the key idea of "personalized" prices.[21] Consequently, we can be rather brief here. (The basic references on public goods were also given in Chapter 11.)

---

21. In fact, the current discussion is more general than the one in Chapter 11 because there we restricted ourselves to a quasilinear setting.

Suppose there are $I$ consumers and two commodities; a "private" good, say labor, and a public good (the theory presented extends without essential modification to any number of private or public goods). A *private good* is like the goods discussed up to now: A unit of the good can be consumed only once, so if consumer $i$ consumes it then it is unavailable for consumption by others. We let $x_{1i}$ denote consumer $i$'s consumption of the private good. But in the case of a (pure) *public good*, its consumption by consumer $i$ does not prevent its availability to other consumers. Thus, if $x_2$ is the total amount of public good produced, then $x_2$ can be made available at no extra cost to *every* consumer.

We assume that every consumer $i$ has the consumption set $\mathbb{R}_+^2$ and continuous, convex, locally nonsatiated preferences $\succsim_i$ defined on pairs $(x_{1i}, x_2)$. The model is completed by having some amount $\bar{\omega}_1$ of the private good as the initial total endowment (there is no endowment of the public good) and a firm that transforms amounts $z \in \mathbb{R}_+$ of the private good into the public good by means of an increasing, concave production function $f(z)$.

An allocation $((x_{11}, \dots, x_{1I}, x_2), (q, z)) \geq 0$ is feasible if

$$q \leq f(z), \quad \sum_i x_{1i} + z = \bar{\omega}_1, \quad \text{and} \quad q = x_2.$$

It is Pareto optimal if there is no other feasible allocation $((x'_{11}, \dots, x'_{1I}, x'_2), (q', z'))$ such that $(x'_{1i}, x'_2) \succsim_i (x'_{1i}, x'_2)$ for all $i$ and $(x'_{1i}, x'_2) \succ_i (x'_{1i}, x'_2)$ for some $i$.

We now describe this model in an artificial but equivalent way, with the advantage, that, formally speaking, it reduces the public commodities to private ones and therefore makes the results of Sections 16.C and 16.D applicable. The "trick" is to define a personalized commodity $x_{2i}$ for every consumer $i$, to be interpreted as "commodity 2 as received by the $i$th consumer." Formally, consumer $i$ cares only about good 1 and the $i$th personalized commodity. We therefore denote her consumption bundle by $x_i = (x_{1i}, x_{2i})$. The single firm is now viewed as producing a *joint* bundle of personalized commodities with a technology that produces these commodities in fixed proportions. Formally, its (convex) production set is

$$Y = \{(-z, q_1, \dots, q_I) \in \mathbb{R}_+^{I+1} : z \geq 0 \text{ and } q_1 = \cdots = q_I = q \leq f(z)\}.$$

With this reinterpretation, the model fits into the structure analyzed throughout the chapter. A price equilibrium with transfers for this artificial economy is known as a *Lindahl equilibrium*.[22]

**Definition 16.G.1:** A *Lindahl equilibrium* for the public goods economy is a price equilibrium with transfers for the artificial economy with personalized commodities. That is, an allocation $(x_1^*, \dots, x_I^*, q^*, z^*) \in \mathbb{R}^{2I} \times \mathbb{R} \times \mathbb{R}$ and a price system $(p_1, p_{21}, \dots, p_{2I}) \in \mathbb{R}^{I+1}$ constitute a Lindahl equilibrium if there is a set of wealth levels $(w_1, \dots, w_I)$ satisfying $\sum_i w_i = \sum_i p_1 x_{1i}^* + (\sum_i p_{2i}) q^* - p_1 z^*$ and such that:

(i) $q^* \leq f(z^*)$ and $(\sum_i p_{2i}) q^* - p_1 z^* \geq (\sum_i p_{2i}) q - p_1 z$ for all $(q, z)$ with $z \geq 0$ and $q \leq f(z)$.

---

22. More properly, we should say a *Lindahl equilibrium with transfers*.

(ii) For every $i$, $x_i^* = (x_{1i}^*, x_{2i}^*)$ is maximal for $\succsim_i$ in the set $\{(x_{1i}, x_{2i}) \in X_i : p_1 x_{1i} + p_{2i} x_{2i} \leq w_i\}$.

(iii) $\sum_i x_{1i}^* + z^* = \bar{\omega}_1$ and $x_{2i}^* = q^*$ for every $i$.

The first and second fundamental welfare theorems tell us that every Lindahl equilibrium is Pareto optimal and every Pareto optimal allocation can be implemented using a Lindahl equilibrium (with appropriate wealth transfers and, perhaps, with the usual quasiequilibrium qualification).[23] There is an important caveat, however: unlike economies where with large numbers of agents each agent becomes small relative to the size of the market, in markets for personalized goods, each consumer is necessarily large with respect to the market in her personalized good. As we multiply the number of consumers, we also multiply, as a matter of definition, the number of commodities. As a result, it is very unlikely that the critical assumption of price taking will be satisfied. Thus, the descriptive content of this equilibrium concept is low.

Nevertheless, the second welfare theorem may still be of some interest. In particular, it tells us that *if* the planning authority has a means to enforce the prices, then we have a mechanism involving voluntary purchases of the public good that achieves the desired Pareto optimal allocation. Even for this purpose, however, further difficulties arise that are inherent to the public goods setting: First, to calculate the personalized supporting prices, statistical information (e.g. information on the distribution of preferences across the economy) will not do; the fact that prices are personalized means that personal, private information is required. This information may be difficult to get because individuals will often not have incentives to reveal this information truthfully (see Chapters 11 and 23 for more on this issue). Second, for a personalized market voluntary mechanism to work, individuals must expect to receive precisely the amount of public good they purchase. This requires that the public good be *excludable*; that is, there must be some procedure to deny total or partial use of the public good to anyone who does not pay for it. In many cases, such exclusion is difficult, if not impossible (consider, for example, national defense). ∎

### Nonconvex Production Technologies and Marginal Cost Pricing

The second welfare theorem runs into difficulties in the presence of nonconvex production sets (in this section, we do not question the assumption of convexity on the consumption side). In the first place, large nonconvexities caused by the presence of fixed costs or extensive increasing returns lead to a world of a small number of large firms (in the limit, production efficiency may require a single firm, a so-called "natural monopoly"), making the assumption of price taking less plausible. Yet, even

---

23. Suppose that the production function $f(\cdot)$ is differentiable and the indifference curves are smooth, and consider a Lindahl equilibrium that is interior. Then preference maximization implies that $p_{2i}/p_1 = -MRS_{21}^i$, where $MRS_{21}^i$ is consumer $i$'s marginal rate of substitution of good 2 for good 1. On the other hand, profit maximization entails $\sum_i p_{2i}/p_1 = -MRT_{21}$, where $MRT_{21}$ is the firm's marginal rate of transformation of good 2 for good 1 (the marginal cost of output in terms of input). Hence, in any Lindahl equilibrium, we must have $\sum_i MRS_{21}^i = MRT_{21}$, which is exactly the Samuelson optimality condition for a public good (see Section 11.G for its derivation in the case of quasilinear preferences).

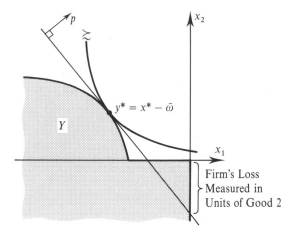

**Figure 16.G.1**

The firm incurs a loss at the prices that locally support the Pareto optimal allocation.

if price taking can somehow be relied on (perhaps because a planning authority can enforce prices), it may still be impossible to support a given Pareto optimal allocation. Examples are provided by Figures 15.C.3(a) and 16.G.1. In Figure 16.G.1, at the only relative prices that could support the production $y^*$ locally, the firm sustains a loss and would rather avoid it by shutting down. In Figure 15.C.3(a), on the other hand, not even local profit maximization can be guaranteed (see the discussion in Section 15.C).

Although nonconvexities may prevent us from supporting the Pareto optimal production allocation as a profit-maximizing choice, under the differentiability assumptions of Section 16.F we can use the first-order necessary conditions derived there to formulate a weaker result that parallels the second welfare theorem (see Exercise 16.G.1).

**Proposition 16.G.1:** Suppose that the basic assumptions of Section 16.F hold[24] and that, in addition, all consumers have convex preferences (so utility functions are quasiconcave). If $(x^*, y^*)$ is Pareto optimal, then there exists a price vector $p = (p_1, \ldots, p_L)$ and wealth levels $(w_1, \ldots, w_I)$ with $\sum_i w_i = p \cdot \bar{\omega} + \sum_j p \cdot y_j^*$ such that:

(i) For any firm $j$, we have

$$p = \gamma_j \nabla F_j(y_j^*) \quad \text{for some } \gamma_j > 0. \tag{16.G.1}$$

(ii) For any $i$, $x_i^*$ is maximal for $\succsim_i$ in the budget set

$$\{x_i \in X_i : p \cdot x_i \leq w_i\}.$$

(iii) $\sum_i x_i^* = \bar{\omega} + \sum_j y_j^*.$

The type of equilibrium represented by conditions (i) to (iii) of Proposition 16.G.1 is called a *marginal cost price equilibrium with transfers*. The motivation for this terminology comes from the one-output, one-input case.[25]

---

24. That is, the assumptions leading up to conditions (16.F.2) and (16.F.3).

25. We point out that for the general case, the term *marginal cost price equilibrium* is, strictly speaking, inappropriate. Exercise 16.G.3 explains why. However, the terminology is by now standard, and we retain it.

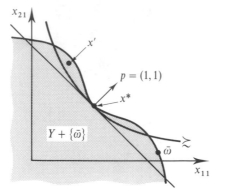

**Figure 16.G.2**

A marginal cost price equilibrium need not be Pareto optimal.

**Exercise 16.G.2:** Suppose there are only two goods: an input and an output. Show that in this case, condition (16.G.1) simply says that the price of the input must equal the price of the output multiplied by the marginal productivity of the input or, equivalently, that the price of the output equals its marginal cost.

As we have noted, condition (16.G.1) does *not* imply that the $(y_1^*, \ldots, y_J^*)$ are profit-maximizing production plans for price-taking firms. The condition says only that small changes in production plans have no first-order effect on profit. But small changes may still have positive second-order effects (as in Figure 15.C.3, where at a marginal cost price equilibrium the firm actually chooses the production that *minimizes* profits among the efficient productions) and, at any rate, large changes may increase profits (as in Figure 16.G.1). Thus, to achieve allocation $(x^*, y^*)$ may require that a regulatory agency prevent the managers of nonconvex firms from attempting to maximize profits at the given prices $p$.[26]

See Quinzii (1992) for extensive background and discussion on the material presented in this section.

---

It should be noted that the converse result to Proposition 16.G.1, which would assert that every marginal cost price equilibrium is Pareto optimal, is *not true*. In Figure 16.G.2, for example, we show a one-consumer economy with a nonconvex production set. In the figure, $x^*$ is a marginal cost price equilibrium with transfers for the price system $p = (1, 1)$. Yet, allocation $x'$ yields the consumer a higher utility. Informally, this occurs because marginal cost pricing neglects second-order conditions and it may therefore happen that, as at allocation $x^*$, the second-order conditions for the social utility maximization problem are not fulfilled. As a result, satisfaction of the first-order marginal optimality conditions (which in the case of Figure 16.G.2 amounts simply to the tangency of the indifference curve and the production surface) does not ensure that the allocaton is Pareto optimal. (See Exercise 16.G.4 for more on this topic.)

---

26. In the context of Figure 16.G.1, the regulator could reach the desired outcome by merely prohibiting the firm from shutting down and otherwise letting it maximize profits at the "supporting" prices (assuming that the firm will act as a price taker; otherwise, the regulator may also need to enforce those prices).

## APPENDIX A: TECHNICAL PROPERTIES OF THE SET OF FEASIBLE ALLOCATIONS

The set of feasible allocations is

$$A = \{(x_1, \ldots, x_I, y_1, \ldots, y_J) \in X_1 \times \cdots \times X_I \times Y_1 \times \cdots \times Y_J : \sum_i x_i = \bar{\omega} + \sum_j y_j\}$$
$$\subset \mathbb{R}^{LI} \times \mathbb{R}^{LJ}.$$

Our economic problem would not be very interesting if there were no feasible allocations for the economy or if we could give every consumer an unboundedly large consumption vector. We might therefore simply assume that $A$ is nonempty, bounded, and, for good measure, closed (i.e., nonempty and compact). In Chapter 17, where this technical point becomes important for the study of the existence of Walrasian equilibria, we assume exactly this. Nonetheless, it is useful to give, once and for all, a set of sufficient conditions for these very basic properties to hold.

**Proposition 16.AA.1:** Suppose that
  (i) Every $X_i$:
     (i.1) is closed;
     (i.2) is bounded below (i.e., there is $r > 0$ such that $x_{\ell i} > -r$ for every $\ell$ and $i$; in words, no consumer can supply to the market an arbitrarily large amount of any good).
  (ii) Every $Y_j$ is closed. Moreover, the aggregate production set $Y = \sum_j Y_j$:[27]
     (ii.1) is convex:
     (ii.2) admits the possibility of inaction (i.e., $0 \in Y$):
     (ii.3) satisfies the no-free-lunch property (i.e., $y \geq 0$ and $y \in Y$ implies $y = 0$):
     (ii.4) is irreversible ($y \in Y$ and $-y \in Y$ implies $y = 0$).

Then the set of feasible allocations $A$ is closed and bounded [i.e., there is $r > 0$ such that $|x_{\ell i}| < r$ and $|y_{\ell j}| < r$ for all $i$, $j$, $\ell$ and any $(x, y) \in A$]. If, moreover, $-\mathbb{R}_+^L \subset Y$ and we can choose $\hat{x}_i \in X_i$ for every $i$ in such a manner that $\sum_i \hat{x}_i \leq \bar{\omega}$, then $A$ is nonempty.

**Proof:** The proof of this proposition is rather technical, and we shall not give it. Nonetheless, we shall say a few words regarding the logic of the result.

The nonemptiness part is clear enough because we have $\hat{x}_i \in X_i$ for every $i$ and $\sum_i \hat{x}_i - \bar{\omega} \in -\mathbb{R}_+^L \subset Y$. Thus, an allocation with individual consumptions $(\hat{x}_1, \ldots, \hat{x}_I)$ and aggregate production vector $\sum_i \hat{x}_i - \bar{\omega}$ is feasible.

Similarly, the closedness of $A$ is a direct consequence of the closedness assumptions on the consumption and production sets (see Exercise 16.AA.1).

What remains is to show that $A$ is bounded. To gain some understanding, suppose that $J = 1$ and $X_i = \mathbb{R}_+^L$ for every $i$ (as long as every $X_i$ is bounded below, the argument for general consumption sets is similar). In Figure 16.AA.1, we represent the set of feasible aggregate consumption bundles $(Y + \{\bar{\omega}\}) \cap \mathbb{R}_+^L$, that is, the set of nonnegative vectors obtained when the origin of $Y$ is shifted to $\bar{\omega} \geq 0$. It is intuitive from the figure that this set can be unbounded above only if $Y$ contains nonnegative, nonzero vectors and so violates the no-free-lunch condition.

---

27. See Section 5.B for a discussion of conditions (ii.1) to (ii.4).

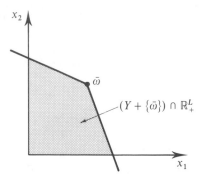

**Figure 16.AA.1**

The set of feasible aggregate consumption vectors is compact.

You should verify, however, that this intuition also depends on three facts: $0 \in Y$, $Y$ is closed, and $Y$ is convex (see Exercise 16.AA.2). Note now that if the set of feasible aggregate consumptions is bounded, then, a fortiori, so are the sets of feasible individual consumptions and the set of feasible productions (because $J = 1$, we get this set by subtracting $\bar{\omega}$ from each feasible aggregate consumption vector). Hence, $A$ is bounded.

The case with several production sets is more delicate, and it is here that the irreversibility assumption comes to the rescue. Very informally, we can derive, as in the preceding paragraph, the boundedness of feasible *aggregate* productions and feasible individual consumptions. Now, the only way that unboundedness would be possible at the individual production level while remaining bounded in the aggregate is if, so to speak, the unboundedness in one individual production plan was to be canceled by the unboundedness of another. However, this would imply that the collection of all technologies in the economy (i.e., the aggregate production set) allows the reversal of some technologies (see Exercise 16.AA.3 for more details). Incidentally, it can also be shown that irreversibility, with the other assumptions, yields the closedness of $Y$, so we do not actually need to assume this separately. ∎

Proposition 16.AA.2 gives an important implication of the compactness of the set of feasible allocations for the form of the utility possibility set.

**Proposition 16.AA.2:** Suppose that the set of feasible allocations $A$ is nonempty, closed, and bounded and that utility functions $u_i(\cdot)$ are continuous. Then the utility possibility set $U$ is closed and bounded above.

**Proof:** Note that $U = U' - \mathbb{R}_+^L$ where

$$U' = \{(u_1(x_1), \ldots, u_I(x_I)): (x, y) \in A\} \subset \mathbb{R}^L.$$

Thus, $U'$ is the image of the compact set $A$ under a continuous function and is therefore itself a compact set (see Section M.F of the Mathematical Appendix). From this, the closedness and the boundedness above of $U = U' - \mathbb{R}_+^L$ follow directly. ∎

**REFERENCES**

Allais, M. (1953). *Traité d'économie pure*. Paris: Publications du CNRS.
Arrow, K., and F. Hahn. (1971). *General Competitive Analysis*. San Francisco: Holden-Day.
Debreu, G. (1959). *Theory of Value*. New York: Wiley.

Koopmans, T. (1957). *Three Essays on the State of Economic Science*. New York: McGraw-Hill.

Lange, O. (1942). The foundation of welfare economics. *Econometrica* 10: 215–228.

Quinzii, M. (1992). *Increasing Returns and Efficiency*. New York: Oxford University Press.

Samuelson, P. (1947). *Foundations of Economic Analysis*. Cambridge, Mass.: Harvard University Press.

## EXERCISES

**16.C.1$^B$** Show that if a consumption set $X_i \subset \mathbb{R}^L$ is nonempty, closed, and bounded and the preference relation $\succsim_i$ on $X_i$ is continuous, then $\succsim_i$ cannot be locally nonsatiated. [*Hint*: Show that the continuous utility function representing $\succsim_i$ must have a maximum of $X_i$; see Section M.F of the Mathematical Appendix on this.]

**16.C.2$^A$** Suppose that the preference relation $\succsim_i$ is locally nonsatiated and that $x_i^*$ is maximal for $\succsim_i$ in set $\{x_i \in X_i : p \cdot x_i \leq w_i\}$. Prove that the following property holds: "If $x_i \succsim_i x_i^*$ then $p \cdot x_i \geq w_i$."

**16.C.3$^B$** In this exercise you are asked to establish the first welfare theorem under a set of assumptions compatible with satiation. Suppose that every $X_i$ is nonempty and convex and that every $\succsim_i$ is strictly convex (i.e., if $x_i' \succsim_i x_i$ and $x_i' \neq x_i$ then $\alpha x_i' + (1 - \alpha) x_i \succ_i x_i$ whenever $0 < \alpha < 1$). Prove the following:

**(a)** Every $i$ can have at most one global satiation point and preferences are locally nonsatiated at any consumption bundle different from the single global satiation point.

**(b)** Any price equilibrium with transfers is a Pareto optimum.

**16.C.4$^A$** Suppose that for each individual there is a "pleasure function" depending on her own consumption only, given by $u_i(x_i)$. Every individual's utility depends positively on her own and everyone else's "pleasure" according to the utility function

$$U_i(x_1, \ldots, x_I) = U_i(u_1(x_1), u_2(x_2), \ldots, u_I(x_I)).$$

Show that if $x = (x_1, \ldots, x_I)$ is Pareto optimal relative to the $U_i(\cdot)$'s, then $(x_1, \ldots, x_I)$ is also a Pareto optimum relative to the $u_i$'s. Does this mean that a community of altruists can use competitive markets to attain Pareto optima? Does your argument depend on the concavity of the $u_i$'s, or the $U_i$'s?

**16.D.1$^A$** Prove that if preferences are locally nonsatiated then the condition: "if $x_i \succ_i x_i^*$ then $p \cdot x_i \geq p \cdot x_i^*$" is equivalent to the condition: "$x_i^*$ is expenditure minimizing for the price vector $p$ in the set $\{x_i \in X_i : x_i \succsim_i x_i^*\}$."

**16.D.2$^B$** Exhibit a one-firm, one-consumer economy in which the production set is convex, the preference relation is continuous and convex, and there is nevertheless a Pareto optimal allocation that can be supported neither as a price equilibrium with transfers nor as a price quasiequilibrium with transfers. Which condition of Proposition 16.D.1 fails?

**16.D.3$^B$** Suppose that we have an economy with continuous and strongly monotone preferences (consumption sets are $X_i = \mathbb{R}_+^L$). Suppose also that a strictly positive production is possible; that is, there are $y_j \in Y_j$ such that $\sum_j y_j + \bar{\omega} \gg 0$. Prove that any price quasiequilibrium with transfers must be a price equilibrium with transfers. [*Hint*: Show first that $w_i > 0$ for some $i$ and then argue that $p \gg 0$.]

**16.D.4$^C$** Consider a two-good exchange economy with $r$ identical consumers. The consumption set is $\mathbb{R}_+^2$, the individual endowments are $\omega \in \mathbb{R}_{++}^2$, and the preferences are continuous and strongly monotone but not necessarily convex. Argue that the symmetric allocation in which every consumer gets her initial allocation is either a Walrasian equilibrium (for some price vector $p$) or, if it is not, then for $r$ large enough it is not a Pareto optimum. [*Hint*: the differentiable case is simpler.]

**16.E.1**[B] Given a utility possibility set $U$, denote by $U' \subset U$ the subset actually achieved by feasible allocations:

$$U' = \{(u_1(x_1), \ldots, u_I(x_I)): \textstyle\sum_i x_i = \sum_j y_j + \bar{\omega} \text{ for some } y_j \in Y_j\}.$$

(Relative to $U'$, the set $U$ allows for free disposal of utility).

**(a)** Give a two-consumer, two-commodity exchange example showing that it is possible for a point of $U'$ to belong to the boundary of $U$ and *not* be a Pareto optimum.

**(b)** Suppose that every $Y_j$ satisfies free disposal and $0 \in Y_j$. Also, assume that for every $i$, $X_i = \mathbb{R}_+^I$ and $\succsim_i$ is continuous and strongly monotone. Show that any boundary point of $U$ that belongs to $U'$ is then a Pareto optimum. [*Hint*: Let $u_i(0) = 0$ for all $i$ and show first that $U' = U \cap \mathbb{R}_+^L$. Next argue that if $u \in U$ is a Pareto optimum and $0 \leq u' \leq u$, $u' \neq u$, then we must be able to reach $u'$ with a surplus of goods relative to $u$.]

**(c)** Consider an exchange economy with consumption sets equal to $\mathbb{R}_+^L$, continuous, locally nonsatiated preferences, and a strictly positive total endowment vector. Show that if $u = (u_1, \ldots, u_I)$ is the utility vector corresponding to a price quasiequilibrium with transfers then $u$ cannot be in the interior of $U$; that is, there is no feasible allocation yielding higher utility to *every* consumer. [*Hint*: Show that $w_i > 0$ for some $i$ and then apply Proposition 16.D.2.]

**16.E.2**[B] Show that the utility possibility set $U$ of an economy with convex production and consumption sets and with concave utility functions is convex.

**16.F.1**[B] In text.

**16.F.2**[A] Derive the first-order conditions (16.F.2) and (16.F.3) of the maximization problem (16.F.1).

**16.F.3**[A] Derive conditions (16.F.4), (16.F.5), and (16.F.6) from the first-order conditions (16.F.2) and (16.F.3).

**16.F.4**[A] Derive the first-order conditions (16.F.4), (16.F.5), and (16.F.6) from problems (16.F.7), (16.F.8), and (16.F.9), respectively.

**16.G.1**[A] Prove Proposition 16.G.1 using the first-order conditions (16.F.2) and (16.F.3).

**16.G.2**[A] In text.

**16.G.3**[B] Exhibit graphically a one-consumer, one-firm economy with two inputs and one output where at the (unique) marginal cost price equilibrium, cost is *not* minimized. [*Hint*: Choose the production function to violate quasiconcavity.]

**16.G.4**[B] Show that under the general conditions of Section 16.G if there is a single consumer (perhaps a normative representative consumer) with convex preferences, then there exists at least one marginal cost price equilibrium that is an optimum.

**16.G.5**[B] In a certain economy there are two commodities, education ($e$) and food ($f$), produced by using labor ($L$) and land ($T$) according to the production functions

$$e = (\text{Min } \{L, T\})^2 \quad \text{and} \quad f = (LT)^{1/2}$$

There is a single consumer with the utility function

$$u(e, f) = e^{\alpha} f^{(1-\alpha)},$$

and endowment $(\omega_L, \omega_T)$. To ease the calculations, take $\omega_L = \omega_T = 1$ and $\alpha = \frac{1}{2}$.

**(a)** Find the optimal allocation of the endowments to their productive uses.

**(b)** Recognizing that the production of education entails increasing returns to scale, the government of this economy decides to control the education industry and finance its operation with a lump-sum tax on the consumer. The consumption of education is competitive in the sense that the consumer can choose any amount of education and food desired at the going prices. The food industry remains competitive in both its production and consumption aspects. Assuming that the education industry minimizes cost, find the marginal cost of education at the optimum. Show that if this price of education were announced, together with a lump-sum tax to finance the deficit incurred when the education sector produces the optimal amount at this price for its product, then the consumer's choice of education will be at the optimal level.

**(c)** What is the level of the lump-sum tax necessary to decentralize this optimum in the manner described in **(b)**?

Now suppose there are two consumers and that their preferences are identical to those above. One owns all of the land and the other owns all of the labor. In this society, arbitrary lump-sum taxes are not possible. It is the law that any deficit incurred by a public enterprise must be covered by a tax on the value of land.

**(d)** In appropriate notation, write the transfer from the landowner as a function of the government's planned production of education.

**(e)** Find a marginal cost price equilibrium for this economy where transfers have to be compatible with the transfer function specified in **(d)**. Is it Pareto optimal?

**16.AA.1**[A] Show that if every $X_i$ and every $Y_j$ is closed, then the set $A$ of feasible allocations is closed.

**16.AA.2**[B] Show that $(Y + \{\bar{\omega}\}) \cap \mathbb{R}_+^L$ is compact if the following four assumptions are satisfied: (i) $Y$ is closed, (ii) $Y$ is convex, (iii) $0 \in Y$, and (iv) if $v \in Y \cap \mathbb{R}_+^L$ then $v = 0$. Exhibit graphically four examples showing that each of the four assumptions is indispensable.

**16.AA.3**[B] Suppose that $Y = Y_1 + Y_2 \subset \mathbb{R}_+^L$ satisfies the assumptions given in Exercise 16.AA.2 and that $0 \in Y_1$, $0 \in Y_2$. Argue that if the irreversibility assumption holds for $Y$ then $\{y_1 \in Y_1 : y_1 + y_2 + \bar{\omega} \geq 0 \text{ for some } y_2 \in Y_2\}$ is bounded.

# The Positive Theory
# of Equilibrium

## 17.A Introduction

In this chapter, we study the theoretical predictive power of the Walrasian equilibrium model. Thus, in contrast with Chapter 16, our outlook here is positive rather than normative.

We begin in Section 17.B by laying the foundations for our analysis. We recall the basic model of a *private ownership economy* and the definition of a *Walrasian equilibrium* presented in Section 16.B. We then introduce the notion of an *aggregate excess demand function* and, in a framework of strong assumptions, we characterize Walrasian equilibria as solutions to a system of aggregate excess demand equations. The analysis of this system of equations serves throughout the chapter as our primary method for the study of Walrasian equilibria. (In Appendix A, we discuss another useful equation system based instead on the welfare properties of Walrasian equilibria.)

In Section 17.C (and with much more generality in Appendix B), we present conditions guaranteeing the existence of a Walrasian equilibrium. The identification of an interesting set of conditions ensuring existence assures us that the object of our study in this chapter is not vacuous. A key condition turns out to be the *convexity* of the decision problems of individual economic agents.

Sections 17.D to 17.H all deal with properties of the set of equilibria. Section 17.D reaches a general conclusion: typically (or in the usual terminology, *generically*), there is a finite number of equilibria, and each equilibrium is therefore "locally isolated." Even more, this number is odd, and the equilibria fall naturally into two categories according to the sign of their "index." Section 17.E brings bad news: without further assumptions on the nature of preferences, endowments, or technologies, we cannot say anything more; the behavior of excess demand functions and hence the properties of Walrasian equilibria are not restricted in any manner that goes beyond the facts established in Section 17.D. This negative message reverberates in Section 17.F on uniqueness, Section 17.G on comparative statics, and Section 17.H on (tâtonnement) stability. The purpose of these three sections is precisely to find interesting sufficient conditions for, respectively, the uniqueness of equilibria, good comparative statics properties, and the stability of equilibria. A common theme of the three sections is the role of two sufficient conditions: the *weak axiom of revealed preference in the aggregate* (a way of saying that wealth effects do not cancel in the aggregate the positive influence of the substitution effects), and the property of *gross substitution* (a way of saying that there are not strong complementarities among the goods in the economy).

In Section 17.I, we return to the role of convexity in guaranteeing the existence of Walrasian equilibrium. We qualify this role by showing that nonconvexities that are "small" relative to the aggregate economy (e.g., the indivisibility represented by a car) are not an obstacle to the (near) existence of equilibria, even if they are "large" from the standpoint of an individual agent.

This chapter is of interest from both methodological and substantive points of view. From a substantive standpoint, it deals with an important theory: that of Walrasian equilibrium. Methodologically, the questions that we ask (e.g., does an equilibrium exist? Are the equilibria typically isolated? Is the equilibrium unique? Is it stable? What are the effects of shocks?) and the techniques that we use are questions and techniques that are of relevance to any theory of equilibrium.

# 17.B  Equilibrium: Definitions and Basic Equations

The concept of a private ownership economy was described in Section 16.B. In such an economy, there are $I$ consumers and $J$ firms. Every consumer $i$ is specified by a consumption set $X_i \subset \mathbb{R}^L$, a preference relation $\succsim_i$ on $X_i$, an initial endowment vector $\omega_i \in \mathbb{R}^L$, and an ownership share $\theta_{ij} \geq 0$ of each firm $j = 1, \ldots, J$ (where $\sum_i \theta_{ij} = 1$). Each firm $j$ is characterized by a production set $Y_j \subset \mathbb{R}^L$. An *allocation* for such an economy is a collection of consumption and production vectors:

$$(x, y) = (x_1, \ldots, x_I, y_1, \ldots, y_J) \in X_1 \times \cdots \times X_I \times Y_1 \times \cdots \times Y_J.$$

The object of investigation in this chapter is the notion of *Walrasian equilibrium*, which we take as a positive prediction for the outcome of a system of markets in which consumers and firms are price takers and the wealth of consumers derives from their initial endowments and profit shares. The formal notion of a Walrasian equilibrium was already introduced in Definition 16.B.3. Definition 17.B.1 repeats it.

**Definition 17.B.1:** Given a private ownership economy specified by

$$(\{(X_i, \succsim_i)\}_{i=1}^I, \{Y_j\}_{j=1}^J, \{(\omega_i, \theta_{i1}, \ldots, \theta_{iJ})\}_{i=1}^I),$$

an allocation $(x^*, y^*)$ and a price vector $p = (p_1, \ldots, p_L)$ constitute a *Walrasian* (or *competitive*, or *market*, or *price-taking*) equilibrium if

(i) For every $j$, $y_j^* \in Y_j$ maximizes profits in $Y_j$; that is,

$$p \cdot y_j \leq p \cdot y_j^* \quad \text{for all } y_j \in Y_j.$$

(ii) For every $i$, $x_i^* \in X_i$ is maximal for $\succsim_i$ in the budget set

$$\{x_i \in X_i : p \cdot x_i \leq p \cdot \omega_i + \sum_j \theta_{ij} p \cdot y_j^*\}.^1$$

(iii) $\sum_i x_i^* = \sum_i \omega_i + \sum_j y_j^*$.

---

1. The terminology "$x_i$ is maximal for $\succsim_i$ in set $B$" means that $x_i$ is consumer $i$'s preference-maximizing choice in the set $B$; that is, $x_i \in B$ and $x_i \succsim_i x_i'$ for all $x_i' \in B$.

For purposes of formal analysis, it is extremely helpful to be able to express equilibria as the solutions of a system of equations. We devote the remainder of this section to the study of how this may be done. In what follows, we aim at being very concrete and impose strong assumptions to simplify the analysis.

### Exchange Economies and Excess Demand Functions

We begin our derivation of equilibrium equations by studying the case of a pure exchange economy. Recall that a pure exchange economy is one in which the only possible production activities are those of free disposal. Formally, we let $J = 1$ and $Y_1 = -\mathbb{R}_+^L$. We take $X_i = \mathbb{R}_+^L$ and we assume at the outset that each consumer's preferences are *continuous*, *strictly convex*, and *locally nonsatiated* (shortly we shall strengthen local nonsatiation to strong monotonicity). We also assume that $\sum_i \omega_i \gg 0$.

For a pure exchange economy satisfying the above assumptions, the three conditions of Definition 17.B.1 can be equivalently restated as: $(x^*, y^*) = (x_1^*, \ldots, x_I^*, y_1^*)$ and $p \in \mathbb{R}^L$ constitute a Walrasian equilibrium if and only if

(i′) $y_1^* \leq 0$, $p \cdot y_1^* = 0$, and $p \geq 0$.
(ii′) $x_i^* = x_i(p, p \cdot \omega_i)$ for all $i$ [where $x_i(\cdot)$ is consumer $i$'s Walrasian demand function].
(iii′) $\sum_i x_i^* - \sum_i \omega_i^* = y_1^*$.

Condition (i′) is the only one that is not immediate. In Exercise 17.B.1, you are asked to show that it is equivalent to condition (i) of Definition 17.B.1.

Conditions (i′) to (iii′) yield the simple result of Proposition 17.B.1.

**Proposition 17.B.1:** In a pure exchange economy in which consumer preferences are continuous, strictly convex, and locally nonsatiated, $p \geq 0$ is a Walrasian equilibrium price vector if and only if:

$$\sum_i (x_i(p, p \cdot \omega_i) - \omega_i) \leq 0. \tag{17.B.1}$$

**Proof:** That (17.B.1) must hold in any Walrasian equilibrium of such an economy follows immediately from conditions (i′) to (iii′). In the other direction, suppose that (17.B.1) holds. If we let $y_1^* = \sum_i (x_i(p, p \cdot \omega_i) - \omega_i)$ and $x_i^* = x_i(p, p \cdot \omega_i)$, then $(x_1^*, \ldots, x_I^*, y_1^*)$ and $p$ satisfy conditions (i′) to (iii′). In particular, note that $p \cdot y_1^* = p \cdot \sum_i (x_i(p, p \cdot \omega_i) - \omega_i) = \sum_i (p \cdot x_i(p, p \cdot \omega_i) - p \cdot \omega_i) = 0$, where the last equality follows because with local nonsatiation we have $p \cdot x_i(p, p \cdot \omega_i) = p \cdot \omega_i$ for all $i$. ∎

The vector $x_i(p, p \cdot \omega_i) - \omega_i \in \mathbb{R}^L$ lists consumer $i$'s net, or *excess*, demand for each good over and above the amount that he possesses in his endowment vector $\omega_i$. Condition (17.B.1) suggests that it may be useful to have a formal representation of this excess demand vector, and of its sum over the $I$ consumers, as a function of prices. This is given in Definition 17.B.2.

**Definition 17.B.2:** The *excess demand function of consumer $i$* is

$$z_i(p) = x_i(p, p \cdot \omega_i) - \omega_i,$$

where $x_i(p, p \cdot \omega_i)$ is consumer $i$'s Walrasian demand function. The (*aggregate*) *excess demand function* of the economy is

$$z(p) = \sum_i z_i(p).$$

The domain of this function is a set of nonnegative price vectors that includes all strictly positive price vectors.

Using the economy's excess demand function $z(p)$, condition (17.B.1) can now be expressed more succinctly as follows:

"$p \in \mathbb{R}^L_+$ is an equilibrium price vector if and only if $z(p) \leq 0$."    (17.B.1′)

Note that if $p$ is a Walrasian equilibrium price vector in a pure exchange economy with locally nonsatiated preferences, then $p \geq 0$, $z(p) \leq 0$, and $p \cdot z(p) = \sum_i p \cdot z_i(p) = \sum_i (p \cdot x_i(p, p \cdot \omega_i) - p \cdot \omega_i) = 0$ (the last equality follows once again from local nonsatiation). Therefore, for every $\ell$, we not only have $z_\ell(p) \leq 0$, but also $z_\ell(p) = 0$ if $p_\ell > 0$. Thus, we see that at an equilibrium a good $\ell$ can be in excess supply (i.e., have $z_\ell(p) < 0$), but only if it is free (i.e., only if $p_\ell = 0$).[2]

To simplify matters even more, we go one step further by assuming that consumer preferences are *strongly monotone*. Thus, for the rest of this section (and, in fact, for all sections of this chapter except Section 17.I and Appendix B), we let $X_i = \mathbb{R}^L_+$ for all $i$ and assume that *all preference relations $\succsim_i$ are continuous, strictly convex, and strongly monotone.*

With strongly monotone preferences, any Walrasian equilibrium must involve a *strictly positive* price vector $p \gg 0$; otherwise consumers would demand an unboundedly large quantity of all the free goods. As a result, we conclude that with strong monotonicity of preferences, *a price vector $p = (p_1, \ldots, p_L)$ is a Walrasian equilibrium price vector if and only if it "clears all markets"; that is, if and only if it solves the system of $L$ equations in $L$ unknowns:*

$$z_\ell(p) = 0 \quad \text{for every } \ell = 1, \ldots, L, \tag{17.B.2}$$

or, in more compact notation, $z(p) = 0$.

Throughout this chapter, we study the properties of Walrasian equilibria largely by examining the properties of the system of equilibrium equations (17.B.2). We should point out, however, that this is not the only system of equations that we could use to characterize Walrasian equilibria. In Appendix A, for example, we discuss an important alternative system that exploits the welfare properties of Walrasian equilibria identified in Chapter 16.

Proposition 17.B.2 enumerates the properties of the aggregate excess demand function, in pure exchange economies with strongly monotone preferences, that are essential to the developments of this chapter.

**Proposition 17.B.2:** Suppose that, for every consumer $i$, $X_i = \mathbb{R}^L_+$ and $\succsim_i$ is continuous, strictly convex, and strongly monotone. Suppose also that $\sum_i \omega_i \gg 0$. Then the aggregate excess demand function $z(p)$, defined for all price vectors $p \gg 0$,

---

2. As a simple example, good $\ell$ might be a "bad." Then, we would expect that good $\ell$'s price would be zero, consumer demand for the good would be zero, and the excess supply $z_\ell(p) = \omega_\ell > 0$ would be eliminated using the disposal technology.

satisfies the properties:

(i) $z(\cdot)$ is continuous.
(ii) $z(\cdot)$ is homogeneous of degree zero.
(iii) $p \cdot z(p) = 0$ for all $p$ (*Walras' law*).
(iv) There is an $s > 0$ such that $z_\ell(p) > -s$ for every commodity $\ell$ and all $p$.
(v) If $p^n \to p$, where $p \neq 0$ and $p_\ell = 0$ for some $\ell$, then
$$\text{Max} \{z_1(p^n), \ldots, z_L(p^n)\} \to \infty.$$

**Proof:** With the exception of property (v), all these properties are direct consequences of the definition and the parallel properties of demand functions.[3] The bound in (iv) follows from the nonnegativity of demand (i.e., the fact that $X_i = \mathbb{R}_+^L$), which implies that a consumer's total net supply to the market of any good $\ell$ can be no greater than his initial endowment. You are asked to prove property (v) in Exercise 17.B.2. The intuition for it is this: As some prices go to zero, a consumer whose wealth tends to a strictly positive limit [note that, because $p \cdot (\sum_i \omega_i) > 0$, there must be at least one such consumer] and with strongly monotone preferences will demand an increasingly large amount of some of the commodities whose prices go to zero (but perhaps not of all such commodities: relative prices still matter). ∎

Finally, note that because of Walras' law, to verify that a price vector $p \gg 0$ clears all markets [i.e., has $z_\ell(p) = 0$ for all $\ell$] it suffices to check that it clears *all markets but one*. In particular, if $p \gg 0$ and $z_1(p) = \cdots = z_{L-1}(p) = 0$, then because $p \cdot z(p) = \sum_\ell p_\ell z_\ell(p) = 0$ and $p_L > 0$, we must also have $z_L(p) = 0$. Hence, if we denote the vector of $L - 1$ excess demands for goods 1 through $L - 1$ by
$$\hat{z}(p) = (z_1(p), \ldots, z_{L-1}(p)),$$
we see that a strictly positive price vector $p$ is a Walrasian equilibrium if and only if $\hat{z}(p) = 0$.

### Production Economies

It is possible to extend the methodology based on excess demand equations to the general production case. Assume, to begin with, that production sets are closed, strictly convex, and bounded above. Then, for any price vector $p \gg 0$, we can let $\pi_j(p)$ and $y_j(p)$ be the maximum profits and the profit-maximizing production vector, respectively, for firm $j$. Defining
$$\bar{z}(p) = \sum_i x_i\big(p, p \cdot \omega_i + \sum_j \theta_{ij} \pi_j(p)\big) - \sum_i \omega_i - \sum_j y_j(p) \tag{17.B.3}$$

as the *production inclusive excess demand function*, we see that $p$ is a Walrasian equilibrium price vector if and only if it solves the system of equations $\bar{z}(p) = 0$. In Exercise 17.B.4, you are asked to show that under a weak hypothesis (that a strictly positive aggregate consumption bundle is producible using the initial endowments), the function $\bar{z}(\cdot)$ satisfies properties (i) to (v) of Proposition 17.B.2.

Note that if the production sets are not bounded above, then $\bar{z}(p)$ may fail to be

---

3. Note, incidentally, that properties (i) to (iv) continue to hold even if preferences are only locally nonsatiated.

defined for some $p \gg 0$ [because we may have $\pi_j(p) = \infty$ for some $j$]. Nevertheless, an equilibrium price vector is still characterized by $\bar{z}(p) = 0$.

When production sets are not strictly convex, matters become more complicated because the correspondences $y_j(p)$ may no longer be single-valued. Indeed, a production situation of considerable theoretical and practical importance—and one that we certainly do not want to rule out by assumption—is the case of constant returns to scale. With constant returns, however, production sets are neither strictly convex nor bounded above (except for the trivial case in which no positive amount of any good can be produced). In principle, we could still view the equilibria as the zeros of a "production inclusive excess demand *correspondence*," defined as in (17.B.3) for a subset of strictly positive prices.[4] Correspondences, however, do not make good equational systems (e.g., they cannot be differentiated). It is therefore usually much more convenient in such cases to capture the equilibria as the solutions of an extended system of equations involving the production and the consumption sides of the economy. We illustrate this idea in the small type discussion that follows.

---

To see how an extended system of equations can be constructed, consider the case in which production is of the linear activity type (this case is reviewed in Appendix A of Chapter 5). Say that, in addition to the disposal technologies, we have $J$ basic activities $a_1, \ldots, a_J \in \mathbb{R}^L$. That is, the aggregate production set is

$$Y = \left\{ y \in \mathbb{R}^L : y \leq \sum_j \alpha_j a_j \text{ for some } (\alpha_1, \ldots, \alpha_J) \geq 0 \right\}.$$

Because preferences are strongly monotone, there can be no free goods at an equilibrium (i.e., we must have $p \gg 0$). Also, productions should be profit maximizing, and because of constant returns, these maximum profits must be zero. Therefore, a pair $(p, \alpha)$ formed by a price vector $p \in \mathbb{R}^L_+$ and a vector of activity levels $\alpha \in \mathbb{R}^J_+$ constitute an equilibrium if and only if they solve

$$z(p) - \sum_j \alpha_j a_j = 0 \tag{17.B.4}$$

and

$$p \cdot a_j \leq 0, \qquad \alpha_j(p \cdot a_j) = 0 \qquad \text{for all } j, \tag{17.B.5}$$

where $z(\cdot)$ is the consumers' aggregate excess demand function of Definition 17.B.2. Note that, if so desired, condition (17.B.5) can be expressed as a system of equations: just replace "$p \cdot a_j \leq 0$, $\alpha_j(p \cdot a_j) = 0$" by "$\alpha_j p \cdot a_j + \text{Max}\{0, p \cdot a_j\} = 0$." Exercise 17.B.5 presents an extension of the current discussion to a more general production case allowing for continuous substitution of activities.

---

It is worth emphasizing that, at least for the case of convex technologies, there would not be much loss of conceptual generality if we assumed that the production sector of the economy was composed of a single firm endowed with a constant returns production technology. To see this, recall from Proposition 5.B.2 that by creating for each firm $j$ an extra, firm-specific, factor of production, we can always assume that every $Y_j$ exhibits constant returns (when we do so, we transform each consumer's ownership shares of the profits of the $j$th firm into endowments of the $j$th new physical resource). Because profits at an equilibrium must then be zero, we see that once this is done there is no need to keep the identity of firms separate in order to compute the wealth of consumers. Moreover, from the point of view of production decisions, again no such need arises. As we saw in Section 5.E, we could as well work with the aggregate "representative firm" $Y = \sum_j Y_j$.

---

4. That is, $p$ would be an equilibrium price vector if and only if $0 \in \bar{z}(p)$.

A single constant returns $Y$ can be interpreted as a description of a long-run state of knowledge that is freely available to every agent in the economy (i.e., to every consumer), for the purpose of setting up firms or simply for household production. In fact, we could go one step further and formally dispense with the separate consideration of firms and of the profit-maximization condition. In Exercise 17.B.6, you are asked to show that a Walrasian equilibrium can be redefined in terms of the following two-stage process: first, consumers choose a vector $v_i \in \mathbb{R}^L$ subject to the budget constraint $p \cdot v_i \leq p \cdot \omega_i$ (the equilibrium market-clearing condition is $\sum_i v_i = \sum_i \omega_i$); second, every $i$ uses $v_i$ and the technology $Y$ for household production of a most preferred consumption bundle.[5]

# 17.C   Existence of Walrasian Equilibrium

When studying a positive theory, the first question to ask is: under what conditions does the formal model possess a solution? That is, is it capable of predicting a definite outcome? This is known as the *existence* problem. Conceptually, the assurance of existence of an equilibrium means that our equilibrium notion passes the logical test of consistency. It tells us that the mathematical model is well suited to the purposes it has been designed for. Although an existence theorem can hardly be the end of the story, it is, in a sense, the door that opens into the house of analysis.[6]

The existence of a Walrasian equilibrium can be established in considerable generality. To maintain the natural flow of exposition, in this section we offer a detailed examination of the existence problem for the particular case that will be our primary focus throughout the chapter: pure exchange economies modeled by means of excess demand functions. In Appendix B, we discuss the existence problem in the general case.

We have seen in Section 17.B that the excess demand function $z(\cdot)$ of an exchange economy with $\sum_i \omega_i \gg 0$ and continuous, strictly convex, and strongly monotone preferences satisfies properties (i) to (v) of Proposition 17.B.2. We now argue that *any* function $z(\cdot)$ satisfying these five conditions admits a solution, that is, a price vector $p$ such that $z(p) = 0$. By doing so, we establish that a Walrasian equilibrium exists under the conditions of Proposition 17.B.2.

To start simply, suppose that there are only two commodities (i.e., $L = 2$). For this case, it is an easy matter to establish the existence of an equilibrium. First, by the homogeneity of degree zero of $z(\cdot)$ (condition (ii) of Proposition 17.B.2), we can normalize $p_2 = 1$ and look for equilibrium price vectors of the form $(p_1, 1)$. Then, by Walras' law (condition (iii) of Proposition 17.B.2), an equilibrium can be obtained as a solution to the single equation $z_1(p_1, 1) = 0$. This one-variable problem is

---

5. This process formally reduces the production economy to an economy where only exchange takes place. But we do not mean to suggest that the induced exchange economy satisfies all of the strong assumptions that we have imposed in this chapter.

6. It should be emphasized that finding a class of conditions that guarantee the existence of a Walrasian equilibrium does not say that this is the outcome that will occur whenever preferences, endowments, and technologies satisfy the assumptions of the existence theorem: the behavioral assumption of price taking and the institutional assumptions of complete markets must also hold. However, when the conditions required for existence are *not* satisfied by preferences, endowments, or technologies, it does suggest that the type of equilibrium under consideration may not be the right one to look for.

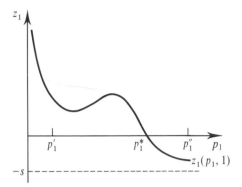

**Figure 17.C.1**

Proof of existence of an equilibrium for the case $L = 2$.

represented in Figure 17.C.1.[7] When $p_1'$ is very small, we must have $z_1(p_1', 1) > 0$; if $p_1''$ is very large, we have $z_1(p_1'', 1) < 0$. These two boundary restrictions follow by using conditions (iv) and (v) of Proposition 17.B.2 to identify the commodity with positive excess demand as the one whose relative price is very low.[8] Because the function $z_1(p_1, 1)$ is continuous [condition (i) of Proposition 17.B.2], there must be an intermediate value $p_1^* \in [p_1', p_1'']$ with $z_1(p_1^*, 1) = 0$ and, hence, an equilibrium price vector must exist.

In the general case of more than two commodities, the proof that a solution exists is more delicate, and involves the use of some powerful mathematical tools. In Proposition 17.C.1, we follow a traditional approach that invokes Kakutani's fixed-point theorem (see Section M.I of the Mathematical Appendix). We should point out that the proof of Proposition 17.C.1 has to deal with the technical complication that excess demand is not defined when the prices of some commodities are zero. The reader may actually gain a more direct insight into the nature of the fixed-point argument from Proposition 17.C.2, which contains a very simple proof for the case of excess demand functions defined for all nonzero, nonnegative prices.

**Proposition 17.C.1:** Suppose that $z(p)$ is a function defined for all strictly positive price vectors $p \in \mathbb{R}_{++}^L$ and satisfying conditions (i) to (v) of Proposition 17.B.2. Then the system of equations $z(p) = 0$ has a solution. Hence, a Walrasian equilibrium exists in any pure exchange economy in which $\sum_i \omega_i \gg 0$ and every consumer has continuous, strictly convex, and strongly monotone preferences.

---

7. Note that we revert to the usual mathematical convention of representing the independent variable $p_1$ on the horizontal axis. The partial equilibrium convention of putting prices on the vertical axis, to which we have adhered throughout Part III, is a vestige of the origins of the theory in Marshall (1920) where, in contrast with Walras (1874), prices are, in fact, dependent variables.

8. In particular, property (iv) implies that the value of intended sales is bounded. By Walras' law, the value of intended purchases must therefore also be bounded. Because, by property (v), intended purchases become unbounded in physical terms for *some* good as $p_1 \to 0$, it follows that it must be good 1 whose demand becomes unbounded as $p_1 \to 0$. Hence, $z_1(p_1', 1) > 0$ for $p_1'$ sufficiently small. By symmetry, as $p_1 \to \infty$ [which, by the homogeneity of degree zero of $z(\cdot)$, is equivalent to $p_2 \to 0$ holding $p_1$ fixed], for $p_1''$ large enough we must have $z_2(p_1'', 1) > 0$, and therefore $z_1(p_1'', 1) < 0$.

**Proof:** We begin by normalizing prices in a convenient way. Denote by

$$\Delta = \left\{ p \in \mathbb{R}^L_+ : \sum_\ell p_\ell = 1 \right\}$$

the unit simplex in $\mathbb{R}^L$. Because the function $z(\cdot)$ is homogeneous of degree zero, we can restrict ourselves, in our search for an equilibrium, to price vectors in $\Delta$. Note, however, that the function $z(\cdot)$ is well defined only for price vectors in the set

$$\text{Interior } \Delta = \{ p \in \Delta : p_\ell > 0 \text{ for all } \ell \}.$$

We shall proceed in five steps. In the first two, we construct a certain correspondence $f(\cdot)$ from $\Delta$ to $\Delta$. In the third, we argue that any fixed point of $f(\cdot)$, that is, any $p^*$ with $p^* \in f(p^*)$, has $z(p^*) = 0$. The fourth step proves that $f(\cdot)$ is convex valued and upper hemicontinuous (or, equivalently, that it has a closed graph). Finally, the fifth step applies Kakutani's fixed-point theorem to show that a $p^*$ with $p^* \in f(p^*)$ necessarily exists.

For notational clarity, in defining the set $f(p) \subset \Delta$, we denote the vectors that are elements of $f(p)$ by the symbol $q$.

*Step 1: Construction of the fixed-point correspondence for $p \in$ Interior $\Delta$.* Whenever $p \gg 0$, we let

$$f(p) = \{ q \in \Delta : z(p) \cdot q \geq z(p) \cdot q' \quad \text{for all } q' \in \Delta \}.$$

In words: Given the current "proposal" $p$, the "counterproposal" assigned by the correspondence $f(\cdot)$ is any price vector $q$ that, among the permissible price vectors (i.e., among the members of $\Delta$), maximizes the value of the excess demand vector $z(p)$. This makes economic sense; thinking of $f(\cdot)$ as a rule that adjusts current prices in a direction that eliminates any excess demand, the correspondence $f(\cdot)$ as defined above assigns the highest prices to the commodities that are most in excess demand. In particular, we have

$$f(p) = \{ q \in \Delta : q_\ell = 0 \text{ if } z_\ell(p) < \text{Max } \{ z_1(p), \ldots, z_L(p) \} \}.$$

Observe that if $z(p) \neq 0$ for $p \gg 0$, then because of Walras' law we have $z_\ell(p) < 0$ for some $\ell$ and $z_{\ell'}(p) > 0$ for some $\ell' \neq \ell$. Thus, for such a $p$, any $q \in f(p)$ has $q_\ell = 0$ for some $\ell$. Therefore, if $z(p) \neq 0$ then $f(p) \subset$ Boundary $\Delta = \Delta \backslash$ Interior $\Delta$. In contrast, if $z(p) = 0$ then $f(p) = \Delta$.

*Step 2: Construction of the fixed-point correspondence for $p \in$ Boundary $\Delta$.* If $p \in$ Boundary $\Delta$, we let

$$f(p) = \{ q \in \Delta : p \cdot q = 0 \} = \{ q \in \Delta : q_\ell = 0 \text{ if } p_\ell > 0 \}.$$

Because $p_\ell = 0$ for some $\ell$, we have $f(p) \neq \varnothing$. Note also that with this construction, no price from Boundary $\Delta$ can be a fixed point; that is, $p \in$ Boundary $\Delta$ and $p \in f(p)$ cannot occur because $p \cdot p > 0$ while $p \cdot q = 0$ for all $q \in f(p)$.

*Step 3: A fixed point of $f(\cdot)$ is an equilibrium.* Suppose that $p^* \in f(p^*)$. As we pointed out in step 2, we must have $p^* \notin$ Boundary $\Delta$. Therefore $p^* \gg 0$. If $z(p^*) \neq 0$, then we saw in step 1 that $f(p^*) \subset$ Boundary $\Delta$, which is incompatible with $p^* \in f(p^*)$ and $p^* \gg 0$. Hence, if $p^* \in f(p^*)$ we must have $z(p^*) = 0$.

*Step 4:* *The fixed-point correspondence is convex-valued and upper hemicontinuous.* To establish convex-valuedness, note that, both when $p \in$ Interior $\Delta$ and when $p \in$ Boundary $\Delta$, $f(p)$ equals a level set of a linear function defined on the convex set $\Delta$ [that is, a set of the form $\{q \in \Delta: \lambda \cdot q = k\}$ for some scalar $k$ and vector $\lambda \in \mathbb{R}^L$], and so it is convex. (Exercise 17.C.1 asks for a more explicit verification.)[9]

To establish upper hemicontinuity (see Section M.M of the Mathematical Appendix for definitions), consider sequences $p^n \to p$, $q^n \to q$ with $q^n \in f(p^n)$ for all $n$. We have to show that $q \in f(p)$. There are two cases: $p \in$ Interior $\Delta$ and $p \in$ Boundary $\Delta$.

If $p \in$ Interior $\Delta$, then $p^n \gg 0$ for $n$ sufficiently large. From $q^n \cdot z(p^n) \geq q' \cdot z(p^n)$ for all $q' \in \Delta$ and the continuity of $z(\cdot)$, we get $q \cdot z(p) \geq q' \cdot z(p)$ for all $q'$; that is, $q \in f(p)$.

Now suppose that $p \in$ Boundary $\Delta$. Take any $\ell$ with $p_\ell > 0$. We shall argue that for $n$ sufficiently large we have $q_\ell^n = 0$ and therefore it must be that $q_\ell = 0$; from this, $q \in f(p)$ follows. Because $p_\ell > 0$, there is an $\varepsilon > 0$ such that $p_\ell^n > \varepsilon$ for $n$ sufficiently large. If, in addition, $p^n \in$ Boundary $\Delta$ then $q_\ell^n = 0$ by the definition of $f(p^n)$. If, instead, $p^n \gg 0$ then the boundary conditions (iv) and (v) of Proposition 17.B.2 come into play. They imply that, for $n$ sufficiently large, we must have

$$z_\ell(p^n) < \text{Max} \{z_1(p^n), \ldots, z_L(p^n)\}$$

and therefore that, again, $q_\ell^n = 0$. To prove the above inequality, note that by condition (v) the right-hand side of the above expression goes to infinity with $n$ (because $p \in$ Boundary $\Delta$, some prices go to zero as $n \to \infty$). But the left-hand side is bounded above because if it is positive then

$$z_\ell(p^n) \leq \frac{1}{\varepsilon} p_\ell^n z_\ell(p^n) = -\frac{1}{\varepsilon} \sum_{\ell' \neq \ell} p_{\ell'}^n z_{\ell'}(p^n) < \frac{s}{\varepsilon} \sum_{\ell' \neq \ell} p_{\ell'}^n < \frac{s}{\varepsilon},$$

where $s$ is the bound in excess supply given by condition (iv).[10] In summary, for $p^n$ close enough to Boundary $\Delta$, the maximal demand corresponds to some of the commodities whose price is close to zero. Therefore, we conclude that, for large $n$, any $q^n \in f(p^n)$ will put nonzero weight only on commodities whose prices approach zero. But this guarantees $p \cdot q = 0$, and so $q \in f(p)$.

*Step 5:* *A fixed point exists.* Kakutani's fixed-point theorem (see Section M.I of the Mathematical Appendix) says that a convex-valued, upper hemicontinuous correspondence from a nonempty, compact, convex set into itself has a fixed point. Since $\Delta$ is a nonempty, convex, and compact set, and since $f(\cdot)$ is a convex-valued upper hemicontinuous correspondence from $\Delta$ to $\Delta$, we conclude that there is a $p^* \in \Delta$ with $p^* \in f(p^*)$. ∎

It is instructive to examine which of properties (i) to (v) of Proposition 17.B.2 fail to hold for the excess demand functions corresponding to the Edgeworth boxes of Figures 15.B.10(a) and (b), where, as we saw, no Walrasian equilibrium existed. In

---

9. Note also that for any $p \in \Delta$, the set $f(p)$ is always a face of the simplex $\Delta$; that is, it is one of the subsets of $\Delta$ spanned by a finite subset of unit coordinates. For $p \in$ Boundary $\Delta$, $f(p)$ is the face of $\Delta$ spanned by the zero coordinates of $p$. For $p \in$ Interior $\Delta$, $f(p)$ is the face spanned by the coordinates corresponding to commodities with maximal excess demand.

10. In words, the last chain of inequalities says that the expenditure on commodity $\ell$ is bounded because it has to be financed by, and therefore cannot be larger than, the bounded value of excess supplies.

the case of Figure 15.B.10(b), preferences are not convex and therefore $z(\cdot)$ is not a function, let alone a continuous one (condition (i)).[11] For Figure 15.B(10(a)), it is property (v) that fails: For any sequence of prices $(p_1^n, p_2^n) \to (1, 0)$, excess demand stays bounded. Note that in the limit there is a single consumer with positive wealth, but the preferences for this consumer, while monotone, are not strongly monotone.

To facilitate a clear understanding of the nature of the fixed-point argument it is helpful to consider Proposition 17.C.2, in which boundary complications are eliminated by studying continuous, homogeneous of degree zero functions $z(p)$ satisfying Walras' law and defined for all nonnegative, nonzero price vectors. Within a framework of continuous and strictly convex preferences, this type of excess demand function is not compatible with monotone preferences but can arise with preferences that are locally nonsatiated. Recall also that the equilibrium condition when zero prices are allowed is $z(p) \le 0$; see expression (17.B.1').

**Proposition 17.C.2:** Suppose that $z(p)$ is a function defined for all nonzero, nonnegative price vectors $p \in \mathbb{R}_+^L$ and satisfying conditions (i) to (iii) of Proposition 17.B.2 (i.e. continuity, homogeneity of degree zero and Walras' law). Then there is a price vector $p^*$ such that $z(p^*) \le 0$.

**Proof:** Because of homogeneity of degree zero we can restrict our search for an equilibrium to the unit simplex $\Delta = \{p \in \mathbb{R}_+^L : \sum_\ell p_\ell = 1\}$.

Define on $\Delta$ the function $z^+(\cdot)$ by $z_\ell^+(p) = \text{Max} \{z_\ell(p), 0\}$. Note that $z^+(\cdot)$ is continuous and that $z^+(p) \cdot z(p) = 0$ implies $z(p) \le 0$.

Denote $\alpha(p) = \sum_\ell [p_\ell + z_\ell^+(p)]$. We have $\alpha(p) \ge 1$ for all $p$.

Define a continuous function $f(\cdot)$ from the closed, convex set $\Delta$ into itself by

$$f(p) = [1/\alpha(p)](p + z^+(p)).$$

Note that, corresponding to intuition, this fixed-point function tends to increase the price of commodities in excess demand. The construction of the function is illustrated in Figure 17.C.2 for the case $L = 2$.

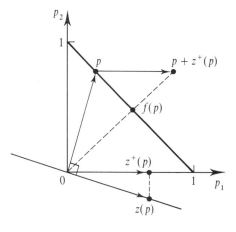

**Figure 17.C.2**

The fixed-point function for Proposition 17.C.2.

---

11. As we shall mention shortly in this section, existence would still obtain if $z(\cdot)$ was a convex-valued and upper hemicontinuous correspondence. In Figure 15.B.10(b), however, excess demand fails to satisfy the convex-valuedness property.

By Brouwer's fixed-point theorem (see Section M.I of the Mathematical Appendix) there is a $p^* \in \Delta$ such that $p^* = f(p^*)$. We show that $z(p^*) \leq 0$.

By Walras' law:

$$0 = p^* \cdot z(p^*) = f(p^*) \cdot z(p^*) = [1/\alpha(p^*)] z^+(p^*) \cdot z(p^*).$$

Therefore, $z^+(p^*) \cdot z(p^*) = 0$. But, as we have already pointed out, this implies $z(p^*) \leq 0$. ∎

The applicability of Proposition 17.C.1 is not limited to exchange economies. We saw, for example, in Section 17.B (and Exercise 17.B.4), that if we allow for production sets that are closed, strictly convex, and bounded above (and if a positive aggregate consumption bundle is producible from the initial aggregate endowments), then the production inclusive excess demand function $\bar{z}(\cdot)$ satisfies conditions (i) to (v) of Proposition 17.B.2. Hence, Proposition 17.C.1 also implies that a Walrasian equilibrium necessarily exists in this case.

We also note for later reference that Proposition 17.C.1 holds as well for a convex-valued and upper hemicontinuous *correspondence* $z(p)$ that satisfies conditions (ii) to (v) (properly adapted) of Proposition 17.B.2. In this case, there exists a $p$ such that $0 \in z(p)$. (See Exercise 17.C.2 for more on this point.)

Although Proposition 17.C.1 tells us that an equilibrium exists, it does not give us the equilibrium price vectors or allocations in an explicit manner. The issue of how to actually find equilibria was first considered by Scarf (1973). By now, a variety of useful techniques are available. They are very important for applied work, where the ability to compute solutions is key. See Shoven and Whaley (1992) for an account of applied general equilibrium.

---

The second welfare theorem of Section 16.D can be seen as a particular case of the current existence result. To see this, suppose that $x = (x_1, \ldots, x_I)$ is a Pareto optimal allocation of a pure exchange economy satisfying the assumptions leading to Proposition 17.C.1. Then, by Proposition 17.C.1, a Walrasian equilibrium price vector $p$ and allocation $\hat{x} = (\hat{x}_1, \ldots, \hat{x}_I)$ exist for the economy in which endowments are $\omega_i = x_i$ for all $i$. Since $x_i$ is affordable at prices $p$ for every consumer $i$, we must have $\hat{x}_i \succsim_i x_i$ for all $i$. Hence, it follows from the Pareto optimality of $x = (x_1, \ldots, x_I)$ that $\hat{x}_i \sim_i x_i$ for all $i$. But since $\hat{x}_i$ is consumer $i$'s optimal demand given prices $p$ and wealth $w_i = p \cdot \omega_i = p \cdot x_i$, $x_i$ must also be an optimal demand for consumer $i$ for price–wealth pair $(p, p \cdot x_i)$. Hence, we see that the price vector $p$ and the wealth levels $w_i = p \cdot x_i$ support the allocation $x$ as a price equilibrium with transfers in the sense of Definition 16.B.4.[12]

---

# 17.D   Local Uniqueness and the Index Theorem

Having established in Section 17.C (and Appendix B) conditions under which a Walrasian equilibrium is guaranteed to exist, we now begin a study of some issues related to its uniqueness or multiplicity.

---

12. The fact that the second welfare theorem can be viewed as a corollary of theorems asserting the existence of Walrasian equilibrium is valid much beyond the economies studied in this section.

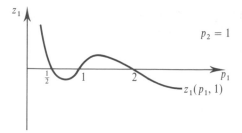

**Figure 17.D.1**

The excess demand function for an economy with multiple equilibria.

For a theorist, the best of the all possible worlds is one in which the social situation being analyzed can be formalized in a manner that, on the one hand, is very parsimonious (i.e., uses as inputs only the most indisputable and sturdy traits of the reality being modeled) and, on the other, manages to predict a unique outcome.

The Walrasian model of perfect competition is indeed very parsimonious. Essentially, it attempts to give a complete theoretical account of an economy by using as fundamentals only the list of commodities, the state of the technology, and the preferences and endowments of consumers. However, the other side of the coin is that the theory is not completely deterministic. We shall see in Section 17.F that the uniqueness of equilibria is assured only under special conditions. The Edgeworth box of Figure 15.B.9 and Example 15.B.2 provides a simple illustration that, under the assumptions we have made, multiplicity of equilibria is possible. Figure 17.D.1 represents the excess demand function for good 1 of Example 15.B.2 as a function of $p_1$ (normalizing to $p_2 = 1$). For another example of multiplicity, see Exercise 17.D.1.

From the theoretical point of view, if uniqueness is not achievable, the next-best property is local uniqueness. We say that an equilibrium price vector is *locally unique*, or *locally isolated*, if we cannot find another (normalized) price vector arbitrarily close to it. If every equilibrium of an economy is locally unique, we say that the *local uniqueness property* holds for the economy. The local uniqueness property is of interest because, if it prevails, then it may not be difficult to complete the theory in any particular application. For example, history may have determined the region where equilibrium lies (it could be the region where equilibrium used to be before a small unanticipated shock to the economy), and in that region we may have a unique equilibrium. In this case, the theory retains its predictive power, albeit only locally. We say that a theory that guarantees the local uniqueness of equilibria is *locally* (as opposed to globally) *determinate*.

The question is then: Is the Walrasian theory locally determinate? The example of Figure 17.D.1 suggests that it is: Every solution to the excess demand equation is locally isolated. But Figures 17.D.2 and 17.D.3 provide a counterexample. The figures depict the offer curves and the excess demand function of an exchange economy with a continuum of Walrasian equilibria. Nonetheless, we should not despair. The situation displayed in Figures 17.D.2 and 17.D.3 has an obvious pathological feel about it; it looks like a coincidence. And indeed, it was shown by Debreu (1970) that such an occurrence is not robust: it can happen only by accident.

We now turn to a formal discussion of these issues. For the sake of concreteness we restrict ourselves, as usual, to the analysis of exchange economies formed by $I$ consumers. Every consumer $i$ is specified by $(\succsim_i, \omega_i)$, where $\succsim_i$ is a continuous,

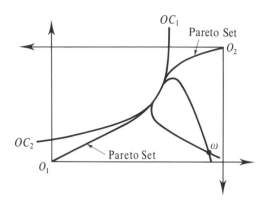

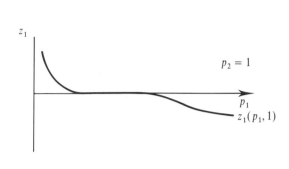

strictly convex, and strongly monotone preference relation on $\mathbb{R}_+^L$ and $\omega_i \gg 0$. As we know, the aggregate excess demand function $z(\cdot)$ then satisfies conditions (i) to (v) of Proposition 17.B.2. We further assume that $z(\cdot)$ is continuously differentiable.[13]

**Figure 17.D.2 (left)**
A continuum of equilibria is possible: Edgeworth box.

**Figure 17.D.3 (right)**
A continuum of equilibria is possible: excess demand.

Because we can only hope to determine *relative* prices, we normalize $p_L = 1$ and, as we did in Section 17.B, denote by

$$\hat{z}(p) = (z_1(p), \ldots, z_{L-1}(p))$$

the vector of excess demands for the first $L-1$ goods.[14] A normalized price vector $p = (p_1, \ldots, p_{L-1}, 1)$ constitutes a Walrasian equilibrium if and only if it solves the system of $L-1$ equations in $L-1$ unknowns:

$$\hat{z}(p) = 0.$$

### Regular Economies

It is useful to begin by introducing the concept stated in Definition 17.D.1.

**Definition 17.D.1:** An equilibrium price vector $p = (p_1, \ldots, p_{L-1})$ is *regular* if the $(L-1) \times (L-1)$ matrix of price effects $D\hat{z}(p)$ is nonsingular, that is, has rank $L-1$. If every normalized equilibrium price vector is regular, we say that the *economy is regular*.

In Figure 17.D.1, every equilibrium is regular because the slope of excess demand, $\partial z_1(p_1, 1)/\partial p_1$, is nonzero at every solution. In contrast, none of the equilibria of Figure 17.D.3 are regular because at any equilibrium price vector the slope of the excess demand function is zero. Later in this section we shall argue that, in a sense that we will make precise, "almost every" economy is regular.

The significance of the technical concept of regularity derives from the fact that a regular (normalized) equilibrium price vector is isolated, and a regular economy can only have a finite number of (normalized) price equilibria. This is formally stated in Proposition 17.D.1.

---

13. In Appendix A to Chapter 3, we discussed conditions for the differentiability of demand functions and therefore of excess demand functions.

14. Nothing in what follows depends on the particular normalization. It can be shown, for example, that if $z(p) = 0$ and the $L \times L$ matrix $Dz(p)$ has rank $L-1$, then the $(L-1) \times (L-1)$ matrix $D\hat{z}(p)$ has rank $L-1$ whichever good we choose to normalize. Even more, the sign of its determinant is independent of the normalization (see Section M.D of the Mathematical Appendix).

**Proposition 17.D.1:** Any regular (normalized) equilibrium price vector

$$p = (p_1, \ldots, p_{L-1}, 1)$$

is *locally isolated* (or *locally unique*). That is, there is an $\varepsilon > 0$ such that if $p' \neq p$, $p'_L = p_L = 1$, and $\|p' - p\| < \varepsilon$, then $z(p') \neq 0$. Moreover, if the economy is regular, then the number of normalized equilibrium price vectors is finite.

**Proof:** The local uniqueness of a regular solution is a direct consequence of the inverse function theorem (see Section M.E of the Mathematical Appendix). Intuitively, this is clear enough. For any infinitesimal change in normalized prices, $dp = (dp_1, \ldots, dp_{L-1}, 0) \neq 0$, the nonsingularity of $D\hat{z}(p)$ implies that $D\hat{z}(p)\, dp \neq 0$. Hence, we cannot remain at equilibrium.

Once we know that every equilibrium is locally isolated, the finiteness of the number of equilibria is a consequence of the boundary condition (v) of Proposition 17.B.2 on the excess demand function. Because of this condition (which, recall, follows from the strong monotonicity of preferences), equilibrium is not compatible with relative prices that are arbitrarily close to zero. That is, there is an $r > 0$ such that if $\hat{z}(p) = 0$ and $p_L = 1$, then $1/r < p_\ell < r$ for every $\ell$. The continuity of $\hat{z}(\cdot)$ adds to this the fact that the set of equilibrium price vectors is a closed subset of $\mathbb{R}^{L-1}$. But a set that is closed and bounded (i.e., compact) in $\mathbb{R}^{L-1}$ and discrete (i.e., with all its points locally isolated) must necessarily be finite (see Section M.F of the Mathematical Appendix). ∎

Our next aim is suggested by reexamining Figure 17.D.1; we see that for a regular economy with two commodities, we can assert more than the finiteness of the number of equilibria. Indeed, the boundary conditions on the excess demand function $z_1(\cdot)$ (excess demand is positive if $p_1$ is very low and negative if it is very high) necessarily imply that, for a regular economy, first, there is an odd number of equilibria and, second, the slopes of the excess demand function at the equilibrium must alternate between being negative and being positive, starting with negative. If we say that an equilibrium with an associated negative slope of excess demand has an *index* of $+1$ and that one with a positive slope has an *index* of $-1$, then, no matter how many equilibria there are, the sum of the indices of the equilibria of a regular economy is always $+1$. With appropriate definitions, it turns out that this invariance of index property also holds in the general case with any number of commodities, where it has some important implications for comparative statics and uniqueness questions.

Let us generalize the definition of the index of a regular equilibrium that we have just suggested for the case $L = 2$ to the case of many commodities.

**Definition 17.D.2:** Suppose that $p = (p_1, \ldots, p_{L-1}, 1)$ is a regular equilibrium of the economy. Then we denote

$$\text{index } p = (-1)^{L-1} \text{sign } |D\hat{z}(p)|,$$

where $|D\hat{z}(p)|$ is the determinant of the $(L-1) \times (L-1)$ matrix $D\hat{z}(p)$.[15]

If $L = 2$, then $|D\hat{z}(p)|$ is merely the slope of $z_1(\cdot)$ at $p$. Hence, we see that for this case the index is $+1$ or $-1$ according to whether the slope is negative or positive.

---

15. For any number $\alpha \neq 0$, sign $\alpha = +1$ or $-1$ according to whether $\alpha > 0$ or $\alpha < 0$.

A regular economy has a finite number of equilibria (Proposition 17.D.1). Therefore, for a regular economy, the expression

$$\sum_{\{p:\, z(p)=0,\, p_L=1\}} \text{index } p$$

makes sense. The next proposition (the *index theorem*) says that the value of this expression is always equal to $+1$.

**Proposition 17.D.2:** (*The Index Theorem*) For any regular economy, we have

$$\sum_{\{p:\, z(p)=0,\, p_L=1\}} \text{index } p = +1.$$

A brief discussion of why this result is true is given at the end of this section. Here we point out some of its implications and why it is useful and significant. Note, first, that it implies that the number of equilibria of a regular economy is odd.[16] In particular, this number cannot be zero; so the existence of at least one equilibrium is a particular case of the proposition. Second, the index concept provides a classification of equilibria into two types. In a sense, Proposition 17.D.2 tells us that the type with positive index is more fundamental because the presence of at least one equilibrium of positive type is unavoidable. In fact, it is typically the case that any search for well-behaved equilibria (what this means depends on the particular application) can be confined to the positive index equilibria. Third, as we shall see in Section 17.F, the index result has implications for the uniqueness and the multiplicity of equilibria. Fourth, as we shall discuss in Section 17.E, part of the importance of the index theorem is that this is all we can hope to derive without imposing (strong) additional assumptions.

We next proceed to argue that typically (or, in the usual jargon, *generically*) economies are regular. Hence, generically, the solutions to the excess demand equations are locally isolated and finite in number, and the index formula holds.[17]

*Genericity Analysis*

To emphasize the wide scope of the methodology to be presented, we discuss it first in terms of a general system of equations. We then specialize our discussion to the economic problem at hand and spell out its consequences for the excess demand equations.

The essence of genericity analysis rests on counting equations and unknowns. Suppose we have a system of $M$ equations in $N$ unknowns:

$$f_1(v_1, \ldots, v_N) = 0,$$
$$\vdots \qquad\qquad\qquad (17.D.1)$$
$$f_M(v_1, \ldots, v_N) = 0,$$

or, more compactly, $f(v) = 0$. The normal situation should be one in which, with $N$ unknowns and $M$ equations, we have $N - M$ degrees of freedom available for the

16. This result was first shown by Dierker (1972).
17. For advanced treatments on the topic of this section, refer to Balasko (1988) or Mas-Colell (1985).

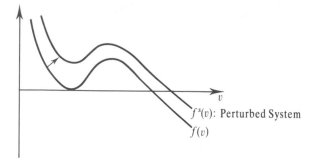

$f^s(v)$: Perturbed System

$f(v)$

**Figure 17.D.4**
The regular case is typical.

description of the solution set. In particular, if $M > N$, the system should be *over-determined* and have no solution; if $M = N$, the system should be *exactly determined* with the solutions locally isolated; and if $M < N$, the system should be *under-determined* and the solutions not locally isolated. Clearly, all these statements are not always true (you can see this just by considering examples with linear equations). So, what does it mean to be in the "normal case"? The implicit function theorem provides an answer: one needs the equations (which we assume are differentiable) to be independent (that is, truly distinct) at the solutions. Definition 17.D.3 captures this notion.

**Definition 17.D.3:** The system of $M$ equations in $N$ unknowns $f(v) = 0$ is *regular* if rank $Df(v) = M$ whenever $f(v) = 0$.

For a regular system, the implicit function theorem (see Section M.E of the Mathematical Appendix) yields the existence of the right number of degrees of freedom. If $M < N$, we can choose $M$ variables corresponding to $M$ linearly independent columns of $Df(v)$ and we can express the values of these $M$ variables that solve the $M$ equations $f(v) = 0$ as a function of the $N - M$ remaining variables (see Exercise 17.D.2). If $M = N$, equilibria must be locally isolated for the same reasons as discussed earlier in this section for the system $\hat{z}(p) = 0$. And if $M > N$, then rank $Df(v) \leq N < M$ for all $v$; in this case, Definition 17.D.3 simply says that, as a matter of definition, the equation system $f(v) = 0$ is regular if and only if the system admits no solution.

It remains to be argued that the regular case is the "normal" one. Figure 17.D.4 suggests how this can be approached. In the figure, the one-equation, one-unknown system $f(v) = 0$ is not regular [because of the tangency point of the graph of $f(\cdot)$ and the horizontal axis]. But clearly this phenomenon is not robust: if we slightly perturb the equation in an arbitrary manner [say that the shocked system is $f^s(\cdot)$], we get a regular system. On the other hand, the regularity of a system that is already regular is preserved for any small perturbation.[18]

This intuitive idea of a perturbation can be formalized as follows. Suppose there are some parameters $q = (q_1, \ldots, q_S)$ such that, for every $q$, we have a system of equations $f(v; q) = 0$, as above. The set of possible parameter values is $\mathbb{R}^S$ (or an open region of $\mathbb{R}^S$). We can then justifiably say that $f(\cdot; q')$ is a perturbation of

---

18. The perturbation should control the values *and* the derivatives of the function. In technical language, it should be a $C^1$ perturbation.

$f(\cdot\,; q)$ if $q'$ is close to $q$. Hence, the notion that the regularity of a system $f(\cdot\,; q) = 0$ is typical, or generic, could be captured by demanding that *for almost every $q$,* $f(\cdot\,; q) = 0$ be regular; in other words, that nonregular systems have probability zero of occurring (with respect to say, a nondegenerate normal distribution on $\mathbb{R}^S$).[19] It stands to reason that some condition will be required on the dependence of $f(\cdot\,; q)$ on $q$ for this to hold. At the very least, $f(\cdot\,; q)$ has to actually depend on $q$. The important mathematical theorem to be presented next tells us that little beyond this is needed.[20]

**Proposition 17.D.3:** (*The Transversality Theorem*) If the $M \times (N + S)$ matrix $Df(v; q)$ has rank $M$ whenever $f(v; q) = 0$ then for almost every $q$, the $M \times N$ matrix $D_v f(v; q)$ has rank $M$ whenever $f(v; q) = 0$.

Heuristically, the assumption of the transversality theorem requires that there be enough variation in our universe. If $Df(v; q)$ has rank $M$ whenever $f(v; q) = 0$, then from any solution it is always possible to (differentially) alter the values of the function $f$ in any prescribed direction by adjusting the $v$ and $q$ variables. The conclusion of the theorem is that, if this can always be done, then whenever we are initially at a nonregular situation an arbitrary random displacement in $q$ breaks us away from nonregularity. In fanciful language, if our universe is nondegenerate, then so will be almost every world in it. Note one of the strengths of the theorem: the matrix $Df(v; q)$ has $M$ rows and $N + S$ columns. Hence, if $S$ is large, so that there are many perturbation parameters, then the assumption of the theorem is likely to be satisfied; after all, we only need to find $M$ linearly independent columns. On the other hand, $D_v f(v; q)$ has $M$ rows but only $N$ columns. It is thus harder to guarantee in advance that at a solution $D_v f(v; q)$ has $M$ linearly independent columns. But the theorem tells us that this is so for almost every $q$. Observe that if $M > N$ (more equations than unknowns), then the $M \times N$ matrix $D_v f(v; q)$ cannot have rank $M$. Hence, the theorem tells us that in this case, generically (i.e., for almost every $q$), $f(v; q) = 0$ has no solution.

Let us now specialize our discussion to the case of a system of $L - 1$ excess demand equations in $L - 1$ unknowns, $\hat{z}(p) = 0$. We have seen by example that nonregular economies are possible. We wish to argue that they are not typical. To

---

19. More formally, we could say that in a system defined by finitely many parameters (taking values in, say, an open set) a property is *generic in the first sense* if it holds for a set of parameters of full measure (i.e., the complement of the set for which it holds has measure zero). The property is *generic in the second sense* if it holds in an open set of full measure. A full measure set is dense but it need not be open. Hence, the second sense is stronger than the first. Yet in many applications (all of ours in fact), the property under consideration holds in an open set, and so genericity in the first sense automatically yields genericity in the second sense. In some applications there is no finite number of parameters and no notion of measure to appeal to. In those cases we could say that a property is *generic in the third sense* if the property holds in an open and dense set. When no measure is available, this still provides a sensible way to capture the idea that the property is typical; but it should be noted that with finitely many parameters a set may be open, dense and have arbitrarily small (positive) measure. In this entire section we deal with genericity in the first sense, and we simply call it *genericity*.

20. For this theorem, we assume that $f(v; q)$ is as many times differentiable in its two arguments as is necessary.

do so, we could resort to a wide variety of perturbation parameters influencing preferences or endowments (or, in a more general setting, technologies). A natural set of parameters are the initial endowments themselves:

$$\omega = (\omega_{11}, \ldots, \omega_{L1}, \ldots, \omega_{1I}, \ldots, \omega_{LI}) \in \mathbb{R}^{LI}_{++}.$$

We can write the dependence of the economy's excess demand function on endowments explicitly as $\hat{z}(p; \omega)$. We then have Proposition 17.D.4.

**Proposition 17.D.4:** For any $p$ and $\omega$, rank $D_\omega \hat{z}(p; \omega) = L - 1$.

**Proof:** It suffices to consider the endowments of a single consumer, say consumer 1, and to show that the $(L - 1) \times L$ matrix $D_{\omega_1}\hat{z}(p; \omega)$ has rank $L - 1$ [this implies that rank $D_\omega \hat{z}(p; \omega) = L - 1$]. To show this, we can either compute $D_{\omega_1}\hat{z}(p; \omega)$ explicitly (Exercise 17.D.3) or simply note that any perturbation of $\omega_1$, say $d\omega_1$, that leaves the wealth of consumer 1 at prices $p$ unaltered will not change demand and therefore will change excess demand by exactly $-d\omega_1$. Specifically, if $p \cdot d\omega_1 = 0$ then, denoting $d\hat{\omega}_1 = (d\omega_{11}, \ldots, d\omega_{L-1,1})$, we have $D_{\omega_1}\hat{z}(p; \omega)\, d\omega_1 = D_{\omega_1}\hat{z}_1(p; \omega)\, d\hat{\omega}_1 = -d\hat{\omega}_1$. Because the condition $p \cdot d\omega_1 = 0$ on $d\omega_1$ places no restrictions on $d\hat{\omega}_1$, it follows that by changing consumer 1's endowments we can move $\hat{z}(p; \omega)$ in any desired direction in $\mathbb{R}^{L-1}$, and so rank $D_{\omega_1}\hat{z}(p; \omega) = L - 1$. ∎

We are now ready to state the main result [due to Debreu (1970)].

**Proposition 17.D.5:** For almost every vector of initial endowments $(\omega_1, \ldots, \omega_I) \in \mathbb{R}^{LI}_{++}$, the economy defined by $\{(\succsim_i, \omega_i)\}_{i=1}^{i=I}$ is regular.[21]

**Proof:** Because of Proposition 17.D.4, the result follows from the transversality theorem (Proposition 17.D.3). ∎

See Exercises 17.D.4 to 17.D.6 for variations on the theme of Proposition 17.D.4.

In Figure 17.D.5, we represent the equilibrium set $E = \{(\omega_1, \omega_2, p_1): \hat{z}(p_1, 1; \omega) = 0\}$ of an Edgeworth box economy with total endowment $\bar{\omega} = \omega_1 + \omega_2$. The set $E$ is the graph of the correspondence that assigns equilibrium prices to economies $\omega = (\omega_1, \omega_2)$.

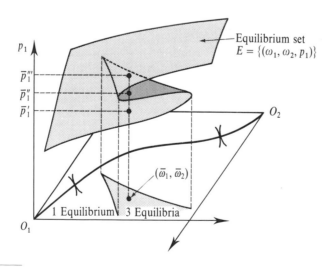

**Figure 17.D.5**

The equilibrium set.

---

21. To be quite explicit, this means that the set of endowments that yield nonregular economies is a subset of $\mathbb{R}^{LI}$ that has ($LI$-dimensional) Lebesgue measure zero, or, equivalently, probability zero for, say, a nondegenerate $LI$-dimensional normal distribution.

Because of the index theorem, this picture, in which the number of equilibria changes discontinuously from 3 to 1 at some points in the space of endowments is typical of the multiple-equilibrium case. A very extensive analysis of this equilibrium set has been carried out by Balasko (1988).

We conclude the discussion of genericity with two observations: First, the generic local determinateness of the theory extends to cases with externalities, taxes, or other "imperfections" leading to the failure of the first welfare theorem. (See Exercise 17.D.6.) This should be clear from the generality of the mathematical techniques which, in essence, rely only on the ability to express the equilibria of the theory as the zeros of a natural system of equations with the same number of equations and unknowns. Second, "finiteness of the number of equilibria" is a blunt conclusion. It is not the same if the "finite" stands for three or for a few million. Unfortunately, short of going all the way to uniqueness conditions (as we do in Section 17.F), we have no technique that allows us to refine our conclusions. We want to put on record, however, that it should not be presumed that in all generality "finite" means "small." In this respect, we mention, tentatively, that there seems to be a distinction between market equilibrium situations for which the first welfare theorem holds (in which, indeed, examples with "many" equilibria seem contrived) and situations with a variety of market failures (where examples are easy to produce). See Exercise 17.D.7 and the discussion on "sunspots" in Section 19.F.

## On the Index Theorem

The index result (Proposition 17.D.2) is, in its essence, a purely mathematical fact. An attempt at a rigorous proof would take us too far afield. Nonetheless, it is instructive to give an argument for its validity. It is an argument, we note incidentally, that can be made into a rigorous proof.

Denote our given, normalized, excess demand function by $\hat{z}(p)$. We begin by availing ourselves of some other excess demand function $\hat{z}^0(p)$ with the properties that (i) there is a unique $\bar{p}$ such that $\hat{z}^0(\bar{p}) = 0$ and (ii) $\text{sign}|D\hat{z}^0(\bar{p})| = (-1)^{L-1}$. For example, $\hat{z}^0(p)$ could be generated from a single-consumer Cobb–Douglas economy (Exercise 17.D.8). The idea is that $\hat{z}^0(p)$ is both simple and familiar to us and that, as a consequence, we can use it to learn about the properties of the unfamiliar $\hat{z}(p)$.

Consider the following one-parameter family (in technical language, a *homotopy*) of excess demand functions:

$$\hat{z}(p, t) = t\hat{z}(p) + (1 - t)\hat{z}^0(p) \qquad \text{for } 0 \le t \le 1.$$

The system $\hat{z}(p, t) = 0$ has $L - 1$ equations and $L$ unknowns: $(p_1, \ldots, p_{L-1}, t)$. Typically, therefore, the solution set $E = \{(p, t): \hat{z}(p, t) = 0\}$ has *one and only one* degree of freedom at any of its points (that is, it looks locally like a segment). Moreover, since this solution set cannot escape to infinite or zero prices (because of the boundary conditions on excess demand) and is closed [because of the continuity of $\hat{z}(p, t)$], it follows that the general situation is well represented in Figure 17.D.6.

In Figure 17.D.6, we depict $E$ as formed, so to speak, by a finite number of circle-like and segment-like components, with the endpoints of the segments at the $t = 0$ and $t = 1$ boundaries. Since there are two endpoints per segment, there is an even number of such endpoints. By construction, $\bar{p}$ is the only endpoint at the $t = 0$ boundary.[22] Therefore, there must be an odd number of endpoints at the $t = 1$ boundary; that is, there is an odd number of solutions to $\hat{z}(p) = \hat{z}(p, 1) = 0$. Suppose now that we follow a segment from end to end. What

---

22. More generally, if $\hat{z}(p; t)$ is an arbitrary homotopy then the typical situation is well represented by any of the Figures 17.G.1(a), (b), or (c).

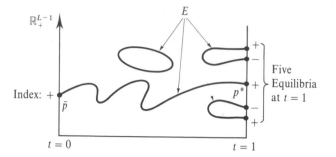

**Figure 17.D.6**

The equilibrium set under a homotopy.

is the relation between the indices at the two ends? A moment's reflection (keeping the implicit function theorem in mind) reveals that as long as we move in a given direction relative to $t$ (i.e., forward or backward), the index, $(-1)^{L-1}$ sign $|D_p \hat{z}(p, t)|$, does not change, and that the index changes sign precisely when we reverse direction.[23] Now, a segment that begins and ends at the same boundary must reverse direction an odd number of times; hence, the indices at the two endpoints have opposite signs. You can verify this in Figure 17.D.6. Therefore, the sum of the indices at $t = 1$ equals the index of the lone equilibrium of $\hat{z}(\cdot)$ connected by a segment to the equilibrium $\bar{p}$ of $\hat{z}^0(\cdot)$ at the boundary $t = 0$. It is represented by $p^*$ in Figure 17.D.6. The segment that connects $\bar{p}$ to $p^*$ in $E$ reverses directions an even number of times (possibly none); therefore, we conclude that the index of this equilibrium at $t = 1$ equals the index of $\bar{p}$ for $\hat{z}^0(\cdot)$, which, by construction, is $+1$. Hence, the sum of the indices at $t = 1$ is $+1$, as Proposition 17.D.2 asserts to be true in complete generality.

# 17.E  Anything Goes: The Sonnenschein–Mantel–Debreu Theorem

We have seen that under a number of general assumptions (of which the most substantial concerns convexity), an equilibrium exists and the number of equilibria is typically finite. Those are important properties, but we would like to know if we could say more, especially for predictive or comparative-statics purposes (see Section 17.G). We may well suspect by now (especially if the message of Chapter 4 on the difficulties of demand aggregation has been well understood) that the answer is likely to be negative; that is, that, in general, we will not be able to impose further restrictions on excess demand than those in Proposition 17.B.2, and therefore that no further general restrictions on the nature of Walrasian equilibria than those already studied can be hoped for. Special assumptions will have to be made to derive stronger implications (such as uniqueness; see Section 17.F).

In this section, we confirm this and bring home the negative message in a particularly strong manner. The theme, culminating in Propositions 17.E.3 and 17.E.4, is: *Anything satisfying the few properties that we have already shown must hold, can actually occur.*

---

23. To see this, think of the case where $L = 2$. Applying the implicit function theorem to $\hat{z}_1(p_1, t) = 0$, verify then that a reversal of direction occurs precisely where $\partial \hat{z}_1(p_1, t)/\partial p_1 = 0$.

The analysis that follows develops the logic of this conclusion through a series of intermediate results that have independent interest. Some readers may wish, in a first reading of this section, to skip these results and examine directly the statements of Propositions 17.E.3 and 17.E.4 and the accompanying discussion of their interpretations.

To be specific, we concentrate the analysis, as usual, on exchange economies formalized by means of excess demand equations. Focusing on exchange economies makes sense because, as we know from Chapter 5, aggregation effects are unproblematic in production. The source of the aggregation problem rests squarely with the wealth effects of the consumption side.

We begin by posing a relatively simple but nonetheless quite important question: To what extent can we derive restrictions on the behavior of excess demand at a given price $p$. In particular, we ask for possible restrictions on the $L \times L$ matrix of price effects $Dz(p)$.[24]

Suppose that $z(p)$ is a differentiable aggregate excess demand function. In Exercise 17.E.1, you are asked to show that

$$\sum_k \frac{\partial z_\ell(p)}{\partial p_k} p_k = 0 \qquad \text{for all } \ell \text{ and } p \ [\text{or } Dz(p)p = 0] \qquad (17.E.1)$$

$$\sum_k p_k \frac{\partial z_k(p)}{\partial p_\ell} = -z_\ell(p) \qquad \text{for all } \ell \text{ and } p \ [\text{or } p \cdot Dz(p) = -z(p)] \qquad (17.E.2)$$

These are the excess demand counterparts of expressions (2.E.1) and (2.E.4) for demand functions. They follow, respectively, from the homogeneity of degree zero and the Walras' law properties of excess demand. More interestingly, from $z(p) = \sum_i (x_i(p, p \cdot \omega_i) - \omega_i)$ we also get

$$Dz(p) = \sum_i [S_i(p, p \cdot \omega_i) - D_{w_i} x_i(p, p \cdot \omega_i) z_i(p)^{\mathrm{T}}] \qquad (17.E.3)$$

where, as usual, $S_i(p, p \cdot \omega_i)$ is the substitution matrix (see Exercise 17.E.2).

Expression (17.E.3) is very instructive. It tells us that if it were not for the wealth effects, $Dz(p)$ would inherit the negative semidefiniteness (n.s.d.) property of the substitution matrices. How much havoc can the wealth effects cause? Notice that the matrix

$$D_{w_i} x_i(p, p \cdot \omega_i) z_i(p)^{\mathrm{T}} = \begin{bmatrix} \dfrac{\partial x_{1i}(p, p \cdot \omega_i)}{\partial w_i} z_{1i}(p) & \cdots & \dfrac{\partial x_{1i}(p, p \cdot \omega_i)}{\partial w_i} z_{Li}(p) \\ & \ddots & \\ \dfrac{\partial x_{Li}(p, p \cdot \omega_i)}{\partial w_i} z_{1i}(p) & \cdots & \dfrac{\partial x_{Li}(p, p \cdot \omega_i)}{\partial w_i} z_{Li}(p) \end{bmatrix}$$

is of rank 1 (any two columns, or rows, are proportional). Therefore, we could informally surmise that the wealth effect of consumer $i$ can hurt in at most one

---

24. Note that $z(p)$ can take any value. You need only specify a consumer with an endowment vector $\omega$ such that $\omega + z(p) \gg 0$ and then choose a utility function that has $\omega + z(p)$ as the demanded point.

direction of price change.[25] Thus, we should expect that if $I < L$ then there are some negative semidefiniteness restrictions left on $Dz(p)$. That this is the case is formalized in Proposition 17.E.1.

**Proposition 17.E.1:** Suppose that $I < L$. Then for any equilibrium price vector $p$ there is some direction of price change $dp \neq 0$ such that $p \cdot dp = 0$ (hence, $dp$ is not proportional to $p$) and $dp \cdot Dz(p) \, dp \leq 0$.

**Proof:** Because $z(p) = \sum_i z_i(p) = 0$, at most $I$ of the $I + 1$ vectors,

$$\{p, z_1(p), \ldots, z_I(p)\} \subset \mathbb{R}^L$$

can be linearly independent. Since $I < L$, it follows that we can find a nonzero vector $dp \in \mathbb{R}^L$ such that $p \cdot dp = 0$ and $z_i(p) \cdot dp = 0$ for all $i$. In words: $dp$ is a nonproportional price change that is compensated (i.e., there is no change in real wealth) for *every* consumer. But then from (17.E.3) we obtain

$$dp \cdot Dz(p) \, dp = \sum_i dp \cdot S_i(p, p \cdot \omega_i) \, dp \leq 0. \qquad \blacksquare$$

Parallel reasoning should make us expect that if $I \geq L$ (i.e., if there are at least as many consumers as commodities), then there may not be any restriction left on $Dz(p)$ beyond (17.E.1) and (17.E.2). After all, the direction of an individual wealth effect vector at a given price is quite arbitrary (and can be chosen independently of the substitution effects of the corresponding individual); and with $I \geq L$ wealth effect vectors to be specified, there is considerable room to maneuver. Proposition 17.E.2 confirms this suspicion.

**Proposition 17.E.2:** Given a price vector $p$, let $z \in \mathbb{R}^L$ be an arbitrary vector and $A$ an arbitrary $L \times L$ matrix satisfying $p \cdot z = 0$, $Ap = 0$ and $p \cdot A = -z$. Then there is a collection of $L$ consumers generating an aggregate excess demand function $z(\cdot)$ such that $z(p) = z$ and $Dz(p) = A$.

---

**Proof:** To keep the argument simple, we restrict ourselves to a search for consumers that at their demanded vectors have a null substitution matrix, $S_i(p, p \cdot \omega_i) = 0$, that is, whose indifference sets exhibit a vertex at the chosen point.[26]

We can always formally rewrite the given $L \times L$ matrix $A$ as

$$A = \sum_\ell e^\ell a^\ell,$$

where $e^\ell$ is the $\ell$th unit column vector (i.e., all the entries of $e^\ell$ are 0 except the $\ell$th entry, which equals 1) and $a^\ell$ is the $\ell$th row of $A$ [i.e., $a^\ell = (a_{\ell 1}, \ldots, a_{\ell L})$].

Suppose now that we could specify $L$ consumers, $i = 1, \ldots, L$, with the property that, for every $i$, consumer $i$ has, at the price vector $p$, an excess demand vector $z_i(p) = -p_i(a^i)^\mathrm{T}$, a wealth effect vector $D_{w_i} x_i(p, p \cdot \omega_i) = (1/p_i) e^i$, and a substitution matrix $S_i(p, p \cdot \omega_i) = 0$ (where $a^1, \ldots, a^L$ and $e^1, \ldots, e^L$ are as defined above). Then we would have both

$$z(p) = \sum_i z_i(p) = -\sum_\ell p_\ell (a^\ell)^\mathrm{T} = -A^\mathrm{T} p = -p \cdot A = z$$

---

25. For example, it cannot hurt in any direction of price change that is orthogonal to the wealth effects vector $D_{w_i} x_i(p, p \cdot \omega_i)$ or to the excess demand vector $z_i(p)$. A more precise argument is given in Proposition 17.E.1.

26. The term "vertex" refers to what is usually called a "kink" in the case $L = 2$.

and

$$Dz(p) = -\sum_i D_{w_i} x_i(p, p \cdot \omega_i) z_i(p)^{\mathrm{T}}$$

$$= \sum_\ell (1/p_\ell) e^\ell (p_\ell a^\ell) = \sum_\ell e^\ell a^\ell = A,$$

and so we would have accomplished our objective.

Can we find these $L$ consumers? The answer is "yes." Begin by choosing a collection of endowments $(\omega_1, \ldots, \omega_I)$ yielding strictly positive consumptions when excess demands are $z_i(p) = -p_i(a^i)^{\mathrm{T}}$; that is, $x_i = \omega_i - p_i(a^i)^{\mathrm{T}} \gg 0$ for every $i$. Observe then that, for every $i = 1, \ldots, L$, the candidate individual excess demand satisfies Walras' law

$$p \cdot z_i(p) = -p_i p \cdot a^i = 0 \quad \text{(because } Ap = 0\text{)},$$

and, also, that the candidate wealth effect vector satisfies the necessary condition of Proposition 2.E.3

$$p \cdot D_{w_i} x_i(p, p \cdot \omega_i) = (1/p_i) p \cdot e^i = 1.$$

Figure 17.E.1 should then be persuasive enough in convincing us that we can assign preferences to $i = 1, \ldots, L$ in such a way that the chosen consumption at $p$ is $x_i$, the wealth effect vector at $p$ is proportional to $e^i$ (and therefore must equal $(1/p_i)e^i$),[27] and the indifference map has a kink at $x_i$. The figure illustrates the complete construction for the case $L = 2$.[28] In Exercise 17.E.3, you are asked to write an explicit utility function. ∎

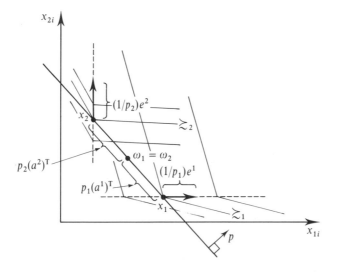

**Figure 17.E.1**

Decomposition of excess demand and price effects at a price vector $p$ (for $L = 2$).

---

27. Indeed, if $Dx_i(p, p \cdot \omega_i) = \alpha_i e^i$, then $1 = p \cdot Dx_i(p, p \cdot \omega_i) = \alpha_i p \cdot e^i = \alpha_i p_i$. Hence, $\alpha_i = 1/p_i$.

28. At no extra cost, we could actually accomplish a bit more. We could also require the substitution matrices of the consumers $i = 1, \ldots, L$ to be any arbitrary collection of $L \times L$ matrices $S_i$ satisfying the properties: $S_i$ is symmetric, negative semidefinite, $p \cdot S_i = 0$, and $S_i p = 0$. The specification of consumers generating excess demand $z(p)$ and excess demand effects $Dz(p)$ at $p$ would proceed in a manner similar to the proof just given except that the argument would now be applied to $A - \sum_i S_i$. By using matrices $S_i$ of maximal rank (i.e., of rank $L - 1$), we could insure that the resulting $L$ consumers display smooth indifference sets at their chosen consumptions.

Up to now, we have studied the possibility of restrictions on the behavior of excess demand at a single price vector. Although the results of Propositions 17.E.1 and 17.E.2 are already quite useful, we can go further. The essence of the negative point being made is, unfortunately, much more general. Consider an arbitrary function $z(p)$, and let us for the moment sidestep boundary issues by having $z(p)$ be defined on a domain where relative prices are bounded away from zero; that is, for a small constant $\varepsilon > 0$, we consider only price vectors $p$ with $p_\ell/p_{\ell'} \geq \varepsilon$ for every $\ell$ and $\ell'$. We could then ask: "Can $z(\cdot)$ coincide with the excess demand function of an economy *for every p in its domain*?" Of course, in its domain, $z(\cdot)$ must fulfill three obvious necessary conditions: it must be continuous, it must be homogeneous of degree zero, and it must satisfy Walras' law. But for any $z(\cdot)$ satisfying these three conditions, it turns out that the answer is, again, "yes."[29]

**Proposition 17.E.3:** Suppose that $z(\cdot)$ is a continuous function defined on

$$P_\varepsilon = \{p \in \mathbb{R}^L_+ : p_\ell/p_{\ell'} \geq \varepsilon \text{ for every } \ell \text{ and } \ell'\}$$

and with values in $\mathbb{R}^L$. Assume that, in addition, $z(\cdot)$ is homogeneous of degree zero and satisfies Walras' law. Then there is an economy of $L$ consumers whose aggregate excess demand function coincides with $z(p)$ in the domain $P_\varepsilon$.[30]

**Proof:** At the end of this section, we offer (in small-type) a brief discussion of the general proof of this result. Here, we limit ourselves to the comparatively simple case where $L = 2$.

Suppose then that $L = 2$ and that an $\varepsilon > 0$ and a function $z(\cdot)$ satisfying the assumption of the proposition are given to us. The continuity and homogeneity of degree zero of $z(\cdot)$ imply the existence of a number $r > 0$ such that $|z_1(p)| < r$ for every $p \in P_\varepsilon$. We now specify two functions $z^1(\cdot)$ and $z^2(\cdot)$ with domain $P_\varepsilon$ and values in $\mathbb{R}^2$, which are also continuous and homogeneous of degree zero, and satisfy Walras' law. In particular, we let

$$z^1_1(p) = \tfrac{1}{2}z_1(p) + r \qquad [\text{accordingly, } z^1_2(p) = -(p_1/p_2)z^1_1(p)]$$

and

$$z^2_1(p) = \tfrac{1}{2}z_1(p) - r \qquad [\text{accordingly, } z^2_2(p) = -(p_1/p_2)z^2_1(p)].$$

Note that $z(p) = z^1(p) + z^2(p)$ for every $p \in P_\varepsilon$. We shall show that for $i = 1, 2$ the function $z^i(\cdot)$ coincides in the domain $P_\varepsilon$ with the excess demand function of a consumer. To this effect, we use the following properties of $z^i(\cdot)$: continuity, homogeneity of degree zero, satisfaction of Walras law, *and* the fact that there is no $p \in P_\varepsilon$ such that $z^i(p) = 0$. In Exercise 17.E.4, you are asked to show by example that this last requirement is needed.

Choose a $\omega_i \gg 0$ such that $\omega_i + z^i(p) \gg 0$ for every $p \in P_\varepsilon$. In Figure 17.E.2, we represent the offer curve $OC_i$ associated with $z^i(\cdot)$ in the domain $P_\varepsilon$. In the figure, for every $p \in P_\varepsilon$,

---

29. The question was posed by Sonnenschein (1973). He conjectured that the answer was that, indeed, on the domain where $p_\ell \geq \varepsilon$ for all $\ell$, the three properties were not only necessary but also sufficient; that is, we could always find such an economy. He also proved that this is so for the two-commodity case. The problem was then solved by Mantel (1974) for any number of commodities. Mantel made use of $2L$ consumers. Shortly afterwards, Debreu (1974) gave a different and very simple proof requiring the indispensable minimum of $L$ consumers. This was topped by Mantel (1976), who refined his earlier proof to show that $L$ homothetic consumers (with no restrictions in their initial endowments) would do.

30. Note, in particular, that this result implies that for any $I \geq L$, there is an economy of $I$ consumers that generates $z(\cdot)$ on $P_\varepsilon$. We need only add to the $L$ consumers identified by the proposition $I - L$ consumers who have no endowments (or, alternatively, whose most preferred consumption bundle at all price vectors in $P_\varepsilon$ is their endowment vector).

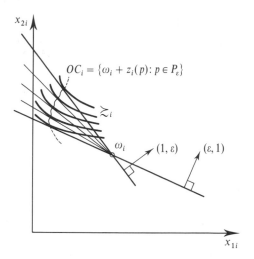

**Figure 17.E.2**

Construction of preferences (in the case $L = 2$) for the offer curve of an excess demand function $z_i(\cdot)$ such that $z_i(p) = 0$ has no solution with $1/\varepsilon < p_1/p_2 < \varepsilon$.

$\omega_i + z^i(p)$ is the intersection point of the offer curve with the budget line perpendicular to $p$. The offer curve is continuous and, because $z^i(p) = 0$ has no solution in $P_\varepsilon$, it does not touch the initial endowment point. We then see in the figure that no matter how complicated the offer curve may otherwise be, we can always fit an indifference map so that for any $p \in P_\varepsilon$ we generate precisely the demands $\omega_i + z^i(p)$. ∎

---

Strictly speaking, Proposition 17.E.3 does not yet settle our original question, "Can we assert anything more about the equilibria of an economy than what we have derived in Sections 17.C and 17.D?" The problem is that Proposition 17.E.3 characterizes the behavior of excess demand away from the boundary, whereas it is the power of the boundary conditions that yields some of the restrictions we have already established: existence, (generic) finiteness, oddness, the index formula.[31] To argue that we cannot hope for more restrictions than these on the equilibrium set, we need to guarantee that if a candidate equilibrium set satisfies them, then the construction of the "explaining" economy will not add new equilibria. The result presented in Proposition 17.E.4, whose proof we omit, provides therefore the final answer to our question.[32]

**Proposition 17.E.4:** For any $N \geq 1$, suppose that we assign to each $n = 1, \ldots, N$ a price vector $p^n$, normalized to $\|p^n\| = 1$, and an $L \times L$ matrix $A_n$ of rank $L - 1$, satisfying $A_n p^n = 0$ and $p^n \cdot A_n = 0$. Suppose that, in addition, the index formula $\sum_n (-1)^{L-1} \operatorname{sign} |\hat{A}_n| = +1$ holds.[33] If $L = 2$, assume also that positive and negative index equilibria alternate.

Then there is an economy with $L$ consumers such that the aggregate excess demand $z(\cdot)$ has the properties:

(i) $z(p) = 0$ for $\|p\| = 1$ if and only if $p = p^n$ for some $n$.
(ii) $Dz(p^n) = A_n$ for every $n$.

---

31. Note, for example, that although a candidate function $z(\cdot)$ defined on $P_\varepsilon$ may not have any solution, we can still successfully generate it from an economy. What happens, of course, is that the equilibria of the economy (which must exist) are all outside of $P_\varepsilon$.

32. For this and more general results, see Mas-Colell (1977).

33. Here, $\hat{A}_n$ is the $L - 1 \times L - 1$ matrix obtained by deleting one row and corresponding column from $A$.

Proposition 17.E.4 tells us that for any finite collection of price vectors $\{p^1, \ldots, p^N\}$ and matrices of price effects $\{Dz(p^1), \ldots, Dz(p^N)\}$, we can find an economy with $L$ consumers for which these price vectors are equilibrium price vectors and $\{Dz(p^1), \ldots, Dz(p^N)\}$, are the corresponding price effects at these equilibria. The result implies that to derive further restrictions on Walrasian equilibria we will need to make additional (and, as we shall see, strong) assumptions. This is the subject of the next three sections. An excellent survey for further reading on the topic of this section is Shafer and Sonnenschein (1982).

---

We should point out that the initial endowments of the consumers obtained by means of Propositions 17.E.2, 17.E.3 or 17.E.4 are not a priori limited in any way. If there are constraints on permissible initial endowments, the nonnegativity conditions on consumption come into play and there may, in fact, be other restrictions on the function $z(\cdot)$. For example, you are asked in Exercise 17.E.5 to verify that the excess demand vectors $z(p)$ and $z(p')$ represented in Figure 17.E.3 cannot be decomposed into individual excess demand functions generated by rational preferences if the amount of any commodity that any consumer may possess as an initial endowment is prescribed to be at most 1 and if consumptions must be nonnegative.

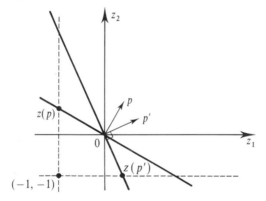

**Figure 17.E.3**

Excess demand choices that cannot be decomposed due to boundary constraints.

**Proof of Proposition 17.E.3 continued:** Although a complete proof of the proposition for the case of any number of commodities would take us too far afield, the essentials of the proof by Debreu (1974) are actually not too difficult to convey. We shall attempt to do so. We note that, when carefully examined, the proof can be seen as a generalization of the argument for the $L = 2$ case presented earlier.

In Section 3.J, we saw that the strong axiom of revealed preference (SA) for demand functions is equivalent to the existence of rationalizing preferences. The same is true for excess demand functions: If an excess demand function $z^i(\cdot)$ satisfies the SA (we will give a precise definition in a moment), then $z^i(\cdot)$ can be generated from rational preferences.[34] It is thus reasonable to redefine our problem as: Given a function $z(\cdot)$ that, on the domain $P_\varepsilon$, is continuous, homogeneous of degree zero, and satisfies Walras' law (for short, we refer to these functions as *excess demand functions*), can we find $L$ excess demand functions $z^i(\cdot)$, each satisfying the SA, such that $\sum_i z^i(p) = z(p)$ for every $p \in P_\varepsilon$?

Before proceeding, let us define the SA for an excess demand function $z^i(\cdot)$. The definition is just a natural adaptation of the definition for demand functions. We say that *p is directly revealed preferred to p′* if

---

34. We refer to the proof of Proposition 3.J.1 for the justification of this claim.

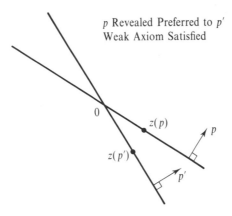

*p* Revealed Preferred to *p′*
Weak Axiom Satisfied

**Figure 17.E.4**
Revealed preference
for excess demand.

$$z^i(p) \neq z^i(p') \qquad \text{and} \qquad p \cdot z^i(p') \leq 0 \qquad \qquad (17.E.4)$$

(see Figure 17.E.4). We say that $p$ is *indirectly revealed preferred to* $p'$ if there is a finite chain $p^1, \ldots, p^N$ such that $p^1 = p$, $p^N = p'$, and $p^n$ is directly revealed preferred to $p^{n+1}$ for all $n \leq N - 1$. The SA then says:

*For every $p$ and $p'$, if $p$ is (directly or indirectly) revealed preferred to $p'$, then $p'$ cannot be (directly) revealed preferred to $p$.*

From now on, we let prices be normalized. A convenient normalization here is $\|p\|^2 = p \cdot p = \sum_\ell (p_\ell)^2 = 1$.

We say that an excess demand function $z^i(\cdot)$ is *proportionally one-to-one* if $p \neq p'$ implies that $z^i(p)$ is not proportional to $z^i(p')$; in particular, we have $z^i(p) \neq z^i(p')$. For proportionally one-to-one excess demand functions (and normalized prices), we can restate the "directly revealed preferred" definition (17.E.4) as

$$p \neq p' \qquad \text{and} \qquad p \cdot z^i(p') \leq 0. \qquad \qquad (17.E.4')$$

Suppose that $\alpha_i(\cdot)$ is an arbitrary real-valued function of $p$ such that $\alpha_i(p) > 0$ for all $p \in P_\varepsilon$. The basic observation of the proof is then the following: *if $z^i(\cdot)$ is a proportionally one-to-one excess demand function that satisfies the SA, then the same properties are true of the function* $\alpha_i(\cdot) z^i(\cdot)$. Indeed, for any $p$ and $p'$ the revealed preference inequalities (17.E.4') hold for $z^i(\cdot)$ *if and only if* they hold for $\alpha_i(\cdot) z^i(\cdot)$, and if $z^i(\cdot)$ is proportionally one-to-one, then so is $\alpha_i(\cdot) z^i(\cdot)$. This observation suggests a way to proceed. We could look for $L$ proportionally one-to-one excess demand functions $z^i(\cdot)$ satisfying the SA and such that, at every $p \in P_\varepsilon$, the vectors $\{z^1(p), \ldots, z^L(p)\}$ constitute a basis capable of spanning $z(p)$ by means of a strictly positive linear combination, that is, such that for every $p \in P_\varepsilon$ we can write $z(p) = \sum_i \alpha_i(p) z^i(p)$ for some numbers $\alpha_i(p) > 0$. This is precisely what we will now do.

For every normalized $p \in P_\varepsilon$, denote $T_p = \{z \in \mathbb{R}^L : p \cdot z = 0\}$ and for every $i = 1, \ldots, L$, let $z^i(p) \in T_p$ be the point that minimizes the Euclidean distance $\|z - e^i\|$ (or, equivalently, maximizes the concave "utility function" $-\|z - e^i\|$ for $z \in T_p$, where $e^i$ is the $i$th unit vector (the column vector whose $i$th entry is 1 with zeros elsewhere). Geometrically, $z^i(p)$ is the perpendicular projection of $e^i$ on the budget hyperplane $T_p$; that is, $z^i(p) = e^i - p_i p$, where $p_i$ is the $i$th component of the vector $p$ (recall that $i \leq L$). Then $z^i(\cdot)$ is proportionally one-to-one (see Exercise 17.E.6) and satisfies the SA (since it is derived from utility maximization; see also Exercise 17.E.7).

Now let $r > 0$ be a large-enough number for us to have $z(p) + rp \gg 0$ for every normalized $p \in P_\varepsilon$ [such an $r$ exists by the continuity of $z(\cdot)$ and the fact that the set of normalized price vectors in $P_\varepsilon$ is compact and includes only strictly positive price vectors]. For every $i = 1, \ldots, L$ and every normalized $p \in P_\varepsilon$, define $\alpha_i(p) = z_i(p) + rp_i > 0$, where $z_i(p)$ is the $i$th component

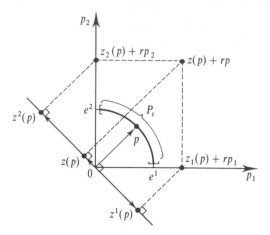

**Figure 17.E.5**

Illustration of the construction of individual excess demand in the proof of Proposition 17.E.3.

of the vector $z(p)$. We claim, that $\sum_i \alpha_i(p)z^i(p) = z(p)$, and this concludes the proof. Indeed,

$$\sum_i (z_i(p) + rp_i)(e^i - p_i p) = \sum_i z_i(p)e^i + \sum_i rp_i e^i - \left(\sum_i p_i z_i(p)\right)p - r\left(\sum_i p_i^2\right)p$$

$$= z(p) \qquad + rp \qquad - 0 \qquad - rp$$

$$= z(p).$$

Geometrically, what we are doing is projecting every $\alpha_i(p)e^i$ on the hyperplane $\{z \in \mathbb{R}^L : p \cdot z = 0\}$. By the definition of $\alpha_i(p)$, we have $\sum_i \alpha_i(p)e^i = z(p) + rp$. Therefore, when we project both sides, we get $\sum_i \alpha_i(p)z^i(p) = z(p)$. The construction is illustrated in Figure 17.E.5. ∎

# 17.F Uniqueness of Equilibria

Up to this point, we have concentrated on the determination of the general properties of the Walrasian equilibrium model. We now take a different tack. We focus on a particular, important property—the uniqueness of equilibrium—and we investigate conditions, necessarily special, under which it obtains.[35]

The presentation is organized into four headings. The first contemplates a general setting with production and discusses conditions on the demand side of the economy that, by themselves (i.e., without the help of further restrictions on the production side), guarantee the uniqueness of equilibrium. The second discusses the gross substitution property, an important class of conditions with uniqueness implications for exchange economies. The third presents a limited result that relies on the Pareto optimality property of equilibrium. The fourth analyzes the role of the index formula as a source of uniqueness and nonuniqueness results.

Throughout Section 17.F, we assume that individual preferences are continuous, strictly convex, and strongly monotone.

---

35. Reviews for this topic are Kehoe (1985) and (1991), and Mas-Colell (1991).

*The Weak Axiom for Aggregate Excess Demand*

Suppose that the production side of the economy is given to us by an arbitrary technology $Y \subset \mathbb{R}^L$ of the constant returns, convex type (i.e., $Y$ is a convex cone). What conditions involving only the demand side of the economy guarantee the uniqueness of equilibrium allocations?[36] From the analysis presented in Section 4.D, we already know one answer: if a welfare authority makes sure that wealth is always distributed so as to maximize a (strictly concave) social welfare function, then the economy admits a (strictly concave) normative representative consumer, and the equilibrium necessarily corresponds to the unique Pareto optimum of this one-consumer economy (as in Section 15.C). In our current framework, however, this is not a promising approach because wealth is derived from initial endowments and only by coincidence can we expect that the induced distribution of wealth maximizes a social welfare function. We will therefore concentrate on a weaker and, for the purpose at hand, more interesting condition: that the *weak axiom of revealed preference* holds for the aggregate excess demand of the consumers.

To begin, suppose that $z(p) = \sum_i (x_i(p, p \cdot \omega_i) - \omega_i)$ is the aggregate excess demand function of the consumers. For this economy with production, Proposition 17.F.1 provides a useful restatement of the definition of Walrasian equilibrium (Definition 17.B.1) in terms of $z(\cdot)$.

**Proposition 17.F.1:** Given an economy specified by the constant returns technology $Y$ and the aggregate excess demand function of the consumers $z(\cdot)$, a price vector $p$ is a Walrasian equilibrium price vector if and only if

(i) $p \cdot y \leq 0$ for every $y \in Y$, and
(ii) $z(p)$ is a feasible production; that is, $z(p) \in Y$.

**Proof:** If $p$ is a Walrasian equilibrium price vector, then (ii) follows from market clearing and (i) is a necessary condition for profit maximization with a constant returns technology. In the other direction, if (i) and (ii) hold, then consumptions $x_i^* = x_i(p, p \cdot \omega_i)$ for $i = 1, \ldots, I$, production vector $y^* = z(p) \in Y$, and price vector $p$ constitute a Walrasian equilibrium. To verify this, the only condition that is not immediate is profit maximization. However, $y^* = z(p) \in Y$ is profit maximizing because $p^* \cdot y \leq 0$ for all $y \in Y$ [since (i) holds] and $p \cdot y^* = p \cdot z(p) = 0$ (from Walras' law). ∎

We next define the weak axiom for excess demand functions.

**Definition 17.F.1:** (*The Weak Axiom for Excess Demand Functions*) The excess demand function $z(\cdot)$ satisfies the weak axiom of revealed preference (WA) if for any pair of price vectors $p$ and $p'$, we have

$$z(p) \neq z(p') \text{ and } p \cdot z(p') \leq 0 \text{ implies } p' \cdot z(p) > 0.$$

---

36. The set $Y$ can be thought as an aggregate production set. The restriction that $Y$ be of constant returns is made merely for convenience of exposition. It allows us, for example, not to worry about the distribution of profits to consumers (since profits are zero in any equilibrium). Note also that the constant returns model includes pure exchange as a special case (where $Y = -\mathbb{R}_+^L$).

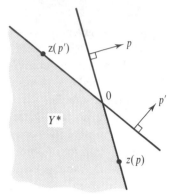

**Figure 17.F.1**

A violation of the weak axiom implies multiplicity of equilibria for some $Y$.

In words, the definition says that if $p$ is revealed preferred to $p'$, then $p'$ cannot be revealed preferred to $p$ [i.e., $z(p)$ cannot be affordable under $p'$]. It is the same definition used in Sections 1.G and 2.F, but now applied to excess demand functions.[37] The axiom is always satisfied by the excess demand function of a single individual, but it is a strong condition for *aggregate* excess demand (see Section 4.C for a discussion of this point).

We first note that, given $z(\cdot)$, the WA is a necessary condition for us to be assured of a unique equilibrium for every possible convex, constant returns technology $Y$ that $z(\cdot)$ is coupled with. To see this, suppose that the WA was violated; that is, suppose that for some $p$ and $p'$ we have $z(p) \neq z(p')$, $p \cdot z(p') \leq 0$, and $p' \cdot z(p) \leq 0$. Then we claim that both $p$ and $p'$ are equilibrium prices for the convex, constant returns production set given by

$$Y^* = \{y \in \mathbb{R}^L : p \cdot y \leq 0 \text{ and } p' \cdot y \leq 0\}.$$

Figure 17.F.1 depicts this production set for the case $L = 2$. Note that we have $z(p) \in Y^*$ and $p \cdot y \leq 0$ for every $y \in Y^*$. Thus, by Proposition 17.F.1, $p$ is an equilibrium price vector. The same is true for $p'$. Since $z(p) \neq z(p')$, we conclude that the equilibrium is not unique for the economy formed by $z(\cdot)$ and the production set $Y^*$.

What about sufficiency? The weak axiom is not quite a sufficient condition for uniqueness, but Proposition 17.F.2 shows that it does guarantee that for any convex, constant returns $Y$, *the set of equilibrium price vectors is convex*. Although this convexity property is certainly not the same as uniqueness, it has an immediate uniqueness implication: if an economy has only a *finite* number of (normalized) price equilibria (a generic situation according to Section 17.D),[38] the equilibrium must be unique.

---

37. A formal, and inessential, difference is that we now define the revealed preference relation on the budget sets (i.e., on price vectors) directly rather than on the choices (i.e., on commodity vectors).

38. Although our discussion in Section 17.D focused on the case of exchange economies, its conclusions regarding generic local uniqueness and finiteness of the equilibrium set can be extended to the present production context.

**Proposition 17.F.2:** Suppose that the excess demand function $z(\cdot)$ is such that, for any constant returns convex technology $Y$, the economy formed by $z(\cdot)$ and $Y$ has a unique (normalized) equilibrium price vector. Then $z(\cdot)$ satisfies the weak axiom. Conversely, if $z(\cdot)$ satisfies the weak axiom then, for any constant returns convex technology $Y$, the set of equilibrium price vectors is convex (and so, if the set of normalized price equilibria is finite, there can be at most one normalized price equilibrium).

**Proof:** The first part has already been shown. To verify the convexity of the set of equilibrium prices, suppose that $p$ and $p'$ are equilibrium price vectors for the constant returns convex technology $Y$; that is, $z(p) \in Y$, $z(p') \in Y$, and, for any $y \in Y$, $p \cdot y \leq 0$ and $p' \cdot y \leq 0$. Let $p'' = \alpha p + (1 - \alpha)p'$ for $\alpha \in [0, 1]$. Note, first, that $p'' \cdot y = \alpha p \cdot y + (1 - \alpha)p' \cdot y \leq 0$ for any $y \in Y$. To show that $p''$ is an equilibrium, we therefore need only establish that $z(p'') \in Y$. Because $0 = p'' \cdot z(p'') = \alpha p \cdot z(p'') + (1 - \alpha)p' \cdot z(p'')$, we have that either $p \cdot z(p'') \leq 0$ or $p' \cdot z(p'') \leq 0$. Suppose that the first possibility holds, so that $p \cdot z(p'') \leq 0$ [a parallel argument applies if, instead, $p' \cdot z(p'') \leq 0$]. Since $z(p) \in Y$ we have $p'' \cdot z(p) \leq 0$. But with $p'' \cdot z(p) \leq 0$ and $p \cdot z(p'') \leq 0$, a contradiction to the WA can be avoided only if $z(p'') = z(p)$. Hence $z(p'') \in Y$.[39] ∎

We are therefore led to focus attention on conditions on preferences and endowments of the $I$ consumers guaranteeing that the aggregate excess demand function $z(p)$ fulfills the WA. To begin with a relatively simple case, suppose that all the endowment vectors $\omega_i$ are proportional among themselves; that is, that $\omega_i = \alpha_i \bar{\omega}$, where $\bar{\omega}$ is the vector of total endowments and $\alpha_i \geq 0$ are shares with $\sum_i \alpha_i = 1$. In such an economy, the distribution of wealth across consumers is independent of prices. Normalizing prices to $p \cdot \bar{\omega} = 1$, the wealth of consumer 1 is $\alpha_i$ and $z_i(p) = x_i(p, \alpha_i) - \omega_i$. The aggregate demand behavior of a population of consumers with fixed wealth levels was studied in Section 4.C. We repeat our qualitative conclusion from there: if individual wealth levels remain fixed, the satisfaction of the WA by aggregate demand (or excess demand), although restrictive, is not implausible.[40]

A proportionality assumption on initial endowments is not very tenable in a general equilibrium context. It is important, therefore, to ask which new effects are at work (relative to those studied in Section 4.C) when the distribution of endowments does not satisfy this hypothesis. Unfortunately, it turns out that nonproportionality of endowments can reduce the likelihood of satisfaction of the weak axiom by aggregate excess demand. To see this, consider the relatively simple situation in which preferences are homothetic. Recall from Sections 4.C and 4.D that, when endowments are proportional, this case is extremely well behaved; not only is the WA satisfied, but the model even admits a representative consumer. Yet, as we proceed to discuss

---

39. Observe that we have established that either $z(p'') = z(p)$ or $z(p'') = z(p')$. Since this is true for any $\alpha \in [0, 1]$, and since the function $z(\cdot)$ is continuous, this implies that $z(p) = z(p')$ for any two equilibrium price vectors $p$ and $p'$; that is, if the WA holds for $z(\cdot)$, then every Walrasian equilibrium for the given endowments must have the same aggregate consumption vector and, hence, the same aggregate production vector.

40. On this point, consult also the references given in Chapter 4, especially Hildenbrand (1994).

below (in small type), even with homothetic preferences, the WA can easily be violated when endowments are not proportional.[41]

---

In Section 2.F we offered a differential version of the WA for the case of demand functions. In a parallel fashion we can also do so for excess demand functions. It can be shown that a sufficient differential condition for the WA is

$$dp \cdot Dz(p) \, dp < 0 \text{ whenever } dp \cdot z(p) = 0 \text{ (i.e., whenever}$$
the price change is compensated) *and dp is not proportional*    (17.F.1)
*to p* (i.e., relative prices change).

Allowing for the first inequality to be weak, expression (17.F.1) constitutes also a necessary condition.[42]

Under the homotheticity assumption, we have

$$D_{w_i} x_i(p, p \cdot \omega_i) = \frac{1}{p \cdot \omega_i} x_i(p, p \cdot \omega_i).$$

Denoting $S_i = S_i(p, p \cdot \omega_i)$, $x_i = x_i(p, p \cdot \omega_i)$, $\bar{x} = \sum_i x_i$ and $\bar{\omega} = \sum_i \omega_i$, this implies (recall 17.E.3)

$$Dz(p) = \sum_i S_i(p, p \cdot \omega_i) - \sum_i \frac{1}{p \cdot \omega_i} x_i(p, p \cdot \omega_i) z_i(p, p \cdot \omega_i)^{\mathrm{T}}$$

$$= \sum_i S_i - \sum_i \frac{1}{p \cdot \omega_i} \left[ x_i - \frac{p \cdot \omega_i}{p \cdot \bar{\omega}} \bar{x} \right] \left[ x_i - \frac{p \cdot \omega_i}{p \cdot \bar{\omega}} \bar{x} \right]^{\mathrm{T}}$$

$$+ \sum_i \frac{1}{p \cdot \omega_i} \left[ x_i - \frac{p \cdot \omega_i}{p \cdot \bar{\omega}} \bar{x} \right] \left[ \omega_i - \frac{p \cdot \omega_i}{p \cdot \bar{\omega}} \bar{\omega} \right]^{\mathrm{T}} - \frac{1}{p \cdot \bar{\omega}} \bar{x} z(p)^{\mathrm{T}}. \quad (17.F.2)$$

For any direction of price change $dp$ with $dp \cdot z(p) = 0$, the first two terms on the right-hand side of equation (17.F.2) generate an effect of the appropriate sign [the $L \times L$ substitution matrices $S_i(p, p \cdot \omega_i)$ and variance matrices

$$- \left[ x_i - \frac{p \cdot \omega_i}{p \cdot \bar{\omega}} \bar{x} \right] \left[ x_i - \frac{p \cdot \omega_i}{p \cdot \bar{\omega}} \bar{x} \right]^{\mathrm{T}}$$

are negative semidefinite], the fourth is null, *but the third is ambiguous.* It is quite possible for this covariance term to have the wrong sign (positive) and even for it to overcome the other two terms.[43] The situation to worry about is when $(1/(p \cdot \omega_i)) x_i(p, p \cdot \omega_i)$ and $\omega_i$ are positively associated within the population of consumers; that is, when the consumers who consume (per dollar) more than the average (per dollar) consumption of some commodities tend to be those that are relatively well endowed (per dollar) with those commodities. It makes sense that this case will cause difficulties: If the price of a good increases, the consumers who are (net) sellers of the good (who are likely to be those relatively well endowed with it) experience a positive wealth effect, whereas the consumers who are (net) buyers experience a negative wealth effect. Hence, an increase in the total demand for the good will ensue if (net) sellers consume relatively more of the good (per dollar) than (net) buyers.

---

41. To reinforce this point, it is also worth mentioning that, in fact, if we are free to choose initial endowments, then the class of homothetic preferences imposes no restrictions on aggregate demand. Indeed, as we noted in Section 17.E, the basic conclusion of Proposition 17.E.2 can still be obtained with the further restriction that preferences be homothetic. See Mantel (1976) and the survey of Shafer and Sonnenschein (1982).

42. Suppose that $\Delta p \cdot z(p) = (p' - p) \cdot z(p) = 0$. Definition 17.F.1 implies then that $\Delta p \cdot \Delta z = (p' - p) \cdot (z(p') - z(p)) \leq 0$. Going to the differential limit and using the chain rule, it follows that $dp \cdot Dz(p) \, dp \leq 0$ whenever $dp \cdot z(p) = 0$.

43. But this cannot happen if the $x_i(p, p \cdot \omega_i)$ are collinear among themselves or if the $\omega_i$ are collinear among themselves. See Exercise 17.F.1.

**Example 17.F.1:** This is an example of a failure of the WA compatible with homotheticity and even with the property of gross substitution, which we will discuss shortly. Consider a four-commodity economy with two consumers. Consumer 1 has preferences and endowments for only the first two goods; that is, he has an excess demand function $z_1(p) = z_1(p_1, p_2)$ that does not depend on $p_3$ and $p_4$ and, further, is such that $z_{31}(p) = z_{41}(p) = 0$ for all $p$. Similarly, consumer 2 has preferences and endowments for only the last two goods.[44] We claim that if there is a price vector $p'$ at which the excess demand of the two consumers is nonzero [i.e., $z_1(p') \neq 0$ and $z_2(p') \neq 0$], then the aggregate excess demand cannot satisfy the WA. To see this, choose $(\hat{p}_1, \hat{p}_2)$ and $(\hat{p}_3, \hat{p}_4)$ arbitrarily, except that $\hat{p}_1 z_{11}(p') + \hat{p}_2 z_{21}(p') < 0$ and $\hat{p}_3 z_{32}(p') + \hat{p}_4 z_{42}(p') < 0$. For $\alpha > 0$, take $q = (p'_1, p'_2, \alpha \hat{p}_3, \alpha \hat{p}_4)$ and $q' = (\alpha \hat{p}_1, \alpha \hat{p}_2, p'_3, p'_4)$. Then if $\alpha > 0$ is sufficiently large, we have $q \cdot z(q') < 0$ and $q' \cdot z(q) < 0$ (Exercise 17.F.2). ∎

See Exercise 17.F.3 for yet another example.

---

*Gross Substitution*

We now investigate the implications of a condition of a different nature from the WA. We shall see that it yields a uniqueness result for situations that are reducible to formalization as exchange economies.

To motivate the concept (and justify its name), consider the demand function of a consumer in a two-commodity situation. At given prices the demand substitution matrix has negative diagonal entries and, as a consequence, positive off-diagonal entries: if the price of one good is raised, the compensated demand for the other good increases. However, if we do not net out the wealth effects (i.e., if we look at the effect of prices on uncompensated demand), then it is possible for an increase in the price of one good to decrease the demand of the two goods: in gross terms, the two goods may be complements. We say that the two goods are *gross substitutes* if this does not happen, that is, if an increase in the price of one good decreases the (uncompensated or gross) demand for that good and increases the (uncompensated or gross) demand for the other good. By extension, the same term is used in the $L$-commodity case for the property that asserts that when a price of one good increases, the demand of *every* other good increases (and, therefore, the demand of that good decreases). For $L > 2$, however, this is not by any means a necessary property of even compensated demand. In fact, the gross substitute property is very restrictive. Nonetheless, it can make sense for problems with a few very aggregated commodities or for those where commodities possess special symmetries (see Exercise 17.F.4).

**Definition 17.F.2:** The function $z(\cdot)$ has the *gross substitute* (GS) property if whenever $p'$ and $p$ are such that, for some $\ell$, $p'_\ell > p_\ell$ and $p'_k = p_k$ for $k \neq \ell$, we have $z_k(p') > z_k(p)$ for $k \neq \ell$.

If, as is the case here, we are dealing with the aggregate excess demand of an economy, then the fact that $z(\cdot)$ is also homogeneous of degree zero has the consequence that with gross substitution we also have $z_\ell(p') < z_\ell(p)$ whenever $p'$ and $p$ are related as in Definition 17.F.2. To see this, let $\bar{p} = \alpha p$, where $\alpha = p'_\ell / p_\ell$. Note that $\bar{p}_\ell = p'_\ell$ and $\bar{p}_k > p'_k$ for $k \neq \ell$. Then the homogeneity of degree zero of $z(\cdot)$

---

44. Thus, this example can also be seen as a case of positive association between endowments and demands.

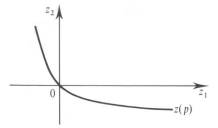

**Figure 17.F.2**

The offer curve of a gross substitute excess demand function.

tells us that $0 = z_\ell(\bar{p}) - z_\ell(p) = z_\ell(\bar{p}) - z_\ell(p') + z_\ell(p') - z_\ell(p)$. However, gross substitution implies that $z_\ell(\bar{p}) - z_\ell(p') > 0$ (change sequentially each price $p'_k$ for $k \neq \ell$ to $\bar{p}_k$, applying the GS property at each step), and so $z_\ell(p') - z_\ell(p) < 0$.

The differential version of gross substitution is clear enough: At every $p$, it must be that $\partial z_k(p)/\partial p_\ell > 0$ for $k \neq \ell$; that is, the $L \times L$ matrix $Dz(p)$ has positive off-diagonal entries. In addition, when $z(\cdot)$ is an aggregate excess demand function, homogeneity of degree zero implies that $Dz(p)p = 0$, and so $\partial z_\ell(p)/\partial p_\ell < 0$ for all $\ell = 1, \ldots, L$: the diagonal entries of $Dz(p)$ are all negative.

If in these definitions the inequalities are weak, one speaks of *weak gross substitution*.[45]

Figure 17.F.2 represents the offer curve of a gross substitute excess demand function $L = 2$. As the relative price of good 1 increases, the excess demand for good 1 decreases and the excess demand for good 2 increases.

An important characteristic of the gross substitute property, which follows directly from its definition, is that *it is additive across excess demand functions*. In particular, if the individual excess demand functions satisfy it, then the aggregate function does also.

**Example 17.F.2:** Consider a utility function of the form $u_i(x_i) = \sum_\ell u_{\ell i}(x_{\ell i})$. If $-[x_{\ell i}u''_{\ell i}(x_{\ell i})/u'_{\ell i}(x_{\ell i})] < 1$ for all $\ell$ and $x_{\ell i}$, then the resulting excess demand function $z_i(p)$ has the gross substitute property for any initial endowments (Exercise 17.F.5). This condition is satisfied by $u_i(x_i) = (\sum_\ell \alpha_{\ell i}x_{\ell i}^\rho)^{1/\rho}$ for $0 < \rho < 1$ (Exercise 17.F.5). The limits of these preferences as $\rho \to 1$ and $\rho \to 0$ are preferences representable, respectively, by linear functions and by Cobb–Douglas utility functions (recall Exercise 3.C.6). As far as the gross substitution property is concerned, Cobb–Douglas preferences constitute a borderline case. Indeed, the excess demand function for good $\ell$ is then $z_{\ell i}(p) = \alpha_{\ell i}(p \cdot \omega_i)/p_\ell - \omega_{\ell i}$. If $\omega_{ki} > 0$, the excess demand for good

---

45. It is worth mentioning that functions satisfying the GS property arise naturally in many economic contexts. For example, if $A$ is an $(L-1) \times (L-1)$ input–output matrix and $c \in \mathbb{R}_+^{L-1}$, then $c - (I - A)\alpha$ satisfies the (weak) GS property as a function of $\alpha \in \mathbb{R}_+^{L-1}$ (see Appendix A of Chapter 5 for the interpretation of these concepts). More generally, the equation system $g(\alpha) - \alpha$ associated with the fixed-point problem [i.e., find $\alpha$ such that $g(\alpha) = \alpha$] of an *increasing* function $g: \mathbb{R}_+^N \to \mathbb{R}_+^N$ [i.e., $g(\alpha) \geq g(\alpha')$ whenever $\alpha \geq \alpha'$] satisfies it (perhaps, again, in its weak version). Note that in these cases there is no homogeneity of degree zero or Walras' law—conditions specific to general equilibrium applications—to complement the GS property. This is significant because these conditions add substantially to the power of the GS property. See Exercise 17.F.16 for an exploration of the implications of the GS property without homogeneity of degree zero or Walras' law.

$\ell$ will respond positively to an increase in $p_k$. But if $\omega_{ki} = 0$, there will be no response.[46] ∎

*In the special case of exchange economies* if the gross substitute property holds for aggregate excess demand then equilibrium is unique.

**Proposition 17.F.3:** An aggregate excess demand function $z(\cdot)$ that satisfies the gross substitute property has at most one exchange equilibrium; that is, $z(p) = 0$ has at most one (normalized) solution.

**Proof:** It suffices that we show that $z(p) = z(p')$ cannot occur whenever $p$ and $p'$ are two price vectors that are not collinear. By homogeneity of degree zero, we can assume that $p' \geq p$ and $p_\ell = p'_\ell$ for some $\ell$. Now consider altering the price vector $p'$ to obtain the price vector $p$ in $L - 1$ steps, lowering (or keeping unaltered) the price of every commodity $k \neq \ell$ one at a time. By gross substitution, the excess demand of good $\ell$ cannot decrease in any step, and, because $p \neq p'$, it will actually increase in at least one step. Hence, $z_\ell(p) > z_\ell(p')$. ∎

One might hope to establish uniqueness in economies with production by applying the GS property to the production inclusive excess demand $\bar{z}(\cdot)$. However, the direct use of the GS property in a production context is limited. Imagine, for example, a situation in which inputs and outputs are distinct goods. If the price of an input increases, the demand for every other input may decrease, not increase as the GS property would require, simply because the optimal level of output decreases. Indirectly, though, the gross substitute concept may still be quite helpful. Recall, in particular, that at the end of Section 17.B, we argued that it is always possible to reduce a production economy to an exchange economy in which, in effect, consumers exchange factor inputs and then engage in home production using a freely available constant returns technology. The aggregate excess demand in this derived exchange economy for factor inputs combines elements of both consumption and production and may well satisfy the GS property.[47]

What is the relationship between gross substitution and the weak axiom? Clearly, the WA does not imply the GS property (the latter can be violated even in quasilinear, one-consumer economies). The converse relationship is not as obvious, but it is nevertheless true that the GS property does not imply the WA. In fact, Example 17.F.1, which violated the WA, could perfectly well satisfy GS.[48] There is, however, one connection that is important. The gross substitute property implies that

$$\text{If } z(p) = 0 \text{ and } z(p') \neq 0, \text{ then } p \cdot z(p') > 0. \tag{17.F.3}$$

We shall not prove condition (17.F.3) here. For the case in which $L = 2$, you are asked for a proof in Exercise 17.F.7. To understand (17.F.3), note that if $p$ is the price vector of an

---

46. See also Grandmont (1992) for an interesting result where a Cobb–Douglas positive representative consumer, and therefore GS excess demand, is derived from a requirement that at any given price, the choice behavior is widely dispersed (in a certain precise sense) across consumers. Grandmont's is an example of a model in which the individual excess demand functions may not satisfy the gross substitute property but the aggregate function does.

47. See Mas-Colell (1991) and Exercise 17.F.6 for further elaborations on this point.

48. Therefore, in view of Proposition 17.F.1, we know that in a constant returns economy the fulfillment of the GS property by the excess demand of the consumers does *not* imply the uniqueness of equilibrium.

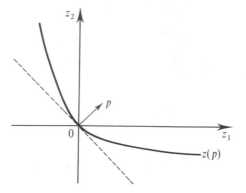

**Figure 17.F.3**

The revealed preference property of gross substitution.

(exchange) equilibrium and $p'$ is not, then, since $z(p) = 0$, we have $p' \cdot z(p) = 0$, and therefore any nonequilibrium $p'$ is revealed preferred to $p$. Hence, the requirement in (17.F.3) that $p \cdot z(p') > 0$ amounts to a restricted version of the WA asserting that no equilibrium price vector $p$ can be revealed preferred to a nonequilibrium price vector $p'$. Geometrically, it says that the range of the excess demand function, $\{z(p'): p' \gg 0\} \subset \mathbb{R}^L$ (i.e., the offer curve), lies entirely above the hyperplane through the origin with normal vector $p$ (see Figure 17.F.3). In parallel to Proposition 17.F.2, condition (17.F.3) implies the convexity of the equilibrium price set of the exchange economy, that is, of $\{p \in \mathbb{R}^L_{++}: z(p) = 0\} \subset \mathbb{R}^L$ (in Exercise 17.F.8, you are asked to show this). Interestingly, condition (17.F.3) is satisfied not only in the WA and the GS cases but also in the no-trade case, to be reviewed shortly.

In the differentiable case, there is a parallel way to explore the connection between the WA and gross substitution. Let $z(p) = 0$. The sufficient differential condition (17.F.1) for the WA tells us that $dp \cdot Dz(p)\, dp < 0$ for any $dp$ not proportional to $p$. Suppose now that instead of the WA, we require that $Dz(p)$ has the gross substitute sign pattern. Because $z(p) = 0$, we have $p \cdot Dz(p) = 0$ and $Dz(p)p = 0$ [recall (17.E.1) and (17.E.2)]. Using these two properties it can then be shown that again we obtain $dp \cdot Dz(p)\, dp < 0$ for any $dp$ not proportional to $p$ (see Section M.D of the Mathematical Appendix). Hence, we can conclude that *at an exchange equilibrium price vector*, the GS property yields every local restriction implied by the WA. This is summarized in Proposition 12.F.4.

**Proposition 17.F.4:** If $z(\cdot)$ is an aggregate excess demand function, $z(p) = 0$, and $Dz(p)$ has the gross substitute sign pattern, then we also have $dp \cdot Dz(p)\, dp < 0$ whenever $dp \neq 0$ is not proportional to $p$.

---

### Uniqueness as an Implication of Pareto Optimality

We now present a result that is not of great significance in itself but that is nonetheless interesting because it highlights a uniqueness implication of Pareto optimality. For simplicity, we restrict ourselves again to an exchange economy (see Exercise 17.F.9 for a generalization allowing for production).

**Proposition 17.F.5:** Suppose that the initial endowment allocation $(\omega_1, \ldots, \omega_I)$ constitutes a Walrasian equilibrium allocation for an exchange economy with strictly convex and strongly monotone consumer preferences (i.e., no-trade is an equilibrium). Then this is the unique equilibrium allocation.

**Proof:** Let an allocation $x = (x_1, \ldots, x_I)$ and price vector $p$ constitute a Walrasian equilibrium when consumers' endowments are $(\omega_1, \ldots, \omega_I)$. Since $\omega_i$ is affordable at price vector $p$ for each consumer $i$, we have $x_i \succsim_i \omega_i$ for all $i$. However, by the assumption of the proposition and the first welfare theorem, $(\omega_1, \ldots, \omega_I)$ is a Pareto optimal allocation and so we must have $x_i \sim_i \omega_i$ for all $i$. But then we can conclude that $x_i = \omega_i$ for all $i$, because otherwise, by the strict convexity of preferences, the allocation $(\frac{1}{2}x_1 + \frac{1}{2}\omega_1, \ldots, \frac{1}{2}x_I + \frac{1}{2}\omega_I)$ would be Pareto superior to $(\omega_1, \ldots, \omega_I)$. ∎

*Index Analysis and Uniqueness (... and Nonuniqueness)*

The index theorem (Proposition 17.D.2) provides a device to test for uniqueness in any given model. The idea is that if merely from the general maintained assumptions of the model we can attach a definite sign to the determinant of the Jacobian matrix of the equilibrium equations at any solution point, then the equilibrium must be unique. After all, the index theorem implies that sign uniformity across equilibria is impossible if there is multiplicity.

As a matter of fact, we could have proceeded by means of this index methodology for many of our previous uniqueness results. Take, for example, an exchange economy. In both the WA and the GS cases, whenever $z(p) = 0$, the matrix $Dz(p)$ is necessarily negative semidefinite [see the small-type discussion of expression (17.F.1) and Proposition 17.F.4]. Moreover, if an equilibrium is regular (i.e., if rank $Dz(p) = L - 1$), the negative semidefiniteness of $Dz(p)$ can be shown to imply that the index of the equilibrium is necessarily $+1$ (see Exercise 17.F.11). Hence, we can conclude that in both the WA and GS cases, any regular economy must have a unique (normalized) equilibrium price vector.

Although the index methodology provides a good research tool, it is often the case that, as here, uniqueness conditions lend themselves to direct proofs. It is a notable fact that some of the more subtle uses of index analysis are not to establish uniqueness but rather to establish nonuniqueness [the first usage of this type was made by Varian (1977)]. This is illustrated in Example 17.F.3.

**Example 17.F.3:** Suppose we have two one-consumer countries, $i = 1, 2$. Countries are symmetrically positioned relative to the home (H) and the foreign (F) good. To be specific, let each country have one unit of the home good as an endowment and none of the foreign good, and utility functions $u_i(x_{Hi}, x_{Fi}) = x_{Hi} - x_{Fi}^{\rho}$ for $-1 < \rho < 0$. Merely from symmetry considerations, it follows that there is a symmetric equilibrium $p = (1, 1)$. But we may be interested in knowing whether there are asymmetric equilibria. One way to proceed is as follows: compute the index of the symmetric equilibrium; a sufficient (but not necessary) condition for the existence of an asymmetric equilibrium is that this index be negative (i.e., $-1$).[49] If we carry out the computation for the present example (you are asked to do so in Exercise 17.F.13), we see that the index is negative if at prices $p = (1, 1)$ the wealth effects in each country are so biased toward the home good that an increase in the price of the good of country 1, say, actually increases the demand for this good in country 1 by more than it decreases the demand from country 2. ∎

---

49. In this, as typically in any example, the excess demand function fails to be differentiable at prices at which demand just "hits" the boundary. Typically (we *could* say "generically"), these prices will not be equilibrium prices and the validity of the index theorem is not affected by these nondifferentiabilities.

# 17.G  Comparative Statics Analysis

Comparative statics is the analytical methodology that concerns itself with the study of how the equilibria of a system are affected by changes (often described as "shocks") in various environmental parameters. In this section, we examine the comparative static properties of Walrasian equilibria.

To be concrete, we consider an exchange economy formalized by a system of aggregate excess demand equations for the first $L - 1$ commodities:

$$\hat{z}(p; q) = (z_1(p; q), \dots, z_{L-1}(p; q)).$$

Here, $q \in \mathbb{R}^N$ is a vector of $N$ parameters influencing preferences or endowments (or both). Throughout, we normalize $p_L = 1$.

Suppose the value of the parameters is given initially by the vector $\bar{q}$ and that $\bar{p}$ is an equilibrium price vector for $\bar{q}$; that is, $\hat{z}(\bar{p}; \bar{q}) = 0$. We wish to analyze the effect of a shock in the exogenous parameters $q$ on the endogenous variable $p$ solving the system. A first difficulty for doing so is the possibility of multiplicity of equilibrium: the system of $L - 1$ equations in $L - 1$ unknowns $\hat{z}(\cdot; q) = 0$ may have more than one solution for the relevant values of $q$, and thus we may need to decide which equilibrium to single out after a shock.

If the change in the values of the parameters from $\bar{q}$ is small, then a familiar approach to this problem is available. It consists of focusing on the *local* effects on $p$, that is, on the solutions that remain near $\bar{p}$. Assuming the differentiability of $\hat{z}(p; q)$, we may determine those effects by applying the implicit function theorem (see Section M.E of the Mathematical Appendix). Indeed, if the system $\hat{z}(\cdot; \bar{q}) = 0$ is regular at the solution $\bar{p}$, that is, if the $(L - 1) \times (L - 1)$ matrix $D_p\hat{z}(\bar{p}; \bar{q})$ has rank $L - 1$,[50] then for a neighborhood of $(\bar{p}; \bar{q})$ we can express the equilibrium price vector as a function $p(q) = (p_1(q), \dots, p_{L-1}(q))$ whose $(L - 1) \times N$ derivative matrix at $\bar{q}$ is

$$Dp(\bar{q}) = -[D_p\hat{z}(\bar{p}; \bar{q})]^{-1} D_q\hat{z}(\bar{p}; \bar{q}). \tag{17.G.1}$$

What can we say about the first-order effects $Dp(\bar{q})$? Expression (17.G.1) and Proposition 17.E.2 [which told us that the matrix of price effects $D_p\hat{z}(\bar{p}; \bar{q})$ is unrestricted when $I \geq L$] strongly suggest that, without further assumptions, the "anything goes" principle applies to the comparative statics of equilibrium in the same manner that in Section 17.E it applied to the closely related issue of the effects of price changes on excess demand. We now elaborate on this point in the context of a specific example.

Let the list of parameters under consideration be the vector $\hat{\omega}_1 = (\omega_{11}, \dots, \omega_{L-1,1})$ of initial endowments of the first consumer for the first $L - 1$ commodities. All of the remaining endowments are kept fixed. As before we assume that $\hat{z}(\cdot; \hat{\omega}_1) = 0$ is regular at the solution $\bar{p}$. It can be shown (see Exercise 17.G.1) that if the demand function of the first consumer satisfies a strict normality condition, then rank $Dp(\hat{\omega}_1) = L - 1$, where $p(\cdot)$ is the locally defined solution function with $p(\hat{\omega}_1) = \bar{p}$. Proposition 17.G.1 tells us that if there are enough consumers then this is all that we can say.

---

50. In a slight abuse of notation, we let $D_p\hat{z}(\bar{p}; \bar{q})$ stand for the matrix obtained from $D_pz(\bar{p}; \bar{q})$ by deleting the last row and column.

**Proposition 17.G.1:** Given any price vector $\bar{p}$, endowments for the first consumer of the first $L - 1$ commodities $\hat{\bar{\omega}}_1 = (\bar{\omega}_{11}, \ldots, \bar{\omega}_{L-1,1})$, and a $(L - 1) \times (L - 1)$ nonsingular matrix $B$, there is an exchange economy formed by $L + 1$ consumers in which the first consumer has the prescribed endowments of the first $L - 1$ commodities, $\hat{z}(\bar{p}; \hat{\bar{\omega}}_1) = 0$, $\hat{z}(\cdot, \hat{\bar{\omega}}_1) = 0$ is regular at $\bar{p}$ and $Dp(\hat{\bar{\omega}}_1) = B$.

**Proof:** Let the first consumer have endowments with the prescribed amounts of the first $L - 1$ commodities, and give to this consumer arbitrary preferences, with the single restriction that $D_{\bar{\omega}_1}\hat{z}_1(\bar{p}; \hat{\bar{\omega}}_1)$ be nonsingular (it suffices for this that the demand function of consumer 1 satisfies a strict normality condition; again see Exercise 17.G.1). Since $D_{\bar{\omega}_1}\hat{z}(\bar{p}; \hat{\bar{\omega}}_1) = D_{\bar{\omega}_1}\hat{z}_1(\bar{p}; \hat{\bar{\omega}}_1)$, expression (17.G.1) tells us that we are looking for an additional collection of $L$ consumers such that the resulting $(L + 1)$-consumer economy has $\hat{z}(\bar{p}; \hat{\bar{\omega}}_1) = 0$ and

$$D_p\hat{z}(\bar{p}; \hat{\bar{\omega}}_1) = -D_{\bar{\omega}_1}\hat{z}_1(\bar{p}; \hat{\bar{\omega}}_1)B^{-1} \tag{17.G.2}$$

Note that the $(L - 1) \times (L - 1)$ matrix defined in (17.G.2) is nonsingular. Thus, we have reduced our problem to the following: can we find $L$ consumers whose aggregate excess demand at $\bar{p}$ is $-\hat{z}_1(\bar{p}; \hat{\bar{\omega}}_1)$ and whose aggregate $(L - 1) \times (L - 1)$ matrix of price effects is $\hat{A} = -D_{\bar{\omega}_1}\hat{z}_1(\bar{p}; \hat{\bar{\omega}}_1)B^{-1} - D_p\hat{z}_1(\bar{p}; \hat{\bar{\omega}}_1)$? It follows from Proposition 17.E.2 that the answer to this question is "yes" (note that the restrictions that Proposition 17.E.2 imposes on the $L \times L$ matrix $A$ place no restriction on the matrix obtained by deleting one row and one column of $A$). ∎

Proposition 17.G.1 shows that any first-order effect is possible. As in Section 17.E (recall Figure 17.E.3), it is also the case here that if there are prior restrictions on initial endowments and if consumption must be nonnegative, then there are again comparative statics restrictions of a global character. [See Brown and Matzkin (1993) for a recent investigation of this point.]

There are a number of comparative static effects that, ideally, we would like to have and that seem economically intuitive: For example, that if the endowment of one good increases, then its equilibrium price decreases. Nevertheless, strong conditions are required for them to hold. By now this should not surprise us: We already know that wealth effects and/or the lack of sufficient substitutability can undermine intuitive comparative static effects. The latest instance we have seen of this occurring has been precisely Proposition 17.G.1.

The analysis of uniqueness in Section 17.E may lead us to suspect that good comparative statics effects can hold if aggregate excess demand satisfies either weak-axiom-like conditions (recall Definition 17.F.1) or gross substitution properties (see Definition 17.F.2). This is in fact so. We consider first the implications of a weak-axiom-like restriction on aggregate excess demand.

**Proposition 17.G.2:** Suppose that $\hat{z}(\bar{p}; \bar{q}) = 0$, where $\hat{z}(\cdot)$ is differentiable. If $D_q\hat{z}(\bar{p}; \bar{q})$ is negative definite,[51] then

$$(D_q\hat{z}(\bar{p}; \bar{q})\, dq) \cdot (Dp(\bar{q})\, dq) \geq 0 \text{ for any } dq. \tag{17.G.3}$$

---

51. This condition is independent of which particular commodity has been labeled as $L$ (see Section M.D of the Mathematical Appendix).

**Proof:** The inverse of a negative definite matrix is negative definite. Therefore $[D_q \hat{z}(\bar{p}; \bar{q})]^{-1}$ is negative definite (see Section M.D of the Mathematical Appendix). Hence, by (17.G.1) we have

$$(D_q \hat{z}(\bar{p}; \bar{q}) \, dq) \cdot (Dp(\bar{q}) \, dq) = -D_q \hat{z}(\bar{p}; \bar{q}) \, dq \cdot [D_p \hat{z}(\bar{p}; \bar{q})]^{-1} D_q \hat{z}(\bar{p}; \bar{q}) \, dq \geq 0$$

which is precisely (17.G.3). ∎

The weak axiom implies the negative semidefiniteness of $D_p \hat{z}(\bar{p}; \bar{q})$ whenever $\hat{z}(\bar{p}; \bar{q}) = 0$ [see expression (17.F.1) and the remark following it]. Therefore, the assumption of Proposition 17.G.2 amounts to a small strengthening of this implication. Its conclusion says that for any infinitesimal shock $dq$ in $q$, the induced shock to excess demand at prices fixed at $\bar{p}$, $D_q \hat{z}(\bar{p}; \bar{q}) \, dq$, and the induced shock in equilibrium prices, $D_q p(\bar{q}) \, dq$, move "in the same direction" (more precisely, as vectors in $\mathbb{R}^{L-1}$ they form an acute angle). For example, a shock that at fixed prices affects only the aggregate excess demand of the first good,[52] say by decreasing it, will necessarily decrease the equilibrium price of this good. Note that this does *not* say that if $\omega_{11}$ increases then the equilibrium price of good 1 decreases. Under an assumption of normal demand, this change in $\omega_{11}$ does indeed decrease the excess demand for good 1 at $\bar{p}$ but it also affects the excess demand for all other goods (see Exercise 17.G.2).

We next consider in Proposition 17.G.3 the implications of gross substitution (or, more precisely, of gross substitution holding locally at $(\bar{p}; \bar{q})$).

**Proposition 17.G.3:** Suppose that $\hat{z}(\bar{p}; \bar{q}) = 0$, where $\hat{z}(\cdot; \cdot)$ is differentiable. If the $L \times L$ matrix $D_p z(\bar{p}; \bar{q})$ has negative diagonal entries and positive off-diagonal entries, then $[D_p \hat{z}(\bar{p}; \bar{q})]^{-1}$ has all its entries negative.

**Proof:** Because of the homogeneity of degree zero of excess demand (recall Exercise 17.E.1), we have $D_p z(\bar{p}; \bar{q})\bar{p} = 0$, and so $D_p \hat{z}(\bar{p}; \bar{q})\hat{\bar{p}} \ll 0$, where $\hat{\bar{p}} = (\bar{p}_1, \ldots, \bar{p}_{L-1})$. Denote by $I$ the $(L-1) \times (L-1)$ identity matrix and take an $r > 0$ large enough for the matrix $A = (1/r)D_p \hat{z}(\bar{p}; \bar{q}) + I$ to have all its entries positive. Then $D_p \hat{z}(\bar{p}; \bar{q}) = -r[I - A]$, and therefore $D_p \hat{z}(\bar{p}; \bar{q})\hat{\bar{p}} \ll 0$ yields $(I - A)\hat{\bar{p}} \gg 0$; that is, the positive matrix $A$, viewed formally as an input–output matrix, is productive (see Appendix A of Chapter 5; the fact that the diagonal entries of $A$ are not zero is inessential). Hence, as we showed in the proof of Proposition 5.AA.1, the matrix $[I - A]^{-1}$ exists and has all its entries positive. From $[D_p \hat{z}(\bar{p}; \bar{q})]^{-1} = -(1/r)[I - A]^{-1}$ we have our conclusion. ∎

It follows from Proposition 17.G.3 and expression (17.G.1) that, given gross substitution, if $D_q \hat{z}(\bar{p}; \bar{q}) \, dq \ll 0$, that is, if the excess demand for all of the first $L - 1$ goods decreases as a consequence of the shock (and therefore the excess demand for the $L$th good increases), then $Dp(\bar{q}) \, dq \ll 0$. That is, the equilibrium prices of the

---

52. What this means is that the excess demand of good 2 to $L - 1$ is not changed. By Walras' law, the excess demand of good $L$ must change.

first $L - 1$ goods (relative to the price of the $L$th good) decrease.[53] In particular, suppose again that consumer 1's initial endowment of some good decreases. By labelling commodities appropriately, we can let this good be commodity $L$. Under the assumption of normal demand for consumer 1, a decrease in $\omega_{L1}$, at the fixed price vector $\bar{p}$, will decrease the excess demand for the first $L - 1$ goods. Therefore, the prices of the first $L - 1$ goods decrease and so we now reach the conclusion that we could not obtain by means of Proposition 17.G.2: if the endowments of a single good decrease then its price (relative to the price of any other good) increases. This suggests, incidentally, that the assumptions of Proposition 17.G.3 are strictly stronger than those of Proposition 17.G.2. Indeed, as we saw in Proposition 17.F.4, if $z(\bar{p}; \bar{q}) = 0$ and the $L \times L$ matrix $D_p z(\bar{p}; \bar{q})$ satisfies the gross substitute property, then $dp \cdot D_p z(\bar{p}; \bar{q}) \, dp < 0$ whenever $dp \neq 0$ is not proportional to $\bar{p}$. In particular, by letting $dp_L = 0$ we have that the matrix $D_p \hat{z}(\bar{p}; \bar{q})$ is negative definite.

---

Expression (17.G.1) allows us to explicitly compute the effects of an infinitesimal shock. In fact, it also offers a practical computational method to estimate the local effects of small (but perhaps not infinitesimal) shocks. Suppose that the value of the vector of parameters after the shock is $\bar{\bar{q}}$ and, for $t \in [0, 1]$, consider a continuous function $\hat{z}(\cdot, t)$ that, as $t$ ranges from $t = 0$ to $t = 1$, distorts $\hat{z}(\cdot; \bar{q})$ into $\hat{z}(\cdot; \bar{\bar{q}})$. An example of such a function, called a *homotopy*, is

$$\hat{z}(\cdot, t) = (1 - t)\hat{z}(\cdot; \bar{q}) + t\hat{z}(\cdot; \bar{\bar{q}}).$$

Denote the solution set by $E = \{(t, p): \hat{z}(p, t) = 0\}$. Then we may attempt to determine $p(\bar{\bar{q}})$ by following a segment in the solution set that starts at $(0, \bar{p})$.[54] If $\bar{\bar{q}}$ is close to $\bar{q}$, and the initial situation $\bar{p}$ is regular, then we are in the simple case of Figure 17.G.1(a): there is a unique segment that connects $(0, \bar{p})$ to some $(1, \bar{\bar{p}})$.[55] Naturally, we then put $p(\bar{\bar{q}}) = \bar{\bar{p}}$.

If $\bar{\bar{q}}$ is not close to $\bar{q}$ but nevertheless $\hat{z}(\cdot, t)$ is a regular excess demand function for every $t$ [this will be the case if, for example, $z(\cdot, t)$ satisfies, for every $t$, any of the uniqueness conditions covered in Section 17.F], then this procedure will still succeed in going from $t = 0$ to $t = 1$ and, therefore, in determining an equilibrium for $\bar{\bar{q}}$.[56] Unfortunately, if the shock is large, we can easily find ourselves in situations such as Figures 17.G.1(b) and 17.G.1(c), where at some $t'$ the economy $\hat{z}(\cdot, t')$ is not regular and at $(t', p_{t'})$ there is no natural

---

53. This conclusion holds for nonlocal shocks as well. To see this let $Dz(p; q)$ have the gross substitute sign pattern throughout its domain and suppose that $\hat{z}(p; \bar{\bar{q}}) \ll \hat{z}(p; \bar{q})$ for all $p$. For $t \in [0, 1]$, define $\hat{z}(p; t) = t\hat{z}(p; \bar{\bar{q}}) + (1 - t)\hat{z}(p; \bar{q})$. Denote by $p(t)$ the solution to $\hat{z}(p; t) = 0$. Note that $D_t \hat{z}(p(t); t) \, dt = \hat{z}(p(t); \bar{\bar{q}}) - \hat{z}(p(t); \bar{q}) \ll 0$ for all $t$ and therefore, by Proposition 17.G.3, $Dp(t) \, dt \ll 0$ for all $t$. But then, for any $\ell = 1, \ldots, L - 1$, we have

$$p_\ell(\bar{\bar{q}}) - p_\ell(\bar{q}) = \int_0^1 \left[ \frac{\partial p_\ell(t)}{dt} \right] dt < 0.$$

In Exercise 17.G.3 you can find a more direct approach to the global theory. See also Milgrom and Shannon (1994) for much more on the latter approach.

54. In practice, "following" a segment involves the application of appropriate numerical techniques; see Garcia-Zangwill (1981), Kehoe (1991), and references therein.

55. Moreover, if the shock is sufficiently small, the $\bar{p}$ so obtained is independent of the particular homotopy used.

56. However, if there are multiple equilibria at $\bar{\bar{q}}$, then which equilibrium we find may now depend on the homotopy.

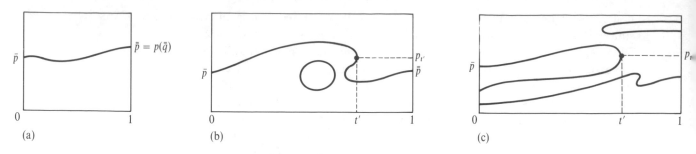

**Figure 17.G.1**   Comparative statics in the large: the general case.

continuation of the path as $t$ increases.[57] To obtain an equilibrium $\bar{p}$ for $\bar{q}$ there is then no real alternative but to appeal to general algorithms for the solution of the system of equations $\hat{z}(\,\cdot\,;\bar{q}) = 0$. It is a sobering thought that which solution we come up with at $\bar{q}$ may be dictated more by our numerical technology than by our initial position $(\bar{p};\bar{q})$. This is most unsatisfactory, and it is a manifestation of a serious shortcoming—the lack of a theory of equilibrium selection.

# 17.H  Tâtonnement Stability

We have, so far, carried out an extensive analysis of equilibrium equations. A characteristic feature that distinguishes economics from other scientific fields is that, for us, the equations of equilibrium constitute the center of our discipline. Other sciences, such as physics or even ecology, put comparatively more emphasis on the determination of dynamic laws of change. In contrast, up to now, we have hardly mentioned dynamics. The reason, informally speaking, is that economists are good (or so we hope) at recognizing a state of equilibrium but are poor at predicting precisely how an economy in disequilibrium will evolve. Certainly there are intuitive dynamic principles: if demand is larger than supply then the price will increase, if price is larger than marginal cost then production will expand, if industry profits are positive and there are no barriers to entry, then new firms will enter, and so on. The difficulty is in translating these informal principles into precise dynamic laws.[58]

The most famous attempt at this translation was made by Walras (1874), and the modern version of his ideas have come to be known as the theory of *tâtonnement stability*. In this section, we review two tâtonnement-style models, one of pure price adjustment and the other of pure quantity adjustment. We should emphasize,

---

57. Note that by reversing the direction of change of $t$ we can continue to move along the segments in these two figures (this is actually quite a general fact). If $\bar{p}$ is the only solution at $t = 0$, as in 17.G.1(b), then the segment necessarily ends with a $(1, \bar{p})$. Thus, in some sense we have succeeded in finding an equilibrium for $\bar{q}$ that is associated with our initial $\bar{p}$. But the association is very weak: it may depend on the particular homotopy and it requires the parameter-reversal procedure. If, as in Figure 17.G.1(c), $\bar{p}$ is not the only equilibrium at $t = 0$, then the procedure may simply not work: the segment that starts at $(0, \bar{p})$ goes back to $t = 0$.

58. Refer to Hahn (1982) for a general review.

however, that those are just two examples. Indeed, one of the difficulties in this area is the plethora of plausible disequilibrium models. Although there is a single way to be in equilibrium, there are many different ways to be in disequilibrium.

## Price Tâtonnement

We consider an exchange economy formalized by means of an excess demand function $z(\cdot)$. Suppose that we have an initial $p$ that is not an equilibrium price vector, so that $z(p) \neq 0$. For example, the economy may have undergone a shock and $p$ may be the preshock equilibrium price vector. Then the demand-and-supply principle suggests that prices will adjust upward for goods in excess demand and downward for those in excess supply. This is what was proposed by Walras; in a differential equation version put forward by Samuelson (1947), it takes the specific form

$$\frac{dp_\ell}{dt} = c_\ell z_\ell(p) \qquad \text{for every } \ell, \tag{17.H.1}$$

where $dp_\ell/dt$ is the rate of change of the price for the $\ell$th good and $c_\ell > 0$ is a constant affecting the speed of adjustment.

Simple as (17.H.1) is, its interpretation is fraught with difficulties. Which economic agent is in charge of prices? For that matter, why must the "law of one price" hold out of equilibrium (i.e., why must identical goods have identical prices out of equilibrium)? What sort of time does "$t$" represent? It cannot possibly be *real* time because, as the model stands, a disequilibrium $p$ is not compatible with feasibility (i.e., not all consumption plans can be simultaneously realized).

Perhaps the most sensible answer to all these questions is that (17.H.1) is best thought of not as modeling the actual evolution of a demand-and-supply driven economy, but rather as a tentative trial-and-error process taking place in fictional time and run by an abstract market agent bent on finding the equilibrium level of prices (or, more modestly, bent on restoring equilibrium after a disturbance).[59]

The hope is that, in spite of its idealized nature, the analysis of (17.H.1) will provide further insights into the properties of equilibria. Even perhaps some help in distinguishing good from poorly behaved equilibria. The analysis is at its most suggestive in the two-commodity case. For this case, Figure 17.H.1 represents the excess demand of the first good as a function of the relative price $p_1/p_2$. The actual dynamic trajectory of relative prices depends both on the initial levels of absolute prices and on the differential price changes prescribed by (17.H.1).[60] But note that, whatever the initial levels of absolute prices, $p_1(t)/p_2(t)$ increases at $t$ if and only if $z_1(p_1(t)/p_2(t), 1) > 0$. In Figure 17.H.1 we see the following two features of the adjustment equations (17.H.1).

(a) Call an equilibrium $(\bar{p}_1, \bar{p}_2)$ *locally stable* if, whenever the initial price vector is sufficiently close to it, the dynamic trajectory causes relative prices to converge to the equilibrium relative prices $\bar{p}_1/\bar{p}_2$ (the equilibrium is *locally totally unstable* if any

---

59. This is, in essence, the idea of Walras (tâtonnement means "groping" in French), who took inspiration from the functioning of the auctioneer-directed markets of the Paris stock exchange. The idea was made completely explicit by Barone (1908) and by Lange (1938), who went so far as to propose the tâtonnement procedure as an actual computing device for a centrally planned economy.

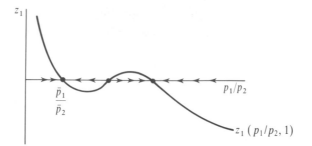

**Figure 17.H.1**

Tâtonnement
trajectories for $L = 2$.

disturbance leads the relative prices to diverge from $\bar{p}_1/\bar{p}_2$). Then a (regular) equilibrium $\bar{p}_1/\bar{p}_2$ is *locally stable or locally totally unstable according to the sign of the slope of excess demand at the equilibrium*, that is, according to the index of the equilibrium (recall Definition 17.D.2). If excess demand slopes downward at $\bar{p}_1/\bar{p}_2$ (as in Figure 17.H.1), then a slight displacement of $p_1/p_2$ above $\bar{p}_1/\bar{p}_2$ will generate excess supply for good 1 (and excess demand for good 2), and therefore the relative price will move back toward the equilibrium level $\bar{p}_1/\bar{p}_2$. The effect is the reverse if excess demand slopes upward at $\bar{p}_1/\bar{p}_2$.

(b) There is *system stability*, that is, *for any initial position* $(p_1(0), p_2(0))$, *the corresponding trajectory of relative prices $p_1(t)/p_2(t)$ converges to some equilibrium arbitrarily closely as $t \to \infty$.*

For regular, two-commodity, economies, properties (a) and (b) give a complete picture of the dynamics. It is very satisfactory picture that accounts for the persistency of tâtonnement stability analysis: a theory yielding properties (a) and (b) must be saying something with economic content.

Unfortunately, as soon as $L > 2$ neither the local conclusions (a) nor the global conclusions (b) of the two-commodity case generalize. This should not surprise us, since the price dynamics in (17.H.1) are entirely driven by the excess demand function, and we know (Propositions 17.E.2 and 17.E.3) that the latter is not restricted in any way (beyond the boundary conditions). Consider an example for $L = 3$ and $c_1 = c_2 = c_3 = 1$. In Figure 17.H.2 we represent the normalized set of prices $S = \{p \gg 0: (p_1)^2 + (p_2)^2 + (p_3)^2 = 1\}$. This normalization has the virtue that, for any excess demand function $z(p)$, the dynamic flow $p(t)$ generated by the differential equation $dp_\ell/dt = z_\ell(p)$, $\ell = 1, 2, 3$, remains in $S$ [i.e., if $p(0) \in S$ then $p(t) \in S$ for all $t$]. This is a consequence of Walras' law:

$$\frac{d(p_1(t)^2 + p_2(t)^2 + p_3(t)^2)}{dt} = 2p_1(t)z_1(p(t)) + 2p_2(t)z_2(p(t)) + 2p_3(t)z_3(p(t)) = 0.$$

Thus, the dynamics of $p$ can be represented by trajectories in $S$, the direction vector of the trajectory at any $p(t)$ being the direction of the excess demand vector $z(p(t))$. We conclude, therefore, that the only restrictions on the trajectories imposed by the general theory are those derived from the boundary behavior of excess demand. In Figure 17.H.2 we represent a possible field of trajectories. In the figure, when the

---

60. Note that although the change in $p_\ell$ at $t$ prescribed by (17.H.1) depends only on the relative prices $p_1/p_2$ for $\ell = 1, 2$, the change in the price ratio $p_1/p_2$ at $t$ depends both on the current price ratio and on the current absolute levels of $p_1$ and $p_2$.

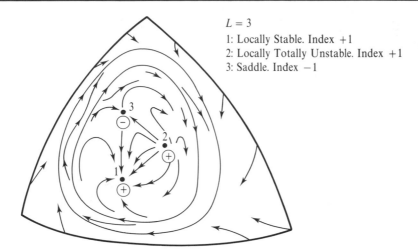

$L = 3$
1: Locally Stable. Index $+1$
2: Locally Totally Unstable. Index $+1$
3: Saddle. Index $-1$

**Figure 17.H.2**

An example of tâtonnement trajectories for $L = 3$.

price of a good goes to zero the excess demand for the good becomes positive (thus, in particular, the trajectories point inward near the boundary). However, properties (a) and (b) are both violated: There are (regular) equilibria that are neither locally stable nor locally totally unstable (they are "saddle points," such as the equilibrium labeled 3 in the figure), and from some initial positions prices may not converge to any equilibrium.[61]

In a more positive spirit, we now argue that for the cases where we have succeeded in proving the uniqueness of Walrasian equilibrium, we are also able to establish the convergence of any price trajectory to this equilibrium (this property is called *global stability*).[62] The next proposition covers, in particular, the weak axiom, the gross substitute, and the no-trade cases studied in Section 17.F.[63] These three cases have in common that they satisfy the weak axiom when we restrict ourselves to comparisons between equilibrium and nonequilibrium prices [see the discussion of condition (17.F.3) in Section 17.F]. That is, for the unique (normalized) equilibrium price vector $p^*$ arising in these cases we have: "If $z(p^*) = 0$ then $p^* \cdot z(p) > 0$ for any $p$ not proportional to $p^*$."

**Proposition 17.H.1:** Suppose that $z(p^*) = 0$ and $p^* \cdot z(p) > 0$ for every $p$ not proportional to $p^*$. Then the relative prices of any solution trajectory of the differential equation (17.H.1) converge to the relative prices of $p^*$.

**Proof:** Consider the (Euclidean) distance function $f(p) = \sum_\ell (1/c_\ell)(p_\ell - p_\ell^*)^2$. For any trajectory $p(t)$ let us then focus on the distance $f(p(t))$ at points $t$ along the trajectory. We have

---

61. We should warn against deriving any comfort when prices converge to a limit cycle. Recall that this price tâtonnement is not happening in real time. The dynamic analysis has a hope of telling us something significant only if it converges.

62. Warning: uniqueness by itself does not imply stability—except for $L = 2$. You should try to draw a counterexample in the style of Figure 17.H.2.

63. For a proof specific to the gross substitute case, see Exercise 17.H.1.

$$\frac{df(p(t))}{dt} = 2 \sum_\ell \frac{1}{c_\ell} (p_\ell(t) - p_\ell^*) \frac{dp_\ell(t)}{dt}$$

$$= \sum_\ell \frac{1}{c_\ell} (p_\ell(t) - p_\ell^*) c_\ell z_\ell(p(t))$$

$$= -p^* \cdot z(p(t)) \leq 0,$$

where the last inequality is strict if and only if $p(t)$ is not proportional to $p^*$. We conclude that the price vector $p(t)$ monotonically approaches the price vector $p^*$ [in fact, since the same argument applies to $\alpha p^*$, $p(t)$ must be monotonically approaching any $\alpha p^*$]. This does not mean that $p(t)$ reaches a vicinity of $p^*$. Typically it will not: the rate of approach of $p(t)$ to $p^*$ will go to zero before $p(t)$ gets near $p^*$. But the rate of approach can go to zero only if $p(t)$ becomes nearly proportional to $p^*$ as $t \to \infty$, in which case the relative prices do converge.[64] ∎

---

We can gain further insight into the dynamics of tâtonnement by carrying out a local analysis. It will be more convenient now if we fix $p_L = 1$ and, consequently, we limit (17.H.1) to the first $L - 1$ coordinates. Accordingly we denote $\hat{z}(p) = (\hat{z}_1(p), \ldots, \hat{z}_{L-1}(p))$. Suppose that $\hat{z}(p^*) = 0$. A standard result of differential equation theory tells us that if the $(L - 1) \times (L - 1)$ matrix $D\hat{z}(p^*)$ is nonsingular (i.e., if the equilibrium is regular), then the behavior of the trajectories in a neighborhood of $p^*$ is controlled by the linearization of the system at $p^*$, that is, by $CD\hat{z}(p^*)$, where $C$ is the $(L - 1) \times (L - 1)$ diagonal matrix whose $\ell$th diagonal entry is the constant $c_\ell$. One says that $p^*$ is *locally stable* if there is $\varepsilon > 0$ such that $p(t) \to p^*$ whenever $\| p(0) - p^* \| < \varepsilon$ (i.e., for small perturbations the equilibrium will tend to restore itself). It then turns out that $p^*$ is locally stable if and only if all the eigenvalues of $CD\hat{z}(p^*)$ have negative real parts. In addition, $p^*$ is locally stable irrespective of the speeds of adjustment[65] (i.e., for all positive diagonal matrices $C$) if $D\hat{z}(p^*)$ is negative definite (see Section M.D of the Mathematical Appendix).[66]

One way to understand why the previous local stability result for the tâtonnement dynamics requires strong conditions on $D\hat{z}(p^*)$ is to note that we are in fact imposing the condition that the price of a commodity reacts *only* to the excess demand or supply for the same commodity. An ideal market agent may want to adjust these prices with an eye also to the effects of the adjustment on the excess demand for the *other* commodities. One concrete possibility is the following: if excess demand at time $t$ is $\hat{z}(p(t))$, then the market agent adjusts prices by some amount $dp/dt = (dp_1/dt, \ldots, dp_{L-1}/dt)$ so as to cause a *proportional* decrease in the magnitude of all excess demands and supplies. That is, $D\hat{z}(p(t))(dp/dt) = -\lambda \hat{z}(p(t))$ for some $\lambda > 0$, or, if the relevant inverse exists,

$$\frac{dp}{dt} = -\lambda [D\hat{z}(p)]^{-1} \hat{z}(p) \tag{17.H.2}$$

This adjustment equation is known as *Newton's method* and is a standard technique of numerical analysis. If $D\hat{z}(p^*)$ is nonsingular, so that $[D\hat{z}(p^*)]^{-1}$ exists, then (17.H.2) always

---

64. Continuous real-valued functions that take decreasing values along any dynamic trajectory and the value zero only at stationary points are known as *Lyapunov functions*.

65. How could we pretend to know much about speeds of adjustments?

66. Note that this fits nicely with Proposition 17.H.1 because the revealed-preference-like property postulated there implies the negative (semi)definiteness of $D\hat{z}(p)$ at the equilibrium price vector $p^*$.

succeeds in restoring equilibrium after a small disturbance. Thus we see the contrast: for tâtonnement stability, we impose few informational restrictions on the adjustment process [to determine the change in $p$ we only need to know $\hat{z}(p)$; in particular, no knowledge of the derivatives of $\hat{z}(\cdot)$ is required], but convergence is guaranteed only in special circumstances. For the Newton method, local convergence always obtains, but to determine the directions of price change at any $p$ we need to know all the excess demands $\hat{z}(p)$ and all the price effects $D\hat{z}(p)$. See Smale (1976) and Saari and Simon (1978) for classic contributions to this type of Newton price dynamics.

### Quantity Tâtonnement

In the analysis so far, prices could be out of equilibrium but quantities, that is to say the amounts demanded and supplied, are always at their equilibrium (i.e., utility and profit-maximizing) values. We now briefly consider a model in which quantities rather than prices may be in disequilibrium.[67] This is best done in a production context.

To be very concrete, suppose that there is a single production set $Y$.[68] At any moment of time, we assume that there is given a single, fixed production vector $y \in Y$. Prices, however, are always in equilibrium in the sense that the general equilibrium system of the economy, conditional on $y$, generates some equilibrium price system $p(y)$ (that is to say, we proceed in the short run as if the short-run production set were $\{y\} - \mathbb{R}_+^L$). This describes the short-run equilibrium of the economy.

What is an appropriate dynamics for this economy? It makes sense to think that, whatever it is, the change in production at time $t$, $dy(t)/dt \in \mathbb{R}^L$, moves production in a direction that increases profits *when the price vector at time $t$, $p(y(t))$, is taken as given*:

**Definition 17.H.1:** We say that the differentiable trajectory $y(t) \in Y$ is *admissible* if $p(y(t)) \cdot (dy(t)/dt) \geq 0$ for every $t$, with equality only if $y(t)$ is profit maximizing for $p(y(t))$ (in which case we could say that we are at a long-run equilibrium).

A difference between the price and the quantity tâtonnement approaches that adds appeal to the second is that feasibility is now insured at any $t$ and that, as a result, we can interpret the dynamics as happening in real time.[69,70]

Will an admissible trajectory necessarily take us to long-run equilibrium? We cannot really explore this matter here in any detail. As usual, the answer is "only

---

67. We could also look at the general case where both could be in disequilibrium; see, for example, Mas-Colell (1986).

68. There is no difficulty in considering several. Also, $Y$ can be interpreted as an individual or as an aggregate production set.

69. Nonetheless, it is important to realize that, even then, this is not a fully dynamic model: The optimization problems of the consumers remain static and free of expectational feedbacks and firms follow naive, short-run rules of adjustment (in a more positive spirit one might call this *adaptive*, rather than naive, behavior). For an extensive analysis of market adjustment procedures in real time, see Fisher (1983).

70. The quantity dynamics of Definition 17.H.1 are reminiscent of Marshall (1920) and are often referred to as *Marshallian dynamics*, especially in a partial equilibrium context. In contrast, the price dynamics are frequently called *Walrasian dynamics*.

under special circumstances." A limited, but important example (it covers the short-run/long-run model of Section 10.F) is described in Proposition 17.H.2.

**Proposition 17.H.2:** If there is a single strictly convex consumer, then any admissible trajectory converges to the (unique) equilibrium.

**Proof:** Consider $u(y(t) + \omega)$ where $u(\cdot)$ and $\omega$ are respectively the utility function and the endowments of the consumer. The unique equilibrium production vector is the single production vector $\bar{y}$ that maximizes $u(y + \omega)$ on $Y$; recall the one-consumer, one-firm example of Section 15.C.

The argument is much simpler if we assume that $u(\cdot)$ is differentiable. We claim that utility must then be increasing along any admissible trajectory. Indeed,

$$\frac{du(y(t) + \omega)}{dt} = \nabla u(y(t) + \omega) \cdot \frac{dy(t)}{dt}$$

$$= \mu(t) p(y(t)) \cdot \frac{dy(t)}{dt} \quad > 0,$$

with equality only at equilibrium. Here we have used the fact that at a short-run (interior) equilibrium, the price vector $p(y(t))$ weighted by the marginal utility of wealth $\mu(t)$ must be equal to the vector of marginal utilities of the consumer. Now, since utility is increasing, we must necessarily reach the production vector $\bar{y}$ at which utility is maximized in the feasible production set (i.e., the equilibrium). This is illustrated in Figure 17.H.3. (We are sidestepping minor technicalities: to proceed completely rigorously, we should argue that the dynamics cannot be so sluggish that we never reach the equilibrium. To do so we would need, strictly speaking, to strengthen slightly the concept of an admissible trajectory). ∎

Note that the single consumer of Proposition 17.H.2 could be a (positive) representative consumer standing for a population of consumers.

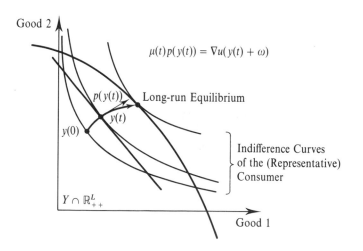

**Figure 17.H.3**

An example of quantity tâtonnement.

# 17.I Large Economies and Nonconvexities

As we have mentioned repeatedly, especially in Chapters 10 and 12, a central justification of the price-taking hypothesis is the assumption that every economic agent constitutes an insignificant part of the whole economy. Literally speaking, however, this cannot be satisfied in the model of this chapter because, formally, we allow for no more than a finite number $I$ of consumers. (This is particularly true of our examples, where we typically have $I = 2$.) A straightforward reinterpretation is possible, however. We illustrate it for the case of a pure exchange economy.

Suppose we consider economies whose consumers have characteristics (preferences and endowments) that fall into $I$ given types, with $r$ consumers of each type (a generalization to unequal numbers per type is possible; see Exercise 17.I.1). That is, the set of consumers is formed by $r$ *replicas* of a basic reference set of consumers. Furthermore, an allocation denoted by $(x_1, \ldots, x_I)$ is understood now to specify that *each* consumer of type $i$ consumes $x_i$ (so the totality of consumers of type $i$ consume $rx_i$). We observe then that the analysis and results presented up to this point are not modified by this reinterpretation; they simply do not depend in any way on the parameter $r$. In this way, we can conclude informally that the theory so far covers cases with an arbitrarily large number, even an infinity, of consumers; in particular, we see that any equilibrium of our earlier model is an equilibrium of the $r$-replica economy (for any integer $r \geq 1$).

There is, however, an important qualification. The ability to interpret the model and results in a manner that is fully independent of the number of consumers depends *crucially* on the convexity assumption on preferences. Without this assumption, it is not justified to neglect allocations that assign different consumption bundles to different consumers of the same type. Consider, for example, the Edgeworth box of Figure 17.I.1. If there is only one consumer of each type, then no equilibrium exists; but if we have two of each type, then there *is* an equilibrium. To see this, give $\omega_2$ to the convex consumers, let one of the two nonconvex consumers receive the bundle $x_1$, and let the other receive the different bundle $x_1'$. Thus, in the nonconvex case, the

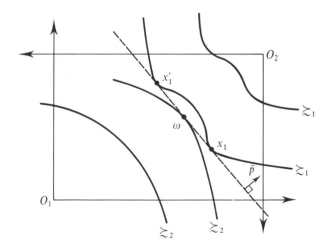

**Figure 17.I.1**

Equilibrium with nonconvex preferences in economies of changing size.

behavior of the economy can depend on the number of replicas: when we replicate an economy, new equilibria may emerge.[71]

The discussion of the previous example suggests an interesting observation: replication may actually *help* in the analysis of economies with nonconvexities, in the sense that an increase in the size of the economy (in terms of the number of replicas) may help insure existence of an equilibrium. Indeed, we devote the rest of this section to develop the argument that, if the economy is large enough, then the existence of an equilibrium is assured, or nearly so, even if preferences are not convex.[72]

To see this, suppose that we have an exchange economy with $I$ types. Consider a consumer of type $i$. If preferences are not convex (perhaps goods are indivisible), then the excess demand of this type is a correspondence $z_i(p)$. For $p \gg 0$, $z_i(p)$ is a compact set that may not be convex (as is the case for consumer 1 at $p = \bar{p}$ in Figure 17.I.1). Measuring in average, *per-replica*, terms, the excess demand correspondence of type $i$ when there are $r$ replicas is

$$z_{ir}(p) = \frac{1}{r}(z_i(p) + \cdots + z_i(p)) \qquad \text{(the sum has } r \text{ terms)}$$

$$= \frac{1}{r}\{z_{i1} + \cdots + z_{ir} : z_{i1} \in z_i(p), \ldots, z_{ir} \in z_i(p)\}.$$

If we examine Figure 17.I.1 again, we see that, as $r \to \infty$, the set $z_{1r}(\bar{p}) + \{\omega_1\}$ fills the entire segment between the demand points $x_1$ and $x_1'$. In particular, for any $\alpha \in [0,1]$ and integer $r$ we can find an integer $a_r \in [0, r]$ such that $|a_r/r - \alpha| \leq 1/r$ (note that the $r$ numbers $\{1/r, \ldots, r/r\}$ are evenly spaced in the interval $[0,1]$). By putting $a_r$ consumers at $x_1$ and $r - a_r$ consumers at $x_1'$, we get a per-replica consumption of

$$\frac{a_r}{r}x_1 + \left(1 - \frac{a_r}{r}\right)x_1' \in z_{ir}(p),$$

which, by taking $r$ large enough, comes as close to $\alpha x_1 + (1 - \alpha)x_1'$ as we wish. It turns out that this convexifying property is completely general. For any $p \gg 0$ and whatever the number of commodities, as $r \to \infty$ the per-replica excess demand $z_{ir}(p)$ of type $i$ converges as a set of the convex hull of $z_i(p)$. In the limit, the average per-replica excess demand correspondence of type $i$ becomes $z_{i\infty}(p) = $ convex hull $z_i(p)$. In the limit, therefore, the excess demand correspondence is convex valued and the existence of an equilibrium can be established as in Section 17.C.[73] In this sense,

---

71. That is, if we let $E(r)$ denote the equilibrium price set of the $r$ replica economy, we have $E(1) \subset E(r)$, but the converse need not be true. Note, moreover, that for arbitrary $r'' > r' > 1$, there need not be any inclusion relationship between $E(r'')$ and $E(r')$ (except if $r'' = mr'$ for some integer $m > 1$, in which case $E(r') \subset E(r'')$).

72. See Starr (1969) for a classic contribution to this topic.

73. See the comment after the proof of Proposition 17.C.2 regarding demand correspondences, and also Exercise 17.C.1.

then, as $r$ grows large, the economy must possess an allocation and price vector that constitute a "near" equilibrium.[74]

---

In the previous reasoning, the convexification of aggregate excess demand, with its existence implication, depends on our ability to prescribe very carefully which of several indifferent consumptions each consumer has to choose. Only in this way can we make sure that the aggregate consumption will be precisely right. Whatever we may think about the possible processes that may lead consumers to select among indifferent optimal choices in the right proportions, there can be little doubt that it would be better if we did not have to worry about this; that is, if, given any price, practically every consumer had a single optimal choice. It is therefore of interest to point out that, while not a necessity, this is a most plausible occurrence if the number of consumers is large. Indeed, *if the distribution of individual preferences is dispersed across the population* (so that, in particular, no two consumers are exactly identical[75]), *then even if the individual excess demands are true correspondences, the limit average may well be a* (continuous) *function*. This is because, at any $p$, only a vanishingly small proportion of consumers may display a nonconvexity at $p$. We commented on this point in Appendix A to Chapter 4 and we illustrate it further in Figure 17.I.2. Consider the Edgeworth box of Figure

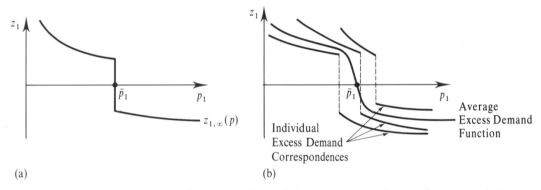

(a)                                       (b)

**Figure 17.I.2** The aggregate demand from dispersed individual demand is a continuous function. (a) Aggregate excess demand for the Edgeworth box of Figure 17.I.1 with a continuum of consumers of each type (i.e., $r = \infty$). (b) Individual excess demands are dispersed.

17.I.1, but with a continuum of consumers of each type. Since in this economy all the consumers of type 1 are identical, all of them exhibit a "consumption switch" (a nonconvexity) at precisely the same $\bar{p}$. The excess demand correspondence for the first good in this economy is represented in Figure 17.I.2(a) as $z_{1,\infty}(\cdot)$.[76] But if tastes of type 1 consumers exhibit variation, even if slight, then we would expect that no significant group of consumers simultaneously switches at any $p$ and therefore that, as in Figure 17.I.2(b), average demand will be well defined at any $p$ and will change only gradually with $p$.

---

74. Roughly speaking, by a "near" equilibrium we mean an allocation and price vector that is close to satisfying the conditions of an equilibrium. A precise technical definition of this concept can be given, but we shall not do so here.

75. We note, as an incidental matter, that in the limit with an infinity of agents this requirement is incompatible with the existence of only a finite number of types. To deal with this case, the formal setting would need to be extended.

76. Precisely, $z_{1,\infty}(\cdot)$ is the correspondence whose graph is the limit graph, as $r$ goes to $\infty$, of the correspondences $z_r(\cdot)$ defined by $z_r(p) = (1/r)(z(p) + \cdots + z(p))$, where the sum has $r$ terms and $z(\cdot)$ is the excess demand correspondence of the two-consumer economy in the Edgeworth box of Figure 17.I.1.

We comment briefly on economies with production. Suppose that the consumption side of the economy is generated, as before, as the $r$-replica of a basic reference set of (possibly nonconvex) consumers. There are also $J$ production sets $Y_j$. Each $Y_j$ is closed, contains the origin, and satisfies free disposal (these are all standard assumptions). In addition, we assume that there is an upper bound (a capacity bound perhaps) on every $Y_j$; that is, there is a number $s$ such that $y_{\ell j} \leq s$ for all $\ell$ and $y_j \in Y_j$. The production sets may be nonconvex.

It is then possible to argue that the economy will possess a near equilibrium if $r$ is large relative to the bound $s$ (i.e., if the size of the consumption side of the economy is large relative to the maximal size of a *single* firm). On the average, the production side of the economy is also being convexified, so to speak (see the small-type discussion of Section 5.E for a related point).[77] Note that the boundedness property of the production sets is important. Suppose, for example, that every firm has the technology represented in Figure 15.C.3. Then no matter how many consumers there are, the potential profits of every firm are infinite (as long as $p_2 > 0$). Thus, there is no reasonable sense in which a near equilibrium exists. For the averaging-out effect to work the nonconvexity in production has to be of bounded size (see Exercise 17.I.2).

---

## APPENDIX A: CHARACTERIZING EQUILIBRIUM THROUGH WELFARE EQUATIONS

We have seen, beginning in Section 17.B, that if our economy satisfies sufficiently nice properties (e.g., strict convexity of preferences) then we can resort, for the purposes of the analysis, to formalizing our theory by means of highly reduced systems of equilibrium equations. In the text of this chapter, we have focused on excess demand equations. But this is not the only possibility. In this appendix, we briefly illustrate a second approach that builds on the welfare properties of equilibria.

We again concentrate on a pure exchange economy in which each consumer $i = 1, \ldots, I$ has the consumption set $\mathbb{R}^L_+$ and continuous, strongly monotone, and strictly convex preferences. We also assume that $\omega_i \geq 0$ for all $i$ and $\sum_i \omega_i \gg 0$.

We know from Chapter 16 that a Walrasian equilibrium of this economy is a Pareto optimum (Proposition 16.C.1). Therefore, to identify an equilibrium, we can as well restrict ourselves to Pareto optimal allocations. To this effect, suppose we fix continuous utility functions $u_i(\cdot)$ for the $I$ consumers with $u_i(0) = 0$. Then to every vector $s = (s_1, \ldots, s_I)$ in the simplex $\Delta = \{s' \in \mathbb{R}^I_+ : \sum_i s'_i = 1\}$ we can associate a unique Pareto optimal allocation $x(s) \in \mathbb{R}^{LI}_+$ such that $(u_1(x_1(s)), \ldots, u_I(x_I(s)))$ is

---

77. Observe that the average is with respect to $r$ (the size of the economy in terms of the number of consumers), not with respect to $J$. If, as $r$ increases, $J$ is made to vary and is kept in some approximate fixed proportion with $r$, then from the qualitative point of view it does not matter how we measure size (this is a possible way to interpret, in the current context, the discussion of Section 5.E). But for the validity of the convexifying effect there is no need to vary $J$ with $r$. The number $J$ may be kept fixed and, thus, $J$ could well be small relative to $r$ (in which case the "averaged" economy is practically one of pure exchange) or it could be large; it could even be that $J = \infty$. The last case corresponds to a model with free entry, where the equilibrium—or the near equilibrium—determines, endogenously, the set of active firms. Typically, with free entry the set of the active firms increases as the number of consumers, measured by $r$, grows (this point has also been discussed in Section 10.F in a partial equilibrium context; there is not much more to add here).

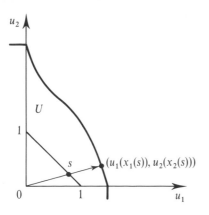

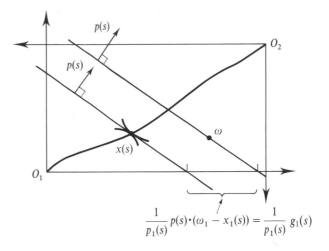

$$\frac{1}{p_1(s)} p(s) \cdot (\omega_1 - x_1(s)) = \frac{1}{p_1(s)} g_1(s)$$

proportional to $s \in \Delta$ (see Exercise 17.AA.1). In words, $s \in \Delta$ stands for the values of utility distribution parameters and the determined allocation distributes "welfare" in accordance with the "shares" $s = (s_1, \ldots, s_I)$. Figure 17.AA.1 illustrates the construction.

An arbitrary $s \in \Delta$ will typically not correspond to an equilibrium. How can we recognize those $s \in \Delta$ that do? To answer this question we can resort to the second welfare theorem. From Propositions 16.D.1 (and the discussion in small type following Proposition 16.D.3), we know that, under our assumptions, associated with $x(s)$ there is a price vector $p(s) \in \mathbb{R}^L$ that supports the allocation in the sense that, for every $i$, $x'_i \succ_i x_i(s)$ implies $p(s) \cdot x'_i > p(s) \cdot x_i(s)$. Therefore, $(x(s^*), p(s^*))$ constitutes a Walrasian equilibrium if and only if $s^* \in \Delta$ solves the system of equations

$$g_i(s^*) = p(s^*) \cdot [\omega_i - x_i(s^*)] = 0 \qquad \text{for every } i = 1, \ldots, I. \quad (17.AA.1)$$

The Edgeworth box example of Figure 17.AA.2 explains the point that we are currently making.

This Pareto-based equation system was first put forward by Negishi (1960), and was the approach taken by Arrow and Hahn (1971) in their proof of existence of equilibrium. It can be quite useful when the number of consumers (say, the number of countries in an international trade model) is small relative to the number of commodities. In contrast, if the number of consumers is large relative to the number of commodities, then an approach via excess demand functions will be superior. A limitation of the Negishi approach is that it is very dependent on the fact that an equilibrium must be a Pareto optimum. The excess demand approach is more easily adaptable to situations where this is not so (for example, because of tax distortions; see Exercise 17.C.3).[78]

**Figure 17.AA.1 (left)**
Construction of the welfare-theoretic equation system: first step.

**Figure 17.AA.2 (right)**
Construction of the welfare-theoretic equation system: second step.

---

78. The systems of equations (17.B.2) and (17.AA.1) can be formally contrasted as follows. In both of them, at any point of the domain of the equations, consumers and firms satisfy the utility maximization conditions for some prices and distribution of wealth. In (17.B.2) this distribution of wealth is always the one induced by the initial endowments, but feasibility (i.e., the equality of demand and supply) is insured only at the solution. In (17.AA.1) it is the other way around: feasibility is always satisfied, but the agreement of the wealth distribution with that induced by the initial endowments is insured only at the solution.

## APPENDIX B: A GENERAL APPROACH TO THE EXISTENCE OF WALRASIAN EQUILIBRIUM

The purpose of this appendix is to offer a treatment of the existence question at the level of generality of the model of Chapter 16. The results presented correspond roughly to those of Arrow and Debreu (1954) and McKenzie (1959).

As when dealing with the second welfare theorem in Section 16.D, and for exactly the same technical reasons, it is useful to concentrate on establishing the existence of a *Walrasian quasiequilibrium*. This is a weaker notion than Walrasian equilibrium in that consumers are required to maximize preferences only relative to consumptions that cost strictly less than the available amount of wealth.

**Definition 17.BB.1:** An allocation $(x_1^*, \ldots, x_I^*, y_1^*, \ldots, y_J^*)$ and a price system $p \neq 0$ constitute a *Walrasian quasiequilibrium* if

(i)   For every $j$, $p \cdot y_j \leq p \cdot y_j^*$ for all $y_j \in Y_j$.

(ii′)  For every $i$, $p \cdot x_i^* \leq p \cdot \omega_i + \sum_j \theta_{ij} p \cdot y_j^*$, and

$$\text{if } x_i \succ_i x_i^* \text{ then } p \cdot x_i \geq p \cdot \omega_i + \sum_j \theta_{ij} p \cdot y_j^*.$$

(iii)  $\sum_i x_i^* = \sum_i \omega_i + \sum_j y_j^*$.

Definition 17.BB.1 is identical to Definition 17.B.1 of a Walrasian equilibrium except that the preference maximization condition (ii) of Definition 17.B.1 has been replaced by the weaker condition (ii′). With local nonsatiation, condition (ii′) is equivalent to the requirement that $x_i^*$ minimizes expenditure for the price vector $p$ in the set $\{x_i \in X_i : x_i \succsim_i x_i^*\}$. The expenditure minimization problem has better continuity properties with respect to prices than does the preference maximization problem. Thus, in Figure 17.BB.1 we have $x_i^n = x_i^n(p^n, p^n \cdot x_i^n)$ and $p^n \cdot x_i^n = e(p^n, u_i(x_i^n))$; that is, $x_i^n$ is preference maximizing relative to the price–wealth pair $(p^n, p^n \cdot x_i^n)$ and expenditure minimizing relative to the price–utility pair $(p^n, u_i(x_i^n))$. However, as $p^n \to p$ and $x_i^n \to \bar{x}_i$, we see that $\bar{x}_i$ fails to maximize $u_i(\cdot)$ relative to $(p, p \cdot \bar{x}_i)$, whereas $\bar{x}_i$ still minimizes expenditure relative to $(p, u_i(\bar{x}_i))$; that is, $p \cdot \bar{x}_i = e(p, u_i(\bar{x}_i))$. Because continuity is an important requirement for existence analysis, it is more convenient to prove the existence of a quasiequilibrium than that of an equilibrium. Ultimately, however, we are interested in equilibrium. As it turns out, it is relatively easy to

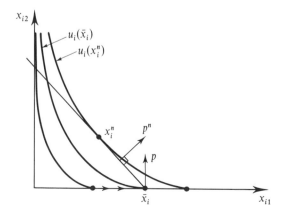

**Figure 17.BB.1**

Discontinuity of preference maximization.

state conditions implying that a quasiequilibrium is automatically an equilibrium. We devote the next few paragraphs to elaborating on this point.

We begin with Definition 17.BB.2

**Definition 17.BB.2:** The Walrasian quasiequilibrium $(x^*, y^*, p)$ satisfies the *cheaper consumption condition for consumer i* if there is $x_i \in X_i$ such that $p \cdot x_i < p \cdot \omega_i + \sum_j \theta_{ij} p \cdot y_j^*$.

We then have Proposition 17.BB.1.

**Proposition 17.BB.1:** Suppose that consumption sets are convex and preferences are continuous. Then any consumer who at the Walrasian quasiequilibrium $(x^*, y^*, p)$ satisfies the cheaper consumption condition must be preference maximizing in his budget set. Hence, if the cheaper consumption condition is satisfied for all $i$, $(x^*, y^*, p)$ is also a Walrasian equilibrium.

**Proof:** Suppose that $i$ satisfies the cheaper consumption condition; that is, there is $x_i \in X_i$ with $p \cdot x_i < p \cdot \omega_i + \sum_j \theta_{ij} p \cdot y_j^*$. If $x_i^*$ fails to be preference maximizing, then there is $x_i'$ such that $x_i' \succ_i x_i^*$ and $x_i'$ is in the budget set of consumer $i$. Denote $x_i^n = (1 - (1/n))x_i' + (1/n)x_i$. Then $x_i^n \in X_i$ and $p \cdot x_i^n < p \cdot \omega_i + \sum_j \theta_{ij} p \cdot y_j^*$ for all $n$, and $x_i^n \to x_i'$ as $n \to \infty$. By continuity of preferences, for large enough $n$ we will have $x_i^n \succ_i x_i^*$. But then consumer $i$ violates condition (ii') of the definition of quasi-equilibrium. ∎

---

Suppose that, for every $j$, $0 \in Y_j$, and for every $i$, $X_i$ is convex and $\omega_i \geq \hat{x}_i$ for some $\hat{x}_i \in X_i$. Suppose, in addition, that the weak condition "$\sum_i \omega_i + \sum_j \hat{y}_j \gg \sum_i \hat{x}_i$ for some $(\hat{y}_1, \ldots, \hat{y}_J) \in Y_1 \times \cdots \times Y_J$" is satisfied. Then the quasiequilibrium $(x^*, y^*, p)$ satisfies the cheaper consumption condition for consumer $i$ in, for example, either of the following situations (Exercise 17.BB.1):

(a) $p \geq 0$, $p \neq 0$, and $\omega_i \gg \hat{x}_i$,
(b) $p \gg 0$ and $\omega_i \neq \hat{x}_i$.

To have $p \geq 0$ at quasiequilibrium it suffices that one production set satisfies the free-disposal condition. Guaranteeing $p \gg 0$ is more difficult. It will happen if, for every $i$, $X_i + \mathbb{R}_+^L \subset X_i$ and preferences are continuous and strongly monotone. To see this, note that by the monotonicity of preferences and the expenditure-minimization property of quasiequilibrium we must have $p \geq 0$, $p \neq 0$, at any quasiequilibrium. It follows that $p \cdot (\sum_i \omega_i + \sum_j y_j^*) \geq p \cdot (\sum_i \omega_i + \sum_j \hat{y}_j) > p \cdot (\sum_i \hat{x}_i)$. Hence, there is at least one consumer with wealth larger than $p \cdot \hat{x}_i$. But this consumer must be maximizing preferences (by Proposition 17.BB.1), which, by the strong monotonicity property, can only occur if every price is positive (i.e., if no good is free).

Although convenient, neither condition (a) nor (b) can be regarded as extremely weak. It would be unfortunate if the validity of the theory were restricted to them. But this is not so: much weaker conditions are available. In particular, McKenzie (1959) has developed a theory of *indecomposable* economies that guarantees that at a quasiequilibrium the cheaper consumption condition is satisfied for every consumer (and therefore the quasiequilibrium is an equilibrium). The basic idea, informally described, is that an economy is indecomposable if, no matter how we partition the economy into two groups, each of the groups has something for which the other group is willing to exchange something of its own. (See Exercise 17.BB.2.)

We now turn to the existence of a Walrasian quasiequilibrium. The aim is to establish the general existence result in Proposition 17.BB.2.

**Proposition 17.BB.2:** Suppose that for an economy with $I > 0$ consumers and $J > 0$ firms we have

(i) For every $i$,
    (i.1) $X_i \subset \mathbb{R}^L$ is closed and convex;
    (i.2) $\succsim_i$ is a rational, continuous, locally nonsatiated, and convex prefer-ence relation defined on $X_i$;
    (i.3) $\omega_i \geq \hat{x}_i$ for some $\hat{x}_i \in X_i$.
(ii) Every $Y_j \subset \mathbb{R}^L$ is closed, convex, includes the origin, and satisfies the free-disposal property.
(iii) The set of feasible allocations

$$A = \{(x, y) \in \mathbb{R}^{LI} \times \mathbb{R}^{LJ} : x_i \in X_i \text{ for all } i, \ y_j \in Y_j \text{ for all } j, \text{ and}$$

$$\sum_i x_i \leq \sum_i \omega_i + \sum_j y_j\}$$

is compact.

Then a Walrasian quasiequilibrium exists.

We comment briefly on the assumptions. As we have repeatedly illustrated (in Chapters 10, 15, and 16), the convexity assumptions on individual preferences and technologies cannot be dispensed with.[79] The Edgeworth box example of Figure 17.BB.2 shows that the local nonsatiation condition is also required.[80] In contrast, the assumption of rational preferences is entirely dispensable (see the comments at the end of this appendix). The free disposal condition $-\mathbb{R}_+^L \subset Y_j$ is also only a matter of convenience.[81] Allowing for negative prices, we could simply drop it from our list of conditions (see Exercise 17.BB.3). The assumption (i.3) says that $\omega_i$ may not belong to the consumption set but that it is possible to reach the consumption set by just eliminating some amounts of commodities from $\omega_i$.[82] Finally, in Appendix A to Chapter 16 we have already investigated the conditions under which the set of feasible allocations is compact.

---

79. Recall, however, the important qualification of Section 17.I, and see also the discussion at the end of this appendix.

80. In Figure 17.BB.2, the second consumer has conventional strongly monotone preferences; but for the first consumer both commodities are bads and, therefore, he is satiated at the origin. Also $\omega_1 \gg 0$ and $\omega_2 \gg 0$. Suppose that $x^* = (x_1^*, x_2^*)$ and price vector $p \neq 0$ constitute a Walrasian quasiequilibrium. Because the preferences of the second consumer are strongly monotone, we must have $p \gg 0$. By profit maximization (using the free-disposal technology) and the possibility of inaction, we have $p \cdot (x_1^* + x_2^* - \omega_1 - \omega_2) \geq 0$. Since $p \cdot x_2^* \leq p \cdot \omega_2$, this yields $p \cdot x_1^* \geq p \cdot \omega_1 > 0$. But then $(x^*, p)$ cannot be a Walrasian quasiequilibrium because consuming nothing costs zero and is preferred by the first consumer to any other consumption.

81. Because $Y_j$ is convex and closed, $-\mathbb{R}_+^L \subset Y_j$ implies $Y_j - \mathbb{R}_+^L \subset Y_j$ (Exercise 5.B.5).

82. A stronger condition would require that $\omega_i \gg \hat{x}_i$ for every $i$. With this assumption, Proposition 17.BB.2 yields the existence of a true equilibrium, not just of a quasiequilibrium. Economically, however, the latter assumption is considerably stronger: $\omega_i \geq \hat{x}_i$ can be interpreted (keeping in mind the possibility of free disposal) simply as saying that consumer $i$ could survive without entering the markets of the economy, while $\omega_i \gg \hat{x}_i$ says that the consumer can supply to the market a strictly positive amount of *every* good.

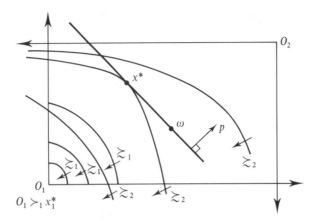

**Figure 17.BB.2**

Equilibrium does not exist: the preferences of the first consumer are satiated.

### Proof of Proposition 17.BB.2

The approach we follow takes advantage of the fact that the reader may already have been exposed in Chapter 8 to the notion of the Nash equilibrium of a normal form game and, more particularly, to the existence results for Nash equilibrium using best-response correspondences contained in Appendix A to Chapter 8. A game-theoretic approach to the existence of Walrasian equilibrium was taken in the classic paper of Arrow and Debreu (1954). Here we follow Gale and Mas-Colell (1975).

**Definition 17.BB.3:** An allocation $(x^*, y^*)$ and a price system $p \neq 0$ constitute a *free-disposal quasiequilibrium* if

> (i)  for every $j$, $p \cdot y_j \leq p \cdot y_j^*$ for all $y_j \in Y_j$.
> (ii')  For every $i$, $p \cdot x_i^* \leq p \cdot \omega_i + \sum_j \theta_{ij} p \cdot y_j^*$, and
>
> $$\text{if } x_i \succ_i x_i^* \text{ then } p \cdot x_i \geq p \cdot \omega_i + \sum_j \theta_{ij} p \cdot y_j^*.$$

> (iii')  $\sum_i x_i^* \leq \sum_i \omega_i + \sum_j y_j^*$ and $p \cdot (\sum_i x_i^* - \sum_i \omega_i - \sum_j y_j^*) = 0$.

Thus, all we have done is replace in Definition 17.BB.1 of a quasiequilibrium the exact feasibility condition "$\sum_i x_i^* = \sum_i \omega_i + \sum_j y_j^*$" by (iii') above. That is, we allow the excess supply of some goods provided that they are free. In Exercise 17.BB.4 you are asked to show that if one production set, say $Y_1$, satisfies the free-disposal property and if $(x_1^*, \cdots, x_I^*, y_1^*, \ldots, y_J^*, p)$ is a free-disposal quasiequilibrium, then there is $y_1'^* \leq y_1^*$ such that $(x_1^*, \cdots, x_I^*, y_1'^*, y_2^*, \ldots, y_J^*, p)$ is a Walrasian quasiequilibrium. Therefore, to establish Proposition 17.BB.2, it is enough for us to show that a free-diposal quasiequilibrium exists.

We proceed to formalize the free-disposal quasiequilibrium notion as a kind of noncooperative equilibrium for a certain game among $I + J + 1$ players. The $I$ and $J$ players are the consumers and the firms, respectively, and their strategies are demand–supply vectors. The extra player is a fictitious *market agent* (a "grand coordinator") having as his strategy the prices of the $L$ different goods.

Since the set $A$ of feasible allocations is bounded, there is $r > 0$ such that whenever $(x_1, \ldots, x_I, y_1, \ldots, y_J) \in A$ we have $|x_{\ell i}| < r$ and $|y_{\ell j}| < r$ for all $i$, $j$, and $\ell$. Because we need to have compactness of strategy sets to establish existence, we begin by replacing every $X_i$ and every $Y_j$ by a truncated version:

$$\hat{X}_i = \{x_i \in X_i \colon |x_{\ell i}| \le r \text{ for all } \ell\},$$

$$\hat{Y}_j = \{y_j \in Y_j \colon |y_{\ell j}| \le r \text{ for all } \ell\}.$$

Note that $A \subset \hat{X}_1 \times \cdots \times \hat{X}_I \times \hat{Y}_1 \times \cdots \times \hat{Y}_J$. Because $(\hat{x}_1, \ldots, \hat{x}_I, \ldots, 0, \ldots, 0) \in A$, it follows that $\hat{x}_i \in \hat{X}_i$ for every $i$, and $0 \in \hat{Y}_j$ for every $j$. In particular, all the strategy sets are nonempty. Lemma 17.BB.1 shows that in our search for a free-disposal quasi-equilibrium we can limit ourselves to the truncated economy.

**Lemma 17.BB.1:** If all $X_i$ and $Y_j$ are convex and $(x^*, y^*, p)$ is a free-disposal quasi-equilibrium in the truncated economy, that is, if $(x^*, y^*, p)$ satisfies Definition 17.BB.3 of free-disposal quasiequilibrium with the consumption and production sets replaced by their truncated versions, then $(x^*, y^*, p)$ is also a free-disposal quasiequilibrium for the original untruncated economy.

**Proof of Lemma 17.BB.1:** Consider a consumer $i$ (the reasoning is similar for a firm). Because $(x^*, y^*) \in A$, we have $|x^*_{\ell i}| < r$ for all $\ell$; that is, the consumption bundle of consumer $i$ is interior to the truncation bound. Suppose now that $x^*_i$ fails to satisfy condition (ii′) of Definition 17.BB.3 in the nontruncated economy, that is, that there is an $x_i \in X_i$ such that $x_i \succ_i x^*_i$, and $p \cdot x_i < p \cdot \omega_i + \sum_j \theta_{ij} p \cdot y^*_j$. Denote $x^n_i = (1 - (1/n)) x^*_i + (1/n) x_i$. For all $n$ we have $p \cdot x^n_i < p \cdot \omega_i + \sum_j \theta_{ij} p \cdot y^*_j$ and, by the convexity of preferences, $x^n_i \succsim_i x^*_i$. Also, we can choose an $n$ large enough to have $|x^n_{\ell i}| < r$ for all $\ell$. By local nonsatiation there must then be an $x'_i \in \hat{X}_i$ such that $x'_i \succ_i x^n_i$ and $p \cdot x'_i < p \cdot \omega_i + \sum_j \theta_{ij} p \cdot y^*_j$. But then $x'_i \in \hat{X}_i$ and $x'_i \succ_i x^n_i \succsim_i x^*_i$, and so in the truncated economy $x^*_i$ fails to satisfy condition (ii′) of Definition 17.BB.3. Thus, $(x^*, y^*, p)$ must not be a free-disposal quasiequilibrium in the truncated economy. This contradiction establishes the result. ∎

We are now ready to set up a simultaneous-move noncooperative game. To do so we need to specify the players' strategy sets and payoff functions. To simplify notation we assign to every consumer $i$, price vector $p$ and production profile $y = (y_1, \ldots, y_J)$, a limited liability amount of wealth

$$w_i(p, y) = p \cdot \omega_i + \text{Max}\left\{0, \sum_j \theta_{ij} p \cdot y_j\right\}.$$

The strategy sets are:

For consumer $i$:  $\hat{X}_i$
For firm $j$:  $\hat{Y}_j$
For the market agent:  $\Delta = \{p \in \mathbb{R}^L \colon p_\ell \ge 0 \text{ for all } \ell \text{ and } \sum_\ell p_\ell = 1\}$.

Given a strategy profile $(x, y, p) = (x_1, \ldots, x_I, y_1, \ldots, y_J, p)$, the payoff functions and best-responses of the different agents are:

Consumer $i$:   Chooses consumption vectors $x'_i \in \hat{X}_i$ such that
(1) $p \cdot x'_i \le w_i(p, y)$ and
(2) $x'_i \succsim_i x''_i$ for all $x''_i \in \hat{X}_i$ satisfying $p \cdot x''_i < w_i(p, y)$.
(Consumer $i$'s payoff function can be thought of as giving a payoff 1 if he chooses a consumption vector satisfying this condition, and 0 otherwise.)

Denote by $\tilde{x}_i(x, y, p) \subset \hat{X}_i$ the set of consumption bundles $x_i'$ so defined.

Firm $j$:     Chooses productions $y_j' \in \hat{Y}_j$ that are profit maximizing for $p$ on $\hat{Y}_j$. (Firm $j$'s payoff function is simply its profit.)

Denote by $\tilde{y}_j(x, y, p) \subset \hat{Y}_j$ the set of production plans $y_j'$ so defined.

Market Agent: Chooses prices $q \in \Delta$ so as to solve

$$\underset{q \in \Delta}{\text{Max}} \left( \sum_i x_i - \sum_i \omega_i - \sum_j y_j \right) \cdot q. \qquad (17.\text{BB}.1)$$

Denote by $\tilde{p}(x, y, p)$ the set of price vectors $q$ so defined.

Only the behavior of the market agent needs comment. Given the total excess demand vector, the market agent chooses prices so as to maximize the value of this vector. Hence, he puts the whole weight of prices (which, recall, have been normalized to lie in the unit simplex) into the commodities with maximal excess demand. As we have already observed when doing the same thing in the proof of Proposition 17.C.1, this is in accord with economic logic: if the objective is to eliminate the excess demand of some commodities, try raising their prices as much as possible.

Lemma 17.BB.2 says that an equilibrium of this noncooperative game yields a free-disposal quasiequilibrium for the truncated economy.

**Lemma 17.BB.2:** Suppose that $(x^*, y^*, p)$ is such that $x_i^* \in \tilde{x}_i(x^*, y^*, p)$ for all $i$, $y_j^* \in \tilde{y}_j(x^*, y^*, p)$ for all $j$, and $p \in \tilde{p}(x^*, y^*, p)$. Then $(x^*, y^*, p)$ is a free-disposal quasiequilibrium for the truncated economy.

**Proof of Lemma 17.BB.2:** We note first that $p \cdot y_j^* \geq 0$ for every $j$ (because $0 \in \hat{Y}_j$). By the definition of $\tilde{x}_i(\cdot)$ and $\tilde{y}_j(\cdot)$, conditions (i) and (ii') of Definition 17.BB.3 are then automatically satisfied. Hence, the only property that remains to be established is (iii'), that is,

$$\sum_i x_i^* - \sum_i \omega_i - \sum_j y_j^* \leq 0 \quad \text{and} \quad p \cdot \left( \sum_i x_i^* - \sum_i \omega_i - \sum_j y_j^* \right) = 0.$$

We have $p \cdot x_i^* \leq w_i(p, y^*) = p \cdot \omega_i + \sum_j \theta_{ij} p \cdot y_j^*$ for all $i$ and therefore

$$p \cdot \left( \sum_i x_i^* - \sum_i \omega_i - \sum_j y_j^* \right) \leq 0.$$

This implies $\sum_i x_i^* - \sum_i \omega_i - \sum_j y_j^* \leq 0$ because otherwise the value of the solution to problem (17.BB.1) would be positive and so $p$ (which as we have just seen has $p \cdot (\sum_i x_i^* - \sum_i \omega_i - \sum_j y_j^*) \leq 0$) could not be a maximizing solution vector, that is, a member of $\tilde{p}(x^*, y^*, p)$. It follows that $(x^*, y^*) \in A$ and so, $x_{\ell i}^* < r$ for all $i$ and $\ell$. From this we get that the budget equations are satisfied with equality (i.e., $p \cdot x_i^* = p \cdot \omega_i + \sum_j \theta_{ij} p \cdot y_j^*$ for all $i$) because otherwise local nonsatiation yields that for some consumer $i$ there is a preferred consumption strictly interior to consumer $i$'s budget set in the truncated economy, implying $x_i^* \notin \tilde{x}_i(x^*, y^*, p)$. We therefore conclude that we also have $p \cdot (\sum_i x_i^* - \sum_i \omega_i - \sum_j y_j^*) = 0$. This completes the proof. ∎

Now, as we discussed in Appendix A to Chapter 8 (see the proof of Proposition 8.D.3 presented there), under appropriate conditions on the best-response correspondences, this noncooperative game has an equilibrium.

**Lemma 17.BB.3:** Suppose that the correspondences $\tilde{x}_i(\cdot)$, $\tilde{y}_j(\cdot)$, and $\tilde{p}(\cdot)$ are nonempty, convex valued, and upper hemicontinuous. Then there is $(x^*, y^*, p)$ such that $x_i^* \in \tilde{x}_i(x^*, y^*, p)$ for all $i$, $y_j^* \in \tilde{y}_j(x^*, y^*, p)$ for all $j$, and $p \in \tilde{p}(x^*, y^*, p)$.

**Proof of Lemma 17.BB.3:** We are simply looking for a fixed point of the correspondence $\Psi(\cdot)$ from $X_1 \times \cdots \times X_I \times Y_1 \times \cdots \times Y_J \times \Delta$ to itself defined by

$$\Psi(x, y, p) = \tilde{x}_1(x, y, p) \times \cdots \times \tilde{x}_I(x, y, p) \times \tilde{y}_1(x, y, p) \times \cdots \times \tilde{y}_J(x, y, p) \times \tilde{p}(x, y, p).$$

The correspondence $\Psi(\cdot)$ is nonempty, convex valued, and upper hemicontinuous. The existence of a fixed point follows directly from Kakutani's fixed point theorem (see Section M.I of the Mathematical Appendix). ∎

Lemmas 17.BB.4 to 17.BB.6 verify that the best-response correspondence of this noncooperative game is nonempty, convex valued, and upper hemicontinuous.[83]

**Lemma 17.BB.4:** For all strategy profiles $(x, y, p)$, the sets $\tilde{x}_i(x, y, p)$, $\tilde{y}_j(x, y, p)$, and $\tilde{p}(x, y, p)$ are nonempty.

**Proof of Lemma 17.BB.4:** For $\tilde{y}_j(x, y, p)$ and $\tilde{p}(x, y, p)$ the claim is clear enough since we are maximizing a continuous (in fact, linear) function on, respectively, the nonempty, compact sets $\hat{Y}_j$ and $\Delta$. For $\tilde{x}_i(x, y, p)$, recall that the continuity of $\succsim_i$ implies the existence of a continuous utility representation $u_i(\cdot)$ for $\succsim_i$.[84] Let $x_i'$ be a maximizer of the continuous function $u_i(x_i)$ on the nonempty compact budget set $\{x_i \in \hat{X}_i: p \cdot x_i \leq w_i(p, y^*)\}$. Then $x_i' \in \tilde{x}_i(x, y, p)$. The budget set is nonempty because $\hat{x}_i \in \hat{X}_i$ and $\hat{x}_i \leq \omega_i$. With $p \geq 0$, this implies that $p \cdot \hat{x}_i \leq p \cdot w_i \leq w_i(p, y^*)$. ∎

**Lemma 17.BB.5:** For all strategy profiles the sets $\tilde{x}_i(x, y, p)$, $\tilde{y}_j(x, y, p)$, and $\tilde{p}(x, y, p)$ are convex.

**Proof of Lemma 17.BB.5:** We establish the claim for $x_i(x, y, p)$. You are asked to complete the proof in Exercise 17.BB.6.

Suppose that $x_i, x_i' \in \tilde{x}_i(x, y, p)$ and consider $x_{i\alpha} = \alpha x_i + (1 - \alpha)x_i'$, for any $\alpha \in [0, 1]$. Note first that $p \cdot x_{i\alpha} \leq w_i(p, y)$. In addition, by the convexity of preferences we cannot have $x_i \succ_i x_{i\alpha}$ and $x_i' \succ_i x_{i\alpha}$ (Exercise 17.BB.5). So suppose that $x_{i\alpha} \succsim_i x_i$. Consider now any $x_i'' \in \hat{X}_i$ with $p \cdot x_i'' < w_i(p, y)$. Then since $x_i \in \tilde{x}_i(x, y, p)$ we have $x_i \succsim_i x_i''$, and so $x_{i\alpha} \succsim_i x_i''$. We conclude that $x_{i\alpha} \in \tilde{x}_i(x, y, p)$. A similar conclusion follows if $x_{i\alpha} \succsim_i x_i'$. Hence, $\tilde{x}_i(x, y, p)$ is a convex set. ∎

**Lemma 17.BB.6:** The correspondences $\tilde{x}_i(\cdot)$, $\tilde{y}_j(\cdot)$, and $\tilde{p}(\cdot)$ are upper hemicontinuous.

**Proof of Lemma 17.BB.6:** Again, we limit ourselves to $\tilde{x}_i(\cdot)$. Exercise 17.BB.7 asks you to complete the proof for $\tilde{y}_j(\cdot)$ and $\tilde{p}(\cdot)$.

---

83. For the firms and the market game this result is covered by Proposition 8.D.3, but for the consumers we need a special argument (as defined, the payoff functions of the consumers are not continuous).

84. This was proved in Proposition 3.C.1 for monotone preferences on $\mathbb{R}_+^L$. As we pointed out there, however, the conclusion actually depends only on the continuity of the preference relation.

Let $p^n \to p$, $y^n \to y$, $x^n \to x$, and $x_i'^n \to x_i'$ as $n \to \infty$, and suppose that $x_i'^n \in \tilde{x}_i(x^n, y^n, p^n)$. We need to show that $x_i' \in \tilde{x}_i(p, x, y)$.

From $p^n \cdot x_i'^n \le w_i(p^n, y^n)$ we get $p \cdot x_i' \le w_i(p^n, y^n)$. Consider now any $x_i'' \in \hat{X}_i$ with $x_i'' \succ_i x_i'$. Then, by the continuity of preferences, $x_i'' \succ_i x_i'^n$ for $n$ large enough. Hence, $p^n \cdot x_i'' \ge w_i(p^n, y^n)$. Going to the limit we get $p \cdot x_i'' \ge w_i(p, y)$. Thus, we conclude that, as we wanted, $x_i' \in \tilde{x}_i(x, y, p)$. It is, incidentally, because of the need to establish this closed-graph property that we have replaced preference maximization by the weaker objective of expenditure minimization in the definition of the objectives of the consumer. ∎

The combination of Lemmas 17.BB.4 to 17.BB.6 establishes that the given best-response correspondences satisfy the properties required in Lemma 17.BB.3 for the existence of a fixed-point, which completes the proof of Proposition 17.BB.2. ∎

---

The assumptions on preferences and technologies can be weakened in an important respect. Our existence argument requires only that the best-response correspondence $\tilde{x}_i(x, y, p)$ and $\tilde{y}_j(x, y, p)$ be convex valued and upper hemicontinuous. Beyond this, the proof imposes no restrictions whatsoever on the dependence of consumers' and firms' choices on the "state" variables $(x, y, p)$. Thus we could allow consumers' tastes, or firms' technologies, to depend on prices (money illusion?), on the choices of other consumers or firms (a form of externalities), or even on own consumption (e.g., tastes could depend on a current reference point—a source of incompleteness or nontransitivity of preferences already illustrated in Chapter 1).[85,86] The following is an example of the sort of generality that can be accommodated: Suppose that consumer preferences are given to us by means of utility functions $u_i(\cdot; x, y, p)$ defined on $X_i$ but dependent, in principle, on the state of the economy. If for every $(x, y, p)$ the conditions of Proposition 17.BB.2 are satisfied, and the parametric dependence on $(x, y, p)$ is continuous, then a Walrasian quasiequilibrium still exists. The proof does not need any change. We can make a similar point with respect to the possibility that firms' technologies depend on external effects, with, then, an added theoretical payoff. It allows us to see that equilibrium exists if the technology of the firm is convex: *it does not matter if the "aggregate" technology of the economy is convex*. See Exercise 17.BB.8 for more on this.

The existence proof we have given in this appendix is an example of a "large space" proof. The fixed-point argument (in our case phrased as a Nash equilibrium existence argument) has been developed in a disaggregated domain where all the equilibrating variables have been listed separately. The advantage of proceeding this way is that the argument remains very flexible and allows us to incorporate the weakest possible conditions without extra effort (as the last paragraph has illustrated). The disadvantage, of course, is that the fixed point may be

---

85. Suppose, for example, that the utility function of a consumer is given to us in the form $u_i(\cdot; x_i)$; that is, the evaluation of possible consumptions depends on the current consumption. Without loss of generality we can normalize $u_i(x_i; x_i) = 0$ for every $x_i$. Define the induced weak and strict preference relations $\succsim_i$ and $\succ_i$ on $X_i$ by, respectively, "$x_i' \succsim_i x_i$ if $u_i(x_i'; x_i) \ge 0$" and "$x_i' \succ_i x_i$ if $u_i(x_i'; x_i) > 0$." Then the relations $\succsim_i$ and $\succ_i$ contain all the relevant information for equilibrium analysis. Note, however, that it is perfectly possible for $\succsim_i$ not to be complete and for neither $\succsim_i$ nor $\succ_i$ to be transitive. See Shafer (1974) and Gale and Mas-Colell (1975) for more on this.

86. Another example of dependence on the overall consumption vector of the economy arises if, for example, we are considering equilibrium at a given point in time. Then current consumptions in the economy (e.g., purchases of physical or financial assets) will typically affect future prices; these, in turn, will influence current preferences via expectations.

hard to compute and cumbersome to analyze. Usually, as we have seen in Section 17.C and in Appendix A of this chapter, it is possible to work with more aggregated, reduced systems. In fact, the general point duly made, it is worthwhile to observe that this is so even under the assumptions of Proposition 17.BB.2.[87] We elaborate briefly on this.

We can prove Proposition 17.BB.2 by setting up a two-player game instead of an $I + J + 1$ one.[88] The first player is an aggregate consumer–firm that has $\sum_i \hat{X}_i - \{\sum_i \omega_i\} - \sum_j \hat{Y}_j$ as its strategy set; the second is, as before, a market agent having $\Delta$ as its strategy set. Given $p \in \Delta$, the first agent responds with the set of vectors $z$ expressible as $z = \sum_i x_i - \sum_i \omega_i - \sum_j y_j$, where $y_j$ is profit maximizing in $\hat{Y}_j$ for every $j$, and $x_i \in \hat{X}_i$ is such that (1) $p \cdot x_i \leq p \cdot \omega_i + \sum_j \theta_{ij} p \cdot y_j$ and (2) $x_i \succsim_i x_i'$ whenever $p \cdot x_i' < p \cdot \omega_i + \sum_j \theta_{ij} p \cdot y_j$. As before, the market agent responds with the set of $q \in \Delta$ that maximize $z \cdot q$ on $\Delta$. Once this two-person game has been set up, the proof proceeds as for Proposition 17.BB.2. You should check this in Exercise 17.BB.9.

If for any $p \in \Delta$ the preference-maximizing choices of consumers, $x_i(p)$, and the profit-maximizing choices of firms, $y_j(p)$, were single valued, we could go one step further and consider a game with a single player (the market agent). Given $p$, we would then let the best response of the market agent be the set of price vectors $q \in \Delta$ that maximizes $[\sum_i x_i(p) - \sum_i \omega_i - \sum_j y_j(p)] \cdot q$ on $\Delta$. In essence, this is what we did in the proof of Proposition 17.C.1.

## REFERENCES

Arrow, K., and G. Debreu. (1954). Existence of equilibrium for a competitive economy. *Econometrica* **22**: 265–90.

Arrow, K., and F. Hahn. (1971). *General Competitive Analysis.* San Francisco: Holden-Day.

Arrow, K., and M. Intriligator, eds. (1982). *Handbook of Mathematical Economics,* vol. II. Amsterdam: North-Holland.

Barone, E. (1908). Il ministro della produzione nello stato collettivista. *Giornali degli economisti.* [Reprinted as: The ministry of production in the collectivist state, in *Collectivist Economic Planning,* edited by F. H. Hayek. London: Routledge, 1935.]

Balasko, Y. (1988). *Foundations of the Theory of General Equilibrium.* Orlando: Academic Press.

Becker, G. (1962). Irrational behavior and economic theory. *Journal of Political Economy* **70**: 1–13.

Brown, D., and R. Matzkin. (1993). Walrasian comparative statics. Mimeograph, Northwestern University.

Chipman, J. (1970). External economies of scale and competitive equilibrium. *Quarterly Journal of Economics* **84**: 347–85.

Debreu, G. (1959). *Theory of Value.* New York: Wiley.

Debreu, G. (1970). Economies with a finite set of equilibria. *Econometrica* **38**: 387–92.

Debreu, G. (1974). Excess demand functions. *Journal of Mathematical Economics* **1**: 15–21.

Dierker, E. (1972). Two remarks on the number of equilibria of an economy. *Econometrica* **40**: 951–53.

Fisher, F. (1983). *Disequilibrium Foundations of Equilibrium Economics.* Cambridge, U.K.: Cambridge University Press.

Gale, D., and A. Mas-Colell. (1975). An equilibrium existence theorem for a general model without ordered preferences. *Journal of Mathematical Economics* **2**: 9–15. [For some corrections see *Journal of Mathematical Economics* **6**: 297–98, 1979.]

Garcia, C. B., and W. I. Zangwill. (1981). *Pathways to Solutions, Fixed Points and Equilibria.* Englewood Cliffs, N.J.: Prentice-Hall.

Grandmont, J. M. (1992). Transformations of the commodity space, behavioral heterogeneity, and the aggregation problem. *Journal of Economic Theory* **57**: 1–35.

Hahn, F. (1982). Stability. Chap. 16 in *Handbook of Mathematical Economics,* vol. II, edited by K. Arrow, and M. Intriligator. Amsterdam: North-Holland.

---

87. But it is not so for the generalizations described in the previous paragraph.
88. This was the approach taken in Debreu (1959).

Hildenbrand, W. (1994). *Market Demand: Theory and Empirical Evidence.* Princeton, N.J.: Princeton University Press.

Hildenbrand, W., and H. Sonnenschein, eds. (1991). *Handbook of Mathematical Economics,* vol. IV. Amsterdam: North-Holland.

Kehoe, T. (1985). Multiplicity of equilibrium and comparative statics, *Quarterly Journal of Economics* **100**: 119–48.

Kehoe, T. (1991). Computation and multiplicity of equilibria. Chap. 38 in *Handbook of Mathematical Economics,* vol. IV, edited by W. Hildenbrand, and H. Sonnenschein. Amsterdam: North-Holland.

Lange, O. (1938). On the economic theory of socialism. In *On the Economic Theory of Socialism,* edited by B. Lippincott. Minneapolis: University of Minnesota Press.

McKenzie, L. (1959). On the existence of general equilibrium for a competitive market. *Econometrica* **27**: 54–71.

Mantel, R. (1974). On the characterization of aggregate excess demand. *Journal of Economic Theory* **7**: 348–53.

Mantel, R. (1976). Homothetic preferences and community excess demand functions. *Journal of Economic Theory* **12**: 197–201.

Marshall, A. (1920). *Principles of Economics,* 8th ed. London: Macmillan.

Mas-Colell, A. (1977). On the equilibrium price set of an exchange economy. *Journal of Mathematical Economics* **4**: 117–26.

Mas-Colell, A. (1985). *The Theory of General Economic Equilibrium: A Differentiable Approach.* Cambridge, U.K.: Cambridge University Press.

Mas-Colell, A. (1986). Notes on price and quantity tatonnement. In *Models of Economic Dynamics,* edited by H. Sonnenschein. Lecture Notes in Economics and Mathematical Systems No. 264. Berlin: Springer-Verlag.

Mas-Colell, A. (1991). On the uniqueness of equilibrium once again. Chap. 12 in *Equilibrium Theory and Applications,* edited by W. Barnett, B. Cornet, C. D'Aspremont, J. Gabszewicz and A. Mas-Colell. Cambridge, U.K.: Cambridge University Press.

Milgrom, P., and C. Shannon. (1994). Monotone comparative statics. *Econometrica* **62**: 157–180.

Negishi, T. (1960). Welfare economics and existence of an equilibrium for a competitive economy. *Metroeconomica* **12**: 92–97.

Rader, T. (1972). *Theory of General Economic Equilibrium.* New York: Academic Press.

Saari, D., and C. Simon. (1978). Effective price mechanisms. *Econometrica* **46**: 1097–125.

Samuelson, P. (1947). *Foundations of Economic Analysis.* Cambridge, Mass.: Harvard University Press.

Scarf, H. (1973). *The Computation of Economic Equilibria* (in collaboration with T. Hansen). New Haven: Yale University Press.

Shafer, W. (1974). The non-transitive consumer. *Econometrica* **42**: 913–19.

Shafer, W., and H. Sonnenschein. (1982). Market demand and excess demand functions. Chap. 14 in *Handbook of Mathematical Economics,* vol. II, edited by K. Arrow and M. Intriligator. Amsterdam: North-Holland.

Shoven, J., and J. Whalley. (1992). *Applying General Equilibrium.* New York: Cambridge University Press.

Sonnenschein, H. (1973). Do Walras' identity and continuity characterize the class of community excess demand functions? *Journal of Economic Theory* **6**: 345–54.

Smale, S. (1976). A convergent process of price adjustment and global Newton methods. *Journal of Mathematical Economics* **3**: 107–20.

Starr, R. (1969). Quasi-equilibria in markets with non-convex preferences. *Econometrica* **37**: 25–38.

Varian, H. (1977). Non-Walrasian equilibria. *Econometrica* **45**: 573–90.

Walras, L. (1874). Eléments d'Économie Politique Pure. Lausanne: Corbaz. [Translated as: *Elements of Pure Economics.* Homewood, Ill.: Irwin, 1954.]

# EXERCISES

**17.B.1**[A] Show that for a pure exchange economy with $J = 1$ and $Y_1 = -\mathbb{R}^L_+$, "$y_1^* \leq 0$, $p \cdot y_1^* = 0$, and $p \geq 0$" if and only if "$y_1^* \in Y_1$ and $p \cdot y_1^* \geq p \cdot y_1$ for all $y_1 \in Y_1$."

**17.B.2$^B$** Prove property (v) of Proposition 17.B.2. The proof of Proposition 17.B.2 in the text contains a hint. Recall also the following technical fact: any bounded sequence in $\mathbb{R}^L$ has a convergent subsequence.

**17.B.3$^B$** Suppose that $z(\cdot)$ is an aggregate excess demand function satisfying conditions (i) to (v) of Proposition 17.B.2. Let $p^n \to p$ with some, but not all, of the components of $p$ being zero.

   **(a)** Show that as $n$ becomes large, the maximal excess demand is always obtained for some commodity whose price goes to zero.

   **(b)** Argue (if possible by example) that a commodity whose price goes to zero may actually remain in excess supply for all $n$. [*Hint*: Relative prices matter.]

**17.B.4$^B$** Suppose that there are $J$ firms whose production sets $Y_1, \ldots, Y_J \subset \mathbb{R}^L$ are closed, strictly convex, and bounded above. Suppose also that a strictly positive consumption bundle is producible using the initial endowments and the economy's aggregate production set $Y = \sum_j Y_j$ (i.e., there is an $\bar{x} \gg 0$ such that $\bar{x} \in \{\sum_i \omega_i\} + Y$). Show that the production inclusive aggregate excess demand function $\bar{z}(p)$ in (17.B.3) satisfies properties (i) to (v) of Proposition 17.B.2.

**17.B.5$^A$** Suppose that there are $J$ firms. Each firm produces a single output under conditions of constant returns. The unit cost function of firm $j$ is $c_j(p)$, which we assume to be differentiable. The consumption side of the economy is expressed by an aggregate excess demand function $z(p)$. Write down an equation system similar to (17.B.4)–(17.B.5) for the equilibria of this economy.

**17.B.6$^C$** [Rader (1972)] Suppose that there is a single production set $Y$ and that $Y$ is a closed, convex cone satisfying free disposal. Consider the following exchange equilibrium problem. Given prices $p = (p_1, \ldots, p_L)$, every consumer $i$ chooses a vector $v_i \in \mathbb{R}^L$ so as to maximize $\succsim_i$ on the set $\{x_i \in X_i : p \cdot v_i \leq p \cdot \omega_i, \text{ and } x_i = v_i + y \text{ for some } y \in Y\}$. The price vector $p$ and the choices $v^* = (v_1^*, \ldots, v_I^*)$ are in equilibrium if $\sum_i v_i^* = \sum_i \omega_i$. Show that, under the standard assumptions on preferences and consumption sets, the price vector and the individual consumptions constitute a Walrasian equilibrium for the economy with production. Interpret.

**17.C.1$^A$** Verify that the correspondence $f(\cdot)$ introduced in the proof of Proposition 17.C.1 is convex-valued.

**17.C.2$^C$** Show that a convex-valued correspondence $z(\cdot)$ defined on $\mathbb{R}_{++}^L$ and satisfying the conditions (i) to (v) listed below (parallel to the corresponding conditions in Proposition 17.C.1) admits a solution; that is, there is a $p$ with $0 \in z(p)$.

   (i) $z(\cdot)$ is upper-hemicontinuous.
   (ii) $z(\cdot)$ is homogeneous of degree zero.
   (iii) For every $p$ and $z \in z(p)$ we have $p \cdot z = 0$ (Walras' law).
   (iv) There is $s \in \mathbb{R}$ such that $z_\ell > -s$ for any $z \in z(p)$ and $p$.
   (v) If $p^n \to p \neq 0$, $z^n \in z(p^n)$ and $p_\ell = 0$ for some $\ell$, then $\text{Max }\{z_1^n, \ldots, z_L^n\} \to \infty$.

[*Hint*: If you try to replicate exactly the proof of Proposition 17.C.1 you will run into difficulties with the upper-hemicontinuity condition. A possible three-step approach goes as follows: (1) Show that for $\varepsilon > 0$ small enough the solutions must be contained in $\Delta_\varepsilon = \{p \in \Delta : p_\ell \geq \varepsilon \text{ for all } \ell\}$; (2) argue then that for $r > 0$ large enough, one has $z(p) \subset [-r, r]^L$ for every $p \in \Delta_\varepsilon$; finally, (3) carry out a fixed-point argument in the domain $\Delta_\varepsilon \times [-r, r]^L$. For an easier result, you could limit yourself to prove the convex-valued parallel to Proposition 17.C.2. The suggested domain for the fixed-point argument is then $\Delta \times [-r, r]^L$.

**17.C.3$^B$** Consider an exchange economy in which every consumer $i$ has continuous, strongly monotone, strictly convex preferences, and $\omega_i \gg 0$. The peculiarity of the equilibrium problem to be considered is that the consumer will now pay a type of tax on his gross consumption; moreover, this tax can differ across commodities and consumers. We will also assume that total tax receipts are rebated equally across consumers and in a lump-sum fashion. Specifically, for every $i$ there is a vector of given tax rates $t_i = (t_{1i}, \ldots, t_{Li}) \geq 0$ and for every price vector $p \gg 0$ the budget set of consumer $i$ is

$$B_i(p, w_i) = \left\{ x_i \in \mathbb{R}^L_+ : \sum_\ell (1 + t_{\ell i}) p_\ell x_{\ell i} \leq w_i \right\}.$$

An *equilibrium with taxes* is then a price vector $p \gg 0$ and an allocation $(x_1^*, \ldots, x_I^*)$ with $\sum x_i^* = \sum_i \omega_i$ such that every $i$ maximizes preferences in $B_i(p, p \cdot \omega_i + (1/I)(\sum_{\ell i} t_{\ell i} p_\ell x_{\ell i}))$.

**(a)** Illustrate the notion of an equilibrium with taxes in an Edgeworth box. Verify that an equilibrium with taxes need not be a Pareto optimum.

**(b)** Apply Proposition 17.C.1 to show that an equilibrium with taxes exists.

**(c)** As formulated here, the taxes are on gross consumptions. If they were imposed instead on net consumptions, that is, on amounts purchased or sold, then (assuming the same rate for buying or selling) the budget set would be

$$B_i(p, T_i) = \left\{ x_i \in \mathbb{R}^L_+ : p \cdot (x_i - \omega_i) + \sum_\ell t_\ell |p_{\ell i}(x_{\ell i} - \omega_{\ell i})| \leq T_i \right\},$$

where the $T_i$ are the lump-sum rebates. In what way does this budget set differ from that described previously for the case of taxes on gross consumptions? Represent graphically. Notice the kinks.

**(d)** Write down a budget set for the situation similar to **(c)** except that the tax rates for amounts bought or sold may be different.

**(e)** (More advanced) How would you approach the existence issue for the modification described in **(c)**?

**17.C.4$^A$** Consider a pure exchange economy. The only novelty is that a progressive tax system is instituted according to the following rule: individual wealth is no longer $p \cdot \omega_i$; instead, anyone with wealth above the mean of the population must contribute half of the excess over the mean into a fund, and those below the mean receive a contribution from the fund in proportion to their deficiency below the mean.

**(a)** For a two-consumer society with endowments $\omega_1 = (1, 2)$ and $\omega_2 = (2, 1)$, write the after-tax wealths of the two consumers as a function of prices.

**(b)** If the consumer preferences are continuous, strictly convex, and strongly monotone, will the excess demand functions satisfy the conditions required for existence in Proposition 17.C.1 given that wealth is being redistributed in this way?

**17.C.5$^B$** Consider a population of $I$ consumers. Every consumer $i$ has consumption set $\mathbb{R}^L_+$ and continuous, strictly convex preferences $\succsim_i$. Suppose, in addition, that every $i$ has a household technology $Y_i \subset \mathbb{R}^L$ satisfying $0 \in Y_i$. We can then define the *induced preferences* $\succsim_i^*$ on $\mathbb{R}^L_+$ by $x_i \succsim_i^* x_i'$ if and only if for any $y_i' \in Y_i$ with $x_i' + y_i' \geq 0$ there is $y_i \in Y_i$ with $x_i + y_i \geq 0$ and $x_i + y_i \succsim_i x_i' + y_i'$ (i.e., whatever can be done from $x_i'$, something at least as good can be obtained from $x_i$).

**(a)** Show that induced preferences are rational, that is, complete and transitive.

**(b)** Show that if $Y_i$ is convex then induced preferences $\succsim_i^*$ are convex.

**(c)** Suppose that goods are of two kinds: marketed goods and nonmarketed household goods. Initial preferences $\succsim_i$ care only about household goods, and initial endowments $\omega_i$ have nonzero entries only for marketed goods. Use the concept of induced preferences to set up the equilibrium problem as one that is formally a problem of pure exchange among marketed goods. Discuss.

**17.C.6$^B$** Let $L = 2$. Consider conditions (i), (iii), and (iv) of Proposition 17.B.2. Exhibit four examples such that in each of the examples only one condition fails and yet the system of equations $z(p) = 0$ has no solution. Why is condition (ii) not included in the list?

**17.D.1$^B$** Consider an exchange economy with two commodities and two consumers. Both consumers have homothetic preferences of the constant elasticity variety. Moreover, the elasticity of substitution is the same for both consumers and is small (i.e., goods are close to perfect complements). Specifically,

$$u_1(x_{11}, x_{21}) = (2x_{11}^\rho + x_{21}^\rho)^{1/\rho} \qquad \text{and} \qquad u_2(x_{12}, x_{22}) = (x_{12}^\rho + 2x_{22}^\rho)^{1/\rho},$$

and $\rho = -4$. The endowments are $\omega_1 = (1, 0)$ and $\omega_2 = (0, 1)$.

Compute the excess demand function of this economy and verify that there are multiple equilibria.

**17.D.2$^A$** Apply the implicit function theorem to show that if $f(v) = 0$ is a system of $M$ equations in $N$ unknowns and if at $\bar{v}$ we have $f(\bar{v}) = 0$ and rank $Df(\bar{v}) = M$, then in a neighborhood of $\bar{v}$ the solution set of $f(\cdot) = 0$ can be parameterized by means of $N - M$ parameters.

**17.D.3$^A$** Carry out explicitly the computations for Proposition 17.D.4.

**17.D.4$^C$** Consider a two-commodity, two-consumer exchange economy satisfying the appropriate differentiability conditions on utility and demand functions. There is a total endowment vector $\bar{\omega} \gg 0$. Show that for almost every $\omega_1 \ll \bar{\omega}$ the economy defined by the initial endowments $\omega_1$ and $\omega_2 = \bar{\omega} - \omega_1$ has a finite number of equilibria. This differs from the situation in Proposition 17.D.2 in that total endowments are kept fixed. [*Hint*: You should use the properties of the Slutsky matrix.]

**17.D.5$^B$** Consider a two-commodity, two-consumer exchange economy satisfying the appropriate differentiability conditions on utility and demand functions. Set the equilibrium problem as an equation system in the consumption variables $x_1 \in \mathbb{R}^2_+$ and $x_2 \in \mathbb{R}^2_+$, the price variables $p \in \mathbb{R}^2_+$, and the reciprocals of the marginal utilities of wealth $\lambda_1 \in \mathbb{R}$ and $\lambda_2 \in \mathbb{R}$ (neglect the possibility of boundary equilibria). The parameters of the system are the initial endowments $(\omega_1, \omega_2) \in \mathbb{R}^4_+$. Prove without further aggregation that (after deleting one equation and one unknown) the system satisfies the full rank condition of the transversality theorem.

**17.D.6$^B$** The setup is identical to Exercise 17.D.5 except that an externality is allowed: The (differentiable) utility function of consumer 1 may depend on the consumption of consumer 2; that is, it has the form $u_1(x_1, x_2)$ where $x_i$ is consumer $i$'s consumption bundle [but we still have $u_2(x_2)$]. Equilibrium is defined as usual, with the proviso that consumer 1 takes consumer 2's consumption as given. Show that, generically on initial endowments $(\omega_1, \omega_2) \in \mathbb{R}^4_+$, the number of equilibria is finite.

**17.D.7$^B$** Suppose the agents of an overall exchange economy are distributed across $N$ islands with no communication among them. Each island economy has three equilibria.

**(a)** Argue that the number of equilibria in the overall economy is $3^N$.

**(b)** Suppose now that the islands' economies are identical and that there is a possibility of communication across the islands: free and costless transportation of commodities. Show that then the number of equilibria is 3.

**17.D.8<sup>A</sup>** Show by explicit computation that the index of the equilibrium of a one-consumer Cobb–Douglas pure exchange economy is $+1$.

**17.E.1<sup>A</sup>** Derive expressions (17.E.1) and (17.E.2).

**17.E.2<sup>A</sup>** Derive expression (17.E.3).

**17.E.3<sup>B</sup>** Provide explicit utility functions rationalizing at a given price vector $p$ the individual excess demands $z_i(p)$ and matrices of price effects $Dz_i(p)$ constructed in the proof of Proposition 17.E.2.

**17.E.4<sup>B</sup>** Consider the two-commodity case. Give an example of a function $z(p)$ defined on $P_\varepsilon = \{(p_1, p_2) \gg 0: \varepsilon < (p_1/p_2) < (1/\varepsilon)\}$, and with values in $\mathbb{R}^2$, that is continuous, is homogeneous of degree zero, satisfies Walras' law, and cannot be generated from a rational preference relation. Represent graphically the offer curve associated with this function. Note that it goes through the initial endowment point and compare with the construction used in Figure 17.E.2.

**17.E.5<sup>A</sup>** Show that the choices represented in Figure 17.E.3 cannot be generated from consumers with endowment vectors bounded above by $(1, 1)$ and nonnegative consumption.

**17.E.6<sup>A</sup>** Show that the excess demand function $z_i(p) = e^i - p_i p$, defined for $\|p\| = 1$, is proportionally one-to-one in the sense used in the general proof of Proposition 17.E.3 (at the end of Section 17.E).

**17.E.7<sup>B</sup>** Show directly that the excess demand function $z_i(p) = e^i - p_i p$ used in the general proof of Proposition 17.E.3 satisfies the strong axiom of revealed preference.

**17.F.1<sup>C</sup>** Show that expression (17.F.2) gives rise to a negative semidefinite matrix of price effects, $Dz(p)$, if initial endowments are proportional among themselves *or* if consumptions are proportional among themselves.

**17.F.2<sup>A</sup>** Complete the requested verification of Example 17.F.1.

**17.F.3<sup>B</sup>** There are four goods and two consumers. The endowments of the consumers are $\omega_1 = (\omega_{11}, \omega_{21}, 0, 0)$ and $\omega_2 = (\omega_{12}, \omega_{22}, 0, 0)$. Consumer 1 spends all his wealth on good 3 while consumer 2 does the same on good 4. Specify some values of $\omega_1$ and $\omega_2$ for which the corresponding excess demand of this economy does not satisfy the weak axiom of revealed preference.

**17.F.4<sup>A</sup>** Suppose that there are $L$ goods but that for every consumer there is a good such that at any price the consumer spends all his wealth on that good (perhaps goods are distinguished by their location). Show that the aggregate excess demand will satisfy the (weak) gross substitute property.

**17.F.5<sup>C</sup>** Complete the missing steps of Example 17.F.2.

**17.F.6<sup>C</sup>** Consider a two-consumption-good, two-factor model with constant returns and no joint production. In fact, suppose that the production functions for the two consumption goods are Cobb–Douglas. Consumers have holdings of factors and have preferences only for the two consumption goods. The economy is a closed economy (at equilibrium, consumption must equal production). Suppose that the two goods are normal and gross substitutes in the *demand function* of the consumers. Define an induced exchange economy for factors of production by assuming that at any vector of factor prices the two goods are priced at average cost and the final demand for them is met. Show that the resulting aggregate excess demand for factors of production has the gross substitute property and, consequently, that there is a unique equilibrium for the overall economy.

**17.F.7$^A$** Prove expression (17.F.3) for $L = 2$.

**17.F.8$^A$** Show that expression (17.F.3) implies that the set of solutions to $z(p) = 0$ is convex.

**17.F.9$^B$** Consider an economy with a single constant returns production set $Y$. Preferences are continuous, strictly convex, and strongly monotone. Suppose that the feasible consumptions $(x_1, \ldots, x_I)$ are associated with a Walrasian equilibrium. Assume, moreover, that no trade is required to attain these consumptions if $Y$ is freely available to all consumers; that is $x_i - \omega_i \in Y$ for all $i$. Show then that those are the only possible equilibrium consumptions.

**17.F.10$^A$** Show that expression (17.F.3) implies that $Dz(p)$ is negative semidefinite at an equilibrium $p$.

**17.F.11$^B$** Show that if $z(p) = 0$, rank $Dz(p) = L - 1$, and $Dz(p)$ is negative semidefinite, then, for any $\ell$, the $(L - 1) \times (L - 1)$ matrix obtained from $Dz(p)$ by deleting the $\ell$th row and column has a determinant of sign $(-1)^{L-1}$. [*Hint:* From Section M.D of the Mathematical Appendix you know that rank $Dz(p) = L - 1$ implies that the $(L - 1) \times (L - 1)$ matrix under study is nonsingular. Consider then $Dz(p) - \alpha I$.]

**17.F.12$^B$** Show that if $z(p) = 0$ and $Dz(p)$ has the gross substitute sign pattern, then the $(L - 1) \times (L - 1)$ matrix obtained from $Dz(p)$ by deleting the $\ell$th row and column has a *negative dominant diagonal* (see Section M.D of the Mathematical Appendix for this concept) and is therefore negative definite.

**17.F.13$^A$** Provide the missing computation for Example 17.F.3.

**17.F.14$^B$** Consider a firm that produces good 1 out of goods $\ell = 2, \ldots, L$ by means of a production function $f(v_2, \ldots, v_L)$. Assume that $f(\cdot)$ is concave, increasing, and twice continuously differentiable. We say that $\ell$ and $\ell'$ are complements at the input combination $v = (v_2, \ldots, v_L)$ if $\partial^2 f(v)/\partial v_\ell \, \partial v_{\ell'} > 0$.

(a) Verify that for the Cobb–Douglas production function $f(v_2, \ldots, v_L) = v_2^{\alpha_1} \times \cdots \times v_L^{\alpha_L}$, $\alpha_2 + \cdots + \alpha_L \leq 1$, any two inputs are complements at any $v$.

(b) Suppose that $f(\cdot)$ is of the constant returns type. Show that at any $v$ and for any $\ell$ there is an $\ell'$ that is a complement to $\ell$ at $v$.

(c) Suppose now that $f(\cdot)$ is strictly concave and that any two inputs are complements at any $v$. Let $v_\ell(p_1, \ldots, p_L)$ be the input demand functions. Show that, for any $\ell$, $\partial v_\ell/\partial p_1 > 0$, $\partial v_\ell/\partial p_\ell < 0$, and $\partial v_\ell/\partial p_{\ell'} < 0$ for $\ell' \neq \ell$.

(d) Discuss the implications of (a) to (c) for uniqueness theorems that rely on the gross substitute property.

**17.F.15$^B$** Consider a one-consumer economy with production and strictly convex preferences. There is a system of ad valorem taxes $t = (t_1, \ldots, t_L)$ creating a wedge between consumer and producer prices; that is, $p_\ell = (1 + t_\ell)q_\ell$ where $p_\ell$ and $q_\ell$ are, respectively, the consumer and producer price for good $\ell$. Tax receipts are turned back in lump-sum fashion. Write the definition of (distorted) equilibrium. Show that the equilibrium is unique if the production sector is of the Leontief type (a single primary factor, no joint production, constant returns) and all goods are normal in consumption. Can you argue by example the nondispensability of the last normality condition? If this is simpler, you can limit your discussion to the case of two commodities (one input and one output).

**17.F.16$^C$** Suppose that $g(p) = (g_1(p), \ldots, g_N(p))$ is defined in the domain $[0, r]^N$ and that $g(0, \ldots, 0) \gg (0, \ldots, 0)$, $g(r, \ldots, r) \ll (0, \ldots, 0)$. Note that we do not assume Walras' law, homogeneity of degree zero, or, for that matter, continuity. The function $g(\cdot)$ could, for example, be the system of excess demands corresponding to a subgroup of markets with the prices of commodities outside the group kept fixed.

**(a)** We say that $g(\cdot)$ satisfies the *strong gross substitute property* (SGS) if for some $\alpha > 0$ every coordinate of the function $\alpha g(p) + p$ is strictly increasing in $p$ and $(\alpha g(p) + p) \in [0, r]^N$ for every $p \in [0, r]^N$. Show that if $g(p)$ has the SGS property then it also has the GS property.

**(b)** Show by example that the GS property does not imply the SGS property. Establish, however, that if $g(\cdot)$ is continuously differentiable and the GS property is satisfied then the SGS property holds.

From now on we assume that $g(\cdot)$ satisfies the SGS property.

**(c)** Show that there is an equilibrium, that is, a $p$ with $g(p) = 0$. Illustrate graphically for the case $N = 1$. [*Hint*: Quote the Tarski fixed point theorem from Section M.I of the Mathematical Appendix, or, if you prefer, assume continuity and apply Brouwer's fixed point theorem.]

**(d)** Give an example for $N = 2$ where the equilibrium is not unique.

**(e)** Suppose that $g(p) = g(p') = 0$. Show that there must be an equilibrium $p''$ such that $p'' \geq p$ and $p'' \geq p'$. Similarly, there is an equilibrium $p'''$ such that $p''' \leq p$ and $p''' \leq p'$. [*Hint*: Apply the argument in **(c)** to the domain $[\text{Max}\{p_1, p_1'\}, r] \times \cdots \times [\text{Max}\{p_N, p_N'\}, r]$.]

**(f)** Argue (you can assume continuity here) that the equilibrium set satisfies a strong and very special property, namely, that it has a maximal and a minimal equilibrium. That is, there are $p^{\max}$ and $p^{\min}$ such that $g(p^{\max}) = g(p^{\min}) = 0$ and $p^{\min} \leq p \leq p^{\max}$ whenever $g(p) = 0$.

**(g)** Assume now that $g(\cdot)$ is also differentiable. Suppose that we know that at equilibrium, that is, whenever $g(p) = 0$, the matrix $Dg(p)$ has a *negative dominant diagonal*; that is, $Dg(p)v \ll 0$ for a $v \gg 0$. Argue (perhaps nonrigorously) that the equilibrium must then be unique.

**(h)** Suppose that $g(\cdot)$ is the usual excess demand system for the first $N$ goods of an economy with $N + 1$ goods in which the last price has been fixed to equal 1 *and* the overall $(N + 1)$-good excess demand system satisfies the gross substitute property. Apply **(g)** to show that the equilibrium is unique.

**17.F.17$^A$** [Becker (1962), Grandmont (1992)] Suppose that $L = 2$ and you have a continuum of consumers. All consumers have the same initial endowments; they are not rational, however. Given a budget set, they choose at random from consumption bundles on the budget line using a uniform distribution among the nonnegative consumptions. Let $z(p)$ be the average excess demand ($=$ expected value of a single consumer's choice). Show that $z(\cdot)$ can be generated from preference maximization of a Cobb–Douglas utility function (thus the economy admits a positive representative consumer in the sense of Section 4.D).

**17.G.1$^B$** Suppose that in an exchange economy (and with the normalization $p_L = 1$) we are given equilibrium prices $p(\hat{\omega}_1)$ as a differentiable function defined as an open domain of the endowments of the first $L - 1$ goods of the first consumer, $\hat{\omega}_1 = (\omega_{11}, \ldots, \omega_{L-1,1})$. All the remaining endowments are kept fixed. Suppose that the demand function of the first consumer is strictly normal in the sense that $D_{w_1} x_1(p, w_1) \gg 0$ through the relevant domain of $(p, w_1)$. Show then that for any $\hat{\hat{\omega}}_1$ and $\bar{p} = p(\hat{\hat{\omega}}_1)$, we have rank $D_{\hat{\omega}_1} \hat{z}_1(\bar{p}; \hat{\hat{\omega}}_1) = L - 1$ and rank $Dp(\hat{\hat{\omega}}_1) = L - 1$, where $\hat{z}_1(p; \hat{\omega}_1)$ is the excess demand function of the first consumer for the first $L - 1$ goods.

**17.G.2$^B$** The setting is as in Exercise 17.G.1 or as in Proposition 17.G.2. Suppose that $\hat{z}(\bar{p}; \hat{\hat{\omega}}_1) = 0$. Show that there are economies with $D_p \hat{z}(\bar{p}; \hat{\hat{\omega}}_1)$ an $(L - 1) \times (L - 1)$ negative definite matrix but where $\partial p_1(\hat{\hat{\omega}}_1)/\partial \omega_{11} > 0$. [*Hint*: Use Proposition 17.G.1 and the arguments employed in its proof.]

**17.G.3$^C$** The setting is as in Exercise 17.F.16, except that now we have two functions $g(p) \in \mathbb{R}^N$ and $\hat{g}(p) \in \mathbb{R}^N$. Each of these functions satisfies the conditions of Exercise 17.F.16 (in particular the SDS property). In addition, we assume that $\hat{g}(\cdot)$ is an upward shift of $g(\cdot)$; that is, $\hat{g}(p) \geq g(p)$ for every $p \in [0, r]^N$. Prove that if $(p^{\min}, p^{\max})$ and $(\hat{p}^{\min}, \hat{p}^{\max})$ are the minimal and maximal equilibrium price vectors (see Exercise 17.F.16) for $g(\cdot)$ and $\hat{g}(\cdot)$, respectively, then $\hat{p}^{\min} \geq p^{\min}$ and $\hat{p}^{\max} \geq p^{\max}$. [You can assume that $g(\cdot)$ and $\hat{g}(\cdot)$ are continuous; if this makes things simpler, assume also that both functions have a unique solution.] Represent graphically for the case $N = 1$.

**17.H.1$^C$** Suppose that the system of excess demand functions $z(p)$ satisfies the gross substitute property. Consider the tâtonnement price dynamics

$$\frac{dp_\ell}{dt} = z_\ell(p) \qquad \text{for every } \ell. \tag{*}$$

For any price vector $p$ let $\psi(p) = \text{Max}\{z_1(p)/p_1, \dots, z_L(p)/p_L\}$.

**(a)** Argue that if $p(t)$ is a solution for the above tâtonnement dynamics (i.e., $dp_\ell(t)/dt = z_\ell(p(t))$ for every $\ell$ and $t$) and $z(p(0)) \neq 0$ then $\psi(p(t))$ should be decreasing through time. [*Hint:* If $z_\ell(p(t))/p_\ell(t) = \psi(p(t))$ then $p_\ell(t)/p_{\ell'}(t)$ cannot decrease at $t$ for any $\ell'$. Hence, $z_\ell(p(t))$ cannot increase, whereas $p_\ell$ surely increases.]

**(b)** Argue that $p(t)$ converges to an equilibrium price as $t \to \infty$. [*Hint:* Recall that for the dynamics (*) Walras' law implies that $\sum_\ell p_\ell^2(t) = \text{constant}$.]

**17.H.2$^B$** There is an output good and a numeraire. The price of the output good is $p$. The data of our problem are given by two functions: The consumption side of the economy provides an excess demand function $z(p)$ for the output good, and the production side an increasing inverse output supply function $p(z)$. Both functions are differentiable. In addition, their graphs cross at $(1, 1)$, which is the equilibrium we will concentrate on in this exercise.

Given this setting we can define two one-variable dynamics:

(i) In *Walras price dynamics* we assume that at $p$ the price increases or decreases according to the sign of the difference between excess demand and (direct) supply at $p$.

(ii) In *Marshall quantity dynamics* we assume that at $z$ production increases or decreases according to the sign of the difference between the demand price (i.e., the inverse excess demand) and the supply price (i.e., $p(z)$) at $z$.

**(a)** Write the above formally and interpret economically.

**(b)** Suppose that the technology is nearly of the constant returns type. Show then that around the equilibrium $(1, 1)$ the system is always Walrasian stable but that Marshallian stability depends on the slope of the excess demand function (in what way?).

**(c)** Write general price and quantity dynamics where prices move à la Walras and quantities à la Marshall. Draw a $(p, z)$ phase diagram and argue that in the typical case dynamic trajectories will spiral around the equilibrium.

**(d)** Go back to the technology specification of **(b)**. Show that the system in **(c)** is locally stable if and only if the equilibrium is Marshallian stable.

**(e)** Consider the simplest price and quantity dynamics in the limit case where there are constant returns and excess demand is also a constant function. Draw the phase diagram. Suppose now that the quantity dynamics is modified by making the quantity responses depend not only on price and cost but also on the "expectation of sales," that is, on the excess demand. Will this have a stabilizing or a destabilizing effect?

**17.H.3$^A$** For $L = 3$ draw an example similar to Figure 17.H.2 but in which there is a single equilibrium that, moreover, is locally totally unstable. Could you make it a saddle?

**17.I.1$^A$** Argue that the replica procedure described at the beginning of Section 17.I does effectively include the case where the numbers of consumers of different types are not the same (assume, for simplicity, that the proportions of the different types are rational numbers). [*Hint*: Redefine the size of the original economy.]

**17.I.2$^A$** Consider for a one-input, one-output problem the production function $q = v^2$, where $v$ is the amount of input. Show that the corresponding production set $Y$ is additive but that the smallest cone containing it, $Y^*$, is not closed. Discuss in what sense the nonconvexity in $Y$ is large. Argue that, whatever the number of consumers, there is no useful sense in which an equilibrium (nearly) exists.

**17.I.3$^B$** There are three commodities: the first is a high-quality good, the second is a low-quality good, and the third is labor. The first and second goods can be produced from labor according to the production functions $f_1(v) = \text{Min} \{v, 1\}$ and $f_2(v) = \text{Min} \{v^\beta, 1\}$ for $0 < \beta < 1$. The economy has one unit of labor in the aggregate. Labor has no utility value. There are two equally sized classes of agents, with a very large number of each. "Rich" and "poor" have identical endowments, but the rich own all the shares in the firms of the economy. The rich spend all their wealth on the high-quality good; the poor must buy either one quality or the other—they cannot buy both. The utility function of the poor is $u(x_1, x_2) = x_1 + \frac{1}{2}x_2$, defined for $(x_1, x_2)$ not both positive.

**(a)** Which standard hypothesis of the general model does this economy fail to satisfy?

**(b)** Show that there can be no equilibria other than one in which both qualities of product are produced.

**(c)** Show that an equilibrium exists.

**17.AA.1$^A$** Consider an exchange economy in which the preferences of consumers are monotone, strictly convex, and represented by the utility functions $(u_1(\cdot), \ldots, u_I(\cdot))$. Show that for any $(s_1, \ldots, s_I) \gg 0$ there can be at most one Pareto optimal allocation $x = (x_1, \ldots, x_I)$ such that $(u_1(x_i), \ldots, u_I(x_I))$ is proportional to $(s_1, \ldots, s_I)$.

**17.AA.2$^B$** Consider the welfare-theoretic approach to the equilibrium equations described in Appendix A (the Negishi approach). The existence of a solution to the system of equations $g(s) = 0$ defined there follows from a fixed-point argument similar to the one carried out in Proposition 17.C.2. Assume that you are in an exchange economy with continuous, strictly convex and strongly monotone preferences, and that $\omega_i \gg 0$ for every $i$. Assume also that $g(s)$ turns out to be a function rather than a correspondence (a sufficient condition for this is that preferences be representable by differentiable utility functions and that at every Pareto optimal allocation at least one consumer gets a strictly positive consumption of every good).

**(a)** Show that $g(s)$ is continuous.

**(b)** Show that $g(s)$ satisfies a sort of Walras' law: "$\sum_i g_i(s) = 0$, for every $s$."

**(c)** Show that if $s_i = 0$ then $g_i(s) > 0$. [*Hint*: If $s_i = 0$ then $u_i(x_i(s)) = 0$ and so $p(s) \cdot x_i(s) = 0$.]

**(d)** Complete the existence proof. (Note that $g(s)$ is also defined for $s$ with zero components. This makes matters simpler.)

**17.AA.3$^B$** Suppose that, in an exchange economy, consumption sets are $\mathbb{R}^L_+$ and preferences are representable by concave, increasing utility functions $u_i(\cdot)$. Let $\Delta = \{\lambda \in \mathbb{R}^L_+ : \sum_i \lambda_i = 1\}$ be a simplex of utility weights. Suggest an equation system for Walrasian equilibrium that proceeds by associating with every $\lambda$ a linear social welfare function.

**17.BB.1$^A$** Give a graphical example (for $L = 2$) of a Walrasian quasiequilibrium with strictly positive prices that is not an equilibrium for an economy in which:

(i)  For every $j$, $Y_j = -\mathbb{R}_+^L$.

(ii)  For every $i$, $X_i$ is nonempty, closed, convex and satisfies $X_i + \mathbb{R}_+^L \subset X_i$.

(iii)  For every $i$, preferences are continuous, convex, and strongly monotone.

(iv)  For every $i$, $\omega_i \in X_i$.

Why does this example not contradict any result given in the text (see the small-type discussion after the proof of Proposition 17.BB.1)?

**17.BB.2**[B] Consider an economy in which every consumer desires only a subset of goods and has holdings of only some goods. For the commodities desired, however, the preferences of the consumer are strongly monotone (they are also continuous) on the corresponding nonnegative orthant. Suppose in addition that $\sum_i \omega_i \gg 0$ and that the economy satisfies the following *indecomposability* condition:

> It is not possible to divide consumers into two (nonempty) groups so that the consumers of one of the groups do not desire any of the commodities owned by the consumers of the other group.

Show then that any Walrasian quasiequilibrium is an equilibrium.

**17.BB.3**[C] Consider an Edgeworth box where preferences are continuous, strictly convex and locally nonsatiated (but not necessarily monotone). Suppose also that free disposal of commodities is not possible. Argue that, nonetheless, the offer curves must cross and, therefore, that an equilibrium exists. Show that at equilibrium the two prices cannot be negative. In fact, at least one price must be positive (this is harder to show).

**17.BB.4**[A] Prove that if $(x^*, y^*, p)$ is a free-disposal quasiequilibrium and $Y_1$ satisfies free disposal, then we can get a true quasiequilibrium by changing only the production of firm 1.

**17.BB.5**[A] Provide the missing step in the proof of Lemma 17.BB.5 (that is, show that the convexity of preferences implies that $x_i \succ_i x_{i\alpha}$ and $x_i' \succ_i x_{i\alpha}$ cannot both occur for $x_{i\alpha} = \alpha x_i + (1 - \alpha) x_i'$).

**17.BB.6**[A] Complete the proof of Lemma 17.BB.5 by verifying the convexity of $\tilde{y}_j(x, y, p)$ and of $\tilde{p}(x, y, p)$.

**17.BB.7**[A] Complete the proof of Lemma 17.BB.6 by verifying the upper hemicontinuity of the correspondences $\tilde{y}_j(\cdot)$ and $\tilde{p}(\cdot)$.

**17.BB.8**[B] [Existence with production externalities; see Chipman (1970) for more on this topic.] There are $L$ goods. Good $L$ is labor and it is the single factor of production. Consumers have consumption set $\mathbb{R}_+^L$, continuous, strongly monotone, and strictly convex preferences, and endowments only of labor. Good $\ell = 1, \ldots, L - 1$ is produced in sector $\ell$, which is composed of $J_\ell$ identical firms. The production function of a firm in sector $\ell$ is $f_\ell(v_\ell) = \alpha_\ell v_\ell^{\beta_\ell}$ for $0 < \beta_\ell \le 1$. The peculiarity of the model is that the productivity coefficient $\alpha_\ell$ will not be a constant but will depend on the aggregate use of labor in sector $\ell$. Precisely,

$$\alpha_\ell = \gamma_\ell \left( \sum_j v_{\ell j} \right)^{\rho_\ell}, \qquad \gamma_\ell > 0 \text{ and } \rho_\ell \ge 0.$$

**(a)** Define the notion of Walrasian equilibrium. Assume in doing so that individual firms neglect the effect on $\alpha_\ell$ of their use of labor. To save on notation, suppose also that profit shares are equal across consumers.

**(b)** Prove the existence of a Walrasian equilibrium for the current model (make the standard additional assumptions that you find necessary). [*Hint*: The general proof of Appendix B needs very few adaptations.]

**(c)** Derive and represent the aggregate production set of each sector. Which conditions on the parameters $\beta_\ell$, $\gamma_\ell$, $\rho_\ell$ guarantee that the aggregate production set of sector $\ell$ exhibits increasing, constant, or decreasing returns to scale?

**(d)** Note that the existence conditions of (b) may be satisfied while the aggregate production set is not convex. What would happen if the externality of sector $\ell$ were internalized by putting all the firms of the sector under joint management?

**(e)** Suppose that $L = 2$, $\beta_\ell = 1$ and individual preferences are quasilinear in labor; that is, they admit a utility function $u_i(x_{1i}) + x_{2i}$. Discuss, both analytically and graphically, the bias of the equilibrium level of production relative to the social optimum.

**17.BB.9$^B$** Carry out the existence argument for the two-player-game approach described at the end of Appendix B.

# 18

# Some Foundations for Competitive Equilibria

## 18.A Introduction

Up to this point of Part IV, the existence of markets in which prices are quoted and taken as given by economic agents has been assumed. In this chapter, we discuss four topics that, in essence, have two features in common: The first is that they all try to single out and characterize the Walrasian allocations from considerations more basic than those stated in its definition. The second is that they all emphasize the role of a large number of traders in accomplishing this task.

In Section 18.B we introduce the concept of the *core*, which can be viewed as embodying a notion of unrestricted competition. We then present the important *core equivalence theorem*.

Section 18.C examines a more restricted concept of competition: that taking place through well-specified trading mechanisms. The analysis of this section amounts to a reexamination in the general equilibrium context of the models of noncooperative competition that were presented in Section 12.F.

The motivation of the remaining two sections is more normative. In Section 18.D we show how informational limitations on the part of a policy authority (constrained to use policy tools relying on *self-selection*, or *envy freeness*) may make the Walrasian allocations the only implementable Pareto optimal allocations.

In Section 18.E the objective is to characterize the Walrasian allocations, among the Pareto optimal ones, in terms of their distributional properties. In particular, we ask to what extent it can be asserted that at the Walrasian allocation everyone gets her "marginal contribution" to the collective economic well-being of society.

A number of the ideas of this chapter (especially those related to the core, but also some in Section 18.E) have come to economics from the cooperative theory of games. This therefore seems a good place to present a brief introduction to this theory; we do it in Appendix A.

## 18.B Core and Equilibria

The theory to be reviewed in this section was proposed by Edgeworth (1881). His aim was to explain how the presence of many interacting competitors would lead to the emergence of a system of prices taken as given by economic agents, and consequently to a Walrasian equilibrium outcome. Edgeworth's work had no immediate impact. The modern versions of his theory follow the rediscovery of his solution concept (known now as the *core*) in the theory of cooperative games. Appendix A contains a brief introduction to the theory of cooperative games; this section, however, is self-contained. For further, and very accessible, reading on the material of this section, we refer to Hildenbrand and Kirman (1988).

The theory of the core is distinguished by its parsimony. Its conceptual apparatus does not appeal to any specific trading mechanism nor does it assume any particular institutional setup. Informally, the notion of competition that the theory explores is one in which traders are well informed of the characteristics (endowments and preferences) of other traders, and in which the members of any group of traders can bind themselves to any mutually advantageous agreement. The simplest example is a buyer and a seller exchanging a good for money, but we can also have more complex arrangements involving many individuals and goods.

Formally, we consider an economy with $I$ consumers. Every consumer $i$ has consumption set $\mathbb{R}^L_+$, and endowment vector $\omega_i \geq 0$, and a continuous, strictly convex, strongly monotone preference relation $\succsim_i$. There is also a publicly available constant returns convex technology $Y \subset \mathbb{R}^L$.[1] For example, we could have $Y = -\mathbb{R}^L_+$, that is, a pure exchange economy. All of these assumptions are maintained for the rest of the section.

As usual, we say that an allocation $x = (x_1, \ldots, x_I) \in \mathbb{R}^{LI}_+$ is *feasible* if $\sum_i x_i = y + \sum_i \omega_i$ for some $y \subset Y$.

With a slight abuse of notation, we let the symbol $I$ stand for both the number of consumers and the *set* of consumers. Any nonempty subset of consumers $S \subset I$ is then called a *coalition*. Central to the concept of the core is the identification of circumstances under which a coalition of consumers can reach an agreement that makes every member of the coalition better off. Definition 18.B.1 provides a formal statement of these circumstances.

**Definition 18.B.1:** A coalition $S \subset I$ *improves upon*, or *blocks*, the feasible allocation $x^* = (x_1^*, \ldots, x_I^*) \in \mathbb{R}^{LI}_+$ if for every $i \in S$ we can find a consumption $x_i \geq 0$ with the properties:

(i) $x_i \succ_i x_i^*$ for every $i \in S$.

(ii) $\sum_{i \in S} x_i \in Y + \{\sum_{i \in S} \omega_i\}$.

Definition 18.B.1 says that a coalition $S$ can improve upon a feasible allocation $x^*$ if there is some way that, by using *only* their endowments $\sum_{i \in S} \omega_i$ and the publicly available technology $Y$, the coalition can produce an aggregate commodity bundle that can then be distributed to the members of $S$ so as to make each of them better off.

---

1. The constant returns assumption is important. With general production sets the difficulty is that we cannot avoid being explicit about ownership shares. However, these have been defined to be *profit* shares, which makes our conceptual apparatus dependent on the very notion of prices whose emergence we are currently trying to explain. Thus we stick here to the case of constant returns. This is not a serious restriction: recall from Section 5.B (Proposition 5.B.2) that it is always possible to reduce general technologies to the constant returns case by reinterpreting the ownership shares as endowments of an additional "managerial" input.

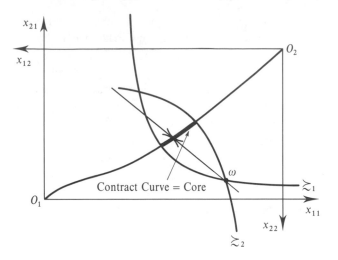

**Figure 18.B.1**

The core equals the contract curve in the two-consumer case.

**Definition 18.B.2:** We say that the feasible allocation $x^* = (x_1^*, \ldots, x_I^*) \in \mathbb{R}_+^{LI}$ has the *core property* if there is no coalition of consumers $S \subset I$ that can improve upon $x^*$. The *core* is the set of allocations that have the core property.

We can see in the Edgeworth box of Figure 18.B.1 that for the case of two consumers the core coincides with the *contract* curve. With two consumers there are only three possible coalitions: $\{1, 2\}$, $\{1\}$, and $\{2\}$. Any allocation that is not a Pareto optimum will be blocked by coalition $\{1, 2\}$.[2] Any allocation in the Pareto set that is not in the contract curve will be blocked by either $\{1\}$ or $\{2\}$. With more than two consumers there are other potential blocking coalitions, but the fact that the coalition of the whole is always one of them means that *all allocations in the core are Pareto optimal*.

We also observe in Figure 18.B.1 that the Walrasian equilibrium allocations, which belong to the contract curve, have the core property. Proposition 18.B.1 tells us that this is true with complete generality. The proposition amounts to an extension of the first welfare theorem. Indeed, in the current terminology, the first welfare theorem simply says that a Walrasian equilibrium cannot be blocked by the coalition of the whole.[3] The following result, Proposition 18.B.1, shows that it also cannot be blocked by any other coalition.

**Proposition 18.B.1:** Any Walrasian equilibrium allocation has the core property.

**Proof:** We simply duplicate the proof of the first welfare theorem (Proposition 16.C.1). We present it for the exchange case. See Exercise 18.B.1 for the case of a general constant returns technology.

Let $x^* = (x_1^*, \ldots, x_I^*)$ be a Walrasian allocation with corresponding equilibrium

---

2. With continuity and strong monotonicity of preferences, if a feasible allocation is Pareto dominated, then it is Pareto dominated by a feasible allocation that strictly improves the utility of *every* consumer. To accomplish this we simply transfer a very small amount of any good from the consumer that is made better off to every other consumer. If the amount transferred is sufficiently small then, by the continuity of preferences, the transferring consumer is still better off, while, by strong monotonicity, every other consumer is made strictly better off.

3. Keep in mind the point made in footnote 2.

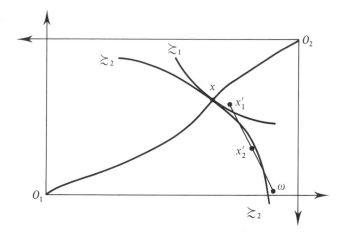

**Figure 18.B.2**

An allocation in the contract curve that can be blocked with two replicas.

price vector $p \geq 0$. Consider an arbitrary coalition $S \subset I$ and suppose that the consumptions $\{x_i\}_{i \in S}$ are such that $x_i \succ_i x_i^*$ for every $i \in S$. Then $p \cdot x_i > p \cdot \omega_i$ for every $i \in S$ and therefore $p \cdot (\sum_{i \in S} x_i) > p \cdot (\sum_{i \in S} \omega_i)$. But then $\sum_{i \in S} x_i \leq \sum_{i \in S} \omega_i$ cannot hold and so condition (ii) of Definition 18.B.1 is not satisfied (recall that we are in the pure exchange case). Hence coalition $S$ cannot block the allocation $x^*$. ∎

The converse of Proposition 18.B.1 is, of course, not true. In the two-consumer economy of Figure 18.B.1 every allocation in the contract curve is in the core, but only one is a Walrasian allocation. The core equivalence theorem, of which we will soon give a version, argues that the converse *does* hold (approximately) if consumers are numerous. Quite remarkably, it turns out that as we increase the size of the economy the non-Walrasian allocations gradually drop from the core until, in the limit, only the Walrasian allocations are left. The basic intuition for this result can perhaps be grasped by examining the Edgeworth box in Figure 18.B.2. Take an allocation such as $x$ where consumer 1 receives a very desirable consumption within the contract curve. Consumer 2 cannot do anything about this: She could not end up better by going alone. But suppose now that the preferences and endowments in the figure represent not individual consumers but *types* of consumers and that the economy is actually composed of four consumers, two of each type. Consider again the allocation $x$, interpreted now as a symmetric allocation, that is, with each consumer of type 1 receiving $x_1$ and each consumer of type 2 receiving $x_2$. Then matters are quite different because a new possibility arises: The two members of type 2 can form a coalition with *one* member of type 1. In Figure 18.B.2, we see that the allocation $x$ can indeed be blocked by giving $x_1'$ to the one consumer of type 1 in the coalition and $x_2'$ to the two consumers of type 2 [note that $-2(x_2' - \omega_2) = (x_1' - \omega_1)$].[4]

---

4. Observe that all this has the flavor of Bertrand competition, as reviewed in Section 12.C. Indeed, we can look at what happens with this three-member coalition as the following: One of the consumers of type 1 bids away the transactions of the consumers of type 2 with the other consumer of type 1. Although this is a topic we shall not get into, we remark that, in fact, there are strong parallels between Bertrand price competition and core competition. Note, in particular, that core competition is as shortsighted as Bertrand competition. By undercutting the other consumer of her type, the consumer of type 1 is only initiating a process of blocking and counterblocking (mutual underbidding in the Bertrand setting) that eventually leads to a result (perhaps the Walrasian allocation) where she will be worse off than at the initial position.

The ability to do this depends, of course, on the way we have drawn the indifference curves. Nonetheless, as we will see, we are always able to form a blocking coalition of this sort if we have sufficiently many consumers of each type.

The version of the core equivalence theorem that we will present is in essence the original of Edgeworth, as generalized by Debreu and Scarf (1963). It builds on the intuition we have just discussed.

To begin, let the set $H = \{1, \ldots, H\}$ stand for a set of *types* of consumers, with each type $h$ having preferences $\succsim_h$ and endowments $\omega_h$. For every integer $n > 0$, we then define the *N-replica* economy as an economy composed of $N$ consumers of each type, for a total number of consumers $I_N = NH$.

We refer to the allocations in which consumers of the same type get the same consumption bundles as *equal-treatment allocations*. Proposition 18.B.2 shows that any allocation in the core must be an equal-treatment allocation. (We hasten to add that this is true for the current replica structure, where there are equal numbers of consumers of each type. It does not hold in general; see Exercise 18.B.2.)

**Proposition 18.B.2:** Denoting by *hn* the *n*th individual of type *h*, suppose that the allocation

$$x^* = (x^*_{11}, \ldots, x^*_{1n}, \ldots, x^*_{1N}, \ldots, x^*_{H1}, \ldots, x^*_{Hn}, \ldots, x^*_{HN}) \in \mathbb{R}^{LHN}_+$$

belongs to the core of the *N*-replica economy. Then $x^*$ has the *equal-treatment property*, that is, all consumers of the same type get the same consumption bundle:

$$x^*_{hm} = x^*_{hn} \qquad \text{for all } 1 \le m, n \le N \text{ and } 1 \le h \le H.$$

**Proof:** Suppose that the feasible allocation $x = (x_{11}, \ldots, x_{HN}) \in \mathbb{R}^{LHN}_+$ does not have the equal-treatment property because, say, $x_{1m} \neq x_{1n}$ for some $m \neq n$. We show that $x$ does not have the core property. In particular, we claim that $x$ can be improved upon by any coalition of $H$ members formed by choosing from every type a worst-treated individual among the consumers of that type. Suppose without loss of generality that, for every $h$, consumer $h1$ is one such worse-off individual, that is, $x_{hn} \succsim_h x_{h1}$ for all $h$ and $n$. Define now the average consumption for each type: $\hat{x}_h = (1/N) \sum_n x_{hn}$. By the strict convexity of preferences we have (recall that consumers of type 1 are not treated identically)

$$\hat{x}_h \succsim_h x_{h1} \quad \text{for all } h \qquad \text{and} \qquad \hat{x}_1 \succ_1 x_{11}. \tag{18.B.1}$$

We claim that the coalition $S = \{11, \ldots, h1, \ldots, H1\}$, formed by $H$ members, can attain by itself the consumptions $(\hat{x}_1, \ldots, \hat{x}_H) \in \mathbb{R}^{LH}_+$. Therefore, by (18.B.1), the original nonequal-treatment allocation can be blocked by $S$.[5] To check the feasibility of $(\hat{x}_1, \ldots, \hat{x}_H) \in \mathbb{R}^{LH}_+$ for $S$, note that, because of the feasibility of $x = (x_{11}, \ldots, x_{HN}) \in \mathbb{R}^{LHN}_+$, there is $y \in Y$ such that $\sum_h \sum_n x_{hn} = y + N(\sum_h \omega_h)$, and therefore

$$\sum_h \hat{x}_h = \frac{1}{N} \sum_h \left( \sum_n x_{hn} \right) = \frac{1}{N} y + \sum_h \omega_h.$$

---

5. Recall that preferences are strongly monotone and continuous, so that if $S$ can achieve an allocation that does strictly better than $x^*$ for some of its members, and at least as well as $x^*$ for all of them, then it can also achieve an allocation that does strictly better for all of its members.

But by the constant returns assumption on $Y$, $(1/N)y \in Y$ and so we conclude that $(\hat{x}_1, \ldots, \hat{x}_H) \in \mathbb{R}_+^{LH}$ is feasible for coalition $S$. ∎

Proposition 18.B.2 allows us to regard the core allocations as vectors of fixed size $LH$, irrespective of the replica that we are concerned with. As a matter of terminology, we call a vector $(x_1, \ldots, x_H) \in \mathbb{R}_+^{LH}$ a *type allocation* and, for any replica $N$, interpret it as the equal-treatment allocation to consumers where each consumer of type $h$ gets $x_h$. A type allocation $(x_1, \ldots, x_H) \in \mathbb{R}_+^{LH}$ is feasible if $\sum_h x_h = y + \sum_h \omega_h$ for some $y \in Y$. Note that for any replica $N$ the corresponding equal-treatment allocation is feasible because

$$\sum_h N x_h = N y + N \left( \sum_h \omega_h \right)$$

and $Ny \in Y$ by the constant returns assumption on $Y$.

By Proposition 18.B.2 the core allocations of a replica economy can be viewed as feasible type allocations. Define by $C_N \subset \mathbb{R}_+^{LH}$ the set of feasible type allocations for which the equal-treatment allocations induced in the $N$-replica have the core property. Note that $C_N$ does depend on $N$. Nonetheless, we always have $C_{N+1} \subset C_N$ because a type allocation blocked in the $N$-replica will be blocked also in the $(N + 1)$-replica by a coalition having exactly the same composition as the one that blocked in the $N$-replica. Thus, as a subset of $\mathbb{R}^{LH}$ the core can only get smaller when $N \to \infty$. At the same time, we know from Proposition 18.B.1 that the core cannot vanish because the Walrasian equilibrium allocations belong to $C_N$ for all $N$. More precisely, the set of Walrasian type allocations is independent of $N$ (see Exercise 18.B.3) and contained in all $C_N$. The core equivalence theorem (which, in the current replica context, is the formal term for the combination of Propositions 18.B.1, 18.B.2 and the forthcoming Proposition 18.B.3) asserts that the Walrasian equilibrium allocations are the only surviving allocations in the core when $N \to \infty$.

**Proposition 18.B.3:** If the feasible type allocation $x^* = (x_1^*, \ldots, x_H^*) \in \mathbb{R}_+^{LH}$ has the core property for all $N = 1, 2, \ldots$, that is, $x^* \in C_N$ for all $N$, then $x^*$ is a Walrasian equilibrium allocation.

**Proof:** To make the proof as intuitive as possible we restrict ourselves to a special case: a pure exchange economy in which, for every $h$, $\succsim_h$ admits a continuously differentiable utility representation $u_h(\cdot)$ [with $\nabla u_h(x_h) \gg 0$ for all $x_h$]. In addition, the initial endowments vector $\omega_h$ is preferred to any consumption $x_h$ that is not strictly positive. This guarantees that any core allocation is interior. We emphasize that these simplifying assumptions are not required for the validity of the result.

Suppose that $x = (x_1, \ldots, x_H) \in \mathbb{R}^{LH}$ is a feasible type allocation that is not a Walrasian equilibrium allocation. Our aim is to show that if $N$ is large enough then $x$ can be blocked.

We may as well assume that $x$ is Pareto optimal (otherwise the coalition of the whole blocks and we are done) and that $x_h \gg 0$ (otherwise a consumer of type $h$ alone could block). Because of Pareto optimality we can apply the second welfare theorem (Proposition 16.D.1) and conclude that $x$ is a price equilibrium with transfers with respect to some $p = (p_1, \ldots, p_L)$. If $x$ is not Walrasian then there must be some $h$, say $h = 1$, with $p \cdot (x_1 - \omega_1) > 0$. Informally, type 1 receives a positive net transfer from the rest of the economy and is thus relatively favored (interpretatively, think of type 1 as the most favored). We shall show that, as long as $N$ is large enough, it would pay for the members of all the other types in the economy to form a coalition with $N - 1$ consumers of type 1 (i.e., to throw out one consumer of type 1).

More precisely, if a member of type 1 is eliminated then to attain feasibility the rest of the economy must absorb her net trade $x_1 - \omega_1$. That, of course, presents no difficulty for the positive entries (those commodities for which the rest of the economy is a net contributor to this consumer of type 1), but it is not so simple for the negative ones (the commodities where the rest of the economy is the net beneficiary). The most straightforward methodology is to simply distribute the gains and losses equally. In summary, our coalition is formed by $(N - 1) + N(H - 1)$ members and, for every type $h$, every member of type $h$ gets

$$x'_h = x_h + \frac{1}{(N - 1) + N(H - 1)} (x_1 - \omega_1).$$

Note that

$$(N - 1)x'_1 + Nx'_2 + \cdots + Nx'_H = (N - 1)x_1 + Nx_2 + \cdots + Nx_H + (x_1 - \omega_1)$$
$$= N\omega_1 + \cdots + N\omega_H - x_1 + x_1 - \omega_1$$
$$= (N - 1)\omega_1 + N\omega_2 + \cdots + N\omega_I.$$

Hence, the proposed consumptions are feasible for the proposed coalition. Note also that the consumptions are nonnegative if $N$ is large enough. For every $h$, every consumer of type $h$ in the coalition moves from $x_h$ to $x'_h$. Is this an improvement or a loss? The answer is that if $N$ is large enough then it is an unambiguous gain. To see this, observe that $p \cdot (x_1 - \omega_1) > 0$ implies $\nabla u_h(x_h) \cdot (x_1 - \omega_1) > 0$ for every $h$ because $p$ and $\nabla u_h(x_h)$ are proportional. As we can then see in Figure 18.B.3 (or, analytically, from Taylor's formula; see Exercise 18.B.4) there is $\bar{\alpha} > 0$ with the property that, for every $h$, $u_h(x_h + \alpha(x_1 - \omega_1)) > u_h(x_h)$ whenever $0 < \alpha < \bar{\alpha}$. Hence, for any $N$ with $(1/[(N - 1) + N(H - 1)]) < \bar{\alpha}$ the coalition will actually be blocking.

Intuitively, we have done the following. The coalition needs to absorb $x_1 - \omega_1$. Evaluated at the marginal shadow prices of the economy, this is a favorable "project" for the coalition since $p \cdot (x_1 - \omega_1) > 0$. If the coalition is numerous then we can make sure that every member will have to absorb only a very small piece of the project. Hence the individual portions of the project will all be "at the margin"

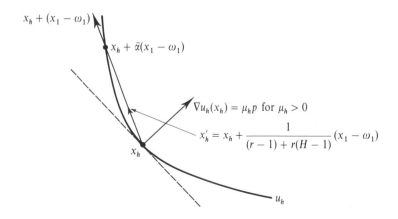

**Figure 18.B.3**

The consumption change of a consumer of type $h$ in the blocking coalition.

and, therefore, will also be individually favorable (recall Section 3.I for similar arguments).[6] ∎

---

We saw in Proposition 18.B.1 that the half of the core equivalence theorem that asserts that Walrasian allocations have the core property generalizes the first welfare theorem. In its essence, the half asserting that, provided the economy is large, core allocations are Walrasian constitutes a version of the second welfare theorem. To understand this it may be useful to go back to the general (nonreplica) setup and formulate the property of a core allocation being Walrasian in terms of the existence of a price support for a certain set. For simplicity, we restrict ourselves to the pure exchange case.

Given a core allocation $x = (x_1^*, \ldots, x_I^*) \in \mathbb{R}_+^{LI}$ then, in analogy with the construction used in the proof of the second welfare theorem (Proposition 16.D.1) we can define the setsy

$$V_i = \{x_i : x_i \succ_i x_i^*\} \cup \{\omega_i\} \subset \mathbb{R}^L$$

$$V = \sum_{i \in I} V_i \subset \mathbb{R}^L$$

We have $\sum_i \omega_i \in V$. But there is more: *the core property for $x^*$ implies that $\sum_i \omega_i$ belongs to the boundary of $V$.* To see this, note that if $\sum_i \omega_i$ is in the interior of $V$ then there is $z \in V$ such that $z \ll \sum_i \omega_i$; that is, there is $x' = (x_1', \ldots, x_I')$ with $x_i' \in V_i$ for every $i$ and $\sum_i x_i' = z \ll \sum_i \omega_i$. Hence, $x'$ is feasible, $x' \neq (\omega_1, \ldots, \omega_I)$, and, for every $i$, either $x_i' \succ_i x_i^*$ or $x_i' = \omega_i$. It follows that the set of consumers $S = \{i : x_i' \neq \omega_i\}$ is nonempty, that $x_i' \succ_i x_i^*$ for every $i \in S$, and that

$$\sum_{i \in S} x_i' \ll \sum_{i \in I} \omega_i - \sum_{i \notin S} x_i' = \sum_{i \in I} \omega_i - \sum_{i \notin S} \omega_i = \sum_{i \in S} \omega_i.$$

Thus $S$ is a blocking coalition.

The next claim is that if $p = (p_1, \ldots, p_L) \neq 0$ supports $V$ at $\sum_i \omega_i$, that is, $p \cdot z \geq p \cdot (\sum_i \omega_i)$ for all $z \in V$, then $p$ must be a Walrasian price vector for $x^* = (x_1^*, \ldots, x_I^*)$. To verify this, note first that, for every $i$, we have $x_i' \succ_i x_i^*$ for some $x_i'$ arbitrarily close to $x_i^*$. Therefore, $x_i' + \sum_{k \neq i} \omega_k \in V$ and so $p \cdot (x_i' + \sum_{k \neq i} \omega_k) \geq p \cdot (\omega_i + \sum_{k \neq i} \omega_k)$. Going to the limit (i.e., letting $x_i' \to x_i^*$), this yields $p \cdot x_i^* \geq p \cdot \omega_i$ for all $i$. Because $\sum_i x_i^* \leq \sum_i \omega_i$, we must therefore have $p \cdot x_i^* = p \cdot \omega_i$ for all $i$. In addition, whenever $x_i' \succ_i x_i^*$ we have $p \cdot (x_i' + \sum_{k \neq i} \omega_k) \geq p \cdot (\omega_i + \sum_{k \neq i} \omega_k)$ and so $p \cdot x_i' \geq p \cdot \omega_i$. If we exploit the continuity and strong monotonicity of preferences as we did in Section 16.D (or in Appendix B of Chapter 17), we can strengthen the last conclusion to $p \cdot x_i' > p \cdot \omega_i$.

The key difference from the case of the second welfare theorem (studied in Section 16.D) is that $V \subset \mathbb{R}^L$ *does not need to be convex* and that therefore a nonzero $p \in \mathbb{R}_+^L$ supporting $V$ at $\sum_i \omega_i$ may not exist. The reason for the lack of convexity is that the individual sets $V_i \subset \mathbb{R}^L$ need not be convex: $V_i$ is the union of the preferred set at $x_i^*$, which is convex, and the initial endowment vector $\omega_i$, which will typically be outside this preferred set and therefore disconnected from it. However, *if the (possibly nonconvex) sets $V_i \subset \mathbb{R}^L$ being added are numerous, then the sum $\sum_i V_i \subset \mathbb{R}^L$ is "almost" convex.* Thus, the existence of (almost) supporting prices for core allocations can be seen as yet another instance of the convexifying effects of aggregation.

We end by mentioning an elegant approach to core theory pioneered by Aumann (1964) and Vind (1964). It consists of looking at a model where there is an actual continuum of consumers and where we replace all the summations by integrals. The beauty of the approach is that all the approximate results then hold exactly. The core equivalence theorem, for example,

---

6. See Anderson (1978) for a different line of proof that makes minimal assumptions on the economy.

takes the form: An allocation belongs to the core if and only if it is a Walrasian equilibrium allocation.

---

# 18.C Noncooperative Foundations of Walrasian Equilibria

The idea of competition that underlies the theory of the core is very unstructured; there are no trading institutions and, in principle, any conceivable profitable opportunity can be taken advantage of. It is because of this, for example, that core allocations are guaranteed to be Pareto optimal.

In many economic applications, however, the structure of competition is given. Trade takes place through some type of market mechanism making explicit use of prices. The set of instruments and the information available to competitors are then limited. Yet, we also expect that price taking will emerge if individual competitors are small relative to the size of the market. We have already investigated this topic in Section 12.F. We reexamine it here because there are a few general equilibrium qualifications worth taking into account.

There are many models of price-mediated competition arising in applications. We will describe three of them, but before doing so, we present an abstract treatment emphasizing the main issues.

Suppose there are $I$ economic agents (abstract competitors, perhaps firms). There are also a set $P \subset \mathbb{R}^L$ of possible price vectors and a set $A$ of "market actions." Every $i$ has a set $A_i \subset A$ and an endowment vector $\omega_i \in \mathbb{R}^L$. For every $a_i \in A_i$ and $p \in P$, a *trading rule* defined on $A \times P$ and with values in $\mathbb{R}^L$, assigns a net trade vector $g(a_i; p)$ to agent $i$, satisfying $p \cdot g(a_i; p) = 0$. Given an array $a = (a_1, \ldots, a_I)$ of actions, there is then a market clearing process that generates a price vector $p(a) \in P$. We also assume that every $i$ has a utility function $u_i(g(a_i; p) + \omega_i)$, thus indirectly defined on $A_i \times P$.

The previous setup suggests treating the problem by the methodology of noncooperative games, as presented in Chapter 8.

**Definition 18.C.1:** The profile of actions $a^* = (a_1^*, \ldots, a_I^*) \in A_1 \times \cdots \times A_I$ is a *trading equilibrium* if, for every $i$,

$$u_i(g(a_i^*; p(a^*)) + \omega_i) \geq u_i(g(a_i; p(a_i, a_{-i}^*)) + \omega_i) \quad \text{for all } a_i \in A_i.[7]$$

The concept of noncooperative equilibrium incorporated in Definition 18.C.1 is the same as the one we used in Chapters 8 and 12. As there, and in contrast to the analysis of the core in Section 18.B, such equilibria need not be Pareto optimal. The question we now pose ourselves is: Under what conditions is it the case that, if individual traders are small relative to the size of the economy, the system of markets approximates a price-taking environment in which, effectively, every trader optimizes given a competitive budget set (and in which, therefore, the equilibria will be nearly Pareto optimal).

---

7. As it has become customary, we follow the notation $(a_i, a_{-i}^*) = (a_1^*, \ldots, a_{i-1}^*, a_i, a_{i+1}^*, \ldots, a_I^*)$.

Given $a = (a_1, \ldots, a_I) \in A_1 \times \cdots \times A_I$, define

$$B_i(a) = \{x_i \in \mathbb{R}_+^L : x_i - \omega_i \leq g(a_i'; p(a_i', a_{-i})) \text{ for some } a_i' \in A_i\}$$

as the *effective budget set* of trader $i$ at $a$. In words, $B_i(a)$ is the set of net trades that trader $i$ can achieve through *some* choice of $a_i$, given that the remaining traders are choosing $a_{-i}$. This set of achievable net trades will be close to the Walrasian budget

$$B(p(a), p(a) \cdot \omega_i) = \{x_i \in \mathbb{R}_+^L : p(a) \cdot x_i \leq p(a) \cdot \omega_i\}$$

if the following two types of conditions both hold:

(1) *Insensitivity of prices to own actions.* For the boundary of $B_i(a)$ to be (almost) contained in a hyperplane, we need the price-clearing function $p(a_i, a_{-i})$ to be very insensitive to $a_i$.[8] Often this will be guaranteed if the economy is large and, consequently, every competitor is of small relative size. Suppose, for example, that $p(a)$ has the form $p((1/r) \sum_i a_i)$ where $r$ is a size parameter (perhaps the number of consumers). It is actually quite common that the problem be given as, or can be transformed into, one in which actions affect price only through some average. At any rate, if this is the case, then the essential fact is clear: *As long as $p(\cdot)$ depends continuously on the average action* $(1/r) \sum_i a_i$ *the dependence of prices on individual actions* (assume the $A_i$ are bounded) *will become negligible as the economy becomes large;* that is, as $r \to \infty$. Continuity of $p(\cdot)$ is therefore a key property.

(2) *Individual spanning.* Even if $p(a)$ is practically independent of the actions of an individual, we could still have a failure of *individual spanning.* That is, the boundary of the set $B_i(a)$, while flat, may be "too short," as in Figure 18.C.1(a), or even lower-dimensional, as in Figure 18.C.1(b) where it reduces to the initial endowment vector (no trade at all is possible). Individual spanning will have to be checked in every case. Verifying it will typically involve showing, first, that $g(a_i, p)$ is sensitive enough to $a_i$ and, second, that $A_i$ is large enough.

We now briefly, and informally, discuss three examples illustrating these ideas.[9]

**Example 18.C.1:** *General Equilibrium, Single-Good Cournot Competition.* This is in essence the same model studied in Section 12.C, except that we now admit a completely general form of "inverse demand function," that is, of the correspondence that assigns market-clearing prices to aggregate production decisions. This is meant to reflect the possibility of wealth effects (a hallmark of the general equilibrium approach).

To be concrete, suppose that we have two goods: the first is a consumption good and the second is "money" (which is also the unit of account with price equal to 1). There are $r$ identical consumers, each endowed with a unit of money. For a price $p \in \mathbb{R}$ of the consumption good the demand of a consumer for this good is $x(p) \in \mathbb{R}$. There are also $J$ firms producing the consumption good out of money. Firms set quantities. Marginal cost, up to a unit of capacity, is zero. To minimize complexity,

---

8. Recall that $p(a_i', a_{-i}) \cdot g(a_i'; p(a_i', a_{-i})) = 0$ for all $a_i'$. Therefore, if $p(a_i', a_{-i})$ is (almost) independent of $a_i'$ then $B_i(a)$ is (almost) contained in the hyperplane perpendicular to $p(a)$.

9. For more on general equilibrium Cournotian models in the style of Examples 18.C.1 and 18.C.2, see Gabszewicz and Vial (1972) and Novshek and Sonnenschein (1978). For a survey of the general area, see Mas-Colell (1982).

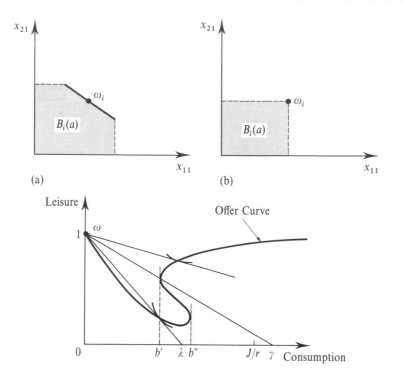

**Figure 18.C.1**

(a) and (b): Two nonspanning effective budget sets.

**Figure 18.C.2**

An economy with no continuous price selection.

assume that the owners of the firms are a separate group of agents interested only in the consumption of money. Therefore, for any total production $q = \sum_j q_j$ and size parameter $r$, the market price of the consumption good must solve the general equilibrium system $rx(p) = q$, or $x(p) = q/r$. We suppose that for any $q/r$ the market selects a solution $p(q/r)$ to this equation.[10]

In the quasilinear, partial equilibrium context of Chapter 12, $x(\cdot)$ is a decreasing continuous function and therefore its inverse $p(\cdot)$ exists and *is continuous* (and decreasing). It then follows that, when $r$ is large, $p(\sum_j q_j/r)$ is quite insensitive to the decision of any particular firm. Hence, firms are almost price takers and, as a consequence, the Cournot equilibria are almost Walrasian. Yet in the current general equilibrium context, $p(\cdot)$ may be unavoidably discontinuous. This is illustrated in Figure 18.C.2, where we represent the offer curve of a consumer. In the figure, there is no way to select money demands, and therefore prices, continuously over the offer curve as consumption per capita $q/r$ ranges from 0 to $J/r$.[11] The location of potential Cournot equilibria will depend on how the market selects $p(\cdot)$ in the domain $[b', b'']$ of consumptions per capita, but the possibility of Cournot equilibria bounded away from the Walrasian equilibrium irrespective of the size of the economy is quite real. A particular price selection $p(\cdot)$ has been chosen in Figure 18.C.3. Note, first, that at the Walrasian equilibria of this model we must have every firm producing at capacity (and so the Walrasian equilibrium price is $p^*$). Yet, provided $r > (J\lambda/\gamma b')$,

---

10. To view this example as a particular case of the abstract trading model described above, you should think of the $J$ firms as the players. Firm $j$ is "endowed" with a unit of the first good and its strategy variable is $q_j \in [0, 1] = A_j$. Finally, the trading rule is $g(q_j; p, 1) = (-q_j, pq_j)$.

11. The example is contrived in that "money" is a Giffen good. If consumers were not identical, this feature would not be required.

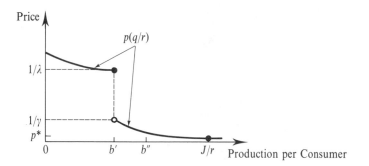

**Figure 18.C.3**

A price equilibrium selection.

every firm producing $rb'/J < 1$ (for a consumption per capita of $b'$) constitutes a Cournot equilibrium: because $p(\cdot)$ is very elastic in the domain $[0, b']$ it will not pay any firm to contract production; and if any firm expands production, no matter how slightly, a precipitous and unprofitable drop in prices ensues.[12] [See Roberts (1980) for more on this point.] ∎

**Example 18.C.2:** *Cournot Competition among Complements.* We modify the previous example in only two respects: (1) There are two consumption goods; (2) firms are producers of either the first or the second of these. The respective number of firms is $J_1$ and $J_2$. To be very simple we assume that the consumer has a quasilinear utility with money as numeraire. If the concave, strictly increasing utility function for the two consumption goods is $\psi(x_1, x_2)$ then, for any total productions $(q_1, q_2)$, market clearing prices are

$$p(q_1, q_2) = \nabla\psi(q_1/r, q_2/r) = \left( \frac{\partial\psi(q_1/r, q_2/r)}{\partial x_1}, \frac{\partial\psi(q_1/r, q_2/r)}{\partial x_2} \right) \gg 0.$$

The Walrasian equilibrium productions are $(J_1, J_2)$. Suppose, now, to take an extreme situation, that the two consumption goods are complements in the sense that the consumption of one is absolutely necessary for the enjoyment of the other, or $\psi(0, x_2) = \psi(x_1, 0) = 0$ for any $x_1$ and $x_2$. Then we claim that lack of activity (i.e., the null production of the two goods) is an equilibrium. The reason is clear enough: If $q_2 = 0$ then any positive supply $q_1 > 0$ of good one can only be absorbed by the market at $p_1 = \nabla_1\psi(q_1/r, 0) = 0$. Thus, no firm has an incentive to produce any amount of good 1 (and similarly for good 2). Economically, the difficulty is that the cooperation of at least two firms is needed to activate a market. Technically, we have a failure of continuity of clearing prices at $(0, 0)$ since $p(\varepsilon, 0) = 0$ for all $\varepsilon > 0$ but the limit of $p(\varepsilon, \varepsilon)$ as $\varepsilon$ goes to zero remains bounded away from zero.[13] ∎

**Example 18.C.3:** *Trading Posts.* This example belongs to a family proposed by Shapley and Shubik (1977). It is not particularly realistic but it has at least three

---

12. When every firm produces $rb'/J$, the profits of one firm are $rb'/J\lambda > 1/\gamma$. But $1/\gamma$ is an upper bound for the profits of any firm that deviates from the suggested production by producing more. Hence an output level of $rb'/J$ for every firm constitutes an equilibrium.

13. The complementarity makes it impossible for $\psi$ to be continuously differentiable at the origin. Therefore, $p(\cdot)$ fails to be continuous. This is the crucial aspect for the example. Note that discontinuity at the origin is a natural occurrence: it will arise, for example, whenever the indifference map of $\psi(\cdot)$ is homothetic (but not linear). See Hart (1980) for more on this issue.

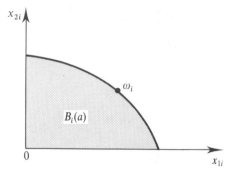

**Figure 18.C.4**

An effective budget set
for the trading post
Example 18.C.3.

virtues: it constitutes a complete general equilibrium model, all of the participants
interact strategically (in the two previous examples, consumers adjust passively), and
it is analytically simple to manipulate.

There are $L$ goods and $I$ consumers. Consumer $i$ has endowment $\omega_i \in \mathbb{R}_+^L$. The
$L$th commodity, to be called "money," is treated asymmetrically. For each of the
first $L - 1$ goods there is a *trading post* exchanging money for the good. At each
trading post $\ell \leq L - 1$, each consumer $i$ can place nonnegative bids $a_{\ell i} = (a'_{\ell i}, a''_{\ell i}) \in \mathbb{R}_+^2$.
The interpretation is that an amount $a'_{\ell i}$ of good $\ell$ is placed at the offer side of the
trading post to be exchanged for money. Similarly, an amount $a''_{\ell i}$ of money is placed
in the demand side to be exchanged for good $\ell$. Accordingly, the bids are also
constrained by $a'_{\ell i} \leq \omega_{\ell i}$ and $\sum_{\ell \leq L-1} a''_{\ell i} \leq \omega_{L i}$.

Given the bids of consumer $i$ in the trading posts $\ell \leq L - 1$ and prices
$(p_1, \dots, p_{L-1}, 1)$ the mechanism is completed by the trading rule:

$$g_\ell(a_{1i}, \dots, a_{L-1,i}; p_1, \dots, p_{L-1}, 1) = \frac{a''_{\ell i}}{p_\ell} - a'_{\ell i}$$

for all $\ell < L - 1$. The trade for the money good is derived from the budget constraint
of the consumer.

Given a vector $a = (a_{11}, \dots, a_{L-1,1}, \dots, a_{1I}, \dots, a_{L-1,I})$ of bids for all consumers,
the clearing prices in terms of money are determined as the ratio of the amount of
money offered to the amount of good offered:

$$p_\ell(a) = \frac{\sum_i a''_{\ell i}}{\sum_i a'_{\ell i}} \qquad \ell = 1, \dots, L - 1. \tag{18.C.1}$$

Note that $p_\ell(a)$ is well defined and continuous *except* when there are no offers at the
trading post $\ell$ [i.e., except when $a'_{\ell i} = 0$ for all $i$].[14]

A typical effective budget set for agent $i$ is convex and, provided that $\sum_{k \neq i} a'_{\ell k} \neq 0$
and $\sum_{k \neq i} a''_{\ell k} \neq 0$ for all $\ell \leq L - 1$, it has an upper boundary containing no straight
segments (you are asked to formally verify this in Exercise 18.C.1). This reflects the
fact that as a consumer increases her bid in one side of a market the terms of trade
turn against her. Figure 18.C.4 gives an illustration for the case $L = 2$.

---

14. For the special, but important, case in which there is a single trading post (i.e., $L = 2$),
we can go a bit farther. When $\sum_i a''_{\ell i} > 0$ and $\sum_i a'_{\ell i} = 0$, the relative price of money is still well
defined: it is zero. The essential difficulty in defining relative prices arises when $\sum_i a'_{\ell i} = 0$ and
$\sum_i a''_{\ell i} = 0$.

It follows from expression (18.C.1) that approximate price taking will prevail in any trading post that is *thick* in the sense that the aggregate positions taken on the two sides of the market are large relative to the size of the initial endowments of any consumer. A necessary condition for thickness is that there be many consumers. But this is not sufficient: it is possible even in a large economy to have equilibrium where some market is *thin* and, as a consequence, a trading equilibrium may be far from a Walrasian equilibrium. In fact, any trading equilibrium for a model where a trading post $\ell$ is closed (i.e., the trading post does not exist) will remain an equilibrium if the trading post is open but stays inactive. That is, if we put $a_{\ell i} = (a'_{\ell i}, a''_{\ell i}) = 0$ for all $i$. Economically, this is related to Example 18.C.2: it takes at least two agents (here a buyer and a seller) to activate a market. Mathematically, the difficulty is again the impossibility of assigning prices continuously when $a_{\ell i} = 0$ for all $i$.

Up to now, in this and previous examples, all of the instances of trading equilibria not approaching a Walrasian outcome when individual competitors are small have been related to failures of continuity of market equilibrium prices. But the current example also lends itself to illustration of the individual spanning problem. Indeed, even if markets are thick and therefore prices, from the individual point of view, are almost fixed, it remains true that the trading post structure imposes the restriction that *goods can only be exchanged for money on hand* (in macroeconomics this restriction is called the cash-in-advance, or the Clower, constraint). Money obtained by selling goods cannot be applied to buy goods. Therefore, for a given individual the Walrasian budget set will be (almost) attainable only if the initial endowments of money are sufficient, that is, only if at the solution of the individual optimization problem the constraint $\sum_{\ell \leq L-1} a''_{\ell i} \leq \omega_{Li}$ is not binding. But there is no general reason why this should be so. Suppose, to take an extreme case, that $\omega_{Li} = 0$. Then consumer $i$ simply cannot buy goods at all. ∎

# 18.D The Limits to Redistribution

In Section 16.D we saw that, under appropriate convexity conditions and provided that wealth can be transferred in a lump-sum manner, Pareto optimal allocations can be supported by means of prices. However, as we also pointed out there, a necessary condition for lump-sum payments to be possible is the ability of the policy authority to tell who is who—that is, to be able to precisely identify the characteristics (preferences and endowments) of every consumer in the economy. In this section, we shall explore the implications of assuming that this cannot be done to any extent; that is, we shall postulate that individual characteristics are private and become public only if revealed by economic agents through their choices. We will then see that under very general conditions the second welfare theorem fails dramatically: the only Pareto optimal allocations that can be supported involve no transfers, that is, they are precisely the Walrasian allocations. Thus, if no personal information of any sort is available to the policy authority, then there may be a real conflict between equity and efficiency: if transfers have to be implemented we must give up Pareto optimality. The nature of this trade-off is further explored in Sections 22.B and 22.C.

We place ourselves in an exchange economy with $I$ consumers. Each consumer $i$ has the consumption set $\mathbb{R}_+^L$, the endowment vector $\omega_i \geq 0$, and the continuous, monotone, and strictly quasiconcave utility function $u_i(\cdot)$.

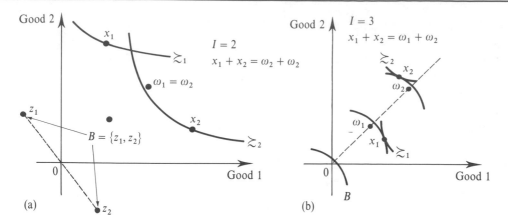

**Figure 18.D.1**

(a) and (b): Two self-selective allocations.

We begin by stating a restriction on feasible allocations designed to capture the possibility that the allocation is the result of a process in which every consumer maximizes utility subject to market opportunities that are identical across consumers.

**Definition 18.D.1:** The feasible allocation $x^* = (x_1^*, \dots, x_I^*) \in \mathbb{R}^{LI}$ if *self-selective* (or *anonymous*, or *envy-free in net trades*) if there is a set of net trades $B \subset \mathbb{R}^L$, to be called a *generalized budget set* or a *tax system*, such that, for every $i$, $z_i^* = x_i^* - \omega_i$ solves the problem

$$\text{Max} \quad u_i(z_i + \omega_i)$$
$$\text{s.t. } z_i \in B,$$
$$z_i + \omega_i \geq 0.$$

Figures 18.D.1(a) and 18.D.1(b) present two examples of self-selective allocations.[15] In the figures the preferences and endowments of the different consumers are depicted in the same orthant.

Note that if $x^* = (x_1^*, \dots, x_I^*)$ is self-selective then it is enough to take $B = \{x_1^*, \dots, x_I^*\}$. Thus, we could read Definition 18.D.1 as saying that no consumer $i$ envies the net trade of any other individual; among all the net trades present in the economy, the consumer is happy enough with the one assigned to her. Expositionally, we have preferred to keep separate the reality of $B$ because we have in mind the limit situation in which there is, on the one hand, a multitude of consumers whose actions are individually imperceptible and, on the other, a policy authority that has perfect statistical information (i.e., knows perfectly the *distribution* of individual characteristics), but no information at all on who is who. In such a world, a viable policy instrument is to choose a set $B$ and let each consumer select her most preferred point in it. Because this is what an income tax schedule amounts to, we also call $B$ a tax system. We remark that, as a policy tool, the notion of a generalized budget presumes the ability to prevent individuals from choosing several times. Hence it models the income tax, adequately, but not a commodity tax.

We now pose a question of the second welfare theorem type: Which Pareto optimal allocations can be supported by means of a common budget? That is, which feasible allocations are simultaneously Pareto optimal and self-selective? This

---

15. The concept of a nonenvy allocation was introduced by Foley (1967) and that of a nonenvy net-trade allocation by Schmeidler and Vind (1972). See Thomson and Varian (1985) for a survey of these notions (with an emphasis on the ethical aspects).

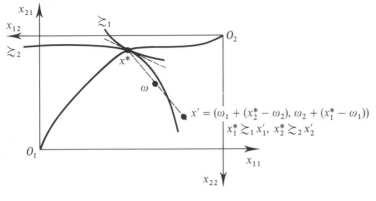

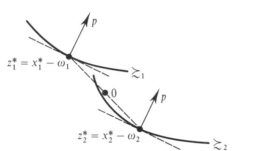

**Figure 18.D.2**

A Pareto optimal,
self-selective allocation
that is not Walrasian.

**Figure 18.D.3**

Another representation
of the example of
Figure 18.D.2.

question is both broader and more limited than the one associated with the second welfare theorem. It is broader because we allow supportability by general (nonlinear) budget sets and not only by linear hyperplanes. It is narrower because it demands that *all* consumers face the *same* budget for their net trades.

The first observation is that if $x^* = (x_1^*, \ldots, x_I^*)$ is a Walrasian allocation with equilibrium price vector $p \in \mathbb{R}^L$, then the allocation is Pareto optimal because of the first welfare theorem, and self-selective because we can take $B = \{z : p \cdot z = 0\}$.

The allocation marked $x^*$ in the Edgeworth box of Figure 18.D.2 provides an example of a self-selective allocation in the Pareto set that is not Walrasian. Figure 18.D.3 shows transparently why $x^*$ is self-selective. In this figure we bring the origin of the consumption sets of the two consumers to their initial endowment vector so that the preferences of the two consumers are expressed over net trades. Then with $z_i^* = x_i^* - \omega_i$, $i = 1, 2$, we see that $z_1^* \succsim_1 z_2^*$ and $z_2^* \succsim_2 z_1^*$.

The previous Edgeworth box example suggests that there may be ample room for anonymous redistribution. The example, however, is special in that there are only two consumers or, more generally, in that all the consumers fall into two preference–endowment types. We will now investigate the situation in which there is a multitude of consumers who *moreover* fall into a rich variety of types. Intuitively, this should make the compatibility of Pareto optimality and transfers more difficult because it is likely that the opportunities for envy will then be many (Pareto optimality will force the net trades to vary across consumers), and therefore the freedom in constructing the generalized budget will be limited.

In Figure 18.D.4 we represent an allocation for an economy with two commodities and a continuum of types (and therefore with a continuum of consumers).[16]

---

16. Approximate versions of the following results exist for economies with a finite but large number of types.

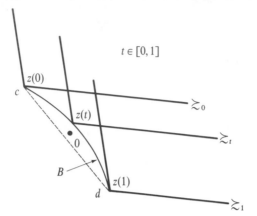

**Figure 18.D.4**

Pareto optimal allocation with a continuum of traders that is self-selective but not Walrasian.

Consumer types are indexed by $t \in [0, 1]$ *and their preferences $\succsim_t$ depend continuously on t.* For simplicity we take their endowments to be the same.[17] An implication of this continuity assumption is that the set of characteristics (preferences–endowment pairs) of the consumers present in the economy cannot be split into two disconnected classes. The consumptions of the different types are distributed along the curvilinear segment $cd$. This allocation has the following properties:

(i)   It is not Walrasian. If it were then all the consumptions would lie in a straight line; in fact, different types end up exchanging the two goods at different ratios.

(ii)  It is self-selective. We see in Figure 18.D.4 that the consumption chosen by each consumer maximizes her utility in the generalized budget set $B$. Note that the frontier of any admissible budget set has to include the segment $cd$ comprised by the consumptions actually chosen by some consumer.

(iii) It is Pareto optimal. Indeed, the price vector $p = (1, 1)$ will make the allocation into a price equilibrium with transfers, hence a Pareto optimum.

Observe that fact (iii) depends crucially on the indifference curves of every consumer exhibiting a kink at the assigned bundle. If we tried to smooth these kinks out then, because $cd$ is curved and the preferences change continuously, the result would be the existence of two consumers with different marginal rates of substitution at their chosen point, which is a violation of Pareto optimality (there would be room for profitable exchange among these two consumers). Only if $B$ were rectilinear could we retain Pareto optimality, but then the allocation would be a Walrasian equilibrium. Thus, it appears that if the indifference curves are smooth at the consumption points then a Pareto optimal, self-selective allocation can be something other than a Walrasian equilibrium only if the characteristics of the consumers present in the economy can be split into disconnected classes. With this motivation we can state Proposition 18.D.1.[18]

---

17.  What is important is that they change continuously with $t$.

18.  For results of this type, see, for example, Varian (1976) or Champsaur and Laroque (1981).

**Proposition 18.D.1:** Suppose we have an exchange economy with a continuum of consumer types. Assume:

(i) The preferences of all consumers are representable by differentiable utility functions.

(ii) The set of characteristics of consumers present in the economy[19] cannot be split into two disconnected classes. Formally, if $(u(\cdot), \omega)$, $(u'(\cdot), \omega')$ are two preference–endowment pairs present in the economy then there is a continuous function $(u(\cdot; t), \omega(t))$ of $t \in [0, 1]$ such that

$$(u(\cdot; 0), \omega(0)) = (u(\cdot), \omega), \quad (u(\cdot; 1), \omega(1)) = (u'(\cdot), \omega),$$

and $(u(\cdot; t), \omega(t))$ is present in the economy for every $t$.

Then any allocation $x^* = \{x_i^*\}_{i \in I}$ that is Pareto optimal, self-selective, and interior (i.e., $x_i^* \gg 0$ for all $i$) must be a Walrasian equilibrium allocation. Here $I$ is an infinite set of names.

---

**Proof:** The proof is far from rigorous. It is also limited to $L = 2$.

Let $p = (p_1, p_2)$ be the price vector supporting $x^*$ as a Pareto optimal allocation. Because of differentiability of the utility functions and interiority of the allocation, the relative prices $p_1/p_2$ are uniquely determined. We want to show that $p \cdot (x_i^* - \omega_i) = 0$ for all $i$.

The first observation is that at $x^*$ the equal-treatment property holds: if $(u_i(\cdot), \omega_i) = (u_k(\cdot), \omega_k)$ then $x_i^* = x_k^*$. Indeed, neither $i$ envies $k$ nor $k$ envies $i$. Hence $x_i^*$ and $x_k^*$ must lie in the same indifference curve of the common preference relation of $i$ and $k$. By the strict convexity of preferences, the price vector $p$ can support only one point in this indifference curve. Hence $x_i^*$ and $x_k^*$ must be equal.

If the set of net trades present in the economy consists of a single point, then this point has to be the vector 0 (otherwise the aggregate of the net trades could not be zero) and the result follows.

Suppose, therefore, that there are at least two different net-trade vectors present in the economy, $z_0$ and $z_1$. In Figure 18.D.5, we represent them as well as the net trades $z(t)$ of all consumers captured by the continuous parametrization given by assumption (ii), where $t = 0, 1$ correspond, respectively, to consumers underlying $z_0$ and $z_1$.

A key fact is that $z(t)$ is continuous as a function of $t$. This is intuitive. We have already seen that the equal-treatment property holds: Identical individuals are treated identically. Technicalities aside, the logic of the continuity of $z(t)$ is the same: If envy is to be prevented, then similar individuals must be treated similarly.

Thus as we go from $t = 0$ to $t = 1$, the net trades are moving continuously from $z_0$ to $z_1$. Hence the frontier of any generalized budget set $B$ must actually connect $z_0$ to $z_1$. If so, then either this frontier is a straight segment with normal $p$ between these two points [in which case $p \cdot (z_0 - z_1) = 0$], or somewhere between them there is one point ($z(t')$ in Figure 18.D.5) where the "slope" of the frontier of $B$, and therefore the $MRS$ of the consumer choosing this point, is different from $p_1/p_2$ [in which case $p$ would not be a supporting price vector].

We conclude that the portion $M$ of the frontier of $B$ containing all the net trades present in the economy is a nontrivial straight segment with normal $p$ (hence, a convex set). Since the net trades add up to zero, we must have $0 \in M$. Thus, $p \cdot z = p \cdot (z - 0) = 0$ for every $z \in M$. In particular, $p \cdot (x_i^* - \omega_i) = 0$ for every $i$. See Figure 18.D.6. ∎

---

19. The expression "characteristics of consumers present in the economy" means technically "contained in the support of the distribution of characteristics induced by the population of consumers."

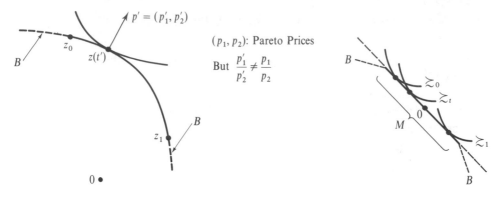

**Figure 18.D.5. (left)**

If the net trade frontier is not flat, then the allocation is not Pareto optimal (assuming self-selectivity).

**Figure 18.D.6 (right)**

A Pareto optimal, self-selective allocation that is Walrasian.

## 18.E  Equilibrium and the Marginal Productivity Principle

In this section, we investigate the extent to which Walrasian equilibria can be characterized by the idea that individuals get exactly what they contribute to the economic welfare of society (at the margin). We will see that, once again, the assumption of a large number of consumers is crucial to this characterization. For an extensive analytical treatment of this topic we refer to the seminal contribution of Ostroy (1980).

To remain as simple as possible, we restrict ourselves to the case of quasilinear exchange economies. The $L$th good is the numeraire.

Suppose that our economy has $H$ types. The concave, differentiable, strictly increasing utility function of type $h$ is

$$u_h(x_h) = \psi_h(x_{1h}, \ldots, x_{L-1,h}) + x_{Lh}.$$

It is defined on $\mathbb{R}_+^{L-1} \times \mathbb{R}$. We take $\psi_h$ to be strictly concave. The initial endowment vector of type $h$ is $\omega_h \geq 0$.

An economy is defined by a profile $(I_1, \ldots, I_H)$ of consumers of the different types, for a grand total of $I = \sum_h I_h$. For any economy $(I_1, \ldots, I_H)$ we define the maximal amount of "social utility" that can be generated, as in Section 10.D.[20]

$$v(I_1, \ldots, I_H) = \text{Max} \quad I_1 u_1(x_1) + \cdots + I_H u_H(x_H) \tag{18.E.1}$$

$$\text{s.t.} \quad \text{(i) } I_1 x_1 + \cdots + I_H x_H \leq I_1 \omega_1 + \cdots + I_H \omega_H,$$

$$\text{(ii) } x_{\ell h} \geq 0 \text{ for all } \ell \leq L - 1 \text{ and } h.$$

The function $v(I_1, \ldots, I_H)$ is homogeneous of degree one in its arguments: $v(rI_1, \ldots, rI_H) = rv(I_1, \ldots, I_H)$ for all $r$. In particular,

$$v(I_1/I, \ldots, I_H/I) = \frac{1}{I} v(I_1, \ldots, I_H).$$

That is, the per-capita social utility only depends on the type-composition and not on the size of the economy. Because of this we can extend the analysis to a situation with a continuum of consumers by defining $v(\mu_1, \ldots, \mu_H)$ for any nonnegative vector

---

20. Because utility functions are concave the maximum utility can be reached while treating consumers of the same type equally.

$\mu = (\mu_1, \ldots, \mu_H) \in \mathbb{R}_+^H$ of masses of the different types. Precisely,

$$v(\mu_1, \ldots, \mu_H) = \text{Max} \quad \mu_1 u_1(x_1) + \cdots + \mu_H u_H(x_H) \tag{18.E.2}$$

$$\text{s.t.} \quad \text{(i)} \quad \mu_1 x_1 + \cdots + \mu_H x_H \leq \mu_1 \omega_1 + \cdots + \mu_H \omega_H,$$

$$\text{(ii)} \quad x_{\ell h} \geq 0 \text{ for all } \ell \leq L - 1 \text{ and } h.$$

If we have a sequence of finite economies $(I_1^n, \ldots, I_H^n)$ such that $I^n = \sum_h I_h^n \to \infty$ and $(1/I^n)I_h^n \to \mu_h$ for every $h$, then we can properly regard $(\mu_1, \ldots, \mu_H)$ as the continuum limit of the sequence of increasingly large finite economies.

**Exercise 18.E.1:** Show that the function $v(\cdot): \mathbb{R}_+^H \to \mathbb{R}$ is concave and homogeneous of degree one.

The function $v(\cdot)$ is a sort of production function whose output is social utility and whose inputs are the individual consumers themselves. Further, in the limit, every individual of type $h$ becomes an input of infinitesimal size. For the time being, we concentrate our discussion on the continuum limit. We assume also that $v(\cdot)$ is differentiable.[21]

**Definition 18.E.1:** Given a continuum population $\mu = (\mu_1, \ldots, \mu_H) \in \mathbb{R}_+^H$ a feasible allocation[22] $(x_1^*, \ldots, x_H^*)$ is a *marginal product*, or *no-surplus*, *allocation* if

$$u_h(x_h^*) = \frac{\partial v(\mu)}{\partial \mu_h} \quad \text{for all } h. \tag{18.E.3}$$

In words: at a no-surplus allocation everyone is getting exactly what she contributes at the margin.

**Proposition 18.E.1:** For any *continuum* population $\bar{\mu} = (\bar{\mu}, \ldots, \bar{\mu}_H) \gg 0$ a feasible allocation $(x_1^*, \ldots, x_H^*) \gg 0$ is a marginal product allocation if and only if it is a Walrasian equilibrium allocation.

**Proof:** If $x^* = (x_1^*, \ldots, x_H^*)$ is a marginal product allocation then, using Euler's formula (see Section M.B of the Mathematical Appendix), we have

$$v(\bar{\mu}) = \sum_h \bar{\mu}_h \frac{\partial v(\bar{\mu})}{\partial \mu_h} = \sum_h \bar{\mu}_h u_h(x_h^*).$$

Hence, $x^*$ solves problem (18.E.2) for $\mu = \bar{\mu}$.

Suppose now that $x^* = (x_1^*, \ldots, x_H^*)$ is a feasible allocation that gives rise to social utility $v(\bar{\mu})$; that is, it constitutes a solution to problem (18.E.2) for $\mu = \bar{\mu}$. Denote by $p_\ell$, $\ell = 1, \ldots, L$, the values of the multipliers of the first-order conditions associated with the constraints $\sum_h \bar{\mu}_h(x_{\ell h} - \omega_{\ell h}) \leq 0, \ell = 1, \ldots, L$, in the optimization problem (18.E.2); see Section M.K of the Mathematical Appendix. By the quasilinear form of $u_h(\cdot)$ we have

$$p_L = 1 \quad \text{and} \quad p_\ell = \nabla_\ell \psi_h(x_{1h}^*, \ldots, x_{L-1,h}^*) \tag{18.E.4}$$

for all $\ell \leq L - 1$ and all $1 \leq h \leq H$.

---

21. This could be derived from more primitive assumptions.

22. We assume that consumers of the same type are treated equally. Feasibility means therefore that $\sum_h \mu_h x_h^* \leq \sum_h \mu_h \omega_h$.

It follows from (18.E.4) that the vector of multipliers $p = (p_1, \ldots, p_L)$ is the vector of Walrasian equilibrium prices of this quasilinear economy (recall the analysis of Section 10.D). In addition, by the envelope theorem (see Section M.L of the Mathematical Appendix), applied to problem (18.E.2), we have (Exercise 18.E.2):

$$\frac{\partial v(\bar{\mu})}{\partial \mu_h} = u_h(x_h^*) + p \cdot (\omega_h - x_h^*). \tag{18.E.5}$$

Therefore, we conclude that $x^*$ is Walrasian if and only if $x^*$ solves problem (18.E.2) for $\mu = \bar{\mu}$ and (18.E.3) is satisfied, that is, if and only if $x^*$ is a marginal product allocation. ∎

Expression (18.E.5) is intuitive. The left-hand side measures how much the maximum sum of utilities increases if we add one extra individual of type $h$. The right-hand side tells us that there are two effects. On the one hand, the extra consumer of type $h$ receives from the rest of the economy the consumption bundle $x_h^*$, and so she directly adds her utility $u_h(x_h^*)$ to the social utility sum. On the other, while receiving $x_h^*$, she contributes her endowment vector $\omega_h$. Hence the net change for the rest of the economy is $\omega_h - x_h^*$. How much is this worth to the rest of the economy? The vector of social shadow prices is precisely $p = (p_1, \ldots, p_L)$, and so the total change for the rest of the economy comes to $p \cdot (\omega_h - x_h^*)$. Note that the Walrasian allocations are thus characterized by this second effect being null: the utility of the consumer equals her entire marginal contribution to social utility.

In Exercise 18.E.4 you are asked to verify that the smoothness assumption on utility functions is essential to the validity of Proposition 18.E.1.

Let us now consider a finite economy $(I_1, \ldots, I_H) \gg 0$. We can define the marginal contribution of an individual of type $h$ as

$$\Delta_h v(I_1, \ldots, I_H) = v(I_1, \ldots, I_h, \ldots, I_H) - v(I_1, \ldots, I_h - 1, \ldots, I_H).$$

Typically, there does not exist a feasible allocation $(x_1^*, \ldots, x_H^*)$ with $u_h(x_h^*) = \Delta_h v(I_1, \ldots, I_H)$ for all $h$. To see this, note that by the concavity of $v(\cdot)$ we have $\Delta_h v \geq \partial v / \partial \mu_h$ [both expressions evaluated at $(I_1, \ldots, I_H)$]. Except for degenerate cases, this inequality will be strict. Moreover, $\sum_h I_h(\partial v / \partial \mu_h) = v(I_1, \ldots, I_H)$ by Euler's formula (see Section M.B of the Mathematical Appendix), and thus we conclude that $\sum_\ell I_h(\Delta_h v) > v(I_1, \ldots, I_H)$; that is, it is impossible to give to each consumer the full extent of her marginal contribution while maintaining feasibility. In contrast with the continuum case, individuals are not now of negligible size: their whole contribution is not entirely at the margin. In particular, you should note that in a finite economy the Walrasian allocation is typically *not* a marginal product allocation. It follows from expression (18.E.5) that an allocation $(x_1^*, \ldots, x_H^*)$ that solves problem (18.E.2) for $(\mu_1, \ldots, \mu_H) = (I_1, \ldots, I_H)$ is a Walrasian equilibrium allocation if and only if

$$u_h(x_h^*) = \frac{\partial v}{\partial \mu_h}(I_1, \ldots, I_H).$$

But we have just argued that normally $\Delta_h v(I_1, \ldots, I_H) > \partial v(I_1, \ldots, I_H)/\partial \mu_h$. In words: At the Walrasian equilibrium consumers are compensated according to prices determined by the marginal unit of their endowments. But they lose the extra social surplus provided by the inframarginal units. This is yet another indication that the concept of Walrasian equilibrium stands on firmer ground in large economies.

We have just seen that in the context of economies with finitely many consumers it is not possible to feasibly distribute the gains of trade while adhering literally to the marginal productivity principle. The cooperative theory of games provides a possibility for a sort of reconciliation between feasibility and the marginal productivity principle. It is known as the *Shapley value*. In Appendix A, devoted to cooperative game theory, we offer a detailed presentation of this solution concept.

For an economy with profile $(I_1, \ldots, I_H)$ the Shapley value is a certain utility vector $(Sh_1, \ldots, Sh_H) \in \mathbb{R}^H$ that satisfies $\sum_h I_h Sh_h = v(I_1, \ldots, I_H)$. For every type $h$, the utility $Sh_h$ can be viewed as an *average of marginal utilities* $\Delta_h v(I_1', \ldots, I_H')$. The average is taken over profiles $(I_1', \ldots, I_H') \leq (I_1, \ldots, I_H)$, where the probability weight given to $(I_1', \ldots, I_H')$ equals $1/I$, interpreted as the probability assigned to sample size $I_1' + \cdots + I_H'$, times the probability of getting the profile $(I_1', \ldots, I_H')$ when independently sampling $I_1' + \cdots + I_H'$ consumers out of the original population with $I$ consumers and profile $(I_1, \ldots, I_H)$. See Appendix A for more on this formula.

An allocation that yields the Shapley value (let us call it a *Shapley allocation*) is not related in any particular way to the Walrasian equilibrium allocation (or for that matter to the core). Except by chance, they will be different allocations. Yet, remarkably, we also have a convergence of these concepts in economies with many consumers: the Walrasian and the Shapley allocations are then close to each other. This result is known as the *value equivalence theorem*. A rigorous proof of this theorem is too advanced to be given here [see Aumann (1975) and his references], but the basic intuition is relatively straightforward.

There are two key facts. First, if the entries of $(I_1', \ldots, I_H')$ are large, then subtracting a consumer of type $h$ amounts to very little, and so

$$\Delta_h v(I_1', \ldots, I_H') \approx \partial v(I_1', \ldots, I_H')/\partial \mu_h.$$

Second, if the entries of $(I_1, \ldots, I_H)$ are large then, by the law of large numbers, most profiles $(I_1', \ldots, I_H')$ constitute a good sample of $(I_1, \ldots, I_H)$ and are therefore almost proportional to $(I_1, \ldots, I_H)$.

Using the homogeneity of degree one of $v(\cdot)$ (hence the homogeneity of degree zero of $\partial v/\partial \mu_h$), the combination of the previous two facts implies

$$\Delta_h v(I_1', \ldots, I_H') \approx \frac{\partial v(I_1', \ldots, I_H')}{\partial \mu_h} \approx \frac{\partial v(I_1, \ldots, I_H)}{\partial \mu_h}$$

for most $(I_1', \ldots, I_H')$. Therefore, $Sh_h \approx \partial v(I_1, \ldots, I_H)/\partial \mu_h$, which is the utility payoff of type $h$ at the Walrasian equilibrium allocation of the economy $(I_1, \ldots, I_H)$.

## APPENDIX A: COOPERATIVE GAME THEORY

In this appendix, we offer a brief introduction to the *cooperative theory of games*. For more extensive recent accounts see Moulin (1988), Myerson (1991), or Osborne and Rubinstein (1994).[23]

In Chapter 7, we presented the normal and the extensive forms of a game. The starting point for the cooperative theory is a classical third description: that of a

---

23. The text by Owen (1982), although not so recent, is nevertheless strong in its coverage of cooperative theory. Another useful reference is Shubik (1984), which is encyclopedic in spirit and contains a wealth of information.

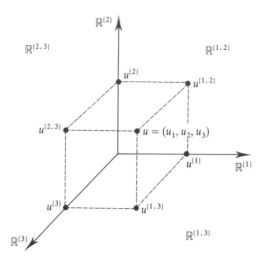

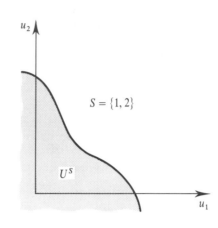

**Figure 18.AA.1 (left)**

Utility outcome $u \in \mathbb{R}^3$ and its projections.

**Figure 18.AA.2 (right)**

A utility possibility set for $S = \{1, 2\}$.

*game in characteristic form.* The characteristic form is meant to be a summary of the payoffs available to each group of players in a context where binding commitments among the players of the group are feasible. Although, in principle, it should be possible to derive the characteristic form from the normal or the extensive forms, the viewpoint of cooperative game theory is that it is often analytically desirable to avoid detail and to go as directly as possible to a summary description of the strategic position of the different groups of players.[24]

After defining the characteristic form, we will discuss two of the main solution concepts of cooperative game theory: the *core* and the *Shapley value.*

The set of players is denoted $I = \{1, \ldots, I\}$. We abuse notation slightly by using the same symbol to denote the set and its cardinality. Nonempty subsets $S, T \subset I$ are called *coalitions.*

An *outcome* is a list of utilities $u = (u_1, \ldots, u_I) \in \mathbb{R}^I$. Given $u = (u_1, \ldots, u_I)$, the relevant coordinates to a coalition $S$ are $u^S = (u_i)_{i \in S}$. Mathematically, $u^S$ is the restriction (or projection) of $u \in \mathbb{R}^I$ to the coordinates corresponding to $S$. We can therefore view $u^S$ as a member of the Euclidean space $\mathbb{R}^S$ spanned by these coordinates. Figure 18.AA.1 shows how outcomes for three players are evaluated by all six proper subsets: $S = \{1\}, \{2\}, \{3\}, \{1, 2\}, \{1, 3\},$ and $\{2, 3\}$.

**Definition 18.AA.1:** A nonempty, closed set $U^S \subset \mathbb{R}^S$ is a *utility possibility set for* $S \subset I$ if it is *comprehensive*:

$$u^S \in U^S \qquad \text{and} \qquad u'^S \le u^S \text{ implies } u'^S \in U^S.$$

See Figure 18.AA.2 for an illustration.[25]

---

24. Nevertheless, we note that there is a school of thought within game theory of the opinion that the condensation of information that a characteristic form represents may not do justice to the strategic complexities inherent in the making of binding commitments. Despite the cogency of this position, the analytical power of games in characteristic forms for the study of normative issues in economics has been amply demonstrated. This is more than enough reason to welcome the parsimony it brings to the analysis.

25. Note that, as we did in Section 16.E, we build free disposability of utility into the definition of a utility possibility set.

**Definition 18.AA.2:** A *game in characteristic form* $(I, V)$ is a set of players $I$ and a rule $V(\cdot)$ that associates to every coalition $S \subset I$ a utility possibility set $V(S) \subset \mathbb{R}^S$.

The elements of $V(S)$ are to be interpreted as the payoffs the players in $S$ can achieve by themselves if they jointly commit to a certain course of action. It is important to observe the expression "can achieve" is not free of subtlety. This is because the course of action undertaken by the members of $I \backslash S$ will typically affect the payoffs of the members of $S$. In applications, therefore, one should be explicit as to how $V(S)$ is constructed.

**Example 18.AA.1:** *Economies*. Consider an economy with $I$ consumers having continuous, increasing, concave utility functions $u_i \colon \mathbb{R}_+^L \to \mathbb{R}$ and endowments $\omega_i \geq 0$. There is also a publicly available convex, constant returns technology $Y \subset \mathbb{R}^L$. We can then define a game in characteristic form by letting

$$V(S) = \left\{ (u_i(x_i))_{i \in S} \colon \sum_{i \in S} x_i = \sum_{i \in S} \omega_i + y, \, y \in Y \right\} - \mathbb{R}_+^S.$$

That is, $V(S)$ is the set of payoffs that the consumers in coalition $S$ can achieve by trading among themselves and using the technology $Y$. Every set $V(S)$ is convex (recall Exercise 16.E.2). Figure 18.AA.3 depicts these sets for the case $I = 3$. ∎

**Example 18.AA.2:** *Majority Voting*. Consider a three-player situation in which any two out of the three players can form a majority and select among a set of social alternatives $A$. If $a \in A$ is selected, the payoffs are $u_i(a) \geq 0$, $i = 1, 2, 3$. In addition, any player $i$ has the right to unilaterally withdraw from the group and get a payoff of zero.

Then we can define a game in characteristic form $(I, V)$ as

$$V(I) = \{ (u_1(a), u_2(a), u_3(a)) \colon a \in A \} - \mathbb{R}_+^I.$$
$$V(\{i, h\}) = \{ (u_i(a), u_h(a)) \colon a \in A \} - \mathbb{R}_+^{\{i, h\}} \quad \text{for all distinct pairs } \{i, h\}.$$
$$V(\{i\}) = -\mathbb{R}_+^{\{i\}}.$$

Figure 18.AA.4 shows this characteristic form for a case with three alternatives, $A = \{a_1, a_2, a_3\}$. In the figure we suppose that the three decisions yield, respectively,

**Figure 18.AA.3 (left)**
A family of utility possibility sets.

**Figure 18.AA.4 (right)**
The utility possibility sets for the majority voting in Example 18.AA.2.

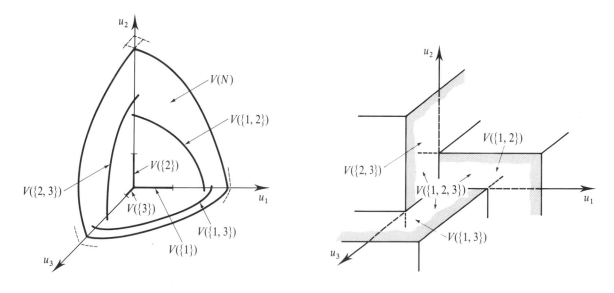

the utility vectors $(2, 1, 0)$, $(1, 0, 2)$, $(0, 2, 1)$. Note that $V(\cdot)$ need not be convex when, as here, decisions are discrete and there are no possibilities for either randomization or any form of side transfers. ∎

**Definition 18.AA.3:** A game in characteristic form $(I, V)$ is *superadditive* if for any coalitions $S$, $T \subset I$ that are disjoint (i.e., such that that $S \cap T = \varnothing$), we have

If $u^S \in V(S)$ and $u^T \in V(T)$, then $(u^S, u^T) \in V(S \cup T)$.

Superadditivity means that coalitions $S$ and $T$ are able to do at least as well acting together as they could do acting separately. It is an assumption we will commonly make (it is satisfied by Examples 18.AA.1 and 18.AA.2). If one of the possibilities open to the union of two disjoint coalitions is to agree to act *as if* they were still separated coalitions, then superadditivity should hold.

It has been a constant theme of this book that often the analysis becomes much simpler when individual utility functions are quasilinear, that is, when there is a commodity ("numeraire") that can be used to effect unit-per-unit transfers of utility across economic agents. The same is true in the theory of cooperative games. Its history is, in fact, replete with instances of concepts first formulated for the transferable utility case that have later been extended to the general setting without an essential loss of intuition and analytical power.

For a situation described by a game in characteristic form, what the quasilinearity, or transferable utility, hypothesis amounts to is the assumption that the sets $V(S)$ are half-spaces (as they were, for example, in Section 10.D); that is, they are sets whose boundaries are hyperplanes in $\mathbb{R}^S$. Moreover, by choosing the units of utility, we can take the hyperplanes defining $V(S)$ to have normals $(1, \ldots, 1) \in \mathbb{R}^S$.[26] Thus, the sets $V(S)$ will now have the form

$$V(S) = \left\{ u^S \in \mathbb{R}^S : \sum_{i \in S} u_i^S \le v(S) \right\}$$

for some $v(S) \in \mathbb{R}$. In other words, we can view coalition $S$ as choosing a joint action so as to maximize the total utility, denoted $v(S)$, which then can be allocated to the members of $S$ in any desired manner through transfers of the numeraire. Figure 18.AA.5 depicts the sets $V(S)$ for the case $I = 3$.

The number $v(S)$ is called the *worth* of coalition $S$. Since the numbers $v(S)$, $S \subset I$, constitute a complete description of $(I, V)$ we provide Definition 18.AA.4.

**Definition 18.AA.4:** A *transferable utility game in characteristic form*, (or *TU-game*), is defined by $(I, v)$, where $I$ is a set of players and $v(\cdot)$ is a function, called the *characteristic function*, that assigns to every nonempty coalition $S \subset I$ a number $v(S)$ called the *worth of S*.

**Example 18.AA.3:** *TU Majority Voting.* Suppose that in Example 18.AA.2 (with the values of Figure 18.AA.4) we add the possibility that utility be freely transferable across players (there may be a numeraire commodity with respect to which

---

26. This choice of units of utility is legitimate because all the solutions to be considered are invariant to normalizations of units. See Chapter 21 for more on this point.

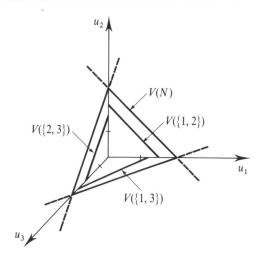

**Figure 18.AA.5**

Utility possibility sets for a transferable utility game.

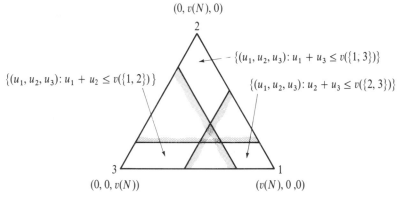

**Figure 18.AA.6**

Using a simplex to represent a three-player TU-game with utilities normalized so that $V(\{i\}) = 0$.

preferences are quasilinear). Then the characteristic function is

$$v(I) = 3, \qquad v(\{1, 2\}) = v(\{1, 3\}) = v(\{2, 3\}) = 3 \qquad \text{and} \qquad v(\{i\}) = 0, \ i = 1, 2, 3. \quad \blacksquare$$

All the developments in this appendix will be invariant to changes in the origins of individual utilities; thus we can fix these arbitrarily. The usual convention is to put $v(\{i\}) = 0$ for every $i$.

In Figure 18.AA.6 we represent a diagrammatic device for the case of three-player games that is particularly useful. Instead of working in three dimensions, we look at the two-dimensional simplex that exhibits all possible divisions of $v(I)$ subject to the condition that $u_i \geq 0$ for all $i$ [which means, in the normalization just discussed, that $u_i \geq v(\{i\})$]. The other sets in the diagram represent, for every two-person coalition $\{i, h\}$, the utility combinations in the simplex satisfying $u_i + u_h \leq v(\{i, h\})$.

We now turn to a presentation of two well-known solution concepts for cooperative games: the *core* and the *Shapley value*.

### The Core

The first solution concept we review is the *core*: the set of feasible utility outcomes with the property that no coalition could on its own improve the payoffs of all its members. An empty core is indicative of competitive instability in the situation being modeled. If the core is nonempty and small, then we could say that coalitional

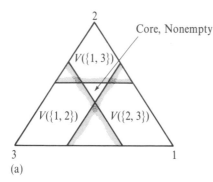
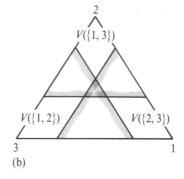

**Figure 18.AA.7**
(a) A TU-game with a nonempty core.
(b) A TU game with an empty core.

competition by itself brings about a sharply determined outcome. If it is nonempty and large, then coalitional competition alone does not narrow down the possible outcomes very much.

**Definition 18.AA.5:** Given a game in characteristic form $(I, V)$, the utility outcome $u \in \mathbb{R}^I$ is *blocked*, or *improved upon*, by a coalition $S \subset I$ if there exists $u'^S \in V(S)$ such that $u_i^S < u_i'^S$ for all $i \in S$.

If the game is a TU game $(I, v)$ then the outcome $u = (u_1, \ldots, u_I)$ is blocked by $S$ if and only if $\sum_{i \in S} u_i < v(S)$.

**Definition 18.AA.6:** A utility outcome $u = (u_1, \ldots, u_I)$ that is feasible for the grand coalition [i.e., $u \in V(I)$] is in the *core* of the characteristic form game $(I, V)$ if there is no coalition $S$ that blocks $u$.

In TU games the core is the set of utility vectors $u = (u_1, \ldots, u_I)$ satisfying the linear inequalities

$$\sum_{i \in S} u_i \geq v(S) \text{ for all } S \subset I \quad \text{and} \quad \sum_{i \in I} u_i \leq v(I).$$

Figure 18.AA.7(a) depicts a three-player game with nonempty core. In contrast, in Figure 18.AA.7(b) the core is empty. See Exercise 18.AA.1 for a set of necessary and sufficient conditions in the TU case for the nonemptiness of the core.

**Exercise 18.AA.2:** Show that any TU game with a nonempty core must satisfy: For any two coalitions $S, T \subset I$ such that $S \cap T = \emptyset$ and $S \cup T = I$, we have $v(S) + v(T) \leq v(I)$.

**Example 18.AA.4:** *Majority Voting, Once Again.* For the majority voting games described in Examples 18.AA.2 and 18.AA.3, the core is empty. In the latter, which is a TU game, this is clear enough: if $u_1 + u_2 + u_3 = 3$ then $u_i + u_h < 3$ for some $i, h$. Hence the coalition $\{i, h\}$ will block. For the former (nontransferable utility) game, note that the outcomes $(2, 1, 0)$, $(1, 0, 2)$, $(0, 2, 1)$ are blocked, respectively, by the coalitions $\{2, 3\}$ using $a_3$, $\{1, 2\}$ using $a_1$, and $\{1, 3\}$ using $a_2$. These examples constitute instances of the so called *Condorcet paradox* (which we have already encountered in Section 1.B and will see again in Section 21.C). They are illustrative of an inherent instability of majority voting. ∎

**Example 18.AA.5:** *Economies, Again.* The economic example in Example 18.AA.1 was extensively studied in Section 18.B. Note that the concept of the core discussed there is identical with the concept considered here for games in characteristic form.[27] We conclude, therefore that if a Walrasian equilibrium exists then the core is nonempty. ∎

**Example 18.AA.6:** *Single-Input, Increasing Returns Production Function.* Consider a one-input, one-output world in which there is a publicly available technology $f(z)$ which is continuous and satisfies $f(0) = 0$. There are $I$ players. Each player $i$ cares only about the consumption of the output good and owns an amount $\omega_i$ of input. Assuming that utility is transferable, we can define a TU characteristic function by $v(S) = f(\sum_{i \in S} \omega_i)$. The core of this game will be nonempty whenever the technology exhibits nondecreasing returns to scale, that is, whenever average product $f(z)/z$ is *nondecreasing*. [In particular, if $f(\cdot)$ is convex, that is, if we have a nondecreasing marginal product, then $f(z)/z$ is nondecreasing.] To verify this, suppose that we distribute the product proportionally:

$$u_h = \frac{\omega_h}{\sum_{i \in I} \omega_i} f\left(\sum_{i \in I} \omega_i\right)$$

for every $h \in I$. Then, for any $S \subset I$ we have

$$\sum_{h \in S} u_h = \frac{\sum_{h \in S} \omega_h}{\sum_{i \in I} \omega_i} f\left(\sum_{i \in I} \omega_i\right) \geq f\left(\sum_{h \in S} \omega_h\right) = v(S),$$

where the inequality follows because average product is nondecreasing. We conclude that this proportional distribution of output belongs to the core. In Exercise 18.AA.3 you are asked to show that if average product is constant then the proportional allocation is the only allocation in the core. It is also intuitively clear that the more pronounced is the degree of increasing returns, the more difficult it will be for proper subgroups to do better by their own means (they will have relatively low average product) and therefore the more we could depart from the proportional allocation while remaining in the core. Hence, for this sort of one-dimensional distribution problem, the larger the degree of increasing returns, the larger the core will be.[28] ∎

*The Shapley Value*

The core tries to capture how the possible outcomes of a game may be shaped by coalitional competitive forces. It is the simplest solution concept in what could be called the *descriptive* side of cooperative game theory. We shall now investigate a solution concept, the *value*, whose motivation is normative. It attempts to describe

---

27. The connection of the solution concept proposed by Edgeworth (1881) with the modern game-theoretic notion of the core was made in Shubik (1959).

28. On the other hand, if $f(\cdot)$ exhibits strictly decreasing returns then it follows from Exercise 18.AA.2 that the core is empty [indeed, $v(S) + v(T) > v(I)$ for any partition of $I$ into two coalitions $S, T$].

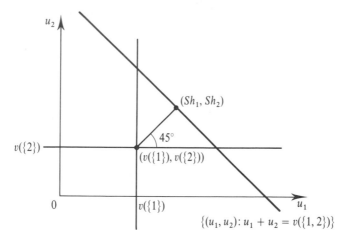

**Figure 18.AA.8**
Egalitarian division for two-player games.

a reasonable, or "fair," way to divide the gains from cooperation, *taking as a given the strategic realities captured by the characteristic form.*[29]

We study only the TU case, for which the theory is particularly simple and well established. The central concept is then a certain solution called the *Shapley value*.[30]

Suppose that individual utilities are measured in dollars and that, so to speak, society has decided that dollars of utility of different participants are of comparable social worth. The criterion of fairness to which value theory adheres is *egalitarianism*: the aim is to distribute the gains from trade equally.

To see what the egalitarian principle could mean in the current TU context let us begin with a two-player game $(I, v) = (\{1, 2\}, v)$. Then the gains (or losses, if super-additivity fails) from cooperation are

$$v(I) - v(\{1\}) - v(\{2\}).$$

Therefore, the obvious egalitarian solution, which we denote $(Sh_1(I, v), Sh_2(I, v))$, is (see Figure 18.AA.8)

$$Sh_i(I, v) = v(\{i\}) + \tfrac{1}{2}(v(I) - v(\{1\}) - v(\{2\})), \qquad i = 1, 2. \qquad (18.AA.1)$$

How should we define the egalitarian solution $(Sh_1(I, v), \ldots, Sh_I(I, v))$ for an arbitrary TU-game $(I, v)$? We have already solved the problem for two-player games. It is suggestive to *rewrite* expression (18.AA.1) as

$$Sh_1(I, v) - Sh_1(\{1\}, v) = Sh_2(I, v) - Sh_2(\{2\}, v),$$

$$Sh_1(I, v) + Sh_2(I, v) = v(I),$$

where we put $Sh_i(\{i\}, v) = v(\{i\})$. In words, this says that utility differences are preserved: *What player 1 gets out of the presence of player 2 is the same as player 2 gets out of the presence of player 1.* This points to a recursive definition: Given $S \subset I$, denote by $(S, v)$ the TU-game obtained by restricting $v(\cdot)$ to the subsets of $S$ [this is called a *subgame* of $(I, v)$]. Then we could say that a family of numbers $\{Sh_i(S, v)\}_{S \subset I, i \in S}$ constitutes an *egalitarian solution* if, for every subgame $(S, v)$ and

---

29. Thus, the redistributional fairness considerations that we will discuss in Sections 22.B and 22.C, based on notions of absolute justice, are alien to the value.

30. It is named after L. Shapley, who proposed it in his Ph.D. dissertation at Princeton (in 1953).

players $i, h \in S$, utility differences are preserved in a manner similar to the two-player case:

$$Sh_i(S, v) - Sh_i(S \setminus \{h\}, v) = Sh_h(S, v) - Sh_h(S \setminus \{i\}, v)$$

$$\text{for all } S \subset I, i, h \in S, \tag{18.AA.2}$$

$$\sum_{i \in S} Sh_i(S, v) = v(S) \qquad \text{for all } S \subset I,$$

Expressions (18.AA.2) determine the numbers $Sh_i(S, v)$, $i \in S$, uniquely. This is clear for $Sh_i(\{i\}, v)$. From here we can then proceed inductively. Suppose that we have defined $Sh_i(S, v)$ for all $S \subset I$, $S \neq I$, $i \in S$. We show that there is one and only one way to define $Sh_i(I, v)$, $i \in I$. To this effect, note that (18.AA.2) allows us to express every $Sh_i(I, v)$ as a function of $Sh_1(I, v)$ and of already determined numbers:

$$Sh_i(I, v) = Sh_1(I, v) + Sh_i(I \setminus \{1\}, v) - Sh_1(I \setminus \{i\}, v) \qquad \text{for all } i \neq 1.$$

Then to determine $Sh_1(I, v)$ use $\sum_{i \in I} Sh_i(I, v) = v(I)$. Specifically,

$$Sh_1(I, v) = \frac{1}{I} \left[ v(I) - \sum_{i \neq 1} Sh_i(I \setminus \{1\}, v) + \sum_{i \neq 1} Sh_1(I \setminus \{i\}, v) \right].$$

**Definition 18.AA.7:** The *Shapley value* of a game $(I, v)$, denoted

$$Sh(I, v) = (Sh_1(I, v), \ldots, Sh_I(I, v)),$$

is the single outcome consistent with expression (18.AA.2).

We can compute $Sh_i(I, v)$ in a direct and interesting manner as follows. For any $S \subset I$ and $i \notin S$ let $m(S, i) = v(S \cup \{i\}) - v(S)$ be the *marginal contribution* of $i$ to coalition $S$.[31] For any ordering $\pi$ of the players in $I$ (technically, $\pi$ is a one-to-one function from $I$ to $I$) denote by $S(\pi, i) \subset I$ the set of players that come before $i$ in the ordering $\pi$ [technically, $S(\pi, i) = \{h : \pi(h) < \pi(i)\}$]. Note that, for any given ordering $\pi$, if we consider the marginal contributions of every player $i$ to the set of the predecessors of $i$ in the ordering $\pi$, then the sum of these marginal contributions must exactly exhaust $v(I)$; that is, $\sum_{i \in I} m(S(\pi, i), i) = v(I)$. It then turns out that $Sh_i(I, v)$ is the *average marginal contribution* of $i$ to the set of her predecessors, where the average is taken over all orderings (held to be equally likely). Since the total number of orderings is $I!$ this gives

$$Sh_i(I, v) = \frac{1}{I!} \sum_{\pi} m(S(\pi, i), i). \tag{18.AA.3}$$

where the sum is taken over all orderings $\pi$ of the players in $I$.

**Example 18.AA.7:** *Glove Market.* Consider the three-player game defined by

$$v(\{1, 2, 3\}) = 1,$$
$$v(\{1, 3\}) = v(\{2, 3\}) = 1, \qquad v(\{1, 2\}) = 0,$$
$$v(\{1\}) = v(\{2\}) = v(\{3\}) = 0.$$

If the utility of a matched pair of gloves is 1, while an unmatched pair is worth nothing, then this game could arise from a situation in which players 1 and 2 own

---

31. Whenever we compute marginal contributions we follow the convention $v(\emptyset) = 0$. Therefore, $m(S, i) = v(\{i\})$ whenever $S = \emptyset$.

one right-hand glove each, while player 3 owns a left-hand glove. Let us compute $Sh_3(I, v)$. There are six possible orderings of the players:

$$\{1, 2, 3\}, \{1, 3, 2\}, \{2, 1, 3\}, \{2, 3, 1\}, \{3, 1, 2\}, \text{ and } \{3, 2, 1\}.$$

The marginal contribution of player 3 to its predecessors in each of these orderings is, respectively: 1, 1, 1, 1, 0, and 0. The average of these numbers is $\frac{2}{3}$; hence $Sh_3(I, v) = \frac{2}{3}$. Similarly, we get $Sh_1(I, v) = Sh_2(I, v) = \frac{1}{6}$. Note that these numbers satisfy (18.AA.2). For example,

$$Sh_3(I, v) - Sh_3(I \setminus \{1\}, v) = \tfrac{2}{3} - \tfrac{1}{2} = \tfrac{1}{6} - 0 = Sh_1(I, v) - Sh_1(I \setminus \{3\}, v). \qquad \blacksquare$$

We can give a more explicit formula than (18.AA.3) for $Sh_i(I, v)$. The probability that in a random ordering a given coalition $T \subset I, i \in T$, arises as the union of $i$ and its predecessors equals the probability that $i$ is in the $T$th place,[32] which is simply $1/I$, multiplied by the probability that $T \setminus \{i\}$ arises when we randomly select $\#T - 1$ members from the population $I \setminus \{i\}$, which is $(I - \#T)!(\#T - 1)!/(I - 1)!$. Hence, we can rewrite (18.AA.3) as

$$Sh_i(I, v) = \sum_{T \subset I, i \in T} [(I - \#T)!(\#T - 1)!/I!](v(T) - v(T \setminus \{i\})). \qquad (18.AA.4)$$

In Exercise 18.AA.4 you are asked to verify that if we were to define the Shapley value by (18.AA.4), or (18.AA.3), then equations (18.AA.2) would be satisfied; this means that, indeed, (18.AA.3) or (18.AA.4) provide correct formulas for the Shapley value.

We now put on record, rather informally, some of the basic properties of the Shapley value.

(a) *Efficiency.* $\sum_i Sh_i(I, v) = v(I)$; that is, no utility is wasted.

(b) *Symmetry.* If the games $(I, v)$ and $(I, v')$ are identical, except that the roles of players $i$ and $h$ are permuted,[33] then $Sh_i(I, v) = Sh_h(I, v')$. In words: The Shapley values do not depend on how we label players; only their position in the game, as summarized by the characteristic function, matters.

(c) *Linearity.* Note from (18.AA.3) or (18.AA.4) that the Shapley values depend linearly on the data, that is, on the coefficients $v(S)$ defining the game.

(d) *Dummy axiom.* Suppose that a player $i$ contributes nothing to the game; that is, $v(S \cup \{i\}) - v(S) = 0$ for *all* $S \subset I$. Then $Sh_i(I, v) = 0$. This important property follows directly from (18.AA.3): The marginal contribution of player $i$ to *any* coalition is null; hence its average is also null.

These four properties fully characterize the Shapley value. Although the proof of this fact is not difficult, we shall not give it here. See Exercises 18.AA.5 and 18.AA.6 for the discussion of some examples.

Given a game, the Shapley value assigns to it a single outcome. In contrast, the core solution assigns a set. We point out that the Shapley value need not belong to the

---

32. The symbol $\#T$ denotes the number of players in a coalition $T$.

33. Precisely, $v(S) = v'(S)$ whenever $i \in S$ and $h \in S$, $v(S) = v'(S)$ whenever $i \notin S$ and $h \notin S$, $v(S) = v'((S \setminus \{i\}) \cup \{h\})$ whenever $i \in S$ and $h \notin S$, and $v(S) = v'((S \setminus \{h\}) \cup \{i\})$ whenever $h \in S$ and $i \notin S$.

core. In a sense, we already know this because the Shapley value is defined for all games and there are games for which the core is empty. But the phenomenon can also occur if the core is nonempty. To see this, let us reexamine the glove market of Example 18.AA.7.

**Example 18.AA.7 continued:** In the glove market example a core utility outcome is $(0, 0, 1)$. Moreover, this is the *only* outcome in the core. Indeed, if $(u_1, u_2, u_3)$ with $\sum_i u_i = 1$ has, say, $u_1 > 0$, then the coalition $\{2, 3\}$ can block by means of $(0, u_2 + \frac{1}{2}u_1, u_3 + \frac{1}{2}u_1)$. In effect, at the core the two owners of right-hand gloves undercut each other until they charge a price of zero. In contrast, the Shapley value, while heavily skewed towards player 3, nonetheless leaves something to the other two players ($\frac{1}{6}$ to each of them). ∎

There is an important class of games for which the Shapley value belongs to the core. They are games characterized by the presence of a type of pronounced increasing returns to scale.

**Definition 18.AA.8:** A game $(I, v)$ is *convex* if for every $i$ the marginal contribution of $i$ is larger to larger coalitions. Precisely, if $S \subset T$ and $i \in I \setminus T$, then

$$v(S \cup \{i\}) - v(S) \le v(T \cup \{i\}) - v(T).$$

**Example 18.AA.8:** *Complementary Inputs.* Let $f(z_1, \ldots, z_N)$ be a production function displaying increasing marginal productivities with respect to all inputs; that is, $\partial^2 f(z)/\partial z_h \, \partial z_k \ge 0$ for all $z$ and $h, k$. Suppose that every player $i \in I$ is endowed with a vector of inputs $\omega_i \in \mathbb{R}_+^n$. Then we can define a TU-game by $v(S) = f(\sum_{i \in S} \omega_i)$. In Exercise 18.AA.8 you are asked to show that this game is convex. A warning on terminology: if $N = 1$ the previous condition simply says that $f(\cdot)$ is convex and, thus, the convexity of $f(\cdot)$ suffices for the convexity of the game; but for $N > 1$ the condition $\partial^2 f(z)/\partial z_h \, \partial z_k \ge 0$ for all $z$ and $h, k$, is neither necessary nor sufficient for the convexity of $f(\cdot)$. In fact, the convexity of $f(\cdot)$ is far from sufficient for the convexity of the game (see Exercise 18.AA.8). ∎

We can then show the result in Proposition 18.AA.1.

**Proposition 18.AA.1:** If a game $(I, v)$ is convex then its Shapley value utility outcome $Sh(I, v) = (Sh_1(I, v), \ldots, Sh_I(I, v))$ belongs to the core (in particular, the core is nonempty).

---

**Proof:** It is enough to show that if $i \in S \subset T$ then $Sh_i(S, v) \le Sh_i(T, v)$. Indeed, for any $S \subset I$ this implies that $v(S) = \sum_{i \in S} Sh_i(S, v) \le \sum_{i \in S} Sh_i(I, v)$ and therefore the coalition $S$ cannot block.

To prove the claimed property it suffices to consider $i \in S$ and $T = S \cup \{h\}$. Given an ordering $\pi$ of $S$ denote by $m(\pi, i)$ the marginal contribution of $i$ to its predecessors in $S$ and according to the ordering $\pi$ by $m'(\pi, i)$ the average marginal contribution of $i$ to its predecessors in $T$ when the average is taken over the $\# T$ orderings of $T$ differing from the given ordering $\pi$ of $S$ only by the placement of $h$. Then

$$Sh_i(S, v) = \frac{1}{\# S!} \sum_\pi m(\pi, i) \qquad \text{and} \qquad Sh_i(T, v) = \frac{1}{\# S!} \sum_\pi m'(\pi, i).$$

Note that for every ordering $\pi$ of $S$ we must have $m'(\pi, i) \ge m(\pi, i)$: If we place $h$ after $i$ then the marginal contribution of $i$ to its predecessors in $T$ is still $m(\pi, i)$; if we place $h$ before $i$ then, by the convexity condition, this marginal contribution is at least $m(\pi, i)$. We conclude that $Sh_i(T, v) \geq Sh_i(S, v)$, as we wanted to show. ∎

## REFERENCES

Anderson, R. (1978). An elementary core equivalence theorem. *Econometrica* **46**: 83–87.

Aumann, R. (1964). Markets with a continuum of traders. *Econometrica* **32**: 39–50.

Aumann, R. (1975). Values of markets with a continuum of traders. *Econometrica* **43**: 611–46.

Champsaur, P., and G. Laroque. (1981). Fair allocations in large economies. *Journal of Economic Theory* **25**: 269–82.

Debreu, G., and H. Scarf. (1963). A limit theorem on the core of an economy. *International Economic Review* **4**: 235–46.

Edgeworth, F. Y. (1881). *Mathematical Psychics*. London: Kegan Paul.

Foley, D. (1967). Resource allocation and the public sector. *Yale Economic Essays* **7**: 45–98.

Gabszewicz, J. J., and J. P. Vial. (1972). Oligopoly 'à la Cournot' in a general equilibrium analysis. *Journal of Economic Theory* **4**: 381–400.

Hart, O. (1980). Perfect competition and optimal product differentiation. *Journal of Economic Theory* **22**: 165–99.

Hildenbrand, W., and A. Kirman. (1988). *Equilibrium Analysis*. New York: North-Holland.

Mas-Colell, A. (1982). The Cournotian foundations of Walrasian equilibrium: an exposition of recent theory. Chap. 7 in *Advances in Economic Theory*, edited by W. Hildenbrand. New York: Cambridge University Press.

Moulin, H. (1988). *Axioms of Cooperative Game Theory*. New York: Cambridge University Press.

Myerson, R. (1991). *Game Theory: Analysis of Conflict*. Cambridge, Mass.: Harvard University Press.

Novshek, W., and H. Sonnenschein. (1978). Cournot and Walras equilibrium. *Journal of Economic Theory* **19**: 223–66.

Roberts, K. (1980). The limit points of monopolistic competition. *Journal of Economic Theory* **22**: 256–278.

Osborne, M. and A. Rubinstein. (1994). *A Course in Game Theory*. Cambridge, Mass.: MIT Press.

Ostroy, J. (1980). The no-surplus condition as a characterization of perfectly competitive equilibrium. *Journal of Economic Theory* **22**: 65–91.

Owen, G. (1982). *Game Theory*, 2nd ed. New York: Academic Press.

Schmeidler, D., and K. Vind. (1972). Fair net trades. *Econometrica* **40**: 637–47.

Shapley, L., and M. Shubik. (1977). Trade using a commodity as a means of payment. *Journal of Political Economy* **85**: 937–68.

Shubik, M. (1959). Edgeworth's market games. In *Contributions to the Theory of Games, IV*, edited by R. D. Luce, and A. W. Tucker. Princeton, N.J.: Princeton University Press.

Shubik, M. (1984). *Game Theory in the Social Sciences*. Cambridge, Mass.: MIT Press.

Thomson, W., and H. Varian. (1985). Theories of justice based on symmetry. Chap. 4 in *Social Goals and Social Organizations*, edited by L. Hurwicz, D. Schmeidler, and H. Sonnenschein. New York: Oxford University Press.

Varian, H. (1976). Two problems in the theory of fairness. *Journal of Public Economics* **5**: 249–60.

Vind, K. (1964). Edgeworth allocations in an exchange economy with many traders. *International Economic Review* **5**: 165–77.

## EXERCISES

**18.B.1**[A] Show that Walrasian allocations are in the core for the model with a constant returns technology described in Section 18.B.

**18.B.2**[B] Exhibit an example of a nonequal-treatment core allocation in a three-consumer exchange economy with continuous, strictly convex, strongly monotone preferences. Can an example be given with only two consumers?

**18.B.3**[A] Give a direct proof (i.e., not using properties of the core) that a Walrasian allocation of an economy with continuous, strictly convex preferences has the equal-treatment property.

**18.B.4**[A] Use Taylor's formula to complete the proof of Proposition 18.B.3.

**18.B.5**[B] Consider an economy composed of $2I + 1$ consumers. Of these, $I$ each own one right shoe and $I + 1$ each own a left shoe. Shoes are indivisible. Everyone has the same utility function, which is Min $\{R, L\}$, where $R$ and $L$ are, respectively, the quantities of right and left shoes consumed.

**(a)** Show that any allocation of shoes that is matched (i.e., every individual consumes the same number of shoes of each kind) is a Pareto optimum, and conversely.

**(b)** Which Pareto optima are in the core of this economy? (This time, in the definition of the core allow for weak dominance in blocking.)

**(c)** Let $p_R$ and $p_L$ be the respective prices of the two kinds of shoes. Find the Walrasian equilibria of this economy.

**(d)** Comment on the relationship between the core and the Walrasian equilibria in this economy.

**18.C.1**[C] Establish the properties of effective budget sets claimed in the discussion of Example 18.C.3. You can restrict yourself to the case $L = 2$.

**18.D.1**[B] Consider an Edgeworth box with continuous, strictly convex and monotone preferences. Show that every feasible allocation where both consumers are at least as well off as at their initial endowments is self-selective.

**18.E.1**[B] In text.

**18.E.2**[A] Use the envelope theorem (see Section M.L of the Mathematical Appendix) to derive expression (18.E.5).

**18.E.3**[B] By considering an example with $L$-shaped preferences for two non-numeraire goods (hence, the utility function cannot be differentiable), argue that it is possible that at a Walrasian allocation with a continuum of traders every trader gets less than her marginal contribution.

**18.AA.1**[B] A collection of coalitions $S_1, \ldots, S_N \subset I$ is a *generalized partition* if we can assign a weight $\delta_n \in [0, 1]$ to every $1 \le n \le N$ such that, for every player $i \in I$, we have $\sum_{\{n:\, i \in S_n\}} \delta_n = 1$. Exhibit examples of generalized partitions, with the corresponding weights.

We say that a TU-game $(I, v)$ is *balanced* if for every generalized partition we have $\sum_n \delta_n v(S_n) \le v(I)$, where $\delta_n$ are the corresponding partition weights. Show that the game has a nonempty core if and only if it is balanced. [*Hint*: Appeal to the duality theorem of linear programming (see Section M.M of the Mathematical Appendix).]

**18.AA.2**[A] In text.

**18.AA.3**[A] Show that the proportional allocation of Example 18.AA.6 is the only allocation in the core if average product is constant.

**18.AA.4**[C] Show that if the Shapley value is defined by formula (18.AA.4)—or, equivalently, by (18.AA.3)—then the preservation of differences expression (18.AA.2) is satisfied.

**18.AA.5$^B$** We say that a game $(I, v)$ is a *unanimity* game if there is a nonempty $S \subset I$ such that $v(T) = v(S)$ if $S \subset T$ and $v(T) = 0$ otherwise. Show then that under the efficiency, symmetry, and dummy axioms we are led to distribute $v(S)$ equally across the members of $S$.

**18.AA.6$^B$** Show that any TU-game $(I, v)$ can be expressed as a linear combination of unanimity games. Then use the Exercise 18.AA.5 and the linearity axiom to show that there is a unique solution satisfying the efficiency, symmetry, dummy, and linearity axioms. Connect your discussion with the Shapley value.

**18.AA.7$^C$** Show that the production game described in Example 18.AA.8 is convex.

**18.AA.8$^B$** In the context of the production example of Example 18.AA.8, give an example of a two-input production function that is convex (as a function) but for which, nonetheless, the core is empty (thus, the induced game cannot be convex).

**18.AA.9$^B$** Consider the game with four players defined by $v(\{i\}) = 0$, $v(\{12\}) = v(\{34\}) = 0$, $v(\{13\}) = v(\{14\}) = v(\{23\}) = v(\{24\}) = 1$, $v(\{ijk\}) = 1$ for all three-player coalitions $\{ijk\}$, and $v(\{1234\}) = 2$.

(a) Show that this is the game that you would get from the utility production technology Min $\{z_1, z_2\}$, where $z_1$ and $z_2$ are the amounts of two factors, if the factor endowments of the four consumers are $\omega_1 = \omega_2 = (1, 0)$ and $\omega_3 = \omega_4 = (0, 1)$.

(b) Show that the core of this game contains all points of the form $(\alpha, \alpha, 1 - \alpha, 1 - \alpha)$ for $\alpha \in [0, 1]$.

(c) Show that if $v(\{134\})$ is increased to 2, holding all other coalition values constant, there is then only one point in the core. Compare the welfare of player 1 at this point to what she would get at all the points in the core before the increase in $v(\{134\})$.

(d) Compute the Shapley value of the game [before the modification in (c)] without using the brute-force enumeration technique. [*Hint:* Use symmetry considerations and other axiomatically based simplifications to go part of the way to the answer.]

(e) How does the Shapley value change under the modification of part (c)?. Discuss the difference between the changes in the Shapley value and in the core.

**18.AA.10$^B$** Consider a firm constituted by two divisions. The firm must provide overhead in the form of space, $(x_1, x_2)$, to each of them. The cost of *aggregate* amounts of space is given by $C(x_1 + x_2) = (x_1 + x_2)^\gamma$, $0 < \gamma < 1$.

(a) Suppose that, whatever the usage of space $(x_1, x_2)$, the total cost must be *exactly* allocated between the two divisions. Propose a cost allocation system based on the Shapley value to accomplish this.

(b) Compute the marginal cost imposed on each of the two divisions [according to the cost allocation system identified in (a)] whenever a division increases its usage of space.

(c) Suppose now that the profits accruing to the two divisions are $\alpha_1 x_1$ and $\alpha_2 x_2$, respectively (we assume that $\alpha_1 > 0$ and $\alpha_2 > 0$), and that each division uses space to the point where marginal profits equal own marginal costs [as determined in (b)]. Will this lead to an efficient (that is, profit-maximizing) choice of overhead?

(d) Is there any distribution rule $\psi_1(x_1, x_2)$, $\psi_2(x_1, x_2)$, with $\psi_1(x_1, x_2) + \psi_2(x_1, x_2) = C(x_1 + x_2)$ for all $(x_1, x_2)$, that leads to efficient decentralized choice [in the sense of (c)] for all $\alpha_1, \alpha_2$? [*Hint:* Consider the externality imposed by each division on the other.]

# General Equilibrium Under Uncertainty

## 19.A Introduction

In this chapter, we apply the general equilibrium framework developed in Chapters 15 to 18 to economic situations involving the exchange and allocation of resources under conditions of uncertainty. In a sense, this chapter offers the equilibrium counterpart of the decision theory presented in Chapter 6 (and which we recommend you review at this point).

We begin, in Section 19.B, by formalizing uncertainty by means of *states of the world* and then introducing the key idea of a *contingent commodity*: a commodity whose delivery is conditional on the realized state of the world. In Section 19.C we use these tools to define the concept of an *Arrow–Debreu equilibrium*. This is simply a Walrasian equilibrium in which contingent commodities are traded. It follows from the general theory of Chapter 16 that an Arrow–Debreu equilibrium results in a Pareto optimal allocation of risk.

In Section 19.D, we provide an important reinterpretation of the concept of Arrow–Debreu equilibrium. We show that, under the assumptions of *self-fulfilling*, or *rational, expectations*, Arrow–Debreu equilibria can be implemented by combining trade in a certain restricted set of contingent commodities with *spot trade* that occurs *after* the resolution of uncertainty. This results in a significant reduction in the number of ex ante (i.e., before uncertainty) markets that must operate.

In Section 19.E, we generalize our analysis. Instead of trading contingent commodities prior to the resolution of uncertainty, agents now trade *assets*; and instead of an Arrow–Debreu equilibrium we have the notion of a *Radner equilibrium*. We also discuss here the important notion of *arbitrage* among assets. The material of this section lies at the foundations of a very rich body of finance theory [good introductions are Duffie (1992) and Huang and Litzenberger (1988)].

In Section 19.F, we briefly illustrate some of the welfare difficulties raised by the possibility of *incomplete markets*, that is, by the possibility of there being too few asset markets to guarantee a fully Pareto optimal allocation of risk.

Section 19.G is devoted to the issue of the objectives of the firm under conditions of uncertainty. In particular, it gives sufficient conditions for shareholders to agree unanimously on the objective of *market value maximization*.

Section 19.H takes a close look at the informational requirements of the theory developed in this chapter. We see that the theory applies well to situations of *symmetric* information across consumers (reviewed in Section 19.H); but its applicability is more problematic in situations of *asymmetric* information. This provides a further argument for the techniques developed in Chapters 13 and 14 for the study of asymmetric information problems.

For additional material and references on the topic of this chapter, see the textbooks of Huang and Litzenberger (1988) and Duffie (1992) already mentioned, or, at a more advanced level, Radner (1982) and Magill and Shafer (1991).

# 19.B  A Market Economy with Contingent Commodities: Description

As in our previous chapters, we contemplate an environment with $L$ physical commodities, $I$ consumers, and $J$ firms. The new element is that technologies, endowments, and preferences are now *uncertain*.

Throughout this chapter, we represent uncertainty by assuming that technologies, endowments, and preferences depend on the *state of the world*. The concept of state of the world was already introduced in Section 6.E. A state of the world is to be understood as a complete description of a possible outcome of uncertainty, the description being sufficiently fine for any two distinct states of the world to be mutually exclusive. We assume that an exhaustive set $S$ of states of the world is given to us. For simplicity we take $S$ to be a finite set with (abusing notation slightly) $S$ elements. A typical element is denoted $s = 1, \ldots, S$.

We state in Definition 19.B.1 the key concepts of a (*state-*)*contingent commodity* and a (*state-*)*contingent commodity vector*. Using these concepts we shall then be able to express the dependence of technologies, endowments, and preferences on the realized states of the world.

**Definition 19.B.1:** For every physical commodity $\ell = 1, \ldots, L$ and state $s = 1, \ldots, S$, a unit of (*state-*)*contingent commodity* $\ell s$ is a title to receive a unit of the physical good $\ell$ if and only if $s$ occurs. Accordingly, a (*state-*)*contingent commodity vector* is specified by

$$x = (x_{11}, \ldots, x_{L1}, \ldots, x_{1S}, \ldots, x_{LS}) \in \mathbb{R}^{LS},$$

and is understood as an entitlement to receive the commodity vector $(x_{1s}, \ldots, x_{Ls})$ if state $s$ occurs.[1]

We can also view a contingent commodity vector as a collection of $L$ *random variables*, the $\ell$th random variable being $(x_{\ell 1}, \ldots, x_{\ell S})$.

With the help of the concept of contingent commodity vectors, we can now describe how the characteristics of economic agents depend on the state of the world. To begin, we let the endowments of consumer $i = 1, \ldots, I$ be a contingent commodity vector:

$$\omega_i = (\omega_{11i}, \ldots, \omega_{L1i}, \ldots, \omega_{1Si}, \ldots, \omega_{LSi}) \in \mathbb{R}^{LS}.$$

---

1. As usual, a negative entry is understood as an obligation to deliver.

The meaning of this is that if state $s$ occurs then consumer $i$ has endowment vector $(\omega_{1si}, \ldots, \omega_{Lsi}) \in \mathbb{R}^L$.

The preferences of consumer $i$ may also depend on the state of the world (e.g., the consumer's enjoyment of wine may well depend on the state of his health). We represent this dependence formally by defining the consumer's preferences over contingent commodity vectors. That is, we let the preferences of consumer $i$ be specified by a rational preference relation $\succsim_i$ defined on a consumption set $X_i \subset \mathbb{R}^{LS}$.

**Example 19.B.1:** As in Section 6.E, the consumer evaluates contingent commodity vectors by first assigning to state $s$ a probability $\pi_{si}$ (which could have an objective or a subjective character), then evaluating the physical commodity vectors at state $s$ according to a Bernoulli state-dependent utility function $u_{si}(x_{1si}, \ldots, x_{Lsi})$, and finally computing the expected utility.[2] That is, the preferences of consumer $i$ over two contingent commodity vectors $x_i, x_i' \in X_i \subset \mathbb{R}^{LS}$ satisfy

$$x_i \succsim_i x_i' \quad \text{if and only if} \quad \sum_s \pi_{si} u_{si}(x_{1si}, \ldots, x_{Lsi}) \geq \sum_s \pi_{si} u_{si}(x_{1si}', \ldots, x_{Lsi}').$$

■

It should be emphasized that the preferences $\succsim_i$ are in the nature of ex ante preferences: the random variables describing possible consumptions are evaluated before the resolution of uncertainty.

Similarly, the technological possibilities of firm $j$ are represented by a production set $Y_j \subset \mathbb{R}^{LS}$. The interpretation is that a (*state-*)*contingent production plan* $y_j \in \mathbb{R}^{LS}$ is a member of $Y_j$ if for every $s$ the input–output vector $(y_{1sj}, \ldots, y_{Lsj})$ of physical commodities is feasible for firm $j$ when state $s$ occurs.

**Example 19.B.2:** Suppose there are two states, $s_1$ and $s_2$, representing good and bad weather. There are two physical commodities: seeds ($\ell = 1$) and crops ($\ell = 2$). In this case, the elements of $Y_j$ are four-dimensional vectors. Assume that seeds must be planted before the resolution of the uncertainty about the weather and that a unit of seeds produces a unit of crops if and only if the weather is good. Then

$$y_j = (y_{11j}, y_{21j}, y_{12j}, y_{22j}) = (-1, 1, -1, 0)$$

is a feasible plan. Note that since the weather is unknown when the seeds are planted, the plan $(-1, 1, 0, 0)$ is not feasible: the seeds, if planted, are planted in both states. Thus, in this manner we can imbed into the structure of $Y_j$ constraints on production related to the timing of the resolution of uncertainty.[3] ■

To complete the description of an economy in a manner parallel to Chapters 16 and 17 it only remains to specify ownership shares for every consumer $i$ and firm $j$. In principle, these shares could also be state-contingent. It will be simpler, however, to let $\theta_{ji} \geq 0$ be the share of firm $j$ owned by consumer $i$ whatever the state. Of course $\sum_j \theta_{ji} = 1$ for every $i$.

---

2. The discussion in Section 6.E was for $L = 1$. It extends straightforwardly to the current case of $L \geq 1$.

3. A similar point could be made on the consumption side. If, for a particular commodity $\ell$, any vector $x_i \in X_i$ is such that all entries $x_{\ell si}$, $s = 1, \ldots, S$, are equal, then we can interpret this as asserting that the consumption of $\ell$ takes place before the resolution of uncertainty.

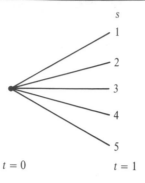

**Figure 19.B.1**

Two periods. Perfect information at $t = 1$.

*Information and the Resolution of Uncertainty*

In the setting just described, time plays no explicit formal role. In reality, however, states of the world unfold over time. Figure 19.B.1 captures the simplest example. In the figure, we have a period 0 in which there is no information whatsoever on the true state of the world and a period 1 in which this information has been completely revealed.

We have already seen (Example 19.B.2) how, by conveniently defining consumption and production sets, we can accomodate within our setup the temporal structure of Figure 19.B.1: a commodity that has as part of its physical description its availability at $t = 0$ should never appear in differing amounts across states.

The same methodology can be used to incorporate into the formalism a much more general temporal structure. Suppose we have $T + 1$ dates $t = 0, 1, \dots, T$ and, as before, $S$ states, but assume that the states emerge gradually through a *tree*, as in Figure 19.B.2. These trees are

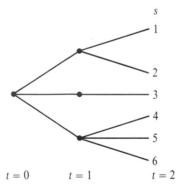

**Figure 19.B.2**

An information tree: gradual release of information.

similar to those described in Chapter 7. Here final nodes stand for the possible states realized by time $t = T$, that is, for complete histories of the uncertain environment. When the path through the tree coincides for two states, $s$ and $s'$, up to time $t$, this means that in all periods up to and including period $t$, $s$ and $s'$ cannot be distinguished.

Subsets of $S$ are called *events*. A collection of events $\mathscr{S}$ is an *information structure* if it is a partition, that is, if for every state $s$ there is $E \in \mathscr{S}$ with $s \in E$ and for any two $E, E' \in \mathscr{S}$, $E \neq E'$, we have $E \cap E' = \varnothing$. The interpretation is that if $s$ and $s'$ belong to the same event in $\mathscr{S}$ then $s$ and $s'$ cannot be distinguished in the information structure $\mathscr{S}$.

To capture formally a situation with sequential revelation of information we look at a *family* of information structures: $(\mathscr{S}_0, \dots, \mathscr{S}_t, \dots, \mathscr{S}_T)$. The process of information revelation makes the $\mathscr{S}_t$ increasingly fine: once one has information sufficient to distinguish between two states, the information is not forgotten.

**Example 19.B.3:** Consider the tree in Figure 19.B.2. We have

$$\mathscr{S}_0 = (\{1, 2, 3, 4, 5, 6\}),$$
$$\mathscr{S}_1 = (\{1, 2\}, \{3\}, \{4, 5, 6\}),$$
$$\mathscr{S}_2 = (\{1\}, \{2\}, \{3\}, \{4\}, \{5\}, \{6\}). \quad \blacksquare$$

The partitions could in principle be different across individuals. However, except in the last section of this chapter (Section 19.H), we shall assume that the information structure is the same for all consumers.

A pair $(t, E)$ where $t$ is a date and $E \in \mathscr{S}_t$ is called a *date-event*. Date-events are associated with the nodes of the tree. Each date-event except the first has a *unique predecessor*, and each date-event not at the end of the tree has one or more *successors*.

With this temporal modeling it is now necessary to be explicit about the time at which a physical commodity is available. Suppose there is a number $H$ of basic physical commodities (bread, leisure, etc.). We will use the double index $ht$ to indicate the time at which a commodity $h$ is produced, appears as endowment, or is available for consumption. Then $x_{hts}$ stands for an amount of the physical commodity $h$ available at time $t$ along the path of state $s$.

Fortunately, this multiperiod model can be formally reduced to the timeless structure introduced above. To see this, we define a new set of $L = H(T + 1)$ physical commodities, each of them being one of these double-indexed (i.e., $ht$) commodities. We then say that a vector $z \in \mathbb{R}^{LS}$ is *measurable* with respect to the family of information partitions $(\mathscr{S}_0, \ldots, \mathscr{S}_T)$ if, for every $hts$ and $hts'$, we have that $z_{hts} = z_{hts'}$ whenever $s, s'$ belong to the same element of the partition $\mathscr{S}_t$. That is, whenever $s$ and $s'$ cannot be distinguished at time $t$, the amounts assigned to the two states cannot be different. Finally, we impose on endowments $\omega_i \in \mathbb{R}^{LS}$, consumption sets $X_i \subset \mathbb{R}^{LS}$ and production sets $Y_j \subset \mathbb{R}^{LS}$ the restriction that all their elements be measurable with respect to the family of information partitions. With this, we have reduced the multiperiod structure to our original formulation.

# 19.C Arrow–Debreu Equilibrium

We have seen in Section 19.B how an economy where uncertainty matters can be described by means of a set of states of the world $S$, a consumption set $X_i \subset \mathbb{R}^{LS}$, an endowment vector $\omega_i \in \mathbb{R}^{LS}$, and a preference relation $\succsim_i$ on $X_i$ for every consumer $i$, together with a production set $Y_j \subset \mathbb{R}^{LS}$ and profit shares $(\theta_{j1}, \ldots, \theta_{jI})$ for every firm $j$.

We now go a step further and make a strong assumption. Namely, we postulate the existence of a market for every contingent commodity $\ell s$. These markets open *before* the resolution of uncertainty, at date 0 we could say. The price of the commodity is denoted $p_{\ell s}$. What is being purchased (or sold) in the market for the contingent commodity $\ell s$ is commitments to receive (or to deliver) amounts of the physical good $\ell$ if, and when, state of the world $s$ occurs. Observe that although deliveries are contingent, the payments are not. Notice also that for this market to be well defined it is indispensable that all economic agents be able to recognize the occurrence of $s$. That is, information should be *symmetric* across economic agents. This informational issue will be discussed further in Section 19.H.

Formally, the market economy just described is nothing but a particular case of the economies we have studied in previous chapters. We can, therefore, apply to our market economy the concept of Walrasian equilibrium and, with it, all the theory developed so far. When dealing with contingent commodities it is customary to call the Walrasian equilibrium an *Arrow–Debreu equilibrium*.[4]

**Definition 19.C.1:** An allocation

$$(x_1^*, \ldots, x_I^*, y_1^*, \ldots, y_J^*) \in X_1 \times \cdots \times X_I \times Y_1 \times \cdots \times Y_J \subset \mathbb{R}^{LS(I+J)}$$

and a system of prices for the contingent commodities $p = (p_{11}, \ldots, p_{LS}) \in \mathbb{R}^{LS}$ constitute an *Arrow–Debreu equilibrium* if:

(i) For every $j$, $y_j^*$ satisfies $p \cdot y_j^* \geq p \cdot y_j$ for all $y_j \in Y_j$.

(ii) For every $i$, $x_i^*$ is maximal for $\succsim_i$ in the budget set

$$\{x_i \in X_i : p \cdot x_i \leq p \cdot \omega_i + \sum_j \theta_{ij} p \cdot y_j^*\}.$$

(iii) $\sum_i x_i^* = \sum_j y_j^* + \sum_i \omega_i$.

The welfare and positive theorems of Chapters 16 and 17 apply without modification to the Arrow–Debreu equilibrium. Recall from Chapter 6, especially Sections 6.C and 6.E, that, in the present context, the convexity assumption takes on an interpretation in terms of risk aversion. For example, in the expected utility setting of Example 19.B.1, the preference relation $\succsim_i$ is convex if the Bernoulli utilities $u_{si}(x_{si})$ are concave (see Exercise 19.C.1).

The Pareto optimality implication of Arrow–Debreu equilibrium says, effectively, that the possibility of trading in contingent commodities leads, at equilibrium, to an efficient allocation of risk.

It is important to realize that at any production plan the profit of a firm, $p \cdot y_j$, is a nonrandom amount of dollars. Productions and deliveries of goods do, of course, depend on the state of the world, but the firm is active in all the contingent markets and manages, so to speak, to insure completely. This has important implications for the justification of profit maximization as the objective of the firm. We will discuss this point further in Section 19.G.

**Example 19.C.1:** Consider an exchange economy with $I = 2$, $L = 1$, and $S = 2$. This lends itself to an Edgeworth box representation because there are precisely two contingent commodities. In Figures 19.C.1(a) and 19.C.1(b) we have $\omega_1 = (1, 0)$, $\omega_2 = (0, 1)$, and utility functions of the form $\pi_{1i} u_i(x_{1i}) + \pi_{2i} u_i(x_{2i})$, where $(\pi_{1i}, \pi_{2i})$ are the subjective probabilities of consumer $i$ for the two states. Since $\omega_1 + \omega_2 = (1, 1)$ there is no aggregate uncertainty, and the state of the world determines only which consumer receives the endowment of the consumption good. Recall from Section 6.E (especially the discussion preceding Example 6.E.1) that for this model [in which the $u_i(\cdot)$ do not depend on $s$], the marginal rate of substitution of consumer $i$ at any point where the consumption is the same in the two states equals the probability ratio $\pi_{1i}/\pi_{2i}$.

In Figure 19.C.1(a) the subjective probabilities are the same for the two consumers (i.e., $\pi_{11} = \pi_{12}$) and therefore the Pareto set coincides with the diagonal of the box (the box is a square and so the diagonal coincides with the 45-degree line, where the marginal rates of substitution for the two consumers are equal: $\pi_{11}/\pi_{21} = \pi_{12}/\pi_{22}$). Hence, at equilibrium, the two consumers insure completely; that is, consumer $i$'s equilibrium consumption does not vary across the two states. In Figure 19.C.1(b)

---

4. See Chapter 7 of Debreu (1959) for a succinct development of these ideas.

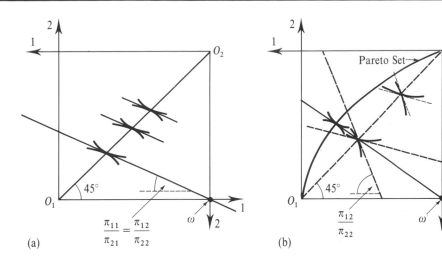

**Figure 19.C.1**

(a) No aggregate risk: same probability assessments.
(b) No aggregate risk: different probability assessments.

the consumer's subjective probabilities are different. In particular, $\pi_{11} < \pi_{12}$ (i.e., the second consumer gives more probability to state 1). In this case, each consumer's equilibrium consumption is higher in the state he thinks comparatively more likely (relative to the beliefs of the other consumer). ∎

**Example 19.C.2:** The basic framework is as in Example 19.G.1. The difference is that now there is aggregate risk: $\omega_1 + \omega_2 = (2, 1)$. The utilities are state independent and the probability assessments are the same for the two traders: $(\pi_1, \pi_2)$. The corresponding Edgeworth box is represented in Figure 19.C.2. We see that at any point of the Pareto set the common marginal rate of substitution is smaller than the ratio of probabilities (see Exercise 19.C.2). Hence at an equilibrium we must have $p_1/p_2 < \pi_1/\pi_2$, or $p_1/\pi_1 < p_2/\pi_2$. If, say, $\pi_1 = \pi_2 = \frac{1}{2}$, then $p_1 < p_2$: The price of one contingent unit of consumption is larger for the state for which the consumption good is scarcer. This constitutes the simplest version of a powerful theme of finance theory: that contingent instruments (in our case, a unit of contingent consumption) are comparatively more valuable if their returns (in our case, the amount of consumption they give in the different states) are negatively correlated with the "market return" (in our case, the random variable representing the aggregate initial endowment). ∎

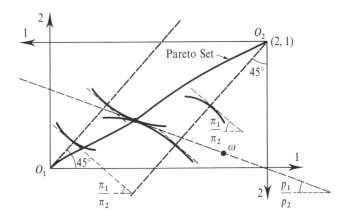

**Figure 19.C.2**

There is aggregate risk: $p_\ell/\pi_\ell$ negatively correlated with total endowment of commodity $\ell$.

# 19.D Sequential Trade

The Arrow–Debreu framework provides a remarkable illustration of the power of general equilibrium theory. Yet, it is hardly realistic. Indeed, at an Arrow–Debreu equilibrium all trade takes place simultaneously and before the uncertainty is resolved. Trade, so to speak, is a one-shot affair. In reality, however, trade takes place to a large extent sequentially over time, and frequently as a consequence of information disclosures. The aim of this section is to introduce a first model of sequential trade and show that Arrow–Debreu equilibria can be reinterpreted by means of trading processes that actually unfold through time.

To be as simple as possible we consider only exchange economies (see Section 19.G for some discussion of production). In addition, we take $X_i = \mathbb{R}^{LS}_+$ for every $i$. To begin with, we assume that there are two dates, $t = 0$ and $t = 1$, that there is no information whatsoever at $t = 0$, and that the uncertainty has resolved completely at $t = 1$. Thus, the date-event tree is as in Figure 19.B.1. Again for simplicity, we assume that there is no consumption at $t = 0$. (We refer to Exercise 19.D.3 for the more general situation.)

Suppose that markets for the $LS$ possible contingent commodities are set up at $t = 0$, and that $(x^*_1, \ldots, x^*_I) \in \mathbb{R}^{LSI}$ is an Arrow–Debreu equilibrium allocation with prices $(p_{11}, \ldots, p_{LS}) \in \mathbb{R}^{LS}$. Recall that these markets are for delivery of goods at $t = 1$ (they are commonly called *forward markets*). When period $t = 1$ arrives, a state of the world $s$ is revealed, contracts are executed, and every consumer $i$ receives $x^*_{si} = (x^*_{1si}, \ldots, x^*_{Lsi}) \in \mathbb{R}^L$. Imagine now that, after this but before the actual consumption of $x^*_{si}$, markets for the $L$ physical goods were to open at $t = 1$ (these are called *spot markets*). Would there be any incentive to trade in these markets? The answer is "no." To see why, suppose that there were potential gains from trade among the consumers. That is, that there were $x_{si} = (x_{1si}, \ldots, x_{Lsi})$ for $i = 1, \ldots, I$, such that $\sum_i x_{si} \leq \sum_i \omega_{si}$ and $(x^*_{1i}, \ldots, x_{si}, \ldots, x^*_{Si}) \succsim_i (x^*_{1i}, \ldots, x^*_{si}, \ldots, x^*_{Si})$ for all $i$, with at least one preference strict. It then follows from the definition of Pareto optimality that the Arrow–Debreu equilibrium allocation $(x^*_1, \ldots, x^*_I) \in \mathbb{R}^{LSI}$ is not Pareto optimal, contradicting the conclusion of the first welfare theorem.[5] In summary, at $t = 0$ the consumers can trade directly to an overall Pareto optimal allocation; hence there is no reason for further trade to take place. In other words, ex ante Pareto optimality implies ex post Pareto optimality and thus no ex post trade.

Matters are different if not all the $LS$ contingent commodity markets are available at $t = 0$. Then the initial trade to a Pareto optimal allocation may not be feasible and it is quite possible that ex post (i.e., after the revelation of the state $s$) the resulting consumption allocation is not Pareto optimal. There would then be an incentive to reopen the markets and retrade.

---

5. Alternatively, consider the Arrow–Debreu equilibrium prices for the $L$ contingent commodities corresponding to state $s$: $p_s = (p_{1s}, \ldots, p_{Ls})$. Then $p_s$, viewed as a system of spot prices at $s$, induces, for the initial endowment vector $(x^*_{s1}, \ldots, x^*_{sI})$, a null excess demand for all traders (and therefore clears markets). Indeed, if $U_i(x_{1i}, \ldots, x_{Si})$ is a utility function for $\succsim_i$ and $(x^*_{1i}, \ldots, x^*_{Si}) \in \mathbb{R}^{LS}$ maximizes $U_i(x_{1i}, \ldots, x_{Si})$ subject to $\sum_s p_s \cdot (x_{si} - \omega_{si}) \leq 0$, then, for any particular $s$, $x^*_{is}$ maximizes $U_i(x^*_{1i}, \ldots, x_{si}, \ldots, x^*_{Si})$ subject to $p_s \cdot (x_{si} - \omega_{si}) \leq p_s \cdot (x^*_{si} - \omega_{si})$, that is, subject to $p_s \cdot (x_{si} - x^*_{si}) \leq 0$.

A most interesting possibility, first observed by Arrow (1953), is that, even if not all the contingent commodities are available at $t = 0$, it may still be the case under some conditions that the retrading possibilities at $t = 1$ guarantee that Pareto optimality is reached, nevertheless. That is, the possibility of ex post trade can make up for an absence of some ex ante markets. In what follows, we shall verify that this is the case whenever at least one physical commodity can be traded contingently at $t = 0$ if, in addition, spot markets occur at $t = 1$ *and* the spot equilibrium prices are correctly anticipated at $t = 0$. The intuition for this result is reasonably straightforward: if spot trade can occur within each state, then the only task remaining at $t = 0$ is to transfer the consumer's overall purchasing power efficiently across states. This can be accomplished using contingent trade in a single commodity. By such a procedure we are able to reduce the number of required forward markets for $LS$ to $S$.

Let us be more specific. At $t = 0$ consumers have *expectations* regarding the spot prices prevailing at $t = 1$ for each possible state $s \in S$. Denote the price vector expected to prevail in state $s$ spot market by $p_s \in \mathbb{R}^L$, and the overall expectation vector[6] by $p = (p_1, \ldots, p_S) \in \mathbb{R}^{LS}$. Suppose that, in addition, at date $t = 0$ there is trade in the $S$ contingent commodities denoted by $11$ to $1S$; that is, there is contingent trade only in the physical good with the label $1$. We denote the vector of prices for these contingent commodities traded at $t = 0$ by $q = (q_1, \ldots, q_S) \in \mathbb{R}^S$.

Faced with prices $q \in \mathbb{R}^S$ at $t = 0$ and expected spot prices $(p_1, \ldots, p_S) \in \mathbb{R}^{LS}$ at $t = 1$, every consumer $i$ formulates a consumption, or trading, plan $(z_{1i}, \ldots, z_{Si}) \in \mathbb{R}^S$ for contingent commodities at $t = 0$, as well as a set of spot market consumption plans $(x_{1i}, \ldots, x_{Si}) \in \mathbb{R}^{LS}$ for the different states that may occur at $t = 1$. Of course, these plans must satisfy a budget constraint. Let $U_i(\cdot)$ be a utility function for $\succsim_i$. Then the problem of consumer $i$ can be expressed formally as

$$\underset{\substack{(x_{1i}, \ldots, x_{Si}) \in \mathbb{R}_+^{LS} \\ (z_{1i}, \ldots, z_{Si}) \in \mathbb{R}^S}}{\text{Max}} \quad U_i(x_{1i}, \ldots, x_{Si}) \tag{19.D.1}$$

$$\text{s.t.} \quad \text{(i) } \sum_s q_s z_{si} \leq 0,$$

$$\text{(ii) } p_s \cdot x_{si} \leq p_s \cdot \omega_{si} + p_{1s} z_{si} \quad \text{for every } s.$$

Restriction (i) is the budget constraint corresponding to trade at $t = 0$. The family of restrictions (ii) are the budget constraints for the different spot markets. Note that the value of wealth at a state $s$ is composed of two parts: the market value of the initial endowments, $p_s \cdot \omega_{si}$, and the market value of the amounts $z_{si}$ of good 1 bought or sold forward at $t = 0$. Observe that we are not imposing any restriction on the sign or the magnitude of $z_{si}$. If $z_{si} < -\omega_{1si}$ then one says that at $t = 0$ consumer $i$ is selling good 1 *short*. This is because he is selling at $t = 0$, contingent on state $s$ occurring, more than he has at $t = 1$ if $s$ occurs. Hence, if $s$ occurs he will actually have to buy in the spot market the extra amount of the first good required for the fulfillment of his commitments. The possibility of selling short is, however, indirectly

---

6. In principle, expectations could differ across consumers, but under the assumption of correct expectations (soon to be introduced) they will not.

limited by the fact that consumption, and therefore ex post wealth, must be nonnegative for every $s$.[7]

To define an appropriate notion of sequential trade we shall impose a key condition: Consumers' expectations must be *self-fulfilled*, or *rational*; that is, we require that consumers' expectations of the prices that will clear the spot markets for the different states $s$ do actually clear them once date $t = 1$ has arrived and a state $s$ is revealed.

**Definition 19.D.1:** A collection formed by a price vector $q = (q_1, \ldots, q_S) \in \mathbb{R}^S$ for contingent first good commodities at $t = 0$, a spot price vector

$$p_s = (p_{1s}, \ldots, p_{Ls}) \in \mathbb{R}^L$$

for every $s$, and, for every consumer $i$, consumption plans $z_i^* = (z_{1i}^*, \ldots, z_{Si}^*) \in \mathbb{R}^S$ at $t = 0$ and $x_i^* = (x_{1i}^*, \ldots, x_{Si}^*) \in \mathbb{R}^{LS}$ at $t = 1$ constitutes a *Radner equilibrium* [see Radner (1982)] if:

  (i) For every $i$, the consumption plans $z_i^*$, $x_i^*$ solve problem (19.D.1).

  (ii) $\sum_i z_{si}^* \leq 0$ and $\sum_i x_{si}^* \leq \sum_i \omega_{si}$ for every $s$.

At a Radner equilibrium, trade takes place through time and, in contrast to the Arrow–Debreu setting, economic agents face a *sequence of budget sets*, one at each date-state (more generally, at every date-event).

We can see from an examination of problem (19.D.1) that all the budget constraints are homogeneous of degree zero with respect to prices. This means that the budget sets remain unaltered if the price of one physical commodity in each date-state (that is, one price for every budget set) is arbitrarily normalized to equal 1. It is natural to choose the first commodity and to put $p_{1s} = 1$ for every $s$, so that a unit of the $s$ contingent commodity then pays off 1 dollar in state $s$.[8] Note that this still leaves one degree of freedom, that corresponding to the forward trades at date 0 (so we could put $q_1 = 1$, or perhaps $\sum_s q_s = 1$).

In Proposition 19.D.1, which is the key result of this section, we show that for this model the set of Arrow–Debreu equilibrium allocations (induced by the arrangement of one-shot trade in $LS$ contingent commodities) and the set of Radner equilibrium allocations (induced by contingent trade in only one commodity, sequentially followed by spot trade) are identical.

---

7. Observe also that we have taken the wealth at $t = 0$ to be zero (that is, there are no initial endowments of the contingent commodities). This is simply a convention. Suppose, for example, that we regard $\omega_{1si}$, the amount of good 1 available at $t = 1$ in state $s$, as the amount of the $s$ contingent commodity that $i$ owns at $t = 0$ (to avoid double counting, the initial endowment of commodity 1 in the spot market $s$ at $t = 1$ should simultaneously be put to zero). The budget constraints are then: (i) $\sum_s q_s(z'_{si} - \omega_{1si}) \leq 0$ and (ii) $p_s \cdot x_{si} \leq \sum_{\ell \neq 1} p_{\ell s}\omega_{\ell 1} + p_{1s}z'_{si}$ for every $s$. But letting $z'_{si} = z_{si} + \omega_{1si}$, we see that these are exactly the constraints of (19.D.1).

8. It follows from the possibility of making this normalization that, without loss of generality, we could as well suppose that our contingent commodity pays directly in dollars (see Exercise 19.D.1 for more on this).

**Proposition 19.D.1:** We have:

(i) If the allocation $x^* \in \mathbb{R}^{LSI}$ and the contingent commodities price vector $(p_1, \ldots, p_S) \in \mathbb{R}^{LS}_{++}$ constitute an Arrow–Debreu equilibrium, then there are prices $q \in \mathbb{R}^S_{++}$ for contingent first good commodities and consumption plans for these commodities $z^* = (z_1^*, \ldots, z_I^*) \in \mathbb{R}^{SI}$ such that the consumptions plans $x^*$, $z^*$, the prices $q$, and the spot prices $(p_1, \ldots, p_S)$ constitute a Radner equilibrium.

(ii) Conversely, if the consumption plans $x^* \in \mathbb{R}^{LSI}$, $z^* \in \mathbb{R}^{SI}$ and prices $q \in \mathbb{R}^S_{++}$, $(p_1, \ldots, p_S) \in \mathbb{R}^{LS}_{++}$ constitute a Radner equilibrium, then there are multipliers $(\mu_1, \ldots, \mu_S) \in \mathbb{R}^S_{++}$ such that the allocation $x^*$ and the contingent commodities price vector $(\mu_1 p_1, \ldots, \mu_S p_S) \in \mathbb{R}^{LS}_{++}$ constitute an Arrow–Debreu equilibrium. (The multiplier $\mu_s$ is interpreted as the value, at $t = 0$, of a dollar at $t = 1$ and state $s$.)

**Proof:** (i) It is natural to let $q_s = p_{1s}$ for every $s$. With this we claim that, for every consumer $i$, the budget set of the Arrow–Debreu problem,

$$B_i^{AD} = \{(x_{1i}, \ldots, x_{Si}) \in \mathbb{R}^{LS}_+ : \textstyle\sum_s p_s \cdot (x_{si} - \omega_{si}) \leq 0\},$$

is identical to the budget set of the Radner problem,

$$B_i^R = \{(x_{1i}, \ldots, x_{Si}) \in \mathbb{R}^{LS}_+ : \text{there are } (z_{1i}, \ldots, z_{Si}) \text{ such that } \textstyle\sum_s q_s z_{si} \leq 0 \text{ and}$$
$$p_s \cdot (x_{si} - \omega_{si}) \leq p_{1s} z_{si} \text{ for every } s\}.$$

To see this, suppose that $x_i = (x_{1i}, \ldots, x_{Si}) \in B_i^{AD}$. For every $s$, denote $z_{si} = (1/p_{1s}) p_s \cdot (x_{si} - \omega_{si})$. Then $\sum_s q_s z_{si} = \sum_s p_{1s} z_{si} = \sum_s p_s \cdot (x_{si} - \omega_{si}) \leq 0$ and $p_s \cdot (x_{si} - \omega_{si}) = p_{1s} z_{si}$ for every $s$. Hence, $x_1 \in B_i^R$. Conversely, suppose that $x_i = (x_{1i}, \ldots, x_{Si}) \in B_i^R$; that is, for some $(z_{1i}, \ldots, z_{Si})$ we have $\sum_s q_s z_{si} \leq 0$ and $p_s \cdot (x_{si} - \omega_{si}) \leq p_{1s} z_{si}$ for every $s$. Summing over $s$ gives $\sum_s p_s \cdot (x_{si} - \omega_{si}) \leq \sum_s p_{1s} z_{si} = \sum_s q_s z_{si} \leq 0$. Hence, $x_i \in B_i^{AD}$.

We conclude that our Arrow–Debreu equilibrium allocation is also a Radner equilibrium allocation supported by $q = (p_{11}, \ldots, p_{1S}) \in \mathbb{R}^S$, the spot prices $(p_1, \ldots, p_S)$, and the contingent trades $(z_{1i}^*, \ldots, z_{Si}^*) \in \mathbb{R}^S$ defined by $z_{si}^* = (1/p_{1s}) p_s \cdot (x_{si}^* - \omega_{si})$. Note that the contingent markets clear since, for every $s$, $\sum_i z_{si}^* = (1/p_{1s}) p_s \cdot [\sum_i (x_{si}^* - \omega_{si})] \leq 0$.

(ii) Choose $\mu_s$ so that $\mu_s p_{1s} = q_s$. Then we can rewrite the Radner budget set of every consumer $i$ *as*

$$B_i^R = \{(x_{1i}, \ldots, x_{Si}) \in \mathbb{R}^{LS} : \text{there are } (z_{1i}, \ldots, z_{Si}) \text{ such that } \textstyle\sum_s q_s z_{si} \leq 0 \text{ and}$$
$$\mu_s p_s \cdot (x_{si} - \omega_{si}) \leq q_s z_{si} \text{ for every } s\}.$$

But from this we can proceed as we did in part (i) and rewrite the constraints, and therefore the budget set, in the Arrow–Debreu form:

$$B_i^R = B_i^{AD} = \{(x_{1i}, \ldots, x_{Si}) \in \mathbb{R}^{LS} : \textstyle\sum_s \mu_s p_s \cdot (x_{si} - \omega_{si}) \leq 0\}.$$

Hence, the consumption plan $x_i^*$ is also preference maximizing in the budget set $B_i^{AD}$. Since this is true for every consumer $i$, we conclude that the price vector $(\mu_1 p_1, \ldots, \mu_S p_S) \in \mathbb{R}^{LS}$ clears the markets for the $LS$ contingent commodities. ∎

**Example 19.D.1:** Consider a two-good, two-state, two-consumer pure exchange economy. Suppose that the two states are equally likely and that every consumer has the same, state-independent, Bernoulli utility function $u(x_{si})$. The consumers differ only in their initial endowments. The aggregate endowment vectors in the two states

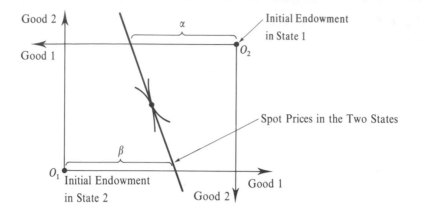

**Figure 19.D.1**

Reaching the Arrow–Debreu equilibrium by means of contingent trade in the first good only.

are the same; however, endowments are distributed so that consumer 1 gets everything in state 1 and consumer 2 gets everything in state 2. (See Figure 19.D.1.)

By the symmetry of the problem, at an Arrow–Debreu equilibrium each consumer gets, in each state, half of the total endowment of each good. In Figure 19.D.1, we indicate how these consumptions will be reached by means of contingent trade in the first commodity and spot markets. The spot prices will be the same in the two states. The first consumer will sell an amount $\alpha$ of the first good contingent on the occurrence of the first state and will in exchange buy an amount $\beta$ of the same good contingent on the second state. (You are asked to provide the details in Exercise 19.D.2.) ■

It is important to emphasize that, although the concept of Radner equilibrium cuts down the number of contingent commodities required to attain optimality (from $LS$ to $S$), this reduction is not obtained free of charge. With the smaller number of forward contracts, the correct anticipation of future spot prices becomes crucial.

---

Up to this point we have discussed the sequential implementation of an Arrow–Debreu equilibrium when there are two dates,[9] that is, for the date–event tree of Figure 19.B.1. Except for notational complications, the same ideas carry over to a tree such as that in Figure 19.B.2 where there are $T + 1$ periods and information is released gradually. (See the small-type discussion at the end of Section 19.B for basic concepts and notation.) We would then have spot markets at every admissible date–event pair $tE$ (i.e., those $tE$ where $E \in \mathscr{S}_t$, the information partition at $t$). With $H$ the set of basic physical commodities, we denote the spot prices by $p_{tE} \in \mathbb{R}^H$. At every $tE$ we could also have trade for the contingent delivery of physical good 1 at each of the successor date–events to $tE$. Denote by $q_{tE}(t + 1, E')$ the price at $tE$ of one unit of good 1 delivered at $t + 1$ if event $E'$ is revealed (of course, we require $E' \in \mathscr{S}_{t+1}$ and $E' \subset E$). The problem of the consumer consists of forming utility-maximizing plans by choosing, at every admissible $tE$, a vector of consumption of goods $x_{tEi} \in \mathbb{R}_+^H$ and, for every successor $(t + 1, E')$, a contingent trade $z_{tEi}(t + 1, E')$ of good 1 deliverable at $(t + 1, E')$. Overall, the budget constraint to be satisfied at $tE$ is

$$p_{tE} \cdot x_{tEi} + \sum_{\{E' \in \mathscr{S}_{t+1}: E' \subset E\}} q_{tE}(t + 1, E') z_{tEi}(t + 1, E') \leq p_{tE} \cdot \omega_{tEi} + p_{1tE} z_{t-1, E^-, i}(t, E)$$

where $E^-$ is the event at the date $t - 1$ predecessor to event $E$ at $t$.

---

9. To be as simple as possible, we have also assumed that there is no consumption at $t = 0$.

One can then proceed to define a corresponding concept of Radner equilibrium and to show that the Arrow–Debreu equilibrium allocations for the model with $H(T + 1)S$ contingent commodity markets[10] at $t = 0$ are the same as the Radner equilibrium allocations obtained from a model with sequential trade in which, at each date-event, consumers trade only current goods and contingent claims for delivery of good 1 at successor nodes. Exercises 19.D.3 and 19.D.4 discuss this topic further.

# 19.E   Asset Markets

The $S$ contingent commodities studied in the previous section serve the purpose of transferring wealth across the states of the world that will be revealed in the future. They are, however, only theoretical constructs that rarely have exact counterparts in reality. Nevertheless, in reality there are *assets*, or *securities*, that to some extent perform the wealth-transferring role that we have assigned to the contingent commodities. It is therefore important to develop a theoretical structure that allows us to study the functioning of these asset markets. We accomplish the task in this section by extending the formal notion of a contingent commodity and then generalizing the theory of Radner equilibrium to the extended environment.[11]

We begin again with the simplest situation, in which we have two dates, $t = 0$ and $t = 1$, and all the information is revealed at $t = 1$. Further, for notational simplicity we assume that consumption takes place only at $t = 1$.

We view an asset, or, more precisely, a unit of an asset, as a title to receive either physical goods or dollars at $t = 1$ in amounts that may depend on which state occurs.[12] The payoffs of an asset are known as its *returns*. If the returns are in physical goods, the asset is called *real* (a durable piece of machinery or a futures contract for the delivery of copper would be examples). If they are in paper money, they are called *financial* (a government bond, for example). Mixed cases are also possible. Here we deal only with the real case and, moreover, to save on notation we assume that the returns of assets are only in amounts of physical good 1.[13] It is then convenient to normalize the spot price of that good to be 1 in every state, so that, in effect, we are using it as numeraire.

**Definition 19.E.1:** A unit of an *asset*, or *security*, is a title to receive an amount $r_s$ of good 1 at date $t = 1$ if state $s$ occurs. An asset is therefore characterized by its *return vector* $r = (r_1, \ldots, r_S) \in \mathbb{R}^S$.

---

10. A contingent commodity is a promise to deliver a unit of physical commodity $h$ at date $t$ if state $s$ occurs. Recall from Section 19.B that the consumption sets have to be defined imbedding in them the information measurability restrictions, that is, making sure that at date $t$ no consumption is dependent on information not yet available.

11. See Radner (1982) and Kreps (1979) [complemented by Marimon (1987)] for treatments in the spirit of this section.

12. As usual "title to receive" means "duty to deliver" if the amount is negative. Although negative returns present no particular difficulty, we will avoid them.

13. This assumption also has an important simplifying feature: At any given state the returns of all assets are in units of the same physical good. Therefore, the relative spot prices of the various physical goods in any given state do not affect the relative returns of the different assets in that state.

**Example 19.E.1:** Examples of assets include the following:

(i) $r = (1, \ldots, 1)$. This asset promises the future noncontingent delivery of one unit of good 1. Its real-world counterparts are the markets for *commodity futures*. In the special case where there is a single consumption good (i.e., $L = 1$), we call this asset the *safe* (or *riskless*) *asset*. It is important to realize that with more than one physical good a futures contract is not riskless: its return in terms of purchasing power depends on the spot prices of all the goods.[14]

(ii) $r = (0, \ldots, 0, 1, 0, \ldots, 0)$. This asset pays one unit of good 1 if and only if a certain state occurs. These were the assets considered in Section 19.D. In the current theoretical setting they are often called *Arrow securities*.

(iii) $r = (1, 2, 1, 2, \ldots, 1, 2)$. This asset pays one unit unconditionally and, in addition, another unit in even-labeled states. ∎

**Example 19.E.2:** *Options.* This is an example of a so-called *derivative asset*, that is, of an asset whose returns are somehow derived from the returns of another asset. Suppose there is a *primary asset* with return vector $r \in \mathbb{R}^S$. Then a (*European*) *call option* on the primary asset at the *strike price* $c \in \mathbb{R}$ is itself an asset. A unit of this asset gives the option to buy, *after the state is revealed* (but before the returns are paid), a unit of the primary asset at price $c$ (the price $c$ is in units of the "numeraire," that is, of good 1).

What is the return vector $r(c)$ of the option? In a given state $s$, the option will be exercised if and only if $r_s > c$ (we neglect the case $r_s = c$). Hence

$$r(c) = (\text{Max } \{0, r_1 - c\}, \ldots, \text{Max } \{0, r_S - c\}).$$

For a primary asset with returns $r = (4, 3, 2, 1)$ specific examples are

$$r(3.5) = (\ .5, \quad 0\ , \quad 0\ , \quad 0),$$
$$r(2.5) = (1.5, \quad 0.5, \quad 0\ , \quad 0),$$
$$r(1.5) = (2.5, \quad 1.5, \quad 0.5, \quad 0). \ \blacksquare$$

We proceed to extend the analysis of Section 19.D by assuming that there is a given set of assets, known as an *asset structure*, and that these assets can be freely traded at date $t = 0$. We postpone to the next section a discussion of the important issue of the origin of the particular set of assets. Each asset $k$ is characterized by a vector of returns $r_k \in \mathbb{R}^S$. The number of assets is $K$. As before, we assume that there are no initial endowments of assets and that short sales are possible. The price vector for the assets traded at $t = 0$ is denoted $q = (q_1, \ldots, q_K)$. A vector of trades in these assets, denoted by $z = (z_1, \ldots, z_K) \in \mathbb{R}^K$, is called a *portfolio*.

The next step is to generalize the definition of a Radner equilibrium to the current environment. In Definition 19.E.2, $U_i(\cdot)$ is a utility function for the preferences $\succsim_i$ of consumer $i$ over consumption plans $(x_{1i}, \ldots, x_{Si}) \in \mathbb{R}_+^{LS}$.

---

14. Strictly speaking, for the term "riskless" to be meaningful we need, in addition to $L = 1$, that utility functions be uniform across states.

**Definition 19.E.2:** A collection formed by a price vector $q = (q_1, \ldots, q_K) \in \mathbb{R}^K$ for assets traded at $t = 0$, a spot price vector $p_s = (p_{1s}, \ldots, p_{Ls}) \in \mathbb{R}^L$ for every $s$, and, for every consumer $i$, portfolio plans $z_i^* = (z_{1i}^*, \ldots, z_{Ki}^*) \in \mathbb{R}^K$ at $t = 0$ and consumption plans $x_i^* = (x_{1i}^*, \ldots, x_{Si}^*) \in \mathbb{R}^{LS}$ at $t = 1$ constitutes a *Radner equilibrium* if:

(i) For every $i$, the consumption plans $z_i^*$, $x_i^*$ solve the problem

$$\underset{\substack{(x_{1i}, \ldots, x_{Si}) \in \mathbb{R}_+^{LS} \\ (z_{1i}, \ldots, z_{Ki}) \in \mathbb{R}^K}}{\text{Max}} \quad U_i(x_{1i}, \ldots, x_{Si})$$

s.t.  (a) $\sum_k q_k \cdot z_{ki} \leq 0$

(b) $p_s \cdot x_{si} \leq p_s \cdot \omega_{si} + \sum_k p_{1s} z_{ki} r_{sk}$  for every $s$.

(ii) $\sum_i z_{ki}^* \leq 0$ and $\sum_i x_{si}^* \leq \sum_i \omega_{si}$  for every $k$ and $s$.

In the budget set of Definition 19.E.2, the wealth of consumer $i$ at state $s$ is the sum of the spot value of his initial endowment and the spot value of the return of his portfolio. Note that, without loss of generality, we can put $p_{1s} = 1$ for all $s$. From now on we will do so. It is convenient at this point to introduce the concept the *return matrix* $R$. This is an $S \times K$ matrix whose $k$th column is the return vector of the $k$th asset. Hence, its generic $sk$ entry is $r_{sk}$, the return of asset $k$ in state $s$. With this notation, the budget constraint of consumer $i$ becomes

$$B_i(p, q, B) = \left\{ x \in \mathbb{R}_+^{LS} : \text{for some portfolio } z_i \in \mathbb{R}^K \text{ we have } q \cdot z_i \leq 0 \text{ and} \right.$$

$$\left. \begin{pmatrix} p_1 \cdot (x_{1i} - \omega_{1i}) \\ \vdots \\ p_s \cdot (x_{Si} - \omega_{Si}) \end{pmatrix} \leq \begin{bmatrix} r_{11}, \ldots, r_{1K} \\ \ddots \\ r_{S1}, \ldots, r_{SK} \end{bmatrix} z_i = R z_i \right\}$$

We now present a very important implication, rich in ramifications, of the assumption that unlimited short sales are possible. Namely, we will establish that knowledge of the return matrix $R$ suffices to place significant restrictions on the asset price vector $q = (q_1, \ldots, q_K)$ that could conceivably arise at equilibrium.

**Proposition 19.E.1:** Assume that every return vector is nonnegative and nonzero; that is, $r_k \geq 0$ and $r_k \neq 0$ for all $k$.[15] Then, for every (column) vector $q \in \mathbb{R}^K$ of asset prices arising in a Radner equilibrium, we can find multipliers $\mu = (\mu_1, \ldots, \mu_S) \geq 0$, such that $q_k = \sum_s \mu_s r_{sk}$ for all $k$ (in matrix notation, $q^T = \mu \cdot R$).

In words, Proposition 19.E.1 says that we can assign values $(\mu_1, \ldots, \mu_S)$ to units of wealth in the different states so that the price of a unit of asset $k$ is simply equal to the sum, in value terms, of the returns across states.[16] Because this is an important

---

15. This assumption can be weakened substantially.

16. As we shall see shortly, the value $\mu_s$ can also be interpreted as the implicit price of the state-contingent commodity that pays one unit of good 1 if state $s$ occurs and nothing otherwise.

result, we shall give two proofs of it. The first, which we give in small type, is based on convexity theory and uses only one implication of equilibrium: the fact that $q$ must be *arbitrage free* (we will give a definition of this concept shortly). The second proof uses the first-order conditions of the utility maximization problem and provides further insight into the nature of the multipliers.

---

**Proof 1 of Proposition 19.E.1:** Call the system $q \in \mathbb{R}^K$ of asset prices *arbitrage free* if there is no portfolio $z = (z_1, \ldots, z_K)$ such that $q \cdot z \leq 0$, $Rz \geq 0$, and $Rz \neq 0$. In words, there is no portfolio that is budgetarily feasible and that yields a nonnegative return in *every state* and a strictly positive return in some state. Note that whether an asset price vector is arbitrage free or not depends only on the returns of the assets and not on preferences.

If, as usual, we assume that preferences are strongly monotone, then an equilibrium asset price vector $q \in \mathbb{R}^K$ must be arbitrage free: if it were not, it would be possible to increase utility merely by adding to any current portfolio a portfolio yielding an arbitrage opportunity. Because there are no restrictions on short sales this addition is always feasible.

In Lemma 19.E.1 we establish a result which in view of the observation just made is formally stronger than the statement of Proposition 19.E.1.

**Lemma 19.E.1:** If the asset price vector $q \in \mathbb{R}^K$ is arbitrage free, then there is a vector of multipliers $\mu = (\mu_1, \ldots, \mu_S) \geq 0$ satisfying $q^{\mathsf{T}} = \mu \cdot R$.

**Proof of Lemma 19.E.1:** Note to begin with that since we deal only with assets having nonnegative, nonzero returns, an arbitrage-free price vector $q$ must have $q_k > 0$ for every $k$. Also, without loss of generality, we assume that no row of the return matrix $R$ has all of its entries equal to zero.[17]

Given an arbitrage-free asset price vector $q \in \mathbb{R}^K$, consider the convex set

$$V = \{v \in \mathbb{R}^S : v = Rz \text{ for some } z \in \mathbb{R}^K \text{ with } q \cdot z = 0\}.$$

The arbitrage freeness of $q$ implies that $V \cap \{\mathbb{R}^S_+ \setminus \{0\}\} = \emptyset$. Since both $V$ and $\mathbb{R}^S_+ \setminus \{0\}$ are convex sets and the origin belongs to $V$, we can apply the separating hyperplane theorem (see Section M.G of the Mathematical Appendix) to obtain a nonzero vector $\mu' = (\mu'_1, \ldots, \mu'_S)$ such that $\mu' \cdot v \leq 0$ for any $v \in V$ and $\mu' \cdot v \geq 0$ for any $v \in \mathbb{R}^S_+$. Note that it must be that $\mu' \geq 0$. Moreover, because $v \in V$ implies $-v \in V$, it follows that $\mu' \cdot v = 0$ for any $v \in V$. Figure 19.E.1(a) depicts this construction for the two-state case.

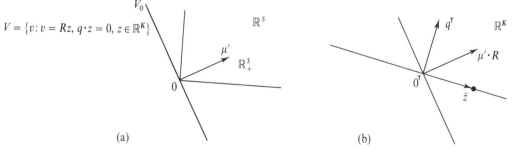

$V = \{v : v = Rz, q \cdot z = 0, z \in \mathbb{R}^K\}$

(a)    (b)

**Figure 19.E.1**
(a) Construction of the no-arbitrage weights.
(b) Existence of an inadmissible $\bar{z}$ if $q^{\mathsf{T}}$ is not proportional to $\mu' \cdot R$.

---

17. If there is such a row, set $\mu_s$ arbitrarily for the state $s$ corresponding to that row, drop $s$ from the list of states, and proceed with the remaining states.

We now argue that the row vector $q^T$ must be proportional to the row vector $\mu' \cdot R \in \mathbb{R}^K$. The entries of $\mu'$ and of $R$ are all nonnegative and no row of $R$ is null. Therefore $\mu' \cdot R \geq 0^T$ and $\mu' \cdot R \neq 0^T$. If $q^T$ is not proportional to $\mu' \cdot R$ then we can find $\bar{z} \in \mathbb{R}^K$ such that $q \cdot \bar{z} = 0$ and $\mu' \cdot R\bar{z} > 0$ [see Figure 19.E.1(b)]. But letting $v = R\bar{z}$, we would then have $v \in V$ and $\mu' \cdot v \neq 0$, which we have just seen cannot happen. Hence $q^T$ must be proportional to $\mu' \cdot R$; that is, $q^T = \alpha\mu' \cdot R$ for some real number $\alpha > 0$. Letting $\mu = \alpha\mu'$, we have the conclusion of the lemma. ∎

As we have already argued, if short sales of assets are possible and preferences are strongly monotone (e.g., if preferences admit an expected utility representation with strictly positive subjective probabilities for the states), then equibrium asset prices must be arbitrage free and, therefore, Proposition 19.E.1 follows from Lemma 19.E.1. ∎

**Proof 2 of Proposition 19.E.1:** For this proof we assume that preferences are represented by utility functions of the expected utility form $U_i(x_{1i}, \ldots, x_{Si}) = \sum_s \pi_{si} u_{si}(x_{si})$ and that the Bernoulli utilities $u_{si}(\cdot)$ are concave, strictly increasing, and differentiable. We denote by $v_{si}(p_s, w_{si})$ the indirect utility function [derived from $u_{si}(\cdot)$] of consumer $i$ in state $s$.

Suppose that in the Radner equilibrium with asset prices $q = (q_1, \ldots, q_K)$ the equilibrium spot prices are $p = (p_1, \ldots, p_S) \in \mathbb{R}^{LS}$. Because unlimited short sales are possible, the optimal portfolio choice $z_i^* \in \mathbb{R}^K$ of any consumer $i$ is necessarily interior and, denoting $w_{si}^* = p_s \cdot \omega_{si} + \sum_k r_{sk} z_{ki}^*$, it must satisfy the following first-order conditions for some $\alpha_i > 0$:

$$\alpha_i q_k = \sum_s \pi_{si} \frac{\partial v_{si}(p_s, w_{si}^*)}{\partial w_{si}} r_{sk} \qquad \text{for every } k = 1, \ldots, K.$$

That is, the vector of expected marginal utilities of the $K$ assets must be proportional to the vector of asset prices.[18] With this we have attained our result, since by taking

$$\mu_{si} = \frac{\pi_{si}}{\alpha_i} \frac{\partial v_{si}(p_s, w_{si}^*)}{\partial w_{si}}$$

we have $q_j = \sum_s \mu_{si} r_{sk}$. Hence, we could determine $\mu = (\mu_1, \ldots, \mu_s)$ by choosing *any* consumer $i$ and letting $\mu_s = \mu_{si}$, the marginal utility of wealth at state $s$ of consumer $i$ weighted by $\pi_{si}/\alpha_i$. The multiplier $\alpha_i$ is the Lagrange multiplier of the budget constraint at $t = 0$ and can therefore be viewed as the marginal utility of wealth at $t = 0$. Hence, for any consumer $i$, $\mu_{si}$ equals the ratio of the (expected) utility at $t = 0$ of one extra unit of wealth at $t = 1$ and state $s$, and the utility of one extra unit of wealth at $t = 0$. See Exercise 19.E.1 for more on this point. Note also that different consumers may lead to different $\mu_i = (\mu_{i1}, \ldots, \mu_{is})$ and therefore to different $\mu$'s. The uniqueness of $\mu$ is assured only when rank $R = S$. ∎

---

18. Recall that we always take $p_{1s} = 1$. Therefore, $r_{sk}$ is the extra amount of wealth in state $s$ derived from an extra unit of asset $k$. The proportionality factor $\alpha_i$ is the Lagrange multiplier of the problem

$$\text{Max} \quad \sum_s \pi_{si} v_{si}(p_s, p_s \cdot \omega_{si} + \sum_k r_{sk} z_{ki})$$

$$\text{s.t. } \sum_k q_k z_{ki} \leq 0.$$

**Example 19.E.3:** Suppose that there is available an asset with noncontingent returns; for example, $r_1 = (1, \ldots, 1)$. Normalize the price of this asset to be 1, that is, $q_1 = 1$. Then if $\mu = (\mu_1, \ldots, \mu_S)$ is the vector of multipliers given by Proposition 19.E.1, we must have $\mu \geq 0$ and $\sum_s \mu_s = \mu \cdot r_1 = q_1 = 1$. For any other asset $k$ we then obtain the intuitive conclusion that $q_k = \sum_s \mu_s r_{sk} \geq \text{Min}_s r_{sk}$ and, similarly, $q_k \leq \text{Max}_s r_{sk}$. ∎

In Section 19.D, we proved that for the set of assets consisting of the $S$ contingent markets in a single physical commodity we have an equivalence result between Arrow–Debreu and Radner equilibrium allocations (Proposition 19.D.1). We now generalize this result. In particular, we show that this equivalence holds for *any* family of $S$ or more assets, *provided* that at least $S$ of them have returns that are linearly independent (i.e., provided the effective number of assets is at least $S$). We begin with Definition 19.E.2.

**Definition 19.E.3:** An asset structure with an $S \times K$ return matrix $R$ is *complete* if rank $R = S$, that is, if there is some subset of $S$ assets with linearly independent returns.

**Example 19.E.4:** In the case of $S$ contingent commodities discussed in Section 19.D, and also in Example 19.E.1(ii), the return matrix $R$ is the $S \times S$ identity matrix. This is the canonical example of complete markets. But there are many other ways for a matrix to be nonsingular. Thus, with three states and three assets, we could have the return matrix

$$R = \begin{bmatrix} 1 & 0 & 0 \\ 1 & 1 & 0 \\ 1 & 1 & 1 \end{bmatrix},$$

which has rank equal to 3, the number of states. ∎

**Example 19.E.5:** *Spanning through Options.* Suppose that $S = 4$ and there is a primary asset with returns $r = (4, 3, 2, 1)$. We have seen in Example 19.E.2 that, for every strike price $c$, the option defined by $c$ constitutes an asset with return vector $r(c) = (\text{Max}\,\{0, r_1 - c\}, \ldots, \text{Max}\,\{0, r_4 - c\})$. Using options we can create a complete asset structure supported entirely on the primary asset $r$. For example, the return vectors $r(3.5)$, $r(2.5)$, $r(1.5)$, and $r$ and linearly independent (the matrix $R$ has all its entries below the diagonal equal to zero). Thus, the asset structure consisting of the primary asset plus three options with strike prices 3.5, 2.5, and 1.5 is complete. More generally, whenever the primary asset is such that $r_s \neq r_{s'}$ for all $s \neq s'$, it is possible to generate a complete asset structure by means of options (see Exercise 19.E.2). If $r_s = r_{s'}$ for some distinct $s$ and $s'$, then we cannot do so: If the primary asset does not distinguish between two states, no derived asset can do so either. ∎

To repeat, the importance of the concept of completeness derives from the fact that with it we can generalize Proposition 19.D.1. With a complete asset structure, economic agents are, in effect, unrestricted in their wealth transfers across states (except, of course, by their budget constraints). Therefore, at the equilibrium, their portfolio choices induce the same second-period consumptions as in the Arrow–Debreu equilibrium, and so full Pareto optimality is reached. This is the content of Proposition 19.E.2.

**Proposition 19.E.2:** Suppose that the asset structure is complete. Then:

(i) If the consumption plans $x^* = (x_1^*, \ldots, x_I^*) \in \mathbb{R}^{LSI}$ and the price vector

$$(p_1, \ldots, p_S) \in \mathbb{R}_{++}^{LS}$$

constitute an Arrow–Debreu equilibrium, then there are asset prices $q \in \mathbb{R}_{++}^K$ and portfolio plans $z^* = (z_1^*, \ldots, z_I^*) \in \mathbb{R}^{KI}$ such that the consumption plans $x^*$, portfolio plans $z^*$, asset prices $q$, and spot prices $(p_1, \ldots, p_S)$ constitute a Radner equilibrium.

(ii) Conversely, if the consumption plans $x^* \in \mathbb{R}^{LSI}$, portfolio plans $z^* \in \mathbb{R}^{KI}$, and prices $q \in \mathbb{R}_{++}^K$, $(p_1, \ldots, p_S) \in \mathbb{R}_{++}^{LS}$ constitute a Radner equilibrium, then there are multipliers $(\mu_1, \ldots, \mu_S) \in \mathbb{R}_{++}^S$ such that the consumption plans $x^*$ and the contingent commodities price vector $(\mu_1 p_1, \ldots, \mu_S p_S) \in \mathbb{R}^{LS}$ constitute an Arrow–Debreu equilibrium. (The multiplier $\mu_s$ is interpreted as the value, at $t = 0$, of a dollar at $t = 1$ and state $s$; recall that $p_{1s} = 1$.)

**Proof:** It is entirely similar to the proof of Proposition 19.D.1.

(i) Define $q_k = \sum_s p_{1s} r_{sk}$ for every $k$. Denote by $\Lambda$ the $S \times S$ diagonal matrix whose $s$ diagonal entry is $p_{1s}$. Then $q^T = e \cdot \Lambda R$, where $e \in \mathbb{R}^S$ is a column vector with all its entries equal to 1. For every $i$ the (column) vector of wealth transfers across states (at the Arrow–Debreu equilibrium) is

$$m_i = (p_1 \cdot (x_{1i}^* - \omega_{1i}), \ldots, p_S \cdot (x_{Si}^* - \omega_{Si}))^T.$$

We have $e \cdot m_i = 0$ for every $i$ and $\sum_i m_i = 0$. By completeness, rank $\Lambda R = S$ and, therefore, we can find vectors $z_i^* \in \mathbb{R}^K$ such that $m_i = \Lambda R z_i^*$ for $i = 1, \ldots, I - 1$. Letting

$$z_I^* = -(z_1^* + \cdots + z_{I-1}^*)$$

we also have $m_I = -(m_1 + \cdots + m_{I-1}) = \Lambda R z_I^*$. Therefore, for each $i$, the portfolio $z_i^*$ allows consumer $i$ to reach the Arrow–Debreu consumptions in the different states at the spot prices $(p_1, \ldots, p_S)$. To verify budget feasibility note that $q \cdot z_i^* = e \cdot \Lambda R z_i^* = e \cdot m_i = 0$. In Exercise 19.E.3 you are asked to complete the proof by showing that the consumption and portfolio plans $x_i^*$ and $z_i^*$ are not just budget feasible but also utility maximizing in the budget set.

(ii) Assume, without loss of generality, that $p_{1s} = 1$ for all $s$. By Proposition 19.E.1 we have $q^T = \mu \cdot R$ for some arbitrage weights $\mu = (\mu_1, \ldots, \mu_S)$. We show that $x^*$ is an Arrow–Debreu equilibrium with respect to $(\mu_1 p_1, \ldots, \mu_S p_S)$. To this effect, suppose that $x_i \in \mathbb{R}^{LS}$ satisfies the Arrow–Debreu single budget constraint, that is, $\sum_s \mu_s p_s \cdot (x_{si} - \omega_{si}) \leq 0$. Then by the completeness assumption there is $z_i \in \mathbb{R}^K$ such that $(p_1 \cdot (x_{1i} - \omega_{1i}), \ldots, p_S \cdot (x_{Si} - \omega_{Si}))^T = R z_i$ and, therefore, $q \cdot z_i = \mu \cdot R z_i \leq 0$. Hence $x_i$ also satisfies the budget constraints of the Radner equilibrium. Observe next that the Radner equilibrium consumption $x_i^*$ is Arrow–Debreu budget feasible since $(p_1 \cdot (x_{1i}^* - \omega_{1i}), \ldots, p_S \cdot (x_{Si}^* - \omega_{Si}))^T \leq R z_i^*$ and $q^T = \mu \cdot R$ yields

$$\sum_s \mu_s p_s \cdot (x_{si}^* - \omega_{si}) \leq \mu \cdot R z_i^* = q \cdot z_i^* \leq 0.$$

Therefore, $x_i^*$ is utility maximizing in the Arrow–Debreu budget constraint. ∎

It is important to realize that in discussing Radner equilibria what matters is not so much the particular asset structure but the linear space,

$$\text{Range } R = \{v \in \mathbb{R}^S : v = Rz \text{ for some } z \in \mathbb{R}^K\} \subset \mathbb{R}^S,$$

the set of wealth vectors that can be *spanned* by means of the existing assets. It is quite possible for two different asset structures to give rise to the same linear space. Our next result, Proposition 19.E.3, tells us that, whenever this is so, the set of Radner equilibrium allocations for the two asset structures is the same.

**Proposition 19.E.3:** Suppose that the asset price vector $q \in \mathbb{R}^K$, the spot prices $p = (p_1, \ldots, p_S) \in \mathbb{R}^{LS}$, the consumption plans $x^* = (x_1^*, \ldots, x_I^*) \in \mathbb{R}_+^{LSI}$, and the portfolio plans $(z_1^*, \ldots, z_I^*) \in \mathbb{R}^{KI}$ constitute a Radner equilibrium for an asset structure with $S \times K$ return matrix $R$. Let $R'$ be the $S \times K'$ return matrix of a second asset structure. If Range $R' =$ Range $R$, then $x^*$ is still the consumption allocation of a Radner equilibrium in the economy with the second asset structure.

**Proof:** By Proposition 19.E.1, the asset prices satisfy the arbitrage condition $q^T = \mu \cdot R$, for some $\mu \in \mathbb{R}_+^S$. Denote $q' = [\mu \cdot R']^T$. We claim that if Range $R =$ Range $R'$ then

$$B_i(p, q', R') = B_i(p, q, R) \qquad \text{for every } i. \tag{19.E.1}$$

We show that if $x_i \in B_i(p, q, R)$ then $x_i \in B_i(p, q', R')$. To see this, let

$$(p_1 \cdot (x_{1i} - \omega_{1i}), \ldots, p_S \cdot (x_{Si} - \omega_{Si}))^T \leq R z_i$$

and $q \cdot z_i \leq 0$. Since Range $R =$ Range $R'$, we can find $z_i' \in$ Range $R'$ such that $R z_i = R' z_i'$. But then $q' \cdot z_i' = \mu \cdot R' z_i' = \mu \cdot R z_i = q \cdot z_i \leq 0$, and therefore we can conclude that $x_i \in B_i(p, q', R')$. The converse statement [if $x_i \in B_i(p, q', R')$ then $x_i \in B_i(p, q, R)$] is proved in exactly the same way.

It follows from (19.E.1) that, for every consumer $i$, $x_i^*$ is preference maximal in the budget set $B_i(p, q', R')$.

To argue that the asset prices $q'$, the spot prices $p = (p_1, \ldots, p_S)$, and the consumption allocation $x^*$ are part of a Radner equilibrium in the economy with an asset structure having return matrix $R'$, it suffices to find portfolios $(z_1', \ldots, z_I') \in \mathbb{R}^{KI}$ such that, first, $\sum_i z_i' = 0$ and, second, for every consumer $i$, the vector of across-states wealth transfers

$$m_i = (p_1 \cdot (x_{1i}^* - \omega_{1i}), \ldots, p_S \cdot (x_{Si}^* - \omega_{Si}))^T$$

satisfies $m_i = R' z_i'$. This is simple to accomplish. By strong monotonicity of preferences we have $m_i = R z_i^*$, for every $i$. Hence, $m_i \in$ Range $R$ and therefore $m_i \in$ Range $R'$ for every $i$. Choose then $z_1', \ldots, z_{I-1}'$ such that $m_i = R' z_i'$ for every $i = 1, \ldots, I - 1$. Finally, let $z_I' = -z_1' - \cdots - z_{I-1}'$. Then $\sum_i z_i' = 0$ and also

$$m_I = -(m_1 + \cdots + m_{I-1}) = -R'(z_1' + \cdots + z_{I-1}') = R' z_I'. \quad \blacksquare$$

One says that an asset is *redundant* if its deletion does not affect the linear space Range $R$ of spannable wealth transfers, that is, if its return vector is a linear combination of the return vectors of the remaining assets. It follows from Proposition 19.E.3 that the set of consumption allocations obtainable as part of a Radner equilibrium is not changed by the addition or deletion of a redundant asset. Another important fact is that a redundant asset can be priced merely by knowing the matrix of returns and the prices of the other assets.

**Exercise 19.E.4:** (*Pricing by Arbitrage*). Suppose that $r_3 = \alpha_1 r_1 + \alpha_2 r_2$. Show that at equilibrium we must have $q_3 = \alpha_1 q_1 + \alpha_2 q_2$. Recall that unlimited short sales are possible. (Assume also that the return vectors are nonnegative and nonzero.)

An implication of Exercise 19.E.4 is that, if the asset structure is complete, then we can deduce the prices of all assets from knowing the prices of a subset formed by $S$ of them with linearly independent returns. A related way to see this is to note that from the prices of $S$ assets with linearly independent returns we can uniquely deduce the state multipliers $\mu = (\mu_1, \ldots, \mu_S)$ of Proposition 19.E.1; indeed, for this we just have to solve a linear system of $S$ independent equations in $S$ unknowns. These multipliers can be interpreted as the (arbitrage) prices of the Arrow securities [Example 19.E.1(ii)]. Once we have these multipliers, we can obtain the price of any other asset $k$ with return vector $r_k$ as $q_k = \sum_s \mu_s r_{sk}$.

**Example 19.E.6:** *Pricing an Option.* Suppose that, with $S = 2$, there is an asset with uncontingent returns, say $r_1 = (1, 1)$ and a second asset $r_2 = (3 + \alpha, 1 - \alpha)$, with $\alpha > 0$. The asset prices are $q_1 = 1$ and $q_2$. We now consider an option on the second asset that has strike price $c \in (1, 3)$. Then

$$r_2(c) = (3 + \alpha - c, 0) = \frac{3 + \alpha - c}{2 + 2\alpha} r_2 - \frac{(1 - \alpha)(3 + \alpha - c)}{2 + 2\alpha} r_1.$$

Therefore, the arbitrage price of the option (the only price compatible with equilibrium in the asset market) must be

$$q_2(c) = \frac{3 + \alpha - c}{2 + 2\alpha} [q_2 - (1 - \alpha)]. \tag{19.E.2}$$

An equivalent way to get the same formula is to note that, since the $2 \times 2$ return matrix $R$ is nonsingular, the multipliers $\mu = (\mu_1, \mu_2)$ of Proposition 19.E.1 can be determined uniquely from $(1, q_2) = \mu \cdot R$. They are $\mu_1 = (q_2 - (1 - \alpha))/(2 + 2\alpha)$ and $\mu_2 = 1 - \mu_1$. But, again from Proposition 19.E.1, we have

$$q_2(c) = \mu \cdot r_2(c) = \mu_1(3 + \alpha - c),$$

which is precisely expression (19.E.2).

Note that if the prices of the two assets $r_1$ and $r_2$ are themselves arbitrage free, then we must have $3 + \alpha \geq q_2 \geq 1 - \alpha$ (recall Example 19.E.3). Therefore, we learn from formula (19.E.2) that $q_2(c)$ is nonnegative, decreasing in $c$, and increasing in $q_2$.

We can also show that if the asset price $q_2$ stays constant but the dispersion parameter represented by $\alpha$ increases, then the option becomes more valuable. Suppose, in effect, that $\alpha' > \alpha$ and $r_2'(c)$, $r_2(c)$ are the corresponding returns of the option. Then $r_3 = r_2'(c) - r_2(c)$ is itself an asset with nonnegative returns. We can also price it by arbitrage from $r_1$ and $r_2$ to get a $q_3 \geq 0$ (typically, $q_3 > 0$). But then, again by arbitrage, $q_2'(c) = q_3 + q_2(c) \geq q_2(c)$. ∎

---

Everything generalizes to the case of $T + 1$ periods and gradual release of information. With several periods, an asset can take many forms. For example, we could have *short-term assets* available for trade in a given period and having positive returns only in the next period. Or we could have *long-term assets* available at $t = 0$, tradeable at every period, and having positive returns only at the final period $t = T$. And, of course, there could be mixed cases of assets tradeable in a subset of periods and providing returns also in a subset of periods (not necessarily the same).

Again, the equivalence result of Proposition 19.D.1 generalizes if the asset structure is *complete*. Suppose, for example, that our asset structure is composed only of collections of short-term assets available and tradeable at any admissible date-event pair $tE$ and paying contingent amounts of physical good 1 at the immediately succeeding date-event pairs. Denote by $S(tE)$ the number of successors at $tE$. If the number of assets available at $tE$ is $K(tE)$ we can view the return matrix at $tE$ as an $S(tE) \times K(tE)$ matrix $R(tE)$. The completeness condition is then the requirement that rank $R(tE) = S(tE)$ for all admissible date–events pairs $tE$. In

Section 19.D, the matrices $R(tE)$ were identity matrices, and so the asset structure there was complete. But, to repeat, the results of Section 19.D generalize to the complete, nondiagonal case.

A very interesting, and new, phenomenon is that if assets are long lived, and therefore repeatedly tradeable as information is gradually disclosed, it may be possible to implement the Arrow–Debreu equilibrium with much fewer than $S$ assets. This is illustrated in Example 19.E.7.

**Example 19.E.7:** Suppose that $T = 2$ and the date–event tree unfolds as in Figure 19.E.2. In

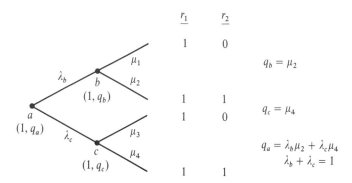

**Figure 19.E.2**

Construction of Arrow–Debreu prices from the equilibrium values of the asset prices of two sequentially traded assets.

the figure we have seven admissible date–events corresponding to the four terminal nodes, or states, to the initial node, denoted $a$, and to two intermediate nodes, denoted $b$ and $c$. In particular, there are no more than two branches from any node. In this case we claim that, typically, two long-lived assets should suffice to guarantee that the Radner and the Arrow–Debreu equilibrium consumption allocations are the same.[19] Suppose, to take a simple instance, that $L = 1$ and that our two assets have return vectors $r_1 = (1, 1, 1, 1)$ and $r_2 = (0, 1, 0, 1)$, payable at the terminal nodes. Consumption takes place only at the terminal nodes, but the assets may be traded both at the node $a$ corresponding to $t = 0$ and at the nodes $b$ and $c$ correponding to $t = 1$. We can normalize the price of the first asset (as well as the price of final consumption) to be 1 at every node.[20] Denote by $q_a$, $q_b$, and $q_c$ the prices of the second asset at the respective nodes. By arbitrage (Proposition 19.E.1), applied at $t = 1$, there are $(\mu_1, \mu_2) \geq 0$ such that $\mu_1 + \mu_2 = 1$, $\mu_2 = q_b$, and $(\mu_3, \mu_4) \geq 0$ such that $\mu_3 + \mu_4 = 1$ and $\mu_4 = q_c$. Again by arbitrage (applied this time at $t = 0$), we must have $(\lambda_b, \lambda_c) \geq 0$ such that $\lambda_b + \lambda_c = 1$ and $q_a = \lambda_b q_b + \lambda_c q_c = \lambda_b \mu_2 + \lambda_c \mu_4$. This suggests considering the following Arrow–Debreu prices:

$$p = (\lambda_b \mu_1, \lambda_b \mu_2, \lambda_c \mu_3, \lambda_c \mu_4).$$

In Exercise 19.E.5 you are asked to show that, under the weak condition $q_b \neq q_c$, the set of final consumptions achievable through sequential trade with asset prices $(q_a, q_b, q_c)$ is indeed the same as the set of final consumptions achievable with the four Arrow–Debreu contingent commodities at prices $p$.[21] ∎

---

19. We say "typically" because the existence of two assets is a necessary condition for completeness at every node but, strictly speaking, not a sufficient condition.

20. Note that, as should be the case, we do not normalize more than one price per budget constraint.

21. Incidentally, the assets prices provide a specific instance of what is called the *martingale property of asset prices*: at any node the price of an asset is the conditional expectation of the final returns, where the expectation is taken with respect to some probabilities, in our case the Arrow–Debreu prices.

# 19.F Incomplete Markets

In this section we explore the implications of having fewer than $S$ assets, that is, of having an asset structure that is necessarily incomplete. We pursue this point in the two-period framework of the previous sections.[22]

Markets may fail to exist for a number of reasons. One class of reasons refers to the informational asymmetries to be covered in Section 19.H: contracts for the delivery of goods can only be made contingent on states whose occurrence can be verified to the satisfaction of all contracting parties. Another class of reasons stems from transaction costs: the availability of a market is, after all, in the nature of a public good. Yet another variety of reasons comes from enforceability constraints: a promise to deliver one unit of good is worthless if delivery cannot be enforced.[23] This said, we shall not delve further into a theory of asset determination. We will rest content for the moment with taking the incomplete situation as a reasonable description of reality.

We begin by observing that when $K < S$ a Radner equilibrium need not be Pareto optimal. This is not surprising: if the possibilities of transferring wealth across states are limited, then there may well be a welfare loss due to the inability to diversify risks to the extent that would be convenient. Just consider the extreme case where there are no assets at all. Example 19.F.1 provides another interesting illustration of this type of failure.

**Example 19.F.1:** *Sunspots.* Suppose that preferences admit an expected utility representation and that the set of states $S$ is such that, first, the probability estimates for the different states are the same across consumers (i.e., $\pi_{si} = \pi_{si'} = \pi_s$ for all $i$, $i'$, and $s$) and, second, that the states do not affect the fundamentals of the economy; that is, the Bernoulli utility functions and the endowments of every consumer $i$ are uniform across states [i.e., $u_{si}(\cdot) = u_i(\cdot)$ and $\omega_{si} = \omega_i$ for all $s$]. Such a set of states is called a *sunspot* set. The question we shall address [first posed by Cass and Shell (1983)] is whether in these circumstances the Radner equilibrium allocations can assign varying consumptions across states. An equilibrium where this happens is called a *sunspot equilibrium.*[24]

Under the assumption that consumers are strictly risk averse, so that the utility functions $u_i(\cdot)$ are strictly concave, *any Pareto optimal allocation* $(x_1, \ldots, x_I) \in \mathbb{R}^{LSI}$ *must be uniform across states (or state independent)*; that is, for every $i$ we must have

---

22. For a general and advanced treatment, see Magill and Shafer (1991).

23. An example of a situation where enforceability would be helped is when we are dealing with the shares of a firm (the total endowments of this asset is, therefore, positive) and no short sales are possible. Enforceability is then guaranteed because the physical shares—the ownership claims to the firm—are actually transacted at $t = 0$. This sort of consideration, which, unfortunately, clashes with the very convenient assumption that unlimited short sales are possible, could explain why some assets may exist and others not: in order for the asset to exist, it helps if the random variable has a physical reality that can be exchanged at $t = 0$.

24. The term "sunspots" is old, but the current meaning is recent. In the XIX century, research on the "sunspot problem" tried to determine the influence on the fundamentals (e.g., on agriculture) that could make an unobservable signal (sunspots) have an effect on prices. The modern problem is to determine how an observable signal with no influence on fundamentals can nonetheless have, via expectations, an effect on prices.

$x_{1i} = x_{2i} = \cdots = x_{si} = \cdots = x_{Si}$. To see this, suppose that, for every $i$ and $s$, we replace the consumption bundle of consumer $i$ in state $s$, $x_{si} \in \mathbb{R}^L_+$, by the expected consumption bundle of this consumer: $\bar{x}_i = \sum_s \pi_s x_{si} \in \mathbb{R}^L_+$. The new allocation is state independent, and it is also feasible because

$$\sum_i \bar{x}_i = \sum_i \sum_s \pi_s x_{si} = \sum_s \pi_s \left( \sum_i x_{si} \right) \leq \sum_s \pi_s \left( \sum_i \omega_i \right) = \sum_i \omega_i.$$

By the concavity of $u_i(\cdot)$ it follows that no consumer is worse off:

$$\sum_s \pi_s u_i(\bar{x}_i) = u_i(\bar{x}_i) = u_i \left( \sum_s \pi_s x_{si} \right) \geq \sum_s \pi_s u_i(x_{si}) \qquad \text{for every } i.$$

Because of the Pareto optimality of $(x_1, \ldots, x_I)$, the above weak inequalities must in fact be equalities; that is, $u_i(\bar{x}_i) = \sum_s \pi_s u_i(x_{si})$ for every $i$. But, if so, then the strict concavity of $u_i(\cdot)$ yields $x_{si} = \bar{x}_i$ for every $s$. In summary: the Pareto optimal allocation $(x_1, \ldots, x_I) \in \mathbb{R}^{LSI}$ is state independent.

From the state independence of Pareto optimal allocations and the first welfare theorem we reach the important conclusion that if a system of complete markets over the states $S$ can be organized, then the equilibria are *sunspot free*, that is, consumption is uniform across states. In effect, traders wish to insure completely and have instruments to do so.

It turns out, however, that if there is not a complete set of insurance opportunities, then the above conclusion does not hold true. Sunspot-free, Pareto optimal equilibria always exist (just make the market "not pay attention" to the sunspot; see Exercise 19.F.1). But it is now possible for the consumption allocation of some Radner equilibria to depend on the state, and consequently to fail the Pareto optimality test. In such an equilibrium consumers expect different prices in different states, and their expectations end up being self-fulfilling. The simplest, and most trivial, example is when there are no assets whatsoever ($K = 0$). Then a system of spot prices $(p_1, \ldots, p_S) \in \mathbb{R}^{LS}$ is a Radner equilibrium if and only if every $p_s$ is a Walrasian equilibrium price vector for the spot economy defined by $\{(u_i(\cdot), \omega_i)\}_{i=1}^{i=I}$. If, as is perfectly possible, this economy admits several distinct Walrasian equilibria, then by selecting different equilibrium price vectors for different states, we obtain a sunspot equilibrium, and hence a Pareto inefficient Radner equilibrium. ∎

We have seen that Radner equilibrium allocations need not be Pareto optimal, and so, in principle, there may exist reallocations of consumption that make all consumers at least as well off, and at least one consumer strictly better off. It is important to recognize, however, that this *need not* imply that a welfare authority who is "as constrained in interstate transfers as the market is" can achieve a Pareto optimum. An allocation that cannot be Pareto improved by such an authority is called a *constrained Pareto optimum*. A more significant and reasonable welfare question to ask is, therefore, whether Radner equilibrium allocations are constrained Pareto optimal. We now address this matter.[25]

_____

25. This is a typical instance of a *second-best* welfare issue. We have already encountered problems of this kind in Chapters 13 and 14, and we shall do so again in Chapter 22.

To proceed with the analysis we need a precise description of the constrained feasible set and of the corresponding notion of constrained Pareto optimality. This is most simply done in the context where there is a single commodity per state, that is, $L = 1$. The important implication of this assumption is that then the amount of consumption good that any consumer $i$ gets in the different states is entirely determined by the portfolio $z_i$. Indeed, $x_{si} = \sum_k z_{ki} r_{sk} + \omega_{si}$. Hence, we can let

$$U_i^*(z_i) = U_i^*(z_{1i}, \dots, z_{Ki}) = U_i(\sum_k z_{ki} r_{1k} + \omega_{1i}, \dots, \sum_k z_{ki} r_{Sk} + \omega_{Si})$$

denote the utility induced by the portfolio $z_i$. The definition of constrained Pareto optimality is then quite natural.

**Definition 19.F.1:** The asset allocation $(z_1, \dots, z_I) \in \mathbb{R}^{KI}$ is constrained Pareto optimal if it is feasible (i.e., $\sum_i z_i \leq 0$) and if there is no other feasible asset allocation $(z_1', \dots, z_I') \in \mathbb{R}^{KI}$ such that

$$U_i^*(z_1', \dots, z_I') \geq U_i^*(z_1, \dots, z_I) \qquad \text{for every } i,$$

with at least one inequality strict.

In this $L = 1$ context the utility maximization problem of consumer $i$ becomes

$$\underset{z_i \in \mathbb{R}^K}{\text{Max}} \quad U_i^*(z_{1i}, \dots, z_{Ki})$$

$$\text{s.t.} \ q \cdot z_i \leq 0.$$

Suppose that $z_i^* \in \mathbb{R}^K$ for $i = 1, \dots, I$, is a family of solutions to these individual problems, for the asset price vector $q \in \mathbb{R}^K$. Then $q \in \mathbb{R}^K$ is a Radner equilibrium price if and only if $\sum_i z_i^* \leq 0$.[26] Note that this has become now a perfectly conventional equilibrium problem with $K$ commodities [see Exercise 19.F.2 for a discussion of the properties of $U_i^*(\cdot)$]. To it we can apply the first welfare theorem (Proposition 16.C.1) and reach the conclusion of Proposition 19.F.1.

**Proposition 19.F.1:** Suppose that there two periods and only one consumption good in the second period. Then any Radner equilibrium is *constrained Pareto optimal* in the sense that there is no possible redistribution of assets in the first period that leaves every consumer as well off and at least one consumer strictly better off.[27,28]

The situation considered in Proposition 19.F.1 is very particular in that once the initial asset portfolio of a consumer is determined, his overall consumption is fully determined: with only one consumption good, there are no possibilities for trade once the state occurs. In particular, second-period relative prices do not matter, simply because there are no such prices. Things change if there is more than one

---

26. Recall that, given $z_i$, the consumptions in every state are determined. Also, the price of consumption good in every state is formally fixed to be 1.

27. We reemphasize that the term *constrained* is appropriate. Wealth can be transferred across individuals and states only by trade in the given set of assets. To see how restrictive this can be, suppose that there are no assets. Then the welfare authority has no policy instrument whatsoever.

28. In our current discussion, all consumption takes place in the second period. This is a simplification that does not affect the validity of the proposition. If the welfare authority can also redistribute consumption that takes place in the first period, then the Radner equilibrium allocations will still be constrained Pareto optimal.

consumption good in the second period, or if there are more than two periods. Consider the two-period case with $L > 1$: Then we cannot summarize the individual decision problem by means of an indirect utility of the asset portfolio. The relative prices expected in the second period[29] also matter. This substantially complicates the formulation of a notion of constrained Pareto optimality. Be that as it may, there appears not to be a useful generalization of the "constrained Pareto optimal" concept in which we could assert the constrained Pareto optimality of Radner equilibrium allocations. Example 19.F.2, due to Hart (1975), makes the point. In it we have an economy with several Radner equilibria where two of them are Pareto ordered. That is, we have a Radner equilibrium that is Pareto dominated by another Radner equilibrium. To the extent that it seems natural to allow a welfare authority, at the very least, to select equilibria, it follows that the first equilibrium is not constrained Pareto optimal.[30]

**Example 19.F.2:** *Pareto Ordered Equilibria.* Let $I = 2$, $L = 2$, and $S = 2$. There are no assets ($K = 0$). The two consumers have, as endowments, one unit of every good in every state. The utility functions are of the form $\pi_{1i}u_i(x_{11i}, x_{21i}) + \pi_{2i}u_i(x_{12i}, x_{22i})$. Note that although the probability assessments are different for the two consumers (these probabilities will be specified in a moment), the spot economies are identical in the two states. Suppose that this spot economy has several distinct equilibria (e.g., it could be the exchange economy in Figure 15.B.9). Let $p'$, $p'' \in \mathbb{R}^2$ be the Walrasian prices for two of these equilibria and let $v_i(p)$ be the spot market utility associated with $u_i(\cdot, \cdot)$ and the spot price vector $p \in \mathbb{R}^2$. Suppose that $v_1(p') > v_1(p'')$. By Pareto optimality in the spot market, $v_2(p') < v_2(p'')$.

We now define two Radner equilibria. The first has equilibrium prices $(p_1, p_2) = (p', p'') \in \mathbb{R}^4$ and the second has $(p_1, p_2) = (p'', p') \in \mathbb{R}^4$. Because there is no possibility of transferring wealth across states, these are indeed Radner equilibrium prices and, moreover, they are so for any probability estimates $\pi_i$. However, the expected utility of these Radner equilibria for the different consumers depends on the $\pi_i$. We can see now that if consumer 1 believes that the first state is more likely than the second, that is, he has $\pi_{11} > \frac{1}{2}$, then he will prefer the first equilibrium to the second. Indeed, $\pi_{11} > \frac{1}{2}$ and $v_1(p') > v_1(p'')$ imply $\pi_{11}v_1(p') + \pi_{21}v_1(p'') > \pi_{11}v_1(p'') + \pi_{21}v_1(p')$. Similarly, if the second consumer believes that the second state is more likely than the first, that is, he has $\pi_{22} > \frac{1}{2}$, then he will *also* prefer the first equilibrium to the second: $\pi_{22} > \frac{1}{2}$ and $v_2(p') < v_2(p'')$ imply $\pi_{12}v_2(p') + \pi_{22}v_2(p'') > \pi_{12}v_2(p'') + \pi_{22}v_2(p')$. Thus, the Radner equilibrium with prices $(p', p'')$ Pareto dominates the one with prices $(p'', p')$. ∎

The consensus emerging in the literature seems to be that failures of restricted Pareto optimality (for natural meanings of this concept) are not only possible but even typical [Geanakoplos and Polemarchakis (1986)]. In Exercise 19.F.3 you are asked to develop a related optimality paradox: it is possible for the set of assets to expand and for everybody to be worse off at the new equilibrium! We shall not pursue the constrained optimality analysis

---

29. Or the relative prices of goods between the second and third period, if we are considering more than two dates.

30. That is, the first equilibrium is not Pareto optimal relative to any set of constrained feasible allocations that includes all Radner equilibrium allocations.

in any greater depth. At some point the analysis runs into the difficulty that it is hard to proceed sensibly without tackling the difficult problem of the determination of the asset structure.

We could also analyze the positive issues studied in Chapter 17 within an incomplete market setting. For existence, there is a new set of complexities related to the fact that unbounded short sales are possible. In some contexts this may lead to existence failures (see Exercise 19.F.4).[31] New subtleties also arise for the issue of the determinacy of equilibria (i.e., the number and local uniqueness of equilibria). As we have seen in Section 17.D, with a complete asset structure we have generic finiteness. But with incomplete markets the nature of the assets (e.g., whether real or financial) matters, as may the size of $S$.

# 19.G Firm Behavior in General Equilibrium Models under Uncertainty

In the previous sections we have concentrated on the study of exchange economies. For once, this has not been just for simplicity. The consideration of production and firms is genuinely more difficult in a context of possibly incomplete markets. The reason relates to the issue of the objectives of the firm.[32]

As before, we consider a setting with two periods, $t = 0$ and $t = 1$, and $S$ possible states at $t = 1$. There are $L$ physical commodities traded in the spot markets of period $t = 1$ and $K$ assets traded at $t = 0$. There is no consumption at $t = 0$. The returns of the assets are in physical amounts of the good 1 (which we call the numeraire). The $S \times K$ return matrix is denoted $R$.

We introduce into our model a firm that produces a random amount of numeraire at date $t = 1$ (perhaps by means of inputs used at time $t = 0$, but we do not formalize this part explicitly). We let $(a_1, \dots, a_S)$ denote the state-contingent levels of production of the firm. There are also shares $\theta_i \geq 0$, with $\sum_i \theta_i = 1$, giving the proportion of the firm that belongs to consumer $i$. We take, for the rest of this section (except in the small-type paragraphs at the end) the natural point of view that the firm is an asset with return vector $a = (a_1, \dots, a_S)$ whose shares are tradeable in the financial markets at $t = 0$.[33]

Suppose now that the firm can actually choose, within a range, its (random) production plan. Say, therefore, that there is a set $A \subset \mathbb{R}^S$ of possible choices of return

31. Unbounded short sales are at the origin of a discontinuity in the dependence on asset returns of the space of attainable wealth transfers across states. No matter how close asset returns (in dollar terms) may be to displaying a linear dependence, consumers can plan to attain, by using trades of very large magnitude, any wealth transfer in the subspace spanned by the asset returns. But when returns become exactly linearly dependent, this attainable subspace suddenly drops in dimension. As indicated, this can lead to an existence failure in some contexts. The model we have analyzed in this chapter is not, however, one of those. If, as here, in every state all assets have returns in a single good, which, moreover, is the same across assets, then the discontinuity does not arise.

32. The classic paper on this topic is Diamond (1967). For a more recent survey see Merton (1982).

33. A minor difference with the setting so far is that the firm does really produce the vector $(a_1, \dots, a_S)$, and therefore the total endowment of this asset is not zero. In fact, by putting $\sum_i \theta_i = 1$ we have normalized this total endowment to be 1.

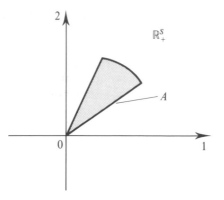

**Figure 19.G.1**

An example of possible production choices of the firm.

vectors $(a_1, \ldots, a_S) \in A$ of the firm. See Figure 19.G.1 for the case where $S = 2$. We assume that the return vector $a \in A$ is chosen before the financial markets of period $t = 0$ open. Thus, the decision is made by the *initial* shareholders (since shares may be sold in period $t = 0$, the shareholders at the end of period $t = 0$ may be a different set). Which production plan should these initial owners choose? It turns out that the answer is very simple if $A$ can be spanned by the existing assets and is very difficult if it cannot.

**Definition 19.G.1:** A set $A \subset \mathbb{R}^S$ of random variables is *spanned* by a given asset structure if every $a \in A$ is in the range of the return matrix $R$ of the asset structure, that is, if every $a \in A$ can be expressed as a linear combination of the available asset returns.

If we assume, first, that $A$ is spanned by $R$ and, second, that we are dealing with a small project (i.e., all the possible productions $a \in A$ are small relative to the size of the economy; e.g., $a_s/\|\sum_i \omega_{si}\|$ is small for all $s$), then we are (almost) justified in taking the equilibrium spot prices $p = (p_1, \ldots, p_S) \in \mathbb{R}^{LS}$ and asset prices $q = (q_1, \ldots, q_K) \in \mathbb{R}^K$ as constants independent of the particular production plan chosen by the firm.[34] For the asset prices $q \in \mathbb{R}^K$ the *market value* $v(a, q)$ of any production plan $a \in A$ can be computed by arbitrage: if $a = \sum_k \alpha_k r_k$ then $v(a, q) = \sum_k \alpha_k q_k$. In Exercise 19.G.1 you are asked to show that if the firm is added as a new asset to the given list of assets, and each production plan $a \in A$ is priced at its arbitrage value $v(a)$, then any budget-feasible consumption plan of any consumer can actually be reached without purchasing any shares of the firm (the fact can be deduced from Proposition 19.E.3). Thus, for fixed asset prices $q \in \mathbb{R}^K$ and spot prices $p = (p_1, \ldots, p_S) \in \mathbb{R}^{LS}$, the budget constraint of consumer $i$ is[35]

---

34. Both assumptions are important for this conclusion. Suppose for a moment that there are zero total endowments of the asset. Then, since the asset is redundant, Proposition 19.E.3 (see also Exercise 19.E.4) implies that at the Radner equilibrium the new asset is absorbed without any change in prices. What we are now assuming is that this remains approximately true if the total endowment of the asset is small (i.e., if the project is small).

35. Note that the value of the initial endowments at $t = 0$ is the value of the shares of the firm $\theta_i v(a, q)$.

$B_{ai} = \{(x_{1i}, \ldots, x_{Si}) \in \mathbb{R}_+^{LS} :$ there is a portfolio $z_i \in \mathbb{R}^K$ such that

$$p_s \cdot (x_{is} - \omega_{is}) \leq \sum_k p_{1s} r_{sk} z_{ki} \text{ for every } s, \text{ and } q \cdot z_i \leq \theta_i v(a, q)\}.$$

(19.G.1)

It follows from the form of this budget constraint that at constant prices every consumer–owner (i.e., any $i$ with $\theta_i > 0$) faced with the choice between two production plans $a, a' \in A$, will prefer the one with higher market value. Indeed, if $v(a, q) \geq v(a', q)$ then $B_{a'i} \subset B_{ai}$. Thus, the objective of market value maximization will be the *unanimous* desire of the firm's initial owners.[36]

If $A$ is not spannable by the given asset structure we run into at least two serious difficulties. The first difficulty has to do with price *quoting* and is common to any commodity innovation problem. Without spanning, the value of a production plan $a \in A$ cannot be computed from current asset prices simply by arbitrage. The value is not, so to speak, implicitly quoted in the economy. Therefore, it would need to be anticipated by the agents of the economy from their understanding of the workings of the overall economy—no mean task.

The second difficulty, more specific to the financial context, has to do with price *taking*. Due to the possibility of unlimited short sales there is a discontinuity in the plausibility of the price-taking assumption. With spanning we can argue, as we did, that if the project is small then the effect of production decisions on asset prices, or on spot prices at $t = 1$, is also small. But if a new asset $a \in A$, no matter how small, is not generated by the current asset structure, then its availability increases the span of available wealth transfers by one whole extra dimension. The impact is therefore substantial, and may well have a dramatic effect on prices.[37] There is then no reason for owners' preferences over different production plans to be dictated merely by the increase in wealth at the prices prior to the introduction of the firm (see Exercise 19.G.2). These two difficulties, to repeat, are serious. There is no easy way out.

---

A variation of the above model entirely eliminates the asset role of the firm at $t = 0$. Let us assume that the firm's shares cannot be traded at $t = 0$.[38] If owners at $t = 0$ choose $a \in A$, this simply means that their endowments at $t = 1$ are modified by the random variable $\theta_i a$ that, recall, pays in good 1 (i.e., the new endowment of consumer $i$ becomes $(\omega_{si} + (\theta_i a_s, 0, \ldots, 0)) \in \mathbb{R}^L$ for every state $s$).

If $a \in A$ can be spanned, then we are as in the previous model. It does not matter whether shares of the firm can be sold or not at $t = 0$. In either case consumers can take positions in the asset markets that will guarantee that the resulting final consumptions at $t = 1$ are the same (Exercise 19.G.3).

If $a \in A$ cannot be spanned, matters are different. The good news is that, because no new tradeable asset is created at $t = 0$, the price-taking discontinuity problem disappears. The bad news is that there is now another difficulty: Because there is no market for the shares at $t = 0$, the value of the asset cannot be computed as a deterministic amount at $t = 0$. It is rather a

---

36. As long as the project is small and, consequently, the prices are almost constant.

37. Recall that short sales are possible. One way out of the dilemma is to put a bound on short sales of roughly the size of the possible production vectors. The cost of this assumption is that we have then to give up the theory of arbitrage pricing.

38. Or perhaps we are now at the end of period $t = 0$ and the financial markets have already closed.

*random variable* at $t = 1$ and therefore the risk attitudes of the consumer–owners will be essential to the determination of the preferred $a \in A$. In particular, unanimity of the consumer–owners should not be expected (see Exercise 19.G.4).

# 19.H Imperfect Information

Up to now we have concentrated the analysis on a model where spot trading for goods occurs under conditions of perfect information about the state of the world. In this section, we relax this feature by considering the possibility that this information is not perfect. In doing so we shall see that there is a key difference between the case of *symmetric* information (all traders have the same information), which is largely reducible to the previous theory, and the case of *asymmetric* information, where a host of new and difficult conceptual problems arise.

To focus on essentials, we deal with trade in a single period. You can think of it as the period $t = 1$ of the previous treatments. In this period, one of several states $s = 1, \ldots, S$ can arise. Once a state occurs, we consider the simplest case in which there is a single spot market. In this market a first commodity (good, service, . . .) is traded against a second good, to be thought of as money (thus, $L = 2$). The price of the second good is normalized to 1. We reserve the symbol $p \in \mathbb{R}$ for the price of the nonmonetary commodity.

There are $I$ consumers. Given probabilities $\pi = (\pi_{1i}, \ldots, \pi_{Si})$ over the states, a random consumption vector $x_i = (x_{1i}, \ldots, x_{Si}) \in \mathbb{R}^{2S}$ is evaluated by consumer $i$ according to an extended von Neumann–Morgenstern utility function:

$$U_i(x_i) = \sum_s \pi_{si} u_{si}(x_{si}),$$

where $u_{si}(\cdot)$ is consumer $i$'s Bernoulli utility function in state $s$. Consumer $i$ also has an initial, state-dependent, endowment vector $\omega_i = (\omega_{1i}, \ldots, \omega_{Si}) \in \mathbb{R}^{2S}$, and a *signal function* $\sigma_i(\cdot)$ assigning a real number $\sigma_i(s) \in \mathbb{R}$ to every state $s \in S$.

The state $s$ occurs at the beginning of the period. We assume that, once this has happened, consumer $i$ receives the initial endowment $\omega_{si}$ and the signal $\sigma_i(s) \in \mathbb{R}$. The interpretation is that consumer $i$ can distinguish two states $s, s' \in S$ if and only if $\sigma_i(s) \neq \sigma_i(s')$.[39] Consistent with this interpretation, we require that the endowments be *measurable* with respect to the signal function, that is, $\omega_{si} = \omega_{s'i}$ whenever $\sigma_i(s) = \sigma_i(s')$ (thus, we can write $\omega_{si}$ as $\omega_{\sigma_i(s)i}$). In this manner the endowments of goods of consumer $i$ do not reveal to him information about the state of the world that is not already revealed by the signal. After every consumer gets his signal, the spot market operates. Finally, at the end of the period, the state is revealed and consumption takes place.[40]

---

39. Equivalently, as we did (in small type) in Section 19.B, we could use *information partitions* instead of explicit signal functions. The information partition $\mathscr{S}_i$ associated with the signal $\sigma_i(\cdot)$ is composed of the events $\{s \in S : \sigma_i(s) = c\}$ obtained by letting $c \in \mathbb{R}$ run over all possible values.

40. In a more general, multistage, situation, some information is revealed at the end of the period and the economy moves on to the next period.

*Symmetric Information*

We say that information is *symmetric* if any two states, $s, s' \in S$, are distinguishable by one consumer $i$ if and only if they are distinguishable by every other consumer $k$; that is, $\sigma_i(s) \neq \sigma_i(s')$ if and only if $\sigma_k(s) \neq \sigma_k(s')$. Thus, with symmetric information we can as well assume that all consumers share the same signal function. We therefore write $\sigma_i(\cdot) = \sigma(\cdot)$ for all $i$. We can think of $\sigma(\cdot)$ as a public signal.

With symmetric information the determination of the spot prices proceeds in a manner entirely parallel to what we have seen so far. Suppose that state $s$ occurs. Then every consumer $i$ receives the signal $\sigma(s)$ and initial endowments $\omega_{\sigma(s)i}$.[41] From the signal and the prior probabilities $\pi_i = (\pi_{1i}, \ldots, \pi_{Si})$, which we take to be strictly positive, he computes his posterior probabilities over the different states $s'$ as

$$\pi_{s'i} \mid \sigma(s) = \frac{\pi_{s'i}}{\sum_{\{s'' : \sigma(s'') = \sigma(s)\}} \pi_{s''i}}$$

for any $s'$ with $\sigma(s') = \sigma(s)$, and $\pi_{s'i} \mid \sigma(s) = 0$ otherwise. The utility of a consumption bundle $x_i \in \mathbb{R}^2$ conditional on the signal $\sigma(s)$ is then

$$u_i(x_i \mid \sigma(s)) = \sum_{s'} (\pi_{s'i} \mid \sigma(s)) u_{s'i}(x_i).$$

Therefore we have, conditional on $s$, a perfectly well-specified spot economy. Under the usual assumption of price-taking behavior, an equilibrium price will be generated. We write this price as $p(\sigma(s)) \in \mathbb{R}$.[42]

The concept of an information signal function lends itself to interesting comparative statics exercises.

**Definition 19.H.1:** The signal function $\sigma': S \to \mathbb{R}$ is *at least as informative* as $\sigma: S \to \mathbb{R}$ if $\sigma(s) \neq \sigma(s')$ implies $\sigma'(s) \neq \sigma'(s')$ for any pair $s, s'$. It is *more informative* if, in addition, $\sigma'(s) \neq \sigma'(s')$ for some pair $s, s'$ with $\sigma(s) = \sigma(s')$.[43]

Two arbitrary signal functions $\sigma(\cdot), \sigma'(\cdot)$ may well not be comparable by the "at least as informative" concept. If they are, it is natural to ask if the more informative signal leads to a welfare improvement. We pose the "improvement" question in an ex ante sense (see Exercise 19.H.1 for an interim and an ex post sense); that is, we want to compare the expected utility of the different consumers under $\sigma(\cdot)$ and under $\sigma'(\cdot)$ when the expectation is evaluated *before* $s$ occurs.

---

41. The endowments could, of course, be the result of the execution of forward trades entered upon in the past. The measurability requirement, namely, the restriction that endowments depend on the state only through the signal, then captures the restriction that a forward contract can only be made contingent on information available at the time of the execution of the contract (strictly speaking, it should be conditional on information available at that time to the contract enforcing authority).

42. Because updated probabilities and utility functions depend only on the values of the signal, we have imposed the natural requirement that the clearing price depends also only on the signal; that is, we write $p(\sigma(s))$ rather than $p(s)$. Indeed, how could the (unmodeled) market mechanism manage to distinguish states that no consumer can distinguish?

43. In terms of the corresponding information partitions, the signal $\sigma'(\cdot)$ is more informative than $\sigma(\cdot)$ if the information partition of $\sigma'(\cdot)$ refines the information partition of $\sigma(\cdot)$.

Consider first the decision problem of a single consumer $i$. Suppose, for simplicity, that the spot price $p \in \mathbb{R}$ and the consumer wealth $w_i \in \mathbb{R}$ are given and are independent of $s$ (a more general case is presented in Exercise 19.H.2). For any signal function $\sigma(\cdot)$ the consumer forms a consumption plan $x_i^{\sigma(\cdot)} \in \mathbb{R}^{2S}$ as follows: Subject to the restriction that $x_{si}^{\sigma(\cdot)} = x_{s'i}^{\sigma(\cdot)}$ whenever $\sigma(s') = \sigma(s)$, the consumer chooses, for every possible state $s$, a consumption $x_{si}^{\sigma(\cdot)}$ in his budget set that maximizes expected utility conditional on the signal $\sigma(s)$. The ex ante utility of the information signal function $\sigma(\cdot)$ is therefore $\sum_s \pi_{si} u_{si}(x_{si}^{\sigma(\cdot)})$.

**Proposition 19.H.1:** In the single-consumer problem, if the signal function $\sigma'(\cdot)$ is at least as informative as the signal function $\sigma(\cdot)$, then the ex ante utility derived from $\sigma'(\cdot)$, $\sum_s \pi_{si} u_{si}(x_{si}^{\sigma'(\cdot)})$, is at least as large as the ex ante utility derived from $\sigma(\cdot)$, $\sum_s \pi_{si} u_{si}(x_{si}^{\sigma(\cdot)})$.

**Proof:** The first observation is that for any $\sigma(\cdot)$, $x_i^{\sigma(\cdot)}$ solves the problem

$$\text{Max} \quad \sum_s \pi_{si} u_{si}(x_{si})$$

$$\text{s.t. } x_i \in B_i^{\sigma(\cdot)} = \{x_i \in \mathbb{R}^{2S} : px_{1si} + x_{2si} \le w_i \text{ for every } s, \text{ and}$$

$$x_{si} = x_{s'i} \text{ whenever } \sigma(s) = \sigma(s')\}.$$

You are asked to verify this formally in Exercise 19.H.3.

The second observation is that if $\sigma'(\cdot)$ is at least as informative as $\sigma(\cdot)$, then $B_i^{\sigma(\cdot)} \subset B_i^{\sigma'(\cdot)}$. Again you should verify this in Exercise 19.H.3.

It follows that moving from $\sigma(\cdot)$ to $\sigma'(\cdot)$ we only expand the constraint set of the consumer's problem. In doing so, the maximum value cannot decrease. ∎

The claim of Proposition 19.H.1 is intuitive: in an isolated single-person decision problem, a more informative signal does not upset the feasibility of any decision plan (hence, it brings about an expansion of the feasible set) because the decision maker always has the option not to act on the extra information provided by $\sigma'(\cdot)$ over $\sigma(\cdot)$. Unfortunately, this line of argument does *not* apply to a system with interacting decision makers. At the equilibrium the budget set of a single consumer may well be affected by the signal, even if the consumer does not use it. It suffices that the other consumers use it and that, as a result, the new information finds its way into the spot prices. Example 19.H.1 shows that, because of this, it is even possible for an increase of information to make *everybody* (ex ante) worse off.

**Example 19.H.1:** Suppose there are two consumers, two commodities, and two equally probable states $s = 1, 2$. In both states the two consumers' endowments of the two physical goods are $\omega_1 = (1, 0)$ for consumer 1 and $\omega_2 = (0, 1)$ for consumer 2. In total, therefore, there is one unit of every commodity in every state. The two consumers have the same von Neumann–Morgenstern expected utility function. Their state dependent Bernoulli utility function is

$$u_{si}(x_{1si}, x_{2si}) = \beta_s \sqrt{x_{1si}} + (1 - \beta_s)\sqrt{x_{2si}}$$

where $\beta_1 = 1$ and $\beta_2 = 0$. Thus, in state 1 the second good is worthless, while in state 2 the first good is worthless.

Suppose first that there is no information (i.e., there is no signal function distinguishing the two states). Then there is a single spot market where every consumer chooses amounts $(x_{1i}, x_{2i})$ of the two commodities so as to maximize the expected utility function

$$\tfrac{1}{2}\sqrt{x_{1i}} + \tfrac{1}{2}\sqrt{x_{2i}}.$$

By symmetry (but nonetheless compute the first order conditions) we see that at equilibrium every consumer will get half of each commodity and have an expected utility of $1/\sqrt{2}$. Hence, in this no-information equilibrium every consumer has managed to insure against the possibility that the good he owns turns out to be worthless.

Suppose that instead we have a perfectly informative signal function revealing the state prior to the opening of the spot market. Then the spot market equilibrium will be different under the two states. What happens now is that in each state one good is known to be worthless and, therefore, there is no possibility of trade in the spot market: Each consumer consumes his endowment, receiving a utility of 1 in one state and of 0 in the other. Ex ante this means that under perfect information every consumer has an expected utility of $\frac{1}{2} < 1/\sqrt{2}$. Thus, we see that the availability of a more informative signal function makes everybody worse off. The reason is that the availability of information destroys insurance opportunities [a possibility first pointed out by Hirshleifer (1973)].[44] ∎

*Asymmetric Information*

Suppose now that information is not symmetric; that is, the signal functions $\sigma_i(\cdot)$ are private and not necessarily the same across consumers. How to proceed then? A first thought is to proceed exactly as before. When $s$ occurs every consumer observes $\sigma_i(s)$ and uses his signal function $\sigma_i(\cdot)$ to update probabilities and utility functions. This defines a spot economy to which we can associate in the usual way a spot market clearing price written as $p(\sigma_1(s), \ldots, \sigma_I(s))$. Note that the price $p(\sigma_1, \ldots, \sigma_S)$ depends on *all* the individual signals: One says that the price *aggregates* the information of the market participants. In particular, the *price function* $p(s) = p(\sigma_1(s), \ldots, \sigma_I(s))$ need not be measurable with respect to the individual signal functions $\sigma_i(\cdot)$; that is, it may be that two states $s, s' \in S$ are *not* distinguishable by consumer $i$ (i.e., $\sigma_i(s) = \sigma_I(s')$), but *are* distinguished by the market [i.e., $p(\sigma_1(s), \ldots, \sigma_I(s)) \neq p(\sigma_1(s'), \ldots, \sigma_I(s'))$]. This raises an important difficulty that we discuss by means of Example 19.H.2.

---

44. Suppose that our period is period 1 and that previous to it there is a period 0 in which forward trade could conceivably take place. Under the no-information scenario there can be no contingent trade at $t = 0$ since the two states cannot be distinguished at $t = 1$. The model considered, therefore, is as complete as it can be (hence, the equilibrium is Pareto optimal relative to the no-information structure). This is not so for the model with perfect information. There is then no informational impediment to the creation of a complete set of contingent markets at $t = 0$. With them the possibility of insurance would be restored. In general, if markets are complete [relative to the information signal function $\sigma(\cdot)$] then the equilibrium is a Pareto optimum [relative to $\sigma(\cdot)$] and, therefore, if information improves (*and the corresponding additional markets are created*) some traders may gain and some may lose (i.e., there may be distribution effects) but overall the new vector of ex ante expected utilities is at the frontier of an expanded utility possibility set. We can conclude, therefore, that if markets are always complete relative to the information signal (i.e., a forward market contingent on every signal takes place at $t = 0$), then not everyone can end up worse off if the information signal function improves.

**Example 19.H.2:** The economy has two goods and two consumers. The two consumers have identical utility functions $u_i(x_{1i}, x_{2i}) = \beta \ln x_{1i} + x_{2i}$. The parameter $\beta$ is the same for the two consumers and it is uncertain. It can take the values $\beta = 1$ and $\beta = 2$ with equal probability. (Hence, we can think that there are two equally probable states: One yields $\beta = 1$ and the other $\beta = 2$.) The two consumers have deterministic endowments of one unit of the first good (because of quasilinearity with respect to the second good we do not need to specify endowments of the latter).

The first consumer has an informative signal $\sigma_1(\beta) = \beta$ that allows him to distinguish the two possible values of $\beta$. The second consumer is not informed: his signal function has $\sigma_2(\beta) = k$ for some constant $k$.

After nature has determined the value of $\beta$ and the information $\sigma_1(\beta)$, $\sigma_2(\beta)$ has been transmitted to the two consumers, a spot market takes place (as usual, the price of the numeraire commodity is fixed to be 1). Since the first consumer knows $\beta$, his demand, given the price $p \in \mathbb{R}$ of the first good, is $x_{11}(p; \beta) = \beta/p$. The second, uninformed, consumer will equalize his expected marginal utility to the price. Hence, his demand function, which does not depend on $\beta$, is

$$x_{12}(p) = \frac{1}{p}\left[\frac{1}{2}1 + \frac{1}{2}2\right] = \frac{3}{2p}. \tag{19.H.1}$$

Solving the market equilibrium equation $x_{11}(p; \beta) + x_{12}(p) = 2$ we get the equilibrium price function

$$p(\beta) = \tfrac{1}{4}(3 + 2\beta).$$

Note now that $p(1) \neq p(2)$. This means *that the price reveals the informed consumer's information.* If so, then it is logical to suppose that the uninformed consumer will try to use the observed market price to infer the unobserved value of $\beta$. There is really no good reason to prevent him from doing so. But, once he does, his demand will no longer be given by (19.H.1), and the price function $p(\beta)$ specified above will no longer clear markets for every possible value of $\beta$. This is the difficulty we wanted to illustrate. It suggests that what is needed is an equilibrium notion embodying a consistency requirement between the information revealed by prices and the information used by consumers. ■

We have argued in Example 19.H.2 that it makes sense to require that the information revealed by prices be taken into account by the consumers in making their consumption plans in the different spot markets. Suppose, therefore, that $p(s) = p(\sigma_1(s), \ldots, \sigma_I(s))$ is an arbitrary price function. Interpret it as a specification of the prices expected to hold by the consumers at the different states. We could now view this price function as a public signal function and let any consumer use it in combination with his private signal. That is, when state $s$ occurs, consumer $i$ knows that the event $E_{p(s), \sigma_i(s)} = \{s' : p(s') = p(s) \text{ and } \sigma_i(s') = \sigma_i(s)\}$ has occurred and updates his probability estimates of any state $s' \in E_{p(s), \sigma_i(s)}$ to

$$\pi_{s'i} \mid p(s), \sigma_i(s) = \frac{\pi_{s'i}}{\sum_{\{s'' : s'' \in E_{p(s), \sigma_i(s)}\}} \pi_{s''i}}.$$

If, for the updated utility functions, the price $p(s)$ clears the spot market for every $s$, then we say that the price function $p(\cdot)$ is a *rational expectations equilibrium price function*.[45,46] This is expressed formally in Definition 19.H.2.

**Definition 19.H.2:** The price function $p(\cdot)$ is a *rational expectations equilibrium price function* if, for every $s$, $p(s)$ clears the spot market when every consumer $i$ knows that $s \in E_{p(s), \sigma_i(s)}$ and, therefore, evaluates commodity bundles $x_i \in \mathbb{R}^2$ according to the updated utility function

$$\sum_{s'} (\pi_{s'i} \mid p(s), \sigma_i(s)) u_{s'i}(x_i).$$

We saw in Example 19.H.2 a situation in which all privately observed information is revealed by the spot market price. This suggests the following approach to the determination of a rational expectations equilibrium price function. Imagine (this is merely a hypothetical experiment) that all the individual signal functions are known to all consumers and that for every state the vector of signal values $(\sigma_1(s), \ldots, \sigma_I(s))$ is made public and is, therefore, usable by all consumers to update probabilities and utilities. The market-clearing price function $\hat{p}(s) = \hat{p}(\sigma_1(s), \ldots, \sigma_I(s))$ thus generated is called the *pooled information equilibrium price function*. If the values of $\hat{p}(\cdot)$ distinguish all possible values of $(\sigma_1, \ldots, \sigma_I)$, that is, if $\hat{p}(s) \neq \hat{p}(s')$ whenever $\sigma_i(s) \neq \sigma_i(s')$ for some $s, s'$, and $i$, then we say the price function $\hat{p}(\cdot)$ is *fully revealing*. In other words, the price function is fully revealing if it distinguishes the occurrence of any two states that can be distinguished by some consumer.

We argue now that if the pooled information equilibrium price function $\hat{p}(\cdot)$ is fully revealing, then it must be a rational expectations equilibrium price function. For any $s$, $\hat{p}(s)$ is determined under the assumption that every $i$ knows that $s \in \{s' : \sigma_k(s') = \sigma_k(s) \text{ for all } k\}$. Because the pooled information equilibrium price function $\hat{p}(\cdot)$ is fully revealing, it follows that $\{s' : \sigma_k(s') = \sigma_k(s) \text{ for all } k\} = \{s' : \hat{p}(s') = \hat{p}(s)\}$. Hence, for any $s$, $\hat{p}(s)$ is a market-clearing price when every $i$ knows that $s \in E_{\hat{p}(s), \sigma_i(s)}$. We conclude that $\hat{p}(\cdot)$ is a rational expectations equilibrium price function. In other words: If a pooled information equilibrium price function is fully revealing, then the pooled information used by consumers need not be obtained by violating any privacy constraint but can simply be derived from the public price signals.

**Example 19.H.2 continued:** If both consumers are fully informed, we have the demand functions $x_{11}(p) = x_{12}(p) = \beta/p$. Thus, in this case, the pooled information equilibrium price function is $\hat{p}(\beta) = \beta$. This pooled information equilibrium price function is fully revealing and therefore a rational expectations equilibrium. ∎

---

45. For the concept of rational expectations equilibrium (including additional references), see Green (1973), Grossman (1977) and (1981), Lucas (1972), and Allen (1986).

46. In this section we concentrate on issues relating to information transmission more than on matters concerning spanning or completeness. But note that, as we pointed out in the case of symmetric information (in footnote 44), there is no conceptual difficulty in imagining that previous to the period $t = 1$ under consideration there has been contingent trade for the delivery at $t = 1$ of amounts of physical good conditional on the values of the public signals at $t = 1$ (we call the overall situation complete if such contingent markets exist for every possible value of the public signals). Observe that because the spot price constitutes a public signal, a possible instrument of contingent trade is an asset with returns conditional on the realized value of the spot market price at $t = 1$; options are instances of such assets.

In Example 19.H.3 the pooled information equilibrium price function is not fully revealing and fails to be a rational expectations equilibrium. In fact, in the example no rational expectations equilibrium price function exists.

**Example 19.H.3:** [Kreps (1977)]  There are two commodities and two consumers with utility functions $u_1(x_{11}, x_{21}) = \beta \ln x_{11} + x_{21}$ and $u_2(x_{12}, x_{22}) = (3 - \beta) \ln x_{12} + x_{22}$. As in Example 19.H.2, there are two states yielding values $\beta = 1, 2$ with equal probability. Consumer 1 is completely informed [i.e., $\sigma_1(1) \neq \sigma_1(2)$] while consumer 2 is uninformed [i.e., $\sigma_2(\beta) = $ constant]. In the two states there is a total endowment of the first good of 3 units.

Given a rational expectations equilibrium price function, which we can write as $p(\beta)$, we have two possibilities. Either $p(1) \neq p(2)$, so that the information is revealed and as a consequence $p(\beta)$ coincides with the pooled information equilibrium price function $\hat{p}(\beta)$, or $p(1) = p(2)$ so that the information is not revealed.

The first possibility cannot arise because, if the information is pooled, then for the values $\beta = 1$ and $\beta = 2$ the utility functions are the same in the two states (except that the utility functions of consumers 1 and 2 are switched) and so the spot equilibrium price is also the same in the two states. In fact, $p = 1$ is the price that clears the market in the two states.

But the second possibility cannot arise either. With a constant, nonrevealing, price function, the uninformed consumer has a demand that is independent of the state, whereas the demand of the first (informed) consumer is state dependent. Hence, the same price cannot clear the market in both states.

In summary: If we assume that information is transmitted at equilibrium, then in fact it is not. And if we assume that it is not transmitted, then it is. As a result, we can only conclude that no rational expectation equilibrium price function exists.  ∎

As we have seen, the concept of a fully revealing equilibrium provides a useful tool for the study of markets with asymmetric information. In applications it is more common that we encounter a slightly weaker and more natural version of the full revelation idea. In effect, in order for the pooled information equilibrium price function $\hat{p}(\cdot)$ to be a rational expectations equilibrium price function, we do not need that, for every $s$, $\hat{p}(\cdot)$ reveals precisely the vector of signals $(\sigma_1(s), \ldots, \sigma_I(s))$; it is enough that it reveals a *sufficient statistic* for this vector [or a statistic that is sufficient for every consumer $i$ in conjunction with the private signal $\sigma_i(\cdot)$]. More generally, all we need is that for every possible state $s$ the expressed demand of every consumer $i$ at the price $\hat{p}(s)$ is the same whether the consumer knows the pooled information signed functions $(\sigma_1(\cdot), \ldots, \sigma_I(\cdot))$, and receives the signal vector $(\sigma_1(s), \ldots, \sigma_I(s))$, or instead knows only the signal function $\hat{p}(\cdot)$ [or only $\hat{p}(\cdot)$ and $\sigma_i(\cdot)$].

**Example 19.H.4:**  The basic economy is as in Example 19.H.2. Now, however, the signal of each consumer $i = 1, 2$ is $\sigma_i = \beta^2 + \varepsilon_i$. The $\varepsilon_i$, for $i = 1$ and 2, are noise variables independently distributed and taking the values $\varepsilon_i = -2, -1, 0, 1, 2$ with equal probability.[47]

---

47. All of this could be expressed in terms of underlying states $s = (\beta, \varepsilon_1, \varepsilon_2)$. We would need $2 \times 5 \times 5 = 50$ of them.

Suppose that information is pooled. Then:

(i)   If $\sigma_i = 4$, 5, or 6 for either $i = 1$ or $i = 2$, we know that $\beta = 2$ with probability 1 and therefore $\hat{p}(\sigma_1, \sigma_2) = \beta/2 = 1$.
(ii)  If $\sigma_i = -1$, 0, or 1 for either $i = 1$ or $i = 2$, we know that $\beta = 1$ with probability 1 and therefore $\hat{p}(\sigma_1, \sigma_2) = \beta/2 = \frac{1}{2}$.
(iii) In the remaining cases, $\sigma_i = 2$ or 3 for both $i = 1$ and $i = 2$, the updated probabilities on the two values of $\beta$ remain $\frac{1}{2}$: No useful information is transmitted. Hence the clearing price is $\hat{p}(\sigma_1, \sigma_2) = \frac{3}{2}$ (Exercise 19.H.4).

The price function $\hat{p}(\cdot)$ defined by (i) to (iii) is not fully revealing: Given the value of $\hat{p}(\cdot)$ we cannot deduce from it the specific values of $\sigma_1$ and $\sigma_2$.[48] Yet, the price function $\hat{p}(\cdot)$ is sufficient to distinguish among cases (i) to (iii), and therefore the knowledge of the single function $\hat{p}(\cdot)$ can replace for every consumer the knowledge of the vector of functions $(\sigma_1(\cdot), \sigma_2(\cdot))$. We can say, therefore, that $\hat{p}(\cdot)$ is a sufficient statistic for the signals, and conclude that $\hat{p}(\cdot)$ is a rational expectations price function. ∎

In Example 19.H.5 price function is not a sufficient statistic but it becomes so when combined with the private signal of any consumer.

**Example 19.H.5:** The basic economy and the signals are as in Example 19.H.4, but with three differences. First, there are $I$ consumers. Second, the noise terms $\varepsilon_i$ are now payoff relevant: in particular, $u_i(x_i) = (\beta + \varepsilon_i) \ln x_{1i} + x_{2i}$. Third, half the consumers have their noise uniformly distributed in the interval $[-\frac{2}{3}, \frac{2}{3}]$, whereas the other half is perfectly informed about $\beta$, that is, $\varepsilon_1 = 0$.

The pooled information equilibrium price function is $\hat{p}(\beta, \varepsilon_1, \ldots, \varepsilon_I) = \beta + (1/I)(\sum_i \varepsilon_i)$. Note that this price function reveals $\beta$ [if $\beta = 1$ then $\hat{p}(\cdot) < 1.5$ with probability 1; if $\beta = 2$ then $\hat{p}(\cdot) > 1.5$ with probability 1] but not the individual values of $\varepsilon_i$. However, a consumer $i$ that knows $\beta$ and $\sigma_i = \beta^2 + \varepsilon_i$ also knows $\varepsilon_i$, and therefore, at any given price, expresses a demand that coincides with the pooled information demand. We conclude that the pooled information equilibrium is a rational expectation equilibrium. It is important to observe that, in contrast with Example 19.H.4, the equilibrium price function alone does not now provide a sufficient statistic. At the rational expectations equilibrium the individual utility maximization problems of half the consumers make essential use of the private signal functions. ∎

Example 19.H.5 allows us to address another issue. Suppose that to our general model we add the feature that acquiring the information signal function $\sigma_i(\cdot)$ costs some small amount of money $\delta > 0$. Suppose also that $I$ is large, so that, plausibly, the pooled information price function $\hat{p}(\cdot)$ is not very sensitive to any single consumer $i$ failing to acquire his signal function $\sigma_i(\cdot)$. Then we have the following paradox [see Grossman and Stiglitz (1976)]: If the price function $\hat{p}(\cdot)$ is fully revealing (or is a sufficient statistic by itself), why will any consumer $i$ pay $\delta$ for the signal function $\sigma_i(\cdot)$? Any one consumer would rather not do so and attempt to free ride on the information transmitted by the price system. But if everybody proceeds in this manner, then the price function cannot be fully revealing (there is nothing to reveal)! Example 19.H.5 suggests one way out of this paradox: it can be verified that in the example there is a sufficiently small $\delta > 0$, not dependent on the number $I$, such that at any fixed price $p$, a consumer $i$ with nontrivial $\varepsilon_i$, even if he already knows $\beta$, has an incentive to pay $\delta$ for the improvement of information provided by his private signal (Exercise 19.H.5). ∎

---

48. Recall that "fully revealing" does not mean that we get to know the value of $\beta$, only that we get to know the value of the signals.

Up to now, prices may have conveyed information about an exogenously ocurring state. But in a world of asymmetric information, prices could also convey information on the consumers' endogenously chosen actions, and those actions could matter for individual utilities. For example, the final utility of a consumer may depend not only of the number of units consumed and on exogenous states but also on some other statistic depending on other consumers' actions. If we regard this statistic as a "state" then it is as if states were determined endogenously. To illustrate this point we consider another example—the market for used cars (also referred to as the "lemons market"). With this, we connect with the analysis of adverse selection in Section 13.B and bring this section to a close.

**Example 19.H.6:** *The Lemons Market.* Suppose that consumers fall into two types: potential buyers and potential sellers (of, say, used cars). There are many consumers and twice as many potential sellers as potential buyers. Potential sellers have one unit of the good and potential buyers buy either one unit or none. The peculiarity of this market is that commodities are of two kinds: good and bad. Half the potential sellers have a good product and half have a bad one. The quality, known to the potential sellers, is unrecognizable to the buyers at the moment of trade. A good commodity is worth 1 to the potential seller and 4 to the buyer. A bad commodity is worth nothing to every consumer.

We could call the *state of the market* the fraction $\alpha \in [0, 1]$ of the commodities supplied that are of good quality. If the state of the market is $\alpha$, then a buyer paying $p$ gets expected utility $4\alpha - p$. The problem is that the state of the market depends on the price (thus, as before, the price provides information about the utility derived from consuming one unit of the good). Indeed, for any $p > 0$, every unit of bad commodity will be supplied to the market. But for $p < 1$ no unit of the good commodity will be supplied, whereas for $p > 1$ every unit of the good commodity will be supplied. Therefore, we must have $\alpha = 0$ for $p < 1$, $\alpha \in [0, \frac{1}{2}]$ for $p = 1$, and $\alpha = \frac{1}{2}$ for $p > 1$. If a pair $(\alpha, p)$ satisfies these inequalities then we say that the pair $(\alpha, p)$ is admissible. Note that the inequalities can be equivalently expressed as $p \le 1$ for $\alpha = 0$, $p = 1$ for $\alpha \in (0, \frac{1}{2})$ and $p \ge 1$ for $\alpha = \frac{1}{2}$.

A potential buyer will deduce $\alpha = 0$ if he observes $p < 1$, and $\alpha = \frac{1}{2}$ if $p > 1$. Potential buyers may or may not express a demand depending on this inference. It is natural to say that if at the admissible pair $(\alpha, p)$ the total demand is not larger than the total supply then we are at a *rational expectations* equilibrium. In fact, in our case any admissible pair $(\alpha, p)$ turns out to be a rational expectations equilibrium. Note, however, that for some $(\alpha, p)$ the supply is larger than the demand (e.g. at $\alpha = \frac{1}{2}$, $p = 3$ no demand is expressed).[49] ∎

---

49. For simplicity we have chosen an example where it is always the case that the forthcoming demand is not larger than the forthcoming supply. It is because of this that all admissible pairs $(\alpha, p)$ may appear as equilibria. More generally, some of these pairs may be eliminated because forthcoming demand is larger than supply. It is also worth observing that it would not be legitimate to impose as an equilibrium condition that demand be larger than or equal to supply. Suppose, for example, that $\alpha = \frac{1}{2}$ and $p = 1.5$. Then total supply is 2 while total demand is 1. The usual argument (underlying the tâtonnement dynamics) for downward pressure on demand is that some frustrated seller would attempt to sell to some buyer at a price $1.5 - \varepsilon$. But, in the current context, how is the buyer to know that the commodity being offered is not of bad quality? Note that things would look different if it were the buyer who approached a random seller (this is the reason why the requirement that the demand be no larger than the supply is a natural equilibrium condition.) In contrast, with symmetric information it is of no consequence who approaches whom when a buyer and a seller meet. The lesson to be learned from this discussion is that with asymmetric information the particular disequilibrium story matters a lot. To push the analysis forward it is therefore appropriate to refer back to Chapter 13 where, in a more limited, partial equilibrium setting, we have already studied asymmetric information problems with the help of a methodology well suited to the consideration of this type of microstructure.

# REFERENCES

Allen, B. (1986). General equilibrium with rational expectations. Chap. 1 in *Contributions to Mathematical Economics*, edited by W. Hildenbrand, and A. Mas-Colell. Amsterdam. North-Holland.

Arrow, K. (1953). Le role des valeurs boursières pour la repartition la meilleure des risques. *Econométrie*, Paris: Centre National de la Recherche Scientifique. [Translated as: Arrow, K. (1964). The role of securities in the optimal allocation of risk-bearing. *Review of Economic Studies* **31**: 91–96.]

Cass, D., and K. Shell. (1983). Do sunspots matter? *Journal of Political Economy* **91**: 193–227.

Debreu, G. (1959). *Theory of Value*. New York: Wiley.

Diamond, P. (1967). The role of a stock market in a general equilibrium model with technological uncertainty. *American Economic Review* **57**: 759–76.

Duffie, D. (1992). *Dynamic Asset Pricing Theory*. Princeton, N.J.: Princeton University Press.

Geanakoplos, J., and H. Polemarchakis. (1986). Existence, regularity and constrained suboptimality of competitive allocations when the asset market is incomplete. In *Essays in Honor of K. Arrow*, vol. III, edited by W. Heller, and D. Starrett. Cambridge, U.K.: Cambridge University Press.

Green, J. (1973). Information, efficiency and equilibrium. Harvard Discussion Paper 284.

Grossman, S. (1977). The existence of future markets, noisy rational expectations and informational externalities. *Review of Economic Studies* **44**: 431–49.

Grossman, S. (1981). An introduction to the theory of rational expectations under asymmetric information. *Review of Economic Studies* **48**: 541–59.

Grossman, S., and J. E. Stiglitz. (1976). Information and competitive price systems. *American Economic Review* **66**: 246–53.

Hart, O. (1975). On the optimality of equilibrium when the market structure is incomplete. *Journal of Economic Theory* **11**: 418–43.

Hirshleifer, J. (1973). Where are we in the theory of information? *American Economic Review, Papers and Proceedings* **63**: 31–40.

Huang, C. F., and R. Litzenberger. (1988). *Foundations of Financial Economics*. Amsterdam: North-Holland.

Kreps, D. (1977). A note on 'fulfilled expectations' equilibria. *Journal of Economic Theory* **14**: 32–43.

Kreps, D. (1979). Three essays on capital markets. Institute for Mathematical Studies in The Social Sciences, Technical Report. v. 298, Stanford University. Reprinted as Kreps, D (1987): Three essays on capital markets. *Revista Española de Economía*, **4**: 111–146.

Lucas, R. (1972). Expectations and the neutrality of money. *Journal of Economic Theory* **4**: 103–24.

Magill, M., and W. Shafer. (1991). Incomplete markets. Chap. 30 in *Handbook of Mathematical Economics*, vol. IV, edited by W. Hildenbrand, and H. Sonnenschein. Amsterdam: North-Holland.

Marimon, R. (1987). Kreps' "Three essays on capital markets" almost ten years later. *Revista Española de Economía* **4**(1): 147–71.

Merton, R. (1982). On the microeconomic theory of investment under uncertainty. Chap. 13 in *Handbook of Mathematical Economics*, vol. II, edited by K. Arrow, and M. D. Intriligator. Amsterdam: North-Holland.

Radner, R. (1982). Equilibrium under uncertainty. Chap. 20 in *Handbook of Mathematical Economics*, vol. II, edited by K. Arrow, and M. D. Intriligator. Amsterdam: North-Holland.

# EXERCISES

**19.C.1[A]** There are $S$ states. A consumer has, in every state $s$, a Bernoulli utility function $u_s(x_s)$, where $x_s \in \mathbb{R}^L_+$. Suppose that, for every $s$, $u_s(\cdot)$ is concave. Show that the expected utility function $U(x_1, \ldots, x_S) = \sum_s \pi_s u_s(x_s)$ defined on $\mathbb{R}^{LS}_+$ is concave.

**19.C.2[A]** For the model described in Example 19.C.2, show that the marginal rates of substitution along the Pareto set are as drawn in Figure 19.C.2; that is, at any point of the Pareto set the marginal rate of substitution is smaller than the ratio of probabilities.

**19.C.3**[A] Consider an Arrow–Debreu equilibrium of the economy described in Section 19.C. Suppose that $L = 1$ and that preferences of every consumer $i$ admit an expected utility representation with continuous, strictly concave, and strictly increasing Bernoulli utility functions (identical across states). For every state $s$ denote by $p_s$, $\pi_{si}$, and $x_{si}$ the equilibrium price for the $s$-contingent commodity, the subjective probability of consumer $i$ for state $s$, and the consumption of consumer $i$ in state $s$, respectively.

Denote by $\bar{p} = \sum_s p_s$ the price of uncontingent delivery of one unit of consumption.

Show that $\sum_s (\pi_{si}\bar{p} - p_s)x_{si} \geq 0$ for every $i$. [*Hint*: Use a revealed preference argument.] Interpret.

**19.C.4**[B] There are a single consumption good, two states, and two consumers. Note that this allows the use of Edgeworth boxes.

Utility functions are of the expected utility form. Bernoulli utility functions are identical across states. That is,

$$U_1(x_{11}, x_{21}) = \pi_{11}u_1(x_{11}) + \pi_{21}u_1(x_{21})$$

and

$$U_2(x_{12}, x_{22}) = \pi_{12}u_2(x_{12}) + \pi_{22}u_2(x_{22}),$$

where $x_{si}$ is the amount of $s$-contingent good consumed by consumer $i$ and $\pi_{si}$ is the subjective probability of consumer $i$ for state $s$. We assume that every $u_i(\cdot)$ is strictly concave and differentiable.

The total initial endowments of the two contingent commodities are $\bar{\omega} = (\bar{\omega}_1, \bar{\omega}_2) \gg 0$. We assume that every consumer gets half of the random variable $\bar{\omega}$, that is, $(\omega_{11}, \omega_{21}) = \frac{1}{2}\bar{\omega}$ and $(\omega_{12}, \omega_{22}) = \frac{1}{2}\bar{\omega}$.

**(a)** Suppose that consumer 1 is risk neutral, consumer 2 is not, and both consumers have the same subjective probabilities. Show that at an interior Arrow–Debreu equilibrium consumer 2 insures completely.

**(b)** Suppose now that consumer 1 is risk neutral, consumer 2 is not, and the subjective probabilities of the two consumers are not the same. Show then that at an interior (Arrow–Debreu) equilibrium consumer 2 will not insure completely. Which is the direction of the bias in terms of the differences in subjective probabilities? Argue also that consumer 1 (the risk-neutral agent) will not gain from trade.

**19.C.5**[A] Consider an economy such as the one introduced in Section 19.C but with only one commodity in each state. There is a number $I$ of risk-averse consumers. Preferences admit an expected utility representation. Suppose that the Bernoulli utility functions of a consumer for the good are identical across states and that subjective probabilities are the same across individuals. Individual endowments vary from state to state. However, we assume that the total endowment is nonstochastic, that is, uniform across states (if, say, $I$ is large and the realizations of individual endowments are identically and independently distributed, then the total endowment per capita is almost nonstochastic).

Set up the Arrow–Debreu trading problem. Show that the allocation in which every individual's consumption in every state is the average across states of his endowments is an equilibrium allocation.

**19.D.1**[A] Consider the model of sequential trade of Section 19.D. The only difference is that we now assume that, for every $s$, the $s$-contingent commodity pays 1 dollar (rather than one unit of physical good 1) if state $s$ occurs (and nothing otherwise). Write down the budget constraints corresponding to this model and discuss which price normalizations are possible.

**19.D.2**[A] Show that in Example 19.D.1 the contingent trades of the two consumers are as claimed in the discussion of the example.

**19.D.3$^A$** Formulate a model similar to the two-period model of Section 19.D with the difference that consumption also takes place at period $t = 0$. Show that the result of Proposition 19.D.1 remains valid.

**19.D.4$^B$** Consider a three-period economy, $t = 0, 1, 2$, in which at $t = 0$ the economy splits into two branches and at $t = 1$ every branch splits again into two. There are $H$ physical commodities and consumption can take place at the three dates.

(a) Describe the Arrow–Debreu equilibrium problem for this economy.

(b) Describe the Radner equilibrium problem. Suppose that at $t = 0$ and $t = 1$ there are contingent markets for the delivery of one unit of the first physical good at the following date.

(c) Argue that the conclusion of Proposition 19.D.1 remains valid.

**19.E.1$^B$** Consider an asset trading model such as that considered in Section 19.E. The only difference is that consumption is also possible at date $t = 0$. Assume for simplicity that the Bernoulli utility functions on consumption are state independent and additively separable across time; that is, $u_i(x_{0i}, x_{1i}) = u_{0i}(x_{0i}) + u_{1i}(x_{1i})$, where $x_{0i}, x_{1i} \in \mathbb{R}^L$.

(a) Argue along the lines of the second proof of Proposition 19.E.1 that the conclusion of Proposition 19.E.1 remains valid.

(b) Suppose now that there is a single physical good in every period. Express the multipliers $\mu_s$ in terms of marginal utilities of consumption.

**19.E.2$^A$** Show that if a primary asset with return vector $r \in \mathbb{R}^S$ *separates* states, that is, if $r_s \neq r_{s'}$ whenever $s \neq s'$, then it is possible to create a complete asset structure by using only options on this primary asset. You can assume that $r_s > 0$ for every $s$.

**19.E.3$^A$** Complete part (i) of the proof of Proposition 19.E.2 in the manner requested in the text.

**19.E.4$^B$** In text.

**19.E.5$^B$** Complete the verification that at the prices specified in Example 19.E.7 the set of consumptions achievable through sequential trade is the same as the set of consumptions achievable through ex ante trade of the four Arrow–Debreu commodities.

**19.E.6$^A$** There are two dates: At date 1 there are three states; at date 0 there is trade in assets. There are two basic assets whose return vectors in current dollars are

$$r_1 = (64, 16, 4) \qquad \text{and} \qquad r_2 = (0, 0, 1).$$

The market prices of these assets are $q_1 = 32$ and $q_2 = 1$, respectively. In the following you are asked to price by arbitrage a variety of derived assets.

(a) Suppose that one unit of a derived asset is described as "One unit of this asset confers the right to buy one unit of asset 1 at 75% of its spot value in period 1 (after the state of the world occurs)." Write the return vector of this asset and price it.

(b) The situation is the same as in (a) except that the asset is modified to read "One unit of this asset confers the right to buy one unit of asset 1 at 75% of its spot value in period 1 (after the state of the world occurs) provided the spot value is at least 10."

(c) Suppose that the asset is as in (b) except that "at least 10" is replaced by "at least 19." Write down the return vector and argue that this asset cannot be priced by arbitrage with the available primary assets.

(d) How would the analysis in (c) differ if we had in addition a riskless asset with a price equal to 1? (You do not need to compute the price explicitly.)

(e) Suppose that now the asset is further complicated to read "One unit of this asset confers, at the choosing of the holder, either 1 dollar in period 1 or the right to buy one unit of asset

1 at 75% of its spot value in period 1 (after the state of the world occurs)." Write the return vector of this asset and price it.

**(f)** The situation is the same as in **(e)** except that the asset is modified to read "One unit of this asset confers, at the choosing of the holder, either 1 dollar in period 1 or the right to buy one unit of asset 1 at 75% of its spot value in period 1 (after the state of the world occurs) provided this value is at least 10."

**19.F.1$^B$** Consider the sunspot model of Example 19.F.1. Argue that, under the standard conditions on preferences, there is a sunspot-free equilibrium, whatever the asset structure.

**19.F.2$^A$** Consider (for the case $L = 1$) the utility function $U_i^*(\cdot)$ on asset portfolios defined in Section 19.F. Give sufficient conditions for $U_i^*(\cdot)$ to be continuous and concave. Show also that if returns are strictly positive then $U_i^*(\cdot)$ is strictly increasing.

**19.F.3$^C$** The aim of this exercise is to show that it is possible in an incomplete market situation for the number of assets to increase while at the same time *everybody* becomes worse off at the new Radner equilibrium. We do this in steps.

**(a)** Construct a two-consumer economy with two equally likely states and in which the distributional effects of trade are so biased that the sum of the utilities at the equilibrium with complete markets is smaller than the sum of the utilities at the equilibrium with incomplete markets.

**(b)** Now construct an economy that has four equally likely states and in which in the first two states the economy is as in **(a)**, while in the other two states it is also as in **(a)** *except* that the roles of the two consumers are reversed.

**(c)** Show then that the asset structure in which there is a single asset allowing a transfer of wealth from the first two states to the other two yields an equilibrium that is better for every consumer than the equilibrium obtained if we add two new assets, one allowing a transfer of wealth between states 1 and 2 and the other doing the same between states 3 and 4.

**19.F.4$^C$** Exhibit an example in which with unlimited short sales a Radner equilibrium may not exist. This example requires returns denominated in more than one commodity. [*Hint*: Recall the no-arbitrage necessary condition.]

**19.F.5$^B$** Consider an economy with a single period, a single consumption good, and a single input (labor). All workers are identical ex ante. Each of them has a probability $\frac{1}{2}$ of being able to work (in which case the production is $k$ units of output and work causes no disutility). With probability $\frac{1}{2}$, the worker is unable to work (is disabled). The utility of an amount $c$ of consumption if able or disabled is $U_a(c)$, $U_d(c)$, respectively. Assume that the probability of disability is independent across workers and that there are sufficient workers that society operates on the expected value production possibility set.

**(a)** If there is a full set of Arrow–Debreu markets that are open before the disability is known, what is the equilibrium allocation of resources? (You may need to allow for the possibility of infinitely many states.)

**(b)** Assume now that it is impossible for others to observe whether an individual really is disabled or just claims to be so and stops working. Assume that insurance markets continue to exist as a competitive industry. Assume also that the condition "$U_a'(c_a) = U_d'(c_d)$ implies $c_a > c_d$" is satisfied and that each individual purchases insurance only from a single company. Show that the competitive equilibrium (you should also define what this means) is the same as the one derived in **(a)**.

**(c)** Continue to assume that it is impossible for others to observe whether a claimed disability is real. But assume now that $U_a'(c_a) = U_d'(c_d)$ implies $c_a < c_d$. Show then that the equilibrium described in the answer to (b) is not reachable. Continuing to assume that each worker can purchase insurance from no more than one insurance company, determine the competitive equilibrium. Is it optimal relative to the allocations the government can achieve, supposing that the government also cannot observe disability?

**19.G.1**[A] Justify expression (19.G.1). That is, suppose that every possible production plan of the firm can be spanned and that prices (in the asset and spot markets) are given. Now introduce the firm as a new asset. Show that any consumption plan of any consumer can be reached without purchasing any shares of the firm.

**19.G.2**[A] Suppose that, in a two-consumer economy with $L = 1$, initially there is a single asset (which, therefore, goes untraded; recall that we do not allow consumption at $t = 0$). Now a firm is introduced that can produce the return vector $\varepsilon a \in \mathbb{R}_+^S$. The firm is owned, with equal shares, by the two consumers. Give an example in which, no matter how small $\varepsilon$ may be (and letting the vector $a \in \mathbb{R}_+^S$ remain fixed), the introduction of the firm as an asset tradeable at $t = 0$ has the property that at the new equilibrium one consumer is significantly better off and the other is significantly worse off.

**19.G.3**[A] Suppose that, in an economy with $L = 1$, a firm is introduced that can produce the single return vector $a \in \mathbb{R}^S$. The ownership share of consumer $i$ is $\theta_i$. Suppose also that the returns $a$ can be spanned by existing assets. Show that the consumption bundles reachable at an equilibrium are the same under the following two scenarios. In the first the shares of the firm are traded at $t = 0$. In the second the asset is not traded and for every $i$ the vector $\theta_i a$ is added to the initial endowments of consumer $i$.

**19.G.4**[A] Suppose there are two consumers and $L = 1$. Initially there are no assets. We now introduce a firm with two possible return vectors $A = \{a^1, a^2\} \subset \mathbb{R}_+^S$. Ownership shares are the same for the two consumers. The firm's shares are not traded at $t = 0$. The production choice of the firm, $a^1$ or $a^2$, is added to the endowments at $t = 1$ (half to each consumer). Show that it is possible for the two consumers not to be unanimous in their preference for $a^1$ or $a^2$.

**19.H.1**[A] We place ourselves in the framework of the single-consumer decision problem considered in Proposition 19.H.1.

(a) Show that if $\sigma(\cdot)$ is completely revealing [i.e., $\sigma(s) \neq \sigma(s')$ whenever $s \neq s'$] then $x_i^{\sigma(\cdot)}$ is ex post optimal in the sense that for every $s \in S$ the consumption allocation in state $s$ is optimal for the spot economy that obtains at state $s$. Show also that this need not be true if $\sigma(\cdot)$ is not completely revealing.

(b) Show that $x_i^{\sigma(\cdot)}$ is interim optimal in the following sense: there is no allocation $x_i$ measurable with respect to $\sigma(\cdot)$ and such that for some possible signal $\sigma(s)$ the expected utility of $x_i$ [conditional on $\sigma(s)$] is larger than that corresponding to $x_i^{\sigma(\cdot)}$.

(c) Show that if $\sigma'(\cdot)$ is at least as informative as $\sigma(\cdot)$ then for every $s$ the expected utility generated by $x_i^{\sigma'(\cdot)}$, conditional on $\sigma'(s)$, cannot be inferior to the expected utility generated by $x^{\sigma(\cdot)}$, conditional on $\sigma'(s)$.

(d) Show, similarly, that if $\sigma'(\cdot)$ is at least as informative as $\sigma(\cdot)$ then for every $s$ the expected utility generated by $x_i^{\sigma'(\cdot)}$, conditional on $\sigma(s)$, cannot be inferior to the expected utility generated by $x^{\sigma(\cdot)}$, conditional on $\sigma(\cdot)$.

**19.H.2**[A] Argue that for the validity of Proposition 19.H.1 we may allow $p$ and $w_i$ to depend on the state. What is required is that, as functions, they be measurable with respect to the original $\sigma(\cdot)$ and that they remain unaltered as $\sigma(\cdot)$ is replaced by $\sigma'(\cdot)$.

**19.H.3**[A] Complete the requested steps of the proof of Proposition 19.H.1.

**19.H.4$^A$** Complete the missing step in Example 19.H.4.

**19.H.5$^B$** Carry out the requested verification in Example 19.H.5.

**19.H.6$^C$** Consider the following two-consumer, two-commodity general equilibrium model. The (Bernoulli) utility functions of the two consumers are

$$u_1(x_{11}, x_{21}) = x_{11} + x_{21},$$

$$u_2(x_{12}, x_{22}) = (x_{12})^{1/2} + x_{22}.$$

Consumer 1's endowment of the second good is $\omega_{21}$. He has no endowment of the first good. Consumer 2 has no endowments of the second good and his endowments of the first good depend on which of three equally likely states occurs. The respective levels in the three states are $\omega_{112}, \omega_{122}, \omega_{132}$.

**(a)** Determine the Arrow–Debreu equilibrium of this economy. You can assume that the parameters are such that the equilibrium is interior.

**(b)** Suppose that the only possible markets are for the noncontingent delivery of the two goods. Set up the equilibrium problem. Is the equilibrium allocation a Pareto optimum?

**(c)** Suppose now that before any trade takes place, and before the endowments are revealed, the two consumers are told whether or not state 1 has occurred. After the revelation of this information (and before the values of the endowments are disclosed) non-contingent trade can take place. Set up the equilibrium problem as it depends on the information available.

**(d)** The setting is as in **(c)**; the only difference is that contingent trade (after the revelation of the information on state 1) is now permitted.

**(e)** Compare ex ante (i.e., before any announcement is known) the expected utilities attained by the two consumers in the equilibria of **(a)**, **(b)**, **(c)**, and **(d)**; assume that all of these equilibria are interior. When can you assert that the information available in parts **(c)** and **(d)** is socially valuable?

**19.H.7$^A$** Suppose that there are two equally likely states. In every state there is a spot market where a consumption good (good 1) is exchanged against the numeraire, which we denote as good 2. There are two consumers. Their utilities are

|              | State 1                      | State 2                         |
|--------------|------------------------------|---------------------------------|
| *Consumer 1* | $2 \ln x_{11} + x_{21}$      | $4 \ln x_{11} + x_{21}$         |
| *Consumer 2* | $4 \ln x_{12} + x_{22}$      | $2 \ln x_{12} \times x_{22}$    |

The total endowment of the first good equals 6 in the first state and $6 + \varepsilon$ in the second state. All the endowments of this good are received by the second consumer. Assume also that the endowments of numeraire for the two consumers are sufficient for us to neglect the possibility of boundary equilibria. The price of the numeraire is fixed to be one in the two states. The prices of the non-numeraire good in the two states are denoted $(p_1, p_2)$.

**(a)** Suppose that when uncertainty is resolved, both consumers know which state of the world has occurred. Determine the spot equilibrium prices $(\hat{p}_1(\varepsilon), \hat{p}_2(\varepsilon))$ in the two states (as a function of the parameter $\varepsilon$).

**(b)** Assume now that when a state occurs, consumer 2 knows the state but consumer 1 remains uninformed (i.e., he must keep thinking of the two states as equally likely). Determine, under this information setup (and assuming that prices cannot be used as signals), the spot equilibrium prices $(\bar{p}_1(\varepsilon), \bar{p}_2(\varepsilon))$ in the two states.

**(c)** The situation is as in **(b)**, except that now we allow consumer 1 to deduce the state of the world from prices. That is, if $p_1 \neq p_2$ then consumer 1 is actually informed, but if $p_1 = p_2$ he is not informed. A pair of spot prices $(p_1^*(\varepsilon), p_2^*(\varepsilon))$ constitute rational expectations equilibrium prices if they clear the two spot markets when consumer 1 derives information from $((p_1^*(\varepsilon), p_2^*(\varepsilon))$ in the manner just described. Suppose that $\varepsilon \neq 0$ and derive a rational expectations equilibrium pair of prices.

**(d)** Show that if $\varepsilon = 0$ then there is no rational expectations equilibrium pair of prices. Compare with Example 19.H.3.

# Equilibrium and Time

## 20.A Introduction

In this chapter, we present the basic elements of the extension of competitive equilibrium theory to an intertemporal setting. In the presentation, we try to maintain a balance between two possible approaches to the theory varying by the degree of emphasis on time.

A first approach contemplates equilibrium in time merely as the particular case of the general theory developed in the previous chapters in which commodities are indexed by time as one of the many characteristics defining them. This is a useful point of view (the display of the underlying unity of seemingly disparate phenomena is one of the prime roles of theory), and to a point we build on it. However, exclusive reliance on this approach would, in the limit, be self-defeating. It would reduce this chapter to a footnote to the preceding ones.

A second approach proceeds by stressing, rather than deemphasizing, the special structure of time. Again, we follow this line to some degree. Thus, every model discussed in this chapter accepts the open-ended infinity of time, or the fact that production takes time. Also, at the cost of some generality, we pursue our treatment under assumptions of stationarity and time separability that allow for a sharp presentation of the dynamic aspects of the theory.

Sections 20.B and 20.C are concerned with the description of, respectively, the consumption and the production sides of the economy.

Section 20.D is the heart of this chapter. It deals with the basic properties of equilibria (including definitions, existence, optimality, and computability) in the context of a single-consumer economy.

Section 20.E (which concentrates on steady states) and Section 20.F (which is general) study the dynamics of the single-consumer model.

Section 20.G considers economies with several consumers. The message of this section is that, as long as the Pareto optimality of equilibrium is guaranteed, the qualitative aspects of the positive theory of Chapter 17 extend to the more general situation and, moreover, that the properties of individual equilibria identified by the single-consumer methodology remain valid in the broader context.

Section 20.H gives an extremely succinct account of overlapping-generations economies, a model of central importance in modern macroeconomic theory. Our interest in it is twofold: on the one hand, we want to display it as yet another instance of a useful equilibrium model; on the other hand, we want to point out that it is an example that, because of the infinity of generations, does not fit the general model of Section 20.G, and one that gives rise to some new and interesting issues having to do with the optimality and the multiplicity of equilibria.

Section 20.I gathers some remarks on nonequilibrium considerations (short-run equilibrium and tâtonnement stability, learning, and so on).

For pedagogical purposes, the entire chapter deals only with the deterministic version of the theory. The unfolding of time is a line, not a tree. A full synthesis of the approaches of Chapter 19 (on uncertainty) and the current one (on time) is possible. However, we view its presentation as advanced material beyond the scope of this textbook. The account of Stokey and Lucas with Prescott (1989) constitutes an excellent introduction to the general theory.

A point of notation: in this chapter $\sum_t$ always means $\sum_{t=0}^{t=\infty}$, that is, $\lim_{T \to \infty} \sum_{t=0}^{t=T}$. When the sum does not run from $t = 0$ to $t = \infty$ the two end-points of the sum are explicitly indicated.

# 20.B Intertemporal Utility

In this chapter, we assume that there are infinitely many dates $t = 0, 1, \ldots$, and that the objects of choice for consumers are *consumption streams* $c = (c_0, \ldots, c_t, \ldots)$ where $c_t \in \mathbb{R}_+^L$, $c_t \geq 0$.[1] To keep things simple, we will consider only consumption streams that are *bounded*, that is, that have $\sup_t \|c_t\| < \infty$.

Rather than proceed from the most general form of preferences over consumption streams to the more specific, we instead introduce first the very special form that we assume throughout this chapter (except for Sections 20.H and 20.I); we subsequently discuss its special properties from a general point of view.

It is customary in intertemporal economies to assume that preferences over consumption streams $c = (c_0, \ldots, c_t, \ldots)$ can be represented by a utility function $V(c)$ having the special form

$$V(c) = \sum_{t=0}^{\infty} \delta^t u(c_t) \tag{20.B.1}$$

where $\delta < 1$ is a *discount* factor and $u(\cdot)$, which is defined on $\mathbb{R}_+^L$, is strictly increasing and concave. This chapter will be no exception to this rule: Throughout it we assume that preferences over consumption streams take this form. However, we comment here, at some length, on six aspects of this utility function. As a matter of notation, given a consumption stream $c = (c_0, \ldots, c_t, \ldots)$, we let $c^T = (c_0^T, c_1^T, \ldots)$ denote the $T$-period "backward shift" consumption stream, that is, the stream $(c_0^T, c_1^T, \ldots)$ with $c_t^T = c_{t+T}$ for all $t \geq 0$.

(1) *Time impatience.* The requirement that future utility is discounted (i.e., that $\delta < 1$), implies *time impatience*. That is, if $c = (c_0, c_1, \ldots, c_t, \ldots)$ is a nonzero consumption stream, then the (forward-) shifted consumption stream $c' = (0, c_0, c_1, \ldots, c_{t-1}, \ldots)$ is strictly worse than $c$ (see Exercise 20.B.1). It is an

---

1. We use the terms "stream," "trajectory," "program," and "path" synonymously.

assumption that is very helpful in guaranteeing that a bounded consumption stream has a finite utility value [i.e., guarantees that the sum in (20.B.1) converges], thus allowing us to compare any two such consumption streams[2] and making possible the application of the machinery of the calculus. There is a strand of opinion that views this technical convenience as the real reason for the fundamental role that the assumption of time discounting plays in economics. This skeptical view on the existence of substantive reasons[3] is excessive. An implication of time discounting is that the distant future does not matter much for current decisions, and this feature seems more realistic than its opposite.

A possible interpretation, and defense, of the discount factor $\delta$ views it as a probability of survival to the next period. Then $V(c)$ is the expected value of lifetime utility. For another interpretation, see (6) below.

(2) *Stationarity.* A more general form of the utility function would be

$$V(c) = \sum_{t=0}^{\infty} u_t(c_t). \tag{20.B.2}$$

The form (20.B.1) corresponds to the special case of (20.B.2) in which $u_t(c_t) = \delta^t u(c_t)$. This special form can be characterized in terms of *stationarity*. Consider two consumption streams $c \neq c'$ such that $c_t = c_t'$ for $t \leq T - 1$: that is, the two streams $c$ and $c'$ are one and the same up to period $T - 1$ and differ only after $T - 1$. Observe that the problem of choosing at $t = T$ between the current and future consumptions in $c$ and $c'$ is the same problem that a consumer would face at $t = 0$ in choosing between the consumption streams $c^T$ and $c'^T$, the $T$ backward shifts of $c$ and $c'$, respectively. Then *stationarity* requires that

$$V(c) \geq V(c') \quad \text{if and only if} \quad V(c^T) \geq V(c'^T).$$

It is a good exercise to verify that (20.B.1) satisfies the stationarity property and that the property can be violated by utility functions of the form $V(c) = \sum_t \delta_t^t u(c_t)$, that is, with a time-dependent discount factor (Exercise 20.B.2).

The property of stationarity should *not* be confused with the statement asserting that if the consumption streams $c$ and $c'$ coincide in the first $T - 1$ periods and a consumer chooses one of these streams at $t = 0$, then she will not change her mind at $T$. This "property" is tautologically true: at both dates we are comparing $V(c)$ and $V(c')$.[4] The stationarity experiment compares $V(c)$ and $V(c')$ at $t = 0$, but at period $T$ it compares the utility values of the future streams shifted to $t = 0$, that is, $V(c^T)$ and $V(c'^T)$. Thus, stationarity says that in the context of the form (20.B.2), the preferences over the future are independent of the *age* of the decision maker.

Time stationarity is not essential to the analysis of this chapter (except for Sections 20.E and 20.F on dynamics), but it saves substantially on the use of subindices.

---

2. Hence, the completeness of the preference relation on consumption streams is guaranteed.

3. Ramsey (1928) called the assumption a "weakness of the imagination."

4. This property is often called *time consistency*. Time inconsistency is possible if tastes change through time (recall the example of Ulysses and the Sirens in Section 1.B!), but, as we have just argued, it must necessarily hold if the preference ordering over consumption streams $(c_0, \ldots, c_t, \ldots)$ does not change as time passes. In line with the entire treatment of Part IV, we maintain the assumption of unchanging tastes throughout the chapter.

(3) *Additive separability.* Two implications of the additive form of the utility function are that at any date $T$ we have, first, that the induced ordering on consumption streams that begin at $T + 1$ is independent of the consumption stream followed from 0 to $T$, and, second, that the ordering on consumption streams from 0 to $T$ is independent of whatever (fixed) consumption expectation we may have from $T + 1$ onward (see Exercise 20.B.3). In turn, these two separability properties imply additivity; that is, if the preference ordering over consumption streams satisfies these separability properties, then it can be represented by a utility function of the form $V(c) = \sum_t u_t(c_t)$ [this is not easy to prove, see Blackorby, Primont and Russell (1978)].

How restrictive is the assumption of additive separability? We can make two arguments in its favor: the first is technical convenience; the second is a vague sense that what happens far in the future or in the past should be irrelevant to the relative welfare appreciation of current consumption alternatives. Against it we have obvious counter-examples: Past consumption creates habits and addictions, the appreciation of a particularly wonderful dish may depend on how many times it has been consumed in the last week, and so on. There is, however, a very natural way to accommodate these phenomena within an additively separable framework. We could, for example, allow for the form $V(c) = \sum_t u_t(c_{t-1}, c_t)$. Here the utility at period $t$ depends not only on consumption at date $t$ but also on consumption at date $t - 1$ (or, more generally, on consumption at several past dates). We can formulate this in a slightly different way. Define a vector $z_t$ of "habit" variables and a *household production technology* that uses an input vector $c_{t-1}$ at $t - 1$ to jointly produce an output vector $c_{t-1}$ of consumption goods at $t - 1$ and a vector $z_t = c_{t-1}$ of "habit" variables at $t$. Then, formally, $u_t$ depends only on time $t$ variables and total utility is $\sum_t u_t(z_t, c_t)$. In summary: additive separability is less restrictive than it appears if we allow for household production and a suitable number (typically larger than 1) of current variables.

(4) *Length of period.* The plausibility of the separability assumption, which makes the enjoyment of current consumption independent of the consumption in other periods, depends on the length of the period. Because even the most perishable consumption goods have elements of durability in them (in the form, for example, of a flow of "services" after the act of consumption), the assumption is quite strained if the length of the elementary period is very short. What determines the length of the period? To the extent that our model is geared to competitive theory, this period is institutionally determined: it should be an interval of time for which prices can be taken as constant. On a related point, note that the value of $\delta$ also depends, implicitly, on the length of the period. The shorter the period, the closer $\delta$ should be to 1.

(5) *Recursive utility.* With the form (20.B.1) for the utility function, we have $V(c) = u(c_0) + \delta V(c^1)$ for any consumption stream $c = (c_0, c_1, \ldots, c_t, \ldots)$. If we think of $u = u(c_0)$ as current utility and of $V = V(c^1)$ as future utility, we see that the marginal rate of substitution of current for future utility equals $\delta$ and is therefore independent of the levels of current and future utility. The *recursive utility model* [due to Koopmans (1960)] is a useful generalization of (20.B.1) that combines two features: it allows this rate to be variable but, as in the additively separable case, it has the property that the ordering of future consumption streams is independent of the consumption stream followed in the past.

The recursive model goes as follows. Denote current utility by $u \geq 0$ and future utility by $V \geq 0$. Then we are given a current utility function $u(c_t)$ and an *aggregator* function $G(u, V)$ that combines current and future utility into overall utility. For example, in the separable additive case we have $G(u, V) = u + \delta V$. More generally we could also have, for example, $G(u, V) = u^\alpha + \delta V^\alpha$, $0 < \alpha \leq 1$. In this case, the indifference curves in the $(u, V)$ plane are not straight lines. The utility of a consumption stream $c = (c_0, \ldots, c_t, \ldots)$ could then be computed recursively from

$$V(c) = G(u(c_0), V(c^1)) = G(u(c_0), G(u(c_1), V(c^2))) = \cdots. \tag{20.B.3}$$

For (20.B.3) to make sense we must be able to argue that the influence of $V(c^T)$ on $V(c)$ will become negligible as $T \to \infty$ [so that $V(c)$ can be approximately determined by taking a large $T$ and letting $V(c^T)$ have an arbitrary value]. This amounts to an assumption of time impatience. In applications, it will typically not be necessary to compute $V(c)$ explicitly. See Exercise 20.B.4 for more on recursive utility.

(6) *Altruism.* The expression $V(c) = u(c_0) + \delta V(c^1)$ suggests a multigeneration interpretation of the single-consumer problem (20.B.1). Indeed, if generations live a single period and we think of generation 0 as enjoying her consumption according to $u(c_0)$, but caring also about the *utility* $V(c^1)$ of the next generation according to $\delta V(c^1)$, then $V(c) = u(c_0) + \delta V(c^1)$ is her overall utility. If every generation is similarly altruistic, then we conclude, by recursive substitution, that the objective function of generation 0 is precisely (20.B.1). The entire "dynasty" behaves as a single individual. With this we also have another justification for $\delta < 1$. The inequality means then that the members of the current generation care for their children, but not quite as much as for themselves. See Barro (1989) for more on these points.

# 20.C   Intertemporal Production and Efficiency

Assume that there is an infinite sequence of dates $t = 0, 1, \ldots$. In each period $t$, there are $L$ commodities. If it facilitates reading, you can take $L = 2$ and interpret the commodities as labor services and a generalized consumption–investment good (see Example 20.C.1). One of the great advantages of vector notation, however, is that in some cases—and this is one—there is no novelty involved in the general case. Thus, while you think you are understanding the simple problem, you are at the same time understanding the most general one.

We shall adopt the convention that goods are *nondurables*. This is a convention because, in order to make a good durable, it suffices to specify a storage technology whose role is, so to speak, to transport the commodity through time.

If we were exogenously endowed with some amount of resources (e.g., some initial capital and some amount of labor every period), we would ask what we could do with them. To give an answer, we need to specify the *production technology*. We already know from Chapter 5 how to do this formally by means of the concept of a *production set* (or a production transformation function, or a production function). With minimal loss of generality, we will restrict our technologies to be of the following form: the production possibilities at time $t$ are entirely determined by the production decisions at the most recent past, that is, at time $t - 1$. If we keep in mind that we can always define new intermediate goods (such as different vintages of a machine), and also that we can always define periods to be very long, we see that the restriction is minor.

Thus, the technological possibilities at $t$ will be formally specified by a production set $Y \subset \mathbb{R}^{2L}$ whose generic entries, or *production plans*, are written $y = (y_b, y_a)$. The indices $b$ and $a$ are mnemonic for "before" and "after." The interpretation is that the production plans in $Y$ cover two periods (the "initial" and the "last" period) with $y_b \in \mathbb{R}^L$ and $y_a \in \mathbb{R}^L$ being, respectively, the production plans for the initial and the last periods. As usual, negative entries represent inputs and positive entries represent outputs.

We impose some assumptions on $Y$ that are familiar from Section 5.B:

(i) $Y$ is *closed and convex*.
(ii) $Y \cap \mathbb{R}^{2L}_+ = \{0\}$ (*no free lunch*).
(iii) $Y - \mathbb{R}^{2L}_+ \subset Y$ (*free disposal*).

An assumption specific to the temporal setting is the requirement that inputs not be used *later* than outputs are produced (i.e., production takes time). This is captured by

(iv) If $y = (y_b, y_a) \in Y$ then $(y_b, 0) \in Y$ (*possibility of truncation*).

In words, (iv) says that, whatever the production plans for the initial period, not producing in the last period is a possibility. A simple case is when $y_{at} \geq 0$ for every $y \in Y$, that is, when all inputs are used in the initial period. Then (iv) is implied by the free-disposal property (iii).

**Example 20.C.1:** *Ramsey–Solow Model.*[5] Assume that there are only two commodities: A consumption–investment good and labor. It will be convenient to describe the technology by a production function $F(k, l)$. To any amounts of capital investment $k \geq 0$ and of labor input $l \geq 0$, applied in the initial period, the production function assigns the *total* amount $F(k, l)$ of consumption–investment good available at the last period. Then

$$Y = \{(-k, -l, x, 0): k \geq 0, l \geq 0, x \leq F(k, l)\} - \mathbb{R}^4_+.$$

Note that labor is a primary factor; that is, it cannot be produced. ∎

**Example 20.C.2:** *Cost-of-Adjustment Model.* Suppose that there are three goods: capacity, a consumption good, and labor. With the amounts $k$ and $l$ of invested capacity and labor at the initial period, one gets $F(k, l)$ units of consumption good output at the last period. This output can be transformed into invested capacity at the last period at a cost of $k' + \gamma(k' - k)$ units of consumption good for $k'$ units of capacity, where $\gamma(\cdot)$ is a convex function satisfying $\gamma(k' - k) = 0$ for $k' < k$ and $\gamma(k' - k) > 0$ for $k' > k$. The term $\gamma(k' - k)$ represents the cost of adjusting capacity upward in a given period relative to the previous period. (Note the marginal cost of doing so increases with invested capacity of the period.) Formally, the production set $Y$ is

$$Y = \{(-k, 0, -l, k', x, 0): k \geq 0, l \geq 0, k' \geq 0, x \leq F(k, l) - k' - \gamma(k' - k)\} - \mathbb{R}^6_+. \quad \blacksquare$$

---

5. See Ramsey (1928) and Solow (1956). The same model was also introduced in Swan (1956).

**Example 20.C.3:** *Two-Sector Model.* We could make a more general distinction between an investment and a consumption good than the one embodied in Examples 20.C.1 and 20.C.2. Indeed, we could let the production set be

$$Y = \{(-k, 0, -l, k', x, 0): k \geq 0, l \geq 0, k' \geq 0, x \leq G(k, l, k')\} - \mathbb{R}_+^6,$$

where $k$, $k'$ are, respectively, the investments in the initial and the last periods. Note that the investment and the consumption good need not be perfectly substitutable [they are produced in two separate sectors, so to speak; see Uzawa (1964)]. If they are [i.e., if the transformation function $G(k, l, k')$ has the form $F(k, l) - k'$] then this example is equivalent to the Ramsey–Solow model of Example 20.C.1. If it has the form $G(k, l, k') = F(k, l) - k' - \gamma(k' - k)$ then we have the cost-of-adjustment model of Example 20.C.2. ∎

**Example 20.C.4:** $(N + 1)$-*Sector Model.* As in Example 20.C.3, we have a consumption good and labor, but we now interpret $k$ and $k'$ as $N$-dimensional vectors. For simplicity of exposition, in Example 20.C.3 we have taken $G(k, l, k')$ to be defined for any $k \geq 0$, $k' \geq 0$. In general, however, this could lead to the production of negative amounts of consumption good. To avoid this it is convenient to complete the specification by means of an admissible domain $A$ of $(k, l, k')$ combinations. Then

$$Y = \{(-k, 0, -l, k', x, 0): (k, l, k') \in A \text{ and } x \leq G(k, l, k')\} - \mathbb{R}_+^{2(N+2)}. \qquad ∎$$

Once we have specified our technology, we can define what constitutes a path of production plans.

**Definition 20.C.1:** The list $(y_0, y_1, \ldots, y_t, \ldots)$ is a *production path*, or *trajectory*, or *program*, if $y_t \in Y \subset \mathbb{R}^{2L}$ for every $t$.

Note that along a production path $(y_0, \ldots, y_t, \ldots)$ there is overlap in the time indices over which the production plans $y_{t-1}$ and $y_t$ are defined. Indeed, both $y_{a,t-1} \in \mathbb{R}^L$ and $y_{bt} \in \mathbb{R}^L$ represent plans, made respectively at dates $t-1$ and $t$, for input use or output production at date $t$. Thus, we have, at every $t$, a net input–output vector equal to $y_{a,t-1} + y_{bt} \in \mathbb{R}^L$ (at $t = 0$, we put $y_{a,-1} = 0$; this convention is kept throughout the chapter).[6] The negative entries of this vector stand for amounts of inputs that have to be injected from the outside at period $t$ if the path is to be realized, that is, amounts of input required at period $t$ for the operation of $y_{t-1}$ and $y_t$ in excess of the amounts provided as outputs by the operation of $y_{t-1}$ and $y_t$. Similarly, the positive entries represent the amounts of goods left over after input use and thus available for final consumption at time $t$.

The situation is entirely analogous to the description of the production side of an economy in Chapter 5. If we think of the technology at every $t$ as being run by a distinct firm (or as an aggregate of distinct firms) and of $\hat{y}_t$ as an infinite sequence with nonzero entries (equal to $y_t$) only in the $t$ and $t + 1$ places, then $\sum_t \hat{y}_t$ is the aggregate production path; and it is also precisely the sequence that assigns the net input–output vector $y_{a,t-1} + y_{bt} \in \mathbb{R}^L$ to period $t$. If we had a finite horizon, the current setting would thus be a particular case of the description of production in

---

6. A minor point of notation: when there is any possibility of confusion or ambiguity in the reading of indices, we insert commas; for example, we write $y_{a,t-1}$ instead of $y_{a\,t-1}$.

Chapter 5. With an infinite horizon there is a difference: we now have a countable infinity of commodities and of firms instead of only a finite number. As we shall see, this is not a minor difference. It will, however, be most helpful to arrange our discussion around the exploration of the analogy with the finite horizon case by asking the same questions we posed in Section 5.F regarding the relationship between efficient production plans and price equilibria.

**Definition 20.C.2:** The production path $(y_0, \ldots, y_t, \ldots)$ is *efficient* if there is no other production path $(y_0', \ldots, y_t', \ldots)$ such that

$$y_{a,t-1} + y_{bt} \leq y_{a,t-1}' + y_{bt}' \quad \text{for all } t,$$

and equality does not hold for at least one $t$.

In words: the path $(y_0, \ldots, y_t, \ldots)$ is efficient if there is no way that we can produce at least as much final consumption in every period using at most the same amount of inputs in every period (with at least one inequality strict). The definition is exactly parallel to Definition 5.F.1.

What constitutes a *price vector* in the current intertemporal context? It is natural to define it as a sequence $(p_0, p_1, \ldots, p_t, \ldots)$, where $p_t \in \mathbb{R}^L$. For the moment we shall not ask where this sequence comes from. We assume that it is somehow given and that it is available to any possible production unit. The prices should be thought of as present-value prices. We shall discuss further the nature of these prices in the next section.

Given a path $(y_0, \ldots, y_t, \ldots)$ and a price sequence $(p_0, \ldots, p_t, \ldots)$, the profit level associated with the production plan at $t$ is

$$p_t \cdot y_{bt} + p_{t+1} \cdot y_{at}.$$

We now pursue the implications of profit maximization on the production plans made period by period.

**Definition 20.C.3:** The production path $(y_0, \ldots, y_t, \ldots)$ is *myopically*, or *short-run*, *profit maximizing* for the price sequence $(p_0, \ldots, p_t, \ldots)$ if for every $t$ we have

$$p_t \cdot y_{bt} + p_{t+1} \cdot y_{at} \geq p_t \cdot y_{bt}' + p_{t+1} \cdot y_{at}' \quad \text{for all } y_t' \in Y.$$

Prices $(p_0, \ldots, p_t, \ldots)$ capable of sustaining a path $(y_1, \ldots, y_t, \ldots)$ as myopically profit-maximizing are often called *Malinvaud prices* for the path [because of Malinvaud (1953)].[7]

Does the first welfare theorem hold for myopic profit maximization? That is, if $(y_0, \ldots, y_t, \ldots)$ is myopically profit maximizing with respect to strictly positive prices, does it follow that $(y_0, \ldots, y_t, \ldots)$ is efficient? In a finite-horizon economy this conclusion holds true because of Proposition 5.F.1, but a little thought reveals that in the infinite-horizon context it need not. The intuition for a negative answer rests on the phenomenon of *capital overaccumulation*. Suppose that prices increase through

---

7. Observe that we do not require that $\sum_t p_t \cdot (y_{a,t-1} + y_{bt}) < \infty$. In principle, a production path may have an infinite present value. We saw in Sections 5.E and 5.F, where we had a finite number of commodities and firms that individual, decentralized profit maximization and overall profit maximization amounted to the same thing. Because of the possibility of an infinite present value, the existence of a countable number of commodities *and* production sets makes this a more delicate matter in the current context. See Exercises 20.C.2 to 20.C.5 for a discussion.

time fast enough. Then it may very well happen that at every single period it always pays to invest everything at hand. Along such a path, consumption never takes place—hardly an efficient outcome.

**Example 20.C.5:** With $L = 1$, let $Y = \{(-k, k'): k \geq 0, k' \leq k\} \subset \mathbb{R}^2$. This is just a trivial storage technology. Consider the path where $y_t = (-1, 1)$ for all $t$; that is, we always carry forward one unit of good. Then $y_{a,-1} + y_{b0} = -1$ and $y_{a,t-1} + y_{bt} = 0$ for all $t > 0$. This is not efficient; just consider the path $y'_t = (0, 0)$ for all $t$, which has $y'_{a,t-1} + y'_{bt} = 0$ for all $t \geq 0$. But for the stationary price sequence where $p_t = 1$ for all $t$, $(y_0, \ldots, y_t, \ldots)$ is myopically profit maximizing. ∎

Efficiency will obtain if, in addition to myopic profit maximization, the (present) value of the production path becomes insignificant as $t \to \infty$. Precisely, efficiency obtains if the (present) value of the period $t$ production plan for period $t + 1$ goes to zero, that is, if $p_{t+1} \cdot y_{at} \to 0$ as $t \to \infty$. This is the so-called *transversality condition*. Note that the condition is violated in the storage illustration of Example 20.C.5.

**Proposition 20.C.1:** Suppose that the production path $(y_0, \ldots, y_t, \ldots)$ is myopically profit maximizing with respect to the price sequence $(p_0, \ldots, p_t, \ldots) \gg 0$. Suppose also that the production path and the price sequence satisfy the *transversality condition* $p_{t+1} \cdot y_{at} \to 0$. Then the path $(y_0, \ldots, y_t, \ldots)$ is efficient.

**Proof:** Suppose that the path $(y'_0, \ldots, y'_t, \ldots)$ is such that $y_{a,t-1} + y_{bt} \leq y'_{a,t-1} + y'_{bt}$ for all $t$, with equality not holding for at least one $t$. Then there is $\varepsilon > 0$ such that if we take a $T$ sufficiently large for some strict inequality to correspond to a date previous to $T$, we must have

$$\sum_{t=0}^{T} p_t \cdot (y'_{a,t-1} + y'_{bt}) > \sum_{t=0}^{T} p_t \cdot (y_{a,t-1} + y_{bt}) + \varepsilon.$$

In fact, if $T$ is very large then $p_{T+1} \cdot y_{aT}$ is very small (because of the transversality condition) and therefore

$$\sum_{t=0}^{T} p_t \cdot (y'_{a,t-1} + y'_{bt}) > p_{T+1} \cdot y_{aT} + \sum_{t=0}^{T} p_t \cdot (y_{a,t-1} + y_{bt}).$$

By rearranging terms—a standard trick in dynamic economics—this can be rewritten as (recall the convention $y_{a,-1} = y'_{a,-1} = 0$)

$$p_T \cdot y'_{bT} + \sum_{t=0}^{T-1} (p_{t+1} \cdot y'_{at} + p_t \cdot y'_{bt}) > \sum_{t=0}^{T} (p_{t+1} \cdot y_{at} + p_t \cdot y_{bt}).$$

We must thus have either $p_{t+1} \cdot y'_{at} + p_t \cdot y'_{bt} > p_{t+1} \cdot y_{at} + p_t \cdot y_{bt}$ for some $t \leq T - 1$ or $p_T \cdot y'_{bT} > p_{T+1} \cdot y_{aT} + p_T \cdot y_{bT}$. In either case we obtain a violation of the myopic profit-maximization assumption [recall that by the possibility of truncation we have $(y'_{bT}, 0) \in Y$]. Therefore, no such path $(y'_0, \ldots, y'_t, \ldots)$ can exist.

Note that the essence of the argument is very simple. The key fact is that if the transversality condition holds, then for $T$ large enough we can approximate the overall profits of the truncated path $(y_0, \ldots, y_T)$ by the sum of the net values of period-by-period input–output realizations (up to period $T$). It does not matter whether we match the inputs and the outputs per period or per firm (that is, "per production plan"). If the horizon is far enough away, either method will come down to Profits = Total Revenue − Total Cost. ∎

Proposition 20.C.1 tells us that a modified version of the first welfare theorem holds in the dynamic production setting. Let us now ask about the second welfare theorem: *Given an efficient path* $(y_0, \ldots, y_t, \ldots)$, *can it be price supported?* In Proposition 5.F.2 we gave a positive answer to this question which applies to the finite-horizon case. In the current infinite-horizon situation we could decompose the question into two parts:

(i) *Is there a system of Malinvaud prices* $(p_0, \ldots, p_t, \ldots)$ *for* $(y_0, \ldots, y_t, \ldots)$, *that is, a sequence* $(p_0, \ldots, p_t, \ldots)$ *with respect to which* $(y_0, \ldots, y_t, \ldots)$ *is myopically profit maximizing?*

(ii) *If the answer to* (i) *is yes, can we conclude that the pair* $(y_0, \ldots, y_t, \ldots)$, $(p_0, \ldots, p_t, \ldots)$ *satisfies the transversality condition?*

*The answer to* (ii) *is* "*not necessarily.*" In Section 20.E we will see, by means of an example, that the transversality condition is definitely not a necessary property of Malinvaud prices.

*The answer to* (i) *is* "*Essentially yes.*" We illustrate the matter by means of two examples and then conclude this section by a small-type discussion of the general situation.

**Example 20.C.6:** *Ramsey–Solow Model Continued.* In this model, we can summarize a path by the sequence $(k_t, l_t, c_t)$ of total capital usage, labor usage, and amount available for consumption. From now on we assume that $k_{t+1} + c_{t+1} = F(k_t, l_t)$ and that the sequence $l_t$ of labor inputs is exogenously given. Then it is enough to specify the capital path $(k_0, \ldots, k_t, \ldots)$. Denoting by $(q_t, w_t)$ the prices of the two commodities at $t$, we have that profits at $t$ are $q_{t+1}F(k_t, l_t) - q_t k_t - w_t l_t$ and, therefore, the necessary and sufficient conditions for short-run profit maximization at $t$ are

$$\frac{q_t}{q_{t+1}} = \nabla_1 F(k_t, l_t) \qquad \text{and} \qquad \frac{w_t}{q_{t+1}} = \nabla_2 F(k_t, l_t).$$

Note that, up to a normalization (we could put $q_0 = 1$), these first-order conditions determine supporting prices for *any* feasible capital path (see Exercise 20.C.6).

The transversality condition says that $q_{t+1}F(k_t, l_t) \to 0$. If the sequence of productions $F(k_t, l_t)$ is bounded, then it suffices that $q_t \to 0$. In view of Proposition 20.C.1, we can conclude that a set of sufficient conditions for efficiency of a feasible and bounded capital path $(k_0, \ldots, k_t, \ldots)$ is that there exist a sequence of output prices $(q_0, \ldots, q_t, \ldots)$ such that

$$\frac{q_t}{q_{t+1}} = \nabla_1 F(k_t, l_t) \qquad \text{for all } t \tag{20.C.1}$$

and

$$q_t \to 0 \qquad (\text{equivalently, } 1/q_t \to \infty). \tag{20.C.2}$$

Because of the possibility of capital overaccumulation, (20.C.1), which is necessary, is not alone sufficient for efficiency. On the other hand, (20.C.2) is not necessary (see Section 20.E). Cass (1972) obtained a weakened version of (20.C.2) that, with (20.C.1), is both necessary and sufficient.[8] The condition is

$$\sum_{t=0}^{\infty} \frac{1}{q_t} = \infty. \tag{20.C.2'}$$

∎

**Example 20.C.7:** *Cost of Adjustment Model continued.* In the cost of adjustment model, a production plan at time $t-1$ involves the variables $k_{t-1}, l_{t-1}, k_t, c_t$. We associate with these variables the prices $q_{t-1}, w_{t-1}, q_t, s_t$. Profits are then

$$s_t(F(k_{t-1}, l_{t-1}) - k_t - \gamma(k_t - k_{t-1})) + q_t k_t - q_{t-1} k_{t-1} - w_{t-1} l_{t-1}.$$

Using the first-order profit-maximization conditions with respect to $k_t$ and $k_{t-1}$ we get the following two conditions:

(i) $q_t = s_t(1 + \gamma'(k_t - k_{t-1}))$; that is, the price of capacity at $t$ equals the investment cost in extra capacity at $t$.

(ii) $q_{t-1} = s_t(\nabla_1 F(k_{t-1}, l_{t-1}) + \gamma'(k_t - k_{t-1}))$; that is, the price of capacity at $t-1$ equals the return at $t$ of one unit of extra capacity at $t-1$ (the return has two parts: the increased production at $t$ and the saving in the cost of capacity adjustment at $t$).

Combining (i) and (ii),

$$\frac{q_{t-1}}{q_t} = \frac{\nabla_1 F(k_{t-1}, l_{t-1}) + \gamma'(k_t - k_{t-1})}{1 + \gamma'(k_t - k_{t-1})}. \tag{20.C.3}$$

Note that if there are no adjustment costs [i.e., if $\gamma(\cdot)$ is identically equal to zero], then (20.C.3) is precisely (20.C.1). Observe also that, in parallel to Example 20.C.6, condition (20.C.3) determines short-run supporting prices for any feasible capital path. ∎

---

In a general smooth model it is not difficult to explain how the supporting prices $(p_0, \dots, p_t, \dots)$ for an efficient path $(y_0, \dots, y_t, \dots)$ can be constructed. Note that, because of efficiency, every $y_t$ belongs to the boundary of $Y$. The smoothness property that we require is that, for every $t$, the production set $Y$ has a single (normalized) outward normal $q_t = (q_{bt}, q_{at})$ at $y_t$ (we could, for example, normalize $q_t$ to have unit length); see Figure 20.C.1. Less geometrically, smoothness means that at $y_t \in Y$ all the marginal rates of transformation ($MRT$) of inputs for inputs, inputs for outputs, and outputs for outputs are uniquely defined.

We claim that the efficiency property implies that for every $t$ we have that $q_{a,t-1} = \beta q_{bt}$ for some $\beta > 0$. Heuristically: for any two commodities their $MRT$ as outputs at $t$ for the production decision taken at time $t-1$ must be the same as their $MRT$ as inputs at $t$ for the production decision taken at time $t$. If this were not so, it would be possible to generate a surplus of goods. The argument is standard (recall the analysis of Section 16.F). Consider, for example, Figure 20.C.2, where in panel (a) we have drawn the output transformation frontier through $y_{a,t-1}$ (i.e., keeping $y_{b,t-1}$ fixed) and in panel (b) the input isoquant through $y_{bt}$ (i.e., keeping $y_{at}$ fixed; recall the sign conventions for inputs). We see that if the slopes at these points are not the same, then it is possible to move from $y_{a,t-1}$ to $y'_{a,t-1}$ and from $y_{bt}$ to $y'_{bt}$ in such a way that $y'_{a,t-1} + y'_{bt} > y_{a,t-1} + y_{bt}$, thus contradicting efficiency.

---

8. Some additional, very minor, regularity conditions on the production function $F(\cdot)$ are required for the validity of this equivalence.

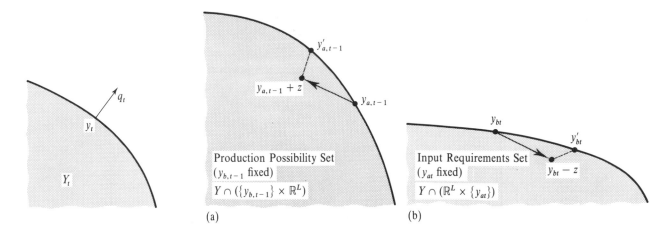

(a)

(b)

We construct the desired price sequence $(p_0, \ldots, p_t, \ldots)$ by induction. Put $p_0 = q_{b0}$ (i.e., the relative prices at $t = 0$ are the $MRT$s between goods at the initial part of the production plan $y_0 \in Y \subset \mathbb{R}^{2L}$). Suppose now that the prices $(p_0, \ldots, p_T)$ have already been determined, and that every $y_t$ up to $t = T - 1$ is myopically profit maximizing for these prices. Because of the first-order conditions for profit maximization at $T - 1$, we have that $p_T = \alpha q_{a, T-1}$ for some $\alpha > 0$. We know that $q_{a, T-1} = \beta q_{bT}$ for some $\beta > 0$. Then $p_T = \alpha \beta q_{bT}$. Therefore, if we put $p_{T+1} = \alpha \beta q_{aT}$, we have that $(p_T, p_{T+1}) = (\alpha \beta q_{bT}, \alpha \beta q_{aT})$ is proportional to $q_T = (q_{bT}, q_{aT})$, which means that $y_T$ is profit maximizing for $(p_T, p_{T+1})$. Hence we have extended our sequence to $(p_0, \ldots, p_{T+1})$ and we can keep going.

Note that, as in Examples 20.C.6 and 20.C.7, the construction of the supporting short-run prices does not make full use of the efficiency. What is used is that the production path is "short-run efficient" (that is, the production path cannot be shown inefficient by changes in the production plans at a finite number of dates).

The above observations can be made into a perfectly rigorous argument for the existence of Malinvaud prices in the smooth case. The proof for the nonsmooth case is more complex. It must combine an appeal to the separating hyperplane theorem (to get prices for truncated horizons) with a limit operation as the horizon goes to infinity. With a minor technical condition (call *nontightness* in the literature), this limit operation can be carried out.

**Figure 20.C.1 (left)**
Smooth production set.

**Figure 20.C.2 (right)**
A production path that is inefficient at $T$.

# 20.D Equilibrium: The One-Consumer Case

In this section, we bring the consumption and the production sides together and begin the study of equilibrium in the intertemporal setting. We shall start with the one-consumer case. As we will see in Section 20.G, the relevance of this case goes beyond the domain of applicability of the representative consumer theory of Chapter 4.

An economy is specified by a *short-term production technology* $Y \subset \mathbb{R}^{2L}$, a *utility function* $u(\cdot)$ defined on $\mathbb{R}_+^L$, a *discount factor* $\delta < 1$, and, finally, a (bounded) sequence of *initial endowments* $(\omega_0, \ldots, \omega_t, \ldots)$, $\omega_t \in \mathbb{R}_+^L$.

We assume that *Y satisfies hypotheses* (i) to (iv) of Section 20.C and that $u(\cdot)$ is *strictly concave, differentiable, and has strictly positive marginal utilities throughout its domain.*

Prices are given to us as sequences $(p_0, \ldots, p_t, \ldots)$ with $p_t \in \mathbb{R}_+^L$. As in Chapter 19 we can interpret these prices either as the prices of a complete system of forward markets occurring simultaneously at $t = 0$ or as the correctly anticipated (present value) prices of a sequence of spot markets. We will consider only bounded price sequences. In fact, most of the time we will have $\| p_t \| \to 0$.[9]

Given a production path $(y_0, \ldots, y_t, \ldots)$, $y_t \in Y$, the induced stream of consumptions $(c_0, \ldots, c_t, \ldots)$ is given by

$$c_t = y_{a,t-1} + y_{bt} + \omega_t.$$

If $c_t \geq 0$ for every $t$, then we say that the production path $(y_0, \ldots, y_t, \ldots)$ is *feasible*: Given the initial endowment stream the production path is capable of sustaining nonnegative consumptions at every period.

To keep the exposition manageable *from now on we restrict all our production paths and consumption streams to be bounded.* Delicate points come up in the general case, which are better avoided in a first approach. Alternatively, we could simply assume that our technology is such that any feasible production path is bounded.

Given a production path $(y_0, \ldots, y_t, \ldots)$ and a price sequence $(p_0, \ldots, p_t, \ldots)$, the induced stream of profits $(\pi_0, \ldots, \pi_t, \ldots)$ is given by

$$\pi_t = p_t \cdot y_{bt} + p_{t+1} \cdot y_{at} \qquad \text{for every } t.$$

Fixing $T$ and rearranging the terms of $\sum_{t \leq T} p_t \cdot c_t = \sum_{t \leq T} p_t \cdot (y_{a,t-1} + y_{bt} + \omega_t)$ we get

$$\sum_{t \leq T} (\pi_t + p_t \cdot \omega_t) - \sum_{t \leq T} p_t \cdot c_t = p_{T+1} \cdot y_{aT} \qquad (20.D.1)$$

Expression (20.D.1) is an important identity. It tells us that *the transversality condition is equivalent to the overall value of consumption not being strictly inferior to wealth* (i.e., there is no escape of purchasing power at infinity).

The definition of a Walrasian equilibrium is now as in the previous chapters. One only has to make sure that a few infinite sums make sense.

**Definition 20.D.1:** The (bounded) production path $(y_0^*, \ldots, y_t^*, \ldots)$, $y_t^* \in Y$, and the (bounded) price sequence $p = (p_0, \ldots, p_t, \ldots)$ constitute a *Walrasian* (or *competitive*) equilibrium if:

(i) $c_t^* = y_{a,t-1}^* + y_{bt}^* + \omega_t \geq 0$ \qquad for all $t$. \hfill (20.D.2)

(ii) For every $t$,

$$\pi_t = p_t \cdot y_{bt}^* + p_{t+1} \cdot y_{at}^* \geq p_t \cdot y_b + p_{t+1} \cdot y_a \qquad (20.D.3)$$

for all $y = (y_b, y_a) \in Y$.

(iii) The consumption sequence $(c_0^*, \ldots, c_t^*, \ldots) \geq 0$ solves the problem

$$\text{Max} \ \sum_t \delta^t u(c_t) \qquad (20.D.4)$$

$$\text{s.t. } \textstyle\sum_t p_t \cdot c_t \leq \sum_t \pi_t + \sum_t p_t \cdot \omega_t.$$

Condition (i) is the *feasibility* requirement. Condition (ii) is the short-run, or myopic, profit-maximization condition already considered in Section 20.C (Definition 20.C.3). The form of the budget constraint in part (iii) deserves comment. Note first that there is a single budget constraint. As in Chapter 19, this amounts to an assumption of *completeness*, which means, in one interpretation, that at time $t = 0$

---

9. Keep in mind that prices are to be thought of as measured in current-value terms.

there is a forward market for every commodity at every date, or, in another, that assets (e.g., money) are available that are capable of transferring purchasing power through time (see Exercise 20.D.1 for more on this). Secondly, observe that the strict monotonicity of $u(\cdot)$ implies that if we have reached utility maximization then, a fortiori, total wealth (denoted $w$) must be finite; that is,

$$w = \sum_t \pi_t + \sum_t p_t \cdot \omega_t < \infty.$$

Moreover, at the equilibrium consumptions the budget constraint of (20.D.4) must hold with equality.

   An important consequence of the last observation is that at equilibrium the transversality condition is satisfied. Formally, we have Proposition 20.D.1.

**Proposition 20.D.1:** Suppose that the (bounded) production path $(y_0^*, \ldots, y_t^*, \ldots)$ and the (bounded) price sequence $(p_0, \ldots, p_t, \ldots)$ constitute a Walrasian equilibrium. Then the transversality condition $p_{t+1} \cdot y_{at}^* \to 0$ holds.

**Proof:** Denote $c_t^* = y_{a,t-1}^* + y_{bt}^* + \omega_t$. By expression (20.D.1) we have

$$\sum_{t \leq T} (\pi_t + p_t \cdot \omega_t) - \sum_{t \leq T} p_t \cdot c_t = p_{T+1} \cdot y_{aT}.$$

Since each of the sums in the left-hand side converges to $w < \infty$ as $T \to \infty$, we conclude that $p_{T+1} \cdot y_{aT}^* \to 0$. ∎

   Another implication of $w < \infty$ is the possibility of replacing condition (ii) of Definition 20.D.1 by

   (ii') The production path $(y_0^*, \ldots, y_t^*, \ldots)$ maximizes total profits, in the sense that for any other path $(y_0, \ldots, y_t, \ldots)$ and any $T$ we have

$$\sum_{t=0}^{t=T} (p_t \cdot y_{bt} + p_{t+1} \cdot y_{at}) \leq \sum_t (p_t \cdot y_{bt}^* + p_{t+1} \cdot y_{at}^*) < \infty.$$

Clearly, (ii') implies (ii), and (ii) with $w < \infty$ implies (ii') (see Exercise 20.D.2). Thus, at equilibrium prices, the test of myopic and of overall profit maximization coincide. Could a similar statement be made for an appropriate concept of myopic utility maximization? We now investigate this question.

**Definition 20.D.2:** We say that the consumption stream $(c_0, \ldots, c_t, \ldots)$ is *myopically*, or *short-run, utility maximizing* in the budget set determined by $(p_0, \ldots, p_t, \ldots)$ and $w < \infty$ if utility cannot be increased by a new consumption stream that merely transfers purchasing power between some two consecutive periods.

   The key fact is presented in Exercise 20.D.3.

**Exercise 20.D.3:** Show that a consumption stream $(c_0, \ldots, c_t, \ldots) \gg 0$ is short-run utility maximizing for $p = (p_0, \ldots, p_t, \ldots)$ and $w < \infty$ if and only if it satisfies $\sum_t p_t \cdot c_t = w$ and the collection of first-order conditions:

   For every $t$ there is $\lambda_t > 0$ such that

$$\lambda_t p_t = \nabla u(c_t) \qquad \text{and} \qquad \lambda_t p_{t+1} = \delta \nabla u(c_{t+1}). \qquad (20.D.5)$$

   It follows from (20.D.5) that $\lambda_t p_t = \nabla u(c_t)$ and $\lambda_{t-1} p_t = \delta \nabla u(c_t)$. Therefore, $\lambda_{t-1} = \delta \lambda_t$ and so $\lambda_0 = \delta^t \lambda_t$. Hence letting $\lambda = \lambda_0$, we see that (20.D.5) is actually equivalent to

$$\text{For some } \lambda, \qquad \lambda p_t = \delta^t \, \nabla u(c_t) \quad \text{for all } t. \qquad (20.D.6)$$

Once we realize that myopic utility maximization in a budget set amounts to (20.D.6), we can verify that overall utility maximization follows. This is done in Proposition 20.D.2.

**Proposition 20.D.2:** If the consumption stream $(c_0, \ldots, c_t, \ldots)$ satisfies $\sum_t p_t \cdot c_t = w < \infty$ and condition (20.D.6), then it is utility maximizing in the budget set determined by $(p_0, \ldots, p_t, \ldots)$ and $w$.

---

**Proof:** We first note that we cannot improve upon $(c_0, \ldots, c_t, \ldots)$ by transferring purchasing power only through a finite number of dates. Indeed, (20.D.6) implies that the first-order sufficient conditions for any such constrained utility maximization problem are satisfied.

Suppose now that $(c'_0, \ldots, c'_t, \ldots)$ is a consumption stream satisfying the budget constraint and yielding higher total utility. Then for a sufficiently large $T$, consider the stream $(c''_0, \ldots, c''_t, \ldots)$ with $c''_t = c'_t$ for $t \le T$ and $c''_t = c_t$ for $t > T$. Because $\delta < 1$, there is $\varepsilon > 0$ such that if $T$ is large enough then there is an improvement of utility of more than $2\varepsilon$ in going from $(c_0, \ldots, c_t, \ldots)$ to $(c''_0, \ldots, c''_t, \ldots)$. Since $w < \infty$, the amount $\sum_{t > T} |p_t \cdot (c_t - c'_t)|$ can be made arbitrarily small. Hence, for large $T$ the stream $(c''_0, \ldots, c''_t, \ldots)$ is almost budget feasible. It follows that it can be made budget feasible by a small sacrifice of consumption in the first period resulting in a utility loss not larger than $\varepsilon$. Overall, it still results in an improvement. But this yields a contradiction because only the consumption in a finite number of periods has been altered in the process. ■

---

**Example 20.D.1:** In this example we illustrate the use of conditions (20.D.6) for the computation of equilibrium prices. Suppose that we are in a one-commodity world with utility function $\sum_t \delta^t \ln c_t$. Given a price sequence $(p_0, \ldots, p_t, \ldots)$ and wealth $w$, the first-order conditions for utility maximization (20.D.6) are

$$\lambda p_t = \frac{\delta^t}{c_t} \quad \text{for all } t, \quad \text{and} \quad \sum_t p_t c_t = w.$$

Hence, $w = \sum_t p_t c_t = (1/\lambda) \sum_t \delta^t = (1/\lambda)[1/(1 - \delta)]$ and so $p_t c_t = \delta^t/\lambda = \delta^t(1 - \delta)w$ for all $t$. Note that this implies a *constant rate of savings* because $p_T c_T / (\sum_{t \ge T} p_t c_t) = 1 - \delta$, for all $T$ (Exercise 20.D.4).[10]

We now discuss three possible production scenarios.

(i) The economy is of the exchange type; that is, there is no possibility of production and we are given an initial endowment sequence $(\omega_0, \ldots, \omega_t, \ldots) \gg 0$. Then the equilibrium must involve $c_t^* = \omega_t$ for every $t$, and therefore, normalizing to $\sum_t p_t \omega_t = 1$, the equilibrium prices should be

$$p_t = \frac{\delta^t(1 - \delta)}{\omega_t} \quad \text{for every } t.$$

---

10. Logarithmic utility functions facilitate computation and are very important in applications. However, they are not continuous at the boundary ($\ln c_t \to -\infty$ as $c_t \to 0$) and therefore violate one of our maintained assumptions. This does not affect the current analysis but should be kept in mind.

(ii) Suppose instead that $\omega_0 = 1$ and $\omega_t = 0$ for $t > 0$. There is, however, a linear production technology transforming every unit of input at $t$ into $\alpha > 0$ units of output at $t + 1$. Because of the boundary behavior of the utility function, consumption will be positive in every period, and therefore the technology will be in operation at every period. The linearity of the technologies then has the important implication that the equilibrium price sequence is completely determined by the technology. Putting $p_0 = 1$, we must have $p_t = 1/\alpha^t$. Wealth is $w = p_0 \omega_0 = 1$, and therefore the equilibrium consumptions must be $c_t^* = [\delta^t(1 - \delta)]/p_t = (\alpha\delta)^t(1 - \delta)$. Note that, as long as $1 \leq \alpha < 1/\delta$, both the price and the consumption sequences are bounded. Observe also the interesting fact that for this example we have been able to compute the equilibrium without explicitly solving for the sequence of capital investments.

(iii) We are as in (ii) except that we now have a general technology $F(k)$ transforming every unit $k_t$, of investment at $t$ into $F(k_t)$ units of output at $t + 1$. This output can then be used indistinctly for consumption or investment purposes at $t + 1$. That is, $c_{t+1} = F(k_t) - k_{t+1}$. The logarithmic form of the utility function allows for a shortcut to the computation of equilibrium prices. Indeed, say that $(p_0, \ldots, p_t, \ldots)$ are equilibrium prices and $(c_0^*, \ldots, c_t^*, \ldots)$, $(k_0^*, \ldots, k_t^*, \ldots)$ equilibrium paths of consumption and capital investment. Then we know that at any $T$ a constant fraction $\delta$ of remaining wealth is invested. That is,

$$p_{T+1}k_{T+1}^* = \delta\left(\sum_{t \geq T+1} p_t c_t^*\right) = \delta p_{T+1}F(k_t^*).$$

Therefore, we must have $k_{t+1}^* = \delta F(k_t^*)$ for every $t$. With $k_0 = \omega_0 = 1$ given, this allows us to iteratively compute the sequence of equilibrium capital investments. The sequence of prices is then obtained from the profit-maximization conditions $p_{t+1}F'(k_t^*) - p_t = 0$. ∎

Since a Walrasian equilibrium is myopically profit maximizing and satisfies the transversality condition (Proposition 20.D.1), we know from Proposition 20.C.1 that it is production efficient (assuming $p_t \gg 0$ for all $t$). Can we strengthen this to the claim that the full first welfare theorem holds? We will now verify that we can. In the current one-consumer problem, Pareto optimality simply means that the equilibrium solves the utility-maximization problem under the technological and endowment constraints:

$$\text{Max} \quad \sum_t \delta^t u(c_t), \tag{20.D.7}$$

$$\text{s.t. } c_t = y_{a,t-1} + y_{bt} + \omega_t \geq 0 \quad \text{and} \quad y_t \in Y \text{ for all } t.$$

**Proposition 20.D.3:** Any Walrasian equilibrium path $(y_0^*, \ldots, y_t^*, \ldots)$ solves the planning problem (20.D.7).

**Proof:** Denote by $B$ the budget set determined by the Walrasian equilibrium price sequence $(p_0, \ldots, p_t, \ldots)$ and wealth $w = \sum_t \pi_t + \sum_t p_t \cdot \omega_t$, where

$$\pi_t = p_t \cdot y_{bt}^* + p_{t+1} \cdot y_{a,t+1}^*$$

for all $t$. That is,

$$B = \{(c'_0, \ldots, c'_t, \ldots): c'_t \geq 0 \text{ for all } t \text{ and } \sum_t p_t \cdot c'_t \leq w\}.$$

By the definition of Walrasian equilibrium, the utility of the stream $(c^*_0, \ldots, c^*_t, \ldots)$ defined by $c^*_t = y^*_{a,t-1} + y^*_{bt} + \omega_t$ is maximal in this budget set. It suffices, therefore, to show that any feasible path $(y''_0, \ldots, y''_t, \ldots)$, that is, any path for which $y''_t \in Y$ and $c''_t = y''_{a,t-1} + y''_{bt} + \omega_t \geq 0$ for all $t$, must yield a consumption stream in $B$. To see this note that, for any $T$,

$$\sum_{t \leq T} p_t \cdot c''_t = \sum_{t \leq T-1} (p_t \cdot y''_{bt} + p_{t+1} \cdot y''_{at}) + p_T \cdot y''_{bT} + \sum_{t \leq T} p_t \cdot \omega_t.$$

By the possibility of truncation of production plans, we have $(y''_{bT}, 0) \in Y$. Therefore, by short-run profit maximization, $p_t \cdot y''_{bT} \leq \pi_T$ and $p_t \cdot y''_{bt} + p_{t+1} \cdot y''_{at} \leq \pi_t$ for all $t \leq T - 1$. Hence,

$$\sum_{t \leq T} p_t \cdot c''_t \leq \sum_{t \leq T} \pi_t + \sum_{t \leq T} p_t \cdot \omega_t \leq w \quad \text{for all } T,$$

which implies $\sum_t p_t \cdot c''_t \leq w$. ∎

Let us now ask for the converse of Proposition 20.D.3 (i.e., for the second welfare theorem question; see chapter 16): Is any solution $(y_0, \ldots, y_t, \ldots)$ to the planning problem (20.D.7) a Walrasian equilibrium? In essence, the answer is "yes," but the precise theorems are somewhat technical because, to obtain a well-behaved price system (i.e., a price system as we understand it: a sequence of nonzero prices), one needs some regularity condition on the path. We give an example of one such result.[11]

**Proposition 20.D.4:** Suppose that the (bounded) path $(y^*_0, \ldots, y^*_t, \ldots)$ solves the planning problem (20.D.7) and that it yields strictly positive consumption (in the sense that, for some $\varepsilon > 0$, $c_{\ell t} = y^*_{\ell a, t-1} + y^*_{\ell bt} + \omega_{\ell t} > \varepsilon$ for all $\ell$ and $t$). Then the path is a Walrasian equilibrium with respect to some price sequence $(p_0, \ldots, p_t, \ldots)$.

**Proof:** We provide only a sketch of the proof. A possible candidate for an equilibrium price system is suggested by expression (20.D.6):

$$p_t = \delta^t \nabla u(c^*_t) \quad \text{for all } t,$$

where $c^*_t = y^*_{a,t-1} + y^*_{bt} + \omega_t$. Because $(c^*_0, \ldots, c^*_t, \ldots)$ is bounded above and bounded away from the boundary (uniformly in $t$) we have $\sum_t \|p_t\| < \infty$, which implies the transversality condition. In turn, by expression (20.D.1) this yields $\sum_t p_t \cdot c^*_t = \sum_t (\pi_t + p_t \cdot \omega_t) = w < \infty$. Therefore, by Proposition 20.D.2, the utility-maximization condition holds.

It remains to establish that short-run profit maximization also holds. To that effect suppose that this is not so, that is, that for some $T$ there is $y' \in Y$ with

$$p_T \cdot y'_b + p_{T+1} \cdot y'_a > p_T \cdot y^*_{bT} + p_{T+1} \cdot y^*_{aT} = \pi_T.$$

Let $(y'_1, \ldots, y'_t, \ldots)$ be the path with $y'_T = y'$ and $y'_t = y^*_t$ for any $t \neq T$. Let $(c'_0, \ldots, c'_t, \ldots)$ be the associated consumption stream. Because of the convexity of $Y$ and the strict positivity property of $(c^*_0, \ldots, c^*_t, \ldots)$ we can assume that $y'_T = y'$ is sufficiently close to $y^*_T$ for us to

---

11. A general treatment would involve, as in Sections 15.C or 16.D, the application of a suitable version (here infinite-dimensional) of the separating hyperplane theorem. The next result gets around this by exploiting the differentiability of $u(\cdot)$. It is thus parallel to the discussion in Section 16.F.

have $c_t' \gg 0$ for all $t$ and, moreover, for it to be legitimate to determine the sign of

$$\sum_t \delta^t(u(c_t') - u(c_t^*)) = \delta^T(u(c_T') - u(c_T^*)) + \delta^{T+1}(u(c_{T+1}') - u(c_{T+1}^*))$$

by signing the first-order term

$$\delta^T \nabla u(c_T^*) \cdot (c_T' - c_T^*) + \delta^{T+1} \nabla u(c_{T+1}^*) \cdot (c_{T+1}' - c_{T+1}^*)$$

$$= p_T \cdot (y_{bT}' - y_{bT}^*) + p_{T+1} \cdot (y_{aT}' - y_{aT}^*)$$

$$= p_T \cdot y_{bT}' + p_{T+1} \cdot y_{aT}' - p_T \cdot y_{bT}^* - p_{T+1} \cdot y_{aT}^* > 0.$$

But this conclusion contradicts the assumption that $(y_0^*, \ldots, y_t^*, \ldots)$ solves (20.D.7). ∎

---

The close connection between the solutions of the equilibrium and the planning problem (20.D.7) has three important implications for, respectively, the existence, uniqueness, and computation of equilibria.

The first implication is that it reduces the question of the *existence* of an equilibrium to the possibility of solving a single optimization problem, albeit an infinite-dimensional one.

**Proposition 20.D.5:** Suppose that there is a uniform bound on the consumption streams generated by all the feasible paths. Then the planning problem (20.D.7) attains a maximum; that is, there is a feasible path that yields utility at least as large as the utility corresponding to any other feasible paths.

The proof, which is purely technical and which we skip, involves simply establishing that, in a suitable infinite-dimensional sense, the objective function of problem (20.D.7) is continuous and the constraint set is compact.

The second implication is that it allows us to assert the *uniqueness* of equilibrium.

**Proposition 20.D.6:** The planning problem (20.D.7) has at most one consumption stream solution.

**Proof:** The proof consists of the usual argument showing that the maximum of a strictly concave function in a convex set is unique. Suppose that $(y_0, \ldots, y_t, \ldots)$ and $(y_0', \ldots, y_t', \ldots)$ are feasible paths with $\sum_t \delta^t u(c_t) = \sum_t \delta^t u(c_t') = \gamma$, where $(c_0, \ldots, c_t, \ldots)$ and $(c_0', \ldots, c_t', \ldots)$ are the consumption streams associated with the two production paths. Consider $y_t'' = \frac{1}{2}y_t + \frac{1}{2}y_t'$. Then the path $(y_0'', \ldots, y_t'', \ldots)$ is feasible and at every $t$ the consumption level is $c_t'' = \frac{1}{2}c_t + \frac{1}{2}c_t'$. Hence, $\sum_t \delta^t u(c_t'') \geq \gamma$, with the inequality strict if $c_t \neq c_t'$ for some $t$. Thus, if $c_t \neq c_t'$ for some $t$, the paths $(y_0, \ldots, y_t, \ldots)$, $(y_0', \ldots, y_t', \ldots)$ could not both solve (20.D.7). ∎

The third implication is that Proposition 20.D.3 provides a workable approach to the *computation* of the equilibrium. We devote the rest of this section to elaborating on this point.

### The Computation of Equilibrium and Euler Equations

It will be convenient to pursue the discussion of computational issues in the slightly restricted setting of Example 20.C.4, the $(N + 1)$-sector model. To recall, we have $N$ capital goods, labor, and a consumption good. We fix the endowments of labor to a constant level through time. A function $G(k, k')$ gives the total amount of consumption good obtainable at any $t$ if the investment in capital goods at $t - 1$ is given by the vector $k \in \mathbb{R}^N$, the investment at $t$ is required to be $k' \in \mathbb{R}_+^N$, and the labor usage at $t - 1$ and $t$ is fixed at the level exogenously given by the initial endowments. We denote by $A \subset \mathbb{R}^N \times \mathbb{R}^N$ the region of pairs $(k, k') \in \mathbb{R}^{2N}$ compatible with nonnegative consumption [i.e., $A = \{(k, k') \in \mathbb{R}^{2N} : G(k, k') \geq 0\}$]. For notational convenience, we write $u(G(k, k'))$ as $u(k, k')$. We assume that $A$ is convex and that $u(\cdot, \cdot)$ is strictly concave. Also, at $t = 0$ there is some already installed capital investment $\bar{k}_0$ and this is the only initial endowment of capital in the economy.

In this economy the planning problem (20.D.7) becomes[12]

$$\text{Max} \quad \sum_t \delta^t u(k_{t-1}, k_t) \tag{20.D.8}$$

$$\text{s.t. } (k_{t-1}, k_t) \in A \text{ for every } t, \text{ and } k_0 = \bar{k}_0.$$

From now on we assume that (20.D.8) has a (bounded) solution. Because of the strict concavity of $u(\cdot, \cdot)$ this solution is unique.

For every $t \geq 1$ the vector of variables $k_t \in \mathbb{R}^N$ enters the objective function of (20.D.8) only through the two-term sum $\delta^t u(k_{t-1}, k_t) + \delta^{t+1} u(k_t, k_{t+1})$. Therefore, differentiating with respect to these $N$ variables, we obtain the following necessary conditions for an interior path $(k_0, \ldots, k_t, \ldots)$ to be a solution of the problem (20.D.8):[13]

$$\frac{\partial u(k_{t-1}, k_t)}{\partial k_n'} + \delta \frac{\partial u(k_t, k_{t+1})}{\partial k_n} = 0 \qquad \text{for every } n \leq N \text{ and } t \geq 1.$$

In vector notation,

$$\nabla_2 u(k_{t-1}, k_t) + \delta \nabla_1 u(k_t, k_{t+1}) = 0 \qquad \text{for every } t \geq 1. \tag{20.D.9}$$

Conditions (20.D.9) are known as the *Euler equations* of the problem (20.D.8).

**Example 20.D.2:** Consider the Ramsey–Solow technology of Example 20.C.1 (with $l_t = 1$ for all $t$). Then, $u(k, k') = u(F(k) - k')$ and $A = \{(k, k'): k' \leq F(k)\}$. Therefore, the Euler equations take the form

$$-u'(F(k_{t-1}) - k_t) + \delta u'(F(k_t) - k_{t+1})F'(k_t) = 0, \quad \text{for all } t \geq 1$$

or

$$\frac{u'(c_t)}{\delta u'(c_{t+1})} = F'(k_t) \qquad \text{for all } t \geq 1.$$

In words: the marginal utilities of consuming at $t$ or of investing and postponing consumption one period are the same. ∎

**Example 20.D.3:** Consider the cost-of-adjustment technology of Example 20.C.2 (except that as in Example 20.D.2 we fix $l_t = 1$ for all $t$ and drop labor as an explicitly considered commodity) and suppose we have an overall firm that tries to maximize the infinite discounted sum of profits by means of a suitable investment policy in capacity. Output can be sold at a constant unitary price that, with a constant rate

---

12. By convention we put $u(k_{-1}, k_0) = 0$.

13. The expression "interior path" means that $(k_t, k_{t+1})$ is in the interior of $A$ for all $t$. For the interpretation of the expression to come, recall also that $k_n$ and $k_n'$ stand, respectively, for the $n$th and the $(N + n)$th argument of $u(k, k')$.

of interest, gives a present value price of $\delta^t$. Thus the problem becomes that of maximizing $\sum_t \delta^t[F(k_{t-1}) - k_t - \gamma(k_t - k_{t-1})]$. The Euler equations are then

$$-1 - \gamma'(k_t - k_{t-1}) + \delta[F'(k_t) + \gamma'(k_{t+1} - k_t)] = 0 \qquad \text{for all } t \geq 1.$$

In words: the marginal cost of a unit of investment in capacity at $t$ equals the discounted value of the marginal product of capacity at $t$ *plus* the marginal saving in the cost of capacity expansion at $t + 1$. Note that, iterating from $t = 1$, we get

$$1 + \gamma'(k_1 - k_0) = \sum_{t \geq 1} \delta^t(F'(k_t) - 1).$$

In words: At the optimum, the cost of investing in an extra unit of capacity at $t = 1$ equals the discounted sum of the marginal products of a *maintained* increase of a unit of capacity.[14] See Exercise 20.D.5 for more detail.[15] ■

Suppose that a path $(k_0, \ldots, k_t, \ldots)$ satisfies the Euler necessary equations (20.D.9). From their own definition, and the concavity of $u(\cdot, \cdot)$, it follows that the Euler equations are also sufficient to guarantee that the trajectory cannot be improved upon by a trajectory involving changes in a single $k_t$. In fact, the same is true if the changes are limited to any finite number of periods (see Exercise 20.D.6). Thus, we can say that the Euler equations are necessary and sufficient for short-run optimization. The question is then: Do the Euler equations (or, equivalently, short-run optimization) imply long-run optimization? We shall see that, under a regularity property on the path (related, in a manner we shall not make explicit, to the transversality condition[16]), they do.

We say that the path $(k_0, \ldots, k_t, \ldots)$ is *strictly interior* if it stays strictly away from the boundary of the admissible region $A$. [More precisely, the path is strictly interior if there is $\varepsilon > 0$ such that for every $t$ there is an $\varepsilon$ neighborhood of $(k_t, k_{t+1})$ entirely contained in $A$.]

**Proposition 20.D.7:** Suppose that the path $(\bar{k}_0, \ldots, k_t, \ldots)$ is bounded, is strictly interior, and satisfies the Euler equations (20.D.9). Then it solves the optimization problem (20.D.8).

---

**Proof:** The basic argument is familiar. If $(\bar{k}_0, \ldots, k_t, \ldots)$ does not solve (20.D.8), then there is a feasible trajectory $(\bar{k}_0, \ldots, k_t', \ldots)$ that gives a higher utility. To simplify the reasoning suppose that this trajectory is bounded. Then, by the concavity of the objective function, the boundedness of $(\bar{k}_0, \ldots, k_t, \ldots)$ and its strict interiority, we can assume that, for every $t$, $k_t'$ is so close to $k_t$ that $(k_t', k_{t+1}) \in A$. We can now take $T$ large enough for $\sum_{t<T} \delta^t u(k_{t-1}', k_t') > \sum_{t<T} \delta^t u(k_{t-1}, k_t)$ and define then a new trajectory $(\bar{k}_0, \ldots, k_t'', \ldots)$ by

---

14. That is to say, the extra unit of capacity available at $t = 1$ produces $F'(k_1)$ at $t = 2$. Of this amount, one unit is devoted to additional investment at $t = 2$. With this, at $t = 2$ the net addition of capacity has not changed (the initial and final capacities at $t = 2$ expand by one unit) and therefore there is no change in the adjustment cost paid. Consequently, the net gain at $t = 2$ in terms of commodity is $F'(k_1) - 1$. But this is not all the gain because the extra unit of capacity available at $t = 2$ produces $F'(k_2)$ at $t = 3$, and so on.

15. The ideas of this example are related to what is known in macroeconomic theory as the $q$-theory of investment. See, for example, Chapter 2 of Blanchard and Fischer (1989).

16. We refer to the storage illustration of Example 20.C.5 for the need to appeal to a regularity property.

$k''_t = k'_t$ for $t \leq T$ and $k''_t = k_t$ for $t > T$. The new trajectory is admissible [note that $(k'_T, k_{T+1}) \in A$]; it coincides with $(\bar{k}_0, \ldots, k'_t, \ldots)$ up to $T$ and with $(\bar{k}_0, \ldots, k_t, \ldots)$ after $T$. Moreover, if $T$ is large enough, it still gives higher utility than $(\bar{k}_0, \ldots, k_t, \ldots)$. But this is impossible because, as we have already indicated, the Euler equations imply short-run optimization, that is, they are the first-order conditions for the optimization problem where we are constrained to adjust only the variables corresponding to a finite number of periods (see Exercise 20.D.6). ∎

It may be helpful at this stage to introduce the concept of the *value function* $V(k)$ and the *policy function* $\psi(k)$. Given an initial condition $k_0 = k$, the maximum value attained by (20.D.8) is denoted $V(k)$, and if $(k_0, k_1, \ldots, k_t, \ldots)$ is the (unique) trajectory solving (20.D.8) with $k_0 = k$, then we put $\psi(k) = k_1$. That is, $\psi(k) \in \mathbb{R}^N$ is the vector of optimal levels of investment, hence of capital, at $t = 1$ when the levels of capital at $t = 0$ are given by $k$.

What accounts for the importance of the policy function is the observation that if the path $(\hat{k}_0, \ldots, \hat{k}_t, \ldots)$ solves (20.D.8) for $k_0 = \hat{k}_0$ then, for any $T$, the path $(\hat{k}_T, \ldots, \hat{k}_{T+t}, \ldots)$ solves (20.D.8) for $k_0 = \hat{k}_T$. Thus, if $(k_0, \ldots, k_t, \ldots)$ solves (20.D.8) we must have

$$k_{t+1} = \psi(k_t) \text{ for every } t, \tag{20.D.10}$$

and we see that the optimal path can be computed from knowledge of $k_0$ and the policy function $\psi(\cdot)$. But how do we determine $\psi(\cdot)$? We now describe two approaches to the computation of $\psi(\cdot)$. The first exploits the Euler equations; the second rests on the method of *dynamic programming*.

The Euler equations (20.D.9) suggest an iterative procedure for the computation of $\psi(k)$. Fix $k_0 = k$ and consider the equations corresponding to $k_1$. With $k_0$ given, we have $N$ equations in the $2N$ unknowns $k_1 \in \mathbb{R}^N$ and $k_2 \in \mathbb{R}^N$. There are therefore $N$ degrees of freedom. Suppose that we try to fix $k_1$ arbitrarily [equivalently, we try to fix $-\nabla_2 u(k_0, k_1)$, the marginal costs of investment at $t = 1$] and then use the $N$ Euler equations at $t = 1$ to solve for the remaining $k_2$ unknowns [equivalently, we adjust the commitments for investment at $t = 2$ so that the discounted marginal payoff of investment at $t = 1$, $\delta \nabla_1 u(k_1, k_2)$, equals the preestablished marginal cost of investment at $t = 1$, i.e. $-\nabla_2 u(k_0, k_1)$]. Suppose that such a solution $k_2$ is found [by the strict concavity of $u(\cdot)$, if there is one solution then it has to be unique]. We can then repeat the process. The $N$ Euler equations for period 2 are now exactly determined: Both $k_1$ and $k_2$ are given, but we still have the $N$ variables $k_3$ corresponding to $t = 3$ with which we can try to satisfy the $N$ equations of period 2. Suppose that we reiterate in this fashion. There are three possibilities. The first is that the process breaks down somewhere, that is, that given $k_{t-1}$ and $k_t$ there is no solution $k_{t+1}$ [or, more precisely, no solution with $(k_t, k_{t+1}) \in A$]; the second is that we generate a sequence that is unbounded (or nonstrictly interior); the third is that we generate a bounded (and strictly interior) sequence $(k_0, k_1, \ldots, k_t, \ldots)$. In the third case, by Proposition 20.D.7 we have obtained an optimum, and since by Proposition 20.D.6 the optimum is unique, we can conclude that *given $k_0$, the third possibility (the trajectory starting at $k_0$ and $k_1$ is strictly interior and bounded) can occur for at most one value of $k_1$. If it occurs, this value of $k_1$ is precisely $\psi(k_0)$.* Thus, the computational method is: Solve the difference equation induced by the Euler equations with initial condition $(k_0, k_1)$ and then for fixed $k_0$ search for an initial condition $k_1$ generating a bounded infinite path.

**Example 20.D.4:** Consider a Ramsey–Solow model with linear technology $F(k) = 2k$ and utility function $\sum_t (1/2)^t \ln c_t$. Then $u(k_{t-1}, k_t) = \ln (2k_{t-1} - k_t)$ and the period-$t$ Euler equation is (see Exercise 20.D.7)

$$k_{t+1} = 3k_t - 2k_{t-1}.$$

This difference equation has the solution $k_t = k_0 + (k_1 - k_0)(2^t - 1)$. If $k_1 < k_0$, then $k_t$ eventually becomes negative. If $k_1 > k_0$, then $k_t$ is unbounded. The only value of $k_1$ generating a bounded $k_t$ is $k_1 = k_0$. Therefore, $\psi(k_0) = k_0$ for any $k_0$. It is instructive to see what happens if we try $k_1 \geq k_0$. Then, the path induced by the difference equation is feasible and, in fact, we have a constant level of consumption $c_t = 2k_{t-1} - k_t = 2k_0 - k_1$. Thus, for $k_1 > k_0$, we have here an example of a path that is compatible with the Euler equations but that is not optimal, because at $k_1 = k_0$ we get a higher level of constant consumption.[17] ∎

The dynamic programming approach exploits the recursivity of the optimum problem (20.D.8), namely, the fact that

$$V(k) = \underset{k' \text{ with } (k, k') \in A}{\text{Max}} u(k, k') + \delta V(k'), \qquad (20.\text{D}.11)$$

and obtains $\psi(k)$ as the vector $k'$ that solves (20.D.11). This, of course, only transforms the problem into one of computing the value function $V(\cdot)$. However, it turns out that, first, under some general conditions [e.g., if $V(\cdot)$ is bounded] the value function is the *only* function that solves (20.D.11) when viewed as a functional equation, that is, $V(\cdot)$ is the only function for which (20.D.11) is true for every $k$, and, second, that there are some well-known and quite effective algorithms for solving equations such as (20.D.11) for the unknown function $V(\cdot)$. (See Section M.M. of the Mathematical Appendix.)

We end this section by pointing out two implications of the definition of the value function (see Exercise 20.D.8):

(i) *The value function $V(k)$ is concave.*
(ii) *For every perturbation parameter $z \in \mathbb{R}^N$ with $(k + z, \psi(k)) \in A$ we have*

$$V(k + z) \geq u(k + z, \psi(k)) + \delta V(\psi(k)). \qquad (20.\text{D}.12)$$

Suppose that $N = 1$ and $(k, \psi(k))$ is interior to $A$. For later reference we point out that from (i), (ii), and $V(k) = u(k, \psi(k)) + \delta V(\psi(k))$ we obtain

$$V'(k) = \nabla_1 u(k, \psi(k))$$

and, if $V(\cdot)$ is twice-differentiable,

$$V''(k) \geq \nabla_{11}^2 u(k, \psi(k)).$$

(See Figure 20.D.1 and Exercise 20.D.9.[18])

---

17. Hence, when $k_1 > k_0$, the Euler equations lead to capital overaccumulation. We note, without further elaboration, that given a path satisfying the Euler equations we could use the equations themselves to determine a myopically supporting price sequence. However, if $k_1 > k_0$ this sequence will violate the transversality condition.

18. The expression $\nabla_{ij}^2 f(\cdot)$ denotes the $ij$ second partial derivative of the real-value function $f(\cdot)$.

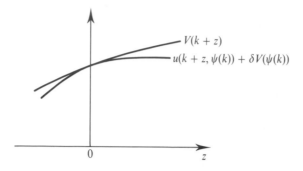

**Figure 20.D.1**

Along an optimal path the value function is majorized by the utilities of single-period adjustments.

# 20.E  Stationary Paths, Interest Rates, and Golden Rules

In this section, we concentrate on the study of steady states. This study constitutes a first step towards the analysis of the dynamics of equilibrium paths. We refer to Bliss (1975), Gale (1973), or Weizsäcker (1971) for further analysis of steady-state theory.

We begin with a production set $Y \subset \mathbb{R}^{2L}$ satisfying the properties considered in Section 20.C. Recall that a production path is a sequence $(y_0, \ldots, y_t, \ldots)$ with $y_t \in Y$ for every $t$.

**Definition 20.E.1:** A production path $(y_0, \ldots, y_t, \ldots)$ is *stationary*, or a *steady state*, if there is a production plan $\bar{y} = (\bar{y}_b, \bar{y}_a) \in Y$ such that $y_t = \bar{y}$ for all $t > 0$.

Abusing terminology slightly, we refer to the "stationary path $(\bar{y}, \ldots, \bar{y}, \ldots)$" as simply the "stationary path $\bar{y}$."

The first important observation is that stationary paths *that are also efficient* are supportable by proportional prices.[19] This is shown in Proposition 20.E.1.

**Proposition 20.E.1:** Suppose that $\bar{y} \in Y$ defines a stationary and efficient path. Then, there is a price vector $p_0 \in \mathbb{R}^L$ and an $\alpha > 0$ such that the path is myopically profit maximizing for the price sequence $(p_0, \alpha p_0, \ldots, \alpha^t p_0, \ldots)$.

**Proof:** A complete proof is too delicate an affair, but the basic intuition may be grasped from the case in which production sets have smooth boundaries. For this case we can, in fact, show that *every* (myopically) supporting price sequence must be proportional.

By the efficiency of the path $(\bar{y}, \ldots, \bar{y}, \ldots)$, the vector $\bar{y}$ must lie at the boundary of $Y$. Let $\bar{q} = (\bar{q}_0, \bar{q}_1)$ be the unique (up to normalization) vector perpendicular to $Y$ at $\bar{y}$. Also, by the small type discussion at the end of Section 20.C, there exists a price sequence $(p_0, \ldots, p_t, \ldots)$ that myopically supports this efficient path. Because $\bar{y} \in Y$ is short-run profit maximizing at every $t$ we must have $(p_t, p_{t+1}) = \lambda_t(\bar{q}_0, \bar{q}_1)$ for some $\lambda_t > 0$. Therefore, $p_t = \lambda_t \bar{q}_0$ and $p_{t+1} = \lambda_t \bar{q}_1$ for all $t$. In particular, $p_t = \lambda_{t-1}\bar{q}_1$ and $p_{t+1} = \lambda_{t+1}\bar{q}_0$. Combining, we obtain $p_{t+1} = (\lambda_t/\lambda_{t-1})p_t$ and

---

19. To prevent possible misunderstanding, we warn that establishing the inefficiency of a given stationary path will typically require the consideration of nonstationary paths.

$p_{t+1} = (\lambda_{t+1}/\lambda_t)p_t$. From this we get $\lambda_t/\lambda_{t-1} = \lambda_{t+1}/\lambda_t$ for all $t \geq 1$. Hence, denoting this quotient by $\alpha$, we have $p_{t+1} = \alpha p_t = \alpha^2 p_{t-1} = \cdots = \alpha^{t+1} p_0$.

The factor $\alpha$ has a simple interpretation. Indeed, $r = (1 - \alpha)/\alpha$ [so that $p_t = (1 + r)p_{t+1}$] can be viewed as a *rate of interest* implicit in the price sequence (see Exercise 20.E.1).

Proposition 20.E.1 is a sort of second welfare theorem result for stationary paths. We could also pose the parallel first welfare theorem question. Namely, suppose that $(\bar{y}, \ldots, \bar{y}, \ldots)$ is a stationary path myopically supported by a proportional price sequence with rate of interest $r$. If $r > 0$, then $p_t = (1/(1 + r))^t p_0 \to 0$ and therefore the transversality condition $p_t \cdot \bar{y}_a \to 0$ is satisfied. We conclude from Proposition 20.C.1 that the path is efficient. If $r \leq 0$, the transversality condition is not satisfied ($p_t$ does not go to zero), but this does not automatically imply inefficiency because the transversality condition is sufficient but not necessary for efficiency. Suppose that $r < 0$ and, to make things simple, let us be in the smooth case again. Consider the stationary candidate paths defined by the constant production plan $\bar{y}_\varepsilon = (\bar{y}_b + \varepsilon e, \bar{y}_a - \varepsilon e)$, where $e = (1, \ldots, 1) \in \mathbb{R}^L$. This candidate path uses fewer inputs (or produces more outputs) at $t = 0$ and generates exactly the same net input–output vector at every other $t$. Therefore, if for some $\varepsilon > 0$, the candidate path is in fact a feasible path; that is, if $\bar{y}_\varepsilon \in Y$, then the stationary path $\bar{y}$ is not efficient (it overaccumulates). But if $Y$ has a smooth boundary at $\bar{y}$, the feasibility of $\bar{y}_\varepsilon$ for some $\varepsilon > 0$ can be tested by checking whether $\bar{y}_\varepsilon - \bar{y} = \varepsilon(e, -e)$ lies below the hyperplane determined by the supporting prices $(p_0, [1/(1 + r)]p_0)$. Evaluating, we have $\varepsilon(1 - 1/(1 + r))p_0 \cdot e < 0$, because $r < 0$. Conclusion: For $\varepsilon$ small enough, the stationary path $\bar{y}$ is dominated by the stationary path $\bar{y}_\varepsilon$. We record these facts for later reference in Proposition 20.E.2.

**Proposition 20.E.2:** Suppose that the stationary path $(\bar{y}, \ldots, \bar{y} \ldots), \bar{y} \in Y$, is myopically supported by proportional prices with rate of interest $r$, then the path is efficient if $r > 0$ and inefficient if $r < 0$.

We have not yet dealt with the case $r = 0$, which as we shall see, is very important.[20] We will later verify in a more specific setup that efficiency obtains in this case.

Let us now bring in the consumption side of the economy and consider *stationary equilibrium paths*. Assuming differentiability and interiority, a stationary path $(\bar{y}, \ldots, \bar{y}, \ldots)$ that is also an equilibrium can be supported only (up to a normalization) by the price sequence $p_t = \delta^t \nabla u(\bar{c})$, where $\bar{c} = \bar{y}_b + \bar{y}_a$; recall Proposition 20.D.4 and expression (20.D.6). That is, *a stationary equilibrium is supported by a price sequence embodying a proportionality factor equal to the discount factor $\delta$*, or, equivalently, with rate of interest $r = (1 - \delta)/\delta$.

**Definition 20.E.2:** A stationary production path that is myopically supported by proportional prices $p_t = \alpha^t p_0$ with $\alpha = \delta$ is called a *modified golden rule path*. A stationary production path myopically supported by constant prices $p_t = p_0$ is called a *golden rule path*.

---

20. Note that 0 is the rate of growth implicit in the path $(\bar{y}, \ldots, \bar{y}, \ldots)$. In a more general treatment we could allow for a constant returns technology and for the production path to be proportional (but not necessarily stationary). Then Proposition 20.E.2 remains valid with 0 replaced by the corresponding rate of growth.

Depending on the technology and on the discount factor $\delta$, there may be a single or there may be several modified golden rule paths (see the small-type discussion at the end of this section). But in any case we have just seen that a *stationary equilibrium path is necessarily a modified golden rule path*. Thus, we have the important implication that the *candidates for stationary equilibrium paths* $(\bar{y}, \ldots, \bar{y}, \ldots)$ *are completely determined by the technology and the discount factor and are independent of the utility function* $u(\cdot)$.

To pursue the analysis it will be much more convenient to reduce the level of abstraction. Consider an extremely simple case, the Ramsey–Solow model technology of Example 20.C.1. We study trajectories with $l_t = 1$ for all $t$ (imagine that there is available one unit of labor at every point in time). We can then identify a production path with the sequence of capital investments $(k_0, \ldots, k_t, \ldots)$.

Given $(k_0, \ldots, k_t, \ldots)$, denote $r_t = \nabla_1 F(k_t, 1) - 1$. Thus, $r_t$ is the *net* (i.e., after replacing capital) *marginal productivity of capital*. Suppose that $k_t > 0$ and that the sequence of output prices $(q_0, \ldots, q_t, \ldots)$ and wages $(w_0, \ldots, w_t, \ldots)$ myopically price supports the given path. Then, by the first-order condition for profit maximization, we have $q_{t+1}(1 + r_t) - q_t = 0$. Hence $r_t$ is the output rate of interest at time $t$ implicit in the output price sequence $(q_0, \ldots, q_t, \ldots)$.

Let us now focus on the stationary paths of this example. Any $k \geq 0$ fixed through time constitutes a *steady state*. With any such steady state we can associate a constant surplus level $c(k) = F(k, 1) - k$ and a rate of interest $r(k) = \nabla_1 F(k, 1) - 1$, also constant through time.[21] Therefore, the supporting price–wage sequence is

$$(q_t, w_t) = \left(\frac{1}{1 + r(k)}\right)^t (q_0, w_0), \qquad \text{with } \frac{w_0}{q_0} = \frac{\nabla_2 F(k, 1)}{\nabla_1 F(k, 1)}.$$

Denote by $w(k)$ the real wage $w_0/q_0$ so determined. It is instructive to analyze how the steady-state levels of consumption $c(k)$, the rate of interest $r(k)$, and the real wage $w(k)$ depend on $k$.

Let $\bar{k}$ be the level of capital at which the steady-state consumption level is maximized [i.e., $\bar{k}$ solves $\text{Max } F(k, 1) - k$]. Note that $\bar{k}$ is characterized by $r(\bar{k}) = \nabla_1 F(\bar{k}, 1) - 1 = 0$. Thus $\bar{k}$ is precisely the *golden rule* steady state. The construction is illustrated in Figure 20.E.1, where we also represent the modified golden rule $k_\delta$ [characterized by $r(k_\delta) = \nabla_1 F(k_\delta, 1) - 1 = (1 - \delta)/\delta$]. Observe that if $k < \bar{k}$ then $r(k) > 0$. As we saw in Proposition 20.E.2, $r(k) > 0$ implies that the steady state $k$ is efficient (thus, in particular, the modified golden rule is efficient: it gives less consumption than the golden rule but it also uses less capital). Similarly, if $k > \bar{k}$ then $r(k) < 0$ and we have inefficiency of the steady state $k$. What about $\bar{k}$?[22] We now argue that *the golden rule steady state $\bar{k}$ is efficient*. A graphic proof will be quickest. Suppose we try to dominate the constant path $\bar{k}$ by starting with $k_0 < \bar{k}$, so that consumption at $t = 0$ is raised. Since the surplus at $t = 1$ must be at least

---

21. Thus, $c(k)$ is the amount of good constantly available through time and usable as a flow for consumption purposes.

22. Recall that the associated price sequence is constant and that the transversality condition is therefore violated.

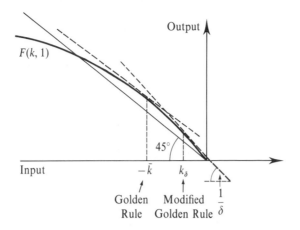

**Figure 20.E.1**

The production technology of the Ramsey–Solow model and the golden rule.

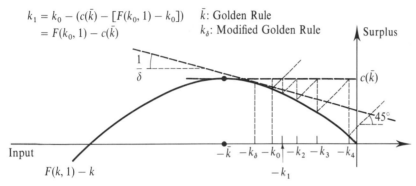

$$k_1 = k_0 - (c(\bar{k}) - [F(k_0, 1) - k_0])$$
$$= F(k_0, 1) - c(\bar{k})$$

$\bar{k}$: Golden Rule
$k_\delta$: Modified Golden Rule

**Figure 20.E.2**

Ramsey–Solow model: the golden rule is efficient.

$c(\bar{k})$, the best we can do for $k_1$ is

$$k_1 = F(k_0, 1) - c(\bar{k}) = F(k_0, 1) - k_0 + k_0 - c(\bar{k}) < k_0,$$

because $F(k_0, 1) - k_0 < c(\bar{k})$. This new best possible value of $k_1$ is represented in Figure 20.E.2. In the figure we also see that as the process of determination of $k_1$ is iterated to obtain $k_2$, $k_3$ and so on we will, at some point get a $k_t < 0$. Hence, the path is not feasible, and we conclude that a constant $\bar{k}$ cannot be dominated from the point of view of efficiency: the attempt to use less capital at some stage will inexorably lead to capital depletion in finite time.

From the form of the production function, three "neoclassical" properties follow immediately (you are asked to prove them in Exercise 20.E.4):

(i) As $k$ increases, the level $c(k)$ increases monotonically up to the golden rule level and then decreases monotonically.

(ii) The rate of interest $r(k)$ decreases monotonically with the level of capital $k$.

(iii) The real wage $w(k)$ increases monotonically with the level of capital. (For the validity of this property you should also assume that production function $F(k, l)$ is homogeneous of degree one.)

---

From the study of the steady states of the Ramsey–Solow model we have learnt at least six new things: First, the rate of interest is equal to the net marginal productivity of capital; second, the golden rule (i.e., zero rate of interest) path is characterized by a surplus-maximizing property among steady states; third, the golden rule is efficient; fourth, fifth, and sixth, we have the three neoclassical properties.

How general is all of this? That is, can we make similar claims for the general model with any number of goods? The answer, in short, is that the three neoclassical properties may or may not hold in a world with several capital goods, but the other three, duly interpreted, remain valid with great generality. Attempting to give proofs of all this would take us into too advanced material [see Bliss (1975) or Brock and Burmeister (1976)], but perhaps we can provide some intuition.

Suppose we consider the general $(N + 1)$-sector technology of Example 20.C.4. That is, $G(k, k')$ is the amount of consumption good available at any period if $k \in \mathbb{R}^N$ is the vector of levels of capital used in the previous period and the investment required in the period is $k' \in \mathbb{R}^N$ (we also let $l_t = 1$ for all $t$). At a steady-state path we have $k' = k$. Denote by $\hat{G}(k) = G(k, k)$ the level of consumption associated with the steady state $k$. If $G(\cdot, \cdot)$ is a concave function then so is $\hat{G}(\cdot)$. In particular, $\nabla \hat{G}(k) = 0$ characterizes the steady state with maximal level of consumption.

Consider a steady steady $k$. By Proposition 20.E.1, this steady state can be myopically supported by a proportional price sequence $s_t \in \mathbb{R}$, $q_t \in \mathbb{R}^N$. Here $s_t$ is the price of the consumption good in period $t$, and $q_t$ is the vector of prices of investment in period $t$. Because of proportionality there is an $r(k)$ such that $s_t = (1 + r(k))s_{t+1}$, $q_t = (1 + r(k))q_{t+1}$ for all $t$. Because of profit maximization,

$$\nabla_1 G(k, k) = \frac{1}{s_t} q_{t-1} \quad \text{and} \quad \nabla_2 G(k, k) = -\frac{1}{s_t} q_t \quad \text{for all } t \quad (20.E.1)$$

(you are asked to verify this in Exercise 20.E.5). Therefore,

$$\nabla \hat{G}(k) = \nabla_1 G(k, k) + \nabla_2 G(k, k) = \frac{1}{s_t} (q_{t-1} - q_t) = \frac{r(k)}{s_t} q_t,$$

that is, at any time *an extra dollar invested in a permanent increase of any capital good yields $r(k)$ dollars in extra value of (permanent) consumption*. In this precise sense the rate of interest measures the marginal productivity of capital. We see again that $\nabla \hat{G}(k) = 0$ (the necessary and sufficient condition for maximum steady-state consumption) is equivalent to $r(k) = 0$. Hence, the golden rule property holds: a steady-state level $k$ yields maximal consumption across steady states if and only if it has associated with it a zero rate of interest. We add that we could also prove that the golden rule path is efficient.

As we have already indicated, the neoclassical properties do not carry over to the general setting. A taste of the possible difficulties can be given even if $N = 1$, that is, for the two-sector model of Example 20.C.3. In Figure 20.E.3 we represent the level curves of $G(k, k')$. The steady states correspond to the diagonal, where $k = k'$. Every steady state $k$ can be myopically

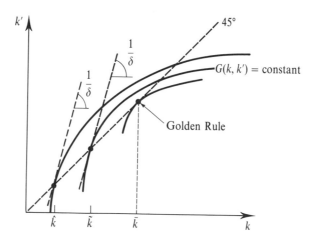

**Figure 20.E.3**

An example with several modified golden rules.

supported by proportional prices $q_t = (1 + r(k))q_{t+1}$ where, to insure profit maximization, $q_t/q_{t+1}$ must be equal to the slope of the level curve through $(k, k)$ (you should verify this in Exercise 20.E.6). Therefore, the efficient steady states, those with $r(k) \geq 0$, correspond to the subset of the diagonal that goes from the origin to the golden rule, where $r(\bar{k}) = 0$. In the special case of the Ramsey–Solow model we have $G(k, k') = F(k, 1) - k'$ and therefore the level curves of $G(k, k')$ admit a quasilinear representation with respect to $k'$ (i.e., they can be generated from each other by parallel displacement along the $k'$ axis). In Exercise 20.E.7 you are asked to show that this guarantees the satisfaction of the neoclassical properties. In general, however, it is clear from Figure 20.E.3 that we may, for example, have two different $\hat{k}, \tilde{k} < \bar{k}$ such that, at the diagonal, the corresponding level curves have the same slope and therefore $r(\hat{k}) = r(\tilde{k})$ (contradicting the second neoclassical property). In particular, while the golden rule is unique [if the function $G(k, k')$ is strictly concave], there may be several modified golden rules [this is the case if, say, the discount factor $\delta$ is equal to the interest rate $r(\hat{k})$].

# 20.F  Dynamics

In this section, we offer a few observations on the vast topic of the dynamic properties of equilibria. The basic framework is as in the previous section: a one-consumer economy with stationary technology and utility.

The arbitrarily given initial conditions[23] will typically not be compatible with a stationary equilibrium situation (e.g., the steady-state level of capital may be higher than the initial availability of capital). Therefore, the typical equilibrium path will be nonstationary. How complicated can the equilibrium dynamics be? Can we, for example, expect convergence to a modified golden rule? This would be nice, as it would tell us that our models carry definite long-run predictions.

We can gain much insight into these matters by considering a variation of the two-sector model of Example 20.C.3. We assume that the technology produces consumption goods (possibly of more than one kind) out of labor and a capital good. There is, as initial endowment, one unit of labor in each period, and we let $u(k, k')$ stand for the maximum utility that can be attained in any given period if in the previous period $k \in \mathbb{R}$ units of capital were installed and the current investment is required to be $k'$ (and, in both periods, a unit of labor is used). There is a positive initial endowment of capital only at t = 0. Also, we take $u(\cdot, \cdot)$ to be strictly concave and differentiable.

We know from Proposition 20.D.3 and 20.D.4 that the equilibrium paths can be determined by means of the following planning problem:

$$\text{Max} \quad \sum_t \delta^t u(k_{t-1}, k_t) \qquad\qquad (20.F.1)$$

$$\text{s.t. } k_t \geq 0 \text{ and } k_0 = k \text{ is given.}$$

Suppose that $V(k)$ and $\psi(k)$ are value and policy functions, respectively, for the problem (20.F.1). These concepts were introduced in Section 20.D. As we explained there, the equilibrium dynamics are entirely determined by iterating the policy function [see expression (20.D.10)]. That is, given $k_0$, the equilibrium trajectory is

$$(k_0, k_1, k_2, \ldots) = (k_0, \psi(k_0), \psi(\psi(k_0)), \ldots).$$

---

23. That is, the initial endowment sequence $(\omega_0, \ldots, \omega_t, \ldots)$.

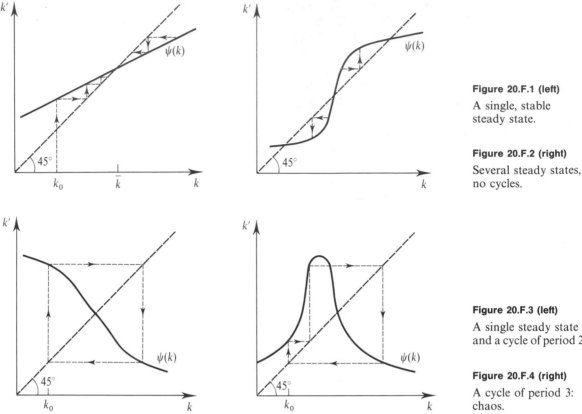

**Figure 20.F.1 (left)**
A single, stable steady state.

**Figure 20.F.2 (right)**
Several steady states, no cycles.

**Figure 20.F.3 (left)**
A single steady state and a cycle of period 2.

**Figure 20.F.4 (right)**
A cycle of period 3: chaos.

Note that a steady-state path $(\bar{k}, \ldots, \bar{k}, \ldots)$ is an equilibrium path (for $k_0 = \bar{k}$), and therefore a modified golden rule steady state path for discount factor $\delta$ (see Definition 20.E.2 and the discussion surrounding it), if and only if $\bar{k} = \psi(\bar{k})$.

Figures 20.F.1 through 20.F.4 represent four mathematical possibilities for this equilibrium dynamics. In Figure 20.F.1, we have the simplest possible situation: a monotonically increasing policy function with a single steady state $\bar{k}$. The steady state is then necessarily globally stable; that is, $k_t \to \bar{k}$ for any $k_0$. In Figure 20.F.2, the policy function is again monotonically increasing, but now there are several steady states. They have different stability properties, but it is still true that from any initial point we converge to some steady state. In Figure 20.F.3, the steady state is unique, but now the policy function is not increasing and cycles are possible. Finally, in Figure 20.F.4 we have a policy function that generates a cycle of period 3. It is known that a one-dimensional dynamical system exhibiting a nontrivial cycle of period 3 is necessarily *chaotic* [see Grandmont (1986) for an exposition of the mathematical theory]. We cannot go here into an explanation of the term "chaotic" in this context. It suffices to say that the equilibrium trajectory may wander in a complicated way and that its location in the distant future is very sensitive to initial conditions. The theoretical possibility of chaotic equilibrium trajectories is troublesome from the economic point of view. How is it to be expected that an auctioneer will succeed in computing them; or even worse, how would a consumer exactly anticipate such a sequence?

Unfortunately, the "anything goes" principle that haunted us in Chapter 17 in the form of the Sonnenschein–Mantel–Debreu theorem (Section 17.E) reemerges here in the guise of the Boldrin–Montruccio theorem [see Boldrin and Montruccio (1986)]: *Any candidate policy function $\psi(k)$ can be generated from some concave $u(k, k')$ and $\delta > 0$.* We will not state or demonstrate this theorem precisely, but the main idea of its proof is quite accessible. We devote the next few paragraphs to it.

Suppose for a moment that for a given $u(\cdot, \cdot)$ our candidate $\psi(\cdot)$ is such that $\psi(k)$ solves, for every $k$, the following "complete impatience" problem:

$$\underset{k' \geq 0}{\text{Max}} \quad u(k, k'). \tag{20.F.2}$$

This would be the problem of a decision maker who did not care about the future. While this is not quite the problem that we want to solve, it approximates it if we take $\delta > 0$ to be very low. Then the decision maker cares very little about the future and therefore its optimal action $k'$ will, by continuity, be very close to $\psi(k)$. Hence, in an approximate sense, we are done if we can find a $u(\cdot, \cdot)$ such that $\psi(k)$ solves (20.F.2) for every $k$.

In order for a $\psi(k) > 0$ to solve (20.F.2), $u(k, \cdot)$ cannot be everywhere decreasing in its second argument (the optimal decision would then be $k' = 0$). In the simplest version of the Ramsey–Solow model (Example 20.C.1), the returns of $k'$, the investment in the current period, accrue only in the next period, and therefore the utility function $u(k, k')$ is decreasing in $k'$. But in the current, more general, two-sector model there is no reason that forces this conclusion. Suppose, for example, that there are two consumption goods. The first is the usual consumption–investment good, while the second is a pure consumption good not perfectly substitutable with the first. Say that with an amount $k$ of investment at time $t - 1$ one gets, jointly, $k$ units of the consumption–investment good at time $t$ and $k$ units of the second consumption good at time $t - 1$. Accordingly, with $k'$ units of the consumption–investment good invested at $t$ one gets, jointly, $k'$ units of the consumption–investment good at $t + 1$ and $k'$ units of the second consumption good at $t$. Thus, if $k$ and $k'$ are the amounts of investment at $t - 1$ and $t$, respectively, then the bundle of consumption goods available at $t$ is $(k - k', k')$. Hence, the utility function $u(\cdot, \cdot)$ has the form $u(k, k') = \hat{u}(k - k', k')$, where $\hat{u}(\cdot, \cdot)$ is a utility function for bundles of the two consumption goods.

Therefore, our problem is reduced to the following: Given $\psi(k)$ can we find $\hat{u}(\cdot, \cdot)$ such that $\psi(k)$ solves $\text{Max}_{k'} \hat{u}(k - k', k')$ for all $k$ in some range? The problem is represented in Figure 20.F.5.[24] We see from the figure that the problem has formally become one of finding a concave utility function with a prespecified Engel curve at some given prices (in our case, the two prices are equal). Such a utility function can always be obtained. It is a well-known, and most plausible fact that the concavity of $\hat{u}(\cdot)$ imposes no restrictions on the shape that a single Engel curve may exhibit (see Exercise 20.F.1).

The news is not uniformly bad, however. In principle, as we have seen, everything may be possible; yet there are interesting and useful sufficient conditions implying a

---

24. We also assume that $\psi(k) < k$ for all $k$.

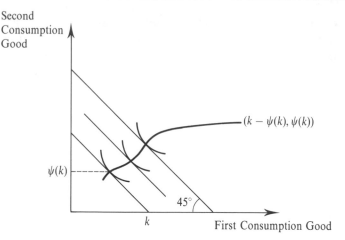

**Figure 20.F.5**

Construction of an arbitrary policy function in the completely impatient case.

well-behaved dynamic behavior. We discuss two types of conditions: a *low discount of time* and *cross derivatives of uniform positive sign.*

*Low Discount of Time*

One of the most general results of dynamic economics is the *turnpike theorem,* which, informally, asserts that *if the one-period utility function is strictly concave and the decision maker is very patient, then there is a single modified golden rule steady state that, moreover, attracts the optimal trajectories from any initial position.*

In the context of the two-sector model studied in this section, we can give some intuition for the turnpike theorem. Suppose that the value function $V(k)$, which is concave, is twice-differentiable.[25] At the end of Section 20.D, we saw that since by definition,

$$V(k + z) \geq u(k + z, \psi(k)) + \delta V(\psi(k))$$

for all $z$ and $k$ (with equality for $z = 0$), we must have

$$V'(k) = \nabla_1 u(k, \psi(k)) \qquad \text{and} \qquad V''(k) \geq \nabla^2_{11} u(k, \psi(k)) \qquad \text{for all } k.$$

Also for all $k$, $\psi(k)$ solves the first-order condition

$$\nabla_2 u(k, \psi(k)) + \delta V'(\psi(k)) = 0. \tag{20.F.3}$$

Differentiating this first-order condition, we have (all the derivatives are evaluated at $k, \psi(k)$ and assumed to be nonzero)

$$\psi'(\cdot) = -\frac{\nabla^2_{21} u(\cdot)}{\nabla^2_{22} u(\cdot) + \delta V''(\cdot)}.$$

Because $\nabla^2_{22} u(\cdot) \leq 0$ and $\delta \nabla^2_{11} u(\cdot) \leq \delta V''(\cdot) \leq 0$, it follows that

$$|\psi'(\cdot)| \leq \left| \frac{\nabla^2_{21} u(\cdot)}{\nabla^2_{22} u(\cdot) + \delta \nabla^2_{11} u(\cdot)} \right|.$$

By the concavity of $u(\cdot)$ we have (see Sections M.C and M.D of the Mathematical Appendix)

$$(\nabla^2_{21} u(\cdot))^2 \leq \nabla^2_{11} u(\cdot) \nabla^2_{22} u(\cdot) < (\nabla^2_{11} u(\cdot) + \nabla^2_{22} u(\cdot))^2.$$

25. For a (very advanced) discussion of this assumption, see Santos (1991).

Hence, if the discount factor $\delta$ is close to 1, it is a plausible conclusion that $|\psi'(k)| < 1$ for all $k$. In technical language: $\psi(\cdot)$ is a *contraction*, and this implies global convergence to a unique steady state.[26] In Exercise 20.F.2 you are invited to draw the policy functions and the arrow diagrams for this case. A particular instance of a contraction is exhibited in Figure 20.F.1.

---

The turnpike theorem is valid for any number of goods. The precise statement and the proof of the theorem are subtle and technical [see McKenzie (1987) for a brief survey], but the main logic is simply conveyed. Consider the extreme case where there is complete patience, that is, "only the long-run matters." A difficulty is that it is not clear what this means for arbitrary paths; but at least for paths that are not too "wild," say for those that from some time become cyclical, it is natural to assume that it means that the paths are evaluated by taking the average utility over the cycle. Observe now that *for any cyclical nonconstant path, the strict concavity of the utility function implies that the constant path equal to the mean level of capital over the cycle yields a higher utility.* It may take some time to carry out a transition from the cycle to the constant path (e.g., it may be necessary to build up capital) but, as long as this can be done in a finite number of periods, the cost of the transition will not show up in the long run. Hence the cyclical nonconstant path cannot be optimal for a completely patient optimizer. By continuity, all this remains valid if $\delta$ is very close to 1. We can conclude, therefore, that if a path tends to a nonconstant cycle then we can always implement a finite transition to a suitable constant "long-run average," for a relatively large long-run gain of utility and a relatively low short-run cost. In fact, this conclusion remains valid whenever a path does not stabilize in the long-run. It follows that the optimal path must be asymptotically almost constant, which can only be the case if the path reaches and remains in a neighborhood of a modified golden rule steady state (recall from Section 20.E that those are the only constant paths that can be equilibria, and therefore optimal).[27]

---

## Cross Derivative of Uniform Positive Sign

We shall concern ourselves here with the particular case of the two-sector model studied so far where $\nabla_1 u(k, k') > 0$ and $\nabla_2 u(k, k') < 0$ for all $(k, k')$. By a *cross derivative of uniform positive sign we mean that $\nabla_{12} u(k, k') > 0$, again at all points of the domain.* In words: An increase in investment requirements at one date leads to a situation of increased productivity (in terms of current utility) of the capital installed the previous date. Examples are the classical Ramsey–Solow model $u(F(k) - k')$ and the cost-of-adjustment model $u(F(k) - k' - \gamma(k' - k))$ (see Exercise 20.F.3). We shall argue that *under this cross derivative condition the policy function is increasing* (as in Figures 20.F.1 or 20.F.2), and therefore the optimal path converges to a stationary path.

To prove the claim, it is useful to express $\psi(k)$ as the $k'$ solution to

$$\underset{(k', V)}{\text{Max}} \quad u(k, k') + \delta V \tag{20.F.4}$$

$$\text{s.t.} \ V \leq V(k'),$$

---

26. We note that $\psi(\cdot)$ need not be monotone and the convergence may be cyclical, although the cycles will dampen through time.

27. Also, with $\delta$ close to 1, the modified golden rule will typically retain the uniqueness property of the golden rule.

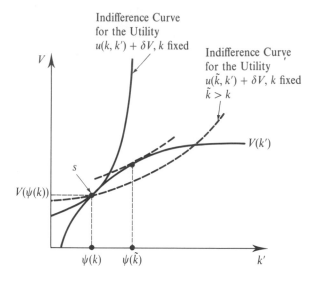

**Figure 20.F.6**
With the uniform positive sign cross derivative condition, the policy function is increasing.

where $V(\cdot)$ is the value function. For fixed $k$, problem (20.F.4) is represented in Figure 20.F.6. The marginal rate of substitution ($MRS$) between current investment $k'$ and future utility $V$ at $s = (\psi(k), V(\psi(k)))$ is $(1/\delta)\nabla_2 u(k, \psi(k)) < 0$. Suppose now that we take $\tilde{k} > k$. Then the indifference map in Figure 20.F.6 changes. Because $\nabla_{12} u(k, \psi(k)) > 0$, the $MRS$ at $s$ is altered in the manner displayed in the figure, that is, the indifference curve becomes flatter. But we can see then that necessarily $\psi(\tilde{k}) > \psi(k)$, as we wanted to show.

The cross derivative condition does not, by itself, imply the existence of a single modified golden rule. Thus, we could be in Figure 20.F.2 rather than in Figure 20.F.1. Note, however, that in many cases of interest it may be possible to show directly that the modified golden rule is unique. Thus, in both the classical Ramsey–Solow model of Example 20.C.1 and in the cost-of-adjustment model [with $\gamma'(0) = 0$] of Example 20.C.2, the modified golden rule is characterized by $F'(k) = 1/\delta$. Hence it is unique and, because the policy function is increasing, we conclude that every optimal path converges to it.

We also point out that if the cross derivative is of uniform *negative* sign, then, by the same arguments, $\psi(\cdot)$ is *decreasing*. While this allows for cycles, the dynamics are still relatively simple. In particular, the nonmonotonic shape associated with the possibility of chaotic paths (Figure 20.F.4) cannot rise. See Deneckere and Pelikan (1986) for more on these points.

---

Figure 20.F.6 is also helpful in illuminating the distinction between *transitory* and *permanent* shocks. One of the important uses of dynamic analysis in general, and of global convergence turnpike results in particular, is in the examination of how an economy at long-run rest reacts to a perturbation of the data at time $t = 1$. In an extremely crude classification, these perturbations can be of two types:

(i) *Transitory* shocks affect the environment of the economy only at $t = 1$; that is, they alter $k_0$ or, more generally, $u(k_0, \cdot)$, the utility function at $t = 1$. Then Figure 20.F.6 allows us to see how the equilibrium path will be displaced. The $(k', V)$ indifference curve of $u(k_0, k') + \delta V$ changes, but the constraint function $V(k')$ remains unaltered. Hence, after the (transitory) shock, the new $k_1^{tr}$ corresponds to the solution of the optimum problem depicted in Figure

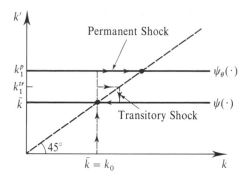

**Figure 20.F.7**

An example of dynamic adjustment under transitional and permanent shocks.

20.F.6 but with the new indifference map. From $t = 2$ on we simply follow the old policy function.

(ii) *Permanent* shocks move the economy to a new utility function $\hat{u}(k, k')$ constant over time. Then the entire policy function changes to a new $\hat{\psi}(\cdot)$. In terms of Figure 20.F.6 there would be a change in both the indifference curves *and* the constraint. The new $k_1^p$ is now harder to determine and to compare with the preshock $k_1$ or, for the same shock at period 1, with $k_1^{tr}$; but it can often be done. We pursue the matter through Example 20.F.1.

**Example 20.F.1:** Consider the separable utility $u(k, k') = g(k) + h(k')$. This could be the investment problem of a firm: $g(k)$ is the maximal revenue obtainable with $k$, and $-h(k')$ is the cost of investment. Then $\nabla_{12}^2 u(k, k') = 0$ at all $(k, k')$. Our previous analysis of Figure 20.F.6, tells us that in this case $\psi(\cdot)$ is constant; that is, from any $k_0$ the economy goes in one step to its steady-state value $\bar{k}$. This is illustrated in Figure 20.F.7.

Suppose now there is a shock variable $\theta$ such that $u(k, k', \theta) = g(k, \theta) + h(k', \theta)$, with the preshock value being $\theta = 0$. The economy is initially at its steady state $\bar{k}$.

If there is a transitory shock to a small $\theta > 0$, then from the analysis of Figure 20.F.6 we can see that $k_1^{tr} \gtreqless \bar{k}$ according to $\partial^2 h(\bar{k}, 0)/\partial k' \, \partial\theta \gtreqless 0$. (Exercise 20.F.4 asks you to verify this.)

To evaluate the effects of a permanent shock to a small $\theta > 0$ (and therefore to a new $\psi_\theta(\cdot)$) the term

$$\partial^2 V(\bar{k}, 0)/\partial k \, \partial\theta = \partial^2 g(\bar{k}, 0)/\partial k \, \partial\theta$$

also matters [the previous equality follows from expression (20.F.3)]. Suppose, for example, that the shock is unambiguously favourable, in the sense that $\partial^2 g(\bar{k}, 0)/\partial k \, \partial\theta > 0$ and $\partial^2 h(\bar{k}, 0)/\partial k' \, \partial\theta > 0$. Then a careful analysis of Figure 20.F.6, would allow us to conclude that $k_1^p > k_1^{tr} > \bar{k}$. (Exercise 20.F.5 asks you to verify this. Note that the indifference map of Figure 20.F.6 is quasilinear with respect to $V$.) Figure 20.F.7 illustrates this case further. ∎

# 20.G Equilibrium: Several Consumers

Up to now we have had a single consumer, or, to be more precise, a single type of consumer. The extension of the definition of equilibrium to economies with several consumers, say $I$, presents no particular difficulty. We simply have to rewrite Definition 20.D.1 as in Definition 20.G.1.

**Definition 20.G.1:** The (bounded) production path $(y_0^*, \ldots, y_t^*, \ldots)$, $y_t^* \in Y$, the (bounded) price sequence $(p_0, \ldots, p_t, \ldots) \geq 0$, and the consumption streams

$(c_{0i}^*, \ldots, c_{ti}^*, \ldots) \geq 0$, $i = 1, \ldots, I$, constitute a *Walrasian* (or *competitive*) equilibrium if:

(i)
$$\sum_i c_{ti}^* = y_{a,t-1}^* + y_{bt}^* + \sum_i \omega_{ti}, \text{ for all } t. \tag{20.G.1}$$

(ii) For every $t$,

$$\pi_t = p_t \cdot y_{bt}^* + p_{t+1} \cdot y_{at}^* \geq p_t \cdot y_{bt} + p_{t+1} \cdot y_{at} \tag{20.G.2}$$

for all $y = (y_{bt}, y_{at}) \in Y$.

(iii) For every $i$, the consumption stream $(c_{0i}^*, \ldots, c_{ti}^*, \ldots) \geq 0$ solves the problem

$$\text{Max} \quad \sum_t \delta_i^t u_i(c_i) \tag{20.G.3}$$

$$\text{s.t.} \sum_t p_t \cdot c_{ti} \leq \sum_t \theta_{ti} \pi_t + \sum_t p_t \cdot \omega_{ti} = w_i.$$

where $\theta_{ti}$ is consumer $i$'s given share of period $t$ profits.

The first, and very important, observation to make is that, in complete analogy with the finite-horizon case (see Section 16.C), the first welfare theorem holds.[28]

**Proposition 20.G.1:** A Walrasian equilibrium allocation is Pareto optimal.

**Proof:** The proof is as in Proposition 16.C.1. Let the Walrasian equilibrium path under consideration be given by the production path $(y_0^*, \ldots, y_t^*, \ldots)$, the consumption streams $(c_{0i}^*, \ldots, c_{ti}^*, \ldots)$, $i = 1, \ldots, I$, and the price sequence $(p_0, \ldots, p_t, \ldots)$. Suppose now that the paths $(y_0, \ldots, y_t, \ldots)$, and $(c_{0i}, \ldots, c_{ti}, \ldots) \geq 0$, $i = 1, \ldots, I$, are feasible [i.e., they satisfy condition (i) of Definition 20.G.1] and are Pareto preferred to the Walrasian equilibrium.

By the utility-maximization condition we have $\sum_t p_t \cdot c_{ti} \geq w_i$ for all $i$, with at least one inequality strict. Hence,

$$\sum_t p_t \cdot \left( \sum_i c_{ti} \right) = \sum_i \left( \sum_t p_t \cdot c_{ti} \right) > \sum_i w_i. \tag{20.G.4}$$

Because of the profit maximization condition we get[29]

$$\sum_t p_t \cdot \left( \sum_i c_{ti} \right) = \sum_t p_t \cdot \left( y_{a,t-1} + y_{bt} + \sum_i \omega_{ti} \right)$$

$$= \sum_t p_t \cdot y_{a,t-1} + \sum_t p_t \cdot y_{bt} + \sum_t \sum_i p_t \cdot \omega_{ti}$$

$$= \sum_{t \geq 1} (p_{t-1} \cdot y_{b,t-1} + p_t \cdot y_{a,t-1}) + \sum_i \sum_t p_t \cdot \omega_{ti}$$

$$\leq \sum_t \pi_t + \sum_i \sum_t p_t \cdot \omega_{ti} = \sum_i w_i.$$

But this conclusion contradicts (20.G.4). ∎

---

28. Note also that, in the terminology of Chapter 19, the market structure is complete: Every consumer has a single budget constraint and, therefore, only prices limit the possibilities of transferring wealth across periods.

29. Recall that, by convention, $y_{a,-1} = 0$.

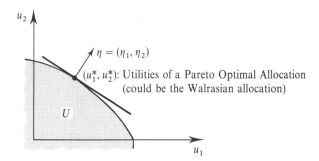

**Figure 20.G.1**
The Walrasian
equilibrium as a
solution of a
planning problem.

We saw in Sections 16.E and 16.F that, under the assumption of concave utility functions, a Pareto optimal allocation of an economy with a finite number of commodities can be viewed as the solution of a planning problem. As described in Figure 20.G.1, the objective function of the planner is a weighted sum of the utilities of the different consumers (the weights being the reciprocal of the marginal utilities of wealth at the equilibrium with transfers associated with the particular Pareto optimum). The arguments of Section 16.E (in particular, Proposition 16.E.2) apply as well to the current infinite-horizon case. Therefore, Proposition 20.G.1 has, besides its substantive interest, a significant methodological implication. It tells us that the prices, productions, and aggregate consumptions of a given Walrasian equilibrium correspond exactly to those of a certain single-consumer economy. We give a more precise statement in Proposition 20.G.2. In it we restrict ourselves to the case of a common discount factor, namely, $\delta_i = \delta$ for all $i$.

**Proposition 20.G.2:** Suppose that $(y_0^*, \ldots, y_t^*, \ldots)$ is the production path and $(p_0, \ldots, p_t, \ldots)$ is the price sequence of a Walrasian equilibrium of an economy with $I$ consumers. Then there are weights $(\eta_1, \ldots, \eta_I) \gg 0$ such that $(y_0^*, \ldots, y_t^*, \ldots)$ and $(p_0, \ldots, p_t, \ldots)$ constitute a Walrasian equilibrium for the one-consumer economy defined by the utility $\sum_t \delta^t u(c_t)$, where $u(c_t)$ is the solution to Max $\sum_i \eta_i u_i(c_{ti})$ s.t. $\sum_i c_{ti} \leq c_t$.

**Proof:** We will not give a rigorous proof, but the result is intuitive from Figure 20.G.1. From there we see (technically this involves, as in Proposition 16.E.2, an application of the separating hyperplane theorem) that there are weights $(\eta_1, \ldots, \eta_I) \gg 0$ such that the equilibrium consumption streams maximize $\sum_i \eta_i (\sum_t \delta^t u_i(c_{ti}))$ over all feasible consumption streams, or, equivalently (it is here that the assumption of a common discount factor matters), the aggregate equilibrium consumption stream, solves the two-step planning problem specified by the definition of $u(c_t)$ and the maximization of $\sum_t \delta^t u(c_t)$. Because we already know (Proposition 20.D.4) that this is tantamount to the one-consumer equilibrium problem, we are done. ■

Proposition 20.G.2 allows us to conclude that the one-consumer theory developed in the last three sections remains highly relevant to the several-consumer case.[30] Somewhat informally, we can distinguish two types of properties of an equilibrium.

---

30. More generally, it remains highly relevant to any equilibrium model that guarantees the Pareto optimality of equilibria.

The *internal* properties are those that refer only to the structure of an equilibrium viewed solely in reference to itself (e.g., convergence to a steady state); the *external* properties refer to how the equilibrium relates to other possible equilibrium trajectories of the economy (e.g., uniqueness or local uniqueness). The message of Proposition 20.G.2 is that, because of Pareto optimality, the internal properties of an equilibrium of an economy with several consumers are those of its associated one-consumer economy. The implications of the one-consumer theory should not, however, be pushed beyond the internal properties. The reason is that *the weights defining the planning problem depend on the particular equilibrium considered.* For example, it is perfectly possible for there to be more than one equilibrium, each a Pareto optimum but supported by different weights.

---

What can be said about the determinacy properties of equilibrium; for example, about the finiteness of the number of equilibria? We will not be able to give a precise treatment of this matter, in part because it is very technical and in part because it is still an active area of research where the ultimate results may not yet be at hand. The basic intuition, however, can be transmitted. We begin by pointing out another implication of Proposition 20.G.1. Formally, our infinite-horizon model involves infinitely many variables (prices, say) and infinitely many equations (Euler equations, say). This is most unpleasant, as the mathematical theory described in Section 17.D applies only (and for good reasons, as we shall see in Section 20.H) to systems with a *finite* number of equations and unknowns. However, Proposition 20.G.1 allows us to view the equilibrium problem as one of finding not equilibrium prices but *equilibrium weights* $\eta$. If we do this then the equilibrium equations in our system are $I - 1$ in number, the same as the number of unknowns. More precisely, the $i$th equation would associate with the vector of weights $\eta = (\eta_1, \ldots, \eta_I)$, $\sum_i \eta_i = 1$, the wealth "gap" of consumer $i$:

$$\sum_t p_t(\eta) \cdot c_{ti}(\eta) - \sum_t (\theta_{ti} \pi_t(\eta) + p_t(\eta) \cdot \omega_{ti}) = 0,$$

where $p_t(\eta)$, $c_{ti}(\eta)$, and $\pi_t(\eta)$ correspond to the Pareto optimum indexed by $\eta$. See Appendix A of Chapter 17 for a construction similar to this. At any rate, once looked at as a wealth-equilibrating problem across a finite number of consumers, the central conjecture should be that, as in Chapter 17, the equilibrium set is nonempty and generically finite. That is, equilibrium exists and, except for pathological cases, there are only a finite number of weights solving the equilibrium equations (we could similarly go on to formulate an index theorem). Technical difficulties[31] aside, this central conjecture can be established in a wide variety of cases [see Exercise 20.G.3 and Kehoe and Levine (1985)].

We end this section with two remarks. The first derives from the question: Is there a relationship, a "correspondence," between internal and external properties? At least in a first approximation the answer is "no." We have seen that in a one-consumer economy the equilibrium is unique, but the equilibrium path may be complicated. Similarly, in a several-consumer economy there may be several equilibria, or even a continuum, each of them nicely converging to a steady state.[32]

---

31. These have to do with guaranteeing the differentiability of the relevant functions.

32. The simplest, trivial, example is the following. Suppose that $L = 2$, $I = 2$ and that there is no possibility of intertemporal production. Individual endowments are constant through time and the utility functions are concave. Then the intertemporal Walrasian equilibria correspond exactly to the infinite, constant repetitions of the one-period Walrasian equilibria (you are asked to prove this in Exercise 20.G.4). Because there are may be several of those, we obtain our conclusion.

The second remark brings home the point that Pareto optimality is key to an expectation of generic determinacy. Consider, as an example, a model of identical consumers but with an externality. The utility function, $u(k, k', e)$, now has three arguments: $k$ and $k'$ are the capital investments in the previous and the current periods, respectively, and $e$ is the level of currently felt externality. Given, for the moment, an exogenously fixed externality path $(e_0, \ldots, e_t, \ldots)$, the (bounded, strictly interior) capital trajectory $k_t$ is an equilibrium if it solves the planning problem for the utility functions $u(\cdot, \cdot, e_t)$, that is, if it satisfies the Euler equations:

$$\nabla_2 u(k_{t-1}, k_t, e_t) + \delta \nabla_1 u(k_t, k_{t+1}, e_{t+1}) = 0 \qquad \text{for all } t.$$

An overall equilibrium must take into account the technology determining the externality. Say that this is $e_t = k_t$; that is, the externality is a side product of current investment. Hence, the equilibrium conditions are

$$\nabla_2 u(k_{t-1}, k_t, k_t) + \delta \nabla_1 u(k_t, k_{t+1}, k_{t+1}) = 0 \qquad \text{for all } t. \tag{20.G.5}$$

Suppose that starting from an equilibrium steady state ($k_t = \bar{k}$ for all $t$), we try, as we did in Section 20.D, to generate a different equilibrium by fixing $k_0 = \bar{k}$, taking $k_1$ to be slightly different from $\bar{k}$, and then iteratively solving (20.G.5) for $k_{t+1}$. A sufficient (but not necessary) condition for this method to succeed is that $|dk_{t+1}/dk_t| < \frac{1}{2}$ and $|dk_{t+1}/dk_{t-1}| < \frac{1}{2}$, where the values $dk_{t+1}/dk_t$ and $dk_{t+1}/dk_{t-1}$ are obtained by applying the implicit function theorem to (20.G.5) and evaluating at the steady state. Indeed, if this condition holds, then the initial perturbation of $k_1$ induces a sequence of adjustments that dampen over time and that will, therefore, never become unfeasible (and, in fact, will remain bounded and strictly interior). Explicitly:

$$\frac{dk_{t+1}}{dk_t} = -\frac{\nabla_{22}^2 u(\cdot) + \nabla_{23}^2 u(\cdot) + \delta \nabla_{11}^2 u(\cdot)}{\delta(\nabla_{12}^2 u(\cdot) + \nabla_{13}^2 u(\cdot))}. \tag{20.G.6}$$

If there are no externalities [i.e., if $\nabla_{23}^2 u(\cdot) = \nabla_{13}^2 u(\cdot) = 0$] then the concavity of $u(\cdot, \cdot)$ implies that expression (20.G.6) is larger than 1 in absolute value (you should verify this in Exercise 20.G.5). Thus, in agreement with the discussion of Section 20.D, we are not then able to find a non-steady-state solution of the Euler equations. But if the externality effects are significant enough, inspection of expression (20.G.6) tells us immediately that $dk_{t+1}/dk_t$ can perfectly well be less than $\frac{1}{2}$ in absolute value. The same is true for $dk_{t+1}/\delta k_{t-1}$, and therefore we can conclude that robust examples with a continuum of equilibria are possible.

# 20.H  Overlapping Generations

In the previous sections we have studied economies that, formally, have an overlapping structure of firms but only one (or, in Section 20.G, several), infinitely long-lived, consumer. We pointed out in Section 20.B that in the presence of suitable forms of altruism it may be possible to interpret an infinitely long-lived agent as a dynasty. We will now describe a model where this cannot be done, and where, as a consequence, the consumption side of the economy consists of an infinite succession of consumers in an essential manner. To make things interesting, these consumers, to be called *generations*, will overlap, so that intergenerational trade is possible. The model originates in Allais (1947) and Samuelson (1958) and has become a workhorse of macroeconomics, monetary theory, and public finance. The literature on it is very extensive; see Geanakoplos (1987) or Woodford (1984) for an overview. Here we will limit ourselves to discussing a simple case with the purpose of highlighting, first, the extent to which the model can be analyzed with the Walrasian equilibrium methodology and, second, the departures from the broad lessons of the previous sections. We shall classify these departures into two categories: issues relating to optimality and issues relating to the multiplicity of equilibria.

We begin by describing an economy that, except for the infinity of generations, is as simple as possible. We have an infinite succession of dates $t = 0, 1, \ldots$ and in every period a single consumption good. For every $t$ there is a generation born at time $t$, living for two periods, and having utility function $u(c_{bt}, c_{at})$ where $c_{bt}$ and $c_{at}$ are, respectively, the consumption of the $t$th generation when young (i.e., in period $t$), and its consumption when old (i.e., in period $t + 1$); the indices $b$ and $a$ are mnemonic symbols for "before" and "after." Note that the utility functions of the different generations over consumption in their lifespan are identical. We assume that $u(\cdot, \cdot)$ is quasiconcave, differentiable and strictly increasing.

Every generation $t$ is endowed when young with a unit of a primary factor (e.g., labor). This primary factor does not enter the utility function and can be used to produce consumption goods contemporaneously by means of some production function $f(z)$.[33] Say that $f(1) = 1$. Under the competitive price-taking assumption, total profits at $t$, in terms of period-$t$ good, will be $\varepsilon = 1 - f'(1)$ and, correspondingly, labor payments will be $1 - \varepsilon$. Thus, we may as well directly assume that the initial endowments of generation $t \geq 0$ are specified to us as a vector of consumption goods $(1 - \varepsilon, 0)$. In addition, we assign the infinite stream of profits to generation 0. That is, the technology $f(\cdot)$ is an infinitely long-lived asset owned at $t = 0$ by the only generation alive in that period and yielding a permanent profit stream of $\varepsilon > 0$ units of consumption good.

Now let $(p_0, \ldots, p_t, \ldots)$ be an infinite sequence of (anticipated) prices. We do not require that it be bounded. For the budget constraint of the different generations we take

$$p_t c_{bt} + p_{t+1} c_{at} \leq (1 - \varepsilon) p_t \qquad \text{for } t > 0 \qquad (20.H.1)$$

and

$$p_0 c_{b0} + p_1 c_{a0} \leq (1 - \varepsilon) p_0 + \varepsilon \left( \sum_t p_t \right) + M. \qquad (20.H.2)$$

These budget constraints deserve comment. For $t > 0$, (20.H.1) is easy to interpret. The value of the initial endowments, available at $t$, is $(1 - \varepsilon) p_t$. Part of this amount is spent at time $t$ and the rest, $(1 - \varepsilon) p_t - p_t c_{bt}$, is saved for consumption at $t + 1$. The saving instrument could be the title to the technology, which would thus be bought from the old by the young at $t$ and then sold at $t + 1$ to the new young (after collecting the period $t + 1$ return). The price paid for the asset is the amount saved, that is, $(1 - \varepsilon) p_t - p_t c_{bt}$. The direct return at $t + 1$ is $\varepsilon p_{t+1}$ and so, if the asset market is to be in equilibrium, the selling price at $t + 1$ should be $(1 - \varepsilon) p_t - p_t c_{bt} - \varepsilon p_{t+1}$. In summary, in agreement with the budget constraint (20.H.1) this leaves $(1 - \varepsilon) p_t - p_t c_{bt}$ to be spent at $t + 1$.

The constraint (20.H.2) for $t = 0$ is more interesting. Its right-hand side is the value of the asset to generation 0. Note that asset market equilibrium requires that

---

33. The assumption that production is contemporary with input usage fits well with the length of the period being long.

this value should be at least the *fundamental* value, that is, $\varepsilon(\sum_t p_t)$.[34] Indeed, the value of the asset at $t = 0$ equals the profit return $\varepsilon p_0$ plus the price paid by the young of generation 1. At any $T$, the price paid by the young of generation $T$ should not be inferior to the direct return $\varepsilon p_{T+1}$. In turn, at $T - 1$ it should not be inferior to the direct return plus the value at $T$; that is, it should be at least $\varepsilon(p_T + p_{T+1})$. Iterating, we get the lower bound $\varepsilon(p_1 + \cdots + p_{T+1})$ for the price paid by generation 1, which, going to the limit and adding $\varepsilon p_0$, gives $\varepsilon(\sum_t p_t)$ as a lower bound for the value to generation 0. Thus, in terms of expression (20.H.2) a necessary condition for equilibrium is $M \geq 0$. In principle, however, we should allow for the possibility of a *bubble* in the value of the asset (i.e., of $M > 0$). We did not do so in Sections 20.D or 20.G because with a *finite* number of consumers, bubbles are impossible at equilibrium. The equality of demand and supply implies that the (finite) value of total endowments plus total profits equals the value of total consumption, and therefore at equilibrium no individual value of consumption can be larger than the corresponding individual value of endowments and profit wealth (you should verify this in Exercise 20.H.1). We will see shortly that under some circumstances bubbles can occur at equilibrium with infinitely many consumers. It would therefore not be legitimate to eliminate them by definition.

The definition of a *Walrasian equilibrium* is now the natural one presented in Definition 20.H.1.

**Definition 20.H.1:** A sequence of prices $(p_0, \ldots, p_t, \ldots)$, an $M \geq 0$, and a family of consumptions $\{(c_{bt}^*, c_{at}^*)\}_{t=0}^{\infty}$ constitute a *Walrasian* (or *competitive*) *equilibrium* if:

    (i) Every $(c_{bt}^*, c_{at}^*)$ solves the individual utility maximization problem subject to the budget constraints (20.H.1) and (20.H.2).

    (ii) The feasibility requirement $(c_{a,t-1}^* + c_{bt}^* = 1)$ is satisfied for all $t \geq 0$ (we put $c_{a,-1}^* = 0$).

In a process reminiscent of the iterative procedure (presented in Section 20.D) for the determination of the policy function from the Euler equations, Figures 20.H.1 and 20.H.2 describe how we could attempt to construct an equilibrium. Normalize to $p_0 = 1$. Suppose that we now try to arbitrarily fix $c_{a0}$. At equilibrium, $c_{b0} = 1$, and thus $p_1$ is determined by the fact that $p_1/p_0$ must equal the marginal rate of substitution of $u(\cdot, \cdot)$ at $(1, c_{a0})$. Also, $c_{b1} = 1 - c_{a0}$. This now determines $p_2$. Indeed, $p_2$, the price at period 2, should be fixed at a value that induces a level of demand by generation 1 in period 1 of precisely $c_{b1}$ [under the budget set given by $p_1, p_2$ and wealth $(1 - \varepsilon)p_1$]. With this, the demand of generation 1 in period 2, and therefore the residual amount $c_{b2}$ left in that period for generation 2, has also been determined. But then we may be able to fix $p_3$ at a value that precisely induces the right amount of demand by generation 2 in period 2, that is, $c_{b2}$. If we can pursue this construction indefinitely so as to generate an infinite sequence $(p_1, \ldots, p_t, \ldots)$, then we have found an equilibrium. In Figure 20.H.1, where $\varepsilon > 0$, there is a single price sequence (with $p_0 = 1$) that can be continued indefinitely, and therefore a single equilibrium path.

---

34. Strictly speaking, we are saying that if the consumption good prices are given by $(p_0, \ldots, p_t, \ldots)$ *and* the asset prices present no arbitrage opportunity, then the price of the asset should be at least as large as its fundamental value.

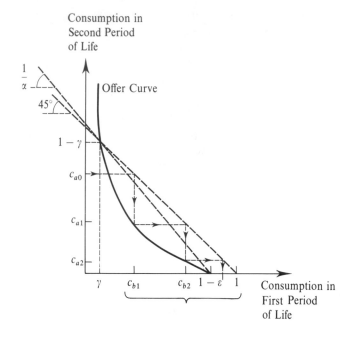

**Figure 20.H.1**

Overlapping generations: construction of the equilibrium (case $\varepsilon > 0$).

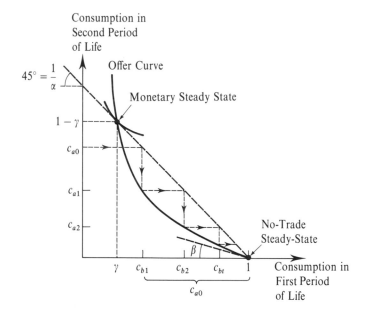

**Figure 20.H.2**

Overlapping generations: construction of equilibria (case $\varepsilon = 0$).

It corresponds to the stationary consumptions $(\gamma, 1 - \gamma)$ and the price sequence $p_t = \alpha^t$, where $\alpha = (1 - \varepsilon - \gamma)/(1 - \gamma) < 1$. Note that the iterates that begin at a value $c_{a0} \neq 1 - \gamma$ unavoidably "leave the picture," that is, become unfeasible. In Figure 20.H.2, where $\varepsilon = 0$, there is a continuum of equilibria: any initial condition $c_{a0} \leq 1 - \gamma$ can be continued indefinitely.

It is plausible from Figures 20.H.1 and 20.H.2 that the existence of an equilibrium can be guaranteed under general conditions. This is indeed the case [see Wilson (1981)].

*Pareto Optimality*

Suppose first that $\varepsilon > 0$. We say then that the asset is *real* (it has "real" returns). At an equilibrium the wealth of generation 0, $(1 - \varepsilon)p_0 + \varepsilon(\sum_t p_t) + M$, must be finite (how could this generation be in equilibrium otherwise?). Therefore, if $\varepsilon > 0$, it follows that $\sum_t p_t < \infty$.[35] An important implication of this is that the *aggregate* (i.e., added over all generations) *wealth of society*, which is precisely $\sum_t p_t$, *is finite*. In Proposition 20.H.1 we now show that, as a consequence, the first welfare theorem applies for the model with $\varepsilon > 0$.

**Proposition 20.H.1:** Any Walrasian equilibrium $(p_0, \dots, p_t, \dots)$, $\{(c^*_{bt}, c^*_{at})\}^{\infty}_{t=0}$, with $\sum_t p_t < \infty$ is a Pareto optimum; that is, there are no other feasible consumptions $\{(c_{bt}, c_{at})\}^{\infty}_{t=0}$ such that $u(c_{bt}, c_{at}) \geq u(c^*_{bt}, c^*_{at})$ for all $t \geq 0$, with strict inequality for some $t$.

**Proof:** We repeat the standard argument. Suppose that $\{(c_{bt}, c_{at})\}^{\infty}_{t=0}$ Pareto dominates $\{(c^*_{bt}, c^*_{at})\}^{\infty}_{t=0}$. From feasibility, we have $c^*_{bt} + c^*_{a,t-1} = 1$ and $c_{bt} + c_{a,t-1} \leq 1$ for every $t$. Therefore, $\sum_t p_t(c^*_{bt} + c^*_{a,t-1}) = \sum_t p_t$ and $\sum_t p_t(c_{bt} + c_{a,t-1}) \leq \sum_t p_t$. Because $\sum_t p_t < \infty$, we can rearrange terms and get

$$\sum_t (p_t c_{bt} + p_{t+1} c_{at}) \leq \sum_t (p_t c^*_{bt} + p_{t+1} c^*_{at}) = \sum_t p_t < \infty.$$

Because the utility function is increasing and $(c^*_{bt}, c^*_{at})$ maximizes utility in the budget set we conclude that $p_t c_{bt} + p_{t+1} c_{at} \geq p_t c^*_{bt} + p_{t+1} c^*_{at}$ for every $t$, with at least one strict inequality. Therefore, $\sum_t (p_t c_{bt} + p_{t+1} c_{at}) > \sum_t (p_t c^*_{bt} + p_{t+1} c^*_{at})$. Contradiction. ∎

Proposition 20.H.1 is important but it is not the end of the story. Suppose now that the asset is purely *nominal* (i.e., $\varepsilon = 0$; for example, the asset could be fiat money, or ownership of a constant returns technology). Then *it is possible to have equilibria that are not optimal*. In fact, it is easy to see that we can sustain autarchy (i.e., no trade) as an equilibrium. Just put $M = 0$ (no bubble, worthless fiat money) and choose $(p_0, \dots, p_t, \dots)$ so that, for every $t$, the relative prices $p_t/p_{t+1}$ equal the marginal rate of substitution of $u(\cdot, \cdot)$ at $(1, 0)$, denoted by $\beta$. This no-trade stationary state (also called *the nonmonetary steady state*) where every generation consumes $(1, 0)$ is represented in Figure 20.H.2. As it is drawn (with $\beta < 1$), we can also see that the no-trade outcome is strictly Pareto dominated by the steady state $(\gamma, 1 - \gamma)$ [or, more precisely, by the consumption path in which generation 0 consumes $(1, 1 - \gamma)$ and every other generation consumes $(\gamma, 1 - \gamma)$]. What is going on is simple: in this example the open-endedness of the horizon makes it possible for the members of every generation $t$ to pass an extra amount of good to the older generation at $t$ and, at the same time, be more then compensated by the amount passed to them at $t + 1$ by the next generation. Note that, in agreement with Proposition 20.H.1, the lack of optimality of this no-trade equilibrium entails $p_t/p_{t+1} = \beta < 1$ for all $t$; that is, prices increase through time.

It is also possible in the purely nominal case for an equilibrium with $M > 0$ not to be Pareto optimal. Note first if $\{(c^*_{bt}, c^*_{at})\}^{\infty}_{t=0}$, $(p_0, \dots, p_t, \dots)$ and $M$ constitute an

---

35. You can also verify this graphically by examining Figure 20.H.1.

equilibrium, then we have (recall that $c_{b0}^* = 1$)

$$p_{t+1}c_{at}^* = p_t(1 - c_{bt}^*) = p_t c_{a,t-1}^* = \cdots = p_1 c_{a0}^* = M \qquad \text{for every } t.$$

Thus, $M = 0$ can occur only at a no-trade equilibrium. In Figure 20.H.2, there is a continuum of equilibria indexed by $c_{b1}$ for $\gamma \le c_{b1} \le 1$. The no-trade equilibrium corresponds to $c_{b1} = 1$. But for every $c_{b1} < 1$ with $c_{b1} > \gamma$ we have a nonstationary equilibrium trajectory with trade (hence $M > 0$) which is also strictly Pareto dominated by the steady state $(\gamma, 1 - \gamma)$. Nonetheless, it is still true that for any equilibrium with $c_{b1} > \gamma$ we have $M/p_t \to 0$; that is, in real terms the value of the asset becomes vanishingly small with time. For $c_{b1} = \gamma$, matters are quite different. We have a steady-state equilibrium (called *the monetary steady state*) in which the price sequence $p_t$ is constant and therefore the real value of money remains constant and positive. This monetary steady state is the analog of the *golden rule* of Section 20.E and, as was the case there, we have that, in spite of $\sum_t p_t < \infty$ being violated, the *monetary steady state is Pareto optimal*. We will not give a rigorous proof of this. The basic argument is contained in Figure 20.H.3. There we represent the indifference curve through $(\gamma, 1 - \gamma)$ and check that any attempt at increasing the utility of generation 0 by putting $c_{b1} < \gamma$ leads to an unfeasible chain of compensations; that is, it cannot be done.

The discussion just carried out of the examples in Figures 20.H.2 and 20.H.3 suggests and confirms the following claim, which we leave without proof: *In the purely nominal case, of all equilibrium paths the Pareto optimal ones are those, and only those, that exhibit a bubble whose real value is bounded away from zero throughout time.*

It is certainly interesting that a bubble can serve the function of guaranteeing the optimality of the equilibria of an economy, but one should keep in mind that this happens only because an asset is needed to transfer wealth through time. If a real asset exists then this asset can do the job. If one does not exist then the economy, so to speak, needs to invent an asset. To close the circle, we point out that if there is a real asset then not only is a bubble not needed but, in fact, it cannot occur.

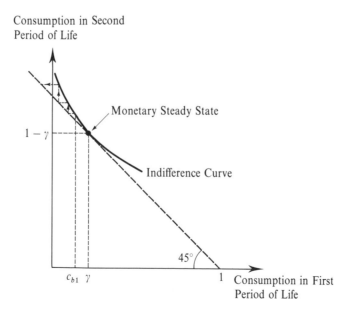

**Figure 20.H.3**

The monetary steady state is Pareto optimal.

**Proposition 20.H.2:** Suppose that at an equilibrium we have $\sum_t p_t < \infty$. Then $M = 0$.

**Proof:** The sum of wealths over generations is $\sum_t p_t + M < \infty$. The value of total consumption is $\sum_t p_t < \infty$. The second amount cannot be smaller than the first (otherwise some generation is not spending its entire wealth). Therefore $M = 0$. ∎

*Multiplicity of Equilibria*

We have already seen, in Figure 20.H.2, a model with a purely nominal asset (i.e., $\varepsilon = 0$) and very nicely shaped preferences (the offer curve is of the gross substitute type) for which there is a continuum of equilibria. Of those, one is the Pareto optimal monetary steady state and the rest are nonoptimal equilibria where the real value of money goes to zero asymptotically. The existence of this sort of indeterminacy is clearly related to the ability to fix with some arbitrariness the real value of money (the "bubble") at $t = 0$, that is $M/p_0$. It cannot occur if bubbles are impossible, as, for example, in the model with a real asset (i.e., $\varepsilon > 0$) where, in addition, we know that the equilibrium is Pareto optimal.

One may be led by the above observation to suspect that the failure of Pareto optimality is a precondition for the presence of a robust indeterminacy (i.e., of a continuum of equilibria not associated with any obvious coincidence in the basic data of the economy). This suspicion may be reinforced by the discussion of Section 20.G, where we saw that the Pareto optimality of equilibria was key to our ability to claim the generic determinacy of equilibria in models with a finite number of consumers. Unfortunately, with overlapping generations the number of consumers is infinite in a fundamental way,[36] and this complicates matters. Whereas with a real asset the Pareto optimality of equilibria is guaranteed and the type of indeterminacy of Figure 20.H.2 disappears, it is nevertheless possible to construct nonpathological examples with a continuum of equilibria.

The simplest example is illustrated in Figure 20.H.4. The figure describes a real-asset model with the steady state $(\gamma, 1 - \gamma)$. Suppose that, in a procedure we have resorted to repeatedly, we tried to construct an equilibrium with $c_{a0}$ slightly different from $1 - \gamma$. Then, normalizing to $p_0 = 1$, we would need to use $p_1$ to clear the market *of period* 0, $p_2$ to do the same for period 1, and so on. In the leading case of Figure 20.H.1, we have seen that this eventually becomes unfeasible. A change in $p_t$ that takes care of a disequilibrium at $t - 1$ creates an even larger disequilibrium at $t$, which then has to be compensated by a change of a larger magnitude in $p_{t+1}$ in an explosive process that finally becomes impossible. But in Figure 20.H.4, the utility function is such that, at the relative prices of the steady state, a change in the price of the second-period good has a larger impact on the demand for the first-period good than on the demand for the second-period good. Hence, the successive adjustments necessitated by an initial disturbance from $c_{a0} = 1 - \gamma$ dampen with each iteration and can be pursued indefinitely. We conclude that an equilibrium exists with the new initial condition. As a matter of terminology, the

---

36. By this vague statement we mean that there is no way we could assert that the infinitely many consumers are sufficiently similar for them to be "approximated" by a finite number of representatives.

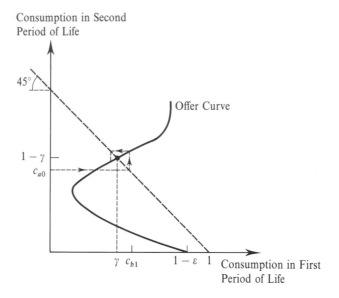

**Figure 20.H.4**

An example of a continuum of (Pareto optimal) equilibria in the real asset case.

locally isolated steady state equilibrium of Figure 20.H.1 is called *determinate*, and the one of Figure 20.H.4 is called *indeterminate*.[37]

It is interesting to point out that the leading case of unique equilibrium (Figure 20.H.1) in a real-asset model corresponds to a gross substitute excess demand function, while Figure 20.H.4 represents the sort of pronounced complementaries that were sources of nonuniqueness in the examples of Sections 15.B (recall also the discussion of uniqueness in Section 17.F). The connection between nonuniqueness and indeterminateness is actually quite close, and you are asked to explore it in Exercise 20.H.2. Here we simply mention that gross substitution is not a necessary condition for uniqueness. It can be checked, for example, that in the real asset model the steady state remains the only equilibrium if consumption in both periods is normal in the demand function of $u(\cdot, \cdot)$ and if the corresponding excess demand $(z_b(p_b, p_a), z_a(p_b, p_a))$ satisfies

$$\nabla_1 z_b(p_b, p_a) < \nabla_1 z_a(p_b, p_a) \qquad \text{for all } p_b, p_a. \tag{20.H.3}$$

Expression (20.H.3) permits a price increase in the first period of life to lead to an increase in demand in this period (a possibility ruled out by gross substitution); but, if so, it requires the increase of demand in the second period of life to be larger. Geometrically speaking, the condition is that the slope of the offer curve in the $(c_b, c_a)$ plane should never be positive and less than 1. Note that in Figure 20.H.4 this is violated at the steady state. Condition (20.H.3) is known as the *determinacy condition*. If the reverse inequality holds at the steady state, then, as in Figure 20.H.4, there is a continuum of equilibria all converging to the steady state (the steady state is therefore *indeterminate*).

---

37. Observe that, at least in the context of the relatively simple model we are now discussing, there is little room for cases intermediate between uniqueness or the existence of a continuum of equilibria.

In Chapter 17 (see Section 17.D and Appendix A of Chapter 17) we argued that, with Pareto optimality, an equilibrium problem with a finite number of consumers could be represented by means of a finite number of equations with the same number of unknowns. From this we claimed that generic determinacy was the logical conjecture to make for this case. In Section 20.G we extended this argument to the model with a finite number of infinitely long-lived consumers. However, the current overlapping generations problem has a basic difference in formal structure: there is no natural trick allowing us to see the equilibrium as anything but the zeros of an infinite system of equations (of the excess demand type, say). Mathematically, this is significant. To give an example, intimately related to the issues we are discussing, suppose that $f: \mathbb{R}^n \to \mathbb{R}^n$ is a linear map that is onto (i.e., $f(x) = Ax$, where $A$ is a nonsingular matrix). Then 0 is the unique solution to $f(x) = 0$. But suppose now that $f(\cdot)$ maps bounded sequences into bounded sequences and that it is linear and onto. Then $f(x) = 0$, or, equivalently, $f_t(x_1, \ldots, x_t, \ldots) = 0$ for all $t$, need not have a unique solution. A simple example is the backward shift, that is, $f_t(x_1, \ldots, x_t, \ldots) = x_{t+1}$, where any $(\alpha, 0, \ldots, 0, \ldots)$ is sent to zero.

What can we say about the dynamics of an equilibrium? We saw that the "anything goes" principle applied to the one-consumer model. It would be surprising if it did not apply here; indeed, in Figures 20.H.5 and 20.H.6 we provide nonpathological examples with cycles.[38] Note

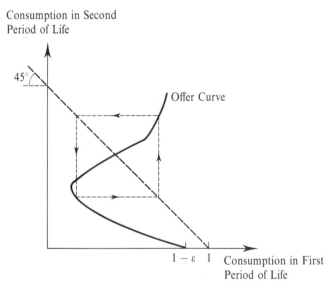

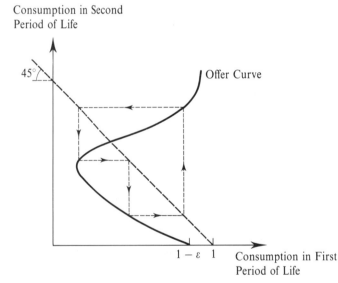

that in Figure 20.H.6 we have a three-period cycle: chaos rears its head. In the gross substitute example of Figure 20.H.1 we have monotone convergence to the steady-state. In a sense, the gross substitute case is the analog of the approach based on the sign of the second derivatives described in Section 20.F. Note that in the overlapping generations situation the factor of discount is not a meaningful concept and, therefore, there is no analog of a dynamic theory based on patience. In Section 20.G we also mentioned, quite loosely, that there did not seem to be, for the case of a finite number of agents with Pareto optimality, a close relation between the determinacy and the dynamic properties of equilibrium. In the current setting the connection is closer, at least in the following sense: If equilibrium trajectories with cycles can occur, then there are infinitely many equilibria.

**Figure 20.H.5 (left)**

Complementary consumptions: example of a period-2 equilibrium path.

**Figure 20.H.6 (right)**

Complementary consumptions: example of a period-3 equilibrium path.

38. In particular, no inferior goods are required for these examples.

# 20.I Remarks on Nonequilibrium Dynamics: Tâtonnement and Learning

The dynamic analysis that has concerned us so far in this chapter is of a different nature from, and should not be confused with, the dynamics studied in Section 17.H. The dynamics here display the temporal unfolding of an equilibrium (an internal property of the equilibrium, in the terminology of Section 20.G), whereas in Section 17.H we were trying to assess the dynamic forces that, in real or in fictional time, would buffet an economy disturbed from its equilibrium (hence, we were looking at an external property). As we saw, nonequilibrium dynamic analysis raises a host of conceptual problems, yet it may offer useful insight into the plausibility of the occurrence of particular equilibria. This remains valid in the setting of intertemporal equilibrium.

Abstracting from technical complexities, the analysis and the results of Section 17.H can be adapted and hold true for the infinite-horizon, finite number of consumers model of Section 20.G. On the other hand, as we have seen, the temporal framework has its own special theory, which could conceivably be illuminated by specific nonequilibrium considerations. We make three remarks in this direction.

*Short-Run Equilibrium and Permanent Income*[39]

Suppose that $(p_0, \ldots, p_t, \ldots)$ is the equilibrium price sequence of an economy with $L$ goods and $I$ consumers. Consumers are as in Section 20.D. Then at the equilibrium consumptions we have (assuming interiority)

$$\delta^t \nabla u_i(c_{ti}) = \lambda_i p_t \qquad \text{for all } t \text{ and every } i. \qquad (20.I.1)$$

This is just (20.D.6). The variable $\lambda_i$ is the marginal utility of income, or wealth, and the vector of reciprocals $(\eta_1, \ldots, \eta_I) = (1/\lambda_1, \ldots, 1/\lambda_I)$ can serve as the weights for which the given equilibrium maximizes the weighted sum of utilities (see Section 20.G).

It follows from (20.I.1) that the short-run demands (i.e., the demands at $t = 0$) are entirely determined by $p_0$ and the marginal utilities of wealth $\lambda_i$. Denote this demand by $c_{0i}(p, \lambda_i)$. In the spirit of tâtonnement dynamics, suppose that $p_0$ is perturbed to some $p_0'$. What will happen to demand at $t = 0$? If the $\lambda_i$ remain fixed, then (20.I.1) implies that short-run demand behaves as the demand for non-numeraire goods in a quasilinear utility model with concave utility functions. In particular, differentiating (20.I.1) we see that the $L \times L$ matrix of short-run price effects

$$D_{p_0} c_{0i}(p_0, \lambda_i) = \lambda_i [D^2 u_i(c_{0i})]^{-1}$$

is negative definite (by the concavity of $u_i(\cdot)$) and, therefore, so is the aggregate $\sum_i D_{p_0} c_{0i}(p_0, \lambda_i)$. In more economic terms, as long as the $\lambda_i$ stay fixed there are no wealth effects present in the short-run demands. Substitution prevails and, consequently, the short-run equilibrium is unique and globally tâtonnement stable.

In reality, however, after a change in $p_0$ we should expect that $\lambda_i$ will have changed at the new consumer optimum. But if the rate of discount is close to 1 (i.e., if agents

---

39. See Bewley (1977) for more on this topic. The term "permanent income" is standard and so we use it rather than "permanent wealth."

are patient) then the change in $\lambda_i$ should be small: The current period is not significantly more important than any other period and, therefore, it will account for only a small fraction of total utility and expenditure. Hence, we could say that partial equilibrium analysis is justified in the short run (recall the discussion of partial equilibrium analysis in Section 10.G). In summary: *If consumers are sufficiently patient, then the short-run equilibrium is unique and globally stable (for the tâtonnement dynamics).*

### The (Short-Run) Law of Demand in Overlapping Generations Models

We now look at the short-run equilibrium of the overlapping generations model of Section 20.H. This is an example of a model where wealth effects matter in the short run and, therefore, the permanent income approach does not apply. We consider the version of the model with a real asset and normal goods and ask whether the stability of the fictional-time tâtonnement dynamics at a given date $t$ helps us to distinguish among types of equilibria. Because there is a single good per period, the stability criterion for a single period is simple enough—it amounts to the law of demand at time $t$. That is, we say that an equilibrium $(p_0, \ldots, p_t, \ldots)$ is tâtonnement stable at time $t$ if an (anticipated) increase in $p_t$, all other prices remaining fixed, results in excess supply in that period (note that only generations $t - 1$ and $t$ will alter their consumption plans).

We know that if the excess demand function of the generations is of the gross substitute type, then there is a unique equilibrium (which is in steady state). (See Figure 20.H.1.) Moreover, the definition of gross substitution tells us that the law of demand is satisfied at any $t$. This gives us a first link between the notions of determinate equilibrium and tâtonnement stability. This link can be pushed beyond the gross substitute case. Take a steady-state equilibrium price sequence $(1, \rho, \ldots, \rho^t, \ldots)$. By the homogeneity of degree zero of excess demand functions $(z_a(\cdot, \cdot), z_b(\cdot, \cdot))$, which implies the homogeneity of degree $-1$ of $\nabla z_a(\cdot, \cdot)$ and $\nabla z_b(\cdot, \cdot)$, we have (you should verify this in Exercise 20.I.1)

$$\nabla_2 z_a(1/\rho, 1) + \nabla_1 z_b(1, \rho) = \rho \nabla_2 z_a(1, \rho) + \nabla_1 z_b(1, \rho) = -\nabla_1 z_a(1, \rho) + \nabla_1 z_b(1, \rho).$$

The negativity of the left-hand side is the tâtonnement stability criterion, that is, the law of demand at a single market,[40] while the negativity of the right-hand side (i.e., the requirement that wealth effects are not so askew that a decrease in the price in one period increases the demand of the young in that period by less than it increases the demand of these same young for their consumption in the next period) is the criterion for the determinacy of the steady state [see expression (20.H.3)]. Recall that determinate means that there is no other equilibrium trajectory that remains in an arbitrarily small neighborhood of the steady state. We conclude that there is an exact correspondence: *a steady-state equilibrium is (short-run, locally) tâtonnement stable at any t if and only if it is determinate.*[41]

---

40. If $p_t$ is changed infinitesimally then the demand of the old changes by $\nabla_2 z_a(\rho^{t-1}, \rho^t)$ while the demand of the young changes by $\nabla_1 z_b(\rho^t, \rho^{t+1})$. Because $\nabla_2 z(\cdot, \cdot)$ and $\nabla_1 z(\cdot, \cdot)$ are homogeneous of degree $-1$, the total change equals $(1/\rho^t) \nabla_2 z_a(1/\rho, 1) + (1/\rho^t) \nabla_1 z_b(1, \rho)$

41. In this "if and only if" statement we neglect borderline cases.

We have confined ourselves to the real asset case to avoid a complication. With a purely nominal asset the previous concept of tâtonnement stability loses the power to discriminate between determinate and indeterminate steady-state equilibria, unless we restrict ourselves a priori to monetary steady states (to see this, consider the simplest gross substitute case). The learning concept to be presented in the remainder of this section does not suffer from this limitation.

## Learning

We now briefly discuss a nonequilibrium dynamics that takes place in real time and that can be interpreted in terms of learning. The framework is that of the over-lapping generations of Section 20.H and, to be as simple as possible, we focus on the purely nominal asset case.

We describe first how the short-run equilibrium (i.e., the equilibrium at a given period $t$) is determined. We suppose that there is a certain fixed amount of fiat money $M$ (denominated, say, in dollars). The excess demand of the older generation at date $t \geq 1$ is then $M/p_t$. The excess demand of the younger generation at the same date depends on $p_t$ but also on the *expectation* $p_{t+1}^e$ of the price at $t + 1$. Given $p_{t+1}^e$, the price $p_t$ is a *temporary equilibrium at time* $t \geq 1$ if $z_b(p_t, p_{t+1}^e) + (M/p_t) = 0$. Thus, given a sequence of price expectations $(p_1^e, \ldots, p_t^e, \ldots)$, we generate a sequence of temporary equilibrium prices $(p_1, \ldots, p_t, \ldots)$.

But, how are expected prices determined? To take them as given does not make much sense. The sequence of realizations should feed back into the sequence of expectations. The self-fulfilled, or rational, expectations approach (which we have implicitly adhered to in this chapter) imposes a correct expectations condition: $p_{t+1}^e = p_{t+1}$ for every $t$.[42] An alternative is to require that $p_{t+1}^e$ (the price expected at $t$ to prevail at $t + 1$) be an extrapolation of the past (and current) realizations $p_0, \ldots, p_t$. In this approach we think of consumers as engaged in some sort of learning and of expectations responding *adaptively* to experienced outcomes.[43]

To be specific, let us take a not very realistic, but very simple, extrapolation rule: $p_{t+1}^e = p_{t-1}$ (i.e., the price at $t + 1$ expected by the young at $t \geq 1$ is the price that ruled in the most recent past). Equivalently (given the fixed amount of fiat money $M$), the young at $t$ expect to consume at $t + 1$, when old, the same amount consumed by the old at $t - 1$. The equation for the determination of $p_t$ is then

$$z_b(p_t, p_{t-1}) = -\frac{M}{p_t}. \tag{20.I.2}$$

By Walras' law, (20.I.2) can equivalently be written as

$$z_a(p_t, p_{t-1}) = \frac{M}{p_{t-1}}. \tag{20.I.3}$$

---

42. The term "self-fulfilled" is justified because the sequence of expectations $(p_1^e, \ldots, p_t^e, \ldots)$ induces a sequence of realizations identical to itself. The term "rational" is justified by the fact that, given $(p_1^e, \ldots, p_t^e, \ldots)$, a member of generation $t$ should, in principle, be able to compute the price realization $p_{t+1}$ and therefore verify the correctness of $p_{t+1}^e$.

43. We should emphasize, first, that all this is a nonequilibrium story and, second, that we cannot rigorously discuss learning without explicitly introducing an uncertain environment.

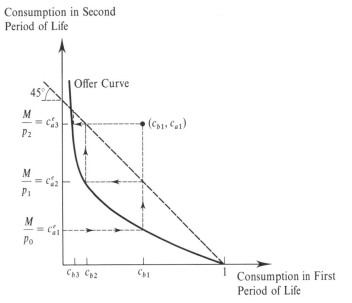

**Figure 20.I.1**
Learning dynamics.

Given an arbitrary initial condition $p_0$, we can then compute the sequence of temporary equilibrium realizations $(p_1, \ldots, p_t, \ldots)$ by iteratively using (20.I.2) or (20.I.3). Note that in doing so, the planned excess demands in (20.I.2) will be realized but those in (20.I.3) may not (because $p_{t+1}$ may not be equal to $p_{t-1}$). We represent the dynamic process in Figure 20.I.1. In the figure, $c_{bt}$ and $c_{at}^e$ stand for the planned consumptions of generation $t$ at times $t$ and $t + 1$, respectively. Given $M/p_{t-1}$ we get $c_{at}^e$ from (20.I.3), and $c_{bt}$ from the fact that planned consumptions are in the offer curve. Finally (20.I.2) moves us to the next value $M/p_t$. For generation 1 we also show the actual consumption vector $(c_{b1}, c_{a1})$.

From Figure 20.I.1 we can see an interesting fact: The learning dynamics exactly reverses the equilibrium dynamics (compare with Figure 20.H.2).[44] For the gross substitute case shown in the figure, this means that all the trajectories tend to the monetary steady state. Hence, in the limit we have a true self-fulfilled expectations equilibrium. Consumers have learned their way into equilibrium, so to speak. For the crude learning dynamics we are considering, this need not be so for the case of a general offer curve (an infinite sequence with systematic prediction error is quite possible), but the property of exact reversal of equilibrium dynamics suffices to provide, once again, a test for the well-behavedness of steady states that reinforces the intuitions developed earlier: *A steady state is (locally) stable for the learning dynamics if and only if it is determinate (i.e., "locally isolated").*

44. More precisely, if $(p_1, \ldots, p_t, \ldots)$ is the sequence of realizations of the adaptive expectations dynamics, then for any $T$ there is an equilibrium sequence $(p_0', \ldots, p_t', \ldots)$ such that $p_t' = p_{T-t}$ for every $t < T$.

## REFERENCES

Allais, M. (1947). *Economie et Interét*. Paris: Imprimérie Nationale.

Barro, R. (1989). The Ricardian approach to budget deficits. *Journal of Economic Perspectives* **3**: 37–54.

Bewley, T. (1977). The permanent income hypothesis: A theoretical formulation. *Journal of Economic Theory* **16**: 252–92.

Blackorby, C., D. Primont, and R. Russell. (1978). *Duality, Separability, and Functional Structure: Theory and Economic Applications*. Amsterdam: North-Holland.

Blanchard, O., and S. Fischer. (1989). *Lectures on Macroeconomics*. Cambridge, Mass.: MIT Press.

Boldrin, M., and L. Montruccio. (1986). On the indeterminacy of capital accumulation paths. *Journal of Economic Theory* **40**: 26–39.

Bliss, C. (1975). *Capital Theory and the Distribution of Income*. Amsterdam: North-Holland.

Brock, W. A., and E. Burmeister. (1976). Regular economies and conditions for uniqueness of steady-states in optimal multisector economic models. *International Economic Review* **17**: 105–20.

Cass, D. (1972). On capital overaccumulation in the aggregative, neoclassical model of economic growth: a complete characterization. *Journal of Economic Theory* **4**: 200–23.

Deneckere, R., and J. Pelikan. (1986). Competitive chaos. *Journal of Economic Theory* **40**: 13–25.

Gale, D. (1973). On the theory of interest. *American Mathematical Monthly* **88**: 853–68.

Geanakoplos, J. (1987). Overlapping generations. Entry in *The New Palgrave: A Dictionary of Economics*, edited by J. Eatwell, M. Milgate, and P. Newman. London: Macmillan.

Grandmont, J. M. (1986). Periodic and aperiodic behavior in discrete one dimensional systems. In *Contributions to Mathematical Economics*, edited by W. Hildenbrand, and A. Mas-Colell. Amsterdam: North-Holland.

Kehoe, T., and D. Levine. (1985). Comparative statics and perfect foresight. *Econometrica* **53**: 433–54.

Koopmans, T. C. (1960). Stationary ordinal utility and impatience. *Econometrica* **28**: 287–309.

Malinvaud, E. (1953). Capital accumulation and efficient allocation of resources. *Econometrica* **21**: 223–68.

McKenzie, L. (1987). Turnpike theory. Entry in *The New Palgrave: A Dictionary of Economics*, edited by J. Eatwell, M. Milgate, and P. Newman. London, Macmillan.

Ramsey, F. (1928). A mathematical theory of saving. *Economic Journal* **38**: 543–49.

Samuelson, P. A. (1958). An exact consumption-loan model of interest without the social contrivance of money. *Journal of Political Economy* **66**: 467–82.

Santos, M. S. (1991). Smoothness of the policy function in discrete time economic models. *Econometrica* **59**: 1365–82.

Solow, R. M. (1956). A contribution to the theory of economic growth. *Quarterly Journal of Economics* **70**: 65–94.

Stokey, N., and R. Lucas, with E. C. Prescott. (1989). *Recursive Methods in Economic Dynamics*. Cambridge, Mass.: Harvard University Press.

Swan, T. W. (1956). Economic growth and capital accumulation. *Economic Record* **32**: 334–61.

Uzawa, H. (1964). Optimal growth in a two-sector model of capital accumulation. *Review of Economic Studies* **31**: 1–24.

Weizsäcker, C. C. von (1971). *Steady State Capital Theory*. New York: Springer-Verlag.

Wilson, C. (1981). Equilibrium in dynamic models with an infinity of agents. *Journal of Economic Theory* **24**: 95–111.

Woodford, M. (1984). Indeterminacy of equilibrium in the overlapping generations model: a survey. Mimeograph, Columbia University.

## EXERCISES

**20.B.1**[B] Adopting the definition of *time impatience* given in comment (1) of Section 20.B, show that a utility function of the form (20.B.1) exhibits time impatience.

**20.B.2**[B] Verify that a utility function of the form (20.B.1) is stationary according to the definition given in comment (2) of Section 20.B. Also, exhibit a violation of stationarity with a utility function of the form $V(c) = \sum_{t=0}^{\infty} \delta_t^t u(c_t)$.

**20.B.3$^B$** With reference to comment (3) of Section 20.B, write $c = (c', c'')$ where $c' = (c_0, \ldots, c_t)$, $c'' = (c_{t+1}, \ldots)$. Suppose that the utility function $V(\cdot)$ is additively separable. Show that if $V(\bar{c}', c'') \geq V(\bar{c}', \hat{c}'')$ for some $\bar{c}'$, then $V(c', c'') \geq V(c', \hat{c}'')$ for all $c'$. Show that if $V(c', \bar{c}'') \geq V(\hat{c}', \bar{c}'')$ for some $\bar{c}''$, then $V(c', c'') \geq V(\hat{c}', c'')$ for all $c''$. Interpret.

**20.B.4$^C$** Show that in a recursive utility model with aggregator function $G(u, V) = u^\alpha + \delta V^\alpha$, $0 < \alpha < 1$, $\delta < 1$, and increasing, continuous one-period utility $u(c_t)$, the utility $V(c)$ of a bounded consumption stream is well defined. [*Hint*: Use (20.B.3) to compute the utility for consumption streams truncated at a finite horizon. Then show that a limit exists as $T \to \infty$. Finally, argue that the limit satisfies the aggregator equation.]

**20.B.5$^A$** Show that the utility function $V(c)$ on consumption streams given by (20.B.1) is concave. Show also that the additively separable form of $V(\cdot)$ is a cardinal property.

**20.C.1$^A$** Given the price sequence $(p_0, p_1, \ldots, p_t, \ldots)$, $p_t \in \mathbb{R}^L$, define for every $t$ and every commodity $\ell$ the rate of interest from $t$ to $t + 1$ in terms of commodity $\ell$ (this is known as the *own rate of interest* of commodity $\ell$ at $t$).

**20.C.2$^A$** Show that if the path $(y_0, \ldots, y_t, \ldots)$, is myopically profit maximizing for $(p_0, p_1, \ldots, p_t, \ldots) \geq 0$, then $(y_0, \ldots, y_t, \ldots)$ is also profit maximizing for $(p_0, p_1, \ldots, p_t, \ldots)$ over any finite horizon, in the sense that, for any $T$, the total profits over the first $T$ periods cannot be increased by any coordinated move involving only these periods.

**20.C.3$^A$** Define an appropriate concept of weak efficiency and reprove Proposition 20.C.1, requiring only that $(p_0, \ldots, p_t, \ldots)$ is a nonnegative sequence with some nonzero entry.

**20.C.4$^B$** Suppose that the production path $(y_0, \ldots, y_t, \ldots)$ is bounded (i.e., there is a fixed $\alpha$ such that $\|y_t\| \leq \alpha$ for all $t$), that $(p_0, \ldots, p_t, \ldots) \gg 0$, and that $\sum_{t=0}^\infty p_t < \infty$. We say that the path $(y_0, \ldots, y_t, \ldots)$ is overall profit maximizing with respect to $(p_0, \ldots, p_t, \ldots)$ if

$$\sum_{t=0}^\infty (p_t \cdot y_{bt} + p_{t+1} \cdot y_{a,t}) \geq \sum_{t=0}^\infty (p_t \cdot y'_{bt} + p_{t+1} \cdot y'_{a,t})$$

for any other production path $(y'_0, \ldots, y'_t, \ldots)$.

**(a)** Show that if $(y_0, \ldots, y_t, \ldots)$ is overall profit maximizing with respect to $(p_0, \ldots, p_t, \ldots) \gg 0$, then it is efficient.

**(b)** Show that if $(y_0, \ldots, y_t, \ldots)$ is myopically profit maximizing with respect to $(p_0, \ldots, p_t, \ldots) \gg 0$, then it is also overall profit maximizing.

**20.C.5$^C$** Say that a production path $(y_0, \ldots, y_t, \ldots)$, is $T$-efficient, for $T < \infty$, if there is no other production path $(y'_0, \ldots, y'_t, \ldots)$ that, first, dominates $(y_0, \ldots, y_t, \ldots)$ in the sense of efficiency and, second, is such that the cardinality of $\{t : y_t \neq y'_t\}$ is at most $T$.

**(a)** Show that if $(y_0, \ldots, y_t, \ldots)$ is myopically profit maximizing with respect to $(p_0, \ldots, p_t, \ldots) \gg 0$, then $(y_0, \ldots, y_t, \ldots)$ is $T$-efficient for all $T < \infty$.

**(b)** Show that if the technology is smooth (in the sense used in the small-type discussion at the end of Section 20.C; assume also that the outward unit normals to the production frontiers are strictly positive), then 2-efficiency implies $T$-efficiency for all $T < \infty$.

**(c)** (Harder) Show that the conclusion of **(b)** fails for general linear activity technologies. Exhibit an example. [*Hint*: Rely on chains of intermediate goods.]

**20.C.6$^A$** Consider the Ramsey–Solow technology of Example 20.C.1, as continued in Example 20.C.6. The exogenous path of labor endowments is $(l_0, \ldots, l_t, \ldots)$. Given a production path $(k_0, \ldots, k_t, \ldots)$, we determine a sequence of consumption good prices $(q_0, \ldots, q_t, \ldots)$ by the requirement that $(q_t/q_{t+1}) = \nabla_1 F(k_t, l_t)$ for all $t$. Show then that a sequence of wages $w_t$ can be found so that the path determined by $(k_0, \ldots, k_t, \ldots)$ is myopically profit maximizing for the price sequence determined by $((q_0, w_0), \ldots, (q_t, w_t), \ldots)$.

**20.D.1$^A$** Consider the budget constraint of problem (20.D.3). To simplify, suppose that we are in a pure exchange situation. Write the budget constraint as a sequence of budget constraints, one for each date. To this effect, assume that money can be borrowed and lent at a zero nominal rate of interest.

**20.D.2$^A$** Show that condition (ii') in Section 20.D (it is stated just before Definition 20.D.2) implies condition (ii) of Definition 20.D.1. Show that, conversely, condition (ii), together with $w = \sum_t p_t \cdot \omega_t + \sum_t \pi_t < \infty$, implies condition (ii').

**20.D.3$^A$** in text.

**20.D.4$^A$** Complete the computations requested in Example 20.D.1.

**20.D.5$^C$** In the context of Example 20.D.3, compute the Euler equations for the optimal investment policy when the production function has the form $F(k) = k^\alpha$, $0 < \alpha < 1$, and the adjustment cost function is given by $g(k' - k) = (k' - k)^\beta$, with $\beta > 1$, for $k' > k$, and by $g(k' - k) = 0$ for $k' \le k$. Say as much as you can about the policy. In particular, determine the steady-state trajectory of investment.

**20.D.6$^B$** Verify the claim made in the proof of Proposition 20.D.7 that the Euler equations (20.D.9) are the first-order necessary and sufficient conditions for short-run optimization. In other words: they are necessary and sufficient for the nonexistence of an improving trajectory differing from the given one at only a finite number of dates.

**20.D.7$^A$** With reference to Example 20.D.4, show that, for the functional forms given, the Euler equations are as indicated in the example: $k_{t+1} = 3k_t - 2k_{t-1}$ for every $t$. Also verify that the solution to this difference equation given in the text is indeed a solution, that is, that it satisfies the equation.

**20.D.8$^A$** Verify that the value function $V(k)$ does satisfy the properties (i) and (ii) claimed for it at the end of Section 20.D.

**20.D.9$^A$** Argue that the properties (i) and (ii) of the value function referred to in Exercise 20.D.8 yield the two consequences, concerning $V'(k)$ and $V''(k)$, claimed at the end of Section 20.D.

**20.E.1$^A$** Discuss in what sense the term $r$ defined after the proof of Proposition 20.E.1 can be interpreted as the rate of interest implicit in the proportional price sequence.

**20.E.2$^B$** Suppose that the production set $Y \subset \mathbb{R}^L$ is of the constant return type and consider production paths that are *proportional* (but not necessarily stationary), that is, paths $(y_0, \ldots, y_t, \ldots)$ that satisfy $y_t = (1 + n)y_{t-1}$ for all $t$ and some $n$.

    **(a)** Argue that the conclusion of Proposition 20.E.1 remains valid for proportional paths.

    **(b)** State and prove the result parallel to Proposition 20.E.2 for proportional paths.

**20.E.3$^B$** Suppose that in the Ramsey–Solow model $\bar{k}$ solves Max $(F(k, 1) - k)$ (see Figure 20.E.2). Show that if $k_t \le \bar{k} - \varepsilon$ for all $t$, then the path determined by $(k_0, \ldots, k_t, \ldots)$ is efficient. [*Hint*: Compute prices and verify the transversality condition.]

**20.E.4$^A$** Prove the three neoclassical properties stated at the end of the regular type part of Section 20.E.

**20.E.5$^A$** Carry out the requested verification of expression (20.E.1).

**20.E.6$^A$** Carry out the verification requested in the discussion of Figure 20.E.3.

**20.E.7$^A$** In the Ramsey–Solow model, two different steady states are associated with different rates of interest. This is not so in the example illustrated in Figure 20.E.3, at first sight very similar. The key difference is that in the Ramsey–Solow model the consumption and investment goods are perfect substitutes in production. Clarify this by proving, in the context of the example underlying Figure 20.E.3, that if the two goods are perfect substitutes then $r(\bar{k}) \neq r(\bar{\bar{k}})$ whenever $\bar{k} \neq \bar{\bar{k}}$. [*Hint*: Their being perfect substitutes means that $G(k, k' + \alpha) = G(k, k') - \alpha$ for any $\alpha < F(k, k')$.]

**20.E.8$^A$** Consider the proportional production paths with rate of growth equal to $n > 0$ (recall Exercise 20.E.2) in the context of a Ramsey–Solow technology of constant returns. Show that among these paths the one that maximizes surplus (at $t = 1$, or, equivalently, normalized surplus or surplus "per capita") is characterized by having the rate of interest equal to $n$. This path is also called the *golden rule steady state path*.

**20.E.9$^A$** Argue that, for the one-consumer model of Section 20.D, the golden rule path cannot arise as part of a competitive equilibrium. [*Hint*: The key fact is that $\delta < 1$.]

**20.F.1$^C$** Consider two arbitrary functions $\gamma_1(w)$ and $\gamma_2(w)$ that are defined for $w > 0$, take nonnegative values, and satisfy $\gamma_1(w) + \gamma_2(w) = w$ for all $w$. Suppose also that they are twice continuously differentiable.

Show that for any $\alpha > 0$ there is a utility function for two commodities, $u(x_1, x_2)$, that is increasing and concave on the domain $\{(x_1, x_2): x_1 + x_2 \leq \alpha\}$ and is such that $(\gamma_1(w), \gamma_2(w))$ coincides with the Engel curve functions for prices $p_1 = 1$, $p_2 = 1$ and wealth $w < \alpha$. [*Hint*: Let $u(x_1, x_2) = (x_1 + x_2)^{1/2} - \varepsilon[(x_1 - \gamma_1(x_1 + x_2))^2 + (x_2 - \gamma_2(x_1 + x_2))^2]$ and take $\varepsilon$ to be small enough. Verify then that $\nabla u(x_1, x_2)$ is strictly positive and $D^2 u(x_1, x_2)$ is negative definite for any $(x_1, x_2)$ such that $0 < x_1 + x_2 \leq \alpha$, and that the Engel curve is as required.]

**20.F.2$^A$** Suppose that, for $k \in \mathbb{R}_+$, the policy function $\psi(k)$ is a contraction (see the definition in the part of Section 20.F headed by "Low discount of time"). Draw several possible graphs for such a policy function and argue that there is always a unique steady state. Also, carry out the graphical dynamic analysis for your graphs and establish in this way that the steady states are always globally stable.

**20.F.3$^A$** Verify that for the classical Ramsey–Solow technology and for the cost-of-adjustment technology the cross derivative of uniform positive sign condition is satisfied.

**20.F.4$^A$** Carry out the verification concerning transitory shocks requested in Example 20.F.1.

**20.F.5$^A$** Carry out the verification concerning permanent shocks requested in Example 20.F.1.

**20.G.1$^B$** Analyze the equilibrium problem for the exchange case with two consumers (i.e., $I = 2$), and a single physical commodity (i.e., $L = 1$). Both consumers have the same discount factor [utility functions are of the form (20.B.1)]. In addition, assume that $\omega_{t1} + \omega_{t2} = 1$ for all $t$. Show in particular that the equilibrium consumption streams must be stationary, that the sequence of equilibrium prices is proportional (what is the rate of interest?), and that therefore there is only one stream of equilibrium consumptions.

**20.G.2$^A$** Consider an exchange model with two consumers. Utility functions are of the form (20.B.1) and both consumers have the same discount factor. There are no restrictions on the number of commodities $L$ or on the total endowments at any $t$. Show that at a Pareto optimal allocation the following holds: for every consumer, the in-period marginal utilities of wealth of the consumer is the same across periods (and equal to the overall marginal utility of wealth of the consumer). Interpret and discuss what this means in terms of intertemporal and interindividual transfers of wealth.

**20.G.3$^B$** The situation is the same as that of Exercise 20.G.2.

**(a)** Parametrize the Pareto frontier of the utility possibility set by the ratio of marginal utilities of wealth of the two consumers.

**(b)** Then express the equations of equilibrium à la Negishi (see Appendix A of Chapter 17). That is, write down one equation in one unknown (the ratio of marginal utilities of wealth) whose zeros are precisely the equilibria of the model.

**(c)** Argue in terms of the methodology discussed in Section 17.D that generically there are only a finite number of equilibria. Be as precise as you can.

**20.G.4$^A$** Prove the claim made in footnote 32. Be explicit about the form of the equilibrium price sequences.

**20.G.5$^B$** Verify that the concavity of the utility function implies that the expression (20.G.6) is larger than one in absolute value if there is no externality (i.e., if $\nabla^2_{23}u(\cdot) = \nabla^2_{13}u(\cdot) = 0$).

**20.H.1$^B$** Show that in the context of Sections 20.D or 20.G (a finite number of consumers) no bubbles can arise at equilibrium.

**20.H.2$^B$** In the framework of Section 20.H do the following (diagrammatic proofs are permissible).

**(a)** Show that if condition (20.H.3) is satisfied then, in the real asset case, the steady state is the only equilibrium.

**(b)** Show that if condition (20.H.3) is satisfied then, in the purely nominal asset case, the monetary steady state is the only equilibrium that is a Pareto optimum.

**(c)** Conversely, suppose that condition (20.H.3) is violated with strict inequality at $p_b = p_a$. Show then that, for the purely nominal asset case, there is more than one Pareto optimal equilibrium.

**(d)** (Harder) Suppose that the utility function is of the form $v(c_b) + \delta v(c_a)$. Investigate which conditions on $v(\cdot)$ and $\delta$ imply that the excess demand function satisfies condition (20.H.3). [*Hint*: Recall Example 17.F.2 for a special case.]

**20.I.1$^A$** Verify the computation requested in the part of Section 20.I headed "The (short-run) law of demand in overlapping generations models."

# Welfare Economics
# and Incentives

Part V is devoted to a systematic presentation of a number of issues related to the foundations of welfare economics, a topic that we have encountered repeatedly throughout the text. The point of view is that of a policy maker engaged in the design and implementation of collective decisions.

In Chapter 21, we review classical social choice theory. The central question of this theory concerns the possibility of deriving the objectives of the policy maker as an aggregation of the preferences of the agents in the economy, and of doing so in a manner that could be deemed as satisfactory according to a number of desiderata. The difficulties of accomplishing this task are dramatically illustrated in *Arrow's impossibility theorem*, which we present and discuss in detail. On a more positive note, we also discuss the assumption of single-peaked preferences and analyze the performance of majority voting under it.

In Chapter 22, we admit, to a variety of extents, the possibility of explicit value judgments as to the comparability of individuals' utility levels. Most of the chapter is devoted to a presentation of welfare economics in the Bergson–Samuelson tradition. Towards this end, we develop the apparatus of utility possibility sets and social welfare functions and emphasize the distinction between first-best and second-best problems. We also offer an account of axiomatic bargaining theory, an approach that emphasizes the compromise, rather than the constrained optimality, nature of social decisions.

In Chapter 23, we recognize that, in actuality, a policy maker rarely knows individuals' preferences with certainty; rather, this information is typically only *privately* known by the individuals themselves. The presence of information that is observed privately by rational, self-interested actors generates severe incentive-compatibility, second-best constraints. We offer a detailed analysis of what can and cannot be implemented collectively when these incentive constraints are taken into consideration. The content of Chapter 23 links with the game theory covered in Part II and revisits a number of themes first broached in Part III.

# Social Choice Theory

## 21.A Introduction

In this chapter, we analyze the extent to which individual preferences can be aggregated into social preferences, or more directly into social decisions, in a "satisfactory" manner—that is, in a manner compatible with the fulfillment of a variety of desirable conditions.

Throughout the chapter, we contemplate a set of possible social alternatives and a population of individuals with well-defined preferences over these alternatives.

In Section 21.B, we start with the simplest case: that in which the set of alternatives has only two elements. There are then many satisfactory solutions to the aggregation problem. In our presentation, we focus on a detailed analysis of the properties of aggregation by means of majority voting.

In Section 21.C, we move to the case of many alternatives and the discussion takes a decidedly negative turn. We state and prove the celebrated *Arrow's impossibility theorem*. In essence, this theorem tells us that we cannot have everything: If we want our aggregation rule (which we call a *social welfare functional*) to be defined for any possible constellation of individual preferences, to always yield Pareto optimal decisions, and to satisfy the convenient, and key, property that social preferences over any two alternatives depend only on individual preferences over these alternatives (the *pairwise independence condition*), then we have a dilemma. Either we must give up the hope that social preferences could be rational in the sense introduced in Chapter 1 (i.e., that society behaves as an individual would) or we must accept dictatorship.

Section 21.D describes two ways out of the conclusion of the impossibility theorem. In one we allow for partial relaxations of the degree of rationality demanded of social preferences. In the other, we settle for aggregation rules that perform satisfactorily on restricted domains of individual preferences. In particular, we introduce the important notion of *single-peaked* preferences and, for populations with preferences in this class, we analyze the role of a *median voter* in the workings of pairwise majority voting as an aggregation method.

Section 21.E sets the aggregation problem more directly as one of aggregating individual preferences into social decisions. It introduces the concept of a *social choice function*, and proceeds to give a version of the impossibility result for the latter. Essentially, this result is obtained by replacing the pairwise independence condition (which is meaningless in the context of this section) by a *monotonicity* condition on the social choice function. This condition provides an important link to the incentive-based theory of Chapter 23.

General references and surveys for the topics of this chapter are Arrow (1963), Moulin (1988), and Sen (1970) and (1986).

# 21.B  A Special Case: Social Preferences over Two Alternatives

We begin our analysis of social choice by considering the simplest possible case: that in which there are only two alternatives over which to decide. We call these alternative $x$ and alternative $y$. Alternative $x$, for example, could be the "status-quo," and alternative $y$ might be a particular public project whose implementation is being contemplated.

The data for our problem are the individual preferences of the members of society over the two alternatives. We assume that there is a number $I < \infty$ of individuals, or *agents*. The family of individual preferences between the two alternatives can be described by a profile

$$(\alpha_1, \ldots, \alpha_I) \in \mathbb{R}^I,$$

where $\alpha_i$ takes the value 1, 0, or $-1$ according to whether agent $i$ prefers alternative $x$ to alternative $y$, is indifferent between them, or prefers alternative $y$ to alternative $x$, respectively.[1]

**Definition 21.B.1:** A *social welfare functional* (or *social welfare aggregator*) is a rule $F(\alpha_1, \ldots, \alpha_I)$ that assigns a social preference, that is, $F(\alpha_1, \ldots, \alpha_I) \in \{-1, 0, 1\}$, to every possible profile of individual preferences $(\alpha_1, \ldots, \alpha_I) \in \{-1, 0, 1\}^I$.

All the social welfare functionals to be considered respect individual preferences in the weak sense of Definition 21.B.2.

**Definition 21.B.2:** The social welfare functional $F(\alpha_1, \ldots, \alpha_I)$ is *Paretian*, or has the *Pareto property*, if it respects unanimity of strict preference on the part of the agents, that is, if $F(1, \ldots, 1) = 1$ and $F(-1, \ldots, -1) = -1$.

**Example 21.B.1:** Paretian social welfare functionals between two alternatives abound. Let $(\beta_1, \ldots, \beta_I) \in \mathbb{R}_+^I$ be a vector of nonnegative numbers, not all zero. Then we

---

1. In the whole of this chapter we make the restriction that only the agents' rankings between the two alternatives matter for the social decision between them. In Section 21.C we will state formally the principle involved. Note, in particular, that this specification precludes the use of any "cardinal" or "intensity" information between the two alternatives because this intensity can only be calibrated (perhaps using lotteries) by appealing to some third alternative. A fortiori, the specification also precludes the comparison of feelings of pleasure or pain across individuals. In Chapter 22, we discuss in some detail matters pertaining to the issue of interpersonal comparability of utilities.

could define

$$F(\alpha_1, \ldots, \alpha_I) = \operatorname{sign} \sum_i \beta_i \alpha_i,$$

where, recall, for any $a \in \mathbb{R}$, sign $a$ equals 1, 0, or $-1$ according to whether $a > 0$, $a = 0$, or $a < 0$, respectively.

An important particular case is *majority voting*, where we take $\beta_i = 1$ for every $i$. Then $F(\alpha_1, \ldots, \alpha_I) = 1$ if and only if the number of agents that prefer alternative $x$ to alternative $y$ is larger than the number of agents that prefer $y$ to $x$. Similarly, $F(\alpha_1, \ldots, \alpha_I) = -1$ if and only if those that prefer $y$ to $x$ are more numerous than those that prefer $x$ to $y$. Finally, in case of equality of these two numbers, we have $F(\alpha_1, \ldots, \alpha_I) = 0$, that is, social indifference. ■

**Example 21.B.2:** *Dictatorship.* We say that a social welfare functional is *dictatorial* if there is an agent $h$, called a *dictator*, such that, for any profile $(\alpha_1, \ldots, \alpha_I)$, $\alpha_h = 1$ implies $F(\alpha_1, \ldots, \alpha_I) = 1$ and, similarly, $\alpha_h = -1$ implies $F(\alpha_1, \ldots, \alpha_I) = -1$. That is, the strict preference of the dictator prevails as the social preference. A dictatorial social welfare functional is Paretian in the sense of Definition 21.B.2. For the social welfare functionals of Example 21.B.1, we have dictatorship whenever $\alpha_h > 0$ for some agent $h$ and $\alpha_i = 0$ for $i \neq h$, since then $F(\alpha_1, \ldots, \alpha_I) = \alpha_h$. ■

The majority voting social welfare functional plays a leading benchmark role in social choice theory. In addition to being Paretian it has three important properties, which we proceed to state formally. The first (symmetry among agents) says that the social welfare functional treats all agents on the same footing. The second (neutrality between alternatives) says that, similarly, the social welfare functional does not a priori distinguish either of the two alternatives. The third (positive responsiveness) says, more strongly than the Paretian property of Definition 21.B.2, that the social welfare functional is sensitive to individual preferences.

**Definition 21.B.3:** The social welfare functional $F(\alpha_1, \ldots, \alpha_I)$ is *symmetric among agents* (or *anonymous*) if the names of the agents do not matter, that is, if a permutation of preferences across agents does not alter the social preference. Precisely, let $\pi: \{1, \ldots, I\} \to \{1, \ldots, I\}$ be an onto function (i.e., a function with the property that for any $i$ there is $h$ such that $\pi(h) = i$). Then for any profile $(\alpha_1, \ldots, \alpha_I)$ we have $F(\alpha_1, \ldots, \alpha_I) = F(\alpha_{\pi(1)}, \ldots, \alpha_{\pi(I)})$.

**Definition 21.B.4:** The social welfare functional $F(\alpha_1, \ldots, \alpha_I)$ is *neutral between alternatives* if $F(\alpha_1, \ldots, \alpha_I) = -F(-\alpha_1, \ldots, -\alpha_I)$ for every profile $(\alpha_1, \ldots, \alpha_I)$, that is, if the social preference is reversed when we reverse the preferences of all agents.

**Definition 21.B.5:** The social welfare functional $F(\alpha_1, \ldots, \alpha_I)$ is *positively responsive* if, whenever $(\alpha_1, \ldots, \alpha_I) \geq (\alpha'_1, \ldots, \alpha'_I)$, $(\alpha_1, \ldots, \alpha_I) \neq (\alpha'_1, \ldots, \alpha'_I)$, and $F(\alpha'_1, \ldots, \alpha'_I) \geq 0$, we have $F(\alpha_1, \ldots, \alpha_I) = +1$. That is, if $x$ is socially preferred or indifferent to $y$ and some agents raise their consideration of $x$, then $x$ becomes socially preferred.

It is simple to verify that majority voting satisfies the three properties of symmetry among agents, neutrality between alternatives, and positive responsiveness (see Exercise 21.B.1). As it turns out, these properties entirely characterize majority voting. The result given in Proposition 21.B.1 is due to May (1952).

**Proposition 21.B.1:** (*May's Theorem*) A social welfare functional $F(\alpha_1, \ldots, \alpha_I)$ is a majority voting social welfare functional if and only if it is symmetric among agents, neutral between alternatives, and positive responsive.

**Proof:** We have already argued that majority voting satisfies the three properties. To establish sufficiency note first that the symmetry property among agents means that the social preference depends only on the total number of agents that prefer alternative $x$ to $y$, the total number that are indifferent, and the total number that prefer $y$ to $x$. Given $(\alpha_1, \ldots, \alpha_I)$, denote

$$n^+(\alpha_1, \ldots, \alpha_I) = \#\{i: \alpha_i = 1\}, \text{ and } n^-(\alpha_1, \ldots, \alpha_I) = \#\{i: \alpha_i = -1\}.^2$$

Then symmetry among agents allows us to express $F(\alpha_1, \ldots, \alpha_I)$ in the form

$$F(\alpha_1, \ldots, \alpha_I) = G(n^+(\alpha_1, \ldots, \alpha_I), n^-(\alpha_1, \ldots, \alpha_I)).$$

Now suppose that $(\alpha_1, \ldots, \alpha_I)$ is such that $n^+(\alpha_1, \ldots, \alpha_I) = n^-(\alpha_1, \ldots, \alpha_I)$. Then $n^+(-\alpha_1, \ldots, -\alpha_I) = n^-(\alpha_1, \ldots, \alpha_I) = n^+(\alpha_1, \ldots, \alpha_I) = n^-(-\alpha_1, \ldots, -\alpha_I)$, and so

$$\begin{aligned}
F(\alpha_1, \ldots, \alpha_I) &= G(n^+(\alpha_1, \ldots, \alpha_I), n^-(\alpha_1, \ldots, \alpha_I)) \\
&= G(n^+(-\alpha_1, \ldots, -\alpha_I), n^-(-\alpha_1, \ldots, -\alpha_I)) \\
&= F(-\alpha_1, \ldots, -\alpha_I) \\
&= -F(\alpha_1, \ldots, \alpha_I).
\end{aligned}$$

The last equality follows from the neutrality between alternatives. Since the only number that equals its negative is zero, we conclude that if $n^+(\alpha_1, \ldots, \alpha_I) = n^-(\alpha_1, \ldots, \alpha_I)$ then $F(\alpha_1, \ldots, \alpha_I) = 0$.

Suppose next that $n^+(\alpha_1, \ldots, \alpha_I) > n^-(\alpha_1, \ldots, \alpha_I)$. Denote $H = n^+(\alpha_1, \ldots, \alpha_I)$, $J = n^-(\alpha_1, \ldots, \alpha_I)$; then $J < H$. Say, without loss of generality, that $\alpha_i = 1$ for $i \leq H$ and $\alpha_i \leq 0$ for $i > H$. Consider a new profile $(\alpha'_1, \ldots, \alpha'_I)$ defined by $\alpha'_i = \alpha_i = 1$ for $i \leq J < H$, $\alpha'_i = 0$ for $J < i \leq H$, and $\alpha'_i = \alpha_i \leq 0$ for $i > H$. Then $n^+(\alpha'_1, \ldots, \alpha'_I) = J$ and $n^-(\alpha'_1, \ldots, \alpha'_I) = n^-(\alpha_1, \ldots, \alpha_I) = J$. Hence $F(\alpha'_1, \ldots, \alpha'_I) = 0$. But by construction, the alternative $x$ has lost strength in the new individual preference. Indeed, $(\alpha_1, \ldots, \alpha_I) \geq (\alpha'_1, \ldots, \alpha'_I)$ and $\alpha_{J+1} = 1 > 0 = \alpha'_{J+1}$. Therefore, by the positive responsiveness property, we must have $F(\alpha_1, \ldots, \alpha_I) = 1$.

In turn, if $n^-(\alpha_1, \ldots, \alpha_I) > n^+(\alpha_1, \ldots, \alpha_I)$ then $n^+(-\alpha_1, \ldots, -\alpha_I) > n^-(-\alpha_1, \ldots, -\alpha_I)$ and so $F(-\alpha_1, \ldots, -\alpha_I) = 1$. Therefore, by neutrality among alternatives:

$$F(\alpha_1, \ldots, \alpha_I) = -F(-\alpha_1, \ldots, -\alpha_I) = -1.$$

We conclude that $F(\alpha_1, \ldots, \alpha_I)$ is indeed a majority voting social welfare functional. ∎

In Exercise 21.B.2, you are asked to find examples different from majority voting that satisfy any two of the three properties of Proposition 21.B.1.

# 21.C The General Case: Arrow's Impossibility Theorem

We now proceed to study the problem of aggregating individual preferences over any number of alternatives. We denote the set of alternatives by $X$, and assume that

---

2. Recall the notation $\#A$ = cardinality of the set $A$ = number of elements in the set $A$.

there are $I$ agents, indexed by $i = 1, \ldots, I$. Every agent $i$ has a rational preference relation $\succsim_i$ defined on $X$. The strict preference and the indifference relation derived from $\succsim_i$ are denoted by $\succ_i$ and $\sim_i$, respectively.[3] In addition, it will often be convenient to assume that no two distinct alternatives are indifferent in an individual preference relation $\succsim_i$. It is therefore important, for clarity of exposition, to have a symbol for the set of all possible rational preference relations on $X$ and for the set of all possible preference relations on $X$ having the property that no two distinct alternatives are indifferent. We denote these sets, respectively, by $\mathscr{R}$ and $\mathscr{P}$. Observe that $\mathscr{P} \subset \mathscr{R}$.[4]

In parallel to Section 21.B, we can define a social welfare functional as a rule that assigns social preferences to profiles of individual preferences $(\succsim_i, \ldots, \succsim_I) \in \mathscr{R}^I$. Definition 21.C.1 below generalizes Definition 21.B.1 in two respects: it allows for any number of alternatives and it permits the aggregation problem to be limited to some given domain $\mathscr{A} \subset \mathscr{R}^I$ of individual profiles. In this section, however, we focus on the largest domains, that is, $\mathscr{A} = \mathscr{R}^I$ and $\mathscr{A} = \mathscr{P}^I$.

**Definition 21.C.1:** A *social welfare functional* (or *social welfare aggregator*) defined on a given subset $\mathscr{A} \subset \mathscr{R}^I$ is a rule $F\!:\!\mathscr{A} \to \mathscr{R}$ that assigns a rational preference relation $F(\succsim_1, \ldots, \succsim_I) \in \mathscr{R}$, interpreted as the social preference relation, to any profile of individual rational preference relations $(\succsim_1, \ldots, \succsim_I)$ in the admissible domain $\mathscr{A} \subset \mathscr{R}^I$.

Note that, as we did in Section, 21.B the problem of social aggregation is being posed as one in which individuals are described exclusively by their preference relations over alternatives.[5]

For any profile $(\succsim_1, \ldots, \succsim_I)$, we denote by $F_p(\succsim_1, \ldots, \succsim_I)$ the strict preference relation derived from $F(\succsim_1, \ldots, \succsim_I)$. That is, we let $x\, F_p(\succsim_1, \ldots, \succsim_I)\, y$ if $x\, F(\succsim_1, \ldots, \succsim_I)\, y$ holds but $y\, F(\succsim_1, \ldots, \succsim_I)\, x$ does not. We say then that "$x$ is socially preferred to $y$." We read $x\, F(\succsim_1, \ldots, \succsim_I)\, y$ as "$x$ is socially at least as good as $y$."

Definition 21.C.2. (which generalizes Definition 21.B.2) isolates the social welfare functionals that satisfy a minimal condition of respect for individual preferences.

---

3. Recall from Section 1.B that $\succ_i$ is formally defined by letting $x \succ_i y$ if $x \succsim_i y$ holds but $y \succsim_i x$ does not. That is, $x$ is preferred to $y$ if $x$ is at least as good as $y$ but $y$ is not as good as $x$. Also, the indifference relation $\sim_i$ is defined by letting $x \sim_i y$ if $x \succsim_i y$ and $y \succsim_i x$. From Proposition 1.B.1 we know that if $\succsim_i$ is rational, that is, complete and transitive, then $\succ_i$ is irreflexive ($x \succ_i x$ cannot occur) and transitive ($x \succ_i y$ and $y \succ_i z$ implies $x \succ_i z$). Similarly, $\sim_i$ is reflexive ($x \sim_i x$ for all $x \in X$), transitive ($x \sim_i y$ and $y \sim_i z$ implies $x \sim_i z$) and symmetric ($x \sim_i y$ implies $y \sim_i x$).

4. Formally, the preference relation $\succsim_i$ belongs to $\mathscr{P}$ if it is reflexive ($x \succsim_i x$ for every $x \in X$), transitive ($x \succsim_i y$ and $y \succsim_i z$ implies $x \succsim_i z$) and *total* (if $x \neq y$ then either $x \succsim_i y$ or $y \succsim_i x$, but not both). Such preference relations are often referred to as *strict preferences* (although *strict-total preferences* would be less ambiguous) or even as *linear orders*, because these are the properties of the usual "larger than or equal to" order in the real line.

5. In particular, there are no individual utility levels and, therefore, there is no meaningful sense in which any conceivable information on individual utility levels could be compared and matched up. We refer again to Chapter 22 (especially Section 22.D) for an analysis of the problem that focuses on the information used in the aggregation process.

**Definition 21.C.2:** The social welfare functional $F: \mathscr{A} \to \mathscr{R}$ is *Paretian* if, for any pair of alternatives $\{x, y\} \subset X$ and any preference profile $(\succsim_1, \ldots, \succsim_I) \in \mathscr{A}$, we have that $x$ is socially preferred to $y$, that is, $x \, F_p(\succsim_1, \ldots, \succsim_I) \, y$, whenever $x \succ_i y$ for every $i$.

In Example 21.C.1 we describe an interesting class of Paretian social welfare functionals.

**Example 21.C.1:** *The Borda Count.* Suppose that the number of alternatives is finite. Given a preference relation $\succsim_i \in \mathscr{R}$ we assign a number of points $c_i(x)$ to every alternative $x \in X$ as follows. Suppose for a moment that in the preference relation $\succsim_i$ no two alternatives are indifferent. Then we put $c_i(x) = n$ if $x$ is the $n$th ranked alternative in the ordering of $\succsim_i$. If indifference is possible in $\succsim_i$ then $c_i(x)$ is the average rank of the alternatives indifferent to $x$.[6] Finally, for any profile $(\succsim_1, \ldots, \succsim_I) \in \mathscr{R}^I$ we determine a social ordering by adding up points. That is, we let $F(\succsim_1, \ldots, \succsim_I) \in \mathscr{R}$ be the preference relation defined by $x \, F(\succsim_1, \ldots, \succsim_I) \, y$ if $\sum_i c_i(x) \leq \sum_i c_i(y)$. This preference relation is complete and transitive [it is represented by the utility function $-c(x) = -\sum_i c_i(x)$]. Moreover, it is Paretian since if $x \succ_i y$ for every $i$ then $c_i(x) < c_i(y)$ for every $i$, and so $\sum_i c_i(x) < \sum_i c_i(y)$. ∎

We next state an important restriction on social welfare functionals first suggested by Arrow (1963). The restriction says that the social preferences between any two alternatives depend only on the individual preferences between the same two alternatives. There are three possible lines of justification for this assumption. The first is strictly normative and has considerable appeal: it argues that in settling on a social ranking between $x$ and $y$, the presence or absence of alternatives other than $x$ and $y$ should not matter. They are irrelevant to the issue at hand. The second is one of practicality. The assumption enormously facilitates the task of making social decisions because it helps to separate problems. The determination of the social ranking on a subset of alternatives does not need any information on individual preferences over alternatives outside this subset. The third relates to incentives and belongs to the subject matter of Chapter 23 (see also Proposition 21.E.2). Pairwise independence is intimately connected with the issue of providing the right inducements for the truthful revelation of individual preferences.

**Definition 21.C.3:** The social welfare functional $F: \mathscr{A} \to \mathscr{R}$ defined on the domain $\mathscr{A}$ satisfies the *pairwise independence condition* (or the *independence of irrelevant alternatives condition*) if the social preference between any two alternatives $\{x, y\} \subset X$ depends only on the profile of individual preferences over the same alternatives. Formally[7], for any pair of alternatives $\{x, y\} \subset X$, and for any pair of preference profiles $(\succsim_1, \ldots, \succsim_I) \in \mathscr{A}$ and $(\succsim_1', \ldots, \succsim_I') \in \mathscr{A}$ with the property that, for every $i$,

$$x \succsim_i y \iff x \succsim_i' y \qquad \text{and} \qquad y \succsim_i x \iff y \succsim_i' x,$$

---

6. Thus if $X = \{x, y, z\}$ and $x \succsim_i y \sim_i z$ then $c_i(x) = 1$, and $c_i(y) = c_i(z) = 2.5$.

7. The expressions that follow are a bit cumbersome, We emphasize therefore that they do nothing more than to capture formally the statement just made. An equivalent formulation would be: for any $\{x, y\} \subset X$, if $\succsim_i|\{x, y\} = \succsim_i'|\{x, y\}$ for all $i$, then $F(\succsim_1, \ldots, \succsim_I)|\{x, y\} = F(\succsim_1', \ldots, \succsim_I')|\{x, y\}$. Here $\succsim|\{x, y\}$ stands for the restriction of the preference ordering $\succsim$ to the set $\{x, y\}$.

we have that

$$x \, F(\succsim_1, \ldots, \succsim_I) \, y \qquad \Leftrightarrow \qquad x \, F(\succsim'_1, \ldots, \succsim'_I) \, y$$

and

$$y \, F(\succsim_1, \ldots, \succsim_I) \, x \qquad \Leftrightarrow \qquad y \, F(\succsim'_1, \ldots, \succsim'_I) \, x.$$

**Example 21.C.1:** *continued.* Alas, the Borda count does not satisfy the pairwise independence condition. The reason is simple: the rank of an alternative depends on the placement of *every* other alternative. Suppose, for example, that there are two agents and three alternatives $\{x, y, z\}$. For the preferences

$$x \succ_1 z \succ_1 y,$$

$$y \succ_2 x \succ_2 z$$

we have that $x$ is socially preferred to $y$ [indeed, $c(x) = 3$ and $c(y) = 4$]. But for the preferences

$$x \succ'_1 y \succ'_1 z,$$

$$y \succ'_2 z \succ'_2 x$$

we have that $y$ is socially preferred to $x$ [indeed, now $c(x) = 4$ and $c(y) = 3$]. Yet the relative ordering of $x$ and $y$ has not changed for either of the two agents.

For another illustration, this time with three agents and four alternatives $\{x, y, z, w\}$, consider

$$z \succ_1 x \succ_1 y \succ_1 w,$$

$$z \succ_2 x \succ_2 y \succ_2 w,$$

$$y \succ_3 z \succ_3 w \succ_3 x.$$

Here, $y$ is socially preferred to $x$ [$c(x) = 8$ and $c(y) = 7$]. But suppose now that alternatives $z$ and $w$ move to the bottom for all agents (which because of the Pareto property is a way of saying that the two alternatives are eliminated from the alternative set):

$$x \succ'_1 y \succ'_1 z \succ'_1 w,$$

$$x \succ'_2 y \succ'_2 z \succ'_2 w, \tag{21.C.1}$$

$$y \succ'_3 x \succ'_3 z \succ'_3 w.$$

Then $x$ is socially preferred to $y$ [$c(x) = 4$, $c(y) = 5$]. Thus the presence or absence of alternatives $z$ and $w$ matters to the social preference between $x$ and $y$. Another modification would take alternative $x$ to the bottom for agent 3:

$$x \succ''_1 y \succ''_1 z \succ''_1 w,$$

$$x \succ''_2 y \succ''_2 z \succ''_2 w,$$

$$y \succ''_3 z \succ''_3 w \succ''_3 x.$$

Now $y$ is socially preferred to $x$ [which, relative to the outcome with (21.C.1), is a nice result from the point of view of agent 3]. ∎

The previous discussion of Example 21.C.1 teaches us that the pairwise independence condition is a substantial restriction. However, there is a way to proceed that will automatically guarantee that it is satisfied. It consists of determining the social preference between any given two alternatives by applying an aggregation rule that uses only the information about the ordering of *these two alternatives* in individual preferences. We saw in Section 21.B that, for any pair of alternatives, there are many such rules. Can we proceed in this pairwise fashion and still end up with social preferences that are rational, that is, complete and transitive? Example 21.C.2 shows that this turns out to be a real difficulty.

**Example 21.C.2:** *The Condorcet Paradox.*[8] Suppose that we were to try majority voting among any two alternatives (see Section 21.B for an analysis of majority voting). Does this determine a social welfare functional? We shall see in the next section that the answer is positive in some restricted domains $\mathscr{A} \subset \mathscr{R}^I$. But in general we run into the following problem, known as the Condorcet paradox. Let us have three alternatives $\{x, y, z\}$ and three agents. The preferences of the three agents are

$$x \succ_1 y \succ_1 z,$$
$$z \succ_2 x \succ_2 y,$$
$$y \succ_3 z \succ_3 x.$$

Then pairwise majority voting tells us that $x$ must be socially preferred to $y$ (since $x$ has a majority against $y$ and, a fortiori, $y$ does not have a majority against $x$). Similarly, $y$ must be socially preferred to $z$ (two voters prefer $y$ to $z$) and $z$ must be socially preferred to $x$ (two voters prefer $z$ to $x$). But this cyclic pattern violates the transitivity requirement on social preferences. ∎

The next proposition is *Arrow's impossibility theorem*, the central result of this chapter. It essentially tells us that the Condorcet paradox is not due to any of the strong properties of majority voting (which, we may recall from Proposition 21.B.1, are symmetry among agents, neutrality between alternatives, and positive responsiveness). The paradox goes to the heart of the matter: with pairwise independence there is no social welfare functonal defined on $\mathscr{R}^I$ that satisfies a minimal form of symmetry among agents (no dictatorship) and a minimal form of positive responsiveness (the Pareto property).

**Proposition 21.C.1:** (*Arrow's Impossibility Theorem*) Suppose that the number of alternatives is at least three and that the domain of admissible individual profiles, denoted $\mathscr{A}$, is either $\mathscr{A} = \mathscr{R}^I$ or $\mathscr{A} = \mathscr{P}^I$. Then every social welfare functional $F:\mathscr{A} \to \mathscr{R}$ that is Paretian and satisfies the pairwise independence condition is *dictatorial* in the following sense: There is an agent $h$ such that, for any $\{x, y\} \subset X$ and any profile $(\succsim_1, \ldots, \succsim_I) \in \mathscr{A}$, we have that $x$ is socially preferred to $y$, that is, $x F_p(\succsim_1, \ldots, \succsim_I) y$, whenever $x \succ_h y$.

**Proof:** We present here the classical proof of this result. For another approach to the demonstration we refer to Section 22.D.

It is convenient from now on to view $I$ not only as the number but also as the *set* of agents. For the entire proof we refer to a fixed social welfare functional $F: \mathscr{A} \to \mathscr{R}$ satisfying the Pareto and the pairwise independence conditions. We begin with some definitions. In what follows, when we refer to pairs of alternatives we always mean distinct alternatives.

---

8. This example was already discussed in Section 1.B.

**Definition 21.C.4:** Given $F(\cdot)$, we say that a subset of agents $S \subset I$ is:

    (i) *Decisive for x over y* if whenever every agent in $S$ prefers $x$ to $y$ *and* every agent not in $S$ prefers $y$ to $x$, $x$ is socially preferred to $y$.

    (ii) *Decisive* if, for any pair $\{x, y\} \subset X$, $S$ is decisive for $x$ over $y$.

    (iii) *Completely decisive for x over y* if whenever every agent in $S$ prefers $x$ to $y$, $x$ is socially preferred to $y$.

The proof will proceed by a detailed investigation of the structure of the family of decisive sets. We do this in a number of small steps. Steps 1 to 3 show that if a subset of agents is decisive for some pair of alternatives then it is decisive for all pairs. Steps 4 to 6 establish some algebraic properties of the family of decisive sets. Steps 7 and 8 use these to show that there is a smallest decisive set formed by a single agent. Steps 9 and 10 prove that this agent is a dictator.

*Step 1:   If for some $\{x, y\} \subset X$, $S \subset I$ is decisive for $x$ over $y$, then, for any alternative $z \neq x$, $S$ is decisive for $x$ over $z$. Similarly, for any $z \neq y$, $S$ is decisive for $z$ over $y$.*

We show that if $S$ is decisive for $x$ over $y$ then it is decisive for $x$ over any $z \neq x$. The reasoning for $z$ over $y$ is identical (you are asked to carry it out in Exercise 21.C.1).

If $z = y$ there is nothing to prove. So we assume that $z \neq y$. Consider a profile of preferences $(\succsim_1, \ldots, \succsim_I) \in \mathscr{A}$ where

$$x \succ_i y \succ_i z \qquad \text{for every } i \in S$$

and

$$y \succ_i z \succ_i x \qquad \text{for every } i \in I \setminus S.$$

Then, because $S$ is decisive for $x$ over $y$, we have that $x$ is socially preferred to $y$, that is, $x\, F_p(\succsim_1, \ldots, \succsim_I)\, y$. In addition, since $y \succsim_i z$ for every $i \in I$, and $F(\cdot)$ satisfies the Pareto property it follows that $y\, F_p(\succsim_1, \ldots, \succsim_I)\, z$. Therefore, by the transitivity of the social preference relation, we conclude that $x\, F_p(\succsim_1, \ldots, \succsim_I)\, z$. By the pairwise independence condition, it follows that $x$ is socially preferred to $z$ whenever every agent in $S$ prefers $x$ to $z$ and every agent not in $S$ prefers $z$ to $x$. That is, $S$ is decisive for $x$ over $z$.

*Step 2:   If for some $\{x, y\} \subset X$, $S \subset I$ is decisive for $x$ over $y$ and $z$ is a third alternative, then $S$ is decisive for $z$ over $w$ and for $w$ over $z$, where $w \in X$ is any alternative distinct from $z$.*

By step 1, $S$ is decisive for $x$ over $z$ and for $z$ over $y$. But then, applying step 1 again, this time to the pair $\{x, z\}$ and the alternative $w$, we conclude that $S$ is decisive for $w$ over $z$. Similarly, applying step 1 to $\{z, y\}$ and $w$, we conclude that $S$ is decisive for $z$ over $w$.

*Step 3:   If for some $\{x, y\} \subset X$, $S \subset I$ is decisive for $x$ over $y$, then $S$ is decisive.*

This is an immediate consequence of step 2 and the fact that there is some alternative $z \in X$ distinct from $x$ or $y$. Indeed, take any pair $\{v, w\}$. If $v = z$ or $w = z$, then step 2 implies the result directly. If $v \neq z$ and $w \neq z$, we apply step 2 to conclude that $S$ is decisive for $z$ over $w$, and then step 1 [applied to the pair $\{z, w\}$] to conclude that $S$ is decisive for $v$ over $w$.

*Step 4:*   *If $S \subset I$ and $T \subset I$ are decisive, then $S \cap T$ is decisive.*

Take any triple of distinct alternatives $\{x, y, z\} \subset X$ and consider a profile of preferences $(\succsim_1, \ldots, \succsim_I) \in \mathscr{A}$ where

$$z \succ_i y \succ_i x \qquad \text{for every } i \in S \backslash (S \cap T),$$
$$x \succ_i z \succ_i y \qquad \text{for every } i \in S \cap T,$$
$$y \succ_i x \succ_i z \qquad \text{for every } i \in T \backslash (S \cap T),$$
$$y \succ_i z \succ_i x \qquad \text{for every } i \in I \backslash (S \cup T).$$

Then $z \, F_p(\succsim_1, \ldots, \succsim_I) \, y$ because $S \, (= [S \backslash (S \cap T)] \cup (S \cap T))$ is a decisive set. Similarly, $x \, F_p(\succsim_1, \ldots, \succsim_I) \, z$ because $T$ is a decisive set. Therefore, by the transitivity of the social preference, we have that $x \, F_p(\succsim_1, \ldots, \succsim_I) \, y$. It follows by the pairwise independence condition that $S \cap T$ is decisive for $x$ over $y$, and so, by step 3, that $S \cap T$ is a decisive set.

*Step 5:*   *For any $S \subset I$, we have that either $S$ or its complement, $I \backslash S \subset I$, is decisive.*

Take any triple of distinct alternatives $\{x, y, z\} \subset X$ and consider a profile of preferences $(\succsim_1, \ldots, \succsim_I) \in \mathscr{A}$ where

$$x \succ_i z \succ_i y \qquad \text{for every } i \in S$$
$$y \succ_i x \succ_i z \qquad \text{for every } i \in I \backslash S.$$

Then there are two possibilities: either $x \, F_p(\succsim_1, \ldots, \succsim_I) \, y$, in which case, by the pairwise independence condition, $S$ is decisive for $x$ over $y$ (hence, by step 3, decisive), or $y \, F(\succsim_1, \ldots, \succsim_I) \, x$. Because, by the Paretian condition, we have $x \, F_p(\succsim_1, \ldots, \succsim_I) \, z$, the transitivity of the social preference relation yields that $y \, F_p(\succsim_1, \ldots, \succsim_I) \, z$ in this case. But then, using the pairwise independence condition again, we conclude that $I \backslash S$ is decisive for $y$ over $z$ (hence, by step 3, decisive).

*Step 6:*   *If $S \subset I$ is decisive and $S \subset T$, then $T$ is also decisive.*

Because of the Pareto property the empty set of agents cannot be decisive (indeed, if no agent prefers $x$ over $y$ and every agent prefers $y$ over $x$, then $x$ is not socially preferred to $y$). Therefore $I \backslash T$ cannot be decisive because otherwise, by step 4, $S \cap (I \backslash T) = \varnothing$ would be decisive. Hence, by step 5, $T$ is decisive.

*Step 7:*   *If $S \subset I$ is decisive and it includes more than one agent, then there is a strict subset $S' \subset S$, $S' \neq S$, such that $S'$ is decisive.*

Take any $h \in S$. If $S \backslash \{h\}$ is decisive, then we are done. Suppose, therefore, that $S \backslash \{h\}$ is not decisive. Then, by step 5, $I \backslash (S \backslash \{h\}) = (I \backslash S) \cup \{h\}$ is decisive. It follows, by step 4, that $\{h\} = S \cap [(I \backslash S) \cup \{h\}]$ is also decisive. Thus, we are again done since, by assumption, $\{h\}$ is a strict subset of $S$.

*Step 8:*   *There is an $h \in I$ such that $S = \{h\}$ is decisive.*

This follows by iterating step 7 and taking into account, first, that the set of agents $I$ is finite and, second, that, by the Pareto property, the set $I$ of all agents is decisive.

*Step 9:*   *If $S \subset I$ is decisive then, for any $\{x, y\} \subset X$, $S$ is completely decisive for $x$ over $y$.*

We want to prove that, for any $T \subset I \backslash S$, $x$ is socially preferred to $y$ whenever every agent in $S$ prefers $x$ to $y$, every agent in $T$ regards $x$ to be at least as good as

$y$, and every other agent prefers $y$ to $x$. To verify this property, take a third alternative $z \in X$, distinct from $x$ and $y$. By the pairwise independence condition it suffices to consider a profile of preferences $(\succsim_1, \ldots, \succsim_I) \in \mathscr{A}$ where

$$x \succ_i z \succ_i y \qquad \text{for every } i \in S,$$
$$x \succ_i y \succ_i z \qquad \text{for every } i \in T,$$
$$y \succ_i z \succ_i x \qquad \text{for every } i \in I \backslash (S \cup T).$$

Then $x \, F_p(\succsim_1, \ldots, \succsim_I) \, z$ because, by step 6, $S \cup T$ is decisive, and $z \, F_p(\succsim_1, \ldots, \succsim_I) \, y$ because $S$ is decisive. Therefore, by the transitivity of social preference, we have that $x \, F_p(\succsim_1, \ldots, \succsim_I) \, y$, as we wanted to show.

*Step 10:* *If, for some $h \in I$, $S = \{h\}$ is decisive, then $h$ is a dictator.*

If $\{h\}$ is decisive then, by step 9, $\{h\}$ is completely decisive for any $x$ over any $y$. That is, if the profile $(\succsim_1, \ldots, \succsim_I)$ is such that $x \succ_h y$, then $x \, F_p(\succsim_1, \ldots, \succsim_I) \, y$. But this is precisely what is meant by $h \in I$ being a dictator.

The combination of steps 8 and 10 completes the proof of Proposition 21.C.1. ■

# 21.D Some Possibility Results: Restricted Domains

The result of Arrow's impossibility theorem is somewhat disturbing, but it would be too facile to conclude from it that "democracy is impossible." What it shows is something else—that we should not expect a collectivity of individuals to behave with the kind of coherence that we may hope from an individual.

It is important to observe, however, that in practice collective judgments are made and decisions are taken. What Arrow's theorem does tell us, in essence, is that the institutional detail and procedures of the political process cannot be neglected. Suppose, for example, that the decision among three alternatives $\{x, y, z\}$ is made by first choosing between $x$ and $y$ by majority voting, and then voting again to choose between the winner and the third alternative $z$. This will produce an outcome, but the outcome may depend on how the agenda is set—that is, on which alternative is taken up first and which is left for the last. [Thus, if preferences are as in the Condorcet paradox (Example 21.C.2) then the last alternative, whichever it is, will always be the survivor.] This relevance of procedures and rules to social aggregation has far-reaching implications. They have been taken up and much emphasized in modern political science; see, for example, Austen-Smith and Banks (1996) or Shepsle and Boncheck (1995).

In this section, we remain modest and retain the basic framework. We explore to what extent we can escape the dictatorship conclusion if we relax some of the demands imposed by Arrow's theorem. We will investigate two weakenings. In the first, we relax the rationality requirements made on aggregate preferences. In the second, we pose the aggregation question in a restricted domain. In particular, we will consider a restriction—*single-peakedness*—that has been found to be significant and useful in applications.

## Less Than Full Social Rationality

Suppose that we keep the Paretian and pairwise independence conditions but permit the social preferences to be less than fully rational. Two weakenings of the rationality of preferences are captured in Definition 21.D.1.

**Definition 21.D.1:** Suppose that the preference relation $\succsim$ on $X$ is reflexive and complete. We say then that:

(i) $\succsim$ is *quasitransitive* if the strict preference $\succ$ induced by $\succsim$ (i.e. $x \succ y \Leftrightarrow x \succsim y$ but not $y \succsim x$) is transitive.

(ii) $\succsim$ is *acyclic* if $\succsim$ has a maximal element in every finite subset $X' \subset X$, that is, $\{x \in X' : x \succsim y \text{ for all } y \in X'\} \neq \varnothing$.

A quasitransitive preference relation is acyclic, but the converse may not hold. Also, a rational preference relation is quasitransitive, but, again, the converse may not hold.[9] Thus the weaker condition is acyclicity. Yet acyclicity is not a drastic weakening of rationality: Note, for example, that the social orderings of the Condorcet paradox (Example 21.C.2) also violate acyclicity. (For more on acylicity see Exercise 21.D.1.)

We will not discuss in detail the possibilities opened to us by these weakenings of social rationality. There are some but they are not very substantial. We refer to Sen (1970) for a detailed exposition. The next two examples are illustrative.

**Example 21.D.1:** *Oligarchy.* Let $I$ be the set of agents, and let $S \subset I$ be a given subset of agents to be called an *oligarchy* (the possibilities $S = \{h\}$ or $S = I$ are permitted). Given any profile $(\succsim_1, \ldots, \succsim_I) \in \mathscr{R}^I$, the social preferences are formed as follows: For any $x, y \in X$, we say that *$x$ is socially at least as good as $y$* [written $x F(\succsim_1, \ldots, \succsim_I) y$] *if there is at least one $h \in S$ that has $x \succsim_h y$*. Hence, $x$ is socially *preferred* to $y$ if and only if *every* member of the oligarchy prefers $x$ to $y$. In Exercise 21.D.2 you should verify that this social preference relation is quasitransitive but not transitive (because social indifference fails to be transitive). This is the only condition of Arrow's impossibility theorem that is violated (the Paretian condition and pairwise independence conditions are clearly satisfied). Nonetheless, this is scarcely a satisfactory solution to the social aggregation problem, as the aggregator has become very sluggish. At one extreme, if the oligarchy is a single agent then we have a dictatorship. At the other, if the oligarchy is the entire population then society is able to express strict preference only if there is complete unanimity among its members. ∎

**Example 21.D.2:** *Vetoers.* Suppose there are two agents and three alternatives $\{x, y, z\}$. Then given any profile of preferences $(\succsim_1, \succsim_2)$, we let the social preferences coincide with the preferences of agent 1 with one qualification: agent 2 can veto the possibility that alternative $x$ be socially preferred to $y$. Specifically, if $y \succ_2 x$ then $y$ is socially at least as good as $x$. Summarizing, for any two alternatives

---

9. Suppose that $\succsim$ is quasitransitive. Assume for a moment that it is not acyclic. Then there is some finite set $X' \subset X$ without a maximal element for $\succsim$. That is, for every $x \in X'$ there is some $y \in X'$ such that $y \succ x$ (i.e., such that $y \succsim x$ but not $x \succsim y$). Thus, for any integer $M$ we can find a chain $x^1 \succ x^2 \succ \cdots \succ x^M$, where $x^m \in X'$ for every $m = 1, \ldots, M$. If $M$ is larger than the number of alternatives in $X'$, then there must be some repetition in this chain. Say that $x^{m'} = x^m$ for $m > m'$. By quasitransitivity, $x^{m'} \succ x^m = x^{m'}$, which is impossible because $\succ$ is irreflexive by definition. Hence, $\succsim$ must be acyclic. An example of an acyclic but not quasitransitive relation will be given in Example 21.D.2. The relation $\succ$ derived from a rational preference relation $\succsim$ is transitive (Proposition 1.B.1). An example of a quasitransitive, but not rational, preference relation is given in Example 21.D.1.

$\{v, w\} \subset \{x, y, z\}$ we have that $v$ is socially at least as good as $w$ if either $v \succsim_1 w$, or $v = y$, $w = x$ and $v \succ_2 w$. In Exercise 21.D.3 you should verify that the social preferences so defined are acyclic but not necessarily quasitransitive. ∎

### Single-Peaked Preferences

We proceed now to present the most important class of restricted domain conditions: single-peakedness. We will then see that, in this restricted domain, nondictatorial aggregation is possible. In fact, with a small qualification, we will see that on this domain pairwise majority voting gives rise on this domain to a social welfare functional.

**Definition 21.D.2:** A binary relation $\geq$ on the set of alternatives $X$ is a *linear order* on $X$ if it is *reflexive* (i.e., $x \geq x$ for every $x \in X$), transitive (i.e., $x \geq y$ and $y \geq z$ implies $x \geq z$) and *total* (i.e., for any distinct $x, y \in X$, we have that either $x \geq y$ or $y \geq x$, but not both).

**Example 21.D.3:** The simplest example of a linear order occurs when $X$ is a subset of the real line, $X \subset \mathbb{R}$, and $\geq$ is the natural "greater than or equal to" order of the real numbers. ∎

**Definition 21.D.3:** The rational preference relation $\succsim$ is *single peaked* with respect to the linear order $\geq$ on $X$ if there is an alternative $x \in X$ with the property that $\succsim$ is increasing with respect to $\geq$ on $\{y \in X : x \geq y\}$ and decreasing with respect to $\geq$ on $\{y \in X : y \geq x\}$. That is,

$$\text{If } x \geq z > y \quad \text{then} \quad z \succ y$$

and

$$\text{If } y > z \geq x \quad \text{then} \quad z \succ y.$$

In words: There is an alternative $x$ that represents a peak of satisfaction and, moreover, satisfaction increases as we approach this peak (so that, in particular, there cannot be any other peak of satisfaction).

**Example 21.D.4:** Suppose that $X = [a, b] \subset \mathbb{R}$ and $\geq$ is the "greater than or equal to" ordering of the real numbers. Then a continuous preference relation $\succsim$ on $X$ is single peaked with respect to $\geq$ if and only if it is *strictly convex*, that is, if and only if, for every $w \in X$, we have $\alpha y + (1 - \alpha)z \succ w$ whenever $y \succsim w$, $z \succsim w$, $y \neq z$, and $\alpha \in (0,1)$. (Recall Definition 3.B.5 and also that, as a matter of definition, preference relations generated from strictly quasiconcave utility functions are strictly convex.) This fact accounts to a large extent for the importance of single-peakedness in economic applications. The sufficiency of strict convexity is actually quite simple to verify. (You are asked to prove necessity in Exercise 21.D.4.) Indeed, suppose that $x$ is a maximal element for $\succsim$, and that, say, $x > z > y$. Then $x \succsim y$, $y \succsim y$, $x \neq y$, and $z = \alpha x + (1 - \alpha)y$ for some $\alpha \in (0, 1)$. Thus, $z \succ y$ by strict convexity. In Figures 21.D.1 and 21.D.2, we depict utility functions for two preference relations on $X = [0, 1]$. The preference relation in Figure 21.D.1 is single peaked with respect to $\geq$, but that in Figure 21.D.2 is not. ∎

**Definition 21.D.4:** Given a linear order $\geq$ on $X$, we denote by $\mathcal{R}_\geq \subset \mathcal{R}$ the collection of all rational preference relations that are single peaked with respect to $\geq$.

Given a linear order $\geq$ and a set of agents $I$, from now on we consider the

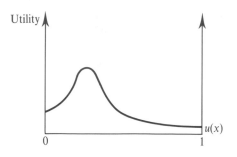

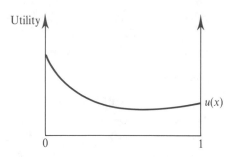

**Figure 21.D.1 (left)**

Preferences are single
peaked with respect
to $\geq$.

**Figure 21.D.2 (right)**

Preferences are not
single peaked with
respect to $\geq$.

restricted domain of preferences $\mathcal{R}_{\geq}^{I}$. This amounts to the requirement that all individuals have single-peaked preferences with respect to the *same* linear order $\geq$.

Suppose that on the domain $\mathcal{R}_{\geq}^{I}$ we define social preferences by means of pairwise majority voting (as introduced in Example 21.B.1). That is, given a profile $(\succsim_1, \ldots, \succsim_I) \in \mathcal{R}_{\geq}^{I}$ and any pair $\{x, y\} \subset X$, we put $x\,\hat{F}(\succsim_1, \ldots, \succsim_I)y$, to be read as "$x$ is socially at least as good as $y$", if the number of agents that strictly prefer $x$ to $y$ is larger or equal to the number of agents that strictly prefer $y$ to $x$, that is, if $\#\{i \in I : x \succ_i y\} \geq \#\{i \in I : y \succ_i x\}$.

Note that, from the definition, it follows that for any pair $\{x, y\}$ we must have either $x\,\hat{F}(\succsim_1, \ldots, \succsim_I)\,y$ or $y\,\hat{F}(\succsim_1, \ldots, \succsim_I)\,x$. Thus, pairwise majority voting induces a complete social preference relation (this holds on any possible domain of preferences).

In Exercise 21.D.5 you are asked to show in a direct manner that the preferences of the Condorcet paradox (Example 21.C.2) are not single peaked with respect to any possible linear order on the alternatives. In fact, they cannot be because, as we now show, with single-peaked preferences we are always assured that the social preferences induced by pairwise majority voting have maximal elements, that is, that there are alternatives that cannot be defeated by any other alternatives under majority voting.

Let $(\succsim_1, \ldots, \succsim_I) \in \mathcal{R}_{\geq}^{I}$ be a fixed profile of preferences. For every $i \in I$ we denote by $x_i \in X$ the maximal alternative for $\succsim_i$ (we will say that $x_i$ is "$i$'s peak").

**Definition 21.D.5:** Agent $h \in I$ is a *median agent for the profile* $(\succsim_1, \ldots, \succsim_I) \in \mathcal{R}_{\geq}^{I}$ if

$$\#\{i \in I : x_i \geq x_h\} \geq \frac{I}{2} \quad \text{and} \quad \#\{i \in I : x_h \geq x_i\} \geq \frac{I}{2}.$$

A median agent always exists. The determination of a median agent is illustrated in Figure 21.D.3.

If there are no ties in peaks and $\#I$ is odd, then Definition 21.D.5 simply says that a number $(I-1)/2$ of the agents have peaks strictly smaller than $x_h$ and another number $(I-1)/2$ strictly larger. In this case the median agent is unique.

**Proposition 21.D.1:** Suppose that $\geq$ is a linear order on $X$ and consider a profile of preferences $(\succsim_1, \ldots, \succsim_I)$ where, for every $i$, $\succsim_i$ is single peaked with respect to $\geq$. Let $h \in I$ be a median agent. Then $x_h\,\hat{F}(\succsim_1, \ldots, \succsim_I)\,y$ for every $y \in X$. That is, the peak $x_h$ of the median agent cannot be defeated by majority voting by any other alternative. Any alternative having this property is called a *Condorcet winner*. Therefore, a Condorcet winner exists whenever the preferences of all agents are singlepeaked with respect to the same linear order.

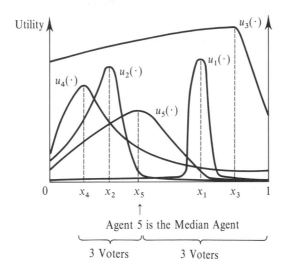

**Figure 21.D.3**

Determination of a median for a single-peaked family.

Agent 5 is the Median Agent

3 Voters    3 Voters

**Proof:** Take any $y \in X$ and suppose that $x_h > y$ (the argument is the same for $y > x_h$). We need to show that $y$ does not defeat $x$, that is, that

$$\#\{i \in I : x_h \succ_i y\} \geq \#\{i \in I : y \succ_i x_h\}.$$

Consider the set of agents $S \subset I$ that have peaks *larger than or equal* to $x_h$, that is, $S = \{i \in I : x_i \geq x_h\}$. Then $x_i \geq x_h > y$ for every $i \in S$. Hence, by single-peakedness of $\succsim_i$ with respect to $\geq$, we get $x_h \succ_i y$ for every $i \in S$. On the other hand, because agent $h$ is a median agent we have that $\#S \geq I/2$ and so $\#\{i \in I : y \succ_i x_h\} \leq \#(I \setminus S) \leq I/2 \leq \#S \leq \#\{i \in I : x_h \succ_i y\}$. ∎

Proposition 21.D.1 guarantees that the preference relation $\hat{F}(\succsim_1, \ldots, \succsim_I)$ is acyclic. It may, however, not be transitive. In Exercise 21.D.6 you are asked to find an example of nontransitivity. Transitivity obtains in the special case where $I$ is odd and, for every $i$, the preference relation $\succsim_i$ belongs to the class $\mathscr{P}^I_{\geq} \subset \mathscr{R}^I_{\geq}$ formed by the rational preference relations $\succsim$ that are single peaked with respect to $\geq$ and have the property that no two distinct alternatives are indifferent for $\succsim$. Note that, if $I$ is odd and preferences are in this class, then, for any pair of alternatives, there is always a strict majority for one of them against the other. Hence, in this case, a Condorcet winner necessarily defeats any other alternative.

**Proposition 21.D.2:** Suppose that $I$ is odd and that $\geq$ is a linear order on $X$. Then pairwise majority voting generates a well-defined social welfare functional $F: \mathscr{P}^I_{\geq} \to \mathscr{R}$. That is, on the domain of preferences that are single-peaked with respect to $\geq$ and, moreover, have the property that no two distinct alternatives are indifferent, we can conclude that the social relation $\hat{F}(\succsim_1, \ldots, \succsim_I)$ generated by pairwise majority voting is complete and transitive.

**Proof:** We already know that $\hat{F}(\succsim_1, \ldots, \succsim_I)$ is complete. It remains to show that it is transitive. For this purpose, suppose that $x\,\hat{F}(\succsim_1, \ldots, \succsim_I)y$ and $y\,\hat{F}(\succsim_1, \ldots, \succsim_I)\,z$. Under our assumptions (recall that $I$ is odd and that no individual indifference is allowed) this means that $x$ defeats $y$ and $y$ defeats $z$. Consider the set $X' = \{x, y, z\}$. If preferences are restricted to this set then, relative to $X'$, preferences still belong to the class $\mathscr{P}^I_{\geq}$, and therefore there is an alternative in $X'$ that is not defeated by any

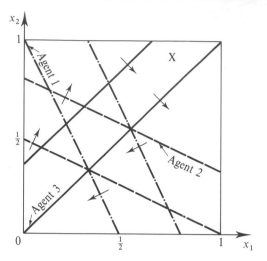

**Figure 21.D.4**

Indifference curves for
the preferences of
Example 21.D.5.

other alternative in $X'$. This alternative can be neither $y$ (defeated by $x$) nor $z$ (defeated by $y$). Hence, it has to be $x$ and we conclude that $x \, \hat{F}(\succsim_1, \ldots, \succsim_I) \, z$, as required by transitivity. ∎

In applications, the linear order on alternatives arises typically as the natural order, as real numbers, of the values of a one-dimensional parameter. Then, as we have seen, single-peakedness follows from the strict quasiconcavity of utility functions, a restriction quite often satisfied in economics. It is an unfortunate fact that the power of quasiconcavity is confined to one-dimensional problems. We illustrate the issues involved in more general cases by discussing two examples.

**Example 21.D.5:** Suppose that the space of alternatives is the unit square, that is, $X = [0, 1]^2$. The generic entries of $X$ are denoted $x = (x_1, x_2)$. There are three agents $I = \{1, 2, 3\}$. The preferences of the agents are expressed by the utility functions on $X$:

$$u_1(x_1, x_2) = -2x_1 - x_2,$$
$$u_2(x_1, x_2) = x_1 + 2x_2,$$
$$u_3(x_1, x_2) = x_1 - x_2.$$

These preferences are represented in Figure 21.D.4. Every utility function is linear and therefore preferences are convex (also, they have a single maximal element on $X$).[10] But, we will now argue that for every $x \in X$ there is a $y \in X$ preferred by two of the agents to $x$. To see this we take an arbitrary $x = (x_1, x_2) \in [0, 1]^2$ and distinguish three cases:

   (i) If $x_1 = 0$, then $y = (\frac{1}{2}, x_2)$ is preferred by agents 2 and 3 to $x$.
   (ii) If $x_2 = 1$, then $y = (x_1, \frac{1}{2})$ is preferred by agents 1 and 3 to $x$.
   (iii) If $x_1 > 0$ and $x_2 < 1$, then $y = (x_1 - \varepsilon, x_2 + \varepsilon) \in [0, 1]^2$ with $\varepsilon > 0$, is preferred by agents 1 and 2 to $x$.

You should verify the claims made in (i), (ii), and (iii). ∎

The situation illustrated in Example 21.D.5 is not a peculiarity. The key property of the

---

   10. The preferences of this example are not strictly convex. This is immaterial. Without changing the nature of the example we could modify them slightly so as to make the indifference curve map strictly convex.

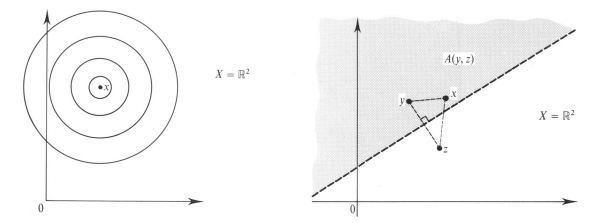

example is that the cone spanned by the nonnegative combinations of the gradient vectors of the three utility functions equals the entire $\mathbb{R}^2$ (see Figure 21.D.4). Exercises 21.D.7 and 21.D.8 provide further elaboration on this issue.

**Figure 21.D.5 (left)**
Euclidean preferences in $\mathbb{R}^2$.

The reason why in two (or more) dimensions, quasiconcavity does not particularly help is that, in contrast with the one-dimensional case, there is no sensible way to assign a "median" to a set of points in the plane. This will become clear in the next, classical, Example 21.D.6 which we now describe.

**Figure 21.D.6 (right)**
The region of Euclidean preferences that prefer $y$ to $z$.

**Example 21.D.6:** *Euclidean Preferences.* Suppose that the set of alternatives is $\mathbb{R}^n$. Agents have preferences $\succsim$ represented by utility functions of the form $u(y) = -\|y - x\|$, where $x$ is a fixed alternative in $\mathbb{R}^n$. In words: $x$ is the most preferred alternative for $\succsim$ and other alternatives are evaluated by how close they are to $x$ in the Euclidean distance. The indifference curves of a typical consumer in $\mathbb{R}^2$ are pictured in Figure 21.D.5.

In the current example, the set $\mathbb{R}^n$ does double duty. On the one hand, it represents the set of alternatives. On the other, it also stands for the set of all possible preferences because every $x \in \mathbb{R}^n$ uniquely identifies the preferences that have $x$ as a peak.[11]

Given two distinct alternatives $y, z \in \mathbb{R}^n$, an agent will prefer $y$ to $z$ if and only if his peak is closer to $y$ than to $z$. Thus, the region of peaks associated with preferences that prefer $y$ to $z$ is

$$A(y, z) = \{x \in \mathbb{R}^n : \|x - y\| < \|x - z\|\}.$$

See Figure 21.D.6 for a representation. Geometrically, the boundary of $A(y, z)$ is the hyperplane perpendicular to the segment connecting $y$ and $z$ and passing through its midpoint.

We will consider the idealized limit situation where there is a continuum of agents with Euclidean preferences and the population is described by a density function $g(x)$ defined on $\mathbb{R}^n$, the set of possible peaks. Then given two distinct alternatives $y, z \in \mathbb{R}^n$, the fraction of the total population that prefers $y$ to $z$, denoted $m_g(y, z)$, is simply the integral of $g(\cdot)$ over the region $A(y, z) \subset \mathbb{R}^n$.

When will there exist a Condorcet winner? Suppose there is an $x^* \in \mathbb{R}^n$ with the property that *any* hyperplane through $x^*$ divides $\mathbb{R}^n$ into two half-spaces each having a total mass of $\frac{1}{2}$ according to the density $g(\cdot)$. This point could be called a *median* for the density $g(\cdot)$; it coincides with the usual concept of a median in the case $n = 1$. A median in this sense is a Condorcet winner. It cannot be defeated by any other alternative because if $y \neq x^*$ then $A(x^*, y)$ is larger than a half-space through $x^*$ and, therefore, $m_g(x^*, y) \geq \frac{1}{2}$. Conversely, if $x^*$

---

11. For an example in the same spirit where the two roles are kept separate, see Grandmont (1978) and Exercise 21.D.9.

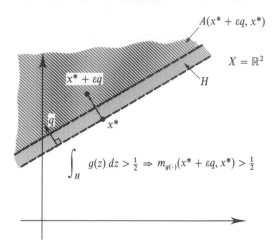

$$\int_H g(z)\,dz > \tfrac{1}{2} \;\Rightarrow\; m_{g(\cdot)}(x^* + \varepsilon q, x^*) > \tfrac{1}{2}$$

**Figure 21.D.7**

If $x^*$ is not a median then it is not a Condorcet winner.

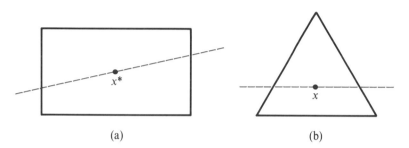

(a)                                        (b)

**Figure 21.D.8**

(a) Uniform distribution over a rectangle: The center point $x^*$ is a median since every plane through $x^*$ divides the rectangle into two figures of equal area. (b) Uniform distribution over a triangle: There is no median.

is not a median then there is a direction $q \in \mathbb{R}^n$ such that the mass of the half-space $\{z \in \mathbb{R}^n : q \cdot z > q \cdot x^*\}$ is larger than $\tfrac{1}{2}$. Thus, by continuity, if $\varepsilon > 0$ is small then the mass of the translated half-space $A(x^* + \varepsilon q, x^*)$ is larger than $\tfrac{1}{2}$. Hence $x^* + \varepsilon q$ defeats $x^*$, and $x^*$ cannot be a Condorcet winner. (See Figure 21.D.7.)

We have seen that a Condorcet winner exists if and only if there is a median for the density $g(\cdot)$. But for $n > 1$ the existence of a median imposes so many conditions (there are many half-spaces) that it becomes a knife-edge property. Figure 21.D.8 provides examples. In Figure 21.D.8(a), the density $g(\cdot)$ is the uniform density over a rectangle [a case first studied by Tullock (1967)]. The center of the rectangle is then, indeed, a median. But the rectangle is very special. The typical case is one of nonexistence. In Figure 21.D.8(b), the density $g(\cdot)$ is the uniform density over a triangle. Then no median exists: Through any point of a triangle we can draw a line that divides it into two regions of unequal area.[12]  ∎

12. See Caplin and Nalebuff (1988) for further analysis. They show that under a restriction on the density function (called "logarithmic concavity" and satisfied, in particular, for uniform densities over convex sets), there are always points ("generalized medians") in $\mathbb{R}^n$ with the property that any hyperplane through the point divides $\mathbb{R}^n$ into two regions, each of which has mass larger than $1/e$. This means that these points cannot be defeated by any other alternative *if* the majority required is not $\tfrac{1}{2}$ but any number larger than $1 - (1/e) > \tfrac{1}{2}$, $64\%$ say. Of course, a $64\%$ rule becomes less decisive than a $50\%$ rule: There will now be many pairs of alternatives with the property that no member of the pair defeats the other.

# 21.E  Social Choice Functions

The task we set ourselves to accomplish in the previous sections was how to aggregate profiles of individual preference relations into a coherent (i.e. rational) social preference order. Presumably, this social preference order is then used to make decisions. In this section we focus directly on social decisions and pose the aggregation question as one of analyzing how profiles of individual preferences turn into social decisions.

The main result we obtain again yields a dictatorship conclusion. The result amounts, in a sense, to a translation of the Arrow's impossibility theorem into the language of choice functions. It also offers a reinterpretation of the condition of pairwise independence, and provides a link towards the incentive-based analysis of Chapter 23.

As before, we have a set of alternatives $X$ and a finite set of agents $I$. The set of preference relations $\succsim$ on $X$ is denoted $\mathscr{R}$. We also designate by $\mathscr{P}$ the subset of $\mathscr{R}$ consisting of the preference relations $\succsim \in \mathscr{R}$ with the property that no two distinct alternatives are indifferent for $\succsim$.

**Definition 21.E.1:** Given any subset $\mathscr{A} \subset \mathscr{R}^I$, a *social choice function* $f : \mathscr{A} \to X$ defined on $\mathscr{A}$ assigns a chosen element $f(\succsim_1, \ldots, \succsim_I) \in X$ to every profile of individual preferences in $\mathscr{A}$.

The notion of social choice function embodies the requirement that the chosen set be single valued. We could argue that this is, after all, in the nature of what a choice is.[13] More restrictive is the fact that we do not allow for random choice.[14]

If $X$ is finite, every social welfare functional $F(\cdot)$ on a domain $\mathscr{A}$ induces a natural social choice function by associating with each $(\succsim_1, \ldots, \succsim_I) \in \mathscr{A}$ a most preferred element in $X$ for the social preference relation $F(\succsim_1, \ldots, \succsim_I)$. For example, if, as in Proposition 21.D.2, $\mathscr{A} \subset \mathscr{P}_{\geq}^I$ is a domain of single-peaked preferences, $I$ is odd, and $F(\cdot)$ is the pairwise majority voting social welfare functional defined on $\mathscr{A}$, then for every $(\succsim_1, \ldots, \succsim_I)$ the choice $f(\succsim_1, \ldots, \succsim_I)$ is the Condorcet winner in $X$.

We now state and prove a result parallel to Arrow's impossibility theorem. Recall that for Arrow's theorem we had two conditions: the social welfare functional had to be Paretian and had to be pairwise independent. Here we require again two conditions: first, the social choice function must be, again, (*weakly*) *Paretian*; and, second, it should be *monotonic*. We define these concepts in Definitions 21.E.2 and 21.E.4, respectively.

---

13. Nevertheless, allowing for multivalued choice sets (that is, allowing there to be more than one acceptable social choice) is natural in some contexts, and certain assumptions on social choice may be more plausible in the multivalued case.

14. Note also the contrast between the definition of choice function here and the similar concept of choice rule in Section 1.C. There we contemplated the possibility of there being several budgets and of the choice depending on the budget at hand. Here the budget is fixed (it is always $X$) but the choice may depend on the profile of underlying individual preferences. Clearly we could, but will not, consider situations that encompass both cases. Another contrast with Section 1.C is that here we limit ourselves to single-valued choice.

**Definition 21.E.2:** The social choice function $f: \mathscr{A} \to X$ defined on $\mathscr{A} \subset \mathscr{R}^I$ is *weakly Paretian* if for any profile $(\succsim_1, \ldots, \succsim_I) \in \mathscr{A}$ the choice $f(\succsim_1, \ldots, \succsim_I) \in X$ is a weak Pareto optimum. That is, if for some pair $\{x, y\} \subset X$ we have that $x \succ_i y$ for every $i$, then $y \neq f(\succsim_1, \ldots, \succsim_I)$.

In order to define monotonicity we need a preliminary concept.

**Definition 21.E.3:** The alternative $x \in X$ *maintains its position from* the profile $(\succsim_1, \ldots, \succsim_I) \in \mathscr{R}^I$ to the profile $(\succsim_1', \ldots, \succsim_I') \in \mathscr{R}^I$ if

$$x \succsim_i y \quad \text{implies} \quad x \succsim_i' y$$

for every $i$ and every $y \in X$.

In other words, $x$ maintains its position from $(\succsim_1, \ldots, \succsim_I)$ to $(\succsim_1', \ldots, \succsim_I')$ if for every $i$ the set of alternatives inferior (or indifferent) to $x$ expands (or remains the same) in moving from $\succsim_i$ to $\succsim_i'$. That is,

$$L(x, \succsim_i) = \{y \in X : x \succsim_i y\} \subset L(x, \succsim_i') = \{y \in X : x \succsim_i' y\}.$$

Note that the condition stated in Definition 21.E.3 imposes no restriction on how other alternatives different from $x$ may change their mutual order in going from $\succsim_i$ to $\succsim_i'$.[15]

**Definition 21.E.4:** The social choice function $f: \mathscr{A} \to X$ defined on $\mathscr{A} \subset \mathscr{R}^I$ is *monotonic* if for any two profiles $(\succsim_1, \ldots, \succsim_I) \in \mathscr{A}$, $(\succsim_1', \ldots, \succsim_I') \in \mathscr{A}$ with the property that the chosen alternative $x = f(\succsim_1, \ldots, \succsim_I)$ maintains its position from $(\succsim_1, \ldots, \succsim_I)$ to $(\succsim_1', \ldots, \succsim_I')$, we have that $f(\succsim_1', \ldots, \succsim_I') = x$.

In words: The social choice function is monotonic if no alternative can be dropped from being chosen unless for some agent its disirability deteriorates.

Are there social choice functions that are weakly Paretian and monotonic? The answer is "yes." For example, in Exercise 21.E.1 you are asked to verify that the pairwise majority voting social decision function defined on a domain of single-peaked preferences is weakly Paretian and monotonic. But what if we have a universal domain (i.e., $\mathscr{A} = \mathscr{R}^I$ or $\mathscr{A} = \mathscr{P}^I$)? A not very attractive class of social choice functions having the two properties in this domain are the *dictatorial* social choice functions.

**Definition 21.E.5:** An agent $h \in I$ is a *dictator* for the social choice function $f: \mathscr{A} \to X$ if, for every profile $(\succsim_1, \ldots, \succsim_I) \in \mathscr{A}$, $f(\succsim_1, \ldots, \succsim_I)$ is a most preferred alternative for $\succsim_h$ in $X$; that is,

$$f(\succsim_1, \ldots, \succsim_I) \in \{x \in X : x \succsim_h y \text{ for every } y \in X\}.$$

A social choice function that admits a dictator is called *dictatorial*.

In the domain $\mathscr{P}^I$, a dictatorial social choice function is weakly Paretian and monotonic. (This is clear enough, but at any rate you should verify it in Exercise 21.E.2, where you are also asked to discuss the case $\mathscr{A} = \mathscr{R}^I$.) Unfortunately, in the universal domain we cannot get anything better than the dictatorial social choice functions. The impossibility result of Proposition 21.E.1 establishes this.

---

15. As in Section 3.B, the sets $L(x, \succsim_i)$ are also referred to as *lower contour sets*.

**Proposition 21.E.1:** Suppose that the number of alternatives is at least three and that the domain of admissible preference profiles is either $\mathscr{A} = \mathscr{R}^I$ or $\mathscr{A} = \mathscr{P}^I$. Then every weakly Paretian and monotonic social choice function $f: \mathscr{A} \to X$ is dictatorial.

**Proof:** The proof of the result will be obtained as a corollary of Arrow's impossibility theorem (Proposition 21.C.1). To this effect, we proceed to derive a social welfare functional $F(\cdot)$ that rationalizes $f(\succsim_1, \ldots, \succsim_I)$ for every profile $(\succsim_1, \ldots, \succsim_I) \in \mathscr{A}$. We will then show that $F(\cdot)$ satisfies the assumptions of Arrow's theorem, hence yielding the dictatorship conclusion.

We begin with a useful definition.

**Definition 21.E.6:** Given a finite subset $X' \subset X$ and a profile $(\succsim_1, \ldots, \succsim_I) \in \mathscr{R}^I$, we say that the profile $(\succsim'_1, \ldots, \succsim'_I)$ *takes $X'$ to the top from* $(\succsim_1, \ldots, \succsim_I)$ if, for every $i$,

$$x \succ'_i y \qquad \text{for } x \in X' \text{ and } y \notin X',$$
$$x \succsim_i y \Leftrightarrow x \succsim'_i y \qquad \text{for all } x, y \in X'.$$

In words: The preference relation $\succsim'_i$ is obtained from $\succsim_i$ by simply taking every alternative in $X'$ to the top, while preserving the internal (weak or strict) ordering among these alternatives. The ordering among alternatives not in $X'$ is arbitrary. For example, if $x \succ_i y \succ_i z \succ_i w$, then the preference relation $\succ'_i$ defined by $y \succ'_i w \succ'_i z \succ'_i x$ takes $\{y, w\}$ to the top from $\succsim_i$. Note also that if $(\succsim'_1, \ldots, \succsim'_I)$ takes $X'$ to the top from $(\succsim_1, \ldots, \succsim_I)$, then every $x \in X'$ maintains its position in going from $(\succsim_1, \ldots, \succsim_I)$ to $(\succsim'_1, \ldots, \succsim'_I)$.

For the rest of the proof we proceed in steps:

*Step 1:* *If both the profiles $(\succsim'_1, \ldots, \succsim'_I) \in \mathscr{A}$ and $(\succsim''_1, \ldots, \succsim''_I) \in \mathscr{A}$ take $X' \subset X$ to the top from $(\succsim_1, \ldots, \succsim_I)$, then $f(\succsim'_1, \ldots, \succsim'_I) = f(\succsim''_1, \ldots, \succsim''_I)$.*

For every $i$ and $x \in X'$ we have

$$\{y \in X: x \succsim'_i y\} = \{y \in X: x \succsim''_i y\} = \{y \in X: x \succsim_i y\} \cup X\backslash X'.$$

By the weak Pareto property, $f(\succsim'_1, \ldots, \succsim'_I) \in X'$. Thus, $f(\succsim'_1, \ldots, \succsim'_I) \in X'$ maintains its position in going from $(\succsim'_1, \ldots, \succsim'_I)$ to $(\succsim''_1, \ldots, \succsim''_I)$. Therefore, by the monotonicity of $f(\cdot)$, we conclude that $f(\succsim'_1, \ldots, \succsim'_I) = f(\succsim''_1, \ldots, \succsim''_I)$.

*Step 2:* *Definition of $F(\succsim_1, \ldots, \succsim_I)$.*

For every profile $(\succsim_1, \ldots, \succsim_I) \in \mathscr{A}$ we define a certain binary relation $F(\succsim_1, \ldots, \succsim_I)$ on $X$. Specifically, we let $x \, F(\succsim_1, \ldots, \succsim_I) \, y$, (read as "$x$ is socially at least as good as $y$") if $x = y$ or if $x = f(\succsim'_1, \ldots, \succsim'_I)$ when $(\succsim'_1, \ldots, \succsim'_I) \in \mathscr{A}$ is any profile that takes $\{x, y\} \subset X$ to the top from the profile $(\succsim_1, \ldots, \succsim_I)$. By step 1 this is well defined, that is, independent of the particular profile $(\succsim'_1, \ldots, \succsim'_I)$ chosen.

*Step 3:* *For every profile $(\succsim_1, \ldots, \succsim_I) \in \mathscr{A}$, $F(\succsim_1, \ldots, \succsim_I)$ is a rational preference relation. Moreover, $F(\succsim_1, \ldots, \succsim_I) \in \mathscr{P}$; that is, no two distinct alternatives are socially indifferent.*

Because $f(\cdot)$ is weakly Paretian, it follows that when $(\succsim'_1, \ldots, \succsim'_I)$ takes $\{x, y\}$ to the top from $(\succsim_1, \ldots, \succsim_I)$ we must have $f(\succsim'_1, \ldots, \succsim'_I) \in \{x, y\}$. Therefore, we conclude that either $x \, F(\succsim_1, \ldots, \succsim_I) \, y$ or $y \, F(\succsim_1, \ldots, \succsim_I) \, x$, *but*, because of step 1, *not both* (unless $x = y$). In particular, $F(\succsim_1, \ldots, \succsim_I)$ is complete.

To verify transitivity, suppose that $x F(\succsim_1, \ldots, \succsim_I) y$ and $y F(\succsim_1, \ldots, \succsim_I) z$. We can assume that the three alternatives $\{x, y, z\}$ are distinct. Let $(\succsim_1'', \ldots, \succsim_I'') \in \mathscr{A}$ be a profile that takes $\{x, y, z\}$ to the top from $(\succsim_1, \ldots, \succsim_I)$. Because $f(\cdot)$ is weakly Paretian, we have $f(\succsim_1'', \ldots, \succsim_I'') \in \{x, y, z\}$.

Suppose that we had $y = f(\succsim_1'', \ldots, \succsim_I'')$. Consider a profile $(\succsim_1', \ldots, \succsim_I') \in \mathscr{A}$ that takes $\{x, y\}$ to the top from $(\succsim_1'', \ldots, \succsim_I'')$. Since $y$ maintains its position from $(\succsim_1'', \ldots, \succsim_I'')$ to $(\succsim_1', \ldots, \succsim_I')$, it follows from monotonicity that $f(\succsim_1', \ldots, \succsim_I') = y$. But $(\succsim_1', \ldots, \succsim_I')$ also takes $\{x, y\}$ to the top from $(\succsim_1, \ldots, \succsim_I)$: the relative ordering of $x$ and $y$, the two alternatives at the top, has not been altered in any individual preference in going from $(\succsim_1, \ldots, \succsim_I)$ to $(\succsim_1', \ldots, \succsim_I')$. Therefore we conclude that $y F(\succsim_1, \ldots, \succsim_I) x$, which contradicts the assumption that $x F(\succsim_1, \ldots, \succsim_I) y$, $x \neq y$. Hence, $y \neq f(\succsim_1'', \ldots, \succsim_I'')$.

Similarly, we obtain $z \neq f(\succsim_1'', \ldots, \succsim_I'')$. We only need to repeat the same argument using the pair $\{y, z\}$ (you are asked to do so in Exercise 21.E.3).

The only possibility left is $x = f(\succsim_1'', \ldots, \succsim_I'')$. Thus, let $(\succsim_1', \ldots, \succsim_I') \in \mathscr{A}$ take $\{x, z\}$ to the top from $(\succsim_1'', \ldots, \succsim_I'')$. Since $x$ maintains its position in going from $(\succsim_1'', \ldots, \succsim_I'')$ to $(\succsim_1', \ldots, \succsim_I')$, it follows that $x = f(\succsim_1', \ldots, \succsim_I')$. But $(\succsim_1', \ldots, \succsim_I')$ also takes $\{x, z\}$ to the top from $(\succsim_1, \ldots, \succsim_I)$. Thus, $x F(\succsim_1, \ldots, \succsim_I) z$, and transitivity is established.

*Step 4:   The social welfare functional $F: \mathscr{A} \to \mathscr{P}$ rationalizes $f: \mathscr{A} \to X$; that is, for every profile $(\succsim_1, \ldots, \succsim_I) \in \mathscr{A}, f(\succsim_1, \ldots, \succsim_I)$ is a most preferred alternative for $F(\succsim_1, \ldots, \succsim_I)$ in $X$.*

This is intuitive enough since $F(\cdot)$ has been constructed from $f(\cdot)$. Denote $x = f(\succsim_1, \ldots, \succsim_I)$ and let $y \neq x$ be any other alternative. Consider a profile $(\succsim_1', \ldots, \succsim_I') \in \mathscr{A}$ that takes $\{x, y\}$ to the top from $(\succsim_1, \ldots, \succsim_I)$. Since $x$ maintains position from $(\succsim_1, \ldots, \succsim_I)$ to $(\succsim_1', \ldots, \succsim_I')$, we have $x = f(\succsim_1', \ldots, \succsim_I')$. Therefore, $x F(\succsim_1, \ldots, \succsim_I) y$.

*Step 5:   The social welfare functional $F: \mathscr{A} \to \mathscr{P}$ is Paretian.*

Clear if $x \succ_i y$ for every $i$ then, by the Paretian property of $f(\cdot)$, we must have $x = f(\succsim_1', \ldots, \succsim_I')$ whenever $(\succsim_1', \ldots, \succsim_I')$ takes $\{x, y\}$ to the top from $(\succsim_1, \ldots, \succsim_I)$. Hence $x F(\succsim_1, \ldots, \succsim_I) y$, and by step 3 we conclude that $x F_p(\succsim_1, \ldots, \succsim_I) y$.

*Step 6:   The social welfare functional $F: \mathscr{A} \to \mathscr{P}$ satisfies the pairwise independence condition.*

This follows from step 1. Suppose that $(\succsim_1, \ldots, \succsim_I) \in \mathscr{A}$ and $(\succsim_1', \ldots, \succsim_I') \in \mathscr{A}$ have the same ordering of $\{x, y\}$ for every $i$ (that is, for every $i$, $x \succsim_i y$ if and only if $x \succsim_i' y$). Suppose that $(\succsim_1'', \ldots, \succsim_I'') \in \mathscr{A}$ takes $\{x, y\}$ to the top from $(\succsim_1, \ldots, \succsim_I)$ and that, say, $x = f(\succsim_1'', \ldots, \succsim_I'')$. Then $x F(\succsim_1, \ldots, \succsim_I) y$. But $(\succsim_1'', \ldots, \succsim_I'')$ also takes $\{x, y\}$ to the top from $(\succsim_1', \ldots, \succsim_I')$. Hence, $x F(\succsim_1', \ldots, \succsim_I') y$, as we wanted to prove.

*Step 7:   The social choice function $f: \mathscr{A} \to X$ is dictatorial.*

By Arrow's theorem (Proposition 21.C.1) there is an agent $h \in I$ such that for every profile $(\succsim_1, \ldots, \succsim_I) \in \mathscr{A}$ we have $x F_p(\succsim_1, \ldots, \succsim_I) y$ whenever $x \succ_h y$. Therefore, $f(\succsim_1, \ldots, \succsim_I)$ [which by step 4 is a most preferred alternative for

$F(\succsim_1, \ldots, \succsim_I)$ in $X$] must also be a most preferred alternative for $h$; that is, $f(\succsim_1, \ldots, \succsim_I) \succsim_h x$ for every $x \in X$. Hence agent $h$ is a dictator. ∎

Finally, we mention the following corollary (Proposition 21.E.2) to hint at the connection between Proposition 21.E.1 and the issue of incentives to truthful preference revelation, a topic that is studied extensively in Chapter 23.

**Proposition 21.E.2:** Suppose that the number of alternatives is at least three and that $f: \mathscr{P}^I \to X$ is a social choice function that is weakly Paretian and satisfies the following *no-incentive-to-misrepresent* condition:

$$f(\succsim_1, \ldots, \succsim_{h-1}, \succsim_h, \succsim_{h+1}, \ldots, \succsim_I) \succsim_h f(\succsim_1, \ldots, \succsim_{h-1}, \succsim'_h, \succsim_{h+1}, \ldots, \succsim_I)$$

for every agent $h$, every $\succsim'_h \in \mathscr{P}$, and every profile $(\succsim_1, \ldots, \succsim_I) \in \mathscr{P}^I$. Then $f(\cdot)$ is dictatorial.

**Proof:** In view of Proposition 21.E.1 it suffices to show that $f: \mathscr{P}^I \to X$ must be monotonic.

Suppose that it is not. Then without loss of generality we can assume that, for some agent $h$, there are preferences $\succsim_i \in \mathscr{P}$ for agents $i \neq h$, and preferences $\succsim''_h$, $\succsim'''_h \in \mathscr{P}$ for agent $h$, such that, denoting

$$x = f(\succsim_1, \ldots, \succsim_{h-1}, \succsim''_h, \succsim_{h+1}, \ldots, \succsim_I)$$

and

$$y = f(\succsim_1, \ldots, \succsim_{h-1}, \succsim'''_h, \succsim_{h+1}, \ldots, \succsim_I),$$

we have that $x \succsim''_h z$ implies $x \succsim'''_h z$ for every $z \in X$, and yet $y \neq x$.

There are two possibilities: Either $y \succ''_h x$ or $x \succsim''_h y$.

If $y \succ''_h x$ then the no-incentive-to-misrepresent condition is violated for the "true" preference relation $\succsim_h = \succsim''_h$ and the misrepresentation $\succsim'_h = \succsim'''_h$.

If $x \succsim''_h y$ then $x \succsim'''_h y$. Therefore, since no two distinct alternatives can be indifferent, $x \succ'''_h y$. But if $x \succ'''_h y$ then the no-incentive-to-misrepresent condition is violated for the "true" preference relation $\succsim_h = \succsim'''_h$ and the misrepresentation $\succsim'_h = \succsim''_h$. ∎

## REFERENCES

Arrow, K. J. (1963). *Social Choice and Individual Values*, 2d ed. New York: Wiley.

Austen-Smith, D., and J. S. Banks. (1996). *Positive Political Theory*. Ann Arbor: University of Michigan Press.

Caplin, A., and B. Nalebuff. (1988). On 64%-majority voting. *Econometrica* **56**: 787–814.

Grandmont, J-M. (1978). Intermediate preferences and majority rule. *Econometrica* **46**: 317–30.

May, K. (1952). A set of independent, necessary and sufficient conditions for simple majority decision. *Econometrica* **20**: 680–84.

Moulin, H. (1988) *Axioms of Cooperative Decision Making*. Cambridge, U.K.: Cambridge University Press.

Sen, A. (1970). *Individual Choice and Social Welfare*. San Francisco: Holden Day.

Sen, A. (1986). Social choice theory. Chap. 22 in *Handbook of Mathematical Economics*, edited by K. Arrow, and M. Intriligator. Amsterdam: North-Holland.

Shepsle, K. A., and M. Boncheck. (1995), *Analyzing Politics*. New York: W. W. Norton.

Tullock, G. (1967). The general irrelevancy of the general possibility theorem. *Quarterly Journal of Economics* **81**: 256–70.

**EXERCISES**

**21.B.1**[A] Verify that majority voting between two alternatives satisfies the properties of symmetry among agents, neutrality between alternatives, and positive responsiveness.

**21.B.2**[A] For each of the three properties characterizing majority voting between two alternatives according to Proposition 21.B.1 (symmetry among agents, neutrality between alternatives, and positive responsiveness) exhibit an example of a social welfare functional $F(\alpha_1, \ldots, \alpha_I)$ distinct from majority voting and satisfying the other two properties. This shows that none of the three properties is redundant for the characterization result.

**21.B.3**[A] Suppose there is a public good project that can take two levels $k \in \{0, 1\}$, where $k = 0$ can be interpreted as the status quo. The cost, in dollars, of any level of the public good is zero. There is a population $I$ of agents having quasilinear preferences (with dollars as numeraire) over levels of the public good and money holdings. Thus, the preferences of agent $i$ are completely described by the willingness to pay $v_i \in \mathbb{R}$ for the level $k = 1$ over the level $k = 0$. The number $v_i$ may be negative (in this case it amounts to the minimum compensation required).

Show that a majority rule decision over the two levels of the public project guarantees a Pareto optimal decision over the set of policies constituted by the two levels of the public project (with no money transfers taking place across agents) but not over the larger set of policies in which transfers across agents are also possible.

Compare and contrast the majority decision rule (a "median") with the Pareto optimum decision rule for the case in which transfers across agents are possible (a "mean").

**21.C.1**[A] Provide the requested completion of step 1 of the proof of Proposition 21.C.1.

**21.C.2**[B] We can list the implicit and explicit assumptions of the Arrow impossibility theorem (Proposition 21.C.1) to be the following:

  (a) The number of alternatives is at least 3.
  (b) Universal domain: To be specific, the domain of the social welfare functional $F(\cdot)$ is $\mathscr{R}^I$.
  (c) Social rationality: That is, $F(\succsim_1, \ldots, \succsim_I)$ is a rational preference relation (i.e. complete and transitive) for every possible profile of individual preferences.
  (d) Pairwise independence (Definition 21.C.3).
  (e) Paretian condition (Definition 21.C.2).
  (f) No dictatorship: That is, there is no agent $h$ that at any profile of individual preferences imposes his strict preference over any possible pair of alternatives (see Proposition 21.C.1 for a precise definition).

For each of these six assumptions exhibit a social welfare functional $F(\cdot)$ satisfying the other five. This shows that none of the conditions is redundant for the impossibility result.

**21.C.3**[A] Show that there are social welfare functionals $F: \mathscr{R}^I \to \mathscr{R}$ defined on $\mathscr{R}^I$ (i.e., individual indifference is possible) satisfying all the conditions of Arrow's impossibility theorem (Proposition 21.C.1) and for which, however, the social preferences are not *identical* to the preferences of any individual. [*Hint*: Try a *lexical dictatorship* in which the $n$th-ranked dictator imposes his preference if and only if every higher ranked dictator is indifferent.]

**21.D.1**[B] Suppose that $X$ is a finite set of alternatives. Construct a reflexive and complete preference relation $\succsim$ on $X$ with the property that $\succsim$ has a maximal element on every strict subset $X' \subset X$, and yet $\succsim$ is not acyclic.

**21.D.2**[A] Verify that the social preferences generated by the oligarchy example (Example 21.D.1) are quasitransitive but that social indifference may not be transitive. Interpret.

**21.D.3**[A] Show that the social preferences generated by the vetoers example (Example 21.D.2) are acyclic but not necessarily quasitransitive. Show also that in spite of the veto power of agent 2 it may happen that alternative $x$ is the only maximal alternative for the social preferences.

**21.D.4**[A] With reference to Example 21.D.4, show that a continuous preference relation $\succsim$ on $X = [0, 1]$ is single peaked only if it is *strictly convex*.

**21.D.5**[A] Give a direct proof that none of the six linear orders possible among three alternatives can make the three preferences involved in the Condorcet paradox (Example 21.C.2) into a single-peaked family.

**21.D.6**[B] Give an example with an even number of agents and single-peaked preferences in which pairwise majority voting fails to generate a fully transitive social preference relation.

**21.D.7**[C] Suppose that $X$ is a convex subset of $\mathbb{R}^2$ with the origin in its interior. There are three agents $i = 1, 2, 3$. Every $i$ has a continuously differentiable utility function $u_i \colon X \to \mathbb{R}$. Assume that the cone in $\mathbb{R}^2$ spanned by the set of gradients at the origin $\{\nabla u_1(0), \nabla u_2(0), \nabla u_3(0)\}$ is the entire $\mathbb{R}^2$. Show the following:

(a) There are three alternatives $x, y, z \in X$ that constitute a Condorcet cycle (i.e., there is a strict majority for $x$ over $y$, $y$ over $z$, and $z$ over $x$).

(b) (Harder) Given any $x \in \mathbb{R}^2$, there is a $y \in \mathbb{R}^2$ such that $\|x - y\| < \|x\|$ and $y$ is preferred by two agents to the origin $0 \in \mathbb{R}^2$. That is, if you think of the origin as the status-quo then for any $x$ we can find a strict majority that prefers, over the status-quo, an alternative that moves us closer to $x$. [*Hint:* You can safely assume that the utility functions are linear.]

**21.D.8**[C] The situation is as in Exercise 21.D.7 except that now, at the origin, the gradients of the utility functions constitute a pointed cone (i.e. the cone does not contain any half-space). Assume also that utility functions are quasiconcave.

(a) Argue that at the origin there is an agent who is a directional median in the sense that any alternative having a strict majority against the origin must make this agent strictly better off.

(b) Suppose now that at every $x \in X$ the cone spanned by $\{\nabla u_1(x), \nabla u_2(x), \nabla u_3(x)\}$ is pointed. Then according to (a) there is a directional median agent at every $x \in X$. Show that this directional median agent can change with $x$ and that Condorcet cycles are possible.

(c) The situation is as in (b). Show that, if the directional median agent is the same at every $x \in X$, then there can be no Condorcet cycle.

**21.D.9**[C] (Grandmont) Consider a set of alternatives $X$. Given three rational preference relations $\succsim, \succsim', \succsim''$ on $X$, one says that $\succsim''$ is *intermediate* between $\succsim$ and $\succsim'$ if $x \succsim y$ and $x \succsim' y$ implies $x \succsim'' y$. That is, for every alternative $y$ the intersection of the upper contour sets for $\succsim$ and $\succsim'$ is contained in the upper contour set for $\succsim''$.

(a) Show that if $u(x)$ and $u'(x)$ are utility functions for preferences on $X$ then, for any positive numbers $\gamma$ and $\psi$, the preference relation represented by $\psi u(x) + \gamma u'(x)$ is intermediate between the preference relations represented by $u(x)$ and $u'(x)$.

(b) Suppose we are given $N$ functions $h_1(x), \ldots, h_N(x)$ defined on $X$. The preferences of agents are represented by utility functions of the form $u_\beta(x) = \beta_1 h_1(x) + \cdots + \beta_N h_N(x)$, where $\beta = (\beta_1, \ldots, \beta_N) \in \mathbb{R}^N_{++}$. Show that for any two alternatives $x, y \in X$, the set $B(x, y) = \{\beta \in \mathbb{R}^N_{++} : u_\beta(x) > u_\beta(y)\}$ is the intersection of $\mathbb{R}^N_{++}$ with a translated half-space.

(c) Argue that the conclusion from (b) is still correct if a parametrization of utility functions $u_\beta(x)$ by a $\beta \in \mathbb{R}^N$ is such that whenever $\beta''$ is a convex combination of $\beta$ and $\beta'$ then the preferences represented by $u_{\beta''}(x)$ are intermediate between the preferences represented by $u_\beta(x)$ and $u_{\beta'}(x)$.

(d) Continuing with the parametrization of (b), suppose that we take the limit situation where the population of agents is represented by a density $g(\beta)$ over $\mathbb{R}^N_{++}$. We say that $\beta^*$ is a *median agent* for $g(\cdot)$ if *every* hyperplane in $\mathbb{R}^N$ passing through $\beta^*$ divides $\mathbb{R}^N$ into two regions having equal mass according to the density $g(\cdot)$. Show that a median agent for an arbitrary $g(\cdot)$ may or may not exist.

(e) In the framework of (d), suppose there is a median agent $\beta^*$, that $g(\beta^*) > 0$, and that $x^*$ is the single most preferred alternative of the median agent. Show then that $x^*$ defeats any other alternative in pairwise majority voting.

(f) Show that the Euclidean preferences in Example 21.D.6 can be put into the framework of this exercise by keeping the sets of alternatives and of agents conceptually separated.

**21.D.10$^B$** The purpose of this exercise is to illustrate the use of single-peakedness in a policy problem. Specifically, we consider the problem of determining by majority voting a tax level for wealth redistribution.

Suppose that there is an odd number $I$ of agents. Each agent has a level of wealth $w_i > 0$ and an increasing utility function over wealth levels. The mean wealth is $\bar{w}$, and the median wealth is $w^*$.

(a) Interpret the distributional significance of a difference between $\bar{w}$ and $w^*$.

(b) Consider a proportional tax rate $t \in [0, 1]$ identical across agents. The set of alternatives is $X = [0, 1]$, the set of possible levels of the tax rate. Tax receipts are redistributed uniformly. Thus, for a tax rate $t$, the after-tax wealth of agent $i$ is $(1 - t)w_i + t\bar{w}$. Show that the preferences over $X$ of all agents are single peaked and that the Condorcet winner $t_c$ is $t_c = 0$ or $t_c = 1$ according to whether $w^* > \bar{w}$ or $w^* < \bar{w}$, respectively. Interpret.

(c) Now suppose that taxation gives rise to a deadweight loss. Being very crude about it, suppose that a tax rate of $t \in [0, 1]$ decreases the pretax level of agent $i$'s wealth to $w_i(t) = (1 - t)w_i$ [thus, the average tax receipts are $t(1 - t)\bar{w}$ and the ex post wealth level of agent $i$ is $(1 - t)^2 w_i + t(1 - t)\bar{w}$]. Show that preferences on wealth levels are again single peaked (but notice that the after-tax wealth level may not be a concave function of the tax rate). Show then that $t_c \leq \frac{1}{2}$. Also, $t_c = 0$ or $t_c > 0$ according to whether $w^* > \frac{1}{2}\bar{w}$ or $w^* < \frac{1}{2}\bar{w}$, respectively. Compare with (b) and interpret.

(d) Let us modify (c) by assuming that the deadweight loss affects individual wealth differently: A tax rate of $t \in [0, 1]$ decreases pretax wealth of agent $i$ to $(1 - t^2)w_i$ [this is theoretically more satisfactory than the situation in (c) since we know from first principles that at $t = 0$ a small increase in $t$ should have a second-order effect on total welfare]. Show then that individual preferences on tax rates need no longer be single peaked.

**21.D.11$^B$** Consider a finite set of alternatives $X$ and a set of preferences $\mathscr{P}_\geq$, single-peaked with respect to some linear order $\geq$ on $X$ (note that we rule out the possibility of individual indifference). The number of agents is odd. As we have seen in Proposition 21.D.2, a possible class of social welfare functionals $F : \mathscr{P}_\geq^I \to \mathscr{P}$ that satisfy the Paretian and pairwise independence conditions are those where we fix a subset $S \subset I$ composed of an odd number of agents (a kind of oligarchy) and let the members of this subset determine social preferences by pairwise majority voting. Show by example that this is *not* the only possible class of social welfare functionals $F : \mathscr{P}_\geq^I \to \mathscr{P}$ that satisfy the Paretian and pairwise independence conditions.

**21.D.12$^A$** Suppose that the total cost $c > 0$ of a project has to be financed by levying taxes from three agents. Therefore, the set of alternatives is $X = \{(t_1, t_2, t_3) \geq 0 : t_1 + t_2 + t_3 = c\}$. The financing scheme is to be decided by majority voting.

(a) Show that no strictly positive alternative $(t_1, t_2, t_3) \gg 0$ can be a Condorcet winner.

(b) Discuss what happens with alternatives $(t_1, t_2, t_3)$ where $t_i = 0$ for some $i$.

**21.D.13$^B$** We have a population of agents (to be simple, a continuum) with Euclidean preferences in $\mathbb{R}^2$. The preferences of the agents fall into a finite number $J$ of types. Each type is indexed by the most preferred point $x_j$. We assume that the $x_j$'s are in "general position," in the sense that no three of the $x_j$'s line up into a straight line. We denote by $\alpha_j \in [0, 1]$ the fraction of the total mass of agents that are of type $j$.

(a) Suppose that $J$ is odd and $\alpha_1 = \cdots = \alpha_J$. Prove that if $y \in \mathbb{R}^2$ is a Condorcet winning alternative, then $y \in \{x_1, \ldots, x_J\}$. That is, the Condorcet winning alternative must coincide with the top alternative of some type. Does this remain true if $J$ is even?

(b) (De Marzo) Suppose now that there is a dominant type, that is, a type $h$ such that $\alpha_h > \alpha_j$ for every $j \neq h$. Prove that if there is a Condorcet winning alternative $y \in \mathbb{R}^2$, then $y = x_h$. That is, only the top alternative of the dominant type can be a Condorcet winning alternative.

**21.D.14$^B$** In this exercise we verify that we cannot weaken the definition of single-peakedness to require only that preference be weakly increasing as the peak is approached.

Suppose we have five agents and five alternatives $\{x, y, z, v, w\}$. The individual preferences are

$$x \succ_1 y \sim_1 z \sim_1 v \sim_1 w,$$

$$y \succ_2 x \succ_2 z \succ_2 v \succ_2 w,$$

$$z \succ_3 y \sim_3 v \sim_3 w \succ_3 x,$$

$$v \succ_4 w \succ_4 x \sim_4 y \sim_4 z,$$

$$w \succ_5 x \sim_5 y \sim_5 z \sim_5 v,$$

(a) Show that there is no Condorcet winner among these alternatives; that is, every alternative is defeated by majority voting by some other alternative.

(b) Show that there is a linear order $\geq$ on the alternatives such that the preference relation of the five agents satisfies the following property: "Preferences are weakly increasing as we approach, in the linear order $\geq$, the most preferred alternative of the agent."

(c) Verify that the alternatives could be viewed as points in $[0, 1]$ and that the preferences of each agent could be induced by the restriction to the set of alternatives of a quasiconcave utility function on $[0, 1]$. [Note: $u_i(t)$ is quasiconcave if $\{t \in [0, 1] : u_i(t) \geq \gamma\}$ is convex for every $\gamma$.]

(d) (Harder) Extend the previous arguments and constructions into an example with the following characteristics: (i) There are five agents; (ii) the space of alternatives equals the interval $[0, 1]$; (iii) every agent has a quasiconcave utility function on $[0, 1]$ with a single maximal alternative; and (iv) there is no Condorcet winner in $[0, 1]$.

**21.E.1$^A$** Consider a finite set of alternatives $X$ and suppose that there is an odd number of agents. The domain of preferences is $\mathcal{A} = \mathcal{P}_{\geq}^I$, where $\geq$ is a linear order on $X$ (i.e., preferences are single peaked and individual indifferences do not arise). Show that the social choice function that assigns the Condorcet winner to every profile satisfies the weak Pareto and the monotonicity conditions.

**21.E.2$^A$** Suppose that the set of alternatives $X$ has $N < \infty$ elements and that the alternatives are given to us with labels that go from 1 to $N$, that is, $X = \{x_1, \ldots, x_N\}$. Consider the social choice function defined on $\mathscr{R}^I$ (i.e., we allow for individual indifference) by letting $f(\succsim_1, \ldots, \succsim_I)$ be the alternative that has the smallest label among all the alternatives that are most preferred by the first agent. Show that this social choice function is dictatorial, weakly Paretian and monotonic. For the sake of completeness, carry out the same verification if the domain of $f(\cdot)$ is $\mathscr{P}^I$.

**21.E.3$^A$** As requested, complete the proof of step 3 of Proposition 21.E.1.

**21.E.4$^A$** Suppose that the number of alternatives is finite and that $F: \mathscr{A} \to \mathscr{P}$ is a social welfare functional satisfying the weakly Paretian and the pairwise independence condition on some domain $\mathscr{A} \subset \mathscr{P}^I$. The *induced social choice function* assigns to every profile the socially most preferred alternative. Give two examples where the induced social choice function is not monotonic. One example should be for the two-alternative case and $\mathscr{A} = \mathscr{P}^I$, and the other should be for a case with more than two alternatives. [*Hint:* Choose $\mathscr{A}$ to be very small.]

# Elements of Welfare Economics
# and Axiomatic Bargaining

## 22.A Introduction

In this chapter, we continue our study of welfare economics. The main difference from Chapter 21 is that here the cardinal aspects of individual utility functions will be at center stage. Moreover, we will not eschew exploring the implications of assuming that utilities are interpersonally comparable.

In Section 22.B, we present the concept of the *utility possibility set*. We also emphasize the distinction between first-best and second-best welfare problems.

In Section 22.C, we first posit the existence of a policy maker, or social planner, endowed with coherent objectives in the form of a *social welfare function*. The role of policy consists, precisely, in the maximization of the social welfare function subject to the constraint represented by the utility possibility set. We then analyze a variety of practically useful examples. The section concludes with a brief discussion of the *compensation criterion*.

In Section 22.D, we probe the extent to which interpersonal comparisons of utility underlie the use of social welfare functions. We do this by analyzing the implications of axioms that postulate the invariance of social preferences to changes in the origins and units of individual utility functions. This section links naturally with Chapter 21 as, again, it relies on the concept of a social welfare functional and, through a different road, it takes us back to Arrow's impossibility theorem.

Sections 22.E and 22.F deal with a somewhat different topic: axiomatic bargaining theory. The aim is now to formulate and analyze reasonable criteria for dividing among several agents the *gains* (or *losses*) from a cooperative endeavor.

In Section 22.E, we study the simplest case: that in which either there is complete cooperation (with the possible outcomes of cooperation described by a utility possibility set) or the outcome is a given *threat point*. We present several solutions for this case, among them the classical *Nash bargaining solution*.

In Section 22.F, we restrict ourselves to the situation in which the utility is transferable among agents. We allow, however, for the possibility of cooperation among subgroups of agents. A classical solution is then the *Shapley value*, of which we give a brief account. We also provide an illustration of an interesting application of the Shapley value to a problem of allocating joint costs to individual projects.

# 22.B Utility Possibility Sets

As a first step in the study of policy decision problems, this section is concerned with the description of the set of options available to a policy maker. The following section will consider the objectives of the policy maker.[1]

The starting point of the analysis is a nonempty *set of alternatives* $X$ and a collection of $I$ agents. In contrast with Chapter 21, where we used preference relations, we will now assume that agents' tastes are given to us in the form of utility functions $u_i: X \to \mathbb{R}$. One may wonder what is the exact meaning of the utility values $u_i(x)$: Do they have cardinal or ordinal significance? Are they comparable across individuals? These questions will be considered in Section 22.D. For current purposes there is no need to answer them.

It is a traditional, and firm, principle of welfare economics that policy making should not be *paternalistic*. At a minimum, this means that alternatives that cannot be distinguished from the standpoint of agents' tastes should not be distinguished by the policy maker either. We are therefore led to the idea that only the agents' utility values for the different alternative should matter and therefore that the relevant constraint set for the policy maker is the *utility possibility set* [introduced by Samuelson (1947)], which we now define.

**Definition 22.B.1:** The *utility possibility set* (UPS) is the set

$$U = \{(u_1, \ldots, u_I) \in \mathbb{R}^I : u_1 \leq u_i(x), \ldots, u_I \leq u_I(x) \text{ for some } x \in X\} \subset \mathbb{R}^L.$$

The *Pareto frontier* of $U$ is formed by the utility vectors $u = (u_1, \ldots, u_I) \in U$ for which there is no other $u' = (u'_1, \ldots, u'_I) \in U$ with $u'_i \geq u_i$ for every $i$ and $u'_i > u_i$ for some $i$.

To gain some insight into the characteristics of UPSs, and in particular, into the important distinction between *first-best* and *second-best* policy problems, we discuss some examples.

**Example 22.B.1:** *Exchange Economies.* Suppose that we focus on the exchange and production economies with $L$ commodities and $I$ consumers studied in Chapter 10 and in Part IV. The set of alternatives $X \subset \mathbb{R}^{LI}$ then stands for the set of feasible consumption allocations $x = (x_1, \ldots, x_I)$. The utility functions of the different consumers have the form $u_i(x) = u_i(x_i)$; that is, consumer $i$'s utility from an allocation depends only on her own consumption. In Exercise 22.B.1 you are asked to show that under standard conditions (including the concavity of the utility functions), the UPS of this economy is a convex set. In the particular case where the utility functions are quasilinear,[2] we saw in Section 10.D that the boundary of $U$ is a hyperplane. The general case and the quasilinear case are illustrated in Figures 22.B.1 and 22.B.2, respectively. ∎

---

1. For general introductions to public economics, see Atkinson and Stiglitz (1980), Laffont (1988), and Starrett (1988). At a more advanced level, see Guesnerie (1995). Phelps (1973) contains a good compilation of basic articles emphasizing conceptual foundations.

2. As usual, in this case we also neglect the nonnegativity constraints on numeraire.

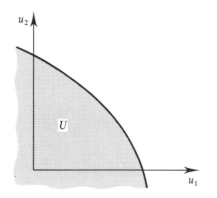

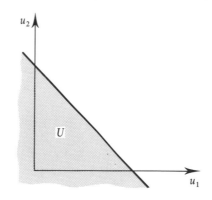

**Figure 22.B.1 (left)**
A utility possibility set.

**Figure 22.B.2 (right)**
A utility possibility set: transferable utility.

Example 22.B.1 corresponds to a first-best situation. A *first-best problem* is one in which the constraints defining $X$ are only those imposed by technology and resources. The policy maker cannot produce from a void and, therefore, must respect these constraints, but otherwise she can appeal to any conceivable policy instrument. If, as is often the case, there are other restrictions on the usable instruments, we say that we have a *second-best problem*. The restrictions can be of many sorts: legal, institutional, or, more fundamentally, informational. The last type were amply illustrated in Chapters 13 and 14 (and will be seen again in Chapter 23). We should warn, however, that the conceptual distinction between first-best and second-best problems is not sharp. In a sense, adverse selection or agency restrictions are as primitive as technologies and endowments.

**Example 22.B.2:** *Ramsey Taxation.* Consider a quasilinear economy with three goods, of which the third is the numeraire. The numeraire good can be freely transferred across consumers (more formally, one of the policy instruments available to the policy maker is the lump-sum redistribution of wealth). The first two goods are produced from the numeraire at a constant marginal cost equal to 1. Consumers face market prices that are equal to marginal cost plus a commodity tax whose level is fixed by the policy maker. Tax proceeds are returned to the economy in lump-sum form. Finally, the amounts consumed are those determined by the demand functions of the different consumers.

We know from the second welfare theorem (Section 16.D) that any utility vector in the first-best UPS can be reached with the above instruments (it suffices to set the tax rates at a zero level and distribute wealth appropriately). But suppose that we now have an unavoidable distortion—the policy maker is constrained to raise a total amount $R$ of tax receipts. This has then become a second-best problem. To determine the corresponding second-best UPS, note first that, since the numeraire is freely transferable across consumers, the boundary of this set is still linear, as in the first-best case (i.e., as in Figure 22.B.2). Hence, to place this boundary it suffices to find the level of prices $p_1, p_2$ that maximizes $v(p_1, p_2)$, the indirect utility function of a representative consumer (which, up to an increasing transformation, equals the aggregate consumer surplus; see Section 4.D and Chapter 10 for these concepts).[3]

Denote by $x_1(p_1, p_2)$ and $x_2(p_1, p_2)$ the aggregate demand functions. Then we must solve the problem

$$\text{Max} \quad v(p_1, p_2)$$

$$\text{s.t.} \quad (p_1 - 1)x_1(p_1, p_2) + (p_2 - 1)x_2(p_1, p_2) \geq R.$$

Suppose, to take the simplest case, that the utility functions of the different consumers are additively separable. This means that the two demand functions can be written as $x_1(p_1)$ and $x_2(p_2)$. Then the first-order conditions satisfied by a solution $(\bar{p}_1, \bar{p}_2)$ of the maximization problem are (carry out the calculation in Exercise 22.B.2):

There is $\lambda < 0$, such that

$$\lambda(\bar{p}_1 - 1)\frac{dx_1(\bar{p}_1)}{dp_1} = (1 - \lambda)x_1(\bar{p}_1)$$

and

$$\lambda(\bar{p}_2 - 1)\frac{dx_2(\bar{p}_2)}{dp_2} = (1 - \lambda)x_2(\bar{p}_2).$$

Denoting by $t_\ell = (\bar{p}_\ell - 1)/\bar{p}_\ell$ the tax rate on good $\ell$, we can write this condition in elasticity form as

$$t_1 = \frac{\alpha}{\varepsilon_1(\bar{p}_1)} \quad \text{and} \quad t_2 = \frac{\alpha}{\varepsilon_2(\bar{p}_2)} \quad \text{for some } \alpha > 0. \quad (22.B.1)$$

Expression (22.B.1) is known as the *Ramsey taxation formula* [because of Ramsey (1927)]. An implication of it is that if the demand for good 1 is uniformly less elastic than that for good 2, then the optimal tax rate for good 1 is higher. This makes sense: For example, if the demand for good 1 is totally inelastic then there is no deadweight loss from taxation of this good (see Section 10.C) and therefore we could reach the first-best optimum by taxing only this good.[4]  ∎

**Example 22.B.3:** *Compensatory Distortion.* The basic economy is as in Example 22.B.2, except that we do not necessarily assume that the utility functions of the consumers are additively separable. The distortion is now of a different type. We

---

3. Because total surplus equals consumer surplus plus the fixed amount of tax revenues $R$, by maximizing consumer surplus we maximize total surplus. We note also that the assumption that the amount $R$ must be raised through commodity taxation is somewhat artificial in a context where lump-sum redistribution is possible. We make the assumption, in this and the next example, merely to be pedagogical. Alternatively, we could rule out the possibility of lump-sum transfers. In this case the exercise carried out in this example (and the next) determines the first-order conditions for the problem of maximizing the sum of individual utilities (the "purely utilitarian social welfare function" in the terminology of Section 22.C)

4. We should warn that the formulas in (22.B.1) constitute only first-order conditions. As we shall see in the forthcoming examples, second-best problems are frequently nonconvex and therefore the satisfaction of first-order conditions does not guarantee that we have determined a true maximum.

assume that $p_1$ is fixed at some level $\hat{p}_1 > 1$.[5] The policy instruments are any transfer of numeraire across agents and the level of a commodity tax on the second good. The net revenue in the two markets is given back to consumers in a lump-sum form. The solution $\bar{p}_2$ of the surplus-maximization problem is then characterized by the first-order conditions (see Exercise 22.B.3)

$$(\hat{p}_1 - 1) \frac{\partial x_1(\hat{p}_1, \bar{p}_2)}{\partial p_2} + (\bar{p}_2 - 1) \frac{\partial x_2(\hat{p}_1, \bar{p}_2)}{\partial p_2} = 0. \tag{22.B.2}$$

Note that except in the separable case, where $\partial x_1(\hat{p}_1, \bar{p}_2)/\partial p_2 = 0$, we have $\bar{p}_2 \neq 1$; that is, even if the initial distortion involves only the first market, second-best efficiency requires creating a compensatory distortion in the second market [this point was emphasized by Lipsey and Lancaster (1956)]. This is an intuitive result: suppose that we were to put $p_2 = 1$; then the last (infinitesimal) unit demanded of the second good makes a contribution $p_2 - 1 = 0$ to the total surplus (recall that $p_2$ will equal the marginal utility for good 2). Therefore, a small tax on good 2 is desirable because its effect is to divert some demand toward good 1, where the contribution to total surplus of the last unit demanded is $\hat{p}_1 - 1 > 0$. ∎

**Example 22.B.4:** *Few Policy Instruments.* In Examples 22.B.2 and 22.B.3 we have assumed that the unrestricted transfer of numeraire across consumers is one of the instruments available to the policy maker. Because of this, in those two examples the UPS had a "full" frontier, that is, a frontier that is an $(I - 1)$-dimensional surface. In addition, quasilinearity insured that this surface was flat (and therefore that the UPS was convex). We now explore the implications of limiting the extent to which the numeraire is transferable.

We assume that we have two goods and that the utility functions of $I$ consumers are quasilinear with respect to the first good (which is untaxed). Arbitrary transfers of numeraire are not permitted, however. The policy maker now has a single instrument: a commodity tax (or subsidy) on the second good. Again, this good can be produced at unit marginal cost. The policy maker's surplus (or deficit) is given back to the consumers *according to some fixed rule* (hence, no arbitrary transfers of numeraire are permitted). Say, to be specific, that this rule is that the surplus–deficit is absorbed by the first consumer. Then the (second-best) UPS is [denoting by $v_i(p_2)$ the indirect utility function of consumer $i$]

$$U = \{u \in \mathbb{R}^I : u \leq (v_1(p_2) + (p_2 - 1) \textstyle\sum_i x_i(p_2), v_2(p_2), \ldots, v_I(p_2)) \text{ for some } p_2 > 0\}.$$

Two points are worth observing. The first is that $U$ does not need to be convex (you should show this in Exercise 22.B.4; recall from Proposition 3.D.3 that the indirect utility functions are quasi-convex. An example is represented in Figure 22.B.3. The second is that $U$ is defined by means of a single parameter, $p_2$, and therefore its Pareto frontier (which, naturally, lies in $\mathbb{R}^I$) is one-dimensional. See Figure 22.B.4 for a case with $I = 3$. This feature is entirely typical. As long as the instruments available to the policymaker are fewer than $I - 1$ in number, the frontier of the UPS cannot be $(I - 1)$-dimensional. Note that when there is free transferability of numeraire across

---

5. More generally, we could think of the market for good 1 as being beyond the control of the policy maker and giving rise, perhaps because of a monopolistic structure, to a price higher than marginal cost.

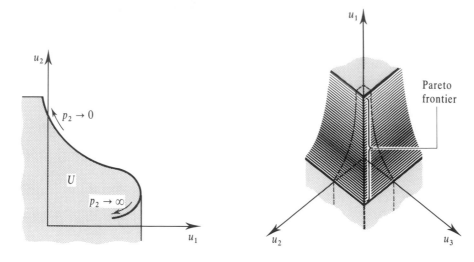

**Figure 22.B.3 (left)**

A nonconvex
second-best utility
possibility set
(Example 22.B.4).

**Figure 22.B.4 (right)**

A second-best utility
possibility set for a
case with few
instruments:
low-dimensional
Pareto frontier
(Example 22.B.4).

the $I$ consumers, this automatically gives us the necessary minimum of $I - 1$ instruments. ∎

**Example 22.B.5:** *First-best Nonconvexities.* In Example 22.B.4 the possible non-convexity of the UPS is due to the second-best nature of this set. If lump-sum transfers of numeraire were allowed, then the corresponding first-best UPS would be convex. Yet a first-best UPS may also be nonconvex. Two familiar sources of nonconvexities in first-best problems are indivisibilities and externalities. As for the first, suppose that there are two locations and two agents with identical locational tastes (in particular, they both prefer the same location). There are only two possible assignments of individuals to locations and therefore the UPS will be as in Figure 22.B.5. As for externalities, suppose that there is a single good and that the utility functions of two consumers are $u_1(x_1) = x_1$ and $u_2(x_1, x_2) = x_2/x_1$. Then the UPS is as in Figure 22.B.6 (see Appendix A of Chapter 11 for more on nonconvexities due to externalities). ∎

Examples 22.B.4 and 22.B.5 have provided instances where the UPS is nonconvex. There is a procedure that permits one, in principle, to convexify the UPS. It consists of allowing the policy maker to randomize over her set of feasible policies. If random outcomes are evaluated by the different agents according to their expected utility (see

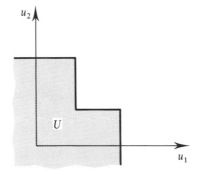

**Figure 22.B.5**

A nonconvex utility
possibility set for a
first-best locational
problem (Example
22.B.5).

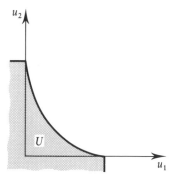

**Figure 22.B.6**

A nonconvex utility possibility set for a first-best problem with externalities (Example 22.B.5).

Chapter 6), then the (expected, or ex ante) UPS is convex since it is just the set of convex combinations of the utility vectors in the UPS associated with deterministic policies. There is no general theoretical reason to prevent the policy making from randomizing. On the other hand, the *practical* admissibility of stochastic policies cannot be decided on a priori grounds either.

We conclude this section with a final example [borrowed from Atkinson (1973)] that highlights the contrast between first-best and second-best problems.

**Example 22.B.6:** *Unproductive Taxation.* Suppose that there are two commodities and two consumers. We call the first commodity "labor", or leisure, and the second the "consumption good." There is a total of one unit of labor which is entirely owned by the first consumer. The consumption good can be produced by the first consumer from labor at a constant marginal cost of 1 (there is also free disposal). The first consumer has a utility function $u_1(x_{11}, x_{21})$ and the second has $u_2(x_{22})$. In Figure 22.B.7 we illustrate the construction of the first-best Pareto frontier for this model. Suppose that $u_1$ is given. Then, subject to attaining the level of utility $u_1$ for consumer 1, we want to give to consumer 2 as much utility as possible. If consumer 1 gets $(\bar{x}_{11}, \bar{x}_{21})$ then the labor supply is $1 - \bar{x}_{11}$ and the amount of consumption good available for consumer 2 is $1 - \bar{x}_{11} - \bar{x}_{21}$. Thus, we should first determine $(\bar{x}_{11}, \bar{x}_{21})$ by minimizing $x_{11} + x_{21}$ subject to $u_1(x_{11}, x_{21}) \geq u_1$, and then let $u_2 = u_2(1 - \bar{x}_{11} - \bar{x}_{21})$.

We now study the second-best problem where consumer 1 cannot be forced to supply labor. The only available policy instrument for providing consumption good

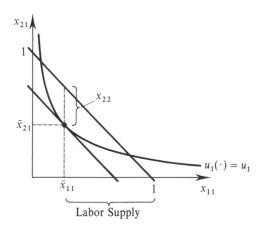

**Figure 22.B.7**

Construction of the first-best Pareto frontier for Example 22.B.6.

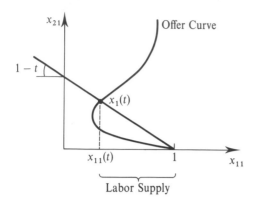

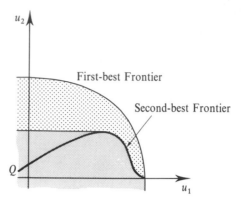

**Figure 22.B.8 (left)**

Construction of the second-best Pareto frontier for Example 22.B.6.

**Figure 22.B.9 (right)**

First-best and second-best utility possibility sets for the unproductive taxation example (Example 22.B.6).

to consumer 2 is a linear tax $t(1 - x_{11})$ on whatever amount of labour the first consumer *decides to supply* given the tax rate. The construction of the second-best frontier is illustrated in Figure 22.B.8. For $t \geq 0$, consumer 1 will choose $x_{11}$ so as to maximize $u_1(x_{11}, (1 - t)(1 - x_{11}))$. Observe that this is as if she had chosen the point in her offer curve corresponding to the price vector $(1, 1/(1 - t))$. Denote this point by $x_1(t) = (x_{11}(t), x_{21}(t))$. The utility of consumer 2 is then $u_2(t(1 - x_{11}(t)))$.

The first-best and second-best UPS are displayed in Figure 22.B.9.[6] In the second-best case the figure also depicts the locus of utility pairs $Q \subset \mathbb{R}^I$ obtained as $t$ ranges from 0 to 1, that is,

$$Q = \{(u_1(x_1(t)), u_2(t(1 - x_{11}(t)))) \in \mathbb{R}^2 : 0 \leq t \leq 1\}.$$

Note that $Q$ does not coincide with the Pareto set of the second-best UPS because it exhibits a characteristic nonmonotonicity. The economic intuition underlying it is clear: if $t$ is low, consumer 2 will get very little of the consumption good; but if $t$ is very high, the situation is not much better. Consumer 2 will now get a large fraction of the labor supplied by consumer 1, but for precisely this reason not much labor will be supplied by consumer 1. ■

We can distill yet another lesson from Example 22.B.6. We see in Figure 22.B.9 that it is quite possible for the first-best and second-best Pareto frontiers to have some points in common; that is, there may well be second-best Pareto optima that are first-best Pareto optima. Yet Figure 22.B.9 tells us that it would be quite silly to select a point in the second-best Pareto frontier merely according to the criterion of proximity to the first-best frontier. The resulting selection may be distributionally very biased.[7] The investigation of more sensible selection criteria will be the purpose of Section 22.C.

---

6. Again, the second-best frontier may or may not be convex.

7. We may add that it may also be uninteresting from the point of view of policy: in Figure 22.B.9 the only second-best policy that yields a first-best result is $t = 0$, that is, no policy at all!

# 22.C Social Welfare Functions and Social Optima

In Section 22.B we described the constraint set of the policy maker, or social planner. The next question is which particular policy is to be selected. The application of the Pareto principle eliminates any policy that leads to utility vectors not in the Pareto frontier. Yet this still leaves considerable room for choice,[8] which, by necessity, must now involve trading off the utility of some agent against that of others. In this section we assume that the policy maker has an explicit and consistent criterion to carry off this task. Specifically, we assume that this criterion is given by a *social welfare function* $W(u) = W(u_1, \ldots, u_I)$ that aggregates individuals' utilities into social utilities. We can imagine that $W(u)$ reflects the distributional value judgments underlying the decisions of the policy maker.[9] In Section 22.E (and subsequent ones) we will discuss a somewhat different approach, one that puts more emphasis on the bargaining, or arbitration, aspects of the determination of the final policy selection.

In the current section, we refrain from questioning the assumption of *interpersonal comparability of utility*, which is implicit in our use of levels of individual utility as arguments in the aggregator function $W(u_1, \ldots, u_I)$. Section 22.D, which links with the analysis of Chapter 21, is devoted to investigating this matter.

Thus, for a given social welfare function $W(\cdot)$ and utility possibility set $U \subset \mathbb{R}^I$, the policy maker's problem is

$$
\begin{aligned}
\text{Max} \quad & W(u_1, \ldots, u_I) \\
\text{s.t.} \quad & (u_1, \ldots, u_I) \in U.
\end{aligned}
\tag{22.C.1}
$$

A vector of utilities, or the underlying policies, solving problem (22.C.1) is called a *social optimum*. If the problem has a second-best nature, and we want to emphasize this fact, then we may refer to a *constrained social optimum*.

We now present and discuss some of the interesting properties that a social welfare function (SWF) may, or may not, satisfy.

(i) *Nonpaternalism.* This first property is already implicit in the concept itself of a SWF. It prescribes that in the expression of social preferences only the individual utilities matter: Two alternatives that are considered indifferent by every agent should also be socially indifferent. The planner does not have direct preferences on the final alternatives.

(ii) *Paretian property.* Granted the previous property, the *Paretian* property is an uncontroversial complement to it. It simply says that $W(\cdot)$ is increasing; that is, if $u_i' \geq u_i$ for all $i$, then $W(u') \geq W(u)$, and if $u_i' > u_i$ for all $i$, then $W(u') > W(u)$. We also say that $W(\cdot)$ is *strictly Paretian* if it is strictly increasing; that is, if $u_i' \geq u_i$ for all $i$ and $u_i' > u_i$ for at least one $i$, then $W(u') > W(u)$. If $W(\cdot)$ is strictly Paretian then a solution to (22.C.1) is necessarily a Pareto optimum.

---

8. Only exceptionally will the Pareto frontier consist of a single point. Recall also that, as we saw in Example 22.B.3, in second-best situations with few instruments, the requirement of Pareto optimality may not succeed in ruling out many policies.

9. This approach to welfare economics was first taken by Bergson (1938) and Samuelson (1947).

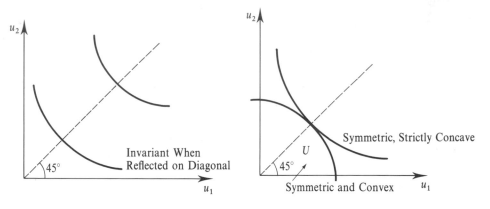

**Figure 22.C.1 (left)**
A symmetric social welfare function.

**Figure 22.C.2 (right)**
The optimum of a symmetric, strictly concave social welfare function on a symmetric and convex utility possibility set is egalitarian.

(iii) *Symmetry.* The *symmetry* property asserts that in evaluating social welfare all agents are on the same footing. Formally, $W(\cdot)$ is symmetric if $W(u) = W(u')$ whenever the entries of the vector $u$ [e.g., $u = (2, 4, 5)$] constitute a permutation of the entries of the vector $u'$ [e.g., $u' = (4, 5, 2)$]. In other words, the names of the agents are of no consequence, only the frequencies of the different utility values matter. The indifference curves of a symmetric $W(\cdot)$ are represented in Figure 22.C.1 for a two-agent case. Geometrically, each indifference curve is symmetric with respect to the diagonal. Note also that, because of this, if the indifference surfaces are smooth then the marginal rates of substitution at any $u = (u_1, \ldots, u_I)$ with identical coordinates are all equal to 1.

(iv) *Concavity.* Finally, a most important property is the *concavity* of $W(\cdot)$. We saw in Chapter 6 that, in the context of uncertainty, the (strict) concavity of a utility function implies an aversion to risk. Similarly, in the current welfare-theoretic context it can be interpreted as an *aversion to inequality* condition. A straightforward way to see this is to simply note that if $W(\cdot)$ is concave and $W(u) = W(u')$, then $W(\frac{1}{2}u + \frac{1}{2}u') \geq W(u)$ [with the inequality strict if $u \neq u'$ and $W(\cdot)$ is strictly concave]. Another is to observe that if the UPS is convex and symmetric, then the utility vector that assigns the same utility value to every agent is a social optimum of any symmetric and concave SWF (see Figure 22.C.2 and Exercise 22.C.1).[10] Thus, with convex UPSs and concave, symmetric SWFs some inequality is called for only if, as will typically be the case, the UPS is not symmetric.

It is to be emphasized that in general, and especially for second-best problems, the UPS may not be convex. This means that even if $W(\cdot)$ is concave the identification of social optima is not an easy task. A utility vector that satisfies the first-order conditions of problem (22.C.1) may not satisfy the second-order conditions or, if it does, it still may not constitute a global maximum.

We can gain further insights by discussing some important instances of social welfare functions.

---

10. The set $U \subset \mathbb{R}^I$ is symmetric if $u \in U$ implies $u' \in U$ for any $u' \in \mathbb{R}^L$ that differs from $u$ only by a permutation of its entries. The interpretation of the symmetry property of a UPS is that there is no bias in the ability to produce utility for different agents. In other words, from the point of view of their possible contributions to social welfare, all agents are identical.

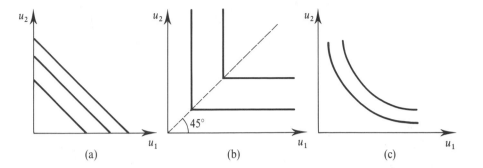

**Figure 22.C.3**
Social welfare
functions.
(a) Purely utilitarian.
(b) Maximin or
Rawlsian.
(c) Generalized
utilitarian.

**Example 22.C.1:** *Utilitarian.* A SWF $W(u)$ is *purely utilitarian* if it has the form $W(u) = \sum_i u_i$ [or, in the nonsymmetric situation, $W(u) = \sum_i \beta_i u_i$]. In this case, the indifference hypersurfaces of $W(\cdot)$ are hyperplanes. They are represented in Figure 22.C.3(a). Note that $W(\cdot)$ is strictly Paretian.

In the purely utilitarian case, increases or decreases in individual utilities translate into identical changes in social utility. The use of the purely utilitarian principle goes back to the very birth of economics as a theoretical discipline. In Exercise 22.C.2 you are asked to develop an interpretation of the purely utilitarian SWF as the expected utility of a single individual "behind the veil of ignorance." Another line of defense, based also on expected utility theory, has been offered by Harsanyi (1955); see Exercise 22.C.3.

Because only the total amount of utility matters, the purely utilitarian SWF is *neutral* towards the inequality in the *distribution of utility*. It is important not to read into this statement more than it says. In particular, it does not say "distribution of wealth." For example, if there is a fixed amount of wealth to be distributed among individuals and these have strictly concave utility functions for wealth, then the purely utilitarian social optimum will be unique and distribute wealth so as to equalize the marginal utility of wealth across consumers. If, say, the utility functions are identical across individuals then this will choose as the unique social optimum the vector in the Pareto frontier that assigns the same utility to every agent (see Exercise 22.C.1 for generalizations). ∎

**Example 22.C.2:** *Maximin.* A SWF is of *maximin* or *Rawlsian type* [because of Rawls (1971)] if it has the form $W(u) = \text{Min}\{u_1, \ldots, u_I\}$ [or, in the nonsymmetric case, $W(u) = \text{Min}\{\beta_1 u_1, \ldots, \beta_I u_I\}$]. In other words, social utility equals the utility value of the worst-off individual. It follows that the social planning problem becomes one of maximizing the utility of the worst-off individual.[11] The (L-shaped) indifference curves of the maximin SWF are represented in Figure 22.C.3(b).

---

11. One could refine this criterion by adopting a *lexical*, or *serial*, maximin decision rule. First maximize the utility of the worst-off, then choose among the solutions of this first problem by maximizing the utility of the next worst-off, and so on. With this, the objectives of the policy maker can still be expressed by a *leximin* social welfare ordering of utility vectors, but the ordering is not continuous and cannot be represented by a SWF (compare with Example 3.C.1). Even so, the refinement is natural and important. For example, we are then guaranteed that the social optimum is a Pareto optimum. You are asked to show all this in Exercise 22.C.4. Note that the maximin SWF is Paretian but not strictly Paretian. This makes for some difficulties. In Figure 22.C.4 the

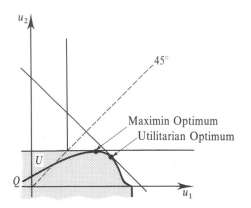

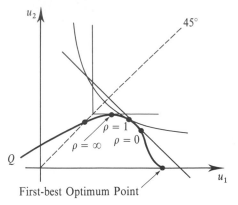

**Figure 22.C.4 (left)**

A maximin optimum for Example 22.B.6.

**Figure 22.C.5 (right)**

Range of generalized utilitarian optima for Example 22.B.6 and the constant elasticity SWF of Example 22.C.4 ($\rho \in [0, \infty]$).

It is reasonably intuitive that this concave SWF will have strong egalitarian implications. In fact, the preference for equality is quite extreme. Suppose, in effect, that $U \in \mathbb{R}^I$ is an arbitrary UPS and that $u \in U$ has all its coordinates equal. Then $u$ fails to be the Rawlsian social optimum only if $u$ is not Pareto optimal. Hence, if there is a $u = (u_1, \ldots, u_I)$ in the Pareto frontier of $U$ with all its coordinates equal, then $u$ is a maximin optimum. Note, in contrast, that for a purely utilitarian SWF we reached the social optimum at complete equality only in the case where $U$ is convex and symmetric. In Figure 22.C.4, which continues the analysis of Example 22.B.6, we depict a situation where maximin optimization leads to the selection of a policy (a tax level) that does not yield complete equality. Nonetheless, even in this case, the purely utilitarian social optimum is significantly more unequal than the maximin optimum. ∎

**Example 22.C.3:** *Generalized Utilitarian.* A SWF is *generalized utilitarian* if it has the form $W(u) = \sum_i g(u_i)$ [or, in the nonsymmetric case, $W(u) = \sum_i g_i(u_i)$], where $g(\cdot)$ is an increasing, concave function. The generalized utilitarian SWF is strictly Paretian and could be regarded as an instance of the purely utilitarian case where the individual utility functions $u_i(\cdot)$ have been replaced by $g(u_i(\cdot))$. This is not, however, a conceptually useful point of view. The point is precisely that, given the individual utility functions, there is a deliberate social decision to attach decreasing social weight to successive units of individual utility. The social indifference curves for this case are represented in Figure 22.C.3(c).

We can also verify in Figure 22.C.4 and 22.C.5 that the equality implications of the generalized utilitarian SWF are intermediate between those of the purely utilitarian and of the maximin SWFs. ∎

**Example 22.C.4:** *Constant Elasticity.* An instance of generalized utilitarian functions that is very useful in applications is provided by the family defined by social utility functions $g(\cdot)$ whose marginal utilities have constant elasticity. This is a family in which attitudes towards inequality can be adjusted by means of a single parameter $\rho \geq 0$.

point at the boundary of $U$ with equal coordinates is a maximin optimum but not a Pareto optimum. In the figure we have selected as "maximin optimum" the leximin optimum (which, by definition, is a maximin optimum itself).

For the rest of the example, individual utility values are restricted to be nonnegative. Then, for any $\rho \geq 0$, we let

and
$$g_\rho(u_i) = (1 - \rho)u_i^{1-\rho} \qquad \text{if } \rho \neq 1,$$
$$g_\rho(u_i) = \ln u_i \qquad \text{if } \rho = 1.$$

Note that, as claimed, the elasticity of $g'_\rho(u_i)$ is constant because we have $u_i g''_i(u_i)/g'_\rho(u_i) = -\rho$ for all values $u_i$. Taking into account that, for $\rho \neq 1$, $h(W) = [1/(1 - \rho)]W^{1/(1-\rho)}$ is an increasing transformation of $W$, we can represent the generalized utilitarian social preferences in a particularly convenient manner as

and
$$W_\rho(u) = (\textstyle\sum_i u_i^{1-\rho})^{1/1-\rho} \qquad \text{for } \rho \neq 1,$$
$$W_\rho(u) = \textstyle\sum_i \ln u_i \qquad \text{for } \rho = 1.$$

Thus, we obtain the CES functions that are well known from demand and production theories (see Exercises 3.C.6 and 5.C.10, respectively). Note that for $\rho = 0$ we get $W_0(u) = \sum_i u_i$, the purely utilitarian case, and as $\rho \to \infty$ we get $W_\rho(u) \to \text{Min}\{u_1, \ldots, u_I\}$, the maximin case. (See Exercise 22.C.5.)

In Figure 22.C.5 we depict the range of solutions to Example 22.B.6 as we vary $\rho$. We see that as the aversion to inequality increases (that is, as $\rho \to \infty$) the optimal tax rate increases. Note, however, that even for very high $\rho$ we do not approach complete equality. On the other hand, none of these second-best solutions corresponds to the point in the Pareto frontier that is also Pareto optimal for the first-best problem. The latter distributes utility so unequally that the equity considerations underlying any symmetric and concave SWF leads us to sacrifice some first-best efficiency for an equity gain. ∎

### The Compensation Principle

We could ask ourselves to what an extent we can do welfare economics *without* social welfare functions. If the purpose of the SWF is the determination of optimal points in a given Pareto frontier, then resorting to them seems indispensable. This is the usage of social welfare functions that we have emphasized up to now; but in practice this is not the only usage. Often, the policy problem is given to us as one of choosing among several different utility possibility sets; these may correspond, for example, to the UPS associated with different levels of a basic policy variable.[12] If we have a social welfare function $W(\cdot)$, then the choice among two utility possibility sets $U$ and $U'$ should be determined by comparing the social utility of the optimum in $U$ with that of the optimum in $U'$. However, even if there is no explicit social welfare function one may attempt to say something meaningful about this problem using revealed preference-like ideas. This is the approach underlying the *compensation principle* (already encountered in Sections 4.D and 10.E).

Let us first take the simplest case: that in which we have two utility possibility sets such that $U \subset U'$. Then one is very tempted to conclude that $U'$ should be preferred to $U$. This would certainly be the case if the points that would be chosen

---

12. Formally, we can reduce this problem to the previous one by considering the overall UPS formed by the union of the UPSs over which we have to choose. But this may not be the most convenient thing to do because it loses the sequential presentation of the problem (first choose among UPS, then choose the utility vector).

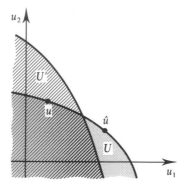

**Figure 22.C.6**

$U'$ passes the weak compensation test over $(U, u)$.

within each of $U$ and $U'$ were the optima of a social welfare function. But even if no social welfare function is available the set $U'$ might still be considered superior to $U$ according to the following *strong compensation test*: For any possible $u \in U$ there is a $u' \in U'$ such that $u_i' \geq u_i$ for every $i$. That is, wherever we are in $U$ it is possible to move to $U'$ and compensate agents in a manner that insures that every agent is made (weakly) better off by the change to $U'$. If the compensation is actually made, so that every agent will indeed be made better off by a switch from $U$ to $U'$, there is no doubt that the switch should be recommended. But if compensation will not occur, matters are not so clear: By choosing $U'$ over $U$ based only on a *potential* compensation we are neglecting quite drastically any distributional implication of the policy change. In fact, it is even possible that the change leads to a purely egalitarian worsening (see Exercise 22.C.6).

Recall from Section 10.D that in the quasilinear case we always have $U \subset U'$ or $U' \subset U$. This is because the boundaries of these sets are hyperplanes determined by the unit vector (hence parallel). In addition, this property also guarantees that the strong compensation criterion (which in Sections 3.D and 10.E we called simply the compensation criterion) coincides with the choice we would make using a purely utilitarian social welfare function. In this quasilinear case, therefore, the strong compensation criterion does not neglect distributional issues to a larger extent than do purely egalitarian social welfare functions.

Matters are more delicate when we compare two utility possibility sets $U$ and $U'$ which are such that one is not included in the other, that is, whose frontiers cross (see Figure 22.C.6). Suppose that we know that the outcome with utility possibility set $U$ is the vector $u \in U$, and that we are considering a move to $U'$.[13] If $u \in U'$, and we were to allocate utility optimally in $U'$ according to a social welfare function, then the move to $U'$ would be advisable. More generally, whenever $u \in U'$, the move from $(U, u)$ to $U'$ passes the following *weak compensation test*: There is a $u' \in U'$ such that $u_i' \geq u_i$ for every $i$. That is, given that we know that the outcome at $U$ is $u$, we could move to $U'$ and compensate every agent in a manner that makes every agent (weakly) better off. In Figure 22.C.6, $U'$ passes the test with respect to $(U, u)$ but not with respect to $(U, \hat{u})$.

Again, if the compensation is actually paid, then the weak compensation criterion

---

13. For example, the original $U$ could correspond to some underlying economy and $u$ could be the utility values of a market equilibrium.

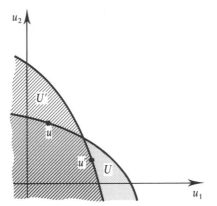

**Figure 22.C.7**

A paradox: $U'$ passes the weak compensation test over $(U, u)$, and $U$ passes the weak compensation test over $(U', u')$.

carries weight. If it is not paid, then it is subject to two serious criticisms. The first is the same as before (it disregards distributional consequences). The second is that it may lead to paradoxes. As in Figure 22.C.7, it is possible to have two utility possibility sets $U$ and $U'$, with respective outcomes $u \in U$ and $u' \in U'$, such that $U'$ passes the weak compensation test over $(U, u)$ and $U$ passes the weak compensation test over $(U', u')$. In Exercise 22.C.7 you are asked to provide a more explicit example of this possibility in an economic context. Further elaborations are contained in Exercise 22.C.8.

# 22.D Invariance Properties of Social Welfare Functions

In this section, we probe deeper into the meaning of the comparisons of individual utilities implicit in the definition of a social welfare function. The significance of the matter derives from the fact that whereas a policy maker may be able to identify individual cardinal utility functions (from revealed risk behavior, say), it may actually do so but only up to a choice of origins and units. Fixing these parameters unavoidably involves making value judgments about the social weight of the different agents. It is therefore worth examining the extent to which such judgments may be avoided. Thus, following an approach to the problem taken by d'Aspremont and Gevers (1977), Roberts (1980), and Sen (1977), we explore such questions as: What are the implications for social decisions of requiring that social preferences be independent of the units, or the origins, of individual utility functions?[14]

To answer these types of questions, we need to contemplate the dependence of social preferences on profiles of individual utility functions. Thus, the social welfare functionals introduced in Chapter 21 provide a natural starting point for our analysis. However, we modify their definition slightly by specifying that individual characteristics are given to us in the form of individual utility functions $\tilde{u}_i(\cdot)$ rather than as individual preference relations.

From now on we are given a set of alternatives $X$. We denote by $\mathcal{U}$ the set of all possible utility functions on $X$, and by $\mathcal{R}$ the set of all possible rational (i.e., complete and transitive) preference relations on $X$.

---

14. In addition to the previous references, you can consult Moulin (1988) for a succinct presentation of the material of this section.

**Definition 22.D.1:** Given a set $X$ of alternatives, a *social welfare functional* $F: \mathscr{U}^I \to \mathscr{R}$ is a rule that assigns a rational preference relation $F(\tilde{u}_1, \ldots, \tilde{u}_I)$ among the alternatives in the domain $X$ to every possible profile of individual utility functions $(\tilde{u}_1(\cdot), \ldots, \tilde{u}_I(\cdot))$ defined on $X$. The strict preference relation derived from $F(\tilde{u}_1, \ldots, \tilde{u}_I)$ is denoted $F_p(\tilde{u}_1, \ldots, \tilde{u}_I)$.[15]

As in Chapter 21, we will concern ourselves only with social welfare functionals that are Paretian.

**Definition 22.D.2:** The social welfare functional $F: \mathscr{U}^I \to \mathscr{R}$ satisfies the (weak) *Pareto property*, or is *Paretian*, if, for any profile $(\tilde{u}_1, \ldots, \tilde{u}_I) \in \mathscr{U}^I$ and any pair $x, y \in X$, we have that $\tilde{u}_i(x) \geq \tilde{u}_i(y)$ for all $i$ implies $x\, F(\tilde{u}_1, \ldots, \tilde{u}_I)\, y$, and also that $\tilde{u}_i(x) > \tilde{u}_i(y)$ for all $i$ implies $x\, F_p(\tilde{u}_1, \ldots, \tilde{u}_I)\, y$.

The first issue to explore is the relationship between these social welfare functionals and the social welfare functions of Section 22.C. A social welfare function $W(\cdot)$ assigns a social utility *value* to profiles $(u_1, \ldots, u_I) \in \mathbb{R}^I$ of individual utility *values*, whereas a social welfare functional assigns social *preferences* to profiles $(\tilde{u}_1, \ldots, \tilde{u}_I)$ of individual utility *functions* (or, in Section 21.C, of individual preference relations). From a social welfare function $W(\cdot)$ we can generate a social welfare functional simply by letting $F(\tilde{u}_1, \ldots, \tilde{u}_I)$ be the preference relation in $X$ induced by the utility function $\tilde{u}(x) = W(\tilde{u}_1(x), \ldots, \tilde{u}_I(x))$. The converse may not be possible, however. In order to be able to "factor" a social welfare functional through a social welfare function, the following necessary condition must, at the very least, be satisfied. Suppose that the profile of utility functions changes, but that the profiles of utility values for two given alternatives remain unaltered; then the social ordering among these alternatives should not change (since the value given by the social welfare function to each alternative has not changed). That is, the social ordering among two given alternatives should depend only on the profiles of individual utility values for these alternatives. Apart from being formulated in terms of utilities, this property is analogous to the pairwise independence condition for social welfare functionals (Definition 21.C.3). We keep the same term and state the condition formally in Definition 22.D.3.

**Definition 22.D.3:** The social welfare functional $F: \mathscr{U}^I \to \mathscr{R}$ satisfies the *pairwise independence condition* if, whenever $x, y \in X$ are two alternatives and $(\tilde{u}_1, \ldots, \tilde{u}_I) \in \mathscr{U}^I$, $(\tilde{u}'_1, \ldots, \tilde{u}'_I) \in \mathscr{U}^I$ are two utility function profiles with $\tilde{u}_i(x) = \tilde{u}'_i(x)$ and $\tilde{u}_i(y) = \tilde{u}'_i(y)$ for all $i$, we have

$$x\, F(\tilde{u}_1, \ldots, \tilde{u}_I)\, y \quad \Leftrightarrow \quad x\, F(\tilde{u}'_1, \ldots, \tilde{u}'_I)\, y.$$

The necessary pairwise independence condition is almost sufficient: In Proposition 22.D.1 we now see that if the number of alternatives is greater than 2, and the Pareto and pairwise independence conditions are satisfied, then we can derive from the social welfare functional a social preference relation defined on profiles $(u_1, \ldots, u_I) \in \mathscr{R}^I$ of utility values.[16] A standard continuity condition then allows us to represent this

---

15. That is, $x\, F_p(\tilde{u}_1, \ldots, \tilde{u}_I)\, y$ if $x\, F(\tilde{u}_1, \ldots, \tilde{u}_I)\, y$ but not $y\, F(\tilde{u}_1, \ldots, \tilde{u}_I)\, x$.

16. In Exercise 22.D.1 you can find examples showing that the Pareto condition and the restriction on the number of alternatives cannot be dispensed with for the result of Proposition 22.D.1.

preference relation by means of a function $W(u_1, \ldots, u_I)$, thereby yielding a social welfare function.

**Proposition 22.D.1:** Suppose that there are at least three alternatives in $X$ and that the Paretian social welfare functional $F: \mathcal{U}^I \to \mathcal{R}$ satisfies the pairwise independence condition. Then there is a rational preference relation $\succsim$ defined on $\mathbb{R}^I$ [that is, on profiles $(u_1, \ldots, u_I) \in \mathbb{R}^I$ of individual utility values] that generates $F(\cdot)$. In other words, for every profile of utility functions $(\tilde{u}_1, \ldots, \tilde{u}_I) \in \mathcal{U}^I$ and for every pair of alternatives $x, y \in X$ we have

$$x\, F(\tilde{u}_1, \ldots, \tilde{u}_I)\, y \quad \Leftrightarrow \quad (\tilde{u}_1(x), \ldots, \tilde{u}_I(x)) \succsim (\tilde{u}_1(y), \ldots, \tilde{u}_I(y)).$$

**Proof:** The desired conclusion dictates directly how $\succsim$ should be constructed. Consider any pair of utility profiles $u = (u_1, \ldots, u_I) \in \mathbb{R}^I$ and $u' = (u'_1, \ldots, u'_I) \in \mathbb{R}^I$. Then we let $u \succsim u'$ if $x\, F(\tilde{u}_1, \ldots, \tilde{u}_I)\, y$ for some pair $x, y \in X$ and a profile $(\tilde{u}_1, \ldots, \tilde{u}_I) \in \mathcal{U}^I$ with $\tilde{u}_i(x) = u_i$ and $\tilde{u}_i(y) = u'_i$ for every $i$. We argue first that the conclusion $u \succsim u'$, is independent of the particular two alternatives and the profile of utility functions chosen. Independence of the utility functions chosen is an immediate consequence of the statement of the pairwise independence condition. Proving independence of the pair chosen is a bit more delicate.

It suffices to show that if we have concluded that $u \succsim u'$ by means of a pair $x, y$ then, for any third alternative $z$ (recall that by assumption there are third alternatives), we obtain the same conclusion using the pairs $x, z$ or $z, y$.[17] We carry out the argument for $x, z$ (in Exercise 22.D.2 you are asked to do the same for $z, y$). To this effect, take a profile of utility functions $(\tilde{u}_1, \ldots, \tilde{u}_I) \in \mathcal{U}^I$ with $\tilde{u}_i(x) = u_i$, $\tilde{u}_i(y) = u'_i$, and $\tilde{u}_i(z) = u'_i$ for every $i$. Because we have concluded that $u \succsim u'$ using the pair $x, y$, we must have $x\, F(\tilde{u}_1, \ldots, \tilde{u}_I)\, y$. By the Pareto property, we also have $y\, F(\tilde{u}_1, \ldots, \tilde{u}_I)\, z$. Hence, by the transitivity of $F(\tilde{u}_1, \ldots, \tilde{u}_I)$, we obtain $x\, F(\tilde{u}_1, \ldots, \tilde{u}_I)\, z$, which is the property we wanted.

It remains to prove that $\succsim$ is complete and transitive. Completeness follows simply from the fact that the preference relation $F(\tilde{u}_1, \ldots, \tilde{u}_I)$ is complete for any $(\tilde{u}_1, \ldots, \tilde{u}_I) \in \mathcal{U}^I$. As for transitivity, let $u \succsim u' \succsim u''$, where $u, u', u'' \in \mathbb{R}^I$. Take three alternatives $x, y, z \in X$ and a profile of utility functions $(\tilde{u}_1, \ldots, \tilde{u}_I) \in \mathcal{U}^I$ with $\tilde{u}_i(x) = u_i$, $\tilde{u}_i(y) = u'_i$, and $\tilde{u}_i(z) = u''_i$ for every $i$. Since $u \succsim u'$ and $u' \succsim u''$, it must be that $x\, F(\tilde{u}_1, \ldots, \tilde{u}_I)\, y$ and $y\, F(\tilde{u}_1, \ldots, \tilde{u}_I)\, z$. Because of the transitivity of $F(u_1, \ldots, u_I)$, this implies $x\, F(\tilde{u}_1, \ldots, \tilde{u}_I)\, z$, and so $u \succsim u''$. Hence, $\succsim$ is transitive. ∎

By the Pareto condition, the social preference relation $\succsim$ obtained in Proposition 22.D.1 is monotone. You are asked to show this formally in Exercise 22.D.3.

**Exercise 22.D.3:** Show that if the social welfare functional $F: \mathcal{U}^I \to \mathcal{R}$ satisfies the Pareto property, then a social preference relation $\succsim$ on utility profiles for which the

---

17. Indeed, suppose that we initially used the pair $(x, y)$. Consider any other pair $(v, w)$. If $v = x$ or $w = y$ then we have just claimed that we get the same ordering between $u$ and $u'$. Hence, let $v \neq x$ and $w \neq y$. If, in addition, $v \neq y$, then we reach the same ordering by the chain of replacements: $(x, y) \to (v, y) \to (v, w)$. Similarly, if $w \neq x$ we can use $(x, y) \to (x, w) \to (v, w)$. There remains the case $(v, w) = (y, x)$. Here we use a third alternative, $z$, and the chain $(x, y) \to (x, z) \to (y, z) \to (y, x)$.

conclusion of Proposition 22.D.1 holds must be monotone in the sense that if $u' \geq u$ then $u' \succsim u$, and if $u' \gg u$ then $u' \succ u$.

The social preference relation $\succsim$ on $\mathbb{R}^I$ obtained in Proposition 22.D.1 need not be continuous or representable by a utility function. Consider, for example, a lexical dictatorship (say that there are two agents and let $u \succ u'$ if $u_1 > u'_1$ or if $u_1 = u'_1$ and $u_2 > u'_2$) and recall from Example 3.C.1 that this type of ordering is not representable by a utility function. Nonetheless, we want to focus on social welfare functions and so from now on we will simply assume that we deal only with social welfare functionals that, in addition to the assumptions of Proposition 22.D.1, yield a continuous social preference relation $\succsim$ on $\mathbb{R}^I$. As in Section 3.C, such a social preference relation can then be represented by a utility function: in fact, a continuous one. This is then our social welfare function $W(u_1, \ldots, u_I)$. Note that any increasing, continuous transformation of $W(\cdot)$ is also an admissible social welfare function.

In summary, we have seen that the existence of a social welfare function generating a given social welfare functional amounts, with some minor qualifications, to the satisfaction of the pairwise independence condition by the social welfare functional. Therefore, we will concern ourselves from now on with a social welfare functional $F: \mathcal{U}^I \to \mathcal{R}$ that can be generated from an increasing and continuous social welfare function $W: \mathbb{R}^I \to \mathbb{R}$, or equivalently, from a monotone and continuous rational preference relation $\succsim$ on $\mathbb{R}^I$. We will discover that, in this context, natural utility invariance requirements on the social welfare functional have quite drastic effects on the form that we can choose for $W(\cdot)$ and, therefore, on the social welfare functional itself.

**Definition 22.D.4:** We say that the social welfare functional $F: \mathcal{U}^I \to \mathcal{R}$ is *invariant to common cardinal transformations* if $F(\tilde{u}_1, \ldots, \tilde{u}_I) = F(\tilde{u}'_1, \ldots, \tilde{u}'_I)$ whenever the profiles of utility functions $(\tilde{u}_1, \ldots, \tilde{u}_I)$ and $(\tilde{u}'_1, \ldots, \tilde{u}'_I)$ differ only by a common change of origin and units, that is, whenever there are numbers $\beta > 0$ and $\alpha$ such that $\tilde{u}_i(x) = \beta \tilde{u}'_i(x) + \alpha$ for all $i$ and $x \in X$. If the invariance is only with respect to common changes of origin (i.e., we require $\beta = 1$) or of units (i.e., we require $\alpha = 0$), then we say that $F(\cdot)$ is *invariant to common changes of origin* or *of units*, respectively.

It is hard to quarrel with the requirement of invariance with respect to common cardinal transformations. Even if the policy maker has the ability to compare the utilities of different agents, the notion of an absolute unit or an absolute zero is difficult to comprehend.

We begin by analyzing the implications of invariance with respect to common changes of origin. Suppose that the social welfare functional is generated from the social welfare function $W(\cdot)$. We claim that the invariance with respect to common changes of origin can hold only if $W(u) = W(u')$ implies $W(u + \alpha e) = W(u' + \alpha e)$ for all profiles of utility values $u \in \mathbb{R}^I$, $u' \in \mathbb{R}^I$ and $\alpha \in \mathbb{R}$, where $e = (1, \ldots, 1)$ is the unit vector. Indeed, let $W(u) = W(u')$ and $W(u + \alpha e) < W(u' + \alpha e)$. Consider a pair $x, y \in X$ and profile $(\tilde{u}_1, \ldots, \tilde{u}_I) \in U^I$ with $\tilde{u}_i(x) = u_i$ and $\tilde{u}_i(y) = u'_i$ for every $i$. Then $x F(\tilde{u}_1, \ldots, \tilde{u}_I) y$. However, $x F(\tilde{u}'_1, \ldots, \tilde{u}'_I) y$ does not hold when $\tilde{u}'_i(\cdot) = \tilde{u}_i(\cdot) + \alpha$, contradicting the invariance to common changes of origin.

Geometrically, the assertion that $W(u) = W(u')$ implies $W(u + \alpha e) = W(u' + \alpha e)$ says that the indifference curves of $W(\cdot)$ are parallel with respect to $e$—they are

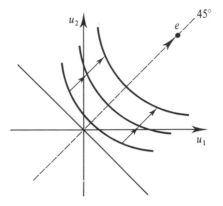

**Figure 22.D.1**

Indifference map of a social welfare function invariant to identical changes of utility origins.

obtained from each other by translations along the $e$ direction (see Figure 22.D.1). In Proposition 23.D.2 [due to Roberts (1980)], we show that this property has an important implication: up to an increasing transformation, the social welfare function can be written as a sum of a purely utilitarian social welfare function and a dispersion term.

**Proposition 22.D.2:** Suppose that the social welfare functional $F: \mathscr{U}^I \to \mathscr{R}$ is generated from a continuous and increasing social welfare function. Suppose also that $F(\cdot)$ is invariant to common changes of origins. Then the social welfare functional can be generated from a social welfare function of the form

$$W(u_1, \ldots, u_I) = \bar{u} - g(u_1 - \bar{u}, \ldots, u_I - \bar{u}), \qquad (22.D.1)$$

where $\bar{u} = (1/I) \sum_i u_i$.

Moreover, if $F(\cdot)$ is also independent of common changes of units, that is, fully invariant to common cardinal transformations, then $g(\cdot)$ is homogeneous of degree one on its domain: $\{s \in \mathbb{R}^I: \sum_i s_i = 0\}$.

**Proof:** By assumption the social welfare functional $F: \mathscr{U}^I \to \mathscr{R}$ can be generated by a continuous and monotone preference relation $\succsim$ on $\mathbb{R}^I$. Moreover the invariance to identical changes of units implies that if $u \sim u'$ then $u + \alpha e \sim u' + \alpha e$ for any $\alpha \in \mathbb{R}$.

We now construct a particular utility function $W(\cdot)$ for $\succsim$. Because of continuity and monotonicity of $\succsim$ there is, for every $u \in \mathbb{R}^I$, a single number $\alpha$ such that $u \sim \alpha e$. Let $W(u)$ denote this number. That is, $W(u)$ is defined by $u \sim W(u)e$. (See Figure 22.D.2 for a depiction.) Because of the monotonicity of preferences, $W(\cdot)$ is a legitimate utility representation for $\succsim$.[18]

The first part of the proof will be concluded if we show that $W(u) - \bar{u}$ depends only on the vector of deviations $(u_1 - \bar{u}, \ldots, u_I - \bar{u}) = u - \bar{u}e$, that is, that if $u - \bar{u}e = u' - \bar{u}'e$ then $W(u) - \bar{u} = W(u') - \bar{u}'$. But this is true because $u \sim W(u)e$ and the invariance to common changes of origin imply that if $u - \bar{u}e = u' - \bar{u}'e$ then

$$u' = u + (\bar{u}' - \bar{u})e \sim W(u)e + (\bar{u}' - \bar{u})e = [W(u) + (\bar{u}' - \bar{u})]e$$

---

18. Up to here this is identical to the parallel construction in consumption theory carried out in Proposition 3.C.1. We refer to the proof of the latter for details.

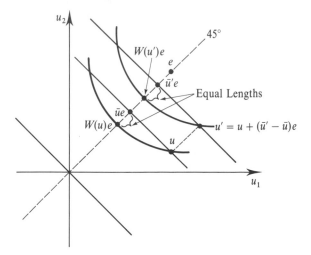

**Figure 22.D.2**

Construction of the social welfare function of form (22.D.1) for the invariant to identical changes of origin case.

and therefore, $W(u') = W(u) + (\bar{u}' - \bar{u})$ as we wanted. The construction is illustrated in Figure 22.D.2.[19]

To prove the second part, suppose that $F(\cdot)$ is also invariant to common changes of units. Because $F(\cdot)$ is generated from $W(\cdot)$, this can only happen if for every $u \sim u'$ and $\beta > 0$ we have $\beta u \sim \beta u'$. But then $u \sim W(u)e$ implies $\beta u \sim \beta W(u)e$, and so $W(\beta u) = \beta W(u)$ for any $u \in \mathbb{R}^I$ and $\beta > 0$. That is, $W(\cdot)$ is homogeneous of degree one, and since $g(\cdot)$ coincides with $-W(\cdot)$ on the domain where $\bar{u} = 0$, we conclude that $g(\cdot)$ is also homogeneous of degree one. ∎

Going further, if the policy maker is not empowered with the ability to compare the absolute levels of utility across consumers, then the social welfare functional must satisfy more demanding invariance notions.

**Definition 22.D.5:** The social welfare functional $F: \mathcal{U}^I \to \mathcal{R}$ *does not allow interpersonal comparisons of utility* if $F(\tilde{u}_1, \ldots, \tilde{u}_I) = F(\tilde{u}'_1, \ldots, \tilde{u}'_I)$ whenever there are numbers $\beta_i > 0$ and $\alpha_i$ such that $\tilde{u}_i(x) = \beta_i \tilde{u}'_i(x) + \alpha_i$ for all $i$ and $x$. If the invariance is only with respect to independent changes of origin (i.e., we require $\beta_i = 1$ for all $i$), or only with respect to independent changes of units (i.e., we require that $\alpha_i = 0$ for all $i$), then we say that $F(\cdot)$ is *invariant to independent changes of origins* or *of units*, respectively.

We have then Proposition 22.D.3.[20]

---

19. We can gain some intuition on the form of this utility function by noticing its similarity to the quasilinear representations in consumer theory. Here we can write any vector $u \in \mathbb{R}^I$ as $u = \bar{u}e + (u - \bar{u}e)$ and indifference sets can be obtained by parallel displacements in the direction $e$. In consumer theory we can write any vector $x \in \mathbb{R}^L$ as $x = (x_1, 0, \ldots, 0) + (0, x_2, \ldots, x_L)$ and indifference sets are parallel in the direction $(1, 0, \ldots, 0)$. Similarly, the conclusion in both cases is that there is a utility function that is linearly additive in the first term (i.e., in the direction in which indifference sets are parallel).

20. See d'Aspremont and Gevers (1977) for more results of this type.

**Proposition 22.D.3:** Suppose that the social welfare functional $F: \mathcal{U}^I \to \mathcal{R}$ can be generated from an increasing, continuous social welfare function. If $F(\cdot)$ is invariant to independent changes of origins, then $F(\cdot)$ can be generated from a social welfare function $W(\cdot)$ of the purely utilitarian (but possibly nonsymmetric) form. That is, there are constants $b_i \geq 0$, not all zero, such that

$$W(u_1, \ldots, u_I) = \sum_i b_i u_i \qquad \text{for all } i. \tag{22.D.2}$$

Moreover, if $F(\cdot)$ is also invariant to independent changes of units [i.e., if $F(\cdot)$ does not allow for interpersonal comparisons of utility], then $F$ is dictatorial: There is an agent $h$ such that, for every pair $x, y \in X$, $\tilde{u}_h(x) > \tilde{u}_h(y)$ implies $x F_p(\tilde{u}_1, \ldots, \tilde{u}_I) y$.

**Proof:** Suppose that $\succsim$ is the continuous preference relation on $\mathbb{R}^I$ that generates the given $F(\cdot)$. For a representation of the form (22.D.2) to exist, we require that the indifference sets of $\succsim$ be parallel hyperplanes. Since we already know from Proposition 22.D.2 that those sets are all parallel in the direction $e$, it suffices to show that they must be hyperplanes, that is, that if we take two $u, u' \in \mathbb{R}^I$ such that $u \sim u'$, then for $u'' = \frac{1}{2}u + \frac{1}{2}u'$ we also have $u'' \sim u \sim u'$.

The invariance of $F(\cdot)$ with respect to independent changes of origins means, in terms of $\succsim$, that for *any* $\alpha \in \mathbb{R}^I$ we have $u + \alpha \succsim u'' + \alpha$ if and only if $u \succsim u''$. Take $\alpha = \frac{1}{2}(u' - u)$. Then $u + \alpha = u''$ and $u'' + \alpha = u'$. Hence, $u \succsim u''$ if and only if $u'' \succsim u'$. If $u \succsim u''$ then $u'' \succsim u'$ and so $u'' \sim u$. If $u'' \succ u$ then $u' \succ u''$ which contradicts $u \sim u'$. We conclude that $u'' \sim u \sim u'$, as we wanted.

Once we know that indifference sets are parallel hyperplanes, the same construction as in the Proof of Proposition 22.D.2 will give us a $W(\cdot)$ of the form (22.D.2). In addition, the Pareto property yields $b_i \geq 0$ for all $i$.

Finally, suppose that $F(\cdot)$ is also invariant to independent changes of units. Then dictatorship follows simply. Choose an agent $h$ with $b_h > 0$. Take $u, u' \in \mathbb{R}^I$ with $u_h > u'_h$. Then, by invariance to independent changes of units, we have that $\sum_i b_i u_i > \sum_i b_i u'_i$ if and only if $b_h u_h + \varepsilon \sum_{i \neq h} b_i u_i > b_h u'_h + \varepsilon \sum_{i \neq h} b_i u'_i$ for any $\varepsilon > 0$. Therefore, since $b_h u_h > b_h u'_h$ we get, by choosing $\varepsilon > 0$ small enough, that $\sum_i b_i u_i > \sum_i b_i u'_i$. Thus, agent $h$ is a dictator (show, in Exercise 22.D.4, that in fact $b_i = 0$ for all $i \neq h$). ∎

We point out that for the dictatorship conclusion of Proposition 22.D.3, it is not necessary that $F(\cdot)$ be generated from a social welfare function. It suffices that it be generated from a social preference relation on $\mathbb{R}^I$.

Proposition 22.D.3 (extended in the manner indicated in the last paragraph) has as a corollary the Arrow impossibility theorem of Chapter 21 (Proposition 21.C.1), which is, in this manner, obtained by a very different methodology. Indeed, suppose that $F(\cdot)$ is a social welfare functional defined, as was done in Chapter 21, on profiles of preference relations $(\succsim_1, \ldots, \succsim_I) \in \mathcal{R}^I$. Then we can construct a social welfare functional $F'(\cdot)$ defined on profiles of utility functions $(\tilde{u}_1, \ldots, \tilde{u}_I) \in \mathcal{U}^I$ by letting $F'(\tilde{u}_1, \ldots, \tilde{u}_I) = F(\succsim_1, \ldots, \succsim_I)$, where $\succsim_i$ is the preference relation induced by the utility function $\tilde{u}_i(\cdot)$. In Exercise 22.D.5 you are asked to verify, first, that $F'(\cdot)$ inherits the Paretian and pairwise independence conditions from $F(\cdot)$, second, that $F'(\cdot)$ does not allow for interpersonal comparisons of utility and, third, that a dictator for $F'(\cdot)$ is a dictator for $F(\cdot)$.

Other invariance properties of social welfare functionals have been found to be of interest. We mention two.

We say that the social welfare functional $F: \mathcal{U}^I \to \mathcal{R}$ is *invariant to common ordinal transformations* if $F(\tilde{u}_1, \ldots, \tilde{u}_I) = F(\tilde{u}'_1, \ldots, \tilde{u}'_I)$ whenever there is an increasing function $\gamma(\cdot)$ such that $\tilde{u}_i(x) = \gamma(\tilde{u}'_i(x))$ for every $x \in X$ and all $i$. The interpretation of this invariance is that although the social planner has no notion of individual utility scales she can, nonetheless, recognize that one individual is better off than another (but the question "by how much?" is meaningless). An example is provided by the social welfare functional induced by the symmetric Rawlsian social welfare function $W(u) = \text{Min} \{u_1, \ldots, u_I\}$. With this SWF, the ordering over policies depends only on the ability to determine the worse-off individual (see Exercise 22.D.8 for further elaboration).

We say that a social welfare function $W(\cdot)$ generating a given social welfare functional $F: \mathcal{U}^I \to \mathbb{R}$ is *independent of irrelevant individuals* if, when we split the set of agents into any two groups, the social preference among utility vectors in one of the groups is independent of the level at which we fix the utilities of the agents in the other group (we should add that, if so desired, the condition can be formulated directly in terms of the social welfare functional). This is a sensible requirement: tt says that the distributional judgments concerning the inhabitants of, say, California, should be independent of the individual welfare levels of the inhabitants of, say, Massachusetts.

As in the formally similar situation in consumer theory (Exercise 3.G.4), a social welfare function for $I > 2$ agents that is continuous, increasing, and independent of irrelevant individuals has, up to an increasing transformation, the *additively separable form* $W(u) = \sum_i g_i(u_i)$; that is, $W(u)$ is generalized utilitarian, possible nonsymmetric. Moreover, under weak conditions it is also true that the only social welfare functions that, up to increasing transformations, both admit an additively separable form and are invariant to common changes of origin are the utilitarian $W(u) = \sum_i b_i u_i$. Thus, from an invariance viewpoint we can arrive at the utilitarian form for a social welfare function by two roads: one, Proposition 22.D.3, is based on invariance to independent changes of origins; the other, just mentioned, is based on independence of irrelevant individuals and invariance to common changes of origins. See Maskin (1978) for more on this.

**Example 22.D.1:** Fix an alternative $x^*$ and define a social welfare functional $F(\cdot)$ by associating to every profile of individual utility functions $(\tilde{u}_1, \ldots, \tilde{u}_I)$ the social preference relation generated by a utility function $V(x) = \sum_i g_i(\tilde{u}_i(x) - \tilde{u}_i(x^*))$. Then, informally, this social welfare functional is both invariant to independent changes of origins and independent of irrelevant individuals, but it is neither utilitarian nor dictatorial. Note, however, that this functional cannot be generated from a social welfare function because it is not pairwise independent: the social preference among two alternatives *may depend on the utility of the third alternative $x^*$.* ∎

# 22.E The Axiomatic Bargaining Approach

In this section, we briefly review an alternative approach to the determination of *reasonable* social compromises. The role of a planner endowed with her own preferences is now replaced by that of an (implicit) *arbitrator* who tries to distribute the gains from trade or, more generally, from cooperation in a manner that reflects "fairly" the bargaining strength of the different agents. The origin of the theory is game-theoretic. However, it sidesteps the construction of explicit noncooperative bargaining games (such as those considered in Appendix A of Chapter 9) by adopting an *axiomatic* point of view. Thus, the approach is more related to ideas of cooperative game theory (as reviewed in Appendix A of Chapter 18).[21]

For current purposes, the description of a *bargaining problem* among $I$ agents is composed of two elements: a *utility possibility* set $U \subset \mathbb{R}^I$ and a *threat*, or *status-quo*, point $u^* \in U$. The set $U$ represents the allocations of utility that can be settled on if there is cooperation among the different agents. The point $u^*$ is the outcome that will occur if there is a breakdown of cooperation. Note that cooperation requires the unanimous participation of all agents, in which case, to repeat, the available utility options are given by $U \subset \mathbb{R}^I$. If one agent does not participate, then the only possible outcome is the vector $u^*$. This setup is completely general with two agents and, because of this, the two-agent case is our central reference case in this section. With more than two agents, the assumption is a bit extreme, since we may want to allow for the possibility of partial cooperation. We take up this possibility in Section 22.F.

Throughout this section we assume that $U \subset \mathbb{R}^I$ is convex and closed and that it satisfies the free disposal property $U - R^I_+ \subset U$ (i.e. if $u' \leq u$ and $u \in U$ then $u' \in U$). As in Definition 22.B.1, $U \subset \mathbb{R}^I$ could be generated from a set of underlying alternatives $X$, which could well include lotteries over deterministic outcomes.[22] For simplicity we also assume that $u^*$ is interior to $U$ and that $\{u \in U: u \geq u^*\}$ is bounded.

**Definition 22.E.1:** A *bargaining solution* is a rule that assigns a solution vector $f(U, u^*) \in U$ to every bargaining problem $(U, u^*)$.[23]

We devote the rest of this section to a discussion of some of the properties one may want to impose on $f(\cdot)$ and to a presentation of four examples of bargaining solutions: the *egalitarian*, the *utilitarian*, the *Nash* and the *Kalai–Smorodinsky solutions*. We should emphasize, however, that a strong assumption has already been built into the formalization of our problem: we are implicitly assuming that the solution depends on the set $X$ of feasible alternatives only through the resulting utility values.

**Definition 22.E.2:** The bargaining solution $f(\cdot)$ is *independent of utility origins* (IUO), or *invariant to independent changes of origins*, if for any $\alpha = (\alpha_1 \ldots, \alpha_I) \in \mathbb{R}^I$ we have

$$f_i(U', u^* + \alpha) = f_i(U, u^*) + \alpha_i \qquad \text{for every } i$$

whenever $U' = \{(u_1 + \alpha_1, \ldots, u_I + \alpha_I): u \in U\}$.

The IUO property says that the bargaining solution does not depend on absolute scales of utility. From now on we assume that this property holds. Note that we therefore always have $f(U, u^*) = f(U - \{u^*\}, 0) + u^*$. This allows us to normalize our problems to $u^* = 0$. From now on we do so and simply write $f(U)$ for $f(U, 0)$.

21. For general introductions to the material of this section, see Roth (1979), Moulin (1988), and Thomson (1995).

22. In principle, the underlying set $X$ and the corresponding utility functions on $X$ could be different for different $U \subset \mathbb{R}^I$. For the theory that follows all that matters is the utility set $U$.

23. Thus, a bargaining solution is a choice rule in the sense of Chapter 1. If an underlying alternative set $X$ is kept fixed and, therefore, the form of $U$, generated as in Definition 22.B.1, depends only on the utility functions, we can also regard the bargaining solution as a choice of function in the sense of Definition 21.E.1.

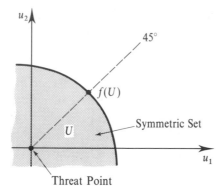

Figure 22.E.1
The symmetry property for bargaining solutions.

It should not be forgotten, however, that a change in the threat point (which will now show up as a change in $U$) will affect the point settled on.

**Definition 22.E.3:** The bargaining solution $f(\cdot)$ is *independent of utility units* (IUU), or *invariant to independent changes of units*, if for any $\beta = (\beta_1, \ldots, \beta_I) \in \mathbb{R}^I$ with $\beta_i > 0$ for all $i$, we have

$$f_i(U') = \beta_i f_i(U) \qquad \text{for every } i$$

whenever $U' = \{(\beta_1 u_1, \ldots, \beta_I u_I): u \in U\}$.[24]

With independence of utility origins (implicitly assumed in Definition 22.E.3), independence of utility units tells us that, although the bargaining solution uses cardinal information on preferences, it does not in any way involve interpersonal comparisons of utilities.

**Definition 22.E.4:** The bargaining solution $f(\cdot)$ satisfies the *Pareto* property (P), or is *Paretian*, if, for every $U$, $f(U)$ is a (weak) Pareto optimum, that is, there is no $u \in U$ such that $u_i > f_i(U)$ for every $i$.

**Definition 22.E.5:** The bargaining solution $f(\cdot)$ satisfies the property of *symmetry* (S) if whenever $U \subset \mathbb{R}^I$ is a symmetric set (i.e., $U$ remains unaltered under permutations of the axes;[25] see Figure 22.E.1), we have that all the entries of $f(U)$ are equal.

The interpretation of the symmetry property is straightforward: if, as reflected in $U$, all agents are identical, then the gains from cooperation are split equally.

**Definition 22.E.6:** The bargaining solution $f(\cdot)$ satisfies the property of *individual rationality* (IR) if $f(U) \geq 0$.

In words: the cooperative solution does not give any agent less than the threat point (recall also that, after normalization, we consider only sets $U$ with $0 \in U$). It is a sensible property: if some agent got less than zero, then she would do better by opting out and bringing about the breakdown of negotiation.

The next property is more substantial.

---

24. Geometrically, $U'$ is obtained from $U$ by stretching the different axes by the rescaling factors $(\beta_1, \ldots, \beta_I)$.

25. More precisely, if $u \in U$ then $u' \in U$ for any $u'$ differing from $u$ only by a permutation of its entries.

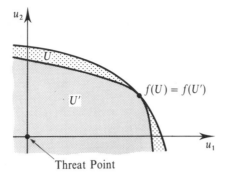

**Figure 22.E.2**

The property of
independence of
irrelevant alternatives
for bargaining
solutions.

**Definition 22.E.7:** The bargaining solution satisfies the property of *independence of irrelevant alternatives* (IIA) if, whenever $U' \subset U$ and $f(U) \in U'$, it follows that $f(U') = f(U)$.

The IIA condition says that if $f(U)$ is the "reasonable" outcome in $U$ and we consider a $U'$ that is smaller than $U$ but retains the feasibility of $f(U)$, that is, we only eliminate from $U$ "irrelevant alternatives," then $f(U)$ remains the reasonable outcome (see Figure 22.E.2). This line of justification would be quite persuasive if we could replace "reasonable" by "best." Indeed, if $f(U)$ has been obtained as the unique maximizer on $U$ of some social welfare function $W(u)$, then the IIA condition is clearly satisfied [if $f(U)$ maximizes $W(\cdot)$ on $U$ then it also maximizes $W(\cdot)$ on $U' \subset U$]. We note that while the converse is not true, it is nonetheless the case that, in practice, the interesting examples where IIA is satisfied involve the maximization of some SWF.

We proceed to present four examples of bargaining solutions. To avoid repetition, we put on record that all of them satisfy the Paretian, symmetry, and individual rationality properties (as well as, by the formulation itself, the independence of utility origins). You are asked to verify this in Exercise 22.E.1. In Exercise 22.E.2 you are asked to construct examples violating some of these conditions.

**Example 22.E.1:** *Egalitarian Solution.* At the egalitarian solution $f_e(\cdot)$, the gains from cooperation are split equally among the agents. That is, for every bargaining problem $U \subset \mathbb{R}^I$, $f_e(U)$ is the vector in the frontier of $U$ with all its coordinates equal. Figure 22.E.3 depicts the case $I = 2$. Note also that, as illustrated in the figure, every $f_e(U)$ maximizes the Rawlsian social welfare function Min $\{u_1, \ldots, u_I\}$ on $U$.

The egalitarian solution satisfies the IIA property (verify this). Clearly, for this olution, utility units are comparable across agents, and so the IUU property is not satisfied.[26] ∎

**Example 22.E.2:** *Utilitarian Solution.* For every $U$ we now let $f_u(U)$ be a maximizer of $\sum_i u_i$ on $U \cap \mathbb{R}^I_+$. If $U$ is strictly convex, then this point is uniquely defined and, therefore, on the domain of strictly convex bargaining problems the IIA property is satisfied. As with the previous example, the solution violates the IUU condition. Figure 22.E.4 illustrates the utilitarian solution in the case $I = 2$. ∎

---

26. Do not forget that the utility values are not absolute values but rather utility differences from the threat point. It is because of this that changes of origins do not matter.

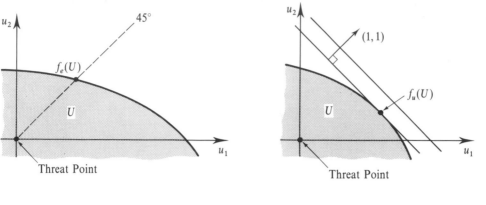

**Figure 22.E.3 (left)**

The egalitarian solution for bargaining problems.

**Figure 22.E.4 (right)**

The utilitarian solution for bargaining problems.

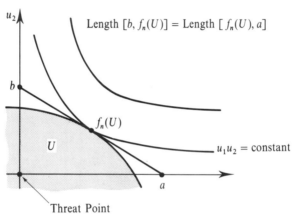

**Figure 22.E.5**

The Nash solution for bargaining problems.

**Example 22.E.3:** *Nash Solution.* For this solution, we take a position intermediate between the two previous examples by requiring that $f_n(U)$ be the point in $U \cap \mathbb{R}_+^I$ that maximizes the product of utilities $u_1 \times \cdots \times u_I$, or, equivalently, that maximizes $\sum_i \ln u_i$ (this corresponds to the case $\rho = 1$ in Example 22.C.4). In Figure 22.E.5, we provide an illustration for $I = 2$. In this case, the Nash solution has a simple geometry: $f_n(U)$ is the boundary point of $U$ through which we can draw a tangent line with the property that its midpoint in the positive orthant is precisely the given boundary point $f_n(U)$; see Exercise 22.E.3.

As with the egalitarian and the utilitarian examples, the Nash solution satisfies the IIA property (because it is defined by the maximization of a strictly concave function). Interestingly, and in contrast to those solutions, *the condition of independence of utility units* (IUU) *holds for the Nash solution.* To see this, note that $\sum_i \ln u_i \geq \sum_i \ln u_i'$ is equivalent to $\sum_i \ln \beta_i u_i = \sum_i \ln u_i + \sum_i \ln \beta_i \geq \sum_i \ln u_i' + \sum_i \ln \beta_i = \sum_i \ln \beta_i u_i'$ for any constants $\beta_i > 0$. The Nash solution is therefore invariant to whatever origins or units we wish to fix. It depends only on the cardinal characteristics of the utility functions of the agents over the underlying set of alternatives.

There is a way to view the Nash solution as a synthesis of the egalitarian and the utilitarian solutions designed to accomplish the invariance to units: *Given a bargaining problem U, the Nash solution is the only utility outcome that, for some rescaling of units of utility, coincides simultaneously with the utilitarian and the egalitarian solutions.* More formally, suppose that

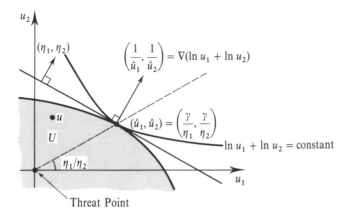

**Figure 22.E.6**

For some rescaling factors $(\eta_1, \eta_2)$ the Nash solution is simultaneously egalitarian and utilitarian.

$\eta_i > 0$ are transformation rates of the given units into new units comparable across agents. If the utilitarian and the egalitarian solutions coincide when applied to the rescaled $U'$ $(= \{(\eta_1 u_1, \ldots, \eta_I u_I) : (u_1, \ldots, u_I) \in U \})$ then the chosen point $\hat{u} \in U$ must be such that, first, it maximizes $\sum_i \eta_i u_i$ on $U$ and, second, for some $\gamma > 0$ it satisfies $\eta_1 \hat{u}_1 = \cdots = \eta_I \hat{u}_I = \gamma$, that is, $\eta_i = \gamma(1/\hat{u}_i)$ for every $i$. Consider now any $u' \in U$. We have $\sum_i \eta_i u_i' \leq \sum_i \eta_i \hat{u}_i$ and therefore $\sum_i (1/\hat{u}_i) u_i' \leq \sum_i (1/\hat{u}_i) \hat{u}_i$. Since $(1/\hat{u}_1, \ldots, 1/\hat{u}_I)$ is the gradient of the concave function $\sum_i \ln u_i$ at $(\hat{u}_1, \ldots, \hat{u}_I)$, this implies $\sum_i \ln u_i' \leq \sum_i \ln \hat{u}_i$ (see Section M.C of the Mathematical Appendix). Hence $\hat{u}$ maximizes $\sum_i \ln u_i$ on $U$, that is, $\hat{u} = f_n(U)$.[27] See Figure 22.E.6 for an illustration of the argument. In Exercise 22.E.3 you should show the converse—that the Nash solution is simultaneously utilitarian and egalitarian for appropriate choice of units.

∎

The Nash solution was proposed by Nash (1950), who also established the notable fact that it is the only solution that satisfies all the conditions so far.

**Proposition 22.E.1:** The Nash solution is the only bargaining solution that is independent of utility origins and units, Paretian, symmetric, and independent of irrelevant alternatives.[28]

**Proof:** We have already shown in the discussion of Example 22.E.4 that the Nash solution satisfies the properties claimed.

To establish the converse, suppose we have a candidate solution $f(\cdot)$ satisfying all the properties. By the independence of utility origins, we can assume, as we have done so far, that $f(\cdot)$ is defined on sets where the threat point has been normalized to the origin. Given now an arbitrary $U$, let $\hat{u} = f_n(U)$ and consider the sets

$$U' = \{u \in \mathbb{R}^I : \sum_i u_i / \hat{u}_i \leq I\} \qquad \text{and} \qquad U'' = \{u \in \mathbb{R}^I : \sum_i u_i \leq I\}.$$

27. To repeat in more geometric terms: the hyperplane with normal $(\eta_1, \ldots, \eta_I)$ passing through $\hat{u}$ leaves $U$ below it (because of the utilitarian property). Thus, it suffices to show that the set $\{u : \sum_i \ln u_i \leq \sum_i \ln \hat{u}_i\}$ lies above the hyperplane. But note that this follows from the fact that, because of the egalitarian property, $(\eta_1, \ldots, \eta_I)$ is proportional to $(1/\hat{u}_1, \ldots, 1/\hat{u}_I)$, which is the gradient of the concave function $\sum_i \ln u_i$ at $\hat{u}$.

28. Note that we do not assume individual rationality explicitly: tt turns out to be implied by the other conditions.

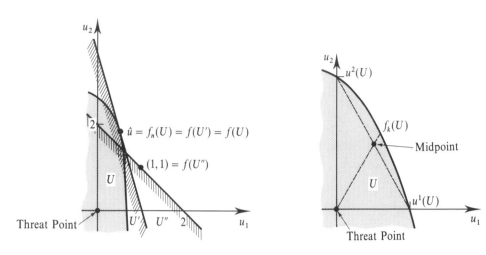

**Figure 22.E.7 (left)**
The Nash solution is determined uniquely from the independence of utility origins and units, symmetry, Pareto, and independence of irrelevant alternatives properties (Proposition 22.E.1).

**Figure 22.E.8 (right)**
The Kalai–Smorodinsky solution for bargaining problems.

See Figure 22.E.7 for an illustration in the case $I = 2$. Note that $U \subset U'$ because the concave function $\sum_i \ln u_i$ has gradient $(1/\hat{u}_1, \ldots, 1/\hat{u}_I)$ at $\hat{u}$, the point where it reaches its maximum value in the convex set $U$. The set $U''$ is symmetric and, therefore, by the symmetry and Paretian properties, we conclude that $f(U'') = (1, \ldots, 1)$. By the independence of utility units, it then follows that $f(U') = (\hat{u}_1, \ldots, \hat{u}_I) = \hat{u}$ [observe that $u \in U''$ if and only if $(\hat{u}_1 u_1, \ldots, \hat{u}_I u_I) \in U'$]. Finally, since $\hat{u} \in U$ and $U \subset U'$, the independence of irrelevant alternatives property yields $f(U) = \hat{u} = f_n(U)$, which is the result we wanted. ∎

**Example 22.E.4:** *Kalai–Smorodinsky Solution.* This will be an example of a solution that does not satisfy the independence of irrelevant alternatives property. It was proposed by Kalai and Smorodinsky (1975). Given a bargaining problem $U \subset \mathbb{R}^I$, denote by $u^i(U) \in \mathbb{R}$ the maximum utility value that agent $i$ could attain by means of some vector in $U \cap \mathbb{R}^I_+$. See Figure 22.E.8 for the case $I = 2$. To motivate the solution suppose that agent $i$ has all the bargaining power (i.e., she can make a take-or-leave offer to the remaining agents). Then the outcome would give $u^i(U)$ to agent $i$ and nothing to the remaining ones.[29] Hence, we could regard the numbers $u^i(U)$ as rough measures of the contributions of the respective agents to the cooperative endeavor and argue, perhaps, that if cooperation takes place then the solution should be the Pareto optimal allocation where the utilities of the different agents are proportional to $(u^1(U), \ldots, u^I(U))$; in other words, where utilities are proportional to the expected utilities that would obtain if we chose with equal probability the agent making a take-or-leave offer. This is precisely the Kalai–Smorodinsky solution $f_k(U)$. Its construction is indicated in Figure 22.E.8.

The Kalai–Smorodinsky solution satisfies the Paretian and the symmetry properties. As with the Nash solution, *it does not involve interpersonal comparisons of utilities.* However, it is different from the Nash solution and, therefore (by Proposition 22.E.1), it cannot satisfy the IIA property. In Exercise 22.E.4 you are asked to verify all this. ∎

---

29. We neglect cases where the utility vector that gives $u^i(U)$ to agent $i$ and nothing to the remaining ones is Pareto dominated.

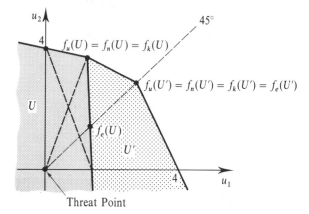

**Figure 22.E.9**

Lack of monotonicity of the utilitarian, Nash, and Kalai–Smorodinsky bargaining solutions.

The conditions summarized so far are by no means an exhaustive list of the properties that have been found to be of interest in the study of the bargaining problem. We conclude with a few informal comments about some others.

(i) *Linearity, or decomposability, properties.* Suppose that given two bargaining problems, $U \subset \mathbb{R}^I$ and $U' \subset \mathbb{R}^I$, we consider $\alpha U + (1 - \alpha)U' \subset \mathbb{R}^I$, for $\alpha \in [0, 1]$; we may think of this as, for example, a randomization between the two problems. Then we may want $f(\alpha U + (1 - \alpha)U') = \alpha f(U) + (1 - \alpha)f(U')$; that is, we may wish that all agents be indifferent between coming to a settlement before or after the resolution of uncertainty. This is a strong requirement, and none of the solutions we have studied satisfies it. In fact, it can be shown that, essentially (i.e., with a few other weak conditions), it is only satisfied by the modified version of the utilitarian solution that does not impose individual rationality. The same conclusion is reached if we consider $U + U'$ and ask that the overall settlement $f(U + U')$ equals the sequential settlement $f(U' + \{f(U)\}, f(U))$. Recall that by the IUO condition the last expression equals $f(U') + f(U)$.

(ii) *Monotonicity properties.* A bargaining solution $f(\cdot)$ is *monotone* if $f(U) \leq f(U')$ whenever $U \subset U'$, that is, if whenever the utility possibility set expands (keeping the threat point fixed at the origin), it is to everyone's advantage. The monotonicity requirement is stronger than may appear at first sight because the utility possibility set may expand in ways that are very asymmetric across agents. In fact, you can verify in Figure 22.E.9 that neither the utilitarian, nor the Nash, nor the Kalai–Smorodinsky solutions satisfy monotonicity. On the other hand, the egalitarian solution clearly does. In Exercise 22.E.5 you are invited to verify that the egalitarian solution is essentially the only symmetric and Paretian bargaining solution that satisfies the monotonicity condition. In Exercise 22.E.6 you can also check that the Kalai–Smorodinsky solution for $I = 2$ is characterized, with the IUO, IUU, P, and S properties, by a certain condition of partial monotonicity.

(iii) *Consistency properties.* This type of property concerns the mutual fit of the bargaining solutions when we apply them to problems with different numbers of agents. Let $f^I(\cdot)$ be a family of bargaining solutions (one for every set of agents $I$). Suppose, to be specific, that we start with $I = \{1, 2, 3\}$. Take any $i$, say $i = 1$, and imagine that, conditional on final cooperation, we give agent 1 the utility level $f_1^I(U)$, but that after making this commitment we reopen the negotiation between the two remaining agents. These two agents then have to find a settlement between themselves in the set $U' = \{(u_2, u_3): (f_1^I(U), u_2, u_3) \in U\} \subset \mathbb{R}^2$. It is then natural to apply the solution in our family, that is, $f^{I\backslash\{1\}}(U')$. Our family is consistent if

$f^{I\setminus\{1\}}(U') = (f_2^I(U), f_3^I(U))$. In words: the renegotiation leads exactly to the outcome of the initial negotiation. The utilitarian and the Nash solution are consistent (in general, any solution obtained by maximizing a generalized utilitarian SWF is consistent; see Exercise 22.E.7). The Kalai–Smorodinski solution is not (verify this in Exercise 22.E.8). It is an interesting, and nontrivial, fact that the consistency axiom can be used instead of IIA in the characterization of the Nash solution [see Lensberg (1987) and Thomson and Lensberg (1992)].

# 22.F  Coalitional Bargaining: The Shapley Value

The analysis of Section 22.E is limited in one important respect: it does not contemplate the possibility of situations intermediate between the full cooperation of all agents and the complete breakdown represented by the threat-point outcome. When there are more than two agents this is definitely restrictive. In this section, we make allowance for the possibility of *partial cooperation* and discuss how this may influence the eventual distribution of the gains from cooperation.

We are given a set $I$ of agents and we proceed by specifying a possible set of utility outcomes to every potential subset of cooperators $S \subset I$. When $S \neq I$ these utility outcomes are interpreted as a description of what may occur if bargaining breaks down and the members of $S$ end up cooperating among themselves. For the purpose of simplicity, we limit ourselves to the case where utility is comparable across agents (we fix individual units to have the same social utility value) and freely transferable among them. We can then represent the total amount of utility available to the members of $S \subset I$, if they cooperate, by a number $v(S)$ or, equivalently, by the utility possibility set $\{u \in \mathbb{R}^S : \sum_{i \in S} u_i \leq v(S)\}$. In cooperative game theory, which we reviewed in Appendix A of Chapter 18, the rule that assigns $v(S)$ to every $S \subset I$ is known as a *game in characteristic form*, a subset $S \subset I$ is usually referred to as a *coalition*, and the number $v(S)$ is known as the *worth* of the coalition $S$.

The situation in which there are no gains from partial cooperation is captured by a characteristic form where $v(S) = \sum_{i \in S} v(i)$ for every $S \neq I$. When we interpret the vector $(v(1), \ldots, v(I))$ as the threat point, this situation reduces to the bargaining problem studied in Section 22.E. In the current world of transferable utility, the egalitarian, Nash, and Kalai–Smorodinsky bargaining solutions[30] lead to the same proposal: The gains from cooperation should be split equally among the agents; that is, agent $i \in I$ should get

$$v(i) + \frac{1}{I}\left(v(I) - \sum_{h \in I} v(h)\right).$$

In fact, any bargaining solution that is independent of utility origins, Paretian, and symmetric makes this recommendation (Exercise 22.F.1).

The question we will try to answer in this section is the following: *Assume that, in an environment of games in characteristic form, all the members of $I$ decide on cooperation, and therefore on distributing $v(I)$ among themselves. What is then the proper generalization of the equal split solution?* It stands to reason that the solution will have to reflect, in some manner, the numbers $v(S)$, $S \subset I$, since these incorporate

---

30. The utilitarian solution is not uniquely defined in the transferable utility case.

the information on how valuable the contribution of a particular agent is compared to that of another.

**Definition 22.F.1:** Given the set of agents $I$, a *cooperative solution* $f(\cdot)$ is a rule that assigns to every game $v(\cdot)$ in characteristic form a utility allocation $f(v) \in \mathbb{R}^I$ that is feasible for the entire group, that is, such that $\sum_i f_i(v) \leq v(I)$.

Reiterating the analytical strategy of Section 22.E, we continue by stating a number of desirable properties for a solution. The first three are merely variations of properties already encountered above.

**Definition 22.F.2:** The cooperative solution $f(\cdot)$ is *independent of utility origins and of common changes of utility units* if, whenever we have two characteristic forms $v(\cdot)$ and $v'(\cdot)$ such that $v(S) = \beta v'(S) + \sum_{i \in S} \alpha_i$ for every $S \subset I$ and some numbers $\alpha_1, \ldots, \alpha_I$, and $\beta > 0$, it follows that $f(v) = \beta f(v') + (\alpha_1, \ldots, \alpha_I)$.

From now on we assume the property of Definition 22.F.2. Because of it we can, in particular, normalize $v(\cdot)$ to $v(i) = 0$ for all $i$.

**Definition 22.F.3:** The cooperative solution $f(\cdot)$ is *Paretian* if $\sum_i f_i(v) = v(I)$, for every characteristic form $v(\cdot)$.

**Definition 22.F.4:** The cooperative solution $f(\cdot)$ is *symmetric* if the following property holds: Suppose that two characteristic forms, $v(\cdot)$ and $v'(\cdot)$ differ only by a permutation $\pi: I \to I$ of the names of the agents; that is, $v'(S) = v(\pi(S))$ for all $S \subset I$. Then the solution also differs only by this permutation; that is, $f_i(v') = f_{\pi(i)}(v)$ for all $i$.

The property defined next, in Definition 22.F.5, underlines the fact that we are trying to solve not the welfare-theoretic problem of distributing total utility equitably but rather the more limited problem of distributing equitably the *surplus* that can be attributed to the cooperation among agents, given the realities of the particular bargaining situation captured by the characteristic form.

**Definition 22.F.5:** The cooperative solution $f(\cdot)$ satisfies the *dummy axiom* if, for all games $v(\cdot)$ and all agents $i$ such that $v(S \cup \{i\}) = v(S)$ for all $S \subset I$, we have $f_i(v) = v(i)$ $(= 0)$. In words: If agent $i$ is a *dummy* (i.e., does not contribute anything to any coalition), then agent $i$ does not receive any share of the surplus.

There are a number of cooperative solutions that satisfy the above properties. The most important is the *Shapley value* [proposed by Shapley (1953)]. We refer to Appendix A of Chapter 18 on cooperative game theory for examples, motivation, and extended discussion of this concept. Here we limit ourselves to offering a definition.

Suppose that we consider an arbitrary ordering of the agents or, formally, an arbitrary permutation $\pi$ of the names $\{1, \ldots, I\}$. Then

$$g_{v,\pi}(i) = v(\{h: \pi(h) \leq \pi(i)\}) - v(\{h: \pi(h) < \pi(i)\})$$

represents how much agent $i$ contributes when she joins the group of her predecessors in the ordering. This is the amount the predecessors would agree to pay $i$ if she had all the negotiating power, that is, if she could make a take-it-or-leave-it offer.[31] Note that $\sum_i g_{v,\pi}(i) = v(I)$ for all permutations $\pi$.

The agents do not come to us ordered. They all stand on the same footing. We may account for this by giving every agent the same chance of being in any position, thereby making all positions equally likely. Equivalently, we could take the (equal weighting) average of agent $i$ contributions over all permutations $\pi$ (there are $I!$ of these). This is precisely the Shapley value solution.

**Definition 22.F.6:** The Shapley value solution $f_s(\cdot)$ is defined by

$$f_{si}(v) = \frac{1}{I!} \sum_\pi g_{v,\pi}(i) \qquad \text{for every } i. \tag{22.F.1}$$

It is simple to verify that $f_s(\cdot)$ satisfies all the properties listed so far (see Exercise 22.F.2). For further discussion, see Exercises 22.F.3 and 22.F.4 (and, to repeat, Appendix A of Chapter 18). In Exercise 22.F.5 we describe another cooperative solution (the nucleolus).

---

### The Cost-Allocation Problem

The following discussion is in the nature of an appendix as there is no immediate conceptual connection with the previous material. The link is that we again make use of the Shapley value.[32]

Suppose that we have a set $I$ of *projects* and that a policy decision to carry them forward has already been taken. For some reason (e.g., accounting or financing rules), the total cost $C(I)$ must be allocated exactly to the different projects; that is, we must specify $(c_1, \ldots, c_I)$ such that $\sum_i c_i = C(I)$. What is a reasonable way to determine such *cost allocation rules*? This is the cost-allocation problem.

We must first of all emphasize that, from the point of view of first-best optimality, the cost allocation rules *should not* be used to guide investment, that is, to decide which projects to carry out. Loosely speaking, we have seen in Section 16.G that the correct efficiency prices for inputs (note that we can think of projects as inputs to the production function for welfare) do not need to cover total cost exactly (see Exercises 22.F.6 and 22.F.7). Because we wish to avoid the temptation to use cost allocation rules in this way we insist that the set of projects to be implemented be exogenously given.

An alternative would be to recognize that the cost-covering constraint confers to the welfare problem a second-best nature. That is, we could attempt to maximize social welfare subject to the condition that input (i.e., project) prices must be fixed at levels that exactly cover costs. This approach was taken by Boiteux (1956) in the context of the theory of the regulated firm, and the solution is closely related to Ramsey pricing (see Example 22.B.2 and Exercise 22.F.6).

Any welfare-theoretic approach, however, would need to use information on individual preferences. If this cannot, or should not, be done, we are still left with an unresolved the problem. A suggested approach proceeds then as follows: suppose that we have information on the cost of every subset of projects (this is far from an innocuous demand); that is, we know $C(T)$ for every $T \subset I$. Then, formally, $C(\cdot)$ is a cooperative game in characteristic form

---

31. In other words, an offer that, if rejected by some predecessor, would permanently preclude the possibility of agent $i$ or any successor from joining the coalition of the predecessors. To verify the informal claim that the offer will be $g_{v,\pi}(i)$, determine how much the last agent in the ordering will get and proceed by backward induction.

32. See Young (1994) for an introductory account to cost-allocation and related problems.

and we could resort to the Shapley value as a way to split $C(I)$ among the different projects. An example may help to clarify the point.

**Example 22.F.1:** This is a favorite example for academics. A professor of economics based in the United States is planning a grand tour of Europe that will take her to three universities, one in Britain (B), one in Spain (S), and one in Germany (G). The total air fare comes to 1600 dollars. How is this to be reimbursed by the three institutions? Suppose that after some research it turns out that $C(\text{B}) = C(\text{S}) = C(\text{G}) = 800$, $C(\text{BS}) = C(\text{BG}) = 1000$, and $C(\text{SG}) = 1400$. The Shapley value calculation (carry it out!) then gives $c_B = 400$ and $c_S = c_G = 600$. This split does indeed seem to reflect well the comparative ease of managing a side trip to Britain if already going to some of the other destinations. ∎

# REFERENCES

d'Aspremont, C., and L. Gevers. (1977). Equity and the informational basis of collective choice. *Review of Economic Studies* **44**: 199–209.

Atkinson, A. (1973). How progressive should income-tax be? In *Economic Justice, Selected Readings*, edited by E. Phelps. London: Penguin Books.

Atkinson, A., and J. Stiglitz. (1980). *Lectures on Public Economics*. New York: McGraw-Hill.

Bergson, A. (1938). A reformulation of certain aspects of welfare economics. *Quarterly Journal of Economics* **52**: 310–34.

Boiteux, M. (1956). Sur la gestion des monopoles publiques astreints à l'équilibre budgétaire. *Econometrica* **24**: 22–40. [Translated in *Journal of Economic Theory* (1991) **3**: 219–40.]

Harsanyi, J. (1955). Cardinal welfare, individual ethics, and interpersonal comparability of utility. *Journal of Political Economy* 61: 309–21. [Also in Phelps (1973).]

Guesnerie, R. (1995). *A Contribution to the Pure Theory of Taxation*, Cambridge, U.K.: Cambridge University Press.

Kalai, E., and M. Smorodinsky. (1975). Other solutions to Nash's bargaining problem. *Econometrica* **43**: 513–18.

Laffont, J.-J. (1988). *Fundamentals of Public Economics*. Cambridge, Mass.: MIT Press.

Lipsey, R. C., and K. Lancaster. (1956). The general theory of the second best. *Review of Economic Studies* **24**: 11–32.

Lensberg, T. (1987). Stability and collective rationality. *Econometrica* **55**: 935–62.

Maskin, E. (1978). A theorem on utilitarianism. *Review of Economic Studies* **42**: 93–96.

Moulin, H. (1988). *Axioms of Cooperative Decision Making*. Cambridge, U.K.: Cambridge University Press.

Nash, J. F. (1950). The bargaining problem. *Econometrica* **28**: 155–62.

Phelps, E., ed. (1973). *Economic Justice, Selected Reading*. London: Penguin Books.

Ramsey, F. (1927). A contribution to the theory of taxation. *Economic Journal* **37**: 47–61.

Rawls, J. (1971). *A Theory of Justice*. Cambridge, Mass.: Harvard University Press.

Roberts, K. (1980). Possibility theorems with interpersonally comparable welfare levels. *Review of Economic Studies* **47**: 409–20.

Roth, A. (1979). *Axiomatic Models of Bargaining*. New York: Springer-Verlag.

Samuelson, P. (1947). *Foundations of Economic Analysis*. Cambridge, Mass.: Harvard University Press.

Sen, A. (1977). On weights and measures: informational constraints in social welfare analysis. *Econometrica* **45**: 1539–72.

Shapley, L. (1953). A value for *n*-person games. In *Contributions to the Theory of Games II. Annals of Mathematics Studies*, 28, edited by H. Kuhn, and A. Tucker. Princeton, N.J.: Princeton University Press.

Starrett, D. A. (1988). *Foundations of Public Economics*. Cambridge, U.K.: Cambridge University Press.

Thomson, W., and T. Lensberg. (1992). *The Theory of Bargaining with a Variable Number of Agents*. Cambridge, U.K.: Cambridge University Press.

Thomson, W. (1995). Cooperative models of bargaining. In *Handbook of Game Theory*, Vol. II, edited by
    R. Aumann, and S. Hart. Amsterdam: North-Holland.
Young, H. P. (1994). *Equity. In Theory and Practice*. Princeton, N.J.: Princeton University Press.

## EXERCISES

**22.B.1**[A] Give sufficient conditions for the convexity of the first-best utility possibility set in the context of the exchange economies of Example 22.B.1.

**22.B.2**[A] Derive the first-order conditions stated in Example 22.B.2.

**22.B.3**[A] Derive the first-order conditions (22.B.2) of Example 22.B.3.

**22.B.4**[B] Show as explicitly as you can that the utility possibility set of Example 22.B.4 may not be convex.

**22.C.1**[A] Suppose that the utility possibility set $U \subset \mathbb{R}^I$ is symmetric and convex. Show that the social optimum of an increasing, symmetric, strictly concave social welfare function $W(\cdot)$ assigns the same utility values to every agent. [Note: A set $U$ is symmetric if $u \in U$ implies $u' \in U$ for any $u'$ obtained from $u$ by a permutation of its entries.] Observe that the same conclusion obtains if $W(\cdot)$ is allowed to be just concave, as in the utilitarian case, but $U$ is required to be strictly convex.

**22.C.2**[A] Suppose that we contemplate a decision maker in an original position (or *ex-ante*, or *behind the veil of ignorance*) before the occurrence of a state of the world that will determine which of $I$ possible identities the decision maker will have. There is a finite set $X_i$ of possible final outcomes in identity $i$. Denote $X = X_1 \times \cdots \times X_I$.

(a) Appeal to the theory of state-dependent utility presented in Section 6.E to justify a utility function on $X$ of the form

$$U(x_1, \ldots, x_I) = u_1(x_1) + \cdots + u_I(x_I).$$

Interpret and discuss the implications of this utility function for the usage of a purely utilitarian social welfare function.

(b) Suppose that $X_1 = \cdots = X_I$ and the preference relation on $X$ defined by the utility function in (a) is symmetric. What does this imply for the form of the utility function? Discuss and interpret.

**22.C.3**[B] We have $N$ final social outcomes and we consider a set of alternatives $X$ that is the set of lotteries over these outcomes. An alternative can be represented by the list of probabilities assigned to the different final outcomes, that is, $p = (p_1, \ldots, p_N)$ where $p_n \geq 0$ for every $n$ and $p_1 + \cdots + p_N = 1$.

We assume that we are given a social preference relation $\succsim$ on $X$ that is continuous and conforms to the independence axiom. Thus, it can be represented by a utility function of the expected utility form

$$U(p) = u_1 p_1 + \cdots + u_N p_N.$$

From now on we assume that this social utility function $U(\cdot)$ defined on $X$ is given.

(a) Suppose that there are two final outcomes and that they are specified by which of two individuals will receive a certain indivisible object. Suppose also that social preferences are symmetric in the sense that there is social indifference between the lottery that gives the object to individual 1 for sure and the lottery that gives the object to individual 2 for sure. Show that all the lotteries must then be socially indifferent. Discuss and interpret this conclusion.

Is it plausible to you? If you wanted to escape from it, how would you do it? What does this all say about the independence axiom as applied to social decisions?

Suppose now that there are $I$ agents and that in addition to the social utility function $U(\cdot)$ we are also given $I$ individual preference relations $\succsim_i$ defined on the same set of lotteries $X$. We assume that they are also represented by utility functions of the expected utility form

$$U_i(p) = u_{1i}p_1 + \cdots + u_{Ni}p_N \qquad \text{for } i = 1, \ldots, I.$$

We say that the social utility function $U(\cdot)$ is *Paretian* if we have $U(p) > U(p')$ whenever $U_i(p) > U_i(p')$ for every $i$.

**(b)** Consider a case with $N = 3$ and $I = 2$ and illustrate, in the 2-dimensional simplex of lotteries, how the indifference map of the utility functions of the two agents and of the social utility function fit together when the social utility function is Paretian.

**(c)** Exhibit a case where the Paretian condition determines uniquely the social indifference map (recall that we are always assuming the independence axiom for social preferences!). Argue, however, that in general the Paretian condition does not determine uniquely the social indifference map. In fact, exhibit an example where any social utility function is Paretian.

**(d)** Argue (you can restrict yourself to $N = 3$ and $I = 2$) that if the social utility function $U(p)$ is Paretian then it can be written in the form

$$U(p) = \beta_1 U_1(p) + \cdots + \beta_I U_I(p)$$

where $\beta_i \geq 0$ for every $i$ and $\beta_i \neq 0$ for some $i$. What does this conclusion say for the usage of a purely utilitarian social welfare function? Interpret the $\beta_i$ weights, as well as the fact that they need not be equal across individuals.

**22.C.4$^A$** The *leximin* ordering, or preference relation, on $\mathbb{R}^I$ has been mentioned in footnote 11 of this chapter when discussing the Rawlsian SWF. It is formally defined as follows. Given a vector $u = (u_1, \ldots, u_I)$ let $u^r \in \mathbb{R}^I$ be the vector that is the *nondecreasing rearrangement* of $u$. That is, the entries of $u^r$ are in nondecreasing order and its numerical values (multiplicities included) are the same as for $u$. We then say that the vector $u$ is at least as good as the vector $\hat{u}$ in the leximin order if $u^r$ is at least as good as $\hat{u}^r$ in the lexicographic ordering introduced in Example 3.C.1.

**(a)** Interpret the definition of the leximin as a refinement of the Rawlsian preference relation.

**(b)** Show that the leximin ordering cannot be represented by a utility function. It is enough to show this for $I = 2$.

**(c)** (Harder) Show that the social optimum of a leximin ordering is a Pareto optimum. You can limit yourself to the case $I = 3$.

**22.C.5$^B$** Consider the constant elasticity family of social welfare functions (Example 22.C.4). Argue that $W_\rho(u) \to \text{Min } \{u_1, \ldots, u_I\}$ as $\rho \to \infty$.

**22.C.6$^A$** Suppose that $U$ and $U'$ are utility possibility sets and that we associate with them Pareto optimal utility outcomes $\bar{u} \in U$ and $\bar{u}' \in U'$, respectively. Show graphically that:

**(a)** It is possible for $U'$ to pass the strong compensation test over $U$ and yet for the outcome with $U'$ to be worse than the outcome with $U$, as measured by the purely utilitarian SWF.

**(b)** If the utility possibility sets are derived from a quasilinear economy and $U'$ passes the weak compensation test over $U$, then it also passes the strong compensation test and, moreover, the outcome for $U'$ is a utilitarian improvement over the outcome for $U$. Is this conclusion valid if we evaluate social welfare by a nonutilitarian SWF?

**22.C.7$^B$** Construct an explicit example of two Edgeworth box economies, differing only in their distributions of the initial endowments, such that the utility possibility set of each one passes the weak compensation test over the utility possibility set of the other, when the utility outcome in the latter is chosen to correspond to one of its competitive equilibria.

**22.C.8$^A$** Suppose we have two utility possibility sets $U, U'$ with respective outcomes $u \in U$ and $u' \in U'$. We say that $(U', u')$ passes the *Kaldor compensation test* over $(U, u)$ if $U'$ passes the weak compensation test over $(U, u)$ and $U$ *does not* pass the weak compensation test over $(U', u')$.

(a) For $I = 2$, represent graphically a situation where Kaldor comparability is possible and one where it is not.

(b) Observe that Kaldor comparability is asymmetric. Define your terms.

(c) Show that Kaldor comparability may not be transitive.

**22.D.1$^B$** In this exercise we verify the indispensability of the assumptions of Proposition 22.D.1.

(a) Suppose there are three agents and only two alternatives, that is, $X = \{x, y\}$. The social welfare functional is given by

$$x\, F(\tilde{u}_1, \tilde{u}_2, \tilde{u}_3)\, y \qquad \text{if and only if} \qquad \tilde{u}_i(x) \geq \tilde{u}_i(y) \text{ for every } i$$

and

$$y\, F(\tilde{u}_1, \tilde{u}_2, \tilde{u}_3)\, x \qquad \text{if and only if} \qquad \tilde{u}_i(y) \geq \tilde{u}_i(x) \text{ for at least one } i.$$

Check that the social preference relation is always complete, that the social welfare functional cannot be represented by means of a social welfare function, and that only the condition on the number of alternatives fails from Proposition 22.D.1.

(b) Now we have three agents and three alternatives, that is, $X = \{x, y, z\}$. The social welfare functional is given by

$$x\, F_p(\tilde{u}_1, \ldots, \tilde{u}_I)\, y\, F_p(\tilde{u}_1, \ldots, \tilde{u}_I)\, z$$

for every $(\tilde{u}_1, \ldots, \tilde{u}_I) \in \mathscr{U}^I$. Show that, again, no representation by means of a social welfare function is possible and that, of the assumptions of Proposition 22.D.1, only the Paretian property fails to be satisfied.

(c) Exhibit an example in which the only condition of Proposition 22.D.1 that fails to be satisfied is pairwise independence.

**22.D.2$^A$** Carry out the verification requested in the second paragraph of the proof of Proposition 22.D.1.

**22.D.3$^A$** In text.

**22.D.4$^A$** A social welfare functional $F$ is *lexically dictatorial* if there is a list of $n > 0$ agents $h_1, \ldots, h_n$ such that the strict preference of $h_1$ prevails socially, the strict preference of $h_2$ prevails among the alternatives for which $h_1$ is indifferent, and so on.

(a) Show that if $F$ is lexically dictatorial then $F$ is Paretian, is pairwise independent, and does not allow for interpersonal comparisons of utility.

(b) Under what conditions can a social welfare functional that is lexically dictatorial be generated from a social welfare function?

(c) Show that if a dictatorial social welfare functional is generated from a social welfare function $W(u) = \sum_i b_i u_i$, then $b_i = 0$ for every $i$ distinct from the dictator.

**22.D.5$^C$** Complete the proof of Arrow's impossibility theorem along the lines suggested in the last paragraph prior to the small-type text at the end of Section 22.D. (Assume that Proposition

22.D.3 is valid under the weakened assumption that $F$ is generated from a social preference relation on $\mathbb{R}^I$.)

**22.D.6$^B$** This exercise is concerned with social welfare functions satisfying expression (22.D.1).

(a) Show that the nonsymmetric utilitarian function $W(u) = \sum_i b_i u_i$ can be written in the form (22.D.1).

(b) Show that if $W(\cdot)$ is symmetric and $g(0) = 0$ then $g(\cdot) \geq 0$.

(c) Show that the symmetric Rawlsian social welfare function $W(u) = \text{Min} \{u_1, \ldots, u_I\}$ can be written in the form (22.D.1). What about nonsymmetric Rawlsian social welfare functions? [*Hint*: Check the condition of invariance to common changes of origins.]

(d) Give other examples satisfying (22.D.1), in particular, examples with $g(\cdot) \geq 0$ and intermediate between the utilitarian and the Rawlsian cases. Interpret them.

(e) Argue that if in (22.D.1) the function $g(\cdot)$ is homogeneous of degree one and differentiable, then it must be linear (and so we are back to the utilitarian case).

**22.D.7$^B$** Consider the constant elasticity family of social welfare functions studied in Example 22.C.4.

(a) Show that the social welfare functionals derived from SWFs in this family are invariant to common changes of units.

(b) Show that the only members of this family which are also invariant to common changes of origins, and therefore admit a representation in the form (22.D.1), are the purely utilitarian (i.e., $\rho = 0$) and the Rawlsian (i.e., $\rho = \infty$).

**22.D.8$^B$** This is an exercise on the property of invariance to common ordinal transformation.

(a) Show that the symmetric, Rawlsian social welfare function satisfies the property.

(b) Show that the anti-Rawlsian function $W(u) = \text{Max} \{u_1, \ldots, u_I\}$ also satisfies it.

(c) Show that the property is satisfied for dictatorial social welfare functionals.

(d) (Harder) Suppose that $I = 2$ and $W(u) = W(u')$ for two vectors $u, u' \in \mathbb{R}^2$, with $u_1' < u_1 < u_2 < u_2'$. Assume also that $W(\cdot)$ is increasing. Show that the induced social welfare functional cannot be invariant to identical ordinal transformations. From this, argue informally (you can do it graphically) that for $I = 2$ a continuous, increasing social welfare function that is also invariant to identical ordinal transformations must be either dictatorial, Rawlsian, or anti-Rawlsian.

**22.E.1$^A$** Verify that the bargaining solutions in Examples 22.E.1 to 22.E.4 are independent of utility origins, Paretian, symmetric, and individually rational. It is enough if you do so for $I = 2$.

**22.E.2$^A$** State nonsymmetric versions of the four bargaining solutions studied in Section 22.E (egalitarian, utilitarian, Nash, and Kalai–Smorodinsky). Motivate them.

**22.E.3$^B$** This is an exercise on the Nash solution.

(a) Verify that for $I = 2$, $f_n(U)$ is the boundary point of $U$ through which we can draw a tangent line with the property that its midpoint in the positive orthant is precisely the given boundary point $f_n(U)$.

(b) Verify that if $U \subset \mathbb{R}^I$ is a bargaining problem then there are rescaling units for the individual utilities with the property that the Nash solution becomes simultaneously egalitarian and utilitarian.

**22.E.4$^A$** Verify that the Kalai–Smorodinsky solution satisfies the property of independence of utility units but violates the property of independence of irrelevant alternatives. You can restrict yourself to $I = 2$.

**22.E.5$^B$** This is an exercise on the monotonicity property.

**(a)** Show that the egalitarian solution is the only bargaining solution that is independent of utility origins, Paretian, symmetric and monotonic. [*Hint*: Consider first a family of symmetric utility possibility sets with linear boundaries. Notice then that for any two sets $U, U'$ we always have $U \cap U' \subset U$ and $U \cap U' \subset U'$.]

**(b)** (Harder) Suppose that $f(\cdot)$ is a bargaining solution that is independent of utility origins, Paretian, and strongly monotonic [if $U \subset U'$ then $f(U) \leq f(U')$ and, in addition, if $f(U)$ is interior to $U'$ then $f(U) \ll f(U')$]. Show that there is a curve in $\mathbb{R}^I$ starting at the origin and strictly increasing such that, for every $U$, $f(U)$ is the intersection point of the boundary of $U$ with this curve. You can restrict yourself to the case $I = 2$.

**22.E.6$^C$** Let $I = 2$. A bargaining solution $f(\cdot)$ is *partially monotone* if when $U \subset U'$ and $u^i(U) = u^i(U')$, that is, $U'$ expands $U$ only in the direction of agent $j \neq i$, we have $f_j(U') \geq f_j(U)$ for $j \neq i$. Argue that the Kalai–Smorodinsky solution is characterized by the following properties: independence of utility origins and units, Pareto, symmetry, and partial monotonicity. [*Hint*: use sets $U$ such that $U' \subset U$ and $u^1(U) = u^1(U')$, $u^2(U) = u^2(U')$].

**22.E.7$^A$** Consider a family of bargaining solutions $f^I(\cdot)$ such that, for every set of agents $I$, $f^I(\cdot)$ is independent of utility origins and is generated by maximizing the social welfare function $\sum_i g(u_i)$ on normalized bargaining problems $U \subset \mathbb{R}^I$, where $g(\cdot)$ is increasing, strictly concave, and independent of the particular $I$ considered. Show that the family $f^I$ is consistent.

**22.E.8$^C$** Show by example that the Kalai–Smorodinsky solution is not consistent. It is enough to consider three agents and its subgroups of two agents.

**22.E.9$^A$** This exercise is aimed at showing the independence of the assumptions of Proposition 22.E.1. To this effect, give five examples such that for each of the five assumptions of Proposition 22.E.1 there is one of the examples that violates this assumption but satisfies the remaining four.

**22.E.10$^A$** Give an example of a utilitarian bargaining solution (Example 22.E.2) that violates the property of independence of irrelevant alternatives. [*Hint*: It suffices to consider $I = 2$. Also, the violation should involve sets $U$ that are convex but not strictly convex.]

**22.E.11$^C$** Go back to the infinite horizon Rubinstein's bargaining model discussed in the Appendix A to Chapter 9 (specifically, Example 9.AA.2). The only modification is that the two agents are risk averse on the amount of money they get. That is, each has an increasing, concave, differentiable utility function $u_i(m_i)$ on the nonnegative amounts of money that they receive. The factor of discount $\delta < 1$ is the same for the two agents. Also $u_i(0) = 0$. The total amount of money is $m$.

**(a)** Write down the equations for a subgame perfect Nash equilibrium (SPNE) *in stationary strategies*. Argue that there is a single configuration of utility payoffs that can be obtained as payoffs of a SPNE in stationary strategies.

**(b)** Consider the utility possibility set

$$U = \{(u_1(m_1), u_2(m_2)) \in \mathbb{R}^2 : m_1 + m_2 = m\} - \mathbb{R}_+^2 \,.$$

Show that if $\delta$ is close to 1 then the payoffs of a SPNE in stationary strategies are nearly equal to the Nash bargaining solution payoffs.

**(c)** (Harder) Argue that every payoff configuration of a SPNE can be obtained as the payoff configuration of a SPNE in stationary strategies. Thus, the uniqueness result presented in Example 9.AA.2 extends to the case in which the agents have strictly concave, possibly different, utility functions for money.

**22.F.1**[A] Show that in the transferable utility case any bargaining solution that is invariant to independent changes of origin, symmetric, and Paretian divides the gains from cooperation equally among the agents.

**22.F.2**[A] Show that the Shapley value cooperative solution presented in Section 22.F satisfies the following properties: invariance to independent changes of utility origins, invariance to common changes of utility units, Paretian, symmetry, and the dummy axiom.

**22.F.3**[A] Suppose that for a given set of agents $I$ we take two characteristic forms $v$ and $v'$ and consider their sum $v + v'$; that is, $v + v'$ is the characteristic form where $(v + v')(S) = v(S) + v'(S)$ for every $S \subset I$.

**(a)** Verify that the Shapley value is *linear* in the characteristic form; that is, $f_{si}(v + v') = f_{si}(v) + f_{si}(v')$ for all $v$, $v'$ and $i$.

**(b)** Interpret the linearity property as a postulate that agents are indifferent to the timing of resolution of uncertainty when we randomize among bargaining situations.

**22.F.4**[C] The linearity property of the previous exercise can be restated in a perhaps more intuitive form. We say that a characteristic form $v(\cdot)$ is a *unanimity game* if for some $T \subset I$ we have that $v(S) = v(T)$ if $T \subset S$, and $v(S) = 0$ otherwise (thus, the bargaining situations of Section 22.E correspond to $T = I$).

**(a)** Show that the independence of utility origins and invariance to common changes of utility units, Pareto, symmetry, and dummy axiom properties imply that, for a unanimity game $v(\cdot)$, any cooperative solution $f(\cdot)$ assigns the values $f_i(v) = (1/T)v(I)$ if $i \in T$, and $f_i(v) = 0$ otherwise.

**(b)** We say that the cooperative solution $f(\cdot)$ is *weakly linear* if for any $v$ and $v'$ differing only by a unanimity game [i.e., there is $T \subset I$ and $\alpha \in \mathbb{R}$ such that $v'(S) = v(S) + \alpha$ if $T \subset S$, and $v'(S) = v(S)$ otherwise] we have that $f_i(v') = f_i(v) + \alpha/T$ if $i \in T$, and $f_i(v') = f_i(v)$ otherwise. Show that if, in addition to the properties listed in (a), the cooperative solution $f(\cdot)$ is weakly linear, then it is fully linear, that is, $f(v + v') = f(v) + f(v')$ for any two characteristic forms $v$ and $v'$.

**(c)** Show that the Shapley value is the only cooperative solution that satisfies the following properties: independence of utility origins and invariance to common changes of utility units, Paretian, symmetry, dummy axiom, and linearity.

**22.F.5**[C] In this exercise we describe another cooperative solution for a game in characteristic form: the *nucleolus*. For simplicity we do it for the particular case in which $I = 3$, $v(1) = v(2) = v(3) = 0$, and $0 \leq v(S) \leq v(I)$, for any group $S$ of two agents.

Given a utility vector $u = (u_1, u_2, u_3) \geq 0$ and an $S \subset I$ the *excess* of $S$ at $u$ is $e(u, S) = v(S) - \sum_{i \in S} u_i$. We define the *first maximum excess* as $m_1(u) = \text{Max } \{e(u, S): 1 < \#S < 3\}$. Choose a two-agent coalition $S$ such that $m_1(u) = e(u, S)$. Then we define the *second maximum excess* as $m_2(u) = \text{Max } \{e(u, S'): 1 < \#S' < 3 \text{ and } S' \neq S\}$.

We say that an exactly feasible [i.e., $\sum_{i \in I} u_i = v(I)$] utility profile $u = (u_1, u_2, u_3) \geq 0$ is in the nucleolus if for any other such profile $u'$ we have either $m_1(u) < m_1(u')$ or $m_1(u) = m_1(u')$ and $m_2(u) \leq m_2(u')$.

**(a)** Show that if $u = (u_1, u_2, u_3)$ is in the nucleolus then either the three excesses for two-agent coalitions are identical or two are identical and the third is larger.

**(b)** Show that there is one and only one utility profile in the nucleolus. [*Hint*: Argue first that there is a two-agent coalition $S$ such that $e(u, S) = m_1(u)$ for every profile in the nucleolus.] From now on we refer to this profile as the *nucleolus solution*.

**(c)** Argue that the nucleolus solution is symmetric.

**(d)** Suppose that agent 1 is a dummy. Then $u_1 = 0$ at the nucleolus solution.

**(e)** Suppose that $\frac{1}{2}v(I) \leq v(S)$ for any coalition $S$ of two agents. Show then that at the nucleolus profile the three excesses for two-agent coalitions are identical.

**(f)** Compute and compare the Shapley value and the nucleolus for the characteristic form: $v(1) = v(2) = v(3) = 0$, $v(\{1, 2\}) = v\{(1, 3)\} = 4$, $v(\{2, 3\}) = 5$, $v(I) = 6$.

**(g)** Show that if the core is nonempty (see Appendix A to Chapter 18 for the definition of the core in this context) then the nucleolus utility profile belongs to the core.

**22.F.6$^B$** Consider a regulated firm that produces an output by means of a cost function $c(q)$. Assuming a quasilinear economy, the consumer surplus generated by $q$ is $S(q)$.

**(a)** Suppose that $c(q)$ is strictly concave (i.e., strictly increasing returns to scale). Show that at the first-best price the firm will not cover costs. Conversely, for any $q$ suppose that the price $p(q)$ is determined so that the cost is covered; that is, $p(q) = c(q)/q$. Show that if $q$ is then determined so as to have $p(q) = S'(q)$, we will not reach the first-best optimum. Illustrate graphically.

**(b)** Suppose that the quantity produced, $q$, has to be determined under the constraint that with $p = S'(q)$ we have $pq \geq c(q)$. Solve this second-best welfare problem. Illustrate graphically.

**(c)** Interpret the units of output as "projects." For any production decision $q$, what is the cost allocation suggested by the Shapley value?

**22.F.7$^C$** This exercise is similar to Exercise 22.F.6, except that the firm now produces two outputs under the separable cost functions $c_1(q_1), c_2(q_2)$. The surplus $S_1(q_1) + S_2(q_2)$ is also separable.

**(a)** The second-best problem [first studied by Boiteux (1956)] is now richer than in Exercise 22.F.6. Suppose that the quantities $q_1, q_2$ have to be determined so that with $p_1 = S'(q_1)$ and $p_2 = S'(q_2)$ we have $p_1q_1 + p_2q_2 \geq c_1(q_1) + c_2(q_2)$ (equivalently, at the chosen prices demand must be served and cost covered). Derive first-order conditions for this problem. Make them as similar as possible to the Ramsey formula of Example 22.B.2.

**(b)** (Harder) Interpret the units of outputs as projects. Suppose that these units are very small, so that a given production decision $(q_1, q_2) \gg 0$ represents the implementation of many projects of each of the two types. Can you guess, given $(q_1, q_2)$, what is an approximate value for the cost allocation suggested by the Shapley value? [*Hint*: For most orderings of projects, any particular project will have preceding it an almost perfect sample of all the projects.]

**(c)** Suppose that for the productions $(\bar{q}_1, \bar{q}_2)$, the Shapley value cost allocation assigns cost per unit of $c_1$ and $c_2$ (note that "projects" of the same type receive the same cost imputation). Suppose also that $c_1 = \partial S_1(\bar{q}_1)/\partial q_1$ and $c_2 = \partial S_2(\bar{q}_2)/\partial q_2$. Interpret. Argue that, in general, these productions will not correspond to either the first-best or the second-best optima of the problem.

# Incentives and Mechanism Design

## 23.A Introduction

In Chapter 21, we studied how individual preferences might be aggregated into social preferences and ultimately into a collective decision. However, an important feature of many settings in which collective decisions must be made is that individuals' actual preferences are not publicly observable. As a result, in one way or another, individuals must be relied upon to reveal this information.

In this chapter, we study how this information can be elicited, and the extent to which the information revelation problem constrains the ways in which social decisions can respond to individual preferences. This topic is known as the *mechanism design problem.*

Mechanism design has many important applications throughout economics. The design of voting procedures, the writing of contracts among parties who will come to have private information, and the construction of procedures for deciding upon public projects or environmental standards are all examples.[1]

The chapter is organized as follows. In Section 23.B, we introduce the mechanism design problem. We begin by illustrating the difficulties introduced by the need to elicit agents' preferences. We also define and discuss the concepts of *social choice functions* (already introduced in Section 21.E), *ex post efficiency*, *mechanisms*, *implementation*, *direct revelation mechanisms*, and *truthful implementation*.

In Section 23.C, we identify the circumstances under which a social choice function can be implemented in *dominant strategy equilibria* when agents' preferences are private information. Our analysis begins with a formal statement and proof of the *revelation principle*, a result that tells us that we can restrict attention to direct revelation mechanisms that induce agents to truthfully reveal their preferences. Using this fact, we then study the constraints that the information revelation

---

1. Simple examples of the last two applications were encountered in Sections 14.C and 11.E, respectively.

problem puts on the set of implementable social choice functions. We first present the important *Gibbard–Satterthwaite theorem*, which provides a very negative conclusion for cases in which individual preferences can take unrestricted forms. In the rest of the section, we go on to study the special case of *quasilinear environments*, discussing in detail *Groves–Clarke mechanisms*.

In Section 23.D, we study implementation in *Bayesian Nash equilibria*. We begin by discussing the *expected externality mechanism* as an example of how the weaker Bayesian implementation concept can allow us to implement a wider range of social choice functions than is possible with dominant strategy implementation. We go on to provide a characterization of Bayesian implementable social choice functions for the case in which agents have quasilinear preferences that are linear in their type. As an application of this result, we prove the remarkable *revenue equivalence theorem* for auctions.

In Section 23.E, we consider the possibility that participation in a mechanism may be voluntary and study how the need to satisfy the resulting *participation constraints* limits the set of implementable social choice functions. Here we prove the important *Myerson–Satterthwaite theorem*, which shows that, under very general conditions, it is impossible to achieve ex post efficiency in bilateral trade settings when agents have private information and trade is voluntary.

In Section 23.F, we discuss the welfare comparison of mechanisms, defining the notions of *ex ante* and *interim incentive efficiency*, and providing several illustrations of the computation of welfare optimal Bayesian mechanisms.

Appendices A and B are devoted to, first, a discussion of the issue of multiple equilibria in mechanism design and, second, the issue of mechanism design when agents know each others' types but the mechanism designer does not (so-called *complete information environments*).

References for further reading are provided at the start of the various sections. We would be remiss, however, not to mention here two early seminal articles: Mirrlees (1971) and Hurwicz (1972).

# 23.B  The Mechanism Design Problem

In this section, we provide an introduction to the *mechanism design problem* that we study in detail in the rest of the chapter.

To begin, consider a setting with $I$ agents, indexed by $i = 1, \ldots, I$. These agents must make a collective choice from some set $X$ of possible alternatives. Prior to the choice, however, each agent $i$ privately observes his preferences over the alternatives in $X$. Formally, we model this by supposing that agent $i$ privately observes a parameter, or signal, $\theta_i$ that determines his preferences. We will often refer to $\theta_i$ as agent $i$'s *type*. The set of possible types for agent $i$ is denoted $\Theta_i$. Each agent $i$ is assumed to be an expected utility maximizer, whose Bernoulli utility function when he is of type $\theta_i$ is $u_i(x, \theta_i)$. The ordinal preference relation over pairs of alternatives in $X$ that is associated with utility function $u_i(x, \theta_i)$ is denoted $\succsim_i(\theta_i)$. Agent $i$'s set of possible preference relations over $X$ is therefore given by

$$\mathscr{R}_i = \{\succsim_i : \succsim_i = \succsim_i(\theta_i) \text{ for some } \theta_i \in \Theta_i\}.$$

Note that because $\theta_i$ is observed only by agent $i$, in the language of Section 8.E we are in a setting characterized by *incomplete information*. As in Section 8.E, we suppose that agents' types are drawn from a commonly known prior distribution. In particular, denoting a profile of the agents' types by $\theta = (\theta_1, \ldots, \theta_I)$, the probability density over the possible realizations of $\theta \in \Theta_1 \times \cdots \times \Theta_I$ is $\phi(\cdot)$. The probability density $\phi(\cdot)$ as well as the sets $\Theta_1, \ldots, \Theta_I$ and the utility functions $u_i(\cdot, \theta_i)$ are assumed to be common knowledge among the agents, but the specific value of each agent $i$'s type is observed only by $i$.[2]

Because the agents' preferences depend on the realizations of $\theta = (\theta_1, \ldots, \theta_I)$, the agents may want the collective decision to depend on $\theta$. To capture this dependence formally, we introduce in Definition 23.B.1 the notion of a *social choice function*, a concept already discussed in Section 21.E.[3]

**Definition 23.B.1:** A *social choice function* is a function $f \colon \Theta_1 \times \cdots \times \Theta_I \to X$ that, for each possible profile of the agents' types $(\theta_1, \ldots, \theta_I)$, assigns a collective choice $f(\theta_1, \ldots, \theta_I) \in X$.[4]

One desirable feature for a social choice function to satisfy is the property of *ex post efficiency* described in Definition 23.B.2.

**Definition 23.B.2:** The social choice function $f \colon \Theta_1 \times \cdots \times \Theta_I \to X$ is *ex post efficient* (or *Paretian*) if for no profile $\theta = (\theta_1, \ldots, \theta_I)$ is there an $x \in X$ such that $u_i(x, \theta_i) \geq u_i(f(\theta), \theta_i)$ for every $i$, and $u_i(x, \theta_i) > u_i(f(\theta), \theta_i)$ for some $i$.

Definition 23.B.2 says that a social welfare function is ex post efficient if it selects, for every profile $\theta = (\theta_1, \ldots, \theta_I)$, an alternative $f(\theta) \in X$ that is Pareto optimal given the agents' utility functions $u_1(\cdot, \theta_1), \ldots, u_I(\cdot, \theta_I)$.

The problem faced by the agents is that the $\theta_i$'s are not publicly observable, and so for the social choice $f(\theta_1, \ldots, \theta_I)$ to be chosen when the agents' types are $(\theta_1, \ldots, \theta_I)$, each agent $i$ must be relied upon to disclose his type $\theta_i$. However, for a given social choice function $f(\cdot)$, an agent may not find it to be in his best interest to reveal this information truthfully. We illustrate this information revelation problem in Examples 23.B.1 through 23.B.4, which range from very abstract to more applied settings.

---

2. The formulation here is restrictive in one sense: in some settings of interest, agents' preferences over outcomes depend not only on their own observed signals but also on signals observed by others (e.g., agent $i$'s preferences over whether to hold a picnic indoors may depend on agent $j$'s knowledge of likely weather conditions). Through most of this chapter, we focus on the case in which an agent's preferences depend only on his own signal, known as the *private values* case. We generalize our analysis in Section 23.F.

3. In Section 21.E an agent's type was equivalent to his ordinal preferences over $X$, and so a social choice function was defined there simply as a mapping from $\mathscr{R}_1 \times \cdots \times \mathscr{R}_I$ to $X$. Moreover, it was assumed there that for all $i$ we have $\mathscr{R}_i = \mathscr{R}$, the set of all possible ordinal preference orderings on $X$.

4. Two points should be noted about this definition. First, it restricts attention to *deterministic* social choice functions. This is largely for expositional purposes; although much of the chapter considers deterministic social choice functions, in Sections 23.D to 23.F we allow social choice functions that assign *lotteries* over $X$. Second, as in Section 21.E, we limit our attention to single-valued choice functions.

**Example 23.B.1:** *An Abstract Social Choice Setting.* In the most abstract case, we are given a set $X$ and, for each agent $i$, a set $\mathscr{R}_i$ of possible rational preference orderings on $X$. To consider a very simple example, suppose that $X = \{x, y, z\}$ and that $I = 2$. Suppose also that agent 1 has one possible type, so that $\Theta_1 = \{\bar{\theta}_1\}$, and that agent 2 has two possible types, so that $\Theta_2 = \{\theta'_2, \theta''_2\}$. The agents' possible preference orderings $\mathscr{R}_1 = \{\succsim_1(\bar{\theta}_1)\}$ and $\mathscr{R}_2 = \{\succsim_2(\theta'_2), \succsim_2(\theta''_2)\}$ are given by

| $\succsim_1(\bar{\theta}_1)$ | $\succsim_2(\theta'_2)$ | $\succsim_2(\theta''_2)$ |
|:---:|:---:|:---:|
| $x$ | $z$ | $y$ |
| $y$ | $y$ | $x$ |
| $z$ | $x$ | $z$ |

[A higher positioned alternative is strictly preferred to a lower positioned one; so, for example, $x \succ_1(\bar{\theta}_1) y \succ_1(\bar{\theta}_1) z$.]

Now suppose that the agents wish to implement the ex post efficient social choice function $f(\cdot)$ with

$$f(\bar{\theta}_1, \theta'_2) = y \qquad \text{and} \qquad f(\bar{\theta}_1, \theta''_2) = x.$$

If so, then agent 2 must be relied upon to truthfully reveal his preferences. But it is apparent that he will not find it in his interest to do so: When $\theta_2 = \theta''_2$, agent 2 will wish to lie and claim that his type is $\theta'_2$.

In abstract social choice settings, a case of central interest arises when $\mathscr{R}_i$ is, for each agent $i$, equal to $\mathscr{R}$, the set of all possible rational preference relations on $X$. In this case, an agent has many possible false claims that he can make and, intuitively, it may be very difficult for a social choice function always to induce the agents to reveal their preferences truthfully. We will see a formal illustration of this point in Section 23.C when we present the Gibbard–Satterthwaite theorem. ∎

**Example 23.B.2:** *A Pure Exchange Economy.* Consider a pure exchange economy with $L$ goods and $I$ consumers in which agent $i$ has consumption set $\mathbb{R}^L_+$ and endowment vector $\omega_i = (\omega_{1i}, \ldots, \omega_{Li}) \gg 0$ (see Chapter 15). The set of alternatives is

$$X = \{(x_1, \ldots, x_I): x_i \in \mathbb{R}^L_+ \text{ and } \sum_i x_{\ell i} \leq \sum_i \omega_{\ell i} \text{ for } \ell = 1, \ldots L\}.$$

In this setting it may be natural to suppose that $\mathscr{R}_i$, each consumer $i$'s set of possible preference relations over alternatives in $X$, is a subset of $\mathscr{R}_E$, the set of individualistic (i.e., depending on $x_i$ only), monotone, and convex preference relations on $X$.

To consider a simple example, suppose that $I = 2$, that consumer 1 has only one possible type, so that $\Theta_1 = \{\bar{\theta}_1\}$ and $\mathscr{R}_1 = \{\succsim_1(\bar{\theta}_1)\}$, and that for consumer 2 we have $\mathscr{R}_2 = \mathscr{R}_E$. Imagine then that we try to implement a social choice function that, for each pair $(\succsim_1(\theta_1), \succsim_2(\theta_2))$, chooses a Walrasian equilibrium allocation (note that this social choice function is ex post efficient). As Figure 23.B.1 illustrates, consumer 2 will not generally find it optimal to reveal his preferences truthfully. In the figure, $f(\bar{\theta}_1, \theta'_2)$ is the unique Walrasian equilibrium when preferences are $(\succsim_1(\bar{\theta}_1), \succsim_2(\theta'_2))$ [it is the unique intersection of the consumers' offer curves $OC_1$ and $OC'_2$ occurring at a point other than the endowment point]. However, by claiming that he has type $\theta''_2$, which has as its offer curve $OC''_2$, consumer 2 can obtain the allocation $f(\bar{\theta}_1, \theta''_2)$ [the unique Walrasian equilibrium allocation when preferences

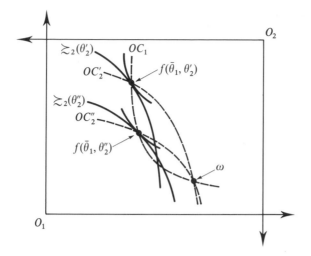

**Figure 23.B.1**
In the social choice function that selects a Walrasian equilibrium for each preference profile, agent 2 has an incentive to claim to be type $\theta_2''$ when he is really type $\theta_2'$.

are $(\succsim_1(\bar{\theta}_1), \succsim_2(\theta_2''))$], an allocation that he strictly prefers to $f(\bar{\theta}_1, \theta_2')$ when his preferences are $\succsim_2(\theta_2')$. ∎

**Example 23.B.3:** *A Public Project.* Consider a situation in which $I$ agents must decide whether to undertake a public project, such as building a bridge, whose cost must be funded by the agents themselves. An outcome is a vector $x = (k, t_1, \ldots, t_I)$, where $k \in \{0, 1\}$ is the decision whether to build the bridge ($k = 1$ if the bridge is built, and $k = 0$ if not), and $t_i \in \mathbb{R}$ is a monetary transfer to (or from, if $t_i < 0$) agent $i$. The cost of the project is $c \geq 0$ and so the set of feasible alternatives for the $I$ agents is

$$X = \{(k, t_1, \ldots, t_I): k \in \{0, 1\}, t_i \in \mathbb{R} \text{ for all } i, \text{ and } \sum_i t_i \leq -ck\}.$$

The constraint $\sum_i t_i \leq -ck$ reflects the fact that there is no source of outside funding for the agents (so that we must have $c + \sum_i t_i \leq 0$ if $k = 1$, and $\sum_i t_i \leq 0$ if $k = 0$). We assume that type $\theta_i$'s Bernoulli utility function has the quasilinear form

$$u_i(x, \theta_i) = \theta_i k + (\bar{m}_i + t_i),$$

where $\bar{m}_i$ is agent $i$'s initial endowment of the numeraire ("money") and $\theta_i \in \mathbb{R}$. We can then interpret $\theta_i$ as agent $i$'s willingness to pay for the bridge.

In this context, the social choice function $f(\theta) = (k(\theta), t_1(\theta), \ldots, t_I(\theta))$ is ex post efficient if, for all $\theta$,

$$k(\theta) = \begin{cases} 1 & \text{if } \sum_i \theta_i \geq c, \\ 0 & \text{otherwise,} \end{cases} \tag{23.B.1}$$

and

$$\sum_i t_i(\theta) = -ck(\theta). \tag{23.B.2}$$

Suppose that the agents wish to implement a social choice function that satisfies (23.B.1) and (23.B.2) and in which an egalitarian contribution rule is followed, that is, in which $t_i(\theta) = -(c/I)k(\theta)$. To consider a simple example, suppose that $\Theta_i = \{\bar{\theta}_i\}$ for $i \neq 1$ (so that all agents other than agent 1 have preferences that are known) and

$\Theta_1 = [0, \infty)$. Suppose also that $c > \sum_{i \neq 1} \bar{\theta}_i > c(I - 1)/I$. These inequalities imply, first, that with this social choice function agent 1's type is critical for whether the bridge is built (if $\theta_1 \geq c - \sum_{i \neq 1} \bar{\theta}_i$ it is; if $\theta_1 < c - \sum_{i \neq 1} \bar{\theta}_i$ it is not), and that the sum of the utilities of agents $2, \ldots, I$ is strictly greater if the bridge is built under this egalitarian contribution rule than if it is not built [since $\sum_{i \neq 1} \bar{\theta}_i - c(I - 1)/I > 0$].

Let us examine agent 1's incentives for truthfully revealing his type when $\theta_1 = c - \sum_{i \neq 1} \bar{\theta}_i + \varepsilon$ for $\varepsilon > 0$. If agent 1 reveals his true preferences, the bridge will be built because

$$\left( c - \sum_{i \neq 1} \bar{\theta}_i + \varepsilon \right) + \sum_{i \neq 1} \bar{\theta}_i > c.$$

Agent 1's utility in this case is

$$\theta_1 + \bar{m}_1 - \frac{c}{I} = \left( c - \sum_{i \neq 1} \bar{\theta}_i + \varepsilon \right) + \bar{m}_1 - \frac{c}{I}$$

$$= \left( \frac{c(I - 1)}{I} - \sum_{i \neq 1} \bar{\theta}_i + \varepsilon \right) + \bar{m}_1.$$

But, for $\varepsilon > 0$ small enough, this is less than $\bar{m}_1$, which is agent 1's utility if he instead claims that $\theta_1 = 0$, a claim that results in the bridge not being built. Thus, agent 1 will prefer not to tell the truth. Intuitively, under this allocation rule, when agent 1 causes the bridge to be built he has a positive externality on the other agents (in the aggregate). Because he fails to internalize this effect, he has an incentive to understate his benefit from the project. ∎

**Example 23.B.4:** *Allocation of a Single Unit of an Indivisible Private Good.* Consider a setting in which there is a single unit of an indivisible private good to be allocated to one of $I$ agents. Monetary transfers can also be made. An outcome here may be represented by a vector $x = (y_1, \ldots, y_I, t_1, \ldots, t_I)$, where $y_i = 1$ if agent $i$ gets the good, $y_i = 0$ if agent $i$ does not get the good, and $t_i$ is the monetary transfer received by agent $i$. The set of feasible alternatives is then

$$X = \{(y_1, \ldots, y_I, t_1, \ldots, t_I) : y_i \in \{0, 1\} \text{ and } t_i \in \mathbb{R} \text{ for all } i, \sum_i y_i = 1, \text{ and } \sum_i t_i \leq 0\}.$$

We suppose that type $\theta_i$'s Bernoulli utility function takes the quasilinear form

$$u_i(x, \theta_i) = \theta_i y_i + (\bar{m}_i + t_i),$$

where $\bar{m}_i$ is once again agent $i$'s initial endowment of the numeraire ("money"). Here $\theta_i \in \mathbb{R}$ can be viewed as agent $i$'s valuation of the good, and we take the set of possible valuations for agent $i$ to be $\Theta_i = [\underline{\theta}_i, \bar{\theta}_i] \subset \mathbb{R}$.

In this situation, a social choice function $f(\theta) = (y_1(\theta), \ldots, y_I(\theta), t_1(\theta), \ldots, t_I(\theta))$ is ex post efficient if it always allocates the good to the agent who has the highest valuation (or to one of them if there are several) and if it involves no waste of the numeraire; that is, if for all $\theta = (\theta_1, \ldots, \theta_I) \in \Theta_1 \times \cdots \times \Theta_I$,

$$y_i(\theta)(\theta_i - \text{Max}\{\theta_1, \ldots, \theta_I\}) = 0 \qquad \text{for all } i$$

and

$$\sum_i t_i(\theta) = 0.$$

Two special cases that have received a great deal of attention in the literature deserve mention. The first is the case of *bilateral trade*. In this case we have $I = 2$; agent 1 is interpreted as the initial owner of the good (the "seller"), and agent 2 is the potential purchaser of the good (the "buyer"). When $\underline{\theta}_2 > \bar{\theta}_1$ there are certain to be gains from trade regardless of the realizations of $\theta_1$ and $\theta_2$; when $\underline{\theta}_1 > \bar{\theta}_2$ there are certain to be no gains from trade; finally, if $\underline{\theta}_2 < \bar{\theta}_1$ and $\underline{\theta}_1 < \bar{\theta}_2$ then there may or may not be gains from trade, depending on the realization of $\theta$.

The second special case is the *auction* setting. Here, one agent, whom we shall designate as agent 0, is interpreted as the seller of the good (the "auctioneer") and is assumed to derive no value from it (more generally, the seller might have a known value $\theta_0 = \bar{\theta}_0$ different from zero). The other agents, $1, \ldots, I$, are potential buyers (the "bidders").[5]

To illustrate the problem with information revelation in this example, consider an auction setting with two buyers ($I = 2$). In the previous examples, we simplified the discussion of information revelation by assuming that only one agent has more than one possible type. We now suppose instead that both buyers' (privately observed) valuations $\theta_i$ are drawn independently from the uniform distribution on $[0, 1]$ and that this fact is common knowledge among the agents. Consider the social choice function $f(\theta) = (y_0(\theta), y_1(\theta), y_2(\theta), t_0(\theta), t_1(\theta), t_2(\theta))$ in which

$$y_1(\theta) = 1 \quad \text{if } \theta_1 \geq \theta_2; \quad = 0 \text{ if } \theta_1 < \theta_2 \tag{23.B.3}$$

$$y_2(\theta) = 1 \quad \text{if } \theta_1 < \theta_2; \quad = 0 \text{ if } \theta_1 \geq \theta_2 \tag{23.B.4}$$

$$y_0(\theta) = 0 \quad \text{for all } \theta \tag{23.B.5}$$

$$t_1(\theta) = -\theta_1 y_1(\theta) \tag{23.B.6}$$

$$t_2(\theta) = -\theta_2 y_2(\theta) \tag{23.B.7}$$

$$t_0(\theta) = -(t_1(\theta) + t_2(\theta)). \tag{23.B.8}$$

In this social choice function, the seller gives the good to the buyer with the highest valuation (to buyer 1 if there is a tie) and this buyer gives the seller a payment equal to his valuation (the other, low-valuation buyer makes no transfer payment to the seller). Note that $f(\cdot)$ is not only ex post efficient but also is very attractive for the seller: if $f(\cdot)$ can be implemented, the seller will capture all of the consumption benefits that are generated by the good.

Suppose we try to implement this social choice function. Assume that the buyers are expected utility maximizers. We now ask: If buyer 2 always announces his true value, will buyer 1 find it optimal to do the same? For each value of $\theta_1$, buyer 1's problem is to choose the valuation to announce, say $\hat{\theta}_1$, so as to solve

$$\underset{\hat{\theta}_1}{\text{Max}} \quad (\theta_1 - \hat{\theta}_1) \operatorname{Prob}(\theta_2 \leq \hat{\theta}_1)$$

or

$$\underset{\hat{\theta}_1}{\text{Max}} \quad (\theta_1 - \hat{\theta}_1)\hat{\theta}_1.$$

---

5. Note that, for ease of notation, we take there to be $I + 1$ agents in the auction setting.

The solution to this problem has buyer 1 set $\hat{\theta}_1 = \theta_1/2$. We see then that if buyer 2 always tells the truth, truth telling is *not* optimal for buyer 1. A similar point applies to buyer 2. Intuitively, for this social choice function, a buyer has an incentive to understate his valuation so as to lower the transfer he must make in the event that he has the highest announced valuation and gets the good. The cost to him of doing this is that he gets the good less often, but this is a cost worth incurring to at least some degree.[6] Thus, we again see that there may be a problem in implementing certain social choice functions in settings in which information is privately held. (For a similar point in the bilateral trade context, see Exercise 23.B.2.)

Although buyers have an incentive to lie given the social choice function described in (23.B.3) to (23.B.8), this is *not* true of *all* social choice functions in this auction setting. To see this point, suppose we try to implement the social choice function $\tilde{f}(\cdot)$ that has the same allocation rule as that above [i.e., in which the functions $y_i(\cdot)$ for $i = 0, 1, 2$ are the same as those described in (23.B.3) to (23.B.5)] but instead has transfer functions

$$t_1(\theta) = -\theta_2 y_1(\theta)$$

$$t_2(\theta) = -\theta_1 y_2(\theta)$$

$$t_0(\theta) = -(t_1(\theta) + t_2(\theta)).$$

In this social choice function, instead of buyer $i$ paying the seller an amount equal to his own valuation $\theta_i$ if he wins the object, he now pays $\theta_j$, where $j \neq i$; that is, he pays an amount equal to the *second-highest valuation*. Consider buyer 1's incentives for truth telling now. If buyer 2 announces his valuation to be $\hat{\theta}_2 \leq \theta_1$, buyer 1 can receive a utility of $(\theta_1 - \hat{\theta}_2) \geq 0$ by truthfully announcing that his valuation is $\theta_1$. For any other announcement, buyer 1's resulting utility is either the same (if he announces a valuation of at least $\hat{\theta}_2$) or zero (if he announces a valuation below $\hat{\theta}_2$). So if $\hat{\theta}_2 \leq \theta_1$, announcing the truth is weakly best for buyer 1. On the other hand, if buyer 2's announced valuation is $\hat{\theta}_2 > \theta_1$, then buyer 1's utility is 0 if he reveals his true valuation. However, buyer 1 can receive only a negative utility by making a false claim that gets him the good (a claim that his valuation is at least $\hat{\theta}_2$). We conclude that truth telling is optimal for buyer 1 regardless of what buyer 2 announces. Formally, in the language of the theory of games, truth telling is a weakly dominant strategy for buyer 1 (see Section 8.B). A similar conclusion follows for buyer 2. Thus, this social choice function *is* implementable even though the buyers' valuations are private information: it suffices to simply ask each buyer to report his type, and then to choose $\tilde{f}(\theta)$.[7] ∎

Examples 23.B.1 to 23.B.4 suggest that when agents' types are privately observed the information revelation problem may constrain the set of social choice functions that can be successfully implemented. With these examples as motivation, we can now pose the central question that is our focus in this chapter: *What social choice functions can be implemented when agents' types are private information?*

---

6. This trade-off is similar to that faced by a monopolist (see Section 12.B): when the monopolist raises his price, he lowers his sales but makes more on his remaining sales.

7. For other examples of implementable social choice functions, see Exercise 23.B.1.

To answer this question, we need in principle to begin by thinking of all the possible ways in which a social choice function might be implemented. In the above examples we have implicitly imagined a very simple scenario in which each agent $i$ is asked to directly reveal $\theta_i$ and then, given the announcements $(\hat{\theta}_1, \ldots, \hat{\theta}_I)$, the alternative $f(\hat{\theta}_1, \ldots, \hat{\theta}_I) \in X$ is chosen. But this is not the only way a social choice function might be implemented. In particular, a given social choice function might be *indirectly* implemented by having the agents interact through some type of institution in which there are rules governing the actions the agents may take and how these actions translate into a social outcome. To illustrate this point, Examples 23.B.5 and 23.B.6 study two commonly used auction institutions.

**Example 23.B.5:** *First-Price Sealed-Bid Auction.* Consider again the auction setting introduced in Example 23.B.4. In a *first-price sealed-bid auction* each potential buyer $i$ is allowed to submit a sealed bid, $b_i \geq 0$. The bids are then opened and the buyer with the highest bid gets the good and pays an amount equal to his bid to the seller.[8]

To be specific, consider again the case where there are two potential buyers ($I = 2$) and each $\theta_i$ is independently drawn from the uniform distribution on $[0, 1]$. We will look for an equilibrium in which each buyer's strategy $b_i(\cdot)$ takes the form $b_i(\theta_i) = \alpha_i \theta_i$ for $\alpha_i \in [0, 1]$. Suppose that buyer 2's strategy has this form, and consider buyer 1's problem. For each $\theta_1$ he wants to solve

$$\underset{b_1 \geq 0}{\text{Max}} \quad (\theta_1 - b_1) \, \text{Prob}(b_2(\theta_2) \leq b_1).$$

Since buyer 2's highest possible bid is $\alpha_2$ (he submits a bid of $\alpha_2$ when $\theta_2 = 1$), it is evident that buyer 1 should never bid more than $\alpha_2$. Moreover, since $\theta_2$ is uniformly distributed on $[0, 1]$ and $b_2(\theta_2) \leq b_1$ if and only if $\theta_2 \leq (b_1/\alpha_2)$, we can write buyer 1's problem as

$$\underset{b_1 \in [0, \alpha_2]}{\text{Max}} \quad (\theta_1 - b_1)(b_1/\alpha_2).$$

The solution to this problem is

$$b_1(\theta_1) = \begin{cases} \frac{1}{2}\theta_1 & \text{if } \frac{1}{2}\theta_1 \leq \alpha_2, \\ \alpha_2 & \text{if } \frac{1}{2}\theta_1 > \alpha_2. \end{cases}$$

By similar reasoning,

$$b_2(\theta_2) = \begin{cases} \frac{1}{2}\theta_2 & \text{if } \frac{1}{2}\theta_2 \leq \alpha_1, \\ \alpha_1 & \text{if } \frac{1}{2}\theta_2 > \alpha_1. \end{cases}$$

Letting $\alpha_1 = \alpha_2 = \frac{1}{2}$, we see that the strategies $b_i(\theta_i) = \frac{1}{2}\theta_i$ for $i = 1, 2$ constitute a Bayesian Nash equilibrium for this auction. Thus, there is a Bayesian Nash equilibrium of this first-price sealed-bid auction that indirectly yields the outcomes specified by the social choice function $f(\theta) = (y_0(\theta), y_1(\theta), y_2(\theta), t_0(\theta), t_1(\theta), t_2(\theta))$

---

8. If there are several highest bids, we suppose that the lowest numbered of these bidders gets the good. We could equally well randomize among the highest bidders if there are more than one, but this would require that we expand the set of alternatives to $\Delta(X)$, the set of all lotteries over $X$. In fact, we do precisely this when we study auctions in Sections 23.D and 23.F.

in which

$$y_1(\theta) = 1 \qquad \text{if } \theta_1 \geq \theta_2; \quad = 0 \text{ if } \theta_1 < \theta_2 \qquad\qquad (23.\text{B}.9)$$

$$y_2(\theta) = 1 \qquad \text{if } \theta_1 < \theta_2; \quad = 0 \text{ if } \theta_1 \geq \theta_2 \qquad\qquad (23.\text{B}.10)$$

$$y_0(\theta) = 0 \qquad \text{for all } \theta \qquad\qquad (23.\text{B}.11)$$

$$t_1(\theta) = -\tfrac{1}{2}\theta_1 y_1(\theta) \qquad\qquad (23.\text{B}.12)$$

$$t_2(\theta) = -\tfrac{1}{2}\theta_2 y_2(\theta) \qquad\qquad (23.\text{B}.13)$$

$$t_0(\theta) = -(t_1(\theta) + t_2(\theta)). \qquad\qquad (23.\text{B}.14)$$

■

**Example 23.B.6:** *Second-Price Sealed-Bid Auction.*[9]   Once again, consider the auction setting described in Example 23.B.4. In a *second-price sealed-bid auction*, each potential buyer $i$ is allowed to submit a sealed bid, $b_i \geq 0$. The bids are then opened and the buyer with the highest bid gets the good, but now he pays the seller an amount equal to the *second-highest* bid.[10]

By reasoning that parallels that at the end of Example 23.B.4, the strategy $b_i(\theta_i) = \theta_i$ for all $\theta_i \in [0, 1]$ is a weakly dominant strategy for each buyer $i$ (see Exercise 23.B.3). Thus, when $I = 2$ the second-price sealed-bid auction implements the social choice function $f(\theta) = (y_0(\theta), y_1(\theta), y_2(\theta), t_0(\theta), t_1(\theta), t_2(\theta))$ in which

$$y_1(\theta) = 1 \qquad \text{if } \theta_1 \geq \theta_2; \quad = 0 \text{ if } \theta_1 < \theta_2$$

$$y_2(\theta) = 1 \qquad \text{if } \theta_1 < \theta_2; \quad = 0 \text{ if } \theta_1 \geq \theta_2$$

$$y_0(\theta) = 0 \qquad \text{for all } \theta$$

$$t_1(\theta) = -\theta_2 y_1(\theta)$$

$$t_2(\theta) = -\theta_1 y_2(\theta)$$

$$t_0(\theta) = -(t_1(\theta) + t_2(\theta)). \quad ■$$

Examples 23.B.5 and 23.B.6 illustrate that, as a general matter, we need to consider not only the possibility of directly implementing social choice functions by asking agents to reveal their types but also their indirect implementation through the design of institutions in which the agents interact. The formal representation of such an institution is known as a *mechanism*.

**Definition 23.B.3:** A *mechanism* $\Gamma = (S_1, \ldots, S_I, g(\cdot))$ is a collection of $I$ strategy sets $(S_1, \ldots, S_I)$ and an outcome function $g \colon S_1 \times \cdots \times S_I \to X$.

A mechanism can be viewed as an institution with rules governing the procedure for making the collective choice. The allowed actions of each agent $i$ are summarized by the strategy set $S_i$, and the rule for how agents' actions get turned into a social choice is given by the outcome function $g(\cdot)$.

Formally, the mechanism $\Gamma$ combined with possible types $(\Theta_1, \ldots, \Theta_I)$, probability density $\phi(\cdot)$, and Bernoulli utility functions $(u_1(\cdot), \ldots, u_I(\cdot))$ defines

---

9. This auction is also called a *Vickrey auction*, after Vickrey (1961).

10. If there is more than one highest bid, we again select the lowest-numbered of these bidders.

a Bayesian game of incomplete information. That is, letting $\tilde{u}_i(s_1, \ldots, s_I, \theta_i) = u_i(g(s_1, \ldots, s_I), \theta_i)$, the game

$$[I, \{S_i\}, \{\tilde{u}_i(\cdot)\}, \Theta_1 \times \cdots \times \Theta_I, \phi(\cdot)]$$

is exactly the type of Bayesian game studied in Section 8.E. Note that a mechanism could in principle be a complex dynamic procedure, in which case the elements of the strategy sets $S_i$ would consist of contingent plans of action (see Chapter 7).[11]

For the auction setting, the first-price sealed-bid auction is the mechanism in which $S_i = \mathbb{R}_+$ for all $i$ and, given the bids $(b_1, \ldots, b_I) \in \mathbb{R}_+^I$, the outcome function $g(b_1, \ldots, b_I) = (\{y_i(b_1, \ldots, b_I)\}_{i=1}^I, \{t_i(b_1, \ldots, b_I)\}_{i=1}^I)$ is such that

$$y_i(b_1, \ldots, b_I) = 1 \quad \text{if and only if} \quad i = \text{Min}\{j : b_j = \text{Max}\{b_1, \ldots, b_I\}\},$$

$$t_i(b_1, \ldots, b_I) = -b_i y_i(b_1, \ldots, b_I).$$

In the second-price sealed-bid auction, on the other hand, we have the same strategy sets and functions $y_i(\cdot)$, but instead $t_i(b_1, \ldots, b_I) = -\text{Max}\{b_j : j \neq i\} y_i(b_1, \ldots, b_I)$.

A strategy for agent $i$ in the game of incomplete information created by a mechanism $\Gamma$ is a function $s_i : \Theta_i \to S_i$ giving agent $i$'s choice from $S_i$ for each possible type in $\Theta_i$ that he might have. Loosely put, we say that a mechanism *implements* social choice function $f(\cdot)$ if there is an equilibrium of the game induced by the mechanism that yields the same outcomes as $f(\cdot)$ for each possible profile of types $\theta = (\theta_1, \ldots, \theta_I)$. This is stated formally in Definition 23.B.4.

**Definition 23.B.4:** The mechanism $\Gamma = (S_1, \ldots, S_I, g(\cdot))$ *implements* social choice function $f(\cdot)$ if there is an equilibrium strategy profile $(s_1^*(\cdot), \ldots, s_I^*(\cdot))$ of the game induced by $\Gamma$ such that $g(s_1^*(\theta_1), \ldots, s_I^*(\theta_I)) = f(\theta_1, \ldots, \theta_I)$ for all $(\theta_1, \ldots, \theta_I) \in \Theta_1 \times \cdots \times \Theta_I$.

Note, however, that we have not specified in Definition 23.B.4 exactly what we mean by an "equilibrium". This is because, as we have seen in Part II, there is no single equilibrium concept that is universally agreed upon as *the* appropriate solution concept for games. As a result, the mechanism design literature has investigated the implementation question for a variety of solution concepts. In Sections 23.C and 23.D we focus on two central solution concepts: dominant strategy equilibrium and Bayesian Nash equilibrium.[12]

Note also that the notion of implementation that we have adopted in Definition 23.B.4 is in one sense a weak one: in particular, the mechanism $\Gamma$ may have *more than one equilibrium*, but Definition 23.B.4 requires only that *one of them* induce outcomes in accord with $f(\cdot)$. Implicitly, then, Definition 23.B.4 assumes that, if multiple equilibria exist, the agents will play the equilibrium that the mechanism designer wants. Throughout the chapter we shall stick to this notion of implementation. Appendix A is devoted to a further discussion of this issue.

---

11. Note also that we are representing the game created by a mechanism using its normal form. For all the analysis that follows in the text this will be sufficient. In Appendix B, however, we consider a case where the extensive form representation is used.

12. Appendix B considers several other equilibrium concepts in the special context of *complete information* settings in which the players observe each others' types.

The identification of all social choice functions that are implementable may seem like a daunting task because, in principle, it appears that we need to consider all possible mechanisms—a very large set. Fortunately, an important result known as the *revelation principle* (to be formally stated and proven in Sections 23.C and 23.D) tells us that we can often restrict attention to the very simple type of mechanisms that we were implicitly considering at the outset, that is, mechanisms in which each agent is asked to reveal his type, and given the announcements $(\hat{\theta}_1, \ldots, \hat{\theta}_I)$, the alternative chosen is $f(\hat{\theta}_1, \ldots, \hat{\theta}_I) \in X.$[13] These are known as *direct revelation mechanisms*, and formally constitute a special case of the mechanisms of Definition 23.B.3.

**Definition 23.B.5:** A *direct revelation mechanism* is a mechanism in which $S_i = \Theta_i$ for all $i$ and $g(\theta) = f(\theta)$ for all $\theta \in \Theta_1 \times \cdots \times \Theta_I$.

Moreover, as we shall see, the revelation principle also tells us that we can further restrict our attention to direct revelation mechanisms in which *truth telling is an optimal strategy for each agent*. This fact motivates the notion of *truthful implementation* that we introduce in Definition 23.B.6 (we are again purposely vague in the definition about the equilibrium concept we wish to employ).

**Definition 23.B.6:** The social choice function $f(\cdot)$ is *truthfully implementable* (or *incentive compatible*) if the direct revelation mechanism $\Gamma = (\Theta_1, \ldots, \Theta_I, f(\cdot))$ has an equilibrium $(s_1^*(\cdot), \ldots, s_I^*(\cdot))$ in which $s_i^*(\theta_i) = \theta_i$ for all $\theta_i \in \Theta_i$ and all $i = 1, \ldots, I$; that is, if truth telling by each agent $i$ constitutes an equilibrium of $\Gamma = (\Theta_1, \ldots, \Theta_I, f(\cdot))$.

To offer a hint as to why we may be able to restrict attention to direct revelation mechanisms that induce truth telling, we briefly verify that the social choice functions that are implemented indirectly through the first-price and second-price sealed-bid auctions of Examples 23.B.5 and 23.B.6 can also be truthfully implemented using a direct revelation mechanism. In fact, for the second-price sealed-bid auction of Example 23.B.6 we have already seen this fact, because the social choice function implemented by the second-price auction is exactly the social choice function that we studied at the end of Example 23.B.4 in which truth telling is a weakly dominant strategy for both buyers. Example 23.B.7 considers the first-price sealed-bid auction.

**Example 23.B.7:** *Truthful Implementation of the Social Choice Function Implemented by the First-Price Sealed-Bid Auction.* When facing the direct revelation mechanism $(\Theta_1, \ldots, \Theta_I, f(\cdot))$ with $f(\theta) = (y_0(\theta), y_1(\theta), y_2(\theta), t_0(\theta), t_1(\theta), t_2(\theta))$ satisfying (23.B.9) to (23.B.14), buyer 1's optimal announcement $\hat{\theta}_1$ when he has type $\theta_1$ solves

$$\underset{\hat{\theta}_1}{\text{Max}} \quad (\theta_1 - \tfrac{1}{2}\hat{\theta}_1) \, \text{Prob}(\theta_2 \le \hat{\theta}_1)$$

or

$$\underset{\hat{\theta}_1}{\text{Max}} \quad (\theta_1 - \tfrac{1}{2}\hat{\theta}_1)\hat{\theta}_1.$$

---

13. Some early versions of the revelation principle were derived by Gibbard (1973), Green and Laffont (1977), Myerson (1979), and Dasgupta, Hammond and Maskin (1979).

The first-order condition for this problem gives $\hat{\theta}_1 = \theta_1$. So truth telling is buyer 1's optimal strategy given that buyer 2 always tells the truth. A similar conclusion follows for buyer 2. Thus, the social choice function implemented by the first-price sealed-bid auction (in a Bayesian Nash equilibrium) can also be truthfully implemented (in a Bayesian Nash equilibrium) through a direct revelation mechanism. That is, the social choice function (23.B.9) to (23.B.14) is incentive compatible. ∎

Because of the revelation principle, when we explore in Sections 23.C and 23.D the constraints that incomplete information about types puts on the set of implementable social choice functions, we will be able to restrict our analysis to identifying those social choice functions that can be truthfully implemented.

Finally, we note that, in some applications, participation in the mechanism may be *voluntary*, and so a social choice function must not only induce truthful revelation of information but must also satisfy certain *participation* (or *individual rationality*) *constraints* if it is to be successfully implemented. In Sections 23.C and 23.D, however, we shall abstract from issues of participation to focus exclusively on the information revelation problem. We introduce participation constraints in Section 23.E.

# 23.C  Dominant Strategy Implementation

In this section, we study implementation in *dominant strategies*.[14] Throughout we follow the notation introduced in Section 23.B: The vector of agents' types $\theta = (\theta_1, \ldots, \theta_I)$ is drawn from the set $\Theta = \Theta_1 \times \cdots \times \Theta_I$ according to a probability density $\phi(\cdot)$, and agent $i$'s Bernoulli utility function over the alternatives in $X$ given his type $\theta_i$ is $u_i(x, \theta_i)$. We also adopt the notational convention of writing $\theta_{-i} = (\theta_1, \ldots, \theta_{i-1}, \theta_{i+1}, \ldots, \theta_I)$, $\theta = (\theta_i, \theta_{-i})$, and $\Theta_{-i} = \Theta_1 \times \cdots \times \Theta_{i-1} \times \Theta_{i+1} \times \cdots \times \Theta_I$. A mechanism $\Gamma = (S_1, \ldots, S_I, g(\cdot))$ is a collection of $I$ sets $S_1, \ldots, S_I$, each $S_i$ containing agent $i$'s possible actions (or plans of action), and an outcome function $g: S \to X$, where $S = S_1 \times \cdots \times S_I$. As discussed in Section 23.B, a mechanism $\Gamma = (S_1, \ldots, S_I, g(\cdot))$ combined with possible types $(\Theta_1, \ldots, \Theta_I)$, density $\phi(\cdot)$, and Bernoulli utility functions $(u_1(\cdot), \ldots, u_I(\cdot))$ defines a Bayesian game of incomplete information (see Section 8.E). We will also often write $s_{-i} = (s_1, \ldots, s_{i-1}, s_{i+1}, \ldots, s_I)$, $s = (s_i, s_{-i})$, and $S_{-i} = S_1 \times \cdots \times S_{i-1} \times S_{i+1} \times \cdots \times S_I$.

Recall from Section 8.B that a strategy is a weakly dominant strategy for a player in a game if it gives him at least as large a payoff as any of his other possible strategies for every possible strategy that his rivals might play. In the present incomplete information environment, strategy $s_i: \Theta_i \to S_i$ is a weakly dominant strategy for agent $i$ in mechanism $\Gamma = (S_1, \ldots, S_I, g(\cdot))$ if, for all $\theta_i \in \Theta_i$ and all possible strategies for agents $j \neq i$, $s_{-i}(\cdot) = [s_1(\cdot), \ldots, s_{i-1}(\cdot), s_{i+1}(\cdot), \ldots, s_I(\cdot)]$,[15]

$$E_{\theta_{-i}}[u_i(g(s_i(\theta_i), s_{-i}(\theta_{-i})), \theta_i)|\theta_i] \geq E_{\theta_{-i}}[u_i(g(\hat{s}_i, s_{-i}(\theta_{-i})), \theta_i)|\theta_i] \qquad \text{for all } \hat{s}_i \in S_i.$$

$$(23.C.1)$$

Condition (23.C.1) holding for all $s_{-i}(\cdot)$ and $\theta_i$ is equivalent to the condition that,

---

14. Good sources for further reading on the subject of this section are Dasgupta, Hammond and Maskin (1979) and Green and Laffont (1979).

15. The expectation in (23.C.1) is taken over realizations of $\theta_{-i} \in \Theta_{-i}$.

for all $\theta_i \in \Theta_i$,

$$u_i(g(s_i(\theta_i), s_{-i}), \theta_i) \geq u_i(g(\hat{s}_i, s_{-i}), \theta_i) \tag{23.C.2}$$

for all $\hat{s}_i \in S_i$ and all $s_{-i} \in S_{-i}$.[16] This leads to Definition 23.C.1.

**Definition 23.C.1:** The strategy profile $s^*(\cdot) = (s_1^*(\cdot), \ldots, s_I^*(\cdot))$ is a *dominant strategy equilibrium* of mechanism $\Gamma = (S_1, \ldots, S_I, g(\cdot))$ if, for all $i$ and all $\theta_i \in \Theta_i$,

$$u_i(g(s_i^*(\theta_i), s_{-i}), \theta_i) \geq u_i(g(s_i', s_{-i}), \theta_i)$$

for all $s_i' \in S_i$ and all $s_{-i} \in S_{-i}$.

We now specialize Definition 23.B.4 to the notion of dominant strategy equilibrium.

**Definition 23.C.2:** The mechanism $\Gamma = (S_1, \ldots, S_I, g(\cdot))$ *implements the social choice function $f(\cdot)$ in dominant strategies* if there exists a dominant strategy equilibrium of $\Gamma$, $s^*(\cdot) = (s_1^*(\cdot), \ldots, s_I^*(\cdot))$, such that $g(s^*(\theta)) = f(\theta)$ for all $\theta \in \Theta$.

The concept of dominant strategy implementation is of special interest because if we can find a mechanism $\Gamma = (S_1, \ldots, S_I, g(\cdot))$ that implements $f(\cdot)$ in dominant strategies, then this mechanism implements $f(\cdot)$ in a very strong and robust way. This is true in several senses. First, we can feel fairly confident that a rational agent who has a (weakly) dominant strategy will indeed play it.[17] Unlike the equilibrium strategies in Nash-related equilibrium concepts, a player need not correctly forecast his opponents' play to justify his play of a dominant strategy. Second, although we have assumed that the agents know the probability density $\phi(\cdot)$ over realizations of the types $(\theta_1, \ldots, \theta_I)$, and hence can deduce the correct conditional probability distribution over realizations of $\theta_{-i}$, if $\Gamma$ implements $f(\cdot)$ in dominant strategies this implementation will be robust even if agents have incorrect, and perhaps even contradictory, beliefs about this distribution. In particular, agent $i$'s beliefs regarding the distribution of $\theta_{-i}$ do not affect the dominance of his strategy $s_i^*(\cdot)$.[18] Third, it follows that if $\Gamma$ implements $f(\cdot)$ in dominant strategies then it does so regardless of the probability density $\phi(\cdot)$. Thus, the same mechanism can be used to implement $f(\cdot)$ for any $\phi(\cdot)$. One advantage of this is that if the mechanism designer is an outsider (say, the "government"), he need not know $\phi(\cdot)$ to successfully implement $f(\cdot)$.

As we noted in Section 23.B, to identify whether a particular social choice function $f(\cdot)$ is implementable, we need, in principle, to consider all possible mechanisms. Fortunately, it turns out that for dominant strategy implementation it suffices to ask

---

16. Condition (23.C.2) follows from (23.C.1) simply by setting $s_{-i}(\theta_{-i}) = s_{-i}$ for all $\theta_{-i} \in \Theta_{-i}$. To see that (23.C.2) implies (23.C.1), consider the case where $S_{-i}$ is a finite set. Then, for any $s_i$,

$$E_{\theta_{-i}}[u_i(g(s_i, s_{-i}(\theta_{-i})), \theta_i)|\theta_i] = \sum_{s_{-i} \in S_{-i}} \text{Prob}(s_{-i}(\theta_{-i}) = s_{-i}) u_i(g(s_i, s_{-i}), \theta_i).$$

Thus, (23.C.2) implies (23.C.1).

17. We leave aside the question of what might happen if an agent has *several* weakly dominant strategies. This is the issue of multiple equilibria that we discuss in Appendix A. Even so, we at least mention one conclusion from that discussion: The problem of multiple equilibria is relatively small when we are dealing with dominant strategy equilibrium.

18. In fact, the implementation of $f(\cdot)$ using $\Gamma$ is also robust to substantial relaxations of the hypothesis that agents maximize expected utility.

whether a particular $f(\cdot)$ is truthfully implementable in the sense introduced in Definition 23.C.3.

**Definition 23.C.3:** The social choice function $f(\cdot)$ is *truthfully implementable in dominant strategies* (or *dominant strategy incentive compatible*, or *strategy-proof*, or *straightforward*) if $s_i^*(\theta_i) = \theta_i$ for all $\theta_i \in \Theta_i$ and $i = 1, \ldots, I$ is a dominant strategy equilibrium of the direct revelation mechanism $\Gamma = (\Theta_1, \ldots, \Theta_I, f(\cdot))$. That is, if for all $i$ and all $\theta_i \in \Theta_i$,

$$u_i(f(\theta_i, \theta_{-i}), \theta_i) \geq u_i(f(\hat{\theta}_i, \theta_{-i}), \theta_i) \tag{23.C.3}$$

for all $\hat{\theta}_i \in \Theta_i$ and all $\theta_{-i} \in \Theta_{-i}$.

The ability to restrict our inquiry, without loss of generality, to the question of whether $f(\cdot)$ is truthfully implementable is a consequence of what is known as the *revelation principle for dominant strategies*.

**Proposition 23.C.1:** (*The Revelation Principle for Dominant Strategies*) Suppose that there exists a mechanism $\Gamma = (S_1, \ldots, S_I, g(\cdot))$ that implements the social choice function $f(\cdot)$ in dominant strategies. Then $f(\cdot)$ is truthfully implementable in dominant strategies.

**Proof:** If $\Gamma = (S_1, \ldots, S_I, g(\cdot))$ implements $f(\cdot)$ in dominant strategies, then there exists a profile of strategies $s^*(\cdot) = (s_1^*(\cdot), \ldots, s_I^*(\cdot))$ such that $g(s^*(\theta)) = f(\theta)$ for all $\theta$ and, for all $i$ and all $\theta_i \in \Theta_i$,

$$u_i(g(s_i^*(\theta_i), s_{-i}), \theta_i) \geq u_i(g(\hat{s}_i, s_{-i}), \theta_i) \tag{23.C.4}$$

for all $\hat{s}_i \in S_i$ and all $s_{-i} \in S_{-i}$. Condition (23.C.4) implies, in particular, that for all $i$ and all $\theta_i \in \Theta_i$,

$$u_i(g(s_i^*(\theta_i), s_{-i}^*(\theta_{-i})), \theta_i) \geq u_i(g(s_i^*(\hat{\theta}_i), s_{-i}^*(\theta_{-i})), \theta_i) \tag{23.C.5}$$

for all $\hat{\theta}_i \in \Theta_i$ and all $\theta_{-i} \in \Theta_{-i}$. Since $g(s^*(\theta)) = f(\theta)$ for all $\theta$, (23.C.5) means that, for all $i$ and all $\theta_i \in \Theta_i$,

$$u_i(f(\theta_i, \theta_{-i}), \theta_i) \geq u_i(f(\hat{\theta}_i, \theta_{-i}), \theta_i)$$

for all $\hat{\theta}_i \in \Theta_i$ and all $\theta_{-i} \in \Theta_{-i}$. But, this is precisely condition (23.C.3), the condition for $f(\cdot)$ to be truthfully implementable in dominant strategies. ∎

The intuitive idea behind the revelation principle for dominant strategies can be put as follows: Suppose that the indirect mechanism $\Gamma = (S_1, \ldots, S_I, g(\cdot))$ implements $f(\cdot)$ in dominant strategies, and that in this indirect mechanism each agent $i$ finds playing $s_i^*(\theta_i)$ when his type is $\theta_i$ better than playing any other $s_i \in S_i$ for any choices $s_{-i} \in S_{-i}$ by agents $j \neq i$. Now consider altering this mechanism simply by introducing a mediator who says to each agent $i$: "You tell me your type, and when you say your type is $\theta_i$, I will play $s_i^*(\theta_i)$ for you." Clearly, if $s_i^*(\theta_i)$ is agent $i$'s optimal choice for each $\theta_i \in \Theta_i$ in the initial mechanism $\Gamma$ for any strategies chosen by the other agents, then agent $i$ will find telling the truth to be a dominant strategy in this new scheme. But this means that we have found a way to truthfully implement $f(\cdot)$.

The implication of the revelation principle is that to identify the set of social choice functions that are implementable in dominant strategies, we need only identify those that are truthfully implementable. In principle, for any $f(\cdot)$, this is just a matter of checking the inequalities (23.C.3).

The inequalities (23.C.3), which are necessary and sufficient for a social choice function $f(\cdot)$ to be truthfully implementable in dominant strategies, can be usefully thought of in terms of a certain *weak preference reversal property*. In particular, consider any agent $i$ and any pair of possible types for $i$, $\theta_i'$ and $\theta_i''$. If truth telling is a dominant strategy for agent $i$, then for any $\theta_{-i} \in \Theta_{-i}$ we must have

$$u_i(f(\theta_i', \theta_{-i}), \theta_i') \geq u_i(f(\theta_i'', \theta_{-i}), \theta_i')$$

and

$$u_i(f(\theta_i'', \theta_{-i}), \theta_i'') \geq u_i(f(\theta_i', \theta_{-i}), \theta_i'').$$

That is, agent $i$'s preference ranking of $f(\theta_i', \theta_{-i})$ and $f(\theta_i'', \theta_{-i})$ must *weakly reverse* when his type changes from $\theta_i'$ to $\theta_i''$, with him weakly preferring alternative $f(\theta_i', \theta_{-i})$ to $f(\theta_i'', \theta_{-i})$ when his type is $\theta_i'$, but weakly preferring alternative $f(\theta_i'', \theta_{-i})$ to $f(\theta_i', \theta_{-i})$ when his type is $\theta_i''$. In the reverse direction, if this weak preference reversal property holds for *all* $\theta_{-i} \in \Theta_{-i}$ and *all* pairs $\theta_i', \theta_i'' \in \Theta_i$, then truth telling is indeed a dominant strategy for agent $i$ (check this in Exercise 23.C.1).

This weak preference reversal property can be succinctly stated using agent $i$'s *lower contour sets*. Define the lower contour set of alternative $x$ when agent $i$ has type $\theta_i$ by (see Section 3.B):

$$L_i(x, \theta_i) = \{z \in X: u_i(x, \theta_i) \geq u_i(z, \theta_i)\}.$$

Using this lower contour set we get the characterization of the set of social choice functions that can be truthfully implemented in dominant strategies that is given in Proposition 23.C.2.

**Proposition 23.C.2:** The social choice function $f(\cdot)$ is truthfully implementable in dominant strategies if and only if for all $i$, all $\theta_{-i} \in \Theta_{-i}$, and all pairs of types for agent $i$, $\theta_i'$ and $\theta_i'' \in \Theta_i$, we have

$$f(\theta_i'', \theta_{-i}) \in L_i(f(\theta_i', \theta_{-i}), \theta_i') \quad \text{and} \quad f(\theta_i', \theta_{-i}) \in L_i(f(\theta_i'', \theta_{-i}), \theta_i''). \quad (23.C.6)$$

The idea behind this preference reversal characterization of the social choice functions that can be truthfully implemented in dominant strategies is illustrated in Figures 23.C.1 and 23.C.2. In Figure 23.C.1, we represent the social choice function $f(\cdot)$ for each possible configuration of types $(\theta_1, \theta_2)$ in a situation in which there are two agents ($I = 2$), two possible values of $\theta_1$, and three possible values of $\theta_2$. Consider agent 1's incentives to tell the truth. If truth telling is a weakly dominant strategy for agent 1, then when his type changes from $\theta_1'$ to $\theta_1''$, he must experience a weak preference reversal between outcomes $f(\theta_1', \theta_2)$ and $f(\theta_1'', \theta_2)$ for each possible value of $\theta_2$. A similar point applies for agent 2.

**Figure 23.C.1**

For agent 1 to find truth telling to be his dominant strategy, he must experience a weak preference reversal between outcomes $f(\theta_1', \theta_2)$ and $f(\theta_1'', \theta_2)$ when his type changes from $\theta_1'$ to $\theta_1''$, for each possible $\theta_2$.

|  | $\theta_2'$ | $\theta_2''$ | $\theta_2'''$ |
|---|---|---|---|
| $\theta_1'$ | $f(\theta_1', \theta_2')$ | $f(\theta_1', \theta_2'')$ | $f(\theta_1', \theta_2''')$ |
| $\theta_1''$ | $f(\theta_1'', \theta_2')$ | $f(\theta_1'', \theta_2'')$ | $f(\theta_1'', \theta_2''')$ |

$\theta_2$ (column header), $\theta_1$ (row header)

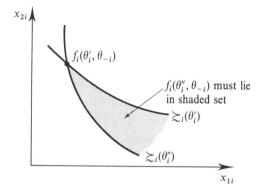

**Figure 23.C.2**

The weak preference reversal property of Proposition 23.C.2 when preferences satisfy the single-crossing property.

Figure 23.C.2 depicts a change in some agent $i$'s type from $\theta_i'$ to $\theta_i''$ in an exchange setting in which agent $i$'s preferences satisfy the *single-crossing property* that we discussed in Sections 13.C and 14.C. In the figure, we denote agent $i$'s allocation in outcome $f(\theta_1, \theta_2)$ by $f_i(\theta_1, \theta_2)$. According to Proposition 23.C.2, $f_i(\theta_i'', \theta_{-i})$ must lie in the shaded region of the figure if truth telling is to be a dominant strategy for agent $i$. Thus, the characterization in Proposition 23.C.2 can be seen as a multiperson extension of the truth-telling constraints that we encountered in Section 14.C (here they must hold for every possible $\theta_{-i} \in \Theta_{-i}$).

In the remainder of this section we explore in more detail the characteristics of social choice functions that can be truthfully implemented in dominant strategies.

### The Gibbard–Satterthwaite Theorem

The Gibbard–Satterwaite theorem was discovered independently in the early 1970s by the two named authors [Gibbard (1973), Satterthwaite (1975)]. It is an impossibility result similar in spirit to Arrow's theorem (Proposition 21.C.1), and has shaped the course of research on incentives and implementation to a great extent. It shows that for a very general class of problems there is no hope of implementing satisfactory social choice functions in dominant strategies.

In what follows, we let $\mathscr{P}$ denote the set of all rational preference relations $\succsim$ on $X$ having the property that no two alternatives are indifferent, and we recall that $\mathscr{R}_i = \{\succsim_i : \succsim_i = \succsim_i(\theta_i)$ for some $\theta_i \in \Theta_i\}$ is agent $i$'s set of possible ordinal preference relations over $X$. We denote by $f(\Theta)$ the image of $f(\cdot)$; that is, $f(\Theta) = \{x \in X : f(\theta) = x$ for some $\theta \in \Theta\}$. In Definitions 23.C.4 and 23.C.5 we also recall two properties of social choice functions introduced and discussed in Section 21.E.

**Definition 23.C.4:** The social choice function $f(\cdot)$ is *dictatorial* if there is an agent $i$ such that, for all $\theta = (\theta_1, \ldots, \theta_I) \in \Theta$,

$$f(\theta) \in \{x \in X : u_i(x, \theta_i) \geq u_i(y, \theta_i) \text{ for all } y \in X\}.$$

In words: A social choice function is dictatorial if there is an agent $i$ such that $f(\cdot)$ always chooses one of $i$'s top-ranked alternatives.

**Definition 23.C.5:** The social choice function $f(\cdot)$ is *monotonic* if, for any $\theta$, if $\theta'$ is such that $L_i(f(\theta), \theta_i) \subset L_i(f(\theta), \theta_i')$ for all $i$ [i.e., if $L_i(f(\theta), \theta_i)$ is weakly included in $L_i(f(\theta), \theta_i')$ for all $i$], then $f(\theta') = f(\theta)$.

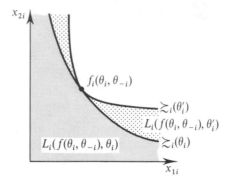

**Figure 23.C.3**

If $f(\cdot)$ is
monotonic, then
$f(\theta'_i, \theta_{-i}) = f(\theta_i, \theta_{-i})$.

Monotonicity requires the following: Suppose that $f(\theta) = x$, and that the $I$ agents' types change to a $\theta' = (\theta'_1, \ldots, \theta'_I)$ with the property that no agent finds that some alternative that was weakly worse for him than $x$ when his type was $\theta_i$ becomes strictly preferred to $x$ when his type is $\theta'_i$. Then $x$ must still be the social choice. The monotonicity property is illustrated in Figure 23.C.3 for an exchange setting. In the figure, $f_i(\theta_i, \theta_{-i})$ represents agent $i$'s allocation in outcome $f(\theta_i, \theta_{-i})$. The figure depicts a change in agent $i$'s type from $\theta_i$ to a $\theta'_i$ having the property that $L_i(f(\theta_i, \theta_{-i}), \theta_i) \subset L_i(f(\theta_i, \theta_{-i}), \theta'_i)$. If $f(\cdot)$ is monotonic, then $f(\theta'_i, \theta_{-i}) = f(\theta_i, \theta_{-i})$.

With these definitions we now state and prove the Gibbard–Satterthwaite theorem.

**Proposition 23.C.3:** *(The Gibbard–Satterthwaite Theorem)* Suppose that $X$ is finite and contains at least three elements, that $\mathscr{R}_i = \mathscr{P}$ for all $i$, and that $f(\Theta) = X$.[19] Then the social choice function $f(\cdot)$ is truthfully implementable in dominant strategies if and only if it is dictatorial.

**Proof:** It is immediate that a dictatorial $f(\cdot)$ is truthfully implementable (check for yourself that every agent will tell the truth). We now show that if $f(\cdot)$ is truthfully implementable in dominant strategies then it must be dictatorial. The argument consists of three steps.

*Step 1:* *If $\mathscr{R}_i = \mathscr{P}$ for all $i$, and $f(\cdot)$ is truthfully implementable in dominant strategies, then $f(\cdot)$ is monotonic.*

Consider two profiles of types $\theta$ and $\theta'$ such that $L_i(f(\theta), \theta_i) \subset L_i(f(\theta), \theta'_i)$ for all $i$. We want to show that $f(\theta') = f(\theta)$. Let us begin by determining $f(\theta'_1, \theta_2, \ldots, \theta_I)$. By Proposition 23.C.2 we know that we must have $f(\theta'_1, \theta_2, \ldots, \theta_I) \in L_1(f(\theta), \theta_1)$. Hence, $f(\theta'_1, \theta_2, \ldots, \theta_I) \in L_1(f(\theta), \theta'_1)$. But Proposition 23.C.2 also implies that $f(\theta) \in L_1(f(\theta'_1, \theta_2, \ldots, \theta_I), \theta'_1)$. Since, by hypothesis, no two alternatives can be indifferent in preference relation $\succsim_1 (\theta'_1)$, this must imply that $f(\theta'_1, \theta_2, \ldots, \theta_I) = f(\theta)$. The same line of argument can be used to show next that $f(\theta'_1, \theta'_2, \theta_3, \ldots, \theta_I) = f(\theta)$. Indeed, proceeding iteratively, we establish that $f(\theta') = f(\theta)$. Thus, $f(\cdot)$ is monotonic.

*Step 2:* *If $\mathscr{R}_i = \mathscr{P}$ for all $i$, $f(\cdot)$ is monotonic, and $f(\Theta) = X$, then $f(\cdot)$ is ex post efficient.*

19. Strictly speaking, finiteness of the set $X$ is not required for the result. But in the absence of finiteness, our assumption that agents are expected utility maximizers may not be compatible with the condition that $\mathscr{R}_i = \mathscr{P}$ (e.g., if $X = \mathbb{R}^L_+$, the lexicographic preference relation studied in Example 3.C.1 is a strict preference relation that is not representable by a utility function). For a proof that Proposition 23.C.3 continues to be true if we let $X$ be an arbitrary set and $\mathscr{R}_i$ be the set of all *continuous* preferences on $X$, see Barberà and Peleg (1990).

To verify this, suppose not. Then there is a $\theta \in \Theta$ and a $y \in X$ such that $u_i(y, \theta_i) > u_i(f(\theta), \theta_i)$ for all $i$ (recall that no two alternatives can be indifferent). Because $f(\Theta) = X$, there exists a $\theta' \in \Theta$ such that $f(\theta') = y$. Now choose a vector of types $\theta'' \in \Theta$ such that, for all $i$, $u_i(y, \theta_i'') > u_i(f(\theta), \theta_i'') > u_i(z, \theta_i'')$ for all $z \neq f(\theta), y$. (Remember that all preferences in $\mathscr{P}$ are possible.) Since $L_i(y, \theta_i') \subset L_i(y, \theta_i'')$ for all $i$, monotonicity implies that $f(\theta'') = y$. But, since $L_i(f(\theta), \theta_i) \subset L_i(f(\theta), \theta_i'')$ for all $i$, monotonicity also implies that $f(\theta'') = f(\theta)$: a contradiction because $y \neq f(\theta)$. Hence, $f(\cdot)$ must be ex post efficient.

*Step 3: A social choice function $f(\cdot)$ that is monotonic and ex post efficient is necessarily dictatorial.*

Step 3 follows directly from Proposition 21.E.1.

Together, steps 1 to 3 establish the result. ∎

It should be noted that the conclusion of Proposition 23.C.3 does *not* follow if $X$ contains two elements. For example, in this case, a majority voting social choice function (see Section 21.E) is both nondictatorial and truthfully implementable in dominant strategies (Exercise 23.C.2).

Note also that when $\mathscr{R}_i = \mathscr{P}$ for all $i$, any ex post efficient social choice function *must* have $f(\Theta) = X$ (verify this in Exercise 23.C.3). Thus, the Gibbard–Satterthwaite theorem tells us that when $\mathscr{R}_i = \mathscr{P}$ for all $i$, and $X$ contains more than two elements, the only ex post efficient social choice functions that are truthfully implementable in dominant strategies are dictatorial social choice functions.

Given this negative conclusion, if we are to have any hope of implementing desirable social choice functions, we must either weaken the demands of our implementation concept by accepting implementation by means of less robust equilibrium notions (such as Bayesian Nash equilibria) or we must focus on more restricted environments. In the remainder of this section, we follow the latter course, studying the possibilities for implementing desirable social choice functions in dominant strategies when preferences take a quasilinear form. Section 23.D explores the former possibility: It studies implementation in Bayesian Nash equilibria.

---

Proposition 23.C.3 is readily extended in two ways. First, the result's conclusion still follows whenever $\mathscr{R}_i$ contains $\mathscr{P}$ (the set of all rational preference relations having the property that no two alternatives are indifferent), and so it extends to environments in which individual indifference is possible. This is stated formally in Corollary 23.C.1.

**Corollary 23.C.1:** Suppose that $X$ is finite and contains at least three elements, that $\mathscr{P} \subset \mathscr{R}_i$ for all $i$, and that $f(\Theta) = X$. Then the social choice function $f(\cdot)$ is truthfully implementable in dominant strategies if and only if it is dictatorial.

**Proof:** It is again immediate that a dictatorial social choice function is truthfully implementable. We now show that under the stated hypotheses $f(\cdot)$ must be dictatorial if it is truthfully implementable.

An implication of Proposition 23.C.3 is that there must be an agent $h$ such that $f(\theta) \in \{x \in X : u_h(x, \theta_h) \geq u_h(y, \theta_h) \text{ for all } y \in X\}$ whenever $\succsim_i(\theta_i) \in \mathscr{P}$ for all $i$ (see Exercise 23.C.4). Without loss of generality, let this be agent $I$. Suppose now that the result is not true. Then there is a profile of types $\theta' \in \Theta$ such that $f(\theta') \notin \{x \in X : u_I(x, \theta_I') \geq u_I(y, \theta_I') \text{ for all}$

$y \in X\}$. Let $z \in \{x \in X : u_I(x, \theta'_I) \geq u_I(y, \theta'_I)$ for all $y \in X\}$. Now consider a profile of types $\theta'' \in \Theta$ such that (i) $\succsim_i(\theta''_i) \in \mathscr{P}$ for all $i = 1, \ldots, I$; (ii) for all agents $i \neq I$, $u_i(f(\theta'), \theta''_i) > u_i(z, \theta''_i) > u_i(x, \theta''_i)$ for all $x \notin \{f(\theta'), z\}$; and (iii) $u_I(z, \theta''_I) > u_I(f(\theta'), \theta''_I) > u_I(x, \theta''_I)$ for all $x \notin \{f(\theta'), z\}$. Consider the profile of types $(\theta''_1, \theta'_2, \ldots, \theta'_I)$. By Proposition 23.C.2, we must have $f(\theta') \in L_1(f(\theta''_1, \theta'_2, \ldots, \theta'_I), \theta'_1)$, and so it must be that $f(\theta''_1, \theta'_2, \ldots, \theta'_I) = f(\theta')$. The same argument can be applied iteratively for all $i \neq I$ to show that $f(\theta''_1, \ldots, \theta''_{I-1}, \theta'_I) = f(\theta')$. Next, note that (by Proposition 23.C.2) we must have $f(\theta''_1, \ldots, \theta''_{I-1}, \theta'_I) \in L_I(f(\theta''), \theta''_I)$. Hence, $f(\theta'') \in \{z, f(\theta')\}$. But (by Proposition 23.C.2) we must also have $f(\theta'') \in L_I(f(\theta''_1, \ldots, \theta''_{I-1}, \theta'_I), \theta'_I)$, and since $u_I(z, \theta'_I) > u_I(f(\theta'), \theta'_I)$ this means we cannot have $f(\theta'') = z$. Hence, $f(\theta'') = f(\theta')$. But, since $u_I(z, \theta''_I) > u_I(f(\theta'), \theta''_I)$, this contradicts agent $I$ being a dictator whenever $\succsim_i(\theta_i) \in \mathscr{P}$ for all $i$. ∎

As our second extension, we can derive a related dictatorship result for social choice functions whose image $f(\Theta)$ is smaller than $X$. We first offer Definition 23.C.6.

**Definition 23.C.6:** The social choice function $f(\cdot)$ is *dictatorial on set* $\hat{X} \subset X$ if there exists an agent $i$ such that, for all $\theta = (\theta_1, \ldots, \theta_I) \in \Theta$, $f(\theta) \in \{x \in \hat{X} : u_i(x, \theta_i) \geq u_i(y, \theta_i)$ for all $y \in \hat{X}\}$.

This weaker notion of dictatorship requires only that $f(\cdot)$ select one of the dictator's most preferred alternatives in $\hat{X}$, rather than in $X$.

**Corollary 23.C.2:** Suppose that $X$ is finite, that the number of elements in $f(\Theta)$ is at least three, and that $\mathscr{P} \subset \mathscr{R}_i$ for all $i = 1, \ldots, I$. Then $f(\cdot)$ is truthfully implementable in dominant strategies if and only if it is dictatorial on the set $f(\Theta)$.

**Proof:** It is immediate that $f(\cdot)$ is truthfully implementable if it is dictatorial on the set $f(\Theta)$, and so we now show that under the stated hypotheses $f(\cdot)$ must be dictatorial on set $f(\Theta)$. If $f: \Theta \to X$ is truthfully implementable in dominant strategies when the set of alternatives is $X$, then the social choice function $\hat{f}: \Theta \to f(\Theta)$ which has $\hat{f}(\theta) = f(\theta)$ for all $\theta \in \Theta$ is truthfully implementable in dominant strategies when the set of alternatives is $f(\Theta)$. By Corollary 23.C.1, $\hat{f}(\cdot)$ must be dictatorial. Hence, $f(\cdot)$ is dictatorial on the set $f(\Theta)$. ∎

The implication flowing from Corollary 23.C.2 is therefore this: When $\mathscr{R}_i \subset \mathscr{P}$ for all $i$, the set of social choice functions which have an image that contains at least three elements and which are truthfully implementable in dominant strategies is exactly the set of social choice functions that can be implemented (indirectly) by restricting the set of possible choices to some subset $\hat{X} \subset X$ and assigning a single agent $i$ to choose from within this set.

---

### Quasilinear Environments: Groves–Clarke Mechanisms

In this subsection we focus on the special, but much studied, class of environments in which agents have quasilinear preferences. In particular, an alternative is now a vector $x = (k, t_1, \ldots, t_I)$, where $k$ is an element of a finite set $K$, to be called the "project choice," and $t_i \in \mathbb{R}$ is a transfer of a numeraire commodity ("money") to agent $i$. Agent $i$'s utility function takes the quasilinear form

$$u_i(x, \theta_i) = v_i(k, \theta_i) + (\bar{m}_i + t_i),$$

where $\bar{m}_i$ is agent $i$'s endowment of the numeraire. We assume that we are dealing with a closed system in which the $I$ agents have no outside source of financing. The set of alternatives is therefore[20]

$$X = \{(k, t_1, \ldots, t_I) : k \in K, t_i \in \mathbb{R} \text{ for all } i, \text{ and } \sum_i t_i \leq 0\}.$$

Note that this environment encompasses the cases studied in Examples 23.B.3 and 23.B.4:

**Example 23.C.1:** *A Public Project.* We can fit a generalized version of the public project setting of Example 23.B.3 into the framework outlined above. To do so, let $K$ contain the possible levels of a public project (e.g., if $K = \{0, 1\}$, then either the project is "not done" or "done") and denote by $c(k)$ the cost of project level $k \in K$. Suppose that $\tilde{v}_i(k, \theta_i)$ is agent $i$'s *gross* benefit from project level $k$ and that, in the absence of any other transfers, projects will be financed through equal contribution [i.e., each agent $i$ will pay the amount $c(k)/I$].[21] Then, we can write agent $i$'s *net* benefit from project level $k$ when his type is $\theta_i$ as $v_i(k, \theta_i) = \tilde{v}_i(k, \theta_i) - (c(k)/I)$. The $t_i$'s are now transfers over and above the payments $c(k)/I$. ∎

**Example 23.C.2:** *Allocation of a Single Unit of an Indivisible Private Good.* Consider the environment described in Example 23.B.4 in which an indivisible unit of a private good is to be allocated to one of $I$ agents. Here the "project choice" $k = (y_1, \ldots, y_I)$ represents the allocation of the private good and $K = \{(y_1, \ldots, y_I) : y_i \in \{0, 1\}$ for all $i$ and $\sum_i y_i = 1\}$. Agent $i$'s valuation function takes the form $v_i(k, \theta_i) = \theta_i y_i$. ∎

A social choice function in this quasilinear environment takes the form $f(\cdot) = (k(\cdot), t_1(\cdot), \ldots, t_I(\cdot))$ where, for all $\theta \in \Theta$, $k(\theta) \in K$ and $\sum_i t_i(\theta) \leq 0$. Note that if the social choice function $f(\cdot)$ is ex post efficient then, for all $\theta \in \Theta$, $k(\theta)$ must satisfy

$$\sum_{i=1}^{I} v_i(k(\theta), \theta_i) \geq \sum_{i=1}^{I} v_i(k, \theta_i) \qquad \text{for all } k \in K. \tag{23.C.7}$$

We begin with a result that identifies a class of social choice functions that satisfy (23.C.7) and that are truthfully implementable in dominant strategies.

**Proposition 23.C.4:** Let $k^*(\cdot)$ be a function satisfying (23.C.7). The social choice function $f(\cdot) = (k^*(\cdot), t_1(\cdot), \ldots, t_I(\cdot))$ is truthfully implementable in dominant strategies if, for all $i = 1, \ldots, I$,

$$t_i(\theta) = \left[ \sum_{j \neq i} v_j(k^*(\theta), \theta_j) \right] + h_i(\theta_{-i}), \tag{23.C.8}$$

where $h_i(\cdot)$ is an arbitrary function of $\theta_{-i}$.

**Proof:** If truth is not a dominant strategy for some agent $i$, then there exist $\theta_i$, $\hat{\theta}_i$, and $\theta_{-i}$ such that

$$v_i(k^*(\hat{\theta}_i, \theta_{-i}), \theta_i) + t_i(\hat{\theta}_i, \theta_{-i}) > v_i(k^*(\theta_i, \theta_{-i}), \theta_i) + t_i(\theta_i, \theta_{-i}).$$

---

20. Observe that $X$ is not a compact set. This explains what might appear as a small paradox: in this setting, there are no dictatorial social choice functions because any agent $i$, when allowed to pick his best alternative in $X$, faces no bound on how much money he can extract from the other agents.

21. Nothing we do depends on this choice for the "base" method of contribution.

Substituting from (23.C.8) for $t_i(\hat{\theta}_i, \theta_{-i})$ and $t_i(\theta_i, \theta_{-i})$, this implies that

$$\sum_{j=1}^{I} v_j(k^*(\hat{\theta}_i, \theta_{-i}), \theta_j) > \sum_{j=1}^{I} v_j(k^*(\theta), \theta_j),$$

which contradicts $k^*(\cdot)$ satisfying (23.C.7). Thus, $f(\cdot)$ must be truthfully implementable in dominant strategies. ∎

A direct revelation mechanism $\Gamma = (\Theta_1, \ldots, \Theta_I, f(\cdot))$ in which $f(\cdot) = (k(\cdot), t_1(\cdot), \ldots, t_I(\cdot))$ satisfies (23.C.7) and (23.C.8) is known as a *Groves mechanism* or *Groves scheme* [after Groves (1973)].[22] In a Groves mechanism, given the announcements $\theta_{-i}$ of agents $j \neq i$, agent $i$'s transfer depends on his announced type only through his announcement's effect on the project choice $k^*(\theta)$. Moreover, the change in agent $i$'s transfer that results when his announcement changes the project decision $k$ is exactly equal to the effect of this change in $k$ on agents $j \neq i$. Put differently, the change in agent $i$'s transfer reflects exactly the *externality* that he is imposing on the other agents. As a result, agent $i$ is led to internalize this externality and make an announcement—namely, truth—that leads to a level of $k$ that maximizes the $I$ agents' joint payoff from the project, $\sum_i v_i(k, \theta_i)$.

A special case of a Groves mechanism was discovered independently by Clarke (1971) and is known as the *Clarke*, or *pivotal*, *mechanism*. This mechanism corresponds to the case in which $h_i(\theta_{-i}) = -\sum_{j \neq i} v_j(k^*_{-i}(\theta_{-i}), \theta_j)$ where, for all $\theta_{-i} \in \Theta_{-i}$, $k^*_{-i}(\theta_{-i})$ satisfies

$$\sum_{j \neq i} v_j(k^*_{-i}(\theta_{-i}), \theta_j) \geq \sum_{j \neq i} v_j(k, \theta_j) \qquad \text{for all } k \in K.$$

That is, $k^*_{-i}(\theta_{-i})$ is the project level that would be ex post efficient if there were only the $I - 1$ agents $j \neq i$. Agent $i$'s transfer in the Clarke mechanism is then given by

$$t_i(\theta) = \left[ \sum_{j \neq i} v_j(k^*(\theta), \theta_j) \right] - \left[ \sum_{j \neq i} v_j(k^*_{-i}(\theta_{-i}), \theta_j) \right].$$

Note that agent $i$'s transfer is 0 if his announcement does not change the project decision relative to what would be ex post efficient for agents $j \neq i$ in isolation [i.e., if $k^*(\theta) = k^*_{-i}(\theta_{-i})$], and is negative if it does change the project decision [i.e., if $k^*(\theta) \neq k^*_{-i}(\theta_{-i})$], that is, if agent $i$ is "pivotal" to the efficient project choice. Thus, in the Clarke mechanism agent $i$ pays a tax equal to his effect on the other agents if he is pivotal to the project decision, and he pays nothing otherwise.[23]

---

22. We will sometimes be a little loose in our terminology and simply refer to a social choice function $f(\cdot)$ satisfying (23.C.7) and (23.C.8) as a Groves mechanism.

23. Note that the social choice function of the Clarke mechanism satisfies the feasibility condition that $\sum_i t_i(\theta) \leq 0$ for all $\theta$. Indeed, examining (23.C.8), we see that a sufficient (but *not* necessary) condition for a Groves scheme to satisfy the condition that $\sum_i t_i(\theta) \leq 0$ for all $\theta$ is that

$$h_i(\theta_{-i}) \leq -\sum_{j \neq i} v_j(k^*_{-i}(\theta_{-i}), \theta_j) \qquad \text{for all } \theta_{-i} \in \Theta_{-i}.$$

It is interesting to note that in the case of allocation of a single indivisible unit of a private good, the Clarke mechanism is precisely the social choice function implemented by the second-price sealed-bid auction (see Example 23.B.6). In particular: (*i*) $k^*(\theta)$ is the allocation rule that gives the item to the agent with the highest valuation; (ii) agent *i* is pivotal precisely when he is the buyer with the highest valuation; and (iii) when he is pivotal his "tax" is exactly equal to the second-highest valuation (in particular, in this case $\sum_{j \neq i} v_j(k^*(\theta), \theta_j) = 0$, and $\sum_{j \neq i} v_j(k^*_{-i}(\theta_{-i}), \theta_j)$ is equal to the amount of the second-highest valuation).

We have seen so far that social choice functions satisfying (23.C.7) and (23.C.8) are truthfully implementable in dominant strategies. Are these the only social choice functions satisfying (23.C.7) that are truthfully implementable? The result given in Proposition 23.C.5 [due to Green and Laffont (1979)] provides one set of conditions under which the answer is "yes."[24] In it, we let $\mathcal{V}$ denote the set of all possible functions $v: K \to \mathbb{R}$.

**Proposition 23.C.5:** Suppose that for each agent $i = 1, \ldots, I$, $\{v_i(\cdot, \theta_i): \theta_i \in \Theta_i\} = \mathcal{V}$; that is, every possible valuation function from $K$ to $\mathbb{R}$ arises for some $\theta_i \in \Theta_i$. Then a social choice function $f(\cdot) = (k^*(\cdot), t_1(\cdot), \ldots, t_I(\cdot))$ in which $k^*(\cdot)$ satisfies (23.C.7) is truthfully implementable in dominant strategies only if $t_i(\cdot)$ satisfies (23.C.8) for all $i = 1, \ldots, I$.

**Proof:** Note first that we can always write

$$t_i(\theta_i, \theta_{-i}) = \sum_{j \neq i} v_j(k^*(\theta_i, \theta_{-i}), \theta_j) + h_i(\theta_i, \theta_{-i}). \tag{23.C.9}$$

What we want to show, then, is that the function $h_i(\cdot)$ must in fact be independent of $\theta_i$ if $f(\cdot)$ is truthfully implementable in dominant strategies. Suppose that it is not; that is, that $f(\cdot)$ is truthfully implementable in dominant strategies but that for some $\theta_i$, $\hat{\theta}_i$, and $\theta_{-i}$, we have $h_i(\theta_i, \theta_{-i}) \neq h_i(\hat{\theta}_i, \theta_{-i})$. We now consider two distinct cases.

(i) $k^*(\theta_i, \theta_{-i}) = k^*(\hat{\theta}_i, \theta_{-i})$: If $f(\cdot)$ is truthfully implementable in dominant strategies, then by (23.C.3) we have

$$v_i(k^*(\theta_i, \theta_{-i}), \theta_i) + t_i(\theta_i, \theta_{-i}) \geq v_i(k^*(\hat{\theta}_i, \theta_{-i}), \theta_i) + t_i(\hat{\theta}_i, \theta_{-i})$$

and

$$v_i(k^*(\hat{\theta}_i, \theta_{-i}), \hat{\theta}_i) + t_i(\hat{\theta}_i, \theta_{-i}) \geq v_i(k^*(\theta_i, \theta_{-i}), \hat{\theta}_i) + t_i(\theta_i, \theta_{-i}).$$

Since, $k^*(\theta_i, \theta_{-i}) = k^*(\hat{\theta}_i, \theta_{-i})$, these two inequalities imply that $t_i(\theta_i, \theta_{-i}) = t_i(\hat{\theta}_i, \theta_{-i})$, and so by (23.C.9) we have $h_i(\theta_i, \theta_{-i}) = h_i(\hat{\theta}_i, \theta_{-i})$: a contradiction.

(ii) $k^*(\theta_i, \theta_{-i}) \neq k^*(\hat{\theta}_i, \theta_{-i})$: Suppose, without loss of generality, that $h_i(\theta_i, \theta_{-i}) > h_i(\hat{\theta}_i, \theta_{-i})$. Consider the type $\theta_i^\varepsilon \in \Theta_i$ such that

$$v_i(k, \theta_i^\varepsilon) = \begin{cases} -\sum_{j \neq i} v_j(k^*(\theta_i, \theta_{-i}), \theta_j) & \text{if } k = k^*(\theta_i, \theta_{-i}) \\ -\sum_{j \neq i} v_j(k^*(\hat{\theta}_i, \theta_{-i}), \theta_j) + \varepsilon & \text{if } k = k^*(\hat{\theta}_i, \theta_{-i}) \\ -\infty & \text{otherwise.} \end{cases} \tag{23.C.10}$$

---

24. For another, see the small-type discussion at the end of this section and Exercise 23.C.10.

We will argue that for a sufficiently small $\varepsilon > 0$, type $\theta_i^\varepsilon$ will strictly prefer to falsely report that he is type $\theta_i$ when the other agents' types are $\theta_{-i}$. To see this, note first that $k^*(\theta_i^\varepsilon, \theta_{-i}) = k^*(\hat{\theta}_i, \theta_{-i})$ since setting $k = k^*(\hat{\theta}_i, \theta_{-i})$ maximizes $v_i(k, \theta_i^\varepsilon) + \sum_{j \neq i} v_j(k, \theta_j)$. Thus, truth telling being a dominant strategy requires that

$$v_i(k^*(\hat{\theta}_i, \theta_{-i}), \theta_i^\varepsilon) + t_i(\theta_i^\varepsilon, \theta_{-i}) \geq v_i(k^*(\theta_i, \theta_{-i}), \theta_i) + t_i(\theta_i, \theta_{-i}),$$

or, substituting, from (23.C.9) and (23.C.10),

$$\varepsilon + h_i(\theta_i^\varepsilon, \theta_{-i}) \geq h_i(\theta_i, \theta_{-i}).$$

But by the logic of part (i), $h_i(\theta_i^\varepsilon, \theta_{-i}) = h_i(\hat{\theta}_i, \theta_{-i})$ because $k^*(\theta_i^\varepsilon, \theta_{-i}) = k^*(\hat{\theta}_i, \theta_{-i})$. This gives

$$\varepsilon + h_i(\hat{\theta}_i, \theta_{-i}) \geq h_i(\theta_i, \theta_{-i}). \tag{23.C.11}$$

By hypothesis we have $h(\theta_i, \theta_{-i}) > h(\hat{\theta}_i, \theta_{-i})$, and so (23.C.11) must be violated for small enough $\varepsilon > 0$. This completes the proof. ∎

---

Thus, when all possible functions $v_i(\cdot)$ can arise for some $\theta_i \in \Theta_i$, the only social choice functions satisfying (23.C.7) that are truthfully implementable in dominant strategies are those in the Groves class.

*Groves mechanisms and budget balance*

Up to this point, we have studied whether we can implement in dominant strategies a social choice function that always results in an efficient choice of $k$ [one satisfying (23.C.7)]. But ex post efficiency also requires that none of the numeraire be wasted, that is, that we satisfy the *budget balance condition*:

$$\sum_i t_i(\theta) = 0 \quad \text{for all } \theta \in \Theta. \tag{23.C.12}$$

We now briefly explore when fully ex post efficient social choice functions [those satisfying *both* (23.C.7) *and* (23.C.12)] can be truthfully implemented in dominant strategies.

Unfortunately, in many cases it is impossible to truthfully implement fully ex post efficient social choice functions in dominant strategies. For example, the result [due to Green and Laffont (1979)] in Proposition 23.C.6, whose proof we omit, shows that if the set of possible types for each agent is sufficiently rich, then no social choice functions that are truthfully implementable in dominant strategies are ex post efficient.[25]

**Proposition 23.C.6:** Suppose that for each agent $i = 1, \ldots, I$, $\{v_i(\cdot, \theta_i): \theta_i \in \Theta_i\} = \mathcal{V}$; that is, every possible valuation function from $K$ to $\mathbb{R}$ arises for some $\theta_i \in \Theta_i$. Then there is no social choice function $f(\cdot) = (k^*(\cdot), t_1(\cdot), \ldots, t_I(\cdot))$ that is truthfully implementable in dominant strategies and is ex post efficient, that is, that satisfies (23.C.7) and (23.C.12).

Thus, under the hypotheses of Proposition 23.C.6, the presence of private information means that the $I$ agents must either accept some waste of the numeraire

---

25. For another negative result, see the small-type discussion at the end of this section and Exercise 23.C.10.

[i.e., have $\sum_i t_i(\theta) < 0$ for some $\theta$, as in the Clarke mechanism] or give up on always having an efficient project selection [i.e., have a project selection $k(\theta)$ that does not satisfy (23.C.7) for some $\theta$].

One special case in which a more positive result does obtain arises when there is at least one agent whose preferences are known. For notational purposes, let this agent be denoted "agent 0", and let there still be $I$ agents, denoted $i = 1, \ldots, I$, whose preferences are private information (so that we are now letting there be $I + 1$ agents in total). The simplest case of this phenomenon, of course, occurs when agent 0 has no preferences over the project choice $k$, that is, when his preferences are $u_i(x) = \bar{m}_0 + t_0$. We saw one example of this kind in Example 23.B.4 when we considered auction settings (agent 0 is then the seller). Another example arises in the case of a public project when the project affects only a subset of the agents in the economy (so that agent 0 represents all of the other agents in the economy).

When there is such an agent, ex post efficiency of the social choice function still requires that (23.C.7) be satisfied; but now ex post efficiency is compatible with *any* transfer functions $t_1(\cdot), \ldots, t_I(\cdot)$ for the $I$ agents with private information, as long as we set $t_0(\theta) = -\sum_{i \neq 0} t_i(\theta)$ for all $\theta$. That is, in this $(I + 1)$-agent setting, the Groves mechanisms identified in Proposition 23.C.4 (in which only agents $i = 1, \ldots, I$ announce their types) are ex post efficient as long as we set the transfer of agent 0 to be $t_0(\theta) = -\sum_{i \neq 0} t_i(\theta)$ for all $\theta$. In essence, the presence of an "outside" agent 0 who has no private information allows us to break the budget balance condition for those agents who do have privately observed types.

We should offer, however, one immediate caveat to this seemingly positive result: Up to this point, we have not worried about whether agents will find it in their interest to participate in the mechanism. As we will see in Section 23.E, when participation is voluntary, it may be that no ex post efficient social choice function is implementable in dominant strategies even when such an outside agent exists.

---

*The differentiable case*

It is common in applications to encounter cases in which $K = \mathbb{R}$, the $v_i(\cdot, \theta_i)$ functions are assumed to be twice continuously differentiable with $\partial^2 v_i(k, \theta_i)/\partial k^2 < 0$ and $\partial^2 v_i(k, \theta_i)/\partial k\, \partial\theta_i \neq 0$ at all $(k, \theta_i)$, and each $\theta_i$ is drawn from an interval $[\underline{\theta}_i, \bar{\theta}_i] \subset \mathbb{R}$ with $\underline{\theta}_i \neq \bar{\theta}_i$. In this case a great deal can be said about the set of social choice functions that can be truthfully implemented in dominant strategies. Exercise 23.C.9 develops this point fully. Here we will simply show how, in this environment, we can easily derive a number of our previous results.

Note first that for any continuously differentiable social choice function $f(\cdot) = (k(\cdot), t_1(\cdot), \ldots, t_I(\cdot))$, if truth telling is a dominant strategy for agent $i$, then agent $i$'s first-order condition implies that, for all $\theta_{-i}$,

$$\frac{\partial v_i(k(\theta_i, \theta_{-i}), \theta_i)}{\partial k} \frac{\partial k(\theta_i, \theta_{-i})}{\partial \theta_i} + \frac{\partial t_i(\theta_i, \theta_{-i})}{\partial \theta_i} = 0 \qquad (23.C.13)$$

at all $\theta_i \in (\underline{\theta}_i, \bar{\theta}_i)$. Integrating (23.C.13) with respect to the variable $\theta_i$, this implies that for all profiles of types $(\theta_i, \theta_{-i})$ we have

$$t_i(\theta_i, \theta_{-i}) = t_i(\underline{\theta}_i, \theta_{-i}) - \int_{\underline{\theta}_i}^{\theta_i} \frac{\partial v_i(k(s, \theta_{-i}), s)}{\partial k} \frac{\partial k(s, \theta_{-i})}{\partial s}\, ds. \qquad (23.C.14)$$

Consider now any social choice function $f(\cdot) = (k^*(\cdot), t_1(\cdot), \ldots, t_I(\cdot))$ that satisfies

(23.C.7). Under our present assumptions $k^*(\cdot)$ must satisfy, for all $\theta$,

$$\sum_{j=1}^{I} \frac{\partial v_j(k^*(\theta), \theta_j)}{\partial k} = 0. \tag{23.C.15}$$

Moreover, using the implicit function theorem and our assumptions on the $v_i(\cdot)$ functions, we see that $k^*(\cdot)$ is continuously differentiable and that it has nonzero partial derivatives, $\partial k^*(\theta)/\partial \theta_i \neq 0$ for all $i$.

We now substitute for $\partial v_i(k^*(s, \theta_{-i}), s)/\partial k$ in (23.C.14) using (23.C.15). Doing so, we derive that, for all profiles $(\theta_i, \theta_{-i})$,

$$t_i(\theta_i, \theta_{-i}) = t_i(\underline{\theta}_i, \theta_{-i}) + \int_{\underline{\theta}_i}^{\theta_i} \left( \sum_{j \neq i} \frac{\partial v_j(k^*(s, \theta_{-i}), \theta_j)}{\partial k} \right) \frac{\partial k(s, \theta_{-i})}{\partial s} \, ds$$

$$= t_i(\underline{\theta}_i, \theta_{-i}) + \int_{k^*(\underline{\theta}_i, \theta_{-i})}^{k^*(\theta_i, \theta_{-i})} \left( \sum_{j \neq i} \frac{\partial v_j(k, \theta_j)}{\partial k} \right) dk$$

$$= t_i(\underline{\theta}_i, \theta_{-i}) + \sum_{j \neq i} v_j(k^*(\theta_i, \theta_{-i}), \theta_j) - \sum_{j \neq i} v_j(k^*(\underline{\theta}_i, \theta_{-i}), \theta_j).$$

But this is true if and only if $t_i(\theta)$ satisfies (23.C.8). Thus, in this setting, Groves mechanisms are the only social choice functions satisfying (23.C.7) that are truthfully implementable in dominant strategies.[26]

Consider now the question of budget balance when there is no outside agent. We will show that satisfying (23.C.15) and budget balance is impossible in this differentiable setting when $I = 2$ [for $I > 2$ see Laffont and Maskin (1980) and Exercise 23.C.10]. By (23.C.13), for all $\theta = (\theta_1, \theta_2)$, we have

$$\frac{\partial t_1(\theta)}{\partial \theta_1} = -\frac{\partial v_1(k^*(\theta), \theta_1)}{\partial k} \frac{\partial k^*(\theta)}{\partial \theta_1}$$

and

$$\frac{\partial t_2(\theta)}{\partial \theta_2} = -\frac{\partial v_2(k^*(\theta), \theta_2)}{\partial k} \frac{\partial k^*(\theta)}{\partial \theta_2}.$$

Thus, for all $\theta = (\theta_1, \theta_2)$,

$$-\frac{\partial^2 t_1(\theta)}{\partial \theta_1 \, \partial \theta_2} = \frac{\partial^2 v_1(k^*(\theta), \theta_1)}{\partial k^2} \frac{\partial k^*(\theta)}{\partial \theta_2} \frac{\partial k^*(\theta)}{\partial \theta_1} + \frac{\partial v_1(k^*(\theta), \theta_1)}{\partial k} \frac{\partial^2 k^*(\theta)}{\partial \theta_1 \, \partial \theta_2} \tag{23.C.16}$$

and

$$-\frac{\partial^2 t_2(\theta)}{\partial \theta_1 \, \partial \theta_2} = \frac{\partial^2 v_2(k^*(\theta), \theta_2)}{\partial k^2} \frac{\partial k^*(\theta)}{\partial \theta_1} \frac{\partial k^*(\theta)}{\partial \theta_2} + \frac{\partial v_2(k^*(\theta), \theta_2)}{\partial k} \frac{\partial^2 k^*(\theta)}{\partial \theta_1 \, \partial \theta_2}, \tag{23.C.17}$$

If we have budget balance, then $t_1(\theta) = -t_2(\theta)$ for all $\theta$, and so we must have $\partial^2 t_1(\theta)/\partial \theta_1 \partial \theta_2 = -\partial^2 t_2(\theta)/\partial \theta_1 \partial \theta_2$. But this would imply, by adding (23.C.16) and (23.C.17), and using (23.C.15), that

$$\left[ \frac{\partial^2 v_1(k^*(\theta), \theta_1)}{\partial k^2} + \frac{\partial^2 v_2(k^*(\theta), \theta_2)}{\partial k^2} \right] \frac{\partial k^*(\theta)}{\partial \theta_1} \frac{\partial k^*(\theta)}{\partial \theta_2} = 0,$$

which is impossible under our assumptions.

---

26. This argument generalizes to any case in which $k^*(\cdot)$ is continuously differentiable.

# 23.D Bayesian Implementation

In this section, we study implementation in *Bayesian Nash equilibrium*.[27] Throughout we follow the notation introduced in Section 23.B: The vector of agents' types $\theta = (\theta_1, \ldots, \theta_I)$ is drawn from set $\Theta = \Theta_1 \times \cdots \times \Theta_I$ according to probability density $\phi(\cdot)$, and agent $i$'s Bernoulli utility function over the alternatives in $X$ given his type $\theta_i$ is $u_i(x, \theta_i)$. We also adopt the notational convention of writing $\theta_{-i} = (\theta_1, \ldots, \theta_{i-1}, \theta_{i+1}, \ldots, \theta_I)$ and $\theta = (\theta_i, \theta_{-i})$. A mechanism $\Gamma = (S_1, \ldots, S_I, g(\cdot))$ is a collection of $I$ sets $S_1, \ldots, S_I$, each $S_i$ containing agent $i$'s possible actions (or plans of action), and an outcome function $g: S \to X$, where $S = S_1 \times \cdots \times S_I$. As discussed in Section 23.B, the mechanism $\Gamma = (S_1, \ldots, S_I, g(\cdot))$ combined with possible types $(\Theta_1, \ldots, \Theta_I)$, density $\phi(\cdot)$, and Bernoulli utility functions $(u_1(\cdot), \ldots, u_I(\cdot))$ defines a Bayesian game of incomplete information (see Section 8.E). We will also often write $s_{-i} = (s_1, \ldots, s_{i-1}, s_{i+1}, \ldots, s_I)$, $s = (s_i, s_{-i})$, and $s(\cdot) = (s_i(\cdot), s_{-i}(\cdot))$ where $s_{-i}(\cdot) = (s_1(\cdot), \ldots, s_{i-1}(\cdot), s_{i+1}(\cdot), \ldots, s_I(\cdot))$.

We begin by defining the concept of a Bayesian Nash equilibrium (see also Section 8.E) and specializing Definition 23.B.4 to the notion of implementation in Bayesian Nash equilibrium.[28]

**Definition 23.D.1:** The strategy profile $s^*(\cdot) = (s_1^*(\cdot), \ldots, s_I^*(\cdot))$ is a *Bayesian Nash equilibrium* of mechanism $\Gamma = (S_1, \ldots, S_I, g(\cdot))$ if, for all $i$ and all $\theta_i \in \Theta_i$,

$$E_{\theta_{-i}}[u_i(g(s_i^*(\theta_i), s_{-i}^*(\theta_{-i})), \theta_i)|\theta_i] \geq E_{\theta_{-i}}[u_i(g(\hat{s}_i, s_{-i}^*(\theta_{-i})), \theta_i)|\theta_i]$$

for all $\hat{s}_i \in S_i$.

**Definition 23.D.2:** The mechanism $\Gamma = (S_1, \ldots, S_I, g(\cdot))$ *implements the social choice function $f(\cdot)$ in Bayesian Nash equilibrium* if there is a Bayesian Nash equilibrium of $\Gamma$, $s^*(\cdot) = (s_1^*(\cdot), \ldots, s_I^*(\cdot))$, such that $g(s^*(\theta)) = f(\theta)$ for all $\theta \in \Theta$.

As with implementation in dominant strategies (see Section 23.C), we will see that a social choice function is Bayesian implementable if and only if it is truthfully implementable in the sense given in Definition 23.D.3.

**Definition 23.D.3:** The social choice function $f(\cdot)$ is *truthfully implementable in Bayesian Nash equilibrium* (or *Bayesian incentive compatible*) if $s_i^*(\theta_i) = \theta_i$ for all $\theta_i \in \Theta_i$ and $i = 1, \ldots, I$ is a Bayesian Nash equilibrium of the direct revelation mechanism $\Gamma = (\Theta_1, \ldots, \Theta_I, f(\cdot))$. That is, if for all $i = 1, \ldots, I$ and all $\theta_i \in \Theta_i$,

$$E_{\theta_{-i}}[u_i(f(\theta_i, \theta_{-i}), \theta_i)|\theta_i] \geq E_{\theta_{-i}}[u_i(f(\hat{\theta}_i, \theta_{-i}), \theta_i)|\theta_i] \tag{23.D.1}$$

for all $\hat{\theta}_i \in \Theta_i$.

The ability to restrict our inquiry, without loss of generality, to the question of whether $f(\cdot)$ is truthfully implementable is a consequence of the *revelation principle for Bayesian Nash equilibrium*.

---

27. Good sources for further reading on the subject of this section are Myerson (1991) and Fudenberg and Tirole (1991).

28. As in Section 8.E, we restrict our attention to pure strategy equilibria.

**Proposition 23.D.1:** (*The Revelation Principle for Bayesian Nash Equilibrium*) Suppose that there exists a mechanism $\Gamma = (S_1, \ldots, S_I, g(\cdot))$ that implements the social choice function $f(\cdot)$ in Bayesian Nash equilibrium. Then $f(\cdot)$ is truthfully implementable in Bayesian Nash equilibrium.

**Proof:** If $\Gamma = (S_1, \ldots, S_I, g(\cdot))$ implements $f(\cdot)$ in Bayesian Nash equilibrium, then there exists a profile of strategies $s^*(\cdot) = (s_1^*(\cdot), \ldots, s_I^*(\cdot))$ such that $g(s^*(\theta)) = f(\theta)$ for all $\theta$, and for all $i$ and all $\theta_i \in \Theta_i$,

$$E_{\theta_{-i}}[u_i(g(s_i^*(\theta_i), s_{-i}^*(\theta_{-i})), \theta_i)|\theta_i] \geq E_{\theta_{-i}}[u_i(g(\hat{s}_i, s_{-i}^*(\theta_{-i})), \theta_i)|\theta_i] \quad (23.D.2)$$

for all $\hat{s}_i \in S_i$. Condition (23.D.2) implies, in particular, that for all $i$ and all $\theta_i \in \Theta_i$,

$$E_{\theta_{-i}}[u_i(g(s_i^*(\theta_i), s_{-i}^*(\theta_{-i})), \theta_i)|\theta_i] \geq E_{\theta_{-i}}[u_i(g(s_i^*(\hat{\theta}_i), s_{-i}^*(\theta_{-i})), \theta_i)|\theta_i] \quad (23.D.3)$$

for all $\hat{\theta}_i \in \Theta_i$. Since $g(s^*(\theta)) = f(\theta)$ for all $\theta$, (23.D.3) means that, for all $i$ and all $\theta_i \in \Theta_i$,

$$E_{\theta_{-i}}[u_i(f(\theta_i, \theta_{-i}), \theta_i)|\theta_i] \geq E_{\theta_{-i}}[u_i(f(\hat{\theta}_i, \theta_{-i}), \theta_i)|\theta_i] \quad (23.D.4)$$

for all $\hat{\theta}_i \in \Theta_i$. But, this is precisely condition (23.D.1), the condition for $f(\cdot)$ to be truthfully implementable in Bayesian Nash equilibrium. ∎

The basic idea behind the revelation principle for Bayesian Nash equilibrium parallels that given for the revelation principle for dominant strategy implementation (Proposition 23.C.1): If in mechanism $\Gamma = (S_1, \ldots, S_I, g(\cdot))$ each agent finds that, when his type is $\theta_i$, choosing $s_i^*(\theta_i)$ is his best response to the other agents' strategies, then if we introduce a mediator who says "Tell me your type, $\theta_i$, and I will play $s_i^*(\theta_i)$ for you," each agent will find truth telling to be an optimal strategy given that all other agents tell the truth. That is, truth telling will be a Bayesian Nash equilibrium of this direct revelation game.

The implication of the revelation principle is, once again, that to identify the set of implementable social choice functions (now in Bayesian Nash equilibrium) we need only identify those that are truthfully implementable.[29]

We can note immediately that the Bayesian implementation concept is a strictly weaker notion than the notion of dominant strategy implementation. Since every dominant strategy equilibrium is necessarily a Bayesian Nash equilibrium, any social choice function that is implementable in dominant strategies is a fortiori implementable in Bayesian Nash equilibrium. Intuitively put, when we compare the requirements for truthful implementation of a social choice function $f(\cdot)$ in dominant strategies and in Bayesian Nash equilibrium given in equations (23.C.3) and (23.D.1), respectively, we see that, with Bayesian implementation, truth telling need only give agent $i$ his highest payoff *averaging over all possible types $\theta_{-i}$ that might arise for the other agents*. In contrast, the dominant strategy concept requires that truth telling be agent $i$'s best strategy *for every possible $\theta_{-i}$*. Thus, we can reasonably hope to be

---

29. Note that Proposition 23.D.1 is what we implicitly relied on in Section 14.C when, in studying the principal–agent problem with hidden information, we restricted our focus to direct revelation mechanisms that induced truth telling by the agent. Formally, Proposition 23.D.1 tells us that the equilibrium outcome arising from any contract between the principal and the agent can be replicated using a direct revelation mechanism that induces the agent to truthfully reveal his type.

able to successfully implement a wider range of social choice functions in Bayesian Nash equilibrium than in dominant strategies. The drawback, of course, is that we can be less confident about this implementation relative to implementation in dominant strategies because it depends on the agents (and any outside mechanism designer) knowing the density $\phi(\cdot)$ of agents' types, as well as on the plausibility of the Nash assumption that the agents' have mutually correct expectations about each others' strategy choices (see Section 8.D).

In what follows in the remainder of this section, we first provide an example that illustrates that we can indeed implement a wider range of social choice functions with Bayesian implementation. Specifically, we show that in the quasilinear environment studied in Section 23.C, whenever the agents' types are statistically independent of one another, we can *always* Bayesian implement at least one ex post efficient social choice function (i.e., one that both has an efficient project choice and satisfies budget balance). In Section 23.C we saw that it may not be possible to accomplish this with dominant strategy implementation (recall Proposition 23.C.6 and the small-type discussion at the end of that section). After showing this, we then examine the properties of Bayesian implementable social choice functions in greater detail, concentrating on the special case in which agents have quasilinear utility functions that are linear in their type. As an application of this analysis, we prove the *revenue equivalence theorem* for auctions.

### The Expected Externality Mechanism

Let us return to the quasilinear setting studied in Section 23.C. In particular, an alternative is now a vector $x = (k, t_1, \ldots, t_I)$, where $k$ is an element of a finite set $K$, and $t_i \in \mathbb{R}$ is a transfer of a numeraire commodity ("money") to agent $i$. Agent $i$'s utility function takes the quasilinear form

$$u_i(x, \theta_i) = v_i(k, \theta_i) + (\bar{m}_i + t_i), \tag{23.D.5}$$

where $\bar{m}_i$ is agent $i$'s endowment of the numeraire.[30] For simplicity, we shall henceforth normalize $\bar{m}_i = 0$ for all $i$. We assume here that the $I$ agents have no outside source of financing, and so $X = \{(k, t_1, \ldots, t_I): k \in K, t_i \in \mathbb{R} \text{ for all } i, \text{ and } \sum_i t_i \leq 0\}$. A social choice function in this environment takes the form $f(\cdot) = (k(\cdot), t_1(\cdot), \ldots, t_I(\cdot))$. Note that if $f(\cdot)$ is ex post efficient then, for all $\theta \in \Theta$,

$$\sum_i v_i(k(\theta), \theta_i) \geq \sum_i v_i(k, \theta_i) \qquad \text{for all } k \in K \tag{23.D.6}$$

and

$$\sum_i t_i(\theta) = 0. \tag{23.D.7}$$

In Proposition 23.C.6 we saw that conditions exist in which no social choice

---

30. Unlike the analysis in Section 23.C (see Exercise 23.C.11), the developments that follow depend not only on preferences over certain outcomes having a quasilinear form but also on the fact that, with this Bernoulli utility function, each agent $i$ is risk neutral with respect to lotteries over his monetary transfer.

function $f(\cdot) = (k(\cdot), t_1(\cdot), \ldots, t_I(\cdot))$ satisfying both (23.D.6) and (23.D.7) is truthfully implementable in dominant strategies. We will now show that it *is* possible to implement such a social choice function in Bayesian Nash equilibrium whenever the agents' types are statistically independent of one another [i.e., when the density $\phi(\cdot)$ has the form $\phi(\theta) = \phi_1(\theta_1) \times \cdots \times \phi_I(\theta_I)$].[31]

To verify this, let $k^*(\cdot)$ satisfy (23.D.6) and consider a social choice function $f(\cdot) = (k^*(\cdot), t_1(\cdot), \ldots, t_I(\cdot))$ in which, for all $i = 1, \ldots, I$,

$$t_i(\theta) = E_{\tilde{\theta}_{-i}}\left[ \sum_{j \neq i} v_j(k^*(\theta_i, \tilde{\theta}_{-i}), \tilde{\theta}_j) \right] + h_i(\theta_{-i}), \qquad (23.D.8)$$

where, for now, we take $h_i(\cdot)$ to be an arbitrary function of $\theta_{-i}$. Note that the expectational term in (23.D.8) represents the *expected benefits* of agents $j \neq i$ when agent $i$ announces his type to be $\theta_i$ and agents $j \neq i$ tell the truth. (As such, it is a function of only agent $i$'s actual announcement $\theta_i$—it is *not* a function of the actual announcements $\theta_{-i}$ of agents $j \neq i$.) Thus, the change in agent $i$'s transfer when he changes his announced type is exactly equal to the *expected externality* of this change on agents $j \neq i$.

We check first that any social choice function $f(\cdot)$ with the form (23.D.8) is Bayesian incentive compatible. To see this, note that when agents $j \neq i$ announce their types truthfully, agent $i$ finds that truth telling is his optimal strategy because (using statistical independence of $\theta_i$ and $\theta_{-i}$)

$$E_{\theta_{-i}}[v_i(k^*(\theta), \theta_i) + t_i(\theta)|\theta_i] = E_{\theta_{-i}}\left[ \sum_{j=1}^{I} v_j(k^*(\theta), \theta_j) \right] + E_{\theta_{-i}}[h_i(\theta_{-i})]$$

$$\geq E_{\theta_{-i}}\left[ \sum_{j=1}^{I} v_j(k^*(\hat{\theta}_i, \theta_{-i}), \theta_j) \right] + E_{\theta_{-i}}[h_i(\theta_{-i})]$$

$$= E_{\theta_{-i}}[v_i(k^*(\hat{\theta}_i, \theta_{-i}), \theta_j) + t_i(\hat{\theta}_i, \theta_{-i})|\theta_i]$$

for all $\hat{\theta}_i \in \Theta_i$, where the inequality follows because $k^*(\cdot)$ satisfies (23.D.6).

What remains is to show that we can choose the $h_i(\cdot)$ functions (for $i = 1, \ldots, I$) so that we also satisfy the budget balance condition (23.D.7). For notational ease, define $\xi_i(\theta_i) = E_{\tilde{\theta}_{-i}}[\sum_{j \neq i} v_j(k^*(\theta_i, \tilde{\theta}_{-i}), \tilde{\theta}_j)]$. We now let

$$h_i(\theta_{-i}) = -\left(\frac{1}{I-1}\right) \sum_{j \neq i} \xi_j(\theta_j), \qquad (23.D.9)$$

for $i = 1, \ldots, I$. With this choice for the $h_i(\cdot)$ functions, we have

$$\sum_i t_i(\theta) = \sum_i \xi_i(\theta_i) + \sum_i h_i(\theta_{-i})$$

$$= \sum_i \xi_i(\theta_i) - \left(\frac{1}{I-1}\right) \sum_i \sum_{j \neq i} \xi_j(\theta_j)$$

$$= \sum_i \xi_i(\theta_i) - \left(\frac{1}{I-1}\right) \sum_i (I-1)\xi_i(\theta_i)$$

$$= 0.$$

---

31. See Fudenberg and Tirole (1991) for a discussion of the case of correlated types and for further references.

Intuitively, the form of the $h_i(\cdot)$ functions in (23.D.9) can be thought of as follows: We have seen that when the agents' types are $(\theta_1, \ldots, \theta_I)$, each agent $i = 1, \ldots, I$ receives a payment equal to $\xi_i(\theta_i)$ [the first term in (23.D.8)]. Now, if each agent contributes an equal $1/(I - 1)$ share of all of the other agents' payments, the payments from a given agent $i$ to each of the other $I - 1$ agents will total $[1/(I - 1)] \sum_{j \neq i} \xi_j(\theta_j)$, and agent $i$ will receive from these agents in return payments that total to $\xi_i(\theta_i)$. Agent $i$'s net transfer will therefore be $\xi_i(\theta_i) - (1/(I - 1)) \sum_{j \neq i} \xi_j(\theta_j)$.

This direct revelation mechanism is known as the *expected externality mechanism* [due to d'Aspremont and Gérard-Varet (1979) and Arrow (1979)]. In summary, we have shown that when agents' Bernoulli utility functions take the form in (23.D.5), and agents' types are statistically independent, there is an ex post efficient social choice function that is implementable in Bayesian Nash equilibrium.

Although this is an interesting result, it is not the end of the story, even when we restrict our attention to Bernoulli utility functions of the form (23.D.5) and a statistically independent distribution of types. The reason is that while the expected externality mechanism implements an ex post efficient social choice function, its transfer functions imply a particular distribution of utility across the various types of the agents, and we may wish to consider other mechanisms, possibly ones involving social choice functions that are not ex post efficient, that alter this distribution.

One reason why this may be important is that, in many applications of interest, agents are free to opt out of the mechanism, and so any mechanism that we wish to implement must not only be incentive compatible in the sense that we have studied so far, but must also satisfy *individual rationality* (or *participation*) *constraints* that assure that each agent $i$ actually wishes to participate in the mechanism. If the expected externality mechanism does not satisfy these constraints, we will need to consider other mechanisms that do. We will have more to say about this issue in Sections 23.E and 23.F, but for now suffice it to say that for this reason, as well as others, we may be interested in identifying *all* of the social choice functions that are Bayesian implementable in this environment.

In the remainder of this section we do this for the special, but often-studied, class of cases in which agents' preferences take a form that is linear in their type, and their types are independently distributed.

## Bayesian Incentive Compatibility with Linear Utility

Suppose now that each agent $i$'s Bernoulli utility function takes the form

$$u_i(x, \theta_i) = \theta_i v_i(k) + (\bar{m}_i + t_i).$$

As before, we shall normalize $\bar{m}_i = 0$ for all $i$. We also suppose that each agent $i$'s type lies in an interval $\Theta_i = [\underline{\theta}_i, \bar{\theta}_i] \subset \mathbb{R}$ with $\underline{\theta}_i \neq \bar{\theta}_i$, and that the agents' types are statistically independent. We let the distribution function of $\theta_i$ be denoted $\Phi_i(\cdot)$, and we assume that it has an associated density $\phi_i(\cdot)$ satisfying $\phi_i(\theta_i) > 0$ for all $\theta_i \in [\underline{\theta}_i, \bar{\theta}_i]$.

We begin by deriving a necessary and sufficient condition for a social choice function $f(\cdot) = (k(\cdot), t_1(\cdot), \ldots, t_I(\cdot))$ to be Bayesian incentive compatible. It is convenient to define $\bar{t}_i(\hat{\theta}_i) = E_{\theta_{-i}}[t_i(\hat{\theta}_i, \theta_{-i})]$; this is agent $i$'s expected transfer given that he announces his type to be $\hat{\theta}_i$ and that all agents $j \neq i$ truthfully reveal their types. Likewise, we let $\bar{v}_i(\hat{\theta}_i) = E_{\theta_{-i}}[v_i(k(\hat{\theta}_i, \theta_{-i}))]$ denote agent $i$'s expected "benefit" conditional on announcing $\hat{\theta}_i$. Because of the form of agents' utility functions, we can write agent $i$'s expected utility when he is type $\theta_i$ and announces his type to be $\hat{\theta}_i$ (assuming that all agents $j \neq i$ tell the truth) as[32]

$$E_{\theta_{-i}}[u_i(f(\hat{\theta}_i, \theta_{-i}), \theta_i) | \theta_i] = \theta_i \bar{v}_i(\hat{\theta}_i) + \bar{t}_i(\hat{\theta}_i). \qquad (23.D.10)$$

It is also convenient to define for each $i$ the function

$$U_i(\theta_i) = \theta_i \bar{v}_i(\theta_i) + \bar{t}_i(\theta_i),$$

giving agent $i$'s expected utility from the mechanism conditional on his type being $\theta_i$ when he and all other agents report their true types.

**Proposition 23.D.2:** The social choice function $f(\cdot) = (k(\cdot), t_1(\cdot), \ldots, t_I(\cdot))$ is Bayesian incentive compatible if and only if, for all $i = 1, \ldots, I$,

(i) $\bar{v}_i(\cdot)$ is nondecreasing. $\qquad (23.D.11)$

(ii) $U_i(\theta_i) = U_i(\underline{\theta}_i) + \displaystyle\int_{\underline{\theta}_i}^{\theta_i} \bar{v}_i(s)\, ds \qquad$ for all $\theta_i$. $\qquad (23.D.12)$

**Proof:** (i) *Necessity.* Bayesian incentive compatibility implies that for each $\hat{\theta}_i > \theta_i$ we have

$$U_i(\theta_i) \geq \theta_i \bar{v}_i(\hat{\theta}_i) + \bar{t}_i(\hat{\theta}_i) = U_i(\hat{\theta}_i) + (\theta_i - \hat{\theta}_i)\bar{v}_i(\hat{\theta}_i)$$

and

$$U_i(\hat{\theta}_i) \geq \hat{\theta}_i \bar{v}_i(\theta_i) + \bar{t}_i(\theta_i) = U_i(\theta_i) + (\hat{\theta}_i - \theta_i)\bar{v}_i(\theta_i).$$

Thus,

$$\bar{v}_i(\hat{\theta}_i) \geq \frac{U_i(\hat{\theta}_i) - U_i(\theta_i)}{\hat{\theta}_i - \theta_i} \geq \bar{v}_i(\theta_i). \qquad (23.D.13)$$

Expression (23.D.13) immediately implies that $\bar{v}_i(\cdot)$ must be nondecreasing (recall that we have taken $\hat{\theta}_i > \theta_i$). In addition, letting $\hat{\theta}_i \to \theta_i$ in (23.D.13) implies that for all $\theta_i$ we have

$$U_i'(\theta_i) = \bar{v}_i(\theta_i)$$

and so

$$U_i(\theta_i) = U_i(\underline{\theta}_i) + \int_{\underline{\theta}_i}^{\theta_i} \bar{v}_i(s)\, ds \qquad \text{for all } \theta_i.$$

(ii) *Sufficiency.* Consider any $\theta_i$ and $\hat{\theta}_i$ and suppose without loss of generality that $\theta_i > \hat{\theta}_i$. If (23.D.11) and (23.D.12) hold, then

$$U_i(\theta_i) - U_i(\hat{\theta}_i) = \int_{\hat{\theta}_i}^{\theta_i} \bar{v}_i(s)\, ds$$

$$\geq \int_{\hat{\theta}_i}^{\theta_i} \bar{v}_i(\hat{\theta}_i)\, ds$$

$$= (\theta_i - \hat{\theta}_i)\bar{v}_i(\hat{\theta}_i).$$

---

32. Observe that the agent's preferences here over his expected benefit $\bar{v}_i$ and expected transfer $\bar{t}_i$ satisfy the single-crossing property that played a prominent role in Sections 13.C and 14.C.

Hence,

$$U_i(\theta_i) \geq U_i(\hat{\theta}_i) + (\theta_i - \hat{\theta}_i)\bar{v}_i(\hat{\theta}_i) = \theta_i\bar{v}_i(\hat{\theta}_i) + \bar{t}_i(\hat{\theta}_i).$$

Similarly, we can derive that

$$U_i(\hat{\theta}_i) \geq U_i(\theta_i) + (\hat{\theta}_i - \theta_i)\bar{v}_i(\theta_i) = \hat{\theta}_i\bar{v}_i(\theta_i) + \bar{t}_i(\theta_i).$$

So $f(\cdot)$ is Bayesian incentive compatible. ■

Proposition 23.D.2 shows that to identify all Bayesian incentive compatible social choice functions in the linear setting, we can proceed as follows: First identify which functions $k(\cdot)$ lead every agent $i$'s expected benefit function $\bar{v}_i(\cdot)$ to be nondecreasing. Then, for each such function, identify the expected transfer functions $\bar{t}_1(\cdot), \ldots, \bar{t}_I(\cdot)$ that satisfy condition (23.D.12) of the proposition. Substituting for $U_i(\cdot)$, these are precisely the expected transfer functions that satisfy, for $i = 1, \ldots, I$,

$$\bar{t}_i(\theta_i) = \bar{t}_i(\underline{\theta}_i) + \underline{\theta}_i v_i(\underline{\theta}_i) - \theta_i v_i(\theta_i) + \int_{\underline{\theta}_i}^{\theta_i} \bar{v}_i(s)\,ds$$

for some constant $\bar{t}_i(\underline{\theta}_i)$. Finally, choose any set of transfer functions $(t_1(\theta), \ldots, t_I(\theta))$ such that $E_{\theta_{-i}}[t_i(\theta_i, \theta_{-i})] = \bar{t}_i(\theta_i)$ for all $\theta_i$. In general, there are many such functions $t_i(\cdot, \cdot)$; one, for example, is simply $t_i(\theta_i, \theta_{-i}) = \bar{t}_i(\theta_i)$.[33]

We now illustrate one implication of this characterization result for the auction setting introduced in Example 23.B.4. Some further implications of Proposition 23.D.2 are derived in Sections 23.E and 23.F.

*Auctions: the revenue equivalence theorem*

Let us consider again the auction setting introduced in Example 23.B.4: Agent 0 is the seller of an indivisible object from which he derives no value, and agents $1, \ldots, I$ are potential buyers.[34] It will be convenient, however, to generalize the set of possible alternatives relative to those considered in Example 23.B.4 by allowing for a *random* assignment of the object. Thus, we now take $y_i(\theta)$ to be buyer $i$'s *probability* of getting the object when the vector of announced types is $\theta = (\theta_1, \ldots, \theta_I)$. Buyer $i$'s expected utility when the profile of types for the $I$ buyers is $\theta = (\theta_1, \ldots, \theta_I)$ is then $\theta_i y_i(\theta) + t_i(\theta)$. Note that buyer $i$ is risk neutral with respect to lotteries both over transfers and over the allocation of the good.

This setting corresponds in the framework studied in Proposition 23.D.2 to the case where we take $k = (y_1, \ldots, y_I)$, $K = \{(y_1, \ldots, y_I): y_i \in [0, 1]$ for all $i = 1, \ldots, I$ and $\sum_i y_i \leq 1\}$, and $v_i(k) = y_i$. Thus, to apply Proposition 23.D.2 we can write $\bar{v}_i(\hat{\theta}_i) = \bar{y}_i(\hat{\theta}_i)$, where $\bar{y}_i(\hat{\theta}_i) = E_{\theta_{-i}}[y_i(\hat{\theta}_i, \theta_{-i})]$ is the probability that $i$ gets the object conditional on announcing his type to be $\hat{\theta}_i$ when agents $j \neq i$ announce their types truthfully, and $U_i(\theta_i) = \theta_i \bar{y}_i(\theta_i) + \bar{t}_i(\theta_i)$.

---

33. However, if we wish the social choice function $f(\cdot) = (k(\cdot), t_1(\cdot), \ldots, t_I(\cdot))$ to satisfy some further properties, such as budget balance, only a subset (possibly an empty one) of the transfer functions generating the expected transfer functions $(\bar{t}_1(\theta_1), \ldots, \bar{t}_I(\theta_I))$ may have these properties.

34. We note that our assumption that the seller in an auction setting derives no value from the object is not necessary for the revenue equivalence theorem. (As we shall see, the result characterizes the expected revenues generated for the seller in different auctions, and so is valid for any utility function that the seller might have.) In the absence of this assumption, however, the seller in an auction will generally care about more than just the expected revenue he receives.

We can now establish a remarkable result, known as the *revenue equivalence theorem*.[35]

**Proposition 23.D.3:** *(The Revenue Equivalence Theorem)* Consider an auction setting with $I$ risk-neutral buyers, in which buyer $i$'s valuation is drawn from an interval $[\underline{\theta}_i, \bar{\theta}_i]$ with $\underline{\theta}_i \neq \bar{\theta}_i$ and a strictly positive density $\phi_i(\cdot) > 0$, and in which buyers' types are statistically independent. Suppose that a given pair of Bayesian Nash equilibria of two different auction procedures are such that for every buyer $i$: (i) For each possible realization of $(\theta_1, \ldots, \theta_I)$, buyer $i$ has an identical probability of getting the good in the two auctions; and (ii) Buyer $i$ has the same expected utility level in the two auctions when his valuation for the object is at its lowest possible level. Then these equilibria of the two auctions generate the same expected revenue for the seller.

**Proof:** By the revelation principle, we know that the social choice function that is (indirectly) implemented by the equilibrium of any auction procedure must be Bayesian incentive compatible. Thus, we can establish the result by showing that if two Bayesian incentive compatible social choice functions in this auction setting have the same functions $(y_1(\theta), \ldots, y_I(\theta))$ and the same values of $(U_1(\underline{\theta}_1), \ldots, U_I(\underline{\theta}_I))$ then they generate the same expected revenue for the seller.

To show this, we derive an expression for the seller's expected revenue from an arbitrary Bayesian incentive compatible mechanism. Note, first, that the seller's expected revenue is equal to $\sum_{i=1}^{I} E[-t_i(\theta)]$. Now,

$$E[-t_i(\theta)] = E_{\theta_i}[-\bar{t}_i(\theta_i)]$$

$$= \int_{\underline{\theta}_i}^{\bar{\theta}_i} [\bar{y}_i(\theta_i)\theta_i - U_i(\theta_i)]\phi_i(\theta_i)\, d\theta_i$$

$$= \int_{\underline{\theta}_i}^{\bar{\theta}_i} \left( \bar{y}_i(\theta_i)\theta_i - U_i(\underline{\theta}_i) - \int_{\underline{\theta}_i}^{\theta_i} \bar{y}_i(s)\, ds \right)\phi_i(\theta_i)\, d\theta_i$$

$$= \left[ \int_{\underline{\theta}_i}^{\bar{\theta}_i} \left( \bar{y}_i(\theta_i)\theta_i - \int_{\underline{\theta}_i}^{\theta_i} \bar{y}_i(s)\, ds \right)\phi_i(\theta_i)\, d\theta_i \right] - U_i(\underline{\theta}_i).$$

Moreover, integration by parts implies that

$$\int_{\underline{\theta}_i}^{\bar{\theta}_i} \left( \int_{\underline{\theta}_i}^{\theta_i} \bar{y}_i(s)\, ds \right)\phi_i(\theta_i)\, d\theta_i = \left( \int_{\underline{\theta}_i}^{\bar{\theta}_i} \bar{y}_i(\theta_i)\, d\theta_i \right) - \left( \int_{\underline{\theta}_i}^{\bar{\theta}_i} \bar{y}_i(\theta_i)\Phi_i(\theta_i)\, d\theta_i \right)$$

$$= \int_{\underline{\theta}_i}^{\bar{\theta}_i} \bar{y}_i(\theta_i)(1 - \Phi_i(\theta_i))\, d\theta_i.$$

Substituting, we see that

$$E[-\bar{t}_i(\theta_i)] = \left[ \int_{\underline{\theta}_i}^{\bar{\theta}_i} \bar{y}_i(\theta_i)\left( \theta_i - \frac{1 - \Phi_i(\theta_i)}{\phi_i(\theta_i)} \right)\phi_i(\theta_i)\, d\theta_i \right] - U_i(\underline{\theta}_i), \quad (23.D.14)$$

---

35. Versions of the revenue equivalence theorem have been derived by many authors; see McAfee and McMillan (1987) and Milgrom (1987) for references as well as for a further discussion of the result.

or, equivalently,

$$E[-\bar{t}_i(\theta_i)] =$$
$$\left[ \int_{\underline{\theta}_1}^{\bar{\theta}_1} \cdots \int_{\underline{\theta}_I}^{\bar{\theta}_I} y_i(\theta_1, \dots, \theta_I)\left(\theta_i - \frac{1 - \Phi_i(\theta_i)}{\phi_i(\theta_i)}\right)\left(\prod_{j=1}^{I} \phi_j(\theta_j)\right) d\theta_I \cdots d\theta_1 \right] - U_i(\underline{\theta}_i).$$

$$(23.D.15)$$

Thus, the seller's expected revenue is equal to

$$\left[ \int_{\underline{\theta}_1}^{\bar{\theta}_1} \cdots \int_{\underline{\theta}_I}^{\bar{\theta}_I} \left[ \sum_{i=1}^{I} y_i(\theta_1, \dots, \theta_I)\left(\theta_i - \frac{1 - \Phi_i(\theta_i)}{\phi_i(\theta_i)}\right)\right]\left(\prod_{j=1}^{I} \phi_j(\theta_j)\right) d\theta_I \cdots d\theta_1 \right]$$
$$- \sum_{i=1}^{I} U_i(\underline{\theta}_i). \quad (23.D.16)$$

By inspection of (23.D.16), we see that any two Bayesian incentive compatible social choice functions that generate the same functions $(y_1(\theta), \dots, y_I(\theta))$ and the same values of $(U_1(\underline{\theta}_1), \dots, U_I(\underline{\theta}_I))$ generate the same expected revenue for the seller. ∎

As an example of the application of Proposition 23.D.3, consider the equilibria of the first-price and second-price sealed-bid auctions that we identified in Examples 23.B.5 and 23.B.6 (where the buyers' valuations were independently drawn from the uniform distribution on [0, 1]). For these equilibria, the conditions of the revenue equivalence theorem are satisfied: in both auctions the buyer with the highest valuation always gets the good and a buyer with a zero valuation has an expected utility of zero. Thus, the revenue equivalence theorem tells us that the seller receives exactly the same level of expected revenue in these equilibria of the two auctions (you can confirm this fact in Exercise 23.D.3). More generally, it can be shown that in any *symmetric auction setting* (i.e., one where the buyers' valuations are independently drawn from identical distributions), the conditions of the revenue equivalence theorem will be met for *any* Bayesian Nash equilibrium of the first-price sealed-bid auction and the (dominant strategy) equilibrium of the second-price sealed-bid auction (see Exercise 23.D.4 for a consideration of symmetric equilibria in these settings). We can conclude from Proposition 23.D.3, therefore, that in any such setting the first-price and second-price sealed-bid auctions generate exactly the same revenue for the seller.

# 23.E Participation Constraints

In Sections 23.B to 23.D, we have studied the constraints that the presence of private information puts on the set of implementable social choice functions. Our analysis up to this point, however, has assumed implicitly that each agent $i$ has no choice but to participate in any mechanism chosen by the mechanism designer. That is, agent $i$'s discretion was limited to choosing his optimal actions within those allowed by the mechanism.

In many applications, however, agents' participation in the mechanism is *voluntary*. As a result, the social choice function that is to be implemented by a mechanism must not only be incentive compatible but must also satisfy certain *participation* (or *individual rationality*) *constraints* if it is to be successfully implemented. In this section, we provide a brief discussion of these additional constraints on the set of implementable social choice functions. By way of motivating our study, Example 23.E.1 provides a simple illustration of how the presence of participation constraints may limit the set of social choice functions that can be successfully implemented.

**Example 23.E.1:** *Participation Constraints in Public Project Choice.* Consider the following simple example of public project choice (recall our initial discussion of public project choice in Example 23.B.3). A decision must be made whether to do a given project or not, so that $K = \{0, 1\}$. There are two agents, 1 and 2. For each agent $i$, $\Theta_i = \{\underline{\theta}, \bar{\theta}\}$, so that each agent either has a valuation of $\underline{\theta}$, or a valuation of $\bar{\theta}$. We shall assume that $\bar{\theta} > 2\underline{\theta} > 0$. The cost of the project is $c \in (2\underline{\theta}, \bar{\theta})$. Suppose that we want to implement a social choice function having an ex post efficient project choice; that is, one that has $k^*(\theta_1, \theta_2) = 1$ if either $\theta_1$ or $\theta_2$ is equal to $\bar{\theta}$, and $k^*(\theta_1, \theta_2) = 0$ if $\theta_1 = \theta_2 = \underline{\theta}$. In the absence of the need to insure voluntary participation, we know from Section 23.C that we can implement some such social choice function in dominant strategies using a Groves scheme.

Suppose, however, that each agent has the option of withdrawing from the mechanism at any time (perhaps by withdrawing from the group), and that, if he does, he will not enjoy the benefits of the project if it is done, but will also avoid paying any monetary transfers. Can we implement a social choice function that achieves voluntary participation and that has an ex post efficient project choice?[36] The answer is "no." To see this, note that if agent 1 can withdraw at any time, then to insure his participation it must be that $t_1(\underline{\theta}, \bar{\theta}) \geq -\underline{\theta}$. That is, it must be that whenever his valuation for the project is $\underline{\theta}$, he pays no more than $\underline{\theta}$ toward the cost of the project. Now consider what agent 1's transfer must be when both agents announce that they have valuation $\bar{\theta}$: If truth telling is to be a dominant strategy, then $t_1(\bar{\theta}, \bar{\theta})$ must satisfy

$$\bar{\theta}k^*(\bar{\theta}, \bar{\theta}) + t_1(\bar{\theta}, \bar{\theta}) \geq \bar{\theta}k^*(\underline{\theta}, \bar{\theta}) + t_1(\underline{\theta}, \bar{\theta}),$$

or, substituting for $k^*(\bar{\theta}, \bar{\theta})$ and $k^*(\underline{\theta}, \bar{\theta})$,

$$\bar{\theta} + t_1(\bar{\theta}, \bar{\theta}) \geq \bar{\theta} + t_1(\underline{\theta}, \bar{\theta}).$$

Since $t_1(\underline{\theta}, \bar{\theta}) \geq -\underline{\theta}$, this implies that $t_1(\bar{\theta}, \bar{\theta}) \geq -\underline{\theta}$. Thus, we conclude that agent 1 must not make a contribution toward the cost of the project that exceeds $\underline{\theta}$ when $(\theta_1, \theta_2) = (\bar{\theta}, \bar{\theta})$. Moreover, by symmetry, we have exactly the same constraint for agent 2's transfer when $(\theta_1, \theta_2) = (\bar{\theta}, \bar{\theta})$, namely, $t_2(\bar{\theta}, \bar{\theta}) \geq -\underline{\theta}$. Hence, $t_1(\bar{\theta}, \bar{\theta}) + t_2(\bar{\theta}, \bar{\theta}) \geq -2\underline{\theta}$. But if this is so, then because $2\underline{\theta} < c$, the feasibility condition $t_1(\bar{\theta}, \bar{\theta}) + t_2(\bar{\theta}, \bar{\theta}) \leq -c$ cannot be satisfied. We conclude, therefore, that it is impossible to implement a social choice function with an ex post efficient project choice when the agents can withdraw from the mechanism at any time.

Note also that the presence of an "outside agent" (say "agent 0") who does not care about the project decision does not help at all here when that agent can also withdraw from the mechanism at any time. This is because, to insure this agent's participation, his transfer $t_0(\theta_1, \theta_2)$ must be nonnegative for every realization of

---

36. Note that any social choice function that *fails* to have both agents participate is necessarily *ex post* inefficient because one of the agents is excluded from the benefits of the project.

$(\theta_1, \theta_2)$. In particular, we must have $t_0(\bar{\theta}, \bar{\theta}) \geq 0$, and so we must fail to satisfy the feasibility condition $t_0(\bar{\theta}, \bar{\theta}) + t_1(\bar{\theta}, \bar{\theta}) + t_2(\bar{\theta}, \bar{\theta}) \leq -c$. ∎

As a general matter, we can distinguish among three stages at which participation constraints may be relevant in any particular application. First, as in Example 23.E.1, an agent $i$ may be able to withdraw from the mechanism at the *ex post stage* that arises after the agents have announced their types and an outcome in $X$ has been chosen. Formally, suppose that agent $i$ can receive a utility of $\bar{u}_i(\theta_i)$ by withdrawing from the mechanism when his type is $\theta_i$.[37] Then, to insure agent $i$'s participation, we must satisfy the *ex post participation* (or *individual rationality*) *constraints*[38]

$$u_i(f(\theta_i, \theta_{-i}), \theta_i) \geq \bar{u}_i(\theta_i) \qquad \text{for all } (\theta_i, \theta_{-i}). \qquad (23.E.1)$$

In other circumstances, agent $i$ may only be able to withdraw from the mechanism at the *interim stage* that arises after the agents have each learned their type but before they have chosen their actions in the mechanism. Letting $U_i(\theta_i|f) = E_{\theta_{-i}}[u_i(f(\theta_i, \theta_{-i}), \theta_i)|\theta_i]$ denote agent $i$'s *interim expected utility* from social choice function $f(\cdot)$ when his type is $\theta_i$, agent $i$ will participate in a mechanism that implements social choice function $f(\cdot)$ when he is of type $\theta_i$ if and only if $U_i(\theta_i|f)$ is not less than $\bar{u}_i(\theta_i)$. Thus, *interim participation* (or *individual rationality*) *constraints* for agent $i$ require that

$$U_i(\theta_i|f) = E_{\theta_{-i}}[u_i(f(\theta_i, \theta_{-i}), \theta_i)|\theta_i] \geq \bar{u}_i(\theta_i) \qquad \text{for all } \theta_i. \qquad (23.E.2)$$

In still other cases, agent $i$ might only be able to refuse to participate at the *ex ante stage* that arises before the agents learn their types. Letting $U_i(f) = E_{\theta_i}[U_i(\theta_i|f)] = E[u_i(f(\theta_i, \theta_{-i}), \theta_i)]$ denote agent $i$'s *ex ante expected utility* from a mechanism that implements social choice function $f(\cdot)$, the *ex ante participation* (or *individual rationality*) *constraint* for agent $i$ is

$$U_i(f) \geq E_{\theta_i}[\bar{u}_i(\theta_i)]. \qquad (23.E.3)$$

Participation constraints are of the ex ante variety when the agents can agree to be bound by the mechanism prior to learning their types. When, instead, agents know their types prior to the time at which they can agree to be bound by the mechanism, we face interim participation constraints.[39] Finally, if there is no way to bind the

---

37. We assume that agent $i$'s utility from withdrawal depends only on his own type.

38. We assume throughout that it is always optimal to insure that each agent is always willing to participate. In fact, however, there is no loss of generality from assuming this: When agents can "not participate," any outcome that can arise when some subset $I'$ of the $I$ agents does not participate, say $x'$, should be included in the set $X$. Because we can always have the mechanism select $x'$ in the circumstances when this subset of agents would have refused to participate, if the set $X$ is defined appropriately we can always replicate the outcome of any mechanism that causes nonparticipation with a mechanism in which all agents are always willing to participate.

39. Recall that the assumption in a Bayesian game that types are drawn from a common prior density is often merely a modeling device for how agents form beliefs about each others' types (see Section 8.E). That is, for analytical purposes we may be representing a setting in which agents' types are already determined but are only privately observed by assuming that there has been a prior random draw of types from a commonly known distribution; but there may not actually be any such prior stage at which the agents could possibly interact.

agents to the assigned outcomes of the mechanism against their will, then we face ex post participation constraints.[40]

Note that if $f(\cdot)$ satisfies (23.E.1), then it satisfies (23.E.2); and, in turn, if it satisfies (23.E.2), then it satisfies (23.E.3). However, the reverse is not true. Thus, the constraints imposed by voluntary participation are most severe when agents can withdraw at the ex post stage, and least severe when they can withdraw only at the ex ante stage.

In summary, when agents' types are privately observed, the set of social choice functions that can be successfully implemented are those that satisfy not only the conditions identified in Sections 23.C and 23.D for incentive compatibility (in, respectively, either a dominant strategy or Bayesian sense, depending on the equilibrium concept we employ) but also any participation constraints that are relevant in the environment under study.

In the remainder of this section, we illustrate further the limitations on the set of implementable social choice functions that may be caused by participation constraints by studying the important *Myerson–Satterthwaite theorem* [due to Myerson and Satterthwaite (1983)].

### The Myerson–Satterthwaite Theorem

Consider again the bilateral trade setting introduced in Example 23.B.4. Agent 1 is the seller of an indivisible object and has a valuation for the object that lies in the interval $\Theta_1 = [\underline{\theta}_1, \bar{\theta}_1] \subset \mathbb{R}$; agent 2 is the buyer and has a valuation that lies in $\Theta_2 = [\underline{\theta}_2, \bar{\theta}_2] \subset \mathbb{R}$. The two valuations are statistically independent, and $\theta_i$ has distribution function $\Phi_i(\cdot)$ with an associated density $\phi_i(\cdot)$ satisfying $\phi_i(\theta_i) > 0$ for all $\theta_i \in [\underline{\theta}_i, \bar{\theta}_i]$. We let $y_i(\theta)$ denote the probability that agent $i$ receives the good given types $\theta = (\theta_1, \theta_2)$, and so agent $i$'s expected utility given $\theta$ is $\theta_i y_i(\theta) + t_i(\theta)$ (we normalize $\bar{m}_i = 0$ for all $i$).

The expected externality mechanism studied in Section 23.D shows that in this setting we can Bayesian implement an ex post efficient social choice function (or what, in this environment, we might call a "trading rule"). A problem arises with the expected externality mechanism, however, when trade is voluntary. In this case, every type of buyer and seller must have nonnegative expected gains from trade if he is to participate. In particular, if a seller of type $\theta_1$ is to participate in a mechanism that implements social choice function $f(\cdot)$, that is, if participation in the mechanism is to be *individually rational* for this type of seller, it must be that $U_1(\theta_1 | f) \geq \theta_1$, because this seller can achieve an expected utility of $\theta_1$ by not participating in the mechanism and simply consuming the good. Likewise, a buyer of type $\theta_2$ can always earn zero by refusing to participate, and so we must have $U_2(\theta_2 | f) \geq 0$. Unfortunately, these interim participation constraints are not satisfied in the expected externality mechanism (you are asked to verify this in Exercise 23.E.1).

The *Myerson–Satterthwaite Theorem* tells us the following disappointing piece of

---

40. For example, if the mechanism can lead an agent into bankruptcy, the provisions of bankruptcy law provide an effective lower bound on ex post utilities.

news: Whenever gains from trade are possible, but are not certain,[41] there is *no* ex post efficient social choice function that is both Bayesian incentive compatible and satisfies these interim participation constraints. Thus, under the conditions of the theorem, the presence of both private information and voluntary participation implies that it is impossible to achieve ex post efficiency. (For an illustration of the result for specific functional forms, see Exercise 23.E.7.)

**Proposition 23.E.1:** (*The Myerson–Satterthwaite Theorem*)  Consider a bilateral trade setting in which the buyer and seller are risk neutral, the valuations $\theta_1$ and $\theta_2$ are independently drawn from the intervals $[\underline{\theta}_1, \bar{\theta}_1] \subset \mathbb{R}$ and $[\underline{\theta}_2, \bar{\theta}_2] \subset \mathbb{R}$ with strictly positive densities, and $(\underline{\theta}_1, \bar{\theta}_1) \cap (\underline{\theta}_2, \bar{\theta}_2) \neq \varnothing$. Then there is no Bayesian incentive compatible social choice function that is ex post efficient and gives every buyer type and every seller type nonnegative expected gains from participation.

**Proof:** The argument consists of two steps:

*Step 1: In any Bayesian incentive compatible and interim individually rational social choice function $f(\cdot) = [y_1(\cdot), y_2(\cdot), t_1(\cdot), t_2(\cdot)]$ in which $y_1(\theta_1, \theta_2) + y_2(\theta_1, \theta_2) = 1$ and $t_1(\theta_1, \theta_2) + t_2(\theta_1, \theta_2) = 0$, we must have*

$$\int_{\underline{\theta}_1}^{\bar{\theta}_1} \int_{\underline{\theta}_2}^{\bar{\theta}_2} y_2(\theta_1, \theta_2) \left[ \left( \theta_2 - \frac{1 - \Phi_2(\theta_2)}{\phi_2(\theta_2)} \right) - \left( \theta_1 + \frac{\Phi_1(\theta_1)}{\phi_1(\theta_1)} \right) \right] \phi_1(\theta_1) \phi_2(\theta_2) \, d\theta_2 \, d\theta_1 \geq 0. \tag{23.E.4}$$

To see this, note first that the same argument that leads to (23.D.15) can be applied here to give [throughout the proof we suppress the argument $f$ in $U_i(\theta_i | f)$ and simply write $U_i(\theta_i)$]:

$$E[-\bar{t}_2(\theta_2)] = \left[ \int_{\underline{\theta}_1}^{\bar{\theta}_1} \int_{\underline{\theta}_2}^{\bar{\theta}_2} y_2(\theta_1, \theta_2) \left( \theta_2 - \frac{1 - \Phi_2(\theta_2)}{\phi_2(\theta_2)} \right) \phi_1(\theta_1) \phi_2(\theta_2) \, d\theta_2 \, d\theta_1 \right] - U_2(\underline{\theta}_2). \tag{23.E.5}$$

Also, because (23.D.12) implies that

$$U_1(\underline{\theta}_1) = U_1(\bar{\theta}_1) - \int_{\underline{\theta}_1}^{\bar{\theta}_1} \int_{\underline{\theta}_2}^{\bar{\theta}_2} y_1(\theta_1, \theta_2) \phi_2(\theta_2) \, d\theta_2 \, d\theta_1,$$

condition (23.D.15) also implies that

$$E[-\bar{t}_1(\theta_1)] = \left[ \int_{\underline{\theta}_1}^{\bar{\theta}_1} \int_{\underline{\theta}_2}^{\bar{\theta}_2} y_1(\theta_1, \theta_2) \left( \theta_1 + \frac{\Phi_1(\theta_1)}{\phi_1(\theta_1)} \right) \phi_1(\theta_1) \phi_2(\theta_2) \, d\theta_2 \, d\theta_1 \right] - U_1(\bar{\theta}_1). \tag{23.E.6}$$

Then, since $y_1(\theta_1, \theta_2) = 1 - y_2(\theta_1, \theta_2)$ we have

$$E[-\bar{t}_1(\theta_1)] = \left[ \int_{\underline{\theta}_1}^{\bar{\theta}_1} \int_{\underline{\theta}_2}^{\bar{\theta}_2} \left( \theta_1 + \frac{\Phi_1(\theta_1)}{\phi_1(\theta_1)} \right) \phi_1(\theta_1) \phi_2(\theta_2) \, d\theta_2 \, d\theta_1 \right]$$

$$- \left[ \int_{\underline{\theta}_1}^{\bar{\theta}_1} \int_{\underline{\theta}_2}^{\bar{\theta}_2} y_2(\theta_1, \theta_2) \left( \theta_1 + \frac{\Phi_1(\theta_1)}{\phi_1(\theta_1)} \right) \phi_1(\theta_1) \phi_2(\theta_2) \, d\theta_2 \, d\theta_1 \right] - U_1(\bar{\theta}_1).$$

---

41. That is, whenever $(\underline{\theta}_1, \bar{\theta}_1) \cap (\underline{\theta}_2, \bar{\theta}_2) \neq \varnothing$ (or equivalently, $\bar{\theta}_2 > \underline{\theta}_1$ and $\bar{\theta}_1 > \underline{\theta}_2$), so that for some realizations of $\theta = (\theta_1, \theta_2)$ there are gains from trade but for others there are not.

But

$$\left[ \int_{\underline{\theta}_1}^{\bar{\theta}_1} \int_{\underline{\theta}_2}^{\bar{\theta}_2} \left( \theta_1 + \frac{\Phi_1(\theta_1)}{\phi_1(\theta_1)} \right) \phi_1(\theta_1) \phi_2(\theta_2)\, d\theta_2\, d\theta_1 \right] = \left[ \int_{\underline{\theta}_1}^{\bar{\theta}_1} [\theta_1 \phi_1(\theta_1) + \Phi_1(\theta_1)]\, d\theta_1 \right]$$

$$= [\theta_1 \Phi_1(\theta_1)]_{\underline{\theta}_1}^{\bar{\theta}_1}$$

$$= \bar{\theta}_1.$$

Thus,

$$E[-\bar{t}_1(\theta_1)] = \bar{\theta}_1 - \left[ \int_{\underline{\theta}_1}^{\bar{\theta}_1} \int_{\underline{\theta}_2}^{\bar{\theta}_2} y_2(\theta_1, \theta_2) \left( \theta_1 + \frac{\Phi_1(\theta_1)}{\phi_1(\theta_1)} \right) \phi_1(\theta_1) \phi_2(\theta_2)\, d\theta_2\, d\theta_1 \right] - U_1(\bar{\theta}_1).$$

$$(23.E.7)$$

Now, the fact that $t_1(\theta_1, \theta_2) + t_2(\theta_1, \theta_2) = 0$ implies that $E[-t_1(\theta_1, \theta_2)] + E[-t_2(\theta_1, \theta_2)] = 0$. So, adding (23.E.5) and (23.E.7) we see that

$$[U_1(\bar{\theta}_1) - \bar{\theta}_1] + U_2(\underline{\theta}_2) =$$

$$\int_{\underline{\theta}_1}^{\bar{\theta}_1} \int_{\underline{\theta}_2}^{\bar{\theta}_2} y_2(\theta_1, \theta_2) \left[ \left( \theta_2 - \frac{1 - \Phi_2(\theta_2)}{\phi_2(\theta_2)} \right) - \left( \theta_1 + \frac{\Phi_1(\theta_1)}{\phi_1(\theta_1)} \right) \right] \phi_1(\theta_1) \phi_2(\theta_2)\, d\theta_2\, d\theta_1.$$

But individual rationality implies that $U_1(\bar{\theta}_1) \geq \bar{\theta}_1$ and $U_2(\underline{\theta}_2) \geq 0$, which establishes (23.E.4).

*Step 2:   Condition (23.E.4) cannot be satisfied if* $y_2(\theta_1, \theta_2) = 1$ *whenever* $\theta_2 > \theta_1$ *and* $y_2(\theta_1, \theta_2) = 0$ *whenever* $\theta_2 < \theta_1$.

Suppose it were. Then the left-hand side of (23.E.4) could be written as

$$\int_{\underline{\theta}_2}^{\bar{\theta}_2} \int_{\underline{\theta}_1}^{\text{Min}\{\theta_2, \bar{\theta}_1\}} \left[ \left( \theta_2 - \frac{1 - \Phi_2(\theta_2)}{\phi_2(\theta_2)} - \theta_1 \right) \phi_1(\theta_1) - \Phi_1(\theta_1) \right] \phi_2(\theta_2)\, d\theta_1\, d\theta_2$$

$$= \int_{\underline{\theta}_2}^{\bar{\theta}_2} \left[ \left( \theta_2 - \frac{1 - \Phi_2(\theta_2)}{\phi_2(\theta_2)} - \theta_1 \right) \Phi_1(\theta_1) \right]_{\underline{\theta}_1}^{\text{Min}\{\theta_2, \bar{\theta}_1\}} \phi_2(\theta_2)\, d\theta_2$$

$$= \int_{\underline{\theta}_2}^{\bar{\theta}_2} \left[ \left( \theta_2 - \frac{1 - \Phi_2(\theta_2)}{\phi_2(\theta_2)} - \text{Min}\{\theta_2, \bar{\theta}_1\} \right) \Phi_1(\text{Min}\{\theta_2, \bar{\theta}_1\}) \right] \phi_2(\theta_2)\, d\theta_2$$

$$= -\int_{\underline{\theta}_2}^{\bar{\theta}_1} [1 - \Phi_2(\theta_2)] \Phi_1(\theta_2)\, d\theta_2 + \int_{\bar{\theta}_1}^{\bar{\theta}_2} [(\theta_2 - \bar{\theta}_1)\phi_2(\theta_2) + (\Phi_2(\theta_2) - 1)]\, d\theta_2$$

$$= -\int_{\underline{\theta}_2}^{\bar{\theta}_1} [1 - \Phi_2(\theta_2)] \Phi_1(\theta_2)\, d\theta_2 + [(\theta_2 - \bar{\theta}_1)(\Phi_2(\theta_2) - 1)]_{\bar{\theta}_1}^{\bar{\theta}_2}$$

$$= -\int_{\underline{\theta}_2}^{\bar{\theta}_1} [1 - \Phi_2(\theta_2)] \Phi_1(\theta_2)\, d\theta_2$$

$$< 0,$$

where the inequality follows because $\bar{\theta}_1 > \underline{\theta}_2$ and $\underline{\theta}_1 < \bar{\theta}_2$. This contradicts (23.E.4) and completes the argument. ∎

Recalling the revelation principle for Bayesian Nash equilibrium (Proposition 23.D.1), the implication of the Myerson–Satterthwaite theorem can be put as follows: Consider *any* voluntary trading institution that regulates trade between the buyer and the seller. This includes, for example, any bargaining process in which the parties can make offers and counteroffers to each other, as well as any arbitration mechanism in which the parties tell a third party their types and this third party then decides whether trade will occur and at what price.[42] By the revelation principle, we know that the social choice function that is indirectly implemented in a Bayesian Nash equilibrium[43] of such a mechanism must be Bayesian incentive compatible. Moreover, since participation is voluntary, this social choice function $f(\cdot)$ must satisfy the interim individual rationality constraints that $U_1(\theta_1 | f) \geq \theta_1$ for all $\theta_1$ and $U_2(\theta_2 | f) \geq 0$ for all $\theta_2$. Thus, the Myerson–Satterthwaite theorem tells us that, under its assumptions, no voluntary trading institution can have a Bayesian Nash equilibrium that leads to an ex post efficient outcome for all realizations of the buyer's and seller's valuations.

# 23.F Optimal Bayesian Mechanisms

In Sections 23.B to 23.E we have been concerned with the identification of implementable social choice functions in environments characterized by incomplete information about agents' preferences. In this section, we shift our focus to the welfare evaluaton of implementable social choice functions. We begin by developing several welfare criteria that extend the notion of Pareto efficiency that we have used throughout the book in the context of economies with complete information to these incomplete information settings. With these welfare notions in hand, we then discuss several examples that illustrate the characterization of optimal social choice functions (and, by implication, the optimal direct revelation mechanisms that implement them). We restrict our focus throughout this section to implementation in Bayesian Nash equilibria, discussed in detail in Section 23.D. Unless otherwise noted, we also adopt the assumptions and notation of Section 23.D. Good sources for further reading on the subject of this section are Holmstrom and Myerson (1983), Myerson (1991), and Fudenberg and Tirole (1991).

For economies in which agents' preferences are known with certainty, the concept of Pareto efficiency (or Pareto optimality) provides a minimal test that any welfare optimal outcome $x \in X$ should pass: There should be no other feasible outcome $\hat{x} \in X$ with the property that some agents are strictly better off with outcome $\hat{x}$ than with outcome $x$, and no agent is worse off.

The extension of this welfare test to social choice functions in settings of incomplete information should read something like the following:

> The social choice function $f(\cdot)$ is efficient if it is feasible and if there is no other feasible social choice function that makes some agents strictly better off, and no agents worse off.

To operationalize this idea, however, we need to be more specific about two things: First, what exactly do we mean by a social choice function being "feasible"? Second,

---

42. Strictly speaking, for a direct application of Proposition 23.E.1, the date of delivery and consumption of the good must be fixed (so the bargaining processes studied in Appendix A of Chapter 9 would not count). But through a suitable reinterpretation Proposition 23.E.1 can be applied to settings in which trade may take place over real time, where not only delivery of the good matters but also the *time of delivery* (see Exercise 23.E.4 for details).

43. And, hence, in any perfect Bayesian or sequential equilibrium (see Section 9.C).

precisely what do we mean when we say that no other feasible social choice function "makes some agents strictly better off, and no agent worse off"?

Let us consider the first of these issues. The identification of the set of feasible social choice functions when agents' preferences are private information has been discussed extensively in Sections 23.D and 23.E. Suppose that we define the set

$$F_{BIC} = \{f: \Theta \to X: f(\cdot) \text{ is Bayesian incentive compatible}\}. \qquad (23.F.1)$$

The elements of set $F_{BIC}$ in any particular application are the social choice functions that satisfy condition (23.D.1), the condition that assures that there is a Bayesian Nash equilibrium of the direct revelation mechanism $\Gamma = (\Theta_1, \ldots, \Theta_I, f(\cdot))$ in which truth telling is each agent's equilibrium strategy.

Likewise, following the discussion in Section 23.E, we can also define the set

$$F_{IR} = \{f: \Theta \to X: f(\cdot) \text{ is individually rational}\}. \qquad (23.F.2)$$

The set $F_{IR}$ contains those social choice functions that satisfy whichever of the three types of individual rationality (or participation) constraints (23.E.1)–(23.E.3) are relevant in the application being studied. If no individual rationality constraints are relevant (i.e., if agents' participation is not voluntary), then we simply have $F_{IR} = \{f: \Theta \to X\}$, the set of all possible social choice functions.

The content of our discussion in Sections 23.D and 23.E is therefore that the set of feasible social choice functions in environments in which agents' types are private information is precisely $F^* = F_{BIC} \cap F_{IR}$. Following Myerson (1991), we call this the *incentive feasible set* to emphasize that it is the set of feasible social choice functions when, because of incomplete information, incentive compatibility conditions must be satisfied.

Now consider the second issue: What do we mean when we say that no other feasible social choice function would "make some agents strictly better off, and no agents worse off"? The critical issue here has to do with the *timing* of our welfare analysis. In particular, is the welfare analysis occurring *before* the agents (privately) learn their types, or *after*? The former amounts to a welfare analysis conducted at what we called in Section 23.E the *ex ante stage* (the point in time at which agents have not yet learned their types); the latter corresponds to what we called in Section 23.E the *interim stage* (the point in time after each agent has learned his type, but before the agents' types are publicly revealed). To formally define the different welfare criteria that arise in these two cases, let us once again denote by $U_i(\theta_i|f)$ agent $i$'s expected utility from social choice function $f(\cdot)$ conditional on being of type $\theta_i$. Also let $U_i(f) = E_{\theta_i}[U_i(\theta_i|f)]$ denote agent $i$'s ex ante expected utility from social choice function $f(\cdot)$. We can now state Definitions 23.F.1 and 23.F.2.

**Definition 23.F.1:** Given any set of feasible social choice functions $F$, the social choice function $f(\cdot) \in F$ is *ex ante efficient in F* if there is no $\hat{f}(\cdot) \in F$ having the property that $U_i(\hat{f}) \geq U_i(f)$ for all $i = 1, \ldots, I$, and $U_i(\hat{f}) > U_i(f)$ for some $i$.

**Definition 23.F.2:** Given any set of feasible social choice functions $F$, the social choice function $f(\cdot) \in F$ is *interim efficient in F* if there is no $\hat{f}(\cdot) \in F$ having the property that $U_i(\theta_i|\hat{f}) \geq U_i(\theta_i|f)$ for all $\theta_i \in \Theta_i$ and all $i = 1, \ldots, I$, and $U_i(\theta_i|\hat{f}) > U_i(\theta_i|f)$ for some $i$ and $\theta_i \in \Theta_i$.

The motivation for the ex ante efficiency test is straightforward: If agents have not yet learned their types, then when comparing two feasible social choice functions we should evaluate each agent's well-being using his expected utility over all of his possible types. However, when our welfare analysis occurs after agents have (privately) learned their types, things are a bit trickier. Although the agents each know their types, we—as outsiders—do not know them. Thus, the appropriate notion for us to adopt in saying that one social choice function $\hat{f}(\cdot)$ welfare dominates another social choice function $f(\cdot)$ is that $\hat{f}(\cdot)$ makes every possible type of every agent at least as well off as does $f(\cdot)$, and makes some type of some agent strictly better off. This leads to the concept of interim efficiency given in Definition 23.F.2.

Proposition 23.F.1 compares these two notions of efficiency.

**Proposition 23.F.1:** Given any set of feasible social choice functions $F$, if the social choice function $f(\cdot) \in F$ is ex ante efficient in $F$, then it is also interim efficient in $F$.

**Proof:** Suppose that $f(\cdot)$ is ex ante efficient in $F$ but is not interim efficient in $F$. Then there exists an $\hat{f}(\cdot) \in F$ such that $U_i(\theta_i \mid \hat{f}) \geq U_i(\theta_i \mid f)$ for all $\theta_i \in \Theta_i$ and all $i = 1, \ldots, I$, and $U_i(\theta_i \mid \hat{f}) > U_i(\theta_i \mid f)$ for some $i$ and $\theta_i \in \Theta_i$. But since, for all $i$, $U_i(f) = E_{\theta_i}[U_i(\theta_i \mid f)]$ and $U_i(\hat{f}) = E_{\theta_i}[U_i(\theta_i \mid \hat{f})]$, it follows that $U_i(\hat{f}) \geq U_i(f)$ for all $i = 1, \ldots, I$, and $U_i(\hat{f}) > U_i(f)$ for some $i$, contradicting the hypothesis that $f(\cdot)$ is ex ante efficient in $F$. ∎

The ex ante efficiency concept is more demanding than is interim efficiency (and so fewer social choice functions $f(\cdot)$ pass the ex ante efficiency test) because a social choice function $\hat{f}(\cdot)$ can raise every agent's ex ante expected utility relative to the social choice function $f(\cdot)$ even though $\hat{f}(\cdot)$ may lead some type of some agent $i$ to have a lower expected utility than he does with $f(\cdot)$.

Putting together the elements developed above, we conclude that when agents' types are already determined at the time we are conducting our welfare analysis, the proper notion of efficiency of a social choice function in an environment with incomplete information is interim efficiency in $F^*$, the set of Bayesian incentive compatible and individually rational social choice functions.[44] On the other hand, if our analysis is conducted prior to agents learning their types, then the proper notion of efficiency is ex ante efficiency in $F^*$.[45] These two notions are often called simply *ex ante incentive efficiency* and *interim incentive efficiency* [the terminology is due to Holmstrom and Myerson (1983)], where the modifier "incentive" is meant to convey the point that the set $F^*$ is being used.[46]

These two welfare notions differ from the ex post efficiency criterion introduced in Definition 23.B.2. To see their relationship to it more clearly, Definition 23.F.3

---

44. These cases often correspond to situations in which our assumption that the agents' types are drawn from a known prior distribution is being used merely as a device to model agents' beliefs about each others' types, as described in Section 8.E, rather than as a description of any actual prior time at which the agents could interact or our welfare analysis might have been done.

45. This case often arises in contracting problems when, at the time of contracting, the agents anticipate that they will later come to acquire private information about their types. Then the natural welfare standard to use in comparing different contracts (i.e., different mechanisms) is the ex ante criterion. The principal–agent model studied in Section 14.C and Example 23.F.1 below is an example along these lines.

46. However, since the relevant individual rationality constraints vary from one application to another, it is usually clearer to describe precisely the set $F$ within which efficiency is being evaluated.

develops the ex post efficiency notion in a manner that parallels Definitions 23.F.1 and 23.F.2.

**Definition 23.F.3:** Given any set of feasible social choice functions $F$, the social choice function $f(\cdot) \in F$ is *ex post efficient in F* if there is no $\hat{f}(\cdot) \in F$ having the property that $u_i(\hat{f}(\theta), \theta_i) \geq u_i(f(\theta), \theta_i)$ for all $i = 1, \ldots, I$ and all $\theta \in \Theta$, and $u_i(\hat{f}(\theta), \theta_i) > u_i(f(\theta), \theta_i)$ for some $i$ and $\theta \in \Theta$.

The ex post efficiency test in Definition 23.F.3 conducts its welfare evaluation at the ex post stage at which all agents' information has been publicly revealed. Using this definition, we see that a social choice function $f(\cdot)$ is ex post efficient in the sense of Definition 23.B.2 if and only if it is ex post efficient in the sense of Definition 23.F.3 when we take $F = \{f: \Theta \to X\}$.

Note that the criterion of ex post efficiency in $\{f: \Theta \to X\}$, or more generally, of ex post efficiency in $F_{IR}$ when individual rationality constraints are present, ignores issues of incentive compatibility. As a result, it is appropriate as a welfare criterion only if agents' types are in fact publicly observable. Because $F^* \subset F_{IR}$, allocations that are ex ante or interim incentive efficient need not be ex post efficient in this sense. Indeed, the Myerson–Satterthwaite theorem (Proposition 23.E.1) provides an illustration of this phenomenon for the bilateral trade setting: under its assumptions, no element of $F^*$ is ex post efficient. Examples 23.F.1 to 23.F.3 provide further illustrations. (For one way in which the notion of ex post efficiency is nevertheless still of interest in settings with privately observed types, see Exercise 23.F.1.)

Note also that even in settings in which agents' types are public information, the use of ex post efficiency in $F_{IR}$ as our welfare criterion is appropriate only when agents' types are already determined. When our welfare analysis instead occurs prior to agents learning their types, the appropriate notion is instead the stronger criterion that $f(\cdot)$ be ex ante efficient in $F_{IR}$. These two notions are sometimes called *ex post classical efficiency* and *ex ante classical efficiency* [again, the terminology is due to Holmstrom and Myerson (1983)] to indicate that no incentive constraints are involved in defining the feasible set of social choice functions.

In the remainder of this section we study three examples in which we characterize welfare optimal social choice functions. In Examples 23.F.1 and 23.F.2, it is supposed that one agent who receives no private information chooses a mechanism to maximize his expected utility subject to both incentive compatibility constraints and interim individual rationality constraints for the other agents. These two examples therefore amount to a characterization of one particular interim incentive efficient mechanism. In Example 23.F.3, we provide a full characterization of the sets of interim and ex ante incentive efficient social choice functions for a simple setting of bilateral trade with adverse selection.

**Example 23.F.1:** *A Principal–Agent Problem with Hidden Information.* In Section 14.C we studied principal–agent problems with hidden information for the case in which the agent has two possible types. Here we consider the case where the agent may have a continuum of types. Recall from Section 14.C that in the principal–agent problem with hidden information, the principal faces the problem of designing an optimal (i.e., payoff maximizing) contract for an agent who will come to possess private information. In doing so, the principal faces both incentive constraints and a reservation utility constraint for the agent. Recall also from Section 14.C that, in the limiting case in which the agent is infinitely risk averse, the agent must be guaranteed his reservation utility for each possible type he may come to have, and so this contracting problem is identical to the contracting problem that would arise if the agent already knew his type at the time of contracting. Here we shall set things up directly in these terms, assuming that the agent already possesses this information when contracting occurs. With this formulation, the principal's optimal contract can be viewed as implementing one particular interim incentive efficient social choice function. (When the agent actually does not know his type at the time of contracting and is infinitely risk averse, then this social choice function is also ex ante incentive efficient.)

To introduce our notation, we suppose that the agent (individual 1) may take some observable action $e \in \mathbb{R}_+$ (his "effort" or "task" level) and receives a monetary payment from the principal of $t_1$. The agent's type is drawn from the interval $[\underline{\theta}, \bar{\theta}]$, where $\underline{\theta} < \bar{\theta} < 0$, according to the distribution function $\Phi(\cdot)$ which has an associated density function $\phi(\cdot)$ that is strictly positive on $[\underline{\theta}, \bar{\theta}]$. We assume that this distribution satisfies the property that $[\theta - ((1 - \Phi(\theta))/\phi(\theta))]$ is nondecreasing in $\theta$.[47]

The agent's Bernoulli utility function when his type is $\theta$ is $u_1(e, t_1, \theta) = t_1 + \theta g(e)$, where $g(\cdot)$ is a differentiable function with $g(0) = 0$, $g(e) > 0$ for $e > 0$, $g'(0) = 0$, $g'(e) > 0$ for $e > 0$, and $g''(\cdot) > 0$; that is, $\theta g(e)$ represents the agent's disutility of effort (recall that $\theta < 0$), with higher effort levels leading to an increasing level of disutility to the agent. Note that a larger (i.e., less negative) level of $\theta$ lowers, at any level of $e$, both the agent's total level of disutility and his marginal disutility from any increase in $e$. As noted above, we suppose that the agent must be guaranteed an expected utility level of at least $\bar{u}$ for each possible type he may have.

The principal (individual 0) has no private information. His Bernoulli utility function is $u_0(e, t_0) = v(e) + t_0$, where $t_0$ is his net transfer and $v(\cdot)$ is a differentiable function satisfying $v'(\cdot) > 0$ and $v''(\cdot) < 0$.

A contract between the principal and the agent can be viewed as specifying a mechanism in the sense we have used throughout this chapter. By the revelation principle for Bayesian Nash equilibrium (Proposition 23.D.1), the equilibrium outcome induced by such a contract, formally a social choice function that maps each possible agent type into effort and transfer levels, can always be duplicated using a direct revelation mechanism that induces truth telling. Thus, the principal can confine his search for an optimal contract to the set of Bayesian incentive compatible social choice functions $f(\cdot) = (e(\cdot), t_0(\cdot), t_1(\cdot))$ that give the agent an expected utility of at least $\bar{u}$ for every possible value of $\theta$. In what follows, we shall (without loss of generality) restrict attention in our search for the principal's optimal contract to contracts that have $t_0(\theta) = -t_1(\theta)$ for all $\theta$ (i.e., that involve no waste of numeraire).

The principal's problem can therefore be stated as

$$\underset{f(\cdot) = (e(\cdot), t_1(\cdot))}{\text{Max}} \quad E[v(e(\theta)) - t_1(\theta)]$$

$$\text{s.t.} \quad f(\cdot) \text{ is Bayesian incentive compatible and}$$
$$\text{individually rational.}$$

---

47. For a discussion of how the analysis changes when this assumption is not satisfied, see Fudenberg and Tirole (1991).

The present model falls into the class of models with linear utility studied in Section 23.D [specifically, in the notation of Proposition 23.D.2, $k = e$, $v_1(k) = g(e)$, and $\bar{v}_1(\theta) = g(e(\theta))$ here]. Letting $U_1(\theta) = t_1(\theta) + \theta g(e(\theta))$ denote the agent's utility if his type is $\theta$ and he tells the truth, Proposition 23.D.2 can be used to restate the principal's problem in terms of choosing the functions $e(\cdot)$ and $U_1(\cdot)$ to solve

$$\underset{e(\cdot), U_1(\cdot)}{\text{Max}} \quad E[v(e(\theta)) + \theta g(e(\theta)) - U_1(\theta)] \qquad (23.\text{F}.3)$$

$$\text{s.t.} \quad \text{(i)} \ e(\cdot) \text{ is nondecreasing}$$

$$\text{(ii)} \ U_1(\theta) = U_1(\underline{\theta}) + \int_{\underline{\theta}}^{\theta} g(e(s)) \, ds \text{ for all } \theta$$

$$\text{(iii)} \ U_1(\theta) \geq \bar{u} \text{ for all } \theta.$$

Constraints (i) and (ii) are the necessary and sufficient conditions for the principal's contract to be Bayesian incentive compatible, adapted from Proposition 23.D.2 [constraint (i) follows because $g(\cdot)$ is increasing in $e$], while constraint (iii) is the agent's individual rationality constraint.

Note first that if constraint (ii) is satisfied, then constraint (iii) will be satisfied if and only if $U_1(\underline{\theta}) \geq \bar{u}$. As a result, we can replace constraint (iii) with

$$\text{(iii}') \quad U_1(\underline{\theta}) \geq \bar{u}.$$

Next, substituting for $U_1(\theta)$ in the objective function from constraint (ii), and then integrating by parts in a fashion similar to the steps leading to (23.D.14), problem (23.F.3) can be restated as

$$\underset{e(\cdot), U_1(\underline{\theta})}{\text{Max}} \quad \left[ \int_{\underline{\theta}}^{\bar{\theta}} \left\{ v(e(\theta)) + g(e(\theta)) \left( \theta - \frac{1 - \Phi(\theta)}{\phi(\theta)} \right) \right\} \phi(\theta) \, d\theta \right] - U_1(\underline{\theta}) \quad (23.\text{F}.4)$$

$$\text{s.t.} \quad \text{(i)} \ e(\cdot) \text{ is nondecreasing}$$
$$\text{(iii}') \ U_1(\underline{\theta}) \geq \bar{u}.$$

It is now immediate from (23.F.4) that in any solution we must in fact have $U_1(\underline{\theta}) = \bar{u}$. Thus, we can write the principal's problem as one of choosing $e(\cdot)$ to solve

$$\underset{e(\cdot)}{\text{Max}} \quad \left[ \int_{\underline{\theta}}^{\bar{\theta}} \left\{ v(e(\theta)) + g(e(\theta)) \left( \theta - \frac{1 - \Phi(\theta)}{\phi(\theta)} \right) \right\} \phi(\theta) \, d\theta \right] - \bar{u} \quad (23.\text{F}.5)$$

$$\text{s.t. (i)} \ e(\cdot) \text{ is nondecreasing.}$$

Suppose for the moment that we can ignore constraint (i). Then the optimal function $e(\cdot)$ must satisfy the first-order condition[48]

$$v'(e(\theta)) + g'(e(\theta)) \left( \theta - \frac{1 - \Phi(\theta)}{\phi(\theta)} \right) = 0 \qquad \text{for all } \theta. \qquad (23.\text{F}.6)$$

But note that, under our assumption that $[\theta - ((1 - \Phi(\theta))/\phi(\theta))]$ is nondecreasing in $\theta$, the implicit function theorem applied to (23.F.6) tells us that any solution $e(\cdot)$ to this relaxed problem must in fact be nondecreasing. Thus, (23.F.6) characterizes the solution to the principal's actual problem (see Section M.K of the Mathematical Appendix). The optimal $U_1(\cdot)$ [and, hence, $t_1(\cdot)$] is then calculated from constraint (ii) of (23.F.3) using this optimal $e(\cdot)$ and the fact that $U_1(\underline{\theta}) = \bar{u}$.

---

48. It can be shown that under our assumptions, the optimal contract is interior, that is, has $e(\theta) > 0$ for (almost) all $\theta$.

It is interesting to compare this solution with the optimal contract for the case in which the agent's type is observable. This contract solves

$$\underset{e(\cdot),t_1(\cdot)}{\text{Max}} \quad E[v(e(\theta)) - t_1(\theta)]$$

$$\text{s.t. } t_1(\theta) + \theta g(e(\theta)) \geq \bar{u} \text{ for all } \theta.$$

Hence, the optimal task level in this complete information contract is the level $e^*(\theta)$ that satisfies, for all $\theta$,

$$v'(e^*(\theta)) + g'(e^*(\theta))\theta = 0.$$

Note that $e^*(\theta)$ is the level that arises in any ex post (classically) efficient social choice function. In contrast, the principal's optimal $e(\cdot)$ when $\theta$ is private information is such that

$$v'(e(\theta)) + g'(e(\theta))\theta \begin{cases} > 0 & \text{at all } \theta < \bar{\theta}, \\ = 0 & \text{at } \theta = \bar{\theta}. \end{cases}$$

We see then that $e(\theta) < e^*(\theta)$ for all $\theta < \bar{\theta}$, and $e(\bar{\theta}) = e^*(\bar{\theta})$. This is a version of the same result that we saw for the two-type case in Section 14.C. In the optimal contract, the type of agent with the lowest disutility from effort (here type $\bar{\theta}$; in Section 14.C, type $\theta_H$) takes an ex post efficient action, while all other types have their effort levels distorted downward. The reason is also the same: doing so helps reduce the amount the agent's utility exceeds his reservation utility for types $\theta > \underline{\theta}$ (his so-called *information rents*). To see this point heuristically, suppose that starting with some function $e(\cdot)$ we lower $e(\hat{\theta})$ by an amount $de < 0$ for some type $\hat{\theta} \in (\underline{\theta}, \bar{\theta})$ and lower this type's transfer to keep his utility unchanged.[49] The decrease in the transfer paid to type $\hat{\theta}$ is $\hat{\theta}g'(e(\hat{\theta})) \, de$, while the direct effect on the principal is $v'(e(\hat{\theta})) \, de$. At the same time, according to constraint (ii), this change in $e(\hat{\theta})$ lowers the utility level, and hence the transfer, that must be given to all types $\theta > \hat{\theta}$ by exactly $g'(e(\hat{\theta})) \, de$. The expected value of this reduction in the transfers paid to these types is $-(1 - \Phi(\hat{\theta}))g'(e(\hat{\theta})) \, de$. If the original $e(\cdot)$ is an optimum, the sum of the first two changes in the principal's profits (those for type $\hat{\theta}$) weighted by the density of type $\hat{\theta}$, $[v'(e(\hat{\theta})) + \hat{\theta}g'(e(\hat{\theta}))]\phi(\hat{\theta}) \, de$, plus the reduction in payments to types $\theta > \hat{\theta}$, $(1 - \Phi(\hat{\theta}))g'(e(\hat{\theta})) \, de$, must equal zero. This gives exactly (23.F.6). ∎

**Example 23.F.2:** *Optimal Auctions.* We consider again the auction setting introduced in Example 23.B.4. Here we determine the optimal auction for the seller of an indivisible object (agent 0) when there are $I$ buyers, indexed by $i = 1, \ldots, I$. Each buyer has a Bernoulli utility function $\theta_i y_i(\theta) + t_i(\theta)$, where $y_i(\theta)$ is the probability that agent $i$ gets the good when the agents' types are $\theta = (\theta_1, \ldots, \theta_I)$. In addition, each buyer $i$'s type is independently drawn according to the distribution function $\Phi_i(\cdot)$ on $[\underline{\theta}_i, \bar{\theta}_i] \subset \mathbb{R}$ with $\underline{\theta}_i \neq \bar{\theta}_i$ and associated density $\phi_i(\cdot)$ that is strictly positive on $[\underline{\theta}_i, \bar{\theta}_i]$. We assume also that, for $i = 1, \ldots, I$,

$$\theta_i - \frac{1 - \Phi_i(\theta_i)}{\phi_i(\theta_i)}$$

is nondecreasing in $\theta_i$.[50]

---

49. We say "heuristically" because to do this rigorously we need to perform this reduction in $e$ over an interval of types and then take limits.

50. For a discussion of the case in which this assumption is not met, see Myerson (1981).

A social choice function in this environment is a function $f(\cdot) = (y_0(\cdot), \ldots, y_I(\cdot)$, $t_0(\cdot), \ldots, t_I(\cdot))$ having the properties that, for all $\theta \in \Theta$, $y_i(\theta) \in [0, 1]$ for all $i$, $\sum_{i \neq 0} y_i(\theta) = 1 - y_0(\theta)$, and $t_0(\theta) = -\sum_{i \neq 0} t_i(\theta)$.[51] The seller wishes to choose the Bayesian incentive compatible social choice function that maximizes his expected revenue $E_\theta[t_0(\theta)] = -E_\theta[\sum_{i \neq 0} t_i(\theta)]$ but faces the interim individual rationality constraints that $U_i(\theta_i) = \theta_i \bar{y}_i(\theta_i) + \bar{t}_i(\theta_i) \geq 0$ for all $\theta_i$ and $i \neq 0$ [as in Section 23.D, $\bar{y}_i(\theta_i)$ and $\bar{t}_i(\theta_i)$ are agent $i$'s probability of getting the good and expected transfer conditional on announcing his type to be $\theta_i$] because buyers are always free not to participate. The seller's optimal choice is therefore a particular element of the set of interim incentive efficient social choice functions.

The seller's problem can be written as one of choosing functions $y_1(\cdot), \ldots, y_I(\cdot)$ and $U_1(\cdot), \ldots, U_I(\cdot)$ to solve

$$\underset{\{y_i(\cdot), U_i(\cdot)\}_{i=1}^I}{\text{Max}} \sum_{i \neq 0} \int_{\underline{\theta}_i}^{\bar{\theta}_i} [\bar{y}_i(\theta_i)\theta_i - U_i(\theta_i)] \phi_i(\theta_i)\, d\theta_i \qquad (23.F.7)$$

s.t.  (i)  $\bar{y}_i(\cdot)$ is nondecreasing for all $i \neq 0$.

(ii)  For all $\theta$: $y_i(\theta) \in [0, 1]$ for all $i \neq 0$, $\sum_{i \neq 0} y_i(\theta) \leq 1$.

(iii)  $U_i(\theta_i) = U_i(\underline{\theta}_i) + \int_{\underline{\theta}_i}^{\theta_i} \bar{y}_i(s)\, ds$ for all $i \neq 0$ and $\theta_i$.

(iv)  $U_i(\theta_i) \geq 0$ for all $i \neq 0$ and $\theta_i$.

We note first that if constraint (iii) is satisfied then constraint (iv) will be satisfied if and only if $U_i(\underline{\theta}_i) \geq 0$ for all $i \neq 0$. As a result, we can replace constraint (iv) with

(iv′)  $U_i(\underline{\theta}_i) \geq 0$ for all $i \neq 0$ and $\theta_i$.

Next, substituting into the objective function for $U_i(\theta_i)$ using constraint (iii), and following the same steps that led to (23.D.16), the seller's problem can be written as one of choosing the $y_i(\cdot)$ functions and the values $U_1(\underline{\theta}_1), \ldots, U_I(\underline{\theta}_I)$ to maximize

$$\int_{\underline{\theta}_1}^{\bar{\theta}_1} \cdots \int_{\underline{\theta}_I}^{\bar{\theta}_I} \left[ \sum_{i=1}^{I} y_i(\theta_1, \ldots, \theta_I) \left( \theta_i - \frac{1 - \Phi_i(\theta_i)}{\phi_i(\theta_i)} \right) \right] \left[ \prod_{i=1}^{I} \phi_i(\theta_i) \right] d\theta_I \cdots d\theta_1 - \sum_{i=1}^{I} U_i(\underline{\theta}_i)$$

subject to constraints (i), (ii), and (iv′). It is evident that the solution must have $U_i(\underline{\theta}_i) = 0$ for all $i = 1, \ldots, I$. Hence, the seller's problem reduces to choosing functions $y_1(\cdot), \ldots, y_I(\cdot)$ to maximize

$$\int_{\underline{\theta}_1}^{\bar{\theta}_1} \cdots \int_{\underline{\theta}_I}^{\bar{\theta}_I} \left[ \sum_{i=1}^{I} y_i(\theta_1, \ldots, \theta_I) \left( \theta_i - \frac{1 - \Phi_i(\theta_i)}{\phi_i(\theta_i)} \right) \right] \left[ \prod_{i=1}^{I} \phi_i(\theta_i) \right] d\theta_I \cdots d\theta_1 \qquad (23.F.8)$$

subject to constraints (i) and (ii).

Let us ignore constraint (i) for the moment. Define

$$J_i(\theta_i) = \theta_i - \frac{1 - \Phi_i(\theta_i)}{\phi_i(\theta_i)}.$$

Then inspection of (23.F.8) indicates that $y_1(\cdot), \ldots, y_I(\cdot)$ is a solution to this relaxed

---

51. Once again we restrict attention, without loss of generality, to social choice functions involving no waste of either the numeraire or the good (there is always an optimal social choice function for the seller with this form).

problem if and only if for all $i = 1, \ldots, I$ we have

$$y_i(\theta) = 1 \qquad \text{if } J_i(\theta_i) > \text{Max}\{0, \text{Max}_{h \neq i} J_h(\theta_h)\}$$

and                                                                                  (23.F.9)

$$y_i(\theta) = 0 \qquad \text{if } J_i(\theta_i) < \text{Max}\{0, \text{Max}_{h \neq i} J_h(\theta_h)\}.$$

[Note that $J_i(\theta_i) = \text{Max}\{0, \text{Max}_{h \neq i} J_h(\theta_h)\}$ is a zero probability event.] But, given our assumption that $J_i(\cdot)$ is nondecreasing in $\theta_i$, (23.F.9) implies that $y_i(\cdot)$ is nondecreasing in $\theta_i$, which in turn implies that $\bar{y}_i(\cdot)$ is nondecreasing. Thus the solution to this relaxed problem actually satisfies constraint (i), and so is a solution to the seller's overall problem (see Section M.K of the Mathematical Appendix). The optimal transfer functions can then be set as $t_i(\theta) = U_i(\underline{\theta}_i) - \theta_i \bar{y}_i(\theta_i)$, where $U_i(\underline{\theta}_i)$ is calculated from constraint (iii).

A few things should be noted about (23.F.9). First, observe that when the various agents have differing distribution functions $\Phi_i(\cdot)$, the agent $i$ who has the largest value of $J_i(\theta_i)$ is *not* necessarily the same as the agent who has the highest valuation for the object. Thus, the seller's optimal auction need not be ex post (classically) efficient.

Second, in the case of *symmetric* bidders in which $\underline{\theta}_i = \underline{\theta}$ and $J_i(\cdot) = J(\cdot)$ for $i = 1, \ldots, I$, when $\underline{\theta} > 0$ is large enough so that $J(\underline{\theta}) > 0$, the optimal auction always gives the object to the bidder with the highest valuation and also leaves each bidder with an expected utility of zero when his valuation attains its lowest possible value. We can therefore conclude, using the revenue equivalence theorem (Proposition 23.D.3), that the first-price and second-price sealed-bid auctions are both optimal in this case.

Third, the optimal auction has a nice interpretation in terms of monopoly pricing. Consider, for example, the case in which $I = 1$ and $\underline{\theta}_1 = 0$. Then conditions (23.F.9) tell us that the optimal auction gives the object to the buyer (agent 1) if and only if $J_1(\theta_1) = [\theta_1 - ((1 - \Phi_1(\theta_1))/\phi_1(\theta_1))] > 0$. Suppose we think instead of the seller in this circumstance simply naming a price $p$ and letting the buyer then decide whether to buy at this price. The seller's expected revenue from this scheme is $p(1 - \Phi_1(p))$, and so the first-order condition for his optimal posted price, say $p^*$, is $(1 - \Phi_1(p^*)) - p^* \phi_1(p^*) = 0$, or equivalently, $J_1(p^*) = 0$. Since $J_1(\cdot)$ is nondecreasing, we see that with this optimal posted price policy a buyer of type $\theta_1$ gets the good with probability 1 if $J_1(\theta_1) > 0$, and with probability 0 if $J_1(\theta_1) < 0$, exactly as in the optimal auction derived above. Indeed, given the revenue equivalence theorem we can conclude that in this case this simple posted price scheme is an optimal mechanism for the seller. [For more on the monopoly interpretation of optimal auctions, see Exercise 23.F.5 and Bulow and Roberts (1989).] ∎

Throughout the chapter, we have restricted attention to "private values" settings in which agents' utilities depend only on their own types. In a number of settings of economic interest, however, an agent $i$'s utility depends not only his own type, $\theta_i$, but also on the types of other agents, $\theta_{-i}$. That is, agent $i$'s Bernoulli utility function may take the form $u_i(x, \theta)$ rather than $u_i(x, \theta_i)$, where $\theta = (\theta_i, \theta_{-i})$. Fortunately, all of the concepts of implementation for Bayesian Nash equilibrium that we have studied in Sections 23.D to 23.F extend readily to this case. For example, we can say that the social choice function $f: \Theta \to X$ is Bayesian incentive compatible if for all $i$

and all $\theta_i \in \Theta_i$,

$$E_{\theta_{-i}}[u_i(f(\theta_i, \theta_{-i}), \theta) | \theta_i] \geq E_{\theta_{-i}}[u_i(f(\hat{\theta}_i, \theta_{-i}), \theta) | \theta_i] \qquad (23.F.10)$$

for all $\hat{\theta}_i \in \Theta_i$. Our third and last example, which studies a simple bilateral trade setting with adverse selection (see Section 13.B for more on adverse selection), falls within this class of models. Another difference from the analysis of Examples 23.F.1 and 23.F.2 is that here we shall characterize the *entire sets* of both ex ante and interim incentive efficient social choice functions.

**Example 23.F.3:** *Bilateral Trade with Adverse Selection* [from Myerson (1991)]. Consider a bilateral trade setting in which there is a seller (agent 1) and a potential buyer (agent 2) of one unit of an indivisible private good. The good may be of high quality or low quality, but only the seller observes which is the case. To model this, we let the seller have two possible types, so that $\Theta_1 = \{\theta_L, \theta_H\}$, and we assume that $\text{Prob}(\theta_H) = .2$. Both the buyer's and the seller's utilities from consumption of the good depend on the seller's type. In particular, letting $y$ denote the probability that the buyer receives the good, and letting $t$ denote the amount of any monetary transfer from the buyer to the seller, we suppose that[52]

$$\begin{aligned} u_1(y, t | \theta_L) &= t + 20(1 - y), & u_1(y, t | \theta_H) &= t + 40(1 - y), \\ u_2(y, t | \theta_L) &= 30y - t, & u_2(y, t | \theta_H) &= 50y - t. \end{aligned} \qquad (23.F.11)$$

A social choice function in this setting assigns a probability of trade and a transfer for each possible value of $\theta_1$, and so can be represented by a vector $(y_L, t_L, y_H, t_H)$. We suppose that trade is voluntary, and that as a result any feasible social choice function must satisfy interim individual rationality constraints for both the buyer and the seller. For the seller this means that, for each type he may have, his expected utility must be no less than his utility from refusing to participate and simply consuming the good. Hence, we must have

$$t_L + 20(1 - y_L) \geq 20 \qquad (\text{IR}_{1L}) \qquad (23.F.12)$$

$$t_H + 40(1 - y_H) \geq 40. \qquad (\text{IR}_{1H}) \qquad (23.F.13)$$

For the buyer, on the other hand, interim individual rationality simply requires that he receive nonnegative expected utility from participation (recall that he does not observe $\theta_1$). Hence, we must have

$$.2(50y_H - t_H) + .8(30y_L - t_L) \geq 0. \qquad (\text{IR}_2) \qquad (23.F.14)$$

Note from (23.F.11) that if $\theta_1$ were publicly observable then, for each value of $\theta_1$, there would be gains from trade between the buyer and the seller. Because of this fact, any ex post (classically) efficient social choice function has $y_H = y_L = 1$ (see Exercise 23.F.8).

Because $\theta_1$ is only privately observed, the set of feasible social choice functions is the incentive feasible set $F^*$, the set of Bayesian incentive compatible and (interim) individually rational social choice functions. In the present context, the social choice

---

52. We assume that there is no waste of either the good or the numeraire, so that the probability that either the buyer or the seller consumes the good is 1, and any transfer from the buyer goes to the seller.

function $(y_L, t_L, y_H, t_H)$ is Bayesian incentive compatible if

$$t_H + 40(1 - y_H) \geq t_L + 40(1 - y_L) \qquad (IC_H) \qquad (23.F.15)$$

and

$$t_L + 20(1 - y_L) \geq t_H + 20(1 - y_H). \qquad (IC_L) \qquad (23.F.16)$$

Condition (23.F.15) requires that truth telling be an optimal strategy for the seller when his type is $\theta_H$; (23.F.16) is the condition for truth telling to be optimal when his type is $\theta_L$. Thus, $(y_L, t_L, y_H, t_H)$ is a feasible social choice function if and only if it satisfies the incentive compatibility constraints (23.F.15)–(23.F.16) and the interim individual rationality constraints (23.F.12)–(23.F.14).

These constraints imply that *any* feasible social choice function possesses the following three properties (Exercise 23.F.9 asks you to establish these points):

(i) No feasible social choice function is ex post (classically) efficient.

(ii) In any feasible social choice function, $y_H \leq y_L$ and $t_H \leq t_L$.

(iii) In any feasible social choice function, the expected gains from trade for a low-quality seller are at least as large as the expected gains from trade for a high-quality seller, that is, $t_L - 20y_L \geq t_H - 40y_H$.

We now proceed to characterize the interim and ex ante incentive efficient social choice functions for this bilateral trade problem. To determine the interim incentive efficient social choice functions, we need to determine the $(y_L, t_L, y_H, t_H)$ that solve, for each possible choice of $\bar{u}_{1H} \geq 0$ and $\bar{u}_2 \geq 0$, the following problem (we have simplified the incentive compatibility and individual rationality constraints by eliminating constants on both sides of the inequalities, and have removed a constant from the objective function as well[53]):

$$\underset{(y_L \in [0, 1], t_L, y_H \in [0, 1], t_H)}{\text{Max}} \quad t_L - 20y_L \qquad (23.F.17)$$

$$\begin{aligned}
\text{s.t.} \quad &\text{(i)} \quad t_H - 40y_H \geq t_L - 40y_L \\
&\text{(ii)} \quad t_L - 20y_L \geq t_H - 20y_H \\
&\text{(iii)} \quad t_H - 40y_H \geq \bar{u}_{1H} \\
&\text{(iv)} \quad .2(50y_H - t_H) + .8(30y_L - t_L) \geq \bar{u}_2.
\end{aligned}$$

Problem (23.F.17) characterizes interim incentive efficient social choice functions by maximizing the interim expected utility of the type $\theta_L$ seller subject to giving the type $\theta_H$ seller an interim expected utility of at least $\bar{u}_{1H} \geq 0$, giving the buyer an interim expected utility of $\bar{u}_2 \geq 0$ (since the buyer acquires no private information, this is equivalent to giving him an ex ante expected utility of $\bar{u}_2$), and satisfying the seller's incentive compatibility constraints.

We now proceed to characterize the solution to problem (23.F.17) through a series of steps.

*Step 1: Any solution to problem (23.F.17) has $y_L = 1$; that is, in any interim incentive efficient social choice function, trade is certain to occur when the good is of low quality.*

To see this, suppose that $(y_L^*, t_L^*, y_H^*, t_H^*)$ solves (23.F.17) but that $y_L^* < 1$. Consider a change to social choice function $(\hat{y}_L, \hat{t}_L, \hat{y}_H, \hat{t}_H) = (y_L^* + \varepsilon, t_L^* + 30\varepsilon, y_H^*, t_H^*)$

---

53. In essence, we have expressed all of these in terms of the agents' *gains from trade*.

where $\varepsilon > 0$. For a sufficiently small $\varepsilon > 0$, this new social choice function satisfies all of the constraints of problem (23.F.17) (check this), and raises the value of the objective function—but this contradicts the optimality of $(y_L^*, t_L^*, y_H^*, t_H^*)$.

*Step 2:    Any solution to problem (23.F.17) has $y_H < 1$; that is, in any interim incentive efficient social choice function, trade does not occur with certainty when the good is of high quality.*

Given step 1, if a solution to (23.F.17), say $(y_L^*, t_L^*, y_H^*, t_H^*)$ has $y_H^* = 1$, then $(y_L^*, t_L^*, y_H^*, t_H^*)$ is ex post (classically) efficient (i.e., it has $y_L^* = y_H^* = 1$). But we have already noted above that no such social choice function is incentive feasible (i.e., is an element of $F^*$).

*Step 3:    In any solution to (23.F.17), constraint (ii) is binding (i.e., holds with equality).*

Suppose that the social choice function $(y_L^*, t_L^*, y_H^*, t_H^*)$ is a solution to (23.F.17) in which constraint (ii) is not binding in the solution. Consider instead the social choice function $(\hat{y}_L, \hat{t}_L, \hat{y}_H, \hat{t}_H) = (y_L^*, t_L^* + \varepsilon, y_H^* + \varepsilon, t_H^* + 45\varepsilon)$ for $\varepsilon > 0$. For small enough $\varepsilon > 0$, this alternative social choice function satisfies all of the constraints of problem (23.F.17) (note that it satisfies $\hat{y}_H < 1$ because, by step 2, $y_H^* < 1$; check the other constraints too). Moreover, it yields a larger value of the objective function of (23.F.17) than $(y_L^*, t_L^*, y_H^*, t_H^*)$—a contradiction. This establishes step 3.

*Step 4:    If constraint (ii) binds and $y_L \geq y_H$, then constraint (i) is necessarily satisfied.*

If constraint (ii) binds then $t_H - t_L = 20(y_H - y_L)$. If $y_L \geq y_H$ then this implies that $t_H - t_L \geq 40(y_H - y_L)$, or, equivalently, $t_H - 40y_H \geq t_L - 40y_L$. Hence, constraint (i) is satisfied.

Given steps 1 to 4, we can simplify problem (23.F.17). In particular, we see that $(y_L, t_L, y_H, t_H)$ is interim incentive efficient if and only if $y_L = 1$ and $(t_L, y_H, t_H)$ solve

$$\underset{(t_L \in [0,1], y_H, t_H \in [0,1])}{\text{Max}} \quad t_L - 20 \qquad (23.F.18)$$

$$\text{s.t. (ii')} \ \ t_L - 20 = t_H - 20y_H.$$
$$\text{(iii)} \ \ t_H - 40y_H \geq \bar{u}_{1H}.$$
$$\text{(iv)} \ \ .2(50y_H - t_H) + .8(30 - t_L) \geq \bar{u}_2.$$

Substituting from constraint (ii') of problem (23.F.18) for $t_L$ in its objective function and in constraint (iv) we see that we can determine the optimal values of $(y_H, t_H)$ by solving

$$\underset{(y_H \in [0,1], t_H)}{\text{Max}} \quad t_H - 20y_H \qquad (23.F.19)$$

$$\text{s.t.} \ \ \text{(ii)} \ \ t_H - 40y_H \geq \bar{u}_{1H}.$$
$$\text{(iv')} \ \ 26y_H - t_H + 8 \geq \bar{u}_2.$$

The solution for a given pair of values of $\bar{u}_{1H} \geq 0$ and $\bar{u}_2 \geq 0$ is depicted in Figure 23.F.1. The pairs $(y_H, t_H)$ that satisfy constraints (ii) and (iv') of (23.F.19) lie in the shaded set. Also drawn are two level sets of the objective function $t_H - 20y_H$. The optimal pair $(y_H, t_H)$ for these values of $\bar{u}_{1H}$ and $\bar{u}_2$ is the point labeled $(y_H^*, t_H^*)$. The corresponding values of $t_L$ and $y_L$ in this interim incentive efficient social choice function are then $y_L^* = 1$ and $t_L^* = 20 + t_H^* - 20y_H^*$.

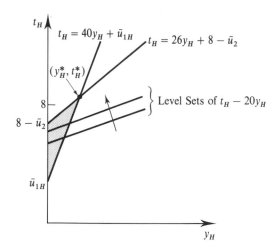

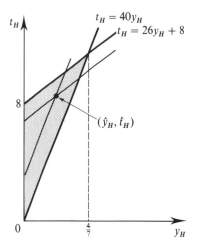

**Figure 23.F.1 (left)**

The optimal level of $(y_H, t_H)$ in problem (23.F.19) for a given pair $(\bar{u}_H, \bar{u}_2) \geq 0$.

**Figure 23.F.2 (right)**

The shaded set contains those pairs $(y_H, t_H)$ arising in interim incentive efficient social choice functions.

The shaded set in Figure 23.F.2, $\{(y_H, t_H): y_H \in [0, 1], t_H \geq 40y_H,$ and $t_H \leq 26y_H + 8\}$, depicts *all* of the pairs $(y_H, t_H)$ that arise in interim incentive efficient social choice functions. These are determined by performing the analysis in Figure 23.F.1 for each possible pair $(\bar{u}_{1H}, \bar{u}_2) \geq 0$ [a sample pair $(\hat{y}_H, \hat{t}_H)$ is also depicted in Figure 23.F.2]. Note that in any interim incentive efficient social choice function we have $y_H \leq 4/7$. As above, for each pair $(\hat{y}_H, \hat{t}_H)$ in this set, we can determine an interim incentive efficient social choice function $(\hat{y}_L, \hat{t}_L, \hat{y}_H, \hat{t}_H)$ by setting $\hat{y}_L = 1$ and $\hat{t}_L = 20 + \hat{t}_H - 20\hat{y}_H$.

Now, out of this set of interim incentive efficient social choice functions, which are ex ante incentive efficient? (Recall that the set of ex ante incentive efficient social choice functions is a subset of the interim incentive efficient set. Note also that although we now employ an ex ante welfare criterion, the set of participation constraints defining $F^*$ continue to be the same interim participation constraints used above.) The buyer's and seller's ex ante expected utilities in an interim incentive efficient social choice function $(y_L, t_L, y_H, t_H)$ are

$$U_1 = .8(t_L + 20(1 - y_L)) + .2(t_H + 40(1 - y_H))$$

and

$$U_2 = .8(30y_L - t_L) + .2(50y_H - t_H).$$

Since $y_L = 1$ and $t_L = 20 + t_H - 20y_H$ in any interim incentive efficient social choice function, these expected utilities can be written as functions of only $(y_H, t_H)$ as follows:

$$U_1 = 24 + t_H - 24y_H, \qquad U_2 = 8 + 26y_H - t_H.$$

In Figure 23.F.3, for an arbitrary point $(\hat{y}_H, \hat{t}_H)$ in set $\{(y_H, t_H): y_H \in [0, 1], t_H \geq 40y_H,$ and $t_H \leq 26y_H + 8\}$, the pairs $(y_H, t_H)$ in the shaded set raise the ex ante expected utilities of both the buyer and the seller. As can be seen from this figure, no pair $(y_H, t_H)$ that is not on the $t_H = 40y_H$ boundary of the set $\{(y_H, t_H): y_H \in [0, 1], t_H \geq 40y_H,$ and $t_H \leq 26y_H + 8\}$ can be ex ante incentive efficient. Moreover, each pair $(y_H, t_H)$ on this boundary *is* part of an ex ante incentive efficient social choice function. The set of $(y_H, t_H)$ pairs in ex ante incentive efficient social choice functions

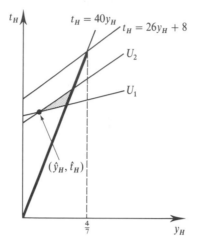

**Figure 23.F.3**

The set of ex ante incentive efficient social choice functions corresponds to those interim incentive efficient social choice functions with $(y_H, t_H)$ lying in the heavily traced line segment.

is therefore precisely the heavily traced line segment in Figure 23.F.3.[54] Notice that in every such social choice function the interim individual rationality constraint for a high-quality seller binds: the high-quality seller receives no gains from trade. ∎

## APPENDIX A: IMPLEMENTATION AND MULTIPLE EQUILIBRIA

The notion of implementation that we have employed throughout the chapter (e.g., in Definition 23.B.4) is weaker in one potentially important respect than what we might want: Although a mechanism $\Gamma$ may implement the social choice function $f(\cdot)$ in the sense of having *an* equilibrium whose outcomes coincide with $f(\cdot)$ for all $\theta \in \Theta$, there may be *other* equilibria of $\Gamma$ whose outcomes do *not* coincide with $f(\cdot)$. In essence, we have implicitly assumed that the agents will play the equilibrium that the mechanism designer wants if there is more than one.[55]

This suggests that if a mechanism designer wishes to be fully confident that the mechanism $\Gamma$ does indeed yield the outcomes associated with $f(\cdot)$, he might instead want to insist upon the stronger notion of implementation given in Definition 23.AA.1 (as in Definition 23.B.4, we are deliberately vague here about the equilibrium concept to be employed).

**Definition 23.AA.1:**   The  mechanism  $\Gamma = (S_1, \ldots, S_I, g(\cdot))$  *strongly implements* social  choice  function  $f: \Theta_1 \times \cdots \times \Theta_I \to X$  if  every  equilibrium  strategy

---

54. Note that $y_H \leq 4/7 < 1$ in any ex ante incentive efficient social choice function. This may seem at odds with our conclusion in Section 13.B that the ex ante efficient outcome that gives firms zero expected profits has all workers accepting employment in a firm (the structure of the model in Section 13.B parallels that here). The difference is that in Section 13.B we did not impose any interim individual rationality constraints on the workers, effectively supposing that the government could compel workers to participate (pay any taxes, etc.). See Exercise 23.F.10.

55. One possible argument for this assumption is that in a direct revelation mechanism that truthfully implements social choice function $f(\cdot)$, the truth-telling equilibrium may be focal (in the sense discussed in Section 8.D).

profile $(s_1^*(\cdot), \ldots, s_I^*(\cdot))$ of the game induced by $\Gamma$ has the property that $g(s_1^*(\theta_1), \ldots, s_I^*(\theta_I)) = f(\theta_1, \ldots, \theta_I)$ for all $(\theta_1, \ldots, \theta_I)$.[56]

Let us consider first the implications of this stronger concept for implementation in dominant strategy equilibria. In Exercise 23.C.8 we have already seen a case where, in the direct revelation mechanism that truthfully implements a social choice function $f(\cdot)$ in dominant strategies, some player has more than one dominant strategy, and when he plays one of these dominant strategies the outcome in $f(\cdot)$ does not result (see also Exercises 23.AA.1 and 23.AA.2). Thus, with dominant strategy implementation we may have mechanisms that implement a social choice function $f(\cdot)$ but that do not strongly implement it.

Nevertheless, there are at least two reasons why the multiple equilibrium problem may not be too severe with dominant strategy implementation. First, whenever each agent's dominant strategy in a mechanism $\Gamma$ that implements $f(\cdot)$ is in fact a *strictly* dominant strategy (rather than just a weakly dominant one), mechanism $\Gamma$ also strongly implements $f(\cdot)$. This is always the case, for example, in any environment in which agents' preferences never involve indifference between any two elements of $X$. Second, when a player has two weakly dominant strategies, he is of necessity indifferent between them for any strategies than the other agents choose. Thus, to play the "right" equilibrium in this case, it is only necessary that each agent be willing to resolve his indifference in the way we desire.

In contrast, with Nash-based equilibrium concepts such as Bayesian Nash equilibrium, if mechanism $\Gamma$ has two equilibria, then in each equilibrium each player may have a strict preference for his equilibrium strategy given that the other agents are playing their respective equilibrium strategies. Having agents play the "right" equilibrium is then not just a matter of resolving indifference but rather of generating expectations that the desired equilibrium is the one that will occur. Example 23.AA.1 illustrates the problem.

**Example 23.AA.1:** *Multiple Equilibria in the Expected Externality Mechanism.* Consider again the expected externality mechanism of Section 23.D. Suppose that we are in a setting with two agents ($I = 2$) in which a decision must be made regarding a public project (see Example 23.B.3). The project may be either done ($k = 1$) or not done ($k = 0$). Each agent's valuation (net of funding the project) is either $\theta_L$ or $\theta_H$ (so $\Theta_i = \{\theta_L, \theta_H\}$ for $i = 1, 2$), where $\theta_H > 0 > \theta_L$ and $\theta_L + \theta_H > 0$. The agents' valuations are statistically independent with Prob $(\theta_i = \theta_L) = \lambda \in (0, 1)$ for $i = 1, 2$.

In the expected externality mechanism, each agent $i$ announces his valuation and agent $i$'s transfer when the announced types are $(\theta_1, \theta_2)$ has the form $t_i(\theta_i, \theta_{-i}) = E_{\tilde{\theta}_{-i}}[\tilde{\theta}_{-i} k^*(\theta_i, \tilde{\theta}_{-i})] + h_i(\theta_{-i})$, where $k^*(\theta_1, \theta_2) = 0$ if $\theta_1 = \theta_2 = \theta_L$, and $k^*(\theta_1, \theta_2) = 1$ otherwise.

As we saw in Section 23.D, in one Bayesian Nash equilibrium of this mechanism, truth telling is each agent's equilibrium strategy. But this truth-telling equilibrium is *not* the only Bayesian Nash equilibrium. In particular, there is an equilibrium in which both agents always claim that $\theta_H$ is their type. To see this, consider agent $i$'s optimal

---

56. The "strong" terminology is not standard; in the literature it is not uncommon, for example, to see the strong implementation concept simply referred to as "implementation."

strategy if agent $-i$ will always announce $\theta_H$. Whichever announcement agent $i$ makes, the project is done. Thus, regardless of his actual type, agent $i$'s direct benefit (i.e., $\theta_i k^*(\theta_1, \theta_2)$) is not affected by his announcement (it is $\theta_L$ if he is of type $\theta_L$, and $\theta_H$ if he is of type $\theta_H$). It follows that agent $i$'s optimal strategy is to make an announcement that maximizes his expected transfer. Now, agent $i$'s expected transfer if he announces $\theta_H$ is $(\lambda\theta_L + (1 - \lambda)\theta_H) + h_i(\theta_H)$, whereas if he announces $\theta_L$ his expected transfer is $(1 - \lambda)\theta_H + h_i(\theta_H)$. Hence, agent $i$ will prefer to announce $\theta_H$ regardless of his type if agent $-i$ is doing the same. It follows that both agents always announcing $\theta_H$, and the project consequently always being done, constitutes a second Bayesian Nash equilibrium of this mechanism. ∎

We shall not pursue here the characterization of social choice functions that can be strongly implemented in Bayesian Nash equilibria. A good source of further reading on this subject is Palfrey (1992). We also refer to Appendix B, where we discuss many of these issues for the special context of complete information environments.

There are, however, two important points about strong implementation that we wish to stress here. First, when trying to strongly implement a social choice function $f(\cdot)$, we *cannot* generally restrict attention to direct revelation mechanisms. The reason is that when we replace a mechanism $\Gamma = (S_1, \ldots, S_I, g(\cdot))$ with a direct revelation mechanism, as envisioned by the revelation principle, we may introduce new, undesirable equilibria. (See Exercises 23.C.8 and 23.AA.1 for an illustration.) Second, because a social choice function $f(\cdot)$ can be strongly implemented only if it can be implemented in the weaker sense studied in the text of the chapter, all of the necessary conditions for implementation that we have derived are *still* necessary for $f(\cdot)$ to be strongly implemented. Thus, for example, the conclusions of the Gibbard–Satterthwaite theorem (Proposition 23.C.3), the revenue equivalence theorem (Proposition 23.D.3), and the Myerson–Satterthwaite theorem (Proposition 23.E.1) all continue to be valid when we seek strong implementation.

---

Throughout the chapter we have restricted attention to single-valued social choice functions. It is sometimes natural, however, to consider social choice *correspondences* that can specify more than one acceptable alternative for a given profile of agent types. In this case, we would say that mechanism $\Gamma = (S_1, \ldots, S_I, g(\cdot))$ strongly implements the social choice correspondence $f(\cdot)$ if every equilibrium $s^*(\cdot)$ of the game induced by $\Gamma$ has the property that $g(s^*(\theta)) \in f(\theta)$, that is, if, for every $\theta$, all possible equilibrium outcomes are acceptable alternatives according to $f(\cdot)$.

---

## APPENDIX B: IMPLEMENTATION IN ENVIRONMENTS WITH COMPLETE INFORMATION

In this appendix we provide a brief discussion of implementation in complete information environments. An excellent source for further reading on this subject is the survey by Moore (1992) [see also Maskin (1985)].

In the complete information case we suppose that each agent will observe not only his own preference parameter $\theta_i$, but also the preference parameters $\theta_{-i}$ of all other agents. However, while the agents will observe each others' preference parameters, we suppose that no outsider does. Thus, despite the agents' abilities to observe $\theta$, there is still an implementation problem: Because no outsider (such as a court) will observe $\theta$, the agents cannot write an enforceable ex ante agreement saying that they will choose outcome $f(\theta)$ when agents' preferences are $\theta$. Rather, they can only agree to participate in some mechanism in which equilibrium play yields $f(\theta)$ if $\theta$ is realized.[57]

Note that a complete information setting can be viewed as a special case of the general environment considered throughout this chapter, in which the probability density $\phi(\cdot)$ on $\Theta$ has the (degenerate) property that each agent's observation of his "type" is completely informative about the types of the other agents.[58]

To begin, observe that the set of social choice functions that are dominant strategy implementable is unaffected by the presence of complete information because an agent's belief about the types of other agents does not affect his set of dominant strategies.[59] [Indeed, recall our comment in Section 23.C that if mechanism $\Gamma$ implements social choice function $f(\cdot)$ in dominant strategies, then it does so for *any* $\phi(\cdot)$.]

This is *not* the case, however, for implementation in Nash-based equilibrium concepts, such as Bayesian Nash equilibrium. Recall that in complete information environments, the Bayesian Nash equilibrium concept reduces to our standard notion of Nash equilibrium. This motivates Definition 23.BB.1.

**Definition 23.BB.1:** The mechanism $\Gamma = (S_1, \ldots, S_I, g(\cdot))$ *implements the social choice function* $f(\cdot)$ *in Nash equilibrium* if, for each profile of the agents' preference parameters $\theta = (\theta_1, \ldots, \theta_I) \in \Theta$, there is a Nash equilibrium of the game induced by $\Gamma$, $s^*(\theta) = (s_1^*(\theta), \ldots, s_I^*(\theta))$, such that $g(s^*(\theta)) = f(\theta)$. The mechanism $\Gamma = (S_1, \ldots, S_I, g(\cdot))$ *strongly implements the social choice function* $f(\cdot)$ *in Nash equilibrium* if, for each profile of the agents' preference parameters $\theta = (\theta_1, \ldots, \theta_I) \in \Theta$, every Nash equilibrium of the game induced by $\Gamma$ results in outcome $f(\theta)$.

The first point to note about implementation in Nash equilibria is that if we are satisfied with the weaker notion of implementation that we have employed throughout the text of the chapter (as opposed to the strong implementation concept discussed in Appendix A), then *any* social choice function can be implemented in Nash equilibrium as long as $I \geq 3$. To see this, consider the following mechanism: each agent $i$ simultaneously announces a profile of types for each of the $I$ agents. If at least $I - 1$ agents announce the same profile, say $\hat{\theta}$, then we select outcome $f(\hat{\theta})$.

---

57. This type of setting is often natural in contracting problems, where it is frequently reasonable to suppose that the parties will come to know a lot about each other that is not verifiable by any outside enforcer of their contract.

58. Thus, we can think of the complete information environment as a case in which agents receive signals that are perfectly correlated. There are several ways to formalize this. Perhaps the simplest is to suppose that each agent $i$'s preference parameter is drawn from some set $\Theta_i$. An agent's *signal* (or *type*), which is now represented by $\bar{\theta}_i = (\theta_{i1}, \ldots, \theta_{iI}) \in \Theta$, is a vector giving agent $i$'s observation of his and every other agent's preference parameters. Thus, the set of possible "types" for agent $i$ in the sense in which we have used this term throughout the chapter, is now $\bar{\Theta}_i = \Theta$ for each $i = 1, \ldots, I$. The probability density $\phi(\cdot)$ on the set of possible types $\bar{\Theta}_1 \times \cdots \times \bar{\Theta}_I$ then satisfies the property that $\phi(\bar{\theta}_1, \ldots, \bar{\theta}_I) > 0$ if and only if $\bar{\theta}_1 = \cdots = \bar{\theta}_I$, and agent $i$'s Bernoulli utility function has the form $u_i(x, \bar{\theta}_i) = \tilde{u}_i(x, \theta_{ii})$.

59. The same is true for strong implementation in dominant strategies.

Otherwise we select outcome $x_0 \in X$ ($x_0$ is arbitary). With this mechanism, for every profile $\theta$, there is a Nash equilibrium in which every agent announces $\theta$, and the resulting outcome is $f(\theta)$, because no agent can affect the outcome by unilaterally deviating.

Although this mechanism implements $f(\cdot)$ in Nash equilibrium, it is obviously not a very attractive mechanism [i.e., its implementation of $f(\cdot)$ is not very convincing] because there are so many other Nash equilibria that do not result in outcome $f(\theta)$ when the preference profile is $\theta$. Indeed, with this mechanism, given the profile of preference parameters $\theta$, there is a Nash equilibrium resulting in $x$ for every $x \in f(\Theta) = \{x \in X: \text{ there is a } \theta \in \Theta \text{ such that } f(\theta) = x\}$. We see then that for Nash implementation with $I \geq 3$, the *entire* problem of satisfactorily implementing a given social choice function revolves around the issue of successfully dealing with the multiple equilibrium problem discussed in Appendix A.

Given this observation, what social choice functions can we strongly implement in Nash equilibrium? The simple but powerful result in Proposition 23.BB.1 comes from Maskin's (1977) path-breaking paper on Nash implementation.

**Proposition 23.BB.1:** If the social choice function $f(\cdot)$ can be strongly implemented in Nash equilibrium, then $f(\cdot)$ is monotonic.[60]

**Proof:** Suppose that $\Gamma = (S_1, \ldots, S_I, g(\cdot))$ strongly implements $f(\cdot)$. Then when the preference parameter profile is $\theta$, there is a Nash equilibrium resulting in outcome $f(\theta)$; that is, there is a strategy profile $s^* = (s_1^*, \ldots, s_I^*)$ having the properties that $g(s^*) = f(\theta)$ and $g(\hat{s}_i, s_{-i}^*) \in L_i(f(\theta), \theta_i)$ for all $\hat{s}_i \in S_i$ and all $i$.[61] Now suppose that $f(\cdot)$ is not monotonic. Then there exists another profile of preference parameters $\theta' \in \Theta$ such that $L_i(f(\theta), \theta_i) \subset L_i(f(\theta), \theta_i')$ for all $i$, but $f(\theta') \neq f(\theta)$. But $s^*$ is also a Nash equilibrium under preference parameter profile $\theta'$, because $g(\hat{s}_i, s_{-i}^*) \in L_i(f(\theta), \theta_i')$ for all $\hat{s}_i \in S_i$ and all $i$. Hence, $\Gamma$ does not strongly implement $f(\cdot)$—a contradiction. ∎

As an illustration of the restriction imposed by monotonicity, Proposition 23.BB.2 records one implication of this result.

**Proposition 23.BB.2:** Suppose that $X$ is finite and contains at least three elements, that $\mathscr{R}_i = \mathscr{P}$ for all $i$, and that $f(\Theta) = X$. Then the social choice function $f(\cdot)$ is strongly implementable in Nash equilibrium if and only if it is dictatorial.

**Proof:** To strongly implement a dictatorial social choice function in Nash equilibrium, we need only let the dictator choose an alternative from $X$. In the other direction, the result follows from steps 2 and 3 of the proof of the Gibbard–Satterthwaite theorem (Proposition 23.C.3). ∎

One lesson to be learned from Propositions 23.BB.1 and 23.BB.2 is that dealing with the multiple equilibrium problem can potentially impose very significant restrictions on the set of implementable social choice functions.

---

60. See Definition 23.C.5.
61. Recall that $L_i(x, \theta_i) \subset X$ is agent $i$'s lower contour set for outcome $x \in X$ when agent $i$'s preference parameter is $\theta_i$.

Maskin (1977) also showed that, when $I > 2$, monotonicity is *almost*, but not quite, a sufficient condition for strong implementation [we omit the proof; see Moore (1992) for a discussion of this and more recent results, including consideration of the case $I = 2$]. Maskin's added condition, known as *no veto power*, requires that if $I - 1$ agents all rank some alternative $x$ as their best alternative then $x = f(\theta)$.

**Proposition 23.BB.3:** If $I \geq 3$, $f(\cdot)$ is monotonic, and $f(\cdot)$ satisfies no veto power, then $f(\cdot)$ is strongly implementable in Nash equilibrium.

No veto power should be thought of as a very weak additional requirement; indeed, in any setting in which there is a desirable and transferable private good, it is trivially satisfied: no two agents then ever have the same top-ranked alternative (each wants to get all of the available transferable private good). Thus, in these commonly studied environments, monotonicity of $f(\cdot)$ is a necessary and sufficient condition for $f(\cdot)$ to be strongly implementable in Nash equilibrium.

A multivalued social choice correspondence $f(\cdot)$ is said to be monotonic if whenever $x \in f(\theta)$ and $L_i(x, \theta_i) \subset L_i(x, \theta_i')$ for all $i$ then $x \in f(\theta')$. The necessary and sufficient conditions for Nash implementation in Propositions 23.BB.1 and 23.BB.3 carry over to the multivalued case. [In fact, for Proposition 23.BB.3, Maskin's result actually establishes that there is a mechanism that has, for each preference profile $\theta$, a set of Nash equilibrium outcomes exactly equal to the set $f(\theta)$; this type of implementation of a social choice correspondence is commonly called *full implementation*.] It may be verified, for example, that if $f(\theta)$ is equal to the Pareto set for all $\theta$ (the set of all ex post efficient outcomes in $X$ given preference profile $\theta$), then $f(\cdot)$ is monotonic. Thus, in any setting with a transferable good, the Pareto set social choice correspondence is strongly implementable in Nash equilibrium.

*Implementation using Extensive Form Games: Subgame Perfect Implementation*

So far we have seen that the need to "knock out" undesirable equilibria (formalized through the notion of strong implementation) can significantly restrict the set of implementable social choice functions. This suggests the possibility that we may be more successful if we use instead a refinement of the Nash equilibrium concept. Indeed, recent work has shown that such refinements can be very powerful. Here we briefly illustrate how, by considering *dynamic* mechanisms and employing the equilibrium concepts for dynamic games discussed in Section 9.B, we can expand the set of strongly implementable social choice functions.

**Example 23.BB.1:** [Adapted from Moore and Repullo (1988)]. Consider a pure exchange economy (see Example 23.B.2) with two consumers in which each consumer has two possible individualistic preference relations: if $\theta_i = \theta_i^C$, then consumer $i$ has Cobb–Douglas preferences; if $\theta_i = \theta_i^L$, then consumer $i$ has Leontief preferences. These two possible preference relations for consumers 1 and 2 are depicted in Figure 23.BB.1.

Suppose that we wish to strongly implement the social choice function

$$f(\theta) = \begin{cases} x^C & \text{if } \theta_1 = \theta_1^C, \\ x^L & \text{if } \theta_1 = \theta_1^L, \end{cases}$$

where $x^C$ and $x^L$ are the allocations depicted in Figure 23.BB.1. Note that consumer 1 always prefers $x^C$ to $x^L$, and the reverse is true for consumer 2. By inspection of

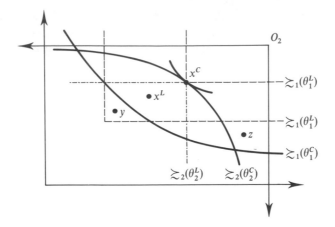

**Figure 23.BB.1**

Preferences and outcomes in Example 23.BB.1.

Figure 23.BB.1, we see that $f(\cdot)$ is not monotonic, because $L_i(x^C, \theta_i^C) \subset L_i(x^C, \theta_i^L)$ for $i = 1, 2$ but $f(\theta_1^L, \theta_2^L) \neq f(\theta_1^C, \theta_2^C)$. Hence, by Proposition 23.BB.1, $f(\cdot)$ cannot be strongly implemented in Nash equilibrium.

Suppose, instead, that we construct the following three-stage dynamic mechanism:

*Stage 1:*   Agent 1 announces either "L" or "C." If he announces "L," $x^L$ is immediately chosen. If he announces "C," we go to stage 2.

*Stage 2:*   Agent 2 says either "agree" or "challenge." If he says "agree," then $x^C$ is immediately chosen. If he says "challenge," then we go to stage 3.

*Stage 3:*   Agent 1 chooses between the allocations $y$ and $z$ depicted in Figure 23.BB.1.

It is straightforward to verify that, for each possible profile of preferences $\theta = (\theta_1, \theta_2)$, the unique subgame perfect Nash equilibrium of this dynamic game of perfect information results in outcome $f(\theta)$ (see Exercise 23.BB.1). Thus, $f(\cdot)$ *can* be strongly implemented if we consider dynamic mechanisms and take subgame perfect Nash equilibrium as the appropriate solution concept for the games induced by these mechanisms. ∎

In fact, Moore and Repullo (1988) [see also Moore (1990)] show that the use of dynamic mechanisms and subgame perfection expands the set of strongly implementable social choice functions dramatically compared to the use of the Nash equilibrium concept. Even stronger results are possible with other refinements; see, for example, Palfrey and Srivastava (1991) for a study of strong implementation in undominated Nash equilibrium (i.e., Nash equilibria in which no agent is playing a weakly dominated strategy).[62]

## REFERENCES

Abreu, D., and H. Matsushima. (1994). Exact implementation. *Journal of Economic Theory* **64**: 1–19.

Arrow, K. (1979). The property rights doctrine and demand revelation under incomplete information. In *Economics and Human Welfare*, edited by M. Boskin. New York: Academic Press.

---

62. Very positive results have also been obtained recently for implementation in iteratively undominated strategies; see, for example, Abreu and Matsushima (1994).

Barberà, S., and B. Peleg. (1990). Strategy-proof voting schemes with continuous preferences. *Social Choice and Welfare* **7**: 31–38.

Baron, D., and R. B. Myerson. (1982). Regulating a monopolist with unknown costs. *Econometrica* **50**: 911–30.

Bulow, J., and J. Roberts. (1989). The simple economics of optimal auctions. *Journal of Political Economy* **97**: 1060–90.

Clarke, E. H. (1971). Multipart pricing of public goods. *Public Choice* **2**: 19–33.

Cramton, P., R. Gibbons, and P. Klemperer. (1987). Dissolving a partnership efficiently. *Econometrica* **55**: 615–32.

Dana, J. D., Jr., and K. Spier. (1994). Designing a private industry: Government auctions with endogenous market structure. *Journal of Public Economics* **53**: 127–47.

Dasgupta, P., P. Hammond, and E. Maskin. (1979). The implementation of social choice rules: Some general results on incentive compatibility. *Review of Economic Studies* **46**: 185–216.

d'Aspremont, C., and L. A. Gérard-Varet. (1979). Incentives and incomplete information. *Journal of Public Economics* **11**: 25–45.

Fudenberg, D., and J. Tirole. (1991). *Game Theory*. Cambridge, Mass.: MIT Press.

Gibbard, A. (1973). Manipulation of voting schemes. *Econometrica* **41**: 587–601.

Green, J. R., and J.-J. Laffont. (1977). Characterization of satisfactory mechanisms for the revelation of preferences for public goods. *Econometrica* **45**: 427–38.

Green, J. R., and J.-J. Laffont. (1979). *Incentives in Public Decision Making*. Amsterdam: North-Holland.

Gresik, T. A., and M. A. Satterthwaite. (1989). The rate at which a simple market becomes efficient as the number of traders increases: An asymptotic result for optimal trading mechanisms. *Journal of Economic Theory* **48**: 304–32.

Groves, T. (1973). Incentives in teams. *Econometrica* **41**: 617–31.

Holmstrom, B., and R. B. Myerson. (1983). Efficient and durable decision rules with incomplete information. *Econometrica* **51**: 1799–1819.

Hurwicz, L. (1972). On informationally decentralized systems. In *Decision and Organization*, edited by C. B. McGuire, and R. Radner. Amsterdam: North-Holland.

Laffont, J.-J., and E. Maskin. (1980). A differential approach to dominant strategy mechanisms. *Econometrica* **48**: 1507–20.

Maskin, E. (1977). Nash equilibrium and welfare optimality. MIT Working Paper.

Maskin, E. (1985). The theory of implementation in Nash equilibrium: A survey. In *Social Goals and Social Organization: Essays in Honor of Elisha Pazner*, edited by L. Hurwicz, D. Schmeidler, and H. Sonnenschein. Cambridge, U.K.: Cambridge University Press.

Maskin, E., and J. Riley. (1984). Monopoly with incomplete information. *Rand Journal of Economics* **15**: 171–96.

McAfee, R. P., and J. McMillan. (1987). Auctions and bidding. *Journal of Economic Literature* **25**: 699–738.

Milgrom, P. R. (1987). Auction theory. In *Advances in Economic Theory: Fifth World Congress*, edited by T. Bewley. Cambridge, U.K.: Cambridge University Press.

Mirrlees, J. (1971). An exploration in the theory of optimal income taxation. *Review of Economic Studies* **38**: 175–208.

Moore, J. (1992). Implementation, contracts, and renegotiation in environments with complete information. In *Advances in Economic Theory: Sixth World Congress*, vol. I, edited by J.-J. Laffont. Cambridge, U.K.: Cambridge University Press.

Moore, J., and R. Repullo. (1988). Subgame perfect implementation. *Econometrica* **56**: 1191–1220.

Myerson, R. B. (1979). Incentive compatibility and the bargaining problem. *Econometrica* **47**: 61–73.

Myerson, R. B. (1981). Optimal auction design. *Mathematics of Operation Research* **6**: 58–73.

Myerson, R. B. (1991). *Game Theory: Analysis of Conflict*. Cambridge, Mass.: Harvard University Press.

Myerson, R. B., and M. A. Satterthwaite. (1983). Efficient mechanisms for bilateral trading. *Journal of Economic Theory* **28**: 265–81.

Palfrey, T. R. (1992). Implementation in Bayesian equilibrium: The multiple equilibrium problem in mechanism design. In *Advances in Economic Theory: Sixth World Congress*, vol. I, edited by J.-J. Laffont. Cambridge, U.K.: Cambridge University Press.

Palfrey, T., and S. Srivastava. (1991). Nash implementation using undominated strategies. *Econometrica* **59**: 479–501.

Satterthwaite, M. A. (1975). Strategy-proofness and Arrow's conditions: Existence and correspondence theorems for voting procedures and social welfare functions. *Journal of Economic Theory* **10**: 187–217.

Vickrey, W. (1961). Counterspeculation, auctions, and competitive sealed tenders. *Journal of Finance* **16**: 8–37.

## EXERCISES

**23.B.1**[A] Consider the setting explored in Example 23.B.1, where $\mathcal{R}_1 = \{\succsim_1(\bar{\theta}_1)\}$ and $\mathcal{R}_2 = \{\succsim_2(\theta_2'), \succsim_2(\theta_2'')\}$. For each of the following social choice functions $f(\cdot)$, will agent 2 be willing to truthfully reveal his preferences?

  **(a)** $f(\bar{\theta}_1, \theta_2') = y, f(\bar{\theta}_1, \theta_2'') = y$.

  **(b)** $f(\bar{\theta}_1, \theta_2') = z, f(\bar{\theta}_1, \theta_2'') = x$.

  **(c)** $f(\bar{\theta}_1, \theta_2') = z, f(\bar{\theta}_1, \theta_2'') = y$.

  **(d)** $f(\bar{\theta}_1, \theta_2') = z, f(\bar{\theta}_1, \theta_2'') = z$.

  **(e)** $f(\bar{\theta}_1, \theta_2') = y, f(\bar{\theta}_1, \theta_2'') = z$.

**23.B.2**[A] Consider a bilateral trade setting (see Example 23.B.4) in which both the seller's (agent 1) and the buyer's (agent 2) types are drawn independently from the uniform distribution on $[0, 1]$. Suppose that we try to implement the social choice function $f(\cdot) = (y_1(\cdot), y_2(\cdot), t_1(\cdot), t_2(\cdot))$ such that

$$y_1(\theta_1, \theta_2) = 1 \text{ if } \theta_1 \geq \theta_2; \ = 0 \text{ if } \theta_1 < \theta_2.$$

$$y_2(\theta_1, \theta_2) = 1 \text{ if } \theta_2 > \theta_1; \ = 0 \text{ if } \theta_2 \leq \theta_1.$$

$$t_1(\theta_1, \theta_2) = \tfrac{1}{2}(\theta_1 + \theta_2)y_2(\theta_1, \theta_2).$$

$$t_2(\theta_1, \theta_2) = -\tfrac{1}{2}(\theta_1 + \theta_2)y_2(\theta_1, \theta_2).$$

Suppose that the seller truthfully reveals his type for all $\theta_1 \in [0, 1]$. Will the buyer find it worthwhile to reveal his type? Interpret.

**23.B.3**[B] Show that $b_i(\theta_i) = \theta_i$ for all $\theta_i \in [0, 1]$ is a weakly dominant strategy for each agent $i$ in the second-price sealed-bid auction.

**23.B.4**[C] Consider a bilateral trade setting (see Example 23.B.4) in which both the seller's and the buyer's types are drawn independently from the uniform distribution on $[0, 1]$.

  **(a)** Consider the *double auction* mechanism in which the seller (agent 1) and buyer (agent 2) each submit a sealed bid, $b_i \geq 0$. If $b_1 \geq b_2$, the seller keeps the good and no monetary transfer is made; while if $b_2 > b_1$, the buyer gets the good and pays the seller the amount $\tfrac{1}{2}(b_1 + b_2)$. (The interpretation is that the seller's bid is his minimum acceptable price, while the buyer's is his maximum acceptable price; if trade occurs, the price splits the difference between these amounts.) Solve for a Bayesian Nash equilibrium of this game in which each agent $i$'s strategy takes the form $b_i(\theta_i) = \alpha_i + \beta_i\theta_i$. What social choice function does this equilibrium of this mechanism implement? Is it ex post efficient?

  **(b)** Show that the social choice function derived in **(a)** is incentive compatible; that is, that it can be truthfully implemented in Bayesian Nash equilibrium.

**23.C.1**[A] Verify that if the preference reversal property [condition (23.C.6)] is satisfied for all $i$ and all $\theta_i'$, $\theta_i''$, and $\theta_{-i}$, then $f(\cdot)$ is truthfully implementable in dominant strategies.

**23.C.2**[B] Show that, for any $I$, when $X$ contains two elements (say, $X = \{x_1, x_2\}$), then any majority voting social choice function [i.e., a social choice function that always chooses alternative $x_i$ if more agents prefer $x_i$ over $x_j$ than prefer $x_j$ over $x_i$ (it may select either $x_1$ or $x_2$ if the number of agents preferring $x_1$ over $x_2$ equals the number preferring $x_2$ over $x_1$)] is truthfully implementable in dominant strategies.

**23.C.3^A** Show that when $\mathcal{R}_i = \mathcal{P}$ for all $i$, any ex post efficient social choice function $f(\cdot)$ has $f(\Theta) = X$.

**23.C.4^A** Show that if $f: \Theta \to X$ is truthfully implementable in dominant strategies when the set of possible types is $\Theta_i$ for $i = 1, \ldots, I$, then when each agent $i$'s set of possible types is $\hat{\Theta}_i \subset \Theta_i$ (for $i = 1, \ldots, I$) the social choice function $\hat{f}: \hat{\Theta} \to X$ satisfying $\hat{f}(\theta) = f(\theta)$ for all $\theta \in \hat{\Theta}$ is truthfully implementable in dominant strategies.

**23.C.5^C** Show that in an environment with single-peaked preferences having the property that no two alternatives are indifferent (see Section 21.D) and an odd number of agents, the (unique) social choice function that always selects a Condorcet winner (see Section 21.D) is truthfully implementable in dominant strategies.

**23.C.6^C** The property of a social choice function identified in Proposition 23.C.2 is called *independent person-by-person monotonicity* (IPM) by Dasgupta, Hammond, and Maskin (1979). In this exercise, we investigate its relationship with the *monotonicity* property defined in Definition 23.C.5.

(a) Show by means of an example that if $f(\cdot)$ satisfies IPM, it need not be monotonic (this can be done with a very simple example).

(b) Show by means of an example that if $f(\cdot)$ is monotonic, it need not satisfy IPM.

(c) Prove that if $f(\cdot)$ satisfies IPM, and if $\mathcal{R}_i \subset \mathcal{P}$ for all $i$, then $f(\cdot)$ is monotonic.

(d) Prove that if $f(\cdot)$ is monotonic, and $\mathcal{R}_i = \mathcal{P}$ for all $i$, then $f(\cdot)$ satisfies IPM.

**23.C.7^C** A social welfare functional $F(\cdot)$ (see Section 21.C) satisfies the property of *nonnegative responsiveness* if for all $x, y \in X$, and for any two pairs of profiles of preferences for the $I$ agents $(\succsim_1, \ldots, \succsim_I)$ and $(\succsim_1', \ldots, \succsim_I')$ such that $x \succsim_i y \Rightarrow x \succsim_i' y$ and $x \succ_i y \Rightarrow x \succ_i' y$ for all $i$, we have

$$x\, F(\succsim_1, \ldots, \succsim_I)\, y \Rightarrow x\, F(\succsim_1', \ldots, \succsim_I')\, y$$

and

$$x\, F_p(\succsim_1, \ldots, \succsim_I)\, y \Rightarrow x\, F_p(\succsim_1', \ldots, \succsim_I')\, y,$$

where $x\, F_p(\cdot)\, y$ means "$x\, F(\cdot)\, y$ and not $y\, F(\cdot)\, x$." Show that if the social choice function $f(\cdot)$ maximizes a social welfare functional $F(\cdot)$ satisfying nonnegative responsiveness [in the sense that for all $(\theta_1, \ldots, \theta_I)$ we have $f(\theta_1, \ldots, \theta_I) = \{x \in X: x\, F(\succsim_1(\theta_1), \ldots, \succsim_I(\theta_I))\, y$ for all $y \in X\}$], then $f(\cdot)$ is truthfully implementable in dominant strategies.

**23.C.8^A** Suppose that $I = 2$, $X = \{a, b, c, d, e\}$, $\Theta_1 = \{\theta_1', \theta_1''\}$, and $\Theta_2 = \{\theta_2', \theta_2''\}$, and that the agents' possible preferences are ($a$–$b$ means that alternatives $a$ and $b$ are indifferent):

| $\succsim_1(\theta_1')$ | $\succsim_1(\theta_1'')$ | $\succsim_2(\theta_2')$ | $\succsim_2(\theta_2'')$ |
|---|---|---|---|
| $a$–$b$ | $a$ | $a$–$b$ | $a$ |
| $c$ | $b$ | $c$ | $b$ |
| $d$ | $d$ | $d$ | $d$ |
| $e$ | $c$ | $e$ | $c$ |
| | $e$ | | $e$ |

Consider the social choice function

$$f(\theta) = \begin{cases} b & \text{if } \theta = (\theta_1', \theta_2'), \\ a & \text{otherwise.} \end{cases}$$

**(a)** Is $f(\cdot)$ ex post efficient?

**(b)** Does it satisfy the property identified in Proposition 23.C.2?

**(c)** Examine the direct revelation mechanism that truthfully implements $f(\cdot)$. Is truth telling each agent's *unique* (weakly) dominant strategy? Show that if an agent chooses his untruthful (weakly) dominant strategy, then $f(\cdot)$ is not implemented.

**23.C.9$^C$** Suppose that $K = \mathbb{R}$, the $v_i(\cdot, \theta_i)$ functions are assumed to be twice continuously differentiable, $\theta_i$ is drawn from an interval $[\underline{\theta}_i, \bar{\theta}_i]$, $\partial^2 v_i(k, \theta_i)/\partial k^2 < 0$, and $\partial^2 v_i(k, \theta_i)/\partial k \partial \theta_i > 0$. Show that the continuously differentiable social choice function $f(\cdot) = (k(\cdot), t_1(\cdot), \dots, t_I(\cdot))$ is truthfully implementable in dominant strategies if and only if, for all $i = 1, \dots, I$,

$$k(\theta) \text{ is nondecreasing in } \theta_i$$

and

$$t_i(\theta_i, \theta_{-i}) = t_i(\underline{\theta}_i, \theta_{-i}) - \int_{\underline{\theta}_i}^{\theta_i} \frac{\partial v_i(k(s, \theta_{-i}), s)}{\partial k} \frac{\partial k(s, \theta_{-i})}{\partial s} \, ds.$$

**23.C.10$^B$** (B. Holmstrom) Consider the quasilinear environment studied in Section 23.C. Let $k^*(\cdot)$ denote any project decision rule that satisfies (23.C.7). Also define the function $V^*(\theta) = \sum_i v_i(k^*(\theta), \theta_i)$.

**(a)** Prove that there exists an ex post efficient social choice function [i.e., one that satisfies condition (23.C.7) *and* the budget balance condition (23.C.12)] that is truthfully implementable in dominant strategies if and only if the function $V^*(\cdot)$ can be written as $V^*(\theta) = \sum_i V_i(\theta_{-i})$ for some functions $V_1(\cdot), \dots, V_I(\cdot)$ having the property that $V_i(\cdot)$ depends only on $\theta_{-i}$ for all $i$.

**(b)** Use the result in part **(a)** to show that when $I = 3$, $K = \mathbb{R}$, $\Theta_i = \mathbb{R}_+$ for all $i$, and $v_i(k, \theta_i) = \theta_i k - (\frac{1}{2})k^2$ for all $i$ an ex post efficient social choice function exists that is truthfully implementable in dominant strategies. (This result extends to any $I > 2$.)

**(c)** Now suppose that the $v_i(k, \theta_i)$ functions are such that $V^*(\cdot)$ is an $I$-times continuously differentiable function. Argue that a necessary condition for an ex post efficient social choice function to exist is that, at all $\theta$,

$$\frac{\partial^I V^*(\theta)}{\partial \theta_1 \dots \partial \theta_I} = 0.$$

(In fact, this is a sufficient condition as well.)

**(d)** Use the result in **(c)** to verify that, under the assumptions made in the small type discussion at the end of Section 23.C, when $I = 2$ no ex post efficient social choice function is truthfully implementable in dominant strategies.

**23.C.11$^A$** Consider a quasilinear environment, but now suppose that each agent $i$ has a Bernoulli utility function of the form $u_i(v_i(k, \theta_i) + \bar{m}_i + t_i)$ with $u_i'(\cdot) > 0$. That is, preferences over certain outcomes take a quasilinear form, but risk preferences are unrestricted. Verify that Proposition 23.C.4 is unaffected by this change.

**23.D.1$^B$** [Based on an example in Myerson (1991)] A buyer and a seller are bargaining over the sale of an indivisible good. The buyer's valuation is $\theta_b = 10$. The seller's valuation takes one of two values: $\theta_s \in \{0, 9\}$. Let $t$ be the period in which trade occurs ($t = 1, 2, \dots$) and let $p$ be the price agreed. Both the buyer and the seller have discount factor $\delta < 1$.

**(a)** What is the set $X$ of alternatives in this setting?

**(b)** Suppose that in a Bayesian Nash equilibrium of this bargaining process, trade occurs immediately when the seller's valuation is 0 and the price agreed to when the seller has valuation $\theta_s$ is $(10 + \theta_s)/2$. What is the earliest possible time at which trade can occur when the seller's valuation is 9?

**23.D.2$^B$** Consider a bilateral trade setting in which each $\theta_i$ ($i = 1, 2$) is independently drawn from a uniform distribution on $[0, 1]$.

    **(a)** Compute the transfer functions in the expected externality mechanism.

    **(b)** Verify that truth telling is a Bayesian Nash equilibrium.

**23.D.3$^A$** Reconsider the first-price and second-price sealed-bid auctions studied in Examples 23.B.5 and 23.B.6. Verify that the revenue equivalence theorem holds for the equilibria identified there.

**23.D.4$^C$** Consider a first-price sealed-bid auction with $I$ symmetric buyers. Each buyer's valuation is independently drawn from the interval $[\underline{\theta}, \bar{\theta}]$ according to the strictly positive density $\phi(\cdot)$.

    **(a)** Show that the buyer's equilibrium bid function is nondecreasing in his type.

    **(b)** Argue that in any symmetric equilibrium $(b^*(\cdot), \ldots, b^*(\cdot))$ there can be no interval of types $(\theta', \theta'')$, $\theta' \neq \theta''$, such that $b^*(\theta)$ is the same for all $\theta \in (\theta', \theta'')$. Conclude that $b^*(\cdot)$ must therefore be strictly increasing.

    **(c)** Argue, using the revenue equivalence theorem, that any symmetric equilibrium of such an auction must yield the seller the same expected revenue as in the (dominant strategy) equilibrium of the second-price sealed-bid auction.

**23.D.5$^C$** For the same assumptions as in Exercise 23.D.4, consider a sealed-bid *all-pay* auction in which every buyer submits a bid, the highest bidder receives the good, and *every* buyer pays the seller the amount of his bid *regardless of whether he wins*. Argue that any symmetric equilibrium of this auction also yields the seller the same expected revenue as the sealed-bid second-price auction. [*Hint*: Follow similar steps as in Exercise 23.D.4.]

**23.D.6$^C$** Suppose that $I$ symmetric individuals wish to acquire the single remaining ticket to a concert. The ticket office opens at 9 a.m. on Monday. Each individual must decide what time to go to get on line: the first individual to get on line will get the ticket. An individual who waits $t$ hours incurs a (monetary equivalent) disutility of $\beta t$. Suppose also that an individual showing up after the first one can go home immediately and so incurs no waiting cost. Individual $i$'s value of receiving the ticket is $\theta_i$, and each individual's $\theta_i$ is independently drawn from a uniform distribution on $[0, 1]$. What is the expected value of the number of hours that the first individual in line will wait? [*Hint*: Note the analogy to a first-price sealed-bid auction and use the revenue equivalence theorem.] How does this vary when $\beta$ doubles? When $I$ doubles?

**23.E.1$^B$** Consider again a bilateral trade setting in which each $\theta_i$ ($i = 1, 2$) is independently drawn from a uniform distribution on $[0, 1]$. Suppose now that by refusing to participate in the mechanism a seller with valuation $\theta_1$ receives expected utility $\theta_1$ (he simply consumes the good), whereas a buyer with valuation $\theta_2$ receives expected utility 0 (he simply consumes his endowment of the numeraire, which we have normalized to equal 0). Show that in the expected externality mechanism there is a type of buyer or seller who will strictly prefer not to participate.

**23.E.2$^A$** Argue that when the assumptions of Proposition 23.E.1 hold in the bilateral trade setting:

    **(a)** There is no social choice function $f(\cdot)$ that is dominant strategy incentive compatible and interim individually rational (i.e., that gives each agent $i$ nonnegative gains from participation conditional on his type $\theta_i$, for all $\theta_i$).

**(b)** There is no social choice function $f(\cdot)$ that is Bayesian incentive compatible and ex post individually rational [i.e., that gives each agent nonnegative gains from participation for every pair of types $(\theta_1, \theta_2)$].

**23.E.3$^B$** Show by means of an example that when the buyer and seller in a bilateral trade setting both have a discrete set of possible valuations, social choice functions may exist that are Bayesian incentive compatible, ex post efficient, and individually rational. [*Hint*: It suffices to let each have two possible types.] Conclude that the assumption of a strictly positive density is required for the Myerson–Satterthwaite theorem.

**23.E.4$^B$** A seller ($i = 1$) and a buyer ($i = 2$) are bargaining over the sale of an indivisible good. Trade can occur at discrete periods $t = 1, 2, \ldots$. Both the buyer and the seller have discount factor $\delta < 1$. The buyer's and seller's valuations are drawn independently with positive densities from $[\underline{\theta}_2, \bar{\theta}_2]$ and $[\underline{\theta}_1, \bar{\theta}_1]$, respectively. Assume that $(\underline{\theta}_2, \bar{\theta}_2) \cap (\underline{\theta}_1, \bar{\theta}_1) \neq \varnothing$. Note that in this setting ex post efficiency requires that trade occur in period 1 whenever $\theta_2 > \theta_1$, and that trade not occur whenever $\theta_1 > \theta_2$. Use the Myerson–Satterthwaite theorem to show that, in this setting with discounting, no voluntary trading process can achieve ex post efficiency.

**23.E.5$^B$** Suppose there is a *continuum* of buyers and sellers (with quasilinear preferences). Each seller initially has one unit of an indivisible good and each buyer initially has none. A seller's valuation for consumption of the good is $\theta_1 \in [\underline{\theta}_1, \bar{\theta}_1]$, which is independently and identically drawn from distribution $\Phi_1(\cdot)$ with associated strictly positive density $\phi_1(\cdot)$. A buyer's valuation from consumption of the good is $\theta_2 \in [\underline{\theta}_2, \bar{\theta}_2]$, which is independently and identically drawn from distribution $\Phi_2(\cdot)$ with associated strictly positive density $\phi_2(\cdot)$.

**(a)** Characterize the trading rule in an ex post efficient social choice function. Which buyers and sellers end up with a unit of the good?

**(b)** Exhibit a social choice function that has the trading rule you identified in **(a)**, is Bayesian incentive compatible, and is individually rational. [*Hint*: Think of a "competitive" mechanism.] Conclude that the inefficiency identified in the Myerson–Satterthwaite theorem goes away as the number of buyers and sellers grows large. [For a formal examination showing that, with a finite number of traders, the efficiency loss goes to zero as the number of traders grows large, see Gresik and Satterthwaite (1989).]

**23.E.6$^B$** Consider a bilateral trading setting in which *both* agents initially own one unit of a good. Each agent $i$'s ($i = 1, 2$) valuation per unit consumed of the good is $\theta_i$. Assume that $\theta_i$ is independently drawn from a uniform distribution on $[0, 1]$.

**(a)** Characterize the trading rule in an ex post efficient social choice function.

**(b)** Consider the following mechanism: Each agent submits a bid; the highest bidder buys the other agent's unit of the good and pays him the amount of his bid. Derive a symmetric Bayesian Nash equilibrium of this mechanism. [*Hint*: Look for one in which an agent's bid is a linear function of his type.]

**(c)** What is the social choice function that is implemented by this mechanism? Verify that it is Bayesian incentive compatible. Is it ex post efficient? Is it individually rational [which here requires that $U_i(\theta_i) \geq \theta_i$ for all $\theta_i$ and $i = 1, 2$]? Intuitively, why is there a difference from the conclusion of the Myerson–Satterthwaite theorem? [See Cramton, Gibbons, and Klemperer (1987) for a formal analysis of these "partnership division" problems.]

**23.E.7$^B$** Consider a bilateral trade setting in which the buyer's and seller's valuations are drawn independently from the uniform distribution on $[0, 1]$.

**(a)** Show that if $f(\cdot)$ is a Bayesian incentive compatible and interim individually rational social choice function that is ex post efficient, the sum of the buyer's and seller's expected utilities under $f(\cdot)$ cannot be less than 5/6.

**(b)** Show that, in fact, there is no social choice function (whether Bayesian incentive compatible and interim individually rational or not) in which the sum of the buyer's and seller's expected utilities exceeds 2/3.

**23.F.1$^C$** Consider the quasilinear setting studied in Sections 23.C and 23.D. Show that if the social choice function $f(\cdot) \in F^*$ is ex post classically efficient in $F_{IR}$ then it is both ex ante and interim incentive efficient in $F^*$. [From this fact, we see that if an ex post classically efficient social choice function *can* be implemented in a setting with privately observed types (i.e., if it is incentive feasible), then no other incentive feasible social choice function can welfare dominate it. Note, however, that there may be *other* ex ante or interim incentive efficient social choice functions that are not ex post efficient; for example, you can verify that in Example 23.F.1 there is an ex post classically efficient social choice function that is incentive feasible, but the particular interim incentive efficient social choice function derived in the example is not ex post efficient.]

**23.F.2$^B$** [Based on Maskin and Riley (1984)] A monopolist seller produces a good with constant returns to scale at a cost of $c > 0$ per unit. The monopolist sells to a consumer whose preference for the product the monopolist cannot observe. A consumer of type $\theta > 0$ derives a utility of $\theta v(x) - t$ when he consumes $x$ units of the monopolist's product and pays the monopolist a total of $t$ dollars for these units. Assume that $v'(\cdot) > 0$ and $v''(\cdot) < 0$. The set of possible consumer types is $[\underline{\theta}, \bar{\theta}]$ with $\bar{\theta} > \underline{\theta} > 0$, and the distribution of types is $\Phi(\cdot)$, with an associated strictly positive density function $\phi(\cdot) > 0$. Assume that $[\theta - ((1 - \Phi(\theta))/\phi(\theta))]$ is nondecreasing in $\theta$.

Characterize the monopolist's optimal selling mechanism to this consumer, assuming that a consumer of type $\theta$ can always choose not to buy at all, thereby deriving a utility of 0.

**23.F.3$^C$** An auction with a *reserve price* is an auction in which there is a minimum allowable bid. Suppose that in the auction setting of Example 23.F.2 the $I$ buyers are symmetric and that $\underline{\theta} = 0$. Argue that a second-price sealed-bid auction with a reserve price is an optimal auction in this case. What is the optimal reserve price? Can you think of a modified second-price sealed-bid auction that is optimal in the general (nonsymmetric) case?

**23.F.4$^B$** Derive the optimal $y_i(\cdot)$ functions in the auction setting of Example 23.F.2 when the seller's valuation for the object is $\theta_0 > 0$.

**23.F.5$^B$** Suppose that a monopolist seller who has two potential buyers has a total of one divisible unit to sell; that is, production costs are zero up to one unit, and infinite beyond that. The demand function of buyer $i$ is the decreasing function $x_i(p)$ for $i = 1, 2$. The monopolist can name distinct prices for the two buyers.

**(a)** Characterize the monopolist's optimal prices.

**(b)** Relate your answer in **(a)** to the optimal auction derived in Example 23.F.2. [For more on this, see Bulow and Roberts (1989).]

**23.F.6$^C$** [Based on Baron and Myerson (1982)]. Consider the optimal regulatory scheme for a regulator of a monopolist who has known demand function $x(p)$, with $x'(p) < 0$, and a privately observed constant marginal cost of production $\theta$. The regulator can set the monopolist's price and can make a transfer from or to the monopolist, so the set of outcomes is $X = \{(p, t): p > 0 \text{ and } t \in \mathbb{R}\}$. The regulator must guarantee the monopolist a nonnegative profit regardless of his production costs to prevent the monopolist from shutting down. The monopolist's marginal cost $\theta$ is drawn from $[\underline{\theta}, \bar{\theta}]$ with $\bar{\theta} > \underline{\theta} > 0$ according to the distribution function $\Phi(\cdot)$, which has an associated strictly positive density function $\phi(\cdot) > 0$. Assume that

$\Phi(\theta)/\phi(\theta)$ is nondecreasing in $\theta$. Denote a type-$\theta$ monopolist's profit from outcome $(p, t)$ by $\pi(p, t, \theta) = (p - \theta)x(p) + t$.

**(a)** Adapt the characterization in Proposition 23.D.2 to this application.

**(b)** Suppose that the regulator wants to design a direct revelation regulatory scheme $(p(\cdot), t(\cdot))$ that maximizes the expected value of a weighted sum of consumer and producer surplus,

$$\int_{p(\theta)}^{\infty} x(s)\, ds + \alpha\pi(p(\theta), t(\theta), \theta),$$

where $\alpha < 1$. Characterize the regulator's optimal regulatory scheme. What if $\alpha \geq 1$?

**23.F.7$^C$** [Based on Dana and Spier (1994)] Two firms, $j = 1, 2$, compete for the right to produce in a given market. A social planner designs an optimal auction of production rights to maximize the expected value of social welfare as measured by

$$W = \sum_{j} \pi_j + S + (\lambda - 1)\sum_{j} t_j,$$

where $t_j$ denotes the transfer from firm $j$ to the planner, $S$ is consumer surplus, $\pi_j$ is the gross (pretransfer) profit of firm $j$, and $\lambda > 1$ is the shadow cost of public funds. The auction specifies transfers for each of the firms and a market structure; that is, it either awards neither firm production rights, awards only one firm production rights (thereby making that firm an unregulated monopolist), or gives production rights to both firms (thereby making them compete as unregulated duopolists).

Each firm $j$ privately observes its fixed cost of production $\theta_j$. The fixed cost levels $\theta_1$ and $\theta_2$ are independently distributed on $[\theta, \bar{\theta}]$ with continuously differentiable density function $\phi(\cdot)$ and distribution function $\Phi(\cdot)$. Assume that $\Phi(\cdot)/\phi(\cdot)$ is increasing in $\theta$. The firms have common marginal cost $c < 1$ and produce a homogeneous product for which the market inverse demand function is $p(x) = 1 - x$ (this is publicly known). If both firms are awarded production rights, they interact as Cournot competitors (see Section 12.C).

Characterize the planner's optimal auction of production rights.

**23.F.8$^A$** Show that any ex post classically efficient social choice function in Example 23.F.3 has $y_L = y_H = 1$.

**23.F.9$^B$** Show that in the model of Example 23.F.3:

**(a)** No feasible social choice function is ex post efficient.

**(b)** In any feasible social choice function, $y_H \leq y_L$ and $t_H \leq t_L$.

**(c)** In any feasible social choice function, the expected gains from trade of a low-quality seller are at least as large as the expected gains from trade of a high-quality seller; that is, $t_L - 20y_L \geq t_H - 40y_H$.

**23.F.10$^B$** Characterize the sets of interim and ex ante incentive efficient social choice functions in the model of Example 23.F.3 when trade is not voluntary for the seller (but it is voluntary for the buyer).

**23.AA.1$^B$** Reconsider Exercise 23.C.8. Exhibit a mechanism $\Gamma = (S_1, \ldots, S_I, g(\cdot))$ that is not a direct revelation mechanism that truthfully implements $f(\cdot)$ in dominant strategies and for which each agent has a *unique* (weakly) dominant strategy.

**23.AA.2$^B$** Let $K = \{k_0, k_1, \ldots, k_N\}$ be the set of possible projects and suppose that, for each agent $i$, $\{v_i(\cdot, \theta_i): \theta_i \in \Theta_i\} = \mathcal{V}$, that is, that every possible valuation function from $K$ to $\mathbb{R}$ arises for some $\theta_i \in \Theta_i$. Do players in a Groves mechanism have a unique (weakly) dominant strategy? Consider instead a mechanism in which each agent $i$ is allowed to announce a *normalized* valuation function, that is, a function such that $v_i(k_0) = 0$. Suppose that $k^*(\cdot)$ and the Groves transfers are calculated using these announcements. Does each agent have a unique (weakly) dominant strategy in this normalized Groves mechanism?

**23.BB.1**[A] Consider the dynamic mechanism in Example 23.BB.1.

**(a)** For each possible preference profile, write down its normal form and identify its Nash equilibria.

**(b)** For each possible preference profile, identify this mechanism's subgame perfect Nash equilibria.

**23.BB.2**[B] Is a social choice function that is implementable in dominant strategies necessarily implementable in Nash equilibrium? What if we are interested in strong implementation instead?

**23.BB.3**[C] Consider a setting of public project choice (see Example 23.B.3) in which $K = \{0, 1\}$. Let $\theta_i$ denote agent $i$'s benefit if the project is done (i.e., if $k = 1$); normalize the value from $k = 0$ to equal zero. Assume that $\Theta_i = \mathbb{R}$. In this setting, the only mechanisms that involve an ex post efficient project choice are Groves mechanisms. Let $k^*(\cdot)$ denote the project choice rule in such a mechanism. Also, suppose that $I \geq 3$. The transfers in a Groves mechanism are characterized by two properties:

(i) if $k^*(\theta_i, \theta_{-i}) = k^*(\theta_i', \theta_{-i})$, then $t_i(\theta_i, \theta_{-i}) = t_i(\theta_i', \theta_{-i})$;
(ii) if $k^*(\theta_i, \theta_{-i}) = 1$ and $k^*(\theta_i', \theta_{-i}) = 0$, then $t_i(\theta_i, \theta_{-i}) - t_i(\theta_i', \theta_{-i}) = \sum_{j \neq i} \theta_j$.

Which, if any, of these two properties must be satisfied by any Nash implementable social choice function that involves an ex post efficient project choice?

# Mathematical Appendix

This appendix contains a quick and unsystematic review of some of the mathematical concepts and techniques used in the text.

The formal results are quoted as "Theorems" and they are fairly rigorously stated. It seems useful in a technical appendix such as this to provide motivational remarks, examples, and general ideas for some proofs. This we often do under the label of the "Proof" of the mathematical theorem under discussion. Nonetheless, no rigor of any sort is intended here. Perhaps the heading "Discussion of Theorem" would be more accurate.

It goes without saying that this appendix is no substitute for a more extensive and systematic, book-length, treatment. Good references for some or most of the material covered in this appendix, as well as for further background reading, are Simon and Blume (1993), Sydsaeter and Hammond (1994), Novshek (1993), Dixit (1990), Chang (1984), and Intriligator (1971).

## M.A Matrix Notation for Derivatives

We begin by reviewing some matters of notation. The first and most important is that formally and mathematically a "vector" in $\mathbb{R}^N$ is a *column*. This applies to any vector; it does not matter, for example, if the vector represents quantities or prices. It applies also to the *gradient* vector $\nabla f(\bar{x}) \in \mathbb{R}^N$ of a function at a point $\bar{x}$; this is the vector whose $n$th entry is the partial derivative with respect to the $n$th variable of the real-valued function $f: \mathbb{R}^N \to \mathbb{R}$, evaluated at the point $\bar{x} \in \mathbb{R}^N$. Expositionally, however, because rows take less space to display, we typically describe vectors horizontally in the text, as in $x = (x_1, \ldots, x_N)$. But the rule has no exception: all vectors are mathematically columns.

The inner product of two $N$ vectors $x \in \mathbb{R}^N$ and $y \in \mathbb{R}^N$ is written as $x \cdot y = \sum_n x_n y_n$. If we view these vectors as $N \times 1$ matrices, we see that $x \cdot y = x^T y$, where $^T$ is the matrix transposition operator. An expression such as "$x \cdot$" can always be read as "$x^T$"; for example, the expression $x \cdot A$, where $A$ is an $N \times M$ matrix, is the same as $x^T A$.

If $f: \mathbb{R}^N \to \mathbb{R}^M$ is a vector-valued differentiable function, then at any $x \in \mathbb{R}^N$ we denote by $Df(x)$ the $M \times N$ matrix whose $mn$th entry is $\partial f_m(x)/\partial x_n$. Note, in particular, that if $M = 1$ (so that $f(x) \in \mathbb{R}$) then $Df(x)$ is a $1 \times N$ matrix; in fact $\nabla f(x) = [Df(x)]^T$. To avoid ambiguity, in some cases we write $D_x f(x)$ to indicate explicitly the variables with respect to which the function $f(\cdot)$ is being differentiated. For example, with this notation, if $f: \mathbb{R}^{N+K} \to \mathbb{R}^M$ is a function whose arguments are the vectors $x \in \mathbb{R}^N$ and $y \in \mathbb{R}^K$, the matrix $D_x f(x, y)$ is the $M \times N$ matrix whose $mn$th entry is $\partial f_m(x, y)/\partial x_n$. Finally, for a real-valued differentiable function $f: \mathbb{R}^N \to \mathbb{R}$, the *Hessian matrix* $D^2 f(x)$ is the derivative matrix of the vector-valued gradient function $\nabla f(x)$; i.e., $D^2 f(x) = D[\nabla f(x)]$.

In the remainder of this section, we consider differentiable functions and examine how two well-known rules of calculus—the chain rule and the product rule—come out in matrix notation.

### The Chain Rule

Suppose that $g: \mathbb{R}^S \to \mathbb{R}^N$ and $f: \mathbb{R}^N \to \mathbb{R}^M$ are differentiable functions. The *composite* function $f(g(\cdot))$ is also differentiable. Consider any point $x \in \mathbb{R}^S$. The chain rule allows us to evaluate the $M \times S$ derivative matrix of the composite function with respect to $x$, $D_x f(g(x))$ by matrix multiplication of the $N \times S$ derivative matrix of $g(\cdot)$, $Dg(x)$, and the $M \times N$ derivative matrix of $f(\cdot)$ evaluated at $g(x)$, that is, $Df(y)$, where $y = g(x)$. Specifically,

$$D_x f(g(x)) = Df(g(x))\, Dg(x). \tag{M.A.1}$$

### The Product Rule

Here we simply provide a few illustrations.

(i) Suppose that $f: \mathbb{R}^N \to \mathbb{R}$ has the form $f(x) = g(x)h(x)$, where both $g(\cdot)$ and $h(\cdot)$ are real-valued functions of the $N$ variables $x = (x_1, \dots, x_N)$ (so that $g: \mathbb{R}^N \to \mathbb{R}$ and $h: \mathbb{R}^N \to \mathbb{R}$). Then the product rule of calculus tells us that

$$Df(x) = g(x)\, Dh(x) + h(x)\, Dg(x). \tag{M.A.2}$$

which, transposing, can also be written as

$$\nabla f(x) = g(x)\, \nabla h(x) + h(x)\, \nabla g(x).$$

(ii) Suppose that $f: \mathbb{R}^N \to \mathbb{R}$ has the form $f(x) = g(x) \cdot h(x)$ where both $g(\cdot)$ and $h(\cdot)$ are vector-valued functions which map the $N$ variables $x = (x_1, \dots, x_N)$ into $\mathbb{R}^M$. Then

$$Df(x) = g(x) \cdot Dh(x) + h(x) \cdot Dg(x). \tag{M.A.3}$$

Note that $h(x) \cdot Dg(x) = [h(x)]^T Dg(x)$ is a $1 \times N$ matrix, as is the other term in the right-hand side. Thus, the vector-valued case (M.A.3) implies the scalar-valued formula (M.A.2).

(iii) Suppose that $f: \mathbb{R} \to \mathbb{R}^M$ has the form $f(x) = \alpha(x)g(x)$, where $\alpha(\cdot)$ is a real-valued function of one variable (i.e., $\alpha: \mathbb{R} \to \mathbb{R}$) and $g: \mathbb{R} \to \mathbb{R}^M$. Then

$$Df(x) = \alpha(x)\, Dg(x) + \alpha'(x)g(x). \tag{M.A.4}$$

(iv) Suppose that $f: \mathbb{R}^N \to \mathbb{R}^M$ has the form $f(x) = h(x)g(x)$ where $h: \mathbb{R}^N \to \mathbb{R}$ and $g: \mathbb{R}^N \to \mathbb{R}^M$. Then

$$Df(x) = h(x)\, Dg(x) + g(x)\, Dh(x). \tag{M.A.5}$$

Note that $g(x)$ is an $M$-element vector (i.e., an $M \times 1$ matrix) and $Dh(x)$ is a $1 \times N$ matrix. Hence, $g(x)\, Dh(x)$ is an $M \times N$ matrix (of rank 1). Observe also that (M.A.4) follows as a special case of (M.A.5).

# M.B Homogeneous Functions and Euler's Formula

In this section, we consider functions of $N$ variables, $f(x_1, \ldots, x_N)$, defined for all nonnegative values $(x_1, \ldots, x_N) \geq 0$.

**Definition M.B.1:** A function $f(x_1, \ldots, x_N)$ is *homogeneous of degree $r$* (for $r = \ldots, -1, 0, 1, \ldots$) if for every $t > 0$ we have

$$f(tx_1, \ldots, tx_N) = t^r f(x_1, \ldots, x_N).$$

As an example, $f(x_1, x_2) = x_1/x_2$ is homogeneous of degree zero and $f(x_1, x_2) = (x_1 x_2)^{1/2}$ is homogeneous of degree one.

Note that if $f(x_1, \ldots, x_N)$ is homogeneous of degree zero and we restrict the domain to have $x_1 > 0$ then, by taking $t = 1/x_1$, we can write the function $f(\cdot)$ as

$$f(1, x_2/x_1, \ldots, x_N/x_1) = f(x_1, \ldots, x_N).$$

Similarly, if the function is homogeneous of degree one then

$$f(1, x_2/x_1, \ldots, x_N/x_1) = (1/x_1) f(x_1, \ldots, x_N).$$

**Theorem M.B.1:** If $f(x_1, \ldots, x_N)$ is homogeneous of degree $r$ (for $r = \ldots, -1, 0, 1, \ldots$), then for any $n = 1, \ldots, N$ the partial derivative function $\partial f(x_1, \ldots, x_N)/\partial x_n$ is homogeneous of degree $r - 1$.

**Proof:** Fix a $t > 0$. By the definition of homogeneity (Definition M.B.1) we have

$$f(tx_1, \ldots, tx_N) - t^r f(x_1, \ldots, x_N) = 0.$$

Differentiating this expression with respect to $x_n$ gives

$$t \frac{\partial f(tx_1, \ldots, tx_N)}{\partial x_n} - t^r \frac{\partial f(x_1, \ldots, x_N)}{\partial x_n} = 0,$$

so that

$$\frac{\partial f(tx_1, \ldots, tx_N)}{\partial x_n} = t^{r-1} \frac{\partial f(x_1, \ldots, x_N)}{\partial x_n}.$$

By Definition M.B.1, we conclude that $\partial f(x_1, \ldots, x_N)/\partial x_n$ is homogeneous of degree $r - 1$. ∎

For example, for the homogeneous of degree one function $f(x_1, x_2) = (x_1 x_2)^{1/2}$, we have $\partial f(x_1, x_2)/\partial x_1 = \frac{1}{2}(x_2/x_1)^{1/2}$, which is indeed homogeneous of degree zero in accordance with Theorem M.B.1.

Note that if $f(\cdot)$ is a homogeneous function of any degree then $f(x_1, \ldots, x_N) = f(x_1', \ldots, x_N')$ implies $f(tx_1, \ldots, tx_N) = f(tx_1', \ldots, tx_N')$ for any $t > 0$; that is, a radial expansion of a level set of $f(\cdot)$ gives a new level set of $f(\cdot)$.[1] This has an interesting implication: the slopes of the level sets of $f(\cdot)$ are unchanged along any ray through the origin. For example, suppose that $N = 2$. Then, assuming that $\partial f(\bar{x})/\partial x_2 \neq 0$, the slope of the level set containing point $\bar{x} = (\bar{x}_1, \bar{x}_2)$ at $\bar{x}$ is $-(\partial f(\bar{x})/\partial x_1)/(\partial f(\bar{x})/\partial x_2)$,

---

1. A *level set* of function $f(\cdot)$ is a set of the form $\{x \in \mathbb{R}_+^N : f(x) = k\}$ for some $k$. A radial expansion of this set is the set of points obtained by multiplying each vector $x$ in this level set by some positive scalar $t > 0$.

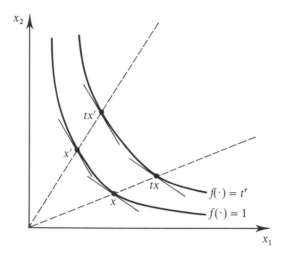

**Figure M.B.1**
The level sets of a
homogeneous function.

and the slope of the level set containing point $t\bar{x}$ for $t > 0$ at $t\bar{x}$ is

$$-\frac{\partial f(t\bar{x})/\partial x_1}{\partial f(t\bar{x})/\partial x_2} = -\frac{t^{r-1}\,\partial f(\bar{x})/\partial x_1}{t^{r-1}\,\partial f(\bar{x})/\partial x_2} = -\frac{\partial f(\bar{x})/\partial x_1}{\partial f(\bar{x})/\partial x_2}.$$

An illustration of this fact is provided in Figure M.B.1.

Suppose that $f(\cdot)$ is homogeneous of some degree $r$ and that $h(\cdot)$ is an increasing function of one variable. Then the function $h(f(x_1, \ldots, x_N))$ is called *homothetic*. Note that the family of level sets of $h(f(\cdot))$ coincides with the family of level sets of $f(\cdot)$. Therefore, for any homothetic function it is also true that the slopes of the level sets are unchanged along rays through the origin.

A key property of homogeneous functions is given in Theorem M.B.2.

**Theorem M.B.2:** (*Euler's Formula*) Suppose that $f(x_1, \ldots, x_N)$ is homogeneous of degree $r$ (for some $r = \ldots, -1, 0, 1, \ldots$) and differentiable. Then at any $(\bar{x}_1, \ldots, \bar{x}_N)$ we have

$$\sum_{n=1}^{N} \frac{\partial f(\bar{x}_1, \ldots, \bar{x}_N)}{\partial x_n}\,\bar{x}_n = rf(\bar{x}_1, \ldots, \bar{x}_N),$$

or, in matrix notation, $\nabla f(\bar{x}) \cdot \bar{x} = rf(\bar{x})$.

**Proof:** By definition we have

$$f(t\bar{x}_1, \ldots, t\bar{x}_N) - t^r f(\bar{x}_1, \ldots, \bar{x}_N) = 0.$$

Differentiating this expression with respect to $t$ gives

$$\sum_{n=1}^{N} \frac{\partial f(t\bar{x}_1, \ldots, t\bar{x}_N)}{\partial x_n}\,\bar{x}_n - rt^{r-1}f(\bar{x}_1, \ldots, \bar{x}_N) = 0.$$

Evaluating at $t = 1$, we obtain Euler's formula. ∎

For a function that is homogeneous of degree zero, Euler's formula says that

$$\sum_{n=1}^{N} \frac{\partial f(x_1, \ldots, x_N)}{\partial x_n}\,\bar{x}_n = 0.$$

As an example, note that for the function $f(x_1, x_2) = x_1/x_2$, we have $\partial f(\bar{x}_1, \bar{x}_2)/\partial x_1 = 1/\bar{x}_2$ and $\partial f(\bar{x}_1, \bar{x}_2)/\partial x_2 = -(\bar{x}_1/(\bar{x}_2)^2)$, and so

$$\sum_{n=1}^{N} \frac{\partial f(x_1, \ldots, x_N)}{\partial x_n} \bar{x}_n = \frac{1}{\bar{x}_2} \bar{x}_1 - \frac{\bar{x}_1}{(\bar{x}_2)^2} \bar{x}_2 = 0,$$

in accordance with Euler's formula.

For a function that is homogeneous of degree one, Euler's formula says that

$$\sum_{n=1}^{N} \frac{\partial f(x_1, \ldots, x_N)}{\partial x_n} \bar{x}_n = f(\bar{x}_1, \ldots, \bar{x}_N).$$

For example, when $f(x_1, x_2) = (x_1 x_2)^{1/2}$, we have $\partial f(\bar{x}_1, \bar{x}_2)/\partial x_1 = \frac{1}{2}(\bar{x}_2/\bar{x}_1)^{1/2}$ and $\partial f(\bar{x}_1, \bar{x}_2)/\partial x_2 = \frac{1}{2}(\bar{x}_1/\bar{x}_2)^{1/2}$, and so

$$\sum_{n=1}^{N} \frac{\partial f(x_1, \ldots, x_N)}{\partial x_n} \bar{x}_n = \frac{1}{2}\left(\frac{\bar{x}_2}{\bar{x}_1}\right)^{1/2} \bar{x}_1 + \frac{1}{2}\left(\frac{\bar{x}_1}{\bar{x}_2}\right)^{1/2} \bar{x}_2$$

$$= (\bar{x}_1 \bar{x}_2)^{1/2}$$

$$= f(\bar{x}_1, \bar{x}_2).$$

# M.C Concave and Quasiconcave Functions

In this section, we consider functions of $N$ variables $f(x_1, \ldots, x_N)$ defined on a domain $A$ that is a convex subset of $\mathbb{R}^N$ (such as $A = \mathbb{R}^N$ or $A = \mathbb{R}_+^N = \{x \in \mathbb{R}^N: x \geq 0\}$).[2] We denote $x = (x_1, \ldots, x_N)$.

**Definition M.C.1:** The function $f: A \to \mathbb{R}$, defined on the convex set $A \subset \mathbb{R}^N$, is *concave* if

$$f(\alpha x' + (1 - \alpha)x) \geq \alpha f(x') + (1 - \alpha)f(x) \qquad \text{(M.C.1)}$$

for all $x$ and $x' \in A$ and all $\alpha \in [0, 1]$. If the inequality is strict for all $x' \neq x$ and all $\alpha \in (0, 1)$, then we say that the function is *strictly concave*.

Figure M.C.1(a) illustrates a strictly concave function of one variable. For this case, condition (M.C.1) says that the straight line connecting any two points in the graph of $f(\cdot)$ lies entirely below this graph.[3] In Figure M.C.1(b), we show a function

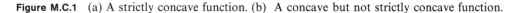

**Figure M.C.1**   (a) A strictly concave function. (b)  A concave but not strictly concave function.

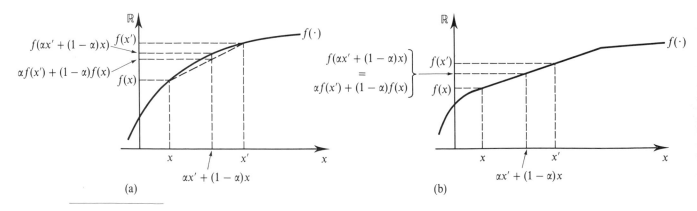

(a)

(b)

---

2. For basic facts about convex sets, see Section M.G.
3. The *graph* of the function $f: A \to \mathbb{R}$ is the set $\{(x, y) \in A \times \mathbb{R}: y = f(x)\}$.

that is concave but not strictly concave; note that in this case the straight line connecting points $x$ and $x'$ lies on the graph of the function, so that condition (M.C.1) holds with equality.

We note that condition (M.C.1) is equivalent to the seemingly stronger property that

$$f(\alpha_1 x^1 + \cdots + \alpha_K x^K) \geq \alpha_1 f(x^1) + \cdots + \alpha_K f(x^K) \qquad \text{(M.C.2)}$$

for any collection of vectors $x^1 \in A, \ldots, x^K \in A$ and numbers $\alpha_1 \geq 0, \ldots, \alpha_K \geq 0$ such that $\alpha_1 + \cdots + \alpha_K = 1$.

---

Let us consider again the one-variable case. We could view each number $\alpha_k$ in condition (M.C.2) as the "probability" that $x^k$ occurs. Then condition (M.C.2) says that the value of the expectation is not smaller than the expected value. Indeed, a concave function $f: \mathbb{R} \to \mathbb{R}$ is characterized by the condition that

$$f\left(\int x \, dF\right) \geq \int f(x) \, dF \qquad \text{(M.C.3)}$$

for any distribution function $F: \mathbb{R} \to [0, 1]$. Condition (M.C.3) is known as *Jensen's inequality*.

---

The properties of *convexity* and *strict convexity* for a function $f(\cdot)$ are defined analogously but with the inequality in (M.C.1) reversed. In particular, for a strictly convex function $f(\cdot)$, a straight line connecting any two points in its graph should lie entirely *above* its graph, as shown in Figure M.C.2. Note also that $f(\cdot)$ is concave if and only if $-f(\cdot)$ is convex.

Theorem M.C.1 provides a useful alternative characterization of concavity and strict concavity.

**Theorem M.C.1:** The (continuously differentiable) function $f: A \to \mathbb{R}$ is concave if and only if

$$f(x + z) \leq f(x) + \nabla f(x) \cdot z \qquad \text{(M.C.4)}$$

for all $x \in A$ and $z \in \mathbb{R}^N$ (with $x + z \in A$). The function $f(\cdot)$ is strictly concave if inequality (M.C.4) holds strictly for all $x \in A$ and all $z \neq 0$.

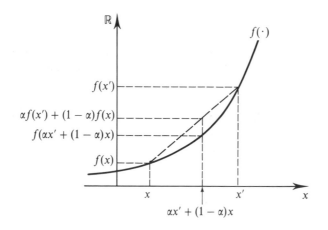

**Figure M.C.2**

A strictly convex function.

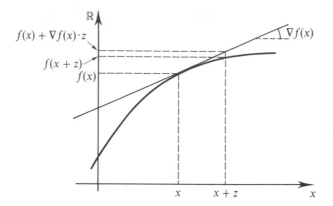

**Figure M.C.3**
Any tangent to the graph of a concave function lies above the graph of the function.

**Proof:** We argue only the necessity of condition (M.C.4) for concave functions. For all $\alpha \in (0, 1]$, the condition $f(\alpha x' + (1 - \alpha)x) \geq \alpha f(x') + (1 - \alpha)f(x)$ for all $x, x' \in A$, can be rewritten (think of $z = x' - x$) as

$$f(x + z) \leq f(x) + \frac{f(x + \alpha z) - f(x)}{\alpha}$$

for all $x \in A$, $z \in \mathbb{R}^N$ (with $x + z \in A$), and $\alpha \in (0, 1]$. Taking the limit as $\alpha \to 0$, we conclude that condition (M.C.4) must hold for a (continuously differentiable) concave function $f(\cdot)$. ■

Condition (M.C.4) is shown graphically in Figure M.C.3. It says that any tangent to the graph of a concave function $f(\cdot)$ must lie (weakly) above the graph of $f(\cdot)$.

The corresponding characterization of convex and strictly convex functions simply entails reversing the direction of the inequality in condition (M.C.4); that is, a convex function is characterized by the condition that $f(x + z) \geq f(x) + \nabla f(x) \cdot z$ for all $x \in A$ and $z \in \mathbb{R}^N$ (with $x + z \in A$).

We next develop a third characterization of concave and strictly concave functions.

**Definition M.C.2:** The $N \times N$ matrix $M$ is *negative semidefinite* if

$$z \cdot Mz \leq 0 \tag{M.C.5}$$

for all $z \in \mathbb{R}^N$. If the inequality is strict for all $z \neq 0$, then the matrix $M$ is *negative definite*. Reversing the inequalities in condition (M.C.5), we get the concepts of *positive semidefinite* and *positive definite* matrices.

We refer to Section M.E for further details on these properties of matrices. Here we put on record their intimate connection with the properties of the Hessian matrices $D^2 f(\cdot)$ of concave functions.[4]

---

4. For theorems M.C.2, M.C.3, and M.C.4, the set $A$ is assumed to be open (see Section M.F) so as to avoid boundary problems.

**Theorem M.C.2:** The (twice continuously differentiable) function $f: A \to \mathbb{R}$ is concave if and only if $D^2 f(x)$ is negative semidefinite for every $x \in A$. If $D^2 f(x)$ is negative definite for every $x \in A$, then the function is strictly concave.

**Proof:** We argue only necessity. Suppose that $f(\cdot)$ is concave. Consider a fixed $x \in A$ and a direction of displacement from $x$, $z \in \mathbb{R}^N$ with $z \neq 0$. Taking a Taylor expansion of the function $\phi(\alpha) = f(x + \alpha z)$, where $\alpha \in \mathbb{R}$, around the point $\alpha = 0$ gives

$$f(x + \alpha z) - f(x) - \nabla f(x) \cdot (\alpha z) = \frac{\alpha^2}{2} z \cdot D^2 f(x + \beta z) z$$

for some $\beta \in [0, \alpha]$. By Theorem M.C.1, the left-hand side of the above expression is nonpositive. Therefore, $z \cdot D^2 f(x + \beta z) z \leq 0$. Since $\alpha$, hence $\beta$, can be taken to be arbitrarily small, this gives the conclusion $z \cdot D^2 f(x) z \leq 0$. ∎

In the special case in which $N = 1$ [so $f(\cdot)$ is a function of a single variable], negative semidefiniteness of $D^2 f(x)$ amounts to the condition that $d^2 f(x)/dx^2 \leq 0$, whereas with negative definiteness we have $d^2 f(x)/dx^2 < 0$ [to see this note that then $z \cdot D^2 f(x) z = z^2 (d^2 f(x)/dx^2)$]. Theorem M.C.2 tells us that in this case $f(\cdot)$ is concave if and only if $d^2 f(x)/dx^2 \leq 0$ for all $x$, and that if $d^2 f(x)/dx^2 < 0$ for all $x$, then $f(\cdot)$ is strictly concave. Note that Theorem M.C.2 does *not* assert that negative definiteness of $D^2 f(x)$ must hold whenever $f(\cdot)$ is strictly concave. Indeed, this is not true: For example, when $N = 1$ the function $f(x) = -x^4$ is strictly concave, but $d^2 f(0)/dx^2 = 0$.

For convex and strictly convex functions the analogous result to Theorem M.C.2 holds by merely replacing the word "negative" with "positive."

The remainder of this section is devoted to discussion of *quasiconcave* and *strictly quasiconcave* functions.

**Definition M.C.3:** The function $f: A \to \mathbb{R}$, defined on the convex set $A \subset \mathbb{R}^N$, is *quasiconcave* if its upper contour sets $\{x \in A : f(x) \geq t\}$ are convex sets; that is, if

$$f(x) \geq t \text{ and } f(x') \geq t \quad \text{implies that} \quad f(\alpha x + (1 - \alpha)x') \geq t \qquad \text{(M.C.6)}$$

for any $t \in \mathbb{R}$, $x$, $x' \in A$, and $\alpha \in [0, 1]$.[5] If the concluding inequality in (M.C.6) is strict whenever $x \neq x'$ and $\alpha \in (0, 1)$, then we say that $f(\cdot)$ is *strictly quasiconcave*.

Analogously, we say that the function $f(\cdot)$ is *quasiconvex* if its *lower* contour sets are *convex*; that is, if $f(x) \leq t$ and $f(x') \leq t$ implies that $f(\alpha x + (1 - \alpha)x') \leq t$ for any $t \in \mathbb{R}$, $x$, $x' \in A$, and $\alpha \in [0, 1]$. For strict quasiconvexity, the final inequality must hold strictly whenever $x \neq x'$ and $\alpha \in (0, 1)$. Note that $f(\cdot)$ is quasiconcave if and only if the function $-f(\cdot)$ is quasiconvex.

The level sets of a strictly quasiconcave function are illustrated in Figure M.C.4(a);

5. For more on convex sets, see Section M.G.

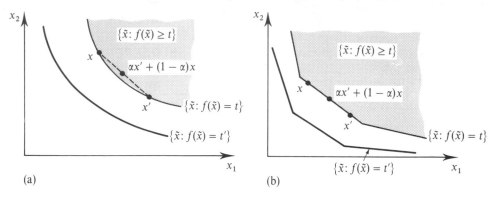

**Figure M.C.4**

(a) The level sets of a strictly quasiconcave function.
(b) The level sets of a quasiconcave function that is not strictly quasiconcave.

in Figure M.C.4(b) we show a function that is quasiconcave, but not strictly quasiconcave.

It follows from Definition M.C.3 that $f(\cdot)$ is quasiconcave if and only if

$$f(\alpha x + (1 - \alpha)x') \geq \text{Min } \{f(x), f(x')\} \qquad \text{(M.C.7)}$$

for all $x, x' \in A$ and $\alpha \in [0, 1]$. From this, or directly from (M.C.6), we see that a concave function is automatically quasiconcave. The converse is not true: For example, *any* increasing function of one variable is quasiconcave. Thus, concavity is a stronger property that quasiconcavity. It is also stronger in a different sense: concavity is a "cardinal" property in that it will *not* generally be preserved under an increasing transformation of $f(\cdot)$. Quasiconcavity, in contrast, will be preserved.

Theorems M.C.3 and M.C.4 are the quasiconcave counterparts of Theorems M.C.1 and M.C.2, respectively.

**Theorem M.C.3:** The (continuously differentiable) function $f : A \to \mathbb{R}$ is quasiconcave if and only if

$$\nabla f(x) \cdot (x' - x) \geq 0 \quad \text{whenever} \quad f(x') \geq f(x) \qquad \text{(M.C.8)}$$

for *all* $x, x' \in A$. If $\nabla f(x) \cdot (x' - x) > 0$ whenever $f(x') \geq f(x)$ and $x' \neq x$, then $f(\cdot)$ is strictly quasiconcave. In the other direction, if $f(\cdot)$ is strictly quasiconcave and if $\nabla f(x) \neq 0$ for all $x \in A$, then $\nabla f(x) \cdot (x' - x) > 0$ whenever $f(x') \geq f(x)$ and $x' \neq x$.

**Proof:** Again, we argue only the necessity of (M.C.8) for quasiconcave functions. If $f(x') \geq f(x)$ and $\alpha \in (0, 1]$ then, using condition (M.C.7), we have that

$$\frac{f(\alpha(x' - x) + x) - f(x)}{\alpha} \geq 0.$$

Taking the limit as $\alpha \to 0$, we get $\nabla f(x) \cdot (x' - x) \geq 0$.

The need for the condition "$\nabla f(x) \neq 0$ for all $x \in A$" in the last part of the theorem is illustrated by the function $f(x) = x^3$ for $x \in \mathbb{R}$. This function is strictly quasiconcave (check this using the criterion in Definition M.C.3), but because $\nabla f(0) = 0$ we have $\nabla f(x) \cdot (x' - x) = 0$ whenever $x = 0$. ∎

Theorem M.C.3's characterization of quasiconcave functions is illustrated in Figure M.C.5. The content of the theorem's condition (M.C.8) is that for any quasiconcave function $f(\cdot)$ and any pair of points $x$ and $x'$ with $f(x') \geq f(x)$, the gradient vector $\nabla f(x)$ and the vector $(x' - x)$ must form an acute angle.

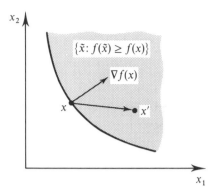

For a quasiconvex function, we reverse the direction of both inequalities in (M.C.8).

**Theorem M.C.4:** The (twice continuously differentiable) function $f: A \to \mathbb{R}$ is quasi-concave if and only if for every $x \in A$, the Hessian matrix $D^2 f(x)$ is negative semidefinite in the subspace $\{z \in \mathbb{R}^N : \nabla f(x) \cdot z = 0\}$, that is, if and only if

$$z \cdot D^2 f(x) z \leq 0 \quad \text{whenever} \quad \nabla f(x) \cdot z = 0 \qquad \text{(M.C.9)}$$

for *every* $x \in A$.[6] If the Hessian matrix $D^2 f(x)$ is negative definite in the subspace $\{z \in \mathbb{R}^N : \nabla f(x) \cdot z = 0\}$ for every $x \in A$, then $f(\cdot)$ is strictly quasiconcave.

**Proof:** Necessity (again, we limit ourselves to this) can be argued exactly as for Theorem M.C.2. The only adjustment is that we restrict $z$ to be such that $\nabla f(x) \cdot z = 0$ and we resort to Theorem M.C.3 instead of Theorem M.C.1. ∎

For a quasiconvex function, we replace the word "negative" with "positive" everywhere in the statement of Theorem M.C.4.

# M.D  Matrices: Negative (Semi)Definiteness and Other Properties

In this section, we gather various useful facts about matrices.

**Definition M.D.1:** The $N \times N$ matrix $M$ is *negative semidefinite* if

$$z \cdot Mz \leq 0 \qquad \text{(M.D.1)}$$

for all $z \in \mathbb{R}^N$. If the inequality is strict for all $z \neq 0$, then the matrix $M$ is *negative definite*. Reversing the inequalities in condition (M.D.1), we get the concepts of *positive semidefinite* and *positive definite* matrices.

Note that a matrix $M$ is positive semidefinite (respectively, positive definite) if and only if the matrix $-M$ is negative semidefinite (respectively, negative definite).

Recall that for an $N \times N$ matrix $M$ the complex number $\lambda$ is a *characteristic value* (or *eigenvalue* or *root*) if it solves the equation $|M - \lambda I| = 0$. The characteristic values of symmetric matrices are always real.

---

6. See Section M.E for a discussion of the properties of such matrices.

**Theorem M.D.1:** Suppose that $M$ is an $N \times N$ matrix.

    (i) The matrix $M$ is negative definite if and only if the symmetric matrix $M + M^T$ is negative definite.

    (ii) If $M$ is symmetric, then $M$ is negative definite if and only if all of the characteristic values of $M$ are negative.

    (iii) The matrix $M$ is negative definite if and only if $M^{-1}$ is negative definite.

    (iv) If the matrix $M$ is negative definite, then for all diagonal $N \times N$ matrices $K$ with positive diagonal entries the matrix $KM$ is *stable*.[7]

**Proof:** Part (i) simply follows from the observation that $z \cdot (M + M^T)z = 2z \cdot Mz$ for every $z \in \mathbb{R}^N$.

The logic of part (ii) is the following. Any symmetric matrix $M$ can be diagonalized in a simple manner: There is an $N \times N$ matrix of full rank $C$ having $C^T = C^{-1}$ and such that $CMC^T$ is a diagonal matrix with the diagonal entries equal to the characteristic values of $M$. But then $z \cdot Mz = (Cz) \cdot CMC^T(Cz)$, and for every $\hat{z} \in \mathbb{R}^N$ there is a $z$ such that $\hat{z} = Cz$. Thus, the matrix $M$ is negative definite if and only if the diagonal matrix $CMC^T$ is. But it is straightforward to verify that a diagonal matrix is negative definite if and only if every one of its diagonal entries is negative.

Part (iii): Suppose that $M^{-1}$ is negative definite and let $z \neq 0$. Then $z \cdot Mz = (z \cdot Mz)^T = z \cdot M^T z = (M^T z) \cdot M^{-1}(M^T z) < 0$.

Part (iv): It is known that a matrix $A$ is stable if and only if there is a symmetric positive definite matrix $E$ such that $EA$ is negative definite. Thus, in our case, we can take $A = KM$ and $E = K^{-1}$. ∎

For positive definite matrices, we can simply reverse the words "positive" and "negative" wherever they appear in Theorem M.D.1.

Our next result (Theorem M.D.2) provides a determinantal test for negative definiteness or negative semidefiniteness of a matrix $M$. Given any $T \times S$ matrix $M$, we denote by $_tM$ the $t \times S$ submatrix of $M$ where only the first $t \leq T$ rows are retained. Analogously, we let $M_s$ be the $T \times s$ submatrix of $M$ where the first $s \leq S$ columns are retained, and we let $_tM_s$ be the $t \times s$ submatrix of $M$ where only the first $t \leq T$ rows and $s \leq S$ columns are retained. Also, if $M$ is an $N \times N$ matrix, then for any permutation $\pi$ of the indices $\{1, \ldots, N\}$ we denote by $M^\pi$ the matrix in which rows and columns are correspondingly permuted.

**Theorem M.D.2:** Let $M$ be an $N \times N$ matrix.

    (i) Suppose that $M$ is symmetric. Then $M$ is negative definite if and only if $(-1)^r |_rM_r| > 0$ for every $r = 1, \ldots, N$.

    (ii) Suppose that $M$ is symmetric. Then $M$ is negative semidefinite if and only if $(-1)^r |_rM_r^\pi| \geq 0$ for every $r = 1, \ldots, N$ *and* for every permutation $\pi$ of the indices $\{1, \ldots, N\}$.

    (iii) Suppose that $M$ is negative definite (not necessarily symmetric). Then $(-1)^r |_rM_r^\pi| > 0$ for every $r = 1, \ldots, N$ and for every permutation $\pi$ of the indices $\{1, \ldots, N\}$.[8]

---

7. A matrix $M$ is stable if all of its characteristic values have negative real parts. This terminology is motivated by the fact that in this case the solution of the system of differential equations $dx(t)/dt = Mx(t)$ will converge to zero as $t \to \infty$ for *any* initial position $x(0)$.

8. A matrix $M$ such that $-M$ satisfies the condition in (iii) is called a $P$ matrix. The reason is that the determinant of any submatrix obtained by deleting some rows (and corresponding columns) is positive.

**Proof:** (i) The necessity part is simple. Note that by the definition of negative definiteness we have that every $_rM_r$ is negative definite. Thus, by Theorem M.D.1, the characteristic values of $_rM_r$ are negative. The determinant of a square matrix is equal to the product of its characteristic values. Hence, $|_rM_r|$ has the sign of $(-1)^r$. The sufficiency part requires some computation, which we shall not carry out. It is very easy to verify for the case $N = 2$ [if the conclusion of (i) holds for a $2 \times 2$ symmetric matrix, then the determinant is positive and *both* diagonal entries are negative; the combination of these two facts is well known to imply the negativity of the two characteristic values].

For (ii), we simply note the requirement to consider all permutations. For example, if $M$ is a matrix with all its entries equal to zero except the $NN$ entry, which is positive, then $M$ satisfies the nonnegative version of (i) but it is not negative semidefinite according to Definition M.D.1.

Notice that in part (iii) we only claim necessity of the determinantal condition. In fact, for nonsymmetric matrices the condition is not sufficient. ∎

**Example M.D.1:** Consider a real-valued function of two variables, $f(x_1, x_2)$. In what follows, we let subscripts denote partial derivatives; for example, $f_{12}(x_1, x_2) = \partial^2 f(x_1, x_2)/\partial x_1 \, \partial x_2$. Theorem M.C.2 tells us that $f(\cdot)$ is strictly concave if

$$D^2 f(x_1, x_2) = \begin{bmatrix} f_{11}(x_1, x_2) & f_{12}(x_1, x_2) \\ f_{21}(x_1, x_2) & f_{22}(x_1, x_2) \end{bmatrix}$$

is negative definite for all $(x_1, x_2)$. According to Theorem M.D.2, this is true if and only if

$$|f_{11}(x_1, x_2)| < 0 \qquad \text{and} \qquad \begin{vmatrix} f_{11}(x_1, x_2) & f_{12}(x_1, x_2) \\ f_{21}(x_1, x_2) & f_{22}(x_1, x_2) \end{vmatrix} > 0,$$

or equivalently, if and only if

$$f_{11}(x_1, x_2) < 0$$

and

$$f_{11}(x_1, x_2) f_{22}(x_1, x_2) - [f_{12}(x_1, x_2)]^2 > 0.$$

Theorem M.C.2 also tells us that $f(\cdot)$ is concave if and only if $D^2 f(x_1, x_2)$ is negative semidefinite for all $(x_1, x_2)$. Theorem M.D.2 tells us that this is the case if and only if

$$|f_{11}(x_1, x_2)| \leq 0 \qquad \text{and} \qquad \begin{vmatrix} f_{11}(x_1, x_2) & f_{12}(x_1, x_2) \\ f_{21}(x_1, x_2) & f_{22}(x_1, x_2) \end{vmatrix} \geq 0,$$

and, permuting the rows and columns of $D^2 f(x_1, x_2)$,

$$|f_{22}(x_1, x_2)| \leq 0 \qquad \text{and} \qquad \begin{vmatrix} f_{22}(x_1, x_2) & f_{21}(x_1, x_2) \\ f_{12}(x_1, x_2) & f_{11}(x_1, x_2) \end{vmatrix} \geq 0.$$

Thus, $f(\cdot)$ is concave if and only if

$$f_{11}(x_1, x_2) \leq 0,$$

$$f_{22}(x_1, x_2) \leq 0,$$

and

$$f_{11}(x_1, x_2) f_{22}(x_1, x_2) - [f_{12}(x_1, x_2)]^2 \geq 0. \qquad\qquad ∎$$

A similar test is available for positive definite and semidefinite matrices: The results for these matrices parallel conditions (i) to (iii) of Theorem M.D.2, but omit the factor $(-1)^r$.[9]

**Theorem M.D.3:** Let $M$ be an $N \times N$ symmetric matrix and let $B$ be an $N \times S$ matrix with $S \leq N$ and rank equal to $S$.

(i) $M$ is negative definite on $\{z \in \mathbb{R}^N : Bz = 0\}$ (i.e., $z \cdot Mz < 0$ for any $z \in \mathbb{R}^N$ with $Bz = 0$ and $z \neq 0$) if and only if

$$(-1)^r \begin{vmatrix} {}_rM_r & {}_rB \\ ({}_rB)^\mathsf{T} & 0 \end{vmatrix} > 0$$

for $r = S + 1, \ldots, N$.

(ii) $M$ is negative semidefinite on $\{z \in \mathbb{R}^N : Bz = 0\}$ (i.e., $z \cdot Mz \leq 0$ for any $z \in \mathbb{R}^N$ with $Bz = 0$ and $z \neq 0$) if and only if

$$(-1)^r \begin{vmatrix} {}_rM_r^\pi & {}_rB^\pi \\ ({}_rB^\pi)^\mathsf{T} & 0 \end{vmatrix} \geq 0$$

for $r = S + 1, \ldots, N$ *and* and every permutation $\pi$, where ${}_rB^\pi$ is the matrix formed by permuting only the *rows* of the matrix ${}_rB$ according to the permutation $\pi$ (${}_rM_r^\pi$ is, as before, a matrix formed by permuting *both* the rows *and* columns of ${}_rM_r$).

**Proof:** We will not prove this result. Note that it is parallel to parts (i) and (ii) of Theorem M.D.2 with the bordered matrix here playing a role similar to the matrix there. ∎

**Example M.D.2:** Suppose we have a function of two variables, $f(x_1, x_2)$. We assume that $\nabla f(x) \neq 0$ for every $x$. Theorem M.C.4 tells us that $f(\cdot)$ is strictly quasiconcave if the Hessian matrix $D^2 f(x_1, x_2)$ is negative definite in the subspace $\{z \in \mathbb{R}^2 : \nabla f(x) \cdot z = 0\}$ for every $x = (x_1, x_2)$. By Theorem M.D.3 the latter is true if and only if

$$\begin{vmatrix} f_{11}(x_1, x_2) & f_{12}(x_1, x_2) & f_1(x_1, x_2) \\ f_{21}(x_1, x_2) & f_{22}(x_1, x_2) & f_2(x_1, x_2) \\ f_1(x_1, x_2) & f_2(x_1, x_2) & 0 \end{vmatrix} > 0,$$

or equivalently, if and only if

$$2f_1(x_1, x_2)f_2(x_1, x_2)f_{12}(x_1, x_2) - [f_1(x_1, x_2)]^2 f_{22}(x_1, x_2) - [f_2(x_1, x_2)]^2 f_{11}(x_1, x_2) > 0.$$

If we apply this test to $f(x_1, x_2) = x_1 x_2$ we get $2x_1 x_2 > 0$ confirming that the function is strictly quasiconcave.

By Theorem M.C.4, $f(\cdot)$ is quasiconcave if and only if the Hessian matrix $D^2 f(x_1, x_2)$ is negative semidefinite in the subspace $\{z \in \mathbb{R}^2 : \nabla f(x) \cdot z = 0\}$ for every $x = (x_1, x_2)$. By Theorem M.D.3 this is true if and only if

$$\begin{vmatrix} f_{11}(x_1, x_2) & f_{12}(x_1, x_2) & f_1(x_1, x_2) \\ f_{21}(x_1, x_2) & f_{22}(x_1, x_2) & f_2(x_1, x_2) \\ f_1(x_1, x_2) & f_2(x_1, x_2) & 0 \end{vmatrix} \geq 0,$$

---

9. Recall that $M$ is positive (semi)definite if and only if $-M$ is negative (semi)definite. Moreover, $|-{}_rM_r| = (-1)^r |{}_rM_r|$.

and (performing the appropriate permutations)

$$\begin{vmatrix} f_{22}(x_1, x_2) & f_{21}(x_1, x_2) & f_2(x_1, x_2) \\ f_{12}(x_1, x_2) & f_{11}(x_1, x_2) & f_1(x_1, x_2) \\ f_2(x_1, x_2) & f_1(x_1, x_2) & 0 \end{vmatrix} \geq 0.$$

Computing these two determinants gives us the necessary and sufficient condition

$$2f_1(x_1, x_2)f_2(x_1, x_2)f_{12}(x_1, x_2) - [f_1(x_1, x_2)]^2 f_{22}(x_1, x_2) - [f_2(x_1, x_2)]^2 f_{11}(x_1, x_2) \geq 0. \quad \blacksquare$$

To characterize matrices that are positive definite or positive semidefinite on the subspace $\{z \in \mathbb{R}^N : Bz = 0\}$, we need only alter Theorem M.D.3 by replacing the term $(-1)^r$ with $(-1)^S$.

**Theorem M.D.4:** Suppose that $M$ is an $N \times N$ matrix and that for some $p \gg 0$ we have $Mp = 0$ and $M^Tp = 0$. Denote $T_p = \{z \in \mathbb{R}^N : p \cdot z = 0\}$ and let $\hat{M}$ be the $(N - 1) \times (N - 1)$ matrix obtained from $M$ by deleting one row and the corresponding column.

    (i) If rank $M = N - 1$, then rank $\hat{M} = N - 1$.
    (ii) If $z \cdot Mz < 0$ for all $z \in T_p$ with $z \neq 0$ (i.e., if $M$ is negative definite on $T_p$), then $z \cdot Mz < 0$ for any $z \in \mathbb{R}^N$ not proportional to $p$.
    (iii) The matrix $M$ is negative definite on $T_p$ if and only if $\hat{M}$ is negative definite.

**Proof:** (i) Suppose that rank $\hat{M} < N - 1$, that is, $\hat{M}\hat{z} = 0$ for some $\hat{z} \in \mathbb{R}^{N-1}$ with $\hat{z} \neq 0$. Complete $\hat{z}$ to a vector $z \in \mathbb{R}^N$ by letting the value of the missing coordinate be zero. Then we have that, first, $z$ is linearly independent of $p$ (recall that $p \gg 0$) and, second, $Mz = 0$ and $Mp = 0$. Thus, rank $M < N - 1$, which contradicts the hypothesis.

    (ii) Take a $z \in \mathbb{R}^N$ not proportional to $p$. For $\alpha_z = (p \cdot z)/(p \cdot p)$ and $z^* = z - \alpha_z p$, we have $z^* \in T_p$ and $z^* \neq 0$. Because $M^Tp = Mp = 0$, we have then

$$z \cdot Mz = (z^* + \alpha_z p) \cdot M(z^* + \alpha_z p) = z^* \cdot Mz^* < 0.$$

    (iii) This is similar to part (ii). In fact, part (ii) directly implies that $\hat{M}$ is negative definite if $M$ is negative definite on $T_p$ (because for any $\hat{z} \in \mathbb{R}^{N-1}$, $\hat{z} \cdot \hat{M}\hat{z} = z \cdot Mz$, where $z$ has been completed from $\hat{z}$ by placing a zero in the missing coordinate, and if $\hat{z} \neq 0$ this $z$ is by construction not proportional to $p$). For the converse, let $n$ denote the row and column dropped from $M$ to obtain $\hat{M}$. If for every $z' \in T_p$ with $z' \neq 0$ we let $z = z' - (z_n'/p_n)p$, then $z_n = 0$ and $z \neq 0$ [if $z$ were equal to zero, then we would have $z' = (z_n'/p_n)p$ in contradiction to $z' \cdot p = 0$]. Moreover, $z' \cdot Mz' = z \cdot Mz = \hat{z} \cdot \hat{M}\hat{z} < 0$. $\quad \blacksquare$

**Definition M.D.2:** The $N \times N$ matrix $M$ with generic entry $a_{ij}$ has a *dominant diagonal* if there is $(p_1, \ldots, p_N) \gg 0$ such that, for every $i = 1, \ldots, N$, $|p_i a_{ii}| > \sum_{j \neq i} |p_j a_{ij}|$.

**Definition M.D.3:** The $N \times N$ matrix $M$ has the *gross substitute sign pattern* if every nondiagonal entry is positive.

**Theorem M.D.5:** Suppose that $M$ is an $N \times N$ matrix.

    (i) If $M$ has a dominant diagonal, then it is nonsingular.
    (ii) Suppose that $M$ is symmetric. If $M$ has a negative and dominant diagonal then it is negative definite.

(iii) If $M$ has the gross substitute sign pattern and if for some $p \gg 0$ we have $Mp \ll 0$ and $M^T p \ll 0$, then $M$ is negative definite.

(iv) If $M$ has the gross substitute sign pattern and we have $Mp = M^T p = 0$ for some $p \gg 0$, then $\hat{M}$ is negative definite, where $\hat{M}$ is any $(N-1) \times (N-1)$ matrix obtained from $M$ by deleting a row and the corresponding column.

(v) Suppose that all the entries of $M$ are nonnegative and that $Mz \ll z$ for some $z \gg 0$ (i.e., $M$ is a *productive input–output* matrix). Then the matrix $(I-M)^{-1}$ exists. In fact, $(I-M)^{-1} = \sum_{k=0}^{k=\infty} M^k$.

**Proof:** (i) Assume, for simplicity, that $p = (1, \ldots, 1)$. Suppose, by way of contradiction, that $Mz = 0$ for $z \neq 0$. Choose a coordinate $n$ such that $|z_n| \geq |z_{n'}|$ for every other coordinate $n'$. Then $|a_{nn} z_n| > \sum_{j \neq n} |a_{nj} z_n| \geq \sum_{j \neq n} |a_{nj} z_j|$, where $a_{ij}$ is the generic entry of $M$. Hence, we cannot have $\sum_j a_{nj} z_j = 0$, and so $Mz \neq 0$. Contradiction.

(ii) If $M$ has a negative dominant diagonal then so does the matrix $M - \alpha I$, for any value $\alpha \geq 0$. Hence, by (i) we have $(-1)^N |M - \alpha I| \neq 0$. Now if $\alpha$ is very large it is clear that $(-1)^N |M - \alpha I| > 0$ (since $(-1)^N |M - \alpha I| = (-1)^N \alpha^N |(M/\alpha) - I|$ and $|-I| = (-1)^N$). Moreover, since $(-1)^N |M - \alpha I|$ is continuous in $\alpha$ and $(-1)^N |M - \alpha I| \neq 0$ for all $\alpha \geq 0$, this tells us that $(-1)^N |M - \alpha I| > 0$ for all $\alpha \geq 0$. Hence, $(-1)^N |M| > 0$. By the same argument, $(-1)^r |_r M_r| > 0$ for all $r$. So, if $M$ is also symmetric then by part (i) of Theorem M.D.2 it is negative definite.

(iii) The stated conditions imply that $M + M^T$ has a negative and dominant diagonal [in particular, note that $Mp \ll 0$ and $M^T p \ll 0$ implies that $p_n(2a_{nn}) < -\sum_{j \neq n} p_j(a_{jn} + a_{nj})$ for all $n$, where $a_{ij}$ is the generic entry of $M$]. Because, by the gross substitute property, $a_{ij} > 0$ for $i \neq j$, this gives us $|p_n(2a_{nn})| > |\sum_{j \neq n} p_j(a_{jn} + a_{nj})|$ for all $n$. Hence, the conclusion follows from part (ii) of this theorem and part (i) of Theorem M.D.1.

(iv) If $M$ satisfies the condition of (iv), then the fact that $M$ has the gross substitute sign pattern implies that $\hat{M}$ does as well and that $\hat{M}p \ll 0$ and $\hat{M}^T p \ll 0$. Hence, $\hat{M}$ satisfies the conditions of (iii) and is therefore negative definite.

(v) This result was already proved in the Appendix to Chapter 5 (see the proof of Proposition 5.AA.1).

# M.E The Implicit Function Theorem

The setting for the *implicit function theorem* (IFT) is as follows. We have a system of $N$ equations depending on $N$ endogenous variables $x = (x_1, \ldots, x_N)$ and $M$ parameters $q = (q_1, \ldots, q_M)$:

$$f_1(x_1, \ldots, x_N; q_1, \ldots, q_M) = 0$$
$$\vdots \qquad\qquad\qquad\qquad \text{(M.E.1)}$$
$$f_N(x_1, \ldots, x_N; q_1, \ldots, q_M) = 0$$

The domain of the endogenous variables is $A \subset \mathbb{R}^N$ and the domain of the parameters is $B \subset \mathbb{R}^M$.[10]

---

10. In what follows, we take $A$ and $B$ to be open sets (see Section M.F) so as to avoid boundary problems.

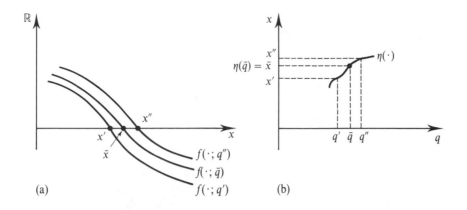

**Figure M.E.1**

A locally solvable
equation.
(a) Solutions of
$f(x; q) = 0$ near $(\bar{x}, \bar{q})$.
(b) The graph of $\eta(\cdot)$.

Suppose that $\bar{x} = (\bar{x}_1, \ldots, \bar{x}_N) \in A$ and $\bar{q} = (\bar{q}_1, \ldots, \bar{q}_M) \in B$ satisfy equations (M.E.1). That is, $f_n(\bar{x}, \bar{q}) = 0$ for every $n$. We are then interested in the possibility of solving for $x = (x_1, \ldots, x_N)$ as a function of $q = (q_1, \ldots, q_M)$ *locally* around $\bar{q}$ and $\bar{x}$. Formally, we say that a set $A'$ is an *open neighborhood* of a point $x \in \mathbb{R}^N$ if $A' = \{x' \in \mathbb{R}^N : \|x' - x\| < \varepsilon\}$ for some scalar $\varepsilon > 0$. An open neighborhood $B'$ of a point $q \in \mathbb{R}^M$ is defined in the same way.

**Definition M.E.1:** Suppose that $\bar{x} = (\bar{x}_1, \ldots, \bar{x}_N) \in A$ and $\bar{q} = (\bar{q}_1, \ldots, \bar{q}_M) \in B$ satisfy the equations (M.E.1). We say that we can *locally solve* equations (M.E.1) at $(\bar{x}, \bar{q})$ for $x = (x_1, \ldots, x_N)$ as a function of $q = (q_1, \ldots, q_M)$ if there are open neighborhoods $A' \subset A$ and $B' \subset B$, of $\bar{x}$ and $\bar{q}$, respectively, and $N$ uniquely determined "implicit" functions $\eta_1(\cdot), \ldots, \eta_N(\cdot)$ from $B'$ to $A'$ such that

$$f_n(\eta_1(q), \ldots, \eta_N(q); q) = 0 \qquad \text{for every } q \in B' \text{ and every } n,$$

and

$$\eta_n(\bar{q}) = \bar{x}_n \qquad \text{for every } n.$$

In Figure M.E.1 we represent, for the case where $N = M = 1$, a situation in which the system of equations can be locally solved around a given solution.

The implicit function theorem gives a sufficient condition for the existence of such implicit functions and tells us the first-order comparative statics effects of $q$ on $x$ at a solution.

**Theorem M.E.1:** (*Implicit Function Theorem*) Suppose that every equation $f_n(\cdot)$ is continuously differentiable with respect to its $N + M$ variables and that we consider a solution $\bar{x} = (\bar{x}_1, \ldots, \bar{x}_N)$ at parameter values $\bar{q} = (\bar{q}_1, \ldots, \bar{q}_M)$, that is, satisfying $f_n(\bar{x}; \bar{q}) = 0$ for every $n$. If the *Jacobian* matrix of the system (M.E.1) with respect to the endogenous variables, evaluated at $(\bar{x}, \bar{q})$, is nonsingular, that is, if

$$\begin{vmatrix} \dfrac{\partial f_1(\bar{x}, \bar{q})}{\partial x_1} & \cdots & \dfrac{\partial f_1(\bar{x}, \bar{q})}{\partial x_N} \\ & \ddots & \\ \dfrac{\partial f_N(\bar{x}, \bar{q})}{\partial x_1} & \cdots & \dfrac{\partial f_N(\bar{x}, \bar{q})}{\partial x_N} \end{vmatrix} \neq 0, \qquad \text{(M.E.2)}$$

then the system can be locally solved at $(\bar{x}, \bar{q})$ by implicitly defined functions $\eta_n : B' \to A'$ that are continuously differentiable. Moreover, the first-order effects of $q$ on $x$ at $(\bar{x}, \bar{q})$ are given by

$$D_q \eta(\bar{q}) = -[D_x f(\bar{x}; \bar{q})]^{-1} D_q f(\bar{x}; \bar{q}). \qquad \text{(M.E.3)}$$

**Proof:** A proof of the existence of the implicit functions $\eta_n : B' \to A'$ is too technical for this appendix, but its common-sense logic is easy to grasp. Expression (M.E.2), a full rank condition, tells us that we can move the values of the system of equations in any direction by appropriate changes of the endogenous variables. Therefore, if there is a shock to the parameters and the values of the equation system are pushed away from zero, then we can adjust the endogenous variables so as to restore the "equilibrium."

Now, given a system of implicit functions $\eta(q) = (\eta_1(q), \ldots, \eta_N(q))$ defined on some neighborhood of $(\bar{x}, \bar{q})$, the first-order comparative static effects $\partial \eta_n(\bar{q})/\partial q_m$ are readily determined. Let $f(x; q) = (f_1(x; q), \ldots, f_N(x; q))$. Since we have

$$f(\eta(q); q) = 0 \qquad \text{for all } q \in B',$$

we can apply the chain rule of calculus to obtain

$$D_x f(\bar{x}; \bar{q}) D_q \eta(\bar{q}) + D_q f(\bar{x}; \bar{q}) = 0.$$

Because of (M.E.2), the $N \times N$ matrix $D_x f(\bar{x}; \bar{q})$ is invertible, and so we can conclude that

$$D_q \eta(\bar{q}) = -[D_x f(\bar{x}; \bar{q})]^{-1} D_q f(\bar{x}; \bar{q}). \qquad \blacksquare$$

Note that when $N = M = 1$ (the case of one endogenous variable and one parameter), (M.E.3) reduces to the simple expression

$$\frac{d\eta(\bar{q})}{dq} = -\frac{\partial f(\bar{x}; \bar{q})/\partial q}{\partial f(\bar{x}; \bar{q})/\partial x}.$$

The special case of the implicit function theorem where $M = N$ and every equation has the form $f_n(x, q) = g_n(x) - q_n = 0$ is known as the *inverse function theorem*.

---

How restrictive is condition (M.E.2)? Not very. In Figure M.E.2 we depict a situation where it fails to hold. [By contrast, in Figure M.E.1 condition (M.E.2) is satisfied.] However, the tangency displayed in Figure M.E.2 appears pathological: it would be removed by any small perturbation of the function $f(\cdot; \cdot)$.

An important result, the *transversality theorem*, makes this idea precise by asserting that, under a weak condition [enough first-order variability of $f(\cdot; \cdot)$ with respect to $x$ *and* $q$], (M.E.2) holds *generically* on the parameters. We present a preliminary concept in Definition M.E.2.

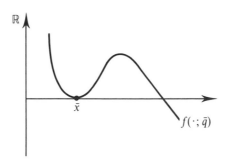

**Figure M.E.2**

Condition (M.E.2) is violated at the solution $(\bar{x}, \bar{q})$.

**Definition M.E.2:** Given open sets $A \subset \mathbb{R}^N$ and $B \subset \mathbb{R}^M$, the (continuously differentiable) system of equations $f(\cdot\,; \hat{q}) = 0$ defined on $A$ is *regular at* $\hat{q} \in B$ if (M.E.2) holds at any solution $x$; that is, if $f(x; \hat{q}) = 0$ implies that $|D_x f(x; \hat{q})| \neq 0$.

With this definition we then have Theorem M.E.2.

**Theorem M.E.2:** (*Transversality Theorem*) Suppose that we are given open sets $A \subset \mathbb{R}^N$ and $B \subset \mathbb{R}^M$ and a (continuously differentiable) function $f: A \times B \to \mathbb{R}^N$. If $f(\cdot\,; \cdot)$ satisfies the condition

The $N \times (N + M)$ matrix $Df(x; q)$ has rank $N$ whenever $f(x; q) = 0$,

then the system of $N$ equations in $N$ unknowns $f(\cdot\,; \hat{q}) = 0$ is regular for *almost every* $\hat{q} \in B$.[11]

---

# M.F  Continuous Functions and Compact Sets

In this section, we begin by formally defining the concept of a continuous function. We then develop the notion of a compact set (and, along the way, the notions of open and closed sets). Finally, we discuss some properties of continuous functions that relate to compact sets.

A *sequence* in $\mathbb{R}^N$ assigns to every positive integer $m = 1, 2, \ldots$ a vector $x^m \in \mathbb{R}^N$. We denote the sequence by $\{x^m\}_{m=1}^{m=\infty}$ or, simply, by $\{x^m\}$ or even $x^m$.

**Definition M.F.1:** The sequence $\{x^m\}$ *converges* to $x \in \mathbb{R}^N$, written as $\lim_{m \to \infty} x^m = x$, or $x^m \to x$, if for every $\varepsilon > 0$ there is an integer $M_\varepsilon$ such that $\|x^m - x\| < \varepsilon$ whenever $m > M_\varepsilon$. The point $x$ is then said to be the *limit point* (or simply the *limit*) of sequence $\{x^m\}$.

In words: The sequence $\{x^m\}$ converges to $x$ if $x^m$ approaches $x$ arbitrarily closely as $m$ increases.

**Definition M.F.2:** Consider a domain $X \subset \mathbb{R}^N$. A function $f: X \to \mathbb{R}$ is *continuous* if for all $x \in X$ and every sequence $x^m \to x$ (having $x^m \in X$ for all $m$), we have $f(x^m) \to f(x)$. A function $f: X \to \mathbb{R}^K$ is continuous if every coordinate function $f_k(\cdot)$ is continuous.

In words: a function is continuous if, when we take a sequence of points $x^1, x^2, \ldots$ converging to $x$, the corresponding sequence of function values $f(x^1), f(x^2), \ldots$ converges to $f(x)$. Intuitively, a function fails to be continuous if it displays a "jump" in its value at some point $x$. Examples of continuous and discontinuous functions defined on $[0, 1]$ are illustrated in Figure M.F.1.

We next develop the notions of open, closed, and compact sets.

**Definition M.F.3:** Fix a set $X \subset \mathbb{R}^N$. We say that a set $A \subset X$ is *open* (relative to $X$) if for every $x \in A$ there is an $\varepsilon > 0$ such that $\|x' - x\| < \varepsilon$ and $x' \in X$ implies $x' \in A$.

---

11. "Almost every" means that if, for example, we choose $\hat{q}$ according to some nondegenerate multinomial normal distribution in $\mathbb{R}^M$, then with probability 1 the equation system $f(\cdot\,; \hat{q}) = 0$ is regular. This is the concept of "genericity" in this context.

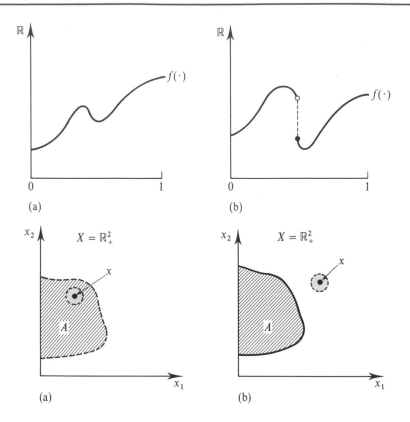

**Figure M.F.1**

Continuous and discontinuous functions.
(a) A continuous function.
(b) A discontinuous function.

**Figure M.F.2**

Open and closed sets.
(a) An open set (relative to $X$).
(b) A closed set (relative to $X$).

A set $A \subset X$ is *closed* (relative to $X$) if its complement $X \backslash A$ is open (relative to $X$).[12] If $X = \mathbb{R}^N$ we simply refer to "open" and "closed" sets.

Given a point $x \in \mathbb{R}^N$, a set $B = \{x' \in \mathbb{R}^N : \|x' - x\| < \varepsilon\}$ for some scalar $\varepsilon > 0$ is called an *open ball around $x$*. With this notion, the idea of an open set can be put as follows: Suppose that the universe of possible vectors in $\mathbb{R}^N$ is $X$. A set $A \subset X$ is open (relative to $X$) if, for every point $x$ in $A$, there is an open ball around $x$ all of whose elements (in $X$) are elements of $A$. In Figure M.F.2(a) the hatched set $A$ is open (relative to $X$). In the figure, we depict a typical point $x \in A$ and a shaded open ball around $x$ that lies within $A$; points on the dashed curve do not belong to $A$. In contrast, the hatched set $A$ in Figure M.F.2(b) is closed because the set $X \backslash A$ is open; note how there is an open ball around the point $x \in X \backslash A$ that lies entirely within $X \backslash A$ [in the figure, the points on the inner solid curve belong to $A$].

Theorem M.F.1 gathers some basic facts about open and closed sets.

**Theorem M.F.1:** Fix a set $X \subset \mathbb{R}^N$. In what follows, all the open and closed sets are relative to $X$.

    (i) The union of any number, finite or infinite, of open sets is open. The intersection of a finite number of open sets is open.

    (ii) The intersection of any number, finite or infinite, of closed sets is closed. The union of a finite number of closed sets is closed.

    (iii) A set $A \subset X$ is closed if and only if for every sequence $x^m \to x \in X$, with $x^m \in A$ for all $m$, we have $x \in A$.

---

12. Given two sets $A$ and $B$, the set $A \backslash B$ is the set containing all the elements of $A$ that are not elements of $B$.

Property (iii) of Theorem M.F.1 is noteworthy because it gives us a direct way to characterize a closed set: a set $A$ is closed if and only if the limit point of any sequence whose members are all elements of $A$ is itself an element of $A$. Points (in $X$) that are the limits of sequences whose members are all elements of the set $A$ are known as the *limit points* of $A$. Thus, property (iii) says that a set $A$ is closed if and only if it contains all of its limit points.

Given $A \subset X$, the *interior* of $A$ (relative to $X$) is the open set[13]

$$\text{Int}_X A = \{x \in A : \text{there is } \varepsilon > 0 \text{ such that } \|x' - x\| < \varepsilon \text{ and } x' \in X \text{ implies } x' \in A\}.$$

The *closure of $A$* (relative to $X$) is the closed set $\text{Cl}_X A = X \backslash \text{Int}_X (X \backslash A)$. Equivalently, $\text{Cl}_X A$ is the union of the set $A$ and its limit points; it is the smallest closed set containing $A$. The *boundary* of $A$ (relative to $X$) is the closed set $\text{Bdry}_X A = \text{Cl}_X A \backslash \text{Int}_X A$. The set $A$ is closed if and only if $\text{Bdry}_X A \subset A$.

**Definition M.F.4:** A set $A \subset \mathbb{R}^N$ is *bounded* if there is $r \in \mathbb{R}$ such that $\|x\| < r$ for every $x \in A$. The set $A \subset \mathbb{R}^N$ is *compact* if it is bounded and closed relative to $\mathbb{R}^N$.

We conclude by noting two properties of continuous functions relating to compact sets. Formally, given a function $f: X \to \mathbb{R}^K$, the *image* of a set $A \subset X$ under $f(\cdot)$ is the set $f(A) = \{y \in \mathbb{R}^K : y = f(x) \text{ for some } x \in A\}$.

**Theorem M.F.2:** Suppose that $f: X \to \mathbb{R}^K$ is a continuous function defined on a nonempty set $X \subset \mathbb{R}^N$.

  (i) The image of a compact set under $f(\cdot)$ is compact: That is, if $A \subset X$ is compact, then $f(A) = \{y \in \mathbb{R}^K : y = f(x) \text{ for some } x \in A\}$ is a compact subset of $\mathbb{R}^K$.

  (ii) Suppose that $K = 1$ and $X$ is compact. Then $f(\cdot)$ has a maximizer: That is, there is $x \in X$ such that $f(x) \geq f(x')$ for every $x' \in X$.

Part (ii) of Theorem M.F.2 asserts that any continuous function $f: X \to \mathbb{R}$ defined on a compact set $X$ attains a maximum. We illustrate this result in Figure M.F.3. A maximum is not attained either in Figure M.F.3(a) or in Figure M.F.3(b). In Figure M.F.3(a), the function is continuous, but the domain is not compact. In Figure M.F.3(b), the domain is compact, but the function is not continuous.

---

Given a sequence $\{x^m\}$, suppose that we have a strictly increasing function $m(k)$ that assigns to each positive integer $k$ a positive integer $m(k)$. Then the sequence $x^{m(1)}, x^{m(2)}, \ldots$ (written $\{x^{m(k)}\}$) is called a *subsequence* of $\{x^m\}$. That is, $\{x^{m(k)}\}$ is composed of an (order-preserving) subset of the sequence $\{x^m\}$. For example, if the sequence $\{x^m\}$ is $1, 2, 4, 16, 25, 36, \ldots$, then one subsequence of $\{x^m\}$ is $1, 4, 16, 36, \ldots$; another is $2, 4, 16, 25, 36, \ldots$.

**Theorem M.F.3:** Suppose that the set $A \subset \mathbb{R}^N$ is compact.

  (i) Every sequence $\{x^m\}$ with $x^m \in A$ for all $m$ has a convergent subsequence. Specifically, there is a subsequence $\{x^{m(k)}\}$ of the sequence $\{x^m\}$ that has a limit in $A$, that is, a point $x \in A$ such that $x^{m(k)} \to x$.

  (ii) If, in addition to being compact, $A$ is also *discrete*, that is, if all its points are isolated [formally, for every $x \in A$ there is $\varepsilon > 0$ such that $x' = x$ whenever $x' \in A$ and $\|x' - x\| < \varepsilon$], then $A$ is finite.

---

13. In what follows in this paragraph, all of the open and closed sets are once again relative to $X$.

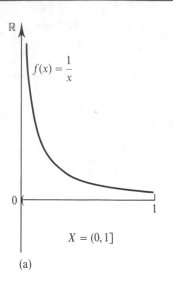

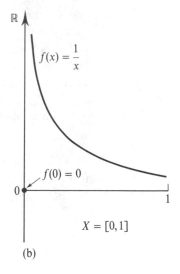

**Figure M.F.3**

Indispensability of the continuity and compactness assumptions for the existence of a maximizer.
(a) A continuous function with no maximizer on a noncompact domain.
(b) A discontinuous function with no maximizer on a compact domain.

# M.G  Convex Sets and Separating Hyperplanes

In this section, we review some basic properties of convex sets, including the important separating hyperplane theorems.

**Definition M.G.1:** The set $A \subset \mathbb{R}^N$ is *convex* if $\alpha x + (1 - \alpha)x' \in A$ whenever $x, x' \in A$ and $\alpha \in [0, 1]$.[14]

In words: A set in $\mathbb{R}^N$ is convex if whenever it contains two vectors $x$ and $x'$, it also contains the entire segment connecting them. In Figure M.G.1(a), we depict a convex set. The set in Figure M.G.1(b) is not convex.

Note that for a concave function $f : A \to \mathbb{R}$ the set $\{(z, v) \in \mathbb{R}^{N+1} : v \leq f(z), z \in A\}$ is convex. Note also that the intersection of any number of convex sets is convex, but the union of convex sets need not be convex.

**Definition M.G.2:** Given a set $B \subset \mathbb{R}^N$, the *convex hull* of $B$, denoted Co $B$, is the smallest convex set containing $B$, that is, the intersection of all convex sets that contain $B$.

Figure M.G.2 represents a set and its convex hull. It is not difficult to verify that the convex hull can also be described as the set of all possible convex combinations of elements of $B$, that is,

$$\text{Co } B = \left\{ \sum_{j=1}^{J} \alpha_j x_j : \text{for some } x_1, \ldots, x_J \text{ with } x_j \in B \text{ for all } j, \right.$$

$$\left. \text{and some } (\alpha_1, \ldots, \alpha_J) \geq 0 \text{ with } \sum_{j=1}^{J} \alpha_j = 1 \right\}.$$

**Definition M.G.3:** The vector $x \in B$ is an *extreme point* of the convex set $B \subset \mathbb{R}^N$ if it cannot be expressed as $x = \alpha y + (1 - \alpha)z$ for any $y, z \in B$ and $\alpha \in (0, 1)$.

---

14. The set $A$ is *strictly convex* if $\alpha x + (1 - \alpha)x'$ is an element of the *interior* of $A$ whenever $x, x' \in A$ and $\alpha \in (0, 1)$ (see Section M.F for a definition of the interior of a set).

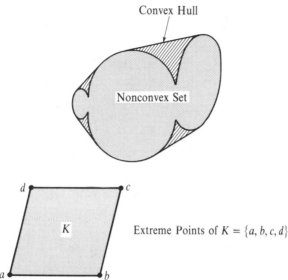

$\alpha x + (1 - \alpha)x'$        $\alpha x + (1 - \alpha)x'$

$x$    $x'$        $x$        $x'$

(a)        (b)

**Figure M.G.1**

Convex and nonconvex sets.
(a) A convex set.
(b) A nonconvex set.

Convex Hull

Nonconvex Set

**Figure M.G.2**

A nonconvex set and its convex hull.

$d$        $c$

$K$        Extreme Points of $K = \{a, b, c, d\}$

$a$        $b$

**Figure M.G.3**

Extreme points of a convex set.

The extreme points of the convex set represented in Figure M.G.3 are the four corners.

A very important result of convexity theory is contained in Theorem M.G.1.

**Theorem M.G.1:** Suppose that $B \subset \mathbb{R}^N$ is a convex set that is also compact (that is, closed and bounded; see Section M.F). Then every $x \in B$ can be expressed as a convex combination of at most $N + 1$ extreme points of $B$.

**Proof:** The proof is too technical to be given here. Note simply that the result is correct for the convex set in Figure M.G.3: Any point belongs to the triangle spanned by *some* collection of three corners. ■

We now turn to the development of the separating hyperplane theorems.

**Definition M.G.4:** Given $p \in \mathbb{R}^N$ with $p \neq 0$, and $c \in \mathbb{R}$, the *hyperplane generated by $p$ and $c$* is the set $H_{p,c} = \{z \in \mathbb{R}^N : p \cdot z = c\}$. The sets $\{z \in \mathbb{R}^N : p \cdot z \geq c\}$ and $\{z \in \mathbb{R}^N : p \cdot z \leq c\}$ are called, respectively, the *half-space above* and the *half-space below* the hyperplane $H_{p,c}$.

Hyperplanes and half-spaces are convex sets. Figure M.G.4 provides illustrations.

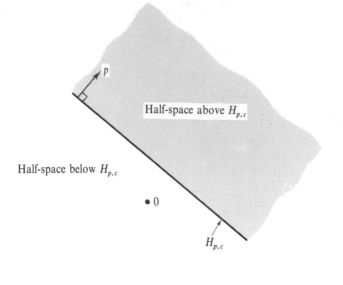

**Figure M.G.4**
Hyperplanes and
half-spaces.

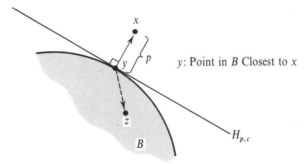

**Figure M.G.5**
The separating
hyperplane theorem.

**Theorem M.G.2:** (*Separating Hyperplane Theorem*)  Suppose that $B \subset \mathbb{R}^N$ is convex and closed (see Section M.F for a discussion of closed sets), and that $x \notin B$. Then there is $p \in \mathbb{R}^N$ with $p \neq 0$, and a value $c \in \mathbb{R}$ such that $p \cdot x > c$ and $p \cdot y < c$ for every $y \in B$.

More generally, suppose that the convex sets $A, B \subset \mathbb{R}^N$ are disjoint (i.e., $A \cap B = \varnothing$). Then there is $p \in \mathbb{R}^N$ with $p \neq 0$, and a value $c \in \mathbb{R}$, such that $p \cdot x \geq c$ for every $x \in A$ and $p \cdot y \leq c$ for every $y \in B$. That is, there is a hyperplane that separates $A$ and $B$, leaving $A$ and $B$ on different sides of it.

**Proof:** We discuss only the first part (i.e., the separation of a point and a closed, convex set). In Figure M.G.5 we represent a closed, convex set $B$ and a point $x \notin B$. We also indicate by $y \in B$ the point in set $B$ closest to $x$.[15] If we let $p = x - y$ and $c' = p \cdot y$, we can then see, first, that $p \cdot x > c'$ [since $p \cdot x - c' = p \cdot x - p \cdot y = (x - y) \cdot (x - y) = \|x - y\|^2 > 0$] and, second, that for any $z \in B$ the vectors $p$ and $z - y$ cannot make an acute angle, that is, $p \cdot (z - y) = p \cdot z - c' \leq 0$. Finally, let $c = c' + \varepsilon$ where $\varepsilon > 0$ is small enough for $p \cdot x > c' + \varepsilon = c$ to hold. ∎

_____

15. We use the familiar Euclidean distance measure. It is to guarantee the existence of a closest point in $B$ that we require $B$ to be closed.

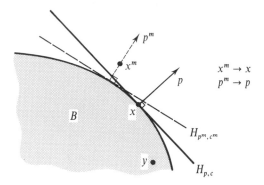

**Figure M.G.6**

The supporting
hyperplane theorem

**Theorem M.G.3:** (*Supporting Hyperplane Theorem*) Suppose that $B \subset \mathbb{R}^N$ is convex and that $x$ is not an element of the interior of set $B$ (i.e., $x \notin \text{Int } B$; see Section M.F for the concept of the interior of a set). Then there is $p \in \mathbb{R}^N$ with $p \neq 0$ such that $p \cdot x \geq p \cdot y$ for every $y \in B$.

**Proof:** Suppose that $x \notin \text{Int } B$. The following argument can be followed in Figure M.G.6. It is intuitive that we can find a sequence $x^m \to x$ such that, for all $m$, $x^m$ is not an element of the closure of set $B$ (i.e., $x^m \notin \text{Cl } B$; see Section M.F for a discussion of sequences and the closure of a set). By the separating hyperplane theorem (Theorem M.G.2), for each $m$ there is a $p^m \neq 0$ and a $c^m \in \mathbb{R}$ such that

$$p^m \cdot x^m > c^m \geq p^m \cdot y \qquad \text{(M.G.1)}$$

for every $y \in B$. Without loss of generality we can suppose that $\| p^m \| = 1$ for every $m$. Thus, extracting a subsequence if necessary (see the small type discussion at the end of Section M.F), we can assume that there is $p \neq 0$ and $c \in \mathbb{R}$ such that $p^m \to p$ and $c^m \to c$. Hence, taking limits in (M.G.1), we have

$$p \cdot x \geq c \geq p \cdot y$$

for every $y \in B$. ∎

Finally, for the important concept of the *support function* of a set and its properties we refer to Section 3.F of the text.

# M.H Correspondences

It is common in economics to resort to a generalized concept of a function called a *correspondence*.

**Definition M.H.1:** Given a set $A \subset \mathbb{R}^N$, a *correspondence* $f : A \to \mathbb{R}^K$ is a rule that assigns a set $f(x) \subset \mathbb{R}^K$ to every $x \in A$.

Note that when, for every $x \in A$, $f(x)$ is composed of precisely one element, then $f(\cdot)$ can be viewed as a function in the usual sense. Note also that the definition allows for $f(x) = \emptyset$, but typically we consider only correspondences with $f(x) \neq \emptyset$ for every $x \in A$. Finally, if for some set $Y \subset \mathbb{R}^K$ we have $f(x) \subset Y$ for every $x \in A$, we indicate this by $f : A \to Y$.

We now proceed to discuss continuity notions for correspondences. Given $A \subset \mathbb{R}^N$ and $Y \subset \mathbb{R}^K$, the *graph* of the correspondence $f : A \to Y$ is the set $\{(x, y) \in A \times Y : y \in f(x)\}$.

**Definition M.H.2:** Given $A \subset \mathbb{R}^N$ and the closed set $Y \subset \mathbb{R}^K$, the correspondence $f : A \to Y$ has a *closed graph* if for any two sequences $x^m \to x \in A$ and $y^m \to y$, with $x^m \in A$ and $y^m \in f(x^m)$ for every $m$, we have $y \in f(x)$.

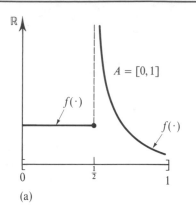

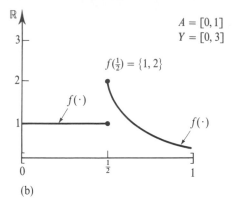

$$A = [0,1]$$
$$Y = [0,3]$$

$$f(\tfrac{1}{2}) = \{1, 2\}$$

**Figure M.H.1**

Closed graphs and upper hemicontinuous correspondences. (a) A closed graph correspondence that is not upper hemicontinuous. (b) An upper hemicontinuous correspondence.

Note that the concept of a closed graph is simply our usual notion of closedness (relative to $A \times Y$) applied to the set $\{(x, y) \in A \times Y : y \in f(x)\}$ (see Section M.F).

**Definition M.H.3:** Given $A \subset \mathbb{R}^N$ and the closed set $Y \subset \mathbb{R}^K$, the correspondence $f : A \to Y$ is *upper hemicontinuous* (uhc) if it has a closed graph and the images of compact sets are bounded, that is, for every compact set $B \subset A$ the set $f(B) = \{y \in Y : y \in f(x) \text{ for some } x \in B\}$ is bounded.[16,17]

In many applications, the range space $Y$ of $f(\cdot)$ is itself compact. In that case, the upper hemicontinuity property reduces to the closed graph condition. In Figure M.H.1(a), we represent a correspondence (in fact, a function) having a closed graph that is not upper hemicontinuous. In contrast, the correspondence represented in Figure M.H.1(b) is upper hemicontinuous.

The upper hemicontinuity property for correspondences can be thought of as a natural generalization of the notion of continuity for functions. Indeed, we have the result of Theorem M.H.1.

**Theorem M.H.1:** Given $A \subset \mathbb{R}^N$ and the closed set $Y \subset \mathbb{R}^K$, suppose that $f : A \to Y$ is a single-valued correspondence (so that it is, in fact, a function). Then $f(\cdot)$ is an upper hemicontinuous correspondence if and only if it is continuous as a function.

**Proof:** If $f(\cdot)$ is continuous as a function, then Definition M.F.2 implies that $f(\cdot)$ has a closed graph (relative to $A \times Y$). In addition, Theorem M.F.2 tells us that images of compact sets under $f(\cdot)$ are compact, hence bounded. Thus, $f(\cdot)$ is upper hemicontinuous as a correspondence.

Suppose now that $f(\cdot)$ is upper hemicontinuous as a correspondence and consider any sequence $x^m \to x \in A$ with $x^m \in A$ for all $m$. Let $S = \{x^m : m = 1, 2, \ldots\} \cup \{x\}$. Then there exists an $r > 0$ such that $\|x'\| < r$ if $x' \in S$.[18] Because $S$ is also closed, it follows that $S$ is compact.

16. See Section M.F for a discussion of bounded and compact sets.

17. It can be verified that Definition M.H.3 implies that the image of a compact set under an upper hemicontinuous correspondence is in fact compact (i.e., closed and bounded), a property also shared by continuous functions (see Theorem M.F.2).

18. To see this, recall that if $x^m \to x$, then for any $\varepsilon > 0$ there is a positive integer $M_\varepsilon$ such that $\|x^m - x\| < \varepsilon$ for all $m > M_\varepsilon$. Hence, for any $r > \text{Max}\{\|x^1\|, \ldots, \|x^{M_\varepsilon}\|, \|x\| + \varepsilon\}$, we have $\|x'\| < r$ if $x' \in S$.

By Definition M.H.3, $f(S)$ is bounded, and so $\text{Cl} f(S)$ (relative to $\mathbb{R}^K$) is a compact set. If, contradicting continuity of the function $f(\cdot)$, the sequence $\{f(x^m)\}$ [which lies in the compact set $\text{Cl} f(S)$] did not converge to $f(x)$, then by Theorem M.F.3 we could extract a subsequence $x^{m(k)} \to x$ such that $f(x^{m(k)}) \to y$ for some $y \in \text{Cl} f(S)$ having $y \neq f(x)$. But then the graph of $f(\cdot)$ could not be closed, in contradiction to the upper hemicontinuity of $f(\cdot)$ as a correspondence. ∎

---

Upper hemicontinuity is only one of two possible generalizations of the continuity notion to correspondences. We now state the second (for the case where the range space $Y$ is compact).

**Definition M.H.4:** Given $A \subset \mathbb{R}^N$ and a compact set $Y \subset \mathbb{R}^K$, the correspondence $f: A \to Y$ is *lower hemicontinuous* (lhc) if for every sequence $x^m \to x \in A$ with $x^m \in A$ for all $m$, and every $y \in f(x)$, we can find a sequence $y^m \to y$ and an integer $M$ such that $y^m \in f(x^m)$ for $m > M$.

Figure M.H.2(a) represents a lower hemicontinuous correspondence.[19] Observe that the correspondence is not upper hemicontinuous—it does not have a closed graph. Similarly, the correspondence represented in Figure M.H.2(b) is upper hemicontinuous but it fails to be lower hemicontinuous (consider the illustrated sequence $x^m \to x$ that approaches $x$ from below and the point $y \in f(x)$). Roughly speaking, upper hemicontinuity is compatible only with "discontinuities" that appear as "explosions" of sets [as at $x = \frac{1}{2}$ in Figure M.H.2(b)], while lower hemicontinuity is compatible only with "implosions" of sets [as at $x = \frac{1}{2}$ in Figure M.H.2(a)].

As with upper hemicontinuous correspondences, if $f(\cdot)$ is a function then the concepts of lower hemicontinuity as a correspondence and of continuity as a function coincide.

Finally, when a correspondence is both upper and lower hemicontinuous, we say that it is *continuous*. An example is illustrated in Figure M.H.3.

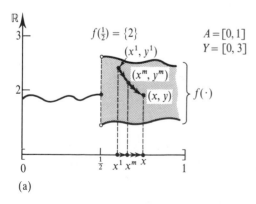

(a)

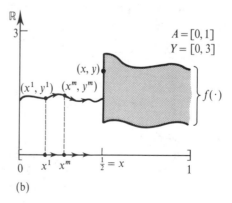

(b)

**Figure M.H.2**

Upper and lower hemicontinuous correspondences. (a) A lower hemicontinuous correspondence that is not upper hemicontinuous. (b) An upper hemicontinuous correspondence that is not lower hemicontinuous.

---

19. For another source of examples, note that any correspondence $f: A \to Y$ with an open graph (relative to $A \times Y$) is lower hemicontinuous.

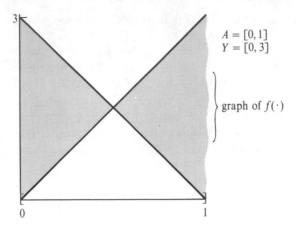

$A = [0, 1]$
$Y = [0, 3]$

graph of $f(\cdot)$

**Figure M.H.3**
A continuous
correspondence.

# M.I Fixed Point Theorems

In economics the most frequent technique for establishing the existence of solutions to an equilibrium system of equations consists of setting up the problem as the search for a *fixed point* of a suitably constructed function or correspondence $f: A \to A$ from some set $A \subset \mathbb{R}^N$ into itself. A vector $x \in A$ is a fixed point of $f(\cdot)$ if $x = f(x)$ [or, in the correspondence case, if $x \in f(x)$]. That is, the vector is mapped into itself and so it remains "fixed." The reason for proceeding in this, often roundabout, way is that important mathematical theorems for proving the existence of fixed points are readily available.

The most basic and well-known result is stated in Theorem M.I.1.

**Theorem M.I.1:** (*Brouwer's Fixed Point Theorem*) Suppose that $A \subset \mathbb{R}^N$ is a nonempty, compact, convex set, and that $f: A \to A$ is a continuous function from $A$ into itself. Then $f(\cdot)$ has a fixed point; that is, there is an $x \in A$ such that $x = f(x)$.

The logic of Brouwer's fixed point theorem is illustrated in Figure M.I.1(a) for the easy case where $N = 1$ and $A = [0, 1]$. In this case, the theorem says that the graph of any continuous function from the interval $[0, 1]$ into itself must cross the diagonal, and it is then a simple consequence of the *intermediate value theorem*. In

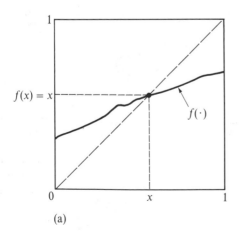

$f(x) = x$

$f(\cdot)$

$x$

(a)

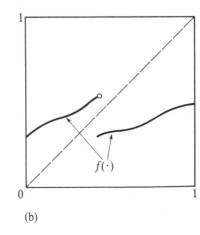

$f(\cdot)$

(b)

**Figure M.I.1**
Brouwer's fixed point
theorem.
(a) A continuous
function from $[0, 1]$ to
$[0, 1]$ has a fixed point.
(b) The continuity
assumption is
indispensable.

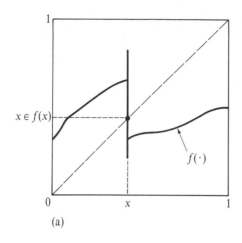

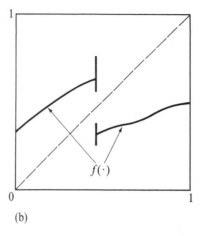

**Figure M.I.2**
Kakutani's fixed point theorem.
(a) A fixed point exists.
(b) The convex-valuedness assumption is indispensable.

particular, if we define the continuous function $\phi(x) = f(x) - x$, then $\phi(0) \geq 0$ and $\phi(1) \leq 0$, and so $\phi(x) = 0$ for some $x \in [0, 1]$; hence, $f(x) = x$ for some $x \in [0, 1]$. In Figure M.I.1(b) we can see that, indeed, the continuity of $f(\cdot)$ is required. As for the convexity of the domain, consider the function defined by a 90-degree clockwise rotation on the circle $S = \{x \in \mathbb{R}^2 : \|x\| = 1\}$: It is a continuous function with no fixed point. The set $S$, however, is not convex.

In applications, it is often the case that the following extension of Brouwer's fixed point theorem to correspondence is most useful.

**Theorem M.I.2:** (*Kakutani's Fixed Point Theorem*) Suppose that $A \subset \mathbb{R}^N$ is a nonempty, compact, convex set, and that $f: A \to A$ is an upper hemicontinuous correspondence from $A$ into itself with the property that the set $f(x) \subset A$ is nonempty and convex for every $x \in A$. Then $f(\cdot)$ has a fixed point; that is, there is an $x \in A$ such that $x \in f(x)$.

The logic of Kakutani's fixed point theorem is illustrated in Figure M.I.2(a) for $N = 1$. Note that the convexity of the set $f(x)$ for all $x$ is indispensable. Without this condition we could have cases such as that in Figure M.I.2(b) where no fixed point exists.

Finally, we mention a fixed point theorem that is of a different style but that is being found of increasing relevance to economic applications.

**Theorem M.I.3:** (*Tarsky's Fixed Point Theorem*) Suppose that $f: [0, 1]^N \to [0, 1]^N$ is a nondecreasing function, that is, $f(x') \geq f(x)$ whenever $x' \geq x$. Then $f(\cdot)$ has a fixed point; that is, there is an $x \in A$ such that $x = f(x)$.

Tarsky's theorem differs from Brouwer's in three respects. First, the base set is not any compact, convex set, but rather a special one—an $N$-product of intervals. Second, the function is required to be nondecreasing. Third, the function is not required to be continuous. The logic of Tarsky's fixed point theorem is illustrated in Figure M.I.3 for the case $N = 1$. In the figure, the function $f(\cdot)$ is not continuous. Yet, the fact that it is nondecreasing forces its graph to intersect the diagonal.

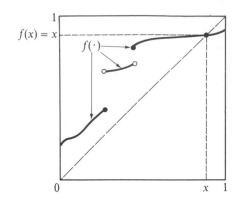

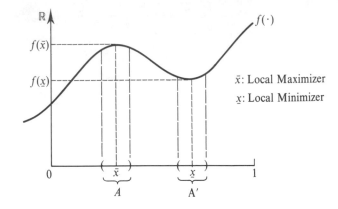

# M.J Unconstrained Maximization

**Figure M.I.3 (left)**
Tarski's fixed point theorem.

In this section we consider a function $f: \mathbb{R}^N \to \mathbb{R}$.

**Definition M.J.1:** The vector $\bar{x} \in \mathbb{R}^N$ is a *local maximizer* of $f(\cdot)$ if there is an open neighborhood of $\bar{x}$, $A \subset \mathbb{R}^N$, such that $f(\bar{x}) \geq f(x)$ for every $x \in A$.[20] If $f(\bar{x}) \geq f(x)$ for every $x \in \mathbb{R}^N$ (i.e., if we can take $A = \mathbb{R}^N$), then we say that $\bar{x}$ is a *global maximizer* of $f(\cdot)$ (or simply a *maximizer*). The concepts of *local* and *global minimizers* are defined analogously.

**Figure M.J.1 (right)**
Local maximizers and minimizers.

In Figure M.J.1, we illustrate a local maximizer $\bar{x}$ and a local minimizer $\underline{x}$ (with open neighborhoods $A$ and $A'$, respectively) of a function for the case in which $N = 1$.

**Theorem M.J.1:** Suppose that $f(\cdot)$ is differentiable and that $\bar{x} \in \mathbb{R}^N$ is a local maximizer or local minimizer of $f(\cdot)$. Then

$$\frac{\partial f(\bar{x})}{\partial x_n} = 0 \qquad \text{for every } n, \tag{M.J.1}$$

or, in more concise notation,

$$\nabla f(\bar{x}) = 0. \tag{M.J.2}$$

**Proof:** Suppose that $\bar{x}$ is a local maximizer or local minimizer of $f(\cdot)$ but that $df(\bar{x})/\partial x_n = a > 0$ (the argument is analogous if $a < 0$). Denote by $e^n \in \mathbb{R}^N$ the vector having its $n$th entry equal to 1 and all other entries equal to 0 (i.e., having $e_n^n = 1$ and $e_h^n = 0$ for $h \neq n$). By the definition of a (partial) derivative, this means that there is an $\varepsilon > 0$ arbitrarily small such that $[f(\bar{x} + \varepsilon e^n) - f(\bar{x})]/\varepsilon > a/2 > 0$ and $[f(\bar{x} - \varepsilon e^n) - f(\bar{x})]/\varepsilon < -a/2$. Thus, $f(\bar{x} - \varepsilon e^n) < f(\bar{x}) < f(\bar{x} + \varepsilon e^n)$. In words: The function $f(\cdot)$ is locally increasing around $\bar{x}$ in the direction of the $n$th coordinate axis. But then $\bar{x}$ can be neither a local maximizer nor a local minimizer of $f(\cdot)$. Contradiction. ∎

The conclusion of Theorem M.J.1 can be seen in Figure M.J.1: In the figure, we have $\partial f(\bar{x})/\partial x = 0$ and $\partial f(\underline{x})/\partial x = 0$.

A vector $\bar{x} \in \mathbb{R}^N$ such that $\nabla f(\bar{x}) = 0$ is called a *critical point*. By Theorem M.J.1, every local maximizer or local minimizer is a critical point. The converse, however,

---

20. An open neighborhood of $\bar{x}$ is an open set that includes $\bar{x}$.

does not hold. Consider for example, the function $f(x_1, x_2) = (x_1)^2 - (x_2)^2$ defined on $\mathbb{R}^2$. At the origin we have $\nabla f(0, 0) = (0, 0)$. Thus, the origin is a critical point, but it is neither a local maximizer nor a local minimizer of this function. To characterize local maximizers and local minimizers of $f(\cdot)$ more completely, we must look at second-order conditions.

**Theorem M.J.2:** Suppose that the function $f: \mathbb{R}^N \to \mathbb{R}$ is twice continuously differentiable and that $f(\bar{x}) = 0$.

   (i) If $\bar{x} \in \mathbb{R}^N$ is a local maximizer, then the (symmetric) $N \times N$ matrix $D^2 f(\bar{x})$ is negative semidefinite.
   (ii) If $D^2 f(\bar{x})$ is negative definite, then $\bar{x}$ is a local maximizer.

Replacing "negative" by "positive," the same is true for local minimizers.

**Proof:** The idea is as follows. For an arbitrary direction of displacement $z \in \mathbb{R}^N$ and scalar $\varepsilon$, a Taylor's expansion of the function $\phi(\varepsilon) = f(\bar{x} + \varepsilon z)$ around $\varepsilon = 0$ gives

$$f(\bar{x} + \varepsilon z) - f(\bar{x}) = \varepsilon \nabla f(\bar{x}) \cdot z + \tfrac{1}{2}\varepsilon^2 z \cdot D^2 f(\bar{x}) z + \text{Remainder}$$

$$= \tfrac{1}{2}\varepsilon^2 z \cdot D^2 f(\bar{x}) z + \text{Remainder},$$

where $\varepsilon \in \mathbb{R}_+$ and $(1/\varepsilon^2)$ Remainder is small if $\varepsilon$ is small. If $\bar{x}$ is a local maximizer, then for $\varepsilon$ small we must have $(1/\varepsilon^2)[f(\bar{x} + \varepsilon z) - f(\bar{x})] \leq 0$, and so taking limits we get

$$z \cdot D^2 f(\bar{x}) z \leq 0.$$

Similarly, if $z \cdot D^2 f(\bar{x}) z < 0$ for any $z \neq 0$, then $f(\bar{x} + \varepsilon z) < f(\bar{x})$ for $\varepsilon > 0$ small, and so $\bar{x}$ is a local maximizer. ∎

In the borderline case in which $D^2 f(\bar{x})$ is negative semidefinite but not negative definite, we cannot assert that $\bar{x}$ is a local maximizer. Consider, for example, the function $f(x) = x^3$ whose domain is $\mathbb{R}$. Then $D^2 f(0)$ is negative semidefinite because $d^2 f(0)/dx = 0$, but $\bar{x} = 0$ is neither a local maximizer nor a local minimizer of this function.

Finally, when is a local maximizer $\bar{x}$ of $f(\cdot)$ (or, more generally, a critical point) automatically a global maximizer? Theorem M.J.3 tells us that a sufficient condition is the concavity of the objective function $f(\cdot)$.

**Theorem M.J.3:** Any critical point $\bar{x}$ of a concave function $f(\cdot)$ [i.e., any $\bar{x}$ satisfying $\nabla f(\bar{x}) = 0$] is a global maximizer of $f(\cdot)$.

**Proof:** Recall from Theorem M.C.1 that for a concave function we have $f(x) \leq f(\bar{x}) + \nabla f(\bar{x}) \cdot (x - \bar{x})$ for every $x$ in the domain of the function. Since $\nabla f(\bar{x}) = 0$, this tells us that $\bar{x}$ is a global maximizer. ∎

By analogous reasoning, any critical point of a *convex* function $f(\cdot)$ is a global *minimizer* of $f(\cdot)$.[21]

---

21. In fact, this follows directly from Theorem M.J.3 because $\bar{x}$ is a global minimizer of $f(\cdot)$ if and only if it is a global maximizer of $-f(\cdot)$, and $-f(\cdot)$ is concave if and only if $f(\cdot)$ is convex.

# M.K Constrained Maximization

We start by considering the problem of maximizing a function $f(\cdot)$ under $M$ equality constraints. Namely, we study the problem

$$\underset{x \in \mathbb{R}^N}{\text{Max}} \quad f(x) \qquad\qquad\qquad (\text{M.K.1})$$

$$\text{s.t. } g_1(x) = \bar{b}_1$$

$$\vdots$$

$$g_M(x) = \bar{b}_M,$$

where the functions $f(\cdot), g_1(\cdot), \dots, g_M(\cdot)$ are defined on $\mathbb{R}^N$ (or, more generally, on an open set $A \subset \mathbb{R}^N$). We assume that $N \geq M$; if $M \geq N$ there will generally be no points satisfying all of the constraints.

The set of all $x \in \mathbb{R}^N$ satisfying the constraints of problem (M.K.1) is denoted

$$C = \{x \in \mathbb{R}^N : g_m(x) = \bar{b}_m \quad \text{for} \quad m = 1, \dots, M\}$$

and is called the *constraint set*. The definitions of a *local constrained* or a *global constrained maximizer* are parallel to those given in Definition M.J.1, except that we now consider only points $x$ that belong to the constraint set $C$. The feasible point $\bar{x} \in C$ is a *local constrained maximizer* in problem (M.K.1) if there exists an open neighborhood of $\bar{x}$, say $A \subset \mathbb{R}^N$, such that $f(\bar{x}) \geq f(x)$ for all $x \in A \cap C$, that is, if $\bar{x}$ solves problem (M.K.1) when we replace the condition $x \in \mathbb{R}^N$ by $x \in A$. The point $\bar{x}$ is a *global constrained maximizer* if it solves problem (M.K.1), that is, if $f(\bar{x}) \geq f(x)$ for all $x \in C$.

Our first result (Theorem M.K.1) states the first-order conditions for this constrained maximization problem.

**Theorem M.K.1:** Suppose that the objective and constraint functions of problem (M.K.1) are differentiable and that $\bar{x} \in C$ is a local constrained maximizer. Assume also that the $M \times N$ matrix

$$\begin{bmatrix} \dfrac{\partial g_1(\bar{x})}{\partial x_1} & \cdots & \dfrac{\partial g_1(\bar{x})}{\partial x_N} \\ & \ddots & \\ \dfrac{\partial g_M(\bar{x})}{\partial x_1} & \cdots & \dfrac{\partial g_M(\bar{x})}{\partial x_N} \end{bmatrix}$$

has rank $M$. (This is called the *constraint qualification*: It says that the constraints are independent at $\bar{x}$.) Then there are numbers $\lambda_m \in \mathbb{R}$, one for each constraint, such that

$$\frac{\partial f(\bar{x})}{\partial x_n} = \sum_{m=1}^{M} \lambda_m \frac{\partial g_m(\bar{x})}{\partial x_n} \qquad \text{for every } n = 1, \dots, N, \qquad (\text{M.K.2})$$

or, in more concise notation [letting $\lambda = (\lambda_1, \dots, \lambda_M)$],

$$\nabla f(\bar{x}) = \sum_{m=1}^{M} \lambda_m \nabla g_m(\bar{x}). \qquad\qquad (\text{M.K.3})$$

The numbers $\lambda_m$ are referred to as *Lagrange multipliers*.

**Proof:** The role of the constraint qualification is to insure that $\bar{x}$ is also a local maximizer in the linearized problem

$$\underset{x \in \mathbb{R}^N}{\text{Max}} \quad f(\bar{x}) + \nabla f(\bar{x}) \cdot (x - \bar{x})$$

$$\text{s.t. } \nabla g_1(\bar{x}) \cdot (x - \bar{x}) = 0$$

$$\vdots$$

$$\nabla g_M(\bar{x}) \cdot (x - \bar{x}) = 0,$$

in which the objective function and constraints have been linearized around the point $\bar{x}$. Thus, the constraint qualification guarantees the correctness of the following intuitively sensible statement: If $\bar{x}$ is a local constrained maximizer, then every direction of displacement $z \in \mathbb{R}^N$ having no first-order effect on the constraints, that is, satisfying $\nabla g_m(\bar{x}) \cdot z = 0$ for every $m$, must also have no first-order effect on the objective function, that is, must have $\nabla f(\bar{x}) \cdot z = 0$ (see also the discussion after the proof and Figure M.K.1). From now on we assume that this is true.

The rest is just a bit of linear algebra. Let $E$ be the $(M + 1) \times N$ matrix whose first row is $\nabla f(\bar{x})^T$ and whose last $M$ rows are the vectors $\nabla g_1(\bar{x})^T, \ldots, \nabla g_M(\bar{x})^T$. By the implication of the constraint qualification cited above, we have $\{z \in \mathbb{R}^N : \nabla g_m(\bar{x}) \cdot z = 0$ for all $m\} = \{z \in \mathbb{R}^N : Ez = 0\}$. Hence, these two linear spaces have the same dimension $M$. Therefore, by a basic result of linear algebra, rank $E = M$. Hence, $\nabla f(\bar{x})$ must be a linear combination of the linearly independent set of gradients $\nabla g_1(\bar{x}), \ldots, \nabla g_M(\bar{x})$. This is exactly what (M.K.3) says. ■

In words, Theorem M.K.1 asserts that, at a local constrained maximizer $\bar{x}$, the gradient of the objective function is a linear combination of the gradients of the constraint functions. The indispensability of the constraint qualification is illustrated in Figure M.K.1. In the figure, we wish to maximize a linear function $f(x_1, x_2)$ in the constraint set $C = \{(x_1, x_2) \in \mathbb{R}^2 : g_m(x_1, x_2) = \bar{b}_m$ for $m = 1, 2\}$ [the figure shows the loci of points satisfying $g_1(x_1, x_2) = \bar{b}_1$ and $g_2(x_1, x_2) = \bar{b}_2$, as well as the level sets of the function $f(\cdot)$]. While the point $\bar{x}$ is a global constrained maximum (it is the only vector in the constraint set!), we see that $\nabla f(\bar{x})$ is *not* spanned by the vectors $\nabla g_1(\bar{x})$ and $\nabla g_2(\bar{x})$ [i.e., it cannot be expressed as a linear combination of $\nabla g_1(\bar{x})$ and $\nabla g_2(\bar{x})$]. Note, however, that $\nabla g_1(\bar{x}) = -\nabla g_2(\bar{x})$, and so the constraint qualification

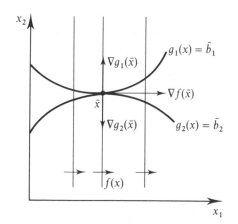

**Figure M.K.1**

Indispensability of the constraint qualification.

is violated. Observe that, indeed, $\bar{x}$ is *not* a local maximizer of $f(\bar{x}) + \nabla f(\bar{x}) \cdot (x - \bar{x})$ $[= f(x)$ since $f(\cdot)$ is linear] in the linearized constraint set

$$C' = \{(x_1, x_2) \in \mathbb{R}^2 : \nabla g_m(\bar{x}) \cdot (x - \bar{x}) = 0 \quad \text{for} \quad m = 1, 2\}.$$

Often the first-order conditions (M.K.2) or (M.K.3) are presented in a slightly different way. Given variables $x = (x_1, \ldots, x_N)$ and $\lambda = (\lambda_1, \ldots, \lambda_N)$, we can define the *Lagrangian function*

$$L(x, \lambda) = f(x) - \sum_m \lambda_m g_m(x).$$

Note that conditions (M.K.2) [or (M.K.3)] are the (unconstrained) first-order conditions of this function with respect to the variables $x = (x_1, \ldots, x_N)$. Similarly, the constraints $g(x) = 0$ are the first-order conditions of $L(\cdot, \cdot)$ with respect to the variables $\lambda = (\lambda_1, \ldots, \lambda_M)$. In summary, Theorem M.K.1 says that if $\bar{x}$ is a local constrained maximizer (and if the constraint qualification is satisfied), then for some values $\lambda_1, \ldots, \lambda_M$ all of the partial derivatives of the Lagrangian function are null; that is, $\partial L(\bar{x}, \lambda)/\partial x_n = 0$ for $n = 1, \ldots, N$ and $\partial L(\bar{x}, \lambda)/\partial \lambda_m = 0$ for $m = 1, \ldots, M$.

Theorem M.K.1 implies that if $\bar{x}$ is a local maximizer in problem (M.K.1), then the $N + M$ variables $(\bar{x}_1, \ldots, \bar{x}_N, \lambda_1, \ldots, \lambda_M)$ are a solution to the $N + M$ equations formed by (M.K.2) and $g_m(\bar{x}) = \bar{b}_m$ for $m = 1, \ldots, M$.

There is also a second-order theory associated with problem (M.K.1). Suppose that at $\bar{x}$ the constraint qualification is satisfied and that there are Lagrange multipliers satisfying (M.K.3). If $\bar{x}$ is a local maximizer, then

$$D_x^2 L(\bar{x}, \lambda) = D^2 f(\bar{x}) - \sum_m \lambda_m \nabla g_m(\bar{x})$$

is negative semidefinite on the subspace $\{z \in \mathbb{R}^N : \nabla g_m(\bar{x}) \cdot z = 0 \text{ for all } m\}$. In the other direction, if the vector $\bar{x}$ is feasible (i.e., $\bar{x} \in C$) and satisfies the first-order conditions (M.K.2), and if $D_x^2 L(\bar{x}, \lambda)$ is negative definite on the subspace $\{z \in \mathbb{R}^N : \nabla g_m(\bar{x}) \cdot z = 0$ for all $m\}$, then $\bar{x}$ is a local maximizer. These conditions can be verified using the determinantal tests provided in Theorem M.D.3.

Finally, note that a local constrained minimizer of $f(\cdot)$ is a local constrained maximizer of $-f(\cdot)$, and therefore Theorem M.K.1 and our discussion of second-order conditions above is also applicable to the characterization of local constrained minimizers.

## Inequality Constraints

We now generalize our analysis to problems that may have inequality constraints. The basic problem is therefore now

$$
\begin{aligned}
\underset{x \in \mathbb{R}^N}{\text{Max}} \quad & f(x) && \text{(M.K.4)} \\
\text{s.t.} \quad & g_1(x) = \bar{b}_1 \\
& \quad\vdots \\
& g_M(x) = \bar{b}_M \\
& h_1(x) \leq \bar{c}_1 \\
& \quad\vdots \\
& h_K(x) \leq \bar{c}_K,
\end{aligned}
$$

where every function is defined on $\mathbb{R}^N$ (or an open set $A \subset \mathbb{R}^N$). We assume that $N \geq M + K$. It is of course possible to have $M = 0$ (no equality constraints) or $K = 0$ (no inequality constraints).

We again denote the constraint set by $C \subset \mathbb{R}^N$, and the meaning of a local constrained maximizer or a global constrained maximizer is unaltered from above.

We now say that the constraint qualification is satisfied at $\bar{x} \in C$ if the constraints *that hold at $\bar{x}$ with equality* are independent; that is, if the vectors in $\{\nabla g_m(\bar{x}) : m = 1, \ldots, M\} \cup \{\nabla h_k(\bar{x}) : h_k(\bar{x}) = \bar{c}_k\}$ are linearly independent.

Theorem M.K.2 presents the first-order conditions for this problem. All of the functions involved are assumed to be differentiable.

**Theorem M.K.2:** (*Kuhn–Tucker Conditions*)  Suppose that $\bar{x} \in C$ is a local maximizer of problem (M.K.4). Assume also that the constraint qualification is satisfied. Then there are multipliers $\lambda_m \in \mathbb{R}$, one for each equality constraint, and $\lambda_k \in \mathbb{R}_+$, one for each inequality constraint, such that:[22]

(i) For every $n = 1, \ldots, N$,

$$\frac{\partial f(\bar{x})}{\partial x_n} = \sum_{m=1}^{M} \lambda_m \frac{\partial g_m(\bar{x})}{\partial x_n} + \sum_{k=1}^{K} \lambda_k \frac{\partial h_k(\bar{x})}{\partial x_n}, \tag{M.K.5}$$

or, in more concise notation,

$$\nabla f(\bar{x}) = \sum_{m=1}^{M} \lambda_m \nabla g_m(\bar{x}) + \sum_{k=1}^{K} \lambda_k \nabla h_k(\bar{x}). \tag{M.K.6}$$

(ii) For every $k = 1, \ldots, K$,

$$\lambda_k(h_k(\bar{x}) - \bar{c}_k) = 0, \tag{M.K.7}$$

i.e., $\lambda_k = 0$ for any constraint $k$ that does not hold with equality.

**Proof:**  We illustrate the proof of the result for the case in which there are only inequality constraints (i.e., $M = 0$).

As with the case of equality constraints, the role of the constraint qualification is to insure that $\bar{x}$ remains a local maximizer in the problem linearized around $\bar{x}$. More specifically, we assume from now on that the following is true: Any direction of displacement $z \in \mathbb{R}^N$ that satisfies the constraints to first order [i.e., such that $\nabla h_k(\bar{x}) \cdot z \leq 0$ for every $k$ with $h_k(\bar{x}) = \bar{c}_k$] must not create a first-order increase in the objective function, that is, must have $\nabla f(\bar{x}) \cdot z \leq 0$.

In Figure M.K.2 we represent a problem with two variables and two constraints for which the logic of the result is illustrated and made plausible. The Kuhn–Tucker theorem says that if $\bar{x}$ is a local maximizer then $\nabla f(\bar{x})$ must be in the cone

$$\Gamma = \{y \in \mathbb{R}^2 : y = \lambda_1 \nabla h_1(\bar{x}) + \lambda_2 \nabla h_2(\bar{x}) \quad \text{for some} \quad (\lambda_1, \lambda_2) \geq 0\}$$

depicted in the figure; that is, $\nabla f(\bar{x})$ must be a nonnegative linear combination of $\nabla h_1(\bar{x})$ and $\nabla h_2(\bar{x})$. Suppose now that $\bar{x}$ is a local maximizer. If starting from $\bar{x}$ we move along the boundary of the constraint set to any point $(\bar{x}_1 + z_1, \bar{x}_2 + z_2)$ with $z_1 < 0$ and $z_2 > 0$, then in the situation depicted we would have

$$h_1(\bar{x}_1 + z_1, \bar{x}_2 + z_2) = \bar{c}_1, \qquad h_2(\bar{x}_1 + z_1, \bar{x}_2 + z_2) < \bar{c}_2,$$

---

22. By convention, if there are no constraints (i.e., if $M = K = 0$), then the right-hand side of (M.K.5) is zero.

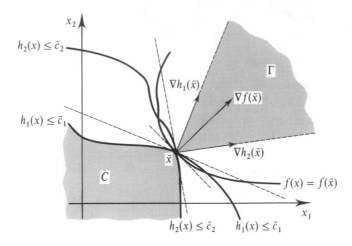

**Figure M.K.2**

Necessity of the Kuhn–Tucker conditions.

and $f(\bar{x}_1 + z_1, \bar{x}_2 + z_2) \leq f(\bar{x})$. Taking limits we conclude that in the direction $z$ such that $\nabla h_1(\bar{x}) \cdot z = 0$ and $\nabla h_2(\bar{x}) \cdot z < 0$, we have $\nabla f(\bar{x}) \cdot z \leq 0$. Geometrically this means that the vector $\nabla f(\bar{x})$ must lie below the vector $\nabla h_1(\bar{x})$, as is shown in the figure. By similar reasoning (moving along the boundary of the constraint set $C$ in the opposite direction), if $\bar{x}$ is a local constrained maximizer the vector $\nabla f(\bar{x})$ must lie above the vector $\nabla h_2(\bar{x})$. Hence, $\nabla f(\bar{x})$ must lie in the cone $\Gamma$. This is precisely what the Kuhn–Tucker conditions require in this case.

The above intuition can be extended to the general case. Suppose that all the constraints are binding at $\bar{x}$ (if a constraint $k$ is not binding, put $\lambda_k = 0$ and drop it from the list). We must show that $\nabla f(\bar{x})$ belongs to the convex cone

$$\Gamma = \left\{ y \in \mathbb{R}^N : y = \sum_k \lambda_k \nabla h_k(\bar{x}) \quad \text{for some} \quad (\lambda_1, \ldots, \lambda_K) \geq 0 \right\} \subset \mathbb{R}^N.$$

Assume for a moment that this is not so, that is, that $\nabla f(\bar{x}) \notin \Gamma$. Then, by the separating hyperplane theorem (Theorem M.G.2), there exists a nonzero vector $z \in \mathbb{R}^N$ and a number $\beta \in \mathbb{R}$ such that $\nabla f(\bar{x}) \cdot z > \beta$ and $y \cdot z < \beta$ for every $y \in \Gamma$. Since $0 \in \Gamma$ we must have $\beta > 0$. Hence, $\nabla f(\bar{x}) \cdot z > 0$. Also, for any $y \in \Gamma$ we have $\theta y \in \Gamma$ for all $\theta \geq 0$. But then $\theta y \cdot z < \beta$ can hold for all $\theta$ (arbitrarily large) only if $y \cdot z \leq 0$. We conclude therefore that $\nabla f(\bar{x}) \cdot z > 0$ and $\nabla h_k(\bar{x}) \cdot z \leq 0$ for all $k$, which contradicts the linearization implication of the constraint qualification. ∎

It is common in applications that a constraint takes the form of a nonnegativity requirement on some variable $x_n$; that is, $x_n \geq 0$. In this case, the appropriate first-order conditions require only a small modification of those above. In particular, we need only change the first-order condition for $x_n$ to

$$\frac{\partial f(\bar{x})}{\partial x_n} \leq \sum_{m=1}^M \lambda_m \frac{\partial g_m(\bar{x})}{\partial x_n} + \sum_{k=1}^K \lambda_k \frac{\partial h_m(\bar{x})}{\partial x_n}, \quad \text{with equality if } \bar{x}_n > 0. \quad \text{(M.K.8)}$$

To see why this is so, suppose that we explicitly introduced this nonnegativity requirement as our $(K + 1)$th inequality constraint [i.e., $h_{K+1}(x) = -x_n \leq 0$] and let $\lambda_{K+1} \geq 0$ be the corresponding multiplier. Note that $\lambda_{K+1}(\partial h_{K+1}(\bar{x})/\partial x_n) = -\lambda_{K+1}$ and $\partial h_{K+1}(\bar{x})/\partial x_{n'} = 0$ for $n' \neq n$. Thus, if we apply condition (M.K.5) of Theorem M.K.2, the only modification to the first-order conditions is that the first-order condition for $x_n$ is now

$$\frac{\partial f(\bar{x})}{\partial x_n} = \sum_{m=1}^{M} \lambda_m \frac{\partial g_m(\bar{x})}{\partial x_n} + \sum_{k=1}^{K} \lambda_k \frac{\partial h_m(\bar{x})}{\partial x_n} - \lambda_{K+1},$$

and we have the added condition that

$$-\lambda_{K+1} x_n = 0.$$

But these two conditions are exactly equivalent to condition (M.K.8). Given the simplicity of the adjustment required to take account of nonnegativity constraints, it is customary in applications not to explicitly introduce the nonnegativity constraint and its associated multiplier, but rather simply to modify the usual first-order conditions as in (M.K.8).

Note also that any constraint of the form $h_k(x) \geq \bar{c}_k$ can be written as $-h_k(x) \leq -\bar{c}_k$. Using this fact, we see that Theorem M.K.2 extends to constraints of the form $h_k(x) \geq \bar{c}_k$. The only modification is that the sign restriction on the multiplier of constraint $k$ is now $\lambda_k \leq 0$. Similarly, because minimizing the function $f(\cdot)$ is equivalent to maximizing the function $-f(\cdot)$, Theorem M.K.2 applies also to local minimizers, with the only change being that the sign restriction on all of the multipliers is now $(\lambda_1, \ldots, \lambda_M) \leq 0$ [assuming that the constraints are all still written as in problem (M.K.4)].

The second-order conditions for the inequality problem (M.K.4) are exactly the same as those already mentioned for the equality problem (M.K.1). The only adjustment is that the constraints that count are those that bind, that is, those that hold with equality at the point $\bar{x}$ under consideration.

Suppose that a vector $x \in C$ satisfies the Kuhn–Tucker conditions, that is, conditions (i) and (ii) in Theorem M.K.2. When can we say that $x$ is a global maximizer? Theorem M.K.3 gives a useful set of conditions.

**Theorem M.K.3:** Suppose that there are no equality constraints (i.e., $M = 0$) and that every inequality constraint $k$ is given by a quasiconvex function $h_k(\cdot)$.[23] Suppose also that the objective function satisfies

$$\nabla f(x) \cdot (x' - x) > 0 \qquad \text{for any } x \text{ and } x' \text{ with } f(x') > f(x). \qquad \text{(M.K.9)}$$

Then if $\bar{x} \in C$ satisfies the Kuhn–Tucker conditions [conditions (i) and (ii) of Theorem M.K.2], and if the constraint qualification holds at $\bar{x}$, it follows that $\bar{x}$ is a global maximizer.[24]

**Proof:** Suppose that this is not so, that is, that $f(x) > f(\bar{x})$ for some $x \in \mathbb{R}^N$ satisfying $h_k(x) \leq \bar{c}_k$ for every $k$. Denote $z = x - \bar{x}$. Then, by (M.K.9) we have $\nabla f(\bar{x}) \cdot z > 0$. If $\lambda_k > 0$, then the Kuhn–Tucker conditions imply that $h_k(\bar{x}) = \bar{c}_k$. Moreover, since $h_k(\cdot)$ is quasiconvex and $h_k(x) \leq \bar{c}_k = h_k(\bar{x})$, it follows that $\nabla h_k(\bar{x}) \cdot z \leq 0$. Hence, we have both $\nabla f(\bar{x}) \cdot z > 0$ and $\sum_k \lambda_k \nabla h_k(\bar{x}) \cdot z \leq 0$, which contradicts the Kuhn–Tucker conditions because these require that $\nabla f(\bar{x}) = \sum_k \lambda_k \nabla h_k(\bar{x})$. ∎

---

23. More generally, equality constraints are permissible if they are linear.

24. If instead we have $\nabla f(x) \cdot (x' - x) < 0$ whenever $f(x') < f(x)$ and the multipliers have the nonpositive sign that corresponds to a minimization problem, then $\bar{x}$ is a global minimizer.

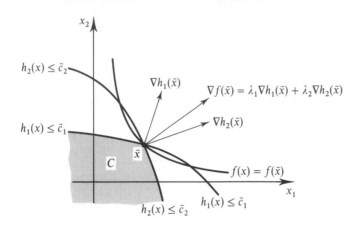

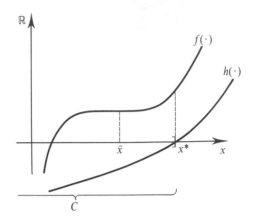

Note that condition (M.K.9) of Theorem M.K.3 is satisfied if $f(\cdot)$ is concave or if $f(\cdot)$ is quasiconcave and $\nabla f(x) \neq 0$ for all $x \in \mathbb{R}^N$. The condition that the constraint functions $h_1(\cdot), \ldots, h_K(\cdot)$ are quasiconvex implies that the constraint set $C$ is convex (check this).[25] In Figure M.K.3, we illustrate the theorem for a case in which $N = K = 2$, $M = 0$, and $f(\cdot)$ is a quasiconcave function with $\nabla f(x) \neq 0$ for all $x$.

The indispensability of condition (M.K.9) in Theorem M.K.3 is shown in Figure M.K.4. There we have $N = M = 1$, and the quasiconcave function $f(\cdot)$ is being maximized on the constraint set $C = \{x \in \mathbb{R} : h(x) \leq 0\}$. In the figure, the point $\bar{x}$ satisfies the Kuhn–Tucker conditions for a multiplier value of $\lambda = 0$, but $\bar{x}$ is not a global maximizer of $f(\cdot)$ on $C$ (the point $x^*$ is the global constrained maximizer). Note, however, that condition (M.K.10) is violated when $x = \bar{x}$ and $x' = x^*$.

We observe finally in Theorem M.K.4 an important implication of the constraint set $C$ being convex and the objective function $f(\cdot)$ being strictly quasiconcave.

**Figure M.K.3 (left)**

With quasiconvex constraint functions and a quasiconcave objective function satisfying $\nabla f(x) \neq 0$ for all $x$, satisfaction of the Kuhn–Tucker conditions at $\bar{x}$ implies that $\bar{x}$ is a global constrained maximizer.

**Figure M.K.4 (right)**

The necessity of condition (M.K.10) for Theorem M.K.3.

**Theorem M.K.4:** Suppose that in problem (M.K.4) the constraint set $C$ is convex and the objective function $f(\cdot)$ is strictly quasiconcave. Then there is a unique global constrained maximizer.[26]

**Proof:** If $x$ and $x' \neq x$ were both global constrained maximizers, then the point $x'' = \alpha x + (1 - \alpha)x'$ for $\alpha \in (0, 1)$ would be feasible (i.e., $x'' \in C$) and by the strict quasiconcavity of $f(\cdot)$, would yield a higher value of $f(\cdot)$ [i.e., $f(x'') > f(x) = f(x')$]. ∎

Suppose that in the case in which only inequality constraints are present we denote by $C_{-k}$ the relaxed constraint set arising when the $k$th inequality constraint is dropped. The following two facts are often useful in applications.

(i) If $f(\bar{x}) \geq f(x)$ for all $x \in C_{-k}$ and if $h_k(\bar{x}) \leq \bar{c}_k$, then $\bar{x}$ is a global constrained maximizer in problem (M.K.4). That is, if we solve a constrained optimization problem ignoring a constraint, and the solution we obtain satisfies this omitted constraint as well, then it must be a solution to the fully constrained problem. This follows simply from the fact that $C \subset C_{-k}$, and so optimizing $f(\cdot)$ on $C$ can at best yield the same value of $f(\cdot)$ as optimizing it on $C_{-k}$.

25. Also, under the conditions of the theorem, a sufficient constraint qualification is that the constraint set $C$ should have a nonempty interior.

26. When $f(\cdot)$ is quasiconcave, but not strictly so, a similar argument allows us to conclude that the set of maximizers is convex.

(ii) Suppose that all of the constraint functions $h_1(\cdot), \ldots, h_K(\cdot)$ are continuous and quasiconvex and that condition (M.K.9) holds. Then if $\bar{x}$ is a solution to problem (M.K.4) in which the $k$th constraint is not binding [i.e., if $h_k(\bar{x}) < \bar{c}_k$], we have $f(\bar{x}) \geq f(x)$ for all $x \in C_{-k}$. That is, under the stated assumptions, if a constraint is not binding at a solution to problem (M.K.4), then ignoring it altogether should have no effect on the solution. To see this, suppose otherwise; i.e., that there is an $x' \in C_{-k}$ such that $f(x') > f(\bar{x})$. Then because the constraint functions $h_1(\cdot), \ldots, h_K(\cdot)$ are quasiconvex, we know that the point $x(\alpha) = \alpha x' + (1 - \alpha)\bar{x}$ is an element of $C_{-k}$ for all $\alpha \in [0, 1]$. Moreover, since the $k$th constraint is not binding at $\bar{x}$, there is an $\bar{\alpha} > 0$ such that $h_k(x(\alpha)) < \bar{c}_k$ for all $\alpha < \bar{\alpha}$. Hence, $x(\alpha) \in C$ for all $\alpha < \bar{\alpha}$. But the derivative of $f(x(\alpha))$ at $\alpha = 0$ is $\nabla f(x) \cdot (x' - \bar{x}) > 0$ [recall that condition (M.K.9) holds and that, by assumption $f(x') > f(\bar{x})$]. Therefore, there must be a point $x(\alpha) \in C$ such that $f(x(\alpha)) > f(\bar{x})$—a contradiction to $\bar{x}$ being a global constrained maximizer in problem (M.K.4).

## Comparative Statics

In our previous discussion we have treated the parameters $\bar{b} = (\bar{b}_1, \ldots, \bar{b}_M)$ and $\bar{c} = (\bar{c}_1, \ldots, \bar{c}_K)$ of problem M.K.4 as given. We will now let them vary.

Suppose that $(b, c) \in \mathbb{R}^{M+K}$ are parameters for which problem (M.K.4) has some solution $\bar{x}(b, c)$ and denote the value of this solution by $v(b, c) = f(\bar{x}(b, c))$. Under fairly general conditions (see the small type at the end of this section), the value $v(b, c)$ depends continuously on the parameters $(b, c)$.

Theorem M.K.5 provides an interpretation for the Lagrange multipliers as the "shadow prices" of the constraints.

**Theorem M.K.5:** Suppose that in an open neighborhood of $(\bar{b}, \bar{c})$ the set of binding constraints remains unaltered and that $v(b, c)$ is differentiable at $(\bar{b}, \bar{c})$.[27] Then for every $m = 1, \ldots, M$ and $k = 1, \ldots, K$ we have

$$\frac{\partial v(\bar{b}, \bar{c})}{\partial b_m} = \lambda_m \qquad \text{and} \qquad \frac{\partial v(\bar{b}, \bar{c})}{\partial c_k} = \lambda_k.$$

**Proof:** This is a particular case of the envelope theorem (Theorem M.L.1) to be presented in the next section. ∎

Consider a more general optimization problem. We maximize a function $f: \mathbb{R}^N \to \mathbb{R}$ subject to $x \in C(q)$ where $C(q)$ is a nonempty constraint set and $q = (q, \ldots, q_S)$ belongs to an admissible set of parameters $Q \subset \mathbb{R}^S$. Suppose that $f(\cdot)$ is continuous and that $C(q)$ is compact for every $q \in Q$. Then we know [from Theorem M.F.2, part (ii)] that the maximum problem has at least one solution. Denote by $x(q) \subset C(q)$ the *set* of solutions corresponding to $q$ and by $v(q)$ [$= f(x)$ for any $x \in x(q)$] the associated maximum value. Theorem M.K.6 concerns the continuity of $x(\cdot)$ and $v(\cdot)$.

**Theorem M.K.6:** (*Theorem of the Maximum*) Suppose that the constraint correspondence $C: Q \to \mathbb{R}^N$ is continuous (see Section M.H) and that $f(\cdot)$ is a continuous function. Then the maximizer correspondence $x: Q \to \mathbb{R}^N$ is upper hemicontinuous and the value function $v: Q \to \mathbb{R}$ is continuous.

---

27. These are simplifying assumptions; a similar result holds more generally but requires the use of directional derivatives at points of nondifferentiability of the function $v(\cdot, \cdot)$.

The result cannot be improved upon. Suppose that we maximize $x_1 + x_2$ subject to $x_1 \in [0, 1]$, $x_2 \in [0, 1]$, and $q_1 x_1 + q_2 x_2 \leq q_1 q_2$ for $q = (q_1, q_2) \in Q = (0, 1)^2$. Then the maximizer correspondence is given by

$$x(q) = \{(q_2, 0)\} \qquad \text{if } q_1 < q_2,$$
$$x(q) = \{(0, q_1)\} \qquad \text{if } q_2 < q_1,$$

and

$$x(q) = \{(x_1, x_2) \in [0, 1]^2 : x_1 + x_2 = q_1\} \qquad \text{if } q_1 = q_2.$$

Both the objective function and the constraint correspondence are continuous (you should check the latter). In accordance with Theorem M.K.6, $x(\cdot)$ is upper hemicontinuous. But it is not continuous (there is an explosion along the line $q_1 = q_2$). On the other hand, suppose that we take $Q = [0, 1]^2$. Then the conclusion of the theorem fails: the maximizer correspondence is not upper hemicontinuous [we have $x(2\varepsilon, \varepsilon) = \{(0, 2\varepsilon)\}$, but $x(0, 0) = \{(1, 1)\}$]. However, the assumptions also fail: at $q = (0, 0)$ the vector $(1, 1)$ belongs to the constraint set, but at $q = (\varepsilon, \varepsilon)$ no vector $x$ with $x_1 + x_2 > \varepsilon$ belongs to the constraint set. Hence the constraint correspondence is not continuous once extended to $Q = [0, 1]^2$.

# M.L  The Envelope Theorem

In this section, we return to the problem of maximizing a function $f(\cdot)$ under constraints, but we suppose that we want to keep track of some parameters $q = (q_1, \ldots, q_S) \in \mathbb{R}^S$ entering the objective function or the constraints of the problem. In particular, we now write the maximization problem as

$$\underset{x \in \mathbb{R}^N}{\text{Max}} \quad f(x; q) \qquad \qquad \text{(M.L.1)}$$

$$\text{s.t. } g_1(x; q) = \bar{b}_1$$
$$\vdots$$
$$g_M(x; q) = \bar{b}_M.$$

We denote by $v(\cdot)$ the *value function* of problem (M.L.1); that is, $v(q)$ is the value attained by $f(\cdot)$ at a solution to problem (M.L.1) when the parameter vector is $q$. To be specific, we suppose that $v(q)$ is well-defined in the neighborhood of some reference parameter vector $\bar{q} \in \mathbb{R}^S$. It is then natural to investigate the marginal effects of changes in $q$ on the value $v(q)$. The *envelope theorem* addresses this matter.[28]

It will be convenient from now on to assume that, at least locally (i.e., for values of $q$ close to $\bar{q}$), the solution to problem (M.L.1) is a (differentiable) function $x(q)$. We can then write $v(q) = f(x(q); q)$.

To start with the simplest case, suppose that there is a single variable and a single parameter (i.e., $N = K = 1$) and that there are no constraints (i.e., $M = 0$). Then, by the chain rule,

$$\frac{dv(\bar{q})}{dq} = \frac{\partial f(x(\bar{q}); \bar{q})}{\partial q} + \frac{\partial f(x(\bar{q}); \bar{q})}{\partial x} \frac{dx(\bar{q})}{dq}. \qquad \text{(M.L.2)}$$

---

28. Formally, we are presenting a case with equality constraints. But note that as long as in a neighborhood of the parameter vector under consideration the set of binding constraints does not change, the discussion applies automatically to the case with inequality constraints.

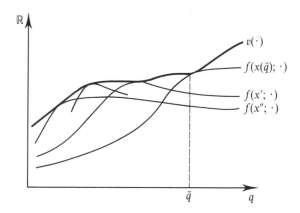

But note, and this is a key observation, that by the first-order conditions for unconstrained maximization (see Section M.J), we must have $\partial f(x(\bar{q}); \bar{q})/\partial x = 0$. Therefore, (M.L.2) simplifies to

$$\frac{dv(\bar{q})}{dq} = \frac{\partial f(x(\bar{q}), \bar{q})}{\partial q}. \tag{M.L.3}$$

That is, the fact that $x(q)$ is determined by maximizing the function $f(\cdot\,; q)$ has the implication that in computing the first-order effects of changes in $q$ on the maximum value, we can equally well assume that the maximizer will not adjust: The only effect of any consequence is the direct effect.

This result is illustrated in Figure M.L.1, which also motivates the use of the term "envelope." In the figure we represent the function $f(x;\,\cdot)$ for different values of $x$. Because at every $q$ we have $v(q) = \text{Max}_x\, f(x; q)$, the value function $v(\cdot)$ is given by the upper envelope of these functions. Suppose now that we consider a fixed $\bar{q}$. Then, denoting $\bar{x} = x(\bar{q})$, we have $f(\bar{x}; q) \leq v(q)$ for all $q$, and $f(\bar{x}; \bar{q}) = v(\bar{q})$. Hence, the graph of $f(\bar{x};\,\cdot)$ lies weakly below the graph of $v(\cdot)$ and touches it when $q = \bar{q}$. So the two graphs have the same slope at that point. This is precisely what condition (M.L.3) says.

We now state the general envelope theorem for a problem with any number of variables, parameters, and constraints. As we will see, its conclusion is similar to (M.L.3), except that Lagrange multipliers play an important role.

**Theorem M.L.1:** (*Envelope Theorem*) Consider the value function $v(q)$ for the problem (M.L.1). Assume that it is differentiable at $\bar{q} \in \mathbb{R}^S$ and that $(\lambda_1, \ldots, \lambda_M)$ are values of the Lagrange multipliers associated with the maximizer solution $x(\bar{q})$ at $\bar{q}$. Then[29]

$$\frac{\partial v(\bar{q})}{\partial q_s} = \frac{\partial f(x(\bar{q}); \bar{q})}{\partial q_s} - \sum_{m=1}^{M} \lambda_m \frac{\partial g_m(x(\bar{q}); \bar{q})}{\partial q_s} \qquad \text{for } s = 1, \ldots, S, \tag{M.L.4}$$

---

29. If we have a case with inequality constraints in which the set of binding constraints remains unaltered in a neighborhood of $\bar{q}$, then expressions (M.L.4) and (M.L.5) are still valid: Accounting for the nonbinding constraints will have no effect either on the left-hand side or on the right-hand side (because its associated multipliers are zero).

or, in matrix notation,

$$\nabla v(\bar{q}) = \nabla_q f(x(\bar{q}); \bar{q}) - \sum_{m=1}^{M} \lambda_m \nabla_q g_m(x(\bar{q}); \bar{q}). \qquad \text{(M.L.5)}$$

**Proof:** We proceed as in the case of a single variable and no constraints. Let $x(\cdot)$ be the maximizer function. Then $v(q) = f(x(q); q)$ for all $q$, and therefore, using the chain rule, we have

$$\frac{\partial v(\bar{q})}{\partial q_s} = \frac{\partial f(x(\bar{q}); \bar{q})}{\partial q_s} + \sum_{n=1}^{N} \left( \frac{\partial f(x(\bar{q}); \bar{q})}{\partial x_n} \frac{\partial x_n(\bar{q})}{\partial q_s} \right).$$

The first-order conditions (M.K.2) tell us that

$$\frac{\partial f(x(\bar{q}); \bar{q})}{\partial x_n} + \sum_{m=1}^{M} \lambda_m \frac{\partial g_m(x(\bar{q}); \bar{q})}{\partial x_n}.$$

Hence (switching the order of summation as we go),

$$\frac{\partial v(\bar{q})}{\partial q_s} = \frac{\partial f(x(\bar{q}); \bar{q})}{\partial q_s} + \sum_{m=1}^{M} \lambda_m \sum_{n=1}^{N} \left( \frac{\partial g_m(x(\bar{q}); \bar{q})}{\partial x_n} \frac{\partial x_n(\bar{q})}{\partial q_s} \right).$$

Moreover, since $g_m(x(q); q) = \bar{b}_m$ for all $q$, we have

$$\sum_{n=1}^{N} \left( \frac{\partial g_m(x(\bar{q}); \bar{q})}{\partial x_n} \frac{\partial x_n(\bar{q})}{\partial q_s} \right) = -\frac{\partial g_m(\bar{x}; \bar{q})}{\partial q_s} \qquad \text{for all } m = 1, \ldots, M.$$

Combining, we get (M.L.4). ∎

# M.M Linear Programming

Linear programming problems constitute the special cases of constrained maximization problems for which both the constraints and the objective function are linear in the variables $(x_1, \ldots, x_N)$.

A general linear programming problem is typically written in the form

$$\underset{(x_1, \ldots, x_N) \geq 0}{\text{Max}} \quad f_1 x_1 + \cdots + f_N x_N \qquad \text{(M.M.1)}$$

$$\text{s.t. } a_{11} x_1 + \cdots + a_{1N} x_N \leq c_1$$

$$\vdots$$

$$a_{K1} x_1 + \cdots + a_{KN} x_N \leq c_K,$$

or, in matrix notation,

$$\underset{x \in \mathbb{R}^N}{\text{Max}} \quad f \cdot x$$

$$\text{s.t. } Ax \leq c,$$

where $A$ is the $K \times N$ matrix with generic entry $a_{kn}$, and $f \in \mathbb{R}^N$, $x \in \mathbb{R}^N$, and $c \in \mathbb{R}^K$ are (column) vectors.[30]

---

30. We say that this is the general form of the linear programming problem because, first, an equality constraint $a \cdot x = b$ can always be expressed as two inequality constraints ($a \cdot x \leq b$ and $-a \cdot x \geq b$) and, second, a variable $x_n$ that is unrestricted in sign can always be replaced by the difference of two variables ($x_{n+} - x_{n-}$), each restricted to be nonnegative.

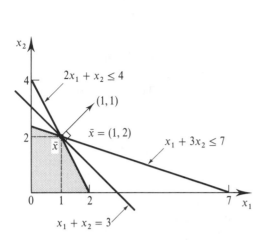

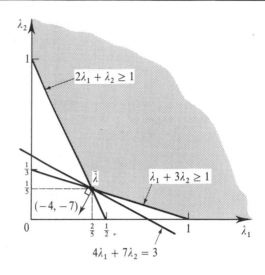

Figure M.M.1 represents a linear programming problem with $N = 2$, the two constraints $2x_1 + x_2 \leq 4$ and $x_1 + 3x_2 \leq 7$, and the objective function $x_1 + x_2$.

A most interesting fact about the linear programming problem (M.M.1) is that with it we can associate another linear programming problem, called the *dual* problem, that has the form of a minimization problem with $K$ variables (one for each constraint of the original, or *primal*, problem) and $N$ constraints (one for each variable of the primal problem):

**Figure M.M.1 (left)**

A linear programming problem (the primal).

**Figure M.M.2 (right)**

A linear programming problem (the dual).

$$\underset{(\lambda_1,\ldots,\lambda_K) \geq 0}{\text{Min}} \quad c_1\lambda_1 + \cdots + c_K\lambda_K \qquad \text{(M.M.2)}$$

$$\text{s.t. } a_{11}\lambda_1 + \cdots + a_{K1}\lambda_K \geq f_1$$
$$\vdots$$
$$a_{1N}\lambda_1 + \cdots + a_{KN}\lambda_K \geq f_N,$$

or, in matrix notation,

$$\underset{\lambda \in \mathbb{R}^K_+}{\text{Max}} \quad c \cdot \lambda$$

$$\text{s.t. } A^{\mathrm{T}}\lambda \geq f,$$

where $\lambda \in \mathbb{R}^K$ is a column vector.

Figure M.M.2 represents the dual problem associated with Figure M.M.1. The constraints are now $2\lambda_1 + \lambda_2 \geq 1$ and $\lambda_1 + 3\lambda_2 \geq 1$, and the objective function is now $4\lambda_1 + 7\lambda_2$.

Suppose that $x \in \mathbb{R}^N_+$ and $\lambda \in \mathbb{R}^K_+$ satisfy, respectively, the constraints of the primal and the dual problems. Then

$$f \cdot x \leq (A^{\mathrm{T}}\lambda) \cdot x = \lambda \cdot (Ax) \leq \lambda \cdot c = c \cdot \lambda. \qquad \text{(M.M.3)}$$

Thus, the solution value to the primal problem can be no larger than the solution value to the dual problem. The *duality theorem of linear programming*, now to be stated, says that these values are actually equal. The key for an understanding of this fact is that, as the notation suggests, the dual variables $(\lambda_1, \ldots, \lambda_K)$ have the interpretation of Lagrange multipliers.

**Theorem M.M.1:** (*Duality Theorem of Linear Programming*) Suppose that the primal problem (M.M.1) attains a maximum value $v \in \mathbb{R}$. Then $v$ is also the minimum value attained by the dual problem (M.M.2).

**Proof:** Let $\bar{x} \in \mathbb{R}^N$ be a maximizer vector for problem (M.M.1). Denote by $\bar{\lambda} = (\bar{\lambda}_1, \ldots, \bar{\lambda}_K) \geq 0$ the Lagrange multipliers associated with this problem (see Theorem M.K.2).[31] Formally, we regard $\bar{\lambda}$ as a column vector. Then, applying Theorem M.K.2, we have

$$A^T\bar{\lambda} = f \qquad \text{and} \qquad \bar{\lambda} \cdot (c - A\bar{x}) = 0.$$

Hence, $\bar{\lambda}$ satisfies the constraints of the dual problem (since $A^T\bar{\lambda} \geq f$) and

$$c \cdot \bar{\lambda} = \bar{\lambda} \cdot c = \bar{\lambda} \cdot A\bar{x} = (A^T\bar{\lambda}) \cdot \bar{x} = f \cdot \bar{x}. \tag{M.M.4}$$

Now, by (M.M.3), we know that $c \cdot \lambda \geq f \cdot \bar{x}$ for all $\lambda \in \mathbb{R}_+^K$ such that $A^T\lambda \geq f$. Therefore $c \cdot \bar{\lambda} \leq c \cdot \lambda$ if $A^T\lambda \geq f$. So (M.M.4) tell us that, in fact, $\bar{\lambda}$ solves the dual problem (M.M.2) and therefore the value of the dual problem, $c \cdot \bar{\lambda}$, equals $f \cdot \bar{x}$, the value of the primal problem. ∎

We can verify the duality theorem for the primal and dual problems of Figures M.M.1 and M.M.2. The maximizer vector for the primal problem is $\bar{x} = (1, 2)$, yielding a value of $1 + 2 = 3$. The minimizer vector for the dual problem is $\bar{\lambda} = (\frac{2}{5}, \frac{1}{5})$, yielding a value of $4(\frac{2}{5}) + 7(\frac{1}{5}) = \frac{15}{5} = 3$.

# M.N  Dynamic Programming

Dynamic programming is a technique for the study of maximization problems defined over sequences that extend to an infinite horizon. We consider here only a very particular and simple case of what is a very general theory [an extensive review is contained in Stokey and Lucas with Prescott (1989)].

Suppose that $A \subset \mathbb{R}^N$ is a nonempty, compact, set.[32] Let $u: A \times A \to \mathbb{R}$ be a continuous function and let $\delta \in (0, 1)$. Given a vector $z \in A$ (interpreted as the initial condition of the variables $\{x_t\}_{t=0}^\infty$), the maximization problem we are now interested in is

$$\underset{\{x_t\}_{t=0}^\infty}{\text{Max}} \quad \sum_{t=0}^\infty \delta^t u(x_t, x_{t+1}) \tag{M.N.1}$$

$$\text{s.t. } x_t \in A \text{ for every } t,$$

$$x_0 = z.$$

It is not mathematically difficult to verify that a maximizer sequence exists for problem (M.N.1) and that, therefore, there is a maximum value $v(z)$. The function $v: A \to \mathbb{R}$ is called the *value function* of problem (M.N.1). As with $u(\cdot, \cdot)$ itself, the value function is continuous. If, in addition, $A$ is convex and $u(\cdot, \cdot)$ is concave, then $v(\cdot)$ is also concave.

---

31. For linear programming problems the constraint qualification is not required. Put another way, the linearity of the constraints is a sufficient form of constraint qualification.

32. The compactness assumption cannot be dispensed with entirely, but it can be much weakened.

It is fairly clear that for every $z \in A$ the value function satisfies the so-called *Bellman equation* (or the *Bellman optimality principle*):

$$v(z) = \underset{z' \in A}{\text{Max}} \quad u(z, z') + \delta v(z').$$

It is perhaps more surprising that, as shown in Theorem M.N.1, the value function is the *only* function that satisfies this equation.

**Theorem M.N.1:** Suppose that $f: A \to \mathbb{R}$ is a continuous function such that for every $z \in A$ the Bellman equation is satisfied; that is,

$$f(z) = \underset{z' \in A}{\text{Max}} \quad u(z, z') + \delta f(z') \tag{M.N.2}$$

for all $z \in A$. Then the function $f(\cdot)$ coincides with $v(\cdot)$; that is, $f(z) = v(z)$ for every $z \in A$.

**Proof:** Successively applying (M.N.2) we have that, for every $T$,

$$f(z) = \underset{\{x_t\}_{t=0}^T}{\text{Max}} \quad \sum_{t=0}^{T-1} \delta^t u(x_t, x_{t+1}) + \delta^T f(x_T)$$

$$\text{s.t. } x_t \in A \text{ for all } t \leq T,$$

$$x_0 = z.$$

But as $T \to \infty$, the term $\delta^T f(\cdot)$ makes an increasingly negligible contribution to the sum. We conclude therefore that $f(z) = v(z)$. $\blacksquare$

Theorem M.N.1 suggests a procedure for the computation of the value function. Suppose that for $r = 0$ we start with an arbitrary continuous function $f_0: A \to \mathbb{R}$. Think of $f_0(z')$ as a trial "evaluation" function giving a tentative evaluation of the value of starting with $z' \in A$. Then we can generate a new tentative evaluation function $f_1(\cdot)$ by letting, for every $z \in A$,

$$f_1(z) = \underset{z' \in A}{\text{Max}} \quad u(z, z') + \delta f_0(z').$$

If $f_1(\cdot) = f_0(\cdot)$, then $f_0(\cdot)$ satisfies the Bellman equation and Theorem M.N.1 tells us that, in fact, $f_0(\cdot) = v(\cdot)$. If $f_1(\cdot) \neq f_0(\cdot)$, then $f_0(\cdot)$ was not correct. We could then try again, starting with the new tentative $f_1(\cdot)$. This will give us a function $f_2(\cdot)$, and so on for an entire sequence of functions $\{f_r(\cdot)\}_{r=0}^\infty$. Does this take us anywhere? The answer is that it does: For every $z \in A$, we have $f_r(z) \to v(z)$ as $r \to \infty$. That is, as $r$ increases, we approach the correct evaluation of $z$.

---

Suppose that the sequence $\{\bar{x}_t\}_{t=0}^\infty$ is a sequence (or a *trajectory*) that solves the maximization problem (M.N.1). A fortiori, for every $t \geq 1$, the decisions taken at $t$ must be optimal. Examining the sum in (M.N.1), we see that $\bar{x}_t$ must solve

$$\underset{x_t \in A}{\text{Max}} \quad u(\bar{x}_{t-1}, x_t) + \delta u(x_t, \bar{x}_{t+1}). \tag{M.N.3}$$

Assuming that $\bar{x}_t$ is in the interior of $A$, (M.N.3) implies that

$$\frac{\partial u(\bar{x}_{t-1}, \bar{x}_t)}{\partial x_{N+n}} + \delta \frac{\partial u(\bar{x}_t, \bar{x}_{t+1})}{\partial x_n} = 0 \tag{M.N.4}$$

for every $n = 1, \ldots, N$.[33] The necessary conditions captured by (M.N.4) are called the *Euler equations* of problem (M.N.1).

---

33. Note that the function $u(\cdot, \cdot)$ has $2N$ arguments, the $N$ variables of the initial period and the $N$ variables of the subsequent period. In condition (M.N.4), the variable $x_n$ is the $n$th component of the initial period, and the variable $x_{N+n}$ is the $n$th component of the subsequent period.

## REFERENCES

Chang, A. C. (1984). *Fundamental Methods of Mathematical Economics*, 3d ed. New York: McGraw-Hill.

Dixit, A. (1990). *Optimization in Economic Theory*, 2d ed. New York: Oxford University Press.

Intriligator, M. (1971). *Mathematical Optimization and Economic Theory*. Englewood Cliffs, N.J.: Prentice-Hall.

Novshek, W. (1993). *Mathematics for Economists*. New York, NY: Academic Press.

Simon, C. P., and L. Blume. (1993). *Mathematics for Economists*. New York: Norton.

Sydsaeter, K. and P. J. Hammond. (1994). *Mathematics for Economic Analysis*. Englewood Cliffs, N.J.: Prentice-Hall.

Stokey, N., and R. Lucas, with E. Prescott (1989). *Recursive Methods in Economic Dynamics*. Cambridge, Mass.: Harvard University Press.

# Index